The Routledge Companion to Leadership

T0313232

Leadership has never been more important – and divisive – than it is today. The idea and discourse of the leader remains a critical factor in organizational and societal performance, but there is evident tension between the persistent focus on the critical importance of individual leaders and the increasing emphasis on collective leadership. *The Routledge Companion to Leadership* provides a survey of the contentious and dynamic discipline of leadership.

This collection covers key themes in the field, including advances in leadership theory, leadership in a range of contexts and geographies, leadership failure, leadership process, and leadership development. Topics range from micro studies to wider political analyses of leadership, taking in unusual but important aspects such as portrayals of leadership in architecture, media, and science fiction. Contributions from 61 internationally renowned authors from 16 countries make available the full range of perspectives, approaches, and insights on the idea of leadership. Providing both a social sciences and a psychological approach, these go beyond common themes to offer diverse perspectives on such topics as emotion and leadership and portrayals of leadership. This volume situates leadership debates and evidence within contemporary leadership crises, while ensuring that the explorations of the issues are of enduring relevance.

With wide and critical coverage of the key topics and potent contextualization of themes in current events, *The Routledge Companion to Leadership* is the ideal resource for graduate study in leadership.

John Storey is Professor of Human Resource Management at The Open University, UK.

Jean Hartley is Professor of Public Leadership at The Open University, UK.

Jean-Louis Denis is Professor of Public Management and Canada Research Chair in Governance and Transformation of Health Organizations and Systems at École nationale d'administration publique (ENAP), Canada.

Paul 't Hart is Professor of Public Administration at Utrecht University, the Netherlands.

Dave Ulrich is the Rensis Likert Professor of Business at the University of Michigan, USA.

"A 'companion' is defined as someone with whom one spends a lot of time and with whom one travels. I anticipate that leadership educators and researchers throughout the world will relish the opportunity to travel intellectually in the company of the most interesting and provocative contemporary leadership thinkers who are gathered together in this intriguing volume."

Brad Jackson, Victoria University of Wellington, New Zealand

"Covering a wide range of topics and written by experts in the field, this collection will be a valuable resource to all students of leadership looking for the most up-to-date and challenging thinking concerning this ubiquitous yet illusive phenomenon."

Donna Ladkin, Plymouth University, UK

"This comprehensive book of leadership essays is an important addition to our understanding of this crucial element of social, economic and political organization in every society. Sophisticated in its framing, wide-ranging in its focus, this is a book that will be useful for every student of leadership, regardless of their field."

Stanley Renshon, City University of New York, USA

"Today, there is no shortage of encyclopedias and handbooks on leadership. Yet this excellent collection of chapters, co-edited by a team of accomplished leadership scholars from various fields, marks a most welcome and important addition to the international literature. While too often editors leave the crucial task of developing meaningful distinctions between, for example, conceptualizing, practicing and evaluating leadership, to their readers, this companion does a marvelous job of bringing clarity, structure and perspective to a burgeoning field that has become notorious for its elusiveness. A truly indispensable resource."

Ludger Helms, University of Innsbruck, Austria

The Routledge Companion to Leadership

*Edited by John Storey, Jean Hartley,
Jean-Louis Denis, Paul 't Hart
and Dave Ulrich*

NEW YORK AND LONDON

First published 2017
by Routledge
605 Third Avenue, New York, NY 10017

and by Routledge
2 Park Square, Milton Park, Abingdon, Oxon OX14 4RN

First issued in paperback 2022

Routledge is an imprint of the Taylor & Francis Group, an informa business

British Library Cataloguing in Publication Data
A catalogue record for this book is available from the British Library

Library of Congress Cataloging in Publication Data
Names: Storey, John, 1947- editor.
Title: The Routledge companion to leadership / [edited by] John Storey,
    Jean Hartley, Jean-Louis Denis, Paul 't Hart, & David O. Ulrich.
Description: 1 Edition. | New York : Routledge, 2016.
Identifiers: LCCN 2016011925 (print) | LCCN 2016012996 (ebook) |
    ISBN 9781138825574 (hbk) | ISBN 9781315739854 (ebk) |
    ISBN 9781317578246 (pdf) | ISBN 9781317578239 (epub) |
    ISBN 9781317578222 (mobi/kindle)
Subjects: LCSH: Leadership.
Classification: LCC HD57.7 .R6898 2016 (print) | LCC HD57.7
    (ebook) | DDC 303.3/4—dc23
LC record available at http://lccn.loc.gov/2016011925

ISBN 13: 978-1-138-82557-4 (hbk)
ISBN 13: 978-1-03-240239-0 (pbk)
ISBN 13: 978-1-315-73985-4 (ebk)

DOI: 10.4324/9781315739854

Typeset in Bembo
by Swales & Willis Ltd, Exeter, Devon, UK

Contents

Contents

Figures

Tables

Contributors

Justin Allen
Principal, The RBL Group, USA

Mats Alvesson
Professor of Business Administration
Lund University, Sweden

Werner Auer-Rizzi
Johannes Kepler University of Linz, Austria

Jack Barentsen
Associate Professor and Chair of Practical
 Theology
Evangelische Theologische Faculteit
Leuven, Belgium

Allan Bird
Professor in Global Business
Northeastern University
Boston, Massachusetts, USA

Peter Bloom
Lecturer in Organization Studies
Faculty of Business and Law
The Open University, UK

Ronald Burke
Professor in the Schulich School of Business
York University
Toronto, Canada

Fredrik Bynander
Associate Professor of Political Science and
 Research Director at Crismart, Stockholm,
 Sweden

Brigid Carroll
Associate Professor
The University of Auckland Business
 School, New Zealand

Melissa Carsten
Associate Professor of Management
College of Business Administration
Winthrop University
South Carolina, USA

Ann Cunliffe
Professor of Organisation Studies
Bradford University School of Management
University of Bradford, UK

Helen Delaney
Senior Lecturer
Department of Management and
 International Business
University of Auckland Business School, New
 Zealand

Jean-Louis Denis
Professor of Public Management and Canada
 Research Chair in Governance and

Transformation of Health Organizations
and Systems, École nationale
d'administration publique (ENAP)
Montreal, Canada

Joshua Firth
Research Fellow
The New Zealand Leadership Institute
The University of Auckland Business School,
New Zealand

Jackie Ford
Professor of Leadership and Organization
Studies
Bradford University School of Management,
UK

Émilie Gibeau
HEC Montréal, Canada

Jonathan Gosling
Professor Emeritus
University of Exeter, UK

Keith Grint
Professor of Public Leadership
Warwick Business School, UK

Peter Gronn
Professor of Education
University of Cambridge, UK

Paul 't Hart
Professor of Public Administration
University of Utrecht, The Netherlands

Jean Hartley
Professor of Public Leadership
The Open University, UK

Michael Hogg
Professor of Social Psychology
Claremont Graduate University
Los Angeles, California, USA

Clare Holt
Warwick Business School
The University of Warwick, UK

Richard Holti
Senior Lecturer in Human Resource
Management
The Open University, UK

Christian Jacobsen
Associate Professor
Department of Political Science
Aarhus University, Denmark

Andrew Kakabadse
Professor of Governance and Leadership
Henley Business School, UK

Nada Kakabadse
Professor of Policy, Governance and Ethics
Henley Business School, UK

Barbara Kellerman
The James McGregor Burns Lecturer in
Leadership
John F. Kennedy School of Government
Harvard University, USA

Nadeem Khan
Lecturer in Governance, Policy and Leadership
Henley Business School, UK

Eva Knies
Associate Professor
Utrecht University, The Netherlands

David Knights
Professor, Organization, Work and
Technology
University of Lancaster, UK

Matthew Laing
Research Fellow in Politics
Monash University, Australia

Ann Langley
Professor, HEC Montréal, Canada

Magnus Larsson
Associate Professor
Copenhagen Business School, Denmark

Alan Lawton
Professor
Federation University, Australia

Mark Mendenhall
J. Burton Frierson Chair of Excellence in
    Business Leadership
College of Business
University of Tennessee, Chattanooga, USA

Michael Minkenberg
Professor of Comparative Politics
Europa-Universität Viadrina
Frankfurt (Oder), Germany

Gary Oddou
Director and Professor of Global Business
    Management
California State University, San Marcos,
    USA

Joyce Osland
Director, Lucas Endowed Professor of Global
    Leadership
School of Global Innovation and Leadership
San Jose State University, USA

David Rast
Assistant Professor of Social Psychology and
    Leadership
University of Alberta
Edmonton, Canada

Gerhard Reber
Professor Emeritus
Johannes Kepler University of Linz, Austria

Sebastian Reiche
IESE
Barcelona, Spain

Wendy Reid
HEC Montréal, Canada

Carl Rhodes
Professor of Organization Studies
UTS Business School
University of Technology
Sydney, Australia

Irma Rybnikova
Technische University Chemnitz, Germany

Viviane Sergi
Professor, Department of Management and
    Technology
University of Quebec at Montreal, Canada

Maja Šimunjak
Lecturer, Department of Media
Middlesex University, UK

Owain Smolović Jones
The Open University, UK

Sverre Spoelstra
Reader in the Department of Business
    Administration
Lund University, Sweden

John Storey
Professor of Human Resource Management
The Open University, UK

John Street
Professor, School of Politics, Philosophy,
    Language and Communication Studies
University of East Anglia, UK

Peter Sun
Associate Professor
Director – Corporate Programmes and Director
    of the Centre for Enterprise and Leadership
University of Waikato, New Zealand

Ian Sutherland
Deputy Dean for Research
IEDC-Bled School of Management, Slovenia

Scott Taylor
Reader in Leadership and Organization
    Studies
University of Birmingham, UK

Dennis Tourish
Professor of Leadership and Organisation
    Studies
Royal Holloway, University of London, UK

Lars Tummers
Associate Professor
School of Governance
Utrecht University, The Netherlands

Mary Uhl-Bien
Professor of Management
Texas Christian University, USA

Dave Ulrich
The Rensis Likert Professor of Business
University of Michigan, USA

James Walter
Professor of Politics
Monash University, Australia

Julie Wilson
Durham University, UK

Kimberly Yost
Visiting Assistant Professor
Lourdes University
Sylvania, Ohio, USA

Preface

John Storey, Jean Hartley, Jean-Louis Denis,
Paul 't Hart and Dave Ulrich

As a practice and as a field of study, 'leadership' is an object of fascination, a source of concern, and an occasion for hope, anticipation, scepticism and aspiration. In consequence of this mix of responses, discussions about leadership are often animated, emotional, vibrant and contested. Leadership, as a process, implies the existence of one or more agents enacting something interpreted as meriting this label. These agents or leaders tend to be of inherent interest because they usually exercise influence and have power; they create, or have created for them, a narrative: how they came to acquire power, how they try to hold on to it, how they exercise it and sometimes how they lose it. Many a legend – indeed numerous examples of story-telling – hinge on the part played by the leader. These central characters may be Emperors, Chieftains, Tsars, Kings and Queens, Presidents, Generals, Chief Executives, Shoguns, Warlords or Sultans. The drama of their interactions with their 'followers', their rivals and other players is the very stuff of theatre, novels, news, and indeed of everyday discourse and gossip.

Leaders of organizations (such as chief executives) and within organizations (such as divisional or departmental heads) share some of the connotations of position power and sometimes of charisma. Moreover, as we will see, even this long list of examples leans towards only one form of leader and leadership. Each of them tends to carry connotations of authority, power, strength and rulership. But there are others who are sometimes recognized as exercising leadership even though they do not occupy a formal position. The focus on organizational leadership is a relatively new phenomenon; the 1990s saw an upsurge in attention, whereas before then organizations were administered or managed. As noted elsewhere (Storey 2011), in response to economic and social challenges, numerous organizations in sectors as diverse as the police, public administration, education, health and local government started to look to 'leadership' as the appropriate answer.

The words 'leader' and 'leadership' trigger fundamental, though very varied, thoughts, emotions and inferences which find reflection in the variety of academic constructs. They often have associations with position in a hierarchy and perhaps even domination; yet they may also trigger ideas of saviour, pathfinder and even messiah. At a psychological level, the terms may prompt feelings associated with loyalty, worship, dependency, parent–child relationships, narcissism, neurosis, projection and splitting. For this range of reasons and more, leadership is an emotionally charged and intellectually challenging construct. At one end of the spectrum is a literature which amounts to hagiography and hero worship; at the other end are sharp critiques. Somewhere in between are multiple approaches, some of which eschew the idea of a charismatic and transformational leader in the traditional sense and instead direct attention to leadership as a skilful, adaptive practice exercised potentially outside the formal authority structure (Heifetz 1994). This realm of practice carries its own potential for excitement as it may challenge extant assumptions and expectations and so its disruptive nature may not always be appreciated or applauded.

In this introduction, we look at the reasons for the continued fascination, the source of the concerns, and the nature of the scepticism and hopefulness, before turning to an outline of the contributions made by this collection of chapters.

Leadership as a Source of Fascination

Despite the many concerns, it is evident that leadership remains a source of persistent and extensive fascination. This fascination stems from a number of sources. Books on leading, leaders and leadership constitute one of the most popular publishing genres. A search for 'leadership' on the web results in many thousands of books and even more journal articles. Many of the books can be seen as ventures in self-improvement – aspiring to leadership and aspiring to self-improvement being seen as close cousins. The genre shades off into the cult of celebrity, with books purporting to impart the secrets of successful leadership from Sir Alex Ferguson (Ferguson and Moritz 2015), Sir Richard Branson (Branson 2015), Steve Jobs (Isaacson 2011) and many others. Close neighbours include books and leadership development seminars featuring explorers, such as Ernest Shackleton (Smith 2015), sportsmen and women, such as cricketer Mike Brearley (Brearley 2015), and former military leaders, such as General McCrystal's extrapolation about leadership from the Iraq campaign to business organizations (McCrystal 2015).

The fascination is found also in the remarkable renaissance of leadership studies among academics and academic institutions. The number of academic journals devoted to leadership and the frequency of their issues continue to grow. Academic and practitioner articles and papers on the subject grow exponentially. A web search for the single term 'leadership' resulted in nearly 3 million articles. And leadership is not only being written about, it is being taught. Business schools throughout the world increasingly present themselves as purveyors of leadership skills. Harvard Business School offers a range of programmes on leadership with the Program for Leadership Development (PLD) being one of the foremost. The prospectus states: 'As global competition intensifies, visionary companies are investing in a pipeline of emerging executives who can help them build and secure a competitive edge.' It suggests that 'You will emerge from the PLD ready to drive change, innovation, and growth in any economy.' For $47,000, participants enjoy two 2-week campus-based sessions plus two distance-learning modules. This would seem to be a valuable learning experience indeed, costing, as it does, nearly $5,000 per day. Harvard is not alone. Numerous business schools have joined the bandwagon and added leadership to their portfolios. For example, the London Business School has a range of offerings. Its prospectus states: 'We're creating a generation of leaders who have a global view, a strong sense of community, and who lead from their heart, as well as their head.' Leaders can 'make the world a better place'. To drive this agenda it has launched a Leadership Institute. The LBS Senior Executive Programme, like Harvard's, offers two 2-week blocks of study for £29,500 ($44,643) – though without the added distance-learning element. One of the course participants, already a success in his chosen field, says that the programme helped him: 'Learn who I am.' A faculty lead on the SEP suggests that they will 'Look at you on a good day, look at you on a bad day and at your values'; they will also uncover 'Your USP' and 'Your Leadership Brand'. Thus, as with any such programme, there is an intriguing and exciting connection between the individual self and the wider world. Both aspects – the individual and the wider context – are apparently open to the exciting possibility of change. Not only that, but work on the one can lead to impact on the other. Little wonder that leadership is a source of fascination: change oneself and change the world.

Nor is this mere bombast. There is a material base to the phenomenon. Graduate training schemes are geared, unashamedly, to finding and nurturing the next generation of top leaders. Thus, graduates aspiring to take up a place on a graduate training programme find that they are signing up to a process which is geared towards the goal of cultivating and sorting and sifting future top leaders. Up or out is the mantra. For ambitious graduates it may be difficult not to enlist on the leadership journey. As McKinsey Consultants make clear: 'We look for people who strive to lead – lead themselves, their teams, their communities – and can foster effective teamwork in order to drive results for clients and positive change in complex organizations.'

More widely, leadership is a hugely significant cultural phenomenon. It is found represented in current popular media such as news, sport and film, and in art, architecture and historiography. It is a subject of conversation among 'ordinary workers'. It is commonplace to hear people on their daily commute, or in the pub, discussing their 'bosses' and in effect evaluating their behaviour and performance. The fascination here may not be based on admiration or respect, but it is often an interest in how 'the leader' (at whatever level) is behaving or is likely to behave. The evaluations are often a mixed brew of criticism, admiration, fear, bemusement and contempt.

Leaders and leadership are a source of fascination also because they may impact heavily on other people's lives. Leaders may maintain and perpetuate the establishment or the regime. Conversely, movements to curtail or even supplant the prevailing regime normally involve and require an 'alternative' leader or set of leaders. Such processes of contestation may develop in different ways – the 'revolutionary' leader may prevail and become part of a new establishment, may be defeated or may be incorporated. On the other hand, the romance of leadership (the belief that leadership matters) may cause reverse attribution, in which people seek to identify the leader who is thought to have caused the success – even where alternative analysis might suggest other causes which do not involve leadership.

There are other reasons for fascination with the idea of leadership that operate on a much more grounded scale. A growing number of works explore the role of everyday informal leaders, the 'ordinary persons' doing extraordinary things. This is the idea of 'learning leadership' through practical action (Antonacopoulou and Bento 2011; Ibarra 2015). The power and pull of this conceptualization are not hard to imagine. It casts leadership in a very different light. It opens up the scope for significant social action; it opens up the potential for almost anyone to 'make a difference' – with potential reverberations across a wide canvas.

Leadership as a Source of Concern

The reasons for unease about leadership stem from a number of different types of concern.

At a practical level, leadership is a common cause for concern because there is a prevalent notion that there is a serious 'shortage' of leadership talent. Numerous global surveys, in both the private and public sectors, persist in reporting that a gap between supply and demand for leaders is supposedly one of the top worries among corporate chiefs. The so-called 'war for talent' is fuelled in part by this perceived scarcity. A perceived lack of leadership talent and capability is found alike in the political sphere and the corporate.

However, the concern is not only about scarcity. There are qualms and fears about the *quality* of leaders. Numerous corporate scandals involving lying, cheating, larceny and greed have followed a trail which points to grievous failures among those supposedly leading (Stein 2007). That such scandals coincide with ever-increasing inequality of reward only adds to the concern and to the sense of injustice and outrage. Reports of committees of inquiry into corporate lapses and catastrophes, whether in healthcare, social care or banking, tend often to conclude that the problems could be traced to failures in leadership and the lack of appropriate leadership quality. In his *Leadership BS*, Jeffrey Pfeffer seeks to expose the underlying reasons for so much reported failure of leadership despite the plethora of courses and materials which are available. He suggests that much of the advice is 'sugar laced but toxic' and that 'the leadership industry has failed' (Pfeffer 2015, p. 4). Indications of failure include the prevalence of workplaces with large numbers of disengaged and dissatisfied workers, and the notable failure to produce sufficient effective leaders.

And there are related concerns about the misuse of power. These regularly accompany a model based on a pyramidal hierarchy of leaders. Such a model often connotes unequal access to resources, to rewards, to power and to status. Leadership often accrues and is equated with position power. Military units require a CO (a commanding officer), business organizations require CEOs (chief executive officers) and schools seek headteachers. The 'someone-in-charge' is frequently seen as 'the leader' albeit it is also often accepted that there may be other leaders, some of whom may act without formal title. Yet there are many examples of leadership undertaken without positional power. These include those people who led movements for change, such as Mahatma Gandhi in India, John Garang in South Sudan, Martin Luther King in the USA and Nelson Mandela in South Africa. There are also other examples, such as the suffragettes, and everyday actions of citizens, such as Caroline Criado Perez who campaigned – in the face of opposition and hostility – to have women on the banknotes of the Bank of England. There are also numerous examples of leadership in the lives of 'ordinary' citizens.

Concerns about the concentration of power can overlap into concerns about the nature and exercise of leadership. Leaders may be narcissistic and egotistical; they may also be arrogant and domineering. As a remedy or alternative, there is increasing interest in 'authentic' and spiritual leadership as opposed to the arrogant and self-serving modes of leadership.

As leadership connects with, and in everyday thinking usually implies, 'followership', the interplay between these can be a further source of concern. Psychological and psychoanalytic perspectives may suggest that deeply held reservations about authority figures may impact on people's views about leaders. Irrespective of evidence about efficacy of outcomes there may simply be an ideological and value preference and desire for shared leadership. There are related avenues of intellectual inquiry which attend to the complexities of mutual influence and the need for collaboration and coalition building.

In the face of these concerns, there continues to be a hope that leaders can influence others in a positive way. Leaders may multiply and build other leaders; lead by positive example and influence; share power to empower others; and create abundant organizations.

Leadership as a Source of Scepticism and Also of Hope

There remains a current of deep scepticism among many academics about leadership both as practised and as studied. Pfeffer's (2015) critique, cited above, is but one of the more developed of the criticisms. The critique stems from a number of sources. Many academic observers work from a values base which is inclined positively towards democratic, emancipatory and shared power, and is disinclined towards, and suspicious of, hierarchy and concentrations of power. Partly, perhaps, as a consequence of working in collegial, scholastic settings, there is a marked preference for distributed and shared leadership. Accordingly, pluralistic leadership modes are a prevalent theme in the spheres of education and health. This inclination tends towards a suspicion of, and indeed an antipathy towards, 'heroic' singular leaders or any perpetuating of the myth of the 'great man' with its associated connotations of paternalism, dependency and inequality. There is often a suspicion of the motives of those who strive to be leaders. Are they seeking to accrue unwarranted access to power, influence and rewards? But if democracy is to offset the exercise of overweening and arbitrary power, society also requires the exercise of leadership to create and implement democratic institutions. Leadership which goes beyond mere populism is needed to tackle strategic challenges.

So, in sum, the field of study is replete with tensions and contradictions. Leaders are viewed with both awe and suspicion. Leadership is viewed as a process of influence that may be concentrated or dispersed. So, while there is a backcloth of controversy, there is also an emergent agenda of intellectually exciting and worthy themes which merit serious attention.

The intellectual challenges are many. For example, there are different conceptualizations of 'leadership'. It is commonly and interchangeably used to denote a person, a position and a process. 'Leader' and 'leadership' are often conflated.

There are also different ontological positions associated with different 'tribes' of researchers. In consequence, the field can be remarkably Balkanized and insular. Like speaks with like, but conversations across boundaries are often limited. For example, even those scholars who publish in the two main leadership journals *Leadership* and *Leadership Quarterly* tend not to interact.

Moreover, different phenomena are all treated as leadership. Thus, small group leadership, leadership of large organizations and leadership of social movements tend to be placed in the same basket. Yet the skills required in the exercise of 'near' leadership may bear little resemblance to those needed in the exercise of 'distant' leadership. Many early studies of leadership were conducted in industrial settings with a focus on supervisors in private firms, and as a result the construct was, and often still is, conflated with a position in a hierarchy. In addition, the context of contemporary organizations provide an intriguing landscape for the expression and study of leadership. Organizations are often populated with autonomous groups and individuals such as professionals or highly skilled manpower. Also, new forms of organizing such as virtual networks may stimulate innovative thinking on what we mean by leadership.

Leadership is a construct and its 'presence' can only be inferred. This inference may draw upon empirical indicators but the empirical data is often variable in quality and quantity.

This volume seeks to make a contribution to the development of these issues.

The Contribution of This Companion

To respond to the scepticism, hope and challenges of leadership, this volumes takes a holistic view of the leadership phenomenon and allows space for examination of the diversity of perspectives in the field. We strongly believe in the benefits of looking at a plurality of approaches to get a better sense of the reality of leadership in societies and organizations.

The chapters, which include analytical assessments of leadership, historical overviews, critical perspectives, psychoanalytic, contextualized and ethical assessments, cultural portrayals and assessments of leadership development, are organized into seven parts.

Part I (Conceptualizing Leadership) allows consideration of a wide view. It includes a fundamental consideration of diverse definitions and understandings of the meanings of leader and leadership. At one extreme, it is noted that leadership has been so widely interpreted that it might be considered a 'floating signifier' – a vessel so open that almost any meaning might be attributed to it. One approach, as shown in Chapter 1, is to regard it as like a quilt which is comprised of diverse approaches and conceptualizations. Part I also contains chapters which conceptualize leadership in different ways, including as a form of capital which could be measured, as a distributed phenomenon and as a process which underpins a group's social identity in times of crisis.

Part II (Studying Leadership) presents a set of chapters which reveal the rich variety of ways in which the leadership phenomenon can be understood and studied. It underscores a set of tensions that structure contemporary studies of leaders and leadership. Leadership can be conceived as a resource that organizations use to achieve their own goals. From a critical standpoint, it is more or less of an ideology that contributes to reproducing models of conduct in organizations. For others, a careful assessment of the scholarship in the field requires a renewal of the thinking around the classics such as the duality of leaders–followers and the study of leadership across various contexts. The reader exits Part II with a variety of concepts that help make sense of various approaches and perspectives on leadership.

Part III (Practising Leadership) examines leadership in practice in politics, in corporate governance settings, in religion and in health services. These chapters highlight that the leadership phenomenon shows up in diverse settings. Leadership is not a given; it is constructed through interactions in context. It is influenced by the type of organizations in which aspiring leaders evolved. It is also a dynamic phenomenon in which leadership positions are never secured forever. Achieving leadership requires work from agents in organizations.

Part IV (Contextualizing Leadership) assesses leadership in the diverse contexts of time, place, type of problem, globalization and the realms of politics and business organizations.

Part V (Evaluating Leadership) comprises a set of chapters which variously address toxic and destructive leadership; ethical leadership; the impact of leadership on performance outcomes; and leaders as spiritual protagonists. Overall, chapters in this part look at the risk and contribution of a cultural figure of leadership that is so often based on individual heroism and power.

Part VI (Imagining Leadership) contains chapters which explore portrayals of leadership in science fiction, portrayals of leadership in other media and the projection of leadership in architecture. It provides alternate prisms to relate leaders and leadership to broader cultural phenomena in society.

Part VII (Nurturing Leadership) contains chapters which address whether and how leadership might be developed, the diverse approaches to leadership development and a chapter examining how aspiring leadership identity is created. These chapters reveal the interplay between what is offered to emergent leaders and how would-be leaders play their own part in growing into the role.

Concluding Comments

In this short preface we hope we have whetted your appetite to read further and more deeply into the range of offerings on the challenges and opportunities of leadership. In the first part of this introduction, the key issues and controversies were laid out. The second part provides a summary overview of how the team of authors gathered together to produce this volume has responded to the implicit agenda outlined. The continuation of the journey is over to you.

References

Antonacopoulou, E. and R. Bento (2011). Learning leadership in practice. In *Leadership in Organizations: Current Issues and Key Trends*. J. Storey. London, Routledge.

Branson, R. (2015). *The Virgin Way: How to Listen, Learn, Laugh and Lead*. London, Virgin Books.

Brearley, M. (2015). *The Art of Captaincy: What Sport Teaches Us About Leadership*. London, Pan.

Ferguson, A. and M. Moritz (2015). *Leading*. London, Hodder & Stoughton.

Heifetz, R. (1994). *Leadership Without Easy Answers*. Cambridge, MA, Harvard University Press.

Ibarra, H. (2015). *Act Like a Leader, Think Like a Leader*. Cambridge, MA, Harvard Business Review Press.

Isaacson, W. (2011). *Steve Jobs*. New York, Little, Brown.

McCrystal, G. S. (2015). *Team of Teams: New Rules of Engagment for a Complex World*. New York, Portfolio Penguin.

Pfeffer, J. (2015). *Leadership Bs: Fixing Workplaces and Careers One Truth at a Time*. New York, HarperBusiness.

Smith, M. (2015). *Shackleton: By Endurance We Conquer*. London, OneWorld.

Stein, M. (2007). Oedipus Rex at Enron: Leadership, Oedipal struggles, and organizational collapse. *Human Relations* 60 (9), 1387–1410.

Storey, J., Ed. (2011). *Leadership in Organizations: Current Issues and Key Trends*. London, Routledge.

Part I
Conceptualizing Leadership

Introduction

Leadership is like the famous movie by Luis Bunuel – it is an obscure object of desire. When things go right or wrong in organizations, commentators all too readily either praise the role played by an exceptional leader or trace the problem to the lack of leadership. 'Leadership', like 'communication', is often used as one of those garbage can ideas used to make sense of a diversity of phenomena in society and organizations.

A variety of related concepts are associated with leadership. It is often used as synonymous with power or influence. The marker of leadership here will be found in the ability to observe empirically how certain individuals influence others in their actions or organizational behaviours. Leadership will thus be visible in action and not in the idealized expression of traits and attitudes. For others, leadership is more of a psychological phenomenon, in which identification and aspiration shape relations among individuals in organizations. The interest in 'charisma' is close to a psychological conceptualization of leadership. The notion of 'authority' also intersects with leadership. Some individuals, apparently more than others, impact on their environment. Of course, any careful observers of organizations will recognize that formal authority conveyed by hierarchical positions is only one piece of the puzzle. Influencing others and contributing to amazing achievements depend on a multitude of factors. While this is very plausible, formal authority has not to be neglected in any thinking about organizational leadership. Formal authority provides the individual with opportunities to be, or become, a leader. It may also, through a complex process of selection, reveal the advantages that some have over others in organizations and societies. Put differently, authority is one dimension of power and may place individuals in formal positions in a privileged niche from which to develop and deploy leadership. These considerations are all influenced by a relatively narrow representation of leadership. Leadership is mostly considered here as something that takes form in an individual – an individual that can be clearly identified and that is the carrier of an idealized and powerful representation of leaders. However, contemporary analyses of organizations have, through various theoretical prisms, called for a much more complex and messy picture of organizations and leadership (Uhl-Bien *et al.* 2007). Here, leadership is not only an obscure object of desire; it is somewhat intractable being located at a network of ramifications, interdependencies and joint production in discourses and actions. Leadership is not the property of individuals; it is the expression of a collective ability to shape organizations.

The four chapters in Part I of the Companion each in their own way explores various conceptions of leadership, showing that this domain of study is à la fois fertile but somewhat fuzzy. Each of the chapters seeks to bring some clarification and boundary about what we will conceive as 'leadership' in organizations.

In Chapter 1, Grint and colleagues review these competing representations of leadership. To navigate the field of leadership studies, the authors ask five questions: Is it WHO 'leaders' are that makes them leaders? Is it WHAT 'leaders' achieve that makes them leaders? Is it WHERE 'leaders' operate that makes them leaders? Is it WHY 'leaders' lead that makes them leaders? Is it HOW 'leaders' get things done that makes them leaders? They suggest refocusing leadership studies on the subject as a way to develop a more productive representation of this important phenomenon.

In Chapter 2, Ulrich and Allen explore three loci of leadership: the person, the organization and external stakeholders. They propose that leadership thinking should move outward and explore how leaders contribute (or not) to fulfil the expectations of these stakeholders. The promotion of such a shift in leadership studies is based on the growing role of intangible assets as represented for example in measuring the role of leadership in the evaluation of firms. Tools and metrics are offered in this chapter which can be used to assess empirically the leadership capital of firms and other organizations. The added value of this perspective is to look at leadership from a result-oriented perspective which departs from an approach in which leadership is considered to have intrinsic value by itself.

In Chapter 3, Sergi and colleagues explore representations and studies that go beyond the individual and heroic bias of the field. They suggest that it is important to bring context back in and to open up new and more collective views on leadership. Pluralistic organizations and networks are arenas where distributed and shared forms of leadership flourish. A more processual approach underlines that leadership is not a given in organizations. Actors have to work to position and reposition themselves as leaders in the organization. The authors conclude that more attention can be paid to atypical contexts such as virtual networks where innovative forms of leadership can develop, often in the periphery of hierarchical relations.

Finally, Chapter 4 by Rast and Hogg deals with the manifestation of leadership in contexts of crisis and uncertainty. In such contexts, landmarks that are used to define boundaries and relations are destabilized or blurred. Leadership tends to be reformulated to take into account attributes of unusual situations. The authors identify key identity and group processes which are required to understand how leadership takes shape and is transformed in the context of crisis. Such contexts offer opportunity for the development of atypical leadership figures; yet paradoxically they may also culminate in pressures for more conservative figures of leadership.

These chapters, taken as a whole, launch the book with a diversity of avenues for thinking about the many meanings of leadership. They also illustrate how leadership studies are pluralistic and in constant flux. The focus and boundaries of the field are in motion.

Reference

Uhl-Bien, M., R. Marion and B. McKelvey (2007). Complexity leadership theory: Shifting leadership from the industrial age to the knowledge era. *The Leadership Quarterly*, 18 (4), 298–318.

1

What Is Leadership

Person, Result, Position, Purpose or Process, or All or None of These?

Keith Grint, Owain Smolović Jones and Clare Holt

What Is Leadership?

Research into leadership – at least in written form – can be traced back to Plato in the West and Sun Tzu in the East, but we do not seem to be any nearer a consensus as to its basic meaning, let alone whether it can be taught or its moral effects measured and predicted, than we were well over two millennia ago. This cannot be because of a dearth of interest or material: on 29 October 2003, when one of the authors first tried to answer the question 'what is leadership?', there were 14,139 items relating to 'leadership' on Amazon.co.uk for sale. Assuming you could read these at the rate of one per day, it would take almost 39 years just to read the material, never mind write anything about leadership or practise it. Just two months later, that number had increased by 3 per cent (471 items) to 14,610. Assuming this increase was annualized, we could look forward to just under 20,000 items by the beginning of 2005, 45,000 by 2010 and 100,000 by 2015. In fact in January 2015 there were 126,149 items, so the increase is exponential. It should be self-evident that we do not need more 'lists' of leadership competences or skills, because leadership research appears to be anything but incremental in its approach to 'the truth' about leadership: the longer we spend looking at leadership, the more complex the picture becomes.

Traditionally, leadership is defined by its alleged opposite: management. Management is concerned with executing routines and maintaining organizational stability – it is essentially concerned with control; leadership is concerned with direction setting, with novelty and is essentially linked to change, movement and persuasion. Another way to put this is that management is the equivalent of déjà vu (seen this before), whereas leadership is the equivalent of vu jàdé (never seen this before). Management implies that managers have seen it all before and simply need to respond correctly to the situation by categorizing it and executing the appropriate process. Leadership implies that leaders have never seen anything like it before and must therefore construct a novel strategy. But this division is often taken to mean that different people are necessary to fill the different roles – hence anyone relegated to the role of 'mere' manager cannot be considered as bringing anything unique to the party – after all, their task is limited to the mechanical one of recognizing situations and applying pre-existing processes. That most roles actually require both recognition and invention should also be clear.

3

Another way of approaching the problem might be to consider what the most popular textbooks have to say on the issue. When one of the authors did this in 2003 (Grint, 2005a), the four best-selling general review texts on leadership were Hughes *et al.* (1999), Northouse (1997), Wright (1996) and Yukl (1998). Apart from noting the variegated properties of their definitions I was, and we are, left more rather than less confused by them. Leadership does seem to be defined differently and, even if there are some similarities, the complexities undermine most attempts to explain why the differences exist. That is to say, we know differences exist but we remain unable to construct a consensus about the concept. However, the dissensus seemed to hang around four areas of dispute: leadership defined as *person, result, position* and *process*. Ten years later, while the fourfold typology has proved useful, the paper by Kempster *et al.* (2011) rightly pointed out that it seemed to omit the very 'purpose' of leadership, and we have included that as a separate element.

The rest of this chapter focuses upon these five approaches and we conclude with an explanation of the problem of diversity and a way of constraining its effects. We hesitate to use the word 'resolution', because the explanation actively inhibits any resolution, but it does enable us to establish some parameters that we might use to understand why the differences exist in the first place. In other words, this does not provide a first step towards a consensus, but a first step towards understanding why a consensus might be unachievable. Moreover, the point is not simply to redescribe the varieties of interpretation, but to consider how this affects the way leadership is perceived, enacted, recruited and supported. For example, if organizations promote individuals on the basis of one particular interpretation of leadership, then that approach will be encouraged and others discouraged – but it may well be that other interpretations of leadership are critical to the organization's success. Hence the importance of the definition is not simply to delineate a space in a language game, and it is not merely a game of sophistry; on the contrary, how we define leadership has vital implications for how organizations work – or do not work.

Let us first generate a taxonomy of leadership that does not claim universal coverage but should encompass a significant proportion of our definitions of leadership. Moreover, the typology is not hierarchical: it does not claim that one definition is more important than another and, contrary to the consensual approach, it is constructed upon foundations that *may* be mutually exclusive. In effect, we may have to choose which form of leadership we are talking about, rather than attempt to elide the differences. It is, however, quite possible that empirical examples of leadership embody elements of all five forms. Thus we are left with five major approaches:

- Leadership as Person: is it WHO 'leaders' are that makes them leaders?
- Leadership as Result: is it WHAT 'leaders' achieve that makes them leaders?
- Leadership as Position: is it WHERE 'leaders' operate that makes them leaders?
- Leadership as Purpose: is it WHY 'leaders' lead that makes them leaders?
- Leadership as Process: is it HOW 'leaders' get things done that makes them leaders?

All these aspects are 'ideal types', following Weber's assertion (see Grint, 1998: 102–103) that no such 'real' empirical case probably exists in any pure form. But this does enable us to understand the phenomenon of leadership better, and its attendant confusions and complexities, because leadership means different things to different people. This is therefore a heuristic model, not an attempt to carve up the world into 'objective' segments that mirror what we take to be reality. We will suggest, having examined these five different approaches to leadership, that the differences both explain why so little agreement has been reached on the definition of leadership and explain why this is important to the execution and analysis of leadership. Finally, we use the work of Lacan to ask whether 'leadership' is so porous in meaning because it is an 'empty-signifier' – a vehicle capable of embodying all kinds of meanings and fantasies – hence its persistence, resilience and contested nature.

Defining Leadership

Person-Based Leadership

Is it who you are that determines whether you are a leader or not? This, of course, resonates with the traditional traits approach: a leader's character or personality. We might consider the best example of this as the charismatic, to whom followers are attracted because of the charismatic's personal 'magnetism'. Ironically, while a huge effort has been made to reduce the ideal leader to his or her essence – the quintessential characteristics or competencies or behaviours of the leader – the effort of reduction has simultaneously reduced its value. It is rather as if a leadership scientist had turned chef and was engaged in reducing a renowned leader to his or her elements by placing them in a saucepan and applying heat. Eventually, the residue left from the cooking could be analysed and the material substances divided into their various chemical compounds. Take, for instance, Wofford's (1999: 525) claim that laboratory research on charisma would develop a 'purer' construct 'free from the influences of such nuisance variables as performance, organizational culture and other styles of leadership'. What a culture-free leader would like is anyone's guess and this attempted purification is literally *reductio ad absurdum*: a pile of chemical residues might have considerable difficulty persuading other people to follow it (although this is what drug addiction is framed around). At its most basic the 'essence' of leadership, qua an individual leader, leaves out the followers, and without followers you cannot be a leader. Indeed, this might be the simplest definition of leadership: 'having followers'.

A complementary or contradictory case can also be made for defining leadership generally as a collective, rather than an individual, phenomenon. In this case the focus usually moves from an individual formal leader to multiple informal leaders. We might, for example, consider how organizations actually achieve anything, rather than being over-concerned with what the CEO has said should be achieved. Thus we could trace the role of informal opinion-leaders in persuading their colleagues to work differently, or to work harder, or not to work at all and so on. This does not necessarily imply that everyone is a leader – though it might do – but rather that a relatively small number of people are crucial for ensuring organizations survive and succeed – and this minority or critical mass may or may not coincide with those in formal leadership positions (Gronn, 2003; Ridderstrale, 2002: 11).

Although person-based theories of leadership may vary in emphasis, they do tend to hold one thing in common: the person the theory is based upon is usually a naked person. Search as one may for a definition of leadership that encompasses anything beyond the human, the most likely trail leads back to the comforting figure of a *homo sapiens*. Latour (1988), for example, makes a robust case for actor–network theory, with his suggestion that a naked Napoleon would have been markedly less effective than a clothed Napoleon, surrounded by clothed soldiers with weapons. Actor–network theory has a history and origin that need not detain us here (see Callon, 1986; Latour, 1993; Law and Hassard, 1999) but it suggests both that wholly social relations are inconceivable – because all humans rely upon and work through non-human forms, through hybrids – and that humans distinguish themselves from animals, among other things, on the basis of the durability or obduracy of their relations. That is, they encase their social relations into material forms. This does not mean that material forms determine things, but that these material forms are an effect of the relations.

Does this imply anything about the link between hybridity and agency? We do not need to enter the debate about whether the future is destined to be dominated by robots or Cyborgs here (see Friedland, 2015; Geary, 2002; Haraway, 1991) to note the increasing degree of hybridity amongst 'people'. In actor–network terms, agency sits in the hybrids, rather than located within either the humans or the non-humans whose relationship forms the hybrid actant.

In 'essence', we might conclude that the search for an essence is irrelevant because the important element is the hybrid, not the elements that comprise the hybrid, nor any alleged network essence. If this is valid, then 'human' leaders should be reconsidering how they can strengthen the links in the hybrid networks, not because non-humans do not embody volition but because non-human leadership is as mythically pure as human leadership. And there lies the (essentially contested) rub – it is not the consciousness of leaders that makes them leaders or makes them effective, it is their hybridity: not how they think but how they are linked.

Result-Based Leadership

It might be more appropriate, however, to take the result-based approach, because whoever is leading and whatever the links, without results there is little support for leadership. There may be thousands of individuals who are 'potentially' great leaders, but if that potential is never realized, if no results of that leadership are forthcoming, then it would be logically difficult to speak of these people as 'leaders' – except in the sense of 'failed' or 'theoretical' leaders': people who actually achieve little or nothing. On the other hand, there is a tendency (e.g. Ulrich *et al.*, 1999) to focus on results as the primary criteria for leadership, but there are two other issues that need further examination here: first, how do we attribute the collective results of an organization to the actions of the individual leader? (Antonakis *et al.*, 2010). Second, assuming that we can causally link the two, do the methods by which the results are achieved play any role in determining the presence of leadership?

The first issue – that we can trace effects back to the actions of individual leaders – is deeply controversial. On the one hand, there are several studies from a psychological approach that suggest it is possible to measure the effect of leaders (e.g. Gerstner and Day, 1997), but more sociologically inclined authors often deny the validity of such measures (e.g. Alvesson and Sveningsson, 2003). A related controversy suggests that this dispute is itself deeply encased within most traditional approaches to leadership and implies that leaders embody agency. Lee and Brown (1994) suggest that to be human is to possess agency, but this, of course, begs the question of agency itself. Volition is the exercise of freewill or conscious choice, as opposed to determinism; hence, if human action is determined (by coercion, biological genes or technology or whatever) then the intentional element of leadership is removed and we may have a problem in determining individual responsibility. In effect, we may have results but no responsibility and therefore no leadership: thus the legal defence of those who regard themselves as acting under duress. In fact, taking this approach to its logical conclusion in the case of biologically inherited characteristics would be to suggest that those leaders with 'criminal genes' are not responsible for their leadership of criminal gangs, even if the results are significant in terms of people killed or money stolen and so on. And if we insist that action is determined by biological requirements over which individuals have no volitional control then we might even consider looking for the leadership gene that is making them act to some degree or other (De Neve *et al.*, 2013).

One could also argue that leadership can be linked to fatalism. For example, Nelson, Churchill, Hitler, Martin Luther King, Joan of Arc and General Patton, to name but a few, are all associated with significant achievements – for better or for worse – but all believed themselves to have been chosen by fate for a particular mission on earth. This fatalism induces enormous self-confidence and facilitates what others would regard as dangerous risk-taking. Yet this stymies our account of leadership – for now leadership is divorced from volition. In effect, if leaders believe themselves to have no choice and no freedom of action, because of a particular belief structure or threat, or religion or whatever, then no matter what we, the observers, might decide, these leaders experience their leadership as non-volitional, as determined by forces beyond their control. In such approaches the role of the leader is not necessarily to cause things to happen but to act as 'hero' when events work out advantageously and to act as 'scapegoat' when things go wrong (Grint, 2010). But might this not be regarded as a form of collective psychosis, a position which holds that we receive our instructions directly from a pure and unmediated source of truth (Lacan, 1997)? In good times, we are sure we have the right messenger; in bad times we can send that person to the proverbial insane asylum and look for the next source of truth.

Meindl *et al.* referred to this as the 'Romance of Leadership', in which followers and onlookers regularly sought – and discovered – 'leadership' when events were going very well or very badly but rarely experienced any leadership when events were relatively calm, mundane and unexceptional (1985; Meindl, 1995). So while Gemmill and Oakley (1997) conclude that leadership is probably just an 'alienating social myth' – an essentially contested concept if ever there was one – it might also be a convenient social myth.

This brings us to the second issue at the heart of result-based leadership – does the process by which the results are achieved actually matter? Most certainly, the office or school bully who successfully 'encourages' followers to comply under threat of punishment becomes a leader under the results-based criteria – providing they are successful in their coercion and its effects. But such a results-based approach to leadership immediately sets it at odds with some perspectives that differentiate leaders according to some putative distinction between leadership – which is allegedly non-coercive – and all other forms of activity that we might regard as the actions of a 'bully' or a 'tyrant' and so on. Northouse (1997: 7–8), for instance, examines 'leaders who use coercion [such as] . . . Adolf Hitler [and] Jim Jones'. But he then suggests that we should distinguish between coercion and leadership and thus writes a large proportion of human 'leadership' out of view by implying that 'Leaders who use coercion are interested in their own goals and seldom interested in the wants and needs of subordinates.' Yet, command, as a decision-style, seems to be entirely appropriate and legitimate in crisis conditions (Grint, 2005b, 2010). A review by Doh (2003) of six leading leadership scholars reflects this line and suggests that the use of 'unethical' methods negates the claim to 'leadership'. Since what counts as 'ethical' behaviour is not discussed, this leaves us stuck in the contestable ethical treacle: it could be argued that Hitler was unethical and therefore was not a leader, or it could be argued, as suggested above, that, since Hitler managed to align his followers' 'ethics' in line with his own, the issue is not the pursuit of some indefinable ethical position but the mutual alignment of what counts as 'ethics'. But, as we suggested above, not everyone accepts that the most important issue is the results rather the methods, so does focusing upon the position by which leadership is recognized offer a radically different perspective?

Position-Based Leadership

Perhaps the most traditional way of configuring leadership is to suggest that it is really concerned with a spatial position in an organization of some kind – formal or informal. Thus we can define leadership as the activity undertaken by someone whose position on a vertical, and usually formal, hierarchy provides them with the resources to lead. These are 'above us', 'at the top of the tree', 'superordinates' and so on. In effect, they exhibit what we might call 'leadership-in-charge'. This is how we normally perceive the heads of vertical hierarchies, whether CEOs or military generals or headteachers or their equivalents. These people lead from their positional control over large networks of subordinates and tend to drive any such required change from the top. That 'drive' also hints at the coercion that is available to those in charge: a general can order executions, a judge can imprison people and a CEO can discipline or sack employees and so on.

A related aspect of this vertical structuring is what appears to be the parallel structuring of power and responsibility. Since the leader is 'in charge', then presumably he or she can ensure the enactment of his or her will. But we should be wary of this parallel universe that irreversibly links a hierarchy of labels to a hierarchy of power, because there are good grounds for linking them both in obverse and in reverse. That is to say that the hierarchy of power simultaneously inverts the hierarchy of labels. While a formal leader may *demand* obedience from his or her subordinates – and normally acquire it because, inter alia, of the resource imbalance – that obedience is never guaranteed. In fact, following Lukes (1979), one could suggest that power encompasses a counterfactual possibility, a subjunctivist verb tense rather than just a verb – it could have been otherwise. Indeed, one could well argue that power is not just a cause of subordinate action but also a consequence of it: if subordinates do as leaders demand then, and only then, are leaders powerful.

The limitations of restricting leadership to a position within a vertical hierarchy are also exposed when we move to consider leadership-in-front, a horizontal approach, in which leadership is largely unrelated to vertical hierarchies and is usually informally constituted through a network or a heterarchy (a flexible and fluid hierarchy). Leadership-in-front might be manifest in several forms, and where it merges into leadership-in-charge might be at the penultimate rank at the bottom of a hierarchy. Indeed, the leadership abilities of low-level leaders may be critical in differentiating the success of armies, both in prior conflicts and in the current focus on 'strategic corporals' in the US Marine Corps (Krulak, 1999).

More commonly, though, we might conceive of leadership-in-front from a fashion leader – someone who is 'in front' of his or her followers, whether that is in trends in clothing, music, business models or whatever. Conversing frequently with undergraduate business students, in our experience this is their most commonly held assumption about leadership and is often embodied in technology and lifestyle business leaders such as Steve Jobs or Mark Zuckerberg. These leaders provide guides to the mass of fashion-followers without any formal authority over them. But leading from the front also encompasses those who guide others, either a professional guide showing the way or simply whoever knows the best way to an agreed destination among a group of friends on a Sunday stroll; both guides exhibit leadership through their role in front, but neither is necessarily formally instituted into an official hierarchy.

Leadership-in-front might also be provided in the sense of legitimizing otherwise prohibited behaviour. For instance, we might consider how Hitler's overt and public anti-Semitism legitimated the articulation of anti-Semitism by his followers. And again it has been suggested that acts such as suicide provide 'permission' by 'leaders-in-front' for others to follow, hence there are often spates of similar acts in quick succession almost as if the social behaviour operates as a biological epidemic (Gladwell, 2002).

Leadership along this positional dimension, then, differs according to the extent to which it is formally or informally structured, and vertically or horizontally constituted. Leadership-in-charge implies some degree of centralizing resources and authority, while leadership-in-front implies the opposite. But, with either position, doesn't the purpose mean more?

Purpose-Based Leadership

The purpose – or point – of leadership is an interesting approach and we are grateful to Kempster *et al.*'s (2011) article for alerting us to this lacuna in one of the author's original works (Grint, 2005a). Its origins might be said to lie in Plato's and Aristotle's teleological suggestions that differentiate between intrinsic purpose – what a thing is designed to do (for example Aristotle suggests an acorn's *telos* is to grow into an oak tree) – and extrinsic purpose – the aim that is ascribed to a thing (a pen is designed to write). Hegel's philosophy suggests that the purpose of humanity is to realize a perfect state – a model refracted in Marx's assumptions about the purpose of the proletariat. However, our 'purpose' here is to consider a leadership model in which the purpose is what differentiates leadership from any other activity. Thus it embodies the possibility that the results may be meagre but the purpose is more important: take Malala Yousafzai, for example, a Pakistani girl shot by the Taliban for promoting education among girls in October 2012. In terms of direct results manifest in an expansion of education for girls across the country, the results are indeed meagre. But in terms of the symbolic significance of her continued activism, the purpose crowds out the results. Moreover, the results approach is always limited by a subsequent temporal question: to misquote Chou en Lai on the significance of the French Revolution two centuries after the event: it is too early to tell the results of Malala's leadership (Yousafzai and Lamb, 2014).

Historically few leadership scholars have focused on purpose as the primary differentiator of leadership – though it forms the frame for much of the debate around transformational and transactional leadership (Burns, 1978) that is ironically one of the key developments in recent scholarship and underpins the work of Moore's (1997) Public Value initiative that sets the purpose of public services as a primary prerequisite for successful leadership.

The purpose of leadership also encompasses an overarching focus on the ethics of leadership. As we have already suggested, ethics are as contested as leadership but this does not mean that ethics are irrelevant. On the contrary, how leaders and followers grapple with the thorny issue of ethics seems to us to be critical. If complying absolutely with a set of absolute ethics was a pre-requisite for successful leadership, then few of us would achieve much in the world because it is precisely when the ethics we abide by do not actually provide clear guidance that we need to consider the role of leadership. This arena, where the black and white dichotomies of ethical guidance shade into grey, is the place where leadership is forged by those willing to engage in the world of leadership practice rather than leadership theory, or, in the words of Sartre (1989), the world of 'dirty hands'.

Process-Based Leadership

The final approach we want to consider is based on an assumption that people that we attribute the term leadership to act differently from non-leaders – that some people 'act like leaders' – but what does this mean? It could mean that the context is critical, or that leaders must be exemplary or that the attribution of difference starts early in the life of individuals, such that 'natural' leaders can be perceived in the school play grounds or on the sports field, etc. But what is this 'process' differential? So are leaders those that allegedly embody the exemplary performance we require to avoid any hint of hypocrisy? And when sacrifice is required or new forms of behaviour demanded from followers is it exemplary leaders that are the most successful?

Perhaps a counter-example is Admiral Nelson, an individual whose military successes were almost always grounded in a paradoxical situation in which he demanded absolute obedience from his subordinates to naval regulations but personally broke just about every rule in that same rulebook (Grabsky, 1993). Yet Nelson's success was not simply a consequence of rule-breaking actions but also a result of his engagement with, and motivation of, his followers, most importantly his fellow officers in his battle fleet, his 'Band of Brothers' (Kennedy, 2001). Hence, at one level this process approach may encompass the specific skills and resources that motivate followers: rhetoric, coercion, bribery, exemplary behaviour, bravery and so on. Leadership under this guise is necessarily a relational concept, not a possessional one. In other words, it does not matter whether you think you have great process skills if your followers disagree with you. Thus it may be that we can recognize leadership by the behavioural processes that differentiate leaders from followers, but this does not mean we can simply list the processes as universally valid across space and time. After all, we would not expect a second-century Roman leader to act in the same way as a twenty-first-century Italian politician, but neither would we expect an American Indian leader to act in a fashion indistinguishable from an American president (Warner, 2003). Yet it remains the case that most of our assumptions about leadership relate to our own cultural context rather than someone else's. In effect, the process approach to leadership is more concerned with how leadership works – the practices through which they lead – their rhetorical skill that entrances the followers, or their inducing of obedience through coercion or whatever happens to work. But is leadership just about securing consent or is dissent just as important?

Within many organizations, the perceived possession of power within the hierarchy is regarded as the principle foundation for leaders to coerce individuals into 'doing the work'. Employees may decide to consent *constructively* – believing it to be right, relevant and appropriate – or *destructively* – because the boss who knows best is telling them to do it, although it might be wrong or irrelevant or inappropriate. Subordinates who do disagree – dissenters – are often regarded as nothing more than 'disturbers of the peace' (Redding, 1985: 247). Despite Perrow (1979: 5–7, 114) identifying a bureaucratic organization as possibly having many advantages for subordinates and society as a whole, he also identifies the potential inefficiencies and ethnocentrism: terms such as 'teamwork', 'morale', 'loyalty' and 'cooperation' often work to inhibit acts of dissent, however constructive. So why do leaders not encourage dissent?

Historically, scholars have defined dissent along a negative trajectory (Graham, 1986; Hegstrom, 1995; Redding, 1985; Stewart, 1980; Westin, 1986), collectively implying that dissent demonstrates dissatisfaction with the status quo; it is a voicing of objections and therefore a form of protest, deemed essentially as confrontational. Those in more senior positions in many organizations are uncomfortable with dissenters, because being openly criticized and questioned about their decisions, policies, processes and strategies reveals that they are not perfect, and they therefore do not have all the answers, possibly revealing their weaknesses.

Other scholars suggest that dissent usually involves personal and principled morals (Dozier and Miceli, 1985; Sprague and Ruud, 1988) and is not always a protest or highly confrontational (Redding, 1985; Sprague and Ruud, 1988). Moreover, dissent can actually be useful, constructive and helpful (Grint, 2005a; Holt, 2015; Redding, 1985; Roberto, 2013), allowing subordinates a voice to enhance the organizational working environment (Sprague and Ruud, 1988) which can, in turn, potentially narrow 'the space between' (Uhl-Bien, 2012: xiv) the individual leaders and individual followers, building relationships alongside improving the organization's performance.

In tackling challenges and organizational change where strong collaboration is required, individuals in positions of leadership require relational interaction, which can be strengthened through appropriate dissent. Those undertaking leadership roles who do not give permission for appropriate dissent are at risk of silencing professional individuals who might have the answer, or part of the solution to improve the context being faced. The answer could already be within the organization, at the 'bottom of *this* box' (Holt, 2015; italics in original), but, without the encouragement of appropriate dissent, it could go unnoticed and ignored.

Silence in organizations may be associated with shyness and respect for others, or an individual's strategy of avoiding embarrassment and confrontation (Perlow and Williams, 2003). However, more commonly, the message – verbally or non-verbally – being delivered from the top usually involves 'if you don't make waves, keep quiet and do your job, you will keep your job and further your career'. These hierarchical responses to individuals expressing dissent only encourage organizations to fall into a pathological culture of blame (Eilerman, 2006; Westrum, 1993), where individuals cover things up – 'sweeping things under the carpet' – ignoring mistakes and resulting in destructive consent (Grint, 2005a).

An infamous example in which employees felt silenced is the Deepwater Horizon disaster on 20 April 2010, which was contracted and managed by BP plc. The culture of blame embedded in the organization caused employees to feel nervous about speaking up about safety issues, scenarios or mistakes in fear of being sanctioned or fired. BP was an organization under the previous leadership of John Browne, and then his protégé Tony Hayward, that appeared on the surface to be a world leader in deep-water oil exploration and production and hugely profitable; however, beneath the surface they were in fact 'drifting into failure' (Dekker, 2011: 4), not focusing on the most important 'p' – the people who actually made the production happen to make the huge profits. On taking up the position of chief executive in 2007, Tony Hayward insisted he was going to reform BP and focus on safety. However, nothing much changed (Sachs, 2012) with regards to the larger and more challenging issues being raised by dissenters, with only the easy part of safety being addressed: for example, hand rails, how to reverse park safely, lids on coffee cups – all visible, easy cheap fixes that were seen to be doing something. But BP was also at the forefront when it came to safety violations (Sachs, 2012), with BP answerable for 97 per cent of all wilful violations of worker safety in the oil industry between June 2007 and February 2010 (Reed and Fitzgerald, 2011: 134). During the investigations into the Deepwater Horizon rig, Henry Waxman led a United States House of Representative Energy and Commerce Committee that scoured over 30,000 BP documents identifying evidence of a variety of risks that had been raised by dissenters on the rig but that had been ignored – swept under the carpet. Waxman reported back to Hayward and the Board of BP, 'There is not a single email or document that shows you paid even the slightest attention to the dangers at the well. You cut corner after corner to save a million dollars here and a few hours there. And now the whole Gulf Coast is paying the price.'[1] In summary, Hayward, and Browne before him, and their senior executives became victims of their own hubris, believing they had all the answers and could not fail, therefore taking more and more extreme risks, and silencing their people into a culture of fear. This is a classic example of Prozac leadership (Collinson, 2012) that metaphorically symbolizes the process of excessive positivity and social addiction between followers and leaders. Collinson argues that it is taken for granted in organizations that leaders are the ones with all the answers, skills and abilities to make the better decisions and provide the answers. Followers, on the other hand, should be submissive and carry out orders, keep quiet and just do their jobs. When these over-positive characteristics are displayed in excess in an organization, there is a risk of a chasm between leader and follower, damaging relationships and therefore enhancing the five underlying principles to Prozac leadership:

- a leader's reluctance to acknowledge and address difficult situations, ignoring bad news, leaving no room for questioning or dissent from followers who could be the expert with the answer;
- if things do go wrong, the leaders are surprised – because they thought everything was going well – and therefore are not prepared;

- followers are discouraged from raising concerns, acknowledging mistakes or voicing opinion or debate;
- leaders who communicate positive narratives that are unrelated to the realities fuel a distrust amongst followers, damaging open communication and learning, encouraging suspicion and scepticism;
- a lack of open communication increases the lack of opportunities for lessons to be learned, with mistakes being repeated time and again, putting the organization at risk of failing.

The hidden costs of individuals feeling silenced and a lack of communication and inclusion in organizational decisions can run into billions of pounds/dollars/euros. BP is still paying fines and a compensation bill of over $70 billion dollars (and rising five years on). Beyond BP, a Gallup survey in 2013[2] found an average of only 13 per cent of the world's working population were actively engaged (fully committed to their role) in their work, costing organizations globally in the region of £52–70 billion per year in the United Kingdom. The issues of disengagement and lack of support for dissenters in organizations are interlinked. Kassing's (1997) work identifies the derivation of the word 'dissent' from the Latin word *dissentire*, with *dis* meaning apart and *sentire* meaning feeling. Therefore, its direct translation references the experience of 'feeling apart'. Within the context of an organization, dissent thus relates to an individual feeling apart from the organization, therefore disengaged. In the dictionary, dissent is explained with the use of synonyms such as disagree, dispute, conflict and nonconcur; however Kassing (1998: 312) suggests that the root meaning of the word as 'feeling apart' transcends the negative concept of conflict and rather suggests a duty to consider different strategies for individuals to express dissent so as to avoid disengagement. Therefore it could be argued that the part of the process to be adopted by leaders in organizations is to give employees permission to be constructive and active in their dissent strategies, to avoid the damaging, hidden costs of silence through destructive and passive dissent (Farrell and Rusbult, 1992).

However, if individuals feel as if they have no voice – no relationships – have a fear of being blamed if things go wrong or a fear of being made an example of, then their contributions become latent and hidden due to passivity: no dissent means a lack of ideas, and a disengaged group of individuals, feeling neglected and therefore resigned that they cannot make a difference. The voicing of dissent is a method allowing individuals to better understand each other (whether as a leader or a follower), the processes and the organization, and to explore actions and outcomes, while being respectful and empathetic.

There is a health warning to be respected with regards to dissent – dissent can be damaging if used inappropriately and not understood. Constant 'inappropriate' dissent has the potential to lead a collective or an organization towards anarchy, with some dissenters intentionally being disruptive. For dissent to be useful, active and constructive, individuals require encouragement to explain why they disagree, possibly along with potential direct 'facts' and potential solutions.

To better understand the effective and ineffective uses of dissent, Kassing's employee dissent model (1997, 1998, 2002, 2005), and work by Redding (1985) and Roberto (2013) in the area of communication studies, have been considered and applied to leadership as a process in The Hill of Upward Dissent (Figure 1.1; Holt, 2015). It is a heuristic model for understanding the role of dissent and how it can facilitate leaders and followers during times of challenge, using a horizontal axis of active and passive and a vertical axis of destructive and constructive to capture the different aspects of dissent. The model demonstrates the different aspects of candour for effective dissent being at the 'top of the hill', with individuals in positions of authority working to encourage these constructive/active attitudes of dissent amongst a collective of subordinates.

Successful leaders that build relationships and support individuals in constructive dissent avoid the organization as a whole 'slipping down the hill' and becoming antagonistic, passive, resisting and resigning from their responsibilities.

Employee dissent is always and will always be present within organizations of all types (Holt, 2015; Kassing, 1997), and so therefore requires the leadership to appreciate the values and objectives of individuals (Tompkins and Chencey, 1985) and the desire of individuals to share opinions and ideas, even when contradictory or challenging (Gorden and Infante, 1987) – what Hirschman (1970) calls 'voice' – in order to avoid what he calls 'exit'. The 'loyalty' of the individual is a moderating variable that influences whether that person stays because they have a voice and feel engaged and included, or they exit (mentally or physically) because they feel silenced, neglected and disengaged (Hirschman, 1970).

The encouragement of active/constructive dissent within the leadership context provides a supportive atmosphere, allowing all involved an opportunity to reflect on the truth of a challenge, consider a wider array of ideas and ensure all voices have an opportunity to be heard through open and more developed relationships – narrowing the space between leaders and followers.

But perhaps there is a more radical take on leadership that goes beyond the problem of dissent and suggests that leadership just acts as a convenient word to explain what appears inexplicable?

Fantasy Leadership: To Fill the Empty Vessel or Find a New Vessel?

Fifty years ago, W. B. Gallie (1955–56) called power an Essentially Contested Concept (ECC) and suggested that many such concepts involved 'endless disputes about their proper uses on the part of the users' to the point where debates appeared irresolvable. For Gallie:

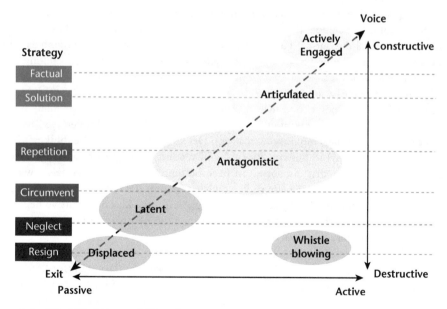

Figure 1.1   The Hill of Upward Dissent

Source: Original, based on the work of: Farrell and Rusbult, 1992; Gorden and Infante, 1987; Grint, 2005a; Hirschman, 1970; Kassing, 1997, 2002 and Perrow, 1979.

> Recognition of a given concept as essentially contested implies recognition of rival uses of it (such as oneself repudiates) as not only logically possible and humanly 'likely', but as of permanent potential critical value to one's own use or interpretation of the concept in question.
>
> *(1964: 187–188)*

Examples of ECCs are multiple, as are the attempts to resolve the contestation: Strine *et al.* (1990) consider performance as an ECC; Kellow (2002) applies it to sustainable development; Bajpai (1999) uses it to analyse security; Cohen (2002) takes civil society as an ECC; and, finally, terrorism is the subject of Smelser and Mitchell's (2002) application of an ECC.

The problem of evaluating leadership is exemplified by Jack Welch: was he 'the best' business leader of the 1990s because GE under his 'leadership' made more money than any other company, or would GE have been this successful anyway and did his methods unnecessarily destroy hundreds of careers? We could equally argue that Sir Peter Bonfield, ex-CEO of BT, was 'the best' because, despite losing over £30 billion, he saved BT from bankruptcy. In other words, it is always possible to devise a way of measuring 'successful leadership', but the measures may not generate a consensus because they are neither objective nor do we all agree on the way to measure success. Our definitions and interpretations of leadership are ECCs.

The case we want to make as the chapter draws to a close is that leadership may actually hold no meaning and *because of this* positively overflows with meaning. Leadership is a great example of what is known in linguistics as a floating signifier, a signifier that in and of itself means very little, or nothing at all, but acts as a form of discursive relay that holds together all kinds of other chains of association (Žižek, 2009).

In this sense, leadership is not even a discourse. A discourse implies a particular form of socio-political meaning expressed via talk and text (Zoller and Fairhurst, 2007). Instead, we invite you to think of leadership metaphorically as a point of stitching in a quilt, the point at which the threads come together, are quilted into one another. Transposed to language, one can think of the quilting operation as potentially weaving together all kinds of different ideological and organizational discourses. This is what fascinated Lacan about floating signifiers – their potential to act as quilting points (or a *point de capiton*, in Lacanese). For Lacan, quilting points played a vital role in any analytical operation, 'this point around which all concrete analysis of discourse must operate' (Lacan, 1997: 267).

Viewed as a quilting point, one may therefore think of 'leadership' (as signifier) holding together regimes of discursive meaning. Laclau (2014) and Laclau and Mouffe (1985) conceptualized these regimes as hegemonic constellations. Drawing on something we think of as quite rigid and fixed (hegemony) in this context is playful yet also salient. What Laclau and Mouffe are conveying is this idea that discourse can become quite stable but nevertheless what we come to think of as stable meaning also shifts slowly over time, and indeed has the potential to explode quite suddenly and radically alter in meaning. Hence the idea of discursive hegemony encapsulates a certain healthy dose of realism concerning the obstinacy of power and yet also incorporates the possibility of radical change.

Leadership is a salient example of a discursive hegemonic constellation. Associated with 'great' traits for so long, the Second World War acted as a kind of disruption for 'leadership'. Previously attached to strong organization and the capacity of individuals to motivate, leadership was now also associated with a chain of 'dark side' associations (Tourish and Pinnington, 2002) – charisma, obedience, worship, manipulation, genocide. In fact one could make a case that leadership enjoyed the dubious distinction of being synonymous with many of the horrors perpetuated within the twentieth century, a period that even by human standards can be thought of as particularly violent (Eagleton, 2011).

It is only relatively recently, and in parallel with the rise in consumerist capitalism and neo-liberal investment in the idea of individuals as autonomous, entrepreneurial subjects, that leadership has enjoyed a reinvention of sorts. In mass market business publications, leadership is now a signifier closely linked with capitalist ideology; the notion is that, if individuals invest in their personal leadership capital, then they will be able to 'transform' their environments, through a range of 'hard' and 'soft' techniques and behaviours (Tomlinson *et al.*, 2013). 'Leadership' might of course imply a different set of associations – in socialism, social democracy or even some form of hegemonic–ideological constellation yet to be imagined.

What differentiates leadership from other organising signifiers, such as management, is its libidinal charge. In other words, the very fact that leadership is so empty as a signifier should act as a clue that it is throbbing and overflowing with (eroticized) meaning. It is a signifier that acts as a receptacle for fantasy, in other words. By now the idea that leadership is a signifier attached to fantasizing is well established. Ford and Harding (2007) and Ford *et al.* (2008), for example, in their study of leadership development programmes, discovered that participants entered development (discursively) stuffed full of heroic and libidinally charged notions of leadership and what it means to be a leader. But of course we do not need academic studies to prove the point, only a very cursory engagement with our own personal and cultural identifications. *Star Wars*, Clint Eastwood, John Wayne, *Lord of the Rings*: we are socialized into consuming images and narratives of heroism–leadership in a way we are not with management. *Lord of the Rings* re-written as a tale of a competent manager designing an efficient and lean transportation system to dispose of a ring of untold power, outsmarting the 'dark' and charismatic, but hopelessly disorganized leadership of Sauron (everyone knows you don't centralize your operations in just Mordor and Isengard – you outsource!) would not make for as intriguing a plotline, perhaps.

It is unlikely that most organizations feature many examples of truly inspirational or heroic acts, but this signifier 'leadership' does allow for fantasies of heroism to be attributed to otherwise fairly decent but mundane people and acts (Alvesson and Sveningsson, 2003).

Returning to Lacan, we might conceptualize fantasy as the narratives and images subjects construct in order to paper over the cracks present in the symbolic fabric of language itself (Lacan, 1966–67). As human beings we have no choice but to be socialized into the world of language, as it is language that governs our basic human relations. And yet language is a flawed concept, incapable of expressing the totality of human feelings or experiences (Driver, 2009). Ultimately, language is always someone else's language, someone else's design. Subjectively, something always escapes language. And for Lacan, this little something is the range and complexity of human desire. Language, via fantasy, can misdirect desire but it can never capture or satisfy desire. That is why fantasies tend to leave subjects slightly dissatisfied – they push us to the edges of the satisfactoriness of language but never deliver completion.

For Lacanians, our contemporary, post-modern universe is one marked by an entreaty to enjoy – consuming the next product, fashion or even social relation that might answer a certain calling of desire (Böhm and Batta, 2010). In leadership terms, the explosion of lists, recipes, pseudo-theories and even human totems of leadership (Jack Welch, Bill Gates, Steve Jobs, Barack Obama and so on) can be explained by the subject's propensity to move from one symbolic fantasy to the next: each one promising, but ultimately failing, to produce satisfaction (Driver, 2013).

We can go further than positing a theory of fantasy in relation to leadership, however, and explore the symbolic content of contemporary leadership fantasy. So when the contemporary capitalist subject dreams of leadership, what is evoked? What springs to mind is the figure of the smart (but not intellectual), health-conscious and 'ethically aware' entre- or intrapreneur, someone fine-tuned in training terms, drawing upon a range of tools and techniques to modify and make more efficient the system, but never to challenge the system itself (Žižek, 2013). Or, in more technical terms, a figure of diluted libidinal appeal: charismatic, but not too much; 'transformational', but not radically so; 'authentic', but only if such authenticity matches norms of liberal–capitalist ethics; collaborative, but only within present ideological–political structures; 'caring', but always informed by the profit motive, and never 'naïve'; committed to policies of equal opportunity, but not the systemic challenging of structures of subordination and oppression.

Perhaps the answer, then, to whether leadership is a matter of person, result, position, purpose or process is that it is all and none of the above. Leadership is whatever a group of subjects makes of it within the symbolic fabric. Such a mobilization of discourse is, of course, very real, holds real material consequences, as well as being rooted in a conception of subjective experience that does nothing other than circling a real – albeit a real that will remain always unattainable. The proper ethical (and professional) stance of the leadership researcher can thus be described in the following terms: studying leadership is deeply flawed at best, problematic and unethical at worst; studying 'leadership' might provide some important insight into the power relations and identifications of organizational and social subjects. In other words, following the fantasy of 'leadership' might be fruitful indeed. To adopt such a research strategy does not mean to belittle the research subject – we are all fantasizing subjects – but to respect the subjectivity of the research subject: to embrace the contradictions and complexities of the enunciating subject, following the discourse and discursive positioning of the subject and respecting this talk in and of itself (Lacan, 1997).

And yet many of us are not solely leadership researchers but also activists and campaigners, at least in our private lives. Some do not accept that division between professional academic pursuit and private activism, seeking to develop a form of socially engaged, critical–academic praxis, putting theoretical insights to use in influencing the world around us (see Grint and Jackson, 2010; Spicer *et al.*, 2009). For these scholars, analysing a discourse, such as leadership, may be one important aspect of scholarly–public life but is also in isolation an unsatisfactory one. Yet how can it be possible to overcome the trap of fantasy: of obfuscating or romanticizing mundane, or even oppressive practice?

One solution might be to dispense with leadership entirely and instead try to deconstruct the fantasy, refusing the shorthand and being incredibly precise and descriptive about what we mean by the term. One might unpack leadership as standing for a range of other signifiers – a certain, explicitly defined conception of ethics; efficient organising; rhetorical flourish; the seeking of new collaborative partnerships; conscientious yet decisive decision-making; conflictual but salient conversation. And so on . . . When leadership is unpacked in this way, it raises the question of whether leadership is needed at all. Wouldn't we inhabit more transparent and accountable organisations were these (and other) organisational and social constructs not poorly expressed, or concealed entirely, under a single signifier?

Another (counter-intuitive) solution might be to return to a person-led conception of leadership, albeit not in the sense of mapping traits and so on. Perhaps one consequence of viewing leadership as a fantastical signifying vessel is to hold people to account for their fantasies, for their desires. Fantasies need not be viewed in the old Marxist sense of false consciousness, as somehow inhibiting access to truth. The central Lacanian lesson is that absolute truth is inaccessible to mere mortals, who will only ever be able to traverse the fantasy, to encircle the real. As Driver (2013) and McGowan (2013) have stated, the realm of fantasy holds great emancipatory, as well as oppressive, potential. Fantasies point to a certain limit in the way in which subjects experience the impersonal and banal of symbolic law: the rules, the norms and mundane control mechanisms that influence their lives (through language). Read in this sense, fantasies do in fact point to both the limits and possibilities of person, result, position, purpose or process in 'leadership', and might signal the possibility of the creation of a new, more accountable leadership.

People do of course act in conformity with their desires and break the constraints of the (symbolically) possible – otherwise, meaningful social change of any sort would likely be impossible, rather than simply a rarity. Bearing this in mind, it is perhaps pertinent that one of the most important, if controversial, philosophers of our time, Slavoj Žižek, has made an impassioned plea for a return of the strong leader in social and political life (Žižek, 2014). The role of the leader, for Žižek, is akin to that of the psychoanalyst in relation to the analysand. Helping the analysand (or followers) make visible the limits and contingency of the present symbolic structures of their lives becomes the core purpose. Such a conception of leading differs of course from a standard transformational/charismatic leadership identity, as the other key act of the analyst is to lead the analysand to a position where he/she sees that the analyst him/herself is a lacking construct, another fantasy. The job of the leader, in other words, is to nullify the need for a leader at all – or at least for a dominant leader-figure. Such a view of leadership bears close resemblance to the role envisaged for leader-figures in Grint's (2005b) and Heifetz's (1994) conception of leadership as a process of negotiating the meaning, importance and potential solutions for intractable problems. These positions ask that the subject breaks from symbolic convention and thinks the unconventional, even the impossible.

Refocusing on the person in leadership, in other words, means that subjects are held accountable – they take responsibility for their own desires and their own discourse as captured in this signifier of leadership. Drawing attention back to the leader-subject (and follower-subject) means a deliberate and conscientious adoption and acceptance of the subjective position: we may never be able to fulfil our desires but we can take responsibility for following and paying heed to our desires. It may be an inevitable consequence of any floating signifier that it becomes filled in with meaning but at least refocusing on the subject(s) means that we become more reflexively aware of why and what is represented by our leadership.

Notes

1 Broder, J. M. and Calmes, J. (2010). 'Chief of BP, contrite, gets a scolding by Congress', *International Herald Times,* 18 June 2010.
2 Gallup report, *State of the Global Workplace Report* (2013),

References

Alvesson, M. and Sveningsson, S. (2003). 'Managers Doing Leadership: The Extra-Ordinarization of the Mundane', *Human Relations*, 56 (12): 1435–1459.

Antonakis, J., Bendahan, S., Jacquart, P. and Laliv, R. (2010). 'On Making Causal Claims: A Review and Recommendations', *The Leadership Quarterly*, 21 (6): 1086–1120.

Böhm, S. and Batta, A. (2010). 'Just Doing It: Enjoying Commodity Fetishism with Lacan', *Organization*, 17 (3): 345–361.

Brooks, R. A. (2002). *Robot*. London: Allen Lane.

Burns, J. M. (1978). *Leadership*. New York: Harper & Row.

Callon, M. (1986). 'The Sociology of an Actor Network'. In M. Callon, J. Law and A. Rip, (eds.), *Mapping the Dynamics of Science And Technology*. London: Macmillan.

Cohen, J. L. (2002). 'Civil Society in Modern Social and Political Philosophy', ca.geocities.com/jazzchul 2000/ glossary/civil_society.htm.

Collinson, D. (2012). 'Prozac Leadership and the Limits of Positive Thinking', *Leadership*, 8 (2): 87–107.

De Neve, J.-E., Mikhaylov, S., Dawes, C., Christakis, N. and Fowler, J. (2013). 'Born to Lead? A Twin Design and Genetic Association Study of Leadership Role Occupancy', *Leadership Quarterly*, 24 (1): 45–60.

Dekker, S. (2011). *Drift into Failure: From Hunting Broken Components to Understanding Complex Systems.* Farnham, Surrey: Ashgate.

Doh, J. P. (2003). 'Can Leadership be Taught? Perspectives From Management Educators', *Academy of Management Learning and Education*, 2 (1): 54–57.

Dozier, J. B. and Miceli, M. P. (1985). 'Potential Predictors of Whistle-Blowing: A Prosocial Behavior Perspective', *Academy of Management Review*, 10: 823–836.

Driver, M. (2009). 'Struggling with Lack: A Lacanian Perspective on Organizational Identity', *Organization Studies*, 30 (1): 55–72.

Driver, M. (2013). 'The Lack of Power or the Power of Lack in Leadership as a Discursively Constructed Identity', *Organization Studies*, 34 (3): 407–422.

Eagleton, T. (2011). *On Evil.* New Haven, CT: Yale University Press.

Eilerman, D. (2006). *Conflict: Cost and Opportunity*, www.mediate.com.

Farrell, D. and Rusbult, C. E. 1992. 'Exploring the Exit, Voice, Loyalty and Neglect Typology: The Influence of Job Satisfaction, Quality of Alternatives and Investment Size', *Employee Responsibilities and Rights Journal*, 4: 283–299.

Ford, J. and Harding, N. (2007). 'Move over Management: We Are All Leaders Now?', *Management Learning*, 38 (5): 475–493.

Ford, J., Harding, N. and Learmonth, M. (2008). *Leadership as Identity: Constructions and Deconstructions.* Basingstoke, Hampshire: Palgrave Macmillan.

Friedland, B. (2015). *Leadership and the Role of Computational Objects.* (Warwick University).

Gallie, W. B. (1955–56). 'Essentially Contested Concepts', *Proceedings of the Aristotelian Society*, 56: 167–198.

Gallie, W. B. (1964). *Philosophy and the Historical Understanding.* London: Chatto and Windus.

Geary, J. (2002). *The Body Electric.* London: Weidenfeld and Nicolson.

Gemmill, G. and Oakley, J. (1997). 'Leadership: An Alienating Social Myth?' In K. Grint (ed.), *Leadership.* Oxford: Oxford University Press.

Gerstner, C. R. and Day, D. V. (1997). 'Meta-Analytic Review of Leader–Member Exchange Theory: Correlates and Construct Issues', *Journal of Applied Psychology*, 82 (6): 827–844.

Gladwell, M. (2002). *The Tipping Point.* London: Abacus.

Gordon, W. I. and Infante, D. A. (1987). 'Employee Rights: Content, Argumentativeness, Verbal Aggressiveness and Career Satisfaction'. In C. A. B. Osigwch (ed.), *Communicating Employee Responsibilities and Rights: A Modern Management Mandate.* Westport, CT: Greenwood Press.

Grabsky, P. (1993). *The Great Commanders.* London: Boxtree.

Graham, J. W. (1986). 'Principled Organizational Dissent: A Theoretical Essay'. In B. M. Staw and L. L. Cummings (eds.), *Research in Organizational Behaviour.* Greenwich, CT: JAI Press.

Grint, K. (1998). *The Sociology of Work.* Chichester: Wiley.

Grint, K. (2005a). *Leadership: Limits and Possibilities.* Basingstoke: Palgrave Macmillan.

Grint, K. (2005b). 'Problems, Problems, Problems: The Social Construction of "Leadership"', *Human Relations*, 58 (11): 1467–1494.

Grint, K. (2010). 'Leadership and the Sacred', *Organization Studies*, 31 (1): 89–107.

Grint, K. and Jackson, B. (2010). 'Towards "Socially Constructive" Social Constructions of Leadership', *Management Communication Quarterly*, 24 (2): 348–355.

Gronn, P. (2003). *The New Work of Educational Leaders.* London: Sage.

Haraway, D. (1991). *Simians, Cyborgs and Women.* New York: Routledge.

Heifetz, R. (1994). *Leadership Without Easy Answers.* Cambridge, MA: Harvard University Press.

Hegstrom, T. G. (1995). 'Focus on Organizational Dissent: A Functionalist Response to Criticism'. In J. Lehtonen (ed.), *Critical Perspective on Communication Research and Pedagogy.* St. Ingbert, Germany: Rohrig University Press.

Hirschman, A. O. (1970). *Exit, Voice, and Loyalty: Responses to Decline in Firms, Organizations and States.* Cambridge, MA: Harvard University Press.

Holt, C. A. (2015). *Moving Beyond the Collective: A Ganzian Analysis of Leader/Follower Relationships in Times of Challenge.* Doctoral Thesis, Warwick University.

Hughes, R. L., Ginnett, R. G. and Curphy, G. J. 1999. *Leadership: Enhancing the Lessons of Experience.* London: McGraw-Hill.

Kassing, J. W. (1997). 'Articulating, Antagonizing, and Displacing: A Model of Employee Dissent', *Communication Studies*, 48: 311–332.

Kassing, J. W. (1998). 'Development and Validation of the Organizational Dissent Scale', *Management Communication Quarterly*, 12 (2): 183–229.

Kassing, J. W. (2002). 'Speaking Up: Identifying Employees' Upward Dissent Strategies', *Management Communication Quarterly*, 16: 187–209.

Kassing, J. W. (2005). 'Speaking up Competently: A Comparison of Perceived Competence in Upward Dissent Strategies', *Communication Research Reports*, 22 (3): 227–234.

Kellow, A. (2002). 'Social Aspects of Sustainability', *Australian Academy of Science Symposium Proceedings: Transition To Sustainability*. Canberra, 3 May 2002.

Kempster, S., Jackson, B. and Conroy, M. (2011). 'Leadership as Purpose: Exploring the Role of Purpose in Leadership Practice', *Leadership*, 7 (3): 317–334.

Kennedy, L. (2001). *Nelson and His Captains*. London: Penguin.

Krulak, C. C. (1999). 'The Strategic Corporal and the Three-Block War', *Marine Corps Gazette*, 83 (1): 18–22.

Lacan, J. (1966–1967) *The Logic of Phantasy: The Seminar of Jacques Lacan Book XIV*. Unedited transcript, translated by Cormac Gallagher.

Lacan, J. (1997). *The Psychoses (1955–1956): The Seminar of Jacques Lacan Book III*. London: Norton.

Laclau, E. (2014). *The Rhetorical Foundations of Society*. London: Verso.

Laclau, E. and Mouffe, C. (1985). *Hegemony and Socialist Strategy: Towards a Radical Democratic Politics*. London: Verso.

Latour, B. (1988). 'The Prince for Machines as Well as Machinations'. In B. Elliot (ed.), *Technology And Social Process*. Edinburgh: Edinburgh University Press.

Latour, B. (1993). *We Have Never Been Modern*. Hemel Hempstead: Harvester/ Wheatsheaf.

Law, J. and Hassard, J. (eds) (1999). *Actor-Network Theory and After*. Oxford: Blackwell.

Lee, N. and Brown, S. (1994). 'Otherness and the Actor Network: The Undiscovered Continent', *American Behavioral Scientist*, 37 (6): 772–790.

Lukes, S. (1979). 'Power and Authority'. In T. Bottomore and R. Nisbet (eds.), *History of Sociological Analysis*. London: Heinemann.

McGowan, T. (2013). *Enjoying What We Don't Have: The Political Project of Psychoanalysis*. Lincoln, NE: University of Nebraska Press.

Meindl, J. R. (1995) 'The Romance of Leadership as a Follower-Centric Theory: a Social Constructionist Approach', *Leadership Quarterly*, 6 (3): 329–341.

Meindl, J. R., Ehrlich, S. B. and Dukerich, J. M. (1985). 'The Romance of Leadership', *Administrative Science Quarterly*, 30: 78–102.

Moore, M. (1997). *Creating Public Value: Strategic Management in Government*. Harvard, CT: Harvard University Press.

Northouse, P.G. (1997). *Leadership*. London: Sage.

Perlow, L. and Williams, S. (2003). 'Is Silence Killing Your Company?' *Harvard Business Review*, May.

Perrow, C. (1979). *Complex Organizations: A Critical Essay* (2nd ed.). Glenview, IL: Scott Foresman.

Redding, C. W. (1985). 'Rocking Boats, Blowing Whistles, and Teaching Speech Communication', *Communication in Education*, 34 (3): 245–258.

Reed, S. and Fitzgerald, A. (2011). *In Too Deep: BP and the Drilling Race That Took It Down*. Hoboken, NJ: J. Wiley and Sons.

Ridderstrale, J. (2002). 'Devising Strategies to Prevent the Flight of Talent', *Financial Times*. 27 August 2002.

Roberto, M. A. (2013). *Managing Conflict and Consensus: Why Great Leaders Don't Take Yes for an Answer* (2nd ed.). Concordville, PA: Soundview Executive.

Sachs, J. (2012). *Winning the Story Wars: Why Those Who Tell – and Live – the Best Stories Will Rule the Future*. Boston, MA: Harvard Business Review Press.

Sartre, J. P. (1989). *Dirty Hands*. London: Vintage Books.

Smelser, N. J. and Mitchell, F. (eds.) (2002). *Terrorism*. Washington, DC: National Academies Press.

Spicer, A., Alvesson, M. and Kärreman, D. (2009). 'Critical Performativity: The Unfinished Business of Critical Management Studies', *Human Relations*, 62 (4): 537–560.

Sprague, J. A. and Rudd, G. I. (1988). 'Boat-Rocking in the High Technology Culture', *American Behavioral Scientist*, 32: 169–193.

Stewart, L. P. (1980). '"Whistleblowing": Implications for Organizational Communication', *Journal of Communication*, 30 (4): 90–101.

Strine, M. S., Long, B. W. and Hopkins, M. F. (1990). 'Research in Interpretation and Performance Studies'. In G. M. Phillips and J. T. Wood (eds.), *Speech Communication*. Carbondale, IL: Southern Illinois University Press.

Tomlinson, M., O'Reilly, D. and Wallace, M. (2013). 'Developing Leaders as Symbolic Violence: Reproducing Public Service Leadership through the (Misrecognized) Development of Leaders' Capitals', *Management Learning*, 44 (1): 81–97.

Tompkins, P. K. and Cheney, G. (1985). 'Communication and Unobtrusive Control in Contemporary Organizations'. In R. D. McPhee and P. K. Tompkins (eds.), *Organizational Communication: Traditional Themes and New Directions*, Beverly Hills, CA: Sage.

Tourish, D. and Pinnington, A. (2002). 'Transformational Leadership, Corporate Cultism and the Spirituality Paradigm: An Unholy Trinity in the Workplace?', *Human Relations*, 55 (2): 147–172.

Uhl-Bien, M. (2012). 'Foreword'. In M. Uhl-Bien and S. M. Ospina (eds.), *Advancing Relational Leadership Research: A Dialogue among Perspectives*. Charlotte, NC: Information Age Publishing.

Ulrich, D., Zenger, J. and Smallwood, N. (1999). *Results-Based Leadership*. Cambridge, MA: Harvard Business School Press.

Warner, L. S. (2003). 'American Indian Leadership'. In D. Collinson and K. Grint (eds.), *New Directions in Leadership Research*. Oxford: Oxford University Press.

Westin, A. F. (1986). 'Professional and Ethical Dissent: Individual, Corporate and Social Responsibility', *Technology in Society*, 8: 335–339.

Westrum, R. (1993). 'Cultures with Requisite Imagination'. In J. A. Wise, V. D. Hopkin and P. Stager (eds.), *Verification and Validation of Complex Systems: Human Factors Issues*. Berlin: Springer-Verlag.

Wofford, J. C. (1999). 'Laboratory Research on Charismatic Leadership', *Leadership Quarterly*, 10 (4): 523–529.

Wright, P. (1996). *Managerial Leadership*. London: Routledge.

Yousafzai, M. and Lamb, C. (2014). *I Am Malala: The Girl Who Stood Up for Education and Was Shot by the Taliban*. London: W&N.

Yukl, G. (1998). *Leadership in Organizations* (4th ed.). London: Prentice Hall.

Žižek, S. (2009). *The Sublime Object of Ideology*. London: Verso.

Žižek, S. (2013). *Demanding the Impossible*. Cambridge: Polity Press.

Žižek, S. (2014). *Trouble in Paradise: From the End of History to the End of Capitalism*. London: Penguin.

Zoller, H. and Fairhurst, G. (2007). 'Resistance Leadership: The Overlooked Potential in Critical Organization and Leadership Studies', *Human Relations*, 60 (9): 1331–1360.

2

Recognizing and Realizing the Market Value of Leadership

Dave Ulrich and Justin Allen

When two disciplines collide, bad or good things can happen. Bad things happen when the collision fragments two disciplines into even more disparate parts. Good things happen when discipline collisions inform and advance each discipline.

The intersection of studies of leadership and firm valuation has the potential to benefit each discipline. Leadership has been one of the most studied topics of social sciences. Google "leader" and discover that there are hundreds of millions of hits; Amazon has hundreds of thousands of books about leaders. While there are some wonderful summaries of the leadership field (Bass, 1990; Bass and Bass, 2008; Norita and Khurana, 2010), the dominant question should be "What makes effective leadership?"

In recent years, investors have learned that defining the market value of a firm may be based on earnings, but goes beyond. For decades, the standards set by the Generally Accepted Accounting Principles (GAAP) and the Financial Accounting Standards Board (FASB) have required financial reporting of earnings, cash flow, and profitability. Recently these financial outcomes have been found to predict about 50 percent of a firm's market value. Investors have shown increased interest in intangibles such as strategy, brand, R&D, innovation, risk, and information flow. These intangibles predict firm profitability. A next step for investors is to analyze the predictors and drivers of intangibles, which shifts to investors recognizing and realizing the market value of leadership. Wise, long-term investors recognize that leadership matters. In our research, we found that investors allocate about 30 percent of their decision making on the quality of leadership. Quality of leadership becomes a predictor of intangible value, which in turn produces financial results.

This chapter shows the value of integrating leadership and firm valuation disciplines by reviewing the evolution of the study of leadership, reviewing the evolution of firm valuation, and offering a proposed approach to evaluating the market value of leadership.

Reviewing Evolution of the Study of Leadership: From Inside Oneself (Personal Style) to Others (Organization Impact) to the External Stakeholders (Investor Value)

It is impossible to synthesize the study of leadership in a few words. In our work, we found that the answer to what makes effective leadership has evolved over time, each new stage building at least in part on its predecessors (Ulrich and Smallwood, 2012). A brief history of modern attempts to understand leadership may be organized around looking inside by leading oneself, looking to others by leading in the organization, and looking outside by creating value to external stakeholders.

Looking Inside by Leading Oneself: Leaders Are Effective because of Who They Are

Early leadership theorists tried to identify a core set of demographic traits according to height, gender, heritage, and speaking style for what characterized an effective leader. They also tried to identify personality traits and backgrounds that made leaders more effective. All to no avail. Successful leaders could have a variety of backgrounds as well as physical and personality traits. The only trait that seemed to consistently differentiate better leaders was that leaders were somewhat (not too much) smarter than their followers (Zaccaro, 2007; Hoffman et al., 2011). Traits eventually combined to form a leadership style, often a trade-off between people and task. Generally, leaders exhibited a preferred style, but the best leaders could be both soft and hard, caring about people and managing tasks. Leaders were given numbers (1–9; 9–1; 9–9) to capture their tendency to care about people or tasks (Blake and Mouton, 1964).

Current evolution of defining effective leadership by looking inside a leader has focused on the core competencies, or knowledge, skills, and values of successful leaders (Boyatzis, 1982; Spencer and Spencer, 1993). Competencies were identified by what leaders said and did and were often tailored not only to the situation but to the business strategy. The world is awash in competency models. We synthesized this competency-based work into what we call the Leadership Code and suggested that leaders master five competency domains to be effective. While many leadership theorists and advisors emphasize one competency area (e.g., authenticity/ emotional intelligence, strategy, execution, talent management, or human capital development), we found that effective leaders master all five competency domains to be effective. Each of these personal approaches to leadership primarily focuses on helping leaders become more attuned to who they are and who they can become to be effective.

Looking to Others by Leading in the Organization: Leaders Are Effective because of the Strategy They Deliver and Organization They Create

Leadership theorists recognized that looking inside the leader was not enough to define effective leadership. Leaders also had to deliver results according to the situation or task at hand. Part of this effort was to determine which leadership approaches worked in which situations. In contingency or situational leadership, effective leadership depends on the requirements of the situation. Situations may vary by maturity of team members, complexity of tasks at hand, time horizon for doing the work, or uncertainty in predicting outcomes of the work. Particular leadership styles worked better in some situations than others (Fiedler, 1964; Hersey and Blanchard, 1969; Vroom and Jago, 1995).

The other part of looking to others is that leadership effectiveness is less about a personality trait and more about how leaders help make organizations more effective. Leaders may drive organization effectiveness through employees, organization cultures, or financial performance (Kaiser et al., 2008). The impact of leadership on employee performance has been studied extensively (Burgoyne et al., 2004). Leaders' actions shape employee affect at work, which may show up as satisfaction, commitment, engagement, or some other positive affect. Literally thousands of studies have shown that leaders drive employee response to work

(Fleck and Inceoglu, 2010; Welbourne and Schlater, 2014; Rucci et al., 1988). Leaders create strategies that differentiate their firms for long-term success (Rowe, 2001). Leaders also shape an organization's culture, or identity. Culture has been represented as the values, norms, beliefs, and unwritten rules of an organization. A culture often takes on the personality of the leader (Schein, 2010; Dennison et al., 2012). Leaders create culture through managing people, performance, information, and work practices (Ulrich and Brockbank, 2006). Culture in turn drives financial performance (Kotter and Heskett, 2011).

Leaders drive financial performance within a firm. Studies also show that leadership competencies affect business performance. Many studies have shown that leadership has about 12 to 14 percent impact on firm performance (Lieberson and O'Conner, 1972; Weiner, 1978; Thomas, 1988; Wasserman et al. 2001; Mackey, 2005).[1] Many cases can be found in which strategic leaders help make choices that better position their organizations for success (Ireland and Hitt, 1999; Rowe, 2001). For example, in her research, Alison Mackey wanted to find out how much CEOs affected firm performance. She looked at 51 firms over 10 years with 92 CEOs. She was able to show that the CEO affected 29.2 percent variance in firm performance, which was higher than corporate affect (7.9 percent) and five times higher than industry affect. In particular, in smaller and faster growing firms, CEOs have more effect (Mackey, 2008).

In each of these approaches, leaders' ability to match skills to situations enables them to deliver success within the organization.

Looking Outside by Creating Value to External Stakeholders

More recently, and a next step in leadership thinking, leadership effectiveness is not just about the person or about the organization outcomes, but about what happens outside the walls of the organization (Ulrich et al., 2012). It is not about whether leaders dress for success or look the part, nor about how leaders build confidence among employees. Effective leadership is not merely what leaders know and do, but how their actions shape the experiences of customers. If a customer buys a Lexus because of the quality and design, then leaders inside Lexus should make sure that their actions drive those desired expectations.

Leadership matters not just because employees are more productive, organization cultures are created, or financial results occur, but because external stakeholders receive value from what leaders do within the firm. For customers, leaders are effective when they link internal organization processes to deliver customer expectations. Culture becomes less focused on the norms and values inside the company and more on making the external identity of the firm (its brand) consistent with internal culture (Ulrich et al., 2009). For leaders, this means not only creating an internal culture consistent with an external identity; building a leadership brand exists when leaders ensure that the behaviors of employees reflect the expectations of customers outside the company (Ulrich and Smallwood, 2009). Work has begun to define leadership effectiveness through the expectations of customers. A next step for defining effective leadership might be to more accurately link leadership actions to investor expectations – what one of the authors has called leadership capital (Deloitte, 2012).

Reviewing Firm Valuation: From Financial to Intangible to Leadership

Leadership may be the next step in firm valuation. Historically, the accounting profession received a major challenge after the stock crash of 1929. Many argued that stock prices misrepresented firm value, because the public information available to investors did not accurately reflect the measure of a firm's assets. In 1934 the Securities Exchange Commission was formed to create standards and regulate how public companies report their financial performance to investors. The large accounting firms who audited organizations at the time (PricewaterhouseCoopers, Deloitte & Touche, KPMG, Ernst & Young, and Arthur Andersen) established a set of accounting standards and principles through the FASB. The standardized accounting rules define uniform standards in an effort to communicate accurate information to investors so they can better measure firm value (GAAP).

The intent of these accounting standards is to offer investors comparable, public, and transparent data that will enable them to make accurate valuation decisions. The ingredients, or financial data, from the accounting standards may then be combined to define a firm's value. An entire industry has been created and evolved to define approaches to measuring a firm's value, which has become increasingly complex (Catty, 2006; Koller et al., 2010; Damodaran, 2001, 2010; Mard et al., 2010). Income approaches to valuation focus on capitalization of current net income or cash flows and discounting future cash flows (e.g., comparable accounting earnings, discounted cash flow, capital asset pricing model). Cost approaches to valuation emphasize the cost of replacement of an asset to determine its value (e.g., real estate appraisal to determine replacement costs). The market approaches value assets based on their current value based on competitive pricing (e.g., if sold, what would the asset be worth). Again, each of these broad approaches to valuation combines the ingredients from the accounting standards data to determine a value of the firm.

Importance of Intangibles for Valuation

In recent years, due to changes and uncertainty in markets, information, and globalization (Baker et al., 2013), the financial data publicly reported by firms does not reflect the accurate value of a firm. As a result, firm valuation has pivoted from a pure focus on financial results to a deeper understanding of the intangibles that cause these results. The reason for increased attention to intangibles is that earnings reported in a variety of forms (net income, operating earnings, core earnings, pro forma earnings, EBITA – earnings before interest, taxes, depreciation, and amortization – and adjusted earnings) have become ever more suspect (Bynes and Henry, 2001). Baruch Lev, an accounting professor who is a thought leader of the intangibles movement, has shown the importance of intangibles as indicated through the market-to-book value (the ratio of capital market value of companies compared to their net asset value) of the Standard & Poor's 500, which has risen from 1 to over 6 in the last 25 years – suggesting that for every $6 of market value, only $1 occurs on the balance sheet (Lev, 2001). What this means is that the balance-sheet number – which is what traditional accounting measures – represents only 10 to 15 percent of the value of these companies (Webber, 2000). This data shows that the value of many firms comes as much from perceived value as from hard assets. Firms such as Coca-Cola and Genentech have high market value from brands and patents. Technology-based firms such as Amazon and Google have high market value with relatively little in the way of cash flow, earnings, hard assets, or patents. And even traditional companies such as 3M are increasing market value by focusing on brands, leveraging the Web, and restructuring. Professor Lev further recommends that managers learn to win investors over by finding ways to more clearly communicate intangibles with them (Lev, 2011).

In recent years, studies of intangibles as a source value have received more attention (BilanciaRSI, 2010). Generally intangibles have been listed as intellectual capital or knowledge as evidenced in patents, trademarks, customer information, software codes, databases, business models, homegrown processes, and employee expertise (Sherman, 2011). Investors have worked to classify lists of intangibles that include intellectual capital, but go beyond. Baruch Lev categorizes intangibles into R&D efforts (e.g., trademarks, patents, copyrights), brand value (e.g., image, reputation), structural assets (e.g., business systems, processes, executive compensation, human resources), and monopoly position (Lev, 2001, 2005; Lev and Radhakrishnan, 2005; Demerjian et al., 2012). In studies of firm value, there is little doubt that intangibles are an increasing source of the overall value of a firm (Hulten and Hao, 2008).

In our previous work, we synthesized the work on intangible value into four domains called the architecture for intangibles (Figure 2.1). We found that intangibles could be clustered into four categories: making and keeping promises, having a clear strategy for growth, managing core competencies, and building organization capabilities (Ulrich and Smallwood, 2003).

- Keeping promises comes when leaders build relationships of trust by doing what they say to employees inside and customers and investors outside, often measured as risk.
- Creating a clear, compelling strategy comes when leaders have strategic capital to define the future and work with customers to deliver value through brand identity and reputation.
- Aligning core competencies increases when leaders invest in R&D and the intellectual capital that comes from patents, copyrights, trademarks, and the like. Creating core competencies also comes when leaders access functional expertise in technology, manufacturing, and operations.
- Building organization capabilities comes when leaders have the ability to create a corporate culture consistent with its mission, which might mean a culture of innovation, collaboration, efficiency, risk management, or information asymmetry.

I propose that leadership is a key underlying factor in organizations being able to keep promises, set clear and compelling strategies, align core competencies, and build organization capabilities. When leaders at all levels of a firm guide these four domains, they create sustainable intangible value. Investors who assess leadership will be more able to fully value a firm's intangible assets and overall market value.

The valuation field has done an incredible job creating ever more granular definitions of asset value. There are two next steps facing the valuation field: information and intangibles. With advanced information and transparency, valuation has come when investors possess increasingly robust and detailed analyses of a company's financial reporting. There are fewer and fewer information asymmetries in financial data. Every interested investor has access to publicly reported data, so, essentially, each investor knows what every other investor knows. Investors need to dig deeper to find new insights, but this is not easy to do.

Leadership is the next step in firm valuation, which goes beyond measuring intangible value. As discussed above, intangibles have become an emerging step in firm valuation by focusing on

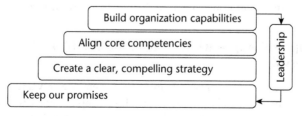

Figure 2.1 Architecture for Intangibles

Source: Ulrich and Smallwood, 2003.

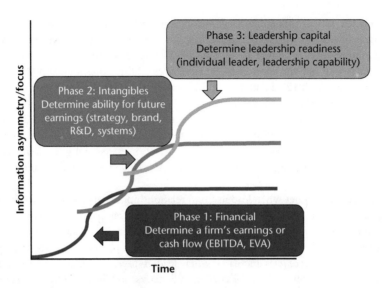

Figure 2.2 Evolution of Firm Valuation

the future more than the past. Figure 2.2 shows that intangibles move beyond financial information. Recent work on intangibles has helped to recognize, validate, and codify intangible value. The next step in valuation may be leadership capital, or quality of leadership, which underlies and creates intangibles and leads to financial results. When assessed, information on leadership capital may give investors information asymmetry that informs their investment choices.

Investors may have common valuation metrics for their financial analysis of a firm, which is the baseline for financial investments. Investors are creating metrics for intangibles. But, investors who do a better job in assessing leadership will create information asymmetry and make better investment decisions. In addition, there is enormous variance of management practices and leadership, across firms and countries (Bloom and van Reenen, 2007). Financial valuation sets the accepted baseline that levels the playing field, but leadership valuation differentiates how investors may determine long-term firm value. Financial vs. intangible valuation is like being certified or licensed (as an accountant, doctor, lawyer, or psychologist), which means you have mastered the basics (financials in firm valuation), but licensing does not assure quality, which requires more subjective judgment (leadership in firm valuation). It is also like betting on a sporting event. Every better knows the past records of both teams. If a gambler has more information about a star player, that information would enable him to make more informed bets. Likewise, a leadership ratings index should help investors make more informed subjective judgments about the quality of leadership as they make their investment choices.

Offering a Proposed Approach to Evaluating the Market Value of Leadership

A leadership capital ratings index should help multiple audiences who want to assess and increase the value of a firm. There is a difference between a leadership rating *index* and a leadership ratings *standard*. Standards (e.g., gold standard) define what is expected; indices (e.g., gold's performance vs. other investments) rate how well an activity performs. For example, *The Economist* has a Big Mac index that adjusts the cost of a Big Mac above or below the average Big Mac price in the US. This index crudely assesses the cost of living in a country. This Big Mac index is not a standard that tells one how much a Big Mac should be priced or how it should taste.

An index guides investors to make more informed choices while a standard defines effectiveness. When a rating agency such as Moody's or Standard & Poor downgrades a company, it is not saying that the company did or did not meet financial reporting requirements. It is offering an opinion about the firm's ability to repay loans in the future. Likewise, a leadership capital index would inform investors about the leadership readiness to meet business challenges. We are not proposing a leadership equivalent of GAAP that codifies all leaders in the same way. Such a leadership standard would be nearly impossible, because leadership is inevitably both a personally subjective activity and a contingent activity based on the unique needs of the company. It is silly to ask who was or is the better leader . . . Lee Iacocca, Bill Gates, Warren Buffet, Steven Jobs, or Jack Welch? In fact, each was very successful using his unique skills appropriate for the circumstance. In the near future, there is not likely to be a uniform standard of leadership, but an investor who recognized the quality of leadership in each of these leaders, and thus invested early in them, would have been well served. A leadership ratings index can give investors and other interested parties a set of guidelines to assess leadership capital.

Many executives recognize the importance of helping investors become more acquainted with and aware of company leaders. But frequently the exposure of investors to company leadership is somewhat haphazard and episodic, often focused on a few leaders with limited information. It is like buying a house by only viewing the information on the internet (pictures, property tax, age, and so forth), but not visiting the house to get additional qualitative information and a feel about the neighborhood, conditions of the house, and the flow of living in the house. While few would buy a house without seriously looking at it and getting more insight about the quality and feel of the house, investors often invest without thorough or thoughtful leadership assessment. When investors define leadership only as the CEO, when they only examine one aspect of effective leadership, or when they assess haphazard views of leadership, they are working in the right direction but with limited information.

Requirements of a Leadership Capital Index

A leadership ratings index will need to synthesize the various and muddled concepts related to leadership capital and provide a discipline to rigorously track these concepts. We propose that a leadership ratings index have two dimensions, or domains: individual and organizational (see Figure 2.3). "Individual" refers to the personal qualities (competencies, traits, characteristics) of the key leaders in the organization. "Organization" refers to the systems (often called human capital) these leaders create to manage leadership throughout the organization and the application of organization systems to specific business conditions. Using these two domains, previous leadership and human capital work may be synthesized into a leadership ratings index that investors can use to inform their valuation decisions.

Domain 1: Individual Leader Competencies

The individual dimension of leadership capital focuses on the qualities of individual leaders within an organization. Leadership obviously begins with the CEO, but also extends to the top team and even the middle managers who assume leadership responsibilities throughout an organization (Ulrich and Smallwood, 2012). Too often investors look only at the CEO to represent the overall quality of leadership. For example, ISS (Institutional Shareholder Services) reports extensive analysis about CEO pay (correlation of CEO pay to performance, CEO base vs. at risk pay, ratio

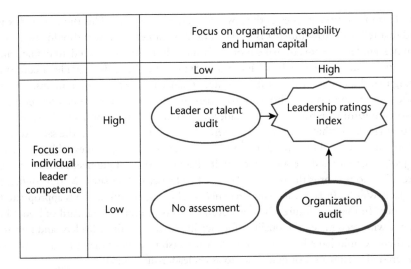

Figure 2.3 Synthesis of Leadership Capital Domains

of CEO pay to next highest officer, and CEO pay vs. peers), because this information is publicly reported in Securities and Exchange Commission reports. Increasingly, collective leadership matters more than individual leaders.

Many studies of leadership acknowledge the general importance of people and overall leadership as the driver of organizational value (Ceridian, 2007). Some have focused on the individual skills of the top and senior leaders as inputs to key investment decisions. Every thoughtful investor interested in long-term investing (portfolio managers, institutional investors, mutual/hedge fund managers, private equity investors, and venture capitalists) would likely recognize that leaders matter in valuing the firm. But when asked about leadership, analysts emphasize more how to get information than what information to look for. Without a guiding framework for what makes an effective leader, each analyst draws on his or her own assumptions.

As discussed above, literally millions of studies have attempted to define the qualities of an effective leader. To cull these studies so that investors can use them to assess leadership, we have defined a metaphor "leadership brand," which consists of code and differentiators. The Leadership Code addresses the question: can leaders in a firm accomplish the basic duties of a leader? The Code includes four factors of leadership that investors can assess (for simplicity in this work, we have combined talent manager and human capital developer). These leadership factors define the individual domain of a leadership ratings index that covers half of leadership capital.

- Personal proficiency: to what extent does the leadership demonstrate the personal qualities required of an effective leader?
- Strategist: to what extent does the leadership articulate a point of view about the future and strategic positioning?
- Executor: to what extent does the leadership make things happen and deliver as promised?
- People manager: to what extent does the leadership build the competence, commitment, and contribution of their people today and tomorrow?[2]

The leadership differentiator addresses the question: to what extent do leaders engage in behaviors that are uniquely suited to the firm given its external brand? In our research we found that about 60 to 70 percent of effective leadership was doing the basics well; 30 to 40 percent was making sure that leaders' actions inside a company reflected customer expectations outside the company. A customer brand becomes a leadership brand when leaders inside a company act in ways customers would expect. This leads to the fifth factor of personal leadership that investors can assess:

- Leadership differentiator: to what extent is leadership behavior consistent with customer expectations?

These five elements offer a framework for what investors should pay attention to in assessing individuals as leaders. Investors who assess individual leaders at the top and throughout the organization will know if they have the personal qualities that define effective leadership.

Domain 2: Organization Capability and Human Capital

Leadership capital not only includes personal or individual leadership traits, but also investments made to build future leaders within the organization. To build future leaders, leaders create organization cultures and invest in human resource practices (often called human capital). Studies have shown the relationship between a firm's investment in human capital practices and financial performance. A number of consulting firms have worked to create human capital, or high performing workplace, assessments, each assessing basic HR practice areas (staffing, training, compensation), then generally emphasizing the strengths of their consulting firm's practice (Bassi and McMurrer, 2009; CIPD, 2007; Filbeck and Preece, 2003; Hay Group, 2008; McBassi and Company, 2007; Mercer, 2006; PricewaterhouseCoopers, 2008; Fulmer et al., 2003). At times these assessments show the relationship between a single practice (e.g., staffing, training, compensation, or succession planning) and financial performance, but more recently efforts have been made to create human capital indices showing how integrated HR investments affect business performance (Fulmer and Ployhart, 2014; Nyberg et al., 2014).

Investors who assess leadership capital should examine the extent to which leaders design and deliver human resource systems to maximize value. Like personal competencies of effective individual leaders, the domain of human capital is very broad, ranging from specific HR practices (e.g., pivotal employees, executive compensation, training investments) to broader issues such as culture. For human capital to be accurately assessed in valuation discussions, the complex domain of processes, practices, metrics, tools, and ideas needs to be simplified. Based on human capital studies such as the above, we can propose that there are five organizational factors that may be part of a leadership ratings index for investors.

1. Culture capability: to what extent has the leadership created a customer focused cultural capability that is shared throughout the organization?
2. Talent: to what extent has the leadership invested in practices that manage the flow of talent into, through, and out of the organization?
3. Performance accountability: to what extent has the leadership created performance management practices (e.g., compensation) that reinforce the right behaviors?
4. Information: to what extent has the leadership managed information flow to gain information asymmetries?
5. Work: to what extent has the leadership created organization and work practices that deal with the increasing pace of change in today's business settings?

Investors can assess the human capital by determining whether leaders wisely invest in these organization practices.

By synthesizing existing leadership capital into individual and organization domains and 10 elements, we can propose a leadership capital ratings index that investors can use to scrutinize quality of leadership (Table 2.1). As suggested, the individual and organization domains serve a purpose similar to the principles that Standard & Poor uses to guide their assessments. This framework is comprehensive in that it synthesizes the range of leadership capital issues investors should pay attention to. It is also simple in that the two domains and 10 elements have both face validity and are easily understood. It also leads to discipline in that investors can examine and codify specific actions and metrics for each of the 10 elements.[3]

Conclusion

The connection of studies of leadership and firm valuation can benefit both. The study of leadership can be improved by examining leadership through investor expectations, and studies of firm valuation can be improved through rigorously examining leadership. Ultimately this leadership ratings index offers investors a more integrated approach to assessing leadership.

A leadership capital index would help multiple stakeholders interested in firm valuation. Investors would have better information on which to make financial commitments. Rating agencies and proxy advisory agencies could offer more granular firm valuation information. Boards of Directors charged with replacing leaders could better evaluate potential candidates. Those charged with building leadership (c-suite executives, HR professionals, consultants) could provide more insightful assessments and development efforts.

Table 2.1 Overview of Leadership Rating Index

Domain	Factor	Question (To what extent do leaders . . .)	Example metric
Individual: What does the individual leader or collection of leaders be, know, and do that would matter most to investors?	1 Personal proficiency	have the required personal characteristics to be effective?	• Has experience in the industry; has been successful in the past • Demonstrates learning agility • Exhibits personal presence (charisma) • Has emotional intelligence (self aware)
	2 Strategist	have a point of view about the future and strategic positioning?	• Articulates a unique point of view about future industry trends • Understands external business drivers (regulatory, technology, demographic shifts) • Enunciates a differentiated strategy for their firm
	3 Executor	make things happen and deliver as promised?	• Has a proven track record of success • Is willing to hold people accountable • Meets commitments

	4 People manager	build the competence, commitment, and contribution of their people?	• Maintains stability of senior team • Able to work with people with different skills • Engages staff (e.g., engagement survey, retention of top talent) • Productivity of staff vs. industry • Has a workforce plan • Empowers others
	5 Leadership differentiator	behave consistently with the desired culture?	• Links firm brand to leadership behaviors (leadership competency model matches firm brand) • Aligns leadership behaviors to strategy • Lives the values • Uses the values to guide decision making
Organization: What do leaders do to build organization capital, which includes capability and human capital, that would matter most to investors?	6 Cultural capability	create a culture that reflects customer expectations?	• Pays attention (time, talk, and money) to defining and delivering desired culture • Connects firm brand to cultural/values statement • Turns cultural/values statement into specific, measureable behaviors • Has a unity of desired culture
	7 Talent	manage the flow of talent into, through, and out of the organization?	• Hiring success rate • Retention of key talent • Training and development investments • Succession planning process
	8 Performance accountability	create performance management processes that reinforce right behaviors?	• Sets clear standards • Aligns executive compensation with performance • Spends time on performance conversations
	9 Information	manage information flow to gain information asymmetries?	• Uses social media • Collects and disseminates external information • Turns data (big data) into insights that inform decisions
	10 Work	create organization and work practices that align with strategy?	• Matches organization structure to strategy • Understands and reengineers key processes for success • Has clear decision-making and governance guidelines

Notes

1 These studies, which capture the impact of leadership and performance, can be summarized in the following table:

Affects	Lieberson and O'Connor	Weiner	Thomas	Wasserman, Nohria, and Anand	Mackey
Year affect	1.8%	2.4%	5.6%	2.6%	1.0%
Industry affect	28.5%	20.5%	n/a	n/a	18.0%
Corporate affect	22.6%	45.8%	82.2%	25.5%	29.5%
CEO affect	14.5%	8.7%	5.7%	14.7%	12.9%
Error	32.6%	22.6%	5.4%	50.9%	38.5%

Using ROA as dependent variable

2 For those who follow our work, in the Leadership Code we separate talent manager, which focuses on managing people for today, and human capital developer, which focuses on investing in people for tomorrow. We have combined these two talent-related leadership skills for simplicity. They both focus on the underlying ability of a leader to manage his or her people, and investors who see this skill in leaders will have more confidence in the firm's ability to deliver intangible and tangible value.
3 We need to be realistic about these 10 factors making up our proposed rating index. If we were asked today, we would say that most investors recognize the need to improve assessments of leadership, but that today's assessments may have a 5 to 10 percent validity because they lack rigor and consistency. The leadership ratings index we propose may move this to 30 to 40 percent validity. Much, much more can and should be done to determine how investors can and should evaluate leadership, but this is an important start.

References

Baker, Scott, Nicholas Bloom, and Steven Davis. 2013. *Measuring Economy Policy Uncertainty*. *Chicago Booth Research Paper* 13–02.

Bass, Bernard. 1990. *Bass and Stogdill's Handbook of Leadership: Theory, Research, and Management Application*. New York: Free Press.

Bass, Bernard and Ruth Bass. 2008. *The Bass Handbook of Leadership: Theory, Research, and Managerial Applications*. New York: Free Press.

Bassi, Laurie J. and Daniel P. McMurrer. 2009. *"A Capital Investment": Learning and Performance*. New York.

BilanciaRSI and AIAF Working Group on Mission Intangibles. 2010. *The Value of Intangibles to Overcome the Systemic Crisis*. Quaderni AIAF, http://www.thevaluegroup.de/fileadmin/documents/Quaderno_AIAF_145-The_value_of_intangibles_to_overcome_the_systemic_crisis.pdf.

Blake, R. and J. Mouton. 1964. *The Managerial Grid: The Key to Leadership Excellence*. Houston, TX: Gulf Publishing Co.

Bloom, Nicholas and John van Reenen. 2007. Management Practices Across Firms and Countries. *The Quarterly Journal of Economics*, 122 (4): 1351–1408.

Boyatzis, Richard. 1982. *The Competent Manager: A Model for Effective Performance*. New York: Wiley.

Burgoyne, John, Wendy Hirsh, and Sadie Williams. 2004. Research Report PR 560. *The Development of Management and Leadership Capability and Its Contribution to Performance: The Evidence, the Prospects and the Research Need*. London: Department for Education and Skills.

Byrnes, Nanette and David Henry. 2001. Confused about Earnings? *Business Week*, November 26.

Catty, James. 2006. *The Professional's Guide to Fair Value*. New York: Wiley.

Ceridian. 2007. Human Capital White Paper, Ceridian UK Ltd, http://www.ceridian.co.uk/hr/downloads/HumanCapitalWhitePaper_2007_01_26.pdf.

Chartered Institute of Personnel and Development (CIPD). 2007. *Human Capital Evolution: Developing Performance Measures*. Human Capital Panel Report. London: CIPD.

Damodaran, Aswath. 2001. *Investment Valuation: Tools and Techniques for Determining Value*. New York: Wiley.

Damodaran, Aswath. 2010. *The Valuation Handbook: Valuation Techniques from Today's Top Practitioners*. New York: Wiley.

Deloitte. 2012. *The Leadership Premium: How Companies Win the Confidence of Investors*. www2.deloitte.com/. . ./Deloitte/. . ./dttl-hc-leadershippremium-8092013.pdf.

Demerjian, Peter, Baruch Lev, and Sarah McVay. 2012. Quantifying Managerial Ability: A New Measure and Validity Tests. *Management Science*, 58 (7): 1229–1248.

Denison, Daniel, Robert Hoojberg, Nancy Lane, and Colleen Lief. 2012. *Leading Culture Change in Global Organizations: Aligning Culture and Strategy*. San Francisco: Jossey-Bass.

Fielder, Fred E. 1964. A Theory of Leadership Effectiveness. In L. Berkowitz (Ed.), *Advances in Experimental Social Psychology*. New York: Academic Press.

Filbeck, Greg and Diane Preece. 2003. Fortune's Best 100 Companies to Work For: Do They Work for Shareholders? *Journal of Business Finance and Accounting*, 30: 771–797.

Fleck, Steven and Ilke Inceoglu. 2010. A Comprehensive Framework for Understanding and Predicting Engagement. In S. L. Albrecht (Eds.), *Handbook of Employee Engagement: Perspectives, Issues, Research and Practice*: 31–42. Cheltenham, UK: Edward Elgar Publishing.

Fulmer, Ingrid Smith and Robert Ployhart. 2014. Our Most Important Asset: A Multidisciplinary/Multilevel Review of Human Capital Valuation for Research and Practice. *Journal of Management*, 40: 371–398.

Fulmer, Ingrid Smith, Barry Gerhart, and Kimberly Scott. 2003. Are the 100 Best Better? An Empirical Investigation of the Relationship between Being a "Great Place to Work" and Firm Performance. *Personnel Psychology*, 56: 965–993.

Hay Group. 2008. What Makes the Most Admired Companies Great: Reward Program Effectiveness, December. www.haygroup.com.

Hersey, Paul and Ken Blanchard. 1969. An Introduction to Situational Leadership. *Training and Development Journal*, 23: 26–34.

Hoffman, Brian J., David J. Woehr, Robyn Maldagen-Youngjohn, and Brian D. Lyons. 2011. Great Man or Great Myth? A Quantitative Review of the Relationship between Individual Differences and Leader Effectiveness. *Journal of Occupational and Organizational Psychology*, 84 (2): 347–381.

Hulten, Charles and Janet Hao. 2008. What Is a Company Really Worth? Intangible Capital and the Market to Book Value Puzzle. Cambridge, MA: NBER Working Paper 14548.

Ireland, R. Duane and Michael A. Hitt. 1999. Achieving and Maintaining Strategic Competitiveness in the 21st Century: The Role of Strategic Leadership. *The Academy of Management Executive*, 13 (1): 43–57.

Kaiser, Robert B., Robert Hogan, and S. Bartholomew Craig. 2008. Leadership and the Fate of Organizations. *American Psychologist* 63 (2): 96.

Koller, Tim, Marc Goerhart, and David Wessels. 2010. *Valuation: Measuring and Managing The Value of Companies* (5th edition). New York: Wiley, McKinsey & Company.

Kotter, John and James Heskett. 2011. *Corporate Culture and Performance*. New York: Free Press.

Lev, Baruch. 2001. *Intangibles: Management, Measurement, and Reporting*. Washington DC: The Brookings Institute.

Lev, Baruch. 2005. Intangible Assets: Concepts and Measurements. In *Encyclopedia of Social Measurement*, Vol 2. Amsterdam: Elsevier.

Lev, Baruch. 2011. *Winning Investors Over: Surprising Truths About Honesty, Earnings Guidance, and Other Ways to Boost Your Stock Price*. Boston: Harvard Business Press.

Lev, Baruch and Suresh Radhakrishnan. 2005. The Valuation Organizational Capital. In Carol Corrado, John Haltiwanger, and Daniel Sichel (Eds.), *Measuring Capital in the New Economy*, Studies in Income and Wealth, Vol. 65. Chicago: The University of Chicago Press, 73–99.

Lieberson, Stanley and James F. O'Connor. 1972. Leadership and Organizational Performance: A Large Study of Corporations. *American Sociological Review*, 37: 117–130.

Mackey, Alison. 2005. How Much Do CEOs Influence Firm Performance – Really? *Available at SSRN 816065*.

Mackey, Alison. 2008. The Effect of CEOs on Firm Performance. *Strategic Management Journal* 29 (12): 1357–1367.

Mard, Michael, James Hitcher, and Steven Hyden. 2010. *Valuation for Financial Reporting*. New York: Wiley.

McBassi and Company. 2007. Human Capital Capability Scorecard™ Human Capital Management (HCM) Index and Factor Definitions. New York: McBassi.

Mercer. 2006. *The Value of People: Insights into Human Capital*. New York: Mercer.

Norita, Nitan and Rakesh Khurana (Eds). 2010. *Handbook of Leadership Theory and Practice*. Boston: Harvard Business Press.

Nyberg, Anthony J., Thomas P. Moliterno, Donald Hale, and David P. Lepak, 2014. Resource-Based Perspectives on Unit-Level Human Capital: A Review and Integration. *Journal of Management*, 40: 316–346.

PricewaterhouseCoopers. 2008. *Managing People in a Changing World. Key Trends in Human Capital: A Global Perspective – 2008*. Saratoga: PWC Human Resource Services.

Rowe, Glen. 2001. Creating Wealth in Organizations: The Role of Strategic Leadership. *Academy of Management Executive*, 15 (1).

Rucci, Anthony J., Steve Kirn, and Richard T. Quinn. 1998. The Employee–Customer–Profit Chain at Sears. *Harvard Business Review*, January–February 1998, 84–97.

Schein, Edgar. 2010. *Leadership and Organizational Culture* (4th edition). San Francisco: Jossey-Bass.

Sherman, Andrew. 2011. *Harvesting Intangible Assets: Uncover Hidden Revenue in Your Company's Intellectual Property*. New York: AMACON.

Spencer, Lyle and Signe Spencer. 1993. *Competence at Work: Modes for Superior Performance*. New York: Wiley.

Thomas, Alan Berkeley. 1988. Does Leadership Make a Difference in Organizational Performance? *Administrative Science Quarterly*, 33: 388–400.

Ulrich, Dave and Wayne Brockbank. 2006. *HR Value Proposition*. Boston: Harvard Business Press.

Ulrich, Dave and Norm Smallwood. 2003. *Why the Bottom Line Isn't: How to Build Value through People and Organization*. New York: Wiley.

Ulrich, Dave and Norm Smallwood. 2009. *Leadership Brand*. Boston: Harvard Business Press.

Ulrich, Dave and Norm Smallwood. 2012. What Is Leadership? In William Mobley, Ming Li, Ying Wang (Eds.), *Advances in Global Leadership, Volume 7*. Bradford: Emerald Publishing Group.

Ulrich, Dave, Justin Allen, Norm Smallwood, Wayne Brockbank, and Jon Younger. 2009. Building Culture from the Outside In. *Strategic HR Review*, 8 (6): 20–27.

Ulrich, Dave, Jon Younger, Wayne Brockbank, and Mike Ulrich. 2012. *HR from the Outside In*. New York: McGraw Hill.

Vroom, Victor and Arthur Jago. 1995. Situation Effects and Levels of Analysis in the Study of Leader Participation. *Leadership Quarterly*, 6: 169–181.

Wasserman, Noam, Nitin Nohria, and Bharat N. Anand. 2001. *What Does Leadership Matter? The Contingent Opportunities View of CEO Leadership*. Harvard Working Paper no. 02–04.

Webber, Allan interviewing Baruch Lev. *New Math for a New Economy: Fast Company*. (January–February 2000).

Weiner, Nan. 1978. Situational and Leadership Influence on Organizational Performance. *Proceedings of the Academy of Management*, 2 (1).

Welbourne, Thersa and Steven Schlater. 2014. *Engaged in What? Role Theory Perspectives for Enhancing Engagement Research and Practice*. Lincoln, NE: University of Nebraska-Lincoln.

Zaccaro, Stephen J. 2007. Trait-Based Perspectives of Leadership. *American Psychologist*, 62 (1): 6–16.

3

Beyond the Hero–Leader

Leadership by Collectives

Viviane Sergi, Jean-Louis Denis and Ann Langley

Introduction

Leadership has always been closely associated with unique, strong individuals. Even today, leadership and leaders tend to be equated with each other. But is this association necessarily valid, and is it possible to transcend this vision? Is it possible to move beyond the close association between leadership and single leaders? In line with a growing number of researchers, we suggest that the answer to the second question is a resounding yes. The central aim of the present chapter will therefore be to explore ways to conceive of leadership beyond traditional unitary models.

Recent research has shown a marked interest in plural forms of leadership. Not only has the number of articles on the topic risen in a notable way in the last ten years, but various journals have devoted special issues to it (e.g., *The Leadership Quarterly* in 2014, *Industrial and Organizational Psychology* in 2012 and *International Journal of Management Reviews* in 2011). Yet, such plural forms are not new: Follett (1924), Gibb (1954) and Hogdson, Levinson and Zaleznik (1965), among others, have each discussed shared conceptions of leadership, and made a case in favour of this approach to leadership years before it became more openly and actively debated in academic circles and used more by practitioners. However, despite their seminal contributions, plural forms of leadership have remained an isolated phenomenon, evoked sparingly by researchers or practiced by marginal leaders. The more widespread interest for these forms is thus quite new. Although still limited in its spread, plural forms of leadership have also started to be mentioned in the general business press: for example, the trio of Sergey Brin, Larry Page and Eric Schmidt was at the head of Google for years, before Eric Schmidt stepped down, leaving a duo in place; Deutsche Bank also had, for some years, a duo at its head, just like Whole Foods and the American restaurant chain Chipotle. However, reading the general press on the possibility of having more than one person in charge of a company quickly reveals how such arrangements are seen: when they are not directly presented as bad decisions,[1] they are discussed with caution. Instances where plural forms have benefited the organization are often contrasted in the same article with cases where the results have been more mixed; many of these articles in the popular press conclude with a more than nuanced view of shared leadership roles, especially in the case of CEOs. Having more than one person in a leadership position may be more openly considered than previously, but it remains a choice and a practice generally seen with a sceptical eye.

Nonetheless, evidence that a single leadership position can be occupied by more than one individual seems to be mounting. Alongside studies that document how such collectives of leaders work, research aimed at documenting the links between these plural forms and various positive benefits for organizations have started to appear. For example, Pearce, Wassenaar and Manz (2014) discuss how shared leadership may enable responsible leadership, linking leadership with corporate social responsibility; other studies are exploring the relationship between plural forms and other benefits for organizations, such as group-level phenomena like caring and solidarity (Houghton, Pearce, Manz, Courtright, & Stewart, 2015), knowledge transfer (Spyridonidis, Hendry, & Barlow, 2015) and management of uncertainty (Jonassen, 2015). More generally, a number of studies published in recent years have attempted to integrate the dispersed literature on forms of plural leadership in order to establish whether there is a link between these forms and team effectiveness or performance (see, for example, the reviews by D'Innocenzo, Mathieu & Kukenberger, 2014; Drescher, Kosgaard, Welpe, Picot, & Wigand, 2014; Dust & Ziegert, forthcoming; and Wang, Waldman, & Zhang, 2014). In particular, the meta-analysis realized by Nicolaides et al. (2014) shows that there are clear links between shared leadership and team performance. Overall, these studies tend to show that there are positive effects. However, Dust and Ziegert (forthcoming) underline that, up to now, structural dimensions of plural forms of leadership have not been assessed with the required precision when it comes to explaining the benefits. They suggest that the number of co-leaders and how they share their leadership roles and responsibilities have to be taken into account to better understand how these modalities function and perform. They nonetheless conclude with a positive appreciation of plural forms of leadership, in a similar vein to the three other recent meta-analyses.

Yet, in reviewing the literature on plural forms of leadership, one realizes that the question of the structure of these teams of leaders has already been investigated in a number of articles: for example, Gronn's work has greatly focussed on the unit, or later on, the configuration of distributed leadership (2002, 2009, 2015), just as studies on the governance of inter-organizational collaborations (e.g., Huxham & Vangen, 2000; Vangen & Huxham, 2003; Vangen, Hayes & Cornforth, 2015) have shed light on the importance of structural concerns in their specific context. In fact, the question of structure can be seen as a backdrop to many studies on plural forms of leadership, as in studies on dual leadership (e.g., Reid & Karambayya, 2009, 2015) or on leadership constellations (Hodgson et al., 1965), where the fact that it is a duo or a trio that occupies the leadership position is the key theme driving the reflection on these plural forms. While these studies, and others, do address the notion of structure, what is currently lacking in the literature on plural forms of leadership is an overview of what the collective entities might actually be. Beyond concerns for the internal structuration of these plural forms, can we identify differences that might exist between all of the instances where leadership is practiced by many individuals?

As we discussed elsewhere (Denis, Langley & Sergi, 2012; Sergi, Denis & Langley, 2012), we start by noting that the notion of "plural leadership" is in fact an umbrella term useful to unify what is otherwise a scattered literature, in which we can find a plethora of labels to designate leadership roles that are shared. In spite of a similar starting point, the growth of interest in this phenomenon is accompanied by a proliferation of labels to describe it, a proliferation that contributes to the fragmentation of research on this topic. Some of these labels have partially stabilized over the years. For example, studies referring to "shared leadership" tend to adopt a similar line of thinking, inspired by organization psychology and behavior, and those using the term "distributed leadership" are still closely associated with the context of schools and education management. Yet, despite the bodies of similar studies that have accumulated around some of these labels, the same labels are used in other contexts, without necessarily acknowledging the context from which they emerged. Other labels are also used in an indistinct fashion. Based on an extensive literature review, our previous work (Denis et al., 2012) was an attempt at ordering the variety of forms "plural leadership" can take, starting from the literature itself to see whether streams of distinct traditions could be identified.

In this chapter, we aim to address the question of what the "collectives" we allude to in the title of our chapter could be. We thus review the variety of forms that such collectives can adopt, with the aim of "pluralizing" leadership. With this aim, the question we explore in these pages is how can such a pluralization of leadership be conceptualized? How has leadership been studied and conceived as a collectively practiced phenomenon? In other words, we will turn our attention to some of the *reasons* that may explain why we can find, both in practice and in research, collective definitions of leadership. The issue at stake here is not the theoretical roots, or the theoretical commonalities between various studies; rather, it is the justifications provided to promote plural forms of leadership, which up to now have rarely been discussed in an all-encompassing way. As we will develop, we propose that collectives in leadership positions can be viewed from three main pluralizing angles: they can result from a structural choice, an ideological commitment and a distinctive theoretical construction. Each of these angles enlarges our understanding of how leadership can be conceived and practiced in or by a collective. We will explore each of these three angles, discussing how they allow us to think about leadership as a phenomenon that is collectively accomplished, and highlight some of the research questions opened up by each angle.

While those studying and investigating plural forms of leadership may be encouraged by the current interest that these forms are attracting, this also opens up another relevant question: why is this interest blossoming now? Could there be changes afoot in today's organizations that call for renewed ways of practicing leadership? Plural forms of leadership may have been long present in specific contexts, such as pluralistic organizations (such as hospitals and artistic organizations), but, as we will also discuss, some changes in more traditional organizations may signal that these plural forms will be on the rise in coming years. We will thus conclude our chapter by proposing some new lines of inquiry that still remain to be empirically studied.

Before we delve into the topic of plural leadership as we have elsewhere defined it (see Denis et al., 2012; Sergi et al., 2012), we believe it is important to address the question that often follows assertions regarding the possibility of sharing, in any form, leadership: what does such a pluralizing of leadership mean for unitary leadership? Does it dilute its relevance; does it call into question its potential beneficial effects for teams and organizations alike? On this topic as on many others, we should eschew binary, dualistic thinking. Plural forms of leadership do not imply a de facto disappearance of unitary leadership. We suggest that pluralizing leadership should first and foremost be understood as an extension of leadership beyond single leaders, but that such an extension should not be understood to happen necessarily at the expense of unitary leaders. Far from it, we contend that extending leadership "out" from single individuals to different groups of individuals complexifies and nuances the picture. We also consider that such an extension has the potential to rejuvenate both thinking and practice. Finally, we argue that singular and plural forms of leadership can – and, in some instances, should – coexist and be simultaneously practiced, depending on the context and on the persons involved.

The remainder of the chapter is structured as follows: we first present three distinct perspectives on plural leadership, each of which can be understood as a set of explanations behind the existence of such collective forms. The first set, "pluralizing by choice," discusses instances where leadership is practiced by collectives for structural reasons, in order to better function in the face of complexity. This category addresses the challenge posed to leadership by pluralistic contexts, and also those stemming from complex interorganizational collaborations. In these settings, opting for plural forms of leadership may help alleviate tensions that tend to arise, given the complexity of decision making or of collaborating across sectors. The second set, "pluralizing by ideal," highlights the various cases where plural forms of leadership derive from adherence to democratic ideals, or from a different organizing philosophy. In these settings, individual actors decide, right from the foundation of their organization, to eschew traditional and hierarchical approaches to leadership to adopt a more open and inclusive conception of it (Raelin, 2005, 2011, forthcoming). The third and final set, "pluralizing by ontological framing," shifts the focus away from organizations and practitioners to researchers. It explores how various researchers, by inscribing their studies in a different ontology than the one commonly found in leadership studies, propose and illustrate a distinct conceptualization of leadership, which in many instances is plural by definition, because of this ontology. Each section starts by presenting the results of studies that belong to the category, and includes a short vignette to illustrate the empirical manifestation of the category.

Instrumental Perspective: Pluralizing by Choice

When considering the literature on plural forms of leadership, a first distinction that appears between different forms and examples relates to structural concerns. This is especially striking in the case of empirical studies of plural forms of leadership: when considering the context in which it is investigated, one can quickly realize that, in some instances, the plural form considered is inscribed in the organization's structure, whereas, in other cases, it stems from mundane collective practices, routine behaviors in terms of decision making or the style of an individual leader who is keen on delegating some of his or her power to followers. Therefore, a first reason explaining why we can find instances of plural leadership is linked to organizational choices made in order to institutionalize formally the collective practice of joint leadership.

Based on our previous work, we can distinguish two forms of plural leadership that result from a decision in terms of a team's structuration. Each of these forms is associated with a different context. The first context is that of pluralistic organizations, where plural leadership is practiced in duos or trios formally defined in the organizational structure, whereas the second refers to interorganizational and cross-sector collaboration, where plural leadership takes the form of a collaborative governance. These two contexts may appear to be quite different, but we see that, in both these situations, organizations have tended to approach leadership in a collective way in order to address the challenges they face, either internally or externally, and have chosen to do so by structuring plural leadership in a formal way. Table 3.1 compares both contexts.

A good example of a pluralistic setting in which collective leadership is often embedded in the structure itself is represented by the performing arts sector: notably, theatres, orchestras, ballet companies (Reid & Karambayya, 2009, 2015). Because the personal qualities needed for high level artistic performance and for strong management are not always compatible, but both are central to these organizations' reputation, viability and performance, many such organizations find it convenient to create leadership structures with an "artistic director" and a "general manager" both reporting to the board of trustees and working together in collaboration in order to ensure that both artistic merit and fiscal responsibility receive equal (and, it is hoped, synergistic) attention. While such structures may sometimes be characterized by tensions and conflicts, they are nevertheless perceived as necessary and effective in many cases (Bhansing, Leenders & Wijnberg, 2012; Reid & Karambayya, 2009, 2015).

Table 3.1 Pluralizing Leadership: Comparison of Two Contexts

	Pluralistic organizations	Interorganizational, cross-sector collaborations
Key characteristics	Knowledge-based work and professional autonomy; diffuse power; competing logics: multiple and often divergent objectives	Combination of multiple organizations collaborating together across organization borders or across sectors
Challenges to overcome	• Difficulty in creating integrated action • Long and arduous negotiation processes • (Denis, Langley & Rouleau, 2007; Fjellvaer, 2010)	• Variety of actors • Coordination of the interorganizational collaboration • Participation issues • (Crosby & Bryson, 2005, 2010; Huxham & Vangen, 2000)
Form that plural leadership adopts	Duos or trios inscribed in the structure of the organization; leadership then takes the form of co-leadership	Complex structuring of the collaboration that may involve no stabilized leadership role as attributed to one individual or one organization; leadership then takes the form of a team structure, of a relay in time or depending on the issue at hand.

Another example of a setting in which plural leadership structures are common is health care where clinical directors (usually trained physicians) may share leadership roles with others with more management training (Denis, Lamothe & Langley, 2001; Baldwin, Dimunation & Alexander, 2011; Koethe & Kroft, 2013; Zismer, Brueggemann & James, 2010). Again it is the complementarity of skills, training and sources of legitimacy that makes such structures attractive. Indeed, wherever advanced professional skills and managerial skills need to be combined, are given equal status, and are rarely present within the same individual, this form of leadership may be desirable (Empson, Cleaver & Allen, 2013; Fjellvaer, 2010). However, as has been noted by some researchers (e.g., Reid & Karambayya, 2009, 2015), these dual structures can also be surrounded by ambiguity in role definition and can generate tensions and conflicts, ultimately leading to dysfunctions that can have a notable impact on the organization. These risks underline the importance of attending to the conditions of co-leadership (see Gibeau, Reid & Langley, Chapter 16, this volume).

As for interorganizational collaborations, a number of studies have shown that this setting may require a collective form of leadership that is distributed across time and space: in other words, the complexity of these collaborations between multiple organizations or stakeholders may be better tackled by structuring leadership roles as a relay between organizations, over time. As Crosby and Bryson (2005, 2010) have underlined, to achieve their common goal, these interorganizational collaborations need a form of collective and integrated leadership to facilitate and maintain communication across partners. As they discuss, these multi-organization or multi-stakeholder collaborations can be effective to address public issues, where such participation can help in fostering change or in solving multifaceted social problems. However, as described in more detail in their 2010 article, Crosby and Bryson highlight the complexity of such collaborations: not only do practices, processes and a specific governance structure associated with the collaboration have to be put in place, but accountability mechanisms have to be developed and implemented. In other words, these interorganizational collaborations require a formal structuration of how leadership will be shared and organized over the organizations involved in the collaboration (see also Huxham & Vangen, 2000, for discussion of what such collaborations require).

In this sense, although positive outcomes may emerge from such interorganizational collaborations, the challenges linked to the practice of this collective form of leadership should not be underestimated. As Vangen, Hayes and Cornforth (2015) have noted, these interorganizational collaborations involve issues related to the "two faces" of their nature: both "collaborative governance" and "governing collaboration" have to be taken into consideration and, more importantly, balanced. Indeed, both terms may refer to the context of complex collaborations, but when considered side by side, the literature on these facets reveals the presence of competing logics that generate tensions. Reflection on how to structure leadership across organizations therefore contributes, among other elements, to alleviating (albeit temporarily) these tensions. Nonetheless, Vangen et al. conclude by underlining the continual challenges of these collaborations:

> [t]he practical implication that we can draw from the conceptualizations and examples presented in this article is that the governance of collaborations is highly resource intensive and requires continuous energy and commitment and a great deal of skill from those who are in charge of them.
>
> *(Vangen et al., 2015: 1258)*

In sum, both the contexts of pluralistic organizations and interorganizational collaborations may call for plural forms of leadership to better face the complexity of their context and to achieve their goals, but this same complexity may explain why in both cases plural leadership is usually structurally and formally defined. However, plural leadership is not always first and foremost a question of structural choice, as we will now discuss.

Ideological Perspective: Pluralizing by Ideal

Following structural arguments in favor of plural forms of leadership, another line of thinking can be found in the literature: that pluralizing leadership reflects a political or an ideological commitment. In this line of reasoning, we find studies of leadership that approach it from a relational understanding, and others that promote a clear democratizing agenda. One of the most notable contributions in this direction is that of Raelin (e.g., 2005, 2011, forthcoming a), who has been advocating a new approach to leadership that he has called "leaderful." In this category, we also find a number of organizations that have, from their inception, defined themselves as "leaderless," such as some orchestras, social movements or organizations that remain hidden such as the hacker collective Anonymous. In these cases, their "leaderlessness" may result from a collective choice, but, fundamentally, this choice proceeds from a strong commitment to specific democratic values and a strong sense of mission. Despite their differences, leaderful and leaderless approaches to leadership all point to a highly pluralized approach to leadership, in which we find groups of individuals who collectively decide, based on ideas, values or philosophies, that leadership roles have to be opened up to all the members of the group or, more radically, have to disappear completely. In these cases, in spite of being reflected in the organization's structure, turning to plural forms of leadership is not an institutionalized way of facing the inherent challenges posed by the context. It is rather a reflection of a specific mission, or a choice to break away from traditional ways of organizing work.

Raelin (2005, 2011, forthcoming a) has argued in favor of a radical change in terms of conceptions of leadership: to move away from traditional definitions of leadership centered on specific individuals, toward a definition based on a democratic and collaborative understanding. His proposition rests on the recognition that current workplaces have changed, and that these changes extend to the practice of leadership, which should now be conceptualized as plural: in his words, "leaders need to co-exist at the same time and all together" (Raelin, 2005: 18). He defines leaderful practice as concurrent (whereas traditional and conventional understanding of leadership is serial), collective (instead of individual), collaborative (rather than controlling) and compassionate (rather than dispassionate). It should also be noted that Raelin proposes a definition of leadership that rests on practice, therefore linking it to the emergent leadership-as-practice stream of research (see, for example, Carroll, Levy & Richmond, 2008; Denis, Langley & Rouleau, 2010; and Raelin, forthcoming b). However, and in contrast to the leadership-as-practice body of research, Raelin's leaderful notion rests on a clear and firmly expressed democratic ideal:

> Leaderful practice is unrepentant in advocating distinctively democratic values. To explain its derivation, think of a time when a team was humming along almost like a single unit. Working together was a joy. Each team member had a specific functional role but seemed able implicitly to support each other when warranted. Any one of the team members could speak for the entire team. How would one characterize such a community? A common reference is that it is leaderless, that there is no need for a leader (see, e.g., Costigan and Donahue, 2009). But it is hardly leaderless because it is not devoid of leadership, it is full of leadership; in other words, leaderful. Everyone is participating in the leadership of the entity both collectively and concurrently; in other words, not just sequentially, but all together and at the same time (Raelin, 2003).
>
> *(Raelin, 2011: 203)*

Raelin is therefore not shy in stating not only that leadership can be conceived as collectively practiced, but that this view is inherently desirable on ethical grounds. Here, traditional hierarchies are contested and emancipation of all actors is promoted. Raelin considers that this approach is more suited to a context in which collaboration, creativity, empathy and ethical behavior, among others, are needed – a context that may correspond to the current challenges organizations face.

In a similar line of thinking, a number of studies on distributed leadership, especially as it has been studied and applied to schools (e.g., Spillane, Halverson & Diamond, 2001, 2004) have presented it as a modality of leadership that may foster more integrative, and less hierarchical, approaches. It should be noted that Woods (2004) has noted that distributed and democratic leadership should not be confused, the former, in his analysis, being more instrumental and functional, while the latter is wider in its social and societal implications. For Woods, democratic leadership extends distributed leadership, but shares with it a view of leadership as a dispersed phenomenon. Jones (2014) has also illustrated, through a case study, that distributed leadership does not necessarily come with more democratic decision-making processes. Yet, as Woods and Gronn (2009) have suggested, because distributed leadership rests on a dispersion of leadership among many organizational actors, it still offers the potential to bring more democracy in workplaces:

> A value of DL [distributed leadership] conceptually is that in its radical form it raises fundamental issues to do with how we understand the relationship between individual and

community: that is, DL as concertive action, where the combined leadership of many individuals in the grouping or organization is greater than the sum of the parts, asserts the inherent interrelationship of person and social structure.

(Woods & Gronn, 2009: 447)

Yet, as Bolden's review (2011) has revealed, the degree to which distributed leadership is truly democratic is open for debate. Other researchers have also criticized how distributed leadership has spread, mainly in the education sector. For example, Mayrowetz (2008) has discussed that the democratic potential of distributed leadership may be more of a stretch of this approach. For their part, Bolden, Petrov and Gosling (2009) contend that distributed leadership corresponds, in the case of the universities they studied, to an effective rhetoric: "Fundamentally, though, we argue that distributed leadership is most influential through its rhetorical value whereby it can be used to shape perceptions of identity, participation and influence but can equally shroud the underlying dynamics of power within universities" (Bolden et al., 2009: 274; on these rhetorical functions, see also Gosling, Bolden & Petrov, 2009). Finally, other researchers go even further, revealing how distributed leadership may in some contexts be closer to a discourse than a real practice, and serve interests that are far from this democratic ideal. For example, as Maxcy and Nguyen (2006) have shown, in some schools distributed leadership has been presented in a way that "employ[s] depoliticized rhetoric that masks an antidemocratic, managerial bias" (p. 188). All of these criticisms – many revealed though empirical studies – point to the importance of recognizing the power issues and the discursive nature of plural forms of leadership that are presented as promoting more democracy in organizations.

Under the opposite label of "leaderlessness" – while sharing with "leaderfulness" a similar ideological commitment – we find studies and organizations that promote plural forms of leadership by refusing completely the idea of having leaders. These organizations include orchestras that choose not to have a conductor (e.g., the Orpheus Chamber Orchestra, see Vredenburgh & He, 2003) to completely distributed networks (e.g., the hackers' collective Anonymous; see Dobusch & Schoeneborn, 2015, for an exploration of how such a collective can function as an organization). In most instances, we find in these organizations a strong culture based on collegiality and open, non-hierarchical participation by all of its members. But going even further, we find collectives, such as social protest movements – where resistance, empowerment and the quest for social justice are at the core of their activities – which explicitly adhere to a leaderless approach to leadership: in other words, where discussion and decision making are based on direct democracy. Eslen-Ziya and Erhart (2015) explored the post-heroic form of leadership that emerged out of the practices of a number of groups in the context of the Gezi protests, revealing that "[together, these groups] exemplified a form of absent leadership where individuals per se were absent but the ideas or common goals served as the leader" (p. 484). Here, it is thus the ideas and objectives that led the actions of these groups. These ideals can also be found in self-management organizations and workers' collectives – again, organizations founded on the ideas of autonomy, horizontality and solidarity, such as the ones studied by Kokkinidis (2015a, 2015b). As he describes:

these self-managed projects are primarily driven by the members' political aspiration to create a space that is open and experimental; a space that would not only challenge the existing forms of work but also put into practice other possibilities that place emphasis on reciprocal relationships and prioritize collective working, egalitarianism and autonomy. [. . .] [When considering the organizations showcased in the article] one of the main features of autonomy is the recognition that individuals are capable of creating their own rules and of governing their affairs as they see fit, which in turn requires a different definition of democracy. One that supports more inclusive models of participation and encourages the construction of rule-creating rather than rule-following individuals, allowing them to determine both the ends and the means, collectively.

(Kokkinidis, 2015b: 868)

As such, these organizations appear as sites where new practices in terms of organizing, decision making and leading are experimented with, all with the aims of fostering social change. Yet, "leaderlessness" is not without issues, as Western (2014) underlines: in protest groups, the discourse (or fantasy, as he calls it) of the absence of leaders can create tensions with the actual practices where leaders emerge out of action. This leads him to recommend to these group to move beyond this anti-leadership discourse, and to talk of autonomist leadership, which he describes as follows: "Autonomist Leadership is a form of individualised collective leadership, i.e. it is embedded in networks and enacted by autonomous individuals and groups" (p. 693). As a form of leadership based on autonomy and mutualism, this conception tries to reconcile leadership with the democratic principles at the heart of these groups.

In sum, these organizations may be relevant sites to explore for researchers aiming at challenging capitalist organizations and management practices, and in exploring alternative workplaces and their transformative potential. Given their will to propose strong and radical alternatives to traditional, hierarchical leadership, they therefore represent an interesting site to study leadership practiced by collectives and to deepen our understanding of it. As Sutherland, Land and Böhm (2014) have noted, "just because an organization is leaderless, it does not necessarily mean that it is also leadershipless" (p. 759) – a provocative statement that can be read as an invitation to conduct more empirical work on these alternative forms of organizing. In sum, while "leaderlessness" may sound as if it is the polar opposite of "leaderfulness," both are in fact more closely related than they may appear, both resting on a strong ideological commitment to equality and democracy.

Ontological Perspective: Pluralizing by Definition

The first two perspectives we explored were first and foremost based on empirical observations: the actual existence of leadership practiced by several individuals, stemming from a formally and *a priori* defined structuration – be it in terms of duos, trios or relays – or from a strong commitment to democratic ideals. In both cases, pluralizing leadership is commanded either by the context (plural forms of leadership as means to manage pluralistic organizations and to collaborate across organizations), or by the principles to which members adhere (plural forms of leadership as a way to embody ideals in daily functioning). With this third angle, we shift from an empirical starting point to a more theoretical one. When surveying the literature, we find a number of studies that develop a plural view of leadership by ontologically and theoretically framing this phenomenon in a different way. While all studies on plural leadership have theoretical grounding, not all stem from a commitment to a particular understanding of reality. Yet, a number of qualitative inquiries, mainly originating from management and organization studies, arrive at a plural conception of leadership, not by counting leaders, but by anchoring their work in a strong process ontology.

Process ontologies postulate that the world is fundamentally in movement, and that change is constant (Rescher, 2012; Helin, Hernes, Hjorth & Holt, 2014; Hernes, 2014). This basic tenet reverses completely the traditional ontological positioning of most research in management and organization studies, which rests on stability, rather than change, as a central and defining characteristic of phenomena. Studies adopting a process ontology place action at the fore of their empirical investigations, as phenomena are reconceptualized as being continually elaborated through action and through social processes, hence the name of this ontological position, situated in a context and happening over time, rather than being "fixed" and established (Chia, 1997). Also, by placing change – and not stability – at their core, studies adopting a process ontology reveal how organizational phenomena, such as leadership, continually require a form of work: seen from this light, leadership continually emerges out of action, and is always being performed. In a process ontology, human phenomena such as leadership are therefore conceptualized not as "possessed" by individuals, but as being constantly elaborated, as actors are acting in a context that is continually evolving: leadership becomes viewed as a question of movement (Wood, 2005), as a process of becoming (Tsoukas & Chia, 2002).

In studies of leadership, this ontological positioning is far from being the norm. But in recent years, organization studies have seen a growing interest in strong process views on phenomena, and a number of researchers have explored leadership using this processual definition. Crevani, Lindgren and Packendorff (2010) have suggested that conceiving leadership as a process facilitates decentering it from individuals – the same move that is at the heart of plural views of leadership. As mentioned previously, a process ontology places action and social processes at the heart of the empirical inquiry. More specifically, when applied to leadership, it has led a number of researchers to propose that leadership is a consequence of social processes and interactions unfolding over time, in which a variety of actors participate (as in most organizational processes). Leadership is therefore constructed as emerging from these interactions.

This third perspective on plural leadership can be understood as a lens through which leadership can be viewed, a lens that produces *by definition* a pluralized conceptualization of leadership. Leadership may or may not, in the settings in which these studies are conducted, be formally defined and consciously practiced by local actors in a collective way. It is rather the way the researcher approaches the phenomenon that leads to them seeing it in a collective way. In this sense, we can place in this third perspective both studies in which the researchers have explicitly stated that their work is anchored in a process ontology, and those in which, while not necessarily making such strong ontological statements, researchers have developed and proposed views of leadership that show a proximity with process ontology. We therefore include in this third perspective all studies on leadership that define leadership as *emerging* out of joint action, interactions and relationships between actors. We emphasize the verb "emerging," as it signals one of the main differences from plural leadership that these studies project: in line with a general process ontology, they all see leadership as produced by the relations and interactions between actors, as they are involved in their daily activities. In this sense, leadership is both collective and processual. This represents a clear difference from the two previous perspectives: in these two perspectives, leadership is defined by practitioners as plural, and the reasons behind this choice are either instrumental or structural, and ideological. From this point, it is a plurality of persons occupying the leadership position – from a structural duo to a leaderless group – that "does" leadership in different circumstances, producing various results. Leadership is still conceived as something that produces effects, results, decisions, etc. – in other words, as a cause. The ontological perspective reverses this way of thinking about leadership. Starting from the social processes in organizational settings, in which a plurality of actors is de facto present, it proposes to identify from all of these interactions those that perform or produce leadership, which then become a resource for pursuing action.

In this line of thinking, the relational theory of leadership has focussed on the situated relational dynamics from which leadership emerges, in many instances proposing a view of leadership as a co-construction. As such, and as discussed by Uhl-Bien and Ospina (2012), process ontology is one of the ontological underpinnings of researchers developing a relational view of leadership. For example, belonging to this perspective, Uhl-Bien (2006) has proposed that these relational dynamics are indeed processual, happening over time, but without identifying the specific onto-logical roots of her work. Cunliffe and Eriksen (2011) have also developed a relational view of leadership, as produced by many actors, much in line with process thinking.

Working in a different tradition, i.e., by attending to what is being said in interactions, Vine, Holmes, Marra, Pfeifer and Jackson (2008) have shown that leadership entails a daily produc-tion, in which interpersonal communication plays a key role. Pushing this idea further, research-ers influenced by the communicative constitution of organization (otherwise known as CCO, a stream of research at the interaction of communication studies and organization studies that posits that organizational phenomena are produced and emerge in and out of communication) have also approached leadership from a processual and plural fashion. But the main contribu-tion of these researchers, as well as that of others that are working in other lines of inquiry, has not been to give a central role to human and interpersonal communication in processes that create leadership: it has rather been in the extension of who – or what – takes part in this pro-cess. Recent studies such as those of Hawkins (2015), Mailhot, Gagnon, Langley and Binette (forthcoming) and Sergi (forthcoming) show how leadership is also materially produced. These researchers tend to view leadership as an assemblage made up of social and material elements, and it is in this sense that leadership is understood as collective.

Finally, as we have discussed elsewhere (Denis et al., 2012), the main risk associated with such a fluid, processual and fully decentered conception of leadership is to dilute it to the point where it can be difficult to conceptually and empirically distinguish it from other social pro-cesses happening in organizational settings. Researchers investigating plural forms of leadership in this line of thinking should therefore be fully aware of this potential risk, and be clear in their definition of what does (and does not) constitute leadership.

Discussion and Conclusion

The overview we have proposed in this chapter is not exhaustive, and justifications other than the one we identified, both in research and in practice, could be found. What we want to suggest here is that it is fruitful not only to consider the "who" and "how" of plural forms of leadership – the configuration of individuals involved in plural leadership and the daily func-tioning of such configurations – but also to consider and to question the "why," the justifica-tions from which these more collective forms may emerge. Our chapter was based on the idea that, by interrogating the ideas and the reasons behind this organizational phenomenon, we could start developing a different typology of forms of plural leadership. In a general context where these plural forms are attracting more and more interest and are increasingly deployed in a variety of organizations, we believe that it is important to have in hand an overview of what this phenomenon involves. Our previous work (Denis et al., 2012) was a first attempt at ordering a body of research that tends to be scattered into a multitude of related concepts, and this chapter should be seen as an extension of that work. As we have revealed with the three categories we presented in these pages, it is possible to see leadership practiced by collectives in a different light, when we consider the reasons advanced for pluralizing leadership. These reasons can have instrumental, ideological or ontological roots, based respectively on organi-zations that require plural forms of leadership to function more effectively, on groups who share a strong commitment to a democratic ideal or on researchers themselves who wish to conceptualize leadership from a different ontological starting point. It is important to consider these reasons, as we suggest that they will impact how plural leadership is practiced and what it creates. Table 3.2 summarizes these implications. We have also included in this table a few issues we see as associated with each perspective. These issues can be seen as opportunities for future research, as they represent challenges – both empirical and conceptual.

As we discussed, the third perspective on plural forms of leadership that we identified stems from researchers themselves, who begin from a different definition of leadership. For their part, the first two perspectives refer to empirical contexts in which plural forms of leadership can be seen. As a first item in an agenda for future research, we propose that the processual understanding of plural leadership that researchers working in the ontological perspective are developing could be applied to the empirical contexts described in the other two perspectives. In organizational settings in which unitary leadership positions are already occupied by more than one actor, how is this plural leadership performed on a daily basis? What are the social processes and the specific patterns of interactions that compose plural leadership in these contexts? We hence suggest that a first extension of research on plural forms of leadership might come from combining the perspectives we identified in this chapter.

As we have demonstrated in this chapter, there are a variety of reasons behind the phenomenon of plural leadership. Rendering these reasons explicit helps us understand why and how the tasks of leadership can be undertaken by a collective rather than a single individual. Moreover, considering the reasons or the justifications behind plural forms of leadership may also help us understand and better apprehend current changes in the workplace. For example,

Table 3.2 Three Perspectives on Plural Leadership

	Instrumental perspective	*Ideological perspective*	*Ontological perspective*
Why pluralize leadership	To address challenges posed by the context	To enact a commitment to a democratic ideal	To conceptualize leadership as a process
How plural leadership is practiced	In a formally defined structure, either as a duo/trio, or as a relay over time	Requires processes of consultation and of negotiation between actors; depending on the context, it can also allow fully distributed action, without consultation	What is being done in specific situation is seen as a collective accomplishment, even if formal leadership is attributed to a single individual
Who participates in plural leadership	Individuals who have been appointed or identified as formal leaders	Extended definition of leadership membership (all or none)	A plurality of actors participate de facto in leadership
Key issues	Finding the right balance inside the duo or trio; making the relay work well for interorganizational collaboration	Maintaining commitment to the democratic ideal in the face of difficult situations	Distinguishing leadership from other social processes: how is leadership different from coordination or decision making?

projects and project management have now clearly spread outside their traditional settings (engineering, construction, IT development, to name a few). Given their temporary nature and their often-interdisciplinary constitution, project teams may represent a relevant context to mobilize plural forms of leadership. Also, it is not unusual for projects to be led by individuals who are not otherwise in a superior hierarchical position compared to other project members. This situation may favor the emergence of a more collaborative approach to decision making, coordination and leadership.

However, while the field of project management has long considered questions pertaining to leadership (see, for example, Gaddis (1959), who was among the first to discuss the characteristics that the project manager must display to effectively manage projects), inquiries into project leadership have mostly been conducted from a unitary view of leadership. Indeed, studies on the leadership of projects or in the context of projects often revolve around the style of leadership (e.g., Müller & Turner, 2007) or the effectiveness and performance of leadership for project success (e.g., Müller, Geraldi & Turner, 2012; for an overview of leadership in the context of projects, see Clarke, 2012a), focusing on elements such as traits, behaviors or competences such as the emotional intelligence of project leaders. Yet, although some studies have noted that the particularities of projects may require adaptations or developments in terms of leadership (Tyssen, Wald & Spieth, 2013), studies on leadership in such contexts tend to remain centered on unitary leaders. It is only recently that a few scholars have started to propose that more collective approaches to leadership might be relevant and appropriate for projects (Clarke, 2012b and Lindgren & Packendorff, 2009), but these ideas still need to be explored empirically. Relevant questions would concern, for example, how projects, as temporary organizations, differ from more permanent organizations, with regards to plural forms of leadership? Does their temporary nature facilitate or hinder plural forms of leadership? Does this limited nature influence how plural leadership is implemented and practiced? Many questions remain to be considered.

Another area in which plural forms of leadership may already be experimented with is virtual work settings. The de facto distributed work setting, where issues of communication, knowledge sharing and alignment are at the forefront, may also offer a fruitful context in which to consider the role of plural forms of leadership. We see in this specific context parallels with interorganizational collaborations that require a structuration of leadership in the form of relays over time and space. Also, when virtual teams are global teams composed of people coming from different cultures, it might also be appropriate to formally implement a collective approach to leadership to better understand the differences that might arise from these differences, again in order to facilitate collaboration. Some studies have addressed plural forms of leadership in virtual settings (e.g., Al-Ani, Horspool & Bligh, 2011; Shuffler, Wiese, Salas & Burke, 2010), discussing how it can be beneficial for team dynamics and what the team achieves. A review of this literature has led Miloslavic, Wildman and Thayer (2015) to recommend combining both shared and vertical leadership in virtual and global teams. These studies are firmly anchored in the first perspective we identified, the instrumental perspective, referring to how leadership is structured in these teams. However, it might be interesting to approach plural leadership in these contexts from the third perspective, whereby plural leadership is defined as emerging from social interactions and communication between actors in the course of their work. How do people taking part in these virtual and sometimes global teams enact a collective form of leadership, through their technology-mediated interactions? Working from this ontological anchoring would offer a different view of plural leadership in this context, which could in turn inspire researchers and practitioners who locate themselves in the instrumental perspective.

Finally, and more broadly, a number of researchers are underlining that work and workplaces are experiencing a wave of change, including changes toward more collaborative workplaces. These new collaborative practices are supported by more general trends that can be witnessed currently in organizations. These trends may or may not be sustained over time; nonetheless, they are feeding a renewed interest in collaboration, collaborative practices and collaboration tools – an interest which in turn may spill over towards more collaborative approaches to leadership. In this sense, this enlarged interest in collaboration may represent a fertile ground for plural forms of leadership, both in terms of empirical experimentations led by practitioners and of research interest. Two issues seem to be arising around this trend. First, we see that, inside traditional organizations, new office spaces are designed and set up for collaboration. These new office spaces are more open, and aim at removing walls (both material and immaterial) inside organizations. Do these spaces create new opportunities for plural forms of leadership? A recent article by De Paoli and Ropo (2015) hints at a positive answer to this question, although much empirical work is still needed. Also, organizational boundaries are increasingly questioned, becoming in some cases more fluid and more porous. Not only are we seeing more collaborations between organizations, but organizations are also developing new relationships with customers and clients. For example, once limited to specific, often design-oriented firms, co-creation practices are becoming more popular. If the involvement of customers, clients or patients do change how new products or services are developed and deployed, this involvement may also give rise to plural forms of leadership in these development activities. Is it happening in practice? And, if so, are these forms different from the ones we already know about, given that they involve actors from both inside and outside the organization? If the scattered evidence we see here and there towards more collaborative practices materializes into a more durable trend in terms of work organization, we believe that plural forms of leadership may also become more than a marginal phenomenon.

Note

1 A quick search on the web with the keywords "companies with multiple CEOs" generates links to articles with titles such as: "With co-CEOs, companies flirt with disaster" (*Fortune*, September 20, 2014) or "With CEOs, two heads aren't better than one" (*Wall Street Journal*, June 8, 2015). But the same search also uncovered links to articles that have a more positive tone towards plural forms of leadership.

References

Al-Ani, B., Horspool, A., & Bligh, M. C. (2011). Collaborating with "virtual strangers": Towards developing a framework for leadership in distributed teams. *Leadership*, 7 (3), 219–249.

Baldwin, K. S., Dimunation, N., & Alexander, J. (2011). Health care leadership and the dyad model. *Physician Exec*, 37 (4), 66–70.

Bhansing, P. V., Leenders, M. A. A. M., & Wijnberg, N. M. (2012). Performance effects of cognitive heterogeneity in dual leadership structures in the arts: The role of selection system orientations. *European Management Journal*, 30 (6), 523–534.

Bolden, R. (2011). Distributed leadership in organizations: A review of theory and research. *International Journal of Management Reviews*, 13 (3), 251–269.

Bolden, R., Petrov, G., and Gosling, J. (2009). Distributed leadership in higher education: Rhetoric and reality. *Educational Management Administration & Leadership*, 37 (2), 257–277.

Carroll, B., Levy, L., & Richmond, D. (2008). Leadership as practice: Challenging the competency paradigm. *Leadership*, 4 (4), 363–379.

Clarke, N. (2012a). Leadership in projects: what we know from the literature and new insights. *Team Performance Management: An International Journal*, 18 (3/4), 128–148.

Clarke, N. (2012b). Shared leadership in projects: a matter of substance over style. *Team Performance Management*, 18 (3/4), 196–209.

Chia, R. (1997). Essai: Thirty years on: From organizational structures to the organization of thought. *Organization Studies*, 18 (4), 685–707.

Crevani, L., Lindgren, M., & Packendorff, J. (2010). Leadership, not leaders: On the study of leadership as practices and interactions. *Scandinavian Journal of Management*, 26, 77–86.

Crosby, B. C., & Bryson, J. M. (2005). A leadership framework for cross-sector collaboration. *Public Management Review*, 7 (2), 177–201.

Crosby, B. C., & Bryson, J. M. (2010). Integrative leadership and the creation and maintenance of cross-sector collaborations. *The Leadership Quarterly*, 21 (2), 211–230.

Cunliffe, A. L., & Eriksen, M. (2011). Relational leadership. *Human Relations*, 64 (11), 1425–1449.

De Paoli, D., & Ropo, A. (2015). Open plan offices: The response to leadership challenges of virtual project work? *Journal of Corporate Real Estate*, 17 (1), 63–74.

Denis, J., Lamothe, L., & Langley, A. (2001). The dynamics of collective leadership and strategic change in pluralistic organizations. *Academy of Management Journal*, 44 (4), 809–837.

Denis, J.-L., Langley, A., & Rouleau, L. (2007). Strategizing in pluralistic contexts: Rethinking theoretical frames. *Human Relations*, 60 (1), 179–215.

Denis, J.-L., Langley, A., & Rouleau, L. (2010). The practice of leadership in the messy world of organizations. *Leadership*, 6 (1), 67–88.

Denis, J.-L., Langley, A., & Sergi, V. (2012). Leadership in the plural. *The Academy of Management Annals*, 6 (1), 211–283.

D'Innocenzo, L., Mathieu, J. E., & Kukenberger, M. R. (2014). A meta-analysis of different forms of shared leadership: Team performance relations. *Journal of Management*, 68 (4), 545–560.

Dobusch, L., & Schoeneborn, D. (2015). Fluidity, identity, and organizationality: The communicative constitution of anonymous. *Journal of Management Studies*, 68 (4), 1005–1035.

Drescher, M. A., Korsgaard, M. A., Welpe, I. M., Picot, A., & Wigand, R. T. (2014). The dynamics of shared leadership: Building trust and enhancing performance. *The Journal of Applied Psychology*, 99 (5), 771–783.

Dust, S. B., & Ziegert, J. C. (2015). Multi-Leader Teams in Review: A Contingent-Configuration Perspective of Effectiveness. *International Journal of Management Reviews*, doi: 10.1111/ijmr.12073.

Empson, L., Cleaver, I., & Allen, J. (2013). Managing partners and management professionals: Institutional work dyads in professional partnerships. *Journal of Management Studies*, 50 (5), 808–844.

Eslen-Ziya, H., & Erhart, I. (2015). Toward postheroic leadership: A case study of Gezi's collaborating multiple leaders. *Leadership*, 11 (4), 471–488.

Fjellvaer, H. (2010). *Dual and unitary leadership: Managing ambiguity in pluralistic organizations* (Unpublished doctoral thesis). Norwegian School of Economics and Business Administration, Bergen, Norway.

Follett, M. P. (1924). *Creative experience*. New York: Longmans, Green.

Gaddis, P. O. (1959). The project manager. *Harvard Business Review*, June, 89–97.

Gibb, C. A. (1954). Leadership. In G. Lindzay (Ed.), *Handbook of social psychology* (Vol. 2, pp. 877–917). Reading, MA: Addison-Wesley.

Gosling, J., Bolden, R., & Petrov, G. (2009). Distributed leadership in higher education: What does it accomplish? *Leadership*, 5 (3), 299–310.

Gronn, P. (2002). Distributed leadership as a unit of analysis. *The Leadership Quarterly*, 13 (4), 423–451.

Gronn, P. (2009). Leadership configurations. *Leadership*, 5 (3), 381–394.

Gronn, P. (2015). The view from inside leadership configurations. *Human Relations*, 68 (4), 545–560.

Hawkins, B. (2015). Ship-shape: Materializing leadership in the British Royal Navy. *Human Relations*, 68 (6), 951–971.

Helin, J., Hernes, T., Hjorth, D., & Holt, R. (2014). *The Oxford handbook of process philosophy and organization Studies*. Oxford: Oxford University Press.

Hernes, T. (2014). *A process theory of organization*. Oxford: Oxford University Press.

Hodgson, R. C., Levinson, D. J., & Zaleznik, A. (1965). *The executive role constellation*. Boston, MA: Harvard Business School Press.

Houghton, J. D., Pearce, C. L., Manz, C. C., Courtright, S., & Stewart, G. L. (2015). Sharing is caring: Toward a model of proactive caring through shared leadership. *Human Resource Management Review*, 25 (3), 313–327.

Huxham, C., & Vangen, S. (2000). Leadership in the shaping and implementation of collaboration agendas: How things happen in a (not quite) joined-up world. *Academy of Management Journal*, 43 (6), 1159–1175.

Jonassen, J. R. (2015). Effects of multi-team leadership on collaboration and integration in subsea operations. *International Journal of Leadership Studies*, 9 (1), 89–114.

Jones, S. (2014). Distributed leadership: A critical analysis. *Leadership*, 10 (2), 129–141.

Koethe, S. M., & Kroft, S. H. (2013). Hospital laboratory leadership and the dyad model of management. *Lab Medicine*, 44 (2), 168–171.

Kokkinidis, G. (2015a). Post-capitalist imaginaries: The case of workers' collectives in Greece. *Journal of Management Inquiry*, 24 (4), 429–432.

Kokkinidis, G. (2015b). Spaces of possibilities: Workers' self-management in Greece. *Organization*, 22 (6), 847–871.

Lindgren, M., & Packendorff, J. (2009). Project leadership revisited: Towards distributed leadership perspectives in project research. *International Journal of Project Organisation and Management*, 1 (3), 285–308.

Mailhot, C., Gagnon, S., Langley, A., & Binette, L. F. (forthcoming). Distributing leadership across people and objects in a collaborative research project. *Leadership*, doi: 10.1177/1742715014543578.

Maxcy, B. D., & Nguyen, T. S. T. (2006). The politics of distributing leadership: Reconsidering leadership distribution in two Texas elementary schools. *Educational Policy*, 20 (1), 163–196.

Mayrowetz, D. (2008). Making sense of distributed leadership: Exploring the multiple usages of the concept in the field. *Educational Administration Quarterly*, 44 (3), 424–435.

Miloslavic, S. A., Wildman, J. L., & Thayer, A. L. (2015). Structuring successful global virtual teams. In J. L. Wildman, & R. L. Griffith (Eds.), *Leading global teams* (pp. 67–87). New York: Springer.

Müller, R., Geraldi, J., & Turner, J. R. (2012). Relationships between leadership and success in different types of project complexities. *IEEE Transactions on Engineering Management*, 59 (1), 77–90.

Müller, R., & Turner, J. (2007). Matching the project manager's leadership style to project type. *International Journal of Project Management*, 25 (1), 21–32.

Nicolaides, V. C., Laport, K. A., Chen, T. R., Tomassetti, A. J., Weis, E. J., Zaccaro, S. J., & Cortina, J. M. (2014). The shared leadership of teams: A meta-analysis of proximal, distal, and moderating relationships. *The Leadership Quarterly*, 25 (5), 923–942.

Pearce, C. L., Wassenaar, C. L., & Manz, C. C. (2014). Is shared leadership the key to responsible leadership? *Academy of Management Perspectives*, 28 (3), 275–288.

Raelin, J. A. (2005). We the leaders: In order to form a leaderful organization. *Journal of Leadership & Organizational Studies*, 12 (2), 18–30.

Raelin, J. A. (2011). From leadership-as-practice to leaderful practice. *Leadership*, 7 (2), 195–211.

Raelin, J. A. (forthcoming a). Imagine there are no leaders: Reframing leadership as collaborative agency. Forthcoming in *Leadership*, doi: 10.1177/1742715014558076.

Raelin, J. A. (forthcoming b). *Leadership-as-practice: Theory and application*. London: Routledge.

Reid, W., & Karambayya, R. (2009). Impact of dual executive leadership dynamics in creative organizations. *Human Relations*, 62 (7), 1073–1112.

Reid, W., & Karambayya, R. (2015). The shadow of history: Situated dynamics of trust in dual executive leadership. *Leadership*. doi: 10.1177/1742715015579931.

Rescher, N. (2012). Process philosophy. In *Stanford Encyclopedia of Philosophy*. Retrieved October 12, 2015 from http://plato.stanford.edu/entries/process-philosophy/.

Sergi, V. (forthcoming). Who's leading the way? Investigating the contributions of materiality to leadership-as-practice. In J. Raelin (Ed.), *Leadership-as-practice: Theory and application*. London: Routledge.

Sergi, V., Denis, J.-L., & Langley, A. (2012). Opening up perspectives on plural leadership. *Industrial and Organizational Psychology*, 5 (4): 403–407.

Shuffler, M. L., Wiese, C. W., Salas, E., & Burke, C. S. (2010). Leading one another across time and space: Exploring shared leadership functions in virtual teams. *Revista de Psicología Del Trabajo Y de Las Organizaciones*, 26 (1), 3–17.

Spillane, J. P., Halverson, R., & Diamond, J. B. (2001). Investigating school leadership practice: A distributed perspective. *Educational Researcher*, 30, 23–28.

Spillane, J. P., Halverson, R., & Diamond, J. B. (2004). Towards a theory of leadership practice: A distributed perspective. *Journal of Curriculum Studies*, 36 (1), 3–34.

Spyridonidis, D., Hendy, J., & Barlow, J. (2015). Leadership for knowledge translation: The case of CLAHRCs. *Qualitative Health Research*, doi: 10.1177/1049732315583268.

Sutherland, N., Land, C., & Böhm, S. (2014). Anti-leaders(hip) in social movement organizations: The case of autonomous grassroots groups. *Organization*, 21 (6): 759–781.

Tsoukas, H., & Chia, R. (2002). On organizational becoming: Rethinking organizational change. *Organization Science*, 13 (5), 567–582.

Tyssen, A. K., Wald, A., & Spieth, P. (2013). Leadership in temporary organizations: A review of leadership theories and a research agenda. *Project Management Journal*, 44 (6), 52–67.

Uhl-Bien, M. (2006). Relational leadership theory: Exploring the social processes of leadership and organizing. *Leadership Quarterly*, 17 (6), 654–676.

Uhl-Bien, M., & Ospina, S. (2012). Paradigm interplay in relational leadership: A way forward. In M. Uhl-Bien & S. M. Ospina (Eds.), *Advancing relational leadership research: A dialogue among perspectives* (pp. 537–580). Charlotte, NC: Information Age Pub.

Vangen, S., Hayes, J. P., & Cornforth, C. (2015). Governing cross-sector, inter-organizational collaborations. *Public Management Review*, 17 (9): 1237–1260.

Vangen, S., & Huxham, C. (2003). Enacting leadership for collaborative advantage: Dilemmas of ideology and pragmatism in the activities of partnership managers. *British Journal of Management*, 14 (s1), S61–S76.

Vine, B., Holmes, J., Marra, M., Pfeifer, D., & Jackson, B. (2008). Exploring co-leadership talk through interactional sociolinguistics. *Leadership*, 4 (3), 339–360.

Vredenburgh, D., & He, I. Y. (2003). Leadership lessons from a conductorless orchestra. *Business Horizons*, 46 (5), 19–24.

Wang, D., Waldman, D. A, & Zhang, Z. (2014). A meta-analysis of shared leadership and team effectiveness. *The Journal of Applied Psychology*, 99 (2), 181–198.

Western, S. (2014). Autonomist leadership in leaderless movements: Anarchists leading the way. *Ephemera*, 14 (4), 673–698.

Wood, M. (2005). The fallacy of misplaced leadership. *Journal of Management Studies*, 42 (6), 1101–1121.

Woods, P. A. (2004). Democratic leadership: drawing distinctions with distributed leadership. *International Journal of Leadership in Education*, 7 (1), 3–26.

Woods, P. A., & Gronn, P. (2009). Nurturing democracy: The contribution of distributed leadership to a democratic organizational landscape. *Educational Management Administration & Leadership*, 37 (4), 430–451.

Zismer, D. K., Brueggemann, J., & James, M. D. (2010). Examining the "dyad" as a management model in integrated health systems. *Physician Exec*, 36 (1), 14–19.

4

Leadership in the Face of Crisis and Uncertainty

David Rast and Michael Hogg

As we planned and wrote this chapter, the worst Ebola epidemic in history ravaged West Africa; the "Islamic State" and its clients continued their barbaric atrocities in and beyond the Middle East; the Ukraine continued to degenerate into civil war; Greece teetered on the brink of exiting the Euro and becoming a failed state within Europe; and across the globe millions of people fleeing war, famine, and poverty formed a tidal wave of immigrants and refugees. The modern world of circumscribed nations, cultures, and economies seemed inexorably to be unraveling. This snapshot of late 2014 and early 2015 highlights that we live in uncertain times, and that these uncertainties may seem inescapable. Of course, these examples of uncertainties and crises are not the only ones we experience. In a less catastrophically life-threatening manner, we all confront accelerating organizational and technological change that nonetheless creates uncertainty and sometimes a sense of crisis.

To deal with these changes and uncertainties, particularly those that ultimately challenge our sense of identity in the world, people look to their leaders. Leaders play a key role, for good and for evil, in initiating and steering us through these events. When experiencing uncertainty we look to our leaders to protect us and shepherd us toward a better future—one that resolves or minimizes these feelings of uncertainty.

Uncertainty and crisis, however, can alter the way in which people think about and respond to their leaders, as well as influence the type of leader they desire. For example, leaders are more likely to be considered charismatic during crises, and charismatic/transformational leadership is more likely to emerge in times of crisis (Trice & Beyer, 1986). Others have shown that a crisis context shifts the typical "think manager—think male" leadership stereotype to "think crisis—think female," therefore making female or minority leaders more desirable in times of uncertainty (Ryan, Haslam, Hersby, & Bongiorno, 2011).

Uncertainty and crisis can also impact how leaders are evaluated. According to the "romance of leadership" perspective (Bligh, Kohles, & Pillai, 2011), accepting a leadership position during an economic crisis or successfully leading an organization out of one can cause the leader to be perceived as confident, effective, or even charismatic, which in turn results in greater support and trust for the leader. An example of this is George W. Bush, who was rated as an extremely uncharismatic leader before 9/11, but immediately following the 9/11 attacks he was rated as being extremely charismatic (e.g., Landau et al., 2004).

In times of uncertainty and crisis, followers look to their leaders to provide an unambiguous vision and direction for the future. This is particularly true for uncertainties implicating one's identity or self-concept. During these periods of crisis, leaders carry the burden of reducing followers' feelings of uncertainty (see Rast, Hogg, & Giessner, 2013), and followers pay attention to their leaders and how leaders react to the uncertainty. A leader's reaction helps followers assess the situation and make sense of it, and signals to followers whether the leader is effective or not (Boin & Hart, 2003; Levay, 2010). To date the majority of research and theorizing on leadership, particularly in times of general crisis and uncertainty, focuses on leaders' characteristics and behaviors, primarily focusing on leaders' charisma (Bligh, Kohles, & Meindl, 2004; Pillai & Meindl, 1998), decision-making style (Mumford, Friedrich, Caughron, & Byrne, 2007), or intelligence (Riggio, Murphy, & Pirozzolo, 2002).

While useful, these approaches fail to capture a fundamental aspect of leadership: leadership is a group process in which leaders construct and communicate people's identity as group members—their social identity (Hogg, 2007a). Leaders must lead an entire collection of people to reduce feelings of crisis and identity uncertainty. In this chapter we redress this oversight by focusing on how leaders impact and how they are impacted by identity processes, group dynamics, and intergroup relations. Our analysis is framed by social identity theory (Tajfel & Turner, 1979; Turner, Hogg, Oakes, Reicher, & Wetherell, 1987) and draws primarily on the social identity theory of leadership (Hogg, 2001; Hogg & Van Knippenberg, 2003; Hogg, Van Knippenberg, & Rast, 2012a). We also introduce uncertainty–identity theory to draw out the logic that identity-related, as opposed to generic, crisis and uncertainty promote follower preference for leadership per se, and for strong, directive, perhaps authoritarian/autocratic leadership (Hogg, 2007b; Rast, in press). Finally, we present an analysis of leadership to resolve an intergroup crisis (e.g., Hogg, Van Knippenberg, & Rast, 2012b).

Social Identity and Influence in Groups

Social identity theory is a social psychological framework that specifies the social, cognitive, and motivational aspects and processes associated with group memberships and intergroup relations. Social identity theory comprises the social identity theory of intergroup relations (Tajfel & Turner, 1979) and the compatible social identity theory of the group (self-categorization theory; Turner et al., 1987)—see comprehensive reviews by Abrams and Hogg (2010) and Hogg (2012, 2013). It starts with the premise that groups are important because they provide their members with sense of self and identity while also providing a feeling of belongingness.

Tajfel (1972) defined social identity as an "individual's knowledge that he belongs to certain social groups together with some emotional and value significance to him of this group membership" (p. 292). Thus, a social identity refers to the cognitive and affective representation of oneself as belonging to a specific group (or the ingroup). Social groups are cognitively represented as prototypes, which are a fuzzy set of interrelated attributes that describe and prescribe the attitudes and behaviors that maximize intragroup similarities and intergroup differences. As an example of these processes, one's social identity as a Democrat or Republican in the US is likely to be salient around a national election. We can readily think about the multitude of attitudes, policy positions, and political ideologies associated with each of these parties, which also distinguish the parties from each other. When we interact with a person from the same party as ours, we view that person as an ingroup member and perceive that person more favorably. When interacting with a person from the opposing party, however, we view him/her as an outgroup member and perceive that person less favorably.

Once a person is categorized, including oneself, then depersonalization occurs. Depersonalization refers to a process by which the self and others are perceived as an embodiment of their group's prototype, rather than as unique individuals—that is, they are seen as a group member rather than an autonomous individual. Because prototypes describe and prescribe the shared social identity-defining attributes of the group, members pay close attention to how well they and others conform to the group's prototype. Members within a group are contrasted with the group's prototype so they can be more or less prototypical compared to other category members. Hence, "group members conform to, and thus are influenced by, the prototype" (Hogg, 2001, p. 189). Because prototypes are context dependent, those who embody the group's prototype in one situation might not in another situation. Thus it is clearly important for people to gain information that they believe is reliable about the group prototype.

Indeed, as people identify more strongly with a particular group, they come to internalize the group's prototype, as well as the associated attitudes and behaviors, as their own. People in groups that are important to self-definition tend to be highly attentive to and aware of differential ingroup prototypicality (Haslam, Oakes, McGarty, Turner, & Onorato, 1995; Hogg, 2005); and thus, in determining what source of norm information is perceived to be most useful and reliable, we tend to prefer highly prototypical ingroup members over both outgroup members and less prototypical ingroup members. Recent developments among social identity researchers explicitly evoke leadership or leadership-related features in subtheories: the social identity theory of leadership (Hogg, 2001; Hogg et al., 2012b), uncertainty–identity theory (Hogg, 2007b), and the social identity theory of intergroup leadership (Hogg et al., 2012a).

Social Identity Theory of Leadership

Leaders are active agents of influence. They influence their followers to achieve a shared collective goal. Leaders are often members of the groups to which they are charged with providing leadership (Hogg, 2010). Similarly, followers are not inactive or passive participants in this relationship. Followers play an active role in defining the group, shaping who can lead the group, and the style and behaviors of group leaders. This active and reciprocal leader–follower relationship has recently garnered attention from social psychologists through social identity theory and the social identity theory of leadership.

The social identity theory of leadership (Hogg, 2001) is based on prototype-based influence from social identity theory described earlier. The theory argues that, as group membership becomes more salient and important to one's self-definition, more effective leadership hinges on the extent to which a leader is perceived as being group prototypical. The more people identify with groups, the more they attend to the group prototype, and thus pay more attention to who is more or less group prototypical.

Highly prototypical leaders are more influential than less prototypical leaders. There are three empirically supported reasons for this, according to social identity theory. First, as described earlier, self-categorization increases conformity to the group prototype due to depersonalization (e.g., Abrams, Wetherell, Cochrane, Hogg, & Turner, 1990). This results in members being more influenced not only by the group prototype, but also by those who embody the group prototype. Second, people prefer and are attracted to similar others (Byrne, 1997). Ingroup members, especially prototypical ingroup members, are more trusted, liked, and popular than outgroup members or non-prototypical members (Hogg, 1993). This affinity translates into prototypical leaders being more influential than non-prototypical leaders. Finally, prototypical members tend to identify more strongly with the group, making it more central and important to their self-definition. As such, they conform and are more invested in the group and its well-being. They engage in greater ingroup favoritism and bias (Abrams & Hogg, 1990), and are seen to be acting in the group's best interest (Tyler & Lind, 1992). All of this results in the conferral of trust and legitimacy. This affords prototypical, compared to non-prototypical, leaders with greater latitude to diverge from the group prototype to be innovative (Abrams, Randsley de Moura, Marques, & Hutchison, 2008).

Research has consistently replicated and supported the basic hypothesis of the social identity theory of leadership using different research paradigms and in various contexts. Reviewing evidence for the leader prototypicality advantage hypothesis, Van Knippenberg (2011) summarized approximately 40 laboratory, field, and observational studies conducted over the past decade. These studies have been carried out with student and non-student (e.g., organizational employee) samples across four continents by numerous research teams. Each of the studies provides support for this basic social identity theory of leadership hypothesis. Recent developments have also explored the impact of a multitude of moderating variables that strengthen the leader prototypicality advantage, including procedural justice (De Cremer, Van Dijke, & Mayer, 2010), leader–follower similarity (Alabastro, Rast, Lac, Hogg, & Crano, 2013), leader successes and failures (Giessner & Van Knippenberg, 2008), charisma (Van Knippenberg & Van Knippenberg, 2005), innovation and change (Abrams et al., 2008), leader rhetoric (Seyranian & Bligh, 2008), and gender (Haslam & Ryan, 2008) to name a few.

Although group members are more likely to emerge as leaders if they are perceived as being prototypical, there is a caveat to this hypothesis. Group prototypicality is tied to social identification, such that the leader prototypicality advantage should be stronger as members identify more strongly with their group. This finding too has been well supported (Fielding & Hogg, 1997; Giessner & Van Knippenberg, 2008; Hogg, Hains, & Mason, 1998; Platow & Van Knippenberg, 2001; Steffens, Haslam, & Reicher, 2014). However, there is evidence indicating that people tend to identify at least a modest amount with core groups that are often salient or accessible (e.g., Oakes, 1987). As such, social identification and leader prototypicality can play an important role in most organizational leadership contexts.

Uncertainty–Identity Theory

The social identity theory of leadership literature paints a relatively bleak picture for non-prototypical or anti-normative group leaders, suggesting they are uninfluential, ineffective, or undesirable. As noted earlier, sometimes followers prefer, desire, and even yearn for strong, anti-normative, or "nasty" leadership (Haller & Hogg, 2014; Hogg, 2007b; Rast, Gaffney, & Hogg, 2013; Rast et al., 2013). Real world events demonstrate that sometimes non-prototypical leaders do emerge and gain influence. For instance, John McCain ran for US president in 2008 in the midst of an economic crisis and war. He successfully won the Republican Party nomination, through a campaign in which he constantly described himself as a "maverick" who regularly disagreed with his own party. In a more business-oriented example, although still underrepresented, women are more likely to be placed into precarious leadership positions (e.g., Haslam & Ryan, 2008). In both examples, the groups or organizations were experiencing a crisis or an uncertainty in which people's leadership preferences changed. Under feelings of uncertainty or crisis, particularly those related to the self, people might change such that they become more supportive of non-prototypical group leaders.

A recent advancement in understanding followers' desire for non-prototypical, unexpected, or even "nasty" leaders is derived through Hogg's uncertainty–identity theory (2007b, 2012). On its own, uncertainty–identity theory does not make explicit predictions about leader preference; however, when combined with the social identity theory of leadership, it allows for novel hypotheses regarding leadership under uncertainty. Uncertainty–identity theory posits that feelings of uncertainty related to one's self-concept or identity are aversive. People are motivated to minimize or reduce their feelings of self-related uncertainty. Self-categorization processes provide an effective and efficient opportunity to reduce these feelings of uncertainty: joining a group or identifying more strongly with a group. Recall that groups provide their members with a social identity that conforms to the group's prototype, and depersonalization occurs. This self-categorization process reduces uncertainty by providing people with a clearly defined sense of social identity that prescribes attitudes, opinions, behaviors, makes the world more predictable, and so forth.

The key tenets of this theory have received substantial empirical support in a wide range of studies (see overviews in Hogg, 2007b, 2012). Studies have also shown that uncertainty motivates group identification with low status groups (Reid & Hogg, 2005) and when accounting for self-esteem as a possible explanation (Hogg & Svensson, 2009). While these studies demonstrate people's natural tendency to identify more strongly with a group when they felt highly uncertain, they also demonstrate that not all groups are equally capable of reducing uncertainty. People prefer highly entitative groups over less entitative groups. Entitativity refers to the features of a group that make it a cohesive entity in the minds of others (Campbell, 1958), such as sharing a common fate, exhibiting clearly defined group boundaries, unambiguous norms, and a clear hierarchy. Indeed, Hogg, Sherman, Dierselhuis, Maitner, and Moffitt (2007) demonstrated that highly distinctive groups (i.e., high entitiativity groups) better reduced the self-uncertainty felt by their members than groups defined vaguely with ambiguous norms and unclear boundaries (i.e., low entitativity groups). This preference for high entitativity groups in times of uncertainty can also motivate people to join or identify more strongly with polarized extremist groups (Sherman, Hogg, & Maitner, 2009). These groups also suppress dissent and have clearly defined power and leadership structures (e.g., Hogg, Meehan, & Faquharson, 2010; Rast et al., 2013). Not surprisingly, these are all features that make non-prototypical, unexpected, and "nasty" leaders more desirable in times of uncertainty.

Uncertainty and Leadership

When integrated, the social identity theory of leadership and uncertainty–identity theory provide clear predictions for leadership in times of uncertainty and crisis. Although still in its infancy, research integrating these two perspectives has produced compelling evidence that uncertainty impacts followers' leader preference, as well as their thoughts, feelings, perceptions, and evaluations of group leaders.

Drawing on the two theoretical frameworks, Pierro, Cicero, Bonaiuto, Van Knippenberg, and Kruglanski (2007) hypothesized that feelings of uncertainty would strengthen the leader prototypicality advantage. That is, the more uncertainty a person feels, the more strongly they will endorse a prototypical compared to a non-prototypical leader. However, rather than focusing on uncertainty itself, they focused on uncertainty-related constructs such as need for closure—the desire to reduce uncertainty and reach closure on judgments, decisions, and actions (Kruglanski & Webster, 1996; Webster & Kruglanski, 1994)—job related stress, and role ambiguity. In an organizational survey, they found that need for closure strengthened the leader prototypicality–effectiveness relationship for established leaders, and this relationship was even stronger among those who identified strongly (vs. weakly) with their organization (Pierro et al., 2007). They found similar results in a separate series of organizational surveys examining job related stress and role ambiguity (Cicero, Pierro, & Van Knippenberg, 2007, 2010): both job related stress and role ambiguity strengthened the leader prototypicality–effectiveness relationship. These studies show that uncertainty-related constructs, such as need for closure and role ambiguity, strengthen the relationship between leader prototypicality and effectiveness or endorsement; thus, by implication, they indicate a motivation to reduce uncertainty.

Focusing explicitly on uncertainty, Rast, Hogg, and colleagues conducted multiple studies focusing on the leader prototypicality–effectiveness relationship for potential leaders in times of uncertainty. Drawing on uncertainty–identity theory, they came up with a novel proposition: uncertainty should weaken or negate the leader prototypicality advantage. Their findings have supported this hypothesis across several studies using multiple methodologies and samples. For instance, Rast, Gaffney, Hogg, and Crisp (2012; Study 1) found that, while prototypical leaders were supported more than non-prototypical leaders, this effect disappeared when participants felt highly uncertain when given only a single leader candidate to evaluate. That is, highly uncertain participants were equally supportive of prototypical and non-prototypical leaders. As uncertainty decreased so did their support for non-prototypical leaders. In a follow-up study (Rast et al., 2012; Study 2) a within-subjects design was employed so that participants could simultaneously evaluate a prototypical and non-prototypical, rather than a single, leader. In this case, their general hypothesis was still supported. Participants still preferred a prototypical leader, but their support for a non-prototypical leader significantly increased when participants felt more uncertain. Based on these findings, Rast and colleagues posited that followers have a need for leadership per se in times of uncertainty. When people feel uncertain, they simply look for the leader who best represents the group (and thus their social identity). If a single leader is available, then it does not matter how prototypical this leader is perceived to be. All that seems to matter is that the leader provides the desired identity-function necessary in times of uncertainty, thus supporting uncertainty–identity theory.

More recently, Rast, Hogg, and Tomory (2015) not only replicated their earlier findings, but also extended them by identifying a potential responsible psychological process. They reasoned that uncertainty might influence people's cognitive processing capacity, which in turn moderates leader preference and evaluation. More specifically, they argued that uncertainty is a cognitive demand (e.g., Proulx & Inzlicht, 2012) that people will respond to differently based on their motivation to process information. Need for cognition is one such motivation to process information. People high in need for cognition enjoy expending cognitive effort to process information and critically examine items, whereas people low in need for cognition avoid expending cognitive resources to process information.

They argued low need for cognition would be expected to encourage greater automatic reliance on how prototypical the leader is (cf. Pierro et al.'s 2005 finding), whereas high need for cognition would encourage less automatic reliance on how prototypical the leader is, and more careful, deliberative, and critical consideration of prototype-related information to ascertain the group's prototype (cf. Rast et al., 2012). This is precisely what they found. This indicates that uncertainty impacts not only peoples' capacity or motivation to process leadership-relevant information, but also the manner in which they process this information (heuristically vs. centrally). We will come back to this point later when we discuss the dark side of leadership.

Gender, Autocrats, and Uncertainty

Leadership preference in times of uncertainty has implications for the selection of women, minority group members, and even autocrats into leadership positions. An example of this is research conducted by Ryan and Haslam (2005, 2007) on the glass–cliff effect. The glass cliff refers to a situation in which women are more likely to be selected for and appointed to precarious leadership positions with a high chance of failure. There is growing evidence for the glass-cliff effect, exhibiting that these precarious leadership situations are associated with uncertainty, threat, and crisis. Compared to men, women are more likely to be placed in leadership positions when their organization experiences poor stock performance (Haslam, Ryan, Kulich, Trojanowski, & Atkins, 2010), during times of crisis or uncertainty (Bruckmüller & Branscombe, 2010), under threat-evoking conditions (Brown, Diekman, & Schneider, 2011), and when gender stereotypic beliefs are reinforced (e.g., Leicht, Crisp, & Randsley de Moura, 2014).

More important in relation to crisis and leadership is the research explaining *why* women are perceived as being better suited than men for crisis leadership. It has long been established that people associate leadership with men. This phenomenon is referred to as the "think manager—think male" paradigm (Schein, 1973). Recently, a seminal meta-analysis by Koenig, Eagly, Mitchell, and Ristikari (2011) confirmed that leadership stereotypes are masculine. In times of uncertainty or crisis, however, this think manager—think male belief is overturned. Instead, leadership stereotypes shift to "think crisis—think female" in times of uncertainty or crisis (Ryan et al., 2011; Ryan, Haslam, & Kulich, 2010). This research indicates that feminine traits and roles typically associated with women make them more desirable in times of uncertainty or crisis (e.g., Gartzia, Ryan, Balluerka, & Aritzeta, 2012). There is another possible explanation, however: in times of uncertainty, people have a need for leadership per se and they are willing to endorse and be more supportive of non-prototypical (e.g., female) leaders. Alternatively, Rast et al. (2013) demonstrated that uncertainty impacts perceptions of leader prototypicality; it is possible that, in times of uncertainty, women are perceived as more group prototypical compared to when uncertainty is lower or absent. These explanations, extrapolating from Rast and colleagues' (2012, 2013, 2015) research has yet to be extended to gender, diversity, and leadership.

The idea that uncertainty alters leadership perceptions and preference does not only have implications for positive aspects of leadership, such as increasing the likelihood of females being selected for leadership roles. This same logic can be extended to predict and explain the emergence of the so-called "dark side of leadership" (Hogg, 2005; Rast, in press; Rast, Gaffney, & Hogg, 2013). Recall that, in times of uncertainty, people look to their leaders to provide them with a clearly articulated and unambiguous vision for their group's future. And in times of uncertainty people prefer highly entitative groups with well-defined group boundaries, hierarchy, and leadership structure.

Drawing on this rationale derived from the social identity theory of leadership and uncertainty–identity theory, Rast et al. (2013) investigated followers' preference for autocratic versus non-autocratic leadership in times of uncertainty. In a survey of 215 organizational employees, their hypotheses were supported: non-autocratic leaders were supported when employees felt less uncertain, while autocratic leaders were preferred when employees felt more uncertain. But, this effect was mediated by the leader's perceived prototypicality. Non-autocratic leaders were perceived as being more prototypical under low uncertainty, which resulted in greater support. However, autocratic leadership was perceived as being more prototypical when uncertainty was high, resulting in employees being more supportive of them. This finding has obvious implications for other leadership styles, such as charismatic or transformational leadership, which ought to emerge or be more effective in times of uncertainty or crisis (Beyer & Browning, 1999; Conger & Kanungo, 1987; Weber, 1947). This is an area ripe for future researchers to explore.

Intergroup Leadership

One of the most significant contemporary challenges facing leaders is how to manage intergroup relations and conflict effectively. Many corporate and organizational environments require teams or departments to collaborate successfully, despite professional, cultural, ethnic, educational, or status differences. For example, in a typical corporate environment, sales, marketing, and engineering teams often "fight" with one another over each group's importance and resources within the larger organization, while simultaneously attempting to work together toward a shared goal. This conflict occurs partly because groups provide their members with a sense of identity that is almost always defined in contrast to other (out)groups (Tajfel & Turner, 1979)—how are "we" different from and thus better than "them"? It is precisely this identity issue that makes effective intergroup leadership extremely difficult.

The consideration of intergroup leadership is new to the study and practice of leadership (Pittinsky, 2009). Effective leadership often requires a leader to lead across deep, tension-fraught, and potentially hostile divisions between self-contained groups that have distinct identities that define their members. Hogg et al. (2012b; see also Hogg, 2015) argue that effective intergroup leadership hinges on successful construction of an *intergroup relational identity*. An intergroup relational identity refers to how the cooperative and mutually promotive relationship between subgroups or teams within a larger group or organization partially defines one's self-concept.

At first blush, intergroup conflict might appear unrelated to organizational and social crisis and uncertainty. However, many of the social and organizational changes and transformations provided throughout this chapter occur in an intergroup context. A recent example is the 2014 referendum for Scottish independence. On September 18, 2014 Scottish voters voted in support of remaining in the United Kingdom. This was a historic vote. For most people, the results of this voting should appear fair and just given it was a democratically held election with an 85 percent turnout rate, of which 55 percent voted against independence and 45 percent in favour of independence. Indeed, even Alex Salmond, the Scottish First Minister, accepted the results, calling them the "verdict of the people" and asked for "all Scots to follow suit in accepting the democratic verdict of the people of Scotland" (Salmond, September 19, 2014).

Many would have suspected this vote would lead to feelings of harmony and one-ness among Scotland, England, and Wales, who could work together to improve the United Kingdom. Indeed, David Cameron urged British people to "unify" following the failed vote. However, the results of the referendum actually appear to have resulted in a backlash, whereby the relationship between Scottish people and those in England and Wales has become more tenuous as Scotland fights for greater devolution of power. For instance, within 24 hours of voting to remain part of the UK, more than 70,000 Scots signed a petition to hold another vote for Scottish independence (Kinder, September 20, 2014). Some argued that English people as well as pro-independence Scots committed voter fraud, and called for a neutral third-party to tally votes; while others argued that the "No" voters were "tricked" into voting against Scottish independence and that the BBC had run a campaign against independence as well (Salmond, September 19, 2014).

This raises an interesting question for British leaders: how can they resolve this conflict before it turns into a major national crisis? This is not an abnormal leadership context, however. Many organizational, societal, and group leaders find themselves caught in the crossfire of intergroup relations. To make matters more difficult, leaders often shift back and forth from intra- to intergroup leadership depending on context demands (Alabastro et al., 2013; Rast, Hackett, Alabastro, & Hogg, in press).

Conclusion

Leadership is one of the most studied constructs in all of the social sciences. The vast majority of leadership research focuses on transformation or charismatic leadership or leader–member exchange theory and their correlates. However, surprisingly little research explores leadership in times of crises and uncertainty (Gardner, Lowe, Moss, Mahoney, & Cogliser, 2010). This is perplexing, because several popular leadership theories, including charismatic leadership theory (e.g., Conger & Kanungo, 1987) argue that uncertainty or crisis strengthens the effect of particular leadership styles, behaviors, or context. This is important because, as we noted earlier, we live in a time rife with uncertainties. And people look to their group leaders to resolve these uncertainties.

In this chapter, we drew on the social identity theory of leadership (Hogg, 2001) and uncertainty–identity theory (Hogg, 2007b) to describe and explain how uncertainty and crises impact leader perceptions, preference, and effectiveness. We argue that identity management is a key leadership function due to social identity processes. That is, people derive a sense of self and identity from their group membership, and in doing so look to their leaders to define their group's identity and prototype. This is especially true when people experience self-related uncertainties and crises. Followers look to their leaders to reduce these feelings of identity-uncertainty. Leaders who are directive, providing a clear vision of the group's future, are particularly well suited and effective at reducing these identity-uncertainties (e.g., Rast, Hogg, & Giessner, 2013).

Identity–uncertainty can also overturn people's typical leader preferences. In times of uncertainty or crisis, followers are also more willing to endorse or support what we refer to as "unexpected leaders" such as women, minorities, non-prototypical group members, deviants, or autocrats. For example, Rast and colleagues (Rast et al., 2012, 2015) integrated social identity theory of leadership and uncertainty–identity theory to creatively predict that uncertainty would weaken or negate the leader prototypicality advantage. In this research, they showed prototypical leaders receive more support than non-prototypical leader when uncertainty is low; however, as uncertainty increases so does support for non-prototypical leaders. Uncertainty does not seem to impact preference for a prototypical leader, but it strengthens preference for non-prototypical leadership. This research also has implications for the emergence of "unexpected" leaders (e.g., the glass-cliff effect, the dark side of leadership). An area ripe for future research is how non-prototypical leaders can capitalize on their followers' uncertainty to incite social or organizational change. Another potential area for exploration revolves around how leaders can use their rhetoric to evoke feelings of uncertainty to their advantage—something successful politicians and business leaders seem particularly astute at doing.

Although not a direct examination of uncertainty and prototypical leadership, research on the glass-cliff effect (Ryan & Haslam, 2007) demonstrates the applied potential of the social identity theory of leadership, and to a lesser extent uncertainty–identity theory. In a situation in which the group experiences a crisis or uncertainty, making leadership success improbable, and thus the leader is likely to fail, support for a non-prototypical (i.e., female) leader increases. That is, failure can be blamed on the leader's poor fit, lack of leader-stereotypic features, etc., rather than on the group's attributes. In this case, the ramifications for blaming the leader can actually make it more difficult for women to be placed in future leadership positions. For example, blaming the failure on a woman because she did not posses the necessary masculine stereotypes associated with successful leaders can result in further negative bias over selecting a female leader in the future.

Finally, an extremely new area of research from the social identity perspective is on theory of intergroup leadership (Hogg et al., 2012b). Leading in an intergroup context is a normal leadership situation, yet it is rarely discussed. How do leaders achieve effective collaboration and communication between groups who do not get along well or where conflict between them is high (e.g., Israelis and Palestinians, or Welsh, Scottish, and English people, or doctors and nurses)? While these intergroup relationships do not necessarily entail leading in a crisis or uncertainty, the relationship between groups can become extremely contentious during uncertainty or times of crisis (e.g., US presidential election), or the uncertainty or crisis can result from the conflict itself (e.g., Israelis and Palestinians). We have shown how delicate and difficult a leadership situation can be in an intergroup context, particularly in times of intergroup hostility (e.g., Alabastro et al., 2013; Hohman, Hogg, & Bligh, 2010; Rast et al., in press). We argue that effective intergroup leadership hinges on successful construction of an *intergroup relational identity*. An intergroup relational identity refers to how the cooperative and mutually promotive relationship between subgroups or teams within a larger group or organization partially defines one's self-concept. We are currently conducting multiple studies to test this hypothesis, and we have initial support for it (Rast, 2013; Rast, Van Knippenberg, & Hogg, 2014).

We believe the social identity theory of leadership provides enormous potential to better understand leadership as a group process, leadership between groups, the identity-function of leadership, and, particularly relevant to this book, leadership in times of uncertainty or crisis. The social identity theory of leadership is still in its infancy compared to mainstream leadership perspectives such as transformational or charismatic leadership (Bass, 1985), contingency theories of leadership (Fiedler, 1964), or leader–member exchange theory (Graen & Uhl-Bien, 1995), yet it has received incredibly reliable and robust support (Hogg et al., 2012a; see also Hogg, 2010). This area of research is ripe for examining boundary conditions for this hypothesis to identify the context in which the leader prototypicality advantage is weakened. In doing so, the social identity theory of leadership revived social psychological research on leaders by connecting it to social influence, social cognition, and group processes. As described in this chapter, there are a number of exciting new developments that will continue to fuel research into the future and further help us understand leadership in times of uncertainty and crisis.

References

Abrams, D., & Hogg, M. A. (1990). Social identification, self-categorization and social influence. *European Review of Social Psychology*, *1*, 195–228.

Abrams, D., & Hogg, M. A. (2010). Social identity and self-categorization. In J. F. Dovidio, M. Hewstone, P. Glick, & V. M. Esses (Eds.), *The SAGE handbook of prejudice, stereotyping and discrimination* (pp. 179–193). London: Sage.

Abrams, D., Randsley de Moura, G., Marques, J. M., & Hutchison, P. (2008). Innovation credit: When can leaders oppose their group's norms? *Journal of Personality and Social Psychology*, *95*, 662–678.

Abrams, D., Wetherell, M. S., Cochrane, S., Hogg, M. A., & Turner, J. C. (1990). Knowing what to think by knowing who you are: Self-categorization and the nature of norm formation, conformity, and group polarization. *British Journal of Social Psychology*, *29*, 97–119.

Alabastro, A. B., Rast, D. E. III, Lac, A., Hogg, M. A., & Crano. W. D. (2013). Intergroup bias and perceived similarity: The effects of successes and failures on support for in- and outgroup political leaders. *Group Processes and Intergroup Relations*, *16*, 58–67. (Special Issue on Leading groups: Leadership as a group process).

Bass, B. M. (1985). *Leadership and performance beyond expectations*. New York: Free Press.

Beyer, J. M., & Browning, L. D. (1999) Transforming an industry in crisis: Charisma, routinization, and supportive cultural leadership. *Leadership Quarterly*, *10*, 483–520.

Bligh, M. C., Kohles, J. C., & Meindl, J. R. (2004). Charisma under crisis: Presidential leadership, rhetoric, and media responses before and after the September 11th terrorist attacks. *The Leadership Quarterly*, *15*, 211–239.

Bligh, M. C., Kohles, J. C., & Pillai, R. (2011). Romancing leadership: Past, present, and future. *The Leadership Quarterly*, *22*, 1058–1077.

Boin, A., & Hart, R. (2003). Public leadership in times of crisis: Mission impossible? *Public Administration Review*, *63*, 544–553.

Brown, E. R., Diekman, A. B., & Schneider, M. C. (2011). A change will do us good: Threats diminish typical preferences for male leaders. *Personality and Social Psychology Bulletin*, *37*, 930–941.

Bruckmüller, S., & Branscombe, N. R. (2010). The glass cliff: When and why women are selected as leaders in crisis contexts. *British Journal of Social Psychology*, *49*, 433–451.

Byrne, D. (1997). An overview (and underview) of research and theory within the attraction paradigm. *Journal of Social and Personal Relationships, 14*, 417–431.

Campbell, D. T. (1958). Common fate, similarity, and other indices of the status of aggregates of person as social entities. *Behavioural Science, 3*, 14–25.

Cicero, L., Pierro, A., & Van Knippenberg, D. (2007). Leader group prototypicality and job satisfaction: The moderating role of job stress and team identification. *Group Dynamics, 11*, 165–175.

Cicero, L., Pierro, A., & Van Knippenberg, D. (2010). Leadership and uncertainty: How role ambiguity affects the relationship between leader group prototypicality and leadership effectiveness. *British Journal of Management, 21*, 411–421.

Conger, J. A., & Kanungo, R. N. (1987). Toward a behavioral theory of charismatic leadership in organizational settings. *Academy of Management Review, 12*, 637–647.

De Cremer, D., Van Dijke, M., & Mayer, D. M. 2010. Cooperating when "You" and "I" are treated fairly: The moderating role of leader prototypicality. *Journal of Applied Psychology, 95*, 1121–1133.

Fiedler, F. E. (1964). A contingency model of leadership effectiveness. *Advanced Experimental Social Psychology, 1*, 149–190.

Fielding, K. S., & Hogg, M. A. (1997). Social identity, self-categorization, and leadership: A field study of small interactive groups. *Group Dynamics: Theory, Research, and Practice, 1*, 39–51.

Gardner, W. L., Lowe, K. B., Moss, T. W., Mahoney, K. T., & Cogliser, C. C. (2010). Scholarly leadership of the study of leadership: A review of *The Leadership Quarterly*'s second decade, 2000–2009. *Leadership Quarterly, 21*, 922–958.

Gartzia, L., Ryan, M., Balluerka, N., & Aritzeta, A. (2012). Think crisis—Think female: further evidence. *European Journal of Work and Organizational Psychology, 21*, 603–628.

Giessner, S. R., & Van Knippenberg, D. (2008). "License to fail": Goal definition, leader group prototypicality, and perceptions of leadership effectiveness after leader failure. *Organizational Behavior and Human Decision Processes, 105*, 14–35.

Graen, G. B., & Uhl-Bien, M. (1995). Relationship-based approach to leadership: Development of leader–member exchange (LMX) theory of leadership over 25 years: Applying a multi-level multidomain approach. *Leadership Quarterly, 6*, 219–247.

Haller, J., & Hogg, M. A. (2014). All power to our great leader: Political leadership under uncertainty. In J.-W. van Prooijen & P. A. M. van Lange (Eds.), *Power, politics, and paranoia: Why people are suspicious of their leaders* (pp. 130–149). Cambridge, UK: Cambridge University Press.

Haslam, S. A., Oakes, P. J., McGarty, C., Turner, J. C., & Onorato, S. (1995). Contextual changes in the prototypicality of extreme and moderate outgroup members. *European Journal of Social Psychology, 25*, 509–530.

Haslam, S. A., & Ryan, M. K. (2008). The road to the glass cliff: Differences in the perceived suitability of men and women for leadership positions in succeeding and failing organizations. *Leadership Quarterly, 19*, 530–546.

Haslam, S. A., Ryan, M. K., Kulich, C., Trojanowski, G., & Atkins, C. (2010). Investing with prejudice: The relationship between women's presence on company boards and objective and subjective measures of company performance. *British Journal of Management, 21*, 484–487.

Hogg, M. A. (1993). Group cohesiveness: A critical review and some new directions. *European Review of Social Psychology, 4*, 85–111.

Hogg, M. A. (2001). A social identity theory of leadership. *Personality and Social Psychology Review, 5*, 184–200.

Hogg, M. A. (2005). Social identity and misuse of power: The dark side of leadership. *Brooklyn Law Review, 70*, 1239–1257.

Hogg, M. A. (2007a). Social psychology of leadership. In A. W. Kruglanski & E. T. Higgins (Eds.), *Social psychology: Handbook of basic principles* (2nd ed., pp. 716–733). New York: Guilford.

Hogg, M. A. (2007b). Uncertainty–identity theory. In M. P. Zanna (Ed.), *Advances in experimental social psychology* (Vol. 39, pp. 69–126). San Diego, CA: Academic Press.

Hogg, M. A. (2010). Influence and leadership. In S. T. Fiske, D. T. Gilbert, & G. Lindzey (Eds.), *Handbook of social psychology* (5th ed., Vol. 2, pp. 1166–1207). New York: Wiley.

Hogg, M. A. (2012). Uncertainty–identity theory. In P. A. M. Van Lange, A. W. Kruglanski, & E. T. Higgins (Eds.), *Handbook of theories of social psychology* (Vol. 2, pp. 62–80). Thousand Oaks, CA: Sage.

Hogg, M. A. (2013). Leadership. In J. M. Levine (Ed.), *Group processes* (pp. 241–266). New York: Psychology Press.

Hogg, M. A. (2015). Constructive leadership across groups: How leaders can combat prejudice and conflict between subgroups. *Advances in Group Processes, 32*, 177–207.

Hogg, M. A., & Svensson, A. (2009). *Uncertainty reduction, self-esteem and group identification*. Unpublished manuscript: Claremont Graduate University.

Hogg, M. A., & Van Knippenberg, D. (2003). Social identity and leadership processes in groups. In M. P. Zanna (Ed.), *Advances in experimental social psychology* (Vol. 35, pp. 1–52). San Diego, CA: Academic Press.

Hogg, M. A., Hains, S. C., & Mason, I. (1998). Identification and leadership in small groups: Salience, frame of reference, and leader stereotypicality effects on leader evaluations. *Journal of Personality and Social Psychology, 75*, 1248–1263.

Hogg, M. A., Meehan, C., & Farquharson, J. (2010). The solace of radicalism: Self-uncertainty and group identification in the face of threat. *Journal of Experimental Social Psychology, 46*, 1061–1066.

Hogg, M. A., Sherman, D. K., Dierselhuis, J., Maitner, A. T., & Moffitt, G. (2007). Uncertainty, entitativity, and group identification. *Journal of Experimental Social Psychology, 43*, 135–142.

Hogg, M. A., Van Knippenberg, D., & Rast, D. E. III (2012a). The social identity theory of leadership: A decade of research and conceptual development. *European Review of Social Psychology, 23*, 258–304.

Hogg, M. A., Van Knippenberg, D., & Rast, D. E. III. (2012b). Intergroup leadership in organizations: Leading across group and intergroup boundaries. *Academy of Management Review, 37*, 232–255.

Hohman, Z. P., Hogg, M. A., & Bligh, M. C. (2010). Identity and intergroup leadership: Asymmetrical political and national identification in response to uncertainty. *Self and Identity, 9*, 113–128.

Kinder, T. (2014). Scottish Independence: 70,000 Nationalists demand referendum be re-held after vote rigging claims. *International Business Times*. Retrieved from: http://www.ibtimes.co.uk/scottish-independence-70000-nationalists-demand-referendum-be-re-held-after-vote-rigging-claims-1466416.

Koenig, A. M., Eagly, A. H., Mitchell, A. A., & Ristikari, T. (2011). Are leader stereotypes masculine? A meta-analysis of three research paradigms. *Psychological Bulletin, 137*, 616–642.

Kruglanski, A. W., & Webster, D. M. (1996). Motivated closing of the mind: "Seizing" and "freezing". *Psychological Review, 103*, 263–283.

Landau, M. J., Solomon, S., Greenberg, J., Cohen, F., Pyszczynski, T., Arndt, J., Miller, C. H., Ogilvie, D. M., & Cook, A. (2004). Deliver us from evil: The effects of mortality salience and reminders of 9/11 on support for President George W. Bush. *Personality and Social Psychology Bulletin, 30*, 1136–1150.

Leicht, C., Randsley de Moura, G., & Crisp, R. J. (2014). Contesting gender stereotypes stimulates generalized fairness in the selection of leaders. *Leadership Quarterly, 25*, 1025–1039.

Levay, C. (2010). Charismatic leadership in resistance to change. *The Leadership Quarterly, 21*, 127–143.

Mumford, M. D., Friedrich, T. L., Caughron, J. J., & Byrne, C. L. (2007). Leader cognition in real-world settings: How do leaders think about crises? *The Leadership Quarterly, 18*, 515–543.

Oakes, P. J. (1987). The salience of social categories. In J. C. Turner, M. A. Hogg, P. J. Oakes, S. D. Reicher, & M. S. Wetherell (Eds.), *Rediscovering the social group: A self-categorization theory* (pp. 117–141). Oxford: Blackwell.

Pierro, A., Cicero, L., Bonaiuto, M., Van Knippenberg, D., & Kruglanski, A. W. (2007). Leader group prototypicality and resistance to organizational change: The moderating role of need for closure and team identification. *Testing, Psychometrics, Methodology in Applied Psychology, 14*, 27–40.

Pillai, R., & Meindl, J. R. (1998). Context and charisma: A "meso" level examination of the relationship of organic structure, collectivism, and crisis to charismatic leadership. *Journal of Management, 24*, 643–664.

Pittinsky, T. (Ed.) (2009). *Crossing the divide: Intergroup leadership in a world of difference*. Cambridge, MA: Harvard Business School Press.

Platow, M. J., & van Knippenberg, D. (2001). A social identity analysis of leadership endorsement: The effects of leader ingroup prototypicality and distributive intergroup fairness. *Personality and Social Psychology Bulletin, 27*, 1508–1519.

Proulx, T., & Inzlicht, M. (2012). The five "A"s of meaning maintenance: Making sense of the theories of sense-making. *Psychological Inquiry, 23*, 317–335.

Rast, D. E. III (2013). *Intergroup leadership: Leading across conflicting social identities* (Doctoral dissertation, Claremont Graduate University).

Rast, D. E. III (in press). Leadership in times of uncertainty: Recent findings, debates, and potential future research directions. *Social and Personality Psychology Compass*.

Rast, D. E. III, Gaffney, A. M., & Hogg, M. A. (2013). The tyranny of normative distance: A social identity account of the exercise of power by remote leaders. In M. C. Bligh & R. E. Riggio (Eds.), *Exploring distance in leader–follower relationships: When near is far and far is near* (pp. 215–240). New York: Taylor and Francis.

Rast, D. E. III, Gaffney, A. M., Hogg, M. A., & Crisp, R. J. (2012). Leadership under uncertainty: When leaders who are non-prototypical group members can gain support. *Journal of Experimental Social Psychology, 48,* 646–653.

Rast, D. E. III, Hackett, J. D., Alabastro, A. B., & Hogg, M. A. (in press). Revoking a leader's "license to fail": Downgrading evaluations of prototypical ingroup leaders following an intergroup failure. *Journal of Applied Social Psychology.*

Rast, D. E. III, Hogg, M. A., & Giessner, S. R. (2013). Leadership under uncertainty: The appeal of strong leaders and clear identities. *Self & Identity, 12,* 635–649.

Rast, D. E. III, Hogg, M. A., & Tomory, J. J. (2015). Prototypical leaders do not always get our support: Impact of self-uncertainty and need for cognition. *Self and Identity, 14,* 135–146.

Rast, D. E. III, Van Knippenberg, D., & Hogg, M. A. (2014, June). *Leaders bridging the divide: Developing and validating a measure of intergroup relational identity.* Invited paper presented at the New Directions in Leadership Research Conference. Rotterdam, the Netherlands.

Reid, S. A., & Hogg, M. A. (2005). Uncertainty reduction, self-enhancement, and ingroup identification. *Personality and Social Psychology Bulletin, 31,* 804–817.

Riggio, R. E., Murphy, S. E., & Pirozzolo, F. J. (2002). *Multiple intelligences and leadership.* Mahwah, NJ: Lawrence Erlbaum.

Ryan, M. K., & Haslam, S. A. (2005). The glass cliff: Evidence that women are over-represented in precarious leadership positions. *British Journal of Management, 16,* 81–90.

Ryan, M. K., & Haslam, S. A. (2007). The glass cliff: Exploring the dynamics surrounding women's appointment to precarious leadership positions. *Academy of Management Review, 32,* 549–572.

Ryan, M. K., Haslam, S. A., Hersby, M. D., & Bongiorno, R. (2011). Think crisis–think female: Using the glass cliff to reconsider the think manager—think male stereotype. *Journal of Applied Psychology, 96,* 470–484.

Ryan, M. K., Haslam, S. A., & Kulich, C. (2010). Politics and the glass cliff: Evidence that women are preferentially selected to contest hard-to-win seats. *Psychology of Women Quarterly, 34,* 56–64.

Salmond, A. (2014). First Minister on referendum outcome. Retrieved from: http://news.scotland.gov.uk/Speeches-Briefings/First-Minister-on-referendum-outcome-106a.aspx.

Schein, V. E. (1973). The relationship between sex role stereotypes and requisite management characteristics. *Journal of Applied Psychology, 57,* 95–100.

Seyranian, V., & Bligh, M. C. (2008). Presidential charismatic leadership: Exploring the rhetoric of social change. *The Leadership Quarterly, 19,* 54–76.

Sherman, D. K., Hogg, M. A., & Maitner, A. T. (2009). Perceived polarization: Reconciling ingroup and intergroup perceptions under uncertainty. *Group Processes and Intergroup Relations, 12,* 95–109.

Steffens, N. K., Haslam, S. A., & Reicher, S. D. (2014). Up close and personal: Evidence that shared social identity is a basis for the "special" relationship that binds followers to their leaders. *The Leadership Quarterly, 25,* 296–313.

Tajfel, H. (1972). Social categorization. English manuscript of "La catégorisation sociale." In S. Moscovici (Ed.), *Introduction à la psychologie sociale* (Vol. 1, pp. 272–302). Paris: Larousse.

Tajfel, H., & Turner, J. C. (1979). An integrative theory of intergroup conflict. In W. G. Austin & S. Worchel (Eds.), *The social psychology of intergroup relations* (pp. 33–47). Monterey, CA: Brooks/Cole.

Trice, H. M., & Beyer, J. M. (1986). Charisma and its routinization in two social movement organizations. *Research in Organizational Behavior, 8,* 113–164.

Turner, J. C., Hogg, M. A., Oakes, P. J., Reicher, S. D., & Wetherell, M. S. (1987). *Rediscovering the social group: A self-categorization theory.* Oxford, UK: Blackwell.

Tyler, T. R., & Lind, E. A. (1992). A relational model of authority in groups. In M. Zanna (Ed.), *Advances in Experimental Social Psychology, 25,* 115–191. New York: Academic Press.

Van Knippenberg, B., & Van Knippenberg, D. (2005). Leader self-sacrifice and leadership effectiveness: The moderating role of leader prototypicality. *Journal of Applied Psychology, 90,* 25–37.

Van Knippenberg, D. (2011). Embodying who we are: Leader group prototypicality and leadership effectiveness. *The Leadership Quarterly, 22,* 1078–1091.

Weber, Max (1947). *The theory of social and economic organization,* translated by A. M. Henderson and Talcott Parsons. New York: Free Press.

Webster, D. M., & Kruglanski, A. W. (1994). Individual differences in need for cognitive closure. *Journal of Personality and Social Psychology, 67,* 1049–1062.

Part II
Studying Leadership

Introduction

We saw in Part I of this Companion that writers in the field of leadership have different views about the meaning of leadership and its significance for organizations and societies. This section presents various approaches to the study of leadership in organizations. Each of the chapters provides in its own way a critical assessment of the scholarship in leadership studies and makes suggestions to push forward the boundaries of the field. By reading these different contributions, we get the sense that the community of researchers in the field feels a need to revitalize the study of leadership. They suggest doing so by proposing new theoretical frames and methodologies and by questioning some fundamental assumptions that have guided inquiry in the field.

Two of the chapters (Alvesson, and Taylor and Ford) take a definitive critical stance on leadership studies. According to the authors, leadership appears to be a concept highly contaminated by the ideology of managerialism. Leadership studies are at risk of reproducing a hierarchical order in organizations that goes against the interests of more disempowered actors. In addition, the fact that leadership is commonly understood as a relation between leaders and followers limits the ability of researchers to develop a more complex and productive view of relationality in organizations. They suggest that researchers should pay more attention to the variety of leadership situations in organizations and to the process of co-construction of leadership. From a critical standpoint, they also underlined that power is key to understanding the manifestation and consequences of leadership for individuals and organizations. Research appears to be an important resource to challenge conventional views of leadership.

The chapter by Carroll and Firth provides an in-depth exploration of the relationship between power and leadership. To do this, they used three metaphors of power in organizations: power as causality, power as mandate, and power as micro-interaction. They then engage in a dialogue between these metaphors and three theories of leadership: transformative, adaptive and process theories. Overall, this chapter underlines the centrality of power in the constitution of leadership phenomena in organizations and provides a language to go beyond simplistic assumptions about these two concepts. They also note that multiple definition of power makes any univocal statement about the relationship between this concept and leadership difficult.

In her chapter, Rybnikova provides an overview of the contribution of psychoanalytical approaches to the study of leadership. Psychoanalytical approaches to leadership have often been identified with the study of leadership pathologies. The author shows how this approach can also provide a solid basis for looking at the emergence of the leader–follower dynamic and the instantiation of leadership in interaction. Despite the richness of this perspective, she suggests that the normative underpinning of psychoanalysis limits its popularity in the field of leadership studies.

In his chapter, Gronn reviews various representations of leadership, from a stand-alone approach to a more collective one. He suggests that the field of leadership studies is at risk of moving from one extreme to the other and of neglecting the importance of individuals in shaping organizational leadership. He proposes instead to take an alternative approach to the individual and collective perspective by looking at leadership configurations. Leadership configurations recognize the co-existence of individuality and collectivism in organizational leadership.

Uhl-Bien and Carsten take a provocative view of the classic distinction between leaders and followers in leadership studies. They suggest looking at leadership as a co-construction between these two sides of the equation. Contexts influence the ways and possibilities that a co-construction of leadership will take place. Innovative followership theories offer a sophisticated view of leadership and open up rich avenues for research. They suggest that such contexts as virtual networks and social media provide opportunities to rethink the leader–follower dynamic.

Bynander and 't Hart make a careful assessment of major works on leadership succession in politics and business and look at the convergence and divergence within these two distinct contexts. They underline the importance of cross-sectoral research (politics, business) to move forward the field of leadership studies. In their analysis, corporate sector and political life appear, at least in the case of leadership succession, more similar than anticipated. Among other considerations, they bring upfront the issue of accountability and its influence on the succession of leaders. This chapter, as with others in this section, shows the importance of relating the manifestation of leadership to context.

Finally, the chapter by Larsson provides an in-depth analysis of the instantiation of leadership in interactions. It illustrates the potential of a practice turn for leadership studies as observed in many others sectors of contemporary studies of organizations. More precisely, the author assesses the contribution of three approaches to the study of leadership as practice: leadership as enactment of a formal role, construction of leader identities in interaction, and accomplishment of influence in interaction. It also explores, through various examples of research in the field, the methodological implications of these various approaches.

This second part of the handbook covers a lot of ground. It is populated by a variety of theoretical prisms and methodological postures. It definitely shows that the field of leadership studies is in a period of critical assessment and scrutiny. It is also a vigorous field of study with continuously moving boundaries. This more reflexive stance within the field of leadership studies takes a diversity of forms. New research trajectories can develop by considering the contribution of alternate theoretical frames such as CMS. Comparative work across sectors is also an occasion to benefit from the diversity of contexts and disciplines. Comparative works have their own challenges and imply working in teams of researchers that originate from different disciplines and sectors. In the end, as in any field of research, theoretical frames and methodological approaches nurture each other and provide a fertile ground from which to generate innovative insights. As we saw, an old concept such as the duality between leaders and followers can also be revisited and reconceptualizes to explore new organizational or social realities. Overall, taking note of the diversity of perspectives found through these chapters, a set of key sensitizing concepts seems to permeate contemporary studies of leadership. To name a few, concepts of identity, power, enactment, practice, and interaction come across in these various chapters and perspectives. The field of leadership studies appears *à la fois* multi-vocal but sharing an interest in a limited set of core concepts that appear promising for the renewal of the field. It is our task now to use this plurality of perspectives and core sensitizing concepts to make a difference in leadership studies.

5

Studying Leadership
Taking Meaning, Relationality and Ideology Seriously

Mats Alvesson

Introduction

There are many different views and definitions of leadership (Barker 1997; Palmer and Hardy 2000). Often there is no definition or even hint of what is meant by leadership – the signifier appears to indicate what CEOs, other senior or even low-level managers (loosely referred to as 'leaders') do. This indicates that the subject matter – if we can see leadership as a specific phenomena or theme for study and not a signifier covering up a wide set of different phenomena falsely unified by the label – is elusive, complex and vague. This is broadly acknowledged, but hardly taken seriously, by most of the researchers in the area(s), typically addressing leadership as if it were a thing. It is too often assumed that instruments for measurement – typically a questionnaire, sometimes an interview – can cut through ambiguity and capture leadership. Research on leadership has been strongly dominated by positivistic/neo-positivistic assumptions, together with an emphasis on rules and procedures for the securing of objectivity in research practice and results (Antonakis *et al.* 2004b; Mumford *et al.* 2009; Kroeck *et al.* 2004). The research ideal is that, through careful measurement and research programs, theories will be verified and reliable knowledge established. The belief is in accumulation. Good new studies add positively to earlier ones. Thousands of studies have been conducted on leadership. But how well do these manage to throw light on the subject matter?

Despite much diversity in the definitions of leadership, there is a loose consensus that leadership is about a relation and a set of interactions involving people in an asymmetrical relation in a social (organizational) context, where, although there is mutual influencing one part ('the leader') is supposed to have a more far-reaching and goal-directed impact than others (the 'followers') (Antonakis *et al.* 2004a; Fiedler 1996; Yukl 1989). But one can raise questions about how well leadership has been studied by the dominating forms of research. Arguably, studying a relation and interactions calls for careful observations and/or empirical material from the *various parties* involved, primarily the manager and the subordinates, in order to be able to address the relationship. Otherwise the understanding produced appears highly partial and unreliable, as if one could understand a marriage or parenting solely through asking only one of the spouses or only the parent or the child. Studying leadership also calls for getting to the core phenomenon one is interested in understanding. This includes the *experience and meaning* of the manager/subordinate relation. A leadership influence process is not a mechanical operation or a matter of simple stimulus–response, but involves interpretation and understanding. Is this relation about leadership or something else? And if the former, in what way? Here it is vital to go beyond the surface (unless one focuses on discourse, i.e. language use) and try to access aspects of reality and ways of relating beyond superficial responses (X-filling behaviours on questionnaires or interview talk taken at face value). There is no reason to assume that responses to questions simply reflect behaviours, experiences or cognitions. All studies risk capturing mainly norms for producing socially acceptable responses and/or folk theories (Alvesson 2011; Silverman 2006). Whether a questionnaire or an interview says more about cultural norms and beliefs, e.g. that good things go hand in hand and something that we dislike leads to something else dislikeable, than about some 'underlying' reality is often an open question, not seriously addressed in most leadership studies. This leads to a need to consider *source critique* (Alvesson and Sköldberg 2009). How can we assess the value of data generated? What do they really tell us? What – apart from perception of reality or subjective states – may inform how subjects deliver 'data'? Implicit leadership theories have been addressed in the method literature (Bryman 2011) but there are many other complications. A key problem here, but also a general one for the study of leadership, is the *issue of ideology*, i.e. idealizing (or demonizing) ideas, naturalizing or legitimizing a particular order (or radical change of order), supporting sectional interests. There is often a strong value bias in talk about leadership; it is difficult to get a good description and sound judgement of something as vague and positively loaded as leadership. The ideology problem needs to be handled in empirical work, as well as how the researcher relates to the subject matter. There is a risk that leadership studies (LS) are more about (naïve) ideology (re)production than well-informed knowledge development of the subject matters addressed (Alvesson and Kärreman 2016).

The overall aim of this chapter is to contribute to more *reflexive research on leadership*, supporting more care in the study of leadership in terms of relationality, meaning, one-source bias and dealing with ideological one-sidedness. These key methodological themes were not addressed that much in the literature on leadership research methods (e.g. not addressed more than marginally in overviews of methodology in LS by Antonakis *et al.* 2004b; Bryman 2011; Mumford *et al.* 2009). Reflexivity concerns critical thinking about assumptions, vocabularies and the researchers' subjective and collective (paradigm-driven) worldview governing the process, producing research results bearing strong imprints of textual conventions, fashions and socio-political interests (including commitment to one's research tribe) (Álvesson *et al.* 2008, 2017). Reflexivity means some challenging of assumptions dominating concerns about method (Alvesson and Sandberg 2011), for example, that the leader–follower distinction and categories can be taken for granted, that leadership is sufficiently tangible that it can be measured or that subjects can simply report 'leadership' in a direct way. A purpose of this chapter is thus to suggest an <u>alternative</u> *methodological framework*, based on:

- careful construction of the relationship involved in manager–subordinate constellations, possibly involving (being productively seen in terms of) leadership;
- focused work unpacking the specific meanings of acts and relations of leadership;
- using source-critique to access broader and richer views of the relation; and
- counter ideology (re-)production in leadership studies.

I should add that this chapter addresses methodology not primarily as mode of data collection or technique, but in the sense of research principles, including the consideration of assumptions and conceptualizations of the phenomena guiding research practices. Methodology is then connected to ideas and guidelines for how to approach, think about and interpret (complex) phenomena (Alvesson and Sköldberg 2009).

I will start by discussing key elements in leadership as broadly defined and emphasize the need to avoid conflating different elements or aspects. The leader–follower categories and distinctions are critically discussed. I then address the issue of meaning, one-source studies and ideology. I show how empirical studies rely on tautologies and halo effects and may reflect language conventions and respondent bias for how 'good' leadership is connected to 'good' results rather than saying that much about reality 'out there'. I then argue that sound leadership research needs to take these issues seriously in theory development and empirical studies, which tend to imply a downgrading of dominating ideals associated with relying on procedures, codification and easy handling of large sets of data ('data dredging'), for many seen as the very essence of (good) research (Antonakis *et al.* 2004a; Mumford *et al.* 2009; Glaser and Strauss 1967; Strauss and Corbin 1994).

Leadership Is a Process and Relationship

The views and definitions of leadership are endless. Various review authors divide up the field in different, more or less arbitrarily produced, ways. Some overviews see traits, information processing, situational–contingency theory and transformational leadership as the four 'big' schools (Antonakis *et al.* 2004c). Others find that too narrow, and an overemphasis on similar types of schools. Fairhurst (2007) talks about business, academic psychology and discourse views. In their handbook, Bryman *et al.* (2011) structure the field into macro and sociological perspectives, political and philosophical perspectives, psychological perspectives and emergent perspectives. Bolden *et al.* (2011) divide the field up into individual, organizational and societal perspectives. Alvesson and Spicer (2012) draw upon Habermas's (1972) idea of knowledge-constitutive interests and refer to functional, interpretive and critical approaches. The major approaches to leadership addressed by the first-mentioned review authors belong to what Fairhurst and Bryman *et al.* refer to as psychology, Bolden *et al.* as an individual perspective and Alvesson and Spicer as functionalism.

Groupings may sometimes appear easy, e.g. there is something called 'transformational leadership' and a number of studies can be plugged into the same camp, but any close look indicates the variety and ambiguity camouflaged by the label (as with most labels used for mapping). Just take the issue of how transformational leadership (TFL) relates to charisma according to various authors: transformational and charismatic leadership are seen by various authors as similar/overlapping (Sashkin 2004), as siblings (Jackson and Parry 2008) or as quite different (Yukl 1999). What a specific grouping includes varies a good deal. There are revisions of TFL 'to include almost any type of effective leadership, regardless of the underlying influence processes' (Yukl 1999: 299). Whether TFL is a theory or direction or just a label for diverse approaches is thus not a straightforward issue. I have two points here: one is that it is important not to take categorizations and ordering conventions for granted, but to carefully reflect upon these and how we impose lines to divide up (and separate) ideas, discourses and communities (Locke and Golden-Biddle 1997). The other is that the value of efforts to sort fields through literature reviews is doubtful.

I will refrain from adding to the numerous reviews and concentrate this chapter on what appears to be broadly shared in the field. Most definitions of leadership include leaders doing something and followers responding to that, thereby shaping some form of influencing process. According to Antonakis and colleagues:

> Most leadership scholars would agree, in principle, that leadership can be defined as the nature of the influencing process – and its resultant outcomes – that occurs between a

leader and followers and how this influencing process is explained by the leaders' dispositional characteristics and behaviours, follower perceptions and attributions of the leader, and the context in which the influencing process occurs.

(2004a: 5)

The 'influencing process' as well as something that 'occurs between' is thus central. The relational aspect is underscored by Fiedler (1996), claiming that:

The most important lesson we have learned over the past 40 years is probably that the leadership of groups and organizations is a highly complex <u>interaction</u> between an individual and the social and task environment.

(1996: 242)

Realizing that 'most' is not all, these statements still capture a sufficient point of departure and focus for this chapter. The descriptor 'most', when used in such a huge and diverse and messy area, is sufficient. This means that some concerns or very radical challenges coming from, e.g. critical theory (Alvesson and Spicer 2014; Collinson 2014) or discourse studies (Fairhurst 2007), are not seriously addressed here. It accepts some of the basic ambitions of 'most' leadership studies, as stated by Antonakis *et al.* and Fiedler above, but then looks seriously at some methodological implications and is, as a consequence, highly critical of how LS is typically conducted, both in quantitative studies and a lot of qualitative work.

The citations above would imply a strong interest in *both* what the leader brings in and does *and* how followers perceive and attribute meaning to (reason about) these inputs and acts. One may assume, as Antonakis *et al.* appear to do, that all this forms a coherent whole, i.e. 'the influencing process'. But one could equally well assume the opposite: that the elements mentioned diverge, dispositions do not necessarily influence behaviour that strongly, attributions may not be triggered closely by the behaviour as intended by the manager, etc. These elements are often conflated in leadership research and seldom targeted for careful scrutiny. A problem here is the typical assumption about the active leader and the passive followers, in which the superiority and strength of the former would lead to alignment of meaning and a coherent influencing process. The act and the outcome should, however, not be seen as more or less by definition the same. An effort to influence does not necessarily lead to an aimed-for outcome. So when leadership – or, and perhaps often better (less mystifying), influencing – is in focus, the intention, the act and the outcome are often coupled and placed in the same box. As Sandelands and Drazin (1989) pointed out, this kind of reasoning is common in organization studies. So is also the case with, for example, research on transformational leadership, making the behaviour and the outcome impossible to separate (Yukl 1999). Transformation as intent and outcome may be two very different issues (Nye 2013). This encourages research with a tendency to produce built-in results and an insensitivity to process and relational issues, i.e. the (only) elements in leadership broadly seen as central. It is important to open up and study what is happening – and not over-pack leadership with a set of possibly quite diverse elements, from intentions to behaviour and to responses and feedback. Here it is important to consider the possibility of discrepancy in the views between the parties involved.

Problematizing the Leader–Follower Categorization

Leadership researchers divide up the world into leaders and followers. This division is seldom discussed, apart from the issue of managers/management vs leaders/leadership (e.g. Zaleznik

1977; Hunt 2004). Typically people in a managerial position are targeted for study, either directly or through subordinates being asked to answer a questionnaire or provide interview responses about the leadership of their manager. Some recent work on shared or distributed leadership broadens the spectrum of those leading and loosens the leader–follower distinction (Gronn 2002; Pearce and Conger 2003), although it sometimes seems to be more about teamwork or peer collaboration than something that benefits from being labelled 'leadership', and it falls outside the scope of this chapter to discuss this in any depth. Work on the dialectics of leadership upgrades the role of followers and draws attention to 'the complex, interactional relationship between leaders and followers' (Collinson 2005: 1425) or talks about leadership as a more relational process (Fletcher and Käufer 2003; Uhl-Bien 2006: 662). All this highlights the need to look at relations, interactions and the mutuality of influencing in what may (or may not) be seen as the leader–follower dyad and also to go beyond that level and consider systemic aspects (Fairhurst 2001; Küpers and Weibler 2008). But it is rare in studies seriously investigating the views of both the manager and the subordinates as parts of the same leadership relation. Rather than taking the relational, and thus socially contingent, character of leadership seriously, the vast majority of studies 'are populated with assessments of various dimensions of leadership by a single individual leader' (Kroeck *et al.* 2004: 93).

But before one uses the categories as the central ones in analysis and research result delivery, irrespective of whether these are bound to formal roles and stable positions or not, it is necessary to investigate the nature of the relationship. Occasionally, LS consider the distinction between managers and leaders (Zaleznik 1977; Hunt 2004; Nichols 1987; Palmer and Hardy 2000). The distinction is problematic. It is regularly set up in such a way that we have boring management and sexy leadership (Bolden *et al.* 2011), with management as regulating and maintaining the status quo, leadership as inspiring and dealing with change (e.g. Barker 1997). Mumford *et al.* (2009) discuss this theme, and claim that the issue of managers vs leaders is something for studies to solve and, in the mean time, it is best or at least good enough to capture (or at least label) those targeted as 'leaders' doing leadership ('to approach leadership broadly', p. 123). It appears increasingly common to neglect any distinction between managers and leaders and favour the use of the second, more sexy or 'grandiose' term. There are two fundamental problems here. One is that those involved may not see each other as leader and follower – often people in formally subordinate positions may not define their formal superior as a 'leader' (in a distinct sense) and do not see themselves as 'followers'. Second, irrespective of the views of those involved, a careful investigation of a relation would lead the researcher, given a specific theoretical idea of what leadership is, to the conclusion that this is badly captured in terms of leader and follower. If so, these labels may be misleading. A study of formal subordinates showed a limited interest in being led and a disinclination to view themselves as followers in need of much leadership (Blom and Alvesson 2014).

It is not necessarily the case either that the labels 'manager' and 'subordinate' are relevant to sensitively capturing the phenomena under study. In contemporary organizations – involving hybrid ingredients, temporary arrangements, project as well as line managers – that deviate from bureaucratic models of a single and stable line of command, both leader–follower and manager–subordinate distinctions may be misleading or at least so crude and clumsy that they work against a sensitive understanding of relations. And even when there is some kind of superior–subordinate relationship associated with a formal hierarchy, talk about leader–follower may still not give a good representation of the object of study. Relations may be collegial, an informal authority base may be stronger than a managerial one, there may be several authority bases, making more than one person appearing as a possible 'non-formal' leader etc. The appropriateness of leader–follower categories and distinctions cannot be established a priori. The relevance and descriptive value of these in individual cases need to be carefully assessed (Alvesson *et al.* 2017). This is very seldom done. Methodologically, researchers find some managers or some people addressed as subordinates/followers and then these are expected to reply on issues related to the manager's leadership (of these people). There is seldom a question of the type 'do you find the terms leader–follower and leadership a precise, broadly reasonable, problematic or misleading way of describing the relationship between you and your formal superior?' Whether people divide up their organizational realities into leaders and followers and/or whether this is a superior way of representing and theorizing relations at work should be seen as a partial and interesting research result, not an unproblematic and robust point of departure. Actually, one could put dominant assumptions and reasoning upside down and say that *if* and *when* it can be demonstrated that people have placed themselves in a clear follower position and expect to be led by a leader, this is an interesting phenomenon calling for explanation. How is it that people emphasize followership to 'the leader' and thus to a significant degree refrain from autonomy and professionalism and relying on peers and other sources – of which one could be the manager – for support, problem-solving, value clarification, mutual adjustment, etc.?

Rigorous research needs to carefully investigate *if* and *when* leadership – defined in a specific way – and leader–follower is actually a good way to describe a phenomenon. Without careful work demonstrating this existence and significance, LS becomes mainly an expression of the *ideological* belief that there are two kinds of people: leaders and followers. That there are, on paper, managers and their subordinates, expected to follow the employment contracts and vertical division of labour, does not mean that there are good reasons to categorize people as leaders or followers. I come back to the issue of ideology below.

The Neglect or Superficiality of Issues of Meaning

Acknowledging that the intention and behaviour of the manager is not necessarily followed by a predictable or expected perception and response from the subordinate leads to an interest in the possible variety and ambiguity of meaning. Many students of leadership view the key quality as management of meaning (Smircich and Morgan 1982; Ladkin 2010), but approaches that are less finely tuned to meaning also need to take the meaning aspect seriously. Even issues (seemingly) 'low' on meaning, such as those typically addressed by questionnaire researchers and other 'non-interpretivists', e.g. 'initiating structure'/'providing direction' questions, include a meaning element, making the counting of responses often problematic. Rather than rely strongly on the adding of standardized questions in order to come up with a single measurement of the aspect of leadership of interest (as if this would be an objective phenomenon) we need to pay careful attention to how people involved understand and relate to a relationship and a situation. The issue of the precise meaning of elements in the influencing process is vital here. Without some convergence and depth in meaning of those involved in terms of what the behaviour of the manager stands for, one may doubt whether this is an influence process that could or should be labelled leadership. (Is it leadership if a manager tries to give an inspiring vision talk, but the subordinates yawn or tell jokes about it afterwards?) What goes on may be seen differently by the people involved. Take typical examples of leadership such as 'consideration' or 'initiating structure' as styles or sets of actions. These are typically treated as objective, measurable phenomena in LS and it is assumed that the leader, the subordinates and the researcher all agree upon the nature of these. But is a certain set of leader behaviour, perhaps intended to show concern, necessarily perceived as such by subordinates? Or is a manager suggesting to the follower what to do, interpreted as a concern only about the task and not about the people? Some people, particularly the young, inexperienced and uncertain, may interpret what for some perhaps appears to be about 'initiating structure' as an expression of consideration and strongly people-oriented (helpful, supportive). The same managerial behaviour may be viewed as being about distrust and control or as support and close contact. Whether I see my manager as concerned/helpful or interfering/controlling may refer to the same behaviour and to corresponding/different intentions by the manager. The distinction may also be inappropriate – often managers may not have a clear intention of focusing on consideration (people) or initiating structure (task) and subordinates may not read their behaviour as possible to plug into these categories, as a lot of manager/subordinate talk or behaviour may not fit neatly into any of them.

Such complications are not discovered through studies that are thin or weak on 'meaning sensitivity', which is the case with most questionnaire studies as well as qualitative research using codification, as in grounded theory (Glaser and Strauss 1967), i.e. those that impose a standard way of sorting data rather than interpreting and exploring the finer grades of empirical indications. Asking one party – the manager or the subordinate – about the issue at hand only through fixed questions and giving space only for limited replies (and not allowing exploration of meaning) risks providing a thin and poor understanding of leadership, e.g. as an influence process within an asymmetrical relation.

Generally there is in LS a preference for approaches – experiments, questionnaires, and codification-oriented qualitative work such as grounded theory – that neglect the complexity of meaning. (Exceptions are a limited number of specifically meaning-focused studies, e.g. Smircich and Morgan 1982; Ladkin 2010; Sandberg and Targama 2007.) The predominant way of studying leadership is through the use of questionnaires (Bryman 2011; Mumford *et al.* 2009). Advocates believe that 'questionnaires have long demonstrated their usefulness, validity and reliability in the measurement of leadership' (Kroeck *et al.* 2004: 85). Sometimes one even gets the impression that leadership 'as such' – practices, interactions, relations – is of less interest to researchers than questionnaire-filling behaviour.

Responses to abstract formulations in questionnaires are usually remotely distanced from the actions, events, feelings, relations, articulations of opinions, etc. emerging in everyday life situations. That a person is asked to put an X in a particular response option from among the five or so possibilities in a questionnaire may say rather little of what or how that person feels or thinks or behaves in the various situations he or she encounters, which the questionnaire tries to reflect. Let us take the example of efforts to measure 'emotional intelligence' (EI). This is investigated through asking people to respond to items such as 'I really understand what I feel' and 'I can always calm down when I am very angry' (emotional intelligence test, referred to in Lindebaum and Cartwright (2010)). These questions are extremely ambiguous, and what a possible answer implies is impossible to tell: presumably it is good to agree with the formulations, but this may instead indicate poor self-understanding. Or if a person says that 'I don't really understand what I feel', is this a sign of low EI or the opposite: an insight acknowledging the complexity of feelings? If a person can always become calm after becoming very angry, is this a proof of ability to regulate emotion or the opposite: getting very angry about something that turns out to be easy to calm down about may indicate a bad temper and thus an inability to regulate emotions.

The point here is not mainly to argue against questionnaires (or other quantitative methods), although I think it is doubtful if we can use them as the only or principal method in a study of leadership. Also much qualitative work, in particular highly structured interview studies or research relying only on observations, is problematic. This point goes directly against many definitions of 'proper science', emphasizing the standardization of data for comparison, aggregation and 'objective' handling, cleansed of too much judgement and interpretation, which is viewed as involving risky subjectivity (e.g. Antonakis *et al.* 2004b; Mumford *et al.* 2009).

Interpretation is, however, key to addressing meaning (Alvesson and Sköldberg 2009). We need to acknowledge and address the complexity and uncertainty of meaning, not avoid it through data management procedures. which may obscure access to important ambiguities. The key issues around leadership need to be opened up to systematic consideration, critical scrutiny and reflection. We should here add that an interest in meaning does not necessarily mean the focus of one, unitary, underlying meaning – meanings may be multiple, situational, inconsistent and processual, as indicated by poststructuralist methods. While 'strong' versions of poststructuralism are into deconstruction and avoid talking about meaning, moderate versions may consider 'unstable', processual meanings (Alvesson 2002).

There are two key issues here: one is the meaning of the elements in the leadership process (if and when it makes sense to talk about such), as addressed above. Another regards meaning in the methodological context and includes the kinds of questions subjects can really answer and the logic behind their responses. As Bryman (2011) notes, observation of the subject matter appears to be a good method, but the problem is that, as leadership potentially includes everything, it is very difficult to know what to observe and the meaning of a certain observable behaviour or verbal interaction (see also Lundholm 2011). The ambiguity and complexity of leadership means that it is often very difficult to know what a specific interaction actually means or assess whether it is vital or not. This is also a great problem for research subjects; it may be almost impossible for people by putting Xs on some items or through interview talk to produce and package clear information about the leadership. But response alternatives such as 'I don't really know' or 'this is so complex and ambiguous that I can't really communicate this in a questionnaire or in a brief interview' are seldom presented to the respondent as legitimate options. Also, in interviews, respondents are expected to 'know' and be able and willing to tell. But what the responses indicate is often highly uncertain and may not reflect 'objective reality' or 'subjective meaning' as much as liking, social desirability, etc. (Bryman 2011; Mumford et al. 2009). Alvesson (2011) shows how interview responses may be influenced. They are not simply providing data indicating the core phenomena the researcher believes is under study, but are informed by eight other 'response logics', e.g. impression management, following a social script, political action and identity work. Leadership talk often appears to reflect social norms for how people should feel about leadership (Sveningsson and Alvesson 2016). 'Data' may be seen as uncertain representations of something, but intensive, rigorous interpretive work is needed before establishing what the meaning and significance behind the Xs and words expressed in inquiries are.

Overreliance on One-Source Studies

Issues around the relational nature of leadership are theoretically complex and are addressed in many different ways (Collinson 2005; Ladkin 2010). It is vital to study the perspectives of the parties involved and go beyond one-source studies, i.e. only getting data from one party in the leadership relationship. A relationship between a manager and the group of subordinates (subordinates here is understood only in a very formal way, not necessarily saying anything about 'real' subordinacy or followership) cannot just be limited to the manager and group, but often also involves a multitude of individuals, groups, networks and institutions acting on the 'core unit'; leadership may for example be an outcome of a dominant discourse or organizational culture putting strong imprints on the manager and the group, but, for reasons of simplicity, I focus here only on manager and subordinates, viewed as the potentially valuable informants about specific cases of leadership relationship.

Many managers are probably inclined to respond to inquiries in such a way that they appear as morally good and/or transformational, but what this actually says about their practices or how other people view them is uncertain. (High scores may indicate self-serving bias or impression management, lower scores modesty.) Laurent (1978) observed that the managers he interviewed claimed to involve their subordinates in change work, while the same managers said that their own superiors did not. Bartolomé and Laurent (1986) asked superior and subordinate managers to describe their expectations of each other and found that these 'differed sharply' (p. 79).

There is a large body of research on TFL and emotional intelligence relying on the same sources and showing strong correlations. But when different sources (e.g. the manager and someone else, such as a subordinate or the manager's own superior) are used, the EI self-ratings of the managers and the TFL ratings of other people (their managers or subordinates) 'do not correlate significantly' (Lindebaum and Cartwright 2010). Some leader–member exchange researchers have investigated variations in perceptions of leader–member exchanges, noting that 'subordinate descriptions of the quality of leader–follower exchanges correlate poorly with their supervisors' descriptions of the same phenomenon' (Zhou and Schriesheim 2010: 827; see also Cogliser et al. 2009; Markham et al. 2010). It is obvious that managers and subordinates do not necessarily see what goes on in 'leadership' in the same or even broadly similar ways. This indicates that one cannot take one respondent's questionnaire responses or interview talk as sufficient data for studying leadership.

The majority of leadership research does not seem to take seriously the idea that there may be considerable discrepancy between the manager and those supposed to follow in terms of their view of leadership behaviour/acts and the relationship. This probably reflects the normative ambition of most leadership research, where the aim is to say something about ideal situations, often at the expense of realism and descriptive precision (Alvesson and Kärreman 2016).

Let me underscore the point on the diversity through connecting to the issue of meanings addressed in the previous section. A common feature of leadership is the leader's 'genuine concern' for the subordinates, briefly addressed above. To understand and assess this calls for careful investigating of the leader's as well as the subordinate's experiences. The leader may have or express such a concern, but this does not guarantee that the subordinates respond in a predictable way. It is here possible to imagine different responses. One is a clear and distinct deviation from the ideals and intentions expressed, e.g. 'no genuine concern for others at all', but 'genuine uninterest' or 'faked concern', or that there is 'genuine concern' but a negative evaluation of this (dislike of the concern). People with a high integrity or preference for autonomy may dislike the manager being too concerned, as they may prefer to avoid inquiries about feelings, well-being, competence, etc., even if the inquiries are 'genuine'. A problem here is that, as 'genuine' sounds good, it is difficult to articulate negative or mixed feelings about this, in particular when filling in questionnaires or responding to pre-structured interview questions. What is genuine and what is not may also be very hard to tell – often the manager may have some instrumental motive, making the 'genuine' interest somewhat ambiguous. A shared assessment of leader and subordinate that the former expresses a genuine concern may indicate that all is good, but if the subordinate does not appreciate the concern, this is not so good. The point here is that we need to have a fairly rich view of the meanings of those involved, from both sides. Studies should allow not only for a fixed measurement of meaning, but provide space for those studied to express ambivalence and ambiguity.

Leadership as interaction and an influence process needs as a minimum to consider the views of both interacting parties. Interactions typically involve a two-way influencing process. 'Followers' do not just follow (Collinson 2006). But, oddly, as Liden and Antonakis (2009) observe, 'research has just touched the surface regarding the many ways in which leaders and followers influence each other' (p. 1598), arguably a key element in the relationship. LS need to address this in order to get a full rather than crippled view of the process/interaction and to exercise source-control over the data material.

Leadership as Ideology

Many leadership researchers strongly embrace the view that leadership is a positive force of great significance. Mumford *et al.* (2009), for example, claim that 'Clearly, leadership makes a difference, a big difference, with respect to the nature of organizational behaviour and the performance of organizations' (p. 111). For people interested in LS, this may be seen as self-evident and at present this kind of conviction seems to be in broad circulation. However, many influential management researchers have expressed strong doubt about the significance of leadership (Drucker 1999; Mintzberg 2004; Pfeffer 1977). Many studies are flawed and the results are unreliable (Van Knippenberg and Sitkin 2013). We should not be uncritically carried away by the current strong fashionability of leadership and conflate popular beliefs with facts and intellectual insight. Given that leadership is defined in an almost endless number of different ways – or not at all – and that the only thing that people can agree upon is that leadership is about influencing something (individuals, groups, behaviours, cultures, emotions . . .), it seems almost impossible to make any definitive statements about its significance. If, then, leadership is defined as somebody influencing, then of course Mumford *et al.* are correct – who can object to influencing making a difference, a big difference – but this is tautological and trivial. A meaningful statement of leadership's impact needs to be based on a specific (not all-embracing) concept of leadership and it cannot be assumed that this delimited phenomenon is so extremely significant.

LS is, however, rich in work based on such assumptions and correspondingly naïve claims. Transformational leadership, the most popular leadership theory during recent decades (Diaz-Saens 2011), is often seen as being about how leadership accomplishes something really extraordinary:

> leaders transform followers. That is, followers are changed from being self-centered individuals to being committed members of a group.
>
> *(Sashkin 2004: 175)*

As remarked by Spoelstra and ten Bos (2011), LS is full of beautiful images of the subject matter. That leadership studies, as is indeed also the case with management (and social science) more generally, are not ideologically neutral is not an original point (Gemmill and Oakley 1992; Knights and Willmott 1992). As Trice and Beyer (1993), for example, have argued, the 'persistence of widespread beliefs in leaders and leadership has ideological overtones' (p. 254).

Social science involves studying value-laden phenomena of which the researcher is a part. The idea of studying effective leadership is hardly neutral. The ideological and political nature of LS and the power effects of discourse must then be taken seriously (Alvesson and Kärreman 2016). Leadership research does not just mirror external realities, but creates ways of seeing and valuing, normalizing subjects, supporting certain interests (normally those labelled 'leaders' and management education providers rather than other people) and has some impact on how leadership behaviour is exercised – through publications and education. (For various views on this matter, see Meindl (1995) and Foucault (1977, 1980)).

Large parts of leadership research have a political and ideological bias – the strengthening of asymmetrical social relations, providing legitimacy to elites and institutions such as business schools and other management education institutes. Leadership ideology naturalizes and reinforces the construction of social relations alongside a leader–follower dichotomy. It provides people with reassuring promises of good, effective leadership, taking care of all problems. Large parts of LS are celebratory in nature. Many authors suggest that, if it is not good, it is not leadership, marrying effectiveness and morality (e.g. Bass and Steidmeier 1999; Jackson and Parry 2008).

Ideology produces consciousness, aspirations and an inclination to see and express coherence and harmony. As such, it has a strong grip on large groups of leadership researchers, eager to portray good leadership in pink and gold, where good things tend to go together (Spoelstra and ten Bos 2011), which they of course in real life do not necessarily do (Grint 2010).

An ideology may have many effects: legitimation, portraying reality in a brighter light, inserting hope, offering clues on what to strive for (Therborn 1980). It offers 'identity material' for managers (and other leader-wannabes), and offers templates for legitimation, in which the mundane, instrumental and operative sides of managerial work are forgotten in favour of far more impressive and ego- and status-boosting activities. Leadership discourse in this sense reduces some of the strains and boredom of managerial work. Managers caught in administrative and technical work in bureaucracies – where the deliveries and the maintenance of the corporate machinery calls for a lot of their efforts to function – can frame, and fantasize about themselves, their work and their contribution through the leadership discourse (Alvesson and Sveningsson 2003; Sveningsson and Larsson 2006). Leadership then fuels (and conceals) a form of escapism, allowing a liberation from awareness of dominating practices, reality becomes bracketed – at least now and then – and a more appealing construction of what and how one 'really' is, somewhere, sometimes, is nicely framed (Sveningsson and Alvesson 2016).

Ideology is not just an issue in terms of how researchers frame the subject matter but also how respondents provide data. Leadership ideology exercises an impact on people in organizations, especially managers whose reports in interview and questionnaire studies may be based on idealized notions of how reality should be, rather than more reflective representations of practices and meanings (Alvesson and Sveningsson 2003; Holmberg and Tyrstrup 2010). When asked about values, practices, motives, relations, etc., it is not unlikely that people express themselves in other ways than how they tend to behave, think or feel in specific everyday work situations. Many studies target managers on or after a training session, when they are probably more affected by leadership ideals than they are otherwise.

The common target for the four aspects addressed is the dominant assumption that there is a unitary, robust leadership phenomenon (behaviour, style, value set, a discourse, some stable meanings) that it is possible to capture through one source of data deliverer (manager or subordinates), giving clear-cut answers (data) reflecting the phenomenon that can be studied in a neutral, ideology-free way. The counter assumption is that these assumptions are potentially misleading and the framework and methodology need to be theoretically and methodologically open about this and include significant theoretically informed checking-points.

Illustrations

Let me point more specifically to how a set of research questions calls for careful consideration in terms of the four methodological ideas discussed above. Mumford *et al.* (2009) exemplify how (good) science should look, by claiming that:

> Differential quality of the relationship formed between leaders and followers is measured through questions such as 'Do you know where you stand with the leader?', 'Does the leader understand your problem and needs?'
>
> *(2009: 112)*

Here we find some basic problems indicated by the four themes above, i.e. when the questions (as Mumford *et al.* seem to suggest) are distributed to a sample of people supposed to provide data on the 'differential quality of the relationship formed between leaders and followers'.

The first problem is on the nature of *the relationship*. It is taken for granted that there is a leader and presumably that there is a specific one (and only one). (There may be a line manager, one or more project managers, one or more informal authority persons complicating the picture, making it difficult to know who is 'the leader' referred to.) It is also assumed that this person, where the respondent stands with them and their understanding of problems and needs are of some or even considerable relevance. All this needs to be critically explored and sorted out, before it may be meaningful to ask the questions or the answers can be assessed. A second issue to be investigated concerns meanings. What do the questions really mean and how can one, as a respondent, interpret them? 'Where do you stand with the leader' in terms of what? Understanding of which problems and needs? Is the criteria for 'good' or whatever a high degree of clarity and precision and stability in terms of where the respondent stands with them? Does 'understand' refer to a high level of personal knowledge based on information about technical skills and work situation or rather empathy and psychotherapeutical understanding? Lack of knowledge and understanding may be related to a dynamic, shifting and ambiguous context and the manager and the respondent being new on the job or having a different task. In a very stable work context and in a long-term relationship, the questions have a very different meaning than under the opposite conditions. And a really skilled professional may be autonomous and not be concerned about spending time and energy on communication with 'the leader' so that s/he understands problems and needs. (Understanding is fine, but may call for the allocation of time and effort facilitating this, time perhaps better spent in other ways.) Often individuals go to people in their network perceived to be knowledgeable about a certain issue rather than to the manager (Blom and Alvesson 2014). But the respondent may interpret the questions as not reflecting the work situation or the 'real' understanding so much as being evaluative of the manager, so the general attitude to the manager may inform the answer. A low or moderate level of understanding may be felt by the respondent to be fine, but anticipation that this may not look good on the questionnaire may then guide the response. As a consequence, one does not know what, if anything, the responses say, even if responses on different questions seem to converge. Third, the questions concern *two parties*. Mumford's questions are very much about a relationship. The person supposed to be capable of answering the questions may have little idea of how the leader 'really' relates to and understands the subordinate. The respondent may believe s/he knows where s/he stands, but the leader may have a different view. Both may feel that the leader understands problems and needs, but the meaning of 'understanding' may differ and the problems and needs addressed may also have little in common. One may of course be interested in the perceptions or guesswork or espoused responses of subordinates about the leader's understanding, but if one is interested in leadership as a relationship and an influencing process (as most leadership researchers are, according to Antonakis *et al.* and Fiedler quoted above), and not just a perception from one angle, this appears insufficient. Fourth, *ideology*: the formulated questions take the idea that there are leaders (and one leader per subordinate/follower) for granted, naturalize the leader–follower distinction and give privilege to the leader. The relationship is indicated to be important, and it is vital that the leader understands the problems and needs of the subordinate, apparently understood to be dependent on the leader's understanding. This reinforces the norm of there being a leader who is significant and superior, that high clarity on where the subordinate stands and good understanding are optimal and that deviations from this indicate imperfections. This may not be wrong, but it is vital to reflect upon this and carefully investigate whether these assumptions steer research in a productive and thoughtful way or whether they, unchecked, may reproduce and reinforce ideology more than good research.

Some advocates of dominating views may feel that valid results have been demonstrated and that 'data' show the value of questionnaire-based studies, thereby downplaying or trivializing the relevance of comments such as those made above. But many correlations showing reliability or support for a theory do not say much (Alvesson 1996). Rather they may be seen as an outcome of norms for how to fill in questionnaire boxes.

This is exemplified by Conger *et al.* (2000). Here, charismatic leadership is expected to be positively related to a follower's sense of collective identity, perceived group performance and feelings of empowerment. The sample was asked to answer a 'questionnaire assessing a supervisor's behaviour' (p. 753). If a person tends to say that 'I hold him/her (the leader) in high respect', they may also agree with statements such as the leader is 'inspirational', 'influences others by developing mutual liking and respect' and 'often expresses personal concern'. And if they do, it would hardly come as a surprise that they tend to agree with statements such as, 'we see ourselves in the work group as a cohesive team' and 'we have high work performance'. And as a single person is the sole data-provider on all questions (on a specific manager), results on the whole confirm expectations are as one would assume. (Conger *et al.* did certain things to reduce the problems mentioned, including handing out two questionnaires, with the second appearing 24 hours after the first had been answered, but the basic problem probably remains.)

This is not a unique example. There is a large literature on transformational leadership that at face value offers much evidence for the theory, but critics have demonstrated that much of this is basically flawed (Alvesson and Kärreman 2016; Van Knippenberg and Sitkin 2013).

A Proposal for Re-orientation: Studying Leadership Seriously

Clarifying Leadership as a Phenomenon and a Relationship

Most of the popular leadership ideas assume that, or at least work as if, the existence of the sole leader forming a stable and robust entity with fixed traits and skills and operating on others to shape and improve them is a function of the leader's essence being put into operation. Without repeating all the critique mentioned earlier, or invoking attributional (follower-focused) or radical constructionist understandings (Meindl 1995), one could say that all these assumptions call for careful scrutiny and for their fairness in specific contexts being investigated.

It is important, in rigorous studies, in opposition to research guided by taken-for-granted assumptions, to postpone imposing a leader–follower categorization on reality. The categorization may make sense, but this is an empirical question. Leaders and followers cannot be starting points to be taken for granted; they are possible (partial) research results. One could even say that if there is a clear leader–follower relationship characterizing a modern, knowledge-intensive workplace, it could be viewed as an interesting deviation from the expectation that managers take care of administration and management, while there is a variety of influencing in which people in more or less symmetrical relations influence each others' understandings and values, through arguments, feedback, jokes, suggestions, stories, advice, exemplary and deviant behaviour, certain performances, etc. Most of this is not necessarily best represented as leadership, even though labels such as shared, distributed, complexity, etc. can broaden the range of 'leadership' in various ways – while easily overstretching and turning 'leadership' into something that captures everything and nothing. LS typically study managers, as 'leaders' are identified through managerial positions, even though this is also quite uncertain in many cases. People with the title may not have or work with subordinates, and formal subordinates may not, in practice, be subordinates, as in many professional organizations, where the manager is rather an administrative person. Also, the nature of the relationship is often ambiguous and sometimes deviates from mainstream understandings. One study found that managers saw their subordinates (co-workers) as the most significant source of feedback, indicating that the influencing process may be almost the opposite to what most LS assume and the relationship is perhaps not so strongly leader-driven (Kairos Futures/Chef 2006). If so, one may have perhaps assumed that the manager's superior would be more significant for feedback – a key influencing mechanism. Sometimes people in (formally) subordinate positions may take initiatives and combine strong elements of leading and subordinateship in relationship to seniors (Courpasson *et al.* 2012).

One key element in LS projects should be to clarify the *sample* in terms of a possible leadership relation, i.e. to explore what is the overall nature of a relationship between a person and a manager (or another potential leader) before deciding that this is a leadership relation (in a specific sense). Here, understanding the context is vital. Is it a stable bureaucracy, in which people tend to stay in their jobs and take formal positions seriously? Is the organizational work and career patterns of such a nature that the senior person is likely to have superior technical competence? Or is it a project-based organization, in which people may be project leader on one project and a member on another, both projects happening simultaneously? As work constellations are shifting all the time, stable leader–follower relationships may be rare or insignificant. Competence-based, more or less issue-specific authority relations may marginalize formal hierarchy, making issues around 'the leader' uncertain. This needs to be clarified in any serious study.

To simply neglect context – or reduce it to a couple of standardized items on a questionnaire – is very common (Antonakis *et al.* 2004b; House and Aditya 1997), but such reductionism leads to poor studies, even though ignorance may be hidden under piles of (poor) data and number-crunching procedures.

Methodologically, this leads to investigating the organizational context and fine-tuning studies based on a qualified pre-understanding of the subject matter. One could interview people about who, if anyone, at the workplace you see as a leader (of importance for you)? Or ask managers or other possible leader characters if they would define themselves as leaders and, if so, in what way and for whom? This would typically imply a qualitative approach, giving people space to express how they see any possible leader–follower relationship. But one can also imagine quantitative work, including questions of the type, 'Do you find the terms leader–follower and leadership to be a precise, problematic or misleading way of describing the relationship between you and your formal superior?' Or 'How would you describe your (formal) superior? As a leader, a manager, an administrator, first among peers or what?' Or 'Does anyone in your workplace exercise a very strong influence on you? If so, who? In what way?'

Investigations like this may lead to the finding that only a part of the sample at present typically defined a priori and without good grounding as 'leaders' doing 'leadership' (i.e. people with managerial jobs) would pass reasonable criteria for fitting the category. Of a number of managers or subordinates initially approached, only some may be worth pursuing for further study of leadership. Also, issues around the possible stability–coherence vs dynamics–fragmentation of manager–subordinate relationships are crucial to sort out.

It may, of course, be tempting for the statistically minded researchers to concentrate on getting the numbers and then using whatever sample are willing to fill in the questionnaires, but scholarship calls for a good understanding of the subject matter, including the context. This calls for careful work on a clearly delimited group, their work situation, their understandings of 'leadership' and possible leadership relations. This calls for a (pre-)study, typically involving at least some qualitative ingredients, as questionnaires and pre-structured interviews may miss key insights that the researcher – caught in his/her and the research tribe's specific worldview – may never have thought of including in the design.

Focused Work Unpacking the Specific Meanings of Acts and Relations of Leadership

Arguably, not much in leadership behaviour and leader–follower relations has a simple, straight-forward meaning. People may use the same words, put Xs in the same boxes on questionnaires or repeat the same words, and still mean something quite different. Specific meanings need to be investigated, clarified and tested before the researcher can make knowledge claims. Critical exploration of the logic behind a specific respondent's data delivery also needs to be clarified. This is to some extent acknowledged through at least passing references to social desirability, personal liking/disliking, etc. (Mumford *et al.* 2009) but is often, in practice, bypassed in studies and not targeted for inquiry, making it impossible for the researcher to make a sound assessment of the nature of the data material.

This calls for a dialogue rather than stimuli-response reasoning and encouragement of the subjects to mobilize their knowledge and experiences about the subject matter, giving space for both breadth and depth. One could ask people how they think about questions, e.g. what their reflections around a questionnaire item are. Getting a holistic view and unpacking meaning complexes around respondents' data deliveries are thus central in determining what knowledge can be pulled out of a study.

Exploring meaning in depth goes strongly against using only questionnaires or standardized/pre-structured interviews and involves giving those studied space to raise their views. It does not mean that one cannot use these methods, but they need to be supplemented with more open-ended, meaning-investigating empirical work. If we take the question, 'My manager provides advice to those who need it' (Seltzer and Bass 1990), one needs to anchor the study in a clear sense of whether this is a relevant and meaningful question, for example by investigating the overall 'advice-giving context': How do you see advice-giving at your workplace? Do you need advice at work? Who is best positioned to give it to you? Do you see advice-giving as an important aspect of your manager's work? Does it function well or badly? After some qualitative inquiries such as this at a workplace, it may be relevant to ask the question by Seltzer and Bass, but if the researcher finds out that the work is technically complex, most managers are not experts and most people have qualified peers that can offer good advice, then the question is not meaningful and the answers may easily be misleading. Managers providing advice – perhaps motivated by a desire to preserve status and demonstrate authority – despite there being people better at it may do a worse job than those not providing much advice. In the absence of such knowledge of the advice-given context, the researchers have no idea of what they are studying or what the results mean.

Using Multiple Parties and Source-Critique to Access Broader and Richer Views of the Relation

A key problem for empirical research is the relationship between representations of reality (including feelings, values, experiences) and the topic of study, which seldom (unless in discourse studies) is how people represent reality. Questionnaire and interview researchers are not happy with only making claims about X-filling behaviour or interview conversations.

Several authors have called for a radical reorientation of the elaboration and measurement of abstracted constructs on the analysis of leadership as a practical accomplishment and social process, defined through interaction and relations, based on a qualitative approach (Alvesson 1996; Bryman 2004; Hosking 1988; Knights and Willmott 1992; Smircich and Morgan 1982). This is probably necessary in order to get good descriptions. But it is here important to go much further than only looking at what managers say in interviews about their own leadership, or subordinates about their leaders. Most qualitative studies only focus on one type of source (Alvesson 2011). As pointed out above, same-source studies are generally to be warned against: getting the views of people involved – managers, subordinates, senior people, colleagues – and the interactions making up leadership is necessary. It is vital to relate leadership issues to social context and social processes involving different parties. Both need to be studied.

This means opening up and studying what is happening – and not over-packing leadership with a set of possibly quite diverse elements, from intentions to behaviour and to responses and feedback, as perceived and expressed only by a set of 'followers' or a set of 'leaders'. The elements in a typical definition of leadership, e.g. by Antonakis *et al.* (2004b) – the leader's dispositional characteristics and behaviours, followers' perceptions of the attributions of the leader, and the context – should be considered separately and relations investigated.

Real-life observations of actions and interactions and understanding of context are crucial, even though the ambiguity and potentially all-embracing nature of leadership often make it difficult to know what to observe (Bryman 2011) and the context can be quite difficult to grasp. Ideally, studies should include interviews with managers (leaders) and those supposed to be led by them, observations of interactions and careful descriptions of the organizational context in which this takes place. In the absence of studies based on qualified data from various sources, ideologies, the wish to avoid cognitive dissonance, tautologies, halo effects, self-serving bias and wishful thinking face little resistance. Researchers need empirical material rich and varied enough to be able to assess whether the ideological scripts (e.g. hero stories) for how to talk/put Xs in questionnaires about leadership (Alvesson 2011) or reasoning informed by implicit leadership theory (Bryman 2011) are at play. Using more than one source is vital here. Of course, the same ideology may inform 'leaders' and 'followers', men and women and various ethnic groups, but there is still some differentiation and some variety in outlook. Given the relational nature of leadership and the need to capture the influencing process, both the leader's and the follower's views need to be documented and compared and then combined into a rich description of the leadership – or whatever comes out of all this, which may trigger interpretations other than in terms of leadership, e.g. conflicts, interpersonal de-coupling or autonomy. Studies should then ask the people involved: how do they see the key phenomena the researcher has picked for study; are there other relevant issues seen as important by those studied that possibly broaden the picture and reframe it in ways not anticipated by the researcher; and critically interpret all statements, making sure that any delivered data is backed up by an additional source (which is not just more items in the questionnaire or adding more respondents of the same type).

De-ideologize Leadership

The fourth key element is to try, as far as possible, to de-ideologize leadership. The idea is not to produce objective, neutral, value-free studies – this is not possible – but to move away from idealized discourses and look at social practices and relations at workplaces in an open and empirically sensitive way. A de-ideologization of leadership – which also involves moves to avoid becoming caught in an 'anti-leadership ideology' – is in one sense very difficult, perhaps impossible (as we are never value-free in social research). One can make serious efforts and at least move far away from ideologically top-scoring examples, such as TFL and other popular approaches. Also, avoiding imposing and naturalizing leader–follower categories and distinctions is fully possible; instead, these should be used when there is clear empirical support.

One specific way forward would be to invoke a much less ideologically positive language in both theorizing and empirical investigations. Tourish and Pinnington (2002), in a critical text on TFL, rely upon insights from studies of cults, which show considerable similarity with the intended outcomes of TFL. They point out that charismatic leadership may mean that the leader is viewed in semi-divine light by followers, the leader is the sole source of key ideas and the leader has privileges far in excess of other group members. A compelling vision may mean that the vision is totalistic in its implication, agreement with the vision vital for group membership, and the vision communicated uni-directionally from top to bottom, with dissent from the vision penalised. Such opposition handling through the use of power is a likely part of getting broad support for a shared vision (Bolden *et al.* 2011).

One could use these formulations instead of (only) the positively biased expressions in TFL, charismatic leadership and other ideological approaches, in which vision is typically captured through statements such as 'provides inspiring strategic and organizational goals', 'consistently generates new ideas', 'inspirational; able to motivate by articulating what organizational members are doing' and 'exciting public speaker' (Conger *et al.* 2000: 759). Here vision is viewed as good vision – the possibility that vision talk may be seen as a sleeping pill or rather abstract and remote from work reality does not surface, nor does the possibility that those that object to the vision talk may be silenced or pushed out. An alternative to this ideological positivity could be to find a language that is as neutral as possible (Alvesson and Kärreman 2016), e.g. asking questions such as 'Do you think people here tend to accept the ideas of the manager without much critical reflection?' or 'Would you say that there is a clear idea of a vision in this organization? If so, is it top-down driven? Does it play a significant or insignificant role in daily work?'

This may be simple and beneficial, but may create complexity and confusion in fieldwork practice – and also make it more difficult for researchers to produce the comforting results that have boosted the standing of leadership studies during recent years, with heavy ideologically biased designs, tolerance for tautologies and overreliance on one-source studies. But unpredictable and non-comforting results may offer interesting opportunities to rethink taken-for-granted assumptions and kick back against the researcher's (ideological) commitments.

New Methodological Principles

The four themes addressed are key themes for the entire research process but may come more specifically into play at the three main elements in the research process.

Fieldwork

Here the idea is to move close to the phenomena claimed to be investigated, trying to produce rich description that allows for a multitude of considerations and allowing the material to kick back at the researcher's (collectively held) assumptions and preconceptions. Using multiple sources is a key aspect, as leadership is (normally defined as) a relation. Close-up studies should be careful in conceptualizing what goes on, how to understand the people involved and the meanings attached to possible leadership acts and interactions, checking claims by research subjects and getting sufficiently rich input to challenge the researcher's (and the research subjects') ideological commitments.

Interpretive Work

This means emphasis on rigour and care in interpretation and reflexivity, based on questioning and suspicion of the 'truth-transmitting' powers of data. This includes reflecting on the key aspects of the relation, getting beneath the surface and digging out underlying meanings, assessing both the logic behind the reporting of 'data' (social conformism, self-serving bias, sincere ambition to tell the truth as one sees it . . .) and the precise meaning of any data seen as valid, given what the researcher is (or during the research process becomes) interested in. Being sceptical to positive-sounding and persuasive formulations dominating ideologically guided representations of leadership is another key part of interpretation.

Theoretical Framing and Problematization Work

Access to theoretical vocabulary and frameworks for conceptualizing and interpreting the material should be broadened. Rather than testing or applying, for example, a specific theory and limiting the framework exclusively to work, and concepts and assumptions within the tradition, it is vital to have access to alternative points of departure, metaphors, discourses, etc., including the idea that contemporary workplace relations in some cases may not include much 'leadership', but rely on other modes of coordination, control and support. One option here is to have access to a set of leadership (and non-leadership) metaphors supporting a set of perspectives and dialogues between them (Alvesson and Spicer 2011).

These three major foci in the research process – fieldwork/data construction, interpretation and use of theory – are all intertwined. It is broadly agreed that all data are theory impregnated; the idea that data are external and neutral to theory is misleading (Kuhn 1970; Alvesson and Sköldberg 2009). They offer various entrance points for the researcher to address the four key methodological concerns emphasized in this chapter.

Conclusion

A lot of leadership research is about the detailed investigation of specific theories. On the whole, a positive view of the state of the art prevails (Parry and Bryman 2006). Authors on methodology briefly notice some shortcomings of the dominating questionnaire studies, but then praise their usefulness (Antonakis *et al.* 2004b; Kroeck *et al.* 2004; Mumford *et al.* 2009).

This chapter offers a much more critical view. LS 'has been imbued with just such intangible qualities for which there are no appropriate methodological measurement tools' (Lakomski 2005: 8). As I have tried to demonstrate, a lot of the so-called findings do not say much – despite positive correlations and support for the hypothesis, it is almost impossible to say what has actually been studied. In-built ideological tendencies and tautologies account for many of the results, and same-source bias is common. Studies can sometimes be seen as exercises in ideology confirmation: good things go together in a harmonious whole. Language rules, social norms and the inclination to avoid cognitive dissonance make predictable 'results' almost guaranteed. Questionnaires with an in-built ideology bias, often filled in by managers when in training (a situation in which they are perhaps most exposed to various persuasive leadership ideas) are of questionable value.

This chapter takes these issues seriously but broadens the critique and addresses four major concerns: the leader–follower categorization and distinction is imposed, not explored or its relevance demonstrated; meanings being the core of the influence process is seldom sensitively addressed; there is an overreliance on one-and-the-same source studies and a shortage of source critique; and the fundamental ideological nature of leadership, informing both research subjects and researchers, is missed. Of course, there are leadership studies that address ambitiously one or several of these issues, e.g. Courpasson *et al.* (2012) and Fu *et al.* (2010), but for the vast majority of all leader research, this critique needs to be taken seriously and radical rethinking seems called for. The chapter addresses normal practice, not the very few exceptional studies that avoid part of the critique.

I have suggested four ways forward. First, researchers should postpone imposing categories, before having good reasons to use a particular 'master vocabulary' (e.g. leader, follower), i.e. to work with a sample that meets the criteria for what is intended to be studied. Second, researchers should explore meanings in depth and go beyond use of standard questions misleadingly assumed to have a uniform meaning and thus being capable of easily tapping subjects on their 'knowledge'. Understanding meaning calls for rich data, a sense of context and careful interpretation. Third, data are always partly an outcome of logics in play other than truth-reporting ambitions and people are often not capable of putting their observations and experiences in words or Xs. There is limited reliability and uncertain value in all efforts to deliver data. This calls for source-critique and use of multiple sources. Before taking the data of a sample of, for example, 'followers' seriously, back-up is called for. Managers' and subordinates' responses need to be compared, critically examined for common bias and good reasons for treating 'data' as Data marshalled. Fourth, to avoid an ideologically biased and often tautological research language and set of assumptions about a 'leader-driven' social world, alternative points of departure representing 'counter-ideological' considerations should be used. In inquiry, interpretation and writing, the researcher can supplement 'positive' and persuasive language (such as transformational, intellectual stimulation, consideration) with a more neutral language, if possible. One can alternate between language uses in interviews/questionnaires and then investigate (in)coherence rather than just aim for patterns and coherence: ambiguity, uncertainty and ambivalence are key aspects of leadership efforts.

All of the above point to the need to do in-depth studies of leadership, getting the views of managers (or others doing the leadership) as well as subordinates, observing practices and interactions, understanding the context and being open-minded (reflexive) about the value and relevance of (specific) leadership vocabulary. It does not imply grounded theory such as inductive studies, as access to frameworks, including alternative theoretical ideas and languages, are crucial in work calling for critical judgement. This is demanding, and calls for quality at the expense of quantity (numbers) and reflexive care rather than procedural and technical rigour, but it is key to understanding leadership as typically defined (an interactive influence process). This does not, however, imply only qualitative work. Questionnaires studies can also be useful in addressing some of the concerns covered here, as part of a mixed-method study (Bryman 2011). Taking the fundamental meaning aspect seriously, however, calls (also) for ambitious qualitative work, so research relying primarily on large numbers is hard to combine with responses to the fundamental critique raised in this chapter.

References

Alvesson, M. (1996) Leadership studies: From procedure and abstraction to reflexivity and situation. *Leadership Quarterly*, 7 (4): 455–485.

Alvesson, M. (2002) *Postmodernism and Social Research*. Buckinghamshire: Open University Press.

Alvesson, M. (2011) *Interpreting Interviews*. London: Sage.

Alvesson, M. and Kärreman, D. (2016) Intellectual failure and ideological success in organization studies: The case of transformational leadership. *Journal of Management Inquiry*, 25 (2): 139–152.

Alvesson, M. and Sandberg, J. (2011) Generating research questions through problematization. *Academy of Management Review*, 36 (2): 247–271.

Alvesson, M. and Sköldberg, K. (2009) *Reflexive Methodology*. London: Sage.

Alvesson, M. and Spicer, A. (eds) (2011) *Metaphors We Lead By: Leadership in the Real World*. London: Routledge.

Alvesson, M. and Spicer, A. (2012) Critical leadership studies. *Human Relations*, 65 (3): 367–390.

Alvesson, M. and Spicer, A. (2014) Critical perspectives on leadership. In Day, D. (ed.) *Oxford Handbook of Organization and Leadership*. Oxford: Oxford University Press.

Alvesson, M. and Sveningsson, S. (2003) The good visions, the bad micro-management and the ugly ambiguity: Contradictions of (non-)leadership in a knowledge-intensive company. *Organization Studies*, 24 (6): 961–988.

Alvesson, M., Hardy, C. and Harley, B. (2008) Reflecting on reflexivity: Reappraising reflexive practice in organisation and management theory. *Journal of Management Studies*, 45 (3): 480–501.

Alvesson, M., Blom, M. and Sveningsson, S. (2017) *Reflexive Leadership*. London: Sage.

Antonakis, J., Cianciolo, A. T. and Sternberg, R. J. (2004a) Introduction. In Antonakis, J., Cianciolo, A. T. and Sternberg, R. J. (eds) *The Nature of Leadership*. Thousand Oaks, CA: Sage.

Antonakis, J., Cianciolo, A. T. and Sternberg, R. J. (2004b) Methods for studying leadership. In Antonakis, J., Cianciolo, A. T. and Sternberg, R. J. (eds) *The Nature of Leadership*. Thousand Oaks: Sage.

Antonakis, J., Cianciolo, A. T. and Sternberg, R. J. (eds) (2004c) *The Nature of Leadership*. Thousand Oaks: Sage.

Barker, R. (1997). How can we train leaders if we don't know what leadership is? *Human Relations*, 50 (4): 343–362.

Bartolomé, F. and Laurent, A. (1986) The manager: Master and servant of power. *Harvard Business Review*, Nov–Dec, 77–81.

Bass, B. M. and Steidlmeier, P. (1999) Ethics, character, and authentic transformational leadership behavior. *Leadership Quarterly*, 10: 181–217.

Blom, M. and Alvesson, M. (2014) Leadership on demand: Followers as initiators and inhibitors of managerial leadership. *Scandinavian Journal of Management*, 30: 344–357.

Bolden, R., Hawkins, B., Gosling, J. and Taylor, S. (2011) *Exploring Leadership*. Oxford: Oxford University Press.

Bryman, A. (2011) Research methods in the study of leadership. In Bryman, A. *et al.* (eds) *The SAGE Handbook of Leadership*. London: Sage.

Bryman, A., Collinson, D., Grint, K., Jackson, B. and Uhl-Bien, M. (eds) (2011) *The SAGE Handbook of Leadership Studies*. London: Sage.

Chef (2006) Bäst på allt och aldrig nöjd. ('Best on everything and never pleased'). Stockholm: Kairos Futures.

Cogliser, C., Schriesheim, C., Scandura, T. and Gardner, W. (2009) Balance in leader and follower perceptions of leader–member exchange: Relationships with performance and work attitudes. *Leadership Quarterly*, 20: 452–465.

Collinson, D. (2005). Dialectics of leadership. *Human Relations*, 58: 1419–1442.

Collinson, D. (2006) Rethinking followership: A post-structural analysis of follower identities. *Leadership Quarterly*, 17: 179–189.

Collinson, D. (2014) Dichotomies, dialectics and dilemmas: new directions for critical leadership. *Leadership*, 10: 36–55.

Conger, J., Kanungo, R. and Menon, S. (2000) Charismatic leadership and follower effects. *Journal of Organizational Behaviour*, 21: 747–767.

Courpasson, D., Deny, F. and Clegg, S. (2012) Resisters at work: Generating productive resistance in the workplace. *Organization Science*, 23: 801–819.

Diaz-Saenz, H. (2011) Transformational leadership. In Bryman, A. Collinson, D., Grint, K., Jackson, B. and Uhl-Bien, M. (eds) *The SAGE Handbook of Leadership*. London: Sage.

Drucker, P. (1999) Managing oneself. *Harvard Business Review*, March–April: 65–74.

Fairhurst, G. T. (2001) Dualisms in leadership research. In Jablin I. F. and Putnam L. L. (eds) *The New Handbook of Organizational Communication: Advances in Theory, Research and Methods*, 379–439. Thousand Oaks, CA: Sage.

Fairhurst, G. T (2007) *Discursive Leadership: In Conversation with Leadership Psychology*. Thousand Oaks, CA: Sage.

Fiedler, F. (1996) Research on leadership selection and training: one view of the future. *Administrative Science Quarterly*, 41: 241–250.

Fletcher, J. K. and Käufer, K. (2003) Shared leadership: Paradoxes and possibility. In Pearce C. I. and Conger J. A. (eds) *Shared Leadership: Reforming the Hows and Whys of Leadership*. Thousand Oaks, CA: Sage.

Foucault, M. (1977). *Discipline and Punish*. Harmondsworth: Penguin.

Foucault, M. (1980). *Power/Knowledge*. New York: Pantheon Books.

Fu, P. P., Tsui, A. S., Liu, J. and Li, L. (2010) Pursuit of whose happiness? Executive leaders' transformational behaviours and personal values. *Administrative Science Quarterly*, 55: 222–254.

Gemmill, G. and Oakley, J. (1992) Leadership: An alienating social myth. *Human Relations*, 45 (2): 113–129.

Glaser, B. and Strauss, A. (1967) *The Discovery of Grounded Theory: Strategies for Qualitative Research*. Chicago: Aldine.

Grint, K. (2010) The sacred in leadership: separation, sacrifice and silence. *Organization Studies*, 31: 89–107.

Gronn, P. (2002) Distributed leadership as a unit of analysis. *Leadership Quarterly*, 13: 423–451.

Habermas, J. (1972) *Knowledge and Human Interests*. London: Heinemann.

Holmberg, I. and Tyrstrup, M. (2010) Well then – what now? An everyday approach to managerial leadership. *Leadership*, 6: 353–372.

Hosking, D. M. (1988) Organizing, leadership and skilful process. *Journal of Management Studies*, 25: 147–166.

House, R. and Aditya, R. (1997) The social scientific study of leadership: Quo vadis? *Journal of Management*, 23 (3): 409–473.

Jackson, B. and K. W. Parry (2008) *A Very Short, Fairly Interesting and Reasonably Cheap Book about Studying Leadership*. London: Sage.

Knights, D. and Willmott, H. (1992) Conceptualizing leadership processes: A study of senior managers in a financial services company. *Journal of Management Studies*, 29: 761–782.

Kroeck, G., Lowe, K. and Brown, K. (2004) The assessment of leadership. In Antonakis, J., Cianciolo, A. T. and Sternberg, R. (eds) *The Nature of Leadership*. Thousand Oaks: Sage.

Kuhn, T. (1970) *The Structure of Scientific Revolutions*. Chicago: University of Chicago Press.

Küpers, W. and Weibler, J. (2008) Inter-leadership: Why and how should we think of leadership and followership integrally? *Leadership*, 4 (4): 443–475.

Ladkin, D. (2010) *Rethinking Leadership: A New Look at Old Leadership Questions*. Cheltenham: Edward Elgar.

Lakomski, G. (2005) *Managing without Leadership*. Amsterdam: Elsevier.

Laurent, A. (1978) Managerial subordinancy. *Academy of Management Review*, 3: 220–230.

Liden, R. and Antonakis, J. (2009) Considering context in psychological leadership research. *Human Relations*, 62 (11): 1587–1606.

Lindebaum, D. and Cartwright, S. (2010) A critical examination of the relationship between emotional intelligence and transformational leadership. *Journal of Management Studies*, 47 (7): 1317–1341.

Locke, K. and Golden-Biddle, K. (1997) Constructing opportunities for contribution: Structuring intertextual coherence and "problematizing" in organizational studies. *Academy Management Journal*, 40 (5): 1023–1062.

Lundholm, S. (2011) *An Act of Balance: Hierarchy in Contemporary Work*. PhD thesis. Lund: Lund Business Press.

Markham, S., Yammarino, F., Murry, W. and Palanski, M. (2010) Leader–member exchange, shared values and performance: Agreement and levels of analysis do matter. *Leadership Quarterly*, 21: 469–480.

Meindl, J. (1995) The romance of leadership as a follower-centric theory: A social constructionist approach. *Leadership Quarterly*, 6: 329–341.

Mintzberg, H. (2004) Enough leadership. *Harvard Business Review*, November: 22.

Mumford, M., Friedrich, T. L., Caughron, J. L. and Antes, A. (2009) Leadership research: traditions, developments, and current directions. In Buchanan, D. and Bryman, A. (eds) *The Sage Handbook of Organizational Research Methods*. London: Sage.

Nicholls, J. (1987) Leadership in organisations: Meta, macro and micro. *European Management Journal*, 6: 16–25.

Nye, S. (2013) Transformational and transactional presidents. *Leadership*, 10: 118–124.

Palmer, I. and Hardy, C. (2000) *Thinking about Management*. London: Sage.

Parry, K. and Bryman, A. (2006) Leadership in organizations. In Clegg, S., Hardy, C. and Nord, W. (eds) *Handbook of Organization Studies* (2nd ed., 447–478). London: Sage.

Pearce, C. and Conger, J. (eds) (2003) *Shared Leadership: Reforming the Hows and Whys of Leadership*. Thousand Oaks, CA: Sage.

Pfeffer, J. (1977) The ambiguity of leadership. *Academy of Management Review*, 2 (1): 104–112.

Sandberg, J. and Targama, A. (2007) *Managing Understanding in Organizations*. London: Sage.

Sandelands, L. and Drazin, R. (1989). On the language of organization theory. *Organization Studies*, 10: 457–458.

Sashkin, M. (2004) Transformational leadership approaches: A review and synthesis. In Antonakis, J., Cianciolo, A. T. and Sternberg, R. J. (eds) *The Nature of Leadership*. Thousand Oaks: Sage.

Seltzer, J. and Bass, B. (1990) Transformational leadership: Beyond initiation and consideration. *Journal of Management*, 16: 693–703.

Silverman, D. (2006) *Interpreting Qualitative Data* (3rd ed.). London: Sage.

Smircich, L. and Morgan, G. (1982) Leadership: The management of meaning. *The Journal of Applied Behavioural Science*, 18 (3): 257–273.

Spoelstra, S. and ten Bos, R. (2011) Leadership. In *Business Ethics and Contemporary Philosophy*. Cambridge: Cambridge University Press.

Strauss, A. and Corbin, J. (1994) Grounded theory. In Denzin, N. and Lincoln, Y. (eds) *Handbook of Qualitative Research*. Thousand Oaks, CA: Sage.

Sveningsson, S. and Alvesson, M. (2016) *Managerial Lives*. Cambridge: Cambridge University Press.

Sveningsson, S. and Larsson, M. (2006) Fantasies of leadership: Identity work. *Leadership*, 2 (2): 203–224.

Therborn, G. (1980) *The Power of Ideology and the Ideology of Power*. London: Verso.

Tourish, D. and Pinnington, A. (2002) Transformational leadership, corporate cultism and the spirituality paradigm: An unholy trinity in the workplace? *Human Relations*, 55: 147–152.

Trice, H. M. and Beyer, J. M. (1993) *The Culture of Work Organizations*. Englewood Cliffs, NJ: Prentice-Hall.

Uhl-Bien, M. (2006) Relational leadership theory: Exploring the social processes of leadership and organizing. *The Leadership Quarterly*, 17 (6): 654–676.

van Knippenberg, D. L. and Sitkin, S. B. (2013) A critical assessment of charismatic–transformational leadership research: Back to the drawing board? *The Academy of Management Annals*, 7: 1–60.

Yukl, G. (1989) Managerial leadership: A review of theory and research. *Journal of Management*, 15: 251–289.

Yukl, G. (1999) An evaluation of conceptual weaknesses in transformational and charismatic leadership theories. *Leadership Quarterly*, 10: 285–305.

Zaleznik, A. (1977) Managers and leaders: Are they different? *Harvard Business Review* (May–June): 67–68.

Zhou, X. and Schriesheim, C. (2010) Quantitative and qualitative examination of propositions concerning supervisor–subordinate convergence in descriptions of leader–member exchange quality. *Leadership Quarterly*, 21: 826–843.

6

Instead of Angels

Leaders, Leadership and *Longue Durée*[1]

Peter Gronn

Introduction

This chapter builds on some ideas articulated initially in Gronn (2010, especially pp. 405–415) in which I was critical of the numerous solo or stand-alone leader approaches that have traditionally asserted such a powerful hegemonic grip on scholarly thinking about leadership. With the number of like-minded critical voices increasing, there are unmistakable indications that, finally, the field may be starting to undergo a makeover. In addition to broad critiques of leadership, for example, there are questions being asked about the leadership industry that helps to legitimize the field while at the same time feeding off it (e.g. Kellerman, 2012). There are initiatives to re-contour the field that employ alternative conceptions of leadership (e.g., Denis *et al.*, 2012). And there are systematic re-appraisals of the assumptions that undergird scholarly (and popular) thinking in key leadership domains (e.g. Brown, 2014). The broad trajectory of this incipient revisionism has been away from what is sometimes referred to by the perhaps disparaging short-hand term "hero paradigm" in the direction of plurality and collectivism. This rethinking of the directions travelled by the field is a sure sign of its vibrancy, although the present author (Gronn, 2015, p. 2; 2011, p. 442) has intruded a note of caution. The possible displacement of an individual (N = 1) by leader pluralities (N = 2+) as the focal unit of analysis risks embedding a dualism (in a field in which binary modes of thinking such as leader–followers already predominate, on which see below) in the guise of pendulum swing-type thinking, as scholarly prominence is accorded successive waves of either individuality or collectivism. One possible way of avoiding such an outcome is to acknowledge that individual and collective instances of leadership co-exist as part of a hybrid mix. For this reason I have proposed previously the idea of a leadership configuration as the preferred unit of analysis (Gronn, 2011).

The particular contribution of this chapter is to indicate that this idea of hybridity is not merely a contemporary phenomenon, but may even have been a persistent feature of leadership that has existed from the earliest societies onwards, so much so that the evidence reviewed below suggests that hybrid leadership patterning is likely to have been a universal historical norm. To make the argument, I begin by providing a brief rationale for a longitudinal or *longue durée* perspective, following which I consider some key leadership terms. The bulk of the chapter is then devoted to a review of (mostly) anthropological and archaeological fieldwork evidence of the development of a range of types of societies and their accompanying leadership formations. Taking as its focus the centrality of human cooperative activity, particularly large-scale cooperation, and the need for it if groups and societies are to survive, scholarly debate about archaic societies in particular has focused on the relationship between egalitarianism and hierarchy. There is one school of thought which suggests, broadly, that the egalitarianism which typified hunter–gatherer band societies and, for the most part, suppressed would-be leaders eventually gave way to inequality and institutionalized modes of stratification when, from an evolutionary point of view, societies began differentiating themselves in the direction of more complex (and successive) polities such as chiefdoms, city states, kingdoms and states. This cultural evolutionism has been contested by a recent body of research findings in which scholars detect varying trajectories towards social complexity, and in which pressures towards egalitarianism and stratification contend or co-exist in emerging polities and societies. Here, scholars have pinpointed two contrasting power strategies (personalized power and corporate power) and evidence of varying degrees of their institutionalization. It is the leadership configurations in which these strategies found expression, I suggest, that provide evidence of historical continuity with respect to my claim about hybridized leadership. I conclude the chapter by considering the significance of that continuity and its implications for the future development of the leadership field.

Longue Durée

The idea of *longue durée* is closely associated with the historian Fernand Braudel (1980, p. 35) who, in an essay first published in 1958, was critical of thinking in "all the social sciences" for being captive of short-term time spans and for having a "constant tendency to evade historical explanation". Evasion, typically, was claimed to occur in two ways: by an over-concentration on current events and real life, or by "transcending time altogether" and conjuring up mathematical formulations of "more or less timeless communications structures". In *The History Manifesto*, Guldi and Armitage (2014) document the eclipse (in the 1970s) of *longue durée* historical scholarship and the rise of a micro-historical alternative that they label as "short past". Essentially, this substitution entailed the replacement of long-term by more immediate time frame thinking, such that by the end of the 1970s the "tendency to go long began to look tarnished" and "something grubby that no self-respecting historian would do" (p. 82). Four decades later, however, they claim that "big is back" (p. 86). Guldi and Armitage's (2014, pp. 61–88) concerns, in counteracting this alleged neglect of time, include time horizons, and the relevance of past events, emergence of institutions and causality for long-term thinking and decision making about current and likely future human problem solving.

Indications of the increasing appeal of longitudinal perspectives are evident in the recent attention accorded by scholars to "bigness" in its various guises, such as big data and data mining in the social sciences, and big history among historians (e.g. Christian, 2005). Bigness, in Guldi and Armitage's sense, however, is not true of leadership where, as a social science, a sense of ahistorical timelessness has long prevailed and has done so (arguably) with theoretically impoverishing consequences. On the other hand, a *longue durée* (or genealogical) approach has a potentially important contribution to make to leadership. This is because one of the features that has set the leadership field apart from other social scientific knowledge domains has been the large weight (or burden) of normative expectations that models and typologies of leadership and leaders themselves have attracted, particularly in the case of the latter with regard to what individual leaders may be deemed able to accomplish. The quintessential manifestation of the exaggerated sense of individual agency typically attributed to leaders has been the field's enduring sub-school of thought, known as the "great man" view of history. This is an essentially romantic set of assumptions derived from a variety of scholarly antecedents (including Carlyle, 1983 [1840]) which, although it has been subjected to substantial critique, continues to prove extraordinarily resilient and has found its most recent expression during leadership's 1980s–1990s resurgence in the popularity (and ubiquity) of charismatic and transformational leadership models. Viewed in this light, one potential outcome of the synthesis of evidence that follows, therefore, might be to inject a long overdue note of realism into lay, professional and scholarly understandings of leadership by documenting the historical vibrancy of leader hybridity, while at the same time managing down grossly inflated expectations of solo leaders. For the purposes of the discussion that follows, a big tent definition of "leadership" is adopted, for it is used to encompass not only leaders as they are understood in the conventional organizational sense but also all historically manifest forms of rulership, monarchy, incumbency of high-level offices and authority positions, and elite membership, both societal and sectoral.

Leadership and Leaders

How have leadership scholars understood their mission? Although sporadic disputation continues about definitions of leadership, overwhelmingly, theorists and researchers have been united in viewing this concept as equivalent to, or a version of, influence (although one notable exception was a doyen of the field, the late James McGregor Burns). Moreover, most of them have justified their existence by describing, analysing, measuring and accounting for such influence, with some colleagues (in sub-fields such as organizational leadership) extending this view of their role to include promulgating and recommending preferred leadership typologies and models as normative prescriptions for desired versions of practice. Regardless of the particular standpoints adopted, however, scholars in virtually all the leadership sub-domains continue to pursue their purposes and projects from within a taken-for-granted terminological binary of leader and followers in a field in which, until recently, a largely solo-focused analytical template has maintained a vice-like grip. There is also probably close to consensual agreement about who gets to be a leader, in the sense that (with contemporary organizations and systems in mind) "leader" is acknowledged as a socio-psychologically attributed status in which persons are perceived as embodying a cognitively defined (and emotionally defined?) prototype of what it means to lead. Moreover, in level terms, allowance is increasingly being made by scholars for the potential manifestation of leaders, leadership and leading in any component part of an organizational whole, not merely at the top.

At the same time, as mentioned at the outset of the chapter, there is a groundswell of interest in forms of leadership other than those seen as monopolized by or focused on (usually) formally positioned individuals. This observation is neither an unsubstantiated assertion nor a mere accident of timing. Among the numerous terms used to try to capture this emerging plurality, Bolden's (2011, pp. 254–255) systematic search in 2011 for the uptake of one such descriptor, distributed leadership (or DL), yielded 187,000 Google hits and identified more than 9,000 publications that referred to DL. Bolden's graph showed an increase in DL's popularity since 2000, including a spike or bounce in publication outputs during 2007–09, and it records a trend which followed (what can only be described as) a two-decades long tsunami of writings about the alleged virtues of charismatic, transformational, authentic and related leader types, especially in the fields of business management, educational leadership and organizational studies. When examined more closely, however, this post-2000 (approx.) emergence of DL is in fact the *re-emergence* of an idea that achieved prominence in social psychology circles in the mid 1950s and was even evident (until its marginalization) in some post-World War II writings on leadership and small groups (see Gronn, 2008, pp. 145–148). Now that DL has re-emerged and can be said to have come into its own, the documenting of forms of plural leadership has travelled so far, particularly since the new millennium, that the most recent comprehensive synthesis (Denis *et al.*, 2012) has sign-posted four streams of ongoing research activity: small group- and team-based shared leadership for outcome effectiveness; the pooling of top-level organizational leadership in dyadic, triadic and similar small constellation groupings; the dispersion and diffusion of leadership (including DL) across organizational levels and boundaries; and, interaction-based activities and processes that manifest leadership. All four streams encompass varying degrees of structurally designed and emergent actions.

Notwithstanding these developments, knowledge advancement in the field continues to be constrained by the orthodox leader–followers binary already referred to – and for that matter by the superordinate–subordinate dualism onto which it is often mapped or for which it provides an alternative form of words. (A notable exception to this binary thinking is anthropology, where most scholars tend to refer to leaders only and make little or no mention of followers.) The major shortcoming of such simplistic binary thinking, however, is that its wording *presumes* a division of labour (i.e. an organization member is labelled as either in this or that category) rather than *demonstrating* empirically an actual division of leadership labour. As a consequence, the leader–followers dualist distinction is impervious to the following considerations: substitution (to what extent can activity outcomes be accounted for by explanations that do not invoke leadership – e.g. such as learned routines?), duration (to what span of time is the presumed leader–followers division of labour meant to apply?), membership and boundary-crossing (is a follower always a follower, or is there the possibility that a follower might become a leader and a leader a follower?), multiple attributions (what happens if more than one person is simultaneously attributed with leader status?) and contradictory attributions (what happens if there is no agreement among organizational members about who is perceived as a leader and who as followers?). In comparison with these difficulties, the notion of hybridity has much to offer. Thus, if a continuum of possibilities is substituted for exclusively classified differences in kind, then rather than viewing leadership conceived of in the singular or the plural as categorical opposites (i.e. as N = 1 or as N = 2+), tendencies toward one or the other polarity are opened up, for the purposes of explanation, along with combinations of degrees of leadership individuality and plurality. It is the resulting sets of elements that constitute leadership configurations. Empirical substantiation of these hybrid possibilities has been provided by researchers in such fields as school education, further education and higher education (see the examples in Gronn, 2011, pp. 442–444), and most recently by Chreim (2015) in her investigation of the configuring of leadership spaces during business unit mergers and acquisitions.

Egalitarianism

The need to accomplish the kinds of cooperative activities mentioned earlier, and therefore to coordinate the harnessing and deployment of energy and information through some form of leadership or decision-making arrangement, is not restricted to human beings. In the case of some living creatures, such as in much of the insect world and among some animal species, however, leadership and leader–followers terminology make little sense where versions of swarm intelligence (e.g. insect hiving, fish schooling or bird flocking as in murmuration) act as the principal mechanisms for behaviour coordination (e.g. for nesting and migration purposes). Among the higher primates, such as gorillas and chimpanzees – with whom humans share 98 per cent of their DNA (Flannery & Marcus, 2012, p. 58) – and to a lesser extent bonobos, by contrast, there are (especially among chimpanzees) distinct male pecking orders of status with dominant alpha males at the top. (There may also be female social dominance hierarchies, although no alphas.) The flipside of the privileges of downward dominance (e.g. access to food, mating opportunities) is upwards submission (Boehm, 2001, pp. 23–25). Yet such dominance is usually tempered because, while a male alpha primate may be tyrannical and terrorize, he is not a coercive group leader and is therefore "far from being a dictator who firmly controls the destinies of others" (Boehm, 2001, p. 27).

In Boehm's (2012, p. 154) hypothesis about shared primate ancestry – in which humans, chimpanzees (*pan troglodytes*) and bonobos (*pan paniscus*) evolved from a common ancestor – life during the epoch of a common ancestral *pan* species (approx. six million years ago) was ordered, and experienced, hierarchically. At some point in time (Boehm estimates it to be probably after 250,000 BP and certainly by 45,000 BP), however, humans "had become decisively egalitarian".[2] The hypothesized trigger for this transition was dependence on sources and types of food (and, therefore, survival), in particular the increased reliance of small human groups on big-game hunting, in which case "the only viable course for efficient meat distribution would have been to suppress alpha behaviour definitively" (Boehm, 2012, p. 155). These human groups were acephalous hunter–gatherer foraging bands. Following his analysis of anthropological data on 50 contemporary band societies (of a total of 150 for which there exists a robust ethnographic evidence base), Boehm (2012, pp. 79–80) suggests that the following characteristics which distinguish current inter-familial bands applied equally to late Pleistocene period foragers (i.e. 125,000 BP to 11,700 BP). Such societies are:

> definitely all mobile, and as nomads, instead of trying to share their large-game meat as individual families, they share it widely. It doesn't matter whether these people live on Arctic tundras or in tropical forests – they never dwell in permanent, year-round villages, and they always combine hunting and gathering to make a living according to what is environmentally available, with an emphasis on eating the relatively fatty meat of large animals.

The point to note here from the perspective of leadership is that, in foraging bands, egalitarian norms trump hierarchy, which means that although hierarchical impulses are not eradicated by small group egalitarianism, potential upstart (male) alphas are collectively disciplined (along with, it has to be said, shirking and free-riding band members) by the utilization of a draconian system of control known as reverse dominance hierarchy. Sanctioning techniques here include direct criticism, gossip, ridicule, ostracism, public shaming, intimidation, expulsion or even, in extreme instances, killing (Boehm, 2001, pp. 43–63, 73–84) – all of which provide cover for status-conscious and competitive susceptibilities on the part of the restraining non-alphas (Seabright, 2013, p. 109). In some bands, there may be a formal or informal leader, although only "as long as the band welcomes him in doing so", otherwise functional leaders with particular expertise come and go as required (Boehm, 2001, p. 69). An example is the Hadza of Tanzania, an egalitarian society in which non-coercive leadership amounted to "no more than the advice of a few respected senior men" (Flannery & Marcus, 2012, p. 37). And yet, despite the prolonged (and likely near to universal) success of such a reverse dominance strategy in containing alpha impulses for more than 100,000 years, such was the strengthening grip of pressures towards stratification that by about 2,500 BCE "virtually every form of inequality known to mankind had been created somewhere in the world, and truly egalitarian societies were gradually being relegated to places no-one else wanted" (Flannery & Marcus, 2012, p. x).

Stratification

Although stratification is evident in a number of ways (e.g. socially, economically and politically), the attribute that its various manifestations have in common is ranked, layered or hierarchical ordering. The dominance hierarchies that were (and remain) exclusive to non-human primate society (Dubreuil, 2013, p. 53), and were resisted by foragers, were mechanisms for the allocation and consumption of (scarce) resources. But dominance hierarchies differ from productive hierarchies, in which there is specialization and a division of labour for the production of goods (Rubin, 2000). Hierarchy (of both varieties) also entails vertically ordered control, the quintessence of which in respect of activities coordinated for instrumental or productive purposes is the idea of unity (or chain) of command, in which "only one position has no superior – the chief executive – and all other positions have exactly one immediate superior" (Mayhew, 1983, pp. 154, 155). A hallmark communication feature of chains of command, regardless of the number of levels that they subsume, is that while information flows up and down the spine and across levels, "no one sends orders up the hierarchy or horizontally within levels" (Mayhew, 1983, p. 158). Degrees of authority are arranged in ranked orders of offices with office incumbents operating under a regime of authority delegation while simultaneously incurring corresponding accountabilities. When the levels and the span of control (i.e. the number of subordinates immediately supervised) increase, the extent of indirect supervision expands proportionately.

The particular version of stratification that was especially apposite to the historically renewed expression of inequality is status hierarchy. While the hominin forerunners of *homo sapiens* – *homo erectus*, *homo heidelbergensis* and *homo neanderthalensis* – may have eradicated dominance hierarchies, it was *homo sapiens* that "paved the way" for hierarchy's re-emergence, although in a different form (Dubreuil, 2013, p. 90). In this regard, numerous accounts of transitions in social formation and leadership have relied on cultural evolutionary explanations of movements between stages, with agriculture emphasized as the key factor in facilitating the establishment of sedentary societies and such pre-state formations as chiefdoms. Some scholars, such as Fukuyama (2011, p. 72), in his account of the emergence of state polities, for example, continue to do so. Where Dubreuil's explanation of hierarchy differs from these evolutionary explanations is in his search for enabling mechanisms. If his thesis in this regard is correct, then it was the cognitive evolution of the human species, in particular changes in its brain morphology, that brought hierarchy back. In his review of a technically complex (and still accumulating) inter-disciplinary body of evidence – genetic and neuro-scientific, combined with archaeological artefact data – that remains provisional and subject to confirmation or disconfirmation, Dubreuil highlights the advanced capacity of *homo sapiens*, ahead of their fellow hominin species, to engage in symbolic behaviour as the key pre-condition for the establishment of a hierarchical social order. Only during the latter part of the middle stone age period (between 130,000 BP and 55,000 BP) – although there is locational variation globally in the timing and dating of evidence (e.g. bone tools, ornaments, abstract engravings, data on network exchange) from which inferences about cognition are drawn – can it be said that advances occurred in human perspective-taking ability. The thesis, in short, is that only "the ability to hold in mind a stable representation of conflicting perspectives on objects" accounts satisfactorily for behaviour modernization and wide-ranging cultural transformation (Dubreuil, 2013, p. 131). The effect of such cognitive changes was to make possible the defining of status categories and the collective ascription of such statuses to individuals (e.g. "chief" or "priest") along with their possible visual representation in, say, cave drawings or other media (Dubreuil, 2013, pp. 136–137).

In light of Dubreuil's cognitive hypothesis, the suggestions of Flannery and Marcus (2012, pp. 59–60) about celestial alphas and betas may assume added plausibility. Hunter–gatherer bands, they argue – although they refrain from pinning their speculations to a precise time period – may well have conceptualized as part of a religious cosmology a dominance hierarchy of invisible supernatural beings (alphas) and invisible ancestors (betas), because there is later evidence (from the Egyptian and Inca civilizations) of would-be hereditary leaders attempting to link themselves with celestial beings and, of course, even later examples of some kings claiming themselves to be deities. Such sacred cosmologies helped to foster inequalities and legitimated lineal leadership descent. Evidence of the extent of the variation in the trajectories taken by different band societies (as well as the timing of their transitions) – not to mention the difficulty of trying to pinpoint cross-cultural regularities – comes from Pacific Northwest cultures. Among the Nootka foragers (on the west coast of Vancouver Island), for example, some individuals became shamans and spiritual healers, and these practices, along with the rights and privileges of chiefly families were claimed to have been acquired by remote ancestors during supernatural experiences. While these kinds of "appropriate changes in social logic" are invoked to explain the creation of inequality out of the previous egalitarianism (Flannery & Marcus, 2012, p. 74), such a claim has little or nothing to say about the mechanism or mechanisms. Other signs of the re-assertion of inequality include tribute giving and feasting (made possible by accumulated food surpluses), which enabled chiefs to establish their generosity and to keep their fellow foragers loyal, although even in these cases with such displays of largesse chiefs did not have matters all their own way because "followers might abandon stingy chiefs and take up residence with their more generous rivals" (Flannery & Marcus, 2012, p. 75). The chiefs referred to here and the behavioural flexibility displayed in respect of shifting chiefly allegiances suggest that, rather than fully developed chiefdoms, *per se*, this evidence of reciprocal behaviour may be more typical of tribes, where tribal leaders possess resource-access privileges but no coercive power (Dubreuil, 2013, p. 43). In fact it is a revised view of the characteristics of chiefdoms proper that has stimulated an alternative hypothesis about pre-state society trajectories and transitions. Before reviewing this, however, it is worth considering an alternative, characterized as the circumscription hypothesis, or the "most ambitious answer" (Dubreuil, 2013, p. 196) to the question of how states originated.

Circumscription

The leading proponent of circumscription Carneiro (1970, p. 734) originally claimed that "only a coercive theory can account for the rise of the state". Force, expressed in warfare, was (for him) the mechanism by which political evolution led "step by step, from autonomous villages to the state". Although warfare and conquest may have been necessary factors, if there is to be a sufficient explanation then a series of enabling conditions had to be in place. Carneiro specified three: circumscribed or delimited areas for agricultural land (illustrated by a comparison of villages in the Amazon basin and Peruvian coastal valleys); resource concentration (once again the Amazon); and social circumscription arising from population density (here his example was the Yanomamö Indians of Venezuela). Compared to the Amazon basin, where there were large amounts of land and low population density, the growth in the number and size of Peruvian villages made the need for land acquisition a motivation for war (a motivation strengthened by an awareness of richly available resources). The resulting pattern of recurrent warfare resulted in an improved level of organization and the integration of villages into more extensive territorial units, and yielded large chiefdoms. The expansion of chiefdoms through conquest further elaborated units politically into kingdoms, consequent on the need to administer added territory and conquered peoples. This responsibility fell primarily to "individuals who had distinguished themselves in war" (Carneiro, 1970, p. 736). With villages subjugated, then, a ruler and his kinsman were able to form an upper ruling class which extracted tribute and taxes. The final stage in this evolutionary pattern was the succession of kingdoms by empires, with the latter being "merely the logical culmination of the process". In short, then, circumscription theory explains (Carneiro, 1970, p. 738): "why states arose where they did, and why they failed to arrive elsewhere. It shows the state to have been a predictable response to certain specific cultural, demographic, and economic conditions."

Three decades after articulating this argument, Carneiro (2000, p. 12,927) had rhetorically glossed it with the generic claim that: "during courses of changes in nature, a quantitative increase in substance once it reaches a critical threshold, results in a qualitative transformation of state." The sole application of this quantity-to-quality idea to which he could point in anthropology – with publication of Dubreuil's (2013) extensive synthesis of research in this area still a decade or more away – was a few sporadic attempts to explain how during hominid evolution "the human brain became able to engage in the symbolling behaviour underlying the production of speech, and with that, to be able to generate culture". Curiously, having mentioned the brain and its importance, Carneiro promptly ignored it altogether and instead fell back on numbers: population. Before drawing general conclusions about population pressure and its significance for state formation, however, he illustrated his point with a couple of examples of temporary leadership structures, including one from earlier research of his own. His study of North American plains tribes comprising about 50 members each indicated that in each case there had been a band head, except that "he had little power and few duties" (2000, p. 12,928). When, however, a couple of dozen bands came together for a summer buffalo hunt, this idyllic scene changed. A tribal council was formed and it elected one of its number as tribal chief, and "in that capacity he enjoyed greatly expanded powers":

> He organized and directed all tribal activities, being assisted by men's societies, which sprang into being as soon as the whole tribe assembled. One of these societies acted as a police force and was charged with keeping order during the buffalo hunt and the Sun Dance ceremony that followed.

With the hunt over, all of these units and functions lapsed during the ensuing fall season, but the qualitative structural response to the pressure of numbers evident in the illustration could be replicated, Carneiro claimed, in societies gearing up for war, such as the city state of Sparta. Indeed, it was (for him) warfare that led to the transcending of village autonomy and the formation of multi-village aggregates known as chiefdoms, with the scale of some chiefdoms warranting their designation as states (Carneiro, 2000, p. 12,930). If, on the other hand, some validity is accorded Dubreuil's view that the key mechanism in accounting for structural emergence was cognition, rather than warfare, then there may be a very different way of understanding the importance of Carneiro's examples (see the section Sanctions below). This argument originated in a quite different view of chiefdoms and their leadership.

Power

In an influential discussion of social organization in early pre-state societies, the archaeologist Renfrew (1974) distinguished two contrasting forms of chiefdom in third millennium BCE Europe (especially southern Britain, early Malta and the Aegean) and Polynesia – with chiefdom being in his view an intermediary social unit between egalitarian tribes and civilizationstates. Disclaiming any implication in his categorization of a commitment to transitional society typographical status and to evolutionary determinism, Renfrew (1974, p. 74) distinguished group-oriented chiefdoms from individualizing chiefdoms, with the former defined as societies in which:

personal wealth in terms of valuable possessions is not impressively documented, but where the solidarity of the social unit was expressed most effectively in communal or group activities

and the latter as those in which:

a marked disparity in personal possessions and in other material indications of prestige appears to document a salient personal ranking, yet often without evidence of large communal meetings or activities.

Over the last decade or so, Renfrew's distinction has provided the impetus for dual-processing (DP) theorists.

Their problem was Mesoamerica. A comparison of leadership in both the central Mexican Mayan and Teotihuacan polities in what is known as the Classic period (300 CE–750 CE) was not thought to be well served by existing classification schemes. For Blanton *et al.* (1996, pp. 1–2), for example, evolutionary theories that highlighted increased political centralization in the guise of chiefdoms and states as a response to socio-environmental stresses had no way of accommodating competitive political strategies devised by actors in ancient civilizations to construct polities and institutions. Feinman (2001, p. 153) likewise resisted what he termed a centralization bias: the idea that hierarchy formation in polities "always entails the stark concentration of power and wealth in the hands of a small number of individuals or specific families". Stimulated, as he said he was, by Renfrew's chiefdom distinction (and also, subsequently, by a clutch of other theorists), Blanton (1998, pp. 150–151) substituted "network" (or exclusionary) and "corporate", respectively, for Renfrew's individualizing and group-oriented categories, to articulate two strategies, because for more than 3,000 years parts of Mesoamerica had "displayed a complex pattern of cycling between more corporate and more overt ruler-centred social formations, rather than a simple evolutionary stage sequence". A network strategy is a ruler-centred approach in which prestige goods and patrimonial rhetoric (e.g. affirmation of kinship, lineage and ranked descent ties) are used to shore up elite privilege and control of exchange systems, networks and wealth. A corporate strategy, by contrast, "always involves the establishment and maintenance of a cognitive code that emphasizes the corporate solidarity of society as an integrated whole, based on a natural, fixed, and immutable interdependence between subgroups and, in more complex societies, between rulers and subjects" (Blanton *et al.*, 1996, p. 6). In Classic Mayan society there were "elite individuals who used their personal networks of ancestors, of affines, exchange partners and personal allies as a basis of their power". With Teotihuacan society, on the other hand, "one is hard pressed to identify a single ruler at Classic period Teotihuacan in burial, text, or graphic depiction". Moreover, Teotihuacan art is noteworthy for "the absence of scenes in which certain humans appear subordinated to other persons" (Feinman, 2001, pp. 164–165). Instead, Teotihuacan was a hierarchical state which manifested collective leadership (in the guise of co-rulership) and power sharing (Feinman, 2001, p. 167).

Proponents of a DP approach are keen to emphasize that, as polarities on a continuum of possibilities, the network–corporate distinction allows for cycles of varying emphasis in different polities. Indeed, pre-Classic Teotihuacan society appears to have had more individualistic rulers, and therefore was more network-like, while socio-political formations in both pre- and post-Classic Maya were much more corporate than in the Classic period. Moreover, "many 'hybrid' cases with features of both strategies can be enumerated", particularly in late pre-Hispanic Aztec society (Feinman, 2001, p. 173). While these network and corporate strategies indicate broadly contrasting ways in which hierarchy became institutionalized, in the interests of accuracy they need to be complemented by evidence of the different pathways taken out of equality by forager societies. In respect of centralization and the network side of the DP duality, the detailed synthesis of evidence by Flannery and Marcus (2012, pp. 86–87) reveals that, for individual leaders, achieved prestige and inherited nobility were not one and the same, and provided different bases of legitimacy. Whereas "prestige accrues to the generous host", nobility, by contrast, "belongs to the child who inherits his father's titles, crests, and sumptuary heirlooms".

Achievement and Inheritance

The evidence surveyed thus far in this chapter indicates that the picture concerning leadership and leaders in pre-state societies is exceedingly varied, with much of this complexity arising out of the interplay between egalitarianism and stratification imperatives. What is more, when Flannery and Marcus (2012, p. 91) can claim that agriculture does not always lead to inequality (contrary to evolutionary explanations of transitions between stages), that "many societies remained egalitarian after thousands of years of farming", and that still other societies "allowed modest amounts of achieved renown but still resisted hereditary rank", the picture risks becoming even less straightforward. Pre-colonial New Guinea is a case in point. At the pinnacle of prestige in densely populated highland Chimbu society, were *yombo pondo* or Big Men who, while they made speeches, initiated or vetoed group activities, participated in regional exchanges and directed the construction of ritual men's houses, possessed nothing more than "strong influence". Occupying no offices that bestowed them with genuine authority, their renown was entirely accomplishment based and they were constantly being challenged by ambitious younger males. Likewise for the Big Men of Mt. Hagen, there was "no authority to give commands and no way to enforce them"; nor could their sons inherit their fathers' prestige, as they "had to earn it on their own" (Flannery & Marcus, 2012, pp. 96, 102).

Flannery and Marcus's review also acknowledges the presence of corporate strategies. Thus, while the Tewa and Hopi peoples, from the American South-West, and the Mandan and Hidatsa, who were plains people, found ways of enabling talented individuals to achieve prestige while also preventing the development of hereditary elites, all four "struck a balance between personal ambition and community spirit" (Flannery and Marcus, 2012, p. 183). Likewise with the Kachin societies of highland Burma, some of which manifested hereditary rank, while others did not, and which also – based on early-twentieth-century fieldwork evidence – cycled back and forth between hereditary privilege, in the guise of *gumsa* chiefs, and equality with *gumlao* chiefs. (For DP scholars such as Blanton *et al.* (1996, p. 60), *gumsa* illustrates a network strategy and *gumlao* is instanced as part of a corporate strategy.) There was a similar cycling in the slave-owning Konyak Naga of Assam, although not in Polynesia (where in Tonga, for example, chiefs shared power with councillors). One important change that was also a hallmark of emerging rank societies was replacement of men's houses (built originally by Big Men for ritual and ceremonial purposes, as well as to enshrine gender segregation for the purposes of sleeping arrangements, particularly to keep young men away from young women, and for men to commune with their ancestors) by temples for worship. Moreover, if a chief in a hereditary ranked society was believed to possess a combination of *mana* (a supernatural life force), *tohunga* (expertise) and *toa* (warrior bravery and toughness), then he was almost as powerful as a king. To complicate matters further, in south-west Pacific Tikopia, where the claim to leadership was based on religious authority and genealogy, there were four chiefs heading up ranked clan lineages, but no unified central authority and no one clan chief was able to impose his will on his fellow chiefs. Yet another strand of pre-state leadership complexity is the opening up of alternative routes to institutionalized leadership. In the Manambu community of New Guinea and among the Ubaid of southern Mesopotamia, for example, there were not only competing secular and religious leadership pathways but also rivalry between both sets of leaders. Finally, there is an alternative form of rank society in which hereditary privilege and wealth co-exist, although there are no chiefs. Here, for example, while the aristocrats of the Apa Tani people of Assam (who were also slave owners) provided community leaders, their elite leadership was collective and exercised by a council, rather than being the preserve of an individual (Flannery & Marcus, 2001, pp. 210, 213, 215, 192, 321, 188, 289 and 258). In fact the Apa Tani councillors, Flannery and Marcus (2012, p. 296) note, were (in Renfrew's terms) "group-oriented members of an oligarchy".

City States and Oligarchies

Oligarchs are individuals empowered by material wealth (in the form of property and income) who are intensely focused on its defence (Winters, 2011, pp. 6–7). As a general rule, by virtue of their command of such resources, oligarchies are able to assert minority power and influence, although they need not be in positions of formal rule. Historically important oligarchies, however, ruled the city states of ancient Rome and Athens, and the Italian cities of Venice and Siena. Most city states, or *poleis*, tended to be small in size and population, and ranged from 2,000 to 10,000 male citizens (Ferguson, 1991, p. 178).

The period of the Roman republic spanned 508 BCE to 27 BCE, followed by the empire: the Principate of 27 BCE to 235 CE and then the Dominate from 235 CE to 476 BCE when the western part of the empire fell and fragmented in feudal Europe. Oligarch wealth derived from vast estates (*latifundia*). The major threat sources to second-century BCE ruling oligarchs were internal, laterally from one another, and below from slaves. The city's total population was just shy of 1,000,000. Of the four landed social strata, the two highest categories of land-owning citizens (senators) comprised a minuscule fraction of the population, although the vast concentration of wealth in their hands was grossly disproportionate. Then followed the *equites* (or knights) and municipal citizens, and then three landless categories: officers and praetorians, soldiers and workers, and slaves and farm labourers. The 600 senators owned between them 250,000 household slaves in Rome (Winters, 2011, pp. 75, 90–101). In what was a system of collective, patriarchal rule, in which the coercive control of slaves was ruthless, an "elaborate architecture of arrangements, rules, regulations and sanctions" was instituted to prevent lateral and external threats (Winters, 2011, p. 101). Offices such as tribune, consul and dictator were variously created and, except in the latter instance (a temporary appointee with unlimited powers for a limited duration and solely to confront emergencies), the authority of office-holders was curtailed. The Roman oligarchy, itself a disarmed elite, instituted a range of protective measures to keep the military in check: as property-holders, generals had shared interests with the oligarchs and severe restrictions were imposed on their movements (and those of the legions that they commanded) both in and out of Rome, and in regard to the carrying of weapons. It was the gradual and eventual violation of "the unwritten commandments of collective oligarchic rule" that finally brought an end to the republic, and ushered into power "first general-dictators and then general-emperors", thereby transforming rather than ending oligarch rule (Winters, 2011, p. 106).

There was a not dissimilar leadership pattern in Athens. In Greek city states generally there was evidence of an extraordinary pattern of leadership diversity: "overlapping, layered, and linked authority patterns – the co-existence and interaction of a great variety of entities which individually might be located at different points along the political evolution continuum" (Ferguson, 1991, p. 192). Archaic Greece existed from 800 to 500 BCE, followed by the Classical period in the fourth and fifth centuries BCE. An authoritarian period then ensued (322–146 BCE) until Greece's absorption by Rome. The population of Athens during the Classical period was about 300,000 of whom the voting adult males numbered about 38,000. The basis of landed wealth in Athens was farming, although the properties were nowhere near the scale of Roman *latifundia*. Twelve hundred trierach oligarchs comprised the wealthiest citizens, immediately beneath whom in the status ranks were (upper and lower) property-owning citizen hoplites (infantry in the Athenian phalanx), then 24,000 thetes (farmers) and finally 120,000 slaves, with the pattern of wealth concentration relatively flat by comparison with Rome. There was no standing army in Athens, nor a regular police force and little bureaucracy. The potential for external threats from other city states was genuine as was the threat of internal oligarch putsches (Winters, 2011, pp. 77–90).

The key points of city state contrast, however, were less between Rome and Athens, but between these two city states and the city of Siena. First, whereas the Roman and Athenian oligarchs policed themselves by and large, for seven decades under collective rule of The Nine (or *Noveschi*), a *podesta* or external person (of landed martial background) was contracted to exercise coercive power in Siena, sufficient to overwhelm an oligarch in the event of intra-oligarchic attacks (Winters, 2011, pp. 124–127). Second, while The Nine comprised a governing council that appointed city officials and made policy, this body was not only an instance of collective leadership, but also (in effect) of collective leadership rotation. Members served for two months only and were unable to serve again for another 20 months, with a consequence of this practice being that over a period of 70 years there was "dizzying leadership turnover" as about 1,000 individuals held office (Winters, 2011, p. 129).

Sanctions

Although these city-state examples illustrate only one of Winters' four types of oligarchies – ruling, as distinct from his warring, civil and sultanistic categories – they provide an interesting sidelight on a problem associated with the emergence of hierarchy, as posed by Dubreuil, i.e. the burden of keeping track of leaders and how to manage their punishment. The consequences arising from the adoption of both the DP strategies summarized earlier illustrates this point (Dubreuil, 2013, p. 185). The effect of locating authority in assemblies, councils or a plurality of competing power centres, as part of a corporate strategy, is to establish a series of diffused checks on the potential actions of a headman, a chief or a leader. With personal networks centralized on a leader, on the other hand, the guarantee of restraints on arbitrariness and that leader's pursuit of aggrandizing self-interest are significantly weakened. Curiously, perhaps with the exception of the Siena example (in its reliance on a *podesta*), the collective surveillance of the oligarchs in the Athenian and Rome cases echoes the joint policing by foragers of potential norm violators among their own band members.

Leaders and rulers are not angels, as James Madison was quoted as saying in the note to the chapter's title, in which case there has to be some form of monitoring. But monitoring between leaders and led operates in both vertical directions, and it becomes costly and difficult when group sizes increase. Here is where Carneiro's earlier example of the temporary leadership structure to manage the foragers' summer buffalo hunt takes on its significance. The handing over of expanded powers to a tribal chief, to be assisted by men's societies – in parallel with the Siena Nine's contracting out to a *podesta* – signals downward checking of norm maintenance and potential violation, the point being that the sheer weight of numbers of hunt participants (a dozen bands of about 50 members each) imposes a severe cognitive constraint on being able to punish potential infringers directly and creates an incentive for the establishment of a delegation of sanction system. After all, the success of such an annual voluntary cooperative venture is otherwise potentially imperilled. In microcosm with this example, then, is to be found Dubreuil's (2013, p. 169) explanation for the emergence of hierarchy in states:

> growing group size depends on the ability to find institutions that relieve the burden on cognition by focusing social monitoring on a few salient individuals. If these individuals are turned into reliable indicators of the trustworthiness of larger groups, the costs of sanctions may be prevented from rising.

In effect, the forager bands in Carneiro's example established what Dubreuil terms a set of secondary rules and an additional layer of norms about their enforcement, albeit for temporary purposes (the duration of the summer hunt). It is resort to secondary rule making that provides the basis of a social division of sanction. This division and the multiplication of corporate groups (i.e. as in the second of the two DP strategies) "allow stateless societies to control the rising costs of sanction and to build groups of thousands of individuals" (Dubreuil, 2013, p. 169). As a hierarchical institutional arrangement, delegation of sanction offers a guarantee of stability, because on the one hand it "multiplies the number of dependents whom salient individuals can count on" and generates benefits for them (Dubreuil, 2013, p. 204, original italicized), while, on the other hand, provided these salient individuals do not violate the norms that they are meant to safeguard, it creates an "emotion of *gratitude* toward the superior" (Dubreuil, 2013, p. 205, original italics).

Conclusion

Part of the purpose of this chapter, by means of *longue durée*, was to highlight the virtues of a historical perspective on leadership. The point here is to be able to get to grips with the fact that, as a core function in securing the success of human cooperative ventures, leadership (and the field of leadership) has a legacy. Like anything else, leadership and leaders become naturalized – taken for granted as simply there and part of the scheme of things or the furniture of the mind, with the internal conversation being something like: just accept them, don't question the need for them, simply get on and do. But what does that legacy have to say? As with other phenomena, leadership and leaders have to come from somewhere, in which case there are reasons for their existence. They do not just happen. The two DP power strategies in combination with Dubreuil's recent mind-based theory of hierarchy, therefore, will have hopefully indicated that a plausible explanation for leadership's existence in its various guises is possible and also, potentially, persuasive. The explanation is possible, although to some extent still hypothetical, because so much of the archaeological (and to a lesser extent the anthropological) evidence base on which this or any alternative explanation for leadership's emergence relies comprises a large body of inferences from limited data rather than direct observation and self-report.

Necessarily, the discussion in the chapter was confined to mostly pre-state examples of leaders and leadership, with the consequence that a vast literature on kingship and states simply could not be included for review. Not only that, but even within the confines of the archaic society focus adopted there were phenomena that could only be alluded to in passing, such as intriguing forms of dual leadership (for more examples and citations see Gronn, 2010, pp. 413–415). That said, the other hope is that the indication provided here of the array of forms taken by leadership as it emerged in early societies will have strengthened my initial claim about the inherent hybridity of this important human function. While one obvious appeal of the linguistic leader–followers template that has had common currency in the field for so long has been to facilitate the simplification of complex (and perhaps unpalatable) realities, in historical terms it simply does not cut the mustard. A similar observation applies to leadership when it is thought of as being pretty much the exclusive preserve of individuals: to marginalize or expunge plural forms of leadership from the way in which it might be configured is to short change knowledge and to not really do justice to the real world. Like so many other things in life, these are inconvenient truths.

Notes

1 "If men were angels, no government would be necessary" (James Madison, *The Federalist Papers*, no. 51).
2 In the research discussed in this chapter, the authors use a number of abbreviations to express periodization. Rather than standardizing these, the original usage has been retained. BP = Before the Present; CE = Common (or Current) Era; BCE = Before the Common (or Current) Era.

References

Blanton, R.E. (1998) Beyond centralization: Steps toward a theory of egalitarian behavior in archaic states, in G.M. Feinman & J. Marcus (Eds), *Archaic States* (Santa Fe: School of American Research Press), pp. 135–172.

Blanton, R.E., Feinman, G.M., Kowalewski, S.A., & Peregrine, P.N. (1996) A dual-processual theory for the evolution of Meso-Amercian civilization, *Current Anthropology*, 37: 1–14.

Boehm, C. (2012) *Moral Origins: The Evolution of Virtue, Altruism, and Shame* (New York: Basic Books).

Boehm, C. (2001) *Hierarchy in the Forest: The Evolution of Egalitarian Behavior* (Cambridge, MA: Harvard University Press).

Bolden, R. (2011) Distributed leadership in organizations: A review of theory and research, *International Journal of Management Reviews*, 13: 251–269.

Braudel, F. (1980) History and the social sciences: The *Longue Durée*, in *On History*, transl. S. Matthews (Chicago: University of Chicago Press), pp. 25–54.

Brown, A. (2014) *The Myth of the Strong Leader: Political Leadership in the Modern Age* (London: Bodley Head).

Carlyle, T. (1983 [1840]) *On Heroes, Hero Worship, and the Heroic in History* (New York: Chelsea House).

Carneiro, R.L. (2000) The transition from quantity to quality: A neglected causal mechanism in accounting for social evolution, *Proceedings of the National Academy of Sciences*, 97 (23): 12,926–12,931.

Carneiro, R.L. (1970) A theory of the origin of the state, *Science*, 169 (3947): 733–738.

Chreim, S. (2015) The (non)distribution of leadership roles: Considering leadership practices and configurations, *Human Relations*, 68 (4): 517–543.

Christian, D. (2005) *Maps of Time: An Introduction to Big History* (Berkeley, CA: University of California Press).

Denis, J.-L., Langley, A., & Sergi, V. (2012) Leadership in the plural, *Academy of Management Annals*, 6: 211–283.

Dubreuil, B. (2013) *Human Evolution and the Origins of Hierarchies: The State of Nature* (Cambridge: Cambridge University Press).

Feinman, G.M. (2001) Mesoamerican political complexity: The corporate–network dimension, in J. Haas (Ed.), *From Leaders to Rulers* (Dordrecht: Kluwer/Plenum), pp. 151–175.

Ferguson, Y.H. (1991) Chiefdoms to city-states: The Greek experience, in T. Earle (Ed.), *Chiefdoms: Power, Economy and Ideology* (Cambridge: Cambridge University Press), pp. 169–191.

Flannery, K., & Marcus, J. (2012) *The Creation of Inequality: How Our Prehistoric Ancestors Set the Stage for Monarchy, Slavery and Empire* (Cambridge, MA: Harvard University Press).

Fukuyama, F. (2011) *The Origins of Political Order: From Prehuman Times to the French Revolution* (London: Profile Books).

Gronn, P. (2015) The view from inside leadership configurations, *Human Relations*, 68 (4): 545–560.

Gronn, P. (2011) Hybrid configurations of leadership, in A. Bryman, D. Collinson, K. Grint, B. Jackson, & M. Uhl-Bien (Eds), *Sage Handbook of Leadership* (London: Sage), pp. 435–452.

Gronn, P. (2010) Leadership: Its genealogy, configuration and trajectory, *Journal of Educational Administration & History*, 42 (4): 405–435.

Gronn, P. (2008) The future of distributed leadership, *Journal of Educational Administration*, 46 (2): 141–158.

Guldi, J., & Armitage, D. (2014) *The History Manifesto* (Cambridge: Cambridge University Press).

Kellerman, B. (2012) *The End of Leadership* (New York: HarperCollins).

Mayhew, B.H. (1983) Hierarchical differentiation in imperatively coordinated associations, *Research in the Sociology of Organizations*, 2: 153–219.

Renfrew, C. (1974) Beyond a subsistence economy: The evolution of social organization in prehistoric Europe, in C.B. Moore (Ed.), *Reconstructing Complex Societies: An Archaeological Colloquium* (Cambridge, MA: Bulletin of the American Schools of Oriental Research, no. 20), pp. 69–85.

Rubin, P.H. (2000) Hierarchy, *Human Nature*, 11 (3): 259–279.

Seabright, P. (2013) The birth of hierarchy, in K. Sterelny, R. Joyce. B. Calcott, & B. Fraser (Eds), *Cooperation and its Evolution* (Cambridge MA: MIT Press), pp. 109–116.

Winters, J.A. (2011) *Oligarchy* (Cambridge: Cambridge University Press).

7

Critical Perspectives on Leadership Studies

A Narrow Normative Programme or a Broad Church?

Scott Taylor and Jackie Ford

Introduction

Critical management studies (CMS) and critical management education (CME) have been used as ways of analysing organisation and management for almost a quarter of a century. Research and education from this perspective shine Marxian, post-structural, and postmodern lights on strategy, marketing, accounting, human resource management, and other managerial activities. Yet leadership as an activity and a field of study has mostly escaped attention from this form of critique. This is an odd neglect, given how central the key critical concept of power has been to both critical analysis and to understanding leadership (Collinson, 2014). The oversight is addressed by recent scholarship which sets out two approaches to critical leadership studies (CLS). One approach suggests a dialectical location of the practice of leadership within organisations, to emphasise the inevitable dilemmas and contradictions produced through the exercise of power (Collinson, 2014). A second approach is more focused on 'deliberated leadership', a form of practice characterised by openness to academic intervention that provokes collective deliberation on the nature of leading (Alvesson and Spicer, 2012). The dialectical is designed to surface tensions and dilemmas in the practice of leadership; the deliberated relies on reflection-in-action during and after the practice of leadership. Both approaches enable better understanding of leading, in that they bring key conceptual issues in CMS and CME to the centre of our understandings of leading and leadership. However, we see more potential and value in the dialectical approach, as it focuses on what leaders do in an everyday sense, and the organisational conditions that all leaders work within. Here, we also suggest that, if closer attention were paid to identity and subjectivity within critical perspectives, this would enable more purposeful research and more meaningful education in this area. This would help respond to a key tenet of 'being critical' in seeking progressive change in leadership practice.

This chapter begins by briefly reviewing the development of CMS and CME over the time of its formal existence (i.e. since it was labelled as such), to identify key theoretical and educational resources members of that community draw on and promote. We note the implications of those resources and their use for the study of leadership. Our argument takes seriously the claim that belonging to the critical community need not, or should not, involve adherence to a specific unitarist theoretical perspective (Willmott, 2013). Indeed, we draw here on the suggestion that one of the key strengths of CMS is its theoretical and educational pluralism, including the tolerance of approaches that apparently contradict or challenge each other. We suggest that CLS as constituted in a normative form is moving towards a somewhat unitarist approach, and so outline an alternative perspective based on a more heterodox understanding of being critical. We draw on other writers' work to do this, bringing issues of identity, subjectivity, and pluralism to the fore (Ford *et al.*, 2008; Collinson, 2011). We work towards framing the proposal that CLS can be a series of 'broad, diverse and heterogeneous perspectives that share a concern to critique the power relations and identity constructions through which leadership dynamics are often produced, frequently rationalised, sometimes resisted and occasionally transformed' (Collinson, 2011: 181). However, we build on this to emphasise that power relations and identity construction is also an aspect of *doing* critical research and education on leadership.

This first section is the foundation for the rest of the chapter. We then explore in more detail the promise and potential of perhaps the highest profile CLS framework as a programmatic approach to research and education on the activities and discourses associated with the 'lead~' terms (Alvesson and Spicer, 2012). In this, we note the extensive research and educational work that has happened on the margins of, or in parallel to, uncritical leadership studies (cf. Willmott (2013) on 'uncritical management studies') that does not qualify for inclusion within this variant of CLS. This focuses on two issues: first, that there has long been a critical literature on leadership which has not used the term; and second, that there is a more recent literature in this area that focuses on critiques of bad leaders, leadership as a means of achieving control over employees, and the performative effects of writing and talking about leading. The studies of leadership and leading we identify, both historical and contemporary, are specifically excluded from a narrowly envisioned and potentially unitarist programmatic CLS approach because of their allegedly negative tone and epistemological positioning as interpretivist. Instead, our reading of this heritage of 'small c' critical studies of leadership suggests that there has long been and continues to be a broad church of scholarship that provides productive, sometimes implicit critiques of leadership and leadership studies, that have considerable value. Above all, we suggest that the studies we identify ask difficult questions of leaders, leading, and leadership, and encourage ethical reflection on practice, performance, and research object. In addition, we argue that these studies are epistemologically reflexive, thereby responding to a key tenet of CMS in their understanding of what it means to seek to generate knowledge.

We conclude the chapter by revisiting the key theoretical bases for CLS, dialectics and performativity, in the light of our argument. We then suggest an alternative perspective on these aspects of being critical in relation to leadership and leadership studies. Our proposal is based on an alternative reading of Judith Butler's (2002) approach to critique, which suggests a closer examination of the reflexive construction of knowledge within its epistemological and ontological power relations. This, we argue, enables better understanding of the formation of an ethical subject, understanding the subject as leader, the subject of leadership studies, and the subject as the leadership researcher.

Critical Management Studies (and Uncritical Management Studies)

There are many accounts of the origins and development of critical management studies (e.g. Adler *et al.*, 2007; Alvesson *et al.*, 2009), as befits an approach to studying management and organisation that is intended to be inherently epistemologically reflexive (Fournier and Grey, 2000). The basic narrative is uncontroversial – Mats Alvesson and Hugh Willmott (1992) first drew together a European and North American group of scholars to set out the possibility of a specific form of critique for analysing marketing, industrial psychology, accounting, and operations research. This initial statement of possibility and intent developed fairly rapidly with the publication of monographs (Alvesson and Wilmott, 1996), methods guidebooks (Alvesson and Deetz, 2000), and finally summative handbooks (Alvesson et al., 2009). The intellectual focus of CMS is often challenged, or sometimes simply dismissed as unoriginal (Perrow, 2008), its links to action are problematised (King and Learmonth, 2015), and the community's cultural practices have also come under scrutiny (Bell and King, 2010; Tatli, 2011). In this section we focus on the conceptual work that has been done to provide theoretical underpinnings for critical analysis and education, particularly positions taken on the creation of knowledge. We see this work as falling into three broad conceptual areas.

First, most prominently, CMS and CME draw on critical theory (Alvesson and Willmott, 2012). This base has a number of consequences. It creates a tendency towards a politically leftist perspective, it takes the damage caused by capitalism as a given, and it combines these two positions in propositions for change (Adler et al., 2007). However, while critical theory is a foundation, proponents frequently caution against interpreting 'it' as an orthodoxy (Adler et al., 2007). Critical theory is therefore suggested as a resource alongside a second key conceptual attitude, represented in the range of epistemological and political positions gathered under the catchall of 'post-' perspectives. These include the post-structural, within which analysis looks to Foucault and Derrida's work above all; postcolonial, drawing from work done at least initially by literary theorists; and postmodern, although this latter is now infrequently invoked, at least as an explicit stance. Finally, most recently and most relevant to us here, CMS has engaged with critical psychoanalytic perspectives, particularly post-Freudian approaches to subjectivity and identity. This work is often located within or alongside feminist analysis (Calás and Smircich, 2006). Alongside the analytical and theoretical work done in the name of CMS, there has also been activity to frame critical approaches to management education. Initially this framing was explicit, and it acquired its own acronym, CME (French and Grey, 1996); latterly, our sense is that CME has developed less clearly, conceptually and empirically, than CMS.[1]

More recently, the ideas and practices associated with CMS and CME have been further, very usefully, differentiated from 'uncritical management studies' (UMS) (Willmott, 2013). UMS is characterised by a 'pervasive but unacknowledged subscription to managerialism in which knowledge is generated and disseminated *for* management, not *of* management' (Willmott, 2013: 283). This further implies, as Willmott goes on to argue, the production of knowledge and provision of education that serves individuals and/or their profession in a narrow sense, as they attempt to secure resources and status in the world-as-is. In this description of a scientistic and careerist field of research and practice, researchers, educators, and learners apparently agree to suspend the empirical realities of discrimination, socially produced inequality, damage enabled by economic theories-in-practice, or the possibility of a non-capitalist economics and ethic. More importantly, however, it seems that studying organisational dynamics from within UMS involves neglect, or outright denial, of power relations in the production, dissemination, and application of knowledge. This is, as Willmott rightly notes, a version of scholarship and learning that falls sadly short of even good conventional scientific practice. That involves intellectual openness, self-doubt, critique of existing theory and practice, and reflexivity in relation to knowledge production, none of which UMS encourages.

Studying Leadership Critically: Conventions from CMS

As Collinson (2011, 2014) argues, it is puzzling that leadership, leaders, and leading have all been neglected by critical researchers and educators. Belatedly, Alvesson and Spicer (2012) provided what would become an influential statement of what it might mean to be critical in relation to leadership and leadership studies. Our argument from this point forward focuses on this statement of intent as simultaneously enabling and problematic. We explore the possibility that this framing of what it is to be critical, which starts by categorising contributions to leadership studies into three approaches (functionalist, interpretive-uncritical, critical-as-negative), is not helpful in developing the field because:

- interpretive research, dismissed as uncritical by Alvesson and Spicer, can, and often has been, critical in the sense that we understand the term;
- there is critical ontological and epistemological work being done in leadership studies to frame the idea of leading that does not fit with their definition of critical-as-negative, but which we believe is central to developing the field (and speaks to a broader understanding of critical);
- through a programmatic selectivity as to what is critical and, more importantly, what is not critical, the possibility of understanding or teaching leadership critically is severely limited to a specific orthodoxy, challenging the convention of CMS and CME as heterodox and open.

Finally, in making their case for CLS, Alvesson and Spicer emphasise from the outset that they want to affirm the importance of leadership. They define it pragmatically, in the sense of practising authority; for them, leadership is simply influence, of individuals, institutions, and other structures. This is obviously a functionalist, individualist definition and perspective, an issue that we return to later.

The programmatic normative approach to critically researching and teaching leadership that Alvesson and Spicer promote is founded on academic intervention into practice as 'critical performativity'. This is based on Spicer et al.'s (2009) interpretation of Butler's work, in which she outlines the idea of performativity and its practice. The logic within the definition of CLS as performative runs as follows: the act of leadership may be emancipatory. However, achieving its radical potential is dependent on interplay with established structures of power (the organisational, social, political, and economic conditions of work and management that CMS developed to challenge). In engaging, however, critical analysis must accept the principle of performance, because we rely on it to be able to develop knowledge and practise critique. Our performances must be subversive as well as performative, but not too challenging to the fundamental structures of everyday life. (One of the examples given by Spicer et al. (2009) is the impossibility that critical research and education faces in critiquing the airline industry, because we are dependent on it to attend international conferences to present the work.) This form of critical performativity is best accomplished, in this argument, by academics as analysts, educators, and leaders, working together to enable leaders to achieve the kind of subversive micro-emancipations that might make collective or systemic change happen.

This is, we think, a very interesting argument that has contributed towards framing critical approaches to understanding leadership studies and teaching leadership. However, we are not comfortable with the conceptual frame that structures the recommended moves to action. The key concern we have is the relationship constructed between critique and performativity, because that is the central contribution of the approach. For that reason, we think it is important to examine both of these terms and their associated implications in everyday action, which we are able to do in a close reading of a statement Butler made on them. This reading has implications for how critique, and therefore CMS, CME, and above all CLS, are accomplished, and through that, the outcomes we can expect of its practice.

Butler's (2002) examination of critique in the context of performativity begins by building on Williams's and Adorno's work, especially Williams's observation that criticism became associated with fault-finding or judgement. Instead, Williams proposed an understanding of criticism as practice in a specific context that implies or demands the practice of a set of values that *does not involve judgement*. If we judge as well, we are assimilating our critique into what Adorno called the 'prevailing constellations of power' that we purport to be in opposition to, because the act of judgement separates the critic from the social world. Rather than simply incorporate the critiqued into existing categories or knowledge through judgement, an alternative form of critique involves questioning the constitution of categories, the construction of knowledge, and what these processes suppress. The primary task of critique is then to bring to the fore the framework of evaluation, rather than judge the object.

Simply the act of asking what critique is, as Foucault did and as Butler does here by engaging with his work in developing her argument, enacts critique. This does not need to be either aesthetic or nihilistic (interpretive or critical-negative, in Alvesson and Spicer's terms). Rather, it opens an epistemological space, or makes clear the epistemological constraints of any space that we attempt to open, so that incoherences and silences can be identified. This in turn demands the practice of virtue, understood as ethics which require something more than following established rules and orders. Morality in this form as a researcher or educator requires a self-transformation through engaging with forms of knowledge that are strange or disturbing, as well as being continually aware of the ethical and normative implications of critiquing, especially its alternative forms of actions or thinking which are presented as better, more effective (in any sense), or more ethical.

The Challenges of Performativity: The Individual Academic in the Social Structure

Butler's exploration of critique is founded on the idea that it can be an institutionalised practice, discourse, episteme, institution, or a more general practice, a philosophy of critique. It is not fault finding or judgement, but a values-based practice founded on suspending judgement. Importantly, this practice does not involve locating critique in or through our existing structural conditions, because critique should seek to expose those as they are practised, including by those positioning themselves as critics. This is because judgement involves separation from the social world, withdrawal from praxis, and construction of a hierarchy based on knowledge and understanding. (In other words, the performance of judgement either explicitly or implicitly implies a lack of reflexivity, as to the social embeddedness of the critic.)

As practice, critique in this form involves reflecting on the kind of question that is being asked, and how responses are framed, including in analysis. This latter is key, because it often involves asking 'what are we to do?' (again, a key issue within CMS as originally formulated, perhaps as a result of Marxist roots). This inevitably means assuming a 'we', and the desirability of having a set of normative goals that we can then work towards. As an alternative, Butler pursues an understanding of the practice of critique by offering a Foucauldian perspective that relocates his arguments in this area as a guide towards engagement with normativity. Her reading of Foucault's work begins from the observation that he proposed that critique could only be understood as relational, a thing or a practice that we can only ever approximate. Critique depends on objects, and those objects delineate the meaning of critique. Critique must be based on understanding the way we evaluate the objects we seek to critique, *not* the production of our own alternative normative guide to action or thought. This in turn allows us to see what is wrong with the way questions are asked, as well as answered, and to begin to generate more interesting ethical and political questions about the object of critique.

This suggests that critical leadership studies, as represented in the programmatic approach proposed by Alvesson and Spicer, is not only asking the wrong question, it is asking the questions in the wrong way altogether. Simply by including the term 'leadership' in the title of the approach, they are failing to ask questions of how they critique the object and the object itself. So what would a more reflexive practice of critique look and feel like, in relation to leading, leaders, and leadership? As we have outlined, there are alternative approaches to being critical of leadership. Based on our reading of Butler's work, we would suggest that CLS might begin from the acceptance that critique is a continuous activity for all involved in the social practice (in our case here, leaders, followers, and researchers/critical commentators), that may not, or should not, result in a normative alternative. In other words, leadership and leading cannot be reconstructed or reconfigured through critique; rather, the epistemologies that bring us to the point of suggesting leadership and leading as inevitably ontologically real should be resisted or avoided, because that produces impossible incoherences and damaging silences (Wood, 2005; Kelly, 2008, 2014).

Second, critique might be understood as an ethical act, that is, as a non-prescriptive form of moral inquiry. This is a description of an ethics that is not circumscribed by *any* established norms of action, behaviour, thought, or knowledge construction. It is, in short, unprescriptive in as many ways as possible, in an attempt to avoid laws, rules, and commands. However, the purpose of this is not simply avoidance. There is a positive aim underlying this practice, to explore what might be changed in practice, thought, and the construction of understanding through knowledge. In particular, knowledge that has been previously un-thought, or unthinkable, may bring the practitioner of critique and her research subjects to a position of difference, perhaps even indicate the possibility of a transformed self. So the answer to the question 'what is to be done?' becomes 'critique' – critique as practice, as non-prescriptive acts of inquiry, and as raising the possibilities of other forms of knowledge that might exist outside the epistemological conventions inhabited to date.

Butler notes the importance of understanding the practice of critique as intentional or voluntary action. In this, the self and prevailing norms of conduct interact, *including problematisation of any normative framework*. It is this, which we understand as a significant extension of performativity and therefore of the normative frame that threatens to frame critical leadership studies as perspective and practice, that forms the basis of the remainder of this chapter. We examine what it might mean for all of those involved in practising and understanding leadership if this form of critique is practised. We do this in three ways: first, by locating critique in relation to a historical classic of critical leadership studies alongside a contemporary interpretive analysis; second, by re-examining the notion of performativity which is so central to CLS; and, third, by raising the possibility that critical analysis of leadership might be a more widespread practice than normative CLS allows.

Critiques of Leadership: The Long View and a Significant Contemporary Exclusion

The Institute of Industrial Relations at the University of California hosted a number of researchers and educators who wrote foundational analyses of work and management. Melville Dalton's 1959 book *Men Who Manage* is one of the most enduring. It is a significant book for anyone interested in learning about the ethical nature of managerial work, as well as a methodological classic that centres on the ethics of the research process. In other words, while researching the managerial work that gives his book its title, Dalton also came to think of himself as an ethical presence during the research process. This may have been provoked by the fact that some of his fieldwork was participant observation, during which Dalton worked as a manager; or it may have been a result of Dalton's working life prior to taking up academic work (Dalton's formal childhood education was short, so he began work early in service jobs such as hotel bellhop, and then moved into heavy industrial work (Stewart, 1979)). That form of research is not inherently reflexive, but it certainly encourages an understanding of data collection and the work being studied as embodied, emotive, and meaningful.

Dalton's book, like his other work, is primarily concerned with the social practices and sociological significance of managing in a large organisation. The analysis presented in *Men Who Manage* centres on conflict and ethical boundaries, always focused on the people who act, but equally cognisant of the structural conditions that an organisation provides. The term 'leadership' is present in the index to the book, but careful reading suggests analysis of it is absent in the text. It is, however, very clear from Dalton's fieldwork that he is concerned with understanding the people who work at the hierarchical peak of the organisation, who are paid in part for their authority, exercise power over colleagues, and are permitted power to make happen or prevent action.

Dalton's book is both deeply negative, in that he identifies many damaging practices (see especially the chapters on the career ladder and informal rewards), and interpretive (as is to be expected from a participant–observational ethnography). These two features, taken with the oblique treatment of leadership and leading, suggest locating Dalton's analysis outside the conventions of CLS, certainly in its more normative form. That would, we believe, be a great shame for two reasons. First, work like Dalton's is closer to the practice of leadership than most contemporary management and organisational research. It provides rare insight, sometimes sympathetically and sometimes critically, to the everyday lives of people who have acquired authority and some form of power. Second, this kind of research is critical in the sense that Butler wrote about many years later. Dalton's narrative continually questions his own judgement, and his right to put himself as a researcher into a position of judgement. In this respect, Dalton puts himself and his analysis *alongside* the people and the contexts that he collected data around.

Notwithstanding, Dalton's research and many similar analyses in that tradition may not be considered critical, especially from a normative CLS perspective. Our second exemplary piece of analysis is similar in being excluded, but for very different reasons. Published almost 50 years later, Amanda Sinclair's *Leadership for the Disillusioned* is, from the title on, almost exclusively concerned with all variations on the 'lead~' term – there are few pages on which it does not appear. It might be read as a guidebook, as it introduces conventional perspectives on leadership, teaching and learning practices commonly used in communicating knowledge about leadership, and then much less well recognised ways of thinking about leading. Chapters on power, bodies, breath and mind, identity, spirit, and ego all provoke thought and incite action.

This book is also essentially empirical. Sinclair draws on classically constructed case studies of individual leaders, based on observation and interview; however, she also takes a considerable risk in drawing on her experiences of teaching and experiences of leading. These aspects of the empirical content of the book, echoing Dalton's risk-taking in conducting covert participant–observational data collection, broaden the meaning of the analysis (as well as making the narrative a lot more intrinsically interesting than most books on leadership).

Sinclair is clear about how and why she presents her analysis as critical. She wants readers to think beyond the individual hero; to consider the self as well as others as an object of analysis and improvement; to question an instrumental focus on ends, to the neglect of means; and to consider purpose (beyond goals, targets, or self-interest). This is a form of critique that resonates strongly with Butler's perspective, as described above. It says little or nothing to a programmatic, normative approach to CLS, which perhaps explains its neglect by those writing that tradition into being. (There might also be, to state the very obvious, a gendered aspect to the exclusion of Sinclair's work, especially as it challenges the masculine norms that frame academic work.)

A Broad Critical Church?

For most of its practitioners, CMS and CME are underpinned by a sense of radical critique (Adler *et al.*, 2007). We are no different in this respect; we encourage our students and our selves to think and act in ways that could be categorised as radical. For us that term signifies a desire to provoke change in and around organisations and organisation theory, such that established social patterns and structures can be disrupted in the service of creating better worlds to work and live in. These patterns of thought and action can include management practices such as performance appraisal or personal development; economic structures such as capitalism; political strategies such as colonialism; or the cultural practices enshrined in belief systems. It is considerably more than just scepticism or routine critical academic thinking. It need not be violent, revolutionary, or even leftist – there are also radical possibilities in a more progressive or liberal model of think-ing and acting. Whatever the politics, radical critique must, for us, involve a degree of reflexivity on the construction of knowledge and authority in academic research and educational work. The main purpose of this chapter has been to suggest that this is a possibility for critical perspec-tives on leadership that has not yet been considered, and that is crucially important if we are to avoid the obvious mistakes that we are so critical of in the practice of leadership we research.

Those self-identifying as participants in the CMS, CME, and CLS communities are often keen to differentiate from mainstream, uncritical analysis and education. This includes those who criticise managers or management research from within 'prevailing structures of domi-nation' (Adler *et al.*, 2007: 121). In other words, in order to be 'properly critical', research and education must look to systemic levels of action, politics, and economy. Here, however, we have concentrated on a further aspect of being critical, in its relationship to knowledge production. We have done this because Butler's notion of performativity forms such a key aspect of being critical in relation to leadership studies and development, as the normative CLS programme makes clear. This is not just a question of reflexivity, central as that must always be to critical research and education. Rather, we have suggested that subject, subjectivity, and subjectivisation wind around the possibility of being critical.

This, we believe, dovetails well with the historical intellectual background that CMS emerged from. Critical analyses can take many forms, from the most radical that propose large-scale political and economic change (Warhurst, 1998), to the more conservative, sometimes based on individual or collective self-interest (Perrow, 2008). There is, however, often a missing subject in these proposals, and for that reason we return in conclusion to the approach to critique that inspired us to attempt this chapter. In particular, we have explored the appropriation of per-formativity into a markedly narrow means through which to research and teach leadership criti-cally. Above all, we want to emphasise in our reading of the programmatic, normative approach to CLS that it neglects the academic subject in that process. Butler interprets Foucault's late writings as an encouragement to reflect on the product of our critique. If critique is closely associated with a specific issue or problem, Butler suggests its practice will very likely coalesce into a particular social ontology and a specific subjectivity. The freedom to critique becomes an exercise of power. Critique, however, may enable considerably more than that, if practised reflexively. This could be especially fruitful if the relationship between self and normative frame is held up to the light, such that the epistemological horizon that delimits practices is brought into question (or at least acknowledged). It is this final, crucial, step that we have argued CLS does not make – indeed, does not even make possible.

Theoretically, we think this can be achieved by much closer engagement with the emerging understanding of leadership or leadership studies as an aspect of negative ontology. This responds to Knights and McCabe's (2015) recent observation that much analysis of the 2008 global financial crisis and its continuing aftermath rests on the same paradigmatic assumptions that underpin the actions and analysis it was built upon. The assumption they expose is the traditional modernist one of instrumental rationality, which in turn produces a disembodied technocratic approach to work and organisation. Here, we have focused on a different form of assumption, related to the nature of knowledge and critique. We have suggested that CLS, as set out in a programmatic narrowly performative form, excludes significant contributions to critiquing leaders and leadership, and restricts the nature of critique to a highly specific form.

Empirically, it is clear that researchers, critical or uncritical, will continue to focus on practising leadership, whether as an essentialised activity and subjectivity, or as a socially constructed reality. However, more attention could be paid to absences in leadership and the absence of leadership in structurally unusual organisational settings (Sutherland et al., 2014). Similarly, research methods that allow for absence or difference, such as grounded theory and more inductive approaches, would provoke the development of different ways of thinking about the act of leading and the people we identify as leaders. Finally, it is worth emphasising that we do see a bright future for CLS. As we noted at the outset, it has taken a relatively long time for leadership studies to discover its critical possibilities. Critique remains, for us, the most insightful way of engaging with the practice and theory of leadership. However, if CLS is to develop in ways that are engaged, we would argue that it urgently needs to acknowledge, and problematise, its own normativity, subjectivity, and epistemology, especially if the practice of critique is intended as an ethical act in its own right.

Note

1 This outline is deliberately short, terse, and representative only at the very broadest level. CMS and to a lesser extent CME are notable in approaches to management and organisational analysis for the volume of review, summary, state-of-the-field pieces – we do not want to reprise those or attempt to reproduce that approach here.

References

Adler, P., Forbes, L., and Willmott, H. (2007) 'Critical management studies', *Academy of Management Annals*, 1: 119–179.

Alvesson, M. and Deetz, S. (2000) *Doing Critical Management Research*. London: Sage.

Alvesson, M. and Spicer, A. (2012) 'Critical leadership studies: The case for critical performativity', *Human Relations*, 65 (3): 367–390.

Alvesson, M. and Willmott, H. ([first edition, 1996] 2012) *Making Sense of Management*. London: Sage.

Alvesson, M. and Willmott, H. (eds) (1992) *Studying Management Critically*. London: Sage.

Alvesson, M., Bridgman, T., and Willmott, H. (eds) (2009) *The Oxford Handbook of Critical Management Studies*. Oxford: Oxford University Press.

Bell, E. and King, D. (2010) 'The elephant in the room: Critical Management Studies conferences as a site of body pedagogics', *Management Learning*, 41 (4): 429–442.

Butler, J. (2002) 'What is critique? An essay on Foucault's virtue', in Ingram, D. (ed) *The Political: Blackwell Readings in Continental Philosophy*. Oxford: Blackwell. pp. 212–228.

Calás, M. and Smircich, L. (2006) 'From "the woman's" point of view: Feminist approaches to organization studies', in Clegg, S., Hardy, C., and Nord, W. (eds) *Handbook of Organization Studies*. London: Sage.

Collinson, D. (2011) 'Critical leadership studies', in Bryman, A., Collinson, D., Grint, K., Jackson, B., and Uhl-Bien, M. (eds) *The Sage Handbook of Leadership*. London: Sage.

Collinson, D. (2014) 'Dichotomies, dialectics and dilemmas: New directions for critical leadership studies', *Leadership*, 10 (1): 36–55.

Dalton, M. (1959) *Men Who Manage*. New York: Wiley.

Ford, J., Harding, N., and Learmonth, M. (2008) *Leadership as Identity: Constructions and Deconstructions*. London: Palgrave Macmillan.

Fournier, V. and Grey, C. (2000) 'At the critical moment: Conditions and prospects for Critical Management Studies', *Human Relations*, 53 (1): 7–32.

French, R. and Grey, C. (eds) (1996) *Rethinking Management Education*. London: Sage.

Kelly, S. (2008) 'Leadership: A categorical mistake?', *Human Relations*, 61 (6): 763–782.

Kelly, S. (2014) 'Towards a negative ontology of leadership', *Human Relations*, 67 (8): 905–922.

King, D. and Learmonth, M. (2015) 'Can Critical Management Studies ever be "practical"? A case study in engaged scholarship', *Human Relations*, 68 (3): 353–375.

Knights, D. and McCabe, D. (2015) 'Masters of the Universe: Demystifying leadership in the context of the 2008 global financial crisis', *British Journal of Management*, 26: 197–210.

Perrow, C. (2008) 'Conservative radicalism', *Organization*, 15 (6): 915–921.

Sinclair, A. (2007) *Leadership for the Disillusioned*. Crows Nest: Allen & Unwin.

Spicer, A., Alvesson, M., and Karreman, D. (2009) 'Critical performativity: The unfinished business of Critical Management Studies', *Human Relations*, 62 (4): 537–560.

Stewart, P. (1979) 'Obituary, Melville Dalton', *ASA Footnotes*, 7 (5): 10.

Sutherland, N., Land, C., and Böhm, S. (2014) 'Anti-leaders(hip) in social movement organizations: The case of autonomous grassroots groups', *Organization*, 21 (6): 759–781.

Tatli, A. (2011) 'On the power and poverty of critical (self) reflection in Critical Management Studies: A comment on Ford, Harding and Learmonth', *British Journal of Management*, 23 (1): 22–30.

Warhurst, C. (1998) 'Recognising the possible: The organization and control of a socialist process', *Administrative Science Quarterly*, 43 (2): 470–497.

Willmott, H. (2013) 'Reflections on the darker side of power analytics', *Academy of Management Perspectives*, 27 (4): 281–286.

Wood, M. (2005) 'The fallacy of misplaced leadership', *Journal of Management Studies*, 42 (6): 1101–1121.

8

Psychoanalytic Perspectives on Leadership

Irma Rybnikova

Introduction

Psychoanalysis in general, and the psychoanalytical perspective on leadership in particular, belong to the approaches challenging the long-standing dominance of the rationality of human behavior. It does this by highlighting the unconscious processes framing organizations, leadership, leaders, and subordinates. In leadership studies, psychoanalytical approaches not only point to the unconsciousness as an integral part of the leadership work, but also highlight the importance of early childhood experience for the behavior of leaders and subordinates. Having its seeds in the work of Sigmund Freud, dating back more than one hundred years, the psychoanalytical perspective on leadership has a barely visible but long-lasting tradition. Instead of considering man as a rational agent, position holder or a wheel of the organizational machinery, psychoanalytical perspectives share the understanding of organizational actors as psychic subjects endowed with individual subjectivity, consisting of their private emotional pasts, fantasies, and idiosyncratic identities (Gabriel and Carr 2002).

In their literature review, Gabriel and Carr (2002: 351) distinguish between two main approaches on how psychoanalytical concepts are used to analyze organizations: the research-oriented approach ("studying organizations psychoanalytically") and the intervention-oriented approach ("psychoanalysing organizations"). Whereas in the first case the main aim is to provide psychoanalytically informed descriptions and explanations of organizational processes, including leadership, in order to gain new theoretical insights, the intervention-oriented approach is much more instrumental and mainly aims at diagnosing organizational dysfunctions and pathologies. Even if this distinction is in some cases arbitrary, in the following I will mainly refer to the psychoanalytically informed analyses on leadership that follow the research-oriented approach. The aim of this chapter is to provide a review of the psychoanalytically informed concepts explicitly addressing leadership issues.

The added value of this review does not lie in its originality, since there already exist seminal reviews of psychoanalytical approaches to leadership, such as Gabriel (2011) or Kets de Vries and Balazs (2011), to mention only the most recent. The aim of the chapter is to provide a review attempt with a slightly differently structured landscape of psychoanalytically informed leadership research than previous reviews, while focusing on the leitmotivs of respective debates, such as the emergence of leadership, leadership interaction, and typologies of leaders. Additionally, the chapter aims at exploring critical tenets of psychoanalytical perspectives on leadership, together with a critical consideration of how these claims have been realized in research up to now.

After a short outline of the main tenets of the psychoanalytical approach, the main attention will then be directed toward the three topics of psychoanalytically informed research on leadership. In the first topic, the *emergence of leadership and followership*, the main attention will be given to Freud's (1967) concepts of "projective identification" and "idealization" as well the ideas proposed by Bion (1959) on psychoanalytical mechanisms of group behavior. The second consideration refers to *leadership as an interaction* from the perspective of psychoanalytically informed transactional analysis according to Berne (1964). The third section concerns the research thread dealing with psychoanalytically informed *typologies of personalities*, especially the typology provided by Maccoby (1976). Special attention will also be given to the discussion of so-called dysfunctional personalities and their consequences for organizations, particularly narcissistic leaders (DuBrin 2012; Kets de Vries and Balazs 2011; Ouimet 2010). The final part of the chapter will carve out the critical kernel of the psychoanalytical perspective on leadership, such as the questioning of rationality and formal instrumentality of leadership, and point to the main current shortcomings of psychoanalytical perspectives on leadership.

Main Tenets of the Psychoanalytical Approach

Despite the fact that psychoanalytical theory in no way represents a monolithic tradition but consists of numerous different theoretical schools, three basic assumptions are shared by all psychoanalytic approaches. The first is the existence of the unconscious as an integral part of the human psyche, which directly or indirectly affects human action (Rosenstiel 2009: 18). Although the understanding of the "unconscious" existed long before Freud, he was the first to consider the unconscious as a social phenomenon deserving special attention (Gabriel and Carr 2002). Freud outlines the topography of the human psyche as consisting of three hierarchically linked and universally valid "areas." First is the id, which is the most archaic and "deepest," consisting of the unconscious physiological impulses and instincts, such as life survival and functioning according to the principle of pleasure (*libido* and *eros*) as well as death (*thanatos*) (Freud, 1950). The second area of the human psyche is the ego, which represents the subconscious and bridges the unconscious and the conscious. In contrast to the id, the ego functions according to the reality principle and ensures adaptation of humans to the environment, especially by providing psychic defense mechanisms, such as projection, identification, or compensation. The third, and chronologically last, area of the human psyche is the superego, which houses culturally transferred expectations, ethical–moral norms and motives. The essential element of the superego is the human conscience whose main function is to control the libidinal impulses of humans (Freud 1949: 73). The second basic assumption shared by all schools of psychoanalysis states a close correspondence between the unconscious with its instinctual impulses and the conscious, which is attempting to restrain them. Freud grants sexual impulses especially "a tremendously large and previously not appreciated role as causes of psychic and mental diseases" (Freud 1950: 16).

The third basic assumption of psychoanalytical sub-schools refers to the idea that the social relations of the present are framed by past experience, especially experience from early childhood with one's own parents (Oglensky 1995: 1036). This assumption is of particular importance for leadership since, drawing from Freud, psychoanalytically informed researchers consider leadership in organizations as a reproduction of the father–child relationship. These three basic assumptions are directly reflected in psychoanalytically informed leadership study. Instead of considering leadership as rational and manageable, it is discussed as a phenomenon consisting of conscious as well as unconscious elements that are highly intertwined. Moreover, from the psychoanalytical point of view, leadership processes in organizations are mainly dominated by unconscious forces, drives, and beliefs, which are rooted either in archetypical experiences of humans or their individual histories. The main ideas on leadership as provided by the psychoanalytically informed literature directly refer to the main tenets of psychoanalysis. Three ideas contour the main corpus of the psychoanalytical study of leadership. These are, first, the issue of leadership emergence, which is considered as a kind of collective outburst of unconscious desires towards the superego; second, the idea of leadership interaction as mainly rooted in and being framed by the unconscious early history of individuals; and, third, several attempts at personality typologies of leaders according to the main unconscious sources of lust and frustration in early childhood. The next sections of the chapter deal with these three main issues in more depth.

Psychoanalytical Consideration of Leadership Emergence

Why do sovereign individuals allow themselves to be led by someone? Psychoanalytical answers to this question deal with the mechanisms of leadership emergence which at the same time represent the main psychoanalytical ideas addressing leadership issues. From the psychoanalytical perspective, the emergence of leadership is mainly an issue of followers. The basic mechanisms describing the psychoanalytical understanding of leadership emergence are Freud's (1967) concepts of "projective identification" and "idealization" on the part of followers, together with ideas proposed by Bion (1959) regarding psychoanalytical mechanisms of group behavior. Both concepts stem from mass psychology. In his work *Group Psychology and the Analysis of the Ego* [Massenpsychologie und Ich-Analyse], Freud (1967) introduces the mechanism of "identification" as an explanation for leadership of the masses. Jaques (1953) complemented it with "projective identification." While explaining "projective identification," both Freud and Jaques refer to the libidinal processes on the one hand and the superego on the other hand. From a psychoanalytic point of view, leadership is a proper expression of the sexual instinct. The leader of a group embodies the ideal of the group members since "every single individual is libidinously bound up to the leader on the one hand and to other members of the mass on the other hand" (Freud 1967: 34). Broadly speaking, members of the group project their own ideal (the superego) on one of the group members, who becomes the leader. Freud calls this process "idealization" and attributes it to the narcissistic tendency of members. According to Freud, the libidinous bounds, which leadership is based on, can be compared with the narcissism of love since:

> The object [of love] serves as replacement for the ego-ideal which could not be achieved. People love this object because of its perfection which they sought for their own ego and which is now projected onto the object loved in order to satisfy own narcissism.
>
> *(Freud, 1967: 51)*

The mechanism of identification is related to the individual's desire to find glamour and recognition by projecting it on the leading person. As a result, individuals identify with this person and accept him or her as leader. The victories of the leader become their own victories, to be celebrated and serve as a source of individual pride. In cases where several members of groups simultaneously identify with the leader, the authors speak of additive projection (e.g. Winkler 2010: 27).

The projective identification is associated with the idealization of the leader. The leader becomes an adored love object. Negative attributes of the leader's personality are ignored. Instead, members focus their expectations on the confirmation of the idealized image of the leader. When leaders fail to meet these idealizations, e.g. in the form of less adorable personality traits becoming obvious or problematic leader behaviors becoming public, they fail as leaders (Neuberger and Kompa 1993: 201) and previous identifications of members with the adored leader turn into the opposite: demonization of the leader. "A leader does not fail because he or she failed as a person, [but] because he or she turned out not to be the God, the ideal which was the fantasy of members" (Neuberger and Kompa 1993: 201). In addition to the projective identification, current scholars deal with the question of which features the emergence of leaders are based on. They point either to the expectations about leaders, which are framed in early childhood (Goethals 2005), or to culturally framed archetypal images of leaders (Lindsey 2011; Neuberger 2002). Goethals (2005) argues that, especially in times of uncertainty, helplessness, and crisis, those persons are able to induce projective identification and become leaders who represent parental figures, such as the "primal father," and are able to provide confidence to group members. Male individuals in particular are able to induce unconscious archaic notions of the strong, powerful father (leader) who provides confidence to and cares for all members, no matter in how despotic a way these persons may operate (Goethals 2005).

In contrast to this, Neuberger (2002) and Lindsey (2011) emphasize the importance of culturally, not individually, anchored archetypal ideas regarding leaders. For example, the archetypes of God, father and teacher seem to be anchored particularly deeply in the collective memory of western European culture, with numerous expressions of them in cultural artifacts, such as paintings (Lindsey 2011), but also in texts and stories (Neuberger 2002). Some scholars associate the success of some leaders with their ability to instrumentalize these archetypical images, such as Rieken (2010) who traces back the political success of Barack Obama to the fact that he incorporates the archetypal American images of success and justice in his political speeches. The study by Gabriel (1997) in which he asked students to reflect on their encounters with the top managers of companies shows the dominance of the father figure and mother figure as archaic images of leaders sharing the omnipotence and godlikeness. According to Gabriel, these figures can be attributed to the unconscious desire for powerful leaders who are able to provide security, albeit an illusionary one. Some authors link the mechanism of projective identification with "corporate madness" (De Board 1978), which can lead to strong leadership but hinder the learning processes of an organization (Brown and Starkey 2000).

Leadership as an Unconsciously Framed Interaction

The structure of interaction between leaders and subordinates is the second field in which the psychoanalytical perspective provides an important contribution to leadership research. The transactional analysis according to Berne (1964) represents the key concept here.

Transactional analysis suggests that social interactions in adulthood, including leadership, are unconsciously framed by individual experience stemming from early childhood. In the case of leadership, the relationship with parents is particularly constitutive, because it represents a prototype of a hierarchical relationship. Drawing on the *transference mechanism* according to Freud, Berne introduces three so-called "ego-states." According to Berne, an ego-state represents a dominant pattern of emotions, experience, and behaviors, which, differently from a personality, are dynamic. An individual possesses a repertoire of different ego-states, which have to be considered not as roles, but as psychological realities (Berne 1964: 25). Berne differentiates between three ego-states of an individual: the child-like, the adult-like, and the parent-like state.

The child-like ego state represents a psychic relict of experience and perceptions in childhood, which is mainly characterized by an impulsive expression of emotions. The adult-like ego state represents a psychic state that is linked to the sovereign behavior of an adult and characterized by rational decision making, including downplaying of emotions. In a metaphorical sense, Berne compares the adult-like ego state with a processor that "orients toward objective perception of reality" (Berne 1964: 27). The last, parent-like, ego state mirrors the parental behavior whose main function is the maintaining of authority. Every human being has all three ego-states, as if three persons were found in one individual: the person he or she was at three years old, his or her own parents, and the person with adult experience. According to Berne, every ego-state fulfills a relevant function in the psychic life of an individual. The child-like state is linked to one's creativity as well as the intuitive and spontaneous drives of one's behavior; the adult-like ego-state enables an adaptive survival and careful decision making when getting on with fast-changing information; and the parent-like ego-state is responsible for routine-oriented decision making (Berne 1964: 28).

Depending on the circumstances, different ego-states dominate in everyday interactions. Incidents reminding an individual of childhood experience are able to activate the child-like ego state with feelings of anxiety, fear, or frustration. According to Berne, individuals are basically able to switch from one ego-state to another, albeit at an individual pace (Berne 1964: 4). In order to describe the ego-state, some authors do not hesitate to use quite trivial instruments, such as the so-called "ego-gram," which maps the current ego-state as three bars whose sizes stand for the expression of each ego-state (Stech 2010: 274).

Berne considers the ego-states as an analytical tool for any form of social interaction, including leadership, in which ego-states experienced in childhood are re-enacted. Given the fact that the behavior of leaders corresponds to that of parents and the subordinates model the behavior of children, the authors distinguish two basic patterns in leaders' transactions: authoritarian and participatory activities. Employees are considered here as being able to respond to the pattern with one of the three behavioral patterns: they show the dependent behavior of obedience and subordination; they may defy and resist the authority claimed by the leaders; and, finally, they may react in a sovereign way while testing limits, creating new spaces of autonomy without openly challenging the leaders. According to Berne, behavioral patterns learned in childhood manifest particularly in stressful situations of adult life, in which conscious reflecting cannot be afforded and a behavioral regression to the primarily learned ego-states can be expected. Similar to Berne, Argyris (1957) differentiates between the so-called mature (adult-like) and immature (child-like) behavior in organizations, while critically pointing to the fact that the immature behavior is ascribed mainly to employees in organizations, whereas the mature behavior is mainly attributed to the leaders. Consequently, while drawing on psychoanalytical ideas, some myths of modern organizations were supported, such as the myth of ontological differences between employees and managers, with employees remaining implicitly equated with children deserving motivation, leadership, and control, whereas leaders were unquestionably attested as being "experienced" adults or parents.

Berne distinguishes between two types of transactions: the so-called complementing and conflicting transactions (Berne 1964: 29ff). From Berne's point of view, complementary transactions represent responses that are "appropriate and expected and follow the natural order of healthy human relationships" (Berne 1964: 33), since this transaction is based on two corresponding ego-states: for example, the parent-like ego-state on the part of the leader and the child-like state on the part of the employee, which results in positive effects such as frictionless communication. Less positively connoted are conflicting transactions in which the ego-states of the leader and employee intersect, with the consequence of numerous conflicts and tensions, as in the case of a parent-like ego-state of a leader which appeals to the child-like ego-state of an employee but is instead facing an adult-like ego state with expressions of sovereign or resisting behavior (Berne 1964: 30).

In contrast to Berne, whose analysis focuses on an individual interaction between leader and subordinate, there are attempts to describe the patterns of leadership interaction in a group. Bion (1959) and, in reference to him, Kets de Vries (2004) consider interaction in a group as an expression of unconscious mental models resulting in psychic regression and shared modes of group functioning. The authors differentiate among three basic patterns of leadership interactions in a group: dependency, fight or flight, and pairing. In the case of the dependency pattern, the relationship is characterized by the fact that employees consider their leader as a safe harbor, similar to the one experienced in childhood, with the leader replacing confidence previously provided by parents. Here, leaders are idealized and glorified; the group members feel themselves to a large extent highly dependent on the omnipotent leader (Kets de Vries 2004). A situation without a leader causes feelings of helplessness and fear; once a leader fails to live up to these high expectations, he or she will be replaced.

The fight or flight mode is reflected by the fact that group members are latently aggressive towards the inner and outer "enemies" (Neuberger and Kompa 1993: 221), which results in an ambivalent attitude towards the environment. The group members at the same time tend to fight against the environment to avoid it or to flee from it. According to Bion, one of the indications for such a pattern can be seen in the constant attempts of the group to draw a separating line between itself and other groups, which is for example expressed by the frequent use of terms such as "we" and "they," or "friends" and "enemies" (Kets de Vries 2004). Instead of actively dealing with the environment, such groups maintain external attributions and blame the environment for problems or failures. The position of the leader in this kind of group is quite precarious, since the leader can be blamed for any failure (Bion 1959). However, leaders who skillfully use fight or flight mechanisms can induce strong group loyalty. In cases in which loyalty to the leaders and identification with them corresponds with a consequent exclusion of different-minded persons from the group, the "fight or flight" pattern can change into an extreme pattern of dependency.

Pairing is the third psychological pattern of group dynamics, which is expressed in the fact that the group seeks coalitions with individuals or groups perceived as powerful and relevant. This behavior draws on the unconscious assumption that one's own individual uncertainty can be avoided by associating with others, even at the risk of fragmentation of the group and jeopardizing its existence (Kets de Vries 2004). As Kets de Vries (2004) shows in his study, the psychological pattern of pairing as well as its consequences can be particularly observed in young technological companies.

Psychoanalytically Informed Typologies of Leaders

Besides the concepts addressing dynamic issues of leadership, there is a range of psychoanalytical attempts to classify human personalities. In the following, I will discuss the typology provided by Maccoby (1976) since, in contrast to several other general personality classifications provided by the psychoanalytical school, such as Jung's (1976), it explicitly deals with leaders.

The typology developed by Michael Maccoby, an American psychoanalytically informed management researcher and consultant, represents one of the most popular psychoanalytical leadership concepts. Maccoby does not explicitly refer to psychoanalytical concepts in his study, which is hardly a surprise, given the fact that he wrote a popular scientific book. Nevertheless, the classification the author has developed relies on an assumption of unconscious needs and desires guiding the organizational behavior of leaders, and thus derives from the core psycho-analytical understanding of the social world.

The typology goes back to a study conducted by the author with 250 American managers (Maccoby 1976) and provides the foundation for four types of leaders: the craftsman, the jungle fighter, the company man, and the gamesman. Each of the four types represents a pattern of individual value-oriented positions and personal identities of the leaders.

The *craftsman* stands in particular for professional quality. The self-esteem of this type of leader is based on professional competence and discipline. Instead of competing with executive colleagues, the craftsman acts in accordance with his or her own objectives of quality and performance, which often results in perfectionist-like aspiration. Colleagues and subordinates are appraised according to the criteria of craftsmanship and performance; because of this, the craftsman often earns the reputation of being a fair manager (Maccoby 1976: 34). Craftmen's high concern for quality finds its expression in over criticism and impatience in the face of errors, both one's own and those of subordinates.

In contrast to the craftsman, the sole aim of the *jungle fighter* is power. This type of leader considers the environment as a jungle, which stands for an arena in which losers are destroyed by the winners. The jungle fighters show an instrumental understanding of their co-workers, with colleagues and subordinates being considered by them as objects ensuring their individual success or hindering it and, consequently, either being their supporters or enemies. Additionally, the activity of the jungle fighters, according to Maccoby, is based on a negative concept of the environment: the jungle fighters encounter their co-workers with high distrust, in order not to be manipulated by them. Hence, while using images of enemies, the jungle fighters as leaders are able to engage subordinates for their own purposes.

The self-esteem of the *company man*, the next type of leader, is based on the fact of being a part of an important and powerful entity, the company, and sharing its glory. The company man is driven by security, not by success; his or her identification with the company is accordingly strong (Maccoby 1976: 74). Given the high relevance of a firm, the company man as a leader is highly concerned with a good working climate in his or her department. Whereas a creative company man is able to establish a climate of cooperation and reciprocity in the team, the weak counterpart tends towards servility, in extreme cases even to masochism due to a fear of job loss (Maccoby 1976: 36). In times of crisis, the company men turn out to be successful leaders, since they tend towards cautiousness and the maintenance of the status quo.

The *gamesman* considers life as a game, the contest as stimulation, and the drive for success as a source of energy. Unlike the jungle fighter, who aims at building his or her own empire, the gamesman lives on competition; his driving force is not power or richness but the sense of glory, joy of leading, and success. The greatest fear of the gamesman is failure. The gamesman earns pleasure from team staffing and inspiring members, using promises of success and not coercion as a motivation source. Polarization of subordinates is the effect of this behavioral pattern: highly performing team members are rewarded strongly, whereas weak, lower performing subordinates or subordinates who are less willing to take risks earn no acknowledgment and tend to be replaced in order not to jeopardize the success of the team. The gamesman is dependent on tensions provided by challenges and new ideas. If the challenges and games cease or disappear, the gamesman begins to be bored; in extreme cases, self-destructive behavior, such as alcohol or drug abuse, can be expected.

In his later publications, Maccoby (1988) provided a new typology with five slightly different types of leaders; however, this attempt did not gain much attention, and the four types described above remain the most popular contribution associated with the author.

Leadership and Narcissism

The psychoanalytical perspective is one of the few approaches which quite early pointed to the dysfunctional aspects of leadership and paved the way for the so-called consideration of the "bad" (Kellerman 2004), "dark" (Tourish 2013) or "shadow" (Kets de Vries and Balazs 2011) side of leadership. Recent leadership scholars not only borrow some of the psychoanalytical terms in order to name certain dysfunctional leadership phenomena, but also more or less draw on psychoanalytical assumptions.

Most attention has been given to the idea of narcissism, which plays a crucial role in the psychoanalytical description of organizational leaders. The term "narcissism" goes back to Narcissus, a figure of Greek mythology, who, according to one of the many versions of the story, was punished by a rejected admirer. He fell in love with his own image mirrored in the water and died while desperately trying to hold onto his image. Psychoanalytically informed scholars share the idea that management positions are particularly prone to attracting narcissist personalities. Kets de Vries and Miller (1984) as well as Maccoby (2000) ascribe narcissism to most historical leaders as well as to leaders of current organizations.

Narcissism, like other functional and dysfunctional personal tendencies, is considered to have its roots in early childhood experiences of powerlessness together with the omnipotence of parents. Dealing with this tension and the kind of care given by the parents results in more or less expressed feelings of one's own grandiosity, which is the source of narcissism (Kets de Vries and Balazs 2011: 389). Essentially, narcissist personalities are characterized by the expressed need for power, prestige, and glamour. Maccoby (2000) describes narcissistic leaders, first, as great visionaries who, instead of analytically dissecting and differentiating complex problems, prefer overall albeit abstract solutions (Maccoby, 2000: 72) and, second, as inspiring persons able to mobilize their subordinates for themselves and their vision, not least because of their rhetorical skills. According to Maccoby (2000), there are at least three weaknesses that distinguish narcissist leaders from others, without necessarily hindering their organizational success: their vulnerability to criticism, inability to have empathy, and relentless desire for competition.

In psychoanalytic terms, narcissism is primarily an analytical category describing and explaining specific human behavior; Freud considered narcissism as a personality tendency (Freud 1946). In leadership literature, narcissism is often used in a quite normative way by either linking the narcissism of leaders with bad, destructive leading behavior, such as authoritarianism (e.g. DuBrin 2012), or by underlining positive effects of leaders' narcissism for organizations, such as innovation and vision (Campbell et al. 2011: 272).

In order to explain these ambivalent effects of leaders' narcissism on organizations, some authors delineate several subcategories of narcissism. For example, Kets de Vries and Balazs (2011: 389) distinguish between constructive and reactive narcissism of leaders. According to the authors, constructive narcissism can be considered as "healthy," whereas reactive narcissism represents an excessive and quite traumatized form. Whereas constructive narcissists draw on positive experience in their childhood, framed by trust and security, reactive narcissistic personalities result from early childhood experience of uncertainty, deprivation, and inconsistent treatment. Consequently, constructive narcissists as leaders are less concerned about their power, but focus on the vision of a better organization while trying to inspire other members. Kets de Vries (2004) points out that a "healthy dose of narcissism" is required for every person who is going to make an organizational career, because the narcissistic imagination of being chosen to achieve great results induces strong loyalty among subordinates. In contrast to this, the reactive type tries to outweigh the feelings of insecurity by self-grandiosity and excessive desire for admiration, which can be accompanied by a lack of empathy and disregard of organizational rules (Kets de Vries and Balazs 2011: 390). Such executives are described as often primarily concerned with their personal status, power, and prestige and consider life as a play-arena between winners and losers.

Meanwhile, there have been further studies going beyond the attempts to classify the narcissism of leaders. Recent authors more often deal with narcissism from a more context-oriented perspective, while addressing organizational circumstances favoring the narcissism of leaders (Ouimet 2010), examining the impact of the narcissism on the organizational behavior of leaders and employees (Ouimet 2010), or differentiating between the contexts that induce effective and ineffective results of leaders' narcissism (Campbell et al. 2011; DuBrin 2012).

Summary: Psychoanalytically Informed Leadership Perspective between Critical Claims and Normative Closure

Looking at the insights gained from the research streams discussed, it becomes evident that psychoanalytical perspectives on leadership comprise a highly heterogeneous research landscape, beginning with the dynamic perspectives on leadership emergence and ending with personality typologies, including dysfunctional personalities of leaders. At the same time, the impression arises that psychoanalytically informed leadership research is trapped between critical claims about mainstream leadership research on the one hand and its own normative closure on the other.

One of the most relevant critical insights of psychoanalytical perspectives lies in the questioning of the instrumentality of leadership. Instead, the psychoanalytical perspective allows for a consideration of leadership as a genuine human encounter, encompassing core human needs, emotions, and often-irresolvable conflicts (Sievers 1994: 167). The psychoanalytic leadership perspective emphasizes that a leadership relationship is more than just rationally based giving and receiving of formal instructions or support for task completion, but rather an expression of the basic – mainly unconscious – human needs of the people involved (Gabriel and Carr 2002). While refusing the assumptions of rationality of human activity and establishing unconsciousness as an important reference of human behavior, the psychoanalytical perspective on leadership paves the way for a critical consideration of leadership in at least two ways. First, the elitist status of leadership phenomena is denied and implicitly becomes a status of ordinary human encounters albeit being embedded in the specific context of organizational hierarchy. Second, while addressing functionalities and dysfunctionalities of human behavior, the psychoanalytical perspective provides approaches and instruments to consider the dark or shadow side of leadership, such as the narcissism of leaders or authoritarian behavior. It is no coincidence that psychoanalytic leadership scholars are at the same time serious critics of modern organizations and leadership, such as Argyris (1957) or Sievers (1994), who point to the fact that modern organizations serve as institutions of infantilization, "perpetuation of immaturity" (Sievers 1994: 157), and glorification of managers and leaders.

Despite the merits mentioned, the psychoanalytic understanding of leadership does not belong to the most popular leadership theories. One possible reason, I would suggest, is the "normative closure" of the psychoanalytical perspective. With this, I refer to the fact that main assumptions of psychoanalysis can neither be tested nor critically discussed by other perspectives since they are considered as given and not questionable, such as the existence of the unconsciousness or the seminal influence of early childhood on adult behavior. One of the consequences of these assumptions is the psychological reductionism which psychoanalytical considerations of leadership are partially based on, with genuine organizational contexts, such as organizational structure or culture, being insufficiently considered. Together with this, numerous concepts provided by the psychoanalytical perspective fall behind its dynamic claims and draw on static and frequently dualistic categories, such as the ego-states by Berne (1964) or reactive and constructive forms of narcissism by Kets de Vries and Balazs (2011). Although of great value, state classifications, particularly those of a dualistic character, remain behind the analytical complexity of original psychoanalytical concepts addressing dynamic processes of leadership emergence, such as projective identification.

References

Argyris, C. (1957): *Personality and organization: The conflict between system and the individual*. New York.

Berne, E. (1964): *Games people play: The psychology of human relationship*. New York.

Bion, W. (1959): *Experiences in groups*. New York.

Brown, A.D.S. and Starkey, K. (2000): Organizational identity and learning: A psychodynamic perspective. *Academy of Management Review* 25 (1), 102–120.

Campbell, K.W., Hoffman, B.J., Campbell, S.M. and Marchisio, G. (2011): Narcissism in organizational contexts. *Human Resource Management Review* 21, 268–284.

De Board, R. (1978): *The psychodynamics of organizations*. London.

DuBrin, A.J. (2012): *Narcissism in the workplace: Research, opinion and practice*. Cheltenham.

Freud, S. (1946): *Zur Einführung des Narzißmus*. London.

Freud, S. (1949): *Neue Folge der Vorlesungen zur Einführung in die Psychoanalyse*. London.

Freud, S. (1950): *Vorlesungen zur Einführung in die Psychoanalyse*. London.

Freud, S. (1967): *Massenpsychologie und Ich-Analyse*. Leipzig.

Gabriel, Y.C. (1997): Meeting god: When organizational members come face to face with the supreme leader. *Human Relations* 50 (4), 315–342.

Gabriel, Y.C. (2011): Psychoanalytical approaches to leadership. In: Bryman, A., Collinson, D.L., Grint, K., Jackson, B. and Uhl-Bien, M. (eds): *The Sage handbook of leadership*. Thousand Oaks, CA, 393–404.

Gabriel, Y.C. and Carr, A. (2002): Organizations, management and psychoanalysis: An overview. *Journal of Managerial Psychology* 17 (5), 348–365.

Goethals, G.R. (2005): The psychodynamics of leadership: Freud's insights and their vicissitudes. In: Messick, D.M. and Kramer, R.M. (eds): *The psychology of leadership: New perspectives and research*. London, 97–112.

Jaques, E. (1953): On the dynamics of social structure: A contribution to the psychoanalytical study of social phenomena deriving from the views of Melanie Klein. *Human Relations* 6, 3–24.

Jung, C.G. (1976): *Aion*. Olten.

Kellerman, B. (2004): *Bad leadership: What it is, how it happens, why it matters*. Boston.

Kets Vries, M.F.R. (2004): Organizations on the couch: A clinical perspective on organizational dynamics. *European Management Journal* 22 (2), 183–200.

Kets Vries, M.F.R. and Balazs, K. (2011): The shadow side of leadership. In: Bryman, A., Collinson, D.L., Grint, K., Jackson, B. and Uhl-Bien, M. (eds): *The Sage handbook of leadership*. Thousand Oaks, CA, 380–392.

Kets de Vries, M.F.R. and Miller, D. (1984): *The neurotic organization: Diagnosing and changing counterproductive styles of management*. San Francisco.

Lindsey, J.L. (2011): Fine art metaphors reveal leader archetypes. *Journal of Leadership & Organizational Studies* 18 (1), 56–63.

Maccoby, M. (1976): *The Gamesman: The new corporate leaders*. New York.

Maccoby, M. (1988): *Why work: Leading the new generation*. New York.

Maccoby, M. (2000): Narcissistic leaders: The incredible pros, the inevitable cons. *Harvard Business Review*, January–February, 69–77.

Neuberger, O. (2002): *Führen und führen lassen*. Stuttgart.

Neuberger, O. and Kompa, A. (1993): *Wir, die Firma. Der Kult um die Unternehmenskultur*. München.

Oglensky, B. D. (1995): Socio-psychoanalytic perspectives on the subordinate. *Human Relations* 48 (9), 1029–1054.

Ouimet, G. (2010): Dynamics of narcissistic leadership in organizations: Towards an integrated research model. *Journal of Managerial Psychology* 25 (7), 713–726.

Rieken, B. (2010): Obamas märchenhafte Wirklichkeit – volkskundlich-psychoanalytische Zugänge. In: Weibler, J. (ed.): *Barack Obama und die Macht der Worte*. Wiesbaden, 142–157.

Rosenstiel von, L. (2009): Grundlagen der Führung. In: Rosenstiel von, L., Regnet, E. and Domsch, M.E. (eds): *Führung von Mitarbeitern. Handbuch für erfolgreiches Personalmanagement.* Stuttgart, 3–27.

Sievers, B. (1994): *Work, death, and life itself.* Berlin.

Stech, E.L. (2010): Psychodynamic approach. In: Northouse, P.G. (ed.) *Leadership: Theory and practice.* London, 271–300.

Tourish, D. (2013): *The dark side of transformational leadership: A critical perspective.* London.

Winkler, I. (2010): *Contemporary leadership theories: Enhancing the understanding of the complexity, subjectivity and dynamic of leadership.* Berlin.

9

Leadership and Power

Joshua Firth and Brigid Carroll

Introduction

Our starting point for this chapter was the puzzling absence of any mention of power in the vast majority of leadership scholarship. On the surface of it, leadership as a concept surely cannot exist without implying or invoking a theory of power, even if skeletal. Given leadership pivots around the fundamental notion of a social process, then regardless of which way this leadership process is theorised, it will either draw upon or redefine an existing theory of power. For us the real question is not whether leadership *implies* power, but why it does not appear to *acknowledge* power. There have been many calls for leadership scholarship to wrestle with a clear and explicit theorisation of power since at least Machiavelli (1908) and Hobbes (1839), and this call is growing ever louder today (Edwards, Schedlitzki, Turnbull, & Gill, 2015; Fletcher, 2004; Gordon, 2002; Ray, Clegg, & Gordon, 2004). Failure to do so risks smuggling in an assortment of assumptions (Gordon, 2002), which will undoubtedly affect not only what we are prepared to call leadership, but where we look, what we will find and what we claim it is for in the first place.

In this vein, we want to unveil the assumptions of power that underpin contemporary leadership theories. Thus we deliberately go deep under the surface of the literature to uncover the dynamics of power that are rarely brought to the surface in leadership research. We hope this offers leadership researchers a way of acknowledging and working with power given that part of the silence on power, we conjecture, may reflect uncertainty about how to work with its vast, entangled and theoretically conflicted terrain. We then aim to characterise the assumptions behind some prominent strands of leadership theory and note what is made possible when power is brought into the open, or conversely what is hidden by its absence.

In light of these objectives, the structure of this chapter is as follows. Rather than attempting to characterise any objective essence or definition of power, we will instead focus on three root metaphors that could be understood as integral in the leadership landscape. In following Rorty (1989), we take root metaphors to be the building blocks with which we construct our knowledge of any concept – in this case leadership. Those three root metaphors are power as causality, power as mandate and power as micro-interaction. We explore each metaphor in terms of power and then in terms of its influence on leadership thinking. We then investigate three contemporary leadership theories – transformational leadership, adaptive leadership and process theory – to show how these root metaphors help us ask critical questions about different dimensions of leadership in them. Our overall objective is to enable a greater reflexivity and criticality on the many ways that power penetrates leadership discourse and scholarship.

Spotlighting Power

We need to acknowledge right from the outset the complexities of working with what must be one of the organisational studies' most salient and debated constructs. We note that researchers and practitioners alike consistently struggle to qualify what they actually mean by power. Even a dictionary search will reveal multiple meanings and interpretations on power. The *Oxford Dictionary* identifies nine different key ideas behind our usage of the word, ranging from an individual capacity, to a variety of relationships, to a synonym for strength, authority, performance, magnification, energy or even as a reference to angels and demons. Indeed our initial search in the ABI/Inform Proquest Database returned 1.4 million articles with power in their abstract alone (and this search was restricted to business publications only). The field of leadership studies displays the same ambiguity where power is given breath amid a range of assumed synonyms, such as influence (e.g. Goncalves, 2013; Kellerman, 2013), authority (e.g. Schweigert, 2007), hierarchy (e.g. Barnes, Humphreys, Oyler, Pane Haden, & Novicevic, 2013), resources (Edmondson, Roberto, & Watkins, 2003, p. 303) or control (e.g. Bennis, Berkowitz, Affinito, & Malone, 1958). Often we note that power is used as a broad unqualified claim that a certain kind of leadership is "powerful" (e.g. Bligh & Hess, 2007; Goleman, Boyatzis, & McKee, 2013; Lisak & Erez, 2015) with no further analysis of power offered. Furthermore, a whole swathe of scholarly research stemmed in the positivist tradition goes so far as to use power as a quantifiable variable in something akin to a leadership equation, for example as in the concept of power–distance (e.g. Mulki, Caemmerer, & Heggde, 2015; Pasa, 2000; Zogjani, Llaci, & Elmazi, 2014). In the vast majority of these references, "power" remains undefined.

In an effort to aid leadership researchers in evoking power in a more explicit and sustained way, we offer three root metaphors that point to a different set of dynamics and emphases in relation to power. We hasten to add that there are numerous ways of conceptualising the field of power and our attempt here is certainly not meant to be definitive or exhaustive in the light of those. We do propose that these three provide a way of approaching power with respect to leadership that we think will be useful and illuminating.

Power as Causality

The first metaphor in our vocabulary is that of causality, and in particular mechanical causality such as the inner workings of a watch. This metaphor is significant for a vocabulary of power because "this seemingly simple definition . . . remains the starting point for a remarkably diverse body of literature" (Hardy & Clegg, 1999, p. 369). This metaphor held sway as the dominant characterisation of power from the seventeenth-century enlightenment philosophy of Hobbes through to its zenith in the mid-twentieth century, especially in political science. Indebted to Clegg (1989) in his *Frameworks of Power*, we can trace power as causality to its modern genesis in the works of Thomas Hobbes. Hobbes was driven by a desire to apply the new advances of Galilean mechanics to human society. Hobbes suggests that:

> Power and Cause are the same thing. Correspondent to cause and effect, are POWER and ACT; nay, those and these are the same things . . . for whensoever any agent has all

those accidents which are necessarily requisite for the production of some effect in the patient, then we say that the agent has the power to produce that effect, if it be applied to a patient . . . Wherefore the power of the agent and the efficient cause are the same thing.

(Hobbes, 1839, ch. X, pp. 127–128, quoted in Ball, 1975, p. 214)

Power, in this metaphor, is not only about producing a desired change effect but also can be seen as originating from a sovereign act. This last point is crucial, for this metaphor relies on the notion that there must be a "who" – an agent (sometimes agents) to whom is attributed the exercise of power. Lastly, it is important to note how this metaphor borrows a sense of predictability from the natural sciences. This serves to allay the nagging fuzziness of power, so that power is consequently reckoned as something empirically observable, quantifiable and predictable.

By the mid-twentieth century the causality metaphor had lost its metaphorical ring and was firmly entrenched as the dominant discourse on power (Ball, 1975). Thus one of its chief proponents, Robert Dahl, could confidently claim his now famous formal definition of power, namely that "A has power over B to the extent that he can get B to do something B would not otherwise do" (1957, pp. 202–203). Dahl used an analogy to precede this formulation, which is worth repeating here, of a situation in which he might stroll out into the middle of the road and try to direct traffic to drive on the opposite side of the road. He contrasts his hypothetical inability to achieve this with the successful efforts of a police officer to do the same thing. This demonstrates what he considers "to be the bedrock idea of power [which is] to say that the policeman acting in this particular role evidently has the power to make automobile drivers turn right or left rather than go on ahead", and thus cause someone ("B") to do something he or she would not otherwise have done (1957, p. 202). This analogy has all three elements of the causal metaphor mentioned by Hobbes: it evokes a representative of the state (sovereignty), who represses a desire to do something and coerces another; it is clearly causally linked both to an observable agent and effect; and it is also amenable to empirical quantification. That is, we can describe the causality as a probability statement; we can quantify the extent of power (i.e. over their traffic patterns but not some other sphere of their lives); and we can identify the bases or resources that invest this power (i.e. traffic laws and penal codes).

Certainty this metaphor, as characterised by Dahl's policeman, resonates with some of our intuitive experiences of power. But it also leads directly to several problems. The first of these is that it introduces the distinction between having and exercising power. This distinction has gone by various names, but the crux of it here is that the policeman appears to *have* the power to stop traffic whether or not he actually exercises this power. This is a problem, because it is internally contradictory to the Humean notion of causality inasmuch as causality requires an observable change effect. If power is by definition the causation of a change in another object, then how can one have power without exercising it? Is it the effect or the capacity to cause an effect? But how does one quantify this capacity prior to its exercise?[1]

The most significant critique of Dahl's formulation (1957) and his subsequent (1961) empirical work on power was levelled against its association of power with elite decision making. This focus was subsequently broadened in two distinct iterations. Bachrach and Baratz (1962, 1963) contended that power is also exercised in *non-decisions*, those occasions in which the exercise of power frustrates the attempts of others to raise a contentious issue for debate. An even more "radical" revision came by way of Lukes (1974), who argued that "*A* may exercise power over *B* by getting him to do what he does not want to do, but he also exercises power over him by influencing, shaping or determining his very wants" (1974, p. 31). Of relevance here is Lukes's attempt to distance himself from individuals as the causal agents of power. In contrast he seemingly posits the responsibility of "the power to control the agenda of politics and exclude potential issues [as being] a function of collective forces and social arrangements" (1974, p. 22).

On the surface it appears that we have stepped out of the A–causes–B model of power, but in fact we have not. Rather what has happened is that Lukes has maintained the same causal notion of power, but merely pushed it out of sight. What betrays Lukes here is the notion of "real interests" (1974, p. 32). His assertion that there is such a thing as "real" interests problematically smuggles causal power back in at some assumed ontologically prior level beyond the recognition of (potentially) either party. *A* in this instance is a set of "collective forces", which *causes B* to do something s/he would not otherwise do, of which *B* may not be fully cognisant. Rather than offer us a radically new metaphor for power, the structuralism behind Lukes's Third Dimension is in fact nothing more than a radically expanded agency, a point which Torfing (2009) makes clearly and of which Lukes's critics were never in doubt (Benton, 1981; Clegg, 1989; Knights & Willmott, 1985). The key point here is that, for as long as the notion of power stays within the metaphor of causality, we cannot escape the primacy of an acting agent, however stretched this "who" may be. Bachrach and Baratz (1962, 1963) and Lukes (1974) rightly recognised the limitations of this view and drew attention to the ways in which power is at work in already constituting who counts as elite and what surfaces in conflict, but none of them succeeded in moving fully beyond this because of the dominant metaphor of causality.

It is no coincidence then that this metaphor sits behind, at least implicitly, much mainstream leadership theory. As the field of leadership was beginning to take off, those who took the time to consider its relationship to power were under no illusions as to its origins. Janda (1960) is an excellent example of this. After complaining at length about the leadership field's failure to acknowledge its power assumptions, he proceeded to point out its significant overlap with power as causality, directly citing Dahl's (1957) definition above. McFarland's (1969) work is another example of exactly this – the direct application of causal power to the concept of leadership. This, we suggest, is the first reason why power is severely under-theorised in the leadership field. That is, it has become axiomatic that leadership equals power which equals causality.

Furthermore, not only does leadership presume causality, it also subscribes to each of the assumptions we saw above. For example, it carries vestiges of sovereignty. More than once, the comparison has made between leadership and the highest sovereignty conceptualised, namely God (Gabriel, 1997; Grint, 2010; Spoelstra & Delaney, 2015). This assumption is most clearly evident in the trait theories of leadership, which continue to flourish under the guise of the modern neuroscience perspective (Taylor, 2015). Here sovereignty is evident, albeit now dressed up as superiority, prowess and endowment. While less obvious elsewhere, it remains the fundamental power assumption behind all leadership theories that presume a leader/follower dyad, including style, contingencies and the "new" (Bryman, 1992) leadership theories (Gordon, 2002). Gordon notes that such theories demonstrate:

> a dualistic orientation in which leaders are given a position of privilege because they are considered to be, either through natural ability or the possession of appropriate attributes, superior to their followers – the argument being that if leaders were not superior, people would not follow them.
>
> *(2002, p. 155)*

Moreover, such theories also frequently associate leadership with positional authority. As we have seen, this same assumption resulted in Dahl's (1961) much criticised focus on elites, an error which has been repeated in the frequent selection of positionally defined managers/leaders as empirical subjects for leadership research (Bedeian & Hunt, 2006); this is also repeated implicitly in the assumptions around the leader's ability to command organisational resources and issue sanctions, as, for example, in leader–member exchange theory (Graen & Uhl-Bien, 1995). And, while there is evidence that the early leadership scholars were aware that position did not equate to leadership (e.g. Morris & Seeman, 1950, p. 152), this awareness has been nevertheless diluted with time, such that Bedeian lamented that "their descendants seem to have forgotten the basis of the early work on which they have built and to be oblivious to the resulting implications for their presumed knowledge" (Bedeian & Hunt, 2006, p. 200).

Most overtly, the causal metaphor smuggles in an assumption of individual agency. This was the assumption that Dahl and his colleagues failed to move beyond, and the same issues are at play in leadership studies. As we have seen, causality relies on an a priori assumption of discrete individuality in order to be able to claim who did what to whom. This commitment has two significant consequences. First, it rules out a thorough consideration of collective leadership, and in its place offers a version of distributed formal responsibility or hidden dominance in which followers/subordinates are given autonomy only so long as they remain compliant (Gordon, 2002). The second consequence is that causality's insistence on individual leaders "causing" an observable effect conveniently renders leadership amenable to scientific analysis. Just as the natural sciences were the original driver of power as causality in Hobbes, the metaphor acts to affix fluid social reality to measurable constructs. Without this fundamental assumption, the very objective of mainstream leadership studies – to know how leadership works best – would need to be reassessed.

Thus leadership pivots upon power as causality – or at least many of its mainstream theories do. But lest we characterise leadership as simply power by another name, it should be pointed out that leadership also tries to distinguish itself from this sort of coercive, top-down power in important ways which our second metaphor picks up on.

Power as Mandate

The causal metaphor had strong origins in the works of Hobbes and prevailed against multiple attempts at stretching it. In contrast, the metaphor of power-as-mandate can be seen to evolve from early hints into a metaphor in its own right. We see these hints as being given shape by Parsons and Follett, but expressed in their fullest form by Arendt.

Parsons is notable inasmuch as he is less interested in the exercise of power and rather focuses on what provides the capacity to exercise power in the first place. This is sometimes referred to as the *power to* side of power in contrast to *power over* (Göhler, 2009). The term itself means various things, but in this sense it refers to the potential or capacity to exercise power. Recalling once again the example of Dahl's policeman directing traffic, this exploration breaks with the notion of power as only about direct causality, and instead wonders why it is that people submit to a policeman in the first place. As a seminal thinker within structural functionalism, Parsons was concerned with the natural evolution of an orderly society by means other than coercion and force. In these terms Parsons defines power as "the generalized medium of mobilizing resources for effective collective action" (Parsons, 1963, p. 108). This definition revolves around the conception of power as being a circulatory medium – in other words currency – that is used to build binding obligations within societies and organisations. Like currency, its value is largely symbolic: it holds because people believe in it. Over time society establishes a body of obligations which are binding insofar as they are associated with authoritative sanctions. Thus the power of Dahl's policeman operates on the symbolic legitimacy that society has placed in its own binding obligations. It is clear that Parsons has not rejected causal notions of power but rather offers inchoate hints of another non-causal dimension to power.

The key difference here is that this power is collective in its origins, rather than stemming from the will of the sovereign.

Follett significantly filled out the metaphor of mandate in offering *power with* in contrast to the *power over* we have so far witnessed. *Power with* is "a jointly developed power, a co-active not coercive power", a distinction she elucidates with the following: "you have rights over a slave, you have rights with a servant" (Follett & Graham, 1995, pp. 103–104). Power must thus be exercised in such a way as to honour and uphold the free choice of its subjects. For her, conflict that results in a victory of one side over the other (cf. Dahl, 1957 above) is an act of domination not power, the consequence of which is the loss of enrichment and learning (Follett & Graham, 1995, p. 86). Rather, the rule of power must seek to utilise conflict as an opportunity to find new and better solutions that honour both sides (Clegg, Courpasson, & Phillips, 2006; Follett & Graham, 1995, p. 74). Follett's theory of power, however, starts from an orientation towards management and thus assumes that the manager already has the mandate to rule (hence the analogy of servants given above). This skews Follett's theory towards something of a warning not to abuse one's "power" by exercising this *over* instead of *with*. It therefore remains unclear whether Follett is redefining power itself or suggesting the right way one ought to wield it.

The last theorist whose work we will review within this metaphor tackles the problem by asserting that power itself can *only* be understood as mandate. Arendt is the key thinker here who critiqued a dangerous tendency to lump words such as strength, force, authority, violence and power all together as if they were synonyms. In contrast, she argues that violence is not an extreme expression of power (cf. causality metaphor, as well as Parsons, 1963), but rather there is an important distinction between the two. Quoting Passerin d'Entrèves (1967), she contends that, if the essence of power is to compel someone to obey one's command, then there is essentially no difference between the commands of a policeman (recall Dahl's example) and that of a gunman (Arendt, 1970, p. 37). Yet, while there is no better means to compel someone than violence, we intuit a significant difference between a policeman and a murderer, which, according to Arendt, we are right to do. So how can we account for this difference if they are on the same continuum?

The answer for Arendt is redefine power in some significant ways. She writes that:

> Power corresponds to the human ability not just to act but to act in concert. Power is never the property of an individual; it belongs to a group and remains in existence only so long as the group keeps together. When we say of somebody that he is "in power" we actually refer to his being empowered by a certain number of people to act in their name. The moment the group, from which the power originated to begin with . . . disappears "his power" also vanishes.
>
> *(1970, p. 44)*

This definition can be regarded as the apex of the mandate metaphor and we would do well to note some of its features. First, we can see that power is inherently collective and thus cannot be referred to without invoking a collectively given mandate. Power is not an individual quality or possession. Thus to use power as an adjective – *A* is "in power" – is to invoke a collective who constitute a person as such. This is significant because it contradicts the usual usage of this word, particularly in reference to the causal metaphor: For Arendt, acts of domination and violence (i.e. coercing B to do otherwise) indicate the *absence* of power rather than its presence, since power is by definition a choice to follow someone who is willingly empowered to rule. Second, power is fundamentally social and needs not reference any particular resources. This is in contrast to violence, argues Arendt, which is always instrumental. The latter lends itself to quantification as resources are measureable, while Arendt's version of power is much fuzzier. Third, power is notably transitory. It may be reified in artefacts such as constitutions or law, but these are secondary to a social relationship at core from which they derive their meaning and authority. In her words, "Power springs up whenever people get together and act in concert" (1970, p. 52).

It is worth noting that Arendt has moved away from a negative conception of power entirely – as have to a lesser extent the other authors in this section. Power is now an entirely positive phenomenon which is wholly oriented towards collective goals. The problem is this runs the risk of dissociating the concept from the everyday experiences we have of power and disempowerment. On this point, Lukes suggests that, while Arendt's theory is "rationally defensible", "by definitional fiat, phenomena of coercion, exploitation, manipulation and so on cease to be phenomena of power – and in consequence disappear from the theoretical landscape" (1974, p. 33–34). In other words, Arendt has defined out of existence any negative connotation related to power. Certainly this is convenient; but it may serve to obscure the inherent tensions of power from those who wield it, even if they are empowered by a collective behind them.

Despite its limitations, the mandate metaphor provides an important addition to our vocabulary of power in that it adds a significant complexity to power. It does this by both offering an alternative to causal coercion and reframing power as the attribute of a collective rather than an individual. These distinctions have been particularly useful for more recent perspectives on leadership, which are redolent, albeit often implicitly, of the mandate metaphor. A similar "definitional fiat" appears to occur in the leadership field, in which leadership is uncritically positioned as a force for collective good, in distinction to lesser forms of coercion such as management (e.g. Kotter, 2001). Such collective auspices are prominent in many of the "new" leadership theories, including spiritual leadership (Palmer, 1994), authentic leadership (Gardner, Avolio, & Walumbwa, 2005), and charismatic leadership (Conger, 1989), and are similarly echoed in other constructs such as collaborative leadership (Chrislip & Larson, 1994) and responsible leadership (e.g. Pless & Maak, 2009; Waldman & Galvin, 2008). The reasoning behind this is understandable, and sometimes explicit. Leadership has a certain romantic quality to it (Meindl, 1995) and mandate's collective and positive conception of power is considerably more attractive than causality's dominance through superiority. Bedeian provides an example of this sentiment. He notes that he:

> happened to re-read Mary [Parker] Follett's 1927 paper "Leader and Expert." In commenting on the "power of leadership," she offered the opinion that "The best leader has not followers but men and women working with him" (p. 235). Now this is an image that I find particularly appealing.
>
> *(Bedeian & Hunt, 2006, p. 191)*

Leadership, it seems, is eager to espouse a different kind of power for itself which is of and for a collective. It is also particularly attracted to the positive associations of a mandate. But there is more to power than a neat dichotomy of positive and negative associations, and to highlight this we will now turn to a third metaphor.

Power as Micro-interaction

In the first metaphor, we were introduced to Dahl's seminal definition that "A has power over B to the extent that he can get B to do something B would not otherwise do" (1957, pp. 202–203).

This was animated in a variety of ways in the causality metaphor, all of which take as an assumption that whatever it is that B "would otherwise do" is or ought to be repressed by A. If we were to persevere with this nomenclature we might say that in the mandate metaphor, B (which would here represent a collective of some sort) empowers A with the mandate to rule, govern or lead – which is a rather striking reversal. In this section we will explore a third metaphor. By way of an introduction to this metaphor, we might say within the terms of this clumsy nomenclature that any attempt to claim such a thing as "what B would otherwise do" is futile: there exists no sphere within human life or thought that is beyond the influence of power. In fact all relations of As and Bs are themselves constituted by the effects of power, while power itself does not originate in the actions of either.

We rely on Foucault for the workings of power in this metaphor. The first key feature of this metaphor is a significant redefinition of what we have so far referred to as "A". For power is neither the possession of the individual nor the collective: "Power is not something that is acquired, seized, or shared, something that one holds on to or allows to slip away; power is exercised from innumerable points, in the inter-play of non-egalitarian and mobile relations" (Foucault, 1978, p. 94), or which Foucault frequently summarises as a "micro-physics of power" (e.g. 1979, p. 22). The first thing we can notice about this metaphor is that it is the inverse of sovereign power. Whereas the latter defined power as by definition top down, this power is bottom up: "Power comes from below; that is, there is no binary and all-encompassing opposition between rulers and ruled at the root of power relations" (Foucault, 1978, p. 94). So this kind of power does not originate from a sovereign. But if power is thus decentralised, what then is its cause?

In fact, Foucault appears to retain only one half of the causal equation, namely effects. Power is inseparable from its effects; indeed power is precisely the aggregate of a vast array of effects strewn throughout the social body. But it has dropped the clearly discernible causal agent we began with. Against the causality metaphor, Foucault asserts that "Power is not built up out of 'wills' (individual or collective), nor is it derivable from interests. Power is constructed and functions on the basis of particular powers, myriad issues, myriad effects of power" (Foucault & Gordon, 1980, p. 188). But crucially, even without a causal agent, Foucault retains a sense of aims and objectives. This point is important and forms the cornerstone of this metaphor. He states that, while power has objectives:

> this does not mean that it results from the choice or decision of an individual subject; let us not look for the headquarters that presides over its rationality; neither the caste which governs, nor the groups which control the state apparatus, nor those who make the most important economic decisions [. . .] the logic is perfectly clear, the aims decipherable, and yet it is often the case that no one is there to have invented them, and few who can be said to have formulated them.
>
> *(Foucault, 1978, p. 95)*

But how can it be that no one is behind these tactics? The actual process of this power is best understood, in Foucault's metaphor, as an aggregate strategy that has resulted from countless capillary power-relations over time. And thus we have the very real effects of power without any discrete causal agent.

There is another insight here, in which power does not operate merely at this level, but also on another meta-analytic level. This is the level of discourse, which is the name given to over-arching strategies formed by, and informing, these micro power-relations. As Foucault puts it: "discourse is not simply that which translates struggles or systems of domination, but is the thing for which and by which there is struggle, discourse is the power which is to be seized"

(1981, pp. 52–53). Put simply, micro-interactions are shaped by discourse and concurrently discourse is constructed through micro-interactions.

But we would be remiss to think that discourse relates only to language. For, as we have seen, discourse is the name given to an ensemble of micro-relations or processes that are in every way tangible. For example, Foucault describes the way that physical arrangements of space facilitate the effects of power, of which his preeminent example is Bentham's (1962) pan-opticon. Here the physical layout isolates individuals from one another while exposing them to constant surveillance. The power of discourse is equally brought to life in practice. Discourses are contingently accomplished as they are enacted or even resisted in practice. Discourses result from "more or less discrete events which, in aggregation, create a new discursive formation" (p. 253). The importance of this point is that it grounds the meta-level concept of discourse firmly within embedded practices: the two are intimately connected.

This insight has been expanded by various methods and theories that focus on the micro-level practices of power relations (e.g., Gordon, Clegg, & Kornberger, 2009; Goss, Jones, Betta, & Latham, 2011; Hardy & Thomas, 2014; Samra-Fredericks, 2005) in that they see power as a tension between agentic reproduction and constraint that is played out in everyday embedded practices, and which is yet part of something much bigger. We therefore see the practice perspectives on power as stretching this metaphor substantially, but arguably staying within it.

The implications of the preceding point leads to one final point within this metaphor, one which is a truly radical departure from the notions above. Recall that the dominant notion of power is repressive, and consequently that its most supreme form is witnessed in the spectacular sovereign execution of an enemy of the state. Foucault argues that such a view of power is "a wholly negative, narrow, skeletal conception of power, one which has been curiously widespread" (Foucault & Gordon, 1980, p. 119). Conversely, Foucault asserts that:

> We must cease once and for all to describe the effects of power in negative terms: it "excludes", it "represses", it "censors", it "abstracts", it "masks", it "conceals". In fact, power produces; it produces reality; it produces domains of objects and rituals of truth.
>
> *(Foucault, 1979, p. 194)*

This productive aspect of power is a novel insight so far in our analysis of power, and is not to be confused with the positive notion expressed by mandate. This is not at all positive. The idea here is that power does not merely alter what people do, it forges what they actually are, or – as it is commonly referred to by Foucault and others – power produces subjectivities. This productive aspect of power reveals its full force, notably by the way it penetrates so many of the assumptions taken for granted in the preceding metaphors.

The significance of this metaphor lies in the insights of how power produces reality, and this is the crux of its contribution. It points to a diffused array of power-effects which loosely align to form a set of objectives. These are discernible at the level of discourse, but their cohesion may be less obvious in their minute manifestations. Such manifestations are sites, or what we are terming micro-interactions of continual struggle over the effects of power, whereby they are enacted, resisted and reproduced. The end result is the constitution of particular subjectivities, of which some are privileged while others are made inferior. This gives the appearance of an A-over-B situation, but this metaphor for power would assert that power is not possessed by A; rather power itself has already constituted A in a position of privilege. Similarly, we can no longer speak of an ontologically prior "what B would otherwise have done" (i.e. Lukes, 1974), since B's possible subjectivities are not natural facts but alternate discourses.

A clear assumption behind this metaphor is that power is everywhere. It is a strength insofar as it makes visible the lines of power that penetrate social life that have been hitherto invisible. Its everydayness brings power down from its elitist heights. It becomes inescapable and thus prompts us to pay attention to it – a point this chapter seeks to address by flushing power out into the open with respect to leadership. Very much in contrast to those we have so far reviewed, leadership perspectives that are underpinned by this metaphor tend to acknowledge power directly. Thus power has been directly theorised in relation to the way leadership is a privileged subjectivity or identity (e.g. Alvesson & Sveningsson, 2003; Carroll & Levy, 2008; Ford, Harding, & Learmonth, 2008; Sveningsson & Larsson, 2006). Further, as was pointed out in Bauman's (1998) critique of Foucault, subjectivities have a certain seductive quality to them, and this has also been said of leadership (Sinclair, 2007). Harding (2014) even described an erotic quality to the power of leadership. Related to this, Driver (2013) has also explored the role of lack in sustaining the leader subjectivity. Last but not least are the those studies which look specifically at the way a leadership identity is constructed through leadership development (Carroll & Levy, 2010) and the technologies of power within these (Carroll & Nicholson, 2014; Gagnon & Collinson, 2014; Nicholson & Carroll, 2013). The strength of these perspectives is a robust denaturalisation of the "leader". We come to find that the leader–follower relationship is not the product of naturally occurring social stratification, but that both positions are themselves already the effects of discourse reproduced by multiple micro-interactions that is sustained and reproduced in everyday interactions.

Reading Leadership Through Root Metaphors of Power

We have proposed that leadership scholarship is actually saturated in theorisations of power and that three root metaphors – causality, mandate and micro-interactions – go a long way in helping us disentangle the tensions of power that our discussions on leadership rely on if not always make explicit. We have tried to show the strengths and weaknesses of each root metaphor and the way they attempt to locate power in very different dimensions of the individual, relational and contextual nature of social processes. We want to turn to three specific theories of leadership – transformational, adaptive and process theory – and attempt an intentional reading of each through the three root metaphors. We should add that there is no simple equation between a leadership theory and any one root metaphor. What we find when we try to read power in leadership is that competing assumptions from different root metaphors co-exist in leadership theories. Acknowledging that co-existence, and working through the tensions should provide a means of bringing more refinement, robustness and nuance to such theories. In doing so, we hope these root metaphors catalyse and expedite leadership theory development.

Transformational Leadership

Transformational theory is widely celebrated as leadership's foremost theorisation of leadership. It would certainly claim the pre-eminent mainstream position in terms of its contemporary canon. Transformational leadership adherents would most likely position this theory squarely in the leadership as mandate territory. Indeed this was the argument of Rusch, Gosetti, and Mohoric (1991) who uncovered surprising links to Follett in Burns's (1978) classic *Leadership*. In an appendix, they detail clear (though unacknowledged) concepts directly borrowed from Follett's work (chiefly Follett, 1949; Follett & Graham, 1995). For example, Burns writes that "Leadership is collective. Leaders, in responding to their own motives, appeal to the motive bases of potential followers. As followers respond, a symbiosis relationship develops that binds leaders and followers together" (1978, p. 426). Burns (1978) also explicates his power metaphor directly, claiming that "power is a relationship among persons" (p. 12). These relationships also define the exercise of power as a collective act" (p. 13). Transformational leadership evinces the mandate metaphor inasmuch as it frames leadership as something that exists of and for a collective, and in its conception of followers as willing participants. It is positioned clearly in distinction to the coercive undertones implicit in causal power, a fact demonstrated in particular by transformational leadership's insistence that it is different to, and considerably better than, transactional leadership (e.g. Waldman, Bass, & Yammarino, 1990).

However, a closer reading of transformational leadership across these metaphors reveals that, while they open up power in ways similar to mandate, this remains very much on the surface, which is a conclusion incidentally reached by both Rusch et al. (1991) and Gordon (2002). Despite its intentions to sidestep the inimical connotations of causal coercion, transformational leadership seems to hold on to the core assumptions of causality even as it speaks a different language. This contradiction can be seen within Burns' original work, in which leaders continue to hold a position of superiority as the individuals who take the initiative, are more skilful, and better at mobilising resources to exercise leadership "over" followers (1978, p. 21). This calls to mind Arendt's observation above that domination is reliant on resources, while power (as mandate) has no need for these. Charisma is particularly notable in this regard, as it does most to obscure transformation leadership's notion of power. Charisma implies the attribution of such from others, and thus suggests the conference of power from a collective (i.e. a mandate). Despite this, charisma remains conceived of in terms of an individual possession or attribute in the new leadership theories, and thus it is yet another resource on which a leader draws in order to influence others.

Most significantly, the notion of "transformation" is essentially another version of A causing B to do otherwise. Here B is now a collective and what A *causes* is their transformation from a lowly state of morality or performance to a "higher" one (Spoelstra & Delaney, 2015). Despite the fact that transformational leadership appears to utilise a more positive conception of power, it remains fundamentally conceptualised and evaluated in terms of causality, so that we can say that this transformational leader caused performance beyond expectations or some other positive "transformation". This is important because it is the assumption that provides the foundation for the scientific certainty espoused in transformational leadership theory. Were these theories to truly embody a genuine mandate metaphor for power, they would also have to forego the same levels of confidence in attributing transformational change to particular individual leaders. The central point here, however, is not a critique of this stance but rather to highlight how a robust and explicit vocabulary of power reveals the assumptions underpinning leadership theory.

Adaptive Leadership

Adaptive Leadership (Heifetz, 1994; Heifetz & Laurie, 1997) would present as having its roots in power as both causality and mandate. Heifetz arrives in this position by outlining the concept of adaptive problems, those being problems for which there is no known solution. These require leadership, rather than the technical orientations of management or expertise. The difference here is that, since the leader does not already know the answer to the problem, leadership must engage the collective to find innovative solutions. Heifetz is thus usefully ambiguous with respect to power: he holds strongly to a language of "the leader" who is clearly drawing on an authority resource (causality). Yet the leader uses this power to create an environment in which another kind of leadership-power can emerge from the collective (e.g. Heifetz, Grashow, & Linsky, 2009, pp. 159–164). Moreover Heifetz notably echoes Follett on conflict and its uses for finding novel solutions (Heifetz et al., 2009, pp. 149–164).

Yet this framing of the use of power as wholesome and collectively empowering actually masks the way "the leader" is clearly holding the reins. As an example, Heifetz promotes the "productive zone of disequilibrium" (Heifetz *et al.*, 2009, pp. 28–32), by which he means increasing people's exposure to the pain of the adaptive problem so that they become engaged. But this masks the dominance of power in two ways. It first suggests a level of manipulation in which a "leader" intervenes against other people's apathy in order to goad them into action. The result may be to engage a collective on its own behalf, but the overwhelming positivity of these aims obscure a hidden dominance in which the leader presumes the mandate to provoke and expose. Second, the "productive zone of disequilibrium" institutes a discourse of engagement and a normalising classification of people (from hot to cold). By asking colleagues/subordinates/followers to declare themselves in terms of their engagement with the issue, a subtle technology of power is at play. That is, people are brought into the open and made to give an account of themselves.

Heifetz argues that this strong leader work is crucial for the accomplishment of collective goals. Indeed Arendt herself concluded that the failure of people to declare their engagement to the issue led in part to the holocaust (1963). But what it does highlight is the way leadership – even when construed as a collective mandate – involves power that cannot be reduced to a purely positive egalitarian phenomenon. It is at this point that the inclusion of the micro-interaction metaphor might actually help, given that, as collectives move to solve adaptive challenges, they initiate a whole series of micro-interactions from which leadership may emerge differently if it is allowed to. The tension between a leader trying to hold the "whole" process and a collective trying to innovate across traditional barriers and constraints would appear a healthy one to make visible. In such micro-interactions discourse, practices, relationships and knowledge become places where power can constitute new realities in theory.

Process Theories of Leadership

Process theories of leadership draw on a process ontology, such as that brought to prominence by Whitehead (1925). In *The Fallacy of Misplaced Leadership*, for example, Martin Wood (2005) demonstrated the strengths of a process-ontological critique, along with a small but growing voice of likeminded scholars (e.g. Crevani, Lindgren, & Packendorff, 2010; Gergen, 2009; Hosking, 1988; Kelly, 2015). Such scholars are dismantling the assumptions we have seen in causality, such as atomistic individuality. Leadership, they argue, is an essentially relational concept which emerges in the context of shared work. Moreover it is a fleeting accomplishment and as such is never possessed by a person; it dissolves as quickly as it appears. Leadership, then, is a constructed phenomenon which animates a social relationship only so long as the collective wills it. Although such theorists seldom explicate power, this conception would appear to be indebted to a micro-interaction metaphor; however, it also clearly echoes the mandate metaphor, especially Arendt. And, given that the power of leadership is thus positioned as a relational construction rather than a natural or personal possession, it tends to acquire the positive flavour of mandate as opposed to the more constitutive power of micro-interaction. Indeed, leadership in such theories is usually positioned precisely as the positive, egalitarian alternative to the mainstream and its assumptions of dominance.

However, a closer reading by way of these metaphors highlights an element of powerlessness in leadership. If leadership hinges on the attribution of power as a mandate from followers, then it may also be observed that leaders are dependent on and subservient to their followers. In other words, leadership is simultaneously a phenomenon of power and powerlessness. Leading is thus a complex and ambiguous position. For example, how does one lead in the face of difficult problems that will require a collective to face failure but without recourse to some other kind of power in moments when a collective wishes to take a more familiar path? Moreover, what is often missing in such accounts of leadership is an acknowledgement of the discourses that underpin what counts as leadership and power, and thus sit behind the attribution and recognition of a leadership mandate in the first place. For leadership is entangled in discourses of patriarchy, masculinity and dominance with the consequence that post-heroic attempts at leading risk being interpreted as passivity and powerlessness (Fletcher, 2004). What is made visible here is the complexity of process theories of leadership, not only in their implicit paradox of power and powerlessness, but also in terms of the micro-interactions of power that already overlay the meaning attributed to interactions. Process theory raises the question of the effect of removing causality from the leadership equation and the degree to which leadership can live with a tension between power and powerlessness which both mandate and, even more so, micro-interaction metaphors raise.

Conclusion

Our readings of three leadership theories would seem to show that power-as-causality is very difficult to move beyond. It chiefly functions to render the social world – including leadership – controllable and agreeable to scientific pragmatism. However, it achieves this at the cost of severe reductionism, and, in its inability to account for the complexity of leadership, it tends to take positional authority as a proxy instead. While leadership may wish to describe its power in terms that hide coercive causality, it is reluctant to stray too far from this metaphor, particularly because it depends upon causality to justify, evaluate and predict leadership effectiveness. Moreover, leadership owes its status not only as a field of scientific inquiry but as a business and social exigency to a claim that is causal at heart. That is, it depends upon the assumption that the leader *causes* B to achieve what it otherwise could not. Recognition of this assumption might be helpful in explaining the vast sums of money that are spent on individual leader development, precisely to develop the efficacy of leaders to succeed at what they are required to undertake. There is a huge challenge here for leadership and leadership development researchers in assessing causality, its reliance on certain channels of power and its limits.

While the simplicity of causality is obviously attractive and deeply embedded in how leadership has been characterised and evolved, we equally see the importance of the mandate metaphor in addressing the collective, constructed nature of leadership. This is a position which appears to be far more fruitful at describing the messy reality of leadership. What this metaphor highlighted was the relationships between leader and led and the positive frame that attention to such a relationship can bring. It similarly accords privileges to certain truths above others, and in this case we saw the temptation to construe leadership as an unqualified positive force for good, which creates a blind spot that conceals the potential for domination in leadership. Lastly we note the analytical utility of the power-as-microinteraction metaphor, particularly in denaturalising what is interpreted as leadership and in seeing leadership as the result of a myriad of micro-moments and interactions, all in turn permeated by overarching discourses that constitute power to certain structures, forms of knowledge, language and practice. While this appears to speak to complexity and hidden sub-texts of power, it also potentially diminishes any hope of identifying leadership within instances which confer power and powerlessness alike on any and all who lead and are led.

Above all, what we have hoped to demonstrate is the importance of power in leadership. The assumptions that each of these metaphors hold are of vital importance for the practice and theory of leadership. In closing we would like to emphasise that none of these metaphors is sufficient by itself. Each reveals, and each hides. What is important therefore is not homogeneity but critical reflexivity. To assume that we mean essentially the same thing by "power" misrepresents the vastly different meanings and root metaphors behind this word and these differences need to be made explicit. As claimed at the beginning of this chapter, power affects what we call leadership, where we look, what we will find, and what we claim it is for in the first place. To that end, we submit these root metaphors as a vocabulary to create a starting place for a richer dialogue on the power(s) of leadership.

Note

1 Note that this problem is resolved by Roy Bhaskar's (Bhaskar, 1975) critical realist conception of causality. Through a stratified ontology, Bhaskar theorises causal power as a real tendency that may or may not bring about an actual effect, due to competing other causal powers in an open system. He further distinguishes any actual effects from what is empirical, meaning that there is no longer a requirement that causality be empirically verifiable. Consequently, the problem dissolves, but nevertheless it remains clear that the underpinning metaphor for power in Bhaskar is still that of causality.

References

Alvesson, M., & Sveningsson, S. (2003). Good visions, bad micro-management and ugly ambiguity: Contradictions of (non-) leadership in a knowledge-intensive organization. *Organization Studies, 24* (6), 961–988.

Arendt, H. (1963). *Eichmann in Jerusalem: A report on the banality of evil.* New York: Viking Press.

Arendt, H. (1970). *On violence.* San Diego, CA: Harcourt, Brace, Jovanovich.

Bachrach, P., & Baratz, M. S. (1962). Two faces of power. *American Political Science Review, 56* (4), 947–952.

Bachrach, P., & Baratz, M. S. (1963). Decisions and nondecisions: An analytical framework. *American Political Science Review, 57* (3), 632–642.

Ball, T. (1975). Models of power: Past and present. *Journal of the History of the Behavioural Sciences, 11* (3), 211–222.

Barnes, B., Humphreys, J. H., Oyler, J. D., Pane Haden, S. S., & Novicevic, M. M. (2013). Transcending the power of hierarchy to facilitate shared leadership. *Leadership & Organization Development Journal, 34* (8), 741–762.

Bauman, Z. (1998). On postmodern uses of sex. *Theory, Culture & Society, 15* (3), 19–33.

Bedeian, A. G., & Hunt, J. G. (2006). Academic amnesia and vestigial assumptions of our forefathers. *The Leadership Quarterly, 17* (2), 190–205.

Bennis, W. G., Berkowitz, N., Affinito, M., & Malone, M. (1958). Authority, power, and the ability to influence. *Human Relations, 11* (2), 143–155.

Bentham, J., & Bowring, J. (1962). *The works of Jeremy Bentham.* New York: Russell & Russell.

Benton, T. (1981). Objective interests and the sociology of power. *Sociology, 15* (2), 161–184.

Bhaskar, R. (1975). *A realist theory of science.* Leeds: Leeds Books Ltd.

Bligh, M. C., & Hess, G. D. (2007). The power of leading subtly: Alan Greenspan, rhetorical leadership, and monetary policy. *The Leadership Quarterly, 18* (2), 87–104.

Bryman, A. (1992). *Charisma and leadership in organizations.* London: Sage Publications.

Burns, J. M. (1978). *Leadership.* New York: Harper & Row.

Carroll, B., & Levy, L. (2008). Defaulting to management: Leadership defined by what it is not. *Organization, 15* (1), 75–96.

Carroll, B., & Levy, L. (2010). Leadership development as identity construction. *Management Communication Quarterly, 24* (2), 211–231.

Carroll, B., & Nicholson, H. (2014). Resistance and struggle in leadership development. *Human Relations, 67* (11), 1413–1436.

Chrislip, D. D., & Larson, C. E. (1994). *Collaborative leadership: How citizens and civic leaders can make a difference.* San Francisco, CA: Jossey-Bass.

Clegg, S. (1989). *Frameworks of power.* London: Sage Publications.

Clegg, S., Courpasson, D., & Phillips, N. (2006). *Power and organizations.* London: Sage Publications.

Conger, J. A. (1989). *The charismatic leader: Behind the mystique of exceptional leadership*. San Francisco, CA: Jossey-Bass.

Crevani, L., Lindgren, M., & Packendorff, J. (2010). Leadership, not leaders: On the study of leadership as practices and interactions. *Scandinavian Journal of Management, 26* (1), 77–86.

Dahl, R. A. (1957). The concept of power. *Behavioral Science, 2* (3), 201–215.

Dahl, R. A. (1961). *Who governs? Democracy and power in an American city*. New Haven, CT: Yale University Press.

Driver, M. (2013). The lack of power or the power of lack in leadership as a discursively constructed identity. *Organization Studies, 34* (3), 407–422.

Edmondson, A. C., Roberto, M. A., & Watkins, M. D. (2003). A dynamic model of top management team effectiveness: Managing unstructured task streams. *The Leadership Quarterly, 14* (3), 297–325.

Edwards, G., Schedlitzki, D., Turnbull, S., & Gill, R. (2015). Exploring power assumptions in the leadership and management debate. *Leadership & Organization Development Journal, 36* (3), 328–343.

Fletcher, J. K. (2004). The paradox of post heroic leadership: An essay on gender, power, and transformational change. *Leadership Quarterly, 15* (5), 647–661.

Follett, M. P. (1949). *Freedom and coordination*. London: Management Publications Trust.

Follett, M. P., & Graham, P. (1995). *Mary Parker Follett – prophet of management: A celebration of writings from the 1920s*. Boston, MA: Harvard Business School Press.

Ford, J., Harding, N., & Learmonth, M. (2008). *Leadership as identity: Constructions and deconstructions*. Basingstoke: Palgrave Macmillan.

Foucault, M. (1978). *The history of sexuality* (R. Hurley, Trans. Vol. 1). New York: Pantheon Books.

Foucault, M. (1979). *Discipline and punish: The birth of the prison* (A. Sheridan, Trans.). New York: Vintage Books.

Foucault, M. (1981). The order of discourse. In R. Young (Ed.), *Untying the text: A post-structuralist reader* (pp. 48–78). Boston, MA: Routledge & Kegan Paul.

Foucault, M., & Gordon, C. (1980). *Power/knowledge: Selected interviews and other writings: 1972–1977*. New York: Pantheon.

Gabriel, Y. (1997). Meeting God: When organizational members come face to face with the supreme leader. *Human Relations, 50* (4), 315–342.

Gagnon, S., & Collinson, D. (2014). Rethinking global leadership development programmes: The interrelated significance of power, context and identity. *Organization Studies, 35* (5), 645–670.

Gardner, W. L., Avolio, B. J., & Walumbwa, F. O. (Eds.) (2005). *Authentic leadership theory and practice Origins, effects and development*. San Diego, CA: Elsevier.

Gergen, K. J. (2009). *Relational being beyond self and community*. New York: Oxford University Press.

Göhler, G. (2009). 'Power to' and 'power over'. In S. R. Clegg & M. Haugaard (Eds.), *The SAGE handbook of power* (pp. 24–40). London: Sage Publications.

Goleman, D., Boyatzis, R., & McKee, A. (2013). *Primal leadership, With a New Preface by the Authors: Unleashing the power of emotional intelligence*. New Haven, CT: Harvard Business Press.

Goncalves, M. (2013). Leadership styles: The power to influence others. *International Journal of Business and Social Science, 4* (4), 1–3.

Gordon, R. (2002). Conceptualizing leadership with respect to its historical–contextual antecedent to power. *Leadership Quarterly, 13* (2), 151–167.

Gordon, R., Clegg, S., & Kornberger, M. (2009). Embedded ethics: Discourse and power in the New South Wales police service. *Organization Studies, 30* (1), 73–99.

Goss, D., Jones, R., Betta, M., & Latham, J. (2011). Power as practice: A micro-sociological analysis of the dynamics of emancipatory entrepreneurship. *Organization Studies, 32* (2), 211–229.

Graen, G. B., & Uhl-Bien, M. (1995). Relationship-based approach to leadership: Development of leader–member exchange (LMX) theory of leadership over 25 years: Applying a multi-level multi-domain perspective. *The Leadership Quarterly, 6* (2), 219–247.

Grint, K. (2010). The sacred in leadership: Separation, sacrifice and silence. *Organization Studies, 31* (1), 89–107.

Harding, N. (2014). Reading leadership through Hegel's master/slave dialectic: Towards a theory of the powerlessness of the powerful. *Leadership*, 1742715014545143.

Hardy, C., & Clegg, S. (1999). Some dare call it power. In S. R. Clegg & C. Hardy (Eds.), *Studying organization: Theory and method* (pp. 368–387). London: Sage.

Hardy, C., & Thomas, R. (2014). Strategy, discourse and practice: The intensification of power. *Journal of Management Studies, 51* (2), 320–348.

Heifetz, R. A. (1994). *Leadership without easy answers*. Cambridge, MA: Belknap Press of Harvard University Press.

Heifetz, R. A., Grashow, A., & Linsky, M. (2009). *The practice of adaptive leadership: Tools and tactics for changing your organization and the world*. Boston, MA: Harvard Business Press.

Heifetz, R. A., & Laurie, D. L. (1997). The work of leadership. *Harvard Business Review, 75*, 124–134.

Hobbes, T. (1839). De Corpore. In W. Molesworth (Ed.), *English Works* (Vol. I). London: John Bohn.

Hosking, D. M. (1988). Organizing, Leadership and Skilful Process. *Journal of Management Studies, 25* (2), 147–166.

Janda, K. F. (1960). Towards the explication of the concept of leadership in terms of the concept of power. *Human Relations, 13*, 345–363.

Kellerman, B. (2013). Leading questions: The end of leadership–redux. *Leadership, 9* (1), 135–139.

Kelly, S. (2015). Leadership and process. In B. Carroll, J. Ford, & S. N. Taylor (Eds.), *Leadership: Contemporary critical perspectives* (pp. 26–44). London: Sage Publications.

Knights, D., & Willmott, H. (1985). Power and identity in theory and practice. *The Sociological Review, 33* (1), 22–46.

Kotter, J. P. (2001). What leaders really do. *Harvard Business Review, 68* (3), 103–111.

Lisak, A., & Erez, M. (2015). Leadership emergence in multicultural teams: The power of global characteristics. *Journal of World Business, 50* (1), 3.

Lukes, S. (1974). *Power: A radical view*. London: Macmillan.

Machiavelli, N. (1908). *The prince*. New York: E.P. Dutton.

McFarland, A. S. (1969). *Power and leadership in pluralist systems*. Stanford, CA: Stanford University Press.

Meindl, J. R. (1995). The romance of leadership as a follower-centric theory: A social constructionist approach. *The Leadership Quarterly, 6* (3), 329–341.

Morris, R. T., & Seeman, M. (1950). The problem of leadership: An interdisciplinary approach. *American Journal of Sociology, 56* (2), 149–155.

Mulki, J. P., Caemmerer, B., & Heggde, G. S. (2015). Leadership style, salesperson's work effort and job performance: The influence of power distance. *The Journal of Personal Selling & Sales Management, 35* (1), 3.

Nicholson, H., & Carroll, B. (2013). Identity undoing and power relations in leadership development. *Human Relations, 66* (9), 1225.

Palmer, P. J. (1994). Leading from within: Out of the shadow, into the light. In J. A. Conger (Ed.), *Spirit at work: Discovering the spirituality in leadership*. San Francisco, CA: Jossey-Bass.

Parsons, T. (1963). On the concept of political power. In S. Lukes (Ed.), *Power* (pp. 94–143). New York: New York University Press.

Pasa, S. F. (2000). Leadership influence in a high power distance and collectivist culture. *Leadership & Organization Development Journal, 21* (8), 414–426.

Passerin d'Entrèves, A. (1967). *The notion of the state: An introduction to political theory*. London: Oxford University Press.

Pless, N., & Maak, T. (2009). Responsible leaders as agents of world benefit: Learnings from "Project Ulysses". *Journal of Business Ethics, 85* (1), 59–71.

Ray, T., Clegg, S. R., & Gordon, R. (2004). A new look at dispersed leadership: Power, knowledge and context. In J. Storey (Ed.), *Leadership in organizations: Current issues and key trends* (pp. 320–337). London: Routledge.

Rorty, R. (1989). *Contingency, irony, and solidarity*. Cambridge: Cambridge University Press.

Rusch, E. A., Gosetti, P. P., & Mohoric, M. (1991, November 7–10). *The social construction of leadership: Theory to praxis*. Paper presented at the Annual Conference on Research on Women and Education, San Jose, CA.

Samra-Fredericks, D. (2005). Strategic practice, "discourse" and the everyday interactional constitution of "power effects". *Organization, 12* (6), 803–841.

Schweigert, F. J. (2007). Learning to lead: Strengthening the practice of community leadership. *Leadership, 3* (3), 325–342.

Sinclair, A. (2007). *Leadership for the disillusioned: Moving beyond myths and heroes to leading that liberates*. Crows Nest, N.S.W: Allen & Unwin.

Spoelstra, S., & Delaney, H. (2015). Transformational leadership: Secularised religion? In B. Carroll, J. Ford, & S. N. Taylor (Eds.), *Leadership: Contemporary critical perspectives* (pp. 26–44). London: Sage Publications.

Sveningsson, S., & Larsson, M. (2006). Fantasies of leadership: Identity work. *Leadership, 2* (2), 203–224.

Taylor, S. N. (2015). Trait theories of leaders and leadership: From Ancient Greece to twenty-first-century neuroscience. In B. Carroll, J. Ford, & S. N. Taylor (Eds.), *Leadership: Contemporary critical perspectives* (pp. 26–44). London: Sage Publications.

Torfing, J. (2009). Power and discourse: Towards an anti-foundationalist concept of power. In S. R. Clegg, & M. Haugaard (Eds.), *The SAGE handbook of power* (pp. 108–125). London: Sage Publications.

Waldman, D. A., Bass, B. M., & Yammarino, F. J. (1990). Adding to contingent–reward behavior the augmenting effect of charismatic leadership. *Group & Organization Management, 15* (4), 381–394.

Waldman, D. A., & Galvin, B. M. (2008). Alternative perspectives of responsible leadership. *Organizational Dynamics, 37* (4), 327–341.

Whitehead, A. N. (1925). *Science and the modern world.* New York: Macmillan.

Wood, M. (2005). The fallacy of misplaced leadership. *Journal of Management Studies, 42* (6), 1101–1121.

Zogjani, A., Llaci, S., & Elmazi, E. M. P. A. (2014). The role of power in effective leadership and follow-ership: The Albanian case. *Romanian Economic and Business Review, 9* (1), 89–102.

10

Followership in Context

A More Nuanced Understanding of Followership in Relation to Leadership

Mary Uhl-Bien and Melissa Carsten

Leadership research is traditionally rooted in hierarchical thinking in which managers (leaders) influence subordinates (followers) in an effort to produce positive results for a work unit and organization (Baker, 2007; Bligh, 2011; Collinson, 2006; Shamir, 2007). This paradigm has resulted in deeply rooted assumptions that only managers can lead and only subordinates can follow (Bedeian & Hunt, 2006; Yukl, 2012). However, today's organizations call for more dynamic relationships in which all organizational members have capabilities to both lead and follow in various situations. To meet this need, and the changing nature of organizations, theoretical and empirical advances in the leadership literature have sparked discussion around new forms of leadership, including distributed leadership (Bolden, 2011; Gronn, 2002), relational leadership (Ospina & Foldy, 2010; Uhl-Bien, 2006; Uhl-Bien & Ospina, 2012), and leadership in networks (Balkundi & Kilduff, 2006).

Inherent in these new ways of thinking is the realization that leadership is about more than leaders—it is also about followers, and how leaders and followers work together in a relational process to co-create leadership (Fairhurst & Uhl-Bien, 2012). These views go beyond treatments of followers as simply recipients of leaders' influence; they consider leadership as occurring in a relational process (Shamir, 2007). Relational (process) views draw attention to the ways in which leaders and followers engage with one another through combined acts of leading and following to co-construct leadership and followership and their outcomes (Uhl-Bien, 2006; Uhl-Bien, Riggio, Lowe, & Carsten, 2014). Identity (process) views describe how, through a series of claiming and granting behaviors, individuals acting in context negotiate relational identities as leaders and followers (DeRue & Ashford, 2010). Both of these views differ from traditional leadership perspectives in that they do not privilege the leader. Instead they position followers as key players (i.e., partners) in the creation, evolution, and impact of leadership and its outcomes. To exaggerate the point, some process researchers even privilege the role of followers, arguing that it is in following that leadership is created (i.e., without followers there can be no leaders) (Uhl-Bien & Ospina, 2012; Uhl-Bien et al., 2014).

Accompanying these new views of leadership is a growing body of research on followership theory (Carsten, Uhl-Bien, West, Patera, & McGregor, 2010; Crossman & Crossman, 2011; Lapierre & Carsten, 2014; Sy, 2010). Followership theory is the study of the nature and impact of followers and following in the leadership process (Uhl-Bien et al., 2014). Some research on followership reverses the lens to consider how leaders view followers (Shamir, 2007; Sy, 2010). Other approaches investigate how subordinates perceive and enact their role with leaders, ranging from traditional definitions of passive and deferent followership (DeCremer & VanDijk, 2005; De Vries & Van Gelder, 2005) to more engaged and proactive views of followership (Carsten et al., 2010; Carsten, Uhl-Bien, & Jayawikrema, 2013; Dvir & Shamir, 2003).

The purpose of this chapter is to delve deeper into our understanding of followership by examining it across different contexts to see how changes in context can illuminate our understanding of followership in relation to leadership. Across the contexts we highlight behaviors, roles, and choices associated with followership. We begin with hierarchy to examine followership in the more classic organizational context. This context represents a position-based perspective that equates managers with leaders and subordinates with followers (Bedeian & Hunt, 2006). A misleading assumption associated with this context is that managers always lead and subordinates always follow. As we will show, this assumption is flawed even in hierarchical structures, in that the most effective leadership relationships occur when managers also follow and subordinates also lead (Graen & Uhl-Bien, 1995).

We then consider followership in two more recently emerging contexts: distributed leadership (Bolden, 2011; Gronn, 2002) and leadership in networks (Balkundi & Kilduff, 2006). In the first, we explore followership and leadership not as position-based phenomena but as negotiated roles and identities constructed in relational and organizational contexts. In the second, we consider followership and leadership in networks, focusing on two special network cases: open source software projects (von Hippel & von Krogh, 2003) and social media (Kumar, Novak, & Tomkins, 2010). Network contexts allow us to extend understanding of followership by showing that, although followership can be both an identity and a behavior, the two are not necessarily aligned. As seen in social media and open source contexts, one can hold a follower identity while engaging in leadership behaviors. In this way, we show the value of a contextual perspective (Osborn, Hunt, & Jauch, 2002), and demonstrate that by changing contexts we can uncover richer, and more deeply nuanced, understandings of followership in relation to leadership.

Followership in a Hierarchical Context

Followership in a hierarchical context is associated with the subordinate position in an organizational hierarchy. The traditional approach to followers in this context is leader-centric, with the actions of the leader (manager) privileged and emphasis placed on how leader characteristics, behaviors, and qualities impact work unit outcomes (Yukl, 2012). These approaches have long identified managers as the best individuals to influence decision-making and change in organizations (Hecksher, 1994). As a result, followers (subordinates) are typically seen as lacking initiative or influence, and acting at the mercy of the leader's direction (Baker, 2007; Bligh, 2011; Chaleff, 2003; Kelley, 1992).

More recent advances in followership theory are moving beyond this more limited view of followership as *subordination* to consider how individuals holding subordinate positions construct their roles and identities in a variety of ways, not just as passive followers (Collinson, 2006; Howell & Mendez, 2008; Kelley, 1992). The most prominent of these is follower role-orientation research (Carsten et al., 2013; Uhl-Bien et al., 2014). This framework, associated with a hierarchical organizational context, emanates from qualitative findings of Carsten et al. (2010) demonstrating that individuals hold a range of followership schema ranging from passive to proactive, and these schema influence social constructions of followership, depending on contextual factors. The findings of Carsten et al. (2010) challenge traditional notions of followership as passive and deferent by showing that followers differentially construct and enact their subordinate position, depending on the schema they hold and the organizational climate.

Building on the concept of schema as they relate to social construction, Carsten and colleagues (2013) draw from role-orientation theory (Parker, 2000) to investigate follower role orientation. Follower role orientation refers to how subordinates define a follower role, how broadly they perceive the tasks associated with the role, and how they believe they should approach a follower role to be effective (Parker, 2007). Follower role orientations develop over time as individuals interact with authority figures in hierarchical contexts (Fiske & Taylor, 1991; Louis, 1980). This research represents a follower-centric approach to followership (Shamir, 2007; Uhl-Bien & Pillai, 2007), viewing followership as a role enactment socially constructed in the context of a subordinate position. Although subordinates maintain followership schema, or deeply seated beliefs, in accordance with their follower role orientations, whether they can act on these schema largely depends on contextual variables, such as leadership style and organizational climate (Carsten et al., 2010).

These contextual factors present dilemmas and choices for subordinates as they enact their roles. For example, a key challenge occurs when one's follower role orientation (i.e., schema) does not match the situation. In these cases, subordinates must decide how they are going to behave. In some cases this can be a choice, such as when proactive followers choose to become passive; in other cases this can be a dilemma, such as passive followers being asked to be proactive when they are not capable of doing so. Another challenge occurs when subordinates must decide whether or not to follow. For those with an anti-authoritarian orientation, not following may be their natural proclivity, in which case they will need to recognize the risk and potential consequences of their actions. In all cases, a key element underlying role enactment is the identity and corresponding behaviors the individual associates with the subordinate position.

Passive Follower Role Orientation: A "Subordinate" Role Enactment

Followership research has begun to identify different types of role orientations followers can adopt (Carsten et al., 2010; Carsten & Uhl-Bien, 2012; Carsten et al., 2013). One type is the passive follower-role orientation, in which subordinates believe that followership is best enacted by being silent, deferent, and obedient to the leader (Carsten et al., 2010; Howell & Mendez, 2008; Kelley, 1992). This role orientation is rooted in bureaucratic beliefs that hierarchy produces legitimate authority figures (i.e., leaders) who are more capable and effective than followers (Weber, 1968). The assumption is that managerial positions carry the responsibility for making decisions, solving problems, gathering information, and setting goals (DeCremer & VanDijk, 2005; De Vries & Van Gelder, 2005; Ravlin & Thomas, 2005). Thus, individuals with a passive follower-role orientation believe that managers are in the best position to "lead" (Hecksher, 1994; Howell & Mendez, 2008; Kelley, 1992), while subordinates are in the best position to "follow" (i.e., a "subordinate" role enactment).

Role orientations are derived from beliefs and schema regarding what it means to follow (Parker, 2000, 2007), but behavior in the follower role is also heavily influenced by context (Carsten et al., 2010; Parker, Wall, & Jackson, 1997). When the context matches a passive role orientation, i.e., when it is highly bureaucratic in nature, subordinates with a passive orientation enact their role using traditional, passive following behaviors. These behaviors represent deference in the form of obedience, compliance, and following without question or challenge. Given that in today's environment support for passive followership styles is waning (Chaleff, 2003; Griffin, Neal, & Parker, 2007; Morgeson, Delaney-Klinger, & Hemingway, 2005), it is likely that the biggest dilemma followers with a passive orientation face is the request to be more proactive (Carsten et al., 2010). Followers with a passive role orientation are likely to find themselves in a context that thrives on participation, or with a leader who encourages collaborative decision-making. Because these subordinates believe that followers should be passive, deferent, and obedient, however, they may find requests to engage and participate uncomfortable (Bjugstad, Thach, Thompson, & Morris, 2006; Carsten et al., 2010; Kelley, 1992; Townsend & Gebhardt, 1997).

For the follower with a passive role orientation, the choice of whether to engage or remain deferent is a difficult one that could cause anxiety or distress. Moreover, their lack of engagement may present challenges to managers who rely on subordinates to contribute valuable knowledge or information. On the other hand, subordinates with a passive role orientation may experience dilemmas associated with following a directive that is deemed unethical or inappropriate (Carsten & Uhl-Bien, 2012; Uhl-Bien & Carsten, 2007). When confronted with an unethical or unreasonable request from a leader, research suggests that approximately 30 percent of subordinates will obey the request, even though they know it is inappropriate (Blass, 2009; Burger 2009; Milgram, 1965). Followers with a passive role orientation, who believe that directives should be followed without question, would be faced with the choice of disobeying a directive (which is in direct violation of their role beliefs) or complying with the unethical request. Subordinates who comply may cause serious harm to others or the organization, whereas subordinates who disobey may incur negative consequences. Thus, the traditional hierarchical context does not allow much flexibility for a subordinate with a passive role orientation, who believes that a manager's directive should be obeyed and followed.

Anti-authoritarian Follower Role Orientation: A "Non-follower" Role Enactment

A second type of follower role orientation is anti-authoritarian orientation (Bennett, 1988). Subordinates with this orientation believe that the follower role involves warding off the leader's attempt to manipulate and subjugate followers (Bennett, 1988; Gregory, 1955; Weitman, 1962). This orientation is the converse of authoritarianism—the belief that superiors are all knowing and all powerful (Gregory, 1955). Individuals with an anti-authoritarian orientation reject the idea that superiors can tell them what to do; they may even have an angry or contemptuous reaction to influence attempts by a superior (Bennett, 1988; Weitman, 1962) (i.e., a "non-follower" role enactment). They prefer to work autonomously and object to power being used to force them into submission (Gregory, 1955).

Individuals with an anti-authoritarian role orientation would be especially challenged in a highly bureaucratic and centralized context where little can be accomplished without approval from the top. In these situation they may become frustrated, and perhaps even aggressive, in their behavior (Bennett, 1988; Kreml, 1977), finding it difficult to remain silent in situations that are especially confining and do not allow for autonomous decision-making. These hierarchical contexts, therefore, present risks for those holding an anti-authoritarian orientation. Hierarchical contexts could prompt them to react in ways that attempt to ward off a sense of powerlessness or engage in desperate attempts to regain power (Fleming & Spicer, 2007).

Such non-following role enactments are likely to impede completion of work assignments, causing frustration for managers and hurting the follower's reputation. In an interesting twist on abusive supervision (Tepper, 2000), these individuals may even be viewed as abusive subordinates due to passive–aggressive or destructive covert behaviors toward the manager (Liu, Kwan, Wu, & Wu, 2010). Hence, those with anti-authoritarian follower orientation must manage this orientation to identify role enactments that avoid potentially negative consequences to themselves and those around them, and that are not detrimental to performance.

Co-production Follower Role Orientation: A "Partnership" Role Enactment

A third type of follower role orientation is a co-production orientation (Carsten & Uhl-Bien, 2012). This orientation is associated with the belief that a strong follower role is necessary for supporting leaders in accomplishing the organizational mission (Chaleff, 2003; Crossman & Crossman, 2011; Dvir & Shamir, 2003; Hollander, 1993; Hollander & Offermann, 1990; Rost, 1993). It is based on the assumption that leaders are better able to solve problems, make decisions, divert crises, and meet objectives *because* of the contribution of followers (Bjugstad et al., 2006; Crossman & Crossman, 2011).

Individuals with a co-production orientation see the follower role as effective and influential, and therefore work to partner with leaders to advance organizational outcomes. They engage with their managers in ways that "advance the mission of their department or organization" (Carsten et al., 2010, p. 556). As a result individuals holding this belief are likely to enact their subordinate role by collaborating constructively with leaders, anticipating problems, thinking ahead, taking initiative to help the unit, and being willing to challenge leaders if they are headed in the wrong direction (Carsten et al., 2010). This view is consistent with Dvir and Shamir's (2003) assertion that followers with critical, independent orientations are active and dominant rather than submissive, making them more likely to contribute actively to the leadership process.

The hierarchical context presents a number of choices and dilemmas for subordinates as they attempt to enact their follower role (Carsten et al., 2010). For example, by engaging in a partnership with the manager and enacting "leadership" behaviors, these subordinates may find themselves overloaded by the increased amount of responsibility and accountability they assume. Given the hierarchical context, they may also find themselves under-rewarded or under-recognized for their contributions. In these situations, subordinates with a co-production orientation may face heightened levels of burnout or exhaustion (Seltzer & Numerof, 1988; Stanley, 2004). If they become frustrated at the lack of acknowledgment of their efforts, they may also withdraw their extra-role behaviors—an action that would likely be accompanied by dissatisfaction, given that withdrawal behavior is not consistent with this orientation.

Individuals with a co-production orientation may face dilemmas when working in an environment that does not support the idea of partnership behaviors from subordinates. A subordinate with a co-production role orientation may become frustrated when the leadership climate discourages participation. For example, Carsten et al. (2010) describe the frustration of a highly proactive follower working for a leader who "over-managed" subordinates. In these situations, it may be easy for subordinates with a co-production orientation to feel disillusioned because their voice and engagement is not acceptable (de Vries, Jehn, & Terwel, 2012). Subordinates are left with the choice of whether to engage (and be perceived as inappropriate) or remain silent and hold back the ideas or suggestions they feel are needed for the betterment of the group. When the environmental pressure associated with "falling in line" and taking a one-down position causes these followers to remain silent, the organization could suffer from missed opportunities or valuable ideas.

A subordinate with a co-production orientation may be equally dismayed when attempting to work with a manager who maintains a more laissez-faire leadership approach (Bass & Stogdill, 1990). Given their belief that followers should engage in partnership and immerse themselves in the leadership process, working with a laissez-faire manager who is not interested in leading may present a real challenge for them (Skogstad, Einarsen, Torsheim, Aasland, & Hetland, 2007). These individuals would likely try to engage with the leader, present ideas and suggestions for improvement, and work to secure information and resources, only to be met with inaction by the manager. In this case, the individuals might even find themselves taking on part of the manager's leadership role, or facing the dilemma of wanting to lead but being constrained by a hierarchical context.

Behavioral (Process) View

An interesting element of a co-production orientation, therefore, is this "partnership" role enactment that it creates. This enactment does not align cleanly with our traditional notions that leaders (managers) lead and followers (subordinates) follow; rather, in a partnership enactment many of the behaviors taken on by the subordinate are more leadership than followership (Graen & Uhl-Bien, 1995). We can see this if we adopt a behavioral (process) view that recognizes leadership and followership in the behaviors that comprise the leadership relationship. In partnership relationships, it is not uncommon for subordinates to take responsibility for leading a project (i.e., subordinate as leader) and for managers to then follow the subordinate (i.e., manager as follower of the subordinate). Managers construct this followership role enactment by deferring to the subordinate's expertise, direction, guidance, and decisions in ways that advance and support successful project performance. In other words, the role of the manager in these situations is to support the subordinate by providing resources, sponsorship, and support.

The use of the term "follower" to describe the subordinate and "leader" to describe the manager is therefore not appropriate in these contexts (Bedeian & Hunt, 2006). This has led some to look for alternative words to describe followership (Rost, 1993). Others describe leadership as "leaderful" (Raelin, 2011) or call for abandoning the term follower altogether (Miller, 1998; Raelin, 2011; Rost, 2008). But eliminating the term follower is not the appropriate response, as it misrepresents the nature of the leader–follower relationship. As described by Shamir (2012), eliminating followers from the leadership equation means we are no longer studying leadership. Leadership is a disproportionate influence relationship—for leadership to occur someone must be willing to follow another at least some of the time, or there is no leadership (Shamir, 2007, 2012; Uhl-Bien et al., 2014).

Our contextual analysis thus reveals the importance of the relational (behavioral process) view. According to the behavioral process view, leadership and followership are co-constructed when individuals engage with one another in combined acts of leading and following (Fairhurst & Uhl-Bien, 2012; Uhl-Bien et al., 2014). In this case, by acceding to the subordinate's decision or expertise, the manager is allowing the subordinate disproportionate influence: the manager is following, the subordinate is leading, and together they are co-constructing followership and, hence, leadership.

Followership in a Distributed Leadership Context

Although we can catch glimmers of the behavioral process view in the hierarchical context, it emerges more clearly in distributed leadership approaches. Distributed leadership approaches view leadership not as the responsibility of just one person but as a social process (Bolden, 2011). They offer an alternative to heroic leadership approaches by arguing that responsibility for leadership is not just in manager positions, but also dispersed throughout the organization (Brown & Hosking, 1986; Bennett, Wise, Woods, & Harvey, 2003). As described by Bennett and colleagues (2003), these approaches view leaders as an emergent property of a group or network of interacting individuals in which varieties of expertise are distributed across the many, not the few. A distributed leadership context, therefore, is one in which leadership and followership are not identified or defined by hierarchical roles but, rather, negotiated in relational interactions between people working together in organizations (Raelin, 2011; Uhl-Bien, 2006).

Interestingly, although distributed leadership approaches are offered as an alternative to leader-centric views of leadership, they share elements of leader-centrism in their privileging of leadership over followership. Rarely in this literature is followership mentioned, and the importance of followership to leadership constructions is not recognized. As described by Gronn (2002), the suggestion in these approaches is to dispense with followership and view organizations instead as a "process of negotiation between leaders" (Gronn, 2002, p. 427 citing Miller, 1998, p. 18). Eliminating followers from consideration, however, means we have moved away from leadership and crossed into some other phenomenon, like teamwork or collaboration (Shamir, 2007, 2012). Although the distributed leadership literature might not acknowledge the importance of followership, by definition, follower identities and/or behaviors must be present for leadership to occur.

A distributed leadership context thus provides a rich opportunity to study leadership and followership unencumbered by formally prescribed positional definitions. By removing leadership and followership from position, distributed approaches require us to consider more precisely what makes a phenomenon leadership (and followership). To answer this, scholars turn to two approaches: the behavioral (process) view and the identity construction view. The first, as described above, considers leadership as a co-creation constructed in leading and following behaviors (Fairhurst & Uhl-Bien, 2012; Ospina & Uhl-Bien, 2012). The second, elaborated below, describes leadership as occurring in a process of negotiated follower and leader identities.

The Identity Construction Process: Follower and Leader Claims and Grants

DeRue and Ashford (2010) advanced their model of leader and follower identity construction process specifically for leadership in distributed contexts. This model draws from research on "identity work" (Snow & Anderson, 1987) and social interactionism (Blumer, 1969) to describe how people form, maintain, strengthen, and revise individual identities. The model considers not only the identity work undertaken by individuals to project particular images but also identity work contributed by others, who mirror back and support (or fail to support) the image being projected. Through identity construction processes, "the ambiguity of organizational membership is resolved" (DeRue & Ashford, 2010, p. 631) when individuals project images that are then matched with either affirming, or disaffirming, responses.

The identity construction model begins with enactment of an identity: the meaning attached to the self (DeRue & Ashford, 2010; Gecas, 1982). The choice to adopt a particular identity depends on three interacting self-construal mechanisms: individual, relational, and collective (Brewer & Gardner, 1996). *Individual* self-construal occurs independently, without input from or interaction with others. It involves seeing oneself and one's own characteristics and behaviors as being more aligned with a particular role or identity (e.g., a follower, a leader). *Relational* self-construal is developed through interaction with others. It involves relying on how others see and treat you (e.g., a follower, a leader). *Collective* construal involves the endorsement of a follower identity from a larger community. This occurs when a larger group collectively bestows a certain identity (follower, leader) on the individual.

Applied to followership, a follower identity is assumed depending on how individuals see themselves and how others see and treat them, which occurs through what DeRue and Ashford (2010) call "claiming" and "granting" behaviors. Claiming behaviors involve the actions people take to establish themselves with a particular identity; "granting" behaviors involve the actions others use to bestow a particular identity on an individual. For example, an individual claims a follower identity by stating or demonstrating that they plan to follow the lead or orders of another. An individual can also claim a follower identity through more subtle behaviors, such as not taking initiative or deferring to another. An individual grants a follower identity when he or she advises another to just follow orders or expects another to do as told. An individual can grant another a follower identity by offering an affirming response to the other's follower claim, such as a follower claim of "I'll follow your lead" being matched with, "Okay good. I'll lead and you follow" (a follower grant). It can also be a more subtle or subversive grant, such as leaving the other out of an important decision-making or brainstorming session.

In a distributed leadership context, when an individual is granted a follower role they are identified by someone else as a follower and urged to take a follower identity. This may happen directly, such as when an individual is told they have to follow another member, or indirectly, such as when another member claims a leader identity and thus grants followership to others. Followership grants, without a reciprocal claim, however, may result in a power struggle. When two individuals attempt to claim leadership without a supporting grant from the other, it could result in counterproductive behaviors that detract from goal achievement (Fleming & Spicer, 2007). This could also damage personal relationships by inciting sabotage or undercutting in an attempt to gain power. In situations where no one is willing to claim a follower identity the resulting power struggles will also drain valuable energy and resources required to complete the work.

An opposite situation could occur when everyone claims a follower identity and no one is willing or able to be a leader. In these cases, groups could struggle due to lack of leadership, or they could end up with individuals being granted leadership who are not necessarily the most competent. An excess of follower claims could also occur on projects or topics that are undesirable, controversial, or risky, where no one wants to assume responsibility. Individuals who claim followership are, in essence, allowing themselves to be influenced by the leader, foregoing privileges that come with being the leader. This is not to say that they abdicate responsibility or fail to contribute to work outcomes. Rather they might fully engage in a work product but fail to gain the recognition and rewards received by leaders. If they do this continually over time, individuals who repeatedly claim a follower identity could eventually be labeled a "follower," and lose potential benefits associated with leadership. DeRue and Ashford (2010) note that repeated claiming of an identity will impact the way that others perceive one's ability to lead or follow (e.g., repeatedly claiming a follower identity could play against individuals when they subsequently attempt to claim a leader identity).

Identity (Process) View

The identity (process) view in a distributed leadership context thus lets us see how identity plays into followership theory. The identity view implies that followership is constructed through a collective negotiation process that results in at least one person taking on a follower identity and at least one person taking on a leader identity. An assumption of this approach is that follower identity is then associated with follower/following behaviors. As we will see in the next context, however, this assumption is not necessarily true: Although individuals in a network context take on a follower identity, this does not necessarily mean their behaviors will reflect what we typically associate with a follower role.

Followership in a Network Context

In recent years, network contexts have become more predominant in our thinking about how individuals coordinate together to accomplish goals. A primary factor behind the emergence of network contexts (e.g., social media, open source software projects) is technological advancements that enable individuals to self-organize around common needs and interests (Baldwin & von Hippel, 2011; Gallivan, 2001). To understand this, a growing body of work is turning attention to how networks are affecting organizational dynamics in informal organizational contexts (Ahuja, 2000; Burt, 2012; Burt, Kilduff, & Tasselli, 2013).

These contexts are not defined by formal structure, or a predetermined set of roles and responsibilities. Instead individuals make choices about when and how to lead and follow and how they will contribute to a project or cause. For example, both online social networking and social media are characterized by members oscillating between "starter" and "follower" roles in an effort to share ideas, content, and expertise (Huberman, Romero, & Wu, 2008; Mathioudakis & Kaudas, 2009). In both examples, leader and follower roles are not enforced by hierarchical positions, and there is no formal organization to ensure that leaders lead and followers follow. Followership in this context is completely voluntary—there is no one to tell you who or how to follow (Yilmaz, 2008). Similarly, open source software projects rely on administrators who begin new innovative projects, and followers who voluntarily join in and contribute to advancing and completing a project (von Krogh, Spaeth, & Lakhani, 2003). Whereas some followers may be directly involved in the effort advanced by the leader (i.e., developers), others may take a more distant role of observer (Kumar et al., 2010).

Compared to hierarchical structures, in which individuals are position bound, in network structures followers have the opportunity to stop following at any time (Roberts, Hann, & Slaughter, 2006; von Hippel & von Krough, 2003). Thus, the choices followers make in this context revolve around whom to follow, how engaged they will be with the leader's movement or project, and whether they will be an advocate to get others involved or passively watch the movement advance. Identifying as a follower of a leader in an open source context is often motivated by a strong sense of belonging that drives collective action (Bagozzi & Dholakia, 2006) or an attraction to a common goal advocated by the leader that creates a sense of shared identity (Haslam & Platow, 2001). As a result, network contexts provide rich environments for studying naturally occurring followership enactments. Without the confines of formal organizational structure, followers in a network context can come and go as they please, share as much or as little information as they want, and make their own decisions regarding which projects they contribute to.

Indeed, in open source software projects followers make up the core work group—leaders would not have a project if it were not for followers. Many such followers contribute to multiple projects at one time (Stam, 2009). Followers choose to engage because they are motivated by the task (Hertel, Niedner, & Herrmann, 2003; Shah 2006), because they believe they have expertise and knowledge to contribute (Roberts et al., 2006), or because they are interested in working with the leader (Hahn, Moon, & Zhang, 2008). In both open source and social media contexts, individuals follow another due to friendship, partnership, or even celebrity worship of the leader (Chesbrough, 2003).

Thus, deciding to be a follower and contribute to an open source project means deciding to be a thought leader, providing expertise and vital information, and ensuring that the project is advanced through one's contributions (Franke & von Hippel, 2003; Lakhani & von Hippel, 2003). Observers who regularly follow a project leader often contribute by spreading news and information to and about the leader. They do this by initiating, sharing, and promoting ideas both within and across project contexts—acting as a bridge to help advance more innovative and effective outcomes (Fleming & Waguespack, 2007; Shah & Tripsas, 2007). Following in this context entails a large amount of work and responsibility, so much so that followers take on many "leader-like" functions, such as sharing vital information and influencing others to get involved and contribute to a project or movement (Chesebrough, 2003). Similarly, in social media contexts, individuals acting as fans help a celebrity become more popular by spreading the word and drawing more fans into the celebrity network.

Paradox: Follower Identity, Leadership Behaviors

In this way, networks provide a unique context for studying followership because they break norms regarding what we believe followers do. Central throughout leadership and followership literature is the belief that followership is identified by some form of deferent or compliant behavior (Uhl-Bien et al., 2014). Although this behavior may range from more passive to more proactive, followers are deferent to leaders in ways that respect the leader's higher status (Kelley, 1992; Yukl, 2012).

In network contexts, deference can be seen in identity but not necessarily in behavior. An individual might be willing to self-identify as a follower to another—granting another a leader identity and claiming for self a follower identity. But rather than being deferent, a follower in this context typically best enacts the role by acting as a leader to enhance, promote, or advance the leader's cause or reputation (Roberts et al., 2006). Followers help spread the word, raise awareness, provide feedback or news, and contribute new knowledge and understanding (Franke & von Hippel, 2003; Lakhani & von Hippel, 2003). When they do this they act as "influencers"—a role typically characterized as defining behaviors of leadership.

In network contexts, therefore, we have self-identified followers acting as leaders. In some ways, this is an extension of the co-production orientation identified in the hierarchical context in which individuals identify their role as partnering with leaders to advance the mission and goals. The difference is that in the hierarchical context followers clearly know their place—they recognize that the hierarchical structure dictates that they ultimately defer to the leader's authority. In network contexts this deference is not embedded in the structure but, instead, is completely voluntary. If anything, these structures mean that leaders are even more dependent on others acting as followers (cf. Kotter, 1977).

This suggests that followership is a more complex phenomenon than previously thought. Rather than assuming we can identify followers clearly by position, behavior, or identity, network contexts call for us to use a combined approach in studying and understanding followership. In networks, such as open source projects and social media, followership is based purely on identity (rather than formal organization); identities and roles can change rapidly; and leaders and followers are truly interdependent (the leader is not a leader without others following, and the follower is not a follower without a leader to identify with). Networks thus represent the most complex and fluid states of leadership and followership of the three contexts.

Conclusion

A key contribution of followership to leadership research and practice is the recognition that followership is inextricably linked to leadership, and as such, followers play just as important a role in leadership as leaders. We have long known this from our understanding of leadership, mutual dependence, and effective management. In his now classic article, Kotter (1977) identified dependency relationships—in which managers are also dependent on subordinates—as an inherent part of the managerial job. Despite this, our dominant line of thinking in leadership research remains rooted in the hierarchical, manager-subordinate relationship of leaders and followers.

A challenge presented by the hierarchical paradigm is that it places followers in a one-down position where they are not expected to contribute much to leadership. We know, however, that leaders increasingly rely on followers for sharing ideas (i.e., voice) (Van Dyne & LePine, 1998), proactively changing the work setting (i.e., taking charge) (Morrison & Phelps, 1999), and contributing in ways that go above and beyond their stated work responsibilities (i.e., issue selling and organizational citizenship behaviors) (Dutton, Ashford, O'Neill, & Lawrence, 2001; Podsakoff & MacKenzie, 1997). Although we expect followers to become more engaged in the leadership process and take more responsibility for work outcomes, our hierarchical thinking about the importance of leaders prevents us from fully understanding the necessity for followership in the co-creation of leadership.

In this chapter we attempt to address this problem by considering followership in context. This contextual analysis reveals three varying views of followership. The first is the classic position (role) view that equates leader with manager, and follower with subordinate (Shamir, 2007). This view is associated with role-based approaches that study followership as a (formal) role enactment (Carsten et al., 2010). The second is a behavioral (process) view that views leadership and followership as co-constructed in combined acts of leading and following (Uhl-Bien et al., 2014). Because this view does not equate position with leadership and followership, it allows us to see that managers can (and often do) engage in following behaviors/roles with subordinates, and subordinates can (and often do) engage in leading behaviors/roles with managers. The behavior view also allows us to see that non-following behaviors can result in no leadership being co-constructed, despite positional roles that might indicate otherwise (Uhl-Bien et al., 2014). The third is an identity (process) view, which says that followership is constructed when, through an interactive social process, individuals take on (or reinforce) a follower identity (DeRue & Ashford, 2010).

When examined across contexts, these views provide a more nuanced understanding of followership than previously considered. Our examination of the hierarchical context supports the view that for some, classic representations of followers as passive and obedient (Kelley, 1992) are valid. For others, however, followership role enactments reflect "partnership" (i.e., co-production) relationships more consistent with leadership than followership. In these partnership relationships, traditional notions of managers as leaders and subordinates as followers break down (Bedeian & Hunt, 2006). The behavioral process view helps us understand this by recognizing followership and leadership as occurring in the behaviors (i.e., following and leading behaviors) individuals use to co-construct these phenomena.

When we move to a distributed leadership context, the behavioral process view becomes more apparent. In a distributed leadership context, leadership and followership are clearly identified by combined acts of leading and following, which together generate the disproportionate influence process that defines leadership (Shamir, 2012). A distributed leadership contexts adds another perspective to followership theory: that of followership as an identity construction process (DeRue & Ashford, 2010). From this perspective, followership occurs when individuals take on a follower identity and act in accordance with this identity in their engagement with leaders. Hence, follower identities are associated with at least some form of deference behavior on the part of the follower (e.g., a leader grant to another and a follower claim for self).

In network contexts, however, we see that none of the perspectives alone explain what is going on—instead we need a combined approach across the behavior and identity perspectives. In network structures, such as social media and open source software projects, individuals take on a follower identity but behave in ways more consistent with leadership. Therefore, we cannot assume that a follower identity is enacted in the same way across contexts. Followership in a hierarchical structure involves strongly embedded norms that do not translate to network environments. Whereas in hierarchical structures the term follower clearly carries with it a negative connotation (hence the desire to abandon the term altogether—Rost, 2008; Raelin, 2011), in network structures following another is carried more like a badge of pride or a vote of approval. In these contexts to say you are following someone is to recognize them in a positive way, and to indicate a desire to want to join with them as a means to elevate one's own sense of status and belonging. Contrary to subordination, followership in a network context conveys a sense of camaraderie, togetherness, and support for attainment of mutually desired needs and outcomes.

In this way, we see an evolution in understanding and meaning of followership as we examine it across contexts. We also see that followership is more nuanced than traditionally understood. Our analysis reveals an urgent need to pay more serious attention to the positioning and importance of followership in leadership and organizational studies. Trends clearly suggest that the nature of work is only going to continue to move toward more distributed and network contexts. As this happens the belief that followership is uninteresting or unimportant is no longer accurate. Rather, the desire by so many in social media and network contexts to self-identify as followers should serve as a clarion call to both scholars and practitioners that followership is among the most important new frontiers in leadership research.

References

Ahuja, G. (2000). Collaboration networks, structural holes and innovation: A longitudinal study. *Administrative Science Quarterly, 45* (3), 425–455.

Bagozzi, R.P., & Dholakia, U.M. (2006). Open source software user communities: A study of participation in Linux user groups. *Management Science, 52* (7), 1099–1115.

Baker, S.D. (2007). Followership. *Journal of Leadership & Organizational Studies, 14* (1), 50–60.

Baldwin, C., & von Hippel, E. (2011). Modeling a paradigm shift: From producer innovation to user and open collaborative innovation. *Organization Science, 22* (6), 1399–1417.

Balkundi, P., & Kilduff, M. (2006). The ties that lead: A social network approach to leadership. *The Leadership Quarterly, 17,* 419–439.

Bass, B.M., & Stogdill, R.M. (1990). *Bass & Stogdill's handbook of leadership: Theory, research, and managerial applications.* New York: Free Press.

Bedeian, A.G., & Hunt, J.G. (2006). Academic amnesia and vestigial assumptions of our forefathers. *The Leadership Quarterly, 17* (2), 190–205.

Bennett, J.B. (1988). Power and influence as distinct personality traits: Development and validation of a psychometric measure. *Journal of Research in Personality, 22* (3), 361–394.

Bennett, N., Wise, C., Woods, P., & Harvey, J. (2003). *Distributed leadership: Full report.* Nottingham, UK: National College for School Leadership.

Bjugstad, K., Thach, E. C., Thompson, K. J., & Morris, A. (2006). A fresh look at followership: A model for matching followership and leadership styles. *Journal of Behavioral and Applied Management, 7* (3), 304–319.

Blass, T. (2009). From New Haven to Santa Clara: A historical perspective on the Milgram obedience experiments. *American Psychologist, 64* (1), 37–45.

Bligh, M.C. (2011). Followership and follower-centred approaches. In A. Bryman, K. Grint, B. Jackson, M. Uhl-Bien, & D. Collinson (Eds.), *The Sage handbook of leadership* (1180–1216). London: Sage Publications.

Blumer, H. (1969). *Symbolic interactionism: Perspective and method.* Englewood Cliffs, NJ: Prentice-Hall.

Bolden, R. (2011). Distributed leadership in organizations: A review of theory and research. *International Journal of Management Reviews, 13,* 251–269.

Brewer, M.B., & Gardner, W. (1996). Who is this "we"? Levels of collective identity and self representations. *Journal of Personality and Social Psychology, 71* (1), 83–93.

Brown, M.H., & Hosking, D.M. (1986). Distributed leadership and skilled performance as successful organization in social movements. *Human Relations, 39* (1), 65–79.

Burger, J.M. (2009). Replicating Milgram: Would people still obey today? *American Psychologist, 64* (1), 1–11.

Burt, R.S. (2012). Network-related personality and the agency question: Multirole evidence from a virtual world. *American Journal of Sociology, 118* (3), 543–591.

Burt, R.S., Kilduff, M., & Tasselli, S. (2013). Social network analysis: Foundations and frontiers on advantage. *Annual Review of Psychology, 64,* 527–547.

Carsten, M.K., & Uhl-Bien, M. (2012). Follower beliefs in the co-production of leadership: Examining upward communication and the moderating role of context. *Journal of Psychology/Zeitschrift Fur Psychologie, 220* (4), 210–220.

Carsten, M.K., Uhl-Bien, M., & Jayawickrema, A. (2013). Reversing the lens in leadership research: Investigating follower role orientations and leader outcomes. Paper presented at the annual conference for the Southern Management Association, New Orleans, LA.

Carsten, M.K., Uhl-Bien, M., West, B.J., Patera, J.L., & McGregor, R. (2010). Exploring social constructions of followership: A qualitative study. *The Leadership Quarterly, 21* (3), 543–562.

Chaleff, I. (2003). *The courageous follower: Standing up to and for our leaders* (2nd ed.). San Francisco, CA: Berrett-Koehler Publishing.

Chesebrough, H.W. (2003). *Open innovation: The new imperative for creating and profiting from technology.* Boston: Harvard Business Press.

Collinson, D. (2006). Rethinking followership: A post-structuralist analysis of follower identities. *The Leadership Quarterly, 17* (2), 179–189.

Crossman, B., & Crossman, J. (2011). Conceptualising followership: A review of the literature. *Leadership, 7* (4), 481–497.

de Cremer, D., & Van Dijk, E. (2005). When and why leaders put themselves first: Leader behaviour in resource allocations as a function of feeling entitled. *European Journal of Social Psychology, 35* (4), 553–563.

DeRue, S., & Ashford, S. (2010). Who will lead and who will follow? A social process of leadership identity construction in organizations. *Academy of Management Review, 35* (4), 627–647.

de Vries, R.E., & van Gelder, J.-L. (2005). Leadership and the need for leadership: Testing an implicit followership theory. In B. Schyns & J.R. Meindl (Eds.), *Implicit leadership theories: Essays and explorations* (277–304). Greenwich, CT: JAI Press.

de Vries, G., Jehn, K.A., & Terwel, B.W. (2012). When employees stop talking and start fighting: The detrimental effects of pseudo voice in organizations. *Journal of Business Ethics, 105,* 221–230.

Dutton, J.E., Ashford, S.J., O'Neill, R.M., & Lawrence, K.A. (2001). Moves that matter: Issue selling and organizational change. *Academy Of Management Journal, 44* (4), 716–736.

Dvir, T., & Shamir, B. (2003). Follower developmental characteristics as predicting transformational leadership: A longitudinal field study. *The Leadership Quarterly, 14* (3), 327–344.

Fairhurst, G.T., & Uhl-Bien, M. (2012). Organizational discourse analysis (ODA): Examining leadership as a relational process. *The Leadership Quarterly, 23* (6), 1043–1062.

Fiske, S.T., & Taylor, S.E. (1991). *Social cognition,* 2nd ed. New York: Mcgraw-Hill Book Company.

Fleming, L., & Waguespack, D.M. (2007). Brokerage, boundary spanning and leadership in open innovation communities. *Organization Science, 18* (2), 165–180.

Fleming, P., & Spicer, A. (2007). *Contesting the corporation: Struggle, power and resistance in organizations.* Cambridge: Cambridge University Press.

Franke, N., & von Hippel, E. (2003). Satisfying heterogeneous user needs via innovation toolkits: The case of Apache security software. *Research Policy, 32* (7), 1199–1215.

Gallivan, M.J. (2001). Striking a balance between trust and control in a virtual organization: A content analysis of open source software case studies. *Information Systems Journal, 11* (4), 277–304.

Gecas, V. (1982). The self-concept. *Annual Review of Sociology, 8,* 1–33.

Graen, G.B., & Uhl-Bien, M. (1995). Relationship-based approach to leadership: Development of a leader–member exchange (LMX) theory of leadership over 25 years: Applying a multi-level multi-domain perspective. *Leadership Quarterly, 6,* 219–247.

Gregory, W.E. (1955). "Authoritarianism" and authority. *The Journal of Abnormal and Social Psychology, 51* (3), 641–643.

Griffin, M.A., Neal, A., & Parker, S.K. 2007. A new model of work role performance: Positive behavior in uncertain and interdependent contexts. *Academy of Management Journal, 50* (2): 327–347.

Gronn, P. (2002). Distributed leadership as a unit of analysis. *The Leadership Quarterly, 13,* 423–451.

Hahn, J., Moon, J.Y., & Zhang, C. (2008). Emergence of new project teams from open source software developer networks: Impact of prior collaboration ties. *Information Systems Research, 19* (3), 369–391.

Haslam, S.A., & Platow, M.J. (2001). The link between leadership and followership: How affirming social identity translates vision into action. *Personality and Social Psychology Bulletin, 27* (11), 1469–1479.

Heckscher, C. (1994). Defining the post-bureaucratic type. In C. Heckscher & A. Donnellon (Eds.), *The post-bureaucratic organization: New perspectives on organizational change* (14–62). Thousand Oaks, CA: Sage Publications.

Hertel, G., Niedner, S., & Hermann, S. (2003). Motivation of software developers in open source projects: An internet-based survey of contributors to the Linux kernel. *Research Policy, 32* (7), 1159–1177.

Hollander, E.P. (1993). Legitimacy, power, and influence: A perspective on relational features of leadership. In M.M. Chemers & R. Ayman (Eds.), *Leadership theory and practice: Perspectives and directions*. San Diego, CA: Academic Press.

Hollander, E.P., & Offermann, L.R. (1990). Power and leadership in organizations: Relationships in transition. *American Psychologist, 45* (2), 179–189.

Howell, J., & Mendez, M. (2008). Three perspectives on followership. In R. Riggio, I. Chaleff, & J. Lipman-Blumen (Eds.), *The art of followership: How great followers create great leaders and organizations* (25–40). San Francisco: Jossey-Bass.

Huberman, B.A., Romero, D.M., & Wu, F. (2008). Social networks that matter: Twitter under the microscope. Available at SSRN 1313405.

Kelley, R. (1992). *The power of followership: How to create leaders people want to follow, and followers who lead themselves*. New York: Broadway Business.

Kotter, J. (1977). Power, dependence and effective management. *Harvard Business Review*, July–August, 125–136.

Kreml, W.P. (1977). *The anti-authoritarian personality*. Oxford: Pergamon Press.

Kumar, R., Novak, J., & Tomkins, A. (2010). Structure and evolution of online social networks. In *Link mining: Models, algorithms, and applications* (337–357). New York: Springer.

Lakhani, K.R., & von Hippel, E. (2003). How open source software works: "Free" user-to-user assistance. *Research Policy, 32* (6), 923–943.

Lapierre, L., & Carsten, M.K. (Eds.) (2014) *Followership: What is it and why do people follow?* Bingly, UK: Emerald.

Liu, J., Kwan, H.H., Wu, L.Z., & Wu, W. (2010). Abusive supervision and subordinate supervisor-directed deviance: The moderating role of traditional values and the mediating role of revenge cognitions. *Journal of Occupational and Organizational Psychology, 83*, 853–856.

Louis, M.R. (1980). Surprise and sense making: What newcomers experience in entering unfamiliar organizational settings. *Administrative Science Quarterly, 25*, 226–251.

Mathioudakis, M., & Koudas, N. (2009, March). Efficient identification of starters and followers in social media. In *Proceedings of the 12th International Conference on Extending Database Technology: Advances in Database Technology* (pp. 708–719). ACM.

Milgram, S. (1965). Some conditions of obedience and disobedience to authority. *Human Relations, 18* (1), 57–76.

Miller, E.J. (1998). The leader with vision: Is time running out? In E.B. Klein, F. Gabelnick, & P. Herr (Eds.), *The psychodynamics of leadership* (3–25). Madison, CT: Psychosocial Press.

Morgeson, F.P., Delaney-Klinger, K.A., & Hemingway, M.A. (2005). The importance of job autonomy, cognitive ability, and job-related skill for predicting role breadth and job performance. *Journal of Applied Psychology, 90*, 399–406.

Morrison, E.W., & Phelps, C.C. (1999). Taking charge at work: Extra role efforts to initiate workplace change. *Academy of Management Journal, 42* (4), 403–419.

Osborn, R.N., Hunt, J.G., & Jauch, L.R. (2002). Toward a contextual theory of leadership. *Leadership Quarterly, 13*, 797–837.

Ospina, S., & Foldy, E.G. (2010). Building bridges from the margins: The work of leadership in social change organizations. *The Leadership Quarterly, 21*, 292–307.

Ospina, S., & Uhl-Bien, M. (2012). *Advancing relational leadership research: A dialogue among perspectives* (xix–xlvii). Charlotte, NC: Information Age Publishers.

Parker, S. (2000). From passive to proactive motivation: The importance of flexible role orientations and role breadth self-efficacy. *Applied Psychology: An International Review, 49* (3), 447–469.

Parker, S.K. (2007). That is my job: How employees' role orientation affects their job performance. *Human Relations, 60* (3), 403–434.

Parker, S.K., Wall, T.D., & Jackson, P.R. (1997). "That's not my job": Developing flexible employee work orientations. *Academy of Management Journal, 40* (4), 899–929.

Podsakoff, P.M., & MacKenzie, S.B. (1997). Impact of organizational citizenship behavior on organizational performance: A review and suggestion for future research. *Human Performance, 10* (2), 133–151.

Raelin, J. (2011). From leadership-as-practice to leaderful practice. *Leadership, 7* (2), 195–211.

Ravlin, E.C., & Thomas, D.C. (2005). Status and stratification processes in organizational life. *Journal of Management, 31* (6), 966–987.

Roberts, J.A., Hann, I.H., & Slaughter, S.A. (2006). Understanding the motivations, participation and performance of open source software developers: A longitudinal study of the Apache projects. *Management Science, 52* (7), 984–999.

Rost, J.C. (1993). *Leadership for the twenty-first century.* New York: Praeger.

Rost, J.C. (2008). Followership: An outmoded concept. In R. Riggio, I. Chaleff, & J. Lipman-Blumen (Eds.), *The art of followership: How great followers create great leaders and organizations* (53–64). San Francisco, CA: Jossey-Bass.

Seltzer, J., & Numerof, R.E. (1988). Supervisory leadership and subordinate burnout. *Academy of Management Journal, 31* (2), 439–446.

Shah, S.K. (2006). Motivation, governance, and the viability of hybrid forms in open source software development. *Management Science, 52* (7), 1000–1014.

Shah, S.K., & Tripsas, M. (2007). The accidental entrepreneur: The emergent and collective process of user entrepreneurship. *Strategic Entrepreneurship Journal, 1*, 123–140.

Shamir, B. (2007). From passive recipients to active co-producers: Followers' roles in the leadership process. In B. Shamir, R. Pillai, M.C. Bligh, & M. Uhl-Bien (Eds.), *Follower-centered perspectives on leadership: A tribute to the memory of James R. Meindl*: ix–xxxix. Greenwich, CT: Information Age Publishing.

Shamir, B. (2012). Leadership research or post-leadership research: Advancing leadership theory versus throwing out the baby with the bath water. In M. Uhl-Bien & S. Ospina (Eds.), *Advancing relational leadership research: A dialogue among perspectives* (477–500). Charlotte, NC: Information Age Publishers.

Skogstad, A., Einarsen, S., Torsheim, T., Aasland, M.S., & Hetland, H. (2007). The destructiveness of laissez-faire leadership behavior. *Journal of Occupational Health Psychology, 12* (1), 80–92.

Snow, D.A., & Anderson, L. (1987). Identity work among the homeless: The verbal construction and avowal of personal identities. *American Journal of Sociology, 92*, 1336–1371.

Stam, W. (2009). When does community participation enhance the performance of open source software companies? *Research Policy, 38* (8), 1288–1299.

Stanley, T.L. (2004). Burnout: A manager's worst nightmare. *Supervision, 65* (5), 11–13.

Sy, T. (2010). What do you think of followers? Examining the content, structure, and consequences of implicit followership theories. *Organizational Behavior and Human Decision Processes, 113* (2), 73–84.

Tepper, B.J. (2000). Consequences of abusive supervision. *Academy of Management Journal, 33*, 261–289.

Townsend, P.L., & Gebhardt, J.E. (1997). *Five-star leadership: The art and strategy of creating leaders at every level.* New York: John Wiley & Sons.

Uhl-Bien, M. (2006). Relational leadership theory: Exploring the social processes of leadership and organizing. *The Leadership Quarterly, 17* (6), 654–676.

Uhl-Bien, M., & Carsten, M. (2007). Being ethical when the boss is not. *Organizational Dynamics, 36* (2), 187–201.

Uhl-Bien, M., & Ospina, S. (2012). *Advancing relational leadership research: A dialogue among perspectives.* Charlotte, NC: Information Age Publishers.

Uhl-Bien, M., & Pillai, R. (2007). The romance of leadership and the social construction of followership. In B. Shamir, R. Pillai, M. Bligh, & M. Uhl-Bien (Eds.), *Follower-centered perspectives on leadership: A tribute to the memory of James R. Meindl* (187–210). Charlotte, NC: Information Age Publishers.

Uhl-Bien, M., Riggio, R.E., Lowe, K.B., & Carsten, M.K. (2014). Followership theory: A review and research agenda. *The Leadership Quarterly, 25*, 83–104.

Van Dyne, L., & LePine, J.A. (1998). Helping and voice extra-role behaviors: Evidence of construct and predictive validity. *Academy of Management Journal, 41* (1), 108–119.

von Hippel, E., & von Krogh, G. (2003). Open source software and the "private–collective" innovation model: Issues for organization science. *Organization Science, 14* (2), 209–223.

Von Krogh, G., Spaeth, S., & Lakhani, K.R. (2003). Community, joining, and specialization in open source software innovation: A case study. *Research Policy, 32* (7), 1217–1241.

Weber, M. (1968). *Economy and society: An outline of interpretative sociology.* New York: Bedminster Press.

Weitman, M. (1962). More than one kind of authoritarian. *Journal of Personality, 30*, 193–208.

Yilmaz, L. (2008). Innovation systems are self-organizing complex adaptive systems. *Proceedings of AAAI Spring Symposium: Creative Intelligent Systems*, Palo Alto, CA, March 26–28.

Yukl, G. (2012). *Leadership in organizations* (8th ed.) New York: Prentice Hall.

11

Leadership Succession in Politics and Business

Converging Logics?

Fredrik Bynander and Paul 't Hart

Building Them Up, Cutting Them Down

In early February 2015, Australian politics was once again rocked by speculation that a third successive incumbent prime minister was about to be dumped by his own party colleagues. It had happened to Australian Labor Party Prime Ministers Kevin Rudd (elected November 2007, toppled June 2010) and his replacement Julia Gillard (toppled June 2013). And now Liberal Party Prime Minister Tony Abbott came perilously close to undergoing the same fate, just fifteen months after having been elected with a large margin by an electorate deeply weary of the unsavory spectacle of three years of factional warfare and political rivalry within the Labor Party. Had all these leaders failed so comprehensively so soon as to compel their colleagues to turn off their political oxygen? What were their colleagues hoping to achieve in making a leadership change? And why keep going down this road in the face of clear evidence that dumping a leader is a self-defeating strategy for a party keen on winning the next election (Tiffen, 2015)?

One can write this example off as merely another illustration of the irrational nature of politics (or of the substandard quality of the people who land in political leadership roles). But it does not take much to find strong indications that remarkably similar practices of leadership succession occur in the allegedly more rational business world too. Business management scholar Rakesh Khurana (2002) studied patterns of CEO recruitment in large publicly traded U.S. companies and found evidence of a persistent, self-defeating pattern of boards recruiting 'charismatic' CEOs: outsiders to the companies they were brought in to lead, highly self-confident communicators, explicitly tasked with, and bent on, 'shaking up' the place. Hailed as corporate 'saviors' at the point of entry, these new leaders set about frantically slashing costs and reorganizing corporate strategies, structures, and business practices. When corporate performance does not improve fast, their momentum stalls as quickly as it was created. The same coalition of forces – investment analysts, institutional investors, recruitment firms, and boards – that brought them in will now dump them, only to surrender the leadership of the company to yet another charismatic outsider (Beck and Wiersema, 2011).

The parallels are striking. In both instances, clever, experienced, and self-interested people authorize and de-authorize leaders in the belief that doing so at the right time and in the right way can change the fate of the organization. In both instances, organizations often claim to embrace 'succession planning,' and sometimes devote noticeable preparatory effort to design orderly processes of elite circulation – akin to cooperative 'relay races,' as opposed to the competitive 'horse races' (Finkelstein et al., 2009). However, more often than not the practice of succession in both business and political organizations is much more 'messy' and 'political' than that (Bynander and 't Hart, 2008; Frederickson et al., 1988). Clearly, in some settings and at least some of the time, the institutional dynamics of leadership selection in politics and business are more similar than one might think. They are certainly a lot more similar than the two virtually completely segmented, self-referential fields of scholarship allow their students and readers to see. By examining both in parallel and showing areas of overlap or potential complementarity, we can enrich leadership studies both theoretically and methodologically. The prize, in short, is to deepen insight into the dynamics of leadership successions in both contexts.

In this chapter, we attempt to build some bridges to cover the chasm. We explore what both disciplines – business studies and political science – have to offer in the way of theory and research about leadership succession. For each, we describe key insights about the causes, processes, and outcomes of leadership succession. In the final part of the chapter, we explore similarities and differences and develop propositions for the kind of comparative cross-sectoral research that can serve to energize both fields of research, which though quite (political science) and extraordinarily (business studies) active and productive in their distinct ways have also become somewhat stale and predictable.

We use the term *leadership succession* to denote changes in the occupation of senior positions within political parties (in or out of government) and firms. The most conspicuous and consequential successions in politics are those of heads of government and party leaders and in business of CEOs and non-executive board chairs. In politics and business alike, successions can proceed in scheduled (popular elections; term limits) or unscheduled (illness/death; ad-hoc resignations and dismissals) fashion. The initiative to end the term of an incumbent can be voluntary (initiated by the incumbent), consensual (mutual agreement between incumbent and selection bodies), or involuntary (dismissals or forced resignations triggered by a breakdown of confidence among key constituents, moves from competitors and their supporters, public calls for resignation, critical media coverage, or intense legal scrutiny). The selection of a successor can likewise be consensual (succession as a 'relay race') or competitive (a 'horse race'; see Bynander and 't Hart, 2006; Finkelstein et al., 2009: 165–168). Business scholars have traditionally focused more on unscheduled CEO departures, whereas political scientists have been equally interested in scheduled (particularly through elections) and unscheduled departures of party leaders.

Perhaps it is good to mention in advance that succession research in both sectors has some key methodological challenges. First, do we conceptualize successions as discrete events or as unfolding processes? The former perspective facilitates straightforward and numerical description of key parameters of these events, their triggers, and their outcomes. It allows for large-N studies. The latter encourages a more in-depth mode of analysis that stays closer to the perceptions and decisions of key actors and picks up on the dramatic twists and turns that are part and parcel of many transition and succession episodes. Its requirements limit the scope for large-N study, and conduce towards the kind of smaller-N 'focused comparison' (Bennett and George, 2005; Blatter and Haverland, 2013). When does a transition or succession episode begin and end? The eventual resignation and replacement of an office-holder is often the product of a long gestation period, whose origins are not easy to determine unequivocally. And when do new CEOs and party leaders stop being 'new' and become 'settled' incumbents? What timelines for institutionalization of the new governance regimes they seek to craft are sensible – and fair – to maintain in assessing their 'performance' and attribute corporate or party performance to their leadership? Or are we content to simply let public opinion polls and shareholder value serve as proxies?

A second methodological challenge is that of dealing with so-called 'non events.' For every leadership change that is made, there may be a number of aborted attempts to remove the incumbent challenges. In politics, these can be very open: an aspirant 'comes out' and the matter is put to a formal vote. When she is repudiated and the incumbent reconfirmed in the role, are such episodes to be simply written off as non-events, or are they in fact consequential – even necessary – steps in the destruction of the political capital of an incumbent? One needs to know much about the political context of the moment and calculations of the actors involved to be able to answer that question sensibly. Likewise, rumor campaigns in the corporate press or quiet words to board chairs can be thought of as exercises in 'testing the waters.' Stakeholder responses allow participants and observers to take stock of potential shifts in the balance of forces in and around the CEO or party leader's 'court.' Such 'non events' impose limits on the ability of traditional large-N dataset studies to fully capture the dynamics of leadership succession. They only emerge on analysts' radars when they really drill down into the inner life of the party/government at the time. So, whilst not denying the considerable virtues and practical possibilities of large-N studies in this field, ideally, studies of leadership succession combine large N, events-focused approaches with small-N, context-sensitive and process-focused approaches in their overall design.

With these challenges and caveats in mind, let us now examine some of the key findings from each field.

Understanding Leadership Succession in Business

Business and organizational studies scholars have spent the last 50 years largely focusing on two types of questions. The first looks at the antecedents of succession: how can one explain (changes in) longevity but specifically the incidence of 'forced dismissals' of CEOs and other senior executives in firms? Scholars look at the role of both exogenous (industry and market characteristics) and endogenous (ownership, age, corporate governance structures, firm performance, decision-making heuristics) factors to try to explain, and presumably predict, the likelihood of dismissal (Bennedsen et al., 2007; Beck and Wiersema, 2011). Less attention is being paid to other forms of CEO exit, but there is a growing body of work seeking to explain CEO recruitment (Mooney et al., 2007; Graffin et al., 2013).

The other line of research looks at the effects of succession. The central question here is: does changing CEOs and/or senior executives make a difference in firm strategy, behavior, organizational change, and performance (Hutzschenreuter et al., 2012)? There is particular interest in the effects of internally versus externally recruited CEOs – Khurana's (2002) study fits that mold (but see also Agrawal et al., 2006 and Jung, 2014). Also, scholars study the impact of new CEOs on the composition of and relations within the corporate management team as well as with the board (Finkelstein et al., 2009; Barron et al., 2011). Another core issue is the integration between new CEOs and their new organizations (Denis et al., 2000).

Research on CEO succession is overwhelmingly of the large-N variety, drawing on publicly available company and industry statistics, often encompassing decades and including thousands of 'succession events' in their datasets, allowing for sophisticated statistical testing and causal modeling. The volume of research is huge, and there are several major meta-reviews consolidating its findings (Kesner and Sebora, 1994; Finkelstein et al., 2009; Giambatista et al., 2005; Hutzschenreuter et al., 2012). Interestingly, the corporate succession research paradigm has begun to be copied and adapted to examine the dynamics of executive succession in public and non-profit agencies (Boyne and Dahya, 2002; Boyne et al., 2011; Froelich et al., 2011; Teodoro, 2013).

To get a flavor of this sizeable body of work, we concentrate on one of its two key strongholds: the study of the effects of succession. Do new CEOs make a difference? The research shows that, at some level, they all do: they may change the tone and style of the company's nerve center. They affect the dynamics – and quite often the composition – of the top management team that leads the company. They may forge new relations with the board, investors, shareholders, and the business press. They allocate their attention to particular areas of firm performance, push pet projects, and have no or little interest in those of their predecessors. But does all of this *matter*, and what for, precisely? It is a question succession researchers wish they could answer, but which to date continues to cause them embarrassment. To their credit, they do not hide the limits of their knowledge: "Five decades of empirical research (1954–2005) does not, unfortunately, provide much insight . . . Scholars have failed to reach a consensus on whether succession events in general, and insider vs. outsider successions in particular, affect firm performance positively, negatively, or insignificantly" (Karaevli, 2007: 682). And: "studies linking CEO succession to organizational performance tend to suffer from a single inescapable fact: organizational performance is a very broad concept and it arises from very complex antecedents" (Finkelstein et al., 2009: 225).

Let us see what they do know. The study of succession impacts on performance has long been dominated by three propositions, emanating from research on coach rotation in sports teams conducted in the 1960s (Grusky, 1963, 1964; Gamson and Scotch, 1964; Rowe et al., 2005). The 'common sense' hypothesis held that the wise choice of a successor, the replacement of a known failure, honeymoon effects accruing to newly appointed coaches and/or managers, and their fresh outlook and zest were likely to induce better performance. Also, in turbulent industries, the competency set of senior executives can be easily outpaced by the swiftly changing rules of the game in the marketplace, at which point a prudent board would find an opportunity to recruit a new, often 'outsider' CEO who provides a better fit (Tushman and Rosenkopf, 1996; Haveman et al., 2001; Finkelstein et al., 2009: 210–211). Other researchers in contrast have suggested that newly appointed executives enjoy all but a honeymoon; rather they are 'extremely vulnerable' in the beginning: being accountable for everything, not having had the time to build up political capital (Frederickson et al., 1988: 258), and given a particular, often narrow license to operate by the appointing board (Finkelstein et al., 2009: 202–204). However, these leaders have strategy options available to them to ingratiate themselves with the organization, primarily by 'affirmative' or 'collaborative' mechanisms, and thus build a platform from which to impose a measure of managerial control of the direction of the organization (Denis et al., 2000: 1093).

The 'vicious circle' hypothesis, in contrast, suggested that teams faring badly are not helped but rather undermined by their frequent rotation of coaches and managers. Each new leader seeks to make their mark under difficult circumstances, which then disrupts routines and lowers morale, hastening further performance decline. Subsequent research beyond the world of sports has shown that the cycle is fueled by board behavior rather than CEO behavior: boards of badly performing companies are more likely to dump their chief executives. They put their new CEOs under bigger pressure to show results fast, and they respond to this pressure by pursuing more dramatic, high-risk initiatives, which are more disruptive of the company's existing structures, strategies, culture, and practices and for this reason have a higher likelihood of eliciting grief, resistance, and uncertainty. When the 'creative destruction' thus pursued does not pay off relatively quickly, the board is more likely to pull the plug than in companies that are in less unforgiving circumstances.

Finally, the 'ritual scapegoating' hypothesis argued that many successions are motivated at least in part to placate frustrated stakeholders and publicly demonstrate awareness of a need for change, but do not lead to any robust performance improvement (or decline). In this way of thinking, CEO resignations and dismissals and presentations of their successors are part of a repertoire of impression management and image repair strategies that have more to do with maintaining and restoring legitimacy than with lifting performance per se.

Five decades later, the argument is still not settled, despite valiant attempts to integrate the hypotheses into a framework with mediating variables such as the timing of executive replacement (Rowe et al., 2005) and whether the departing CEO is a founding figure (Carroll, 1984).

It is easy to see why the question of impact is so hard to settle. New CEOs land in existing company governance structures. They inherit the company's existing product mix and production lines, its staff and management, its sales and market shares, its business processes, its cost structure, and its profitability. Each of those parameters they can start to influence reasonably directly by their decisions. Or so it seems. In reality, they also inherit the firm's traditions, its (sub)cultures, and its reputation. These are crucial mediators of the firm's overall performance, but they are far more opaque and sticky, and in any case take time to transform, time that contemporary CEOs do not necessarily get given by their authorizing environments. In contrast, there is some evidence to support Jim Collins's (2001) contention that successful firms tend to be led by what others have later dubbed 'socialized' CEOs who respect, work with, and gently rather than abruptly seek to transform company DNA (Poulin et al., 2007). Whatever their stylistic inclinations and appetite for delivering change, new CEOs will see their ambitions constrained (but also enabled) by the wider context in which the company operates: placid or turbulent market conditions, government regulation and tax regimes, the strategies and strength of competitors.

Assessment and Prospects

An enormous amount of research time and resources have been invested in corporate succession research. Have its results justified the effort? Succession researchers are the first to criticize where the field has come to. For example, at the end of their meta-review, Giambatista et al. (2005: 981) observe: "If the current status of theory in succession literature could be described in one phrase, that phrase would be *fragmented and variable*" (orig. italic). They coolly note that no discernible progress has been made in the decade of work – several dozen of studies – they reviewed: "we are no closer to finding a general theory for either the antecedents leading to leader succession or the impact of leader succession on performance and/or strategic change consequences than we were" (ibid.). They attribute the lack of theoretical convergence to the multidisciplinary nature of succession research: scholars from corporate strategy, finance, organizational behavior, and leadership backgrounds each bring their own theoretical baggage, and stick to it. Much succession research is relatively theory-poor, and stuck in the now rather stale 'debate' between the three more-than-half-a-century-old hypotheses emanating from the sports team studies (Giambatista et al., 2005: 982). To break the stalemate, engagement is needed with broader theories of organizational behavior, institutionalization, leadership, life-cycles, and ecologies (e.g. Ocasio, 1994, 1999; Ocasio and Kim, 1999).

But there is another cause for the relatively modest progress of the field: the bulk of researchers focus on the data they can get rather than they data they should want to have. They study succession 'events' and their 'impacts,' but not the processes through which successions come about, and new CEOs settle in and try to make their mark. Corporate succession researchers thus largely 'black box' what actually goes on within and between the players involved in succession dramas. They rely on archival information and publicly available succession and performance data. They overwhelmingly eschew the kind of interview, observation, and even survey data-gathering methods that could help us open that black box, and produce knowledge that would no doubt be of much greater practical use than the stale and risk-avoiding practical inferences about 'when to make a leadership change' they have produced to date (but see Grunberg, 2002). The field suffers from a rather tragic stand-off: the more hands-on prescriptive books are more often than not largely 'fact-free' in their empirical underpinnings (rooted as they are in story-telling), and the great bulk of empirical studies has little of any relevance to say to those who live in the real world of corporate management. Instead, they have earnestly endeavored to keep compounding evidence for such trite hypotheses as, "When organizational performance is poor there will be a greater likelihood of CEO dismissal" (Boeker, 1992: 401). As a result, we learn practically nothing notable about leadership from plowing through the ever-growing pile of CEO succession studies. Notable exceptions can be found in the small but growing number of social–constructivist, process-oriented studies (Haddadj, 2006; Dalpiaz et al., 2014), and rich single-case studies that give us a much better insight into the nuances of firm context, firm politics, and the personalities at play (e.g. Lederman, 2007/2008).

With such a modest yield, why does this field continue to elicit so much effort? The cynical answer would be that it is a relatively easy game to play: get a research assistant to do the legwork, build the dataset, bring in the advanced statistics, and go for the least publishable unit. Perhaps it is more pertinent to wonder what role path dependencies, imitation, and publication pressures play in sustaining such inward-looking research communities. In any case, it is clear that we will not learn what is really worth noting about corporate succession until its students come out of their self-created shell, and reposition both the theoretical and methodological pillars upon which they have built their subfield. We need less study of succession as its own cause, and more study of succession as part of a bigger picture theorizing about organizational behavior and leadership dynamics. And empirically we need a greater willingness to take risks: more determination to open the corporate 'black box' through use of close-up, 'messy' methods; fewer numbers, more voices. Less effort to 'explain' in terms of causal modeling and more effort to 'understand' the lived realities and subjective experiences of the leaders who get fired, succeed, and seek to make a difference whilst they are in the chair, as well as of those who put them there and remove them from it.

Understanding Leadership Succession in Politics

Orderly transfers of power are the litmus test for liberal democracies. Usually, we think of the concession of electoral or parliamentary defeat by a ruling regime and its handing the reins of power to the leader(s) of opposition. Leadership succession deals with the change of leadership within a party or a coalition, which can be a more convoluted process and subject to passions less public but no less intense. An incumbent leader is usually the subject of appreciation as well as jealousy, idolatry as well as contempt. The closest colleagues are the most likely to succeed and rebellion is usually one scandal or poor election result away.

Political scientists have built datasets or used cross-national comparative designs to study succession in particular types of parties, party systems, and polities (democracies and non democracies), or to examine the impact of particular institutional rules and mechanisms of leader succession (Bille, 2001; Kenig, 2009). Examples include Calvert's (1978) early survey, and Davis's (1998) comparative analysis of six, Cross and Blais's (2012b) of five, Pilet and Cross's (2014) of twelve, and Laing and 't Hart's (2011) of twenty-three democracies. Beyond that, there are even more comprehensive dataset studies encompassing both democratic and non-democratic polities, such as Bueno de Mesquita et al.'s (2003) wide-ranging analysis of the institutional, situational, political, and behavioral correlates of leader survival in office.

In addition, students of political successions produce intensive 'thick description'-style narrative accounts of succession processes in single cases or focused comparisons across low-N samples. These in-depth, qualitative studies open up the 'black box' of the factional politics that is often at the heart of contested successions. Examples include Punnett (1992), Stark (1996), Denham and O'Hara (2008), and Heppel (2008, 2010), all on the UK main parties alone. They also produce theory-driven studies on, e.g., the economic and political impact of successions (Bunce, 1981; MacAuley and Carter, 1986), and the impact of (changes in) leader selection rules on leader survival, electoral performance, and party culture (Weller 1983, 1994; Rahat and Hazan, 2001; Quinn, 2005; 't Hart and Uhr, 2011). Finally, even the 'after-lives' of defeated or retired political leaders have become an object of study (Theakston and De Vries, 2012).

Let us explore what political scientists have found about the triggers, processes, and effects of party leader succession. Political leadership is enabled and destroyed by the political capital an incumbent is granted by their authorizing environment: those actors within and outside their parties whose support or at least acquiescence is necessary to prevent rivals from challenging them for the position (Bennister et al., 2015). Motivated leaders with a strong position both in the party and with the potential electorate are hard to unseat and tend to deter overt challengers. Laing and 't Hart (2011: 122) offer the following typology to characterize the relative strength of an incumbent.

The first years of leadership are crucial for building up that capital. If leaders manage to survive their first term and/or their first electoral test, their chances for a much longer incumbency increase markedly (Laing and 't Hart, 2011). Leadership capital does tend to erode over time. The wear and tear of leadership forces incumbents to prioritize and make enemies internally as well as externally (Renshon, 2000; Bueno de Mesquita et al., 2003; Bennister et al., 2015).

The relative vulnerability of an incumbent is partly a product of institutional factors, particularly the nature of the body that selects them ('selectorate') and its rules of engagement. At one extreme (high vulnerability), parties can hire and fire leaders by means of informal 'inner circles' of party elders or factional power brokers; at the other (low vulnerability), leaders are chosen for fixed terms by secret ballot among all party members. A wealth of research demonstrates the impact of the nature and size of such institutional characteristics as selectorates, term limits, and voting rules (Quinn, 2005; Kenig, 2009; Cross and Blais, 2012a; Pilet and Cross, 2014). The trend in Western democracies has been for the pre-eminence of the parliamentary parties as selectorates to give way to rank-and-file member ballots. Posing the leadership question to the rank and file carries risk of jeopardizing the balance of the party factions. Members from outside the party elite can raise a challenge and force insider candidates into unwanted positions.

Table 11.1 A Typology of Incumbent Leaders' Positions vis-à-vis Succession Challenges

		Level of external support	
Hold over own party		Strong	Weak
	Firm	Winner (Untouchable)	Oligarch (Vulnerable to changing party support)
	Weak	Maverick (Vulnerable to changing public opinion)	Loser (Untenable)

Source: adapted from Laing and 't Hart 2011: 122.

Once elected by direct member ballot, party leaders do not have to be as meticulously obser-vant of their parliamentary colleagues' needs and views as they must be when the selectorate is comprised of their parliamentary colleagues.

Leader vulnerability is, however, not a static product of institutional structures alone. It can increase at certain moments in the political business cycle: election defeats, internal policy dif-ferences on high-stakes issues, 'relegation' to opposition, negative publicity about the leader's performance. Particular succession triggers tend to carry meaning as they play to the strengths and (more often) weaknesses of a leader. For example, when a 'maverick' leader suffers a big drop in the opinion polls it deflates her claim of being an electoral magnet, and leaves her less immune to the internal opposition her maverick posture is sure to generate (Costa Lobo, 2008). Whispering campaigns commence, challenges are mounted, and even if they are not fully pur-sued or not immediately won in formal contest, their very existence depletes the incumbent's political capital. A 'vicious cycle' – not dissimilar to that which may take hold of firms and their leaders – of further lackluster performance, rising discontent, and support seeping away can get in motion, and is extremely difficult to break. Sometimes a big external crisis can provide an embattled leader with an opportunity to 'perform authority' (Hajer, 2009) when it is needed most, and thus regain stature. The 2015 Paris attacks did just that for embattled French president Francois Hollande.

The increasingly leader-centric character of modern politics and the advent of marketing and branding techniques in U.S. and European politics have turned leaders into political prizefight-ers: core assets for a party in its need to win elections. Entire campaigns are centered on lead-ers; party brand and personal brand have effectively merged (Lees-Marshment, 2012). This has further raised the stakes of leadership selection (Blondel and Thibault, 2009; Karvonen, 2010; Calise, 2011). Under such a leadership model, the actions of party colleagues, especially when in government, are all attributed to the leader. When the party fails, the natural culprit is thus the leader, who may deflect that blame by firing underperforming associates, reshuffle their top team, or take symbolic remedial action. But they cannot escape the fact that the personalization of politics has come with greater instability at the top (Dowding, 2013).

Party culture is a key factor determining eligibility for leadership. It influences what kind of values leadership candidates should espouse and embody. In essence, the test for a new leader is whether to conform or transform the party's sense of 'who "we" are' (Turner and Haslam, 2001; Subašić and Reynolds, 2011).

One telling example is the revolutionary brand of leadership exercised by Tony Blair as he entered the top job of the British Labour Party in 1994 and forged a clean break with a number of party orthodoxies (e.g. the 'clause 4' nationalization commitment in the party constitution, and the power of the union movement within the party's institutions) (Minkin, 2014; Russell, 2005). This was made possible by the eighteen years spent in opposition and the realization that changes touching the core of the party were needed in order to improve the electability of the party.

When an incumbent's weakness becomes clear, a *succession episode* unfolds. Case-study research across a number of parties and epochs has allowed us to draw up a synthetic picture of the process that is set in motion. An incumbent needs to decide, first of all, whether to resist the challenge that is to come, or to throw in the towel. Both these options come with a sec-ondary strategy of resisting change or cooperating with the forces driving a bid for succession (see further Table 11.2).

Succession episodes are one-off contests. The context of succession develops and internalizes the strengths and weaknesses of the two or more contenders (Foley, 2013). An incumbent's position can be softened up by a farfetched challenge from the fringes of the party that creates expectations of overwhelming victory for the incumbent. Anything short of that will cause

Table 11.2 Incumbent Options When Faced with a Succession Trigger

a.	Deny exit →	(Unconscious) use of psychological defense mechanisms in order to avoid facing the prospect of impending loss of office/power	
b.	Resist exit →	*Consensus-seeking*	*proactive*: trying to rebuild political support by 'trying harder' to 'do better'
			reactive: hoping that succession issue will blow over ('it's a passing fad')
		Conflict-accepting	*proactive*: open and covert 'warfare' to silence critics and eliminate contenders
			reactive: retaliate attacks made by critics and contender
c.	Accept exit →	*Consensus-seeking*	*proactive*: instigating successor selection process without pushing own candidate
			reactive: non-interfering in ongoing successor selection process and accepting its results
		Conflict-accepting	*proactive*: unilateral designation of successor
			reactive: trying to influence ongoing successor selection process to push preferred candidate

Source: Bynander and 't Hart, 2006: 713.

serious problems for the leader and make the unlikely contender a lightning rod for internal passions against the incumbent and/or activate other, heavier competition. Restoring a semblance of internal unity now becomes imperative for the incumbent (Ceron, 2014). This may require U-turns on contentious policies, reshuffling key personnel, or transformation of the party's structure or platform. Successful survivors of serious succession triggers have often been effective in fielding the 'better the devil you know' defense. Party organizations generally value stability; appetite for major reform can dwindle quickly in the face of a messy succession battle. The standard incumbency strategy is to keep stability more attractive than change among the power brokers within the party. This may also include the overt or covert threat of retaliation and destabilization of any new leadership that might eventuate (Konrad and Skaperdas, 2007).

The strategic calculus of the incumbent is mirrored by those of the challengers, who initially need to consider whether to field an open contest or wait for the incumbent to be further weakened (see Table 11.3). The purpose of the latter strategy is not to expose ambition too soon and risk retribution, but also to come across as loyal to a point but ready to accept responsibility. The downside of this strategy is the risk that other contenders will get a head start in staking their leadership claims and that erstwhile internal supporters will see the (potential) candidate as weak and indecisive (Punnett, 1992).

The strategic game that then unfolds between incumbent, challengers, and secondary stakeholders can take a number of forms. It can be short and sharp or protracted and destabilize the party for months or more. Core internal and external constituents need to be won. Performance tests – key parliamentary or television appearances, new policy announcements, direct debates – are part and parcel of the vetting and bargaining processes that ultimately determine where the momentum goes. At the tail end of every succession episode is an arduous task for the person left standing: to heal the battle wounds that may have resulted and stake a path that can inject a sense of direction and new credibility for the party. If the new leader does not deliver the new departure with enough vigor and speed, unrest fueled by resumption of factional hostilities, defections from the new leadership team, and parliamentary rebellions may follow.

For political leaders themselves, the *impacts* of succession are tangible – their ability to maneuver has a direct relationship to the way in which they were selected and the context in which

Table 11.3 Challenger Options When Faced with a Succession Trigger

Pre-succession			
Aspiring leader confronted with succession trigger	a. Forego candidacy		→ 'nay sayer'
	b. Seek candidacy	→ covertly	→ harmonious posture: 'spectator'
			→ confrontational posture: 'plotter'
		→ overtly	→ harmonious posture: 'crown prince'
			→ confrontational posture: 'critic'
Post-succession			
New leader's posture vis-à-vis departed leader	a. Embrace heritage		→ 'heir'
	b. Selective support for heritage		→ 'shopper'
	c. Repudiation of heritage		→ 'reformer'

Source: Bynander and 't Hart 2006: 719.

succession occurred. In effect, the succession process is a primary factor in the mandate that a newly elected (or reconfirmed) party leader enjoys. This mandate then needs to be managed in a way that consolidates their position and provides them latitude to design successful election campaigns.

The most straightforward measures of succession impact are leader survival and party (electoral) performance. A key factor determining whether a new leader survives and the party thrives is the level of conflict during the succession process. Research suggests that the connection is counterintuitive (Laing and 't Hart, 2011). Having triumphed in a high-conflict contest with an internal rival (and faction) allows the new leader to exercise a Machiavellian blend of mercy and brutality in a way that realigns internal loyalties and creates a new mandate. Low-conflict succession leaders on the other hand have to some extent tied themselves to the mast by accepting a scenario endorsed by the existing dominant coalition, which may not break the downward electoral spiral that triggered the succession in the first place.

Assessment and Prospects

There are still blind spots in the study of party leadership succession. What we know about political systems, political culture, and party structures is not always lining up with what we need to shed more light on leadership succession. More integration between the subfields that explore these complex areas is needed if there is to be major inroads into the understanding of the significance and impacts of different modes of leadership succession (Foley, 2013). As political leadership succession analysis comes of age, it needs to nurture the budding comparative perspective, integrate with other more established fields of leadership studies, and develop the scope and boundary conditions for its explanatory ambitions. During the last decade, the field has proposed and tested generalizations about when, why, and how successions occur, and what effects they may have on the key protagonists' careers, the performance of the party, and the policies it pursues. We believe that the methodological diversity that it has come to display is part of the strength of this subfield. There is a nascent interplay between the in-depth and the large-N, the causal and the interpretive, the bird's eye view and the down in the dirt view. Such diversity and multi-method approaches need to be nurtured. It is now time to switch the focus of recent times – the impact of changing rules for leader selection on leader legitimacy and longevity – towards the next horizon: examining the implications of the weakening of established cadre parties with 'democratized' rules for leader (de)selection and the rise of a new wave of movement parties of the populist, proto-charismatic variety whose entrepreneurial founder–leaders are less constrained by internal checks and balances (Mair, 2013).

Towards Convergence

It has long been customary to treat the corporate and political sectors as distant universes, and therefore business and political leadership as entirely different crafts. But today it is easy to overstate those differences. Small and medium-sized firms, large corporations, political parties, and governments are all facing the same set of megatrends that challenge their common roots as modernist projects of instrumental rationality through order, design, control, and hierarchy. These trends include: accelerating and disruptive technological change; globalization and connectivity of markets, social problems, and governance structures; greater public demand for transparency and accountability from any type of entity, profession, or authority figure whose actions affect their lives; and mass media, social media, and mobile devices permanently shaping people's cognitive and emotional frames, creating web-empowered customers and citizens with 'liquid' tastes, preferences, values, and life-styles ('t Hart, 2014). The world in which business and political leaders operate has become 'flat': demanding, changeable, boundary-less, fast-paced. They feel the pinch: their longevity in office has gone down while the percentage of forced departures has gone up. Business and political leaders thus face a similar paradox: satisfying a romantic longing for 'charismatic' leadership that provides protection, direction, and order in a complex and volatile world where nothing can be taken for granted anymore, and at the same time being constrained in exercising that leadership by a thickening of governance structures and accountability requirements that enable their authorizing environment to contain them and get rid of them more effectively. There is appetite for transformational leadership, yet the dominant rules of the game governing both business and political leadership conduce towards transactional leadership (cf. Burns, 1978).

Given this unfolding institutional isomorphism, what might be some productive lines for comparative, cross-sectoral inquiry? We propose three theoretical points of departure that could inspire such work. These are paths to distinct but mutually reinforcing understandings of what makes leaders effective in running their organizations. In order to do the job, they need to retain a measure of control, be able to stick around long enough to make a difference, and lastly leave at such a time and in such a manner so as to provide their successors with a fair shot at continuing to develop the organization in a sustainable direction.

Our choice of theoretical departure has methodological consequences. The richness reported in this study suggests that, in order to advance leadership succession studies, multi-method approaches are necessary, not only to be able to pose relevant questions and reach viable conclusions, but also to be able to foster cross-fertilization between researchers that to a large degree have been operating on starkly different conceptual and methodological canvases. By 'mixing and mashing' both concepts, propositions, and research design, we may be able to convince scholars from both niche fields in business studies and political science that there is added value in taking notice of and utilizing what the others are doing. It will require a sustained effort to birth and consolidate a more integrated field of leadership succession analysis, but here are some questions that could be at its core.

First, from a *power perspective* on succession, the lens can be turned on the question of who controls whom. A power perspective on political succession invites us to analyze successions as products of strategic and tactical choices, as well as signaling, impression management, and bargaining. It sees the rise, tenure, actions, impact, and departure of leaders in terms of the ongoing pulling and hauling between leaders and those who can select, empower, de-authorize, and remove them within the relevant governance structure. Political scientists should take note of the elite circulation versus institutionalization of power models that have been used and refined in the study of CEO dismissals (Ocasio, 1994). Likewise, the 'power game' of incumbent–challenger(s) interaction as modeled by Bynander and 't Hart (2006, 2008) might inspire students of corporate successions to go beyond penetrating the succession politics within firms more effectively. Likewise, Finkelstein et al.'s (2009) synopsis of the big body of work on the politics of top management teams can be usefully fused with Dowding et al.'s (2013) work on the politics of ministerial survival and cabinet reshuffles to provide an integrative perspective on the power dynamics that produce both corporate and political successions and influence their outcomes.

Second, an *accountability perspective* on succession generates a set of related, but analytically distinct, questions (Mulgan, 2003; Uhr, 2005). Which mechanisms are in place to ensure that CEOs and party leaders, who are put there to act as 'agents' on behalf of some constituency and/or set of values and interests, are induced to render account of their behavior to the 'principals' who put them there? Who are in effect the relevant principals for, say, party leaders, cabinet ministers, or departmental secretaries, and how are the accountability relationships between principals and agents constituted? The many instances of change to party rules of leadership selection and removal that we have seen across the democratic world in the last three decades have in large part been motivated by the idea of opening these pivotal leadership processes up to broader scrutiny and indeed participation, even down to the level of ordinary party members. Likewise, the thickening of corporate governance structures is aimed at strengthening the checks and balances around corporate executives. A key question generated by the accountability perspective on succession is to what extent these aims have been realized, and succession episodes are a good place to conduct such inquiry. What can the course and outcomes of succession episodes teach us about the real terms of the principal–agent relationships between owners, shareholders, boards, and CEOs within corporations, and between party members, auxiliary organizations, parliamentarians, and party leaders within political parties?

This leads into a third area of comparative inquiry, guided by a *normative perspective* on succession. How do we know a 'good,' 'well-managed' succession if we see it? The academic literature has been largely silent on this, preoccupied as it has been with the when, how, and why questions that suit its empirical toolkit. But, as a result, it has left the job of assessing and advising about successions to the largely theory-deprived and 'fact-free' world of self-help succession planning guides (e.g. Rothwell, 2010). There is no normative theory of succession, but should there be? What ought to be the values that parties and companies seek to maximize when they design their leadership succession rules, and when key actors within both consider replacing incumbent senior office-holders? How to institutionalize succession norms and practices that effectively navigate the tension between the need for continuity and predictability of corporate, party, and government strategy and the need for responsiveness to electoral or market signals, new leaders' need for distinctive political capital, and indeed the need for periodic 'creative destruction' and course changes in the life of institutions? At a minimum, we would want key decisions about leader selection and removal to be taken in a transparent, inclusive fashion. More ambitiously, successions should select office-holders in such a manner as to have the authority necessary not just for surviving in the role but for actually exercising leadership.

These are just ruminations of course. What we need is a field of research that does not eschew but embraces the challenges of evaluating successions. This would provide it with the much-needed impetus to transform itself from what to date has been two sets of largely uncoordinated academic parlor games into a more ambitious and more relevant endeavor that is both transdisciplinary and applied.

References

Agrawal, A., Knoeber, C. R., and Tsoulouhas, T. (2006). Are outsiders handicapped in CEO successions? *Journal of Corporate Finance* 12 (3): 619–644.

Barron, J. M., Chulkov, D. V., and Waddell, G. R. (2011). Top management team turnover, CEO succession type, and strategic change. *Journal of Business Research* 64 (6): 904–910.

Beck, J. B. and Wiersema, M. F. (2011). 15 CEO dismissal: The role of the broader governance context. In: M. A. Carpenter (ed.) *The Handbook of Research on Top Management Teams*. Cheltenham: Edward Elgar, pp. 396–414.

Bennedsen, M., Nielsen, K. M., Perez-Gonzalez, F., and Wolfenzon, D. (2007). Inside the family firm: The role of families in succession decisions and performance. *The Quarterly Journal of Economics* 122 (2): 647–691.

Bennett, A. and George, A. L. (2005). *Case Studies and Theory Development in the Social Sciences*. Cambridge: MIT Press.

Bennister, M., 't Hart, P., and Worthy, B. (2015). Assessing the authority of political office-holders: The Leadership Capital Index. *West European Politics* 38 (3): 417–440.

Bille, L. (2001). Democratizing a democratic procedure: myth or reality? Candidate selection in Western European parties, 1960–1990. *Party Politics* 7 (3): 363–380.

Blatter, J. and Haverland, M. (2013). *Designing Case Studies: Explanatory Approaches in Small-N Research*. Basingstoke: Palgrave.

Blondel, J. and Thibault, J.-L. (2009). *Political Leadership, Parties and Citizens: The Personalisation of Leadership*. London: Routledge.

Boeker, W. (1992). Power and managerial dismissal: Scapegoating at the top. *Administrative Science Quarterly* 37 (3): 400–421.

Boyne, G. and Dahya, J. (2002). Executive succession and the performance of public organizations. *Public Administration* 80 (1): 179–200.

Boyne, G. A., James, O., John, P., and Petrovsky, N. (2011). Top management turnover and organizational performance: A test of a contingency model. *Public Administration Review* 71 (4): 572–581.

Bueno de Mesquita, B., Smith, A., Siverson, R. M., and Morrow, J. D. (2003). *The Logic of Political Survival*. Cambridge, MA: MIT Press.

Bunce, V. (1981). *Do New Leaders Make a Difference? Executive Succession and Public Policy Under Capitalism and Socialism*. Princeton, NJ: Princeton University Press.

Burns, J. M. (1978). *Leadership*. New York: Harper and Row.

Bynander, F. and 't Hart, P. (2006) When power changes hands: The political psychology of leadership succession in democracies. *Political Psychology* 27 (5): 707–729.

Bynander, F. and 't Hart, P. (2008). The art of handing over: (Mis)managing party leader successions. *Government and Opposition* 43 (2): 385–404.

Calise, M. (2011) Personalization of politics. In: B. Badie (ed.) *International Encyclopedia of Political Science*. Thousand Oaks, CA: Sage.

Calvert, P. (ed.) (1978). *The Process of Political Succession*. Basingstoke, Hampshire: Macmillan.

Carroll, G. R. (1984). The dynamics of publisher succession in newspaper organizations. *Administrative Science Quarterly* 16 (3): 416–428.

Ceron, A. (2014). Inter-factional conflicts and government formation: Do party leaders sort out ideological heterogeneity? *Party Politics*, published online on December 16, 2014.

Collins, J. (2001). *Good to Great*. New York: Harper.

Costa Lobo, M. (2008). Parties and leader effects: Impact of leaders in the vote for different types of parties. *Party Politics* 14 (3): 281–298.

Cross, W. and Blais, A. (2012a). Who selects the party leader? *Party Politics* 18 (2): 127–150.

Cross, W. and Blais, A. (2012b). *Politics at the Centre: The Selection and Removal of Party Leaders in the Anglo Parliamentary Democracies*. Oxford: Oxford University Press.

Dalpiaz, E., Tracey, P., and Phillips, N. (2014). Succession narratives in family business: The case of Alessi. *Entrepreneurship Theory and Practice* 38: 1375–1393.

Davis, J. W. (1998). *Leadership Selection in Six Western Democracies*. Westport, CT: Greenwood Press.

Denham, A. and O'Hara, K. (2008). *Demcratising Conservative Leadership Selection: From Grey Suits to Grass Roots*. Manchester: Manchester University Press.

Denis, J.-L., Langley, A., and Pineault, M. (2000). Becoming a leader in a complex organization. *Journal of Management Studies* 37 (8): 1063–1100.

Dowding, K. (2013). Prime-ministerial power: Institutional and personal factors. In: P. Strangio, P. 't Hart, and J. Walter (eds) *Understanding Prime Ministerial Performance: Comparative Perspectives*. Oxford: Oxford University Press.

Dowding, K., Berlinski, S., and Dewan, T. (2013). *Accounting for Ministers: Scandal and Survival in British Government, 1945–2007*. Cambridge: Cambridge University Press.

Finkelstein, S., Hambrick, D. C. and Cannella, A. A. (2009). *Strategic Leadership: Theory and Research on Executives, Top Management Teams, and Boards*. Oxford: Oxford University Press.

Foley, M. (2013). *Political Leadership: Themes, Contexts, and Critiques*. Oxford: Oxford University Press.

Frederickson, J. W., Hambrick, D. C., and Baumrin, S. (1988). A model of CEO dismissal. *The Academy of Management Review* 13 (2): 255–270.

Froelich, K., McKee, G., and Rathge, R. (2011). Succession planning in non profit organizations. *Nonprofit Management and Leadership* 22 (1): 3–20.

Gamson, W. A. and Scotch, N. A. (1964). Scapegoating in baseball. *American Journal of Sociology* 70 (1): 69–72.

Giambatista, R. C., Rowe, W. G., and Riaz, S. (2005). Nothing succeeds like succession: A critical review of leader succession literature since 1994. *The Leadership Quarterly* 16 (5): 963–991.

Graffin, S. D., Boivie, S., and Carpenter, M. A. (2013). Examining CEO succession and the role of heuristics in early-stage CEO evaluation. *Strategic Management Journal* 34 (4): 383–403.

Grunberg, J. (2002). *Problematic Departures: CEO Exits in Large Swedish Publicly Traded Corporations*. Doctoral Thesis no. 93. Uppsala: Department of Business Studies.

Grusky, O. (1963). Managerial succession and organizational effectiveness. *American Journal of Sociology* 69 (1): 21–31.

Grusky, O. (1964). Reply to scapegoating in baseball. *American Journal of Sociology* 70 (1): 72–76.

Haddadj, S. (2006). Paradoxical process in the organizational change of the CEO succession. *Journal of Organizational Change Management* 19 (4): 447–456.

Hajer, M. (2009). *Authoritative Governance*. Oxford: Oxford University Press.

Haveman, H. A., Russo, M. V., and Meyer, A. D. (2001). Organizational environments in flux: The impact of regulatory punctuations on organizational domains, CEO succession and performance. *Organization Science* 12 (3): 253–273.

Heppell, T. (2008). *Choosing the Tory Leader: Conservative Party Leadership Elections from Heath to Cameron*. London: Taurus.

Heppell, T. (2010). *Choosing the Labour Leader: Labour Party Leadership Elections from Wilson to Brown*. London: Taurus.

Hutzschenreuter, T., Kleindienst, I., and Greger, C. (2012). How new leaders affect strategic change following a succession event: A critical review of the literature. *The Leadership Quarterly* 23 (4): 729–755.

Jung, J. (2014). Political contestation at the top: Politics of outsider succession at U.S. corporations. *Organization Studies* 35 (5): 727–764.

Karaevli, A. (2007). Performance consequences of new CEO 'Outsiderness': Moderating effects of pre- and post-succession contexts. *Strategic Management Journal* 28 (7): 681–706.

Karvonen, L. (2010). *The Personalisation of Politics: A Study of Parliamentary Democracies*. Colchester: ECPR Press.

Kenig, O. (2009). Democratization of party leadership selection: Do wider selectorates produce more competitive contests? *Electoral Studies* 28 (2): 240–247.

Kesner, I. F. and Sebora, T. C. (1994). Executive succession: Past, present and future. *Journal of Management* (20) 2: 327–372.

Khurana, R. (2002). *Searching for a Corporate Savior: The Irrational Quest for Charismatic CEOs*. Princeton, NJ: Princeton University Press.

Konrad, K. A. and Skaperdas, S. (2007). Succession rules and leadership rents. *The Journal of Conflict Resolution* 51 (4): 622–645.

Laing, M. and 't Hart, P. (2011). Seeking and keeping the hot seat: A comparative analysis of party leader succession. In: P. 't Hart and J. Uhr (eds) *How Power Changes Hands*. Basingstoke, Hampshire: Palgrave, pp. 111–132.

Lederman, L. (2007/2008). Disney examined: A case study in corporate governance and CEO succession. *New York Law School Review* 52 (2): 557–582.

Lees-Marshment, J. (2012). Political marketing and opinion leadership. In: L. Helms (ed.) *Comparative Political Leadership*. Basingstoke, Hampshire: Palgrave, pp. 165–185.

Mair, P. (2013). *Ruling the Void: The Hollowing of Western Democracy*. London: Verso.

McCauley, M. and Carter, S. (eds) (1986). *Leadership and Succession in the Soviet Union, Eastern Europe and China*. London: Macmillan.

Minkin, L. (2014). *The Blair Supremacy: A Study in the Politics of Labour's Party Management*. Manchester: Manchester University Press.

Mooney, C. H., Dalton, D. R., Dalton, C. M., and Certo, S. T. (2007). CEO succession as a funnel: The critical, and changing, role of inside directors. *Organizational Dynamics* 36 (4): 418–428.

Mulgan, R. (2003). *Holding Power to Account: Accountability in Modern Democracies*. Basingstoke: Palgrave Macmillan.

Ocasio, W. (1994). Political dynamics and the circulation of power: CEO successions in U.S. industrial corporations, 1960–1990. *Administrative Science Quarterly* 39 (2): 285–212.

Ocasio, W. (1999). Institutionalised action and corporate governance: The reliance on rules of CEO succession. *Administrative Science Quarterly* 44 (2): 384–416.

Ocasio, W. and Kim, H. (1999). The circulation of corporate control. *Administrative Science Quarterly* 44 (3): 532–562.

Pilet, J.-B. and Cross, W. (eds) (2014). *The Selection of Political Party Leaders in Contemporary Democracies*. London: Routledge.

Poulin, B. J., Hackman, M. Z., and Barbarasa-Mihai, C. (2007). Leadership succession: The challenge to succeed and the vortex of failure. *Leadership* 3 (3): 301–324.

Punnett, R. M. (1992). *Selecting the Party Leader: Britain in Comparative Perspective*. London: Harvester Wheatsheaf.

Quinn, T. (2005). Leasehold or freehold? Leader eviction rules in the British Conservative and Labour parties. *Political Studies* 53 (4): 793–815.

Rahat, G. and Hazan, R. Y. (2001). Candidate selection methods: An analytical framework. *Party Politics* 7 (3): 297–322.

Renshon, S. (2000). Political leadership as social capital: Governing in a divided national culture. *Political Psychology* 21 (1): 199–226.

Rothwell, W. J. (2010). *Effective Succession Planning: Ensuring Leadership Continuity and Building Talent from Within*. New York: Amacom.

Rowe, W. G., Cannella Jr., A. A., Rankin, D., and Gorman, D. (2005). Leader succession and organizational performance: Integrating the common-sense, ritual scapegoating, and vicious-circle succession theories. *The Leadership Quarterly* 16 (2): 197–219.

Russell, M. (2005). *Building New Labour: The Politics of Party Organisation*. Basingstoke, Hampshire: Palgrave.

Stark, L. (1996). *Choosing a Leader: Party Leadership Contests in Britain from Macmillan to Blair*. London: Macmillan.

Subašić, E. and Reynolds, K. J. (2011). Power consolidation in leadership change contexts: A social identity perspective. In: P. 't Hart and J. Uhr (eds) *How Power Changes Hands*. Basingstoke, Hampshire: Palgrave, pp. 174–190.

't Hart, P. (2014). *Understanding Public Leadership*. Basingstoke, Hampshire: Palgrave.

't Hart, P. and Uhr, J. (eds) (2011) *How Power Changes Hands: Transition and Succession in Government*. Basingstoke, Hampshire: Palgrave.

Teodoro, M. (2013). Moving in, managing up: Executive job formation and political behaviour. *Journal of Public Policy* 33 (2): 137–164.

Theakston, K. and De Vries, J. (eds) (2012). *Former Leaders in Modern Democracies: Political Sunsets*. Basingstoke, Hampshire: Palgrave.

Tiffen, R. (2015). Thinking of dumping a prime minister? History isn't encouraging. *Inside Story*, February 8, 2015. http://insidestory.org.au/thinking-of-dumping-a-prime-minister-history-isnt-encouraging, consulted February 10, 2015.

Turner, J. C. and Haslam, S. A. (2001). Social identity, organizations, and leadership. In: M. E. Turner (ed.) *Groups at Work: Theory and Research*. Mahwah, NJ: Lawrence Erlbaum Associates, pp. 25–65.

Tushman, M. L. and Rosenkopf, L. (1996). Executive succession, strategic reorientation and performance growth. *Management Science* 42 (7): 939–953.

Uhr, J. 2005. *Terms of Trust*. Sydney: UNSW Press.

Weller, P. (1983). The vulnerability of prime ministers: A comparative perspective. *Parliamentary Affairs* 36 (1): 96–117.

Weller, P. (1994). Party rules and the dismissal of prime ministers: Comparative perspectives from Britain, Canada and Australia. *Parliamentary Affairs* 47 (2): 133–143.

12

Leadership in Interaction

Magnus Larsson

Introduction

A chapter on leadership in interaction might appear to address an odd topic, because many observers would contend that interaction is integral to all leadership. However, empirical studies of the processes of interaction are relatively rare in the leadership field. In recent years, though, this perspective has been emerging; therefore, this chapter will present and discuss this emergent work while also clarifying its contribution to date to our understanding of leadership and the potential paths forward.

Object of Study

Here, interaction is taken to mean verbal as well as non-verbal exchanges in real life organizational situations. Studies of leadership interaction generally rest on the assumption that, for leadership to exist and have actual consequences, it needs to be "visible" in some form in organizational practice. Discussing the wider field of organizational studies, Hindmarsh and Llwewllyn (2010, p. 13) argue as follows:

> If one of the problematics of the discipline [organization studies] is to show and analyze, rather than theoretically stipulate or presume, the reproduction of organizational settings, at some point the discipline will have to analyze how organization is apparent in, and sustained through, ordinary work practice.

In line with this argument, studies of leadership interaction rest on the idea that we need to be able to locate leadership in everyday organizational practice for research to credibly grant it any role in the shaping of organizational reality. We are thus interested in:

> investigating, and problematizing, the practices of leadership rather than how ideas about leadership are attributed, by academics or lay persons, to particular individuals or forms of behavior.
> *(Knights & Willmott, 1992, p. 765)*

Such an approach has the potential to complement other approaches to leadership studies in important ways (Fairhurst, 2007a; Knights & Willmott, 1992; Uhl-Bien & Ospina, 2012). Through studies of interaction, we might for instance achieve a deeper understanding of leadership competences (Carroll, Levy, & Richmond, 2008; Lord & Hall, 2005; Mumford, Zaccaro, Harding, Jacobs, & Fleishman, 2000) as they are drawn on and utilized in practice, and we might achieve a deeper understanding of the dynamic process of accomplishing influence (Clifton, 2009; Larsson & Lundholm, 2010). Such studies clearly move away from a focus on the leader as a person to more of a process perspective on leadership (Crevani, Lindgren, & Packendorff, 2010; Grint, 2005a).

Interaction clearly includes behaviors, but studies of leadership interaction typically have a different focus than studies of leadership behaviors. While the latter focus on identifying classes of behaviors (Courtright, Fairhurst, & Rogers, 1989; Yukl, 2012), often identified through self-report questionnaires, the former tend to focus on specific acts in specific interactional contexts. Rather than working to decontextualize behaviors (Fairhurst, 2007a, 2009; Osborn, Hunt, & Jausch, 2002), studies of interaction instead direct the analytical gaze to how behaviors and actions are deeply situated in the immediate context. Further, instead of only focusing on the actions of one part of the leadership relationship—the leader—studies of interaction necessarily involve and acknowledge contributions from all parties.

Studies of interaction generally draw upon a discursive orientation to leadership (Fairhurst, 2007a), including the assumption that leadership, as well as its consequences, is established in interaction and thus in some sense is socially constructed. Fairhurst (2011) contrasts this interest in the social arena to the dominant tendency in leadership research to focus on a "mental theater" (Cronen, 1995, as cited in Fairhurst, 2011), in which the essential phenomena are cognitive, affective or behavioral processes that are internal to the actor(s). With such a perspective, interaction as well as language use tends to be seen as a secondary route, at best, to obtaining information about the more important cognitive phenomena. In contrast, a discursive and interactional perspective takes the social arena as a distinct ontological and empirical field in its own right and assumes that this is where leadership, as well as where an organization more generally (Hindmarsh & Llewellyn, 2010), is shaped and realized.

What is most clearly distinct in studies of interaction is the choice of empirical material. Rather than being based on surveys or interviews, these studies utilize observations and typically audio or video recordings of interactions. Further, the focus is on interactions occurring as part of the ongoing work and life in an organization, rather than on interactions produced by the researcher (such as experiments or interview situations). Analyses of such interactions are typically (but not exclusively) qualitative and may draw upon a vast range of methodological traditions, with attention on different levels of abstraction. Studies with a greater ethnographic orientation tend to focus on the somewhat larger themes and structures in the observed situations, while studies drawing on interactional sociolinguistics or conversation analysis tend to focus on more micro-level mechanisms of the interaction as it evolves turn by turn.

Overall, these differences in approach mean that questions of validity and generalizability need to be addressed somewhat differently from in a standard hypothetical–deductive study. Studies of interaction tend to aim towards what Yin (1994) calls theoretical generalization, meaning that knowledge is gained by using well-chosen cases to test and develop theory. For instance, by demonstrating the influence of the "machinery" of leadership, a deeper theoretical knowledge can by gained that is relevant to our general understanding of leadership.

The existing studies with a focus on the micro-level of interaction cover a wide variety of themes and pose a number of different research questions. In the following, I will discuss them, organized in three broad themes: how a designated leader enacts his or her role; how identities relevant to the leadership process are constructed in interaction; and what influence and organizing processes exist in interaction. The aim with this is both to create an overview of the literature and to discuss the major contributions that this emerging research field offers to the broader field of leadership studies. However, I acknowledge that there are other ways to organize the literature that might bring other features to center stage.

The formal structure and division of roles within an organization, such as between leaders and subordinates, form an important part of the context in which organizational interaction is embedded. Studies of interaction demonstrate how these roles are enacted and realized: that is, how the somewhat abstract organizational structures are brought to life, given the situated meaning and how consequences are produced (Boden, 1994). Two major themes in the existing studies are a focus on the role of the chair in meetings and how a designated leader performs his or her role through various leadership styles.

The Role of the Chair

Meetings are a crucial aspect of the management of organizations (Boden, 1994), and central aspects of the function of meetings are connected to the role of the chair: "The chair provides a means of coordinating turns at talk, of operationalising an (agreed) structure, and represents the voice of contextualised authority" (Holmes, Marra, & Vine, 2011, p. 61). According to the everyday understanding of how meetings work, the chair is endowed with certain exclusive discursive rights (Asmuss & Svennevig, 2009; Clifton, 2006, 2009) that might be utilized to accomplish influence and generally to perform organizational work. Although it is not always the formally highest-ranking leader who chairs a meeting, being the chair is a natural part of most leadership roles (Svennevig, 2011; Van Praet, 2009).

Even if the role of the chair is endowed with certain discursive and interactional rights, these need to be accepted and treated as legitimate by the other participants. The formal authority held by the person acting as chair is one important legitimizing resource. Studying a clearly hierarchical situation, Van Praet (2009) shows an ambassador, with clear formal authority, enacting his role by "supervising, directing and streamlining team performance" (p. 86), verbally emphasizing the importance of the task and role of the team and being explicitly evaluative of team performance. In contrast, Pomerantz and Denvir (2007) showed how a chair who was not the formal manager was constantly oriented toward the need to secure legitimacy for his decisions from the president of the firm (see Extract 1).

Extract 1

1014 Sam S:	That's why you're here tonight=[1]
1015 Harry S:	= Well eh Jim in the view of the eh (0.5) we agree to adjourn
1016	at nine I don't think there's much sense in starting the next
1017	item on the agenda, which is succession (.) With your
1018	agreement, I suggest we adjourn (.) here and now gives us a
1019	good night's rest
1023 (. . .):	((4 lines omitted))
1024 Harry S:	I think we'll all sleep on it.
1025	Alright, we'll all sleep on it (0.5) ((someone starts to speak))
1026 Harry S:	(1.0)
	Alright the (.) meeting is adjourned 'til tomorrow morning at (.) nine o'clock when we'll discuss succession

(Pomerantz & Denvir, 2007, p. 37; transcription simplified)

In this extract, Harry S. acts as chair, while Sam S. is the president of the organization and thus has the highest hierarchical position. In lines 1017–1018, the decision to adjourn the meeting is formulated as a suggestion, placing the right to decide in the hands of the participants including the president of the organization. Harry thus displays awareness that his own authority is dependent on the president and crafts his contributions to secure the necessary support. This is an example of how establishing and maintaining legitimacy, even in such a scripted role as the chair, is a practical problem for the incumbent that is naturally attended to in interaction.

Apart from managing the agenda, the role of the chair is important for at least two other tasks in a meeting: managing decision making and managing conflict. To discuss the role of the chair in decision making, we first need to consider how decision making in meetings is performed in practice. Studying actual interactions, those interactions retrospectively treated as a clear decision turn out to be rather fuzzy and difficult to precisely identify. As noted by several researchers, decision making is an incremental process, and it is often not immediately obvious that a decision has been made (Boden, 1994; Clifton, 2009). In Extract 2 from Huisman (2001), Jaap is the senior manager and chair, and the other participants are managers. One of the managers, Henk, asks whether the people who will attend a management presentation in the evening can claim overtime for it, and it is agreed that they cannot.

Extract 2

Henk:	h-ok<u>ay</u> (.) eh tonight is a presentation uh (region b) and uh Thursday in (region a), (.)[1] where it has come to my <u>ears</u> [that a number of people
Jaap:	[((opens the door, comes in, sits down))
Henk:	ask whether there can be written overtime hours (.) how do we go about this. what is the tradition of this uh division.
Jaap:	for what?
Henk:	for the presentations upcom- or today and Thursday. (.) in the evening hours (1.6)
Karel:	oh for those presentations whether you fir those you {can write} overtime hours
Henk:	mechanics uh it particularly come from the mechanics groups that there uh (1.2)
Jaap:	the answer is no
Henk:	[((chin upwards))
Jaap:	[((looks at Jan))
Jan:	((looks at Jaap, lateral head shake))
Jaap:	((looks at Henk))
Jaap:	what do you think?
Henk:	well I completely [agree
Geert:	[((nods, agreeing gesture))
Henk:	but well if it was, [if [it was the case in the past
Karel:	[((shakes head))
Jan:	[no
Henk:	[then I found it a bit difficult to uh
Marcel:	[((lateral head shake))

(Huisman, 2001, p. 78, transcription simplified)

Even though in this extract there is clearly consensus about the question, there is no specific point when the decision is "made." It could have been when Jaap (the chair) says "the answer is no," or with Jan's nonverbal confirmation (the head shake), or after each subsequent agreement, verbal or non-verbal, but the conversation on the topic continues. Despite the consensus on the issue, there is no clear closure to this episode and no announcement of a decision being or having been made. Nevertheless, the participants (and probably the reader) easily understand the situation as a decision being made. This understanding is displayed in their later treatment of it and in references to the decision. The point here is that this understanding does not rest on any identifiable element in the interaction but rather on a retrospective sensemaking of the sequence as a whole.

Instead of decisions, Huisman calls such interactional sequences "decision-making episodes," that is:

> an interactional process in which participants jointly construct the formulation of states of affairs, and through further assessment and formulation build commitment to particular future states of affairs.
>
> *(2001, p. 75)*

In the extract above, the managers construct a description of the issue of overtime in relation to the management presentation: that is, there will be (and already are) questions about the possibility of claiming overtime. This is followed by the development of a positive assessment to decline future claims on overtime.

This perspective on decision making has important consequences for our understanding of leadership. Rather than focusing only on the process of *making* decisions (influencing others to agree), attention should also be turned to leadership as a process of convincing others that a decision *has been* made: that is, shaping the collective sensemaking of what has been going on.

The role of the chair provides powerful resources both for shaping the decision-making process and for claiming that a decision has been made. The chair is typically endowed with the right to shift topics: that is, with managing the agenda (Svennevig, 2012). Treating a topic as closed and moving on to another is one way to claim that a decision has been made. When a decision cannot be produced—that is, when it is difficult to find an outcome that is positively assessed by the relevant people—the chair might try to change the interaction order. Turns can be distributed differently, for instance by reaching out to participants who have been reticent about their views, or the discussion might be moved to another occasion and possibly involve other participants.

In building consensus around states of affairs and assessments, summaries—which conversation analysts call formulations—play an important role. Formulations are "repeat utterances that display a characterization of prior talk for confirmation or disconfirmation" (Barnes, 2007, p. 275), or, more generally, they are summaries of the gist of what has been said before (Heritage & Watson, 1979). Barnes (2007) and Clifton (2006) both show how formulations build and stabilize consensus, thereby functioning as "harbingers of decisions" (Barnes, 2007, p. 292). Formulations might be produced by anyone, but the chair normally has both a particular right and an obligation to summarize and thereby to influence the decision-making events.

Broadening the perspective somewhat, Wodak, Kwon and Clarke (2011) identified five different discursive strategies employed by leaders in the process of building consensus: bonding, encouraging, directing, modulating and re/committing. Bonding concerns the construction of a group identity that supports the motivation to reach consensus and decisions and is accomplished, for instance, by the skilled use of the pronoun "we." Encouraging concerns involving speakers, thus furthering participation and "buy-in" to a decision. Directing concerns bringing the discussion toward closure and resolution, while modulating concerns regulating the perception of external threats or internal imperatives to act. Re/committing, finally, concerns a move from consensus around an issue toward a commitment to action. *

The diametric opposite of consensus is conflict, and the management of conflict is another conventional expectation for the role of the chair. While furthering consensus is a way to prevent conflict, clear conflict management strategies can also be identified. In a study by Holmes and Marra (2004), four discursive strategies for managing conflict in meetings were identified: conflict avoidance by asserting "the agenda"; conflict diversion; conflict resolution, using negotiation; and conflict resolution using authority by imposing a decision (p. 441). In their study, individual leaders engaged in different strategies in different contexts, showing that the exercise of authority is complex and highly situated.

Clearly, the role of the chair includes managing several sensitive interactional issues. The studies discussed above not only show various tactics employed by the chair but also demonstrate the contextual dependence of both the issues and their management. While there is a range of more general rights and obligations endowed on the chair, the actual enactment of this role is highly varied and to a large degree dependent on the evolving interaction with other participants.

Leadership Styles

Focusing on the actions of a designated leader offers the possibility of more closely examining concepts such as style. Most of the studies that use the concept of leadership style draw on a classification of leader actions along a dimension between centralized and clear authority on the one hand, called authoritarian (Svennevig, 2011; Wodak et al., 2011), hierarchical (Van Praet, 2009; Wodak et al., 2011) or transactional (Holmes & Marra, 2004; Holmes, 2005), and a more decentralized and shared authority on the other hand, called egalitarian (Svennevig, 2011), laissez-faire, transformational (Holmes & Marra, 2004; Holmes, 2005) or bottom up (Yeung, 2004a).

A somewhat more elaborate analysis of leadership style is proposed by Walker and Aritz (2014). Using a framework suggested by Coates (2004), they analyze five aspects of communication: the meaning of questions; links between speaker turns; topic shifts; listening; and simultaneous speech. The authors identify three different styles, which vary in their degree of collaboration between leader and subordinates: directive, cooperative and collaborative. The directive style is characterized by one-way communication, with questions used to direct members, few links between turns and abrupt topic shifts. In contrast, in the collaborative style, questions are used to frame the interaction and check for agreement, topic shifts are smooth and there are frequent cooperative overlaps of speech. The cooperative style is located between these: turns are linked through the acknowledgment of contributions, and listening is active, but relatively little speech overlaps.

The conceptualization of leadership styles along the dimension of centralized versus decentralized authority, or authoritarian versus egalitarian style, captures a central aspect of leadership (see for instance DeRue & Ashford, 2010). Studies demonstrating how such styles are realized in live interaction clearly contribute to the existing literature. However, it is somewhat striking that the studies mainly focus on the dimension of centralized versus decentralized authority, leaving other aspects unexplored, such as charismatic[2] (Conger & Kanungo, 1998), visionary (Bryman, 1992), authentic (Avolio & Gardner, 2005) or shared leadership (Pearce & Conger, 2003).

Most of the studies examining styles build on the assumption that styles are consequential for interactions. For instance, in the previously cited study by Wodak et al. (2011), the authors argue that an egalitarian leadership style, as opposed to a more authoritarian or "hierarchical" style, has a clear positive influence on building a durable consensus. Similarly, Holmes, Schnurr and Marra (2007), in studying changes in leadership style and team culture, suggest that "[a] detailed analysis of leadership performance may thus provide valuable insights into the impact leaders actually have on the construction, maintenance, and change of workplace culture" (p. 448).

Clearly, such a claim has much face validity. However, as the notion of romance of leadership (Meindl, Ehrlich, & Dukerich, 1985) implies, the tendency to see leadership as a causal factor might be as much a consequence of our sensemaking processes as of actual causal relationships. Obviously, a formal leader has access to specific symbolic resources that can be used to influence the interaction, including access to information and formal authority to make decisions with material consequences (such as, for instance, hiring and firing subordinates). The way that formal authority is enacted is therefore obviously important in shaping the interaction. However, it needs to be shown rather than assumed that the causal relationship runs in the direction from leadership to interaction. At least in some situations, it is possible to see a certain leadership style as an alignment with the evolving interaction instead of as a force shaping it. For instance, a style might emerge as a response to a developing conflict (Holmes & Marra, 2004) or as an alignment with cultural expectations providing legitimacy (Yeung, 2004a, 2004b).

In summary, the studies focusing on leadership as an enactment of a formal role bring a range of phenomena into focus, not least the complexities of such an apparently scripted and common role as chairing meetings.

The Ontological Status of Roles and Structures

This line of studies also makes some more general comments relevant. Taking a formal role as the starting point for studies of interaction raises questions of how the relationship between structure and interaction is to be understood and about the ontological assumptions about what an organization "is." At least two different interpretations of a role are available. Following an essentialist assumption, the role can be seen as a structural context that is ontologically real and existing prior to the interaction. Interaction is the arena in which this context is enacted and becomes visible (the bucket theory of context, Heritage & Clayman, 2010), and the analysis focuses on the variations and contingencies in the actual enactment. Causality runs from the role to the interaction.

The second, more constructionist, interpretation is that the role does not exist in any sense other than its accomplishment. Interaction is here seen to have ontological primacy, and the resulting roles are something emerging from the interaction. Causality then runs from the interaction to the structure, and structure is seen as created and re-created in interaction (through what Garfinkel (1967) calls the "documentary method of interpretation": that is, creating the impression that a structure exists by treating the interaction as evidence of it) and is denied any ontological existence outside of this.

Clearly, many of the studies cited demonstrate that, even though the role as leader or as chair of a meeting rests on certain assumptions regarding pre-existing structures, any enactment of this role needs to be recognized as such by the participants in the interaction. As most clearly expressed by Huisman (2001), decision making depends on a consensus among (at least the relevant) participants to "be" a decision, and what the participants actually hear as a decision varies with the context and culture of the group. Despite drawing on somewhat different assumptions about the ontological status of roles, the cited studies taken together provide strong support for the importance of the dynamics in the interactional arena for the outcomes of the actions of the role's incumbent. As argued for instance by Grint (2005a), although both a formal position and the person holding it are important, leadership reasonably consists of a complex interplay between a number of aspects, including the processes of the evolving interactional dynamic.

Leadership and Identity

A second theme in the studies of leadership interaction concerns identity. Within the field of leadership research, identity has been seen as important for, among other things, taking on leadership roles and the performance of leadership, and as an important aspect of developing leadership capacities. Using the common distinction between individual, relational and collective identities (Brewer & Gardner, 1996; DeRue & Ashford, 2010), most studies of leadership identity can be seen to focus on the individual level. For instance, Lord and colleagues (Lord, Brown, & Freiberg, 1999; Lord & Hall, 2005) draw on the concept of a cognitive self-concept to explore leadership relations, while Shamir and Eilam (2005) describe the importance of leadership self-narratives. Another range of studies, drawing on social identity theory, tends to focus on collective identity in the sense of self-categorization as a member of a certain collective (without necessarily interacting with this collective; Ellemers, De Gilder, & Haslam, 2004; Haslam, Reicher, & Platow, 2011; Van Knippenberg, Van Knippenberg, De Cremer, & Hogg, 2004).

Studies of leadership interaction, however, tend instead to focus on relational identities. Here, identity is typically seen as negotiated and constructed in interaction rather than as an individually held concept or self-categorization. Identities are thus always at stake, fragile and potentially rapidly shifting (Antaki & Widdicombe, 1998; de Fina, Schiffrin, & Bamberg, 2006).

Identity as a leader might be inferred through the staging of the situation (Rosen, 1985, 1988; Van Praet, 2009), in which the formal leader is positioned at the end of a table or given a stand in front of subordinates. Such physical arrangements shape the expectations of the participating actors, thus creating a specific interaction order (Goffman, 1983): that is, specific "rules of the game."

Of more interest to us here, however, is how identity is negotiated in interaction. Aspects such as control over the agenda (Svennevig, 2012; Van Praet, 2009), control over topic shifts (Walker & Aritz, 2014) and access to symbolic resources such as knowledge (Nielsen, 2009) have all been shown to be used to claim and establish a leader identity. Further, the interactional functions of humor have received considerable attention. For instance, Schnurr (2009) showed how the use of teasing humor helps to provide interactional identities for leaders in relation to their groups. By using teasing humor, leaders display their power and their right to criticize their subordinates, while simultaneously adhering to the group norms for such humor use. An identity is created of someone who has more power but still belongs to the group.

Within membership categorization analysis (at times considered a part of conversation analysis; Hester & Eglin, 1997; Schegloff, 2007), identities are seen as the categories that individuals and collectives are interactively placed in (Antaki & Widdicombe, 1998). Such categorizations are consequential, because they are associated (by the participants of the interaction) with certain characteristics, actions, relationships and so forth. For instance, categorizing a woman as a mother brings expectations of her being adult, having a child and displaying caretaking of the child.

Drawing on this methodology, Nielsen (2009) showed how leaders in interaction claimed a variety of identities associated with authority and how these identities were accepted and responded to by the participants in the meetings. For instance, by explicating how things should be labeled and explaining why, a manager is seen to claim an interactional identity as an "interpreter" (see Extract 3).

Extract 3

```
 2 Lone:     and there one can say that that project which Sigurd is responsible for¹
 3           .h (.) he has in effect ONE such page
 4           (.)
 5 Kirsten:  hm
 6           (0.4)
 7 Lone:     and there he has managed eighty percent of his marks
 8           (1.0)
 9 Per:      [no] (. ) [that's not] that's not [correct [right] because
10 Lone:     [one could] [say right] [OH] that's
11 ?:        [no] [that's not - -
12 Lone:     not correct ei[ther]
13           Ki: [no]
14           (0.2)
15 Per:      you may say (. ) you may say there could be a project here
16           that was called [(0.2)] for instance (0.8) e: :h (.)
17 Lone:     [h]
18 Lone:     hrm
19           (0.2)
20 Per:      ad(.)justment that's y'know the words to use right,
21           [(0.4)]
22 Lone:     [hh m]
23 Per:      adjustment of the department of development
24           (0.9)
25 Lone:     and that then stands as one project
```

(Nielsen, 2009, pp. 34–35, transcription simplified)

This extract is from a meeting in which the manager Per and two HR consultants Lone and Kirsten discuss a layoff process and more specifically how to translate this process into the vocabulary of projects used in the organization. In lines 20–25, Per calls the process a project concerning adjustment and notes that "adjustment" is the correct term to use in this organization. He interprets the process in the available language and, in doing so, implicitly categorizes himself as an "interpreter." This illustrates the notion of category-associated actions (Hester & Eglin, 1997; Schegloff, 2007), meaning that certain categories of actors are associated with certain actions (a teacher explains, a thief steals, and so on). Performing a category-associated action interactively categorizes the actor accordingly. Identity in interaction can thus not only be verbally claimed but also accomplished in action. However, such categorizations need to be accepted by other participants for any interactional consequences to be accomplished (Schegloff, 2007). In this extract, Lone's comment in line 25 works as a completion of Per's in line 25, thus demonstrating alignment with his interpretation. She thereby accepts his interactive identity as an "interpreter," and Per manages to fulfill the important leadership task of communicating the organizational vocabulary to his subordinates.

Of course, interactively establishing identities as leader and follower is not always a straightforward process. Schnurr and Chan (2011) used the notion of face to analyze episodes of disagreement among co-leaders, that is "two leaders in vertically contiguous positions who share the responsibilities of leadership" (Jackson & Parry, 2008, p. 82). Face is here understood as the positive social value a person claims for him- or herself. Disagreement not only constitutes threats to face but also challenges the relative power balance between the two co-leaders:

> [B]y orienting to or challenging each others' face, members of co-leadership constellations at the same time portray themselves (and each other) as more or less powerful and in charge, and thereby construct their intertwined professional identities as leader and co-leader.
>
> *(Schnurr & Chan, 2011, p. 204)*

Disagreements caused rapidly shifting identities between leader and co-leader as the discussion unfolded. The interactional identity as "leader" emerges as a fragile and complex achievement, closely tied to interpersonally sensitive issues, such as face.

Instead of focusing on the individual identity of a "leader," Larsson and Lundholm (2013) emphasized how the participants in an interaction sequence in a bank were occupied with negotiating the task at hand and finding ways to work on this task. In this process, task-based interactional identities were constructed, such as being account manager attending to potential risks with the customer in question. Their analysis supports Fairhurst's (2007b) earlier observation that close attention to interaction tends to show how leadership in practice is engaged with advancing the task at hand rather than being "something that floats ethereally above task accomplishment as some metalevel commentary" (p. 59), as is common in approaches relying more on interviews or surveys.

Further, Larsson and Lundholm (2013) suggest that the process involves construction of not only individual but also situated collective identities. For instance, in their analysis, the small collective consisting of the group manager and the account manager together analyzing a problem with a customer is constructed by using the pronoun "we" with reference to the interacting parties and by using subtle categorization moves indicating membership in this small collective. Similarly, Djordjilovic (2012) utilized a multimodal analysis (analyzing both linguistic and non-linguistic interaction) to show how two group members "team up" and act as a unit with shared accountability in relation to a task area. By co-constructing their contributions to the team and being addressed as a unit by other units, the two team members were endowed with epistemic authority over their task: that is, shared authoritative knowledge. It is to be noted that this type of interactional collective identity is distinct from Brewer and Gardner's (1996) concept of collective identity, indicating self-categorization to a group without necessarily interacting with it. The collective identities described by Djordjilovic (2012) and Larsson and Lundholm (2013) are instead established in interaction as a "we who are in this together."

However, interactional identities are also constructed in larger scale contexts, such as more general discourses (Alvesson & Willmott, 2002; Collinson, 2003, 2006) and organizational contexts. Using positioning theory, Clifton (2014) analyzed storytelling in meetings and showed a complex interplay between identities constructed in the stories (e.g., identity of the company), in the ongoing interaction and in relation to large-scale discourses. The local practice of storytelling thus allowed the manager to claim and establish an interactional position from which strategic organizational issues might be managed.

Which Identities Are Relevant to Leadership?

Although studies of leadership in interaction generally focus on interactional and relational identities in contrast to the dominating interest in individual and collective (in the sense of membership in larger collectives) identities, some of the studies clearly share an interest in the labels of leader and follower. The studies by Schnurr (2009) and Schnurr and Chan (2011) cited above provide two such examples. These studies resonate closely with the general theory for identity construction proposed by DeRue and Ashford (2010), in which leader and follower identities are seen as being established through an iterative process of claiming and granting respective identity.

Other studies, however, demonstrate the interactional significance of other types of identities. Svennevig (2011) suggests that epistemic authority—that is, the claim of having authoritative knowledge—is an important identity dimension. Similarly, Nielsen (2009) showed how identities such as "interpreter" and "expert" were constructed in interaction and worked to move the organizational agenda forward. Larsson and Lundholm (2013) argue that negotiation of situated, task-bound identities are conducive to problem solving. Leadership is here accomplished through the construction of identities that further the task at hand rather than through the identities of leader and follower as such.

Using the language of ethnomethodology, the emphasis on leader/follower versus other identities might be seen as illustrating the difference between participant and analyst concerns. In many of the studies, the label of leadership is an analytically driven concept rather than something that the participants visibly orient toward. Participants often appear to be more occupied with the task at hand, be it organizing the interaction or solving problems with customer accounts, than with sorting out more abstract labels such as leader and follower.

The interest in identities, of course, rests on the assumption that these are important to the leadership process. Within cognitively and social-cognitively oriented research traditions (Lord et al., 1999; Shamir, House, & Arthur, 1993; Van Knippenberg et al., 2004), it has been shown that follower self-concepts exert significant influence on follower motivation and behavior. These theories say less, however, about the processes through which identities are shaped and constructed or the processes through which established self-concepts in turn influence performance and leadership effectiveness.

An interactional perspective on identity suggests that identities might be of importance for the leadership process beyond their role in shaping self-concepts. Establishing an identity in interaction allows certain subsequent moves and makes others less available. For instance, it is crucial for the manager in the last extract that his interactional identity as "interpreter" is established for him to be able to fulfill the task of communicating the organizational vocabulary. This perspective allows an understanding of the leadership process more as a shaping of the local context of available moves by molding interactional identities than as the establishment of leader and follower identities as such.

Clearly, the relevance of the study of identity depends on the relationship between identities and core aspects of the leadership process. In the next section, we turn to a closer examination of how the studies of interaction to date have thrown light on interpersonal influence, which is probably the most central aspect of the leadership process.

Interpersonal Influence and Organizing

A third area in which studies of interaction contribute to our understanding of leadership concerns the core processes of exerting interpersonal influence and organizing action. Influence is generally understood as the process through which power is realized (Pfeffer, 1992, p. 30). Influence might in practice be accomplished in a variety of ways. In an early study, Kipnis, Schmidt and Wilkinsoon (1980) identified eight dimensions of influence. This list of tactics was gradually refined by later research (e.g., Yukl & Falbe, 1990), until Yukl, Seifertz and Chavez

(2008) finally extended the list to 11 types of tactics: rational persuasion, apprising, inspirational appeals, consultation, collaboration, ingratiation, personal appeals, exchange, coalition tactics, legitimating tactics and pressure.

Such dimensions and classes of behavior might in practice be realized in a number of ways, with attention to the specific situation, its possibilities and its constraints. In interaction, a range of practical problems need to be managed, such as creating legitimacy for a demand or finding ways to ensure that proposed actions will be carried out, while managing face (Brown & Levinson, 1987; Clifton, 2009) for all participants and following the norms inherent in the local culture (Holmes, 2007).

A number of studies demonstrate that influence might be accomplished in interaction through a large number of interactional moves that are also found in many other contexts. For instance, Samra-Fredericks (2003), studying how a strategist managed to influence his colleagues to agree to a certain understanding of the company's strategic situation, observed that the strategist's talk included six important features. These were the ability: to speak forms of knowledge (knowledge embedded in social interaction, for instance, displayed in the skilled use of relevant categories and labels); to mitigate and observe the protocols of human interaction; to question and query; to display appropriate emotion; to deploy metaphors; and finally to put "history" to work. These tactics were all used in varied ways to put his case forward and convince others, but none of these tactics are distinct to strategists' talk, or to talk that accomplishes influence.

Acknowledging the flexible and situated nature of influence, a number of specific mechanisms used to accomplish influence have been examined in more detail. First and foremost are formulations (summaries of the gist of what has been said previously), which were already discussed in relation to decision making. Formulations have an influence function: they fix the meaning of what has transpired before and thereby define the available interactional moves for the participants (Clifton, 2006; Huisman, 2001; Larsson & Lundholm, 2013).

Laughter might also have important influence functions. Holmes (2007) shows how humor and laughter can work to establish cohesion and community, thereby influencing commitment and the available range of interactional moves. Distinguishing between "laughing with" and "laughing at" humor might also work to exclude and make certain positions and arguments less legitimate. Clifton (2009) shows how the treatment of one participant's contribution as "laughable" (something to which laughter is a reasonable response) constructed it as deviant and as reflecting sub-standard performance and excluded its influence on the further treatment of the topic. Laughter might thus work to shape the boundaries for acceptable contributions in addition to performing an inclusive function.

The management of meaning (Smircich & Morgan, 1982) and sensemaking (Pye, 2005) are generally seen as central to leadership. Some of the practical mechanisms for accomplishing this in interaction include labeling and reframing issues in terms of organizationally relevant concepts and discourses, thereby linking local concerns to organizationally strategic issues. Clifton (2012) showed how the assessment of a previous decision was influenced by the introduction of a political, as opposed to artistic, frame and by portraying the organization as primarily a political entity.

Similarly, Larsson and Lundholm (2013) as well as Nielsen (2009) showed how labeling and introducing a specific vocabulary shaped not only the understanding of the current and future situations but also held identity implications for the participants. Working on a task that is semantically linked to broader organizational concerns links individual identity to organizational identity. Framing, translating and labeling thus have potentially broad-ranging consequences, echoing the importance tied to categorizations within ethnomethodologically oriented research (Hester & Eglin, 1997) and broader organizational theory (for instance, Tsoukas & Chia, 2002).

In Larsson and Lundholm's (2010, 2013) work, influence is closely tied to negotiation of the task at hand and to the organizing of actions. For instance, they show how a group manager persuades a subordinate to see the task at hand in a new way (Larsson & Lundholm, 2013; see Extract 4).

Extract 4

50	Roy:	so if we look at (.) the <u>full</u> <u>picture</u>
51	Harriet:	there's no risk associated with him[1]
52		but I'd <u>like</u> you to have a <u>look</u> at the <u>security</u> (.) do you need
53		(.) do you <u>nee:d</u> (.) eh he has a credit limit of <u>four</u> (.) <u>hund</u>red
54	Roy:	mm
55	Harriet:	does he (0.8) does he <u>need</u> to have (0.5) do you <u>nee:d</u>
56		(0.5) <u>four</u> <u>hund</u>red (.) as the value for <u>this</u> (2.0) <u>security</u>
57	Roy:	what does it <u>look</u> like then (.) doesn't he have ((inaudible))
58		<u>security</u>
59		(0.8)
60	Harriet:	but you <u>have</u> (.) because you have reserved <u>four</u> <u>hund</u>red there
61		right
62	Roy:	yes
63	Harriet:	and he has a <u>credit</u> of <u>four</u> <u>hundred</u>
64	Roy:	yes (.) yes[((inaudible))
65	Harriet:	[so] I mean as soon as <u>he</u> <u>touches</u> it (.)
66		then he'll be <u>overdrawn</u> (0.5) since he doesn't have any (.)
		he has no other shares ((inaudible))
		(1.1) it seems he <u>had</u> that <u>before</u>, right
	Roy:	yesyes he's had (.) about a million there (1.1)
	Harriet:	so I mean (.) to have it like this will be difficult right (.)
		that he has a limit of <u>four</u> (1.2) and a collateral eng<u>ag</u>ement
		of <u>four</u> <u>hund</u>red (.) for as soon as he uses any of it he'll be
		<u>overdrawn</u>
		unusually stupid
	Harriet:	yes (0.9) ((both Ha and Ro looks at the screen))
	Roy:	.hhyes
	Harriet:	it doesn't <u>work</u> because I mean the <u>shares</u> <u>never</u> have <u>full</u>
		<u>collat</u>eral value
	Roy:	no

(Larsson & Lundholm, 2013, pp. 1114–1115; transcription simplified)

In this extract, the group manager Harriet performs a step-wise elaboration of her understanding of the issue at hand. She starts out at line 51 by asking about the credit and continues through turns 53, 55, 57, 59 and 61 by developing the understanding that there is something wrong with the construction of the credit. Of importance here is that she does not develop this in one long turn, but stops several times and allows the subordinate, Roy, to contribute (turns 52, 54, 56, 58) and even to add some substantial information (turn 58). Through his active involvement, he becomes an active part of the developing understanding and is finally placed in a position where his only reasonable choice of action is to accept her argument (turns 62, 64, 66). He thus moves from an understanding of the issue as being related to risk (turn 50) to an understanding that it is a question of the construction of the credit (and thereby of profitability). The task at hand shifts from managing risks to constructing credit. The step-wise character of the elaboration thus has a strong persuasive effect on Roy by gradually shaping his viable interactional options.

This extract further illustrates how leadership might have organizing properties. Although leadership is often seen as closely related to organizing (Fairhurst, 2007b; Hosking & Morley, 1988), organizing processes are rarely demonstrated empirically. In one of the few studies attempting this (without discussing leadership), Cooren and Fairhurst (2004) show organizing to be accomplished on a turn-by-turn basis in discursive interaction.

Larsson and Lundholm (2013) argue that leadership might have organizing properties by shaping the obligations of the participants: that is, as a consequence of shaping identities. In the extract above, the persuasion results in new rights and obligations for Roy. He now has an obligation to act according to his new understanding and to provide a better construction of the credit.[3] These obligations are constructed in relation to Harriet, as the other party in the "we working on the credit" team (a situated collective identity, as discussed earlier). The influence process thereby shapes both the understanding of the task at hand and the commitment to act accordingly. Similarly, Clifton (2009) argues that decisions include a commitment to action and that the decision-making episodes described earlier therefore have a certain influence and organizing aspect.

Clearly, attempts to influence another are a sensitive interpersonal issue. Persuasion attempts are regularly coupled with a number of mitigating moves and tactics to preserve the interpersonal context and to preserve face for the interacting parties (Walker & Aritz, 2014). For instance, the use of discourse markers such as "but" softens any suggestions for action (Samra-Fredericks, 2003), and, when requests for action are made, these are designed with attention to and respect for the recipient's situation and other constraints (Curl & Drew, 2008; Larsson & Lundholm, 2013).

These studies clearly demonstrate that, although leaders perform influence attempts, the accomplishment of influence is a collaborative achievement. Subordinates actively contribute by challenging and offering new ideas (Clifton, 2009, 2014), by using the labels and categories offered by leaders (Nielsen, 2009; Larsson & Lundholm, 2013) and generally by collaborating to produce influence effects. Leadership as influence is thus placed firmly in the arena of interaction and relation rather than as an individual attribute or action on behalf of the leader.

Summary and Contributions to Leadership Knowledge

The studies of leadership in interaction discussed here together provide a number of unique contributions to the existing body of leadership knowledge. First, studies of actual work interactions obviously portray leadership as deeply situated and embedded in a local context. While this is hardly surprising, it is in stark contrast to much of the theorizing in the leadership literature. This lack of attention to context has repeatedly been lamented by scholars (Bryman, Stephens, & Campo, 1996; Fairhurst, 2007a; Liden & Antonakis, 2009; Porter & McLaughlin, 2006). However, these scholars mostly focus on the lack of attention to the wider organizational context, while the studies reviewed here bring attention to another type of context. Focusing on talk-in-interaction as the central means of exercising authority and performing leadership (Gronn, 1983) reveals that the leader is highly dependent on actual interactional opportunities and available situations. Contributions need to be tailored to the specific interactional "slot" in which they are produced and to connect to the topic as well as the relational context.

The embedded nature of leadership is shown in the illustrations throughout the chapter. In Extract 3, the manager Per engages with an emerging discussion about how to interpret and label a lay-off process, positions himself as an "interpreter" and explicates how the organizational vocabulary is to be used. The detailed understanding of this particular version of an identity (as shown in Nielsen, 2009) brings a different type of insight compared with studies of frequencies and variation. Similarly, the analysis of influence performed through the stepwise elaboration of an understanding of a task, shown in Extract 4, offers unique insights into the particulars of the actual performance of influence. As argued by Fairhurst (2007a) and also Conger (1998), variable-based quantitative studies might establish causal relationships but are less useful for clarifying the mechanisms through which the observed effects are established, that is "the 'cellular biology' that . . . explicates the mechanisms linking the outcomes [to] . . . the variables which assertedly engender those outcomes" (Schegloff, 2001, p. 315, as cited in Fairhurst 2007a, p. 16). Studies of interaction throw some light on these mechanisms, not least by suggesting that the identities of leader and follower might not be the most important factor from the perspective of the participants.

This deeply embedded nature of human interaction explains some of the variability in the phenomena under study and possibly the fact that leadership has often been described as difficult to observe. Alvesson and Sveningsson (2003) talk about "the great disappearing act" and Kan and Parry (2004) discuss leadership as repressed in practice. These difficulties in observing leadership can to a certain extent be understood as a question of attempting to identify specific acts, recognizable through ordinary observation, while the phenomenon in reality is far more varied. The studies presented together here forcefully demonstrate that leadership is clearly observable but primarily as a situated accomplishment at the micro level of interaction, which normally requires a careful analysis of recorded interaction to be made visible.

The studies presented here all build on observations and recordings of live workplace interactions. In contrast to interviews and surveys, such recordings do not rely on the participants' own sensemaking of interactions and relationships. The participants' sensemaking process is turned into an object of study rather than a window providing access to the central phenomenon. As shown by Huisman (2001) and illustrated in Extract 2, decisions are more a question of the participants' retrospective sensemaking than of any particular interactional action as such. Leadership, then, concerns at least as much the shaping of this later understanding that a decision has been made (for instance, through the use of summaries—so-called formulations) as the *making* of decisions. As noted by Clifton (2006), decisions are clearly relevant to leadership, as decisions work to fix the organizational reality.

Studies of leadership in interaction further contribute to the interest in identity within leadership studies. The focus on identity as being negotiated and accomplished in interaction supplements the dominating focus on individual (Lord & Brown, 2004; Lord & Hall, 2005; Shamir & Eilam, 2005) and social (Ellemers et al., 2004; Knippenberg, Knippenberg, Cremer, & Hogg, 2004). The interest in interactional identities resonates strongly with the framework proposed by DeRue and Ashford (2010), who argue that the negotiation of relational identities is fundamental to both individual and collective identities and to leaders and followers. In Extract 3, Nielsen (2009) shows an identity claim by a leader that is acknowledged by a follower. Extract 4 shows a more elaborate process of influence, in which a specific follower identity is offered to the subordinate (Roy) and gradually accepted by him as he aligns with the perspective developed by the leader. This type of analysis contributes to the understanding of identity negotiation as proposed by DeRue and Ashford (2010) by demonstrating some of the mechanisms and dynamics involved.

Even more importantly, these studies suggest that the focus on leader and follower identities might not be the most important concern for the participants. As earlier noted by Fairhurst

(2007a, 2007b), close attention to actual practice reveals that engagement with the task at hand is a dominant concern, making work a central context to consider (Barley & Kunda, 2001) in leadership processes. Advancing the task at hand often requires identities other than leader and follower that are more focused on practical problems and their management. To the extent that leadership is seen as concerned with advancement of the task at hand (Fairhurst, 2007b), construction of such problem-oriented identities would be a central aspect of the leadership process. In essence, studies of interaction suggest that an occupation with the identity labels of leader and follower might be as much a consequence of the analyst's interest in leadership as a necessary element in the practical work. Focusing instead on the identities relevant to the participants of the interaction opens the potential for a deeper understanding of the mechanisms linking identities to effects and outcomes (Fairhurst, 2007a).

Studies of interaction further provide a unique window into the central processes of influence. Rather than being distinct tactics, influence is here shown to be accomplished through the skilled use of ordinary discursive mechanisms (Samra-Fredericks, 2003). As shown in the discussion of Extract 4, influence is partly accomplished through the turn construction, in which pauses allow the follower to engage with an evolving new understanding of the task. This goes beyond the typologies of influence (Clifton, 2009) by showing that the effect here is less a question of which "type" of influence is employed and more a question of how it is produced in the actual interactional situation. Studies of interaction thus contribute a process-oriented understanding of influence to leadership knowledge in which, for instance, identities and turn construction (Larsson & Lundholm, 2013), stories (Clifton, 2014) and use of knowledge (Samra-Fredricks, 2003) might play important roles.

Finally, the study presented here offers a perspective on the leadership process as basically shared and distributed. Decisions emerge as collaborative achievements (Clifton 2009, 2012; Huisman, 2001), as do identity construction (Nielsen, 2009; Holmes et al., 2011; Walker & Aritz, 2014) and influence attempts (Clifton, 2009; Larsson & Lundholm, 2013). To be legitimate, leaders need to connect to and build on cultural values within as well as surrounding the organization (Jones, 2005) and to visibly engage these cultural values in their interactions (Holmes et al., 2007). In essence, acknowledgment of these constraints on leadership works to shift attention to more distributed (Gronn, 2002; Pearce & Conger, 2003), relational (Uhl-Bien, 2006) and contextually oriented (Fairhurst, 2007b; Grint, 2005b) perspectives.

Ways Forward

Clearly, studies of leadership in interaction are demanding, as they require the analysis of messy empirical material. They require access to analytical resources, such as conversation analysis and interactional sociolinguistics, that currently are not standard methodologies in organizational behavior or organization studies and that are seldom found in the curriculum for doctoral studies in these areas. Moving this research field forward thus heavily depends on doctoral students being brave enough to take on new fields and on collaborative research between scholars with different disciplinary backgrounds. This gap is also reflected in the fact that many studies of leadership in interaction are found in discourse- and language-oriented journals, such as *Discourse & Society*, *Pragmatics* and *Text & Talk*, rather than in traditional leadership journals (although some are found in *Leadership* and *Human Relations*). Fortunately, a certain amount of work has already been published that makes this approach better known and more accepted among organizational and leadership scholars (Llewellyn, 2008; Llewellyn & Hindmarsh, 2010; Samra-Fredericks, 2000).

Studies of leadership in interaction also face a number of analytical challenges. Although a fair amount of work has already been undertaken to operationalize leadership at an interactional level, more work is needed to connect the empirical analysis to theoretical problems in the leadership field. An illustrative case is the studies of leadership style. While drawing on central concepts, such as transformational and transactional leadership, the analysis here tends to focus on the single dimension of the centrality versus the distribution of authority. Here is a clear opportunity for a deeper engagement with the existing theoretical challenges facing, for example, the theory of transformational leadership.

In essence, the import of studies of leadership in interaction could be increased by a stronger problematization of leadership theory than is currently found in many studies. The relatively low level of problematization of leadership theory, of course, resonates with the outlets chosen. Publication in discourse- and language-oriented journals naturally places these phenomena at center stage, leaving engagement with leadership theory less central. However, as this review illustrates, these studies hold the potential to constitute a far stronger contribution to leadership theory than is currently the case. Of course, publication in leadership and organizationally oriented journals also depends on the general knowledge and acceptance of the methodologies used here (Clifton, 2006; Llewellyn & Hindmarsh, 2010; Llewellyn, 2008).

One such area in which studies of interaction has a strong potential for contribution concerns influence and organizing, processes that are often seen as being central to leadership (Fairhurst, 2007a, 2007b; Hosking & Morley, 1988; Rost, 1991; Yukl, 2013). Studies of interaction offer the ability to examine these processes at a level of detail far beyond surveys and interviews. Further, as argued by Fairhurst (2007a), to the extent that we really are interested in interpersonal processes as the ontological object, taking these same interpersonal processes also as the analytical object holds promise for a deeper understanding. The potential to do this has already been demonstrated in studies attempting to study influence, but far more work remains to be done.

Notes

1 Transcription symbols:

[ ]	Overlapping speech
=	Latching on to previous or next turn
(.)	Short pause
(0.5)	Pause in seconds
<u>over</u>	Underlined: emphasis

2 Despite using the label "transformational," Holmes and Marra (2004) and Holmes (2005) mainly focus on the degree of subordinate involvement and of collaboration rather than on elements of charismatic or visionary leadership in the interaction.

3 Of course, this says nothing about what Roy thinks or whether he believes what Harriet says. The interaction is not a shortcut to individual cognitive processes (the "mental theater" discussed earlier). His overt display of understanding, however, produces an obligation toward Harriet, and his potential lack of belief could later become problematic in terms of her trust in him.

References

Alvesson, M., & Sveningsson, S. (2003). The great disappearing act: Difficulties in doing "leadership." *The Leadership Quarterly, 14*, 359–381.

Alvesson, M., & Willmott, H. (2002). Identity regulation as organizational control: Producing the appropriate individual. *Journal of Managment Studies, 39* (5), 619–644.

Antaki, C., & Widdicombe, S. (1998). *Identities in talk*. London: Sage.

Asmuss, B., & Svennevig, J. (2009). Meeting talk: An introduction. *Journal of Business Communication, 46* (1), 3–22.

Avolio, B. J., & Gardner, W. L. (2005). Authentic leadership development: Getting to the root of positive forms of leadership. *The Leadership Quarterly, 16*, 315–338.

Barley, S. R., & Kunda, G. (2001). Bringing work back in. *Organization Science, 12* (1), 76–95.

Barnes, R. (2007). Formulations and the facilitation of common agreement in meetings talk. *Text & Talk, 27* (3), 273–296.

Boden, D. (1994). *The business of talk: Organizations in action.* Cambridge: Cambridge Polity Press.

Brewer, M. B., & Gardner, W. L. (1996). Who is this "we"? Levels of collective identity and self-representations. *Journal of Personality and Social Psychology, 50*, 543–549.

Brown, P., & Levinson, S. (1987). *Politeness.* Cambridge: Cambridge University Press.

Bryman, A. (1992). *Charisma and leadership in organizations.* London: Sage Publications.

Bryman, A., Stephens, M., & Campo, C. à. (1996). The importance of context: Qualitative research and the study of leadership. *Leadership Quarterly, 7* (3), 353–370.

Carroll, B., Levy, L., & Riochmond, D. (2008). Leadership practice: Challenging the competency paradigm. *Leadership, 4* (4), 363–379.

Clifton, J. (2006). A conversation analytical approach to business communication: The case of leadership. *Journal of Business Communication, 43* (3), 202–219.

Clifton, J. (2009). Beyond taxonimies of influence: "Doing" influence and making decisions in management team meetings. *Journal of Business Communication, 46* (1), 57–79.

Clifton, J. (2012). A discursive approach to leadership: Doing assessments and managing organizational meanings. *Journal of Business Communication, 49* (2), 148–168.

Clifton, J. (2014). Small stories, positioning, and the discursive construction of leader identity in business meetings. *Leadership, 10* (1), 99–117.

Coates, J. (2004). *Women, men, and language: A sociolinguistic account of gender differences in language.* London: Pearson Education.

Collinson, D. (2006). Rethinking followership: A post-structuralist analysis of follower identities. *The Leadership Quarterly, 17* (2), 179–189.

Collinson, D. L. (2003). Identities and insecurities: Selves at work. *Organization, 10* (3), 527–547.

Conger, J. A. (1998). Qualitative research as the cornerstone method for understanding leadership. *The Leadership Quarterly, 9* (1), 107–121.

Conger, J. A., & Kanungo, R. N. (1998). *Charismatic leadership in organizations.* Thousand Oaks, CA: Sage.

Cooren, F., & Fairhurst, G. T. (2004). Speech timing and spacing: The phenomenon of organizational closure. *Organization, 11* (6), 793–824.

Courtright, J. A., Fairhurst, G. T., & Rogers, L. E. (1989). Interaction patterns in organic and mechanistic system. *Academy of Management Journal, 32* (4), 773–802.

Crevani, L., Lindgren, M., & Packendorff, J. (2010). Leadership, not leaders: On the study of leadership as practices and interactions. *Scandinavian Journal of Management, 26*, 77–86.

Curl, T. S., & Drew, P. (2008). Contingency and action: A comparison of two forms of requesting. *Research on Language & Social Interaction, 41* (2), 129–153.

De Fina, A., Schiffrin, D., & Bamberg, M. (Eds.). (2006). *Discourse and identity.* Cambridge: Cambridge University Press.

DeRue, D. S., & Ashford, S. J. (2010). Who will lead and who will follow? A social process of leadership identity construction in organizations. *Academy of Management Review, 35* (4), 627–647.

Djordjilovic, O. (2012). Displaying and developing team identity in workplace meetings: A multimodal perspective. *Discourse Studies, 14* (1), 111–127.

Ellemers, N., De Gilder, D., & Haslam, S. A. (2004). Motivating individuals and groups at work: A social identity perspective on leadership and group performance. *Academy of Management Review, 29* (3), 459–478.

Fairhurst, G. T. (2007a). *Discursive leadership: In conversation with leadership psychology.* Los Angeles: Sage.

Fairhurst, G. T. (2007b). Liberating leadership. In F. Cooren (Ed.), Mahwah, NJ: Lawrence Erbaum Associates.

Fairhurst, G. T. (2009). Considering context in discursive leadership research. *Human Relations, 62* (11), 1607–1633.

Fairhurst, G. T. (2011). *Discursive approaches to leadership* (pp. 495–507). London: Sage.

Garfinkel, H. (1967). *Studies in ethnomethodology.* Englewood Cliffs, NJ: Prentice Hall.

Goffman, E. (1983). The Interaction Order: American Sociological Association, 1982 Presidential Address. *American Sociological Review, 48* (1), 1–17.

Grint, K. (2005a). *Leadership: Limits and possibilities.* New York: Palgrave Macmillan.

Grint, K. (2005b). Problems, problems, problems: The social construction of "leadership." *Human Relations*, *58* (11), 1467–1494.

Gronn, P. (2002). Distributed leadership as a unit of analysis. *The Leadership Quarterly*, *13*, 423–451.

Gronn, P. C. (1983). Talk as the work: The accomplishment of school administration. *Administrative Science Quarterly*, *28* (1), 1–21.

Haslam, S. A., Reicher, S. D., & Platow, M. J. (2011). *The new psychology of leadership: Identity, influence and power*. New York: Psychology Press.

Heritage, J., & Clayman, S. (2010). *Talk in action: Interactions, identities, and institutions* (Vol. 44). Oxford: John Wiley & Sons.

Heritage, J., & Watson, R. (1979). Formulations as conversational objects. In G. Psathas (Ed.), *Everyday language: Studies in ethnomethodology* (pp. 123–162). New York: Irvington.

Hersey, P., & Blanchard, K. H. (1969). *Management of organizational behavior: Utilizing human resources* (Vol. 1077). Englewood Cliffs, NJ: Prentice-Hall.

Hester, S., & Eglin, P. (1997). *Culture in action: Studies in membership categorization analysis*. Washington, DC: International Institute for Ethnomethodology and Conversation Analysis & University Press of America.

Hindmarsh, J., & Llewellyn, N. (2010). Finding organisation in detail: Methodological orientations. In J. Hindmarsh & N. Llewellyn (Eds.), *Studies in ethnomethodology and conversation analysis* (pp. 24–46). Cambridge: Cambridge University Press.

Holmes, J. (2005). Leadership talk: How do leaders "do mentoring" and is gender relevant? *Journal of Pragmatics*, *37*, 1779–1800.

Holmes, J. (2007). Humour and the construction of Maori leadership at work. *Leadership*, *3* (1), 5–27.

Holmes, J., & Marra, M. (2004). Leadership and managing conflict in meetings. *Pragmatics*, *14* (4), 439–462.

Holmes, J., Marra, M., & Vine, B. (2011). *Leadership, discourse, and ethnicity*. New York: Oxford University Press.

Holmes, J., Schnurr, S., & Marra, M. (2007). Leadership and communication: Discursive evidence of a workplace culture change. *Discourse & Communication*, *1* (4), 433–451.

Hosking, D.-M., & Morley, I. E. (1988). The skills of leadership. In J. G. B. Hunt, B. R. Baliga, H. P., Dachler, & C. A. Schriesheim (Eds.), *Emerging leadership vistas* (pp. 89–106). Lexington, MA: Lexington Books.

Huisman, M. (2001). Decision-making in meetings as talk-in-interaction. *International Studies of Management and Organization*, *31* (3), 69–91.

Jackson, B., & Parry, K. (2008). *A very short, fairly interesting and reasonably cheap book about studying leadership*. Los Angeles: Sage.

Jones, A. M. (2005). The anthropology of leadership: Culture and corporate leadership in the American South. *Leadership*, *1* (3), 259–278.

Kan, M. M., & Parry, K. W. (2004). Identifying paradox: A grounded theory of leadership in overcoming resistance to change. *The Leadership Quarterly*, *15*, 467–491.

Kipnis, D., Schmidt, S. M., & Wilkinson, I. (1980). Intraorganizational influence tactics: Explorations in getting one's way. *Journal of Applied Psychology*, *65* (4), 440.

Knights, D., & Willmott, H. (1992). Conceptualizing leadership processes: A study of senior managers in a financial services company. *The Journal of Management Studies*, *29* (6), 761–783.

Knippenberg, D. Van, Knippenberg, B. Van, Cremer, D. De, & Hogg, M. A. (2004). Leadership, self, and identity: A review and research agenda, *15*, 825–856.

Larsson, M., & Lundholm, S. (2010). Leadership as work-embedded influence: A micro-discursive analysis of an everyday interaction in a bank. *Leadership*, *6* (2), 159–184.

Larsson, M., & Lundholm, S. E. (2013). Talking work in a bank: A study of organizing properties of leadership in work interactions. *Human Relations*, *66* (8), 1101–1129.

Liden, R. C., & Antonakis, J. (2009). Considering context in psychological leadership research. *Human Relations*, *62* (11), 1587–1605.

Llewellyn, N. (2008). Organization in actual episodes of work: Harvey Sacks and organization studies. *Organization Studies*, *29* (5), 763–791.

Llewellyn, N., & Hindmarsh, J. (2010). *Organisation, interaction and practice: Studies of ethnomethodology and conversation analysis*. Cambridge: Cambridge University Press.

Lord, R. G, & Brown, D. J. (2004). *Leadership process and follower self-identity*. Mahwah, NJ: Lawrence Erlbaum.

Lord, R. G., Brown, D. J., & Freiberg, S. J. (1999). Understanding the dynamics of leadership: The role of follower self-concepts in the leader/follower relationship. *Organizational Behavior and Human Decision Process*, *78*, 167–203.

Lord, R. G., & Hall, R. J. (2005). Identity, deep structure and the development of leadership skill. *The Leadership Quarterly*, *16*, 591–615.

Meindl, J. R., Ehrlich, S. B., & Dukerich, J. M. (1985). The romance of leadership. *Administrative Science Quarterly*, *30* (1), 78–102.

Mumford, M. D., Zaccaro, S. J., Harding, F. D., Jacobs, T. O., & Fleishman, E. A. (2000). Leadership skills for a changing world: Solving complex social problems. *The Leadership Quarterly*, *11*, 11–35.

Nielsen, M. F. (2009). Interpretative management in business meetings: Understanding managers' interactional strategies through conversation analysis. *Journal of Business Communication*, *46* (1), 23–56.

Osborn, R. N., Hunt, J. G., & Jausch, L. R. (2002). Toward a contextual theory of leadership. *The Leadership Quarterly*, *13*, 797–837.

Pearce, C. L., & Conger, J. A. (Eds.). (2003). *Shared leadership: Reframing the hows and whys of leadership*. Thousand Oaks, CA: Sage.

Pfeffer, J. (1992). *Managing with power: Politics and influence in organizations*. Boston, MA: Harvard Business Press.

Pomerantz, A., & Denvir, P. (2007). Enacting the institutional role of chairperson in upper management meetings: The interactional realization of provisional authority. In F. Cooren (Ed.), *Interacting and organizing: Analyses of a management meeting* (pp. 31–52). Mahwah, NJ: Lawrence Erlbaum.

Porter, L. W., & McLaughlin, G. B. (2006). Leadership and the organizational context: Like the weather? *The Leadership Quarterly*, *17*, 559–576.

Pye, A. (2005). Leadership and organizing: Sensemaking in action. *Leadership*, *1* (1), 31–50.

Rosen, M. (1985). Breakfast at Spiro's: Dramaturgy and dominance. *Journal of Management*, *11* (2), 31.

Rosen, M. (1988). You asked for it: Christmas at the bosses' expense. *Journal of Management Studies*, *25* (5), 463–480.

Rost, J. C. (1991). *Leadership for the twenty-first century*. Westport, CT: Praeger.

Samra-Fredericks, D. (2003). Strategizing as lived experience and strategists' everyday efforts to shape strategic direction. *Journal of Management Studies*, *40* (1), 141–174 (January).

Schegloff, E. A. (2007). A tutorial on membership categorization. *Journal of Pragmatics*, *39* (3), 462–482.

Schnurr, S. (2009). Constructing leader identities through teasing at work. *Journal of Pragmatics*, *41*, 1125–1138.

Schnurr, S., & Chan, A. (2011). Exploring another side of co-leadership: Negotiating professional identities through face-work in disagreements. *Language in Society*, *40* (2), 187–209.

Shamir, B., & Eilam, G. (2005). A life-stories approach to authentic leadership development. *The Leadership Quarterly*, *16* (3), 395–417.

Shamir, B., House, R., & Arthur, M. (1993). The motivational effects of charismatic leadership: A self-concept based theory. *Organization Science*, *4* (4), 577–594.

Smircich, L., & Morgan, G. (1982). Leadership: The management of meaning. *The Journal of Applied Behavioral Science*, *18* (3), 257–273.

Svennevig, J. (2011). Leadership style in managers' feedback in meetings. In J. Angouri & M. Marra (Eds.), (pp. 17–39). London: Palgrave.

Svennevig, J. (2012). The agenda as resource for topic introduction in workplace meetings. *Discourse Studies*, *14* (1), 53–66.

Tsoukas, H., & Chia, R. (2002). On organizational becoming: Rethinking organizational change. *Organization Science*, *13* (5), 567–582.

Uhl-Bien, M. (2006). Relational leadership theory: Exploring the social processes of leadership and organizing, *17*, 654–676.

Uhl-Bien, M., & Ospina, S. M. (2012). *Advancing relational leadership research: A dialogue among perspectives*. Charlotte, NC: IAP.

Van Knippenberg, D., van Knippenberg, B., De Cremer, D., & Hogg, M. A. (2004). Leadership, self, and identity: A review and research agenda. *The Leadership Quarterly*, *15* (6), 825–856.

Van Praet, E. (2009). Staging a team performance: A linguistic ethnographic analysis of weekly meetings at a British embassy. *Journal of Business Communication*, *46* (1), 80–99.

Walker, R. C., & Aritz, J. (2014). *Leadership talk: A discourse approach to leader emergence*. New York: Business Expert Press.

Wodak, R., Kwon, W., & Clarke, I. (2011). "Getting people on board": Discursive leadership for consensus building in team meetings. *Discourse & Society*, *22* (5), 592 –644.

Yeung, L. (2004a). The paradox of control in participative decision-making: Facilitative discourse in banks. *Text*, *24* (1), 113–146.

Yeung, L. (2004b). The paradox of control in participative decision-making: Gatekeeping discourse in banks. *International Journal of the Sociology of Language*, *2004* (166), 83–104.

Yin, R. K. (1994). *Case study research: Design and methods*. Thousand Oaks, CA: Sage.

Yukl, G. (2012). Effective leadership behavior: What we know and what questions need more attention. *Academy of Management Perspectives*, *26* (4), 66–85.

Yukl, G. (2013). *Leadership in organizations* (8th ed.). Englewood Cliffs, NJ: Prentice Hall.

Yukl, G., & Falbe, C. M. (1990). Influence tactics and objectives in upward, downward, and lateral influence attempts. *Journal of Applied Psychology*, *75* (2), 132–140.

Yukl, G., Seifert, C. F., & Chavez, C. (2008). Validation of the extended Influence Behavior Questionnaire. *The Leadership Quarterly*, *19* (5), 609–621.

Part III
Practising Leadership

Introduction

In a normal workday, how many 'leaders' will you likely run into? Some of this obviously depends on how you define 'leader' and 'run into'. Leadership might include family members, restaurant (or store) owners, bosses at work, bosses' bosses, media reports on political or social leaders, and so forth. With any definition, the list is long. The processes that define leadership captured in other parts of this book exist in many settings. The chapters in this part talk about types of leadership in different settings. While some of the basic premises of leadership traverse settings, each setting may require unique leadership insights and actions.

Hartley reminds us that sometimes terms may have positive or negative connotations which get in the way of really understanding the practice of leadership. For example, the term 'politics' often has a pejorative undertone and leaders who practise politics or who are political may not be effective or good leaders. By looking at politics through the political science literature, Hartley views politics as a way of creating consensus out of diversity of opinion. Leaders who understand and manage political astuteness more effectively focus their organizations on ways to achieve consensual goals of differences. Five dimensions of political skill offer leaders a positive and useful way to improve leadership theory and practice.

Laing and Walter recognize that, in the modern political era, there is a leadership paradox. On the one hand, citizens seek heroic, strong, and transformational leaders who build confidence by their stature and confidence. Many study the biographies of these esteemed hero leaders to distil secrets they can follow. In surveys lamenting leadership, there may be a lack of these heroic leaders. On the other hand, information ubiquity leads to more democratic or collective leadership, through which people feel empowered to make their own choices. These leaders facilitate and build consensus to engage others in the leadership process. Wise leaders recognize this paradox and learn to manage both political individualism and institutional governance.

Leadership comes both in different settings (e.g. politics vs business) and in different types. Sometimes leaders act alone and sometimes leadership is a distributed or collective activity. Gibeau, Reid, and Langley share the context, configuration, and conditions for the success of co-leadership, where two individuals share a leadership role. Co-leadership is more likely to exist in pluralistic settings, large and complex corporations, transitioning organizations, and family businesses.

Co-leadership may take a number of forms (distribution, dominance, duplication, or disconnection) depending on the requirements of the leadership role. There are a number of conditions for success of co-leadership (e.g. individual skills, relationship building, organizational factors, and environmental setting).

Generally, leaders are visible through their formal positions, roles, and titles. Sometimes, leaders have enormous influence, less through formal position and more through personal credibility. Kakabadse, Khan, and Kakabadse offer a thorough explanation of the history, relevance, and leadership role of the company secretary. Less visible and public than the chairman, CEO, or board member, the company secretary has a profound impact on how information is shared and decisions made on the board.

Barentsen shows that leadership not only shapes political and business organizations, but also religious organizations. Religion refers both to the institutions which govern how spirituality is practised and the rise of personal spirituality. With the come-back of organized religions, Barentsen offers insights on nine dimensions of how postmodern leaders in mostly Christian religious settings fulfil their stewardship. He also reviews ways to create more professionalism among religious leaders so that they can shape culture and identity. Finally, he captures the unique tasks of religious leaders and offers guidance on how to prepare leaders to accomplish these tasks.

In almost every society, there is an increasing attention to health care, partly because of ageing populations, but also medical advances and higher patient expectations. Storey and Holti offer deep insights into the unique requirements of clinical leaders, or leaders who work in the health care system. Clinical leadership is both a political and a business agenda. Traditionally, leadership principles from the private sector are adapted for health-care settings. In this chapter, we learn about some of the unique aspects of clinical leadership, in which leaders are part of a constellation rather than occupying an isolated position. They also offer specific guidelines for clinical leaders to fulfil their unique role.

Across these chapters, we learn that leadership principles – of building personal proficiency, setting a shared agenda, delivering on goals, managing people, and investing in organizations over time – permeate leadership in political, religious, and clinical settings. While each setting requires differentiated and unique insights, there are convergent and common principles that can be adapted to improve leadership. As leaders in any setting master the common principles and adapt to the unique requirements of their setting, it is hoped that we will experience effective leadership no matter what setting we are in. As we run into leaders and leadership throughout our daily meanderings, we should be aware of the leadership principles that can be applied in almost every setting.

13

Politics and Political Astuteness in Leadership

Jean Hartley

How far and in what ways is politics represented, theorised and researched in generic leadership studies? I will argue that there is surprisingly little attention to politics, or that where it is considered it is largely viewed in a dysfunctional way. However, I will also present evidence that there is a growing recognition of the importance of politics in a wide range of leadership settings. I will suggest that this is not a specialist interest or perspective in leadership, but something which needs to be fundamental to the conceptualisation of leadership. To incorporate the existence of politics dramatically shifts the understanding of the purposes of leadership and the social processes involved in exercising leadership.

There are of course, many and varied definitions of leadership (Grint, 2005; Yukl, 2006) but, traditionally, leadership studies have tended to emphasise the pursuit or the creation of common goals and have therefore implicitly often obscured or denied the existence of politics (which starts from the assumption of diverse rather than common interests). For example, Kouzes and Posner (1995) write of leadership involving "shared aspirations" and Bolden (2004) notes the existence of "group goals". An early definition is still highly influential in the field: "Leadership may be considered as the process (act) of influencing the activities of an organized group in its efforts towards goal setting and goal achievement" (Stogdill, 1950, p. 3). Underlying these conceptualisations of leadership is a sense of shared, common or mutual activities and goals. Other definitions emphasise shared values, developing commitment across a group and so on. Within the generic leadership literature, including that deriving from business and management, there is fascination with a sense of shared purpose. It can be argued that this assumes a unitarist rather than pluralist view of organisations and societies (Fox, 1966; Coopey, 1995) whereby those who are within the sphere of influence of a leader have common interests and purposes, which it is the task of the leader to articulate and to mobilise people around.

There are writers in the generic leadership literature who emphasise plurality of interests and perspectives in leadership processes but they have tended to be a minority. Politics is hinted at in definitions such as "Leadership inevitably requires using power to influence the thoughts and actions of other people" (Zaleznik, 1977, p. 67) or in conceptualisations of leadership as being about sense-giving or sense-making (e.g. Smircich and Morgan, 1982) but even here politics or diverse interests are not directly addressed. By contrast, Drath *et al.* (2008) have argued that leadership studies have been based on an inappropriate ontology about what leadership is, which has hampered the development of the field. They suggest that the assumption of commonality of purpose is misplaced in many settings, whether concerned with small groups or with large strategic purposes. Instead, they argue for a conceptualisation of leadership which takes place in a pluralist social setting and therefore direction, alignment and commitment become key tasks for those exercising leadership, because commonality of interests cannot be assumed. It has to be created through leadership to foster sufficient degree of commonality to get things done. Sufficient degree of commonality to achieve purposes is very different from complete consensus (Leftwich, 2004).

In part, unitarist assumptions in the traditional generic leadership literature may have been reinforced by the conflation, in many circumstances, of authority with legitimacy (as noted by Heifetz (1994) and Hartley and Benington (2010, 2011)). Many leadership studies, particularly in the management field, focus on leadership in formal business (often private sector) organisations, where leadership is presumed to be exercised by line management (whether supervisor, chief executive or other formal roles) and where formal authority and hierarchy in Weberian-style bureaucracies can be largely taken for granted. Even here, 'office politics' can be present, though is largely seen as an unfortunate phenomenon which can be overcome through compelling or charismatic leadership which creates a unity of purpose and spirit (a view which is challenged by some academics, e.g. Butcher and Clarke, 1999; Hartley and Fletcher, 2008). However, legitimacy becomes increasingly important where leaders have to mobilise others in circumstances without authority (Heifetz, 1994) or beyond authority (Hartley and Benington, 2011). This can occur where leaders are trying to mobilise or influence others who are not subordinate to them – indeed, in partnerships between organisations may even be senior to them. So leadership which recognises different, diverse and sometimes competing interests may be very valuable. The following section examines how politics is analysed in organisational leadership.

Politics in and around Organisations

The concepts of politics and political skill are increasingly being researched and analysed in relation to leading and managing organisations (Allen *et al.*, 1979; Barley, 2010; Buchanan, 2008; Ferris *et al.*, 2002; Vigoda-Gadot and Drory, 2006). In addition, the contribution of critical management theory, post-modernism and Foucauldian studies have all enhanced the interest in power in relation to organising, and the role of politics as one of the means by which power is exercised (Brunsson, 1985; Grey, 2005; Spicer, 2005; Townley, 2008).

In the realm of practice, as senior and middle managers increasingly spend time not only in their own organisation but also working external to the organisation in strategic alliances, in partnerships and in public affairs, political 'savvy' – astuteness, awareness or having political antennae – is seen to be important in leadership (Hartley *et al.*, 2015; Alford *et al.*, 2016; Barley, 2010; Solace, 2005). Some UK organisations now include 'political acuity', 'political astuteness' or 'political skills' in their competency (or capability) frameworks for leadership.

Yet, despite the salience (and to some degree acceptance) of informal politics in and around organisations, the field is startlingly ambiguous and diverse in the conceptualisation of politics and hence also political skill. Buchanan (2008) notes that "the absence of a common definition of organizational politics is a long-standing concern" (p. 50) (see also Drory and Romm, 1990). Yet whether and how politics is conceptualised goes to the heart of leadership studies.

Politics has been a strand of organisation and management theory in its early history (e.g. March and Simon, 1958) though taking a back seat while Taylorist ideas were in the ascendancy. Simon (1959) had argued that rationality in decision making only takes place under very limited conditions and that most decisions contain a political angle. This theme was elaborated, particularly by those interested in organisational change (e.g. Block, 1987; Burns, 1961; Mangham, 1979; Pettigrew, 1975; Kumar and Thibodeaux, 1990). From the 1980s onwards, two writers in particular helped to bring organisational politics to prominence. Mintzberg (1985) highlighted the existence of organisational politics and the need for political will and skill. Pfeffer (1992) linked power and politics, showing that they were endemic in organisations, and particularly prominent in periods of organisational uncertainty.

Yet, generic leadership theory in organisational settings has neglected the existence and treatment of both formal and informal politics on several counts, and this has impoverished leadership theory. The chapter will later examine ways to remedy these problems.

First, the predominant approach to politics in organisational settings, until fairly recently, has been to view them as illegitimate activity, in the sense of not sanctioned by formal authority (Farrell and Petersen, 1982; Mintzberg, 1983, 1985). Such a perspective is frequently encountered, but does not take account of those organisations where formal, legitimate politics is integral to the purposes, accountability and decision making of the organisation. For example, public service organisations in Western societies contain legitimate and formal politics, in the form of elected members who are chosen through largely free and fair elections to represent citizens in particular jurisdictions (Stoker, 2006). Political leaders at federal, state, devolved or local level are an essential part of many public organisations (whether integral as in local government or governing at a distance in the case of the National Health Service in the UK). Public services represent a significant proportion of organisations and employment in many countries. So leaders may themselves be political representatives and, in addition, leaders in public management may need to take account of formal politics and elected politicians in their work (Manzie and Hartley, 2013; Hartley *et al.*, 2015; Alford *et al.*, 2016).

In addition, some of the activities of private firms, such as political lobbying and corporate affairs, are both legal and prevalent (Barley, 2010; Hillman *et al.*, 1999). Recently, the identification of political skills for those working in political lobbying and policy domains has been analysed (e.g. Woo *et al.*, 2015). Some writers accept that politics can be both legitimate and illegitimate, depending on organisational and social context (e.g. Baddeley and James, 1987; Buchanan, 2008; Butcher and Clarke, 1999, 2008; Farrell and Petersen, 1982). In this chapter, I take the view that politics can be either legitimate or not, depending on context, and it is not assumed to be either one or the other alone.

A second concern is that some scholars define politics in terms of self-interest, and therefore leadership which takes account of politics must, by this chain of logic, be self-serving and therefore problematic and 'bad leadership'. Self-interest may be personal, career based or sectional, such as engaging in turf wars (Buchanan and Badham, 1999; Valle and Perrewé, 2000). The self-interest view of organisational politics is closely related to the illegitimacy perspective, but is conceptually distinct. There are problems with self-interest as the defining characteristic of organisational politics. There is the essentialist and categorical one of defining what constitutes self-interest and how it can be recognised and operationalised – a problem which has defeated philosophers. By contrast, a number of writers (Baddeley and James, 1987; Buchanan, 2008; Butcher and Clarke, 2008; Farrell and Petersen, 1982; Ferris *et al.*, 2005a, b) argue that organisational politics may reflect either self-interest or organisational interest, or indeed both concurrently.

Connotations of illegitimacy and self-interest have contributed, in some writing, to the view that organisational politics is inherently dysfunctional – for those on whom (or against whom) politics is practised, for the organisation and for organisational leaders. In this view, politics is frequently conflated with 'politicking' (e.g. Mintzberg, 1985) and with devious Machiavellian behaviours (at least, those from *The Prince* rather than from *The Discourses*; Machiavelli, trans. 2003a, b) such as overtly blaming, attacking, scapegoating and more covertly manipulating, blocking, distorting, concealing and exploiting (Allen *et al.*, 1979; Bower and Weinberg, 1988; Eiring, 1999).

However, on the other hand, some writers have noted highly functional consequences of political behaviours: for example, greater clarity through contention of ideas; forging a degree of consensus and agreement to action out of difference; and managing complex organisational change (Block, 1987; Holbeche, 2004; Mangham, 1979). Perrewé *et al.* (2004, 2007) construe politics as part of the 'positive organizational behaviour' movement, and Buchanan (2008) notes that over half of the middle and senior leaders and managers in his sample thought that politics contributed to organisational effectiveness. In any case, the outcomes of politics should not, per se, constitute part of the conceptualisation of politics, which needs to be defined in root terms.

A fourth concern with the organisational politics literature and of the leadership literature is that it is still overwhelmingly about politics inside the organisation rather than politics in and around the organisation (e.g. Brouer *et al.*, 2009; Ferris *et al.*, 2005a, b; Kacmar and Carlson, 1997; Parker *et al.*, 1995). Few writers on political skill have commented on politics being concerned with inter-organisational relations (though see Barley, 2010; Farrell and Petersen, 1982; Hartley and Fletcher, 2008; Woo *et al.*, 2015). Particularly for more senior leaders and managers, their strategic leadership work is likely to bring them into contact with a range of organisations in the external environment which they try to shape. Resource dependency theory (Pfeffer and Salancik, 1978), neo-institutional theory (Scott, 2008) and stakeholder theory (Freeman and Reed, 1983) each underline the interaction between actors inside and outside the organisation.

A fifth consideration is the processes which characterise and define organisational politics. Here, there is a range of issues. Some have described politics as non-rational activities and behaviours (e.g. Pettigrew, 1975). Others would argue that politics has its own rationalities concerned with power and mobilisation (e.g. Brunsson, 1985; Townley, 2008) based on constructing consent (Morrell and Hartley, 2006). Others have described politics as influence, which takes place through persuasion, manipulation and negotiation (e.g. Ammeter *et al.*, 2002). The problem with defining politics as influence without a wider theoretical framework in place is that it can be argued that most leadership is about influence in one way or another and so the area of politics is not delimited through this approach, a point also noted by Buchanan (2008).

This chapter argues that, to conceptualise the processes of politics and hence political skill in and around organisations, there is a need to look beyond the generic leadership and management literature to the political science literature. Dunn has argued that it is the:

> struggles which result from the collisions between human purposes: most clearly when these collisions involve large numbers of human beings . . . it takes in, too, the immense array of expedients and practices which human beings have invented to cooperate, as much as to compete with one another.
>
> *(quoted in Stoker, 2006, p. 4)*

It may be considered as all activities of conflict, negotiation or co-operation over the use and distribution of resources (Leftwich, 2004; Stoker, 2006). Bernard Crick's (2000) influential definition of politics in society is that it is the mobilisation of support for a position, decision or action because it is "a way of ruling divided societies without undue violence – and most societies are divided" (p. 33). Other political scientists share this view of mobilising support for particular actions by reconciling different interests and values, in a diverse society with different interests, values and goals among its peoples (e.g. Minogue, 1994; Stoker, 2006). Transposing these ideas from the societal to the organisational and inter-organisational levels of analysis requires viewing organisations in a pluralist perspective of diverse and sometimes competing interests and goals (Fleming and Spicer, 2007; Hoggett, 2006) and leadership as about grappling with diverse interests among those whom the leader is aiming to mobilise. Baddeley and James (1987) echo this approach in arguing that "being politically skilled means being able to manage the requisite variety of your organization" (p. 5).

A final consideration about the theoretical base of politics is who 'does' politics in and around organisations. The idea of politics as pervasive in organisations means that, potentially, all organisational members may engage in politics to defend, advance or reconcile interests and goals in relation to other interests (Buchanan, 2008). However, while the activity of politics may be universal, the skills and resources to engage in politics are likely to be different according to role and level in the organisation, with senior leaders, by and large, having greater capacity and opportunity in this respect than ordinary employees. The opportunities and skills involved in the practice of politics and power is likely to vary by rank and role (e.g. Deetz, 1992; Lukes, 1974).

In summary, the field of politics in leadership has been under-developed and under-theorised and is still largely unexplored. There is now widespread agreement amongst academics that politics in organisations exists (e.g. Buchanan, 2008; Ferris *et al.*, 2005a, b; Perrewé *et al.*, 2004) and by extension this means the need to recognise constructive as well as destructive politics in leadership.

Political Astuteness Skills in Leadership

If politics is accepted as an endemic and integral feature of organisations, partnerships, social movements and societies, then there are significant implications for how leadership is conceptualised, researched, analysed and developed. Processes of leadership involve, in this perspective, recognising and addressing diverse interests, rather than assuming that these are shared goals. Whether leadership is exercised in single or in distributed leadership, it requires leaders (and academic scholars) to think about different stakeholders and what they are seeking to achieve (or avoid) in particular contexts, and to recognise that leadership takes place in arenas where ideas may be contested, disputed or resisted (Hartley and Benington, 2011).

Over the last decade, there has been greater recognition of the role of politics and political skill in leadership, and this has come about in two ways in particular. First, there is a growing literature derived from studies of public organisations, where politics is both formal and integral, and where public officials, particularly at more senior levels, report the value of political astuteness in their work in leadership alongside political representatives (Manzie and Hartley, 2013; Hartley *et al.*, 2015; Baddeley and James, 1987; James and Arroba, 1990). The second is the re-emergence of an interest in leadership in political science ('t Hart and Rhodes, 2014; Couto, 2010), where arguably there is much to learn about leading and managing across different interests and stakeholders from this literature (Hartley and Benington, 2011). However, even research on private sector leadership increasingly emphasises the value of astuteness (Beu and Buckley, 2004) and associated terms such as political nous (Squires, 2001), political acumen (Perrewé and Nelson, 2004; Hackman and Wageman, 2005; Dutton *et al.*, 2001) and political savvy (Ferris *et al.*, 2005a, b) are more common. Hartley *et al.* (2015) define political astuteness as "deploying political skills in situations involving diverse and sometimes competing interests and stakeholders, in order to create sufficient alignment of interests and/or consent in order to achieve outcomes" (p. 24). This conceptualisation is based on a view of politics as being about constructing consent out of different interests, which sometimes require competition and sometimes collaboration (Leftwich, 2004). It is more than 'office politics' alone, and can have an external as well as internal orientation. This definition is neutral about outcomes. It is assumed that political astuteness can be used to pursue personal or sectional interests, as well as formal organisational or societal interests. Political astuteness is conceptualised as a set of skills and judgements exercised in context for a range of legitimate or illegitimate purposes. It follows that, if leaders are inevitably involved in politics, some will display greater skills than others: they are more astute. It is important to note that this definition of political astuteness can cover a range of circumstances where there is contention, or potential contention, over purposes, priorities and resources. Thus 'political' is not just about formal institutions and actors. It encompasses the 'small p' as well as 'big p' politics – the informal as well as the formal – that can take place among the wider citizens and stakeholders who may also form part of the authorising environment. Finally, it includes the machinations of cliques and factions operating within and across as well as outside organisations.

Writers such as Baddeley and James (1987), Butcher and Clarke (2008) and Hartley *et al.* (2013, 2015) all conceptualise politics as able to play a constructive role in organisations, because organisations contain divergent interests and politics (in the sense of trying to find a consensual way forward in a situation with divergent interests). However, the 'dark side' of leadership with political astuteness is always possible – that political arts are used to promote self-serving or sectional interests. The point is that this is not inevitable. There is increasing recognition of the constructive role which political astuteness plays in many organisations and partnerships.

Despite the increasing acceptance of the value of political skills in leadership (taking skill in its widest sense as a short hand for a range of capabilities and interactive and relational social processes), three frameworks for understanding the skills of political astuteness are relevant to leadership in organisational and societal settings.

A body of work from Ferris and colleagues (e.g. Ferris *et al.*, 2005b, 2007) has outlined a quantitative measure of political skill, based on cognitive, affective and behavioural features. This framework has spurred US and also international research (e.g. Ahearn *et al.*, 2004; Douglas and Ammeter, 2004; Kolodinsky *et al.*, 2004). The measure is particularly located in a view of politics as being deceptively manipulative (for example, one of their dimensions is "apparent sincerity") though later writing recognises that political skill can be constructive (e.g. Brouer *et al.*, 2013). Their work tends to be focused on small group leadership but it suggests that political capability may be a critical skill for leadership.

Baddeley and James (1987) argued that political awareness (what this chapter calls political astuteness) is vital in leadership and management, and that leadership requires the development of political skills to be able to act effectively and with integrity. They proposed a model of political skill comprising the two dimensions of reading (the skills an individual uses to understand the context and the stakeholders) and carrying (the skills an individual uses to exercise self-control, from acting with integrity based on accepting oneself and others as they are to psychological game playing and being self-oriented). This is conceptual work which led to characterisation of leaders and managers in four quadrants based on the two dimensions of reading and carrying. This work accepts that political astuteness can be used constructively or destructively.

Finally, work by Hartley and colleagues developed and tested a framework for conceptualising leadership with political astuteness. The original research was conducted in the UK across the public, private and voluntary sectors (Hartley *et al.*, 2007; Hartley and Fletcher, 2008) with a focus on political *awareness*. Later research reconceptualised capabilities in terms of astuteness, not awareness, because the conceptual framework is behavioural as well as cognitive and affective. Research was conducted in Australia, New Zealand and the UK with mainly senior public leaders (Hartley *et al.*, 2013; Hartley *et al.*, 2015; Manzie and Hartley, 2014; Alford *et al.* 2016). This research proposed, constructed and statistically tested a five-dimensional framework of political astuteness skills, which sought to conceptualise political astuteness skills beyond the narrower account of 'political skills as self-interest' extant in some of the literature. The five dimensions (ascending from the 'micro' personal level to the 'macro' strategic level) are as follows.

Personal Skills

Self-awareness of one's own motives and behaviours, and the ability to exercise self-control, form an essential foundation for leading with political astuteness. The personal-skills dimension is also about being open to alternative views, so that it is possible to listen and reflect on the views of others. And it is about having a proactive disposition, initiating rather than waiting for things to happen. Understanding motives, interests and influence is central to effective management with political astuteness; without a firm underpinning of personal skills, the 'higher' skills will not be effective.

Interpersonal Skills

This dimension concerns the interpersonal capacity to influence the thinking and behaviour of others, get buy-in from people over whom the skill user has no direct authority, and make people feel valued. These are 'tough' as well as 'soft' skills, because the ability to negotiate, to stand up to pressures from other people and to handle conflict in ways to achieve constructive outcomes is important. They may be viewed as core management and certainly core leadership skills, but they also constitute foundational skills for political astuteness. Some elements of this dimension go beyond direct leadership skills, such as cultivating relationships which have potential rather than immediate value, and knowing when to rely on position and authority and when to rely on less direct methods of exerting influence. The dimension also includes coaching or mentoring individuals to develop their own political sensitivities and skills.

Reading People and Situations

This factor has a strong analytical aspect to it, and is based on thinking and intuition about the dynamics that can occur when stakeholders and agendas come together. It includes recognising the differing interests and agendas of a variety of people and their organisations, and discerning what may be the underlying, as opposed to espoused, agendas. This entails thinking through the likely standpoints of varying interest groups in advance of dealing with them, and using a wider knowledge of institutions, political processes and social systems to understand what might happen. Finally, it includes recognising where one may be seen as a threat to others and their interests. This dimension lies at the heart of political astuteness skills, as it concerns the power, influence and interests of different groups. This dimension is primarily concerned with analytical rather than influencing skills.

Building Alignment and Alliances

This dimension is a crucial skill of action, which requires the previous elements of skill in order to be effective. Building alignment out of different interests, goals and motives requires a detailed understanding and appreciation of the context, the players and the objectives of each stakeholder. It is about forging differences in outlook or emphasis into collaborative action. This dimension goes beyond that part of the literature on partnerships, which privileges consensus and commonality over dealing with difference. Instead, this dimension involves working with difference and with conflicts of interest in order to foster new opportunities. It builds on the proactivity of personal skills in actively seeking out alliances and partnerships rather than relying on those which are already in existence. It includes being able to bring out and deal with differences between stakeholders, not conceal them or hope that if they are ignored they will somehow go away. Tough negotiation skills (from interpersonal skills) may underpin the capacity to build a realistic and useful consensus without ending up with the lowest common denominator.

Strategic Direction and Scanning

Finally, we reach the important question of purpose: what these political astuteness skills are being used for. This dimension includes two major elements. The first is strategic thinking and action in relation to organisational purpose, so that the understanding of power, interests and influence is set within a strategic aim. This includes thinking long term and having a road map of where the leader wants to go so that he or she is not diverted by short-term pressures. Second, this dimension requires strategic scanning – thinking about longer-term issues that may have the potential to have an impact on the organisation, not just on the horizon, but over the horizon. It requires analytical capacity to think through scenarios of possible futures, to think about small changes which may herald bigger shifts in society and the economy, and to find ways to analyse and manage (as far as possible) the uncertainty that lies outside the organisation. This last includes being able to keep options open rather than reaching for a decision prematurely.

These dimensions of political astuteness are interconnected and therefore together may be considered as a meta-competency, rather than as single dimensions of capability. This research suggests that a leader needing to manage complex set of interrelationships across organisations will require skills in each of these dimensions in order to lead with political astuteness. While personal and interpersonal skills are the foundation of building trust and understanding the needs and interests of other people and organisations, there is also a need for the skills of building alliances across those differences and the ability to detect wider changes in the external environment that may have an impact on plans and objectives.

However, the political astuteness framework emphasises the value of understanding divergent and sometimes competing interests, which brings new insights to understanding the tasks of leadership. Traditional leadership theory still focuses too much on a unitary view of the organisation and its partners – that building complete consensus and commitment, and 'selling' the vision to 'followers' is what counts as effective leadership. Increasingly, commentators are raising questions about this small-group view of leadership applied to larger organisations or to society (e.g. Drath *et al.*, 2008), where multiple interests exist and where influence may need to be directed not to followers (who may already be committed) but to the sceptical and disengaged who are needed to achieve outcomes (Heifetz, 2011). Pluralistic views of leadership are likely to become more common, and to understand pluralism one needs to have an understanding of politics.

Indeed, it is arguable that all leaders, whether in private, public or voluntary sectors, are likely to be more effective to the extent that they supplement their analytical, organisational and operational skill sets with a more textured view of the varied interests and stakeholders in their environments. Academics researching leadership also need to develop theory which more adequately reflects diverse and pluralistic organizations and societies.

Conclusions

Paying greater attention to politics and to political astuteness in leadership processes is likely to pay high dividends in the development of leadership theory and empirical research. First, it helps to create recognition that leadership is often concerned with achieving outcomes in a pluralistic context (see Crosby and Bryson, 2005) where conflict and contestation may be central to the exercise of leadership because interests, goals, values, opinions and attitudes may be diverse and sometimes may be conflicting. Generic leadership theory has often taken a more unitarist view of leadership, based on a leader having a 'compelling vision' which leads to completely shared goals and a consensus about action and approach to a task or purpose. However, an alternative and arguably more compelling perspective recognises the existence of diverse interests which also means that leadership legitimacy may be fragile and can be lost at any moment. So the action of leadership to mobilise attention, resources and people to a purpose has to be continually analysed and if necessary re-won. This is reminiscent of Moore's (1995, 2013) authorising environment in his strategic management framework for public managers: that legitimacy and support is dynamic for a public leader and may change as stakeholders as well as 'followers' review their commitment to the leader. This insight is as relevant to the private as to the public and voluntary sectors.

Politics still needs considerable unpacking analytically in leadership studies. It is surprising how often studies are either silent about politics in leadership or there is a passing reference but little analysis. As noted, there is a bias towards viewing politics as illegitimate, self-serving, dysfunctional or all of these, and this has limited the interest in the role of politics and political astuteness in leadership studies. However, this is now changing (indeed, there has always been a quiet undercurrent of interest in politics in organisational and leadership contexts but only recently has politics become more 'mainstream'). The growing interest in critically examining politics and seeing its double-sided nature (potentially both constructive and destructive, and influenced strongly by attributional processes) has helped to bring politics in leadership more into the open, for more detailed analysis.

Understanding of the role of politics in leadership means that theorising and researching leadership processes have to pay more attention to reading the context, understanding the motives of stakeholders, building alignment and alliances and constructing coalitions (whether temporary or longer term). This requires a careful and sophisticated 'reading' of context and of stakeholders. While context has been noted as a key element of leadership (Alvesson and Sveningsson, 2012; Porter and McLaughlin, 2006), there has perhaps been less attention to how exactly leaders pay attention and what they pay attention to in the environment. It is known that leaders can get better at 'reading context' over time and with relevant experience (Leach et al., 2005; Hartley et al., 2015) but there is more research needed to fully understand these processes.

The 'reading' of stakeholders is also dynamic and complex. These are generally not the passive 'followers' so frequently assumed in the leadership literature, but they may be exercising leadership in their own right, with their own constituents or sources of power. Leadership in some circumstances may be more like 'herding cats' than creating orderly and compelling one-off sensemaking. In a context with higher levels of collaborative governance (Huxham and Vangen, 2000) there are increasing numbers of situations where leaders must lead beyond their formal authority (Hartley and Benington, 2010). Again, we need more research to understand the issues of creating and fostering alignment in a context where there is diversity of interests, views, values and sensemaking.

Political astuteness is being researched as a key capability of leadership. There is still too little understanding of these skills. It is possible to learn a great deal from those who practise political astuteness in their work, whether this is in the formal arenas of democratic politics, in the work of public managers grappling with complex and 'wicked' problems or in the work of accomplished private sector leaders. Political astuteness is found in all sectors, though leaders vary in the extent to which they are comfortable with, and wise in their use of, these skills. To some extent these can be seen as individual skills or capabilities, but they require high levels of relational and strategic skills which go beyond the idea that leadership is simply an individualistic set of traits or behaviours. Working across diverse and sometimes competing interests is a social process, not just a set of individual skills, requiring close reading, understanding and acting in the 'dance' of leadership processes.

References

Ahearn K, Ferris G, Hochwater W, Douglas C and Ammeter A (2004) Leader political skill and team performance. *Journal of Management, 30* (3), 309–27.

Alford J, Hartley J, Yates S and Hughes O (2016) Into the purple zone: Deconstructing the politics/administration dichotomy. *American Review of Public Administration,* doi: 10.1177/0275074016638481

Allen R, Madison D, Porter L, Renwick P and Mayes B (1979) Organizational politics: Tactics and characteristics of its actors. *California Management Review, 22* (1), 77–83.

Alvesson M and Sveningsson S (2012) Un- and re-packing leadership: Context, relations, constructions, and politics. In Uhl-Bien M and Ospina S (eds) *Advancing relational leadership research: A dialogue among perspectives.* Charlotte NC: Information Age Publishing.

Ammeter, A, Douglas C, Gardner W, Hochwater W and Ferris, G (2002) Toward a political theory of leadership. *Leadership Quarterly, 13,* 751–96.

Baddeley S and James K (1987) Owl, fox, donkey or sheep: Political skills for managers. *Management Education and Development, 18* (1), 3–19.

Barley S (2010) Building an institutional field to corral a government: A case to set an agenda for organization studies. *Organization Studies, 31* (6), 777–805.

Beu D S and Buckley M R (2004) This is war: How the politically astute achieve crimes of disobedience through the use of moral disengagement. *Leadership Quarterly, 15,* 551–68.

Block P (1987) *The empowered manager: Positive political skills at work.* San Francisco: Jossey-Bass.

Bolden R (2004) What is leadership? *Research Report 1.* Exeter, UK: Leadership South West.

Bower J and Weinberg M (1988) Statecraft, strategy and corporate leadership. *California Management Review, 30* (2), 39–56.

Brouer R, Duke A, Treadway D and Ferris G (2009) The moderating effect of political skill on the demographic dissimilarity: Leader-member exchange quality relationship. *The Leadership Quarterly, 20,* 61–9.

Brouer R, Douglas C, Treadway D and Ferris G (2013) Leader political skill, relationship quality and leadership effectiveness: A two study-model test and constructive replication. *Journal of Leadership and Organizational Studies, 20* (2), 185–98.

Brunsson N (1985) *The irrational organization.* Chichester: Wiley.

Buchanan D A (2008) You stab my back, I'll stab yours: Management experience and perceptions of organization political behaviour. *British Journal of Management, 19,* 49–64.

Buchanan D and Badham R (1999) *Power, politics and organizational change: Winning the turf game.* London: Sage.

Burns T (1961) Micropolitics: Mechanisms of institutional change. *Administrative Science Quarterly, 55,* 257–81.

Butcher D and Clarke M (1999) Organizational politics: The missing discipline of management? *Industrial and Commercial Training, 31* (1), 9–12.

Butcher D and Clarke M (2008) *Smart management* 2nd ed. Basingstoke: Palgrave Macmillan.

Coopey J (1995) The learning organization: Power, politics and ideology. *Management Learning, 26* (2), 193–213.

Couto R (2010) *Political and civic leadership.* Thousand Oaks, CA: Sage.

Crosby B and Bryson J (2005) *Leadership for the common good.* San Francisco: Jossey-Bass.

Crick B (2000) *In defence of politics* 4th ed. Chicago: Chicago University Press.

Deetz S (1992) Disciplinary power in the modern corporation. In Alvesson M and Wilmott H (eds) *Critical management studies.* London: Sage, pp. 21–45.

Douglas C and Ammeter A (2004) An examination of leader political skill and its effect on ratings of leader effectiveness. *Leadership Quarterly, 15* (4), 537–50.

Drath W, McCauley P C, Van Velsor E, O'Connor P and McGuire J (2008) Direction, alignment, commitment: Toward a more integrative ontology of leadership. *Leadership Quarterly, 19,* 635–53.

Drory A and Romm T (1990) The definition of organizational politics: A review. *Human Relations, 43* (11), 1133–1154.

Dutton J, Ashford B, O'Neill R and Lawrence K (2001) Moves that matter: Issue selling and organizational change. *Academy of Management Journal*, *44* (4), 716–36.

Eiring H (1999) Dynamic office politics: Powering up for programme success. *The Information Management Journal*, *33* (1), 17–25.

Farrell D and Petersen J (1982) Patterns of political behavior. *Academy of Management Review*, 7 (3), 403–12.

Ferris G, Adams G and Kolodinsky R (2002) Perceptions of organizational politics: Theory and research directions. In Yammarino F and Dansereau F (eds) *Research in multi-level issues* vol 1, pp. 179–254.

Ferris G, Davidson S and Perrewé P (2005a) *Political skill at work*. Mountain View, CA: Davies-Black Publishing.

Ferris G, Treadway D, Kolodinsky R, Hochwater, W, Kacmar C, Douglas C and Frink D (2005b) Development and validation of the political skill inventory. *Journal of Management*, *31* (1), 126–52.

Ferris G, Treadway D, Perrewé P, Brouer R, Douglas C and Lux S (2007) Political skill in organizations. *Journal of Management*, *33* (3), 290–320.

Fleming P and Spicer A (2007) *Contesting the corporation: Struggle, power and resistance in organizations*. Cambridge: Cambridge University Press.

Fox A (1966) Industrial sociology and industrial relations. Research paper 3. Royal Commission on Trade Unions and Employers' Associations. London: HMSO.

Freeman E and Reed D (1983) Stockholders and stakeholders: A new perspective on corporate governance. *California Management Review*, *25* (3), 88–106.

Grey C (2005) Critical management studies: Towards a more mature politics. In Howcroft D and Trauth E (eds) *Handbook of critical information systems research*. Cheltenham: Edward Elgar.

Grint K (2005) *Leadership: limits and possibilities*. London: Palgrave Macmillan.

't Hart P and Rhodes R A W (2014) *Oxford handbook of political leadership*. Oxford: Oxford University Press.

Hartley J and Benington J (2010) *Leadership for healthcare*. Bristol: Policy Press.

Hartley J and Benington J (2011) Political leadership. In Bryman A, Jackson B, Grint K and Uhl-Bien M (eds) *Sage handbook of leadership*. London: Sage, pp. 201–12.

Hartley J and Fletcher C (2008) Leading with political awareness: Leadership across diverse interests inside and outside the organization. In James K and Collins J (eds) *Leadership perspectives: Knowledge into action*. London: Palgrave, pp. 163–76.

Hartley J, Fletcher C, Wilton P, Woodman P and Ungemach C (2007) *Leading with political awareness*. London: Chartered Management Institute.

Hartley J, Alford J, Hughes O and Yates S (2013) *Leading with political astuteness: A study of public managers in Australia, New Zealand and the United Kingdom*. Melbourne: Australia and New Zealand School of Government.

Hartley J, Alford J, Hughes O and Yates S (2015) Public value and political astuteness in the work of public managers: The art of the possible. *Public Administration*, *93* (1), 195–211.

Heifetz R (1994) *Leadership without easy answers*. Cambridge, MA: Harvard University Press.

Heifetz R (2011) Leadership and authority. *Public Money and Management*, *31* (5), 305–8.

Hillman A, Zardkoohi A and Bierman L (1999) Corporate political strategies and firm performance: Indications of firm-specific benefits from personal service in the US government. *Strategic Management Journal*, *20* (1), 67–81.

Hoggett P (2006) Conflict, ambivalence and the contested purpose of public organizations. *Human Relations*, *59* (2), 175–94.

Holbeche L (2004) *The power of constructive politics*. Horsham: Roffey Park Institute.

Huxham C and Vangen S (2000) Leadership in the shaping and implementation of collaboration agendas: How things happen in a (not quite) joined-up world. *Academy of Management Journal*, *43* (6), 1159–75.

James K and Arroba T (1990) Politics and management: The effect of stress on the political sensitivity of managers. *Journal of Managerial Psychology*, *5* (3), 22–7.

Kacmar K and Carlson D (1997) Further validation of the perception of politics scale (POPS): A multiple sample investigation.. *Journal of Management*, *23* (5), 627–58.

Kolodinsky R, Hochwarter W and Ferris G (2004) Non-linearity in the relationship between political skill and work outcomes: Convergent evidence from three studies. *Journal of Vocational Behavior*, *65* (2), 294–308.

Kouzes J and Posner B (1995) *The leadership challenge: How to keep getting extraordinary things done in organisations*. San Francisco: Jossey-Bass.

Kumar K and Thibodeaux M (1990) Organizational politics and planned organizational change. *Group and Organization Studies*, *15* (4), 357–65.

Leach S, Hartley J, Lowndes V, Wilson D and Downe J (2005) *Local political leadership in England and Wales.* York: Joseph Rowntree Foundation.

Leftwich A (2004) *What is politics?* Cambridge: Polity Press.

Lukes S (1974) *Power: A radical view.* Basingstoke: Macmillan.

Machiavelli N (trans. 2003a) *The Prince.* London: Penguin.

Machiavelli N (trans. 2003b) *The Discourses.* London: Penguin.

Mangham I (1979) *The politics of organizational change.* Westport, CT: Greenwood Press.

Manzie S and Hartley J (2013) *Dancing on ice: Leadership with political astuteness by senior public servants in the UK.* Milton Keynes: Open University.

March J and Simon H (1958) *Organizations.* New York: Wiley.

Minogue K (1994) *Politics: A very short introduction.* Oxford: Oxford University Press.

Mintzberg H (1983) *Power in and around organizations.* Upper Saddle River, NJ: Prentice Hall.

Mintzberg H (1985) The organization as political arena. *Journal of Management Studies, 22* (2), 133–54.

Moore M (1995) *Creating public value.* Cambridge, MA: Harvard University Press.

Moore M (2013) *Recognizing public value.* Cambridge, MA: Harvard University Press.

Morrell K and Hartley J (2006) A model of political leadership. *Human Relations, 59* (4), 483–504.

Parker C, Dipboye R and Jackson S (1995) Perceptions of organizational politics: An investigation of antecedents and consequences. *Journal of Management, 21* (5), 891–912.

Perrewé P and Nelson D (2004) Gender and career success: The facilitative role of political skill. *Organizational Dynamics, 33,* 366–78.

Perrewé P, Zellars K, Ferris G, Rossi A, Kacmar C and Ralston D (2004) Neutralising job stressors: Political skill as an antidote to the dysfunctional consequences of role conflict stressors. *Academy of Management Journal, 47,* 141–52.

Perrewé P, Ferris G, Stoner J and Brouer R (2007) The positive role of political skill in organizations. In Nelson D and Cooper C (eds) *Positive organizational behaviour.* London: Sage.

Pettigrew A (1975) Towards a political theory of organizational intervention. *Human Relations, 28* (3), 191–208.

Pfeffer J (1992) *Managing with power: Politics and influence in organizations.* Boston, MA: Harvard Business School Press.

Pfeffer J and Salancik G (1978) *The external control of organizations: A resource dependence perspective.* Stanford, CA: Stanford University Press.

Porter L and McLaughlin G (2006) Leadership and the organizational context: Like the weather? *Leadership Quarterly, 17,* 559–76.

Scott W (2008) *Institutions and organizations.* Thousand Oaks, CA: Sage.

Simon H (1959) Theories of decision-making in economics and behavioural science. *American Economic Review, 49,* 253–83.

Smircich L and Morgan G (1982) Leadership: The management of meaning. *Journal of Applied Behavioral Science, 18* (3), 257–73.

Solace (Society of Local Authority Chief Executives and Senior Managers) (2005) *Managing in a political environment.* London: Solace.

Spicer A (2005) The political process of inscribing a new technology. *Human Relations, 58* (7), 867–90.

Squires G (2001) Management as a professional discipline. *Journal of Management Studies, 38* (4), 473–87.

Stogdill R (1950) Leadership, membership and organization. *Psychological Bulletin, 47,* 1–14.

Stoker G (2006) *Why politics matters.* Basingstoke: Palgrave Macmillan.

Townley B (2008) *Reason's neglect.* Oxford: Oxford University Press.

Valle M and Perrewé P (2000) Do politics perceptions relate to political behaviours? Tests of an implicit assumption and expanded model. *Human Relations, 53* (3), 359–86.

Vigoda-Gadot E and Drory A (2006) *Handbook of organizational politics.* Cheltenham: Edward Elgar.

Woo J, Ramesh M and Howlett M (2015) Legitimation capacity: System-level resources and political skills in public policy. *Policy and Society.* http://dx.doi.org/10.1016/j.polsoc.2015.09.008.

Yukl G (2006) *Leadership in organizations (6th edition).* Upper Saddle River, NJ: Pearson Prentice Hall.

Zaleznik A (1977) Managers and leaders: Are they different? *Harvard Business Review, 55,* 67–78.

14

Great Expectations and Great Limitations

Walking the Tightrope of Political Leadership in the Twenty-First Century

Matthew Laing and James Walter

In times of rapid social change such as the present, people look for decisive leaders, with the capacity to meet contemporary challenges, as a hedge against the uncertainties they face. At the same time, those unsettled by change can interpret it as a failure of the old order. Thus existing conventions come into question, giving rise to a paradox: heightened expectations are paired with cynicism about contemporary institutions, including leadership practices. In this chapter, we review the nature of this paradox as it is manifest in both popular sentiment towards, and in contemporary research on, our elected political leaders. Here we consider key developments in theoretical and pragmatic debates regarding contemporary democratic leadership, with a focus on the divergence between the public and academic discourses on democratic leadership in the twenty-first century. We relate these to the tightrope modern leaders must walk if they are to balance the need to provide decisive executive leadership on the one hand and responsiveness to the demos on the other. In particular, we explore the contemporary interest in both 'heroic' leaders and 'collaborative' leaders, to ask how these competing ideals might be reconciled in the modern democratic context.

We argue that, while the sources of the preoccupation with leadership and the rationale for 'strong leader' ideals are understandable, they are bound to lead to disappointment. There are grounds vigorously to contest the myth of the strong leader (Brown, 2014) and the pessimism to which it gives rise. Attention to institutional design that constrains individual leader caprice while encouraging and embedding orchestrators and facilitators into democratic governance is needed. This could both help leaders manage the leadership tightrope, and ensure the creation of distributed leadership across coalitions that can actually do something about the challenges we face.

A striking feature of the twenty-first century thus far has been the emergence of anti-elitist movements demanding greater democracy and popular freedoms. The Occupy and anti-Globalisation movements, the Arab Spring, the Tea Party movement, the rise of Euroscepticism and revolutions in the former Eastern Bloc have definitively put such demands on the agenda, and have done so frequently by directing ire from both left and right against global and national elites and leadership. The dissatisfaction of such social movements with elites seemingly unable to meet their expectations has been matched by a body of research (discussed below) that concludes that contemporary leadership is sorely deficient. It lacks the deliberative, collective and transparent character that is desirable in a modern democracy; there has been an incremental growth in executive control versus representative debate; and power has migrated to the top as political elites have engaged in global networks that distance them from the people and interests they are intended to serve (Foley, 2013; Gill, 2011; Gray, 1998; Helms, 2014; Lipman-Blumen, 2006).

The concerns identified above have also been evident in a surge in the interest in and teaching of leadership. As Jan Pakulski and Andreas Körösényi argue, the media and the public have shifted their attention to our leaders as parties have ceded their former roles of opinion aggregation and policies have been subsumed by celebrity politics (Pakulski and Körösényi, 2012). The contemporary 'personalisation of politics' arises from the centralisation of political attention around a narrow band of political elites (McAllister, 2007). It is, remarked one commentator, 'as if politics and its leaders have to fill a space left by God and religion' (Little, 1988: 2). Perhaps unsurprisingly, this has generated the growth of an industry in leadership training. Leadership qualifications abound in every field and are offered by all types of educational institutions. Despite this explosion of the industry supporting and seeking to convey the qualities of leadership to aspirants, Barbara Kellerman concludes that:

> the tireless teaching of leadership has brought us no closer to leadership nirvana than we were previously . . . we don't have much better an idea of how to grow good leaders, or of how to stop or at least slow bad leaders, than we did a hundred or even a thousand years ago.
>
> *(Kellerman, 2012: xiv)*

Notwithstanding such pessimism, the demand for strong, competent and decisive leaders is seemingly rising in tandem with expectations of openness, networking and greater public participation in the way government is run. How can political leadership manage this balance? Can Kellerman's critique be addressed? How have theorists and analysts of leadership interpreted the problem? What strategies might reconcile the competing demands on modern democratic government? And what skills, values and approaches should underpin the coherent and successful contemporary politician?

Heroic Leaders: The Search Continues

Few actors in modern political life have the power to engage the public imagination like the archetypal strong leader (Little, 1988). The myth of the strong leader (Brown, 2014) still influences our views of leadership and pervades our collective expectations of politics. This is 'heroic leadership' – the sentiment that leaders are central to the rise and fall of nations and the business of politics. The duality of the powerful, individualistic leader versus a consensual, facilitating leader is a dichotomy that goes to the very heart of how we understand the relationship between leadership and history (Edwards and Wayne, 2013: 18–22). But in contemporary Western polities two further factors have come into play. As the mass parties that once served to organise and aggregate opinion have declined, issues rather than ideology have determined voter choice and leaders have come to 'stand in' for parties as the signifiers of issue orientation (Pakulski and Körösényi, 2012: 51–80; Blondel and Thiebault, 2009). Second, with the emergence of the 'risk society' (Beck, 1992), with its associated uncertainties, leaders who can tolerate cognitive complexity are needed, but paradoxically it is the strong leader – who typically eschews complexity for unambiguous solutions – who may benefit by appearing to offer cognitive closure and unequivocal authority as a hedge against uncertainty (Golec de Zavala, 2012).

Defining the boundaries between categories of leadership is an ongoing exercise, but the long-dominant strong leader stereotype owes much to historical expositions of the heroic properties of leaders from Machiavelli, Thomas Hobbes and Carl von Clausewitz, as well as the Weberian concept of charismatic authority – authority that derives from subordinates' perceptions of and devotion to extraordinary qualities in a leader. Although this leadership tradition has been used in many ways over the subsequent century, it dovetails neatly with Thomas Carlyle's famous conjecture that history is the story of 'great men', and has fostered the development of a tradition in leadership studies of focusing on singular transformational leaders (Burns, 1978; Bass, 1985). Although transformational leadership may find its realisation in both individualistic leaders and facilitating leaders, the approach serves to strengthen the overall ideal of heroic leadership, which directs public and elite attention towards singular leaders and the analysis of their strengths and failures (Meindl et al., 1985; Yukl, 1999), notwithstanding Burns's own criticism that the leadership genre in politics 'projects heroic leaders against drab, powerless masses' (Burns, 1978: 3). The transformational leadership model remains one of the most popular frameworks for analysing and considering the efforts of political leaders, and decades after its introduction Burns's work on the subject remains among the best selling in the leadership genre (Dinh et al., 2014).

Other works, particularly those that enter into psychological analysis (e.g. Little, 1988), have noted both the dangerous potential and the particular and enduring appeal of the 'strong' leader for followers and voters alike. This builds upon and supplements the traditional image of the heroic political leader with 'the kind of myth that promises the earth' (Little, 1988: 3). The strong leader tradition advocates a variety of leadership qualities that complement the heroic leader canon, such as decisiveness, toughness, individualism and conviction (Foley, 2013: 79–80). A comprehensive and sustained defenestration of 'the myth of the strong leader' (Brown, 2014) has been a necessary but not yet a sufficiently influential intervention to engender an appropriately critical apprehension of strong leadership. Strong, heroic and transformational leadership, although terms invoked in different bodies of the leadership literature, become somewhat interchangeable as highly individual-centric accounts of the role of leadership in public life and the advancement of the polis. Broadly speaking, these approaches to leadership now fit within the 'neo-charismatic' school of leadership theories (see Winkler, 2009).

Arguably, the heroic leader stereotype still continues to manifest most strongly in public expectations of leadership, notwithstanding an increasing scepticism among academic analysts. The personalisation of politics (discussed further below) appears to have been a decisive factor in engendering the popular renaissance of Carlyle's proposition about how history is made, though the tendency is more pronounced in the majoritarian than in the consensus democracies (see Boumans et al., 2013). What crude measures exist to measure public sentiment towards leadership point towards a lionisation of leaders, particularly those considered to have 'strong' characteristics. In the United Kingdom, for example, the *100 Greatest Britons*, a popular public poll and television programme inviting the public to rank their nation's historical heroes, saw stereotypical 'strong' leaders – Winston Churchill, David Lloyd-George and Margaret Thatcher – the highest ranked of the prime ministers. Academic ranking exercises have produced similar results, with Clement Attlee the only consensus-style leader routinely to join the other three in topping the polls (Theakston and Gill, 2005). The United States public is similarly enamoured of heroic leaders, with presidents conforming to the strong leader mould, such as Franklin Roosevelt, Theodore Roosevelt, George Washington, Andrew Jackson and Ronald Reagan, tending to dominate annual ranking exercises (C-SPAN, 2009; Siena College, 2010;

USPC, 2011). Public and expert polls in other countries routinely produce similar results and celebrate strong leaders in the traditional sense, from Indira Gandhi as the greatest prime minister of India (BBC, 1999; *India Today*, 2001) to Charles De Gaulle as the greatest president of France (*Le Nouvel Observateur*, 2009). Put simply, prime ministers and presidents conforming to the traditional conception of the strong and heroic leader continue to wield significant pull over public sentiment and often align most closely to the realisation of public expectations of political leadership. Polling routinely reveals 'strong' and 'decisive' as amongst the most desirable, if not the most desirable, traits that political leaders should possess (Gallup, 2007, 2009). Accordingly, the lexicon and style of the strong leader continues to receive a great deal of airplay in modern politics, from the 'Iron Chancellor' Angela Merkel in Germany (*The Economist*, 2011a) to the caricature of Vladimir Putin as the rugged saviour of Russia.

The popularity of biography – a genre regarded with scepticism by political scientists (Walter, 2014) – is another indicator of public sentiment. A review of Amazon's top-selling books on political and public leadership in recent years suggests that most adhere to the framework of heroic leadership. Biographies of strong leaders abound, such as Deng Xiaoping (Vogel, 2011), Richard Nixon (Ambrose, 2014), Winston Churchill (Johnson, 2014; Smith, 2014), Margaret Thatcher (Shephard, 2013), Lee Kuan Yew (Yew, 2014) and Vladimir Putin (Hill and Gaddy, 2012). Even when authoritarianism and dictatorship in the context of modern leadership is the subject (e.g. Lipman-Blumen, 2006; Bueno de Mesquita and Smith, 2011), and the question is what can we learn from 'bad leadership', this still dovetails with the penchant for emphasising the role and importance of domineering individuals in public life. The case is much the same with general volumes of leadership advice concentrating on the pursuit of that elusive quality of 'greatness' (e.g. Isaacson, 2010) – here again the 'great' leaders in question are generally those who conform closely to the strong leader stereotype.

Upon closer examination of this public sentiment, scholars have found no shortage of reasons to explain why, despite the increasingly democratic, inclusive and globalised nature of politics, the public still looks to the strong leader. The 'age of fracture' (Rodgers, 2011), in which the public and elites have witnessed declining predictability and control over political and social processes as the world becomes smaller and more interconnected, has given rise to changes in the political order and a renewed emphasis on strong leaders and leader-centric government – the solution to uncertainty is decisive action (Pakulski and Körösényi, 2012). The resort to specialist advice in the face of the challenges of globalisation has introduced a form of 'knowledge politics' common to political elites but from which the electorate is excluded: the leader must serve as the conduit between the decisions that have to be made (Thatcher famously proclaimed of her regime's decisions, 'there is no alternative') and public support. These and accompanying developments have placed leadership at the very heart of public life.

One of the most widely discussed forms of impetus, as mentioned earlier, has been the personalisation of politics, 'a process in which the political weight of the individual actor in the political process increases over time, while the centrality of the political group (i.e. political party) declines' (Rahat and Shaefer, 2007: 65). Studies across jurisdictions and scenarios have repeatedly observed this phenomenon, giving rise to the contention that increasingly elections and policy battles are won and lost on the backs of their leaders and advocates rather than on broader social or political debates (Blondel and Thiebault, 2009; Garzia, 2011, 2014). By its very nature, the personalisation of politics draws us back towards the 'great men' (and now women) sentiment and focuses our attention more narrowly on leaders and their individual characteristics rather than leaders in their broader historical, social and political contexts.

Although this transformation of leader–party–electorate relations was recognised in earnest in the 1980s and 1990s (Wattenberg, 1991), subsequent analyses have noted the trend continuing and amplifying over recent decades. One of the key driving factors identified is the nature of contemporary media coverage of politics: personalisation of politics has been impelled by the shift in focus of the media from campaigns to candidates, policies to personalities, which has played a large part in the transformation we have identified and the increasing centrality of leadership (McAllister, 2007; Campus, 2010; Balmas and Sheafer, 2013; Aarts *et al.*, 2013: 21–30). The media's role is no less influential when it comes to reinforcing typified images of leaders in the public imagination. Mauro Barisione identifies four typical images projected onto public leaders by the media – the 'strong leader', the 'everyman', the 'outsider' and the 'post-ideological' – all of which implicitly reinforce either the heroic or the individualist dimensions of political leadership (Barisione, 2009). These developments have contributed to the emphasis in contemporary political leadership on the creation and maintenance of a leadership brand (Just and Crigler, 2000; Littlefield and Quenette, 2007; Scammell, 2007). In turn, that conscious brand creation by political leaders falls back on strong leadership tropes that have persisted for millennia, from heroic images of the leader in warzones and in times of crisis to dramatic posturing against alleged enemies, both internal and external.

In summary, comparative analysis of political leadership across democracies reveals contingent and institutional reasons behind the elevation of leadership expectations. Globalisation, some argue, has generated more complex problems, demanding specialist knowledge (beyond the ken of the electorate) and urgent attention: does the leader, driven to act and the possessor of privileged knowledge, have time to consult and explain, or must he or she simply decide (Rost and Smith, 1992; cf. Luttwak, 1998)? In conjunction, in Western polities, as we have noted, the hollowing out of parties, attrition of the party membership base and professionalisation of party organisation (now focused on 'the brand') along with changes in media practice have been significant institutional drivers in elevating leaders. Further, several indexes measuring executive power and legislature power, when stratified according to the relative age of the democratic structures, demonstrate consistently that newer democratic systems have tended to adopt presidential or semi-presidential structures, and that within these presidents and executive leaders have assumed a greater share of power than in long-established democracies, effectively reinforcing the trend towards personalisation of politics and political parties in emerging democracies (Samuels and Shugart, 2010).

All of these measures, when taken together, point towards a general electorate that is not only inclined, but also encouraged, towards the heroic leadership and the great-man canon, at least insofar as politics and public life is concerned. In rating our political leaders, commenting on our political leaders and studying to become or to better understand political leaders, we continue to abide by the notion that strong, individualistic leaders with the traits of greatness and decision hold the key to success in public life and national salvation. Furthermore, the social structures of our society are increasingly focused on leaders as the defining elements of day-to-day politics, and prevailing media images have a tendency to reinforce the need for leaders to brand themselves in the tradition of strong leadership.

And yet all is not well: there is a disjunction between what has come to be the expected leadership repertoire, and perceptions of leaders in action. The most recent report of the Davos World Economic Forum identifying the ten major challenges facing the global community listed as number three a 'crisis of leadership' – a lack of direction, energy, initiative and efficacy on the part of the political class. In a global survey of attitudes towards leadership, no less than 86 per cent of respondents agreed with the assessment that their community, nation or region was facing a crisis of leadership. Tellingly there was no significant variation in responses across regions, with respondents in North America equally despondent as respondents in Sub-Saharan Africa (Shahid, 2014). The latest Edelman Barometer of Trust tells a similar story.

Its survey of 33,000 respondents noted that trust in government and political leadership is at the lowest point since the survey's inception, with more than 70 per cent of countries surveyed expressing net distrust in their leaders and governments (Edelman Insights, 2015). Professional commentators across the globe routinely decry a lack of leadership, whether as a general trend of domestic politics (*The Guardian*, 2010; *The Economist*, 2011b; Westen, 2011; *Daily Mail*, 2013) or in relation to specific issues such as climate change and the global economy (Council on Foreign Relations, 2013; *The Independent*, 2013). Even beyond narratives of national leadership, on the global stage we seem to be facing a plethora of crises with a global reach and yet a dearth of compelling and trusted leaders to handle them (see Gill, 2011).

Countervailing Tendencies: The Evolution of Leadership Thinking

A quantitative review of leadership research speaks not only to the diversity of the field and the disparate array of conceptual frameworks within which such research is now being conducted, but also to the increasing weight of inquiry into alternative approaches that depart from the more traditional individualistic and charismatic emphases. (For an excellent quantitative table summarising the literature, see Dinh *et al.*, 2014.) Though we cannot summarise the extensive field of leadership theory, we draw out here some of the recurring tensions, contradictions and disagreements between various popular leadership schools with respect to the normative roles and practical consequences of political leadership within democracies. We contend that many of the emerging and newly popular threads of leadership theory diverge from the 'neo-charismatic' tradition, and instead present an increasingly collaborative ideal of leadership that sharply departs from the conventions of heroic leadership.

Scholarly analysis of leadership is attentive to the disjunction between expectations and performance. Despite our continuing leadership fetishism, as Michael Foley remarks on the state of contemporary political leadership:

> far from the pantheon of heroic leaders . . . most liberal democracies are characterised by a landscape of frustrated leaders and broken leaderships . . . The passage of political time can almost be marked by the regular cycle of unlikely ascents followed by the normal anticlimax of deep descents with ex-leaders complaining about precarious support bases, capricious publics, and the limits of politics.
>
> *(Foley, 2013: 16)*

The appearance of continued faith and interest in heroic leaders is misleading: the twenty-first century has been notably tumultuous for political leadership and has put domineering leadership on notice. Across the developed world, a spate of revolutions has unseated leader-centric regimes, from the Arab Spring in the Middle East, to democratic protest movements in Thailand, Turkey, former nations of the Soviet Union and across Africa. In the developed world too, ire has been directed against political elites, and movements of both left and right, such as the Tea Party, Occupy Wall Street and anti-Globalisation, have taken specific aim at world leaders and the leader class. Yet the legacy of these movements has oft been schizophrenic. In Egypt, the revolution that removed virtual autocrat Hosni Mubarak convulsed through a democratically elected ideologue in Muhammad Morsi, before returning to a heroic 'saviour' of the nation in the form of military strongman Abdel Fattah el-Sisi. As Stephen Medvic postulates, the public obsession with leaders and the heroic mythology of their capacities has given rise to the 'expectations trap' in modern politics, where a series of paradoxical expectations have become particularly pronounced. We expect our leaders to be exceptionally talented and yet have the common touch. They must be pragmatic achievers and yet uncompromisingly principled and honest. They must be decisive and yet also be consultative and democratic (Medvic, 2013: 9–20). Thus as attention to leaders has continued and amplified throughout the twenty-first century, so too have rival expectations about the quality of democracy, ethical scrutiny and the valence issues of leadership arisen.

If there are contradictory expectations of leadership in the public arena, the problem seems to be very much amplified in the context of democratic theory. Despite a large and healthy industry dedicated to studying leadership, and a public intensely interested in it, for political scientists interested in democracy the role of leaders continues to be problematic. The wielding of power and influence by a single individual frequently clashes with contemporary visions of collective democratic deliberation. As Kenneth Ruscio puts it, the dilemma comes down to 'the inescapable need for leadership of some sort, if only for the pragmatic reason of organising a collective effort, and the unavoidable way in which leadership threatens the highest values of democracy' (Ruscio, 2004: 3). The more leaders in democracies are scrutinised from a broad standpoint, the more complex and fraught their position becomes, inducing ever greater efforts to find the necessary conceptual compromises to resolve the individual–collective dilemma (Kane and Patapan, 2012: 10–29; also Hendriks and Karsten, 2014).

One body of academic opinion, alert to the decay of traditional parties, the rise of issue- rather than class-based politics and the influence of 'mediatisation' (Hjarvard, 2008) accepts what is described as 'leader-centric democracy' and focuses on how we might live with it (Pakulski and Körösényi, 2012). A contradictory trend, both within leadership studies and the practice of democratic theory, directs attention away from the heroic conception of leadership, not only by demonstrating its perils (Brown, 2014), but also by showing it to be inadequately attuned to social reality. The complexity of global, network society (Castells, 2010), it is argued, demands leadership models starkly contrasting with the strong leader, and a shift of focus from leaders themselves to the broader contexts in which they operate (see Avolio et al., 2009). Effective leaders are represented in this debate as 'facilitators', 'networkers', 'adjudicators' or 'convenors'. The supposition – central to complexity theory analyses of leadership – is that no one individual can deal with the multiple challenges of the 'wicked' policy problems (Head and Alford, 2015) that bedevil contemporary society: the leadership task is rather to orchestrate the diverse contributors who can, together, do something about them.

Those arguing for leaders as facilitators and consensus builders suggest that the problem of the strong leader is not simply that of narcissism, premature cognitive closure in the face of complexity, or (potential) megalomania. It goes beyond that: in the context of networks and dispersal of power in contemporary democracy, the heroic leader is a liability who will fail to create coalitions of action strong enough or popular enough to create change. Since leadership is dispersed across networks, public leadership (opinion aggregation leading to action) has to be essentially collective: it emanates from many points, from politicians, to community activists, to CEOs to celebrities (Uhr, 2008; Kane et al., 2009). Given this, leaders must necessarily be conciliators and co-operators to coordinate outcomes across these networks. This is the world of network governance, in which no individual can forge outcomes alone, where collaboration and consensus become the hallmarks of successful leadership in government (Klijn, 2014: 405–9), and where the structure of modern democratic institutions may not tolerate strong and heroic leaders for any length of time (Kellerman and Webster, 2001: 487–8).

This paradox then emerges: democratic electorates seem ever more beholden to the promise of the heroic leader and yet political institutions cannot accept them. For example, in Australia, two prime ministers of recent years have fallen victim to this state of affairs. Despite coming into power through electoral campaigns that were explicitly focused on electing a leader rather than electing a party, both Kevin Rudd and Tony Abbott – each of whom presented as strong leaders – soon suffered intense criticism for their lack of consultation and collaboration with colleagues, with both ultimately losing their jobs in party-room coups. And yet arguably, starting from the opposite end of the spectrum has produced results no more successful. Barack Obama famously pitched himself as collaborative and bipartisan, and put his money where his mouth was in attempting extensively to negotiate and consult with the Republican Party over his landmark objectives, such as the Patient Protection and Affordable Care Act. Yet opponents would not play, and criticism over his consultative style and the perceived failure to deliver on core promises led to a marked change in style. Thus the president's heroic individualism came to the fore, culminating with a flurry of executive decisions in 2013 and 2014 in areas such as the environment and immigration that bypassed Congress altogether. This seems an apposite exemplification of the problem facing contemporary leaders: Obama was open to consultation, negotiation and complexity, yet in the context of increasing polarisation and incivility (Shea and Sproveri, 2012) this was at odds with the decisive, cut-through action expected.

Another take on the public's fixation on heroic leaders, and the academic critique of the field, is the *romance of leadership* perspective, which takes a critical view of why the public and elites alike are so prone to attributing the successes and failures of organisations and governments to individual leaders (Meindl *et al.*, 1985). This perspective has given rise to *follower-centric* approaches, which look instead at the complex needs of followers, how these are satisfied by leaders and how perceptions and constructions of leadership roles are learned and spread amongst followers (Little, 1985). Recent research in social psychology has even more forcefully disputed individualistic emphases by stressing the primary importance of social identity factors in explaining follower attachment to leaders (e.g. Haslam *et al.*, 2010).

The cult of the great leader is also challenged by analyses of the ethical dimensions of leadership. An image of leadership that runs counter to our strong leader trope is the exemplar of the 'servant leader', first espoused by Robert Greenleaf in the 1970s but increasingly popular in academic and public discourse of the past two decades. Servant leadership rests on the tenets of empowering people, providing direction, stewardship, interpersonal acceptance, authenticity and humility. Servant leaders seek first to empower their followers to grow and ultimately to govern themselves (Van Dierendonck, 2011: 1231–4). The model of the servant leader is joined by many emphasising similar principles, such as *authentic leadership* (Avolio and Gardner, 2005), *ethical leadership* (Brown *et al.*, 2005; Ciulla, 2014) and *self-sacrificing leadership* (De Cremer and van Knippenberg, 2004). The concern of all these theories, increasingly popular in both the academic and public domain, is with the ethical and values dimensions of leadership, which are the heart of inspiring trust and empowerment in followership. Indeed, many aspects of the ethical leadership canon directly criticise the tradition of charismatic and heroic leadership (Solomon, 2014: 104–26; also Keeley, 2014), again bringing into question the wisdom of a focus on individual leaders at the expense of the needs and rights of followers.

In professional contexts such as business and management, the popularity of authentic and ethical leaders as role models for strategic leadership success has surged (e.g. Pearce, 2013; Schoemaker, 2014). More broadly, international recognition and praise has, in recent decades, fallen particularly on leaders espousing this particular role. The Elders, a prominent group of international elder statesmen involved in brokering solutions to international conflicts, consists of leaders who have been defined in the public eye as ethical, authentic and collaborative – Nelson Mandela, Kofi Annan, Gro Harlem Brundtland and Martti Ahtisaari to name a few. One such group member, Jimmy Carter, was roundly unpopular during his own term as president and routinely characterised as weak and vacillating, yet shifts in leadership attitudes some decades later have seen his leadership style come into vogue. Indeed, the rehabilitation of Jimmy Carter's leadership reputation has itself been observed and studied over the past two decades (Rozell, 1993). Some leaders who seemed representative of the ethical and authentic leadership model, such as Vaclav Havel and Lech Walesa, have mixed legacies in more mundane leadership contexts: they failed to connect with their own electorates during their terms of office.

Leadership is under constant scrutiny from democratic theorists in ways that are often inimical to the assertion of heroic leadership roles. Take, for instance, the debate on *monitory democracy* (Keane, 2009) in which civil society structures are said to have proliferated and, in concert with the intense personalisation of politics, have created a maelstrom in which leaders are constantly subjected to checks and balances. Others have joined this chorus: scholars have taken to placing much greater scrutiny on why leaders fail to live up to expectations, and how followers and observers can be more vigilant in detecting and calling it out. In consequence, an increasingly popular stream of leadership thought has been the attention to 'bad' or 'toxic' leadership – a popular subject in both biographies and academic contributions in recent decades (e.g. Kellerman, 2004; Lipman-Blumen, 2006; Helms, 2014).

Normatively and prescriptively, democratic theories have posited solutions to contemporary leadership paradoxes by advocating increased citizen participation and further diminution of the role of leaders. Deliberative democracy, one of the most prominent and well-known movements in democratic theory, prescribes a very much circumscribed (though seldom discussed) role for leaders, generally pushing such considerations into the background while bringing genuine citizen participation to the fore as an alternative method of resolving political conflict and creating decision-making structures (Dryzek, 2000; Gutmann and Thompson, 2009). As the deliberative democratic movement moves onto its 'third phase' of directing its attention to how deliberative democracy can be implemented on a systemic scale (e.g. Parkinson and Mansbridge, 2013), the legitimacy and place of leaders and leadership itself seem to be on ever shakier ground: heroic leaders are almost completely out of place in such conceptions.

Other prescriptive frameworks, such as that of civic leadership, dismiss the precepts of traditional heroic leadership. Civic leadership attempts to break the dyad of authority and leadership, choosing to focus much more closely on inclusive and democratic structures of decision making and citizen interaction that resolve the tensions inherent in democracy and leadership by making the latter a function that enables and augments the former, rather than a coercive or power-based element (Couto, 2014: 352–8). Indeed, there are many supporting voices that wish to decouple leadership from power and authority as a fundamental first step to resolving normative issues with leadership in a democratic society (Tucker, 1995: 67–76; Heifetz, 2007: 32–41).

Between a Rock and a Hard Place: Modern Democratic Leadership

What we are left with is an unresolved tug-of-war between divergent public and academic discourses on democratic leadership. They are rife with complex contradictions. On one side, much of the public and many commentators outside the world of political science seem to be intensifying their focus on the heroic leader as the salve to the world's ills, despite expectations constantly being disappointed and distrust in leaders ever increasing. Yet on the other, much of the research and science of leadership vigorously contests this tradition, and some of it rejects it altogether, arguing instead for new models of network leadership as integral to good democratic stewardship. This tug-of-war abounds with real world examples. We have seen Obama snared by the inability to pursue his preferred approach and retreating to the default position of executive action. The leadership of the European Union after the creation of new leadership posts by the Treaty of Lisbon is another proving ground of this problem. On the one hand,

the selection of Herman Van Rompuy as president was a clear nod to a background of concili-
ation, negotiation and facilitation that fits with many of the prevailing academic prescriptions
for such a position and indeed was supported by many in formal analysis (Van Assche, 2009;
Maythorne and Petersen, 2010; also Puetter, 2014: 111–33). And yet Rompuy was readily
characterised by the European public and media as weak and ineffective, was lampooned by
commentators seeing the choice as emblematic of a weak European Union, and was circum-
vented in many key respects by a continuing domination of EU politics by a cluster of 'strong'
national leaders (such as Nicholas Sarkozy and Angela Merkel) who presented narrower but far
stronger conceptions of European politics that much more readily met with public acceptance
(*The Economist*, 2009; Kaczynski, 2011: 201; *Eyes on Europe*, 2014).

How do modern leaders resolve this inherent tension over the differing elite and public
expectations placed upon their role? And how might institutions counter leadership caprice?

In *Good Democratic Leadership*, John Kane and Haig Patapan recognise not only the relative
lack of exploration of what good leadership is in a contemporary democratic context, but also
the significant constraints and conflicting expectations that democratic leaders are expected
to address (Kane and Patapan, 2014: 1–7). Thad Williamson, in that same volume, studies
three varied examples of mayoral leadership in Richmond, Virginia, and finds the fundamental
paradox of democratic leadership to be even more problematic – a mayor adhering closely to
democratic norms and facilitative leadership lacked the authority and control to deal with deep
structural problems, while a mayor in the traditional heroic mould who tackled issues forcefully
soon felt a backlash from stakeholders and was drawn into a political quagmire (Williamson,
2014: 32–50). At stake are not just the symbolism of power in leadership, but the very question of how democratic leaders can be effective and get things done when both heroism and
consensus are problematic as leadership watchwords.

One resolution is a careful execution of modern leadership theatre, as modern democratic
authority increasingly requires *acting like* a leader rather than *acting as* a leader. As Thomas Dumm
argues, leadership authority in the public domain is increasingly a product of received images
and popular culture, and acting to the script of being a heroic leader has now become a key
aspect of democratic leadership that the public expects (Dumm, 1999: 143–5). This is the 'drama
democracy', in which a political leader must assume the leading role in staged performances to
capture the public's heart (Fischer, 2003: 58–9; Klijn, 2014: 411–12). Such performances must
appear to be authentic, yet somehow executed without alienating the broad networks of other
actors critical to leading a functional government in a complex multi-stakeholder environment
(Klijn, 2014: 412–13). Or alternatively, the leader must be so successful on the front-stage as
to cow potential opponents backstage. For a compelling instance of this type of leadership, one
can look to Ronald Reagan, whose media-friendly embodiment of the heroic leader, bolstered
by an acting background, has spawned a small industry studying Reagan's perfection of the narrative of politics and cutting through the contemporary political quagmire without alienating
necessary political and public allies in the process (e.g. Stuckey, 1990; Hanska, 2012). In other
words, the solution is not to fight the problem of the personalisation and mediatisation of democratic politics but to embrace and play to it, maintaining a fidelity to heroic leadership images
without necessarily embodying them in the endeavours of government. This is to recognise that
the work of policy deliberation – the work of orchestrating across networks all those whose
contributions are essential to robust decisions – is quite distinct from the rhetorical performance
of leadership. Of course, as argued in *The Myth of the Strong Leader*, to believe in and act through
those images encourages the temptation that is the ultimate downfall of many a heroic leader:
'The leader's advertised strength is often an artifice or illusion' (Brown, 2014: 3) and the most
successful leaders are those who can play up to the myth of the heroic leader without becoming

deluded by it. Brown offers the prominent example of Harry S. Truman as the epitome of the successful resolution of the dilemma, playing the strong-man in public and proudly proclaiming 'the buck stops here', yet behind the scenes in his administration acting as the consummate delegator and collegial leader (Brown, 2014).

Yet rhetoric must be accompanied by delivery: promises of decisive action made must be promises kept. Authenticity and effectiveness must quickly accompany heroic rhetoric in order for the stratagem to have impact with the public. Indeed, this is the chief danger for leaders believing in their own rhetoric. Australia's Tony Abbott, whose personal performance of leadership incorporated strong rhetoric and heroic platitudes, soon found himself unpopular with the public because unequivocal promises could not be honoured, but also within government because colleagues and key stakeholders were disheartened by his frequent invocation of personal prerogatives and a lack of consultation. It culminated in an initial backbench revolt just over a year into his premiership and final loss of the leadership within two years. The leader who can foreshadow decisions, not only from conviction, but also because he or she understands distributed leadership and has already thought through action and enlisted (or knows how to engage) the support of those disparate others needed to bring matters to fruition might both satisfy public expectations and deliver the outcomes that maintain trust. Even though one can think of such examples – on Doris Kearns-Goodwin's account, Abraham Lincoln was one such (Kearns-Goodwin, 2009) – the widespread, cross-national indications of distrust, indeed crises of leadership, noted earlier suggest that such leaders are very rare.

Might the problem be counter-acted by screening to exclude troublesome leadership types, increasing the probability of those with Lincoln-style attributes? The long history of trying to identify and encourage 'the democratic personality' (Almond and Verba, 1963; Lasswell, 1951) does not give cause for optimism – much indicates that those driven by 'power chances' (Lasswell, 1948) continue to predominate in leader roles. Even studies of leaders with largely positive characteristics – Barber's 'active-positive' category, for instance (Barber, 1972) – indicate that they may generate problems, usually by over-rating their capacities and over-reaching. Nevertheless, some political parties themselves have lately turned to psychologists and organisational analysts to develop measures to vet candidates for the 'right qualities' (Silvester, 2012), evaluating 'social skills' and even proposing leaders undertake 360° feedback surveys (Bull, 2012). For all their worthy intentions, such approaches idealise and homogenise political types, ignoring context and taking too little account of the very different roles a politician might play: as thinker, administrator, fixer, constituency advocate, warrior, conciliator, negotiator, power broker. They seem oblivious to circumstances where a particular personality whom one could never imagine satisfying their performance indicators (let alone taking 360° surveys seriously) might be absolutely appropriate. Would the narcissism of some of the great 'active-positive' leaders (e.g. F. D. Roosevelt) rule them out? What about the archetypal 'strong leader', Winston Churchill, reckless, dangerous and politically suspect in the interwar period, an indifferent prime minister after the war, but precisely the right leader in a crisis?

Rather, then, than waiting for another Lincoln, we should acknowledge the likely frailty of individuals and work towards institutional practices that can constrain excess or caprice and that might encourage the sort of distributed network leadership that seems most appropriate to the challenges of contemporary society. Institutionalising processes of deliberative democracy in policy determination would be one move in this direction (Dryzek, 2000), ensuring that consensus on key issues is negotiated rather than being asserted by a domineering leader. Voting systems, too, have their effects: majoritarian democracies (such as the US, the UK, Canada, Australia) are notably more prone to return 'strong' leaders than are the Scandinavian consensus democracies where successful leaders are, perforce, coalition builders (Boumans et al., 2013). More rigorous attention might be paid to what John Uhr called 'the lattice of leadership' – leadership diffused *across* institutional spheres, but constrained to work collectively for the common good, with each élite challenged to do its best by being held to account by leaders in another sphere (Uhr, 2005). Transparent codes of accountability and regulation should ensure that when one element, typically executive government, becomes too dominant, stakeholders will be aware that the ethical constraint of the lattice is under threat and act to demand restoration of its integrity. This leads on to the extensive research on governance, another growth industry, one purpose of which is also to ensure the exercise of leadership within proper bounds and one stream within which has emphasised 'self-organising inter-organisational networks' characterised by trust and mutual adjustment (Rhodes, 1996). There will be patterns of behaviour and agreed operational codes – much governance research is concerned with identifying these and assessing their efficacy. But no one element among these autonomous but interdependent organisations (even government, or its leader) will dominate, since all need to 'exchange resources (for example, money, information, expertise) to achieve their objectives, to maximise their influence over outcomes, and to avoid becoming dependent on other players in the game' (Rhodes, 1996: 658). The effective actor in this context is bound, then, to play a facilitative role.

The point of briefly rendering these institutional options (some of which would be seen by their proponents as in a different domain to that of leadership) is simply to draw out their congruence. All make reference to networks (rather than individuals), to coalition building (rather than tribal discipline), to trust and mutual adjustment (rather than competitive strength), to facilitation (rather than direction), to negotiated outcomes (rather than command and control). They resolve the problem of democratic leadership by reminding us that the most serious challenges must be addressed collectively: the swift decision on a complex problem will almost certainly be wrong; such issues will demand the application of many minds and disparate skills; the successful leader will excel at orchestration.

The greatest challenge lies however in creating institutional structures that support and encourage orchestration, and yet allow for the public desire for acts of leadership heroism to be fulfilled, and indeed for exceptional individuals in times of crisis (think, again, of Lincoln and Churchill in times of war). It was the Anti-Federalists opposed to the US Constitution who foresaw in the 1780s that even a president, theoretically constrained by checks and institutionalised power sharing, would nonetheless eclipse the technically more powerful Congress in time, as the public would always demand a leader to personify and act as the focus of government. As we have shown, there is no sign such public desires are diminishing. Even in the Netherlands, home of the consensus-driven 'polder model' of democratic government, increasingly leaders are perceived more positively, and as more important, than their respective parties (Andeweg and Irwin, 2014: 133–5), and populist 'strong' leaders (e.g. Pim Fortuyn and Geert Wilders) have reaped significant electoral gains in the last decade as agent provocateurs, manifestly rejecting the system. Finding the delicate balance between institutional design that encourages and embeds orchestrators and facilitators into democratic governance and the public demand for leadership heroism, political individualism, and a focus of government, remains one of the great challenges for twenty-first-century political science.

References

Aarts, K., A. Blais and H. Schmitt. (2013). *Political Leaders and Democratic Elections*. Oxford: Oxford University Press.

Almond, G. and S. Verba. (1963). *The Civic Culture: Political Attitudes and Democracy in Five Nations*. Princeton, NJ: Princeton University Press.

Ambrose, S. (2014). *Nixon Volume I: The Education of a Politician 1913–1962*. New York: Simon & Schuster.

Andeweg, R. and G. A. Irwin. (2014). *Governance and Politics of the Netherlands*. London: Palgrave Macmillan.

Avolio, B. J. and W. L. Gardner. (2005). 'Authentic Leadership Development: Getting to the Root of Positive Forms of Leadership'. *The Leadership Quarterly* 16 (3): 315–38.

Avolio, B. J., F. O. Walumbwa and T. J. Weber. (2009). 'Leadership: Current Theories, Research, and Future Directions'. *Annual Review of Psychology*, 60 (1): 421–49.

Balmas, M. and T. Sheafer. (2013). 'Leaders First, Countries After: Mediated Political Personalization in the International Arena'. *Journal of Communication* 63 (3): 454–75.

Barber, J. D. (1972). *The Presidential Character: Predicting Performance in the White House*. Englewood Cliffs, NJ: Prentice Hall.

Barisione, M. (2009). 'Valence Image and the Standardisation of Democratic Political'. *Leadership* 5 (1): 41–60.

Bass, B. M. (1985). *Leadership and Performance Beyond Expectations*. New York: Free Press.

BBC. (1999). 'Indira Gandhi "Greatest Woman"'. *BBC World Service*, 1 December. http://news.bbc.co.uk/2/hi/543743.stm.

Beck, U. (1992). *Risk Society: Towards a New Modernity*. London: Sage.

Blondel, J. and J.-L. Thiebault. (2009). *Political Leadership, Parties and Citizens: The Personalisation of Leadership*. London: Routledge.

Boumans, J., H. Boomgaarden and R. Vliegenthart. (2013). 'Media Personalisation in Context: A Cross-National Comparison between the UK and the Netherlands, 1992–2007'. *Political Studies* 61 (April): 198–216.

Brown, A. (2014). *The Myth of the Strong Leader: Political Leadership in the Modern Age*. London: The Bodley Head.

Brown, M., L. Treviño and D. Harrison. (2005). 'Ethical Leadership: A Social Learning Perspective for Construct Development and Testing'. *Organizational Behavior and Human Decision Processes* 97 (2): 117–34.

Bueno de Mesquita, B. and A. Smith. (2011). *The Dictator's Handbook: Why Bad Behavior Is Almost Always Good Politics*. New York: PublicAffairs.

Bull, P. (2012). 'What Makes a Successful Politician? The Social Skills of Politics'. In A. Weinberg (ed.), *The Psychology of Politicians*, 61–75. Cambridge: Cambridge University Press.

Burns, J. M. (1978). *Leadership*. New York: Harper & Row.

Campus, D. (2010). 'Mediatization and Personalization of Politics in Italy and France: The Cases of Berlusconi and Sarkozy'. *The International Journal of Press/Politics* 15 (2): 219–35.

Castells, M. (2010). *The Rise of the Network Society: The Information Age: Economy, Society, and Culture, Volume I*. (2nd edition). Chichester: Wiley-Blackwell.

Ciulla, J. (2014). *Ethics, the Heart of Leadership*. Santa Barbara, CA: ABC-CLIO.

Council on Foreign Relations. (2013). *The Global Climate Change Regime*. New York: Council on Foreign Relations. http://www.cfr.org/climate-change/global-climate-change-regime/p21831.

Couto, R. A. (2014). 'Civic Leadership'. In R. A. W. Rhodes and P. 't Hart (eds.), *Oxford Handbook of Political Leadership*, 347–61. Oxford: Oxford University Press.

C-SPAN. (2009). 'Historians Presidential Leadership Survey'. *C-SPAN Polls*. http://legacy.c-span.org/PresidentialSurvey/Overall-Ranking.aspx.

Daily Mail. (2013). 'A Crisis of Leadership in the Western World'. 22 January. http://www.dailymail.co.uk/debate/article-2266170/A-crisis-leadership-western-world.html.

De Cremer, D. and D. van Knippenberg. (2004). 'Leader Self-Sacrifice and Leadership Effectiveness: The Moderating Role of Leader Self-Confidence'. *Organizational Behavior and Human Decision Processes* 95 (2): 140–55.

Dinh, J., R. Lord, W. L. Gardner, J. D. Meuser, R. Liden and J. Hu. (2014). 'Leadership Theory and Research in the New Millennium: Current Theoretical Trends and Changing Perspectives'. *The Leadership Quarterly* 25 (1): 36–62.

Dryzek, J. (2000). *Deliberative Democracy and Beyond: Liberals, Critics, Contestations*. Oxford: Oxford University Press.

Dumm, T. L. (1999). *A Politics of the Ordinary*. New York: NYU Press.

Edelmen Insights. (2015). 'Trust around the World'. *2015 Edelman Trust Barometer*. New York: Edelmen Insights. http://www.edelman.com/insights/intellectual-property/2015-edelman-trust-barometer/trust-around-world/.

Edwards, G. and S. Wayne. (2013). *Presidential Leadership: Politics and Policy Making*. Boston, MA: Cengage Learning.

Eyes on Europe. (2014). 'Herman Van Rompuy's Legacy'. *Des Regards Croises Ser L'Europe*. 20 December. http://www.eyes-on-europe.eu/herman-van-rompuys-legacy/.

Fischer, F. (2003). *Reframing Public Policy: Discursive Politics and Deliberative Practices*. Oxford: Oxford University Press.

Foley, M. (2013). *Political Leadership: Themes, Contexts, and Critiques*. Oxford: Oxford University Press.

Gallup. (2007). 'Wanted in Next President: Honesty, Strong Leadership'. *Election 2008*, 4 April. http://www.gallup.com/poll/27085/wanted-next-president-honesty-strong-leadership.aspx.

Gallup. (2009). 'Obama's Leadership Qualities Stand Out to Americans'. *Political Polling*, 21 September. http://www.gallup.com/poll/123104/Obama-Leadership-Qualities-Stand-Out-Americans.aspx.

Garzia, D. (2011). 'The Personalization of Politics in Western Democracies: Causes and Consequences on Leader–Follower Relationships'. *The Leadership Quarterly* 22 (4): 697–709.

Garzia, D. (2014). *Personalization of Politics and Electoral Change*. London: Palgrave Macmillan.

Gill, S. (2011). *Global Crises and the Crisis of Global Leadership*. Cambridge, MA: Cambridge University Press.

Golec de Zavala, A. (2012). 'Cognitive Skills and Motivation to Adapt to Social Change among Polish Politicians'. In A. Weinberg (ed.), *The Psychology of Politicians*, 76–96. Cambridge: Cambridge University Press.

Gray, J. (1998). *False Dawn: The Delusions of Global Capitalism*. New York: The New Press.

Gutmann, A. and D. Thompson. (2009). *Why Deliberative Democracy?* Princeton, NJ: Princeton University Press.

Hanska, J. (2012). *Reagan's Mythical America: Storytelling as Political Leadership*. New York: Palgrave Macmillan.

Haslam, S., S. Reicher and M. Platow. (2010). *The New Psychology of Leadership: Identity, Influence and Power*. Hove, UK: Psychology Press.

Head, B. W. and Alford, J. (2015). 'Wicked Problems Implications for Public Policy and Management'. *Administration & Society* 47, 711–39.

Heifetz, R. (2007). 'The Scholarly/Practical Challenge of Leadership'. In R. A. Couto (ed.), *Reflections on Leadership*, 31–44. Lanham, MD: University Press of America.

Helms, L. (2012). 'Democratic Political Leadership in the New Media Age: A Farewell to Excellence?' *British Journal of Politics and International Relations* 14 (4): 651–70.

Helms, L. (2014). 'When Leaders Are Not Good: Exploring Bad Leadership in Liberal Democracies Across Time and Space'. In J. Kane and H. Patapan (eds.), *Good Democratic Leadership: On Prudence and Judgement in Modern Democracies*, 51–69. Oxford: Oxford University Press.

Hendriks, F. and N. Karsten. (2014). 'Theory of Democratic Leadership'. In R. A. W. Rhodes and P. 't Hart (eds.), *Oxford Handbook of Political Leadership*, 41–56. Oxford: Oxford University Press.

Hill, F. and C. Gaddy (2012). *Mr. Putin: Operative in the Kremlin*. Washington, DC: Brookings Institution Press.

Hjarvard, S. (2008). 'The Mediatization of Society: A Theory of the Media as Agents of Social and Cultural Change'. *Nordicom Review* 29 (2): 105–34.

India Today. (2001). 'Who Has Been the Best Prime Minister of India?' *India Today Online*. http://india today.intoday.in/gallery/india-today-nielson-best-prime-minister-survey/1/5315.html.

Isaacson, W. (2010). *Profiles in Leadership: Historians on the Elusive Quality of Greatness*. New York: W. W. Norton & Company.

Johnson, B. (2014). *The Churchill Factor: How One Man Made History*. London: Hodder & Stoughton.

Just, M. and A. Crigler. (2000). 'Leadership Image-Building: After Clinton and Watergate'. *Political Psychology* 21 (1): 179–98.

Kaczynski, P. M. (2011). 'Towards a President of the European Union'. *Brown Journal of World Affairs* 17 (2): 193.

Kane, J. and H. Patapan. (2012). *The Democratic Leader: How Democracy Defines, Empowers and Limits Its Leaders*. Oxford: Oxford University Press.

Kane, J. and H. Patapan. (2014). *Good Democratic Leadership: On Prudence and Judgment in Modern Democracies*. Oxford: Oxford University Press.

Kane, J., H. Patapan and P. 't Hart. (2009). *Dispersed Democratic Leadership: Origins, Dynamics, and Implications*. Oxford: Oxford University Press.

Keane, J. (2009). *The Life and Death of Democracy*. London: Simon and Schuster.

Kearns-Goodwin, D. (2009). *Team of Rivals: The Political Genius of Abraham Lincoln*. London: Penguin.

Keeley, M. (2014). 'The Trouble with Transformational Leadership: Toward a Federalist Ethic for Organizations'. In J. Ciulla (ed.), *Ethics, the Heart of Leadership*, 179–207. Santa Barbara, CA: ABC-CLIO.

Kellerman, B. (2004). *Bad Leadership: What It Is, How It Happens, Why It Matters*. Boston: Harvard Business Review Press.

Kellerman, B. (2012). *The End of Leadership*. New York: HarperCollins.

Kellerman, B. and S. W. Webster. (2001). 'The Recent Literature on Public Leadership – Reviewed and Considered'. *The Leadership Quarterly* 12 (4): 485–514.

Klijn, E.-H. (2014). 'Political Leadership in Networks'. In R. A. W. Rhodes and P. 't Hart (eds.), *Oxford Handbook of Political Leadership*, 403–17. Oxford: Oxford University Press.

Lasswell, H. D. (1948). *Power and Personality*. New York: W.W. Norton & Company.

Lasswell, H. D. (1951). 'Democratic Character'. In *The Political Writings of Harold D. Lasswell*, 465–525. Glencoe, IL: The Free Press.

Le Nouvel Observateur. (2009). 'Charles de Gaulle, Ex-Président Préféré Des Français'. *Le Nouvel Observateur*, 4 November. http://tempsreel.nouvelobs.com/politique/20091104.OBS6765/charles-de-gaulle-ex-president-prefere-des-francais.html.

Lipman-Blumen, J. (2006). *The Allure of Toxic Leaders: Why We Follow Destructive Bosses and Corrupt Politicians – and How We Can Survive Them*. New York: Oxford University Press.

Little, G. (1985). *Political Ensembles*. Melbourne, VIC: Oxford University Press.

Little, G. (1988). *Strong Leadership: Thatcher, Reagan and an Eminent Person*. Melbourne, VIC: Oxford University Press.

Littlefield, R. S. and A. M. Quenette. (2007). 'Crisis Leadership and Hurricane Katrina: The Portrayal of Authority by the Media in Natural Disasters'. *Journal of Applied Communication Research* 35 (1): 26–47.

Luttwak, E. (1998). *Turbo Capitalism: Winners and Losers in the World Economy*. London: Weidenfeld & Nicholson.

Maythorne, L. and J. Petersen. (2010). *New Model Leadership in a New European Union*. SSRN Scholarly Paper, No. 1690989. Rochester, NY: Social Science Research Network. http://papers.ssrn.com/abstract=1690989.

McAllister, I. (2007). 'The Personalization of Politics'. In R. J. Dalton and H. D. Klingemann (eds.), *The Oxford Handbook of Political Behavior*, 571–88. Oxford: Oxford University Press.

Medvic, S. K. (2013). *In Defense of Politicians: The Expectations Trap and Its Threat to Democracy*. London: Routledge.

Meindl, J., S. Ehrlich and J. Dukerich. (1985). 'The Romance of Leadership'. *Administrative Science Quarterly* 30 (1): 78–102.

Pakulski, J. and A. Körösényi. (2012). *Toward Leader Democracy*. London: Anthem Press.

Parkinson, J. and J. Mansbridge. (2013). *Deliberative Systems: Deliberative Democracy at the Large Scale*. Cambridge: Cambridge University Press.

Pearce, T. (2013). *Leading Out Loud: A Guide for Engaging Others in Creating the Future*. San Francisco, CA: Jossey-Bass.

Puetter, U. (2014). *The European Council and the Council: New Intergovernmentalism and Institutional Change*. Oxford: Oxford University Press.

Rahat, G. and T. Sheafer. (2007). 'The Personalization(s) of Politics: Israel, 1949–2003'. *Political Communication* 24 (1): 65–80.

Rhodes, R. A. W. (1996). 'The New Governance: Governing without Government'. *Political Studies* 44 (4): 652–67.

Rodgers, D. T. (2011). *Age of Fracture*. Cambridge, MA: Harvard University Press.

Rost, J. and A. Smith. (1992). 'Leadership: A Post-industrial Approach'. *European Management Journal* 10 (2): 193–201.

Rozell, M. (1993). 'Carter Rehabilitated: What Caused the 39th President's Press Transformation?' *Presidential Studies Quarterly* 23 (2): 317–30.

Ruscio, K. P. (2004). *The Leadership Dilemma in Modern Democracy*. Boston, MA: Edward Elgar Publishing.

Samuels, D. and M. Shugart. (2010). *Presidents, Parties, and Prime Ministers*. London: Cambridge University Press.

Scammell, M. (2007). 'Political Brands and Consumer Citizens: The Rebranding of Tony Blair'. *The ANNALS of the American Academy of Political and Social Science* 611 (1): 176–92.

Schoemaker, P. J. (2014). 'Nelson Mandela as a Strategic Leader'. *The European Business Review*. http://www.europeanbusinessreview.com/?p=477.

Shahid, S. (2014) 'Lack of Leadership'. *Outlook on the Global Agenda 2015*. Davos, CH: World Economic Forum. http://reports.weforum.org/outlook-global-agenda-2015/top-10-trends-of-2015/3-lack-of-leadership/.

Shea, D. and A. Sproveri. (2012). 'The Rise and Fall of Nasty Politics in America'. *PS: Political Science and Politics* 45 (3): 416–21.

Shephard, G. (2013). *The Real Iron Lady: Working with Margaret Thatcher*. London: Biteback Publishing.

Siena College Research Institute. (2010). *Siena Poll No. 5: American Presidents*. Loudonville, NY: Siena College. http://www.siena.edu/pages/179.asp?item=2566.

Silvester, J. (2012). 'Recruiting Politicians: Designing Competency Based Selection for UK Parliamentary Candidates'. In A. Weinberg (ed.), *The Psychology of Politicians*, 21–38. Cambridge: Cambridge University Press.

Smith, D. (2014). *How to Think Like Churchill*. London: Michael O'Mara.

Solomon, R. (2014). 'Emotions and Trust: Beyond "Charisma"'. In J. Ciulla (ed.), *Ethics, the Heart of Leadership*, 104–26. Santa Barbara, CA: ABC-CLIO.

Stuckey, M. E. (1990). *Playing the Game: The Presidential Rhetoric of Ronald Reagan*. New York: Praeger.

The Economist. (2009). 'The Pity of Herman Van Rompuy'. *The Economist*, 7 November. http://www.economist.com/blogs/charlemagne/2009/11/_normal_0_false_false_4.

The Economist. (2011a). 'A Crisis of Leadership, Too'. *The Economist*, 24 March. http://www.economist.com/node/18441143.

The Economist. (2011b). 'The New Iron Chancellor'. *The Economist*, 26 November. http://www.economist.com/node/21540283.

The Guardian. (2010). 'Lack of Leadership Is Driving Britain to Despair'. 11 January. http://www.theguardian.com/commentisfree/2010/jan/10/leadership-despair-positioning-public-weary.

The Independent. (2013). 'A Lack of Leadership in Africa Threatens Economic Progress'. 18 October. http://www.independent.co.uk/voices/comment/a-lack-of-leadership-in-africa-threatens-economic-progress-8889974.html.

Theakston, K. and M. Gill. (2005). *Rating 20th Century British Prime Ministers*. POLIS Working Paper 19. Leeds, UK: University of Leeds.

Tucker, R. C. (1995). *Politics as Leadership*. Columbia, MO: University of Missouri Press.

Uhr, J. (2005). *Terms of Trust: Arguments over Ethics in Australian Government*. Sydney, NSW: University of New South Wales Press.

Uhr, J. (2008). 'Distributed Authority in a Democracy: The Lattice of Leadership Revisited'. In P. 't Hart and J. Uhr (eds.), *Public Leadership: Perspectives and Practices*, 37–44. Canberra, ACT: ANU E Press.

United States Presidency Centre. (2011). *UK Survey of US Presidents*. London: Institute for the Study of the Americas. http://www.community-languages.org.uk/US-presidency-survey/overall.htm.

Van Assche, T. (2009). *Herman Van Rompuy: Calm Resolve in the European Union. Media, Movements and Politics*. Antwerp, BE: University of Antwerp. http://uahost.uantwerpen.be/m2p/publications/1257767957.pdf.

Van Dierendonck, D. (2011). 'Servant Leadership: A Review and Synthesis'. *Journal of Management* 37 (4): 1228–61.

Vogel, E. (2011). *Deng Xiaoping and the Transformation of China*. Cambridge, MA: Harvard University Press.

Walter, J. (2014). 'Biographical Analysis'. In R. A. W. Rhodes and P. 't Hart (eds.), *The Oxford Handbook of Political Leadership*, 314–27. Oxford: Oxford University Press.

Wattenberg, M. (1991). *The Rise of Candidate-Centered Politics: Presidential Elections in the 1980s*. Cambridge, MA: Harvard University Press.

Westen, D. (2011). 'What Happened to Obama's Passion?' *The New York Times*, 6 August. http://www.nytimes.com/2011/08/07/opinion/sunday/what-happened-to-obamas-passion.html.

Williamson, T. (2014). 'The Tangled Relationship of Democracy, Leadership and Justice in Urban America: A View from Richmond'. In J. Kane and H. Patapan (eds.), *Good Democratic Leadership: On Prudence and Judgement in Modern Democracies*, 32–50. Oxford: Oxford University Press.

Winkler, I. (2009). *Contemporary Leadership Theories*. Heidelberg, BW: Physica-Verlag.

Yew, L. K. (2014). *The Singapore Story: Memoirs of Lee Kuan Yew*. Singapore: Marshall Cavendish International.

Yukl, G. (1999). 'An Evaluative Essay on Current Conceptions of Effective Leadership'. *European Journal of Work and Organizational Psychology* 8 (1): 33–48.

15

Co-leadership

Contexts, Configurations and Conditions[1]

Émilie Gibeau, Wendy Reid and Ann Langley

The idea of co-leadership – that two people might successfully share an organizational leadership role on an equal footing – has been received skeptically by management scholars from Henri Fayol (1949) to Edwin Locke (2003), and also by the popular press, as evidenced in recent blog titles such as "With co-CEOs, companies flirt with disaster" (Zillman, 2014) and "The co-CEO model is officially dead" (Frisch, 2012). Skeptics cite the potential for confusion, conflict, ambiguity and lack of accountability as reasons why such an arrangement is likely to fail. Yet, co-leadership is nevertheless alive and well. It is quite frequent in certain sectors (e.g., the arts, health care) and there have been several co-CEO pairs at the summit of high-profile business firms (e.g., Google, Goldman-Sachs, Deutsche Bank, and Whole Foods) who have managed to sustain collaboration over many years even though, at some point, these arrangements may eventually dissolve, or break down (but single CEOs leave too).

Scholars have recently become more interested in plural forms of leadership (Denis et al., 2012) where more than one individual contributes in some way to leadership tasks. Terms such as "shared leadership" (Pearce and Conger, 2002), "distributed leadership" (Gronn, 2002) and "collective leadership" (Denis et al., 2001) have emerged to describe variants of this phenomenon. In this chapter, we will focus on a very specific type of plural leadership in which two people act jointly as leaders for others lower in the organizational hierarchy, pooling leadership tasks that are more usually attributed to a single person (Denis et al., 2012). This co-leadership form is particularly interesting both because it is quite common, and because of its particularities. Certain authors have discussed "pooled leadership" configurations at the top in which two or three leaders share the top job (Alvarez and Svejenova, 2002; Hodgson et al., 1965). However, co-leadership dyads arguably have certain characteristics that are different from triads. When three people form a leadership group together, there is always the possibility of majority decision in case of disagreements. When there are only two, this possibility is missing, suggesting a more egalitarian mode of functioning. Note that, in this chapter, we do not consider contexts where one member can fire the other even though some authors apply the term "co-leadership" to such situations, notably in relation to CEO-COO pairs (Heenan and Bennis, 1999). Clearly, there is more interest in exploring the issues and challenges associated with co-leadership arrangements involving at least nominally equal partnerships. We include here co-CEO arrangements, as well as co-leadership pairs that may operate below the strategic apex.

To explore the co-leadership phenomenon, we first draw on the literature to review the *contexts* in which co-leadership appears to be most prevalent, in an attempt to understand what drives organizations to consider this form despite some of its apparent disadvantages indicated above. Second, we explore the particular *configurations* that co-leadership may take in terms of division of roles and responsibilities. Third, we consider the *conditions for success*, examining successively individual, relational, organizational and institutional factors. Finally, we draw attention to important opportunities for further research on this phenomenon. Our overall purpose is to draw together and synthesize the rather eclectic and disparate body of work dealing with co-leadership, to better understand what is known and what is not known, and to establish a basis to move forward.

Contexts for Co-leadership

The literature tends to suggest that co-leadership arrangements are especially prevalent and suitable in four types of contexts: pluralistic settings, large and complex corporations, transitioning organizations and family businesses. They may also occur in a variety of other settings, often driven by ideological concerns related to democracy and sharing, although precise data on prevalence is hard to come by.

Bridging Competing Logics in Pluralistic Settings

Pluralistic settings are characterized by the coexistence of multiple institutional demands or logics. Institutional logics refer to "the socially constructed, historical pattern of material practices, assumptions, values, beliefs, and rules by which individuals produce and reproduce their material subsistence, organize time and space, and provide meaning to their social reality" (Ocasio and Thornton, 1999: 804). When logics compete and tensions result, co-leadership can be seen as a strategy to facilitate coexistence, to ensure that the logics are represented in strategic debates and to mobilize different groups toward overarching objectives (Fjellvaer, 2010). Creative organizations, healthcare organizations, professional service firms as well as organizations in the education and media sectors constitute pluralistic settings. Note that most of these settings involve professionals.

Fjellvaer (2010) described in particular how co-leadership can allow organizations in these sectors to cope with multiple logics. For her study, she drew on a sample of 27 pluralistic organizations in Norway of which she found that 13 had official dual leadership structures. For example, in creative organizations such as theaters, orchestras and museums, the author identified the tension between artistic excellence and commercial success as underlying the need for co-leadership. The combination of an artistic director promoting artistic expression and an executive director concerned with financial viability can enable each to focus on their areas of expertise, allowing the simultaneous pursuit of different objectives (Bhansing et al., 2012; Reid, 2015; Reid and Karambayya, 2009; Antrobus, 2009). This kind of structure is widely discussed and fairly common in these sectors. For example, a quick survey by one of the authors confirmed that six out of seven ballet companies in Canada had formal co-leadership structures, as did almost all symphony orchestras. Moreover, an informant at the Professional Association of Canadian Theatre indicated that their membership is predominantly characterized by dual leadership. The structure may be less prevalent in other subsectors of the arts, or in other countries. However, in the Netherlands, Bhansing et al. (2012: 528) found that, of 84 members of the Dutch Association of Performing Stage Art, "69 (82 percent) had a dual leadership structure that was clearly divided along artistic and business goals," suggesting that, at least in the performing arts, the form is far from rare.

In hospitals, co-leadership arrangements are sometimes used as a strategy to deal with the tensions between mission (patient care) and managerial logics (Fjellvaer, 2010; Steinert et al., 2006). Exploring the case of the Sunnybrook Hospital, MacTavish and Norton (1995) explained how co-leadership arrangements allowed medical professionals to lead major re-engineering efforts while continuing their clinical practice. We observe multiple references to governance arrangements in health care in which co-leadership dyads composed of a doctor and a non-medical professional with management training jointly manage programs of care at senior management level below the CEO (Baldwin et al., 2011; Ponte, 2004; Zismer et al., 2010). When they work well, these arrangements enable co-leadership teams to effectively combine and bridge their respective sources of expertise, authority and legitimacy. Health care organizations as prestigious as the Mayo Clinic (Berry, 2004) have adopted such structures. Co-leadership at the level of clinical programs (though not at the CEO level) is a principle that has been put forward in recent structural reforms in the Quebec health care system,[2] and has inspired health system reforms at different times in Denmark and France (Neogy and Kirkpatrick, 2009).

In professional service firms, Empson et al. (2013) highlighted the tensions resulting from the increasing competition between the professional and managerial logics caused by the recent trend toward the "corporatization" of partnerships in law and consulting. The need to retain high performers demonstrating exceptional revenue generation capabilities can also be a driving force for the implementation of co-leadership structures in this field (Arnone and Stumpf, 2010). Empson et al. (2013) note, however, that, despite the growing trend to bring in professional managers to work in dyadic relationships with managing partners in law firms, the partners still tended to retain some hierarchical control and veto power. Co-leadership is not quite egalitarian in this sector.

Finally, Fjellvaer (2010) noted that some higher education institutions rely on co-leadership to cope with the conflict between research and teaching missions, while, in the media sector in Norway, she observed that co-leadership was used to deal with potential tension between maintaining editorial values (associated with freedom of the press) and promoting commercial success. Co-leadership has also been studied quite extensively in the case of schools in public education systems, another professionalized setting (Court, 2004; Gronn and Hamilton, 2004). However, the motivations for having co-leaders in schools may be less about logics and more about ideology. We return to these settings later.

Coping with Complexity in Large Corporations

Many large organizations are not necessarily embedded in environments associated with competing institutional demands to the same extent as the professional settings mentioned above. However, their needs in terms of the sheer size of the job and the range of skills required may still be substantial, and can sometimes lead them to consider co-leadership arrangements at the top. For example, O'Toole et al. (2002) concluded that two heads are better than one when one individual cannot possess the broad range of skills required to cope with the challenges an organization is facing, and Arnone and Stumpf (2010) suggested that the range of leadership styles, skills and competencies possessed by co-leaders can better equip companies to face challenges. Certainly, when co-CEO arrangements are described in the popular press, this is the justification that tends to be emphasized. Similarly, in a wide-ranging study of co-leadership arrangements, Alvarez and Svejenova (2002) suggest that the range and complexity of top management tasks can justify the use of co-leadership.

More specifically, Arnone and Stumpf (2010) reported how co-heads were used to ease geographic expansion by assigning regional responsibilities based on cultural considerations, while Arena et al. (2011) explained how multinational corporations might benefit from having two CEOs, one responsible for domestic operations and another for international operations. The authors also highlighted how the complementary expertise of co-CEOs who possess skills and knowledge in different industries might make co-leadership an interesting arrangement for diversified companies. This complementary expertise can allow the co-leaders to complement or replace advising by board members, while the collaboration of co-CEOs can ensure mutual monitoring when the board is unable to do so (Arena et al., 2011). The complexity, diversity, size and geographical dispersion of some post-merger organizations also create a context in which co-leadership could be an interesting option (Troiano, 1999).

Quite how common such arrangements are in large firms is, however, difficult to assess. In their study of co-leadership arrangements at CEO level in publicly listed firms in the US, Krause et al. (2014) were able to identify 71 cases of formal co-leadership arrangements by trawling publicly available information. This is a not insignificant number, but it remains small compared with the total number of firms listed, for example, on the New York Stock Exchange (2800).[3]

Managing Continuity and Change during Transitions

Transitions also appear to be particularly propitious contexts for the emergence of co-leadership arrangements. We have seen before that the complexity and scope of post-merger organizations can justify co-leadership. However, co-leadership is also seen as an arrangement that can facilitate merger and acquisition processes (Arena et al., 2011; Dennis et al., 2009; Jaklevic, 1999; Krause et al., 2014; O'Toole et al., 2002). Arnone and Stumpf (2010) explain how assigning a leader from each firm to work as co-heads can ease integration, encourage collaboration and ensure that both firms are represented in decision processes. Troiano (1999) sees co-CEO arrangements as a temporary way to facilitate merger transactions. The author also highlights how such arrangements reflect some firms' preference for friendly integrations as opposed to hostile buyouts, as well as a commitment to build a partnership aiming at the success of the whole group instead of a particular faction. The morale of organizational members is consequently more likely to remain intact. Nguyen and Siedel (2000) also believe that a co-CEO model can ease the tensions associated with integrating two organizations, especially in a merger of equals in which no firm is dominant. Co-CEO arrangements also contribute to avoiding conflicts at least for a time over which organization should be dominant and can constitute an interesting power-sharing arrangement when both CEOs are reluctant to relinquish their position.

Besides easing the strain of integrating two organizations in mergers and acquisitions, co-leadership arrangements have been used to facilitate the processes of splitting firms (Krause et al., 2014) as well as succession processes. For instance, Arnone and Stumpf (2010) discussed how some companies use co-CEO structures to ease the transition between a retiring CEO and a new incumbent. It is possible that such an intention may lie behind a recent announcement by the CEO of Oracle to cede the CEO position to two new co-CEOs (Zillman, 2014). This could also be construed, however, as a means for departing executives to retain power, despite formal succession. Finally, co-leadership may sometimes be installed to deal with temporary situations. For example, De Voogt (2006) observed that some museums decided to place a dual leadership structure in place in response to a financial or legal crisis, to allow the board to have more direct control of the business side through a managerial leader working in parallel with the artistic director. Almost by definition, however, these transitional arrangements, whatever their origins, are likely to be temporary, and may simply postpone inevitable power struggles around which individual (and which firm in the case of mergers) will eventually dominate.

Maintaining Control and Sharing the Load in Family Business

Family businesses are also propitious contexts for co-leadership arrangements. Three cases of co-leadership in family businesses have been discussed in the literature: the transfer of executive leadership to two siblings, the overlap between generations as a child is preparing to replace a parent as business leader and the co-leadership of a family firm by a family member and a non-family CEO. In the first case, two siblings are the equal successors to the family business and jointly exercise co-leadership (Alvarez and Svejenova, 2002; Arena et al., 2011; Dennis et al., 2009; Rahael, 2012). Viewing successions as a process rather than an event, Rahael (2012) discussed the second case in which a parent co-leads a family business with a member of the next generation over a few years. Miller et al. (2014) studied the third case in which a family member and a non-family manager act as co-CEOs of a family business. Such co-leadership arrangements are used by family business owners unable to find talented executives within their pool of relatives. In this model, the non-family CEO and an influential member of the controlling family have equivalent formal power and administrative responsibilities. Overall, in a study of ethnic entrepreneurship in Canada, Paré et al. (2008) found that 36 percent of entrepreneurial ventures involved some form of co-leadership, but that the form was more popular with some ethnic communities (notably Italians) than with others, possibly for cultural reasons.

Other Settings and Motivations

Beyond pluralistic settings, complex organizations, transition periods and family firms, co-leadership has been found in other organizational settings that have received less attention in the scientific literature (Dennis et al., 2009). For instance, many descriptive accounts of co-leadership couples can be found in the practitioner literature. Accounts often deal with co-founders of high-tech start-ups (such as Sapient Technologies and Google) who have good relationships during early stages of the creation of the organization but may or may not end in the departure of one of the founders as the enterprise grows (Alvarez et al., 2007; Arena et al., 2011; Krause et al., 2014). Co-leadership in political organizations has also received some attention. These can be used to assign tasks to individuals that are difficult to accomplish simultaneously, such as inspiring and disciplining, or internal (control within the party) and external (relationship with electors) functions (Alvarez and Svejenova, 2002). Hartshorn-Sanders (2006) report how co-leadership of the Green Party in New Zealand allowed increased media coverage and presence at events, and how mutual challenging within the dyad reinforced the team approach of the party.

Co-leadership in such cases and in the case of certain non-profits, schools in public education systems or feminist organizations may be partly driven by ideological commitments to democratic organizational forms as much as by instrumental concerns (Fischbach et al., 2007). Another motivation may lie in enabling people with different perspectives to enter leadership roles. For example, many in the educational sector have argued that opening the organization to shared principal roles has enabled women to enter these roles where they were rarely seen previously (Court, 2004; Dass, 1995).

In summary, co-leadership arrangements are present in a variety of contexts, but are more likely to occur when organizations are subject to multiple institutional demands (as in pluralistic organizations), when the top job is too large or complex to be mastered easily by a single individual, under conditions of transition and in family firms concerned about maintaining control within the family, or solving particular family issues. In such contexts, it appears that there is more chance that "two heads might be better than one" (O'Toole et al., 2002), in other words, that co-leadership might provide solutions to the problems of complexity.

Configurations of Co-leadership

Having identified the contexts in which co-leadership is more or less prevalent, our next question concerns *how* two individuals might organize themselves to share roles, or, put differently, how they may jointly occupy the "shared role space" (Gronn and Hamilton, 2004) created by their collaboration. Hodgson et al.'s 1965 study of the "executive role constellation" developed to describe collective leadership teams suggests three dimensions ("specialization," "differentiation" and "complementarity") that together offer a first useful framework for considering co-leadership configurations. The dimension of specialization refers to the degree to which roles taken by each individual are broad and all encompassing, occupying large areas of the shared role space, or narrow and specialized, focusing on more specific areas. The dimension of differentiation refers to the degree to which roles overlap, creating (or not) zones of mutual substitution or duplication within the shared role space. The dimension of complementarity has two subcomponents: the degree to which the roles occupied by the two individuals adequately cover the shared role space; and the degree to which the two individuals are able to coordinate their work within the space (Denis et al., 2001).

Hodgson et al. (1965) argued that the three features were all important for effective functioning. To see this, Table 15.1 illustrates schematically four configurations of co-leadership roles (see also Gaudreau, 2007). In the table, the large oval represents the overall shared role space while the small ovals represent the terrains occupied by the two individuals A and B. According to Hodgson et al. (1965), an effective configuration would imply that the zones covered by A and B would be relatively equivalent in size (specialized), limited in terms of overlap (differentiated) and would cover the whole of the shared role space while remaining connected. Configuration 1 ("Distribution") fully represents Hodgson et al.'s vision of an effective configuration.

The other three configurations illustrate situations where at least one of the three critical features (specialization, differentiation and complementarity) is missing. For example, the first potentially problematic configuration called "dominance" (metaphor: the "elephant and the mouse"; see Column 2) implies that one of the two co-leaders occupies far more terrain than the other. Essentially, this configuration transforms what is in theory a relatively egalitarian arrangement to a more hierarchical relationship where one player is essentially subordinate to the other. In most circumstances, it would appear that such an arrangement would be inherently unstable

Table 15.1 Co-leadership Role Configurations

1. *Distribution* (Equilibrium: The perfect couple)	2. *Dominance* (No specialization: The elephant and the mouse)	3. *Duplication* (No differentiation: Two-in-a-box)	4. *Disconnection* (No complementarity: Two solitudes)
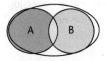	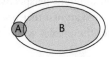	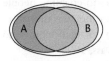	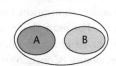
Characteristics	**Characteristics**	**Characteristics**	**Characteristics**
– Specialization	– Overload (for B)	– Rivalry, competition	– Falling through cracks
– Differentiation	– Dissatisfaction	– Conflict	– Ineffectiveness
– Complementarity	– Inefficiency	– Playing A against B	– Bypassing
– 1 + 1 > 2	– 1 + 1 = 1	– 1 + 1 = %!*&$/@?	– 1 + 1 < 2

with the lesser partner likely to drop out (i.e., resign or be dismissed). Interestingly however, in some circumstances, notably in professional organizations, the size of the terrain occupied may not fully reflect the power relationships between the two individuals. For example, in health care studies, Gaudreau (2007) and Langley et al. (2014) found that doctor–administrator dyads could often take on this form, with doctors playing apparently secondary consultative roles and partner-administrators doing the bulk of the more routine work in terms of management of resources. Yet the doctor's influence could nevertheless sometimes be significant for key strategic concerns. The higher professional status of one of the partners in a dyad might result in this configuration being quite common in such settings, without becoming highly problematic. In many arts organizations in Australia, executive directors expressed how they supported the artistic director and the artistic mission, and this less visible role was comfortable for them (MacNeill and Tonks, 2009).

The third configuration of Table 15.1 ("duplication" or "two-in-a-box"; O'Toole et al., 2002) implies that both members of the partnership cover similar areas of interest and expertise. At first sight, this situation seems to offer great potential for conflict and rivalry as well as potentially dysfunctional behaviors from peers, superiors and subordinates who may attempt to play off one of the leaders against the other. No doubt this type of situation lies behind many catastrophic examples of co-leadership identified in the business press (Frisch, 2012; Zillman, 2014). For example, Castaldo (2012) describes overlapping responsibilities between co-CEOs Mike Lazaridis and Jim Balsillie as partly responsible for the failure of Research in Motion (creators of the Blackberry) to defend its market against competitors.

And yet, as Gronn and Hamilton (2004) note in their study of co-principalship in schools, in some circumstances this arrangement could be a strength depending on the quality of the relationship between the two individuals. They note in particular its potential advantages. Redundancy may allow mutual substitutability, which can be advantageous when time is the most critical resource. In addition, having two views on every problem may generate fewer mistakes. The conditions for this type of arrangement to work, however, are likely to be quite rare. While strong mechanisms of communication are likely to be important in any kind of co-leadership (see below), this particular configuration will be particularly demanding in this regard as it seems to require what Dass (1995: 306) describes as "a creation with two bodies and one mind" (noted by Gronn and Hamilton, 2004). This degree of cohabitation apparently does exist in some situations, but this is probably exceptional for co-leader pairs as we discuss further later.

Finally, the last configuration presented in Table 15.1 ("disconnection") appears to have few redeeming features. It implies a mode of functioning in which the co-leaders essentially go their separate ways covering distinct and specialized areas of the role space but failing to connect and leaving key issue areas unaddressed. This pattern seems most likely to emerge over time in co-leadership pairs for rapidly growing companies as new problems and concerns appear that do not fall within the traditional domains of the two protagonists. It seems likely to be unstable and the vacuum at the top appears likely to attract other leadership contenders.

Little research exists on the relative prevalence of these different configurations. Moreover, in practice, configurations may be fluid and evolve during the life of a partnership. However, in her study of 27 pluralistic settings in Norway, Fjellvaer (2010) found that, of the thirteen formal dual leadership structures she observed, two were characterized by the effective dominance of one partner and five involved considerable overlap (duplication), with all these being in the education field. The other six were characterized by clearly separate functions that mainly seemed to reflect the distributed configuration noted above.

Overall, this analysis suggests that navigating in a shared role space is far from simple. Moreover, the apparently "optimal" configuration in which the two individuals each occupy specialized, differentiated and complementary roles may itself take a variety of forms in terms of the *way* roughly equal roles are distributed and connected. Perhaps co-leadership in pluralistic settings offers the simplest solutions in this regard, because there is a natural divide between the roles of professional leaders (focusing on mission-related goals) and managerial leaders (focusing on financial/resource concerns). In other types of settings, we may see one leader focusing on external stakeholders while the other focuses on operational issues, or roles may be distributed according to functional areas, geographies or other mutually agreed arrangements. The precise distribution of roles cannot, however, entirely explain on its own what makes co-leadership more or less successful in particular cases. Other factors clearly enter into the equation. The next section examines some of these conditions for success.

Conditions for Co-leadership

Those who have studied the dynamics of co-leadership in a range of contexts have made many suggestions for how it might work successfully, sometimes partly because they are ideologically committed to its continued existence as a more democratic or humanistic form, but often for instrumental reasons too (Denis et al., 2012). These suggestions do not necessarily guarantee its long-term stability, but examples in several sectors suggest that co-leadership is increasingly necessary and present in certain situations, and that certain winning conditions are possible to find. We consider these possibilities, by examining the conditions for success according to different levels of analysis: individual, relational, organizational and institutional or environmental. Co-leaders are most often situated at the boundary of organizations and so interact with a range of influences. For those concerned with deciding whether to be involved in co-leadership or for those who wish to make co-leadership successful, this section may provide a clearer understanding of how to choose partners, and what is needed to make these partnerships work.

Individual Factors

While scholars of co-leadership tend to focus much of their inquiry on the dynamics between the two players in the dyad, some have pinpointed certain individual abilities and characteristics necessary to enable individuals to function well in such an arrangement. Given that open conflict and split perspectives on the organization's direction are major concerns for all involved, for those doing the hiring, evidence of a collaborative work style and successful negotiating skills would be very useful individual traits (Reid and Karambayya, 2009). As well, a demonstrated ability to trust is helpful to identify likely candidates (Reid and Karambayya, 2015). Individual personal integrity and professional maturity seem to be valuable for individual leadership in most pluralistic and complex contexts (Arnone and Stumpf, 2010; Dass, 1995; Deschamps and Cisneros, 2012). The challenges of the dyadic relationships in such contexts demand such traits. Founders of organizations may find the adjustment to a dual structure difficult, due to the novelty of the experience. Often, the first attempt may not be particularly successful (Reid and Karambayya, 2009, 2015).

Further, a capacity for frank honesty and personal reflection can aid the navigation of differences when they occur (Hartshorn-Sanders, 2006) and generate authenticity in the leadership relationship (MacNeill et al., 2012). Self-awareness, the courage to face weaknesses and allow vulnerability even in a "winner-takes-all" environment such as financial services businesses would aid the development of the relationship, according to Arnone and Stumpf (2010: 18). In such environments, these authors suggest that competitive psychology and desire to win, with supreme confidence while taking risks are elements of a leadership culture that need to be overcome personally by those entering into a co-leadership role. A different sense of self that is open to collaboration becomes important. Note that these positive characteristics of co-leaders have been extensively observed in the arts and education sectors, where personal values and emotions may be closer to the surface (Court, 2004; Dass, 1995; MacNeill et al., 2012), and where competitive corporate cultures might arguably be less pervasive.

Relational Factors

For many scholars studying the phenomenon of co-leadership, the focus falls on the relational dynamics of the duo. Presumably in hopes of avoiding debilitating conflict, the prescriptive literature focuses principally on how to function effectively as a partnership. Trust is considered an essential element of the relationship (Alvarez and Svejenova, 2002; Gronn, 2002; Miles and Watkins, 2007) and how to achieve it is an important scholarly preoccupation in the literature (Reid and Karambayya, 2015). A number of considerations for developing coherence and trust have been noted by observers of co-leader dynamics. Regular communication that resolves problems (Alvarez and Svejenova, 2002), reflection and listening (MacNeill et al., 2012) and keeping differences and disagreements within the couple are all inter-relational skills that support a positive experience within the dyad and, it is hoped, generate trust. The particular importance of avoiding the dissemination of tensions beyond the duo is revealed in Reid and Karambayya's (2009) case study research on eight leadership couples in the arts. The authors found that, when the members of the duo were unable to preserve a common front and began to draw in other players (e.g., by calling on the board), their credibility was seriously undermined, generally with negative consequences both for the organization and the leaders themselves. Serious attention to organization including scheduling time together will certainly help coordinate the work of the co-leaders and may help develop personal trust which will be more enduring (Reid and Karambayya, 2015). Another study by De Moyer and De Schmidt (2015) used a repertory grid technique with fourteen performing arts leaders operating in a dual leadership arrangement to identify ten conflict resolution techniques that they might adopt with their partners. These ranged from simple and non-threatening techniques based on trust and communication, through techniques based on formal clarification and negotiation, to more expensive and risky internal or external mediation, and ultimately dissolution.

Schnurr and Chan (2011) offer a thoughtful analysis of conversations between co-leaders in Hong Kong that reveal speech patterns that save face or not, and thus may contribute to a potentially conflict-free relationship. Etzioni (1965) discusses the combination of instrumental and emotional leadership roles found in the small group dynamics literature that could be applicable to understanding how to achieve mutually supportive relationships between co-leaders. The distinction between instrumental and emotional leadership could be particularly important where the two formal roles are not structured with clearly different and well-defined responsibilities (for example, as in configuration 2 described above).

Observers of co-leadership arrangements disagree as to whether commonality, cognitive similarity and coherence (Alvarez and Svejenova, 2005; Miles and Watkins, 2007) are important to a relationship or whether complete 'opposites' might actually be preferred for stronger decisions and strategy making (Bhansing et al., 2012; Fjellvaer, 2010; Gronn, 1999). However, Groover (1989) cautions that rigidly defined roles or a strongly held point of view by one partner can create stress in the duo's relationships. Others claim that dyads composed of individuals with strongly held individual orientations derived from a cognitive style (Bhansing et al., 2012), a professional orientation (Reid and Karambayya, 2009) or a personality trait (Dass, 1995) can provide a diversity of perspectives and result in robust and resilient leadership duos. These diversified duos typically respond to complex environments where a range of stakeholders need attention (Alvarez and Svejenova, 2005; O'Toole et al., 2002; Bhansing et al., 2012). Fjellvaer (2010) describes numerous practices and mechanisms for duo members to sooth the tension of differing logics within the organizations studied. For example, effective co-leaders tended to familiarize themselves with their partner's tasks, engaged in regular communication and were prepared to confront each other in case of disagreement.

Related to personal differences or coherence are concerns as to whether role-definitions might be better differentiated by functional purposes (as in configuration 1 in Table 15.1 above) which often occur in professionally oriented organizations (Fjellvaer, 2010; Gronn, 2002; Reid and Karambayya, 2009) or 'two-in-a-box' relationships (as in configuration 3, Table 15.1) where the two share essentially the same leadership role and need to use personal strengths or preferences in order to share the role space (Arnone and Stumpf, 2010). Some of the issues related to these two options have been discussed above.

In situations where responsibility and accountability are important, alternating the ultimate responsibility within the duo has been attempted, as reported, for example, in the education (Hagen and Court, 1998) and investment banking sectors (Arnone and Stumpf, 2010). However, there may be negative consequences when delayed responses to a particular decision occur and the new person is in charge (Hagen and Court, 1998). This practice has also been studied for small non-profit theater companies in Finland and it appeared to work well in this context (Järvinen et al., 2015), perhaps partly because of the small size of these organizations. Arnone and Stumpf (2010) suggest that, where the duo shares the same leadership role, they should make it clear who evaluates all the employees of the firm in order to avoid political issues falling between the two leaders.

In a different context, Svejenova and colleagues (Alvarez and Svejenova, 2002; Svejenova et al., 2010) studied co-leaders who typically founded an organization and shared the same career throughout (usually artists or a duo that was personally connected as in the family business situation described above), thus solving issues of difference and complementarity. It appears that personal and role differences that emerge during a career tend to intertwine. Yves St. Laurent and Pierre Bergé are a celebrated example of this, where the fashion firm grew and thrived but the relationship waned, and then later grew back together.

The notion of "conjoint work" was originally suggested by Gronn (2002) to mean that the co-leadership duo shares a joint understanding of leadership in the particular organization involved. Others have mobilized this notion to explain how co-leaders need to share the leadership space (MacNeill et al., 2012; Woods et al., 2004) and provide checks and balances and mutual counseling (Harper, 2008; Hartshorn-Sanders, 2006). Dass (1995) observed that having broader organizational objectives jointly in mind enabled the co-principals that she studied to work effectively together. Numerous other scholars invoke a shared vision of the organization as essential to the effective functioning of co-leadership pairs, regardless of how they share roles (Gronn and Hamilton, 2004; Harper, 2008; Miles and Watkins, 2007).

While clarity in job descriptions and role definitions have been suggested by some as being important to co-leadership (O'Toole et al., 2002), others have found that these may not be necessary where the conjoint nature of the role is well accepted and practiced, and developed through mutual adjustment. Ambiguity of authority within the role space may provide a buffer to maneuver and avoid conflict (Denis et al., 1996). As well, perceived power differences that are not too large appear to support firm performance and generate a sense of success related to co-leadership. However when perceived power differences are too large, they can undermine successful performance, according to one of the rare quantitative studies of co-leadership (Krause et al., 2014).

Organizational Factors

The organizational context can play an important role in the dynamics and success of the co-leadership duo, particularly at the beginning of the relationship. In a number of cases studied, duo members were separately chosen and independently mandated by a third party, either the board of directors (Reid and Karambayya, 2009) or a school superintendent (Dass, 1995). Certainly where the roles are separately chosen and co-leaders are imposed on each other, the chances for longevity appear more limited (Reid and Karambayya, 2009, 2015). Others argue that mutual choice and an appointment as a couple provide better chances for a positive relational experience (Alvarez and Svejenova, 2002; Glenny et al., 1996; Järvinen et al., 2015; O'Toole et al., 2002).

Further, a non-intervention policy by boards of directors (Reid and Karambayya, 2015) or a context that allows independence from government authorities and superintendents in school systems (Glenny et al., 1996; Court, 2003, 2004) will provide a climate that will both force (Arnone and Stumpf, 2010) and allow (Court, 2004) the couple to resolve their own issues and develop a deeper and more reliable relationship. Arnone and Stumpf (2010) argue that an organizational history and culture that rewards collaboration and encourages conflict resolution responsibly will provide support for a healthy relationship. Reid and Karambayya (2015) observed that a history of negative conflict casts a shadow on the subsequent relationships that might be solved by the incoming member. The solutions found by a new partner (in this case a new executive director joining an existing artistic director in a cultural organization) generated a level of trust in the newly constituted duo for some time. Of course, it was also important for the board to leave the couple to solve the issue themselves and not intervene before the new duo member arrived. As well, a designated board member, consultants and family stakeholder members can coach members of co-leadership duos about conflict resolution and enable a good working relationship before or when conflict occurs (Arnone and Stumpf, 2010; Deschamps et al., 2014; Reid and Karambayya, 2015).

Another organizational level intervention might involve developing a contract that includes an exit strategy for each of the members. Negotiating this kind of contract facilitates an understanding of the possibilities that might arise in the co-leadership arrangement from the beginning (Arnone and Stumpf, 2010). Relatedly, Arnone and Stumpf (2010) suggest that having the duo in place for a pre-determined period of time allows them and the organization to understand the nature of the endgame dynamics, which is a useful approach for managing risks inherent in these relationships.

Working with a number of physical and symbolic elements related to power can also help with the success of the co-leadership. Physical space that is either proximate or shared can enable communication and ensure that a symbolic message of coherence is provided for the organization as a whole (Arnone and Stumpf, 2010). It also helps with the organization of the couple's life in the organization. Finally, informal power differences between the pair are often present (Alvarez and Svejenova, 2005) and analyzing these differences and understanding them can help with a better, more reflective, relationship (MacNeill et al., 2012).

Environment and Institutional Factors

Because our study of co-leadership relates mainly to those at the executive level, environmental factors can also influence the success of co-leadership. For example, the institutionalized legitimizing environment of the non-profit arts were instrumental in establishing the presence of 'arts administrators' in cultural organizations in the US in the 1970s and 1980s, thus generating a dual structure as common (DiMaggio and Powell, 1983; Peterson, 1986). Consequently, as organizations grow from a founder status, they eventually find their way to a co-leadership structure, understanding that the structure may support governance and efficient functioning. The pressure of a supportive institutional environment motivates the placement of co-leadership and generates expectations of good performance as a result.

On the other hand, the presence of co-leadership in the educational field has been resisted by the superstructure environment around schools for legal and accountability reasons in New Zealand and the US (Court, 2003, 2004; Groover, 1989). Perceived as a move to the left as part of a larger concept of distributed leadership (Court, 2004), the potential ambiguity of co-principalship with regards to accountability structures has been perceived as difficult to overcome and those in favor of it have had to negotiate with force and care.

The understanding and embracing by key stakeholders in the environment of both co-principalship in the educational system and co-leadership in the private sector have also played a role in successful innovation of newly developed co-leadership structures. Unions and their concerns for traditional careers and salaries have opposed the implementation of the structure in the past (Court, 2004). On the other hand, when a co-leadership structure has been implemented, the stock market appears to respond positively (Arena et al., 2011; Dennis et al., 2009), thus encouraging such leadership structures.

However, recently shareholder ethics groups objected to the co-CEO and co-chairmanship at Research in Motion during the precipitous decline of share value in 2010 and 2011. These groups perceived collusion in the co-leadership structure, suggesting that the legitimacy of this form is fragile. Shareholders voted to allow a six-month period for the co-leaders to prove the value of their leadership structure, but, in January 2012, the two retired and the organization has since been led by a single CEO with a separate chair (Austin, 2012). In a somewhat similar fashion, the confusion of parents and students (users) about the clarity of accountability and value of co-principalship in a school district in South Carolina ultimately resulted in a gradual decline of the practice after about ten years of success. It was felt that the phenomenon had had its day and was phased out. Organizing explanatory public meetings about co-leadership with stakeholders such as parents and students has been suggested as a useful means of ensuring ongoing support and encouragement for this kind of structure (Groover, 1989).

Clearly, the success of co-leadership is the result of many individual and dyad-related issues, but the larger environment of organizations and beyond can also have an important influence on its durability and effectiveness. Scholars have found co-leadership to be useful for many reasons, especially when it offers responses to the complex and pluralistic nature of the organizational context in which it is found. But it can be very fragile and many of the critiques concerning its potential instability and conflicted dysfunctionality may be well founded. More study is needed to understand better how it works and whether and when it fails, since it is being increasingly adopted across a range of sectors.

Looking Ahead: An Agenda for Future Research

This chapter has described the phenomenon of co-leadership, examining the contexts where it is most prevalent, the configurations it may take and the conditions for success based on the existing literature. It has to be recognized, however, that, although there has been some serious scholarly work on this phenomenon, many writings about co-leadership appear in practitioner-oriented outlets, the grey literature or specialized sectoral journals suggesting that there is room for stronger, deeper and more systematic research in mainstream management publications on the issues covered in this review.

Research into co-leadership is possibly hampered by the relative rarity of the phenomenon. This means that it is quite difficult to accumulate large enough sample sizes for strong quantitative studies. For instance, Krause et al.'s (2014) study of co-CEO arrangements and performance included 77 firms, a sample size that is quite low to detect significant effects. Meanwhile, case-study research can greatly enrich understanding of the phenomenon, but detailed comparative work is most easily conducted only in sectors where co-leadership arrangements are quite common (e.g., in the arts or health care). While the in-depth study of the phenomenon in large corporations would be extremely valuable, access issues (Pettigrew, 1992) of course make this difficult and so far only Alvarez and Svejenova (2005) have come close to developing a large systematic study of this context, with most other contributions relying greatly on more limited or sometimes anecdotal evidence.

Beyond this, however, a number of aspects of co-leadership have been studied hardly at all. One of these concerns patterns in the evolution of co-leadership structures over the long term in particular firms. Another issue concerns how moments of transition such as succession events involving one or both of the partners in a co-leadership relationship are or should be managed. We see hints concerning the succession dynamics of co-leader pairs from Reid and Karambayya's (2015) research in arts organizations mentioned above, but more work is needed in this area to better understand whether and how co-leadership can actually be made to pass from one generation of leaders to another, or whether it is in fact more of an idiosyncratic phenomenon that may be "magical" when it happens to work, but is not really sustainable as an institutionalized organizational arrangement that can remain in place when new individuals are substituted.

Another critical area that is barely touched on in most of the existing research concerns power. Clearly, power is the elephant in the room in situations of co-leadership, or indeed in situations of leadership more generally. However, few scholars have attempted to theorize its role in co-leadership arrangements. We see the beginnings of some attention to power issues in leadership configurations in certain studies (Denis et al., 2001; Empson et al., 2013; Lawrence et al., 2012; Krause et al., 2014), but these are few and far between. Several do not look at co-leadership directly, and others do not draw on well-developed theoretical frameworks for considering and capturing power dynamics.

Finally, more needs to be done to investigate how co-leadership pairs jointly achieve influence with respect to other actors in and beyond the organization; here we refer mainly to subordinates, but also to board members and peers. The particular challenges of preserving a common front and of synergistically consolidating influence (rather than fragmenting it as others try to play off one against the other) deserve more attention.

In conclusion, co-leadership remains a fascinating phenomenon for research because it tends to challenge taken-for-granted assumptions about how direction, collaboration and coordination in organizations are or should be organized. To some degree no doubt, scholars seek knowledge about it because it seems to offer a different, perhaps richer and perhaps more humanistic, way of leading and managing. More research is needed to develop a clearer understanding of how, where and when such aspirations can be successfully realized.

Notes

1 The authors would like to thank Jean-Louis Denis, John Storey and David Ulrich for helpful comments on an earlier version of this chapter.
2 See the organizational charts for the newly created Integrated Health and Social Services Centers at http://www.msss.gouv.qc.ca/reseau/reorganisation/portrait, consulted September 16, 2015.
3 See for example: http://www.advfn.com/nyse/newyorkstockexchange.asp, consulted September 16, 2015.

References

Alvarez, J. L. and Svejenova, S. 2002. Pairs at the top: From tandems to coupled careers. *Harvard Business School Conference on Careers*. London.

Alvarez, J. L. and Svejenova, S. 2005. *Sharing executive power: Roles and relationships at the top*. Cambridge University Press.

Alvarez J. L., Svejenova S. and Vives, L. 2007. Leading in pairs. *MIT Sloan Management Review*, 48 (4): 10–14.

Antrobus, C. 2009. Two heads are better than one: What art galleries and museums can learn from the joint leadership model in theatre. Unpublished manuscript, London. http://www.claireantrobus.com/wp/wp-content/uploads/2009/11/twoheadsbetter.pdf.

Arena, M. P., Ferris, S. P. and Unlu, E. 2011. It takes two: The incidence and effectiveness of co-CEOs. *Financial Review*, 46, 385–412.

Arnone, M. and Stumpf, S. A. 2010. Shared leadership: From rivals to co-CEOs. *Strategy & Leadership*, 38, 15–21.

Austin, I. 2012. Bowing to critics and market forces, RIM's co-chiefs step aside. *The New York Times*, January 22, 2012.

Baldwin, K. S., Dimunation, N. and Alexander, J. 2011. Health care leadership and the dyad model. *Physician Executive*, 37, 66–70.

Berry, L. L. 2004. The collaborative organization: Leadership lessons from Mayo Clinic. *Organizational Dynamics*, 33, 228–242.

Bhansing, P. V., Leenders, M. A. A. M. and Wijnberg, N. M. 2012. Performance effects of cognitive heterogeneity in dual leadership structures in the arts: The role of selection system orientations. *European Management Journal*, 30, 523–534.

Castaldo, J. 2012. How management has failed at RIM. *Canadian Business* [Online]. Available from: http://www.canadianbusiness.com/technology-news/how-management-has-failed-at-rim/2015.

Court, M. 2003. Towards democratic leadership: Co-principal initiatives. *International Journal of Leadership in Education*, 6, 161–183.

Court, M. 2004. Using narrative and discourse analysis in researching co-principalships. *International Journal of Qualitative Studies in Education*, 17, 579–603.

Dass, S. 1995. *Inside the co-principalship: A naturalistic study*. Ph.D., University of Oregon.

De Moyer, J. and De Smidt, S. 2015. Dual executive leadership and conflict resolution methods: An analysis using repertory grid. *European Academy of Management (EURAM)*. Warsaw, Poland.

De Voogt, A. 2006. Dual leadership as a problem-solving tool in arts organizations. *International Journal of Arts Management*, 17–22.

Denis, J.-L., Langley, A. and Cazale, L. 1996. Leadership and strategic change under ambiguity. *Organization Studies*, 17, 673–699.

Denis, J.-L., Lamothe, L. and Langley, A. 2001. The dynamics of collective leadership and strategic change in pluralistic organizations. *Academy of Management Journal*, 44, 809–837.

Denis, J. L., Langley, A. and Sergi, V. 2012. Leadership in the plural. *Academy of Management Annals*, 6, 211–283.

Dennis, S. A., Ramsey, D. and Turner, C. 2009. Dual or duel: Co-CEOs and firm performance. *Journal of Business & Economic Studies*, 15, 1–25.

Deschamps, B. and Cisneros, L. 2012. Co-leadership en succession familiale: un partage à définir. *Entreprendre & innover*, 14, 49–57.

Deschamps, B., Cisneros, L. and Barès, F. 2014. PME familiales québécoises: impact des parties prenantes externes à la famille dans les co-successions en fratrie. *Management international/International Management/Gestiòn Internacional*, 18, 151–163.

Dimaggio, P. and Powell, W. W. 1983. The iron cage revisited: Collective rationality and institutional isomorphism in organizational fields. *American Sociological Review*, 48, 147–160.

Empson, L., Cleaver, I. and Allen, J. 2013. Managing partners and management professionals: Institutional work dyads in professional partnerships. *Journal of Management Studies*, 50, 808–844.

Etzioni, A. 1965. Dual leadership in complex organizations. *American Sociological Review*, 688–698.

Fayol, H. 1949. *General and industrial administration*. New York: Pitman.

Fischbach, L. M., Smerz, C., Findlay, G., Williams, C. and Cox, A. 2007. Co-CEOs: A new leadership paradigm for social service agencies. *Families in Society: The Journal of Contemporary Social Services*, 88, 30–34.

Fjellvaer, H. 2010. *Dual and unitary leadership: Managing ambiguity in pluralistic organizations*. Norwegian School of Economics and Business Administration, Bergen, Norway.

Frisch, B. 2012. The co-CEO model is officially dead. *Business Insider* [Online]. Available from: http://www.businessinsider.com/the-co-ceo-model-is-officially-dead-2012-2 2015.

Gaudreau, M. 2007. *Réussir la cogestion: étude exploratoire sur le partage des rôles au sein des tandems de gestionnaires*. M.Sc., HEC Montréal.

Glenny, M., Lewis, D. and White, C. 1996. Power sharing at Selwyn College-Auckland, New Zealand: The coprincipalship model. *Management in Education*, 10, 32–33.

Gronn, P. 1999. Substituting for leadership: The neglected role of the leadership couple. *The Leadership Quarterly*, 10, 41–62.

Gronn, P. 2002. Distributed leadership as a unit of analysis. *The Leadership Quarterly*, 13, 423–451.

Gronn, P. and Hamilton, A. 2004. "A bit more life in the leadership": Co-principalship as distributed leadership practice. *Leadership and Policy in Schools*, 3, 3–35.

Groover, E. C. 1989. *Perceptions of the co-principalship as implemented in High Point, North Carolina*. Ph.D., University of North Carolina at Greensboro.

Hagen, U. and Court, M. 1998. Shared leadership in schools: The Norwegian case in the light of the New Zealand experience. *NZARE Annual Conference*. Dunedin, NZ.

Harper, D. A. 2008. Towards a theory of entrepreneurial teams. *Journal of Business Venturing*, 23, 613–626.

Hartshorn-Sanders, E. 2006. Co-leadership and the Green Party: A New Zealand case study. *Political Science*, 58, 43–53.

Heenan, D. A. and Bennis, W. G. 1999. *Co-leaders: The power of great partnerships*. New York: John Wiley & Sons.

Hodgson, R. C., Levinson, D. J. and Zaleznik, A. 1965. *The executive role constellation*. Harvard University, Division of Research, Graduate School of Business Administration.

Jaklevic, M. C. 1999. Leading jointly: Two executives at Minnesota's Allina Health System show that co-leadership can work. *Modern Healthcare*, 29 (19), 33–36.

Järvinen, M., Ansio, H. and Houni, P. 2015. New variations of dual leadership: Insights from Finnish theatre. *International Journal of Arts Management*, 17.

Krause, R., Priem, R. and Love, L. 2014. Who's in charge here? Co-CEOs, power gaps, and firm performance. *Strategic Management Journal*, 36 (13).

Langley, A., Van Schendel, N., Gibeau, É., Denis, J. L. and Pomey, M.-P. 2014. *Vers de nouvelles pistes de partenariat médico-administratif*. Montréal: Association québécoise d'établissements de santé et de services sociaux.

Lawrence, T. B., Malhotra, N. and Morris, T. 2012. Episodic and systemic power in the transformation of professional service firms. *Journal of Management Studies*, 49, 102–143.

Locke, E. A. 2003. Leadership: Starting at the top. In: Pearce, C. L. and Conger, J. A. (eds.) *Shared leadership*. Thousand Oaks, CA: Sage Publications.

MacNeill, K. and Tonks, A. 2009. Co-leadership and gender in the performing arts. *The Asia Pacific Journal of Arts and Cultural Management*, 6 (1), 392–404.

MacNeill, K., Tonks, A. and Reynolds, S. 2012. Authenticity and the Other: Coleadership in arts organizations. *Journal of Leadership Studies*, 6, 6–16.

MacTavish, M. and Norton, P. 1995. Redesign of a health science centre: Reflections on co-leadership. *Healthcare Management Forum/Canadian College of Health Service Executives = Forum gestion des soins de sante/College canadien des directeurs de services de sante*, 8, 45–48.

Miles, S. A. and Watkins, M. D. 2007. The leadership team. *Harvard Business Review*, 85, 90–98.

Miller, D., Le Breton-Miller, I., Minichilli, A., Corbetta, G. and Pittino, D. 2014. When do non-family CEOs outperform in family firms? Agency and behavioural agency perspectives. *Journal of Management Studies*, 51, 547–572.

Neogy, I. and Kirkpatrick, I. 2009. *Medicine in management: Lessons across Europe*. Leeds, Centre for Innovation in Health Management, University of Leeds.

Nguyen, J. and Siedel, G. 2000. Co-leadership in a merger of equals. PhD thesis. University of Michigan Business School.

O'Toole, J., Galbraith, J. and Lawler, E. E. 2002. When two (or more) heads are better than one: The promise and pitfalls of shared leadership. *California Management Review*, 44, 65–83.

Ocasio, W. and Thornton, P. H. 1999. Institutional logics and the historical contingency of power in organizations: Executive succession in the higher education publishing industry, 1958–1990. *American Journal of Sociology*, 105, 801–843.

Paré, S., Menzies, T. V., Jacques Filion, L. and Brenner, G. A. 2008. Social capital and co-leadership in ethnic enterprises in Canada. *Journal of Enterprising Communities: People and Places in the Global Economy*, 2, 52–72.

Pearce, C. L. and Conger, J. A. 2002. *Shared leadership: Reframing the hows and whys of leadership*. London: Sage Publications.

Peterson, R. A. 1986. From impresario to arts administrator: Formal accountability in nonprofit cultural organizations. In: *Nonprofit enterprise in the arts: Studies in mission and constraint*. Oxford University Press.

Pettigrew, A. M. 1992. On studying managerial elites. *Strategic Management Journal*, 13, 163–182.

Ponte, P. R. 2004. Nurse–physician co-leadership: A model of interdisciplinary practice governance. *Journal of Nursing Administration*, 34, 481–484.

Rahael, A. 2012. *Co-CEOs: An exploratory case study of shared leadership in a family owned and operated business*. Doctor of Education, George Washington University.

Reid, W. 2015. *Board-staff relationships in nonprofit arts and dual executive leadership: Implications for governance*. Academy of Management. Vancouver, Canada.

Reid, W. and Karambayya, R. 2009. Impact of dual executive leadership dynamics in creative organizations. *Human Relations*, 62, 1073–1112.

Reid, W. and Karambayya, R. 2015. The shadow of history: Situated dynamics of trust in dual executive leadership. *Leadership*. Published online before print, doi: 10.1177/1742715015579931.

Schnurr, S. and Chan, A. 2011. Exploring another side of co-leadership: Negotiating professional identities through face-work in disagreements. *Language in Society*, 40, 187–209.

Steinert, T., Goebel, R. and Rieger, W. 2006. A nurse-physician co-leadership model in psychiatric hospitals: Results of a survey among leading staff members in three sites. *International Journal of Mental Health Nursing*, 15, 251–257.

Svejenova, S., Vives, L. and Alvarez, J. L. 2010. At the crossroads of agency and communion: Defining the shared career. *Journal of Organizational Behavior*, 31, 707–725.

Troiano, P. 1999. Sharing the throne. *Management Review*, 88, 39.

Woods, P. A., Bennett, N., Harvey, J. A. and Wise, C. 2004. Variabilities and dualities in distributed leadership findings from a systematic literature review. *Educational Management Administration & Leadership*, 32, 439–457.

Zillman, C. 2014. With co-CEOs, companies flirt with disaster. *Fortune* [Online]. Available from: http://fortune.com/tag/sharing-power/2015.

Zismer, D. K., Brueggemann, J. and James, M. 2010. Examining the "dyad" as a management model in integrated health systems. *Physician Executive*, 36, 14–19.

16

Leadership on the Board

The Role of Company Secretary

Andrew Kakabadse, Nadeem Khan and Nada Kakabadse

Introduction

This chapter explores how the role, power and influence of the company secretary[1] relates to other board members (chairman, chief executive officer (CEO), senior independent director (SID), non-executive director (NED)) in helping the board make better decisions. An analytical framework is developed that depicts this role's heterogeneity and characteristics pertaining to effective leadership practices.

So: why the company secretary? The roles and responsibilities of chairman, CEO, chief financial officer (CFO), SID and NED are legislatively more developed, formally recognised and regularly evolved within governance, and are widely researched as leadership practices. Indeed, individuals in these corporate roles often become household names in media headlines on business successes or failures. Typically the chairman–CEO relationship has received much attention, while, emerging from the recent financial crisis of 2008, the NED role has re-gained prominence. In contrast, the company secretary role remains legislatively less well defined and subject to limited regulatory evolution. This role's relationship to leadership practice is hardly researched (Cadbury, 2002; Roberts, 2002; Muller *et al.*, 2007) and lacks empirical investigations (Erismann-Peyer *et al.*, 2008). Can you name or recognise a company secretary in media circles? Yet, in this chapter, it will become clear that the company secretary not only has a long and majestic history, but is now also likely to be the longest-serving person in the boardroom. The company secretary is usually the first to know, and be closest to, the most up-to-date critical information; ideally placed as the key link between board/executive and chairman/other board members; and centrally involved in board processes (Finkelstein and Mooney, 2003) and agendas. If the company secretary role's relationship to board leadership practices can be better understood as the 'building block' or 'genesis' for addressing the problematic, then the other roles are more easily aligned in achieving consensus. Illustrating the main question through a company secretary lens, two wider questions are brought into focus: why are the expectations from other board members about the company secretary role unclear, and how should boards relate to leadership practice?

To address the main question and two wider problematic issues of the role's link to leadership practice, this chapter will explore the role, power and influence of company secretaries through in-depth semi-structured interviews from mainly FTSE250 boards. These interviews took place in 2014 and reflected on the post-financial crisis developments in the role and leadership practices of the company secretary.

Role within a Board

What does a company secretary do? Typical existing studies outline the role of company secretary as having formal responsibilities such as organising board meetings; supporting the chairman/CEO, directors and stakeholders; inducting or training non-executive directors; dealing with latest governance developments; board evaluations; annual reporting; statutory compliance issues; administrative duties; accurate Companies House filing; and stock exchange listing. However, the focus in this chapter is more on the informal aspects of the role. The company secretary has to adopt additional higher-order skills when relating to leadership practice. The company secretary's challenge is to resolve tension between being the invisible *power behind the throne*, i.e. in the shadow of the chairperson, and knowing how to diplomatically challenge individual board member effectiveness towards higher collective board performance. This includes resolving dilemmas, dealing with complexity, making judgements, acting as advisor and/or confidante and maintaining high levels of trust. The breadth of knowledge and diplomatic skilfulness of the company secretary must balance crafting of relations with, and between, self-assured personalities (chair, CEO, CFO, SID, NEDs) and not expressing ego in oneself.

Few would doubt that boards are an established governance mechanism, protecting the principals' interests (Fama and Jensen, 1983) and acting as 'large, elite, and episodic decision-making group/s' that are networked to perform complex tasks in the realm of corporate strategy (Forbes and Milliken, 1999). This makes the role of company secretary particularly critical, as it is the crucial link that binds the other board roles together as a body; it always protects the interest of the company and tries to seek consensus amongst the board members as a leadership practice. This becomes even more critical when excessive 'prozac leadership' (Collinson, 2012) often conceals power asymmetries and top-down control as a contribution to toxic or destructive behaviours (Schyns and Hansbroughn, 2010; Padilla *et al.*, 2007). Although, within post-heroic leadership practices (Briskin, 2011) the more 'heroic, charismatic and egoistic' leadership roles may receive prominent attention (Fletcher and Kaufer, 2003), it is the more invisible (Ladkin, 2013), facilitative, interpersonal relational power of the company secretary that becomes politically critical in a major change or crisis situation (Van Essen *et al.*, 2013).

Presently, in the Anglo-Saxon context, the 'company secretary' (UK) is legally perceived as an 'officer' of the company. It is an executive position that usually reports directly to the chairman and is the key point of contact for other board members. Actually, this occupation is an old art that can be traced back to its earliest predecessors of some 5,000 years ago in terms of its activities, such as registration, administration and organisation (Schlott, 1989). Despite this, today we typically more often refer to the East India Company (1600–1833/57) as the first joint-stock entity, with Seth's (2012: 222) analysis asserting that 'the past has the capacity to explain the present' contemporary corporate behaviours and issues. However, the inner workings of boards are mostly confined to those participating in their meetings, rendering empirical research limited. Within this sanctum, the company secretary has always been present but is largely ignored (McNulty and Stewart, 2014; Hilb, 2011) resulting in a paucity of research on this role.

Invisible Leadership Practices

In pursuing a study of the role in relation to leadership practice, we use a broad-minded lens of power (Pettigrew, 1992). This is a subjective approach that overcomes the limitations of confining leadership to formal attributes only, such as a simple legal role, managerial thinking or boxed quantitative rationalisations. It allows for a more holistic, meaningful understanding of the higher-order skills, competencies and informal attributes that are needed by the company secretary in practising governance and leadership. Pettigrew (1992) argues for considering the board as an open system and that studies of board roles should not be separated from studies of power in institutions and society, nor from studies of the composition and attributes of top management teams. Others argue that research should expose the hidden dynamics of boardrooms (Van der Walt and Ingley, 2003). Understanding the role via this lens allows for both formal/informal practices and multi-level influences on the role to be considered as behaviours (van Ees et al., 2009). Other studies have adopted a spatial governance perspective (McNulty and Stewart, 2014); our emphasis, however, is on interpreting organisations as being more complex, and consisting of people with less predictable attributes, particularly in the range of leadership roles (Balkundi and Kilduff, 2006).

As such, in this study the definition of leadership practice is focused on how the company secretary uses 'role, power and influence' (Pettigrew, 1992; Lukes, 1974) to affect board decision-making. This broader definition enables the exploration of the informal, discrete, third-dimensional aspects of power, which can influence policy and board outcomes. These leadership practices take place behind the scenes; they are political or relational aspects beyond the typical formal role. Our findings explore the subtle, moral and relational dilemmas that the company secretary faces. The semi-structured interviews we conducted demonstrate how variably company secretaries operate, exercise power and influence dynamics at board level within and outside the boardroom. We term these practices invisible leadership.

Attention is given to how the company secretary deals with power plays within the board and organization. In so doing, how is the company secretary's role exposed to the decision-making processes within the board? We analyse the notion of discretion in the company secretary's role, and take account of structure and processes in relation to influencing the board of directors, helping them make better decisions.

Historical Development of the Role

The position of company secretary has a rich history. Ancient scribes, who were involved in all matters of writing, embodied functions which are precursors to those of the modern company secretary (Boylan, 1922). From an organisational perspective, the role's ancient, informal origins can be traced to the Egyptians (3000 BCE) although it did not achieve formal legal status until 1841. The most significant recorded company secretary developments stem from the colonisation period of 1550 to 1650, which saw the rise of the English Levant and East India Companies (Kaye, 1853; Adams, 1996; Gepken-Jager et al., 2005). The *Pontifex v Bignold* case of 1841 set a precedent related to the power of the company secretary. More recently, the duties and responsibilities of the role were more closely defined (Monsted and Garside, 1991; Cadbury Report, 1992), followed by a phase of wider legal and regulatory enhancements (Daigneault, 2006).

In the English Levant Company (formed in 1581), the company secretary held considerable powers, such as commanding actions to be performed in Her Majesty's name (Epstein, 1908: 74). In the East India Company (formed in 1600), the secretary post at its London-based headquarters became the 'Secretary of State', with the power to control the proceedings of the company. The secretary post on the trading side was responsible for the administration, registration and implementation of acts of parliament, and was given the task of exercising the stipulations from the Supreme Court of Judicature (Kaye, 1853: 131; Ramaswami, 1983: vi–viii). In the Dutch East India Company (formed in 1602), the company secretary at headquarters held a dual role as secretary of the board and as the board's advocate and advisor on legal matters (Schmidt *et al.*, 1988: 58; Gepken-Jager *et al.*, 2005: 52). At the same time, the secretary at the trading company held extensive and concentrated legislative and executive powers (Naval, 1920: 248–249).

The collapse of the Levant and East India Companies marked the end of the monopolistic trading company with powers to execute sovereign rights (Schmidt *et al.*, 1988: 6), which dramatically reduced the power exercised by the company secretary. No longer did this role combine the affairs of state and company. The powerful political duties of the company secretary, granted by the state and parliament, were decoupled from the duties covering company affairs. From then on, the role of company secretary has focused on narrower commercial, economic and legal affairs.

During the period 1750–1850, the company secretary resumed the role of 'servant' of the corporation and 'secretary of the society' with specialised tasks (transferring company shares; seconding resolutions; registering share transfers; acting on behalf of the company; handling unclaimed dividends; and deleting member names from the company registers) but without the authorisation and responsibility to represent the company externally (*Pontifex v Bignold*, 1841; Severn & Wye & Severn Bridge Railway Co, 1896). In the period 1900 to 1950, judicial outcomes such as *Panorama Developments, Guildford, Ltd v Fidelis Furnishing Fabrics Ltd*, 1971 redefined the company secretary as an officer of the company connected with administrative affairs, thus determining the 'profession's duties and responsibilities' (Monsted and Garside, 1991: 4).

The corporate scandals of the 1980s led to renewed stress on regulation and corporate governance (Cadbury Report, 1992), thereby expanding the duties of the company secretary. Around 2000, the role expanded to include certain corporate governance responsibilities (Murphy, 2003; Monks and Minow, 2004; Daigneault, 2006). The company secretary today has responsibilities as outlined in the introduction. These responsibilities – include ensuring that the corporate entities meet governance requirements (Companies House reporting); following procedures set out in law (formal board meetings; appointments; reporting); and ensuring stakeholder satisfaction (shareholders/directors/media) – become critical to company interests in major change or crises situations. In highly regulated and competitive environments such as that of the UK (Burton, 2000), boards as top teams are always under pressure to perform well and meet shareholder and wider stakeholder expectations. The company secretary has to learn to deal with and manage power relations at this level within and outside the organisation as a form of leadership practice.

The company secretary as corporate governance officer (Steger and Bottger, 2008; Filiz 2013) has the responsibility to raise the question 'What is the right thing to do?' (Gallagher, 2002: 41) and is 'in a prime position to make these judgments and then advocate them with management and the board' (Gallagher, 2002: 42). These days, the professional bodies such as the Institute of Chartered Secretaries and Administrators (ICSA)[2] (Armour, 2012) and other associations, such as the Institute of Directors, UK (Ashton, 2008) are politically critical to the standing of the role amongst the board members and the development of the role and its responsibilities.

The history of the development of the company secretary role suggests that it has influential importance, particularly post-crisis when there has been renewed attention paid to its responsibilities. There is criticism, however, that the power of the role remains constrained, under-utilised and/or misunderstood.

Power of Company Secretary

Lamm (2003: 24) argues for the company secretary's dual role, being 'inclusive of corporate governance function', as the optimal position in the organisation. The law defines the company secretary as an officer with administrative duties and responsibilities, but because of its foundation in law, this role sets the tone for, and is central to, the provision of an underlying internal framework for corporate governance structures (Filiz, 2013). Hence, the company secretary is required to provide administrative and legal governance support to the board of directors and the CEO (Lamm, 2003).

In order to be effective, the company secretary must maintain direct relations with these two different sets of actors at the 'apex of the firm's decision control system' (Fama and Jensen, 1983) to act as a protector of the interests of the principals (board directors) and the management (agents). Scholars posit that powerful boards are desirable as this increases their ability to monitor and control the CEO's actions (Chen, 2007; Petra, 2005) as part of overseeing corporate governance execution (Finkelstein *et al.*, 2009). Due to more frequent interactions, the prevailing relationships of the company secretary are more likely to be with the board of directors. This positioning does not diminish the influential link the company secretary provides between the board, individual board members and executive management, often acting as the impartial moderator or mediator.

It is further recognised that the nature of the company secretary's role and activities is influenced by external (i.e. statutory and regulatory requirements) and internal (i.e. procedures such as company-specific articles of association/by-laws; company policies; employment contracts) factors. The extent of these interactions depends upon the individual in the role of company secretary and how he/she responds to changes in formal structures and to new requirements as demanded by the role (Beattie, 1980), along with how the role itself fits, and has been developed, within the company. The unique behavioural demand lies in balancing information requirements and communication effectiveness. The company secretary needs to engage with internal and external stakeholders; negotiate critical and asymmetric information between different interests; and balance the board and management interface in a way that avoids undue antagonism, placates differences and achieves alignment between the demands of two, and often more, bipolar cultures.

The role is mandatory for publicly listed companies, which are obliged to follow statutory and reporting requirements (Dubs, 2006). Beyond that, there is flexibility and discretionary capacity. Characteristics and required competencies include administration, business awareness, communication skills, compliance, guidance, information impact, knowledge shaping, maintenance, management, organisation, process, procedure, qualification, relationship, and shareholder and stakeholder engagement (Vance, 1983; Hannigan, 2009). Activities include keeping the company register, filing, recording, monitoring, supervising, educating, advising, managing and co-ordinating. The combination of characteristics and activities forms the unique and specific company secretary role and its related functions (Vance, 1983; ICSA, 2012). Although the 'precise duties of the company secretary are not generally prescribed by statute – they will usually need to be set out in his/her contract of employment' (Morris *et al.*, 2009: 223).

As it channels information flows between the board of directors and executive management, the role is significant to board members as an 'up to date source of information' (Kakabadse *et al.*, 2014). The company secretary manages the information flow. Planning formal communications with board members requires an understanding of who needs to be informed; what information is needed; how to present it; and the frequency and form of communication (Herbert, 1977). The process is designed to influence opinions, perceptions and relationships, and/or to initiate board and management team actions. It is the company secretary who is most likely to be closest to the dynamic holistic agenda and who understands the more subtle informal individual preferences, personalities and likely reactions.

Although the company secretary often has a low profile in the boardroom, the role is critical to board resolutions and actions. In the majority of cases, it is the preparatory work in advance of board meetings that influences outcomes, enabling the conversion of strategy into implementable action plans (Arnold, 1987). Preparatory work influences the frequency, venue and duration of board meetings; interactions between the CEO and the board; finding solutions to issues; ensuring a level of consensus among directors; the form and technicalities of board proceedings; and involvement of boards in self-evaluation (Zahra and Pearce, 1989; Vance, 1983). It is the company secretary who facilitates timely meetings; ensures the discussion of issues to the required depth; respects disagreements between directors; ensures that directors participate in the decision-making process rather than just ceding the decision to the CEO; and ensures that minutes are well formulated and documented to monitor progress (Zahra and Pearce, 1989: 310; Vance, 1983: 24–27).

Recent research identifies the company secretary as the lynchpin in the communication process between the CEO and the board (Kakabadse *et al.*, 2014; Baron and Kenny, 1986), overcoming inadequacies, manipulation, reliability issues or delays that may impede board effectiveness (Zahra and Pearce, 1989; Kakabadse *et al.*, 2010). This often extends to the company secretary being the third person in the CEO–chairman relationship. Whereas the CEO has hierarchical authority, the chairman is *primus inter pares*, the first among equals (Levrau and Van den Burghe, 2013: 108) as head of a collegial body. This allows the company secretary's extensive discretionary influence to exercise relational power. This may be in the way that information is presented and communicated, catering to different preferences or needs. Or it may be in the way information is prioritised/selected as being important enough to warrant discussion in a board meeting.

Macro-analysis focuses attention on sources of power such as position, expertise, access to information, motivation and rewards (Pettigrew, 1972). More subtly, the ability of an individual or group to realise their intended effects is related to their capability of leveraging relational/micro-aspects of power, which are contingent on the degree of dependency (French and Raven, 1959) or currency to make connections and appropriately influence others (Pettigrew, 1972). Thus, the power capability of the company secretary requires behavioural analysis (Cyert and March, 1963; Huse, 2005) of those involved, coupled with structural positioning of roles held (van Ees *et al.*, 2009; Dalton and Daily, 1997; Roberts *et al.*, 2005).

The power of individuals within a group is primarily derived from five sources: reward, punishment (coercion), legitimacy, knowing other people (referent) and having expert skill or knowledge (French and Raven, 1959; Raven, 2008). More widely, Giddens (1984) asserts that power is of central, if not exclusive, importance to the 'Constitution of Society', a component of social structure exercised by human agents with the capacity to enable or constrain each other. Consequently, knowledge is not objective, but an outcome of continuous negotiation between individuals, reflecting an inseparable link between subject and object (Sandberg, 2005). As such, the company secretary possesses knowledge not only of processes and procedures, but of associated 'corporate memory', enabling greater indirect ability to influence board-level decision-making through less observable behaviours, and acts of consensus-building and prevention of conflict (Kakabadse *et al.*, 2014).

Steven Lukes's (1974) typology of the three dimensions of power is a useful analytic for demonstrating a fundamental distinction between decisional and non-decisional exercises of power within the boardroom. Lukes (1974: 23) observes that 'the most effective and insidious use of power is to prevent conflict from arising in the first place'. Importantly, a lack of conflict and the appearance of consensus do not equal the absence of power relations. That is, those subject to power can be 'socialised' into a false appreciation of their real interests, and thereby act against them, whilst believing that they are acting according to their preferences (Young, 1978).

Third-Dimensional 'Smart Power'

Exploring the dynamics of power within the boardroom elite and episodic decision-making in group interactions provides new insight into informal leadership practices such as managing information flow, dealing with personalities, negotiating the possible outcomes, and managing company interests and individual expectations, all as views of power. The discrete, informal processes of elite communication, socialisation, acculturation and fraternisation are central to any understanding of board consensus (Pettigrew, 1992). Power relations within elite settings such as the boardroom tend to reinforce and perpetuate the dominant logic. However, it is important to recognise that the legitimised constructions that form the social context of boardroom interactions are far from absolute; individuals have strengths, weaknesses and different agendas, making decision-making politically complex (van Ees *et al.*, 2009).

Drawing on Lukes's (1974: 2005) concept of third-dimensional power, this study considers the discrete mechanisms of preference formation at play within boardroom elite interactions. How does the company secretary deal with power plays within the board and the organisation? How is the company secretary's role exposed to the decision-making process within the board?

Lukes (2005) argues that we need to think about power broadly and pay attention to those aspects of power that are least accessible to observation. Power is an imposition of internal constraints; those subject to it acquire beliefs that result in their consent, or their adaptation, to domination, in its either coercive or non-coercive forms.

The first dimension of power is actual observable behaviour (Dahl, 1957; Polsby, 1963) in situations in which the powerful prevail. The second dimension of power has observable instances of control through 'soft initiatives' and is about control over non-decision-making, i.e. 'where demands for change . . . can be suffocated before they are even voiced, or kept covert' (Bachrach and Baratz, 1970: 44). This introduces 'mobilisation of bias' (Bachrach and Baratz, 1962: 948) as a prevailing set of subjectivities (values, beliefs) of one group over another, e.g. strategic agenda setting grounded in matters outside the boardroom. Such pre-decisional activities are of critical importance in determining the decisions that will, ultimately, be made down the line (Cobb, 1983; Rose-Ackerman and Long, 1982).

The third dimension is where 'the supreme exercise of power is to get others to have the desires you want them to have' (Lukes, 1974: 23). The powerful can symbolically or covertly shape agents' awareness of their interest and ability to act. This operates at an ideological, normative level, at which interests remain concealed. This may be at work somewhere within, and between, the structural determinants of the boardroom and the issue definition and agenda-setting activities as a boardroom process (Table 16.1).

Applying Lukes's (1974) third-dimensional or 'smart power' to the company secretary role provides insights into the less obvious, subtle, relational and political aspects that are usually behind the more formal overt elite boardroom interactions and their consensus-formation activities. Smart power is exercised through sensitive diplomatic dialogue, in which endurance is underpinned to build trust, which should be at the core of effective boardroom interactions. Consensus building emerges as covert, informal, massaging, positioning and posturing of strategies that unlock or reinforce structural resistances to dynamic change. The company secretary, with unique direct relations to board members and executives, has discrete power over the desires and beliefs that shape boardroom dynamics. Thus, this radical conceptual mechanism suits the exploration of the questions of whether, and how, the preferences of elite participants have been influenced without their knowledge.

In her commentary on boardroom practice, Baroness Kingsmill (2008: 24) notes that the company secretary is 'the best guide to board etiquette', through their role of servant of the board and employee of the company. The company secretary has often served under a number of CEOs and chairmen and as such 'can be an important source of information and guidance' (Kingsmill, 2008: 24). The company secretary takes the minutes, so if a board member wants to ensure that his/her points are recorded elegantly, they need to 'become their friend' (Kingsmill, 2008: 24). At a deeper level, the company secretary's invisible leadership as lessons of 'service' stands out from following meagre rules and hierarchical titles, to help others create meaning and purpose by engaging moral and human dimensions to the bigger picture and in not allowing leadership to 'begin and end with themselves' (Sena *et al.*, 2013: 41).

Here we draw upon evidence from a study that was informed by 40 one-to-one semi-structured qualitative interviews with company secretaries, chairmen, CEOs, NEDs and independent

Table 16.1 Three Dimensions of Power

Characteristics	First Dimension of Power: Hard/Formal Power	Second Dimension of Power: Soft Power	Third Dimension of Power: Smart/Informal Power
Synonyms	• Material or structural	• Normative (or value) or civilian	• Elite networks
Primary leavers	• Economic • Structures • Military/technology • Policy outcomes	• Economic • Bureaucratic • Collaborative institutions • Different subjective interests in policy outcomes	• Media • Voluntary intuitions • Multinational corporations (MNEs) • Knowledge for control • Single interest policy
Secondary leavers	• Institutions • Normative	• Structures • Co-operation for interest	• Economics • Politics
Perceived effect	• Coercive • Observable • Institutional building • Behavioural	• Collaboration/co-operation • Strategic Partnership, Engagement • Organisation building • Decision-making and non-decision making • Grievances	• Consensus building • Emergent • Invisible/pre-positional • Framed debate (delineated parameters for debate) • Issues and potential issues
Empirical inquiry	Observable power – Decision situation and exercises of power are a product of conflict of interests over political preferences (overt)	Observable power – power located within the decision process (overt and covert)	Power is situated in controlled preferences (i.e. not directly observable) Latent conflict Subjective and real agenda (covert)

Conceptualisation of power	'The ability of A to get B to do something he or she would otherwise not do' (Dahl, 1957: 202)	'Is also exercised when A devotes his energies to creating or reinforcing social and political values and institutional practices that limit the scope of the political process to public consideration of only those issues which are comparatively innocuous to A' (Bachrach and Baratz, 1962: 948)	'A may exercise power over B by getting him to do what he does not want to do, but he also exercises power over him by influencing, shaping or determining his very wants. Indeed, is it not the supreme exercise of power to get another or others to have the desires you want them to have?' (Luke, 1974: 23)
Influential authors	Dahl (1957); Polsby (1963)	Bachrach and Baratz (1962)	Schattschneider (1975); Lukes (2005)

Source: compiled by the authors.

consultants, which were facilitated through focus group sessions (12) and distributed questionnaires. The one-to-one interviews lasted, on average, 70 minutes each, whilst the focus group sessions were designed for two hours each and consisted of between 5 and 20 people per session. Participants were purposefully selected from the ICSA register. A total of 206 participants provided detailed accounts (Harre and Secord, 1972; Kakabadse and Louchart, 2012) of their beliefs about and experiences and perceptions of the company secretary.

The unit of analysis is the individual company secretary. All interviews and focus group sessions were recorded and transcribed; the less detailed questionnaire responses were taken as written responses. The inquiry process interpretively analysed interviews/focus groups/questionnaires reflectively, seeking the deeper inter-subjective meanings of the third-dimensional 'smart power' that underpins boardroom elite interaction and consensus formation.

The primary interest was to achieve understanding of a company secretary's exercise of power, rather than to explain and predict their future behaviours. With this perspective, the view was taken that nothing was trivial in company secretary interactions with relevant others, and that everything they do has the potential for unlocking understanding about the exercise of their power (Janesick, 1994).

Qualitative data analysis (Miles and Huberman, 1994) by the Henley Business School research team used open coding techniques to assign descriptive phrases. Several themes emerged within the interview narratives (Corbin and Strauss, 1990). Discrepancies were resolved through intensive discussions within the team as part of the iterative development process. This allowed for how company secretaries perceive themselves and how other board members perceive and define the company secretary at the board level.

Finally, a focus group session with study participants was convened, which verified the findings through presentation and participative discussion.

Three major themes, each with sub-themes, emerged from our analysis, namely: company secretary's role, power and influence as invisible leadership or third-dimensional power.

Company Secretary's Power

In this section, the themes that impact on the third-dimensional invisible role, power and influence of the company secretary are shared.

Role

Each organisation and board is unique. A company secretary's power depends on their ability to negotiate structure and position the role in a way that is effective for them within the team:

> You're not a member of the executive team, you're not a member of the board, you're the interface between board and executive, you've got to have independence.
>
> *Co. sec.*

A higher level of self-confidence and assuredness within the elite cadre is required, particularly as board members often misunderstand or lack awareness of the role of the company secretary:

> You have the same liabilities as executive directors, but you don't sit on the board but are trusted to sign everything . . . I'm not someone's secretary, I am the Company Secretary which is different.
>
> *Co. sec.*

The associated history and self-moulding of the role affects the power the individual wields within the group context, and to what extent personal skillsets drive duality or wider commitments:

> As general counsel you are heavily involved in the running of the business and are the chief executive's right hand. This is different to being the chairman's right hand as company secretary.
>
> *Co. sec.*

The company secretary's power depends on managing and coping with ethical dilemmas and issues of trust and in putting the best interest of the organisation first:

> I enjoy the moral ethical dilemmas, I am always trying to work out what is the best thing to do in this situation. You need to be a diplomat, have thick skin, be resilient and for this you need independence.
>
> *Co. sec.*

> It goes to chairman and chief executive, but maybe the chief executive wants to change it and chairman doesn't.
>
> *Co. sec.*

Many respondents note that the nature of the role is changing due to developments in reporting requirements, governance, board processes and stakeholder engagement post-financial crisis (2008). The findings illustrate that high-performing company secretaries help to build trust, which results in good governance. Examples may be preparedness for regulatory changes that affect the corporation; being accessible/available to all board members equally; being seen to be transparent in business matters, but dealing sensitively with personal director matters (e.g. the NED facing legal issues on another board, or indicating that they wish to step down).

Power

A company secretary's discretionary power, and to some extent their authority, is defined by how much power the chairman chooses to give:

> What you do as company secretary can principally depend on what chairman wants you to do . . . company secretary is there to support the chairman.
>
> *Chairman*

Respondents note that the company secretary has to mould him/her self to fit the relationship with the chairman, but they are also an invisible leader and close trusted advisor to board members. Thus, the company secretary needs to be a good follower–leader in knowing how and when to speak up.

Another power factor for the company secretary stems from knowing the individual board members at a more personal level:

> You need to be able to relate to people. The board and executive both trust you . . . you act as confidante, advisor, sounding board . . . things they might not want to say directly to each other.
>
> *Co. sec.*

But, at the same time, the company secretary's power demands an ability to be impartial and unbiased in finding the balance between private and public, or challenging board members for effectiveness:

> I use the term Switzerland . . . my role is one of neutrality.
>
> *Co. sec.*

> Judgement is sometimes exercised behind the scenes, helping to steer the right direction.
>
> *Co. sec.*

The nature of demands placed on the company secretary requires their ability to move from the detail to considering the holistic issue in a broader context:

> You need to think very quickly on your feet . . . and be proactive and reactive all the time.
>
> *Co. sec.*

Consequently, the company secretary benefits from experience and knowledge in being able to exert power:

> Understanding the business is vital, you don't operate in a vacuum, you need to know what the drivers are.
>
> *Co. sec.*

Many respondents note that the power of the company secretary comes to the fore in a crisis, major change situation or when directors fall out with each other. In such cases, the company secretary's power to avoid conflict and find consensus makes the difference between successful outcomes and risk of failure. Examples from high-performing company secretaries may be when the chairman and CEO do not get on, knowing where the expertise lies within the boardroom and getting the right know-how about what to do quickly, or being the independent party between board members that have strong, different, views. The crafting of relations for effectiveness is a continuous process.

Influence

The majority of respondents agree that being organised and efficient enables the ability to influence and facilitate alliances, even as an observer:

> It can be quite powerful to observe and then have a quiet word on the side. . . . Company secretaries can add value by precisely observing dynamics and how it affects decision making.
>
> *Co. sec.*

> Each time a new member enters the board there is a new balance of power.
>
> *Co. sec.*

The power of highly skilled company secretaries emerges in being the primary point of information and its quality for board and governance matters:

> You are not only a conduit of information across and between levels, but make sure they get the right information.
>
> *Co. sec.*

Agenda setting can be a trade off between different priorities. The power of the company secretary in organising pre-meetings, taking minutes and guiding board members' thinking is a subtle process:

> Agenda setting is straight forward in that the directors know what they want to say, but you also know what they don't want to talk about and what needs to be discussed . . . you can get board and management to talk.
>
> *Co. sec.*

> The board says no but it does not necessarily mean No.
>
> *Co. sec.*

The ability of the company secretary to influence also arises in that, more often, they are the stability factor and have corporate memory of the issues:

> Corporate memory of the change through good times and bad . . . the tenure of company secretary tends to be longer than CEO these days . . . suddenly people are looking at you for a view.
>
> *Co. sec.*

Underlying this influential power is the fact that the role of the company secretary can be a lonely position, as only they have the depth and understanding of the issue. Further, if they take a stand for the company's interests, it can go against some board members' views. Highly effective company secretaries demonstrate an ability to exercise independent views. Examples may be their active vocal opinions/engagement in board meetings rather than through the chairman; their ability to say 'No' to taking on additional responsibilities; or knowing the inner conversations of different committee meetings, but also knowing the boundaries between them.

Communication and use of language is a critical feature of being able to influence. The majority of respondents agree that company secretaries adopt a non-confrontational, non-threatening, and more subdued and cautious approach to matters:

> You've got to be discrete, diplomatic, have integrity . . . subtle use of language . . . there is a difference between discuss, debate, debate at length, challenge and question.
>
> *Co. sec.*

> I tend to avoid conflict and try and find other ways rather than confrontational.
>
> *Co. sec.*

> You need to be able to read people, understand them and speak their language.
>
> *Co. sec.*

Highly effective company secretaries generally avoid strong language and are diplomatic in what they say and how they frame it. This even extends to their ability to read people's personalities and body language, and deal with each person in a different way that is comfortable to the other party.

Company Secretaries' Invisible Leadership as Third-Dimensional Power

The third-dimensional power of the company secretary emerges as a combination of role, power and influence that combine in giving the company secretary a powerful and unique position as the pivotal role between board and executive management (Table 16.2 below).

In Table 16.2, each company secretary's capacity for the 15 characteristics determines their overall level of power heterogeneity that establishes their discretionary power capacity and credibility as part of the team.

In third-dimensional form, power is highly dependent on subtle communication. Human communication is not limited to the message conveyed only by written (Treece, 1972) or chosen spoken words, but embraces paralinguistic characteristics such as voice inflection, acceleration and deceleration, body language and emotional articulation (Watzlawick *et al.*, 2011). The common elements to most communication models are the message senders (i.e. encoder), the message, the channel and the message receiver (i.e. decoder) (Arnold, 1987: 33–34). The company secretary's depth and diversity of communication skills enable better relations to the other board roles as leadership practice. By understanding the other board members as people with personalities first and then engaging with each board member differently to suit their needs, the company secretary is important to building trust amongst board members. The effective company secretary then may support, over a period of time, more openness and quality of dialogue at the board level. This role is therefore always asking how information helps knowledgeable decision-making, and what is best and right for the organisation.

Table 16.2 Third-Dimensional Discretionary Power of Company Secretary

Characteristics	Role	Power	Influence
Invisible leadership and power heterogeneity	Clarity of understanding (i)	*Chairman's desire and relations (i)	*Forging alliances (i)
	Structure/position and standing (i)	Board member relations (i)	Right and quality information (i/e)
	*Self-confidence (i)	Private/public (i)	Corporate memory (i)
	Ethical resilience (i)	Detail/holistic (i/e)	Agenda steering (i)
	Adaptability and preparedness (e)	Experience/knowledge (i/e)	Diplomacy in language and conduct (i)
Power tension	Shaping regulation (e)	Tension as outward facing (e)	Equitable status (e)
How role can better relate to others for leadership practice	Building trust	Crafting relations	Having independence

Source: designed by authors from interviews applied to Lukes (1974, 2005).

(*Table key*: i – internally focused; e – externally focused; * – dominant characteristic)

The dominant characteristics within Table 16.2, from our research, are *role – self-confidence; power – chairman desires and relations; influence – ability to forge alliances*. These are most commonly critical to company secretaries' power and, interestingly, are all derived within the organisation. Research suggests that the company secretary context is influenced as powerful CEOs or powerful boards prefer engaging similar directors, whereby boards may be more passive or active (Westphal and Zajac, 1995; Westphal and Stern, 2006).

The gaps or tensions in power for the company secretary are that they have less power to shape regulation; lower power on externally facing capacity/stakeholder engagement; and their ability to influence may be constrained due to lack of equitable status amongst the other board members and executives. Interestingly, the power constraints are all derived externally to the organisation.

In board cadres, the quality of individual leadership capacity is commonly observable amongst peers (chair, CEO, SID, NED) as IQ (intelligence) and PQ (political acumen) within the group decision-making setting. Where invisible leadership and follower–leader combine, the company secretary uniquely and consistently engages higher order EQ (emotional) and moral (MQ) skills to a greater level in leadership decision-making. However, power is perceived differently with board members seeing words as most important and the company secretary seeing more subtle actions as important (Odhiambo and Hii, 2012). This power often remains as 'invisible leadership' to the observing stakeholder group. This is why the expectations of other board members of the role of company secretary are often unclear. Our findings indicate that the chairman must actively support and visibly promote the role of the company secretary to other board members on more equitable terms to enable credibility.

Our findings indicate that the role of the company secretary can relate better to other board members, where highly effective company secretaries are able to do a better job by building trust, crafting relations and exercising independence in the role. Where we have focused on the company secretary to illustrate the point, these links between role and leadership also require other board members to engage in such practices through regular contact, meeting face to face, bringing wider experiences and expert knowledge to bear, new suggestions and ideas, defending what is right, seeking and adopting best practices, getting to know each other and the organisation, and knowing the strategy and direction in context. It is the daily routines and individual habits that leaders should be improving, adapting and constantly applying to enhance their leadership practices.

Conclusion

In conclusion, the discretionary capacity and reputation of the company secretary as third-dimensional power is derived internally to the organisation and remains largely 'invisible leadership'. Regardless of the historical narrowing of the powerful secretary role, its renewed corporate form in the ASCG[3] framework is emerging with extensions to governance responsibilities (towards CGO[4]). Thus, there is an opportunity to bridge the power tensions between the internal and external demands of the role and the invisible and visible power play in group decision-making; and to recognise that all regulatory requirements stretch the nature of power demands. After all, the company secretary is the *invisible power behind the throne*!

This covert leadership may be preferred by other board members. However, company secretaries may offer more effectiveness through tempered leadership (Roberts *et al.*, 2008) with more visible power. The informal, covert 15 'invisible leadership' characteristics are presently dominated by self-confidence (role), chairman desires (power) and forging alliances (influence). The move towards greater visible power requires the company secretary to seek greater transparency and equitable trust as embodied power in understanding self as part of others (Arja *et al.*, 2013). Without trust, there is a low level of relationship and the company secretary role cannot have the independence to develop itself to the context or as part of a team. Particularly in a crisis or difficult situation, the board is tested and individuals under pressure may revert to their individual type/role rather than focusing on the board as an entity, which can impact on the effectiveness of the board. In consequence, it is more often that the least visible roles within the board become the most critical and their invisible leadership practices contribute more towards consensus in decision-making. As such, the company secretary role is able to retain a broader board focus as part of making an individual contribution to the board.

In this chapter, the company secretary has illustrated the link between role and leadership, but this also applies to the rest of the board, as a group of individuals working together. Each role engages with the other roles and the board collectively is effective where the output of the whole leadership team is greater than the output of the sum of the parts. It is this value added that the board should be pursuing as a potential rather than realised contribution and effective performance.

In reality, the company secretary is more likely to be the 'calm amongst the storm', in offering a board contribution that not only resolves conflict issues, but also solves problems of co-operation and co-ordination within the politically contested, powerful arena of board governance and leadership. Ultimately, the independent discretionary mindset of the company secretary as a leader is a necessity that contributes to other board members' perceptions of value, adding to highly effective leadership teams. This is an internally powerful 'invisible leadership' role in the elite corporate board that deserves greater peer and external recognition.

Notes

1 The term 'company secretary' in the UK and other Commonwealth countries is an equivalent to the US term 'corporate secretary' and to the term 'board secretary' in China.
2 Institute of Chartered Secretaries (ICSA) https://www.icsa.org.uk/
3 Anglo-Saxon corporate governance.
4 Corporate governance officer.

References

Adams, J. (1996). Principals and Agents, Colonialists and Company Men: The Decay of Colonial Control in the Dutch East Indies. *American Sociological Review, 61 (1),* 12–28.

Arja, R., Sauer, E. and Salovaara, P. (2013). Embodiment of Leadership through Material Place. *Leadership Journal, 9 (3),* 378–395.

Armour, D. (2012). *The ICSA Company Secretary's Handbook* (9th ed.). London: ICSA.

Arnold, V. (1987). The Concept of Process. *The Journal of Business Communication, 24 (1),* 33–35.

Ashton, H. (2008). *The Company Secretary's Handbook: A Guide to Statutory Duties and Responsibilities* (5th ed.). London: Kogan Page.

Bachrach, P. and Baratz, M. S. (1970). *Power and Poverty: Theory and Practice.* New York: Oxford University Press.

Bachrach, P. and Baratz, M. S. (1962). The Two Faces of Power. *American Political Science Review, 56 (4),* 947–952.

Balkundi, P. and Kilduff, M. (2006). The Ties that Lead: A Social Network Approach to Leadership. *The Leadership Quarterly, 17 (4),* 419–439.

Baron, R. M. and Kenny, D. A. (1986). The Moderator–Mediator Variable Distinction in Social Psychological Research: Conceptual, Strategic, and Statistical Considerations. *Journal of Personality and Social Psychology, 51 (6),* 1173–1182.

Beattie, D. (1980). *Company Administration Handbook: A Working Companion for General Management and the Company Secretary.* A Gower Handbook (4th ed.). Farnborough, Hampshire: Gower Publishing.

Boylan, P. M. A. (1922). *Thoth: The Hermes of Egypt.* London: Oxford University Press.

Briskin, L. (2011). Union Renewal, Postheroic Leadership, and Women's Organizing: Crossing Discourses, Reframing Debates. *Labor Journal, 36 (4),* 508–537.

Burton, P. (2000) Antecedents and Consequences of Corporate Governance Structures. *Corporate Governance: An International Review, 8 (3),* 194–204.

Cadbury, A. (2002). *Corporate Governance and Chairmanship: A Personal View.* Oxford: Oxford University Press.

Cadbury, A. (1992). *Report of the Committee on the Financial Aspects of Corporate Governance* [Electronic version]. London: Gee.

Chen, D. (2007). The Behavioural Consequences of CEO-Board Trust and Power Relationships in Corporate Governance. *Business Renaissance Quarterly, 2 (4),* 59–75.

Cobb, R. W. (1983). *Participation in American Politics: The Dynamics of Agenda-Building.* Baltimore, MD: Johns Hopkins University Press.

Collinson, D. (2012). Prozac Leadership and the Limits of Positive Thinking. *Leadership Journal, 8 (2),* 87–102.

Corbin, J. M. and Strauss, A. (1990). Grounded Theory Research: Procedures, Canons, and Evaluative Criteria. *Qualitative Sociology, 13 (1),* 3–21.

Cyert, R. M. and March, J. G. (1963). *A Behavioral Theory of the Firm.* Englewood Cliffs, NJ: Prentice Hall.

Dahl, R. A. (1957). The Concept of Power. *Behavioural Science, 2 (3),* 201–214.

Daigneault, M. G. (2006). Innovative Governance: Expand the Nominating Committee's Role to Include Crucial Governance Responsibilities. *Credit Union Magazine, January 2006,* 44–46.

Dalton, D. R. and Daily, C. M. (1997). CEO and Board Chair Roles Held Jointly or Separately: Much Ado About Nothing? *Academy of Management Executive, 11 (3),* 11–20.

Dubs, R. (2006). *Verwaltungsrat-Sitzungen: Grundlegung und Sitzungstechnik.* Bern: HauptVerlag.

Epstein, M. (1908). *The Early History of the Levant Company.* London: George Routledge & Sons Limited.

Erismann-Peyer, G., Steger, U. and Salzmann, O. (2008). *The Insider's View on Corporate Governance: The Role of Company Secretary.* Hampshire: Palgrave.

Fama, E. F. and Jensen, M. C. (1983). Separation of Ownership and Control. *Journal of Law and Economics, 26,* 301–325.

Filiz, A. (2013). *The Company Secretary within the Corporate Governance Framework*. Dissertation No. 4145, University of St. Gallen.

Finkelstein, S., Hambrick, D. C. and Cannella, A. A. (2009). *Strategic Leadership: Theory and Research on Executives, Top Management Teams, and Boards*. New York: Oxford University Press.

Finkelstein, S. and Mooney, A. C. (2003). Not the Usual Suspects: How to Use Board Process to Make Boards Better. *Academy of Management Executive, 17*, 101–113.

Fletcher, J. and Kaufer, K. (2003). Shared Leadership. In C. L. Pearce and J. A. Conger (Eds.), *Shared Leadership: Reframing the Hows and Whys of Leadership* (pp. 21–47). Thousand Oaks, CA: Sage.

Forbes, D. P. and Milliken, F. J. (1999). Cognition and Corporate Governance: Understanding Boards of Directors as Strategic Decision-Making Groups. *Academy of Management Review, 24 (3)*, 489–505.

French, J. R. and Raven, B. (1959). Bases of Social Power. In D. Cartwright (Ed.), *Studies in Social Power* (pp. 15–167). Ann Arbor, MI: Institute of Social Research.

Gallagher, T. J. (2002). The Ethical Case for Chief Governance Officers after 'Enron'. *The Corporate Governance Advisor, 10 (4)*, 41–42.

GepkenJager, E., van Solinge, G. and Timmerman, L. (2005). VOC 1602–2002: 400 Years of Company Law. *Law of Business and Finance* (Vol. 6). The Netherlands: Kluwer Legal Publishers.

Giddens, A. (1984). *The Constitution of Society: Outline of the Theory of Structuration*. Los Angeles: University of California Press.

Hannigan, B. (2009). *Company Law* (2nd ed.). Oxford: Oxford University Press.

Harré, R. and Secord, P. F. (1972). *The Explanation of Social Behaviour*. Oxford: Blackwell.

Herbert, T. T. (1977). Toward an Administrative Model of the Communication Process. *The Journal of Business Communication, 14 (4)*, 25–35.

Hilb, M. (2011). *Integrierte Corporate Governance: Ein neues Konzept der wirksamen Unternehmens-Führung und Aufsicht*. Vierteüberarbeitete Auflage. Berlin: Springer-Verlag.

Huse, M. (2005). Accountability and Creating Accountability: A Framework for Exploring Behavioural Perspectives of Corporate Governance. *British Journal of Management, 16*, S65–S79.

ICSA. (2012). *Institute of Chartered Secretaries & Administrators: Best Practice Guide: Duties of a Company Secretary*. ICSA, United Kingdom. http://www.icsa.org.uk/resources/guidance/980803 (accessed 20 January 2014).

Janesick, V. J. (1994). The Dance of Qualitative Research Design: Metaphor, Methodology and Meaning. In N. K. Denzin and Y. S. Lincoln (Eds.), *Handbook of Qualitative Research* (pp. 209–235). Thousand Oaks, CA: Sage.

Kakabadse, A., Kakabadse, N. and Khan, N. (2014). *The Company Secretary: Building Trust through Governance*. Joint research project and report between Henley Business School and Institute of Company Secretaries and Administrators UK.

Kakabadse, A., Kakabadse, N. and Knyght, R. (2010). The 'Chemistry Factor' in the Chairman/CEO Relationship. *European Management Journal, Special Issue: New Leadership Themes, 28 (4)*, 285–296.

Kakabadse, N. and Louchart, E. (2012). Practical Approach to Elite Interviewing. In A. Kakabadse and N. Kakabadse (Eds.), *Elite: The Opaque Nature of Transnational Policy Determination* (pp. 286–307). London: Palgrave.

Kaye, J. W. (1853). *The Administration of The East India Company*. London: Richard Bentley.

Kingsmill, D. (2008). Navigating the Board. *Management Today*, November 2008, 24.

Ladkin, D. (2013). From Perception to Flesh: A Phenomenological Account of the Felt Experience of Leadership. *Leadership Journal, 9 (3)*, 320–334.

Lamm, R. (2003). What's in a Name? *CFO – EBSCO Publishing*, September 2003, 24.

Levrau, A. and Van den Berghe, L. (2013). Perspectives on the Decision-Making Style of the Board Chair. *International Journal of Disclosure and Governance, 10 (2)*, 105–121.

Lukes, S. (2005). Three Dimensional Power. In S. Lukes (Ed.), *Power: A Radical View* (2nd ed.) (pp. 137–151). Basingstoke: Palgrave Macmillan.

Lukes, S. (1974). *Power: A Radical View*. London: MacMillan Press.

McNulty, T. and Stewart, A. (2014). Developing the Governance Space: A Study of the Role and Potential of the Company Secretary in and around the Board of Directors. *Organization Studies, 36 (4)*, 515–535.

Miles, M. B. and Huberman, A. M. (1994). *Qualitative Data Analysis: An Expanded Sourcebook*. Thousand Oaks, CA: Sage.

Monks, R. A. G. and Minow, N. (2004). *Corporate Governance* (3rd ed.). Padstow, Cornwall: TJ International Ltd., Blackwell Publishing.

Monsted, P. and Garside, G. (1991). *The Role of the Company Secretary: A Practical Guide*. Institute of Corporate Managers Secretaries and Administrators. Australia: Prentice Hall of Australia Pty Ltd.

Morris, G. D., McKay, S. and Oates, A. (2009). *Finance Director's Handbook* (5th ed.). Burlington, VA: CIMA Publishing.

Muller, R., Lipp, L. and Pluss, A. (2007). *Der Verwaltungsrat: Ein Handbuch fur des Paraxis*. Zurich: Schluthess Juristische Medien AG.

Murphy, C. (2003). Radical Company Law Reform: Implications for Researching Companies. *Business Information Review, 20 (1)*, 42–50.

Naval Staff, Intelligence Division (1920). *A Manual of Netherlands India*. London: Oxford University Press.

Odhiambo, G. and Hii, A. (2012). Key Stakeholders' Perceptions of Effective School Leadership. *Education, Management and Leadership, 40 (2)*, 232–247.

Padilla A., Hogan, R. and Kaiser R. (2007). The Toxic Triangle: Destructive Leaders, Susceptible Followers, and Conducive Environments. *The Leadership Quarterly, 18 (3)*, 176–194.

Panorama Developments (Guildford) Ltd v Fidelis Furnishing Fabrics Ltd (1971). *Queen's Bench*, Vol. 2, 711.

Petra, S. (2005). Do Outside Independent Directors Strengthen Corporate Boards? *Corporate Governance, 5 (1)*, 55–64.

Pettigrew, A. M. (1992). On Studying Managerial Elites. *Strategic Management Journal, 13 (Winter)*, 162–182.

Pettigrew, A. M. (1972). Information Control as a Power Resource. *Sociology, 6 (2)*, 187–204.

Polsby, N. W. (1963). *Community Power and Political Theory: A Further Look at the Problems of Evidence and Inference*. New Haven, CT: Yale University Press.

Pontifex v Bignold (1841). *British Columbia Reports*, Vol. 3, 63; *English Reports*, Vol. 133, 1058.

Pontifex v Bignold (1841). *Manning & Granger's Common Pleas Reports* (England and Wales), Vol. 3, 63; *English Reports*, Vol. 133, 1058.

Ramaswami, N. S. (1983). *The Chief Secretary: Madras Diaries of Alexander Falconar, 1790–1809*. Madras: New Era Publications.

Raven, B. H. (2008). The Bases of Power and the Power/Interaction Model of Interpersonal Influence. *Analyses of Social Issues and Public Policy, 8 (1)*, 1–22.

Roberts, D. D., Roberts, L. M., O'Neil. R. M. and Blake-Beard, S. D. (2008). The Invisible Work of Managing Invisibility for Social Change: Insights from the Leadership of Reverend Dr. Martin Luther King Jr. *Business Society Journal, 47 (4)*, 435–456.

Roberts, J. (2002). Building the Complementary Board: The Work of the plc Chairman. *Long Range Planning, 35 (5)*, 493–520.

Roberts, J., McNulty, T. and Stiles, P. (2005). Beyond Agency Conceptions of the Work of the Non-Executive Director: Creating Accountability in the Boardroom. *British Journal of Management, 16*, S5–S26.

Rose-Ackerman, S. and Long, C. (1982). Winning the Contest by Agenda Manipulation. *Journal of Policy Analysis and Management, 2 (1)*, 123–125.

Sandberg, J. (2005). How Do We Justify Knowledge Produced within Interpretive Approaches? *Organizational Research Methods, 8 (1)*, 41–68.

Schattschneider, E. E. (1975). *Semi-Sovereign People: A Realist's View of Democracy in America*. Hinsdale, IL: The Dryden Press.

Schlott, A. (1989). *Writing and Writers in Ancient Egypt* (*Schrift und Schreiber im Alten Ägypten*). München: Beck.

Schmidt, E., Schleich, T. and Beck, T. (1988). Merchants as Colonial Masters: Trading World of Dutch at the Cape of Good Hope to Nagasaki, 1600–1800. (Kaufleute als Kolonialherren: Die Handelswelt der Niederländer vom Kap der Guten Hoffnung bis Nagasaki, 1600–1800). Bamberg: C. C. Buchners Verlag.

Schyns, B. and Hansbroughn, T. (Eds.) (2010). *When Leadership Goes Wrong*. Charlotte, NC: IAP.

Seth, V. K. (2012). The East India Company: A Case Study in Corporate Governance. *Global Business Review, 13 (2)*, 221–238.

Severn & Wye & Severn Bridge Railway Co (1896). *The Times Law Reports*, Vol. 12, Chapter 1, p. 262.

Sister Sena, R., Schoorman, D. and Bogotch, I. (2013). Leadership: Doing the Seemingly Impossible. *Journal of Cases in Educational Leadership, 16 (2)*, 33–43.

Steger, U. and Bottger, P. (2008). The Corporate Governance Officer: From Company Secretary to Manager of Governance Processes. In P. Bottger (Ed.), *Leading in the Top Team: The CXO Challenge* (p. 247). Cambridge: Cambridge University Press.

Treece, M. C. (1972). Business Communications Practices and Problems of Professional Secretaries. *Journal of Business Communication, 9 (4)*, 25–32.

Van der Walt, N. and Ingley, C. (2003). Board Dynamics and the Influence of Professional Background, Gender and Ethnic Diversity of Directors. *Corporate Governance, 11*, 218–234.

Van Ees, H., Gabrielsson, J. and Huse, M. (2009). Toward a Behavioral Theory of Boards and Corporate Governance. *Corporate Governance: An International Review, 17 (3)*, 307–319.

Van Essen, M., Engelen, P. J. and Carney, M. (2013). Does 'Good' Corporate Governance Help in a Crisis? The Impact of Country- and Firm-Level Governance Mechanisms in the European Financial Crisis. *Corporate Governance: An International Review, 21 (3)*, 201–224.

Vance, S. C. (1983). *Corporate Leadership: Boards, Directors, and Strategy*. New York: McGraw-Hill.

Watzlawick, P., Bavelas, J. B. and Jackson, D. D. (2011). *Pragmatics of Human Communication: A Study of Interactional Patterns, Pathologies and Paradoxes*. New York: WW Norton & Company.

Westphal, J. D. and Stern, I. (2006). The Other Pathway to the Boardroom: Interpersonal Influence Behavior as a Substitute for Elite Credentials and Majority Status in Obtaining Board Appointments. *Administrative Science Quarterly, 51 (2)*, 169–204.

Westphal, J. D. and Zajac, E. J. (1995). Who Shall Govern? CEO/Board Power, Demographic Similarity, and New Director Selection. *Administrative Science Quarterly, 40 (1)*, 60–83.

Young, R. A. (1978). Steven Lukes's Radical View of Power. *Canadian Journal of Political Science, 11 (3)*, 639–649.

Zahra, S. A. and Pierce J. A. (1989). Boards of Directors and Corporate Financial Performance: A Review and Integrative Model. *Journal of Management, 15*, 291–334.

17

Practising Religious Leadership

Jack Barentsen[1]

Introduction

Religious leadership is changing face. In the Western world, decades of religious decline, renewed interest in spirituality and the rise of extremist religious groups have created a different world with vital challenges to religious communities and their leaders. It raises questions such as: how is religious leadership changing, how do religious leaders shape their communities of faith and how do they influence their followers? These are vital questions since religious leadership continues to have a significant, worldwide impact, but its face has changed and its effect is sometimes dramatically destructive. So what are some of the important models of religious leadership? What are the key dimensions of such leadership? Even more vital, what makes religious leaders successful and how should they be trained? This chapter, then, aims to develop an understanding of the context, development, dimensions and key issues of religious leadership, in order to provide the tools to assess the effectiveness of religious leaders, and to design educational strategies for training and deploying them.

The most basic question is simply, 'what is religious leadership?' In this chapter, it is understood as leadership in religious contexts by people who identify themselves with that particular context. This may refer to church or denominational leaders in various Christian traditions, but also to leaders of other religious communities or of non-profit organizations with an explicitly religious purpose. This description locates religious leaders within various organizational and institutional contexts, in their turn embedded within the broader institutions of a society, so we first turn towards a brief description of societal changes and their challenges for religious leadership.

First, though, a note about the limitations of this chapter. It draws primarily from research on Christian leadership as exercised within Christian churches and organizations. This reflects in part the personal biography and commitments of the author. More significantly, it reflects the fact that most research on religious leadership has been carried out within particular Christian traditions, with little knowledge thereof outside its own domains. Relatively little research is done on religious leadership in other religions – although occasionally a famous religious leader like Gandhi or Martin Luther King is studied – and very few organizational or leadership specialists focus on the study of religious leadership. This chapter therefore is an attempt to present findings to a broader public on religious leadership that are admittedly limited to certain traditions as a more general model, in the hope that it will encourage familiarity with and study of religious leadership on a much broader scale.

From Modern to Postmodern Context

Changes in Religiosity in the West

To the surprise of many, religion has made a comeback in the public domain of Western societies. Since the 1960s, mainline churches in the West have declined dramatically, losing millions of members and closing thousands of church buildings. Liberal secularism became the dominant ideology in many segments of Western society, while an increasingly dominant evolutionary paradigm led many to speculate that religion would soon become extinct. The so-called secularization hypothesis proposed that the intimate connection between religion and society of the nineteenth century would gradually be replaced by a more fragmented society in which religion would play only a marginal role. The trends of increasing social differentiation and fragmentation, coupled with the ascendency of a scientific worldview, pushed this process inexorably forward. The result, inevitable according to many scholars, was church and religious decline, as the statistics bear out (Knippenberg, 1998: 209–220; Bruce and Glendinning, 2010: 107–126).

However, analyses of this secularization hypothesis have not offered the expected support for it. It is doubtful on historical and empirical grounds that the twentieth century is less Christian than preceding centuries (Raedts, 2003: 38–40). And even though statistics of church decline in Europe and North America are hardly optimistic (Weems, 2010), a new demographic analysis of northern European countries suggests that religious decline has for the most part halted (Kaufmann *et al.*, 2012: 69–91). Instead of further decline, recent decades have seen a broadening of interest in spirituality, shifting from institutional forms of (mostly) Christianity in the 1950s to a broader range of (frequently non-institutionalized) religions (Wuthnow, 1998: 129–130; Hicks, 2003). For instance, the financial crises starting in 2008 led to a broad realization that neo-liberalism, for all the material wealth that it has brought, fails to offer long-term solutions to the moral, social and spiritual dilemmas of our planet. In response, a significant market has developed even in secular business and organizational leadership studies for 'spiritual leadership', including serious academic studies of the subject (see Fernando, 2007; Fry and Nisiewicz, 2013).

The comeback of religion often takes the form of a renewed quest for spirituality as that which makes life valuable and meaningful. This is defined mostly in terms of personal choices and experiences, not necessarily with reference to religious institutions or even to a transcendent being (Saane, 2014: 46–50). Similarly, newer leadership models such as transformational leadership, servant leadership and authentic leadership are based on values, integrity and personal significance, which are often associated with spirituality (Northouse, 2012: 185–199, 219–132 and 253–166, respectively). In addition, renewed religious presence is broader, more fluid: US officials proposed government support of faith-based initiatives,[2] new religious leaders meet with civic magistrates to engage in community support (Branson and Warnes, 2014; Goodhew *et al.*, 2012), Pope Francis has become surprisingly popular, while Islamic leaders exercise an inescapable worldwide influence.

Thus, in spite of several generations of church decline, the resurgence of religiosity strongly impacts civic society, but its forms have changed. Religiosity was primarily embedded within revered institutions, represented by an appointed leadership. Now, however, religiosity flows increasingly through fluid networks, to which people connect based on their personal sense of and need for spirituality (Ward, 2002). Thus, changes in religiosity take place along at least two dimensions: (a) deinstitutionalization, moving from institutional allegiance to personal spirituality; and (b) religious diversification, which refers to both the increased presence of various world religions, and to the mixing of various religious beliefs and practices in personal forms of spirituality. This postmodern face of religion is quite different from its earlier modern forms.

Changes in Leadership

The exercise of leadership has also been impacted significantly by the shift towards postmodernism. Academic leadership studies no longer focus only on the leader, but also on the followers and the leader's relationship with them, as well as on group dynamics in a particular social context, as considered from a social constructivist perspective (Uhl-Bien and Ospina, 2012).

Societal pressures on leaders have risen significantly in the last few decades. In a world characterized by Wikipedia and Facebook, organizational and institutional leaders no longer have privileged access to information, nor do they have privileged access to follower motivations. Organizations and their leaders are challenged to move from an industrial, control-based form of organization to a more fluid network model of the learning organization (Marquardt, 2011: 2).[3] Simultaneously, the world has been enveloped in a number of high impact crises – climate and food, banking and credit, terrorism and warfare – contributing to a sense of threat which leaders are expected to neutralize quickly and effectively through the use of proven scientific methods. And yet, the complexity of these crises resists easy solutions, and forces leaders to collaborate across various social and corporate networks. The intense political and media scrutiny of leaders amidst a crisis heightens the demand for public accountability and transparency (Boin et al., 2005: 72ff.).

However, some leaders have proven notoriously difficult to hold accountable. This was evident in the aftermath of the banking crisis, where million-dollar bonuses continued to be paid in the midst of the crisis; clearly corporate executives were unable or unwilling to tackle the thorny ethical problems of their business (see also Heinckiens, 2014: 21–24). The ethical and even spiritual dimensions of leadership demand attention as leaders struggle to adapt to these new realities.

Challenges for Religious Leadership

How have religious leaders adapted to the changing place and role of religion in late-modern Western contexts?

The Need for Public Accountability and Transparency

Today, religious leaders cannot simply lead from a hierarchical position or as an institutional representative. The religious scene has become more complex through religious diversification, immigration and global communication. Religious leaders find themselves participating in a religious market where their particular religious tradition is simply a niche – and often an obscure one at that – amidst an overwhelming religious diversity. In addition, some religious leaders have been exposed for their involvement in moral scandals, hate speech and even violence, so that many people view religious leaders with suspicion. Public accountability and transparency are no less needed for religious leaders than for leaders in business or politics.

Pressure from Diversity and Autonomy

Religious diversity is not only a broad social phenomenon; even within their own religious communities, religious leaders face a greater variety of followers. Today, followers tend to adopt and adapt pieces from various religious traditions and beliefs into a bricolage of personal religiosity (Deuze, 2006: 70–71; Barentsen, 2015a). Moreover, thoroughgoing individualism creates a sense of autonomy, so that people feel entitled to their own bricolage; obedience to or identification with a religious institution is no longer the standard response. Thus, religious leaders cannot simply proclaim time-honoured traditions or represent established institutions, from which many members feel increasingly estranged; instead they need to engage with the spiritual journeys and individual sensemaking processes of followers in order to mobilize them for religious communities (Cormode, 2006).

Religious Leadership as Spiritual Guidance

Religious leadership is now less practised through harnessing people's commitment to a particular religious community, for instance by motivating members to faithfully attend and sponsor community activities, often in competitive mode with other religious or non-religious communities. Rather, religious leaders motivate people to participate by engaging in their spiritual journey, focusing on spiritual experience and life meaning through participation. That is, the institutional and organizational focus of religious leadership is decreasing in significance, while the role of spiritual guide to enable people to make spiritual sense of life and to build coalitions for particular religious causes is on the increase. These challenges for the religious leadership are summarized in Table 17.1.

The Development of the Roles and Tasks of Religious Leaders

Professionalization: The Psychological Dimension of Religious Leadership

Until about the middle of the twentieth century – depending on one's geographical and religious context – the main task of religious leadership was to maintain loyalty to the traditional interpretations of one's religious sources.[4] These interpretations were furnished by the religious leaders themselves, who had in turn been securely embedded within their tradition during their years of religious training. This classical model involved upholding one's religious tradition and the 'care of souls' within a small geographical region designated as a 'parish', upholding the symbolic world that made sense of the whole of life.

In the second half of the twentieth century, the growing scientific development of psychology and psychotherapy, and the strong societal drive towards increasing professionalization (Freidson, 1999), shifted the way religious leadership viewed pastoral care. Care focused increasingly on the individual and his or her religious coping mechanisms. Forms of Christian psychotherapy were developed, and religious leaders were immersed in clinical pastoral training as part of their professional education (Boisen, 1955; Aden, 1990). This created new professional standards for the practice of and training in pastoral–psychological care in the 1960s and 1970s, in vogue especially among pastors of mainline churches. The substantial dependence on psychological models drew criticism in some parts for creating distance between the pastor's professional counselling practice and his or her role as representative of the religious tradition.

Professionalization is here understood in the classic sense: the religious leader is formally autonomous in relation to the religious community served; the leader has specific university

Table 17.1 Challenges for Religious Leadership in a Postmodern Context

Modern context	Postmodern context
Focus on the leader (position, calling, tasks, appointment)	Focus on the team and the community
Privileged access to information and institutional interpretation of religious sources	Open access to religious tradition; individualized interpretation of religious sources
Lead from hierarchical or institutional position	Lead as authentic example to guide people's spiritual journey
Followers identify with institution	Followers claim autonomy for a personal spiritual bricolage
Top down, command-and-control style of leadership	Collaborative and transparent leadership
Respect for moral and religious integrity of religious leaders	Religious leaders subject to public scrutiny and accountability
Diversity challenges institutional homogeneity	Diversity as valuable characteristic of the religious community
Orientation towards tradition in competition with other traditions	Market orientation amidst religious diversity
Mobilize followers to contribute and maintain institutional vitality	Empower followers to build a learning organization in a fluid network
Religious identity given by tradition	Religious identity constructed in social networks
Religious leader discourse mostly ideological, internally focused	Religious leader discourse mostly in terms of psychology and leadership, externally focused

training for a theological body of knowledge and skills; and control of the profession is ascertained through denominational accreditation and ordination exams. This distinguishes the religious leader from other types of workers within the religious organization (Freidson, 1999; Brouwer, 1995). For instance, the practice of denominational supervision is supplemented and sometimes overshadowed by pastoral supervision through outside experts (Leach and Paterson, 2010), which points to the value of self-regulation and standardization of professional functioning.

Further indications of professionalization in a pastoral–psychological paradigm are presented by a set of concerns that religious leaders share with the other professions. Religious leaders have difficulty in clearly distinguishing between different fields of work. They have difficulty with the work–private balance and consequently work very long hours (55–60 hours a week). They report health issues, lack of social support, emotional exhaustion and burnout (Brouwer, 1995; Evers and Tomic, 2003).

Professionalization: The Organizational Dimension of Religious Leadership

Due to the continuing decline of church membership, by the 1980s religious leaders were confronted with the need to invest substantially in institutional maintenance, which prioritized their tasks in organizational leadership. Religious leaders turned to organizational studies and adopted this new leadership language to address their communities. They spoke of numerical growth, patterns of growth and the need for strategic planning in reaching one's target audience.

Vision and mission statements became commonplace in many models of congregational leadership and renewal (McGavran, 1980; Warren, 1995; Hybels, 2002; Malphurs, 2005).

This development opened new venues for academic dialogue. For instance, from the late 1990s, US theological educators concerned with teaching religious leadership met regularly to build a common understanding of leadership. In 2002, they initiated the *Journal of Religious Leadership* to study the use of leadership models in religious leadership (Frank, 2002; Callahan, 2002). Over the years, key leadership themes have featured as special *JRL* issues: leadership education (2005), polity and governance (2006), authority and power (2007), change management (2008), charisma (2010), women in leadership (2012), spirituality (2013), emotions (2014) and innovation (2015).

In adopting the vocabulary of other leadership studies, religious leaders positioned themselves, not among the helping professions, as previously, but among the CEOs and other key leaders. It enabled religious leaders to gain self-confidence in leadership, and added to their status (and sometimes salary) as professional experts.

The Impact of Professionalization on Religious Leadership

Professionalization has increased the quality of psychological care and of leadership in many religious organizations, but it has also created some tensions.

Questions about the Identity of Religious Leaders

Some religious leaders served in contexts such as medicine, mental health or social activism (Taylor *et al.*, 2000). Here, they functioned as helping professionals among other professionals in medicine, law or public welfare. This maintains their autonomy over against the members of their own religious community, but poses new questions about the professional identity of the religious leader towards these new colleagues whose understanding of religion has all but disappeared. How does help by a religious professional complement the help offered from the other disciplines? Should religiosity or religious coping count as *professional* rather than *pastoral* skill, comparable to psychotherapy, legal counsel and public policymaking?

Other religious leaders found themselves in contexts where they were forced to cooperate with volunteer 'lay' leaders. This may occur in a large (growing) church with many volunteer workers (Hybels, 2004), but also in a declining church where fewer professionals must share the work with more volunteer lay leaders (Sonnberger, 1996). These lay leaders serve in many different areas that were traditionally the domain of the religious leader, such as in liturgy, pastoral care, small group leadership, organizing events, Christian education, social involvement and more. Here, the religious leader emerges as manager and team worker alongside many volunteers without formal academic training and without formal appointment or ordination (Hoge *et al.*, 1988). The legitimacy of such lay leaders is often not institutionally embedded, and again poses questions about the professional identity of the religious leader. What is his or her role if volunteers do the same job?

Thus, the psychological as well as the organizational paradigms created new opportunities, skills and status for religious leaders. It enabled them to navigate social and cultural shifts that affected religiosity, loyalty and participation in religious communities. Simultaneously, these new social contexts brought new challenges to their self-understanding as religious leader. They functioned as professionals amidst other helping professionals or (lay) leaders, but how did the religious dimension of their leadership complement their professional status?

Questions about the Legitimation of Religious Leadership

Traditionally, the self-understanding of religious leaders is anchored within their religious community. For instance, many Roman Catholic and mainline Protestant leaders are legitimated on the basis of a 'theology of ministry'[5] that focuses on the concept of mission: God the Father sends Jesus Christ, who in turn sends others to bring salvation to the world (Borght, 2007; Witte, 2009, 2010). The religious leader fulfils an essential role in this mission by representing and proclaiming the sacred to the followers, which sets the leader apart within his or her own community. Leaders within evangelical traditions focus more on the concept of charisma, portraying leadership as one among many divinely granted gifts, so that all can contribute to the community through a diversity of talents (Hybels, 2004). This positions the leader as peer within the community.

Whether emphasizing representation of the sacred or divine charisma, this religious legitimation often raises doubts as to whether it is legitimate to consider religious leadership as simply one profession among many. Advocates of a professional ministry emphasize the skills and expertise needed to exercise religious leadership, as well as the ethical codes of conduct. Others warn that emphasis on professional status threatens the peculiar religious dimension in its focus on the divine mystery and obscures the need for a sense of call and proper ordination for such leadership. They point out that religious leadership does not easily align with the sociological dimension of profession.

Here, questions about the identity of the leader arise, not only about one's professional status, but also about one's religious authenticity. Can one truly count as a *religious* leader, if what 'really' counts are the *professional* skills derived from psychology and organizational studies?

Hybrid Professionalization: The Religious Leader as Shaper of Culture and Identity

From Classic to Hybrid Professionalization

The move towards professionalization since the 1980s has left its mark on the shape of religious leadership. Evidently, the answer of professionalization to social change is ambivalent, providing new opportunities for service, but also raising new questions about one's professional status or religious identity. Even so, the professionalization of religious leadership did not stem the tide of continuing church decline. At the turn of the twenty-first century, it became evident that Christianity had shifted permanently from institutional establishment to marginal presence. This development encouraged and even necessitated new forms of community formation and religious leadership (Zscheile, 2012).

At the same time, professionalism had developed from its classic form, where the professional was firmly in control of the content, competence and accreditation of his work, to a hybrid form where the professional loses substantial control to either the customer or the manager or both. For instance, in the field of health care, professionals need to respond ever more quickly to consumers who scour the internet for remedies and medicines, while they must also respond to health care managers who restrict professional autonomy by imposing cost control measures (Noordegraaf, 2007). Similarly, religious leaders interact with followers who behave like religious consumers, shopping locally or digitally for religious experience and insight, while the dynamics of church decline cause severe economic restrictions, with thousands of church buildings closing annually, sweeping layoffs in many denominational headquarters and the loss of many clergy positions (Gaede, 2002; Bisseling *et al.*, 2011).

New forms of religious leadership develop to respond to reduced professional autonomy in a network society. Religious communities are no longer primarily perceived as institutions with a long and respected tradition, within which leaders are the professional experts who know what is to be done. Instead, these communities are becoming learning organizations that navigate their way through the complexities of life and society, with leaders in the role of guide or coach. Due to greater transparency and media scrutiny in a digital age, religious leaders find themselves wrestling with new public roles in unexpected networks of power.

In this new context, models of public and political leadership offer needed insights into these new public dimensions of religious leadership, while models of organizational leadership may become less useful in an era of institutional decline. Table 17.2 represents key leadership characteristics and their relevance for religious leadership, comparing an institutional with a network context.

Table 17.2 Key Characteristics of Religious Leadership, Shaped by Institutional versus Network Contexts

Characteristic	Institutional style of religious leadership	Network style of religious leadership
Legitimacy	By institutional appointment	By continuing personal persuasion and example
Unity	Denominational and institutional unity closed off over against other (inter) national religious institutions	Local religious unity with open borders towards other (non-religious, local) social movements and causes
Authority	By position through institutional authority	By inspiration through example and empowerment
Accountability	Formal accountability at key moments such as board or member meetings	Public scrutiny (from members, media, government) of financial management, good governance, non-discriminatory practices, etc.
Transparency	Limited disclosure of leadership and decision-making processes	Leadership processes, including voice and dissent, open to general observation and inquiry
Authenticity	Office is more important than the person of the leader	The leader embodies personally and visibly the values and strategies that are significant for the organisation
Collaborative	Members passive or as agents for the leader's vision	Members empowered to carry out their own vision
Identity	Conserving: aligned with tradition and institution	Innovative: aligned with individual spiritual journey of members as well as with social and religious causes
Loyalty	Loyal to the religious community, its message and its values	Loyal to one's network and favourite causes, following lines of personal affinity
Diversity	Emphasis on internal unity along a particular dimension, overlooking other differences	Emphasis on respect for internal diversity and relative member autonomy, while seeking a new sense of internal unity to maintain distinction from outgroups

This table combines readings in the field of organizational and leadership studies, and draws particularly (but not exclusively) on the writings of 't Hart on public leadership (2014), of Marquardt on the learning organisation (2011) and of Witte on the impact of the network society on the church (2014). Moreover, empirical research on pastoral leadership suggests a number of these characteristics, such as the studies by Brouwer (1995), Vermeulen (1998) and Doornenbal (2012), including my own (yet unpublished) empirical research in interviewing religious leaders.

Within this new context of marginalization, religious leaders are expected to lead with authenticity and transparency, engaging followers in respectful dialogue to empower them in their religious quest. Communities of faith become less oriented towards tradition and inter-denominational competition; they focus more on making spiritual sense of life and contributing meaningfully to civic society. In this context, the culture-shaping and identity-forming dimensions of religious leadership take on new significance, both for existing communities and for new communities founded by religious entrepreneurial leaders.

The Religious Leader as Entrepreneur

Within this context of hybrid professionalization, the entrepreneurial mode of religious leadership is attractive for many religious leaders. They realize that in many contexts the traditional tasks in liturgy, proclamation and pastoral care will not lead to revitalization, and so they experiment with new forms of community formation and with new ways to recover the lost societal relevance of their communities. New religious communities are started or dying ones are revitalized by connecting with people who were unassociated with religion – perhaps because of previous disappointments or because of a complete absence of religion in their lives. Entrepreneurial leaders attempt to include these people by developing a new sense of community that is both religiously and socially based, often making place for a variety of personal spiritual experiences. They are purposely engaging with contextual factors such as religious background, network loyalty, and ethnic and socio-economic diversity. Yet, by the nature of the entrepreneurial role, such experiments rely heavily on the vision, communication and professionalism of the pioneer leader, who often enjoys a form of (external) institutional legitimation and financial support, creating a leadership gap that makes succession and continuity a very challenging process in this setting (Goodhew *et al.*, 2012; Volland, 2013).

In religious discourse, entrepreneurial leadership is often represented as missional leadership. The mission of religious communities is reconceived with an external focus on contributing to social justice and the civic community, instead of the older focus on building up the faith community (Van Gelder, 2009). This shift in emphasis is presented as a major paradigm change, requiring new forms of leadership that are as yet undefined (Roxburgh, 2010). Furthermore, religious training institutes cannot assume that equipping graduates for clearly delineated religious roles within particular religious traditions will be effective, since the role of religious leaders is shifting to match these shifts in religious and social identity (Doornenbal, 2012).

These forms of religious entrepreneurship position the religious leader within the framework of hybrid professionalism. On the one hand, the religious leader is dependent on patterns of religiosity from potential followers, approaching them as religious consumers. On the other hand, they depend on external legitimation and financing which carry both mandate and restrictions for these entrepreneurs.

The Religious Leader as Sensemaking Guide

Another model of religious leadership that is clearly situated within hybrid professionalism is the leader as interpretive or sensemaking guide (Cormode, 2006). The religious leader is to guide people in interpreting situations or life events in religious terms to appropriate a sense of divine involvement or closeness in the situation. This approximates discursive leadership where a leader (re)frames certain situations or events so that they 'make sense' within the context of the organization (Pye, 2005), except that sensemaking now focuses on one's personal spiritual journey, often but not always connected to a religious community. This leadership model emphasizes collaboration and transparency. The leader is legitimated by personal authenticity rather than institutional identity, and he or she leads through inspiration and empowerment rather than through mobilizing followers through institutional loyalty.

Religious leadership in a multicultural setting is an illustration of such interpretive leadership. Religious leaders encounter increasing cultural variety within their religious communities, and sometimes deliberately seek to be ethnically inclusive. It takes particular skills to unite people of diverse cultural and ethnic backgrounds into one encompassing community. Such models of multicultural religious leadership consistently support collaboration amidst diversity. The potential for cross-cultural tensions requires transparent communication and accountability, as well as transparent ways to distribute power among the various groups (Branson and Martínez, 2011; Murray and Murray-Williams, 2012; DeYmaz and Li, 2013).

The Religious Leader as Shaper of Culture

A closely related model portrays religious leaders as shapers of congregational culture. Realizing that culture shapes our perceptions and expectations, religious leaders are called upon to interpret new situations and events in such a way that they can be woven together with the existing cultural repertoire. A proposed course of action is most likely to be fruitful if it closely follows pre-legitimated paths of meaning (Cormode, 2006). Religious leaders not only interact with these organizational cultural patterns, they also interact with and actively shape the unique blend of history, beliefs, practices and symbols as the cultural pattern of the particular local religious community they lead (Carroll, 2006; Branson and Martínez, 2011). The leader's task in shaping culture implies sensitivity to cultural pressures on loyalty and identity, aiming for increased collaboration. The position of the leader is culturally embedded, and the leader needs to embody the values and vision of the community, demonstrating leader authenticity.

The Religious Leader as Identity Constructor

The identity-constructing role of religious leadership goes largely unnoticed, with some notable exceptions (Carroll, 2006; Roxburgh, 2010). With the loss of institutional respect and identity, many religious communities actively experiment with new forms of religious and social identity. Religious leaders adapt and reshape the identity of the communities they lead, to maintain or upgrade their societal place and relevance. These leaders succeed in rooting the adapted version of religious identity in the hearts and minds of their community members, while empowering them to practise their religion in the affairs of daily life. The process of identity formation is particularly sensitive to social identity and individual loyalties as outcomes of group processes. Religious leaders must authentically embody the values and beliefs of the community to function as prototypical community members, which inspires members to identify with and participate in the community. The model is open towards institutional anchoring of leadership and followership, but does not require it (Haslam et al., 2011; Hogg et al., 2012; Barentsen, 2011).

While adapting the community's socio-religious identity, religious leaders also negotiate their own religious and professional identity. Some religious leaders succeed in adapting their own identity to match the identity shift of the community they lead, so that they maintain their leadership position and influence during the time of change. Other leaders may realize that their community is changing its socio-religious identity in a way that they cannot or do not wish to match – which will result in conflict or in the departure of the leader. Or again, the leader may wish to adapt the community's identity to match his or her own vision, and finds that sometimes the community is willing to adapt while at other times it is inclined to resist (Barentsen, 2015a; Hermans, 2001).

Summary

The religious leader as entrepreneur, as sensemaking guide, as shaper of culture and as identity artist – these and similar models of religious leadership are a feature of hybrid professionalization, since the autonomy, knowledge and control of the professional are considerably restricted by the priority given to facilitating and empowering members to shape their own vision and direct their own participation within or outside the religious community. In addition, the organizational and financial constraints of declining religious communities seriously limit classic professional control and give greater power to the denominational hierarchy or to local lay leaders. This parallels hybrid forms of professionalization in other fields where customer and/or managerial control severely restrict classic professional autonomy (Noordegraaf, 2007).

Summarizing more broadly, the role and tasks of religious leaders have thus developed from religious or denominational representative to professional counsellor to organizational leader, and finally to spiritual sensemaking guide. This evolution is rather simplified. For some communities, this development moves from one model of religious leadership to another. Other communities resist change, becoming more 'fundamental' in an effort to stay true to received religious traditions. Sometimes, different models function concurrently, as religious leaders from different generations and with different forms of religious training function side by side. These models are not exclusive and religious leaders may operate according to one or several models, sometimes by conscious choice, but more often guided by their intuition on how to lead in a particular context with particular people. Evidently, religious communities and their leaders respond in intricate ways to their social context, adopting, adapting and resisting various tendencies in shaping their own sense of community and religious identity.

Dimensions of Religious Leadership

Is it now possible to construct a general model of religious leadership? This question is often answered in the affirmative, usually based on a normative religious perspective from within a particular tradition (Howell, 2003; Strauch, 2003). Others have attempted to include insights from organizational sciences in such a general model, while remaining anchored within one particular Christian tradition (Bekker, 2009). However, it is doubtful that this is possible, considering the large number of contextual variables that determine the shape of religious leadership at any given time and place.

The significant diversity in religious leadership contexts is beautifully illustrated in Callahan's reference handbook on religious leadership (2013). It features nearly 100 chapters over 750 pages, describing leadership in Christian, Jewish, Islamic and Asian religious communities. *Each* tradition offers a *spectrum* of leadership models, framed by intra-religious tradition, by country and ethnicity, by particular issues and by focus – ranging from religious community-building to civic engagement to political action. The book's 18 brief biographies of famous religious leaders further illustrate this diversity.

Another insightful work about the diversity of leadership contexts is an empirical study of the development of religious communities by several Dutch practical theologians (Brouwer et al., 2007). Drawing on organizational literature, they identified several phases of organizational life: start-up, growth, continuity, decline, revitalization or closure. Rather than attempting to define one broad model of religious leadership for all of these phases of organizational life, the authors describe the particular needs of the community and the matching tasks of leadership that apply in each distinct phase.

Additional variables significantly impact the practice of religious leadership:

- location, size, age and demography of a particular religious community;
- personality, training, age and experience of the religious leader;
- culture and ethnicity of the community, its leaders and its social context.

As in all forms of leadership, only a contextual approach to religious leadership can begin to do justice to the complex needs and dynamics of religious leadership in various social, organizational, cultural and ethnic contexts.

A taxonomy of leadership behaviours helps to group various leader behaviours from these diverse contexts in a manageable way. Familiar meta-categories in leadership studies include task-oriented, relations-oriented and change-oriented behaviours (Michel et al., 2010), sometimes supplemented by ethics-oriented behaviours. These meta-categories function at a highly abstract level that does not immediately provide much insight into a particular form of leadership. Considering the overview of religious leadership provided above, another set of meta-categories suggests itself as an appropriate and insightful taxonomy (see Table 17.3).

Table 17.3 furnishes a set of meta-categories that highlights various leader behaviours and clusters of tasks that can be distinguished in the practice of religious leadership – even if there is some overlap between various dimensions. Each dimension would need its own chapter for a full explanation, which is a task for another occasion. However, Table 17.3 is a useful tool to understand and situate religious leadership, both in the general field of leadership, as well as in the specific contexts and types of religious leadership.

First, Table 17.3 points out similarities with other forms of leadership. I would suggest that religious leadership shares with political leadership: *proclaiming publicly* (dim. 8) and *engaging socially* (dim. 9), and also *reconciling differences* (dim. 7). It shares with educational leadership: *modelling spirituality* (3) and *stewarding tradition* (4), perhaps also *reconciling differences* (7) and *engaging socially* (9). And it shares with corporate or business leadership: *leading the organization* (6), *reconciling differences* (7) and *proclaiming publicly* (8). Common dimensions for all these forms of leadership appear to be *celebrating community* (2) and *leading the organization* (6). The driving force for religious leadership is a vision of the sacred; for the other forms of leadership it is political ideology (a vision for society), educational philosophy (a vision of personal development) or business strategy (a vision for products and services).

Second, the table highlights the unique functions of religious leadership. The first four dimensions indicate that religious leaders enable followers to participate meaningfully in the religious worship, rituals and traditions of the community. These four are core dimensions that inform the other dimensions ideologically. Relationships with other followers are nurtured for meaningful, effective and harmonious participation in worship and ritual (dims 5, 6 and 7). Relationships with those outside the religious community are nurtured by the desire to have all people share in worship and ritual (dim. 8) or at least to experience the common good as an outcome of faith (dim. 9). Thus, worship and ritual do not provide goods and services for society, but participation in worship and ritual is the primary good of the community, to which insiders and outsiders are continually invited.

Third, Table 17.3 situates various types of religious leadership. The classical role of the religious leader as representative of a particular tradition and its institutions scores high on *stewarding tradition* (dim. 4) and *tending the community* (dim. 5), and low on *proclaiming publicly* (8) and *engaging socially* (9). The religious entrepreneur, however, generally scores high on dimensions 8 and 9;

Table 17.3 Dimensions, Roles and Tasks of Religious Leadership

Dimensions	Roles	Tasks
Core dimensions that qualify leadership as religious		
1. Representing the sacred	Mystic, visionary priest	Represents and/or mediates the sacred to the followers
2. Celebrating community	Impresario, symbolic leader, liturgist, presider	Draws community together in celebrating the community's (organizational) culture and identity
3. Modelling spirituality	Role model, disciple, spiritual guide	Lives a transparent, authentic spiritual life, embodying the community's identity, inspiring and empowering followers to live similarly
4. Stewarding tradition	Interpreter, theologian preacher, teacher .	Interprets and actualizes religious tradition to engage followers in experiencing its relevance in daily life
Dimensions that focus on relationships within the religious community		
5. Tending the community	Pastoral counsellor, crisis counsellor, diaconal helper	Cares for the spiritual needs of followers, often in loss and grief, to foster meaning-making within and belonging to the community and its traditions
6. Leading the organization	Visionary, strategic planner, organizer, change manager	Mobilizes followers for a common goal, empowering them for a variety of contributions in team settings
7. Reconciling differences	Reconciler, conflict manager, crisis coper	Enables the community to cope with differences, tension, conflict, disaster and scandal, through meaning-making, rendering account, peace-making and change
Dimensions that focus on relationships with those outside the religious community		
8. Proclaiming publicly	Advocate, community representative, evangelist, apologist	Speaks out publicly on behalf of the religious community and its tradition, leading followers to do the same in their sphere of influence; represents the religious community in civic settings
9. Engaging socially	Community organizer, activist, liberator, prophet	Leads followers to engage in the social needs of the public, to serve the common good and liberate people from oppressive social and political conditions

in the start-up phase, scores are likely to be high in *representing the sacred* (1) and *modelling spirituality* (3), while, in the revitalization phase, *celebrating community* (2) and *leading the organization* (6) are probably high scores. The leadership models of 'sensemaking guide', 'shaper of culture', and 'artist of identity' probably score lowest on *stewarding tradition* (4) and *leading the organization* (6), and highest on *representing the sacred* (1), *celebrating community* (2), and *modelling spirituality* (3). Each leadership model has its own peculiar balance of these nine dimensions.

Fourth, Table 17.3 can be used to evaluate religious leadership. The balance of the nine dimensions indicates something of the religious quality of leadership. Religious leadership can be assessed as 'good' or 'bad' depending on whether the core dimensions are sufficiently prominent, whether they are in harmony with other expressions of their particular religious tradition, whether these core dimensions nurture the other dimensions in a transparent and authentic manner, and whether attention to both internal and external relations is in balance. The balance of these nine dimensions thus indicates how a particular style of leadership fits with the religious self-understanding of the community, which in turn indicates the levels of legitimacy and accountability that a leader obtains within that community. Moreover, the effectiveness of religious leadership depends on whether it fits appropriately in the phase of organizational life of the religious community. For instance, the start-up and revitalization phases need models of entrepreneurial leadership, the growth and continuity phases need visionary, organizational, or institutional leadership, while the decline or even closure phases probably need models that excel in personal care and crisis management. It appears that the models focusing on sensemaking, culture-shaping and identity construction are more general, not necessarily fitting a particular organizational phase, but reflecting the postmodern, pluralistic context of religious leadership.

These measures of balance and fit enable an assessment of religious leadership in terms of its own self-understanding and in terms of its own contextual fit, while using general organizational and leadership categories (see also 't Hart, 2014: 229–234).

Key Issues for the Future of Religious Leadership

Our survey of the context, development and dimensions of religious leadership is nearly complete. It remains to briefly mention some key issues for the future of religious leadership.

The Deployment of Religious Leaders

In a multicultural and multireligious society, religious leaders are key agents (1) to shape the culture of their own religious communities, while adapting and resisting a diversity of outside influences and (2) to construct a relevant socio-religious identity that enables the religious community to play a meaningful role in civic society beyond its own religious commitments. Although religion has been marginalized for decades, the public role of religious leaders is once again a significant factor for social justice and peace, or alternatively for discord and even violence. Religious leaders need to recover their public role, without necessarily creating partisan political movements such as the Moral Majority in the 1980s in the US.

At the same time, the deployment of religious leaders faces serious economic and demographical challenges. The average age of religious leaders increases, partly because of an ageing population, partly because of increasing proportions of second career leaders. More women enter the ranks of religious leaders, while part-time, bi-vocational and interim forms of religious leadership increase. These leaders will serve increasingly amidst a growing team of lay leaders (Carroll, 2006: 61ff.).

Clearly, the economic and demographical challenges are in tension with the demands for a greater public and professional role for religious leaders. The tendencies towards entrepreneurial, missional forms of religious leadership may well generate the creativity needed to answer these challenges, so that religious leaders can play a vital role amidst the diversity and life fragmentation of our network society.

Educating Religious Leadership for a Network Society

Traditional education for religious leadership focused on personal development and vocational training to embed religious leaders firmly in their particular religious tradition and to develop theological wisdom and discernment to faithfully represent the sacred to their religious communities (Banks, 1999). With the movement post-Second World War towards professionalization, university training and academic orientation became increasingly important for the self-understanding of religious leaders and for gaining access to positions of religious leadership, while the effects of secularization resulted in lower student numbers and decreasing financial support. Many teaching institutions wrestle with the effects of secularization and the transition to the (digital) network society, since their systems assumed the cultural dominance of Christianity and the continued academic relevance of the Enlightenment vision of rationality and scholarship (Cunningham, 2004).

Significant debate now takes places around the goals, methods and curriculum for religious leadership training institutions. A new balance is needed between spiritual development, professional training and academic excellence. Furthermore, a more missional and entrepreneurial training model is needed to focus not only on institutional vitality and maintenance but also on the leader's public role in social involvement and civic society (Banks, 1999; Foster *et al.*, 2006; Doornenbal, 2012).

Interdisciplinary Research on Religious Leadership

Interdisciplinary research on religious leadership is a major challenge, since religious leadership scholars and academic leadership specialists hardly overlap in their work and research paradigms. Yet, awareness of the need for interdisciplinary academic work is growing.

The professionalization of the religious leadership of the late twentieth century benefitted primarily from organizational and leadership studies, although older psychological and psychoanalytic paradigms remained in vogue (Nauta, 2006). The hybrid professionalism of the early twenty-first century saw the rise of social psychology as an important source for understanding group and identity dynamics of religious communities in a network society where the value of community and loyalty is shifting (Barentsen, 2015b). The domain of public and political leadership offers new ways to understand how to lead in a culture where transparency, voice and dissent have become primary values and where institutional boundaries have become fuzzy or simply irrelevant ('t Hart, 2014). The disciplines of the sociology of religion and cultural anthropology have become fruitful sources to investigate the life and leadership of religious communities through the use of ethnography and other qualitative research methods (Scharen and Vigen, 2011). Finally, the approach of social constructivism enables new perspectives on the development of religious communities and their leaders in particular contexts (Cameron, 2010).

Interdisciplinary research is needed amidst the growing specialization and differentiation of religious leadership, which requires new ways of legitimating religious leaders, new ways of building communities for religious and social involvement and new structures for authority and effectiveness. The range of contexts for religious leadership broadens from traditional churches and Christian organizations to include both institutional and fluid forms of organization that are rooted in various world religions or regional religious movements. Each religion and each context requires its own types of religious leadership. Thus, typologies of religious leadership should be developed to evaluate the legitimacy, accountability and organizational fit of a particular type of religious leadership in a particular socio-religious context. The nine dimensions of religious leadership and the various phases of organizational life provide a helpful guide to developing a limited set of typologies for religious leadership (Kluge, 2000). Such scholarship is direly needed, since it is evident that the practice of religious leadership will remain a vital constituent of a pluriform and just civic society.

Notes

1 I want to express my gratitude to professors Peter-Ben Smit (Theology) and Paul 't Hart (Organizational Sciences) at the University of Utrecht for their feedback and cooperation in a project financed under the theme 'Institutes'.
2 http://georgewbush-whitehouse.archives.gov/government/fbci/.
3 Marquardt identifies eight major forces of change: globalization and the global economy; technology and the Internet; radical transformation of the world of work; increased customer power; emergence of knowledge and learning as major organizational assets; changing roles and expectations of workers; workplace diversity and mobility; rapidly escalating change and chaos. 't Hart describes the following trends: increased networking, focus on empowerment, greater demands for transparency, immediacy, accountability, increased fluidity and glocalization ('t Hart, 2014: 182–183).
4 For additional historical surveys of the development of religious leadership models, see Heitink, 2001; Holifield, 2007.
5 A 'theology of ministry' is a description of leadership within a religious community or organization in religious or theological terminology. It functions as an internal philosophy of leadership with its own rationale for defining, legitimating and delimiting the office and character of the organization's leaders.

References

Aden, L. R. (1990). *Turning Points in Pastoral Care: The Legacy of Anton Boisen and Seward Hiltner*. Grand Rapids, MI: Baker.

Banks, R. J. (1999). *Reenvisioning Theological Education: Exploring a Missional Alternative to Current Models*. Grand Rapids: Eerdmans.

Barentsen, J. (2011). *Emerging Leadership in the Pauline Mission: A Social Identity Perspective on Local Leadership Development in Corinth and Ephesus*. Princeton Theological Monograph Series (Vol. 168). Eugene: Wipf & Stock.

Barentsen, J. (2015a). The Moral Challenge of Diversity Leadership. In P. Nullens and S. v. d. Heuvel (eds.), *The Moral Challenge of Leadership*. Leuven: Peeters.

Barentsen, J. (2015b). Church Leadership as Adaptive Identity Construction in a Changing Social Context. *Journal of Religious Leadership*, 15 (2), Forthcoming.

Bekker, C. J. (2009). Towards a Theoretical Model of Christian Leadership. *Journal of Biblical Perspectives in Leadership*, 2 (2), 142–152.

Bisseling, H., Roest, H. d., and Valstar, P. (2011). *Meer dan hout en steen: Handboek voor sluiting en herbestemming van kerkgebouwen*. Zoetermeer: Boekencentrum.

Boin, A., 't Hart, P., Stern, E., and Sundelius, B. (2005). *The Politics of Crisis Management: Public Leadership under Pressure*. Cambridge: Cambridge University Press.

Boisen, A. T. (1955). *Religion in Crisis and Custom: A Sociological and Psychological Study*. New York: Harper.

Borght, E. A. J. G. v. d. (2007). *Theology of Ministry: A Reformed Contribution to an Ecumenical Dialogue*. Leiden: Brill.

Branson, M. L. and Martínez, J. F. (2011). *Churches, Cultures, and Leadership: A Practical Theology of Congregations and Ethnicities*. Downers Grove: IVP Academic.

Branson, M. L. and Warnes, N. (eds.). (2014). *Starting Missional Churches: Life with God in the Neighborhood*. Downers Grove: InterVarsity.

Brouwer, R. (1995). *Pastor tussen macht en onmacht. Een studie naar de professionalisering van het hervormde predikantschap*. Zoetermeer: Boekencentrum.

Brouwer, R., Groot, K. d., Roest, H. d., Sengers, E., and Stoppels, S. (2007). *Levend lichaam: Dynamiek van christelijk gemeenschappen in Nederland*. Kampen: Kok.

Bruce, S. and Glendinning, T. (2010). When Was Secularization? Dating the Decline of the British Churches and Locating Its Cause. *The British Journal of Sociology*, 61 (1), 107–126.

Callahan, S. H. (2002). Shifting Images of Church Invite New Leadership Frames. *Journal of Religious Leadership*, 1 (1), 55–82.

Callahan, S. H. (ed.). (2013). *Religious Leadership: A Reference Handbook*. Los Angeles: Sage.

Cameron, H. (ed.). (2010). *Talking about God in Practice: Theological Action Research and Practical Theology*. London: SCM Press.

Carroll, J. W. (2006). *God's Potters: Pastoral Leadership and the Shaping of Congregations*. Grand Rapids: Eerdmans.

Cormode, S. (2006). *Making Spiritual Sense: Christian Leaders as Spiritual Interpreters.* Nashville: Abingdon.

Cunningham, D. S. (ed.). (2004). *To Teach, To Delight, and To Move: Theological Education in a Post Christian World.* Eugene: Cascade.

Deuze, M. (2006). Participation, Remediation, Bricolage: Considering Principal Components of a Digital Culture. *The Information Society,* 22 (2), 63–75.

DeYmaz, M. and Li, H. (2013). *Leading a Healthy Multi-ethnic Church: Seven Common Challenges and How to Overcome Them.* Grand Rapids: Zondervan.

Doornenbal, R. J. A. (2012). *Crossroads: An Exploration of the Emerging-Missional Conversation with a Special Focus on 'Missional Leadership' and Its Challenges for Theological Education.* Delft: Eburon.

Evers, W. and Tomic, W. (2003). Burnout among Dutch Reformed Pastors. *Journal of Psychology & Theology,* 31 (4), 329–338.

Fernando, M. (2007). *Spiritual Leadership in the Entrepreneurial Business: A Multifaith Study.* Cheltenham: Edward Elgar.

Foster, C. R., Dahill, L. E., Golemon, L. A., and Tolentino, B. W. (eds.). (2006). *Educating Clergy: Teaching Practices and the Pastoral Imagination.* San Francisco, CA: Jossey-Bass.

Frank, T. E. (2002). The Discourse of Leadership and the Practice of Administration. *Journal of Religions Leadership,* 1 (1), 7–30.

Freidson, E. (1999). Theory of Professionalism: Method and Substance. *International Review of Sociology,* 9 (1), 117–129.

Fry, L. W. and Nisiewicz, M. S. (2013). *Maximizing the Triple Bottom Line through Spiritual Leadership.* Stanford: Stanford Business Books.

Gaede, B. A. (2002). *Ending with Hope: A Resource for Closing Congregations.* Lanham, MD: Rowman & Littlefield.

Goodhew, D., Roberts, A., and Volland, M. (2012). *Fresh! An Introduction to Fresh Expressions of Church and Pioneer Ministry.* London: SCM.

't Hart, P. (2014). *Understanding Public Leadership.* Hampshire: Palgrave Macmillan.

Haslam, S. A., Reicher, S., and Platow, M. J. (2011). *The New Psychology of Leadership: Identity, Influence and Power.* New York: Psychology Press.

Heinckiens, P. (2014). The Impasse of Leadership. In J. Barentsen and P. Nullens (eds.), *Leadership, Spirituality and Innovation,* pp. 15–30. Leuven: Peeters.

Heitink, G. (2001). *Biografie van de dominee.* Baarn: Ten Have.

Hermans, H. J. M. (2001). The Dialogical Self: Toward a Theory of Personal and Cultural Positioning. *Culture & Psychology,* 7 (3), 243–281.

Hicks, D. A. (2003). *Religion and the Workplace: Pluralism, Spirituality, Leadership.* Cambridge: Cambridge University Press.

Hoge, D. R., Carroll, J. W., and Scheets, F. K. (1988). *Patterns of Parish Leadership: Cost and Effectiveness in Four Denominations.* Kansas City: Sheed & Ward.

Hogg, M. A., Knippenberg, D. v., and Rast, D. E. (2012). The Social Identity Theory of Leadership: Theoretical Origins, Research Findings, and Conceptual Developments. *European Review of Social Psychology,* 23 (1), 258–304.

Holifield, E. B. (2007). *God's Ambassadors: A History of the Christian Clergy in America.* Grand Rapids: Eerdmans.

Howell, D. N. (2003). *Servants of the Servant: A Biblical Theology of Leadership.* Eugene: Wipf & Stock.

Hybels, B. (2002). *Courageous Leadership.* Grand Rapids: Zondervan.

Hybels, B. (2004). *The Volunteer Revolution: Unleashing the Power of Everybody.* Grand Rapids: Zondervan.

Kaufmann, E., Goujon, A., and Skirbekk, V. (2012). The End of Secularization in Europe? A Socio-demographic Perspective. *Sociology of Religion,* 73 (1), 69–91.

Kluge, S. (2000). Empirically Grounded Construction of Types and Typologies in Qualitative Social Research. *Forum Qualitative Sozialforschung/Forum Qualitative Social Research,* 1 (1), art. 14.

Knippenberg, H. (1998). Secularization in the Netherlands in Its Historical and Geographical Dimensions. *GeoJournal,* 45 (3), 209–220.

Leach, J. and Paterson, M. (eds.). (2010). *Pastoral Supervision: A Handbook.* London: SCM.

Malphurs, A. (2005). *Advanced Strategic Planning: A New Model for Church and Ministry Leaders* (2nd ed.). Grand Rapids: Baker Books.

Marquardt, M. J. (2011). *Building the Learning Organization: Achieving Strategic Advantage through a Commitment to Learning* (3rd ed.). Boston: Nicholas Brealey.

McGavran, D. A. (1980). *Understanding Church Growth* (fully revised ed.). Grand Rapids: Eerdmans.

Michel, J. W., Lyons, B. D., and Cho, J. (2010). Is the Full-Range Model of Leadership Really a Full-Range Model of Effective Leader Behavior? *Journal of Leadership & Organizational Studies*, 18 (4), 493–507.

Murray, S. R. and Murray-Williams, S. (2012). *Multi-voiced Church*. Milton Keyes: Paternoster.

Nauta, R. (2006). *Paradoxaal leiderschap. Schetsen voor een psychologie van de pastor*. Nijmegen: Valkhof Pers.

Noordegraaf, M. (2007). From 'Pure' to 'Hybrid' Professionalism: Present-Day Professionalism in Ambiguous Public Domains. *Administration & Society*, 39 (6), 761–785.

Northouse, P. G. (2012). *Leadership: Theory and Practice* (6th ed.). Thousand Oaks, CA: Sage.

Pye, A. (2005). Leadership and Organizing: Sensemaking in Action. *Leadership*, 1 (1), 31–49.

Raedts, P. (2003). De secularisatie voorbij. In C. A. M. Hermans (ed.), *Is er nog godsdienst in 2050?*, pp. 35–45. Budel: Damon.

Roxburgh, A. J. (2010). *Missional Map-Making: Skills for Leading in Times of Transition*. San Francisco: Jossey-Bass.

Saane, J. v. (2014). Spirituality and the Psychology of Leadership Credibility: An Analysis from the Psychology of Religion. In J. Barentsen and P. Nullens (eds.), *Leadership, Spirituality and Innovation*, pp. 41–56. Leuven: Peeters.

Scharen, C. B. and Vigen, A. M. (eds.). (2011). *Ethnography as Christian Theology and Ethics*. London: Continuum.

Sonnberger, K. (1996). *Die Leitung der Pfarrgemeide: Eine empirisch-theologische Studie unter niederländischen und deutschen Katholiken*. Kampen: Kok.

Strauch, A. (2003). *Biblical Eldership: An Urgent Call to Restore Biblical Church Leadership* (Revised and expanded ed.). Colorado Springs: Lewis and Roth.

Taylor, R. J., Ellison, C. G., Chatters, L. M., Levin, J. S., and Lincoln, K. D. (2000). Mental Health Services in Faith Communities: The Role of Clergy in Black Churches. *Social Work*, 45 (1), 73–87.

Uhl-Bien, M. and Ospina, S. (Eds.). (2012). *Advancing Relational Leadership Research: A Dialogue among Perspectives*. Charlotte, NC: Information Age.

Van Gelder, C. (ed.). (2009). *The Missional Church and Leadership Formation: Helping Congregations Develop Leadership Capacity*. Grand Rapids: Eerdmans.

Vermeulen, F. (1998). *Patronen van pastoraal leiderschap. Studies over kerkopbouwkunde* (Vol. 7). Baarn: Gooi en Sticht.

Volland, M. (2013). *An Entrepreneurial Approach to Priestly Ministry in the Parish: Insights from a Research Study in the Diocese of Durham*. Unpublished Ph.D. Dissertation, Durham University, Cranmer Hall, Durham.

Ward, P. (2002). *Liquid Church: A Bold Vision of How to Be God's People in Worship and Mission*. Exeter: Paternoster.

Warren, R. (1995). *The Purpose Driven Church: Growth without Compromising Your Message and Mission*. Grand Rapids: Zondervan.

Weems, L. H. (2010, September 22). No Shows: The Decline in Worship Attendance. *Christian Century*, 127 (20).

Witte, H. P. J. (2009). The Local Bishop and Lay Pastoral Workers: A Newly Created Function in the Church and Its Impact on Episcopal Collegiality. *The Jurist*, 69 (1), 84–115.

Witte, H. P. J. (2010). Der Diözesanbischof und die Kooperation der Laien in der Seelsorge: Amtstheologische Reflexionen. In B. Kranemann and M. Wijlens (eds.), *Gesendet in den Weinberg des Herrn, Laien in der katholischen Kirche heute und morgen*, pp. 77–92. Würzburg: Echter Verlag.

Witte, H. P. J. (2014). Bestuurlijke transities in de rooms-katholieke kerk. *Tijdschrift voor Religie, Recht en Beleid*, 5 (2), 70–83.

Wuthnow, R. (1998). *After Heaven: Spirituality in America since the 1950s*. Berkeley, CA: University of California Press.

Zscheile, D. J. (2012). *People of the Way: Renewing Episcopal Identity*. Harrisburg: Morehouse.

18

Practising Clinical Leadership
What Is It and How Does It Work?

John Storey and Richard Holti

Introduction

For some time now, there has been a huge emphasis within healthcare policy debate on the importance and value of 'clinical leadership'. Observers, participants and policy-makers advocate the notion. Indeed, clinical leadership is often put forward as a 'solution' to many pressing problems in healthcare. In many instances, this is an exercise in simple advocacy and prescription, with little detail or evidence about how clinical leadership operates in practice or how it adds value.

The underlying reasons for this kind of advocacy are relatively easy to understand. The rising costs of healthcare, ageing populations and increasing expectations lead to declarations that current models of care are simply 'unsustainable' and a perceived need to devise, shape and sell new models of care. These changes are contentious; they may well entail reconfiguration of existing services and the closure of local hospitals. A suspicious public often requires a clinician to reassure them that proposed changes are for reasons of patient safety and better care rather than just cost savings. As demand outstrips supply, some radical changes in the nature of the service provision appear to be accepted as essential. The common assumptions are that it is clinicians who are best placed to devise such radically new models; and that it is their leadership that is necessary to convince others – the public and other groups working within healthcare – to implement them.

The stakes have been raised. The final report of an HSJ-led commission on the 'crisis in NHS leadership' stated that: 'Today's debate on healthcare leadership, nationally and internationally, is all about integration and system leadership – perhaps a reinvention of consensus management, but this time between organisations rather than within them' (Naylor 2015 p. 1).

Despite the considerable prescriptive and policy literature advocating the importance of clinical leadership, what is lacking are empirical studies which reveal the social processes involved in the practice of clinical leadership and the challenges to be overcome.

In this chapter we address five main questions: Why is clinical leadership so strongly advocated? What is potentially distinctive about clinical leadership, its typical attributes and nature? What are the main challenges entailed and obstacles to its realization? What has been learned to date about its effective practice? And finally, what wider implications can be drawn for other domains of leadership? These five questions are reflected in the five sections into which this chapter is organized. Our perspective is a process-based one, whereby we focus on what actors do in practice and how these actions are related to context. Explication of the nature of clinical leadership and clarification of the lessons to be drawn from it may be expected to shed light on leadership processes more generally.

Policy and Pragmatic Advocacy of Clinical Leadership

The idea of clinical leadership is high on the political agenda and is also a central theme in health service policy literature (Ham and Dickinson 2008; Mountford and Webb 2009; Spurgeon *et al.* 2011; Naylor 2015). On the day that the Health and Social Care Bill passed its final reading in the House of Commons, the prime minister stated: 'The point of our health reforms is to *put doctors in charge*, give patients greater choice and heal the divide between health and social care' (HoC 8 September 2011, emphasis added). This is but one of many restatements of the general idea that leadership by clinicians is a crucial part of the 'answer' to the many challenges facing the National Health Service.

Under the previous Labour administration, the notion of an expanded leadership role for clinicians was also heavily pressed – most notably in the Darzi Review (Darzi 2008). It has also been promulgated by the administrations of Scotland (NHS Scotland 2009), Northern Ireland (Northern Ireland Department of Health Social Services and Public Safety 2009) and Wales (Faculty for Healthcare Improvement 2010).

Much of the literature on clinical leadership is normative and prescriptive. Influential frameworks of an essentially prescriptive nature have been advanced by leading academics at Harvard. For example, in *Redefining Healthcare*, Michael Porter and his colleague make a persuasive case that significant gains in the healthcare industry can best be achieved if healthcare is re-defined from the perspective of 'just another industry' (Porter and Teisberg 2006). This fresh perspective, they maintain, allows an escape from the usual limited attempts to make efficiency savings within individual segments (such as a GP practice or an emergency room) and to substitute a perspective which encourages a more radical review of the value chain. Such a perspective would, for example, involve leaders in relocating routine services from high-cost specialist 'jobbing shops' to more appropriate settings where advantages could be taken of economies of scale as patient needs are met in service areas designed for such purposes.

In *The Innovator's Prescription*, Clayton Christensen similarly argues the merits of borrowing insights from other industries in order to rethink the design of healthcare (Christensen 2009). He offers a framework or, as he puts it, a 'roadmap', for those seeking a way to derive innovative solutions in this sector. His work provides a vision and a set of tools for those who might want to rise to the challenge of rethinking healthcare from first principles. It is a prescription based on formal rationality. It does not address how leaders in a complex context such as the NHS might set about turning such ideas into a practical reality.

From an operations management perspective, Bohmer (2009) argues that healthcare professionals provide two very different types of care – sequential and iterative. With sequential care, a patient can be quickly diagnosed and given predictable, reliable and low-cost care. But, in the case of iterative care, a patient's condition is unknown, and huge resources may be required for diagnosis and treatment, often with uncertain outcomes. Bohmer argues that, to reduce costs and manage care effectively, sequential and iterative care situations require different management systems.

Traces of these influential sources can be found in policy documents issued by the Department of Health in the UK. For example, in *Inspiring Leaders: Leadership for Quality* (Department of

Health 2009), which followed on from Lord Darzi's *Next Stage Review* which championed clinical leadership (Darzi 2008), the scale of ambition for service transformation is evident, using clinical leadership as a key agent of change:

> The essence of clinical leadership is to motivate, to inspire, to promote the values of the NHS, to empower and to create a consistent focus on the needs of the patients being served. Leadership is necessary not just to maintain high standards of care but *to transform services* to achieve even higher levels of excellence.
>
> *(Department of Health 2009, emphasis added)*

This expresses a higher level of ambition than is evident in the related idea of 'clinical engagement', which concerns the ways in which doctors and other clinicians can be 'involved' in decision-making. The re-positioning of doctors and other clinicians as leaders represents a further step.

It is possible to conceive of different degrees or levels of 'clinical leadership' – represented as a journey from 'engagement' at one end through to transformational leadership at the other. The Medical Leadership Competencies Model (NHS Institute for Innovation and Improvement Academy of Royal Colleges 2010), with its levels from junior doctor to senior leader, expresses this idea in terms of career stages. This idea of 'progression' can also be used as a means to conceptualize the proposition into stages towards clinicians becoming the key leaders.

All this conveys a picture of clinical leadership as currently bound up with the need to transform how much of healthcare takes place. In this context, we can further identify a number of reasons why clinicians are held up as protagonists in the leadership that is required.

First, it is argued that clinicians enjoy the natural advantages of credibility deriving from their professional status. They are not perceived to be acting with an accountancy logic to the fore but with some base in professional ethics. Relatedly, they are recognized as having access to special knowledge as a result of lengthy training, supplemented by front-line experience with patients. This experience can also be used to claim a special relationship with patients. These characteristics are often taken as an accumulated capability to initiate and justify change. Adherence to professional ethics – especially the notion of above all acting in the interests of clients – offers special potential for leadership.

A second rationale driving the idea of clinical leadership is the utilization of their unique technical expertise to ensure that change plans are feasible and beneficial from a patient safety point of view. This leads to another rationale – to help reassure patients and public that changes are underpinned and meritorious from a clinical standpoint. The reverse side of this coin on reassurance is that, as with other leadership positions, clinical leaders are being invited to risk scapegoating if things go wrong or are perceived to have gone wrong.

Third, clinical leaders are expected to influence, enlist and convince their professional colleagues; this can be interpreted as part of a workforce strategy. One way to conceive of this is to regard clinical leadership as a form of peer regulation or 'soft governance' (Sheaff *et al.* 2003), a concept related to 'soft bureaucracy' (Courpasson 2000). An expression of this soft bureaucracy may be found in the mechanisms and processes of clinical governance. These preserve the essence of professional autonomy while introducing a modicum of oversight through the use of standards and their monitoring. Clinical leaders may be needed in order to bring clinicians into this regime and to sustain their engagement. Whilst clinical governance usually refers to mechanisms for bringing clinicians into a regime of peer regulation concerning their clinical or technical practice, the idea of clinical leadership can be seen as translating this kind of principle into other areas of practice, concerning decision-making on resources and how health services are delivered to patients (Mountford and Webb 2009). Clinical leadership involves clinicians considering options for how to organize services and improve them, taking into account managerial perspectives such as cost effectiveness as well as the experience of patients and clinical outcomes. It involves some clinicians crossing functional boundaries to discuss such issues and persuading other clinicians that the results of such interchanges amount to valid rationales for change.

Finally, when the intention is to seek integration of care in place of fragmented, individual clinician-to-patient encounters, this requires a shift from clinical autonomy and individuality to a different conception of practices which is facilitated by transparency, agreed protocols and concerted action (Ham 2008a; Woodward and Weller 2011).

Clark *et al.* contend that the time for clinical autonomy from managerial matters is past and that nowadays doctors and other clinicians need to be at the forefront of transforming services to meet patient needs more fully (Clark *et al.* 2008). They use the findings of two reports on the changing nature of medical professionalism – a King's Fund report (Dewar *et al.* 2008) and an earlier Royal College of Physicians report (Royal College of Physicians 2005). Both reports argue that organizational skills of leadership and 'followership' need to become part of the medical training and medical professionalism, and even that managerial skills could become incorporated into fitness to practise requirements. Clark *et al.* make the case for the medical leadership competency framework developed in collaboration between the joint Academy of Royal Medical Colleges and the NHS Institute for Innovation and Improvement. Below, we seek to clarify what such behaviours would look like in practice.

Of course the leadership phenomenon in its wider generic sense is itself problematic (Storey 2016). There are numerous perspectives on its nature. Leadership understood as individual practice often translates into a focus on an individual leader – indeed tending also towards the charismatic or heroic leader. This conceptualization differs from others such as 'distributed leadership', and 'organizational leadership', which may involve a more complex array of attributes (Tate 2016). This last conceptualization highlights the wider system and thus attends to organizational development elements such as identifying obstacles to the practice of leadership, whether by people in formal positions of authority or by those without formal authority (Heifetz 2006; Heifetz *et al.* 2009). In consequence of these multiple interpretations, in our research (Storey and Holti 2012) we attend to clinical leadership as a *process* and this means we are as much concerned with the organizational conditions enabling or blocking the practice of leadership as with leadership as individual performance.

The Nature of Clinical Leadership

One approach to thinking about clinical leadership is in terms of understanding the role of people commonly identified as clinical leaders. Who are these clinicians? The term includes doctors, nurses, physiotherapists, pharmacists and other qualified professionals allied to medicine. It does not therefore include everyone who happens to work in healthcare; it alludes to a specialist with training and qualifications in some aspect of patient care. The term 'clinical leader' therefore indicates that some of these qualified professionals take on an extra dimension to their expected normal clinician-to-patient role. This is the normal meaning – the practising clinician supplementing their role with 'extra-curricular' activities (beyond the call of duty). The lines can be blurred when a retired doctor who no longer practises takes on a role as a medical representative – as for example sitting as a secondary care doctor on a clinical commissioning group board.

The 'extra dimension' to the exercise of the clinical role relates to the array of performance attributes normally associated with the concept of leadership. This includes some sense of a vision of change to healthcare, a display of intent to find ways to realise the associated changes and a willingness to persuade others of the merits of these changes. This set of behaviours implies the array of characteristics often associated with leadership: courage, resilience, determination and energy. At least this is how the phenomenon is normally understood within this setting (Ham 2008b).

From the above, we can see that one distinctive feature of being a 'clinical leader' is that the actors involved have dual roles: they have their 'normal' clinical practice which usually entails day-to-day engagement with individual patients and service users but, in addition, they also engage in 'extra' duties which go beyond the clinic and extend to the imagining and urging of new, alternative processes and provision. This may include new patient pathways, new protocols and new alternative service offerings, which are likely to involve withdrawal from and even closure of existing services. Clinical leaders occupying formal positions such as medical director for a doctor or ward manager for a nurse can thus be seen as occupying a hybrid role: they are both professional practitioner and 'manager'.

Stating the nature of clinical leadership in these terms starts to indicate some of the key challenges. First, the clinical leader who is engaged in the kind of changes indicated will need to enlist support from their own professional group, which can be challenging enough; in addition they are also likely to need the support of other professional groupings outside their own specialism and profession. Hence, they will require skills in cross-boundary working. The changes being sought are likely to require shifts in practices and responsibilities. Some of these may be perceived as threatening established hierarchies, ways of doing and even professional identities. Second, clinical leaders are almost never, if ever, in clear, unambiguous authority positions; they are normally participants in a complex pattern of authorities including chief executives of health organizations, external regulators, professional bodies and national and regional authorities who ultimately control access to resources including money and also legitimacy to operate. Given this array of forces, clinical leaders require considerable political skills alongside related skills of planning, motivating and reshaping.

The contextual element – as seen most especially in the third point above – is exemplified by a consideration of how clinical leaders are invariably caught up in a web of other leaders. The typical healthcare organizational setting is characterized by diffuse power, multiple pressures and competing institutional logics. There may well be complex domains of distributed leadership throughout the organization. Indeed, even this is to simplify somewhat, because a hospital – to take just one significant type of healthcare organization – will usually have porous boundaries, which require working with associated healthcare professionals and organisations. At the top of the 'single' healthcare organizations (say a single hospital or collection of hospitals), the leadership formation is very likely to be of a collective kind.

In a series of studies of hospitals in Quebec, Jean-Louis Denis and colleagues (2001) describe and analyse what they term the 'leadership constellation'. This refers to the kind of collective leadership group they invariably found operating in these Quebec hospitals. In formal leadership terms, the typical pattern was a chief executive as appointed by a board of directors; a set of directors such as the Director of Finance, of Human Resources, of Nursing and of Professional Services (the administration sub-group); and a medical executive. These three poles together comprise an organizational leadership group. We can conceive of this as a 'dominant coalition', to use a term popularized by Cyert and March (1963). So, a key lesson to be drawn is that a notional clinical or medical leader located at the strategic apex is invariably only one player in a much more complex and pluralistic power structure.

As Denis *et al.* (2001) go on to describe, this strategic apex is itself only one player in a wider domain in which national political leaders, regional authorities, regulators and others also seek to influence the course of events. Strategic change attempts in such pluralistic settings tend to unfold in unpredictable ways as successive phases reveal creative opportunities as well as counter-movements and restrictions. The key findings from the Quebec studies offer salutary lessons about the attempted exercise of clinical leadership. First, across their cases, the only substantive change of any significance that was achieved was the formalization of a merger, and this itself, they observe, was not the result of unified leadership constellation but stemmed from the determination of a powerful government. Second, as the organizations overlapped with the environment, leaders are drawn into operating at a super-organizational field level. In this setting, leaders struggle with attempts to reconcile multiple goals and tensions; leadership processes and the associated coupling of elements are exposed as fragile. Third, their cases revealed the cyclical nature of change in these healthcare settings. They note that:

> leaders' credibility rises and falls depending on process tactics and strategic alignment with various interests, and this variation in turn affects their capacity to act in the future . . . vast amounts of energy are consumed in processes that produce tiny effects that are then over-turned or overwhelmed. The many opposing tensions to be reconciled again seem to lie behind this pattern.
>
> *(201: 832)*

Some conceptions of clinical leadership seem to assume the enactment of a traditional heroic individualistic mode of leading. The search for clinical leadership from this perspective would amount to the search for the clinical leader or leaders. From there it is a short step into analyses which seek to reveal the unique characteristics, traits, behaviours and biographies of these leaders; a well trodden route in leadership research; see the summary and critique in Storey (2011).

A significant alternative strand in the literature attends to the idea of 'distributed', 'dispersed' or 'shared leadership' (Gronn 2000, 2002; Spillane 2004). These themes are further explored in a special issue of the *International Journal of Management Reviews* (Thorpe 2011). The distributed leadership research agenda attends first to issues concerning the nature and degree of alignment between different parties to the leadership process, and second to the extent to which distributed leadership is planned or emergent (Leithwood 2007; Thorpe 2011). Drawing on this kind of perspective, Currie and Lockett (2011) assess the concept of distributed leadership in the context of health and social care. Using existing literature, they map a spectrum of variants – from individualistic leadership, through collaborative leadership (Huxham 2000), shared leadership (Pearce and Conger 2003), collective leadership (Denis *et al.* 2001), team leadership (Katzenbach 1993) and 'pure distributed leadership' (Gronn 2002). An important distinction is between distributed leadership modes, which depend on and may be sponsored by a managerial hierarchy, and forms which are more bottom up and which may challenge or bypass the hierarchy.

The phenomenon of clinical leadership can therefore also be seen as having significance in a way that is distinct from the roles of clinicians in formal leadership roles. Clinicians in general are now expected to play a role in collective or distributed leadership for improving the services they work in. For example, the UK General Medical Council includes this expectation in its conditions for registering doctors. There are also large-scale programmes in leadership and service improvement within the NHS targeted at working clinicians, whether or not they aspire to a formal leadership role. Such distributed clinical leadership can be thought of as involving individuals taking on informal leadership roles, often focussing on improving or reshaping services, above all addressing inconsistencies, problems in communication, poor patient flow and long waiting times that arise from the way that different clinical units work together in treating patients.

The rationale for service redesign typically stems from the joint clinical benefits and over-all cost savings that are promised through reworking the boundary between primary-based, community-based and acute hospital-based health services. This is argued primarily with regard to long-term conditions, such as cardiovascular disease, asthma, dementia and diabetes. The potential benefits of this approach were articulated by Feacham *et al.* (2002) who compared the acute in-patient treatment focus of the NHS with the integrated chronic care model of Kaiser Permanente in California. Ham describes the Kaiser model in terms of locating special-ists relevant to common long-term conditions within primary care clinics, combined with risk assessment of the patient population served. This provides the basis for early diagnosis and involvement of patients in life-style changes and treatment that will manage or arrest the devel-opment of more serious morbidity. The intention is to significantly reduce or even eliminate costly unplanned hospital admissions.

Numerous studies have reported the benefits of schemes to provide integrated health and social care for the elderly within community-based teams (for example, Ham 2010; KPMG 2010) and the idea underpins core schemes in the NHS with programmes such as the Pioneers, Vanguards and the Better Care Fund. Such arrangements can be thought of as offering a kind of 'horizontal integration' across established boundaries of health and social care. This comple-ments the 'vertical integration' between primary and acute care central to the Kaiser Permanente model. However, this distinction may be very hard to discern in practice.

Care pathway redesign to bring primary and acute clinicians into closer collaboration is often advocated because of its potential for saving cost, or for increasing coverage without commen-surate increase in costs. Early intervention has also been advocated by clinicians independently of government – the Royal College of Physicians has pressed for greater collaboration between specialists and general practice in 'an integrated model of care, where multi-professional teams work in a managed network across the interfaces and manage patients in a care pathway designed by local clinicians' (Royal College of Physicians 2008 p. 4). This prefigured the major initiative from NHS England and its associated national bodies with their new models of care, as outlined in the 'Five Year Forward View' (NHSE 2014; RCP 2008 p. 4).

It is useful to contrast the typical sphere of action of those engaged in informal distributed leadership to achieve improved care pathways with that of clinicians in formal leadership roles. Formal clinical leaders can be thought of as exercising leadership primarily in a vertical direc-tion, shaping and representing organizational goals to others, but needing to work skilfully with lateral relationships. Those involved in informal clinical leadership for service improvement or redesign can in contrast be thought of as working primarily with lateral influence, but needing to engage skilfully in vertical relationships with hierarchical authority.

Clinicians engaging in informal leadership may have a degree of independence from formal managerial authority, which can give them some freedom to challenge established assumptions and prevailing models for delivering care. Respected clinicians who do not have formal mana-gerial roles have licence to contemplate and instigate what Heifetz (2006) calls 'adaptive chal-lenges'. This is where existing templates and solutions have reached the end of their potential, and leadership involves 'naming' the nature of the search for new models, which usually need to be developed in collaboration between the parties involved. Such 'adaptive leadership' stresses the need for new solutions and common endeavour in finding them, rather than simply provid-ing the new template and persuading others to follow.

Recognized clinical leaders and those engaged in broader processes of informal leadership face broadly the same challenges; many of these stem not from the characteristics of the lead-ers or clinicians themselves but from the context in which they need to operate. These con-texts are often organizations described by Mintzberg (1979) as 'professional bureaucracies'.

Such organizations are inherently pluralistic: they have multiple goals and multiple power structures. The conditions described in Quebec by Denis *et al.* (2001) share many similarities with current healthcare in the UK and elsewhere. The implication is that, while much credibility attaches to those seeking to exercise clinical leadership because of their professional standing, they tend to operate in settings which are difficult to handle. These healthcare settings are complex, pluralistic, ambiguous and beset with competing objectives and competing interests. These are some of the features which represent the obstacles to clinical leadership – the theme of the next section.

Challenges and Obstacles to Clinical Leadership

As noted already, clinicians who seek or are invited to go beyond their normal clinical duties are drawn into a complex world of competing priorities and interests. Working with other professions, clinicians can be seen to enjoy some advantage. However, one of the features of professional work is a notion of professional autonomy; some clinicians seek to cleave to this in a manner which can impede clinical leadership.

Clinical leadership practice needs to maintain its legitimacy and autonomy through demonstrating accountability simultaneously in three directions: to the management of health service organisations; to a system of professional standards and expectations; and to service users. Health service redesign presents challenges for clinicians in each of these directions.

Cross-boundary service redesign tends to be in tension with existing authority structures in existing organizations such as hospitals, which have hierarchical reporting structures (Guthrie *et al.* 2010). From a more critical perspective, clinical leadership as currently advocated is in danger of making clinicians agents of the financial and consumer-driven perspectives of the new public management (Hasselbladh and Bejerot 2007) embraced by senior health service management. This suggests that those involved in clinical leadership need to weigh up different kinds of accountability: for example, accountability to patients and accountability to use public funding effectively and equitably. Arguably such tensions are an inherent ethical component of clinical leadership.

Likewise, collaborative cross-boundary initiatives may disturb professional boundaries (Abbott 1988; Friedson 2001). Processes of clinical leadership often require a process of opening up and then closing down of spheres of practice, knowledge and influence between professional groups. Different degrees of professional defensiveness or openness lead to different levels of pessimism and optimism (Hudson 2007).

Finally, accountability to service users increasingly requires engagement of patients and carers at a much earlier stage and in a sustained way. User engagement in service redesign has assumed a much larger presence in recent years. Sometimes it is more rhetorical than real but in some instances it has been significant. In general, clinical leadership now involves considering how the role of users in healthcare can be extended and how user representatives can be involved in service redesign in order to achieve this.

The stance of the professional bodies can be significant in terms of helping or hindering the productive engagement of those involved in clinical leadership with these three directions of accountability. The chair of the HSJ's commission on clinical leadership (Naylor 2015) said professional bodies 'have not supported clinicians going into leadership as much as they should have done'. He argues that that the rewards for clinicians to go into leadership were not sufficient and the downsides of failure are greater. He added: 'It's so difficult to make changes that leaders who are responsible for making these changes are disincentivised because of the sheer complexity of the processes they have to go through.' The same kind of disincentives can be applied to those who might consider taking up an informal role in leading service improvement. The issue is what recognition they will receive for doing this, in comparison to the skill and application needed to achieve results.

Part of the problem is that the size of the challenge facing would-be clinical leaders can be high. A clinician who takes on a service lead role may find themselves nominally responsible for a complex multi-million pound business. Yet the degree of associated authority is likely to be ambiguous and open to challenge to an extent rarely found in an equivalent conventional business organization. Furthermore, the incumbent will normally have received minimal if any training for the role. Finally, the time allowance is likely to be minimal – usually just a few hours per week.

In their empirical studies of clinical leadership in London and Manchester, Storey and Holti (2012) found many pitfalls awaiting the unwary. Some clinicians seeking to take up informal improvement leadership reported that their senior managers rebuffed their attempts to get involved in issues outside their normal job tasks. In other words, the hierarchal and siloed characteristic of the NHS may act as a barrier to the potential for the more distributed variant of clinical leadership. The NHS at times can act in a schizophrenic way: it can talk the talk about the importance of clinical leadership while organising itself in a manner which impedes it.

Storey and Holti (2012) found that large-scale change can be more easily achieved in some contexts than others. Informants referred to the obstacles presented by some 'large egos' and their considerable reputational power. These factors made change management more intrinsically complex in these settings – as experienced by clinical leaders as well as by project and programme managers. The more complex cases required much more leadership effort and much more project facilitation.

The cases also revealed how difficult clinical leadership can be at a personal level. Willingness to change by some clinicians and unwillingness by others prompted some fraught inter-personal relationships. Interviewees who had taken up prominent formal leadership roles talked about critical phases of change which were 'dreadful', 'horrible' and led to 'tears'. Collaboration between primary care and initiatives in the acute sector appears particularly difficult, apparently because of the pressure on primary care over the last few years and difficulties for GPs in finding the opportunity to take part in wider initiatives.

Service redesigns that involve increased *user participation* or self-management may involve some rethinking of professional boundaries, implying greater collaboration and input in decision-making from the service user, their representative or advocate. However, the tendency across the cases studied by Storey and Holti seems to be to focus on increasing accessibility of services rather than user self-management. There is a suggestion here of ingrained professional resistance to user involvement. Clinical leaders need to be aware of the possibility of threats to professional remits and attentive to the need to find new conceptions of what professionals are there to do and perhaps no longer do, and so work with finding revised 'closure' as well as 'opening up' of professional roles. Increased collaboration between medical and third sector 'care assistant' type staff, for example in mental health and dementia care, may pose particular challenges, with qualified clinicians providing initial diagnosis and periodic review but a great deal of therapeutic activity increasingly occurring through community involvement facilitated by people not conventionally recognised as 'clinicians'.

These developments in professional roles mean that *training and workforce development* are likely to be focal concerns of clinical leadership. Lack of resources for this can be a major barrier to achieving the fruits of clinical leadership for service innovation. For example nurses and healthcare assistants who are expected to take on broader roles may need both on-the-job training and some additional study and competence assessment if they are to be ready for this.

This in turn requires sufficient staffing levels to allow staff to be released for training and the timely engagement of some form of training or educational provision.

Clinical Leadership in Practice: Processes Which Seem to Work

We turn now to what has been learned about how clinical leaders and wider clinical leadership processes appear to function effectively in bringing about improvement and innovation in the delivery of healthcare. Storey and Holti (2012) found that public health rationales and national strategies played a key role in bridging the concerns of clinicians and managers involved in instigating change, and that innovating cabals of clinicians influenced others to follow. In effect, public health goals and national strategies provide a common matrix that can meld together the thinking and action of clinicians in hierarchical roles and 'lateral leaders' in senior practice roles who are oriented towards service innovation. The process of change involved renegotiations of professional spheres, as well as clinicians taking advantage of various managerial initiatives to reshape hierarchical structures and practices to support more integrated services.

Top-down inspired transformation (not the same as fully planned) can be achieved through funding trials and pioneer sites that draw in clinicians and operational level managers from different parts of the care system to design and then plan implementation (Greenhalgh *et al.* 2009). Similar processes are at play with the new models of care sponsored by NHS England (2015).

Storey and Holti (2012) suggest that a clearly articulated national strategy backed by purposeful senior management adhering to a public health rationale can be part of the recipe for kickstarting significant change. However, they also suggest that this kind of top-down approach needs to connect at an early stage with communities of activist clinicians who are interested in redesigning services rather than preserving the status quo. Sometimes, the situation appears to be best described as a managerial initiative that finds clinicians who are 'waiting to be enrolled' (Czarniawska 2009). At other times, it may be activist clinician–innovators who identify and recruit support offered by official priorities, programmes or initiatives in order to bring new service models into being.

Storey and Holti found that all this worked best when clinicians worked with managers who could offer support with technology and with the many administrative support systems required to make a new service work in practice. Likewise, local leadership worked best when it was able to tap into wider national priorities, especially if these carried funding. Local managers were inclined to support clinical initiatives when their priorities aligned with the key measures being used by regulators and higher authorities.

Studies of medical work (Levay and Waks 2009) appear to confirm that doctors can respond to the public sector drive for transparency of performance while retaining significant control over their work – above all by taking a lead within their own professional bodies for defining which performance standards should be used. So, clinical leadership in engaging with management involves being open to techniques that have previously been seen as the province of managers, such as setting performance standards and maintaining comparative records of clinic and individual performance.

This leads to the idea of periodic cycles of *opening up* of professional boundaries and subsequent *closure* on modified terms. The boundary may, for example, be drawn in terms of professionals retaining control over treatment protocols whilst agreeing with managers some explicit and detailed performance requirements for their particular service. These might include increases in the number of patients treated, coupled with reductions in particularly expensive procedures.

Fitzgerald *et al.* (2007) studied service improvements within the boundaries of established organisations and services. They concluded that, even for these circumscribed service improvements, distributed and multi-professional change leadership was necessary – clinical and managerial leaders needed to engage with each other.

We have already described how cross-boundary service redesign is likely to disturb established patterns of influence, authority and control between different kinds of clinician – hospital doctors, general practitioners, nurses, allied healthcare professionals and healthcare assistants. Inter-professional dynamics will be foregrounded and consciously negotiated. Thus, care pathway redesign and the drafting of protocols for the various clinical roles involved are practices which require clinical professionals to rework the relationship between their established spheres of influence.

However, Storey and Holti in their detailed studies of service redesign in dementia and sexual health found that renegotiation of professional roles can be turbulent and conflictual. Doctors in the innovating cabal faced some colleagues who clung tenaciously and defensively to existing conceptions of their role, drawing on arguments based on the crucial and irreplaceable nature of their professional expertise, and who were prepared to mobilize power to undermine innovative leadership. In one case, such an opposition group successfully removed one original member of the innovating cabal.

Thus, the literature points to a number of innovative ideas for redesigning services and for the potential engagement of clinicians as formal and informal leaders in such changes. These include ideas about the need for clinicians and managers to work in tandem, user-centred redesign, user involvement, the enablement of users through telemedicine, early intervention and personalisation. But, while all these ideas offer potentially useful ways to cut across traditional boundaries and to produce more effective modes of treatment, they do not attend to the practical matters which may inhibit their use. In Figure 18.1, we show the elements that we think are necessary to re-think and re-conceptualise the process of clinical leadership and what would be entailed by its realisation.

The diagram indicates that clinicians who seek to exercise leadership are involved in a multi-pronged set of social processes. The first requires some open clarifying statement on the purposes and nature of appropriate care as newly conceived. This relates to Heifetz's notion of naming a required adaptive change. The second sub-process is to secure some room for manoeuvre in bringing about such a change to existing embedded and taken-for-granted practices. The third normally means collaborating with other professionals and also supporting agents such as IT managers. The fourth sub-process entails addressing the normally intricate array of practices, which are likely to require changing in tandem. The fifth requires clarifying and establishing new sets of acceptable working roles and relationships. And the final sub-process requires locating the necessary resources to support the new redesigned service.

So what does all this indicate as to the key capabilities or skills required for those who wish to engage successfully in clinical leadership in order to bring about innovation in how healthcare is delivered?

There are of course the established models we have already referred to for thinking about leadership competencies in healthcare and more generally. These provide one kind of answer to this question. Here, we offer another, perhaps simpler, one that stems directly from the various studies we have reviewed here. We conceptualize the capabilities not in terms of individual competencies but in terms of three guiding perspectives on organizational practice that individuals need to engage with and become skilled in. Identifying these also helps cast light on instances where things appear not to work well, where clinical leadership appears not to be delivering the benefits that many have promised. We briefly describe these three crucial guiding perspectives below.

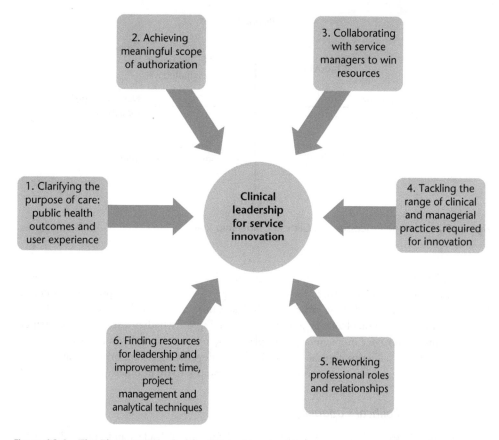

Figure 18.1 The Elements Needed for Clinical Leadership

Maintaining a Scale of Ambition for Change That Goes Beyond Improving Established Clinical Sub-units

The key issue here is that, whether working in formal leadership roles or not, clinicians need to bear in mind how healthcare could be delivered more effectively by imagining and then creating different kinds of patient journey. Failing to do so may still mean that a clinician provides excellent care for patients within the terms of the established approach. They may also be very effective at making their established clinic, ward, department or practice function well, and also manage established interfaces with other parts of the overall system of care with finesse and humanity. But a lack of ambition to move beyond established notions of what happens in particular hospital or community settings limits the sense in which clinicians can be said to provide the leadership needed to address the challenges now faced by healthcare systems.

Engaging with Both Planned and Emergent Approaches to Change

Engaging with clinical leadership seems to involve an ability to bring together top-down planned change and change that emerges from everyday clinical or professional practice. Practising clinicians driven by ambition to transform services beyond what is possible within their established sphere can effectively build links with clinical and managerial colleagues who are formally in

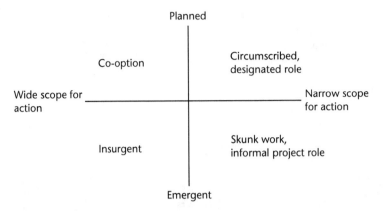

Figure 18.2   Change Processes and Clinical Leadership Roles

charge of larger-scale transformation initiatives, and vice-versa. It is tempting to see a schema such as that shown in Figure 18.2 as a static typology of kinds of change process and clinical leadership roles. We would argue rather that clinicians may find themselves initially in a leadership role in one of the quadrants or another – depending on whether a service improvement initiative appears to have a more emergent or planned genesis, and whether it is narrow or broad in scope. However, effective clinical leadership that achieves service transformation at scale will tend to involve engaging with and moving into leadership activity in other quadrants.

Demonstrating Political Capability

We have already stressed at several points the need for clinical leaders and clinical leadership more generally to negotiate complex power structures and multiple objectives. This inevitably involves the classic work and skills of organizational politics, of building alliances and using available bases of power to achieve objectives, sometimes in the face of opposition. But our own research and our reading of the work of others suggest that a key domain in which clinical leaders specifically need to demonstrate their political prowess concerns the renegotiation of professional remits and inter-professional relations. Building on these ideas, we can further differentiate certain 'modes' of clinical leadership, distinguished by the effectiveness of those involved in first challenging existing divisions of practice and then negotiating new terms of closure. The two do not necessarily go together, and it is possible to understand how setbacks to progress result when one dominates the other. In Figure 18.3, four modes of behaviour are shown. These essentially reflect the degree of skilled deployment of the behaviours we have identified as enabling clinical leadership. They also illustrate what happens when less skilled attempts are made.

The top left cell shows 'reckless' practice – these practitioners rush forward with enthusiasm and vision for the end goal, but they fail to carry their professional colleagues and they also fail to establish a sense of new professional spheres and boundaries between them. The bottom left cell denotes a closed approach in which change is neither sought nor resisted very strongly, with the result that professional autonomy may become seriously compromised when others, for example managers, seize the initiative. The top right cell combines an openness to engage in new ways with the knowledge and practices of others with an awareness that some revised form of professionalism needs to be established. The bottom right cell depicts 'defensive leadership'

Figure 18.3 Modes of Behaviour

in which there is high sensitivity to professional identity but at the expense of openness to new combinations of knowledge and ways of working.

Summary and Wider Relevance

In this chapter, we have so far sought to answer four main questions: Why is clinical leadership so strongly advocated? What is potentially distinctive about clinical leadership? What are the main obstacles to the realisation of clinical leadership? What has been learned about the effective practice of clinical leadership? We have adopted a process-based perspective with a focus on what actors do in practice and how these actions are related to context.

Clinical leadership was shown to be widely advocated. The reasons were many but the main ones related to knowledge, credibility and compliance. Clinicians are needed for their insights and their cooperation in change.

The distinctive attributes of clinical leadership were seen to be regarded as stemming from the natural advantages of credibility deriving from professional status and adherence to professional codes of ethics. This is supplemented with possession of special knowledge as a result of lengthy training and front-line experience with patients. These elements help reassure patients and public that service changes advocated by clinicians are likely to be justified in terms of quality and safety. As a corollary, clinical leaders are in a better position than managers to influence, enlist and convince their professional colleagues. When the intention is to seek integration of care, this requires a shift from clinical autonomy and individuality to a different conception of practices, which is facilitated by transparency, agreed protocols and concerted action. Here again, leadership from clinicians tends to be invaluable.

We revealed a number of different types of clinical leadership in action. We distinguished between the formal role of identified clinical leaders and wider processes of distributed clinical leadership, whilst also explaining that these two fundamental kinds of leadership generally need to work together.

The obstacles and challenges facing clinicians in leadership have been shown to be extensive and complex. If anything, they are increasingly becoming more so as expectations are raised that 'whole systems' leadership is required. Clinical leaders tend to lack training and development for this aspect of their role. They find themselves in complex leadership constellations where numerous other players exert influence: these others are found both within and without the formal organization in which the clinical leader is located. The plurality of objectives and the competing institutional logics are overlaid with extensive and complex regulatory and compliance procedures, which require extended time and huge persistence to overcome. The higher levels of leadership also expose incumbents to challenge from multiple quarters. The high vacancy rates at the most senior levels seem to reflect the vulnerabilities associated with these posts and these roles, while the scarcity which informal leaders make significant impacts also reflects the scale of the challenges facing would-be clinical leaders.

Our discussion of lessons learned about the effective practice of clinical leadership in the face of such complexity leads to the identification of three desirable perspectives that inform the practice of formal and informal leaders alike: maintaining a scale of ambition for change that goes beyond the established clinical sub-unit; bringing together planned and emergent elements of change; and demonstrating political capabilities above all in problematizing and then resolving changes to professional remits and divisions of labour.

We suggest that the lessons identified and three guiding principles are relevant to other domains of organizing characterized by high levels of professional autonomy in tension with increasing and evolving demands for some form of user participation, on the one hand, and financial pressures on the other. This is likely to be the case in many public services, such as social work, education or infrastructure provision. But these features are also arguably present in some private sector industries, such as construction and engineering. Understanding the challenges of clinical leadership may well enrich our understanding of the nature of formal and informal leadership in a range of complex, professionalized organizational settings.

References

Abbott, A. (1988). *The System of Professions: An Essay on the Division of Expert Labour*. Chicago, University of Chicago Press.

Bohmer, R. (2009). *Designing Care: Aligning the Nature and Management of Health Care*. Boston, Harvard Business School Press.

Christensen, C. M. (2009). *The Innovator's Prescription: A Disruptive Solution for Health Care*. New York, McGraw Hill.

Clark, J., P. Spurgeon and P. Hamilton (2008). 'Medical Professionalism: Leadership Competency – an Essential Ingredient'. *International Journal of Clinical Leadership* 16: 3–16.

Courpasson, D. (2000). 'Managerial Strategies of Domination: Power in Soft Bureaucracies'. *Organization Studies* 21 (1): 141–162.

Currie, G. and A. Lockett (2011) 'Distributing Leadership in Health and Social Care: Concertive, Conjoint or Collective'. *International Journal of Management Reviews*, 13, 286–300.

Cyert, R. M. and J. G. March (1963). *A Behavioural Theory of the Firm*. Englewood Cliffs, NJ, Prentice Hall.

Czarniawska, B. (2009). 'Emerging Institutions: Pyramids or Anthills?' *Organization Studies* 30 (4): 423–441.

Darzi, L. (2008). *High Quality Care for All: NHS Next Stage Review, Final Report*. London, DH.

Denis, J.-L., L. Lamothe and A. Langley (2001). 'The Dynamics of Collective Leadership and Strategic Change in Pluralistic Organizations'. *Academy of Management Journal* 44 (4): 809–837.

Department of Health (2009). *Inspiring Leaders: Leadership for Quality*. London, DH.

Faculty for Healthcare Improvement (2010). *The Journey So Far*. Cardiff, Faculty for Healthcare Improvement.

Feacham, R. G. A., N. Sekhri and K. L. White (2002). 'Getting More for Their Dollar: A Comparison of the NHS with California's Kaiser Permanente'. *British Medical Journal*, 324: 135–143.

Fitzgerald, L., E. Ferlie, R. Addicott, J. Baeza, D. Buchanan and M. Gerry (2007). 'Service Improvement in Healthcare: Understanding Change Capacity and Change Context'. *Clinician in Management* 15 (2): 61–74.

Friedson, E. (2001). *Professionalism: The Third Logic*. Cambridge, Polity Press.

Greenhalgh, T., C. Humphrey, J. Hughes, F. Macfarlane, C. Butler and R. A. Y. Pawson (2009). 'How Do You Modernize a Health Service? A Realist Evaluation of Whole-Scale Transformation in London'. *Milbank Quarterly*, 87 (2): 391–416.

Gronn, P. (2000). 'Distributed Properties: A New Architecture for Leadership'. *Educational Management Administration & Leadership* 28: 317–338.

Gronn, P. (2002). 'Distributed Leadership as a Unit of Analysis'. *Leadership Quarterly* 13: 423–451.

Guthrie, B., H. Davies and G. Greig (2010). *Delivering Healthcare Through Managed Clinical Networks (MCNs): Lessons from the North. Report for the National Institute for Health Research Service Delivery and Organisation Programme.*

Ham, C. (2008a). 'Doctors in Leadership: Learning from the International Experience'. *International Journal of Clinical Leadership*, 16: 11–16.

Ham, C. (2008b). 'Integrated NHS Care: Lessons from the Front Line'. *Briefing Paper.* 11. London, The Nuffield Trust.

Ham, C. (2010). 'Working Together for Health: Achievements and Challenges in the Kaiser NHS Beacon Sites Programme'. *Health Services Management Centre Policy Paper Number 6.* University of Birmingham.

Ham, C. and H. Dickinson (2008). 'Engaging Doctors in Leadership: What We Can Learn from International Practice and Research'. NHS Institute for Innovation and Improvement.

Hasselbladh, H. and E. Bejerot (2007). 'Webs of Knowledge and Circuits of Communication: Constructing Rationalized Agency in Swedish Health Care'. *Organization* 14 (2): 175–200.

Heifetz, R. (2006). 'Anchoring Leadership in the Work of Adaptive Progress'. In: F. Hesselbein and M. Goldsmith (eds) *The Leader of the Future: Visions, Strategies and Practices for the New Era.* New York, Jossey-Bass.

Heifetz, R., A. Grashow and M. Linsky (2009). *The Practice of Adaptive Leadership: Tools and Techniques for Changing Your Organization and Your World.* Boston, Harvard Business School Press.

Hudson, B. (2007). 'Pessimism and Optimism in Inter-professional Working: The Sedgefield Integrated Team'. *Journal of Interprofessional Care*, 21 (1): 3–15.

Huxham, C. a. V., S. (2000). 'Leadership in the Shaping and Implementation of Collaborative Agendas: How Things Happen in a Not Quite Joined Up World'. *Academy of Management Journal* 43: 1159–1175.

Katzenbach, J. R. and D. K. Smith (1993). *The Wisdom of Teams: Creating the High Performance Organization.* Boston, Harvard Business School Press.

KPMG (2010). 'A Better Pill to Swallow.' http://www.kpmg.com/Global/en/IssuesAndInsights/Articles Publications/Documents/A-better-pill-to-swallow.pdf:_KPMG International.

Leithwood, K., C. Day, P. Sammons, A. Harris and D. Hopkins (2007). *Leadership and Student Learning Outcomes.* London, DCSF.

Levay, C. and C. Waks (2009). 'Professions and the Pursuit of Transparency in Healthcare: Two Cases of Soft Autonomy'. *Organization Studies*, 30 (5): 509–527.

Mintzberg, H. (1979). *The Structuring of Organizations.* Englewood Cliffs, NJ, Prentice Hall.

Mountford, J. and C. Webb (2009). 'When Clinicians Lead'. *The McKinsey Quarterly*, February.

Nadler, D. and M. Tushman (1980). 'A Model for Diagnosing Organizational Behaviour'. *Organizational Dynamics* 9: 35–51.

Naylor, R. (2015). *Ending the Crisis in NHS Leadership: A Plan for Renewal.* London, HSJ.

NHS Institute for Innovation and Improvement Academy of Royal Colleges (2010). *Medical Leadership Competency Framework: Enhancing Engagement in Medical Leadership.* 3rd edition. London.

NHS Scotland (2009). *NHS Scotland Leadership Development Strategy: Delivering Quality Through Leadership.* Edinburgh, NHS Scotland.

NHSE (2014). *Five Year Forward View.* London, NHS England.

Northern Ireland Department of Health, Social Services and Public Safety (2009). *A Workforce Learning Strategy for Health and Social Services 2009–2014.* Belfast.

Pearce, C. L. and J. A. Conger, (2003). *Shared Leadership: Reframing the Hows and Whys of Leadership.* Thousand Oaks, CA, Sage.

Porter, M. and E. O. Teisberg (2006). *Redefining Health Care.* Boston, Harvard Business School Press.

RCP (2008). *Teams without Walls: The Value of Medical Innovation and Leadership.* Report of a Working Party of the Royal College of Physicians, the Royal College of General Practitioners and the Royal College of Paediatrics and Child Health. London, Royal College of Physicians: 1–12.

Sheaff, R., A. Rogers, S. Pickard, M. Marshall, S. Campbell, B. Sibbald, S. Halliwell and M. Roland (2003). 'A Subtle Governance: "Soft" Medical Leadership in English Primary Care'. *Sociology of Health and Illness* 25 (5): 408–428.

Spillane, J. P. and R. Halverson (2004). 'Towards a Theory of Leadership Practice: A Distributed Perspective'. *Journal of Curriculum Studies* 36 (1): 3–34.

Spurgeon, P., J. Clark and C. Ham (2011). *Medical Leadership: From the Dark Side to Centre Stage*. Oxford, Radcliffe Press.

Storey, J. (2011). *Leadership in Organizations: Current Issues and Key Trends*. London, Routledge.

Storey, J. (2016). *Leadership in Organizations: Current Issues and Key Trends*. London, Routledge.

Storey, J. and R. Holti (2012). *Possibilities and Pitfalls for Clinical Leadership in Improving Service Quality, Innovation and Productivity*. Southampton, NIHR Service Delivery and Organisation.

Tate, W. (2016) 'Linking Leadership Development with Business Needs: From Individual to Organization'. In: John Storey (ed.) *Leadership in Organizations: Current Issues and Key Trends*. London, Routledge.

Thorpe, R. (2011). 'Distributed Leadership Special Issue'. *International Journal of Management Reviews* 13 (239–328).

Woodward, F. and G. Weller (2011). 'An Action Research Study of Clinical Leadership, Engagement and Team Effectiveness in Working across Boundaries'. *Work Based Learning e-Journal* 1 (2): 80–114.

Part IV
Contextualizing Leadership

Introduction

It is a truth universally acknowledged that academic scholars, in search of a good theory, must be in want of context. It would be a rash scientist, social scientist or arts and humanities scholar who would deny this. Some may choose to largely ignore but not deny the context of leadership and focus their attention on agency. Other scholars are intensely interested either in how context shapes leadership and/or how leadership is able to sense and shape context.

But what do we mean by context and what is important in context? These questions are much harder. There are so many factors which constrain or enable leadership action and its perceived legitimacy. It is relatively easy to put one's hand into the lucky dip of assorted explanatory contextual factors and pull out those which have most resonance in a particular leadership time and place. Being predictive or comparative is much harder. Various scholars have attempted categories to help examine context – macro, meso and micro is widely used; the PESTO or EPESTO analysis (environmental, political, economic, social, technological and organizational factors) of strategic management is a useful mnemonic but can end up being a listing. However, those can emphasise current context whereas the chapters here cover these issues but also add time (history, epochs) and place (different countries and sectors). The chapters add to our understanding of when, where and to some extent how context creates both opportunities for, and constraints on, particular types of leadership or particular leadership actions to come to the fore and become accepted. Also, they help us understand how leaders 'read' and shape context. Together, they are a fascinating set of essays, empirical research and theorising, which takes leadership out of the narrow focus on 'here and now' (popular in the micro leadership as practice current fashion) and which sets leadership in its wider philosophical and intellectual landscape.

The chapter by Auer-Rizzi and Reber examines the impact of social institutions on leadership styles and explores this empirically in a longitudinal analysis of leadership styles across four countries. Each of the four countries was profoundly affected by the Second World War but the consequences of the macro-institutional arrangements were different and the correlates of this can be tracked in studies of leadership style. Germany and Austria lost the war and were fundamentally restructured politically and economically in order to weaken autocracy and strengthen democracy in society and in business organizations. This can be tracked in measures of leadership culture. On the other hand, the Czech Republic and Poland experienced different major changes (new borders and under the control of autocratic Russia). Again, the correlates can be seen in leadership styles. The data in this chapter are mainly about individual leaders and managers but set in epochal time spans, and aiming to incorporate elements of context at the institutional, organizational, group and individual level.

Kellerman continues the investigation of leadership context through recent epochal time in her examination of political leadership in Russia in particular but also the USA. She cogently argues that leadership needs to be seen as a system – of leaders, followers and context – and she examines each component of this system and also their interactions. She illustrates how there is a shift in the balance of power between leaders and followers that needs to be explained in contextual, not just interactional, terms. She uses history, ideology, politics and the economy to show the role not only of leaders but also of followers. She reminds us that hardly anyone saw two major contextual shifts which are still playing out in the world: the collapse of the Soviet Union in 1991 and the collapse of oil prices in 2014. It is a reminder that contextual factors which influence the leadership system are far from predictable.

The part then turns to examine leadership in particular 'sectors' – first leadership in the context of religion and religious studies, and second in the context of the recent global financial crisis. Spoelstra brings fascinating insights and reflections by examining the extent to which leadership study relies on religious concepts and ideas, though not often explicitly. Charisma, spiritual leadership, servant leadership all remind us of the religious roots of concepts in leadership studies. Even hierarchy has a religious etymological base. However, he argues that too often leadership scholars have used religious ideas as metaphors only and have repressed the spiritual or religious element of leadership. He shows how religion provides a binding, or bridging, between the ordinary and the extraordinary, the mundane and the spiritual and that is partly what leadership achieves in organizational settings. This chapter reminds us of the richness of insight coming from outside the 'mundane' management field.

The chapter by Knights is a close analysis of leadership processes in one particular context, that of the financial services sector and the events and influences which led up to the global financial crisis of 2008 and its aftermath. Knights examines both agency and context as relevant and intertwined explanations – the 'greedy bankers and bonus mania' versus 'the neoliberal nightmare of deregulation and financialisation'. He shows the need to add two further themes in explanation: that of the ethics of leadership, which, he argues, needs to be embodied and human, not disembodied in rules or consequences; and the need to understand the construction and maintenance of masculine identities which drove the attempts to achieve the largest salaries and the biggest bonuses and which created a masculine mono-culture in banking and finance. Knights argues for greater awareness of ethics and a more socially diverse set of leaders and institutions as a way forward.

Bird, Mendenhall, Osland, Oddou and Reiche tackle the question of global leadership and ask whether global leadership represents a unique context in which 'traditional' leadership competencies and processes can be observed or whether this is a new phenomenon which requires a new conceptualization of leadership. Overall, they lean towards the latter perspective and in this sense they decontextualize leadership within or across particular countries and cultures but instead aim to take an overarching view of what competencies and experiences most prepare leaders to take up global leadership positions. Their overview of this field helpfully maps this new domain. The influence of local context still comes across in some insights from the field – for example that an extended period of expatriate assignment (in whatever country) helps prepare the leader for global leadership by shifting mental scheme and cognitive functioning. Also, it is interesting that the predictors of high performance in-country are not necessarily the same as those for working out of country. This suggests that context still matters.

The chapter by Bloom and Rhodes examines 'the new business of political leadership' and shows how the wider cultural and political economy context of neo-liberalism is changing both leaders' and citizens' conceptions of what makes an effective political leader. They show how, across a number of countries, corporate leaders are laying claim to having the skills, experiences and outlook to run countries in the way that they have run companies. The authors examine the underlying ideological values in neoliberalism, which concern transferring power and resources from the public to the private. The mirroring of this in conceptions of ideal candidates for high political office is carefully charted. They show that there has been a shift from the ideal political leader combining populism (attuned to the citizen) and forward thinking (leading the citizenry) towards a focus on a political leader who can rally financial and economic markets and sustain economic growth. The CEO political leader shifts the focus from serving citizens to serving the market and the role of citizens themselves to being shareholder citizens. They finish the chapter by suggesting some opportunities to challenge this state of affairs as well as recognize it.

19

How Does Institution Matter?

Leadership Behaviour in Eastern and Western Europe

Werner Auer-Rizzi and Gerhard Reber

Leadership behaviour (by which we mean both the work of leaders and followers) is often characterized as a simple outcome of individual volition and choice of style. But patterns of behaviour at societal level suggest that other forces are at play. In this chapter we use a range of data to inquire into the nature and impact of these higher-level forces.

When remembering history classes in high school, we will recall heroes who were able to lead mankind. Many examples come to mind, starting from Alexander the Great to Eisenhower and Gorbachev. Perhaps Darwin was mentioned in the area of natural sciences with his idea that changes in the environment selected animals and human beings for survival. The life of those who could not adjust to situational changes came to an end. Both approaches can be found in organizational/leadership theories, with the latter known as "social Darwinism" or "social ecology theory" (Hannan and Freeman, 1977; Singh, 1990), the "path dependency approach" (Ackermann, 2001; Schreyögg and Sydow, 2011) or "quantum approach" (Miller and Friesen, 1984). This leads to the question: "Do leaders move the world or are they moved by the environment?" (Reber, 1995; Auer-Rizzi and Reber, 2013).

The end of the Second World War and the revolutions in Eastern Europe were tremendous changes which now give us the opportunity to investigate the role of leadership within these time spans. For this examination, serious theories and empirical studies are available, for example the pioneering work by Geert Hofstede (1980) and the GLOBE project initiated by Robert J. House (House *et al.*, 2004). Also the Vroom/Yetton model of leadership behaviour (Vroom and Yetton, 1973) was applied by Jago *et al.* (1986) for cross-cultural comparisons in which a high correlation between Hofstede's power distance indicator and the "mean level of participation" was demonstrated. Smith and Peterson enriched the field of comparative cross-cultural leadership behaviour by using their event management method. Szabo (2007) used all three approaches in her investigation of participation in selected European countries and also added qualitative methods.

All these approaches are based on the work of Fred Fiedler's (1967) "contingency approach" as "situational leadership" theories and are accompanied by considerable theoretical and methodological controversies (Vroom and Jago, 2007), especially concerning the different levels of influential consequences.

According to Douglas North (1990), change and adaption to situational demands can happen on the institutional, the organizational and the individual level, and these also influence each other:

> Institutions are the rules of the game in a society or, more formally, are the humanly devised constraints that shape human interaction. In consequence they structure incentives in human exchange, whether political, social, or economic. Institutional change shapes the way societies evolve through time and hence is the key to understanding historic change.
>
> *(North, 1990: 3)*

North defines "formal" and "informal" elements as institutions: formal ones are constitutions, laws and contracts; informal ones are social norms and beliefs, conventions and codes of conduct:

> Organizations include political bodies (political parties, the Senate, a city council, a regulatory agency), economic bodies (firms, trade unions, family farms, cooperatives), social bodies (churches, clubs, athletic associations) and educational bodies (schools, universities, vocational training centres). They are groups of individuals bound by some common purpose to achieve objectives. Modelling organizations is analysing governance structures, skills, and how learning by doing will determine the organization's success over time. Both, what organizations come into existence and how they evolve are fundamentally influenced by the institutional framework. In turn they influence how the institutional framework evolves.
>
> *(North, 1990: 5)*

According to North (1996: 3), individual "[l]earning . . . is a cumulative process of cultural conditioning in which the experiences of each generation are filtered through the existing belief system and result in its incremental modification". The definitions demonstrate the existence of inertia within the different cultures and the path dependency in the development of historic cultures. Furthermore, North notes the degree of stability between the elements of his framework:

> [T]he fundamental source of change is learning by entrepreneurs of organizations. . . . Change is typically incremental, reflecting ongoing ubiquitous evolving perceptions of the entrepreneurs of organizations in the context of an institutional matrix that is characterized by network externalities, complementarities and economies of scope among the existing organizations. Moreover since the organizations owe their existence to the institutional matrix, they will be an ongoing interest group to assure the perpetuation of that institutional structure – thus assuring path dependence. Revolutions do occur, however, when organizations with different interests emerge (typically as a result of dissatisfaction with the performance of existing organizations) and the fundamental conflict between organizations over institutional change cannot be mediated within the existing institutional framework. Path dependence means that history matters; that the choices we make today and tomorrow are constrained by the past evolution of the belief systems and institutions of the society.
>
> *(North, 1996: 10f)*

All the empirical data of the above-mentioned studies about intercultural differences in leadership behaviour are conducted at the individual level or, as an exception, at the group level (in the case of Fiedler's contingency model). Nevertheless, the empirical data reflect the influence of the institutional and organizational development in the different studies. This data is provided by Hofstede (116,000 questionnaires in 72 countries within the IBM company in the first edition of *Culture Consequences* in 1980 and 140 other studies in 5 to 39 companies in the second edition in 2001). The GLOBE project includes data from 17,000 middle managers collected by 170 scholars in 62 cultures. Both empirical studies use the same classical quantitative instruments. In spite of this, the interpretation of the results led to controversial discussions between the authors and within the community of researchers in the field. Smith (2006) tried to cool down this conflict and points out the positive value of both studies, which can later be used in the presentation of the data. One limitation is that the Czech Republic is not included in the GLOBE project. As far as Poland is concerned, J. Macynski can provide data based on the GLOBE project (very recent) and the Vroom/Yetton model.

The extension of the Vroom/Yetton model into the intercultural arena was initiated by Arthur Jago, and we can deliver data for both countries and, for the purpose of comparison, also from Austria and Germany. The Vroom/Yetton model is based on the provision of learning for leaders. It follows the concept of bounded rationality (Simon, 1960) and the "close-to-action" concept of Locke and Latham (1990). The empirical instrument is unique in providing 30 cases to stimulate responses of active leaders. Based on this concept, empirical data is available from managers in the Czech Republic and Poland and will be compared with the reactions of managers in Austria and Germany. The research of Smith and Peterson (1988) and Szabo (2007) also provides relevant quantitative and qualitative data.

The extension of the theoretical and empirical research about the effectiveness of participation leads to the simple insight that participation has to be connected to other qualities in order to achieve positive results (French *et al.*, 1960; Locke and Schwaiger, 1979; Miller and Monge, 1986). To demonstrate this, Vroom and Yetton (1973) based their model on Maier's (1955) differentiation between quality and acceptance. They combined both terms in the formula: Organizational Effectiveness (OE) is a function of Quality (Q) multiplied by Acceptance (A) (OE = f(Q x A)). According to this formula, participants have to understand and accept the goals of the organization and provide qualified contributions. With a value of zero for one of the two variables, participation does not lead to organizational effectiveness at all. The GLOBE study defines participative leadership as "the degree to which managers involve others in making and implementing decisions" (House and Javidan, 2004, p. 14).

Empirical Findings

There are several empirical cross-cultural studies, which show significant differences between Western and Eastern European countries. Table 19.1 shows the results of some of these studies, which include dimensions referring to participation in leadership decision making. They all point to the preference of Polish and Czech managers for more autocratic leadership styles, in contrast to Austrian and German managers, who would rather have a participative approach.

In Hofstede's classical study (1980), Austria and Germany score significantly lower on the power distance dimension than Poland and the Czech Republic. Hofstede defines power distance as the degree to which members in a society expect power to be unequally shared among its members. High power distance is a synonym for autocratic and paternalistic decision making with subordinates not disagreeing with their bosses, whereas low power distance stands for employees expecting to be included in the decision-making process.

In the GLOBE study, House *et al.* (2004) included a modified version of the power distance indicator for societal culture and also differentiated between societal practices ("as is") and values ("as should be"). All in all, the GLOBE findings – although less pronounced – point in the same direction. House *et al.* (2004) also tried to shed some light on the question of which leadership attributes/behaviours are culture bound, with one of them being "participative leadership".

Table 19.1 Leadership Studies

Study and dimension		Scale	Austria	Germany	Czech Republic	Poland	Russia
Hofstede[1]	Power Distance	0–100	11	35	57	68	93
GLOBE[2]	Power Distance Societal Practice	1–7	4.95	5.25		5.1	5.52
GLOBE[2]	Power Distance Societal Values	1–7	2.44	2.54		3.12	2.62
GLOBE[2]	Leadership: Participative	1–7	6	5.7		5.04	4.67
Vroom Yetton Model[3]	Mean Level of Participation	0–10	5.33	5.4	4.29	4.47	4.19

Source:
[1] Hofstede (1980, 2001)
[2] House *et al.* (2004)
[3] Reber *et al.* (2000), data for Russia: Kaltenbrunner (2010)

The results for this dimension show a consistent picture, with Austria and Germany preferring leaders who practise more participative behaviour than their Polish counterparts. As already mentioned, GLOBE data is not available for the Czech Republic; hence no conclusion can be reached concerning its results. Based on the GLOBE study, Bakacsi *et al.* (2002) confirm the tendency for less participative leadership for the whole Eastern European cluster.

Moreover, as a result of their event management study, Smith *et al.* (2000, p. 317) also conclude that subordinates in Central/Eastern European countries are considered as a source of guidance for handling events to a lesser extent than other sources.

In a cross-cultural comparison including seven European countries employing the Vroom/Yetton model, Reber *et al.* (2000) also show that Austrian and German managers use more participative leadership styles than Czech and Polish managers.

In a longitudinal analysis of the data in six countries on preferred leadership behaviours (autocratic, consultative, group oriented), Reber and Jago (1997) – using the Vroom/Yetton model for data collection – found that leadership behaviour has been highly stable over time. Table 19.2 shows the development of the mean level of participation in Austria, Germany, the Czech Republic and Poland over time, based on a continuing data collection. It can be seen that in Austria and Germany it was stable until 2000. The mean participation then dropped and subsequently remained at this lower level. Auer-Rizzi *et al.* (2005) and Auer-Rizzi and Reber (2007) made an attempt to interpret these changes in leadership behaviour in Austria and Germany but could only speculate that it had to do with a slight deterioration in the social partnership/co-determination model and globalization tendencies in both countries.

In the case of the Czech Republic, the mean level of participation did not change from 1991 to 1996 (Reber and Jago, 1997). Auer-Rizzi and Reber (2013) confirmed this finding with yearly data ranging from 1991 to 2011.

Jago *et al.* (1996) demonstrate in their study, which compared leadership styles of Polish managers before and after the fall of communism, that although there was a slight incremental change toward greater subordinate consultation on a one-on-one basis, the mean level of participation remained constant at a low level. They conclude that "[d]ata collected from 146 managers in 1988 and 253 managers in 1993 and 1994 reveal managerial practices to remain relatively autocratic" (p. 107). Maczynski *et al.* (2010) conducted a longitudinal analysis based on the GLOBE

Table 19.2 Leadership Behaviours

Period	85–90	91–95	96–00	01–05	06–10	11–13	ANOVA F-Value
Austrian Manager[1] n =	1016	927	1168	935	480	206	
Mean Level of Participation (MLP)	5.39 c	5.29 c	5.28 c	5.04 b	4.80 a	4.73 a	27,31***
% Violations Quality Rules (R1–3)	16.09	15.85	15.47	16.05	16.11	15.39	n.s.
% Violations Acceptance Rules (R4–7)	31.37 a	31.85 a	30.56 a	33.95 b	35.19 b	39.04 c	17,18***
German Manager[1] n =		361	328	397	423	154	
Mean Level of Participation (MLP)		5.42 c	5.28 c	5.07 b	4.81 b	4.82 a	17,68***
% Violations Quality Rules (R1–3)		14.92	14.74	14.79	15.50	15.39	n.s.
% Violations Acceptance Rules (R4–7)		29.53 a	32.38 a	35.29 b	37.11 c	36.86 c	15,69***
Czech Manager[2] n =		370	188	328	259	54	
Mean Level of Participation (MLP)		4.25	4.39	4.30	4.22	3.97	n.s.
% Violations Quality Rules (R1–3)		18.15	18.24	17.23	18.16	20.25	n.s.
% Violations Acceptance Rules (R4–7)		44.40	45.67	47.23	48.59	50.62	4,11**
Polish Manager[3] n =	146	253					
Mean Level of Participation (MLP)	4.40	4.51					n.s.
% Violations Quality Rules (R1–3)	22.19	21.34					n.s.
% Violations Acceptance Rules (R4–7)	48.37	48.37					n.s.

* $p < 0.05$ ** $p < 0.01$ *** $p < 0.001$; the periods with the same superscript do not differ significantly from each other

Source:
[1] data recalculated from 1985–2013 based on Auer-Rizzi and Reber (2007) – new data from 2006–2013 not yet published
[2] data recalculated from 1990–2013 based on Auer-Rizzi and Reber (2013) – new data from 2012–2013 not yet published
[3] Jago et al. (1996)

dimensions and compared data from Polish managers from the original study in 1996–1997 and a replication in 2008–2009. They found that the power distance indicator even increased as well as the value for autocratic orientation and conclude:

> that the introduction of a market economy in Poland has shown little effects so far on the leadership behaviour of Polish managers. It would mean that profound changes in political, social, economic and institutional systems are not sufficient (satisfactory) factors that would modify organizational values and subsequent attitudes and behaviours. It means that deep changes in the mentality of people are needed to make necessary, beneficial changes in the cultural values and subsequent (succeeding) attitudes and behaviours.
>
> *(Maczynski et al., 2010, p. 131)*

Interpretation

Based on the data, we can differentiate the influence of institutions, organizations, groups and individuals. The influence of the institutional level is obvious in the case of Germany and Austria. These nations lost the Second World War and their inner structure was completely destroyed. They were forced to find a new way, and the political and economic power groups came to the insight that only cooperation could reunite their country. This worked with the help of the Marshall plan. In Germany, the introduction of co-determination in the mining and steel industry at the request of the Allies under the leadership of Great Britain had the consequence that, in the supervisory boards of those companies, both the capital and labour side had parity of seats. The idea of co-determination was then transferred to the whole economy, but with the reduction to one third of the employee seats on the supervisory board. These institutional changes had consequences at the organizational level of the firms but also at the organizational level of the social and economic systems, beginning with labour relations, the social security system, etc.

In Austria, based on the extremely weak economy, completely new institutions had to be built. Immediately after the end of the war, the two big parties (social democrats and conservatives) worked on a system of social partnership.

> It was in 1956 that institutions of social partnership were finally established in Austria, though without any legal foundation, neither for the panels nor for the procedures which were chosen. The whole system was working and, to the extent it has persisted – is still working exclusively on the basis of the consensus reached by the parties concerned. For the panels, equal representation of employers and employees was ensured. For the wage earners representatives of the Austrian Trade Union Association and the Federal Chamber of Labour were nominated, and for the employers representatives on the Federal Economic chamber and the Chamber of Agriculture of Austria were appointed. Until the early 90s of the past century, the Federation of Austrian Industries, the most important organization of private entrepreneurs, had virtually the status of an expert organization on the employers' side.
>
> *(Preinfalk, 2010, p. 9)*

The social partnership in Austria penetrated all areas of social and economic interactions, including having a strong anchor in organizations.

We can hypothesize that these changes in the institutional and organizational levels over time are mirrored in the individual leadership behaviour of managers, which explains the relatively high mean level of participation in both countries. The first indications that the partnership system is on the way to change are based on the internationalization of the economy and the establishment of the European Union. Subsequently, Austria and Germany were confronted with a majority of members who did not incorporate the Austrian/German form of social partnership and co-determination. This became very obvious with the introduction of the European Company (Societas Europaea). Although the door for co-determination and employee participation is open in this corporate form, Casey *et al.* (2015, p. 1) conclude that "the utilization of this corporate form by labour and management actors is in general underdeveloped".

Preinfalk (2010) argues that the power of the employers has steadily increased and that the trade unions are trapped in a complicated and conflicting process of adapting their organization to the changed economic and social structure. In Germany, Matzig (2005) provides clues that the "consensus society" is endangered by severe fights about the distribution of wealth. This tendency was not so obvious during the time of recession of 2013–2014, but after the recovery in 2015 the number of severe strikes in several sectors in Germany has increased. We can conclude that the decrease of participation shown in our empirical studies seems to be a reaction to the institutional and organizational change.

The Czech Republic and Poland experienced a very different path after the Second World War. They were reconstructed based on the agreement of Jalta, in which the four allies realigned the borders of Europe. Both countries got new borders and were incorporated into the Soviet Empire with its autocratic leadership style. They regained their independence only after 1989 and were then able to erect a democratic system. But this institutional change seems not to have changed the individual leadership behaviour of the managers. Objectively, they did not have the same political and social disaster as those countries on the losing side of the Second World War. Therefore, they did not have the necessity to alter their behaviour within organizations as radically as managers had in Austria and Germany. It appears that they need more time to get rid of the traditions of their former Russian dominators.

Nevertheless, there are signs of the existence of change processes. Our data in the Czech Republic points to a very interesting development at the level of an organizational change process. Within Skoda, a special matrix-structure called "Tandem" was implemented at the organizational and group level in order to facilitate the integration process after the takeover by Volkswagen. A Czech *and* a German (expatriate) manager were appointed to each important hierarchical position from the management board downwards, and each person in the tandem had the same formal power and responsibility. Only on the agreement of both partners could a decision be considered as finalized; without agreement both got into trouble. As the company takeover was completed in a very short period (Dorow/Varga von Kibed 1997, 2006), the managers of both nationalities were ill prepared for tasks and duties of this nature. The tandem's challenging mission was accompanied by numerous conflicts, as there was not much trust and acceptance, due to the negative historical prejudices concerning relations between Czechs and Germans, as well as a long tradition of pride in both companies. Skoda, in particular, was and is a company with a long history and a high reputation in the Czech Republic. The tandem model was discontinued as soon as the integration process had become successful and the partners in the model had learned to cooperate with each other. Despite the higher labour cost – especially in the integration phase – compared to any other VW plant worldwide, the new generation of Skoda vehicles proved to be very profitable and the Skoda subsidiary became a well-respected unit within the Volkswagen corporation.

The tandem model provided a specific situation, where "social support" for learning was included in the form of "forced compliance". Auer-Rizzi and Reber (2013) compared Czech

Table 19.3 Czech and German Managers

	Czech manager	Skoda manager	German manager	ANOVA F-Value
Mean Level of Participation (MLP)	4.30	4.90	5.35	15,7***
% Violations Quality Rules (R1–3)	17.80	15.40	14.80	4,5*
% Violations Acceptance Rules (R4–7)	45.70	43.00	30.90	n.s.

* $p < 0,05$ ** = $p < 0,01$ *** $p < 0,001$

Skoda managers (a generation of managers from after the point at which the tandem model was discontinued) with Czech managers from other companies and German managers. The data for the other organizations was collected as a preparation for executive training at the executive programme of the Prague University of Economics. The results in Table 19.3 show that the mean level of participation of the Skoda managers was significantly higher than that of managers in other organizations in the country and was right in the middle between German and (other) Czech managers.

The development of the four countries seems to demonstrate that the situational variables can lead to fast dramatic changes – for example, the disaster of the Second World War – or need time for learning and adjustment. They can markedly change the societies in a short-term period, but can also be started at the organizational and group level, as in the case of Skoda.

The institutional changes after the Second World War led to organizational changes. In Austria this initiative was based on the reordering of social and economic partnership, which was originated by the political powers of Austria and tolerated by the Allies. In Germany, the initial "coaching" by the Western Allies at the institutional level was later implemented within the democratic constitution at the organizational level. In the Czech Republic and in Poland there were serious institutional changes after the revolutions; however, the political powers were not able to effectively implement support at the organizational level. In the Czech Republic, this became especially apparent through the failed policy of voucher privatization (Kost, 1994). In Poland, organizational impact did not happen until the country joined the European Union, and has not (yet) manifested at the individual level.

Does institution matter for leadership behaviour? We can answer this question with yes. However, to change arrangements at the institutional level only is not enough. In the ideas of North (1990), all the situational forces have to be integrated, from institution to organization to charismatic leaders (entrepreneurs) finding acceptance to initiate and implement change.

References

Ackermann, R. (2001). *Pfadabhängigkeit, Institutionen und Regelformen*. Tübingen: Mohr Siebeck.

Auer-Rizzi, W. and Reber, G. (2007). "Zusammenhang zwischen Corporate Governance Strukturen und Führungsverhalten – Empirische Befunde und Erklärungsansätze". In U. Jürgens, G. F. Schuppert, D. Sadowski and M. Weiss (eds), *Perspektiven der Corporate Governance*, Baden-Baden: Nomos, pp. 182–206.

Auer-Rizzi, W. and Reber, G. (2013). "Leadership Styles: Inertia and Changes in the Czech Republic". *Journal for East European Management Studies*, 18 (1): 9–35.

Auer-Rizzi, W., Reber, G. and Szabo, E. (2005). "Governance-Strukturen und Führungsverhalten: Symptome von Entsolidarisierung in Deutschland und Österreich". *Industrielle Beziehungen*, 12 (3): 231–251.

Bakacsi, G., Takács, S., Karácsonyi, A. and Viktor, I. (2002). "Eastern European Cluster: Tradition and Transition". *Journal of World Business*, 37 (1): 69–80.

Casey, C., Fiedler, A. and Fath, B. (2016). "The European Company (SE): Power and Participation in the Multinational Corporation". *European Journal of Industrial Relations*, 22 (1), 73–90.

Dorow, W. and Varga von Kibed, G. (1997). "Market Entry in Eastern Europe as a Challenge for Expatriates – Case Study: The Volkswagen-Skoda Joint Venture in the Czech Republic". In: D. Wagner (ed.), *Bewältigung des ökonomischen Wandels*, München: Mering, pp. 208–216.

Dorow, W. and Varga von Kibed, G. (2006). "Transformation von Unternehmenskulturen im Spannungsfeld west-europäischer Wertedifferenzen: Zwei Fallbeispiele für Lösungsansätze deutscher Konzerngesellschaften". In T. Beichelt, B. Choluj, G. C. Robe, H.-J. Wagner and T. Lange (eds.), *Europa-Studien: Eine Einführung*, Wiesbaden: VS Verlag für Sozialwissenschaften, pp. 415–432.

Fiedler, F. E. (1967). *A Theory of Leadership Effectiveness*. New York: McGraw-Hill.

French, J. R. P, Israel, J. and As, D. (1960). "An Experiment in Participation in a Norwegian Factory". *Human Relations*, 13 (1): 3–19.

Hannan, M. T. and Freeman, J. (1977). "The Population Ecology of Organizations". *American Journal of Sociology*, 82 (5): 929–964.

Hofstede, G. (1980). *Culture's Consequences: International Differences in Work-Related Values*. Beverly Hills, CA: Sage Publications.

Hofstede, G. (2001). *Culture's Consequences: Comparing Values, Behaviors, Institutions, and Organizations across Nations*. Second edition, Thousand Oaks, CA: Sage Publications.

House, R. J. and Javidan, M. (2004). "Overview of GLOBE". In R. J. House, P. L. Hanges, M. Javidan, P. W. Dorfman and V. Gupta (eds.), *Culture, Leadership, and Organizations: The GLOBE Study of 62 Societies*, Thousand Oaks, CA: Sage, pp. 9–22.

House, R. J., Hanges, P. J., Javidan, M., Dorfman, P. W. and Gupta, V. (eds.) (2004). *Culture, Leadership, and Organizations: The GLOBE Study of 62 Societies*. Thousand Oaks, CA: Sage Publications.

Jago, A. G., Reber, G. and Böhnisch, W. (1986). *"Power Distance" Predictions of Austrian, Mexican, and US Leadership Styles*. Paper presented at the 18th Annual Meeting of the Decision Science Institute, Honolulu.

Jago, A. G., Maczynski, J. and Reber, G. (1996). "Evolving Leadership Styles? A Comparison of Polish Managers Before and After Market Economy Reforms". *Polish Psychological Bulletin*, 27 (2): 107–115.

Kost, M. (1994). *Analyse der Industrieprivatisierung in Polen, Ungarn und der CSFR*. Frankfurt am Main: Peter Lang.

Locke, E. A. and Latham, G. P. (1990). "Work Motivation: The High Performance Cycle". In U. Kleinbeck, H. Quast, H. Thierry and H. Häcker, (eds.), *Work Motivation*, Hillsdale, NJ: Lawrence Erlbaum, pp. 3–25.

Locke, E. A. and Schweiger, D. M. (1979). "Participation in Decision Making: One More Look". In B. Staw (ed.), *Research in Organizational Behaviour* (vol. 1, 265–339). Greenwich, CT: JAI Press.

Maczynski, J., Lobodzinski, A., Wyspianski, D. and Kwiatkowski, P. (2010). "Differences on Organizational Practices and Preferred Leader Attributes between Polish Managers Investigated in 1996/1997 and 2008/2009". *Polish Psychological Bulletin*, 41 (4): 127–132.

Maier, N. R. F. (1955). "Psychology in Industry". Second edition, Boston, MA: Houghton Mifflin.

Matzig, G. (ed.) (2005). "Der große Graben: Das Ende der Konsensgesellschaft". München: Süddeutsche Zeitung.

Miller, D. and Friesen, P. H. (1984). *Organizations: A Quantum View*. Englewood Cliffs, NJ: Prentice-Hall.

Miller, K. and Monge, P. R. (1986). "Participation, Satisfaction, and Productivity: A Meta-analytic Review". *Academy of Management Journal*, 29 (4): 727–753.

North, D. C. (1990). *Institutions, Institutional Change and Economic Performance*. Cambridge: Cambridge University Press.

North, D. C. (1996). *Institutions, Organizations and Market Competition*. Working Paper, EconWPA – Economic History, Nr. 9612005, URL: http://129.3.20.41/eps/eh/papers/9612/9612005.pdf.

Preinfalk, H. (2010). "Aspects of Social Partnership in Austria". *WISO Wirtschafts- und Sozialpolitische Zeitschrift*, 33 (Sonderheft): 5–19.

Reber, G. (1995). "Führung: Bewegt sie oder wird sie bewegt? Antworten auf die Frage auf der Grundlage der Evaluierung von Wirkungen von Führungstrainings". In R. Wunderer (ed.), *Betriebswirtschaftslehre als Management- und Führungslehre*. Third edition, Stuttgart: Schäffer-Poeschel, pp. 395–415.

Reber, G. and Jago A. G. (1997). "Festgemauert in der Erde . . . Eine Studie zur Veränderung oder Stabilität des Führungsverhaltens von Managern in Deutschland, Frankreich, Österreich, Polen, Tschechien und der Schweiz zwischen 1989 und 1996". In R. Klimecki and A. Remer (eds.), *Personal als Strategie: Mit flexiblen und lernbereiten Human-Ressourcen Kernkompetenzen aufbauen*, Bern: Haupt, pp. 158–184.

Reber, G., Jago, A. G., Auer-Rizzi, W. and Szabo, E. (2000). "Führungsstile in sieben Ländern Europas: Ein interkultureller Vergleich". In E. Regnet and L. M. Hofmann (eds.), *Personalmanagement in Europa*, Göttingen: Verlag für Angewandte Psychologie, pp. 154–173.

Schreyögg, G. and Sydow, J. (2011). "Organizational Path Dependence: A Process View". *Organization Studies*, 32 (3): 321–335.

Simon, H. A. (1960). *The New Science of Management-Decision*. New York: Harper.

Singh, J. V. (1990). *Organizational Evolution*. Newbury Park: Sage.

Smith, P. B. (2006). "When Elephants Fight, the Grass Gets Trampled: The GLOBE and Hofstede Projects". *Journal of International Business Studies*, 37 (6): 916–921.

Smith, P. B. and Peterson M. F. (1988). *Leadership, Organizations and Culture*. London: Sage.

Smith, P. B., Kruzela, P., Groblewska, B., Halasova, D., Pop, D., Czegledi, R. and Tsvetanova, S. (2000). "Effective Ways of Handling Work Events in Central and Eastern Europe". *Social Science Information*, 39 (2): 317–333.

Szabo, E. (2007). *Participative Management and Culture: A Qualitative and Integrative Study in Five European Countries*. Frankfurt am Main: Peter Lang.

Vroom, V. H. and Jago, A. G. (2007). "The Role of the Situation in Leadership". *American Psychologist*, 62 (1): 17–24.

Vroom, V. H. and Yetton, P. W. (1973). "Leadership and Decision Making". Chicago: University of Pittsburgh Press.

20

Consequences of Context

Political Leadership and Followership

Barbara Kellerman

This chapter explores aspects of political leadership through a close analysis of leadership and followership in two large countries, both prominent on the world stage. Its focus is upon the importance of context and the role of followership.

There have been very visible changes in leadership and followership during the past quarter century, since the fall of the Wall, the collapse of the Soviet Union, and the decline if not the demise of Communism in Europe. During part of this period, there was increasing *conver-*gence between democracies and autocracies; and yet during part of this period there was also increasing *divergence*. This chapter will explore this apparent contradiction by taking a *systemic* approach to leadership. Specifically, three different variables – leaders, followers, and context – will be discussed in order to explore leadership and change in the United States and Russia, both countries that during the four-and-a-half decades (1945–1990) subsequent to the Second World War, dominated what for the duration was a bipolar world.

Key to this discussion is context, especially, here, as it pertains to Russia. Some leadership experts confirm the importance of context, but most do so only in passing. Context remains by and large a stepchild in Leadership Studies, second not only obviously to leaders, but lately even to followers, who increasingly are considered components of change. Context, though, remains widely ignored, its impact on leadership and followership widely underestimated and in consequence widely underappreciated. It is one of the reasons we fail even to distinguish among the different sorts of contexts, for example, context *within*, as in, say, a particular company, and context *without*, as in, say, the particular industry within which the company is located.

The systemic approach, which I have come to consider *sine qua non*, implies that changes in leadership and followership – or, for that matter, the lack of such changes – are contingent on context. Thus, leadership and followership in the United States must be viewed in the democratic context that constitutes the framework for American history and ideology. Similarly, leadership and followership in Russia must be viewed in the autocratic context that constitutes the framework for Russian history and ideology. This is, not incidentally, another way of saying that, whatever the challenges facing American leaders since 1990, in important ways they are similar to those facing leaders of other democracies, say, France and Brazil. And, whatever the challenges facing Russian leaders since 1990, in important ways they are similar to those facing leaders of other autocracies, say, China and Egypt.

To understand the trajectory of convergence and divergence between the United States and Russia during the last quarter century, it is not, therefore, sufficient to fixate on any single leader, even on so dominant a figure as Vladimir Putin, who for going on two decades has been Russia's undisputed lord and master. Followers equally are variables, independent variables, as are the contexts within which leaders and followers in the United States and Russia are located. I address each in turn, beginning with followers or, perhaps more precisely, with whoever are the other actors. For it is followership that best explains the brief convergence between the United States and Russia – just as it is context that best explains the ensuing, arguably inevitable, divergence.

Convergence

One of my recent books, *The End of Leadership* (Kellerman, 2012) was devoted in large part to the changing balance of power between leaders and followers, the former generally losing power, authority, and influence over time; the latter generally gaining power and influence over time, if not, by definition, authority. In that book I pointed out that this generally has been the historical trajectory. Certainly, since the Enlightenment and the American and French Revolutions, for many millions of people the trend has been away from being led by a small powerful elite, whether royal or religious, and toward being led by large groups, for example, legislatures composed of representatives who are commoners (as opposed to royals) and secularists. Democracies generally, and even some democratic organizations, have a golden rule of sorts, one that during previous periods of human history was inconceivable: governance of the people, by the people, and for the people.

This growing democratization – this growing participation in determining collective outcomes – has, in consequence of two phenomena in particular, accelerated even in the last half century. The first was an increasingly expansive anti-authority mentality, which became a hallmark, certainly of Western culture, in the late 1960s and early 1970s. In the United States particularly pressures were from the bottom-up, pressures exerted by various social and political protest movements, including but by no means limited to those that were anti-war and pro civil rights, women's rights and, some years later, gay and lesbian (and now transgender) rights. The so-called "world the sixties made" has never reverted. The sedate, conformist, "Eisenhower generation" that immediately preceded it was gone forever, and in its place, not only in America but in the West more generally, was a brave new world in which leaders saw their power and authority gradually diminished, and followers, ordinary people, saw their power and influence gradually enhanced. This trend was by no means confined only to the political sphere. The gradual disappearance or at least decline of the "command and control" management style, and the gradual transition to, for example, flatter hierarchies, confirms that patterns of leadership and followership in the private sector generally adhered to those in the public one (Kellerman, 2008).

The second explanation for the changing balance of power between leaders and followers in recent years is actually a contextual one – that is, it has nothing to do with leaders per se or with followers per se. Rather it refers to a change in the context within which they are located – within which there was a revolution in information technology. Social media in particular are nothing if not great equalizers, giving ordinary people goods and services to which previously they had scant access, including information and the capacity to communicate and connect to a degree that historically is unprecedented. We cannot know exactly the impact of the internet on how people relate, and on how they respond to the exercise of power, authority, and influence, especially over the long term. What we can say though is this: the internet engages hundreds of millions of people in collective conversations the world over. No single individual or even group of individuals can completely, reliably, and indefinitely control these conversations. As a result, the internet can and does, some of the time, enable the have-nots (followers) of any given group or society to defy or at least circumvent the haves (leaders). So far in any case, the internet has, in other words, tended to disseminate and distribute power and influence, not to concentrate them.

To comingle the general historical trajectory, that is, increasing democratization, with these two more recent phenomena, increasing anti-authoritarianism and the advent of social media, is to understand why, during approximately the last half century, patterns of leadership and followership have changed so dramatically. Whatever the existing social contract between those in positions of authority and those who are not, it has frayed. Whatever the existing understandings of cultural norms, the overall thrust of this most recent transformation is in keeping with those that were previous: the expansion of individual autonomy and self-expression at the expense of the ruling class.

This does not mean, of course, that followers have refused, necessarily, to follow. But it does mean that they, we, have tended to follow less because we want to and more because we have to, either because we are obliged to, literally, or because it is simply the most expedient thing to do. In the workplace, for example, we usually go along with leaders and managers for any number of self-interested reasons, ranging from the benefits of material reward to the fear of professional punishment. And in the community more generally, as in the nation-state, we tend similarly to accommodate to members of the leadership class, not necessarily because we believe particularly in their integrity and competence, but because it is the path of least resistance. To go along is, nearly always, easier than not going along. But it does not imply between leaders and followers either agreement or affection. In fact, for the last half-century, Americans' estimations of political leaders have relentlessly declined. According to virtually every poll, our opinions of leaders – leaders in politics, in business, in finance, in education, in the media, in the military, in religion, you name it – have gone down, way down, arguably dangerously down.

What I argue here is that, contrary to the conventional wisdom, the changing relationship between leaders and followers is by no means only a Western phenomenon. To the contrary, it is a global one, one from which nearly no country has been entirely exempt. In fact, as suggested, one of the defining geopolitical trends of the last quarter century has been the continuing if inconsistent and imperfect expansion of democracy. The collapse of communism not only in the Soviet Union but across Eastern Europe was typical: it was in consequence of a democratic thrust that, while complicated and compromised by dismally failed economies (to wit, recently in Ukraine), nevertheless was evidence of a far-flung historical momentum. When legendary activists such as Lech Walesa and Vaclav Havel pressed for change in Poland and Czechoslovakia respectively, they did so as democrats in autocratic systems. (Walesa originally was a trade-union activist; Havel was a writer and public intellectual.) Similarly, even in recent years, some of the most noteworthy political upheavals were stunning demonstrations of the power of the people. Whatever the outcomes of the Arab Spring, which to date have been, with the fragile exception of Tunisia, disheartening to the point of depressing, the original impulse for change was a democratic one. When Facebook revolutionists pressed for change in Tunisia and Egypt, they did so as democrats in autocratic systems. Even the catastrophic civil war in Syria was triggered by democratic activists protesting the over-forty-year rule first of the father Hafez al-Assad and then, now, of the son Bashar al-Assad.

What we can say then is that the empowerment of followers at the expense of leaders, however spasmodic and episodic, has been a worldwide phenomenon. It has been a natural consequence of the revolutions and evolutions to which I previously alluded, including in the twenty-first century, the revolution in information technology. Many millions of Americans are online – but so are many millions of Russians and, for that matter, many more millions of Chinese. The US has nearly 280 million internet users and a penetration rate of 86 percent. (That is, 86 percent of Americans have internet access.) Russia in turn has over 84 million internet users, and a penetration rate of nearly 60 percent. In fact, though Russia is not nearly as populous as China, it nevertheless ranks sixth in the world in terms of absolute number of internet users. China in turn has more internet users by far than any other country in the world, some 641 million, a penetration rate of nearly half the population.

In part as a consequence of this connectedness, there have been, in both Russia and China, levels of activism that were previously unthinkable (Sakwa, 2014; China Digital Times, 2015; Elfstrom, 2015). During the last decade, furious followers in both countries were willing to experiment with resistance, if not to upend the existing leadership class, then at least to upset it to the point of obliging it to change. In China this trend has been evidenced in, for example, environmental activism: countless Chinese participating in countless protests to demonstrate against air, soil, and water pollution so egregious it degrades the quality of everyday life. In Russia, which under Soviet rule had tolerated no public protests whatsoever, there were, for a brief moment in time, remarkable expressions of public outrage, notably though not exclusively in late 2011 and early 2012 when, around the time of parliamentary elections, loosely aligned groups of oppositionists and dissidents took to the streets to protest against President Vladimir Putin.

One of the most significant of demonstrations took place in Moscow in December 2011: some 100,000 people participated, many of them carrying signs and placards hostile to the government and shouting slogans that previously were unthinkable, such as "Russia Without Putin" and "Putin is a Thief." One of the stalwarts of the Russian opposition was, presumably still is, Aleksei Navalny, who was using the internet to connect and communicate well before using the internet became the norm. It was Navalny, as much as any other single figure, who personified Russian resistance to Putin for at least five years, telling a BBC interviewer at one point that his goal was no less than the transformation of Russia into a normal democratic state, where power is always achieved by honest democratic elections. Of course Navalny was himself only capitalizing on what briefly was the public mood. A 2011 report by the Pew Research Center found that, while they were still ambivalent about Western style liberalism, Russians' attitudes toward democracy, free markets, and political leadership were changing (Pew, 2011).

Here then was the *convergence*, the brief convergence, to which I allude. In the last quarter century in the United States – and in many other countries around the world – were signs and symptoms that the relationship between leaders and followers had changed. It had deteriorated and been diminished. In the US, public sector indicators included a decline in trust in government; a decline in trust in government leaders; a decline in trust that government can cure whatever it is that ails us; increased voter alienation; a Congress that is dysfunctional to the point of national scandal; a succession of presidencies beset by scandal (Bill Clinton), war (George W. Bush), and the worst financial crisis since the depression (George W. Bush and Barack Obama); a troubled if not destructive relationship between the executive and the legislature; and a decrease in centrism as well as an increase in divisiveness, as evidenced especially by the Tea Party, which for at least the last five years has played an outsized role in American politics, especially but not exclusively in the Republican Party.

One effect of all this has been a more level playing field, a more equal if not equitable relationship between leaders and followers. Followers, ordinary people, feel entitled and emboldened to demean and denigrate their leaders, turning to new media and old to engage in constant carping and criticism of those in positions of power and, or, authority. Democratic leaders, in turn, struggle to lead. They struggle to persuade followers to follow.

In the wake of the collapse of the Soviet Union, Russia, like other countries in Europe and elsewhere, was headed in a direction that was vaguely similar. It was headed toward the contentiousness that is characteristic of democracies. Had the impulse to change not been slowed and finally stopped, it would have leveled the relationship between leaders and followers, certainly to a degree that in Russian history was unprecedented. Two times Russians flirted with increased public participation and decreased state control. The first was just before and after the dissolution of the Soviet Union, in 1989 and 1990, when elections were held that were a break with the past – they were relatively free – and when nascent signs of genuine democratic participation were regularly in evidence. In 1991, for example, there were huge public demonstrations in Moscow, up to a half million people enthusiastically supporting Boris Yeltsin's struggle against the old Soviet order. The second such moment was the one already referenced, in late 2011 and early 2012, when it briefly seemed that Putin had overstepped himself, that he and his government had been so obviously greedy and corrupt that ordinary Russians were turning against them.

This raises several questions. Why did Russians turn so sharply away from nascent democracy? Why did they return, twice over, to autocracy? And why did the growing convergence between the United States and Russia revert to growing divergence?

Divergence

British professor of politics Richard Sakwa has written that "one of the great conundrums of our time is why it has been so hard to establish the rudiments of a working democratic system in Russia." After all, he continued, the middle class (such as it was) supported Yeltsin's struggle against the old Soviet system, and "in the late perestroika period the first relatively free elections, for the Soviet parliament in spring 1989 and for the Russian legislature in spring 1990, were greeted with enormous popular enthusiasm" (Sakwa, 2014). Moreover a few years later, in 1993, was held what American political scientist William Zimmerman referred to as a "founding election." All the relevant actors accepted the outcome and none of the "inevitable errors" substantially distorted the results. Zimmerman went on to add that, by the elections of 1996, the Russian people had evolved still further. By then they displayed the three attributes that are central to a functioning democracy: they were reasonably well informed about the various candidates; they were reasonably coherent about their policy preferences; and they cast their votes accordingly (Zimmerman, 2014).

However fragile, then, the democratic impulse in Russia was real. And of course it surfaced again a decade later, in 2011 and 2012, in mass demonstrations that clearly were pro-democracy. So why the regression after the progression? By and large the answer to this question – the explanation for the conundrum to which Sakwa alludes – has been simple. By and large the finger has been pointed at Putin. This is not to say that Putin is the only reason for Russia's inability to "establish the rudiments of a working democratic system." Other explanations have surfaced as well, including American foreign policy, which has been taken to task for being short-sighted and harsh, when what Russia really needed after communism's collapse was the diplomatic equivalent of a helping hand. Still, because our explanations for why things happen the way they do tend to be leader-centric, and because Putin has loomed so large for what has already been so long, it is Putin to whom we turn to explain why Russia remains rigidly autocratic.

Putin came to power thanks to his benefactor, Boris Yeltsin, who as president of the Russian Federation nominated him (in 1999) to head a new government, and who subsequently declared publicly that he considered Putin his logical successor. So, though he technically surrendered power to Dmitry Medvedev in 2008 by turning over to him for one (four-year) term the Russian presidency, Putin has, in effect, exercised one-man rule over Russia since Yeltsin left the political scene. To be sure, Medvedev's four years in the presidency left their mark – but only temporarily. He was more interested than Putin in legitimizing the state, in liberalizing it, and in modernizing it. He was also more disposed than Putin, certainly the Putin of recent years, to work with the West. It is highly unlikely, for instance, that Medvedev would ever have done what Putin did in 2014: seize Crimea and invade Ukraine or, if you prefer, aggressively insert Russia into Ukrainian politics. There is no disputing, then, that Putin per se – his persona, proclivities, preferences, and policies – have left their stamp not only on Russia but on the international system. Still, questions remain. Why was he able to stop democracy in its tracks, even after two bursts of democratic activism? Why was he able to stop Russians from more closely resembling most of their European (East as well as West) counterparts? And why was he able to reduce recent efforts at Russian activism to an enfeebled and endangered semblance of what they were only relatively recently? (In January 2015, a small crowd protesting the conviction of Navalny on charges of fraud was so quickly and thoroughly dispersed that by nightfall its numbers had dwindled to two dozen.)

For the answers to these questions we turn to *context*. For the explanations of how Putin has been able apparently nearly single-handedly to stop Russians from heading in a direction different from the one that he ordained we must extend our gaze beyond any single Russian in particular – even beyond the Russian people more generally. We must extend our gaze to the larger stage, to the state that is Russia itself.

I have argued for the necessity of putting leadership and followership in context. Context can be defined variously as, for example, distal or proximate, macro or micro. The point in any case is that *leadership is a system* and that to fixate on leaders at the expense of followers, and at the expense of contexts, is to fail fully to understand how history happens. In the book, *Hard Times: Leadership in America*, I developed a checklist that described 24 different components of context (Kellerman, 2014). As the subtitle makes clear, I focus in the book on leadership in the United States. But the checklist has wider application; it is equally relevant to the United Kingdom and, for that matter, to the United Arab Emirates as to the United States. Here I will take just four items from the checklist and apply them to Russia. My purpose is to clarify how key is context to comprehending why Russia has failed so far meaningfully to democratize – and why the large majority of Russians continue to be satisfied with being governed, being ruled, by a single autocratic, even tyrannical individual. To be sure, Putin is not Stalin. But by and large Putin's grip has been strong and, in the last couple of years, has gotten stronger still.

History

Russia has had no experience with democracy. Until Lenin and the Russian Revolution in 1917, it was a monarchy. And just a few years after the Revolution it, by now part of the Union of Soviet Socialist Republics, was under the boot of Joseph Stalin, who by every measure was a dictator, a brutal one. Between about 1924 and 1956 (three years after Stalin's death) the Soviet Union was the quintessential totalitarian state, the Soviet people virtually entirely at its mercy. The total number of civilians killed under Stalin is now estimated to be six million; many millions more (the numbers vary) were sent away to Gulags (Soviet prison camps). Between 1956 and the collapse of communism some 35 years later, the Soviet Union continued as a totalitarian state that, while less fearsome than under Stalin, nevertheless maintained something resembling complete control. In short, the Russian people have never had anyone resembling a democratic leader. And they have never had anything resembling a democratic state.

Ideology

Although Russia's foundational ideologies have changed over time – communism in particular deviating from what it was before the Soviet Union and then again after – nevertheless there are themes in Russian thought that have endured, and that Putin proselytizes to this day. They include patriotism characterized by a strong belief in the superiority of Russia and Russian civilization; alienation from what is perceived to be the hostile and voracious West; alienation from the ideals of liberal democrats, such as individualism and freedom of expression; nationalism and expansionism; centralized control (sometimes primarily religious, sometimes primarily secular); and paternalism – that is, control from the top down, not, never, from the bottom up. (Lenin himself was an ardent elitist. See, for example, his 1903 pamphlet, "What Is to Be Done," which makes clear that the upheaval he envisioned was to be led by a small, secret band of revolutionists, who were highly educated and thoroughly trained.) What some have recently tagged a new Cold War stems to an extent from differences in underlying ideologies. On the one side are accountable bureaucracies, democratic elections, and stability in Europe. And on the other side are a strong centralized state, a small controlling leadership class, and instability in Europe.

Politics

Russia's past has prepared it for the present: for one-man, one-party rule that brooks no genuine, permanent opposition. To be sure, present-day Russia has some of the trappings of democratic institutions, such as a parliament, but these have never been embedded in a democratic political culture or supported by a democratic ideology. Since the collapse of the Russian monarchy in 1917, the Soviet Union and, later, again Russia, have been led successively by a series of strong-men – Lenin, Stalin, Khrushchev, Brezhnev, Andropov, Chernenko, Gorbachev, Yeltsin, and Putin – who, to varying degrees, were intent on controlling the action. The glaring exception to this general rule was Mikhail Gorbachev, who, ironically, was hoisted on his own petard – gradually growing democracy. Gorbachev was done in by perestroika and glasnost, and by the idea that both individuals and individual soviet socialist republics could play a part in determining their own political fortunes. After the Soviet Union, after Gorbachev, his successor, Yeltsin, tried in his way to perpetuate the fledgling democratic impulse. But he was overwhelmed finally by his own personal problems (especially alcoholism), by a miserably failed economy, and by the lack of a democratic foundation on which to build.

Economics

Even in this realm there have been only weak signs of anything resembling a democratic impulse, a market economy. Before the Russian Revolution, Russia was among the most backward and least developed countries in Europe. It remained a largely agrarian country, with no urban or middle class to speak of, and few market incentives to spur individual economic enterprise. After the Revolution came communism, forced centralization, and five-year plans that by many measures failed. When the Soviet Union collapsed, it was not only because of political weakness, but because of economic destitution – poverty, a demographic collapse, and social decay – which persisted until Putin came to power. Yeltsin did in fact implement some radical market reforms. But because there were no legal structures to undergird them, the most striking result was not a growing middle class but a growing oligarchical class, in which a few individuals took advantage of a system that was nearly entirely unregulated. Ironically, Putin came to power promising to rein in the oligarchs, but he did just the opposite. He himself became one, and was surrounded in short order with cronies engaging in the same rapacious practices. The fact that Russia was able under Putin to develop an emergent middle class was due largely to the high prices of commodities, particularly oil, which more recently of course have plummeted.

In her book titled *The Putin Mystique: Inside Russia's Power Cult*, which as its title implies is all about Putin's one-man rule, author Anna Arutunyan nevertheless credits context with explaining the phenomenon:

> Within the patrimonial state, where social roles are reduced to the relative strength or weakness of an individual, the central government, ever distant and perennially autocratic in its constant efforts to ensure order over such a vast land, is ascribed near supernatural powers, even in cases when it is actually weak and inefficient. This is not deification in the common understanding . . . Rather it is the acceptance of a force beyond influence, beyond logic. . . . "State power, not law, holds a sacred status in Russia."
>
> *(Arutunyan, 2015)*

Emergence

Most social scientists would admit, if reluctantly, to being poor prognosticators. In this chapter alone, I have touched on two cataclysmic events that virtually no one, including none of the experts, foresaw. The first is the collapse of the Soviet Union in 1991, and the second is the collapse of oil prices in 2014. So, far be it from me to guesstimate what the United States and/ or Russia will look like five or ten years from now. What I will do, though, is provide a few concluding comments that could be clues to the future.

First the United States. There is little disagreement that the sea change to which I previously alluded – for various reasons leaders getting weaker and followers stronger – has led to democratic discontents, to discontents with, and within, democracies. This is reflected in the polls. And it is echoed by experts. Francis Fukuyama has described "America in Decay," an America in which a "combination of intellectual rigidity and the power of entrenched political actors" is rendering it "increasingly dysfunctional" (Fukuyama, 2014). Seyla Benhabib et al. have observed a "yawning *democratic disconnect*, a gap between citizens and those institutions . . . tasked to answer to the challenges of governance" (Benhabib et al., 2013; italics in original.). Stein Ringen has concluded that "America has declined to the model of dysfunctional democracy" (Ringen, 2013). And William Galston has asked if there is a "fundamental tension between leadership and the democratic principle of popular sovereignty" (Galston, 2014).

Nor are these signs and symptoms of "decay" limited to the United States. As I made clear, whatever the problems that bedevil the US – for instance increased income inequality – they bedevil other Western democracies as well. The primary point is that there is no quick fix. In fact, there is no fix at all, at least not a politically viable one, which is precisely why some of the best and brightest, such as Fukuyama, come to the conclusion that nothing much will change, that the US and other Western democracies will continue on a downward trajectory unless and until there is a "major shock to the political order." Put another way, the future of America looks rather like the recent past, only more so. To be sure, in the last few years the American economy has grown stronger, which means that, in comparison with other Western democracies, the US is doing reasonably well. Still, the democratic discontents are too simmering, too many in number, and too widely shared to predict that they will be effectively ameliorated any time soon.

Russians, in turn, show no significant signs of deviating from past practices. For the moment at least they continue to surrender their power and influence to an autocrat. Putin has effectively eliminated entirely all political and economic opposition. In fact, to all appearances it was precisely the drift toward convergence with the United States, with Western democracy, especially in the winter of 2011–2012, which finally pushed Putin to decimate his opponents, to become more autocratic, not less. The last nail in the coffin of Russia's fledgling democratic movement, at least for the time being, was on May 6, 2012, the eve of Putin's reelection as president, when between 50,000 and 100,000 people gathered for demonstrations just across from the Kremlin. Scuffles erupted, disrupting what were intended to be protests that were peaceful. As a result, soon after the rally Putin's repression began in earnest. Within weeks police had raided the homes of scores of activists. Nearly a thousand people were arrested, several dozen of whom are still in prison (Ioffe, 2015). And the moment that he was back in the Kremlin (after having surrendered the presidency for four years to Medvedev), Putin introduced three major bills: the first toughened criminal penalties for inciting mass unrest; the second forced NGOs with foreign financing to register as foreign agents; and the third set up a registry which had the power to shut down any website deemed extremist. Whatever the hopes for democracy in Russia raised by the collapse of the Bolshevik state, for the time being if not the indefinite future they were dashed.

Still, we know by now that things change, sometimes surprisingly rapidly. Whatever the democratic discontents – which I do not for a moment dismiss – in many ways Americans are doing well, better than most of their counterparts elsewhere in the world. And whatever the Russian context – the impact of which I obviously take seriously – Russia itself is situated in a larger, global context from which it cannot be completely isolated. Whether or not Russians and Americans will again converge – and if yes, when – I cannot foretell. In fact, at this present time relations between the two countries are more conflictual than cooperative: NATO forces in east Europe are being strengthened for fear of further Russian aggression. But what I do know is that Russians have flirted with democracy on more than one occasion; that, according to one study, on average Russians spend more hours on social media than people in any other country; that for all his bluster Putin was scared to make of Navalny a martyr (instead of jailing him, Putin jailed his brother); that, in short order, protests in neighboring Ukraine toppled President Viktor Yanukovych; that Western sanctions and the dramatic decline in the price of oil have negatively impacted Russia's weak economy; and that in spite of the weight of the past there is no evidence that Russians are in some ineffable way unsuited to democracy.

It is not that the United States specifically and Western democracies more generally are irresistible models of good governance. To the contrary – we have seen that the West is beset by democratic discontents. Rather it is that followers worldwide have become more restive, which means that, if leaders are disposed more completely to control them they must suppress, even oppress anyone in opposition. We see this of course not only in Russia, but in other countries as well, such as China, Egypt, and Turkey. So the question of whether over, say, the next decade Russians will continue to tolerate a semblance of a tyrant remains an open one. But, given their history, and given the larger geopolitical context within which Russia itself is situated, the odds seem to point to continued divergence.

Conclusions

In this chapter I have argued that, in order to understand current changes in political leadership, it is necessary to take a systematic approach. The actions of leaders need to be interpreted in context and in relation to the behavior of followers. For purposes of illustration, the chapter focused on Russia and the United States during the period from the fall of the Berlin Wall to the present time, but the argument is relevant also to other periods and other places.

Certain global tendencies were noted which impacted on followership. Most notably these concern the access to and use of information and communications technology and the movement towards widespread participation and the related disenchantment with leaders. There were periods of convergence in the relationship between leaders and followers in both Russia and the United States and this found reflection in many other countries such as Poland, Egypt, and elsewhere. There were moments when there were widespread shifts in power away from leaders. Global phenomena including technology, communications, and anti-authoritarian movements underpinned this trend. But, as argued in the chapter, there was also the phenomenon of the resurgence of leader-centric political behavior in Russia. This was explained in terms of context. That country has a long history of autocratic rule. In such a context, where democratic institutions, expectations, and culture are not firmly embedded, a strong and determined leader has, for the time being at least, been able to push-back the forces of democratization and thus a period of divergence was once again enabled.

References

Arutunyan, Anna (2014) *The Putin Mystique: Inside Russia's Power Cult*. Northampton, MA: Olive Branch Press.

Benhabib, Seyla, Richard Youngs, David Cameron, Anna Dolidge, Gabor Hamai, Gunther Hellmann and Kateryna Pishchikova (2013) *The Democratic Disconnect: Citizenship and Accountability in the Transatlantic Community*. Washington, DC: Transatlantic Academy.

China Digital Times (2015) "Four Views on Activism", July 18, 2015, http://chinadigitaltimes.net/2015/04/four-views-on-activism-in-china/

Elfstrom, Manfred (2015) "Wither China's New Worker Militancy?" *China Policy Institute Blog*, http://blogs.nottingham.ac.uk/chinapolicyinstitute/2015/03/31/whither-chinas-new-worker-militancy/

Fukuyama, Francis (2014) "America in Decay: The Sources of Political Dysfunction", *Foreign Affairs*. September/October, 2014.

Galston, William (2014) "Populist Resentment, Elitist Arrogance: Two Challenges to Good Democratic Leadership" in John Kane and Haig Patapan, eds. *Good Democratic Leadership: On Prudence and Judgement in Modern Democracies*. New York: Oxford University Press.

Ioffe, Julia (2015) "Remote Control", *The New Yorker*, January 5.

Kellerman, Barbara (2008) *Followership: How Followers Are Creating Change and Changing Leaders*. Cambridge, MA: Harvard Business School Press.

Kellerman, Barbara (2012) *The End of Leadership*. New York: HarperCollins.

Kellerman, Barbara (2014) *Hard Times: Leadership in America*. Stanford, CA: Stanford University Press.

Pew Research Center (2011) "Confidence in Democracy and Capitalism Wanes in the Former Soviet Union", December 5.

Ringen, Stein (2013) *Nation of Devils: Democratic Leadership and the Problem of Obedience*. New Haven, CT: Yale University Press.

Sakwa, Richard (2014) *Putin Redux: Power and Contradiction in Contemporary Russia*. Abingdon, Oxon: Routledge.

Zimmerman, William (2014) *Ruling Russia: Authoritarianism from the Revolution to Putin*. Princeton, NJ: Princeton University Press.

21

Leadership and Religion

Sverre Spoelstra

Introduction

The link between leadership studies and religion is both obvious and puzzling. It is obvious in the sense that one needs little more than a glance at the field's most popular concepts to know that leadership has a great deal to do with religion. After all, much of what happens in the field today falls under umbrella concepts with explicitly religious roots, such as charismatic leadership, spiritual leadership, and servant leadership. Other popular concepts have somewhat less obvious religious roots, such as transformational leadership and authentic leadership, but the religious connotations are not difficult to reveal here also. The popular business literature on leadership, meanwhile, is flooded with books of the 'leadership lessons from Jesus' type (e.g. Adair, 2011; Blanchard and Hodges, 2005; Manz, 1998).

But the relation between religion and leadership studies is also puzzling because the connection is rarely addressed within the academic community of leadership scholars (a few exceptions notwithstanding, e.g. Grint, 2010; Sliwa *et al.*, 2013; Spoelstra, 2013b; Thomas *et al.*, 2015; Tourish, 2014). In the rare instances when religion is addressed, leadership scholars have often been content to discuss it at the level of metaphor (e.g. Alvesson, 2010; Hatch *et al.*, 2005), thereby sidestepping the question of whether or not leadership itself may be seen as a religious phenomenon. The absence of an explicit interest in the relation between leadership and religion goes so far that one might be tempted to speak of a repression of the religious dimension of leadership amongst leadership scholars.

This chapter is structured as follows. In the first section, starting with an etymological account of religion, I make the case that leadership can be understood as a religious phenomenon. In the two sections that follow, I show how this religious dimension of leadership plays out in some of the most popular concepts of leadership, first in relation to the concept of charismatic leadership and then, more briefly, in relation to the concepts of transformational leadership, spiritual leadership, servant leadership, authentic leadership, and distributed leadership. These examples serve as illustrations of the overall argument (that leadership is a religious phenomenon) but they also show how and where these leadership concepts overlap and where they are modelled on different religious themes. In the final section I ask what the recognition of leadership as a religious phenomenon may mean for the study of leadership.

Leadership as a Religious Phenomenon

It is a commonplace to say that leadership is hard to define (e.g. Stogdill, 1974). The same has been said about religion (King, 1954). This may suggest that a discussion of the links between these two terms could be a tricky exercise. In an attempt to narrow the focus, I will use a philological starting point, in particular the question of whether the term 'religion' stems from the Latin *religare*, 'to bind', or from the Latin *relegere*, 'to go through', 're-read' (Hoyt, 1912). The first, *religare*, points in the direction of a bond: the religious person is the person who maintains a bond with the divine. The latter, *relegere*, emphasizes the continuous efforts of the religious person to follow the norms of the deities; it points towards 'obligation', or 'strict observance of law' (Hoyt, 1912: 128). The opposite of religion is, in this reading, *neglegere* (negligence): 'An *irreligious* Jew *neglects* the Law' (Hoyt, 1912: 128).

We shall refrain from following one etymological explanation over the other. Instead, I shall use these two possible etymological roots to form a general conception of religion that guides the discussion to come.[1] This basic understanding will allow us to draw parallels with contemporary understandings of leaders and leadership. First, the religious person may be said to be someone who maintains a relation (to establish a bond, *religare*) with a realm outside of the ordinary. This realm is sacred in the sense that it is separated (sacred: 'to set apart') from the ordinary. We may therefore say that religion minimally assumes a separation of two spheres, a natural and a supernatural sphere. We may further say that religious inhabitants of the mundane sphere have established a connection with this higher sphere and that, depending on the religious system, inhabitants of the divine sphere may or may not appear or take action in the natural sphere. In other words, the two spheres are two worlds apart, yet there are many border crossings in both directions, upwards and downwards, by a number of religious figures and through a number of religious practices.

The etymology of *relegere*, in turn, highlights the difficulties in forming this bond, as well as the sustained work that this involves: one must 'go through' again and again (e.g. to follow the liturgy rigorously or to withstand one's earthly desires). According to Smith (1998: 270) the English 'religiously', 'designating a conscientious repetition such as "She reads the morning paper religiously"' captures this meaning. While etymologically distinct, this latter meaning of the term religion does not need to go against the interpretation of religion as *religare*. As Jean-Luc Nancy observes, the difficulty of being religious (to form a bond with the divine) comes with the sacred status of the divine, which, in a sense, appears to foreclose the possibility of forming a bond: 'The sacred is what, of itself, remains set apart, at a distance, and with which one forms no bond (or only a very paradoxical one)' (Nancy, 2005: 1). One may further think of the notion of self-sacrifice (popular in leadership discourse): to give up parts of oneself (or one's entire self) in order to gain a divine (sacred) status.

In some religious systems the border between the natural and the supernatural can be crossed by means of certain practices. For instance, in Buddhism, human beings live in a realm where rebirth in a higher realm is possible by means of meditation and other practices. 'Nirvana' means literally 'blown out' (as a flame may blow out) and refers to a state where one no longer suffers from the earthly 'flames' of greed, aversion and delusion, a state that can be reached by means of sustained practice. In other systems, deities assume themselves earthly forms. Within Christianity, Christ is said to be simultaneously the Son of Man and the Son of God. Jesus Christ (as the second person in the Trinity) shows that 'God has truly assumed manhood and thus is at the same time true man and true God in Jesus' (Ratzinger, 2004: 29). Moses, even though he is seen as a prophet rather than God, occupies a similar position in Judaism: he is understood as the 'primordial cult founder who mediated the details of the inside while standing irrevocably outside' (Hutton, 1994: 36). Next to methods by which humans ascend or deities descend, in virtually all religions we find mediators: figures that allow some form of communication or transfer between the higher and lower spheres. For instance, prophets have been in contact with the divine and can therefore speak on behalf of the deities, apostles are literally 'messengers' who spread the teachings of a particular religion, priests mediate the relation between believers and their deities by administering religious rituals, saints are seen as holy or have been made holy, fallen angels have been cast down to earth, and so on. Each of these figures offers a partial 'solution' to a problem that may seem logically impossible: to legitimately touch what may not be touched, or to partake in a divine world while remaining in this world.

Against this background, let us now turn to the question of to what extent leadership may be understood as a religious phenomenon. First of all, leadership is arguably *not* a religious phenomenon if it simply refers to a (high or highest) function in a formal organization. This is because such a position may be thought about without a separated sphere that transcends the organizational realm. In other words, there is – in principle – nothing religious about the creation of different roles and responsibilities in a functional chart. Having said that, we should not lose sight of the fact that the very concept of hierarchy is itself a secularized theological concept (Parker, 2009). Indeed, it can be difficult to conceive of those at the top of the organizational chart as being in no way connected to the sacred. This tendency is also captured in Weber's concept of the charisma of office, with the figure of the priest, who derives his charisma from his function, as the paradigmatic example.

In the context of this chapter I will not elaborate on the religious dimension of formalized positions. The reason for this is that few people today, whether in leadership studies or in popular culture, understand leadership primarily as a function. Even if leadership authors often turn to the study of top managers when they claim to study leadership (e.g. Waldman *et al.*, 2006) and continue to speak of 'positional leaders' (in contrast to informal or distributed leaders, e.g. Spillane *et al.*, 2001), they tend to emphasize that leadership is not principally function-based. In other words, if authors speak of 'positional leadership' (or similar notions such as 'formal leadership', 'functional leadership', and also 'transactional leadership') they tend to also speak of a non-positional form of leadership, which is the one that is considered superior. Leadership studies is today fundamentally based on a split between two spheres, the sphere of ordinary organization (business) and a higher sphere. The most familiar form that this split takes is the distinction between the manager, who occupies a function within the organization, and the leader, a person who transcends the organization and is therefore capable of doing something fundamental to it (e.g. 'transforming' it, infusing it with meaning). Leadership is seen as a force that transcends, redeems, or complements 'ordinary' management and business. At times this results in the depiction of two different kinds of people: low ones (managers) and high ones (leaders) (e.g. Zaleznik, 1977). More commonly it results in the distinction between (high) leadership and (low) management, leaving open the possibility that organizational members partake in both spheres (e.g. a manager/knowledge worker/production line worker, etc., who is *also* a leader, or who *also* takes part in some form of collective leadership). Leadership, in short, is the name given to that which mediates between the sphere of mundane organization and the extraordinary.

Some have attributed these religious roots of leadership thinking to so-called 'Great Man' theories of leadership, of which Thomas Carlyle is the most famous exponent. Carlyle (1993 [1840]) understood the course of history largely as driven by exceptional men. In line with this, some strands of leadership studies, including charismatic leadership, have been described as 'heroic', in the sense that leaders are portrayed as mythical, larger than life. What is again captured in the labelling of leadership studies as 'heroic' is the movement between a higher and a lower sphere. As Joseph Campbell (1969: 30) notes, in the archetypical hero-narrative:

> a hero ventures forth from the world of common day into a region of supernatural wonder: fabulous forces are there encountered and a decisive victory is won: the hero comes back from this mysterious adventure with the power to bestow boons on his fellow man.

In other words, the hero is capable of bringing something extraordinary to the ordinary, due to their virtues obtained in a different sphere. Another obvious reference here is Plato's philosopher–king, who is fit to rule because he got his hands on a return ticket to the realm of ideas. According to Barker (2001), this is still the model that informs most of leadership studies at the dawn of the twenty-first century.

However, the hero is just one religious archetype that can be read into contemporary leadership studies. As I will show further in this chapter, leadership studies is best read as offering different solutions to the problem of how to bridge the ordinary world of management with the extraordinary world of leadership. In other words, it is in the business of producing images of leadership that would allow business organizations to establish a bond with a realm that is fundamentally outside of business (Spoelstra, 2013a). It frequently draws, implicitly in academic articles and often explicitly in popular leadership books, on theological concepts and religious figures to shape these images. So next to Campbell's description of the hero, we also find concepts of leadership that draw on other forms of religious mediation, such as the prophet or the apostle. It is worth noting (and will become clear in what follows) that the prime inspiration for the construction of leadership concepts is the Judeo-Christian tradition. This is not a surprise, given that contemporary leadership discourse has predominantly Western roots.

Leadership and Charisma

In understanding the relation between leadership and religion, the concept of charisma has become of central importance. Indeed, leadership studies as an academic field has taken an explicit interest in religion since it developed an interest in charismatic leadership in the 1970s and 1980s (e.g. House, 1977; Conger and Kanungo, 1987). The concept of charismatic leadership merits attention in its own right because it may be regarded as the paradigmatic concept of leadership studies in its contemporary form: all other leadership concepts may be seen as variations of the exemplary case of charismatic leadership – an argument which is illustrated in the next section.

The religious, more specifically Christian, roots of the concept of charismatic leadership (literally 'gift of grace') are well known through Max Weber's popularization of the term in the early twentieth century. For Weber (1978: 241), charisma refers to 'a certain quality of an individual personality by virtue of which he is considered extraordinary and treated as endowed with supernatural, superhuman, or at least specifically exceptional power qualities'. Charismatic authority, following Weber's definition, refers to the situation in which a person is considered to be special due to a mysterious gift and for that reason worth following. Crucially, for Weber, charisma, in its ideal form, amounts to an outright 'rejection of economic conduct' (1968: 21). Charisma 'is the opposite of all ordered economy', and even 'the very force that disregards economy' (1968: 21). The prophet exemplifies the non-economic nature of charisma: prophecy is professed for its own sake, not for any material reward (Weber, 1968: 255). This non-economic nature of charisma, i.e. the sacred, is what separates it from the economic concerns of ordinary life, from which it is important for the leader to remain separate.

Within leadership studies, the source of the 'gift' of charismatic leadership is understood in different ways, and not always in line with Weber. Some consider charisma as a mysterious quality coming from above, in line with Weber's definition (and also reminiscent of Carlyle's Great Man descriptions). For others charisma is rather a natural gift, given to certain individuals in the form of a trait by birth. Yet others see charisma as something that can be acquired through learning, which would make it a social gift rather than a natural or supernatural gift. In any of these readings, however, charismatic leaders hover above 'ordinary' people, with the figure of the manager tending to stand for the ordinary. Interestingly, the point of virtually all studies of charismatic leadership in organizations is to show that charismatic leadership is good for organizational performance. In other words, charismatic leadership ought to be welcomed and perhaps even developed in organizations because it is good for the economy of the organization. In some definitions of charisma, the religious sense and economic benefits come together. For instance, charisma has been understood as 'a fire that ignites followers' energy and commitment, producing results above and beyond the call of duty' (Klein and House, 1995: 183).

Despite the one-sided emphasis on the economic and organizational benefits of charisma, it would be a mistake to understand the analysis of charisma in economic terms as going against Weber's ideal type of charismatic leadership as a non-economic phenomenon. The claim of leadership scholars is not that charismatic leaders think in terms of economic benefits for the organization. The claim is rather that charismatic leadership, in Weber's non-economic form, *happens* to be good for organizations. This model can, for instance, be recognized in Chrysler's former CEO Lee Iacocca's reduction of salary, so often celebrated in texts on charismatic leadership (e.g. Conger and Kanungo, 1987): for true business charismatics, as with Weber's prophet, money does not matter. The 'discovery' of charismatic leadership scholars therefore is that *not* thinking in terms of business is good for business (Spoelstra, 2013a). Furthermore, what is separated from business (the sacred) not only makes business prosper but also redeems it from its moral failures (Spoelstra, 2013a). With the business scandals, environmental crisis, and the 2008 financial crisis, business is no longer considered a redeeming power in its own right – at least not by a majority. The religion of business (the market as the hand of God, the capitalist entrepreneur, etc.) has lost its support (Sørensen and Spoelstra, 2013). For non-believers in business, something different is needed: something that does not hamper business as we know it (as that would be 'unrealistic') but a force from the outside that not only makes business prosper but also redeems it.

As Weber writes (1968: 21), 'In order to do justice to their mission, the holders of charisma must stand outside the ties of the world, outside of routine occupations'. It is in this sense that we may understand charismatic leadership as the paradigmatic case for virtually all leadership concepts that have been produced since: servant leadership, authentic leadership, distributed leadership, responsible leadership, and so on. All of these concepts refer to something that stands outside of the economic sphere, which is why that particular form of leadership is deemed capable of intervening from above in business. Leadership as a religion tells the story of the breakdown of the paradigm of management (or systems thinking, control, functions, rules, standards, etc.). Management can only bring the organization so far. What is needed is something higher, and the leader inhabits this higher sphere while also being a part of the organization. Weber's emphasis on the anti-institutional nature of charisma (seen by Weber as a downside) is celebrated in leadership discourse. One could even argue that the leadership/ management distinction is a rearticulation of Weber's distinction between charismatic and formal authority.

If the concept of charismatic leadership may be seen as a paradigm for all popular contemporary leadership concepts, this is not to say that the figure of the charismatic leader still dominates leadership studies. Indeed, research on charismatic leadership has decreased significantly since its heyday in the 1980s and 1990s, and much of what is left explores its 'dark side' (e.g. Tourish, 2014).

This dark side, as Rieff (2008) has argued, has everything to do with the fact that the charismatic is understood as someone who breaks with the rules of this world, but *not* by following the laws of a higher world (as charisma was understood by Paul in the New Testament). In this sense, charismatic leadership is in opposition to religion as *relegere* (i.e. obeying the laws of a higher order). Or, rather, the leader is not seen as an intermediary but as a lawgiver: he is modelled after God the Creator rather than God the Redeemer. For Rieff this is a grave distortion of Paul's notion of charisma, as 'the act of God in the present, a transforming power that is experienced by the believer' (Potts, 2009: 34). What Rieff takes issue with is that Weber's concept of charisma is no longer based on a creed. What makes Jesus charismatic, according to Rieff, is not his miracle making, as Weber suggests, but the fact that 'he accepts without question the authority of the law' (Potts, 2009: 69). This also explains why, in Rieff's view, it would be a mistake to call Hitler charismatic: '[Hitler] is the leader of an anti-credal organization' (Potts, 2009: 118).[2]

In light of the dangers of charismatics (understood as leaders who break earthly laws without following higher laws), most leadership scholars today look for a more modest figure: a mediator rather than a creator–commander. It is against this background that other leadership concepts have been suggested that minimally offer a different emphasis, and often offer a different solution to the problem of how to bridge profane business with the sacred. I will suggest such a reading in the next section for the concepts of transformational leadership, servant leadership, spiritual leadership, authentic leadership, and distributed leadership.

Religious Connotations of Some Central Leadership Concepts

In this section I briefly discuss some of the most popular leadership concepts within leadership studies today. Two of these concepts, transformational leadership and servant leadership, have entered leadership studies in the late 1970s/early 1980s; the three others, spiritual leadership, authentic leadership, and distributed leadership, have become fashionable more recently. This is by no means a complete overview; there are other leadership concepts with (more) obvious religious connotations, such as self-sacrificial leadership (Choi and Mai-Dalton, 1999), transcendental leadership (Cardona, 2000), or visionary leadership (Nanus, 1992). However, the concepts below have – I believe – some of the largest followings within leadership studies today. Together they give a good impression of the way religion plays out, to a greater or lesser extent, in contemporary approaches to leadership.

Transformational Leadership

As already mentioned, transformational leadership is closely affiliated with charismatic leadership. Both concepts came to prominence in the 1970s and 1980s and are often mentioned in the same breath (e.g. Bryman, 1992; Van Knippenberg and Sitkin, 2013). Initially charisma was one of the four dimensions of transformational leadership in the work of Bernard M. Bass (1985). It is therefore not surprising that much of what been said in the previous section about charismatic leadership also holds for transformational leadership. For instance, transformational leaders are, much like charismatic leaders in Weber's ideal type, understood as non-economic (their counter-figure is the transactional leader, who thinks in terms of economic exchange). Furthermore, as Tourish (2014) argues, transformational leadership often assumes the cult-like character that one also finds in Weber's ideal type of the charismatic. If there is a reason to discuss transformational leadership separately from charismatic leadership, then this must stem from the concept of 'transformation' itself, which – perhaps surprisingly – is rarely discussed in the literature on transformational leadership (Delaney and Spoelstra, 2015).

At first sight, transformational leadership is less obviously a religious concept than charismatic leadership. The word 'transformation', in contrast to charisma, is not of religious origin. Indeed, in an anthology of religious concepts, Lawrence (1998) feels he needs to justify the inclusion of the term 'transformation' alongside terms such as 'God', 'sacrifice', and also 'religion' itself. However, as Lawrence continues to show, there is a substantial religious discourse on transformation, including transfiguration, transubstantiation, and conversion. According to Lawrence (1998: 338), this discourse is 'largely individual', 'markedly voluntary', and 'avowedly positive'. This is to say that transformations in religious discourses tend to refer to individuals who out of their own will embrace a higher order. From this perspective, it could be argued that transformational leadership, in comparison to the concept of charismatic leadership, puts (slightly) more emphasis on the follower: it suggests that individual workers voluntarily undergo a transformation where they come to embody higher values for the good of the company. Connotations of the religious concept of conversion are particularly strong (Delaney and Spoelstra, 2015). The transformational leader is the figure that has the capacity of realizing these conversions in others. He or she is perhaps best understood as a secularized version of the prophet: the prophets depicted in the Old Testament's Book of Kings have a 'transformational power' in that they 'change the way people think, their words are effective, almost creative [like God the creator]' (Towey, 2013: 55).

Spiritual Leadership

The concept of spiritual leadership has gained traction since the 1990s (Conger, 1994; Fairholm, 1996; Fry, 2003; Reave, 2005). The term 'spirit' is originally 'a metaphor for the "wind" or "breath" whereby God creates and empower living beings' (Pye, 1994: 253). To be inspired or to be spiritual is to be under the influence of a deity. When leaders are referred to as 'inspirational' or 'inspiring' (one of the most common associations with the term 'leadership', alongside charisma and vision), they appear as secularized deities, i.e. as God-like people who breathe life into others. The concepts of charismatic and transformational leadership often build on this imagery. For instance, Bass (1985) has identified 'inspiration' as one of the four dimensions of transformational leadership. Likewise, Kanungo and Mendonça (1994: 184) conclude that 'it is only when leadership takes on a truly transformational form that the spiritual dimension comes to the fore'. Like the transformational leader, the spiritual leader hovers above the organization and infuses the organization with meaning through their 'vision' and even provides the organization with a 'soul' (Leavitt, 1986).[3] Some of the imagery, even more than transformational leadership writings, reminds one of Carlyle's Great Men prose. For instance, Kanungo and Mendonça write that 'the spiritual dimension [of leadership] . . . is expressed in the sense of the profound consciousness of the eternal values of truth, beauty and goodness represented by the vision of the leader' (Kanungo and Mendonça, 1994: 185). We can further recognize a typical hero-narrative in some renderings of spiritual leadership. For instance, according to Palmer (1994: 28), one can become a spiritual leader only by means of a 'downward journey [into the self] through violence and terror', until one touches 'the deep place where we are in community with each another', which forms the basis of leading others to that happy place.

In some forms, then, spiritual leadership is best understood as an off-shoot of transformational leadership, one that puts more emphasis on the need of the leader's self-transformation.

The basic idea is that the spiritual leader has to engage in self-transformation before transforming others (Fairholm, 1996; Reave, 2005). However, there are also versions of spiritual leadership that blend in with the work of spirituality literature (see Oswick, 2009). The basic idea here is that all workers (whether or not they are designated as 'leaders') ought to establish a relation with a deity or transcendental force so that both humanity and profitability may prosper. From this perspective, the celebration of the vision of the transcendental leader is seen as a danger to spiritual leadership rather than as a defining characteristic (Reave, 2005). The main source for these more 'modest' versions of spiritual leadership is mysticism, i.e. 'personal religion' (James, 1985) rather than institutional religion.

Servant Leadership

Like spiritual leadership, the religious roots of servant leadership are fairly obvious and often the explicit focus of books on the topic (e.g. Wilkes, 1998). However, unlike spiritual leadership, these religious roots are rarely acknowledged in journal publications (exceptions are Sendjaya and Sarros, 2002; Wallace, 2007). The concept of servant leadership has been popular since the late 1970s, following the publication of Greenleaf's (1977) book with the same title. Greenleaf, a Quaker, was obviously influenced by the portrayal of Jesus as servant in Matthew and Mark: 'The Son of Man came not to be served but to serve, and to give His life a ransom for many' (Matt. xx. 28 and Mark x. 45). Jesus is for Greenleaf the archetypical leader (Banks and Ledbetter, 2004), in the sense that he puts the interests of his followers first, as exemplified in the story of Jesus washing his disciples' feet (John xiii. 1–17).

Less often mentioned than Jesus as a model for servant leadership is Paul. But there is a case to be made that servant leadership is modelled on the figure of Paul as much as Jesus: Paul serves God (as Jesus Christ), whereas Jesus, as the second person in the Trinity, is God. Indeed, the famous first ten words of Paul's Letter to the Romans read: 'Paul, a servant of Jesus Christ, called to be an apostle, separated to the gospel of God'. This line may also suggest that servant leadership is best understood as apostolic: the servant leader is an apostle in the sense that he or she is a messenger of God. Also the notion of a calling is crucial in this sentence: one is called to be a servant and it is this calling that binds (*religare*) the religious person to God.

It is useful to compare this image of the servant leader to the concepts of charismatic leadership and spiritual leadership. In contrast to the charismatic (and transformational) leader, the servant leader is not seen as the authoritative source: he or she acts on behalf of God (but does not take the place of God). This is essentially the notion of charisma that Rieff has sought to restore in relation to Weber's (transgressive) charismatic (which has been the model for the organizational versions of charismatic leadership). The charisma derives from God, and one is charismatic only to the extent that one serves God. However, servant leadership resonates closely with less heroic notions of spiritual leadership. As Greenleaf mentions, the 'Spirit is the driving force behind the motive to serve' (cited in Banks and Ledbetter, 2004: 110).

We may finally note that Christianity was not the only point of reference for Greenleaf; he was also inspired by Herman Hesse's short novel *Journey to the East*, whose protagonist Leo was a leader without being recognized as a leader. This is the key motive in the concept of servant leadership: the (best) leader is not someone who stands in the limelight, but someone who is hardly visible because he lets others shine. The servant leader is a mediator in the sense that he or she transmits a spirit that lifts followers up to a higher plane. Out of all leadership concepts popular today, servant leadership is perhaps the most 'humble' in that it draws attention away from the authority of single individuals. This modesty nicely shows in the reversal that 'what we need today are not . . . more *servant leaders* but . . . *leading servants*' (Banks and Ledbetter, 2004: 111).

Authentic Leadership

The concept of authentic leadership has become fashionable in the 2000s with the popular leadership books of Bill George (2003, 2007) as well as scholarly work by Avolio and his colleagues (e.g. Avolio and Gardner, 2005). These authors stress the importance of knowing yourself, being true to yourself (sincerity), and being true to others (transparency).

As Guignon (2004) has shown, contemporary ideas of authenticity can partly be traced back to the Protestant critique of religious hierarchy. For Luther, 'what is all important . . . is the individual's one-to-one relation to God. Luther rejects the church hierarchy, the practice of confessing one's sins to a priest, and every form of worldly intermediary standing between oneself and God' (Guignon, 2004: 15). Lutheranism involves a turn towards inwardness: pure intentions are more important than actions. The task for the religious person is to become true to oneself. Authentic leadership is arguably an expression of this Lutheran ideal of taking part in the divine world by means of inwardness. This is also the main difference from charismatic leadership: if charismatic leadership, in the tradition of Weber, amounts to the loss of inwardness, as Rieff (2008) argues, the concept of authentic leadership is an attempt to bring inwardness back in.

This has the great advantage that leadership becomes in principle open to all: leadership, in line with other fashionable leadership concepts such as self-leadership and distributed leadership, is not limited to extraordinary characters that are created in the image of the prophet or apostle. Every single person in the organization can work on establishing a deeper relation with him or herself. For some this is as difficult as Luther thought it was (in line with *relegere*). For others, however, it is a pretty straightforward matter: 'So what should we do? It is simple, just do what is the right thing in your judgement and be completely transparent about why you are doing it' (Avolio, 2005: 131). In fact, being an authentic leader is even said to be easier than pretending to be one: 'To manage the impression of transparency versus to simply do it is more complicated and the risk of failure is way too high today with the broad availability of information' (Avolio, 2005: 132).

Distributed Leadership

The concept of distributed leadership has become particularly influential in school leadership via the work of Gronn (2000) and Spillane (2006). Out of the concepts discussed so far, the religious bearings of distributed leadership are no doubt the most speculative. Indeed, the word 'distribution' has no religious connotations, at least not to my knowledge. Neither do affiliated concepts such as shared leadership, collective leadership, or team leadership – all concepts that try to move away from so-called 'leader-centred' approaches to leadership (though these concepts often maintain an important role for 'vertical leaders'; see, for example, Pearce, 2004). It has also become the custom to refer to these concepts as 'postheroic', which again suggests a move away from the religious roots of contemporary leadership thinking in the tradition of Carlyle's Great Man hero-worship.

It seems to me that the concept of distributed leadership (and affiliated concepts mentioned above) offer no new contents to the meaning of leadership. All distributed leadership proclaims is that leadership ('as we know it') ought to be distributed. In other words, concepts such as transformational leadership or servant leadership remain present in the idea of distributed leadership, albeit in 'distributed' form (i.e. no longer located in a single individual). This is at times acknowledged by distributed leadership scholars. For instance Spillane, Halverson, and Diamond (2001: 24; see also Harris, 2004; Pearce, 2004) note how their understanding of leadership is in line with transformational leadership.

If this is correct, then the question remains what is left of leadership when the leading characters have left the scene. The obvious answer is that we would encounter a leaderless form of spiritual leadership, where the spirit (or 'the wind of God') moves through different people and different situations. Perhaps distributed leadership points in the direction of a pre-Abrahamic concept of religion: 'In many languages, the words signifying spirit, soul and God relate to ancient words for wind, breadth and light: perceivable fluxes whose message-bearing circulation transforms and reorganizes bodies and their environment' (Serres, 1995: 34). But in the Abrahamic religions too one can find the idea that God's spirit ought to be distributed. One passage may be of particular interest: in the Old Testament (Numbers xi. 16–30), God takes some of the spirit of Moses and distributes it over seventy elders of Israel, who then start prophesizing. When Joshua protests to Moses that he should stop the prophesy of these elders, Moses answers that he wishes that God's spirit would be distributed to all people.

In comparison to other leadership concepts, distributed leadership consists of messengers only: distributed leadership is a mediated form of leadership where the medium is no longer understood as a particular individual (i.e. 'the leader'). This may be connected to its partial roots in activity theory, which sees social life as 'a continuous flow of mediated activity' (Woods, 2004: 5). Drawing on Serres (1995: 9), we may even characterize distributed leadership as angelic: 'the job of angels is only to bring messages'.

Implications for Leadership Studies

A standard narrative in leadership studies claims that the field was in crisis in the late 1970s, a 'doom and gloom' period (Hunt, 1999) in which a number of commentators recommended abandoning the study of leadership altogether for a lack of clear results (e.g. Miner, 1975). The happy ending came in the 1980s when 'the study of transformational and charismatic leadership came in to save (sic) the day' (Hunt, 1999: 130). The arrival of these new concepts amounted to nothing less than 'a transformation of the field' (Hunt, 1999). Since the 1980s, it has been said that leadership studies live in times of 'New Leadership' (capitalized, as in 'New Testament') (Bryman, 1992). This turn has also been described as the invention of a 'new genre of leadership theory', which focuses 'on exceptional leaders who have extraordinary effects on their followers and eventually on social systems' (Shamir et al., 1993: 577).[4]

According to Kuhn (1970), a paradigm shift in the sciences is akin to a religious conversion, where the members of the scientific community come to see the world anew. Rarely, however, do scholars use such an overtly religious idiom to describe a paradigm shift. Indeed, what is interesting in this narrative is that leadership scholars themselves appear as God-like characters who have saved leadership studies from an earthly existence of unconfirmed hypotheses. With the arrival of 'New Leadership', all hypotheses are confirmed, which – within the narrative – signals scientific progress.

But one may question to what extent leadership studies since what we may call the 'religious turn' amounts to a *study* of leadership. Much of what happens in the field is perhaps better understood as apostolic: as messengers of a particular (leadership) religion. The silence on the religious nature of leadership no doubt helps leadership researchers in maintaining their self-identity as scientists (Atwater et al., 2014), but it has come at the expense of the study of leadership.

If leadership is indeed best understood as a religious phenomenon, then there are two obvious possibilities for studying leadership. The first is the theological approach, i.e. to take the religious bearings of leadership seriously and subject them to faith-based analysis. Similar to Odo Casel's (1962: 5) thesis that, '[God's] revelation remains a mystery, because it is not open to the profane world, but hides itself, shows itself only to the believers, the ones whom he has chosen', true leadership may also be said only to show itself to faith-based scholarship. A great example of this, outside of the community of leadership scholars, is Philip Rieff's (2008) book on charisma which I have occasionally drawn on in this chapter: in his book Rieff shows how a theological concept, namely charisma, has come to be corrupted and he offers a powerful critique of contemporary manifestations of leadership on the basis of this critique. From within the community of organizational leadership scholars, Banks and Ledbetter (2004) also come to mind as an example of scholars who subject leadership to faith-based analysis. The second possibility is to study leadership from a religious studies perspective. This would involve studying leadership as a religion without being committed to that religion oneself. The work of Dennis Tourish (2014) on the links between transformational leadership and cults may serve as an example. In my view, both avenues hold great potential for leadership studies.[5]

Notes

1 One may of course question if this etymological exercise is best suited to capture contemporary meanings of 'religion'. Pye (1994: 224) goes as far as saying that 'the modern use of the term [religion] is not dependent on its etymology', which is echoed by Smith who holds that many of the etymological connotations are 'irrelevant for contemporary usage' (1998: 269). In particular, 'religion' is often seen as an institution, which is also captured in anthropological definitions (e.g. Spiro, 1966). However, it seems to me that the most fundamental question underpinning religious institutions is precisely how the border between the sacred and the profane is crossed, which directly pertains to the two etymological roots discussed.

2 Following Rieff's critique of Weber, one may also critique contemporary leadership discourses for their simplistic distinction between the routine nature of management and the anti-institutional nature of leadership. Many religious concepts, including the concept of charisma, offer a much more nuanced picture of the interplay between, and even the simultaneity of, the goals of organizational maintenance and organizational revolution (next to Rieff, 2008, see Hutton, 1994).

3 Among business scholars, the idea that organizations have a soul is, without exception, seen as a positive thing. However, not all celebrate the infusion of spirit in business. Gilles Deleuze (1995: 181), for instance, declares: 'We're told businesses have souls, which is surely the most terrifying news in the world'.

4 One may question to what extent 'New Leadership' is, in fact, new. It may be more precise to speak of a rediscovery of the religious dimension of leadership, given that many leadership texts prior to World War Two also draw on religious themes (see Humphreys and Einstein, 2003).

5 Many thanks to Christian Borch, Nick Butler, Helen Delaney, Josh Firth, Bent Meier Sørensen, and Stefan Tramer for their helpful feedback on an earlier version of this chapter.

References

Adair, J. (2011) *The Leadership of Jesus: And Its Legacy Today*. Norwich: Canterbury Press.

Alvesson, M. (2010) 'Leaders as saints: Leadership through moral peak performance', in *Metaphors We Lead By*, eds. M. Alvesson and A. Spicer. London: Routledge.

Atwater, L. E., Mumford, M. D., Schriesheim, C. A., and Yammarino, F. J. (2014) Retraction of leadership articles: Causes and prevention. *The Leadership Quarterly*, 25 (6), 1174–1180.

Avolio, B. (2005) *Leadership Development in Balance: MADE/Born*. New York: Psychology Press.

Avolio, B. J. and Gardner, W. L. (2005) Authentic leadership development: Getting to the root of positive forms of leadership. *The Leadership Quarterly*, 16 (3), 315–338.

Banks, R. J. and Ledbetter, B. M. (2004) *Reviewing Leadership: A Christian Evaluation of Current Approaches*. Grand Rapids, MI: Baker Academic.

Barker, R. A. (2001) The nature of leadership. *Human Relations*, 54 (4), 469–494.

Bass, B. M. (1985) *Leadership and Performance beyond Expectations*. New York: Free Press.

Blanchard, K. and Hodges, P. (2005) *Lead Like Jesus: Lessons from the Greatest Leadership Role Model of All Time*. Nashville, TN: Thomas Nelson.

Bryman, A. (1992) *Charisma and Leadership in Organisations*. London: Sage.

Campbell, J. (1969) *The Hero with a Thousand Faces*. Princeton, NJ: Princeton University Press.

Cardona, P. (2000) Transcendental leadership. *Leadership & Organization Development Journal, 21* (4), 201–207.

Carlyle, T. (1993). *On Heroes, Hero-Worship, and the Heroic in History.* Berkeley, CA: University of California Press.

Casel, O. (1962) *The Mystery of Christian Worship.* New York: Herder & Herder.

Choi, Y. and Mai-Dalton, R. R. (1999). On the leadership function of self-sacrifice. *The Leadership Quarterly, 9* (4), 475–501.

Conger, J. A. and Kanungo, R. N. (1987) Toward a behavioral theory of charismatic leadership in organizational settings. *Academy of Management Review, 12* (4), 637–647.

Conger, J. A. (1994) *Spirit at Work: Discovering the Spirituality in Leadership.* San Francisco, CA: Jossey-Bass.

Delaney, H. and S. Spoelstra (2015) 'Transformational leadership: Secularized theology?', in *Leadership: Contemporary Critical Perspectives,* eds. B. Carroll, J. Ford and S. Taylor. London: Sage.

Deleuze, G. (1995) 'Postscript on control societies', in *Negotiations 1972–1990,* ed. G. Deleuze. New York: Columbia University Press.

Fairholm, G. W. (1996) Spiritual leadership: Fulfilling whole-self needs at work. *Leadership & Organization Development Journal, 17* (5), 11–17.

Fry, L. W. (2003) Toward a theory of spiritual leadership. *The Leadership Quarterly, 14* (6), 693–727.

George, B. (2003) *Authentic Leadership: Rediscovering the Secrets to Creating Lasting Value.* San Francisco, CA: John Wiley & Sons.

George, B. (2007). *True North: Discover Your Authentic Leadership.* San Francisco, CA: John Wiley & Sons.

Greenleaf, R. K. (1977) *Servant Leadership: A Journey into the Nature of Legitimate Power and Greatness.* Mahwah, NJ: Paulist Press.

Grint, K. (2010) The sacred in leadership: Separation, sacrifice and silence. *Organization Studies, 31* (1), 89–107.

Gronn, P. (2000). Distributed properties: A new architecture for leadership. *Educational Management Administration & Leadership, 28* (3), 317–338.

Guignon, C. B. (2004) *On Being Authentic.* London: Routledge.

Harris, A. (2004) Distributed leadership and school improvement leading or misleading? *Educational Management Administration & Leadership, 32* (1), 11–24.

Hatch, M. J., Kostera, M. and Kozminski, A. K. (2005). *The Three Faces of Leadership: Manager, Artist, Priest.* Malden, MA: Blackwell.

House, R. J. (1977) 'A 1976 theory of charismatic leadership', in *Leadership: The Cutting Edge,* eds. J. G. Hunt and L. L. Larson. Carbondale, IL: Southern Illinois University Press.

Hoyt, S. F. (1912) The etymology of religion. *Journal of the American Oriental Society, 32* (2), 126–129.

Humphreys, J. H. and W. O. Einstein (2003) Nothing new under the sun: Transformational leadership from a historical perspective. *Management Decision, 41* (1): 85–95.

Hunt, J. G. (1999) Transformational/charismatic leadership's transformation of the field: An historical essay. *The Leadership Quarterly, 10* (2), 129–144.

Hutton, R. R. (1994) *Charisma and Authority in Israelite Society.* Minneapolis, MN: Fortress Press.

James, W. (1985 [1902]) *The Varieties of Religious Experience.* Cambridge, MA: Harvard University Press.

Kanungo and Mendonça (1994) 'What leaders cannot do without: The spiritual dimensions of leadership', in *Spirit at Work: Discovering the Spirituality in Leadership,* ed. J. A. Conger. San Francisco, CA: Jossey-Bass.

King, W. L. (1954) *Introduction to Religion.* New York: Harper & Row.

Klein, K. J. and House, R. J. (1995) On fire: Charismatic leadership and levels of analysis. *The Leadership Quarterly, 6* (2), 183–198.

Kuhn, Thomas S. (1970) *The Structure of Scientific Revolutions.* (2nd ed.). Chicago: University of Chicago Press.

Lawrence, B. B. (1998) 'Transformation', in *Critical Terms for Religious Studies,* ed. M. C. Taylor. Chicago: University of Chicago Press.

Leavitt, H. (1986) *Corporate Pathfinders.* Homewood, IL: Dow-Jones Irwin.

Manz, C. C. (1998) *The Leadership Wisdom of Jesus: Practical Lessons for Today.* San Francisco, CA: Berrett-Koehler Publishers..

Miner, J. B. (1975) 'The uncertain future of the leadership concept: An overview', in *Leadership Frontiers,* eds. J. G. Hunt and L. L. Larson. Kent: Kent State University Press.

Nancy, J. L. (2005) *The Ground of the Image.* New York: Fordham University Press.

Nanus, B. (1992) *Visionary Leadership: Creating a Compelling Sense of Direction for Your Organization.* San Francisco, CA: Jossey-Bass.

Oswick, C. (2009) Burgeoning workplace spirituality? A textual analysis of momentum and directions. *Journal of Management, Spirituality and Religion, 6* (1), 15–25.

Palmer, P. J. (1994) 'Leading from within: Out of the shadow, into the light', in *Spirit at Work: Discovering the Spirituality in Leadership*, ed. J. A. Conger. San Francisco, CA: Jossey-Bass.

Parker, M. (2009) Angelic organization: Hierarchy and the tyranny of heaven. *Organization Studies, 30* (11), 1281–1299.

Pearce, C. L. (2004) The future of leadership: Combining vertical and shared leadership to transform knowledge work. *The Academy of Management Executive, 18* (1), 47–57.

Potts, J. (2009) *A History of Charisma*. Basingstoke, UK: Palgrave Macmillan.

Pye, M. (1994) *The Continuum Dictionary of Religion*. New York: Continuum.

Ratzinger, J. (2004) *Introduction to Christianity*. San Francisco, CA: Ignatius Press.

Reave, L. (2005) Spiritual values and practices related to leadership effectiveness. *The Leadership Quarterly, 16* (5), 655–687.

Rieff, P. (2008) *Charisma: The Gift of Grace, and How It Has Been Taken Away from Us*. New York: Vintage.

Sendjaya, S. and Sarros, J. C. (2002) Servant leadership: Its origin, development, and application in organizations. *Journal of Leadership & Organizational Studies, 9* (2), 57–64.

Serres, M. (1995) *Angels: A Modern Myth*. Paris: Flammarion.

Shamir, B., House, R. J., and Arthur, M. B. (1993). The motivational effects of charismatic leadership: A self-concept based theory. *Organization Science, 4* (4), 577–594.

Sliwa, M., Spoelstra S., Sørensen B. M., and Land, C. (2013) Profaning the sacred in leadership studies: A reading of Murakami's *A Wild Sheep Chase. Organization, 20* (6): 860–880.

Smith, J. Z. (1998) 'Religion, religions, religious', in *Critical Terms for Religious Studies*, ed. M. C. Taylor. Chicago: University of Chicago Press.

Sørensen, B. M. and Spoelstra, S. (2013) 'Faith', in *Handbook of the Philosophical Foundations of Business Ethics*, ed. C. Lütge. Dordrecht: Springer.

Spillane, J. P. (2006) *Distributed Leadership*. San Francisco, CA: Jossey-Bass.

Spillane, J. P., Halverson, R., and Diamond, J. B. (2001) Investigating school leadership practice: A distributed perspective. *Educational Researcher, 30* (3): 23–28.

Spiro, M. E. (1966) 'Religion: Problems of definition and explanation', in *Anthropological Approaches to the Study of Religion*, ed. M. Banton. London: Tavistock.

Spoelstra, S. (2013a) 'Leadership studies: Out of business', in *Critical Perspectives on Leadership: Emotion, Toxicity and Dysfunction*, ed. J. Lemmergaard and S. L. Muhr. Northampton, MA: Edward Elgar.

Spoelstra, S. (2013b) Is leadership a visible phenomenon? On the (im)possibility of studying leadership. *International Journal of Management Concepts and Philosophy, 7* (3): 174–188.

Stogdill, R. M. (1974) *Handbook of Leadership: A Survey of the Literature*. New York: Free Press.

Thomas, C. H., Hebdon, A. S., Novicevic, M. M., and Hayek, M. J. (2015) Fluid leadership in dynamic contexts: A qualitative comparative analysis of the biblical account of Nehemiah. *Journal of Management History, 21* (1), 98–113.

Tourish, D. (2014) *The Dark Side of Transformational Leadership: A Critical Perspective*. London: Routledge.

Towey, A. (2013) *An Introduction to Christian Theology: Biblical, Classical, Contemporary*. London: Bloomsbury.

Van Knippenberg, D. and Sitkin, S. B. (2013) A critical assessment of charismatic: Transformational leadership research. Back to the drawing board? *The Academy of Management Annals, 7* (1): 1–60.

Waldman, D. A., Siegel, D. S., and Javidan, M. (2006) Components of CEO transformational leadership and corporate social responsibility. *Journal of Management Studies, 43* (8), 1703–1725.

Wallace, J. R. (2007) Servant leadership: A worldview perspective. *International Journal of Leadership Studies, 2* (2), 114–132.

Warren, B. (1989) *On Becoming a Leader*. Boston, MA: Addison-Wesley Publishing.

Weber, M. (1968) *On Charisma and Institution Building: Selected Papers*. Chicago: University of Chicago Press.

Weber, M. (1978) *Economy and Society: An Outline of Interpretative Sociology*. Berkeley, CA: University of California Press.

Wilkes, C. G. (1998) *Jesus on Leadership: Discovering the Secrets of Servant Leadership from the Life of Christ*. Wheaton, IL: Tyndale House Publishers.

Woods, P. A. (2004) Democratic leadership: Drawing distinctions with distributed leadership. *International Journal of Leadership in Education, 7* (1), 3–26.

Zaleznik, A. (1977) Managers and leaders: Are they different? *Harvard Business Review, 55* (May–June): 67–78.

22

Ethics in Denial

Leadership and Masculinity in the Financial Sector[1]

David Knights

Introduction

Despite numerous signs of imminent disaster at the turn of the century, the global banking crisis of 2007–08 can be traced to the collapse of the wholesale market for credit once Lehman Brothers filed the largest bankruptcy in US history (Li *et al.*, 2012; Knights and McCabe, 2015). No doubt, the crisis and the enormity of the government bailout for what previously were mighty corporations shocked the world, as its global impact and severity was felt on post-war, taken-for-granted, affluent livelihoods. Ordinarily this would result in radical departures from the conditions of life that made such painful traumas possible. However, this seems not to have happened several years after the events of 2007–08, for the sector including its governmental guardians/regulators remains in denial about the scale of the ethical transformations that are needed. Many of the conditions that made the crisis possible were the neoliberal culture/ideology and its faith in 'free markets', economic growth and heroic leaders. This combination of beliefs set the scene for the economic deregulations of the 1970s and 1980s that were perceived as the catalyst for unleashing a proliferation of entrepreneurial creativity, imagination and leadership.

Of course, deregulation did not have a wholly free rein since a limited range of regulatory controls especially in relation to the financial sector were deemed necessary accompaniments to the 'free market' movement in Western economies (Morgan and Knights, 1997). These new regulations were designed, however, to facilitate the growth and development of market relations, *not* to restrain them. So, for example, in UK financial services, regulations at the point of consumption not at the point of production were introduced since these were deemed to protect retail consumers from unscrupulous selling (Knights, 1997) without repressing innovative leadership and strategies. Product innovations of the kind that simply facilitated the circulation of wholesale market financial instruments, without adding value, were not constrained by the new regulations. Indeed, according to Finance Maps of the World,[2] one of the most important objectives of the financial regulatory bodies was to sustain confidence in the financial markets, thus fuelling the proliferation of what turned out to be toxic financial trades. Nor were there any obstacles placed in the paths of the new heroes of the age – entrepreneurial leaders (Kuratko, 2007; White *et al.*, 2007). Yet clearly the crisis demonstrated that the regulators fell well short of achieving their objectives of encouraging entrepreneurial leadership within a context of financial stability. What is interesting is that, despite this failure to protect society from financial mismanagement, the cost of regulation grew '15-fold since 1986 and the number of regulators grew between 1980 and 2010 from one for every 11,000' to one for every 300 people employed in the financial sector (Booth, 2015). Just as in the banks themselves, failure in regulation results in rewards rather than penalties and more of the same as the conventional rule-based regulation continues to remain the principal post-crisis intervention (Bernstein, 2011).

It can be argued that many of the common explanations for, but more importantly solutions to, the global financial crisis of 2008 derive precisely from the same mode of thinking that led to the crisis in the first place (Knights and McCabe, 2015). At present, the media, regulators, politicians and government are providing these explanations and feeding or diverting the public anger about the appalling risks that the bankers put on their organizations and ultimately the global economy. In particular, there is anger that these excessively high-rewarded senior executives can walk away with massive payouts even though they may have had to resign from their jobs. What is interesting is that, while apologizing, the CEOs and chairmen of banks do not accept responsibility. Instead they make the claim that no one could have predicted the collapse of the wholesale market for credit. Yet as early as 2006 many were anxious about the number of defaults on subprime mortgages in the US and how these mortgages had already been packaged into secondary assets that were being traded in global wholesale markets. What is clear is that, partly encouraged by the belief in financial services as an economic panacea, leaders in banking failed to administer due care or undertake adequate risk assessments prior to the crisis. In effect, they were fuelled by a growth mentality from which they personally benefited in terms of large bonuses, as banks expanded their loan book and participated in the trading of securitized products that were becoming increasingly more insecure.

The understandable response of governments in the economies where the crisis was most acute was to refinance these failed markets and to propose stronger and stricter regulatory constraints. However, as has been suggested, these attempts to 'solve the problems with the same thinking that created them' (Thomas, 2009) does not transform behaviour largely because it bypasses reflection on ethical possibilities (a topic I return to later in this chapter). For example, there is no focus on transforming the culture to render it conducive to the development of a leadership that is ethically engaged rather than instrumentally preoccupied with contradictory notions of economic self-interest (Roberts and Jones, 2009). Of the numerous explanations for the financial crisis that has wreaked havoc in global economies – economic deregulation, subprime mortgages, securitized loans, complex derivatives, consumer indebtedness, inadequate regulations, economic dependence on financial services, undue faith in the property boom, short-termism, bonus culture, greedy bankers, contagion of optimism, irrational hubris, poor regulation, neo-liberal consensus and government complacency – none seemed to problematize leadership and its ethical failures. That is, not until further bank scandals were exposed – the mis-selling of mortgage payment protection insurance (Ashton and Hudson, 2012) and the Libor scandal (Malloch and Mamorsky, 2013) – was the Chairman of the Bank of England prompted to declare that: 'the basic social contract at the heart of capitalism was breaking down amid rising inequality' . . . [and that] . . . 'individuals and their firms must have a sense of their responsibilities for the broader system' (Carney, 2014).

This message concerning social responsibility and ethics was also reinforced by the Head of the International Monetary Fund in a speech about unacceptable social inequality (Lagarde, 2014). Following these speeches, a further three banking scandals transpired[3] but little more has been said about ethics in banking or in business more broadly since.

While these interventions in favour of greater social responsibility are welcome, they are unlikely to have impact. This, because they simply reflect politically conservative notions of codes of ethics and social capital that provide little challenge to the status quo. Indeed it is one of the arguments of this chapter that the resort to codes of ethics takes moral responsibility or ethical choice away from the subject, whether individual or corporate entity, and replaces it with an imperative to be compliant or subordinate to some 'higher' order of rules. Consequently leaders do not so much lead through example by 'bearing witness' to what is an ascetic and ethical life but simply reflect and reproduce an unquestioning obedience and subordination. The chapter also seeks to illustrate how the material pursuits of bankers to achieve the largest salaries, target-driven bonuses and pensions can be identified to be a part of the construction and maintenance of their masculine identities. The chapter will suggest that, in the absence of a more ethical and self-reflexive approach, the repair to the markets and reform of the system may be to reproduce the very problems that led to this damaging financial crisis in the first place. In short, rule-based ethics and forms of leadership that fail to escape the domination of masculine senses of identity are part of the problem of financial scandals, not their solution (Knights and Tullberg, 2012). While the precariousness of masculine identity drives leaders to seek ever-increasing material and symbolic rewards, the rules become a challenge to test their creative and innovative skills in finding profitable loopholes in the regulations. Of course, the drive for, and promise of, success can often result in a breach of the rules as in those bank scandals that have been exposed since the crisis of 2008, but these are tiny in comparison with the finding of loopholes where it would seem that, as yet, nothing illegal occurred.

The chapter is organized into three sections followed by a brief conclusion. The first reports on the global financial crisis and examines a broad range of explanations that are divided into two types: those relating to individual and those concerned with contextual conditions. The second section turns to matters of ethical leadership, arguing that the regulation solution to financial mismanagement is highly problematic, not least because, insofar as it works as a constraint, it tends to stifle creativity and innovation. More importantly, however, is its failure to generate ethical behaviour as opposed to mere compliance or deviance where creative leadership is diverted towards finding loopholes in the rules. The third section explores other non-regulatory obstacles to the development of ethical leadership and, in particular, gendered preoccupations with masculine identities. Finally there is a summary and conclusion where the implications of this analysis and suggestions for further research are explored.

The Global Financial Crisis

Banks have never been the most popular of institutions but in 2008 they exceeded themselves in offending almost everyone through their irresponsible lending policies and their reckless accumulation of a large number of re-securitizations of debt in the form of Collateralized Debt Obligations (CDOs) and Credit Default Swaps (CDS) that eventually became toxic assets. No one could imagine that institutions, having traditionally been seen as following the standards of probity, risk aversion, and stability, could find themselves in such a financial crisis. Forced to accept government aid and, in some cases, full public ownership was seemingly the final humiliation, except that more scandal was to follow in the succeeding years.

The crisis had its genesis in the rise of defaults in subprime mortgages in the US, which exposed the loans that had been bundled into securitized packages of loans traded worldwide and fuelling an enormous growth of credit. While banks have traditionally lent around ten times their assets, this debt/asset ratio has multiplied massively as a result of institutions selling their debts as securitized products in a global market. As a result, large numbers of banks throughout the West came close to bankruptcy and had to rely on state funds to survive. Once a default on subprime debts occurred and the securitized packages that had fuelled the economic boom became unmarketable, the money markets dried up as a source of funds and it was clear that the banks were under-capitalized and in need of a massive bail-out through the taxpayer. The US government brought the crisis to a head when in September 2008 it allowed the investment bank Lehman Brothers to go into administration and almost immediately afterwards was forced to bail out several large financial institutions such as the largest mortgage lenders Freddie Mac and Fannie Mae, which were taken into public ownership. Later the government had to support, to the tune of $20bn, Bank of America's $50bn acquisition of Merrill Lynch and then had to purchase the insurer AIB at a cost of $85bn, and provide financial support for many of the retail banks. In total the financial crisis has absorbed $9.7 trillion of taxpayers' funds in the US (Lee, 2009).

While the default of subprime mortgages was not a major issue in the UK, levels of personal debt had reached unsustainable proportions of over £1 trillion and UK banks had participated in reckless lending partly fuelled by trading packaged securitized mortgages both as sellers and buyers. Some of the banks had relied on the money markets rather than personal deposits as a source of finance and, when these dried up in the early days of the credit crunch, they had insufficient funds to trade. Northern Rock had to be taken into public ownership and later Bradford & Bingley, Royal Bank of Scotland, Halifax Bank of Scotland and LloydsTSB had to turn to the government for finance at a total cost to the taxpayer approaching £1 trillion (Boden et al., 2009).

While there are numerous accounts of the crisis, all of which offer some degree of plausibility, in this chapter I will treat these merely as providing background context for an exploration of ethics and gender in relation to leadership in the financial sector. I divide the conventional explanations between those that target individuals and those that focus more on culture and constraints.

Greedy Bankers and Bonus Mania

Because of its effects on the wellbeing of most people, there has been much public anger with the banks, fuelled also by the media and politicians blaming and shaming those that can be identified as the perpetrators of the crisis – CEOs of the major financial institutions that have either gone into administration or been saved only by the injection of huge taxpayer funds. In both the US and UK, the bankers and associated chief executives have been subjected to embarrassing investigation, respectively by congressional and parliamentary committees, that provided the media with scapegoats around which they could write excellent copy.

Since the crisis there have been numerous scandals reported in the media about the way that, despite being rescued by public funds, many of the financial institutions have rewarded failure in the form of exit payments and continued large bonuses to senior executives. Explaining the crisis in terms of a psychology of individual greed or selfishness may be necessary since it is clear that the pursuit of economic self-interest in securing high salaries and huge bonuses had moved into the stratosphere and beyond all reasonable levels of reward for performance. Of course, managers legitimize their high salaries and bonuses in terms of a claim to expert knowledge and in relation to market-level salaries necessary to attract and retain such expertise. However, the failures lend to these claims a sense of ideology and empty rhetoric that reflect the views of many students of business who question the existence of any genuine management expertise or knowledge (MacIntyre, 1981). This will be returned to later when discussing masculinity in management, but it may be argued that there is a tautology working here such that high salaries and bonuses are as much, if not more, about validating the claim to knowledge as the reward for it. Is it not by differentiating themselves from the majority of workers through high income that senior managers can claim the expertise that is then used to justify the stratospheric levels of remuneration?

The media attention to managerial greed and the expectation that they should be rewarded even in the face of gross failure and incompetence does have the cathartic effect of dissipating public anger but it is not helpful in seeking to fully understand the development of either the financial crisis or how to transform social relations to avoid something similar re-occurring. Is it then better simply to identify the crisis to be a function of technical weaknesses in regulation, for perhaps what is needed is a tougher regulatory regime to constrain the kind of excesses that seems to have infected many of our financial institutions?

The Neo-liberal Nightmare of Deregulation and Financialization

In the 1980s there was in Western economies a quiet revolution of neoliberalism where the political consensus embraced the 'free market' with unquestioning demands for economic deregulation, in the belief that markets should be the primary if not sole arbiters of economic transactions (Knights, 1997). Alongside this faith in markets was a parallel conviction that the financial sector could be the salvation for sluggish or declining economies in an era of deindustrialization. The exponential growth of credit that reflected and reproduced the boom in housing prices transformed populations into financialized subjects for whom social relationships are reduced to transactions (Dembinksi, 2009) deprived of content that is not economically instrumental (Palley, 2013), and financial logic and practice begins to intrude into every aspect of life (Froud et al., 2006; Ertürk et al., 2008; Beverungen et al., 2013). The advantage that finance has is that the trader makes a turn on every transaction regardless of outcomes (Ingham, 1984) whereas other businesses can only make a profit when the products are worth more to the consumer than it costs to produce them. At the height of the boom the circulation and recycling of financial assets had reached such proportions that we even witnessed manufacturers and retailers making more profit through financial trade than from their conventional business activities (Dembinski, 2009).

It is the case that a large number of political leaders have become rather late subscribers to the view that markets are *not* the self-regulating and efficient mechanisms that the New Right (Washington or Anglo-Saxon) liberal consensus presumed.[4] However, this brief unease concerning markets following the global financial crisis has been comparatively short lived or perhaps rather superficial, for there is rarely any questioning of the ideology of elites who justify obscene levels of financial reward on the basis of market rates and 'getting the best talent for the job'. While there is acknowledgement that the regulations have to be tighter, this is largely concerned with bringing back confidence to 'free markets' but, as will be argued below, the regulations have almost nothing to do with ethics.

However, a further question is whether regulation is at the heart of the problem in financial services. Clearly, on the back of a deregulatory consensus since the 1980s, the demand for 'light touch' regulation on the part of the industry and some politicians has contributed to the crisis. Yet this cannot be the source of the problem if the chairman of the UK regulator was correct in 2009 when he argued that there had been a fundamental intellectual failure. His argument was that the regulator had focused on processes and procedures in individual companies such as lines of authority and had not recognized that the problem was much more related to a suspect business model that finance capital had created (BBC 1, 2009). While through this means he was following the trend of many of the authorities in passing the blame onto someone else – in this case an anonymous group of intellectuals who should have warned the authorities of the dangers of this business model – it is somewhat fallacious given that it is rare to find business people changing direction at the behest of intellectual academics.[5] One example that he would have been better to speak about is principal–agency theory in finance,[6] which was successful in promoting the single-minded pursuit of shareholder value and advocating managerial bonuses as the only way to motivate managers to secure it. But again this theory had a perfect fit with the 'free' market consensus that was rarely challenged then or now.

However, the intellectual failure does not reside in some amorphous and anonymous set of academics so much as in the establishment where thinking remains locked into a narrow paradigm that shifts between varying levels of market liberalization or regulatory control. While the present crisis clearly pushes the consensus towards increased regulatory intervention, the problem is that too much regulation stifles innovation and, regardless of the levels of intervention, there is never a possibility of covering all permutations such that market excess is always under control. The bonus culture and the scandals over expense claims reveal the gap between legal rules/regulations and ethical behaviour. There is another problem, however, for the greater the degree of regulation, the less justification there is for the financial sector to remain private. It may be possible for the banks to have much more restrictive regulation than other industries since the tacit understanding that the state cannot allow banks to collapse is now explicit but it is difficult to accept *private* rather than public profits being allowed in such circumstances. Nor is it reasonable to have income differentials of the kind that we have seen exposed by this crisis. Some such arrangements may evolve but the politicians do not seem inclined to go to the point of full-scale public ownership of the financial sector despite presently suffering the costs without enjoying the full benefits of doing so. However, the argument of this chapter is that the proposed changes and interventions do not remove the necessity to consider other issues such as business and leadership ethics in relation to the crisis we have witnessed.

Leadership and Ethics

The term leadership cannot be deployed without recognizing how meaning is historically contingent and that we examine the term historically from a position of contemporary concerns or a 'history of the present' (Foucault, 1979; Case et al., 2011: 246). It is then always dangerous to contextualize any contemporary conception of leadership by seemingly tracing it to a historical past because that has already been reconstructed in terms of our current interests (Foucault, 1979; Case et al., 2011). Consequently we have to resist popular views of leadership as deriving from the ancient Greek philosophers Aristotle and Plato, and perhaps even more so, the fifteenth-century Machiavelli whose book *The Prince* (1961) seemingly justified some of the most ruthless and tyrannical tactics of many later leaders. For in the case of the Greeks, the terms they used had more of a correspondence with excellence and facilitating others to pursue what they already knew and our current translation of Machiavelli relates to its inconsistency with contemporary democratic values.

In contrast to personal reflections of either one's own or others' leadership styles (Nohria and Khurana, 2010), leadership studies were really an invention of the mid-twentieth century when empirical research (Khurana, 2007) began to challenge the idiosyncratic personal experience and reminiscences of past leaders. From this time until the latter part of the twentieth century, these studies were dominated by the disciplines of psychology and social psychology and tended to subscribe to individualistic and deterministic approaches that reflected and reproduced the autonomous subject of Enlightenment thinking (Knights and O'Leary, 2006). Research of this kind was preoccupied with identifying the characteristics or traits of individual leaders and this was so even when, as often was the case, other variables were taken into account such as the nature of the group and followers to be led, the context/situation in which leadership was enacted or other contingencies such as collective aspects of leadership and its overall function (Bryman, 1986). Increasingly in the late twentieth century, these individualistic and psychologistic approaches were subject to considerable criticism, largely focusing on their positivist attempts to generate models that promised, yet failed to produce, generalizable knowledge with the power of prediction and control (Case et al., 2011: 243). The field of leadership studies seemed to suffer a period of demise, but this was short lived.

For at the turn of the century there was a revival in academic studies of leadership, partly because of a parallel interest among practitioners who had recently witnessed a collapse of the panacea promised by the systems and information technology revolution, when the dot.com bubble burst (Lowenstein, 2004). At this time, systems solutions that tended to eschew a focus on leadership went into decline, presaging a return to human intervention wherein leadership once again became a fad and fashion.[7] This practitioner interest could have a number of reasons, some of which may simply reflect the historical cycle of fads and fashions and others that relate to the comparative failure of systems, markets or micro-electronic interventions to deliver on their promise to improve performance, productivity and professionalism in practitioner–client relations. A return, therefore, to human intervention was not long in gaining ground as practising managers recognized that, while easier to manage, systems or technology are not guaranteed to deliver productivity and performance. Such outcomes, it was understood, required there to be an adequate management of people so as to encourage, stimulate or inspire rather than simply instruct them to comply with decisions from 'above' (Knights and Willmott, 1999).

This revival took a variety of different forms within the mainstream, largely in the direction of advancing transformational and followership approaches to leadership (Baker, 2007; Carsten et al., 2010) but which has been criticized from a post-structuralist position by Collinson (2006) and others (Wood, 2008; Wood and Ladkin, 2008). This literature formed part of a new development within the revival of studies of leadership that could be seen as taking a critical, ethical and philosophical turn (Case et al., 2011; Lemmergaard and Muhr, 2013; Collinson, 2011, 2014; Schedlitzki and Edwards, 2014; Carroll et al., 2015), pursuing issues of gender and ethnic diversity, emotion, power and identity, the body and ethics in ways that the traditional literature failed to do. Much of the mainstream has taken an amoral approach in which leadership is seen as little more than the instrumental pursuit of commercial 'profit or material gain' (Case et al., 2011: 247). This was a medium and outcome of philosophical orientations ranging from the presumed 'hidden hand' consequences of individual or corporate economic self-interest to Enlightenment beliefs in individual autonomy, reason and a personal responsibility imperative for self-improvement and realizing one's potential (Costea et al., 2012) that has generated a culture of performativity (Craft and Jeffrey, 2008).[8]

This is not to argue that mainstream academic studies or 'how to do it' texts have disappeared, but the field has become more diverse and open to challenge than before. Nor does focusing on topics traditionally excluded from leadership studies necessarily leave the individualistic and heroic traditions behind, as we shall see below when considering virtue ethics. Nonetheless, there is a growing body of research which positions leadership as having a central role and responsibility in constituting organizational or business ethics. For example, Arjoon (2000) argues that the crises that business and society face today are the crises of leadership and ethics. Minkes, Small and Chatterjee (1999: 328) argue that conformity to ethical requirements is a responsibility of, and depends on, leadership in the organization, and Maier (2002) proposes that leadership approaches should be more collaborative than controlling and more values-based than outcome-focused. Sen (2009: 3) suggests that we have neglected to recognize that even the best-known free market economist – Adam Smith – believed that the market leaves a lot of things *undone*. The state has to provide public services such as education, health and welfare, especially for those who are made unemployed by the market. Sen argues that we need an economic system that draws on a variety of institutions chosen pragmatically, and is based on social values that can be defended ethically (Sen, 2009: 1). One of these social values has to be ethical leadership (Sims and Brinkmann, 2002: 327) and they illustrate their case by referring to John Gutfreund, the leader of Salomon Brothers, who, not unlike many of the banking leaders in 2008, created an organizational culture that resulted in unethical and illegal behaviour by its members. Gutfreund, they argue, behaved unethically in his absolute attention to a short-term business focus, his willingness to cover up illegal behaviour and the ease with which he allegedly betrayed his mentor in his rise to power. There is little question but that the swathe of bankers who have been forced to stand before congressional or parliamentary inquiries and offer public apologies have followed precisely the same, and perhaps an even more aggressively masculine, pursuit of short-term bonuses and profits.

The Failure of Ethics in Leadership within Finance[9]

Insofar as the leaders in regulation within financial services draw on ethical discourse and this is not always obvious, they do so indirectly or unconsciously through adhering to a version of deontology or consequentialism.[10] Their main concern is to establish a set of universal rules to which the financial corporations must comply. This appeal to universal principles (e.g. promise-keeping and truth-telling), for example, emphasizes the use of reason to work out a consistent set of moral principles that cannot be overridden. The categorical imperative has two elements: first, it insists that we act in accordance with what can be seen as reasonable principles that can be applied universally; second, we should not be instrumental in the sense of treating others as a means to an end (Kant, 1879). In endorsing universal principles, deontology provides an almost perfect rationale for the regulators, although within the financial sector there may be more difficulties in complying with the non-instrumental principle. In subscribing to a neoliberal free market ideology, the regulators are sympathetic to the consequentialist ethics surrounding Adam Smith's egoistic theory in which morality is attributed to actions that are based on the pursuit of individual self-interest because, through what is seen as the 'hidden hand' of market exchange, the aggregated consequences are seen to have collective benefits (Smith, 1793/1976) if only in the form of increasing overall economic growth. The regulators do, however, see their role as constraining this egoism where it is thought to result in behaviour detrimental to consumers and society. They tend therefore to subscribe to a consequentialist ethics of utili-tarianism in which the rules they create are expected to have positive, or at least not negative, communal or collective consequences. Many of their rules are directed toward enforcing good business conduct through transparency and information disclosure, and fair treatment for customers (see http://www.fsa.gov.uk/) but the success of these rules are grounded more in faith than in evidence.

There are many problems associated with both deontological and consequential ethics, which I now consider in turn. A major problem with the universalism of deontology is that it is impossible for rules and obligations to cover every possible contingency and so there will always be a need for continuous deliberations, given the complexity of moral life. Of course, the biggest problem in relation to the financial sector is that the rule makers are almost always one step behind the practitioners, usually having to close the barn door once the horse has bolted. Rules are often introduced as a means of preventing some action that has been identified as damaging to the industry. However, from an ethical point of view, the most serious problem with deontology is how it produces an unreflexive compliance with rules, and thereby actually removes the moral dilemma of making a choice between alternative actions independently of external constraints (Derrida, 1992) and in this sense de-sensitizes us all to our own moral judgements. For Derrida (1992), moral choice only exists when there are situations of what he calls 'undecidability', i.e. when there is no clear external guide on how we are to behave. By bureaucratizing morality, deontology has the effect of displacing it with rituals and routines with which we either comply or become deviants. It may also be argued that deontology separates the ethics of the act from the ethics of the agent and focuses on the act to the neglect of the agent. Thus, acts of rewarding managers excessively even in the midst of the crisis were possible under the rules; governments had to act in a more draconian fashion to stop bonuses being paid, to shame those who had instead rewarded themselves with huge pay awards and, for example, to withdraw the knighthood of Sir Fred Goodwin who had received a doubling of his pension pot on resignation from the bank that he almost destroyed.

Equally there are problems with consequentialist ethics in its focus almost exclusively on outcomes and in particular its commitment to hedonism. In terms of its focus on outcomes, it assesses whether or not an act is right or wrong wholly in terms of its consequences in relation to the interests of individuals (egoism) or those of a majority in society (utilitarianism) and in relation to the hedonistic principle it assumes the pursuit of pleasure and the avoidance of pain to be universal aspects of the human condition. First a focus on the results that transpire from moral behaviour is problematic insofar as, in matters of human behaviour, we do not have a science that can establish efficient causes in terms of a simple linear relationship between moral acts and their consequences. This is because, unlike natural objects, humans are meaning-creating and transforming subjects, such that there is a double hermeneutic of interpretation on the part of both the subject under observation and the observer (Giddens, 1979). Furthermore, even if the interpretive dilemma did not exist, the complexity of social relations would make it difficult if not impossible to isolate a moral decision from all the other factors that bore on the eventual consequences. Turning to the hedonistic (behaviourist) principle, it is tautological insofar as the pleasurable or painful consequences (responses) are not independent of the ethical act (stimulus) that is deemed to be their cause (Chomsky, 1970). This is partly a function of the impossibility of establishing a universal concept of pleasure, since what can be seen as enjoyable to one person can be seen as hell to another and the idea that pain is to be avoided is routinely contradicted and not just by the existence of masochists. Moreover, there is an additional problem with both the majority and the hedonistic principles insofar as, in situations of majority rule, minorities are disenfranchised or suffer for the sake of the pleasure of the largest group. This is why in establishing the American constitution, there was some acknowledgement of De Tocqueville's (1895/1998) view that a democracy needs to ensure a respect and voice for minorities.

An alternative ethics of leadership that would seem to overcome the objections to deontological and consequential ethics could derive from the theories of virtue originally inspired by Aristotle (MacIntyre, 1981). There has been a growing support for some form of virtue ethics within the literature on ethics and leadership (see e.g. Arjoon, 2000; Whetstone, 2001; Molyneaux, 2003; Case et al., 2011). Although there is not homogeneity between the various authors, generally morality is seen as internal to the subject and the key to 'good' rests, not in rules or rights, but in the classic notion of character (honesty, fairness, compassion and generosity). Virtue ethics is concerned with what we become as subjects rather than moral imperatives to behave according to particular rules and regulations or in terms of specified outcomes. It centres on the agent, the character and the dispositions of persons. Virtue-based ethics seeks to produce excellent persons who both act well (out of spontaneous goodness) and serve as examples to inspire others, and in this sense it is closely aligned with leadership. And given the examples provided earlier, financial sector management has failed miserably to inspire ethical behaviour through leadership.

However, as was hinted at earlier, one of the problems identified in the literature on leadership was its tendency to support individualistic notions of leaders as heroes or occasionally heroines. Unfortunately, the literature on ethical leadership does not escape this tendency for it can be equally as individualistic as the earlier leadership literature, especially when it has a strong focus on the character of leaders or is driven by *virtue* ethics. While virtue ethics does challenge the domination of deontological and utilitarian rules in discussions of ethics, it does so within leadership studies at the cost of retaining a belief in the individual, virtuous and often heroic leader. Whereas the former concentrate on what are the positive consequences of complying with deontological (duty) or utilitarian (greatest good to the greatest number) rules, virtue ethics focuses on *being* a moral subject and displaying good character and disposition. There is some irony here in that, if virtue ethics is adopted in leadership studies, it is in danger of emulating the very trait approach that critical leadership studies have sought to discard. Insofar as morality is founded on a 'relatively arbitrary and almost in-exhaustive list of character traits' that are independent of the context in which leadership might be undertaken (Knights and O'Leary, 2006: 130), it is equally as problematic as the universalized rules of deontology and the consequentialist norms of utilitarianism. It might then be said that the failure of ethical leadership in finance or elsewhere resides in the inadequacy of ethics but there is another problem that, it could be argued, presents major obstacles: namely, the preoccupation of many leaders with their identities, often embedded in discourses of masculinity.

These discourses of masculinity are quite clearly embedded in leadership studies that embrace conceptions of heroism that stretch back as far as Homer's epic and possibly mythic tale of Odysseus's ten-year voyage back home from his heroic battle of Troy. Bankers have never struggled with the elements and war in the way that Odysseus is proclaimed to have done, yet they often display similar kinds of claims to masculine leadership whereby technically rational, disembodied, performance-oriented, highly instrumental, aggressive competition for privileged material and symbolic positions is combined with homosocial bonding and social exclusiveness (Blomberg, 2009; Knights and Tullberg, 2012). Of course, leaders within the financial sector do not exhibit universal or identical sets of behaviour. So, for example, patriarchs in the boardroom will differ significantly from macho dealers on the trading floor (McDowell, 1997), and clearly masculinities differ across a wide range of other distinctive subjectivities such as ethnicity, age, culture and other socio-political contexts (Gilmore, 1990). Nonetheless, throughout the build-up to and following the financial crisis, a certain form of macho masculinity has been in evidence, encouraging the competitive pursuit of astronomically high salaries and bonuses as part of their preoccupation with conquest and control (Seidler, 1989).

While leaders in banking will claim that they are just paying the market rate, these remuneration packages are decided by a predominantly male community of similarly wealthy executives such that they are always indirectly voting for their own pay increases. It has comparatively little to do with an efficient and free market in labour that results in salaries simply reconciling the supply and demand of expertise. It could be argued that this is a systemic problem in which corporate governance has failed to question the interlocking directorships and a self-advancing community of the 'great and the good' who support each others' material and symbolic advancement.

Part of the crisis in the sector then could be seen as relating to the domination of masculinity. The finance industry might then benefit from a broader diversity programme to prevent the cloning effect of white, elderly male managers who tend to think alike and often act in unison, and, in recent history, have followed each other like lemmings into the financial abyss. For this predominant white male culture reflects and reinforces a masculine single-mindedness or tunnel vision that could be seen as fuelling the pursuit of short-term profits without adequate consideration for risk and the longer-term future. As with many of the arguments of this chapter, however, eroding the domination of masculine discourses and practices can only be seen as a necessary not a sufficient condition of diverting financial organizations away from their tendency toward self-destruction.

As we have seen, the global financial crisis has wreaked havoc on most Western economies, forcing them into austerity. The resulting recession has been the subject of much analytical commentary, with different specialists competing with one another to provide the most definitive account of, or explanation for, the events. However, almost all of the explanations are steeped in precisely the same cognitive paradigm that could be said to have generated the crisis in the first place. Perhaps its severity and implications for us all leave some space, therefore, for a radical challenge to that paradigm. Throughout this chapter, a failure of ethical leadership has been suggested as an alternative or complementary means of understanding the events for, as Santoro and Strauss (2013) put it, the 'financial crisis was fundamentally a crisis of ethics and values' (p. 19). Unfortunately the literature on ethical leadership does not provide us with a very optimistic scenario for the future in terms of transforming the financial sector. This is partly because the ethics that are available to inform leadership are dependent on one or other of the three traditional kinds of ethics – consequential, deontological or virtue – all of which arouse some misgivings, because they rely either on a passive compliance with rules or norms or on celebrations of the virtuous individual. The latter tends only to reproduce the heroism of earlier discredited individualistic and psychologistic theories of leadership and the former have been seen as incompatible with modern conceptions of ethics, insofar as they displace any moral dilemma and thereby remove the responsibility of decisive ethical action from the subject (Derrida, 1992). If this were not problematic enough, there is the additional burden within the financial sector of a dominant masculine, technical rationality that sustains an ethics that remains concentrated on constraining misbehaviour rather than transforming the sense of what it is to be ethical. In the following discussion, therefore, I speculate on an alternative embodied ethics that could break from existing paradigms.

Leadership Ethics as Embodied Engagement

At present the financial sector is paradigmatically grounded in a technical rationality that denies or ignores the social embeddedness of its programmatic routines and consequently becomes wholly detached from the bodily, material and tangible aspects of lived experience. No better example of this dematerialization of relations can be found than in the trading of mortgage and other credit securities created by complex derivatives and the (re)bundling of a diverse range of loans into tradable commodities. Conventional explanations for the crisis that followed the proliferation of innovative intangible products vary from, at one extreme, blaming the engineering, mathematics or science graduates that created them to the other, of attributing the cause to the excesses of those seeking to buy property beyond their means of servicing the loan. In between these extremes, however, greedy bankers and intermediaries or sales staffs are blamed for their failure to assess risk properly in pursuit of their own financial interests, either in the form of the growth in value of their stock options or their bonuses and commissions. While these explanations may appear to revolve around attributing some failure to real live human beings, this is something of an illusion insofar as we can see that it is their particular cognitive, instrumental and technical pursuit of economic interests that underlies the decision-making in almost all these cases. This instrumental rationality is, of course, not ordinarily directly a topic for reflection, since it is just taken for granted as normal and unremarkable behaviour.

Unfortunately the literature on leadership in general and ethical leadership in particular does little to shake the foundations of this paradigm. However, there is a different set of literatures that focuses on the possibility of developing an embodied and engaged mode of ethical leadership. This involves challenging the faith in disembodied, instrumental rationality and attributing a major condition of the possibility of financial failure precisely to this ideology (Knights and McCabe, 2015). By adopting this alternative, we would avoid seeking solutions to the crisis in the very technical and instrumental rational pursuits that were important conditions of its possibility. As many commentators have pointed out, those largely regulatory strategies attempt to salvage economic growth out of the embers of the 'burn out', but simply store up problems for tomorrow and/or for future generations. Maybe it is time to restore materiality to finance and the body to those leaders responsible for its development. Of course the intangible nature of financial products and services can never be eradicated, since money as a medium of exchange, unit of account and store of value is abstract and at some distance from the materiality which is its condition and consequence.[11] However, we should never forget that its continuity is inseparable from the trust that real embodied human beings have in one another to accept money as a substitute for the goods and services concerning which it is a mere proxy. As many commentators have remarked, the very term credit has its origins in the Latin term *credo* meaning belief, faith and trust, and yet this is precisely what is now in short supply, given the risks with other people's money that our banking leaders took in order to advance their own personal careers and finances, albeit legitimated by an equally disreputable ideology of corporate greed dressed up as corporate growth.

If there is an ethical leadership question to answer here, given the apparent inadequacy of current discourses, what is to be done? A first step has to be the resuscitation of ethical leadership, and one way to begin this is by turning away from the 'preconceived ideas and institutionalized norms' or established ways of speaking about ethics (Pullen and Rhodes, 2014: 4) that are reflected in deontological, consequential and virtue approaches. For, when there is an appeal to morality through notions of rule compliance, a 'hidden hand' or the unintended consequence of everyone pursuing their own individual material (economic) or symbolic (identity) self-interests, ethics becomes precarious as it is always a poor second that readily falls down the cracks in the pavements of everyday life. Instead we can look to promote an ethics of active bodily engagement with others, whereby leadership could then bear witness to an organizational life beyond passive compliance and subordination or the preoccupation with identity that only reflects and reproduces (often masculine) ideologies of individualism and individual self-interest. Ethical leadership can only advance through discourses and practices of embodied engagement, in which members of organizations are actively involved in their relations to the point at which individual preoccupations with, and indifference towards, that which is not perceived to embellish the self begin to disappear. An analogy to ethical leadership might well be the idea of rhythm that Levinas (1987) describes as that which is imposed and yet we consent to in our very 'participation' (p. 4) for we are 'carried away by a song to the point of dancing involuntarily to it . . . [I]t entails a loss of one's identity, "a passage of oneself to anonymity"' (Levinas, 1987; Sparrow, 2013: 467). As embodied engagement, ethical leadership could be seen at least partly to reflect the philosophy of Spinoza (1955) whose valorization of 'the joyful passage from passivity to activity' is seen as a necessary condition of ethical behaviour (Gatens, 1996: 7).

Of course, talking about ethical and embodied engagement does not necessarily bring it about, but a good part of the conditions that might make it possible is to reflect more critically on why, despite a forlorn and failed history, organizations and institutions keep returning to traditional conceptions of ethics. As has been argued, these involve deontological systems of rules and regulations that stifle innovation or direct it towards finding legal loopholes;

speculative yet nonetheless quantitative utilitarian calculations of the ethical consequences of behaviour; or resort to a notion of good character in the virtuous leader. The implications of this analysis are that in the first instance education in business schools including leadership development and executive education programmes needs first to ensure that ethics is not only embedded in the curriculum but that it reflects, as here, on the practical failure of its applications when drawing on traditional discourses of deontological, consequential or virtue ethics. Embracing an ethics of embodied engagement would have practical benefits well beyond recent leadership developments, whether of a mainstream or critical inclination.

Conclusion

The financial crisis has been examined in terms of a range of attempts to understand its development, of which there are four main variants. Psychological attributions of greed or selfishness, on the one side, or failure of the regulatory regime on the other, are the most common accounts. Two alternative yet in some senses complementary approaches to understanding the crisis draw upon discourses of ethics and masculinity, but these have had little exposure in the post-crisis debates. Whereas conventional thinking sees the pursuit of personal material and symbolic advantage through high bonuses, for example, or the failure of the rules to constrain the banks as final explanations, these alternatives go further to explore the conditions that make it possible for the pursuit of excessive rewards to seem legitimate and why regulations fail. In relation to regulation, rules can never be sufficiently exhaustive to cover all contingencies and if they were they would destroy the very potential for market-driven production to be innovative. An alternative is to advance a conception of leadership that would render unethical behaviour contradictory to what it is to be human. It involves recognizing how disembodied forms of cognitive rationality that inform many of the prevailing conceptions of ethics and leadership can result in ignorance or the glossing over of responsibility to, and engagement with, the other. In this sense, leadership informed by traditional ethics can be seen at best to restrain rather than remove unethical leadership and behaviour, and for this reason, is in denial. The pursuit of excessive material (economic) and symbolic (identity) advantage can be seen to be a major part of the construction and maintenance of a masculine identity, which might be ameliorated were the sector to have a more socially diverse management. For then it might begin to understand how an active embodied and engaged ethical leadership could transform the financial sector in the direction of commitment to the community that they were designed to serve. However, while a more equal gender balance within the higher ranks of the financial sector may be necessary, it is not a sufficient condition for developing ethical leadership. This is because, in climbing the hierarchy, women frequently have little choice but to adopt the norms and values of masculine assertive and aggressive competition, whereby the control of others overrides any sense of ethical and social responsibility (Wajcman, 1998). Consequently there has to be a concerted effort to ensure that, first, ethical leadership is embedded in financial organizations and, second, that it departs from traditional conceptions of ethics so as to develop an embodied sense of engagement with others in relations of common commitment. Ethical leadership has to escape from relying on codes of compliance and ideals of utility or virtue and instead bear witness to embodied engagements that embed relations in feelings, affects and responsibility to others, rather than cognitive calculations of self-interest.

Notes

1 I thank Peter Case for providing very useful comments on an earlier draft of this chapter.
2 http://finance.mapsofworld.com/financial-institutions/regulations.html, consulted 3 August 2013.

3 See http://www.channel4.com/news/five-other-banking-scandals-since-2008, consulted 25 March 2015.

4 Brown, for example, said 'a new economic philosophy would replace the "unbridled free market dogma" which had been discredited by the financial crisis' (http://www.dailymail.co.uk/news/article-1103662/ Well-rise-challenges-year-says-Gordon-Brown.html, consulted 25 March 2009).

5 While not directly related to the current crisis, a consultant colleague and I have personal experience of our challenges to the consensus contributing to the IT bubble in 1998, being summarily dismissed or ignored by managers caught up in the whirlwind of their own and the media hype (see Knights *et al.*, 2002).

6 The theory is designed to analyse conflicts of interest between principals (e.g. shareholders) and agents (e.g. managers) and seek solutions such as managerial bonuses or other rewards based on profit and performance so that interests coincide.

7 I am using this language in a commonsensical manner rather than in the technical manner deployed by Abrahamson and Eisenman (2008), partly as they do not consider singular isolated fashions but also because leadership is too broad a category to be included in their analysis of management fashions. Having said that, my example complies with the distinction between rational and normative swings as underlying elements of fashion.

8 The idea of performativity being used here is pejorative since it is associated with audit and accountability of measurable performance outcomes that have displaced other evaluations of activity through managerialist developments, particularly in public sector organizations such as education. I am aware that the concept is also used in a laudatory fashion when it is contrasted with linguistically dominated representational epistemologies that grant language too much 'power in determining our ontologies' (Barad, 2003: 802).

9 There are parts of this section that draw on our discussion of ethics in Knights and O'Leary (2006).

10 Deontology is a technical term used to describe duty and moral obligation to a set of rules from above. It is primarily associated with the philosopher Kant. Consequentialism simply refers to an ethics that focuses on outcomes rather than their conditions of possibility.

11 There is not space here to examine the complexities of conceptions of money, but for a detailed and radical analysis, see Ingham (2004).

References

Abrahamson, E. and Eisenman, M. (2008) Employee-management techniques: Transient fads or trending fashions? *Administrative Science Quarterly*, 53 (4): 719–744.

Arjoon, S. (2000) Virtue theory as a dynamic theory of business, *Journal of Business Ethics*, 28: 159–178.

Ashton, J. K. and Hudson, R. S. (2012) 'The mis-selling of payments protection insurance in mortgage and unsecured lending markets' in de Guevara Radoselovics, J. F. and Monsálvez, J. P. (eds) *Bank Behaviour in Modern Banking*. Basingstoke: Palgrave Macmillan.

Baker, S. D. (2007) Followership: The theoretical foundation of a contemporary construct, *Journal of Leadership & Organizational Studies*, 14 (1): 50–60.

Barad, K. (2003) Posthumanist performativity: Toward an understanding of how matter comes to matter, *Signs: Journal of Women in Culture and Society*, 28 (3): 801–820.

BBC 1 (2009) *The Andrew Marr Show*, Interviews with Sir Adair Turner and Vince Cable, 15 February 2009.

Bernstein, J. (2011) Capital reserves are the key to financial reform, http://www.csmonitor.com/Business/On-the-Economy/2011/1025/Capital-reserves-are-the-key-to-financial-reform Guest blogger / October 25, consulted 3 August 2013.

Beverungen, A., Dunne, S. and Hoedemaekers, C. (2013) The financialisation of business ethics, *Business Ethics: A European Review*, 22 (1): 102–117.

Blomberg, J. (2009). Gendering finance: Masculinities and hierarchies at the Stockholm stock exchange, *Organization*, 16: 203–222.

Boden, N., Chapman, J. and Drury, I. (2009) 'Darling warns economy could collapse if bailout fails', *Daily Mail*, 19 January. http://www.thisismoney.co.uk/news/article.html?in_article_id=467909&in_page_id=2, consulted 2 March 2009.

Booth, P. (2015) 'How Thatcher's Big Bang may have swept away a better form of regulation', *The Daily Telegraph Business Section*, 26 May, p. B2.

Bryman, A. (1986) *Leadership and Organization*. London: Routledge & Kegan Paul.

Carney, M. (2014) Keynote at *Conference on Inclusive Capitalism*, London, 27 May. See http://www.theguardian.com/business/2014/may/27/capitalism-critique-bank-of-england-carney, consulted 25 March 2015.

Carroll, B., Ford, J. and Taylor, S., editors (2015) *Leadership: Contemporary Critical Perspectives*. London: Sage.

Carsten, M. K., Uhl-Bien, M., Bradley, J., West, B. J., Jaime, L., Patera, J. L. and McGregor, R. (2010) Exploring social constructions of followership: A qualitative study, *The Leadership Quarterly*, 21 (3): 543–562.

Case, P., French, R. and Simpson, P. (2011) 'Philosophy of leadership' in Bryman, A., Collinson, D. L., Grint, K., Jackson, B. and Uhl-Bien, M. (eds) *The Sage Handbook of Leadership*. London: Sage, pp. 242–254.

Chomsky, N. (1970) 'Recent contributions to a theory of innate ideas' in Hudson, L. (ed.) *The Ecology of Human Intelligence*. Harmondsworth: Penguin.

Collinson, D. L. (2006) Rethinking followership: A post-structuralist analysis of follower identities, *The Leadership Quarterly*, 17 (2): 179–189.

Collinson, D. L. (2011) 'Critical leadership studies' in Bryman, A., Collinson, D. L., Grint, K., Jackson, B. and Uhl-Bien, M. (eds) *The Sage Handbook of Leadership*. London: Sage, pp. 179–192.

Collinson, D. (2014) Dichotomies, dialectics and dilemmas: New directions for critical leadership studies? *Leadership*, 10 (1): 36–55.

Costea, B., Amiridis, K. and Crump, N. (2012) Graduate employability and the principle of potentiality: An aspect of the ethics of HRM, *Journal of Business Ethics*, 111 (1): 25–36.

Craft, A. and Jeffrey, B. (2008) Creativity and performativity in teaching and learning: Tensions, dilemmas, constraints, accommodations and synthesis, *British Educational Research Journal*, 34 (5): 577–584.

Dembinski, P. H. (2009) *Finance: Servant or Deceiver*, Observatoire de la Finance, trans. K. Cook. Basingstoke, UK: Palgrave Macmillan.

Derrida, J. (1992) *The Gift of Death*, trans. D. Wills. Chicago: Chicago University Press.

De Tocqueville, A. (1835/1998) *Democracy in America*. Hertfordhire: Ware.

Ertürk, I., Froud, J., Sukhdev, J., Leaver, A. and Williams, K. (2008) *Financialization At Work: Key Texts and Commentary*. London: Routledge.

Foucault, M. (1979) *The History of Sexuality Volume 1: An Introduction*. London: Allen Lane.

Froud, J., Sukhdev, J., Leaver, A. and Williams, K. (2006) *Financialization and Strategy: Narrative and Numbers*. London: Routledge.

Gatens, M. (1996) *Imaginary Bodies: Ethics, Power and Corporeality*. London: Routledge.

Giddens, A. (1979) *New Rules of Sociological Method*. Cambridge: Polity Press.

Gilmore, D. C. (1990) *Manhood in the Making: Cultural Concepts of Masculinity*. Yale: Yale University Press.

Ingham, G. (2004) *The Nature of Money*. Cambridge: Polity Press.

Kant, I. (1879/1949) *Fundamental Principles of the Metaphysic of Morals*, trans Abbott. New York: Liberal Arts Press.

Khurana, R. (2007) *From Higher Aims to Hired Hands*. Princeton, NJ: Princeton University Press.

Knights, D. (1997) 'An industry in transition: Regulation, restructuring and renewal' in D. Knights and T. Tinker (eds) *Financial Service Institutions and Social Transformations: International Studies of a Sector in Transition*. London: Macmillan, pp. 1–27.

Knights, D. and McCabe, D. (2015) 'Masters of the Universe': Demystifying leadership in the context of the 2008 Financial Crisis, *British Journal of Management*, 26 (2): 197–210.

Knights, D. and O'Leary, M. (2006) Leadership, ethics and responsibility to the other, *Journal of Business Ethics*, 67 (2): 125–137.

Knights, D. and Tullberg, M. (2012) Managing masculinity/mismanaging the corporation, *Organization*, 19 (4): 385–404.

Knights, D. and Willmott, H. (1999/2003) *Management Lives! Power and Identity in Work Organisations*. London: Sage.

Knights, D., Noble, F., Vurdubakis, T. and Willmott, H. (2002) 'Allegories of creative destruction: Technology and organisation in narratives of the e-Economy' in Woolgar, S. (ed.) *Virtual Society? Technology, Cyberbole, Reality*. Oxford: Oxford University Press, pp. 99–114.

Kuratko, D. F. (2007) Entrepreneurial leadership in the 21st century, *Journal of Leadership and Organizational Studies*, 13 (4): 1–12.

Lagarde, C. (2014) IMF Meeting Washington: 8th Oct, see http://news.asiaone.com/news/singapore/imf-chief-targets-problem-inequality, consulted 25 March 2015.

Lee, M. (2009) 'The credit crisis has the US taxpayer on the hook for $9.7 trillion', http://www.dailymarkets.com/economy/2009/02/09/the-credit-crisis-has-the-us-taxpayer-on-the-hook-for-97-trillion/, consulted 2 March 2009.

Lemmergaard, J. and Muhr, S. L. (2013) *Critical Perspectives on Leadership: Emotion, Toxicity, and Dysfunction*. London: Edward Elgar.

Levinas, E. (1987) 'Reality and its shadow', in *Collected Philosophical Papers*, trans. A. Lingis. The Netherlands: Kluwer Academic Publishers, pp. 1–14.

Li, J., Leung, A. S. M., Young, M., Xin Y., Cai, Z. and Jun, H. (2012) A *Yin/Yang* Perspective on the 2008 global financial crisis, *British Journal of Management*, 23, S1, S119–S125.

Lowenstein, R. (2004) *Origins of the Crash: The Great Bubble and Its Undoing*, Harmondsworth, UK: Penguin Books.

Machiavelli, N. (1961) *The Prince*, trans. G. Bull. London: Penguin.

MacIntyre, A. (1981) *After Virtue*. London: Duckworth.

Maier, M. (2002) Ten years after a major malfunction . . . Reflections on the challenger syndrome, *Journal of Management Inquiry*, 11 (3).

McDowell, L. (1997) *Capital Culture: Gender at Work in the City*. Oxford: Blackwell.

Minkes, A., Small, M. W. and Chatterjee, S. R. (1999) Leadership and business ethics: Does it matter? Implications for management, *Journal of Business Ethics*, 20, 327–335.

Molyneaux, D. (2003) Blessed are the meek, for they shall inherit the earth: An aspiration applicable to business? *Journal of Business Ethics*, 48: 347–363.

Morgan, G. and Knights, D. (1997) *Deregulation and European Financial Services*. London: Macmillan.

Nohria, N. and Khurana, R. (eds) (2010) *Handbook of Leadership Theory and Practice*. Boston, MA: Harvard Business School Publishing Corporation.

Palley, T. I. (2013) *Financialization: The Economics of Finance Capital Domination*. London: Palgrave Macmillan.

Pullen, A. and Rhodes, C. (eds) (2014) *The Routledge Companion to Ethics, Politics and Organizations*. London: Routledge.

Roberts, J. and Jones, M. (2009) Accounting for self interest in the credit crisis, *Accounting, Organizations and Society*, 34: 856–867.

Santoro, M. A. and Strauss. R. J. (2013) *Wall Street Values: Business Ethics and the Global Financial Crisis*. New York: Cambridge University Press.

Schedlitzki, D. and Edwards, G. (2014) *Studying Leadership: Traditional and Critical Approaches*. London: Sage.

Seidler, V. J. (1989) *Rediscovering Masculinity*. London: Routledge.

Sen, A. (2009) 'Capitalism Beyond the Crisis', *The New York Review of Books*, 56 (5), 26 March.

Sims, R. and Brinkmann, J. (2002) Leaders as role models: The case of John Gutfreund at Solomon Brothers, *Journal of Business Ethics*, 35, 327–339.

Smith, A. (1793/1976) *An Inquiry into the Nature and Causes of the Wealth of Nations*, Campbell, R. H. and Skinner, A. S. (eds). London: Clarendon Press.

Sparrow, T. (2013) *Levinas Unhinged*. Zero Books, Kindle Edition.

Spinoza, B. (1955) *On the Improvement of Human Understanding: The Ethics and Selected Letters*, trans. Elwes, R. H. M. New York: Dover.

Thomas, M. (2009) BBC *Newsnight*, 1 April.

Wajcman, J. (1998) *Managing like a Man: Women and Men in Corporate Management*. University Park, Pennsylvania: The Pennsylvania University Press.

Whetstone, J. (2001) How virtue ethics fits within business ethics, *Journal of Business Ethics*, 33: 101–114.

White, R. E., Thornhill, S. and Hampson, E. (2007) A biosocial model of entrepreneurship: The combined effects of nurture and nature, *Journal of Organizational Behavior*, 28 (4): 451–466.

Wood, M. (2008) 'Process philosophy' in Thorpe, R. and Holt, R. (eds) *Dictionary of Qualitative Management Research*. London: Sage, pp. 171–173.

Wood, M. and Ladkin, D. (2008) 'The event's the thing: Brief encounters with the leaderful moment' in Turnbull James, K. and Collins, J. (eds) *Leadership Perspectives: Knowledge Into Action*. Houndmills: Palgrave Macmillan.

23

Global Leadership in Perspective

Allan Bird, Mark Mendenhall, Joyce Osland,
Gary Oddou and Sebastian Reiche

Introduction

Global leadership, with its beginnings in the late 1980s, is a relatively new area of research in the broader field of international business and international management. Its emergence coincided with, and indeed arose from, the rapid acceleration of the globalization of business in the late twentieth century (Evans, Pucik, & Barsoux, 2002; Hedlund, 1986). This rapid transformation of the global business world—from being country-to-country in nature to a milieu where "for commercial and practical purposes, nations do not exist and the relevant business arena [is] something like a big unified home market"—left companies scrambling to find executives and managers who possessed the skills to operate in this new global world (Black, Morrison, & Gregersen, 1999; Mendenhall, 2001).

Companies responded to this deficit in global leadership skills in their executive and managerial cadres by developing leadership development programs designed to upgrade the skill portfolios of their leaders. The results of these programs were underwhelming: despite their best efforts, companies found developing *global* leadership skills in their existing people to be an elusive outcome (Von Glinow, 2001). In the 1990s, scholars working in the field of international management became aware of this problem, and began conducting research on global leadership in order to better understand its nature in the hope that such understanding would enable firms to design and implement more effective development programs (Mendenhall, 2013).

One of the first challenges these scholars wrestled with was the question of whether or not there was something fundamentally different about global leadership compared to traditional leadership; in other words, is global leadership simply leadership conducted in a unique context or is there something about global leadership that necessitates it being studied as a separate phenomenon? Most scholars working in the field would agree with Osland and Bird's (2006: 123) argument that global leadership:

> differs from domestic leadership in degree in terms of issues related to connectedness, boundary spanning, complexity, ethical challenges, dealing with tensions and paradoxes, pattern recognition, and building learning environments, teams, and community and leading large-scale change efforts across diverse cultures.

In other words, global leadership involves simultaneously leading people from multiple national, organizational, team, and ethnic cultures in real time. It transcends even the challenges faced by expatriates, for the majority of expatriates operate in a bilateral cross-cultural context. Global leaders, conversely, operate in complex and paradoxical multilateral contexts, and many scholars argue that the leadership challenges that are produced from such contexts render global leadership, for all intents and purposes, different in kind from traditional leadership (Mendenhall, 2013).

We review in this chapter how scholars undertook the study of this uncharted phenomenon and summarize their findings. We delineate their work by categorizing the field into four domains: (1) multidisciplinary influences on the study of global leadership; (2) the content domain of global leadership competencies; (3) global leadership development processes and programs; and (4) future directions in the field.

Multidisciplinary Influences on the Study of Global Leadership

To date, the field of leadership has played a surprisingly small role in our current understanding of global leadership. With few exceptions, the earliest researchers approached global leadership as a new phenomenon and focused on understanding the global context and its challenges and demands. By contrast, when traditional or domestic leadership scholars globalized their research, they branched out into comparative leadership, identifying indigenous leadership styles, applying existing leadership theories across cultural borders, or incorporating cultural dimensions into their studies. Thus, global leadership and comparative leadership are different, if complementary, fields (Adler, 2001). Given its meta-level and multidimensional nature, the field of global leadership benefitted from being treated as a new paradigm with a multidisciplinary heritage. Based on a review of the global leadership literature, Osland (2013) identified four fields that have contributed extensively to global leadership: intercultural communication competence, expatriation, global management, and comparative leadership. The following paragraphs briefly identify their contributions.

Intercultural Communication Competence

Intercultural communication competence (ICC) is "the ability to effectively and appropriately execute communication behaviors that negotiate each other's cultural identity or identities in a culturally diverse environment" (Chen & Starosta, 1999: 28). It comprises knowledge, skills, attitudes, and awareness (Fantini, 2000). According to Gudykunst (1994), the most important intercultural skills are: mindfulness, tolerance of ambiguity, cognitive flexibility, cross-cultural empathy, and behavioral flexibility. *Mindfulness* is the process of thinking in new categories, being open to new information, and recognizing multiple perspectives (Thich, 1991). *Cognitive flexibility* is the ability to understand, consider, and weigh multiple frameworks, or schemas (Endicott, Bock, & Narvaez, 2003). *Tolerance of ambiguity* is the way people process information about ambiguous situations and stimuli when confronted with an array of unfamiliar, complex, or incongruent clues (Furnham & Ribchester, 1995: 179). *Empathy* is the ability to experience some aspect of reality differently from what is "given" by one's own culture (Bennett, 1993). These four are cognitive competencies. They inform the global mindset construct (Levy, Beechler, Taylor, & Boyacigiller, 2007) that figures prominently in global leadership research as well as cultural intelligence (see Thomas, 2006). *Behavioral flexibility*—a willingness to adopt and use different styles appropriately—is often termed "code-switching" or "frame-shifting" by global leadership scholars (see Gundling, Hogan, & Cvitkovich, 2011). Overcoming ethnocentrism and acquiring the ability to communicate and cooperate across cultural boundaries (Fennes & Hapgood, 1997) and the ability to decode both cultural values and communication styles when working globally (Bennett, 2009) are other components of ICC.

Intercultural communication competencies have surfaced repeatedly in global leadership competency studies, and many are included in assessment instruments, such as the Global Competencies Inventory, which measure the intercultural competency domain of global leadership (Stevens, Bird, Mendenhall, & Oddou, 2014). Both ICC and leadership development share this caveat: competencies cannot be developed easily or quickly without transformational experiences, careful design, and a strong motivation for personal development.

Expatriation

As companies considered effective ways to develop global leaders, sending an individual on an expatriate assignment emerged as the best way to develop them (Gregersen, Morrison, & Black, 1998; McCall & Hollenbeck, 2002). Expatriate experience, selection, adjustment, and transformation research hold important lessons for global leadership. The challenging nature of an international assignment spurs personal growth and transformation in crucial areas. For example, wrestling with the paradoxes inherent in an international assignment aids the development of cognitive complexity, tolerance of ambiguity, and behavioral flexibility—all aspects of global leadership (Osland, 2001). With respect to selection, past performance in a domestic setting is not a good predictor of excellent performance overseas (Black et al., 1999; Miller, 1973). Characteristics that lead to high potentials being noticed in the US may be liabilities in another country (Ruben, 1989; Spreitzer, McCall, & Mahoney, 1997). Similarly, global leaders often have to unlearn behaviors to be effective globally. Mendenhall (2001a) compared expatriate adjustment characteristics with global leadership competencies, revealing a great deal of overlap. One final caveat is Caligiuri and Di Santo's (2001) discovery that personality traits such as flexibility and level of ethnocentrism did not change as a result of expatriation—a lesson for global leadership selection.

Global Management

A global manager is:

> someone who is assigned to a position with a cross-border responsibility, who needs to understand business from a worldwide rather than from a countrywide perspective, needs to balance potentially contradictory demands in the global environment and who must be able to work with multiple cultures simultaneously rather than with one culture at a time.
>
> *(Cappellen & Janssens, 2005: 348)*

The difference between global managers and global leaders is the latter's status as change agents, in keeping with Kotter's (1990) distinction between managers and leaders. A major criticism of early global leadership research was the interchangeable use of terms and the evolving nature of their roles, particularly in sample selection (Osland, Bird, Mendenhall, & Osland, 2006). Researchers found both similarities and differences in comparisons of domestic and global managers and attributed the differences to global environmental complexity (Dalton, Ernst, Deal, & Leslie, 2002) and culture (McBer, 1995). The primary differences in domestic versus global managers stem from how they perform their roles and from which characteristics are related to effectiveness. This research helped scholars make a conceptual argument for the differences and similarities between domestic and global leaders (Osland, Bird, & Oddou, 2012).

Comparative Leadership

The field of comparative leadership studies the differences and similarities in the indigenous leadership styles of different countries or regions (see House, Hanges, Javidan, Dorfman, & Gupta, 2004). The word "leader" has different connotations in different languages, and national differences have been found in leadership characteristics, such as leader status, goals, role, communication, influence, decision making, and perceived effectiveness (see Dickson, Den Hartog, & Castaño, 2009).

The major contribution of comparative management to the field of global leadership is the understanding that national leadership styles have certain aspects in common as well as differences that are rooted in a country's unique background and culture. Global leaders with followers from different cultures have to consider how and when they need to switch leadership styles to be effective (Gill & Booth, 2003) and when culture does and does not matter.

The lengthy research trajectory of the multidisciplinary roots of global leadership—intercultural communication competence, expatriation, global management, and comparative leadership—have helped the field clarify several of its foundational questions (Osland, Li, & Wang, 2014a). Nevertheless, given our current understanding of what global leadership is and is not, the field could benefit from research that integrates concepts, theory, and process models from traditional leadership (Osland, Li, & Wang, 2014b).

Mapping the Content Domain of Global Leadership Competencies

As the field has grown, scholars have attempted to delineate the competencies that are critical to global leaders' success. Reviews of this literature (Bird & Osland, 2004; Jokinen, 2005; Mendenhall, 2001b; Mendenhall & Osland, 2002; Osland, 2008; Bird & Stevens, 2013) found that social scientists have delineated over 160 competencies that influence global leadership effectiveness; however, many of these competencies overlap conceptually and are often separated only by semantic differences (Jokinen, 2005; Osland, 2008).

A decade previously, Mendenhall and Osland (2002) initially documented this trend of proliferation when they identified 56 different competencies. Since then, there has been a nearly three-fold expansion in competencies identified. Mendenhall and Osland's (2008) initial efforts at cultivating and ordering the list of competencies consisted of grouping the many dimensions into six broad categories, reflecting the type of competency—traits and values, cognitive orientation, global business expertise, global organizing expertise, cross-cultural relationship skills, and visioning. Consideration of the six categories raises several questions about the organizing structure. For example, the six categories are not of the same qualitative type and conceptually overlap. For example, skills are qualitatively different from values, and some types of expertise may overlap with certain types of cognitive orientation.

Subsequently, Jokinen (2005) suggested synthesizing competencies into three broad "layers"—the *fundamental core*, *mental characteristics*, and *behavioral skills*. This conceptualization, however, is overly focused on within-person and interpersonal competencies, leaving business and organizational capabilities largely unaddressed.

To comprehend the proliferation of identified global leader competencies, Bird and Stevens (2013) reviewed theoretical and empirical studies published from 1993 to 2012. Over that time period, they identified a total of 160 separate competencies associated with global leadership as identified in journal articles and books.

Bird (2013) proposed an integration and synthesis that grouped competencies into three broad categories: *business and organizational savvy*; *managing people and relationships*; and *managing self*. In doing so, he drew attention to a pattern that has emerged in earlier research (see Rhinesmith, 1993; Yeung and Ready, 1995; Brake, 1997; Rosen, Digh, Singer, & Phillips, 2000). We consider his integration in greater depth, but, before doing so, note several features that emerge from a consideration of the various lists of competencies and their groupings. First, global leadership competencies appear to span a range of qualitatively different types. These include *predispositional characteristics of personality, attitudinal orientations, cognitive capabilities, motivational inclinations, knowledge bases*, and *behavioral skills*. This leads to a conclusion that global leadership is a multi-faceted phenomenon and the competencies associated with performing at a high level are multi-faceted as well. Second, competencies are distributed roughly equally across the three categories—*business and organizational savvy* grouping, *managing people and relationships*, and *managing self*. Third, there is considerable variation among scholars with regard to focus. For example, Wills and Barham (1994) focus only on competencies related to managing self, while Yeung and Ready (1995) concentrate primarily on business and organizational savvy, to the exclusion of competencies involving the management of self. In some cases this focus appears to be intentional. Bird, Mendenhall, Stevens, and Oddou (2010) explicitly center their attention on interpersonal and self competencies, noting that their exclusion of business or organizational competencies is conscious.

Competencies of Business and Organizational Acumen

Global leadership competencies that relate to the realities of business and organizational functioning can be grouped together in a category that emphasizes implementation and execution. They reflect global leadership as applied primarily to a strategic business unit or to the entire organization. Business and organizational acumen encompasses five competencies: *vision and strategic thinking, business savvy, organizational savvy, managing communities*, and *leading change*. Each of these may be considered an "umbrella" competency that comprises a variety of more specific skills, abilities, knowledge bases, or orientations.

Vision and strategic thinking encompass capabilities involving the comprehension of the complexity of the environment and think about it in strategic ways. *Business savvy* reflects an integration of industry knowledge and an ability to identify efficient solutions. *Managing communities* is the ability of leaders to work effectively within the broader network of relationships in which a unit or firm is embedded. *Organizational savvy* consists of the ability to design organizational structures and processes in ways that facilitate global effectiveness. Finally, *leading change* represents a set of capabilities that enable global leaders to implement change.

Competencies of Managing People and Relationships

The second set of competencies is directed toward people and relationships. They represent leadership of those with whom the leader interacts directly. Bird (2013) identifies five composite competencies: *cross-cultural communication, interpersonal skills, valuing people, empowering others*, and *teaming skills*. *Valuing people* is a foundational competency in that the others in this category are predicated on it. It encompasses a respect for people and their differences, and an orientation toward and an ability to create and maintain trusting relationships. *Interpersonal skills* include a range of predispositional, attitudinal, cognitive, motivational, and behavioral dimensions that allow for interpersonal engagement and social flexibility. *Cross-cultural communication* entails capacity for high-level mindfulness, i.e., a conscious awareness of contextual, cultural, and individual differences and the way in which these differences influence how messages are encoded, transmitted, received, and interpreted, as well as the reciprocal feedback process. *Empowering others* reflects the ability of leaders to energize direct reports, colleagues, and superiors by increasing their sense of personal self-efficacy. Lastly, *teaming skills* is the ability to work effectively in multicultural and global virtual teams.

Competencies of Managing Self

The final group of competencies include predispositional, cognitive, and attitudinal processes that involve aspects of personal management. Leading in a global context is personally challenging and requires a special mix of capabilities for managing oneself. *Resilience* refers to a set of dimensions that relate to a global leader's ability to cope with the highly stressful challenges of leading across multiple time zones, large distances, myriad cultures, and widely varying national, international, political, and regulatory systems. Sometimes described as honesty, courage, or integrity, *character* can be defined as an admixture of integrity, maturity, and conscientiousness. Character also entails a sense of self-awareness and clarity around personal values as well as a measured sense of one's place in the world. *Inquisitiveness* is the most cited competency in this group. It encompasses an innate curiosity, an openness to learning, and humility. *Global mindset* is a cognitive orientation that can be broken down into two facets: *cognitive complexity* (a highly contextualized, multi-faceted, multi-layered approach to the environment) and *cosmopolitanism* (an interest in and knowledge of the world—nations, social and political institutions, cultures, and people). Finally, *flexibility* refers to a willingness to adapt and adjust to varied situations. It includes a cognitive component, *intellectual flexibility*, and a behavioral component, *behavioral flexibility*.

Developing Global Leaders

The managerial talent that firms need, and what they have, are not always the same. A study in 1999 (Black et al.) concluded that 85 percent of the multinational firms they queried did not have adequate numbers of capable global leaders. A study by Development Dimensions International (2009) found that "75 percent of executives identified improving or leveraging global talent as a top business priority; however, only 50 percent of the organizations had a process to identify high-potential leaders and only 39 percent had a program to accelerate their development" (Oddou & Mendenhall, 2013: 216). Firms lack adequate numbers of qualified global leaders and so they must develop them—but how?

Learning Context of Global Leadership Development Methods

The competencies needed for global leaders cannot be easily had through classroom training alone. Rather, the most effective training is through simulations and actual leadership assignments in a cross-cultural context. The most effective medium appears to be real-life situations, with real people and real consequences, where lessons are not easily forgotten. Consequently, as noted previously, firms rely heavily on international assignments, reinforced with targeted training and coaching (Oddou & Mendenhall, 2013).

Conceptual Process and Outcome of Effective GLD Programs

Designing the *process* to learn competencies is critical to the development of global leadership. For GLD programs to be effective, they must include some form of Mezirow's (1978) model of *contrast, confrontation and replacement*. This process proceeds in a sequence: first, encountering an event that is disorienting, paradoxical, or challenging in nature (contrast); second, self-examination of one's worldview/mindset and proactive learning regarding the variables associated with the event (confrontation); third, experimenting with taking on new roles "and building competence and self-confidence in those roles in order to arrive at a stage of reintegration based on one's new perspective (replacement or remapping)" (Oddou & Mendenhall, 2013: 220). Consider the following example:

> One of the author's brother-in-law and sister came to stay with him and his wife in France recently. A dinner, to include the French neighbors, took place. Because the French don't usually invite others for dinner until 7pm, and it's often not until 7:30pm or 8:00pm that the meal actually starts, dinner often goes until 11pm or later. Meals in France are a time to socialize and renew friendships. Eating can be secondary, although the food is always a topic of conversation. This meant that the author's relatives and accompanying teenagers did not get to bed until much later than usual. So the teenagers got up late as well—to the consternation of the brother-in-law. Why did we have to start so late? Why does it have to go so late? He would try to move things along faster and get us to start the dinner earlier. Despite explanations for why the French eat later than Americans and why they prolong the meal late into the evening, he could not internally accept it and it became a source of frustration for him the entire time. He was, in essence, unwilling to confront his mental map that eating was mainly to replenish one's energy supply and not develop deeper relationships. Without confronting his culturally determined mental map about the purpose of a meal, there was no possibility of replacing his views or changing his perspective.
>
> *(Oddou & Mendenhall, 2013: 221)*

Enablers of Transformation

For employees and executives to change and develop—to move through this process of contrast, confrontation, and remapping—is easier if they have certain foundational competencies: being nonjudgmental, tolerating uncertainty, being an aggressive learner, being flexible, having good interpersonal skills, and being able to maintain an even equilibrium in the face of many challenges (Oddou & Mendenhall, 2013). When confronting a contrasting belief, value, or perspective, an individual can react defensively or dismissively and essentially abort the new sense-making process. "This might involve judging, stereotyping, or otherwise evaluating in a way that negates any value to the experience. In those circumstances, nothing is learned and behavior is unchanged. Hence, being *nonjudgmental* is helpful to the process of transformation" (Oddou & Mendenhall, 2013: 223). Similarly, being able to tolerate ambiguity is key. In the process of contrast and confrontation, the manager is not always going to have all the necessary information to understand the differences. Sometimes, it requires patience and initiating learning to discover the "whys."

Strategies for Globalizing Personnel

The key to globalizing managers is to construct processes and programs that require them to engage in the transformation process (contrast–confrontation–replacement/remapping). Oddou, Gregersen, Derr, and Black (1998) found there were five practices that were critical in developing intercultural competencies associated with global leadership, and these remain relevant today: (1) international business travel, (2) international business seminars with in-company personnel,

(3) international business seminars with non-company personnel, (4) international project teams/ task forces, and (5) international assignments (both expatriation and inpatriation) or "hardship" type assignments where global competencies are tested and further developed.

Each of these methods has pros and cons but much of it centers on the degree to which the executive is open to risk vs. being protected from mistakes. Often, executives are met at the airport, chaperoned throughout their travel stay and in a "bubble" that buffers the process of "contrast–confrontation–replacement." The contrasts are minimal, there may be little to no confrontation, and, therefore, little remapping of the executive's perspective and little or no development of GL competencies (Oddou & Mendenhall, 2013: 225). This stands in stark contrast to the more *experiential* experience that involves one's emotional, behavioral, and intellectual self. Caligiuri and Tarique (2011) found that "high contact" experiences (e.g., extended expatriate assignments) fostered the development of global leadership competencies in participants. In addition to the type of experience, research shows the greater the number of *sources* of feedback about whether decisions made in the experience were appropriate, the more impact the contrasting experience will also have (Oddou & Mendenhall, 2013).

Where to Next? The Future of Global Leadership Research

In summary, global leadership is a nascent field that emerged out of the need to understand intercultural leadership processes in more complexity, beyond the comparison of leadership values, norms, and patterns between two or more cultures, the delineation of corporate leadership norms of single countries, and the intercultural adjustment/performance processes of expatriate managers operating within a single, host culture. Rather, the global leadership field focuses on the study of "the process of achieving relevant [leadership] outcomes across borders by influencing constituents from multiple cultures and accommodating the necessary levels of global complexity and global connectivity that the context demands" (Reiche, Bird, Mendenhall, & Osland, 2015: 8). Global leadership is thus distinguished from other forms of leadership in that global leadership involves simultaneous leader involvement in multiple jurisdictions as well as working with internal and external constituents from multiple cultures (Reiche et al., 2015).

Despite the substantial progress that researchers in global leadership have achieved, it is also important to acknowledge the conceptual shortcomings that remain. Initial research efforts have developed fundamental building blocks (e.g., Mendenhall, Reiche, Bird, & Osland, 2012; Reiche & Mendenhall, 2012). Common to this work has been a differentiation of the global leadership construct into a dimension related to the wider task environment in which global leaders fulfill their roles and responsibilities, and a dimension concerning the characteristics of interactions in which global leaders engage to fulfill their roles and responsibilities. The first dimension has been conceptualized as complexity, building on and refining Lane, Maznevski, and Mendenhall's (2004) conceptualization of complexity along the four interrelated facets of multiplicity, interdependence, ambiguity, and flux.

The second dimension highlights the relational demands associated with global leadership, both in terms of the structural or geographical nature of interactions and the type of resources that flow through these ties (Mendenhall et al., 2012). This is commonly referred to as boundary spanning, defined as an individual's linking, integration, and coordination activities by allocating ideas, information, decisions, talent, and resources across functional, organizational, and geographic boundaries (Beechler, Sondergaard, Miller, & Bird, 2004).

The two dimensions of complexity and boundary spanning, although basic in nature, provide scholars with a guiding frame for distinguishing between different types of global leaders according to the unique configuration of the global contexts in which they operate. Using such an approach would aid scholars in building appropriate and more refined, accurate, and valid research samples. Currently, the field lacks such a qualification in the operationalization of global leaders altogether, as reflected in the use of rather vague sampling criteria that simply consider global leaders as "having a global position (working only with global teams) and being responsible for leading these teams" (Story, Youssef, Luthans, Barbuto, & Bovaird, 2013: 2542) or as "business managers representing different cultures and having had different exposures to international work experiences" (Li, Mobley, & Kelly, 2013: 38). By contrast, the two-dimensional framework places an assessment criterion on scholars to make a case for inclusion into their sample based on complexity and boundary spanning. If all researchers were to follow this approach, this in and of itself would constitute a major step forward.

References

Adler, N.J. (2001) "Global leadership: Women leaders." In M. Mendenhall, T. Kuhlmann, & G. Stahl (eds) *Developing Global Business Leaders: Policies, Processes and Innovations*. Westport, CT: Quorum Books. pp. 73–97.

Beechler, S., Sondergaard, M., Miller, E.L., & Bird, A. (2004) "Boundary spanning." In H. Lane, M. Maznevksi, M.E. Mendenhall, & J. McNett (eds) *The Blackwell Handbook of Global Management: A Guide to Managing Complexity*. London: Blackwell. pp. 121–133.

Bennett, J.M. (2009) "Cultivating intercultural competence: A process perspective." In D. Deardorff (ed.) *The SAGE Handbook of Intercultural Competence*. Thousand Oaks, CA: Sage. pp. 121–140.

Bennett, M.J. (1993) "Towards ethnorelativism: A developmental model of intercultural sensitivity." In R.M. Paige (ed.) *Education for the Intercultural Experience*, 2nd ed. Yarmouth, ME: Intercultural Press. pp. 21–71.

Bird, A. (2013) "Mapping the content domain of global leadership competencies." In M.E. Mendenhall, J.S. Osland, A. Bird, G. Oddou, M. Maznevski, G. Stahl, & M. Stevens, (eds) *Global Leadership: Research, Development and Practice*, 2nd ed. London: Routledge. pp. 80–96.

Bird, A., & Osland, J. (2004) "Global competencies: An introduction." In H. Lane, M. Maznevski, M. Mendenhall, & J. McNett (eds) *Handbook of Global Management*. Oxford: Blackwell. pp. 57–80.

Bird, A., & Stevens, M. (2013) "Assessing global leadership competencies." In M.E. Mendenhall, J.S. Osland, A. Bird, G. Oddou, M. Maznevski, G. Stahl, & M. Stevens, (eds) *Global Leadership: Research, Practice and Development*, 2nd ed. London: Routledge. pp. 113–140.

Bird, A., Mendenhall, M., Stevens, M., & Oddou, G. (2010) "Defining the content domain of intercultural competence for global leaders." *Journal of Managerial Psychology*, 25 (8): 810–828.

Black, J.S., Morrison, A., & Gregersen, H. (1999) *Global Explorers: The Next Generation of Leaders*. New York: Routledge.

Brake, T. (1997) *The Global Leader: Critical Factors for Creating the World Class Organization*. Chicago, IL: Irwin Professional Publishing.

Caligiuri, P.M. (2006) "Developing global leaders." *Human Resource Management Review*, 16, 219–228.

Caligiuri, P., & Di Santo, V. (2001) "Global competence: What is it and can it be developed through global assignments?" *Human Resource Planning*, 24 (3): 37–43.

Caligiuri, P., & Tarique, I. (2011) "Dynamic competencies and performance in global leaders: Role of personality and developmental experiences." SHRM Foundation Research Grant. Last accessed on August 5, 2011 at: http://www.shrm.org/about/foundation/research/Pages/SHRMFoundationResearch Caligiuri.asp.

Cappellen, T., & Janssens, M. (2005) "Career paths of global managers: Towards future research." *Journal of World Business*, 40: 328–360.

Chen, G.M., & Starosta, W.J. (1999) "A review of the concept of intercultural awareness." *Human Communication*, 2: 27–54.

Dalton, M., Ernst, C., Deal, J., & Leslie, J. (2002) *Success for the New Global Manager: What You Need to Know to Work Across Distances, Countries and Cultures*. San Francisco, CA: Jossey-Bass and the Center for Creative Leadership.

Development Dimensions International, Inc. (2009) "Global leadership forecast 2008–2009: Overcoming the shortfalls in developing leaders." http://www.ddiworld.com (accessed September 22, 2010).

Dickson, M.W., Den Hartog, D.N., & Castaño, N. (2009) "Understanding leadership across cultures." In R. Bhagat & R. Steers (eds) *Handbook of Culture, Organization, and Work*. New York: Cambridge University Press. pp. 219–244.

Endicott, L., Bock, T., & Narvaez, D. (2003) "Moral reasoning, intercultural development, and multicultural experiences: Relations and cognitive underpinnings." *International Journal of Intercultural Relations*, 27: 403–419.

Evans, P., Pucik, V., & Barsoux, J.-L. (2002) *The Global Challenge: Frameworks for International Human Resource Management*. Boston, MA: McGraw-Hill.

Fantini, A.E. (2000) "A central concern: Developing intercultural competence." http:// www.sit.edu/ publications/docs/competence.pdf (accessed January 3, 2003).

Fennes, H., & Hapgood, K. (1997) *Intercultural Learning in the Classroom*. London: Cassell.

Furnham, A., & Ribchester, T. (1995) "Tolerance of ambiguity: A review of the concept, its measurement and applications." *Current Psychology*, 14 (3): 179–199.

Gill, A., & Booth, S. (2003) "Identifying future global leaders." *Strategic HR Review*, 2 (6): 20–25.

Gregersen, H.B., Morrison, A.J., & Black, J.S. (1998) "Developing leaders for the global frontier." *Sloan Management Review*, 40: 21–32.

Gudykunst, W.B. (1994) *Bridging Differences: Effective Intergroup Communication*, 2nd ed. London: Sage.

Gundling, E., Hogan, T., & Cvitkovich, K. (2011) *What Is Global Leadership: 10 Key Behaviors That Define Great Global Leaders*. Boston, MA: Nicholas Brealey Publishing.

Hedlund, G. (1986) "The hypermodern MNC: A heterarchy?" *Human Resource Management*, Spring: 9–35.

House, R.J., Hanges, P.J., Javidan, M., Dorfman, P.W., & Gupta, V. (eds) (2004) *Culture, Leadership and Organizations: The GLOBE Study of 62 Societies*. Thousand Oaks, CA: Sage.

Jokinen, T. (2005) "Global leadership competencies: A review and discussion." *Journal of European Industrial Training*, 29 (2/3): 199–216.

Kotter, J.P. (1990) "A force for change: How leadership differs from management." *CA Magazine*, 123 (10): 22.

Lane, H.W., Maznevski, M.L., & Mendenhall, M.E. (2004) Hercules meets Buddha. In H.W. Lane, M.L. Maznevski, M.E. Mendenhall & J. McNett (eds) *The Handbook of Global Management: A Guide to Managing Complexity*. Oxford, UK: Blackwell. pp. 3–25.

Levy, O., Beechler, S., Taylor, S., & Boyacigiller, N. (2007) "What do we talk about when we talk about global mindset? Managerial cognition in multinational corporations." *Journal of International Business Studies*, 38: 231–258.

Li, M., Mobley, W. H., & Kelly, A. (2013). "When do global leaders learn best to develop cultural intelligence? An investigation of the moderating role of learning style." *Academy of Management Learning & Education*, 12 (1), 32–50.

McBer & Company (1995) *Mastering Global Leadership: Hay/McBer International CEO Leadership Study*. Boston, MA: Hay/McBer Worldwide Resource Center.

McCall, M.W. Jr., & Hollenbeck, G.P. (2002) *Developing Global Executives: The Lessons of International Experience*. Boston, MA: Harvard Business School Press.

Mendenhall, M.E. (2001a) "New perspectives on expatriate adjustment and its relationship to global leadership development." In M. Mendenhall, T. Kuhlmann, & G. Stahl (eds) *Developing Global Business Leaders: Policies, Processes and Innovations*. Westport, CT: Quorum Books. pp. 1–16.

Mendenhall, M.E. (2001b) "Global assignments, global leaders: Leveraging global assignments as leadership development programs." Paper presented at the Research Colloquium on Expatriate Management, Cranfield Business School, Cranfield, UK, March 15.

Mendenhall, M. (2013). "Leadership and the birth of global leadership." In M.E. Mendenhall, J.S. Osland, A. Bird, G. Oddou, M. Maznevski, G. Stahl, & M. Stevens (eds) *Global Leadership: Research, Development and Practice*, 2nd ed. London: Routledge. pp. 1–20.

Mendenhall, M., & Osland, J.S. (2002) "Terrain of the Global Leadership Construct." Paper presented at the Academy of International Business, Puerto Rico, June 29.

Mendenhall, M., Reiche, B.S., Bird, A., & Osland, J. (2012) "Defining the 'global' in global leadership." *Journal of World Business*, 47 (4). http://dx.doi.org/10.1016/j.jwb.2012.01.003

Mezirow, J. (1978) "Perspective transformation." *Adult Education*, 28 (2): 100–110.

Miller, E.L. (1973) "The international selection decision: A study of some dimensions of managerial behavior in the selection decision process." *Academy of Management Journal*, 16: 239–252.

Oddou, G., & Mendenhall, M. 2013. "Global leadership development." In M. Mendenhall, J.S. Osland, A. Bird, G.R. Oddou, M.L. Maznevski, G.K. Stahl, & M.J. Stevens (eds) *Global Leadership: Research, Practice, and Development*. London: Routledge.

Oddou, G., Gregersen, H., Derr, B., & Black, J.S. (1998) "Internationalizing human resources: Strategy differences among European, Japanese and U.S. multinationals." In M. Mendenhall, T. Kühlmann, & G. Stahl (eds) *Developing Global Business Leaders: Policies, Processes, and Innovations.* Westport, CT: Quorum Books. pp. 99–116.

Osland, J.S. (2001) "The quest for transformation: The process of global leadership development." In M. Mendenhall, T. Kühlmann, & G. Stahl (eds) (2001) *Developing Global Business Leaders: Policies, Processes and Innovations.* Westport, CT: Quorum Books. pp. 137–156.

Osland, J.S. (2008) "An overview of the global leadership literature." In M.E. Mendenhall, J.S. Osland, A. Bird, G.R. Oddou, M.L. Maznevski, G.K. Stahl, & M.J. Stevens (eds) (2008) *Global Leadership: Research, Practice and Development.* London: Routledge. pp. 34–63.

Osland, J. (2013). "The multidisciplinary roots of global leadership." In M.E. Mendenhall, J.S. Osland, A. Bird, G.R. Oddou, M.L. Maznevski, G.K. Stahl, & M.J. Stevens (eds) *Global Leadership: Research, Development and Practice,* 2nd ed. London: Routledge. pp. 21–39.

Osland, J.S., & Bird, A. (2006) "Global leaders as experts." In W. Mobley & E. Weldon (eds) *Advances in Global Leadership, Volume 4.* Stamford, CT: JAI Press. pp. 123–142.

Osland, J., Bird, A., Mendenhall, M.E., & Osland, A. (2006) "Developing global leadership capabilities and global mindset: A review." In G.K. Stahl & I. Björkman (eds) *Handbook of Research in International Human Resource Management.* Cheltenham, UK: Edward Elgar Publishing. pp. 197–222.

Osland, J., Bird, A., & Oddou, G. (2012) "The context of expert global leadership." In W.H. Mobley, Y. Wang, & M. Li (eds) *Advances in Global Leadership, vol. 7.* Oxford: Elsevier.

Osland, J., Li, M., & Wang, Y. (2014a). "Introduction: The State of Global Leadership Research." In J. Osland, M. Li, & Y. Wang (eds) *Advances in Global Leadership, vol. 8.* Bingley, UK: Emerald. pp. 1–18.

Osland, J., Li, M., & Wang, Y. (2014b). "Conclusion: Future Directions for Advancing Global Leadership Research." In J. Osland, M. Li, & Y. Wang (eds) *Advances in Global Leadership, vol. 8.* Bingley, UK: Emerald. pp. 365–376.

Reiche, B.S., & Mendenhall, M.E. 2012. "Looking to the future." In M.E. Mendenhall, J.S. Osland, A. Bird, G. Oddou, M.L. Maznevski, G.K. Stahl, & M.J. Stevens (eds) *Global Leadership: Research, Practice, and Development,* 2nd ed. New York: Routledge. pp. 260–268.

Reiche, B.S., Bird, A., Mendenhall, M.E., & Osland, J.S. (2015) *Towards a theory of global leadership types.* Unpublished manuscript.

Rhinesmith, S. (1993) *A Manager's Guide to Globalization: Six Skills for Success in a Changing World.* New York: McGraw-Hill.

Rosen, R., Digh, P., Singer, M., & Phillips, C. (2000) *Global Literacies: Lessons on Business Leadership and National Cultures.* New York: Simon and Schuster.

Ruben, B.D. (1989) "The study of cross-cultural competence: Traditions and contemporary issues." *International Journal of Intercultural Relations,* 13: 229–239.

Spreitzer, G.M., McCall, M.W. Jr., & Mahoney, J.D. (1997) "Early identification of international executive potential." *Journal of Applied Psychology,* 82 (1): 6–29.

Stevens, M., Bird, A., Mendenhall, M., & Oddou, G. (2014) "Measuring global leader intercultural competence: The development and validation of the Global Competencies Inventory." *Advances in Global Leadership,* 8: 115–154.

Story, J.S.P., Youssef, C.M., Luthans, F., Barbuto, J.E., & Bovaird, J. 2013. "Contagion effect of global leaders' positive psychological capital on followers: Does distance matter and quality of relationship matter?" *International Journal of Human Resource Management,* 24, 2534–2553.

Thich, N.H. (1991) *Peace Is Every Step: The Path of Mindfulness in Everyday Life.* New York: Bantam Books.

Thomas, D.C. (2006) "Domain and development of cultural intelligence: The importance of mindfulness." *Group and Organization Management,* 31: 78–99.

Von Glinow, M.A. (2001) "Future issues in global leadership development." In M.E. Mendenhall, T.M. Kühlmann, & G.K. Stahl (eds) *Developing Global Leaders: Policies, Processes and Innovations.* Westport, CT: Quorum Books. pp. 264–271.

Wills, S., & Barham, K. (1994) "Being an international manager." *European Management Journal,* 12 (1): 49–58.

Yeung A.K., & Ready D.A. (1995) "Developing leadership capabilities of global corporations: A comparative study in eight nations." *Human Resource Management,* 34 (4): 529–547.

24

Political Leadership in the Twenty-First Century

Neo-Liberalism and the Rise of the CEO Politician

Peter Bloom and Carl Rhodes

Introduction

On Monday May 4, 2015 former Hewlett-Packard CEO Carly Fiorina launched her campaign as a candidate for the United States presidency. While her candidature was path breaking as the first female to ever run as a Republican for this position, her campaign had focused first and foremost on her experience as a business leader. The previous February she declared: "HP requires executive decision-making, and the presidency is all about executive decision-making" (Lee, 2015). This echoed the abiding theme that she believed would resonate with voters: the message that "what she did for HP, she can do for America" (Carroll & Neate, 2015). Nevertheless, Fiorina's record as CEO has been severely criticized. Hers was a tenure "marked by layoffs, outsourcing, conflict, and controversy – so much so that several prominent former HP colleagues recoil at the idea of Fiorina managing any enterprise again, let alone the executive branch" (Corn, 2015). While such criticisms are important, they perhaps miss a more fundamental issue. Does being a CEO, even a successful one, serve as a good and proper background for political leadership? What does it reflect about the potentially dangerous change in popular attitudes regarding the relation of leadership to democracy in the twenty-first century?

Leadership remains a pre-eminent concern of twenty-first-century life. The new millennium has brought with it renewed discussions of what it means to be a proper leader as well as the deeper social values this demands. Underpinning these debates are shifting notions of political and social responsibility. Conventional assumptions of the public and private are quickly evaporating as the function of the state has receded on account of neo-liberalism and globalization. Prompted by a political consensus of the value of markets to hitherto non-commercial realms, and by a more general economization of ever broadening dimensions of life, economics has eclipsed politics as the central governing discourse. By now, everything from education, to healthcare, to prisons, and even to one's personal social relationships are conceived of in terms of competition, exchange, financial self-interest, and personal advantage (Brown, 2015). Corporations, in turn, have taken on, at least rhetorically, a more active role in providing for social welfare, as well as being direct players in global politics (Scherer & Palazzo, 2011).

In light of these changes, practices of perceptions of public and private leadership are being dramatically transformed.

The changes to leadership heralded through neo-liberalism are witnessed in the evolving image of it adopted by elected politicians and by corporate managers. The ideal politician is increasingly one who embodies business values of 'efficiency' and 'profitability.' Referred to popularly at times as the 'CEO President,' this emerging model of political authority reflects the government's perceived role in maximizing their country's economic competiveness within a volatile global market. By contrast, corporate authority figures are progressively touting their 'social responsibility' as well as freely advising politicians on how they should go about governing the nation-cum-economy; chief executives present their businesses as not simply profit driven but able to provide for larger public goods such as environmental sustainability, social justice linked to diversity, and helping prepare workers for a twenty-first-century job market.

The convergence of corporate and political leadership is indeed ironic in that it tends towards a reversal of roles. The private has become public and vice versa. On one level, this paradox of current leadership representations simply reflects existing socio-political realities. However, popular discourses are also influential in constituting and reinforcing such ideological shifts. This chapter aims to explore the dynamic and ironic shift, focusing specifically on the way that corporate leadership has come to infuse the meaning and practice of political leadership. In proffering politicians as fulfilling the role of corporate executives, this new leadership strengthens marketed perceptions of the state's function heralded by neo-liberalism. This is a trend that extends to the well-established practices of new public management for managing public services (Dahl & Soss, 2014) and extends the dominance and ubiquity of corporate models to the 'management' of nations themselves.

The changes we outline are not benign; they mark the further embedding of the triumph of neo-liberalism over democracy. The rise of the CEO politician is part of a broader cultural change in the expected social role of government both in the model of and in service of corporations. Rather than being responsible and accountable servants of the electorate, politicians are expected to be active decision makers in pursuit of effectiveness, efficiency, and competitiveness. This represents the deeper transformation in the functions of public leadership with politicians progressively expected to maintain a country's economic solvency in a competitive capitalist global economy. Hence, central to this analysis is how these representations of leadership are helping to facilitate and strengthen neo-liberalism ideologically, and the weakening of democracy practically. Such an investigation also opens the space for interrogating how these leadership discourses create new opportunities for challenging this emerging neo-liberal status quo.

The Politics of the Heroic CEO

The use of the term chief executive officer, together with its acronym CEO, as a title for a corporation's most senior official is relatively new. According to Merriam-Webster's dictionary, the first usage of the abbreviation in business dates to the mid-1970s. Although now CEO is almost exclusively used in reference to corporate leadership, its earlier usage referred to political or military leaders. Ulysses S. Grant, the president of the United States, stated in his annual message of 1876 that:

> It was my fortune, or misfortune, to be called to the office of Chief Executive without any previous political training. From the age of 17 I had never even witnessed the excitement

attending a Presidential campaign but twice antecedent to my own candidacy, and at but one of them was I eligible as a voter.

(Grant in Richardson, 1911: 399)

In his 1850 novel *White Jacket* Herman Melville referred to a navy official as a chief executive, and in Alexander I. Peterman's 1891 instructional manual *Elements of Civil Government* a chief executive was a president or mayor.

By today the CEO has outgrown its origins in politics and the military and has become an established cultural icon of corporate power and leadership. To be a CEO is to be "surrounded by an aura of high achievement, leadership positions, power, huge bank accounts, stretch limousines and luxury" (Hansen, 1996: 36). In the wake of the outbreak of neo-liberalism in the 1970s and 1980s, it is perhaps unsurprising that the cultural valorization of business and economy resulted also in corporate leaders being pitched in heroic terms. Indeed prior to that heads of organizations were largely unknown to the public, imagined to be conservative, conformist, and detached figures who had the job of managing a cadre of other men in grey flannel suits (see Wilson, 1956). By the 1990s, the 'cult of the CEO' (Haigh, 2003) was well established with individual leaders being lauded as stock market superheroes who could, in a single bound, guide the corporation they manage to new heights of achievement and excellence. Along with this came massive rewards, with CEO salaries relative to average workers skyrocketing. In the Unites States in 1983, average CEO compensation was 46 times that of ordinary workers. This rose to a multiple of 195 in 1993, 301 in 2003, and 331 in 2013 (AFL-CIO, 2015).

With new cultural salience, the media enhanced the image of the corporate leader with the creation of what came to be known as the 'celebrity CEO' who has a high public profile through press coverage. Moreover, the nature of this coverage tends to attribute firm performance exclusively to the actions of the CEO (Hayward, Rindova & Pollock, 2004) such that "CEO acquires celebrity status when media sources attribute a firm's positive performance to the CEO's actions in a way that generates a powerful impression of renown and credibility for that CEO" (Sinha, Inkson & Barker, 2012: 224). No longer seen as 'fat cat' exploiters, profiteers and personal wealth maximizers, the new celebrity CEO was a 'cool cat' who legitimated neo-liberal capitalism and reinforced corporate power and brand image (Littler, 2007).

As the twentieth century came to a close, the CEO had been mythologized as a new hero for neo-liberal times, a kind of super-leader whose personal charisma, aptitude, and determination could single-handedly drive organizations to hitherto unknown levels of success and prosperity. So ubiquitous was the image of CEO excellence, the idea of the CEO has become a metaphor for success in all aspects of life. Weight loss can be achieved by becoming the 'CEO of your own body' (Dean, 2011), men can be romantically successful by learning how to 'date like a CEO' (Atwood, 2015), and the good life can be achieved by becoming the 'CEO of me' (Kossek & Luatsch, 2007).

The development of the popular perception of the values and virtues associated with CEOs saw the forms of charismatic authority traditionally associated with political leaders become translated into the business domain. As Weber defined it long ago:

The term 'charisma' [is] applied to a certain quality of an individual personality by virtue of which he is set apart from ordinary men and treated as endowed with supernatural, super-human, or at least specifically exceptional powers or qualities. These are such as are not accessible to the ordinary person, but are regarded as of divine origin or as exemplary, and on the basis of them, the individual concerned is treated as a leader.

(Weber, 1947: 358)

Political leaders have conventionally been judged, at least within liberal democracies, according to political values of consensus building and policy acumen. The ideal leader was one who could craft and implement effective policies and garner the support of the citizenry. Moreover, their success was also linked to their capacity to foster and maintain ruling coalitions as well as foster inclusiveness. They did so commonly, or at least ideally, through inspiring the mass sections of the population with the very charisma that Weber identified, acting as 'spellbinders' for pursuing specific ideologies and policy goals (Willner, 1985). Their success hinged, furthermore, on the delicate balance of presenting a clear alternative to rivals while maintaining a close affinity to the voter's existing political positions (Iverson, 1994).

At a more prosaic level, perhaps, politicians were deemed successful based on their continual electoral viability. Outside of normative concerns of ideology or valence judgments of effectiveness, there resided a general view that a political leader was only as strong as their ability to win power. While not always ethically esteemed, in this regard, there is a certain respect granted to the political actor who can navigate the cutthroat waters of modern democratic politics. Combined, this reflects the traditional 'great man' view of political leadership, whereby politicians are rendered publicly into 'heroes' inspiring individuals to follow them in an almost mythical way (see for instance Kellerman, 1986). The image of the celebrity CEO leader drew on this epic tradition, transforming the business manager from an effective administrator to a charismatic and transformational business hero.

As charismatic leadership became a catch-cry for corporate management in the 1980s and 1990s, it was also infused into the 'new' politics of the 1990s as traditional political values of inspirational consensus building took on a new life, particularly within much of the West such as the US and UK. President Bill Clinton and Prime Minister Tony Blair exemplified this potent mixture of seemingly charismatic appeal, effective policy making, and electoral success. Clinton's leadership style was described, in this regard, as connecting with voters personally through his charisma:

> Bill Clinton was a political genius in a lot of ways. But his brilliance was not in framing issues or governing or formulating policy; he had advisors for those things. Bill's genius was in positioning himself in the public's eye. His dazzling personal skills gave him the ability to make a member of any audience feel that he was speaking directly to them, that he was one of them.
>
> *(Rowley, 2014)*

The ideology of the 'third way' (Giddens, 1998) was characterized by popular presentations of a leader that while centrist – and to many ideologically conservative – were emboldened by conventional ideals of political leadership. These ideas reflected a desire both to win and to achieve tangible social results linked to an inclusive and widespread coalition politics. Just as importantly, they connected this rather moderate pro-market agenda with established political tropes of individual and collective uplift. One famous chronicler of political leadership observed a passionate appeal made by Clinton to an African American audience in support of his centrist agenda:

> In March, I happened on a telecast of Clinton addressing an African American church congregation that could scarcely have been more responsive if Martin Luther King had been in the pulpit. Speaking with ease and self-assurance, Clinton issued a call for policies that would enable citizens to lift themselves by their bootstraps rather than relying on

government handouts. Explaining that he was making the same proposal to audiences of whites, Clinton called on all Americans to put aside their differences and recognize their common bonds.

(Greenstein, 2000)

Thus even as the political class increased their commitment to economic management and development, political authority remained dominantly wedded to the established paradigms of the charismatic and effective 'political leader', the very paradigm that business leaders themselves were being urged to emulate.

The Political Leader as CEO

The popular perception of political leaders has undergone a profound shift in the twenty-first century. While business managers were trying to be charismatic and transformational, political leaders had started to emulate traditional business qualities of 'efficiency', 'productivity' and 'profitability' conventionally associated with corporate executives. There has thus been a direct shift away from charismatic authority towards hardnosed economic management. Ironically this has occurred through political leaders trying to be more like CEOs, the very same CEOs who were adopting charismatic political leadership a short time before. The difference is, however, that the dimensions of CEO leadership that were repatriated into politics did not include charisma and popular appeal, focusing instead on business management acumen.

A witness to this is the rise of what can be called the 'CEO Model of Political Leadership' (Date, 2009). The view of Rajeev Gowda, chair of the Centre for Public Policy at IIM-Bangalore, exemplified this new business model of political leadership:

As democracies mature, you need different types of people. You go from wanting people who can lead political agitations and write constitutions, to people who can manage a budget and improve the efficiency of programmes. That's where an MBA training comes in useful.

(Schiller, 2011)

CEOs had become celebrities and politicians sought to imitate them just as the CEOs had emulated an idealized image of the charismatic political leader before. What politics took from the 'cult of the CEO' (Haigh, 2003), however, was not the image of a leader with a captivating persona unleashing people's talent, but rather the CEO as the person who was an effective manager whose single-handed determination could get things done. In many cases politicians were expected to be a type of business 'man' who managed for financial success. If neo-liberalism is taken to involve "converting the distinctly *political* character, meaning, and operation of democracy's constituent elements into *economic* ones" (Brown, 2015: 17), the political leader became more a leader of the economy than a leader of the polis or the populace. What was taking shape with the dawn of the new millennium was a fresh vision of the ideal politician as constituted in a particular image of the CEO. Importantly, this is not just a metaphoric shift. Contemporary times have seen numerous examples in which former corporate leaders have taken on political careers, for better or for worse. Italy's Silvio Berlusconi came from Finivest, founder of Hyundai Chung Yu Jung became a South Korean statesman, and former UN Secretary General Kofi Annan has a management degree from MIT and headed up the Ghana Tourist Development Company (Haigh, 2003).

The election of George W. Bush to the US presidency in 2001 was perhaps the biggest signal of the rise of the so-called 'CEO President.' In his initial campaign he heralded his business-based education and experience, specifically his MBA from Harvard Business School. Voicing an opinion that seemed at the time common to many, a former classmate of Bush's at Harvard asked pointedly: "The lawyers and the generals have had their chance. Why not give an M.B.A. a shot?" (Cannon & Cannon, 2007: 219). He described his proposed leadership style as akin to that of a top corporate executive. He maintained that as president, "My job is to set the agenda and tone and framework, to lay out the principles by which we operate and make decisions, and then delegate much of the process to them" (quoted in Allen, 2004). Bush's administration followed suit with an impeccable business pedigree. Vice President Dick Cheney, Secretary of Defense Donald Rumsfeld, Commerce Secretary Don Evans, Labor Secretary Elaine Chao, Chief of Staff Andrew Card Jr., and Treasury Secretary John Snow were all former corporate CEOs (Haigh, 2003).

Bush's presidency prioritized values of decisiveness, efficiency, and productivity. Hence, he was trumpeted as "the very model of an MBA president" (Kettl, 2003: 31). He was also singled out as being the embodiment of a novel type of 'CEO President' (Kessler, 2004). These qualities were not confined to – nor discredited by – the presidency of George W. Bush. In the 2012 election Mitt Romney was similarly valorized for his business background, experience that it was assumed would translate well to politics. As Pfiffner observes:

> Voters like to think that business people are efficient and that they can bring good practices to government. But they only think about the best run companies and the worst run agencies. They forget about the thousands of start-ups that go broke every year.
>
> *(quoted in Schiller, 2011)*

This marked a pronounced change in how the so-called 'CEO President' was popularly framed as a transformation and reduction of the celebrity CEO. Initially, a business approach was judged critically in terms of its advantages and disadvantages for political leadership. Pfiffner (2007), for instance, rigorously analyzed Bush and his decision making as the first MBA president. However, by the early twenty-first century the new CEO approach to political leadership was being portrayed almost universally as unquestionably positive. To this end, political and business leadership traits were increasingly conflated as one and the same.

In one sense it has been argued that politicians and CEOs need to display similar leadership qualities of "vision," "getting followers," "emotional intelligence," "listen(ing)," and "confidence" (Strauss, 2013). Despite this, as we have been arguing, the new CEO political leadership focused less on these charismatic qualities, and more on practical matters of economic management. The now exiled former prime minister of Thailand Thaksin Shinawatra was perhaps the most explicit in framing his leadership role as being a corporate executive. Prior to his entry into politics, Shinawatra's business activities, especially in the Thai telecommunications industry, had made him one of the country's wealthiest people. Moreover, he sought to transfer this success directly to political governance. Elected in 2001, he stated that:

> A company is a country. A country is a company. They are the same. The management is the same. It is management by economics. From now onwards, this is the era of management by economics, not management by other means. Economics is the deciding factor.
>
> *(in Phongpaichit & Laker, 2004: 101)*

Shinawatra did not dilute his view: the analogy of country with company brought with it the idea that citizens were employees, other countries were market rivals. Most tellingly the head of government was declared as the 'CEO leader' whose primary goal was to foster economic growth (Phongpaichit & Laker, 2004). Shinawatra was a popular politician, winning elections with landslide victories; victories that were won at least partly on account of "his image as a decisive 'CEO' leader who would act quickly to solve problems" (McCargo, 2005: 512). What we have here is no longer a matter of just bringing leadership skills and attributes to bear on politics, but rather the whole scale economization of society such that it is regarded as a business.

Leading the Economy

The idea that corporate leadership embodies a more decisive, unilateral, and effective means to govern than traditional political leadership, while explicit in Shinawatra's rhetoric, reflects more general tendencies in the changing discourse of politics. Symbolizing this change, corporate leaders were increasingly hailed as having the leadership skills necessary for steering the economy – a view especially resonant in the wake of the 2008 financial crisis. In the United States, 2010 was labeled as the "high water mark for the CEO as candidate"; more than 40 business magnates ran for seats that year, many of whom won convincingly (Briggs, 2013). This reflected a deeper shift in what was expected of politicians. They were meant to embody the skills thought to be the property of the successful businessman. According to Susan MacManus, professor of political science at the University of South Florida, voters "are looking for financial acumen, and they associate that with CEOs. They can talk with credibility when they talk about real financial issues" (quoted in Briggs, 2013).

Similar indicators can be found with the current prime minister of Australia Tony Abbott. Elected to office in 2013, Abbott epitomizes the contemporary neo-liberal politician to the point of virtual caricature. Upon being elected he quickly set about implementing a series of pro-business policies including removing the carbon tax on corporations, negotiating international trade agreements, repealing laws that protect workers, and privatizing the last of the government-owned corporations. In pursuing this agenda on the night of his election he announced that: "Australia is under new management and is once more open for business." Again here we see political leadership being recast as a form of business management, coupled with issues of commerce, and economy taking precedence as the primary function of government. Such changes echo not just in political pronouncements, but also in terms of electoral expectations. With his popularity flailing in 2015, the news media did not only question Abbott's political savvy, but asked: "if Tony Abbott was CEO, would he be sacked for his performance?" In considering this, Richard Dennis, the Executive Director of the left-leaning think tank The Australia Institute, suggested that we might "think of government in terms of a business structure" with the prime minister being the CEO, the party room being the board of directors, and the voters being the shareholders. By implication, Dennis opined:

> any CEO who does a poor job of keeping their board informed and aligning their agenda with that of their board is sailing into dangerous waters. Tony Abbott has made much of his right to make 'captain's calls' on key decisions, but no prime minister should forget that their party room has the right to replace a PM whose judgment they don't support.
>
> *(in Ma, 2015)*

The 'captain's calls' that Dennis is referring to concern a phrase that Abbott has used to defend unilateral decisions without consulting his cabinet ministers. Examples range broadly from delisting Tasmanian forests as world heritage areas rendering them open for logging, to the awarding of an Australian knighthood to Britain's Prince Philip. This unilateral approach reflects on key differences in political leadership conceived as managerial rather than democratic. It suggests that the advent of the CEO politician is in fact a retreat from democracy towards more single-minded forms of decision making that are more economical than political. This is a similar criticism to that faced by Thailand's Thaksin Shinawatra, in that the CEO style is seen to be one based on authoritarianism and a centralization of power around the leader.

It is not surprising then that the recent decade has seen the rise of 'MBA in Politics' degrees, representing the application of corporate leadership principles to guiding how future politicians think and act. Hence, politics has become increasingly more business-like not only in its priorities but also its popular representation. The perfect politician mirrored that of the hard-nosed business executive. Reflected in Abbott's 'open for business' approach is also the idea that business and economy are on the top of the CEO politician's agenda. This tendency, albeit not as crude as in Abbott and Shinawatra's cases, can be seen also in the presidency of Barack Obama. As Brown (2015) elucidates, Obama came to power in 2008 on the back of a 'hope and change' campaign that promised him to be the transformational leader that could unite the people of United States and guide the nation out of a war-torn recent past towards a new era of justice, opportunity, and progress.

By the time of Obama's second term in office, however, things had changed. In his State of the Union address in 2013, he was still calling for political change associated with tax reform, health care, clean energy, home ownership, education, increases to the minimum wage, and various forms of social justice, but this time "each of these issues was framed in terms of its contribution to economic growth and American competitiveness" (p. 25). "The North Star that guides our efforts," he claimed, is "a growing economy that creates good, middle class jobs" (Brown, 2015) The focus was primarily economic – guided by job creation from foreign investors, training people to do those jobs, and ensuring adequate reward for doing them. The situation, as Brown describes it, is one where "Attracting investors and developing an adequately remunerated workforce – these are the goals of the world's oldest democracy led by a justice-minded president in the twenty-first century" (Brown, 2015). The situation is one in which all forms of change can only be justified politically if they can be seen to drive economic growth. The president is there not to ensure freedom, equality, and justice, but rather to formulate "social justice, government investment, and environmental protection as fuel for economic growth [. . .], competitive positioning, and capital enhancement" such that "the conduct of government and the conduct of firms are now fundamentally identical" (pp. 26–27).

The CEO Politician and the 'Neo-Liberalization' of Democratic Leadership

This intimate association of political and business leadership arguably reflects a more fundamental shift within representations of democratic leadership. Traditionally, elected politicians are meant, at least ideally, to serve and respond to the needs of their constituency. Their main priority was for ensuring the present and future welfare of those they represented. Democratic leadership was thus viewed as being simultaneously populist – attuned to popular opinions and desires – and, if required, courageously forward thinking – willing to go against short-term political gains in the name of ensuring voters' long-term interests. While these ideals have been far from ever realized in practice, they did set out the broad co-ordinates for what 'good' democratic leadership was and should be. The present age of the CEO politician, however, has reconfigured this ideal – giving primacy to the demands of 'the market' over people.

This evolution can be termed the 'neo-liberalization' of democratic leadership. In general terms, neo-liberalism is defined as the transferring of power from the public to private sphere. The function of the government in this transition is to promote "a programme of deliberate intervention . . . in order to encourage particular types of entrepreneurial, competitive and commercial behaviour in its citizens" (Gilbert, 2013: 9). Not surprisingly, such a change has potential dramatic consequences for democratic norms and practices. Wendy Brown (2015), in this regard, speaks of the concurrent neo-liberal political transformation of Homo Politicus to Homo Oeconomicus, "wherein an image of man as an entrepreneur of himself" (p. 80) now reigns supreme. This embrace of the 'economic man' extends to what is expected of the ideal political leader as well, emphasizing the necessity of entrepreneurism and good business sense.

This process of neo-liberalization is exemplified in the merging of fiscal and political responsibility. Championed is the image of a 'responsible' democratic leader who is able to act decisively to guarantee a robust market and economic growth. Such responsibility is directly and strategically connected to neo-liberal values of austerity and expanded financialization (Blyth, 2013a). The 'danger' of such ideologies is not only that they uniformly do not work but also, according to Blyth (2013b: 2), that:

> Ideologically, it is the intuitive appeal of the idea of austerity – of not spending more than you have – that really casts its spell. Understanding how austerity came to be the standard policy in liberal economic thought when states get into trouble can reveal why it is so seductive and so dangerous.

The CEO leader is similarly dangerous and seductive to present-day democracies and voters in their promise to lead the country responsibly in accordance with established corporate values.

To this end, the CEO politician is meant first and foremost to serve the market rather than citizens. Their popular responsibility is therefore largely indirect, to meet the needs of voters but attending to the market and its needs. For this reason, scholars such as Roberts (2010) cast neo-liberal fiscal regulations as a form of 'anti-politics.' However, it also signals the advent of a novel type of ideal democratic leader – one able to impose these reforms on an often-time unwilling population, seemingly for their own good. Here, a politician can heroically resist populist but irresponsible demands by citizens. In particular, they must be politically resilient and tactical in order that they justify these reforms. In this neo-liberal era:

> savvy political leaders have proved adept at framing deficit reduction as an economic growth program. They are able to lay economic problems such as high interest rates and inflation at the doorstep of high deficits. The sacrifices involved in fiscal consolidation must be justified by pointing to prospective economic gains in the near term, whether it be easing credit market pressures or staving off the potential for a full-scale exogenous debt crisis.
>
> *(Posner & Blöndal, 2012: 28)*

Present, in turn, is less a democratic decision over values and more an election over who is 'strong, decisive and disciplined enough' to 'responsibly' manage the economy. A novel political 'hero' willing to do what is 'economically necessary' to preserve neo-liberalism is arising (Thorndike, 2013). In the US, organizations such as the Council for Citizens Against Government and Fix the Debt give politicians actual 'hero awards' based on the degree of their fiscal conservatism. Undoubtedly, the wake of the 2008 financial crisis has put this view in question – especially as austerity has seemed to cause greater economic problems than it is solving. Nevertheless, democratic discourse still plays on the ability of a strong leader to enact 'responsible reforms' that will 'cure' capitalism and restore it to health (Bloom, 2014). In this way, it espouses a desire for a leader who can 'steer the country through economic downturn' similar to a change management executive at a corporation.

This neo-liberalization of leadership affects how voters are understood as well. The popularity of the CEO politician has accompanied and helped to produce the 'shareholder citizen.' This type of citizen stands as the inverse of so-called 'citizen shareholders' who "don't have a direct voice in governance but who are intimately affected by it," therefore highlighting "the relationship between economic interests in corporate actions and social and political interests of investors as members/citizens of society" (Tucker, 2012). By contrast, the 'shareholder citizen' is expected to understand the market effects of their political decisions and vote accordingly. It mirrors Philips and Ilcan's (2004: 397) description of the ways neo-liberalism expects individuals to "become self-regulating . . . and market-knowledgeable." As such, in this new era it is not only that the CEO politician is democratically desirable, but even more so that increasingly it is the democratic obligation of each shareholder citizen to vote for such business-like leadership.

Conclusion: The New Business of Political Leadership

This chapter has sought to highlight the relationship between public and private sector leadership as they have changed through the development of neo-liberalism from the 1980s until the present day. We have illustrated that political leadership is increasingly linked to conventional business values of efficiency, profitability, and productivity. By contrast, private leadership is more and more found in public ideals traditionally ascribed to politicians. These changing images of leadership reflect broader shifts in the twenty-first-century configuration of socio-political power as being subservient to the values of capitalism over the values of democracy, the latter being at best a tool through which to achieve economic goals. Politicians, in this vein, still retain their status in the public imagination, at least in part, as the main drivers of social change; it is just that the social change that is demanded is largely focused on financial and economically related matters.

Of course, the association of political sovereignty to business values is not necessarily new. Indeed, as early as the 1920s, scholars were complaining of the dangers of the politician as a 'personnel manager,' akin to a business tycoon, who used his or her power to bestow on their friends favors and influence (White, 1926). Even more presciently, there is a tradition of theorizing and advocating for what Lewis (see in Kellerman, 1986) calls "the political leader as entrepreneur." Here, an ideal political leader was one who "creates or profoundly elaborates a public organization so as to alter greatly the existing pattern of allocation of scarce resources" (quoted in Kellerman, 1986: 250). Neo-liberalism has provided the ideological scaffolding for these ideas to take hold as a central part of politico-economic discourse. At a structural level, politicians are expected to mirror the traits and behavior of their business counterparts in order to ensure that private markets maximize their efficiency and profitability (Boyett, 1996). By contrast, the CEO is viewed as the most credible and dynamic force for producing innovative and socially beneficial transformations. Speaking to the pressing issue of climate change, Toffel and Schendler (2014) recently note that:

> CEOs are well positioned to educate the public and policymakers that climate policy is critical for stable long-term economic growth. Much more than political figures, Americans see CEOs as rock stars. They could play an especially valuable role if they choose to debunk the opposition's claims that regulating greenhouse gases will lead to economic catastrophe.

Again we see that the politically important issue (in this case climate change) can only be discussed in relation to positive economic growth. This heralds that we are at a fully developed stage of neo-liberalism where even the democratic leadership of nation has been 'economized.' One might question "what happens to the constituent elements of democracy – its culture, subjects, principles and institutions – when neoliberal rationality saturates political life" (Brown, 2015: 27) up to a point where that saturation reaches the very top?

Significantly, the switch in cultural expectation of private and public leadership reinforces neo-liberalism at the expense of democracy. It does more than reflect this ideology; it also helps to constitute it. More precisely, it can be said that it is facilitative of neo-liberalism. Brenner (1997) argues for instance that discourses of globalization facilitated what he referred to as a "normative re-ordering" of international politics to reflect neo-liberal ideologies. Analogously, witnessed in these emerging popular representations of leaderships is the facilitation of market values.

Neo-liberalism has normatively re-ordered the cultural landscape related to leadership. The dominant portrayal of politicians as having to be like business people, strengthens this normative reconfiguration of power. More positively, this also opens up new possibilities for resisting this quickly solidifying status quo. Politically, the predominant linking of leadership to business values and concerns increasingly becomes the primary function of politicians in this era. It makes visible their pro-market priorities as well as the limits of political action within this broader neo-liberal environment. This enhanced visibility creates the potential basis for questioning this marketization of politics. Further, through such critiques, novel and less market-based models of leadership can begin to emerge. Such efforts were already glimpsed, for instance, in the global rise of the Occupy movements in the wake of the 2008 financial crisis.

In the present age, the ideal political leader is analogous to a particular image of the CEO. To wit, the business of politics is business and the politics of business is politics. This reflects a potentially dangerous trend away from democracy and public rule towards private control. However, it also provides novel opportunities for challenging the very basis of this neo-liberal order and the paradoxical leadership it relies upon.

References

AFL-CIO (2015). Executive pay watch. Online: http://edit.aflcio.org/Corporate-Watch/Paywatch-2014

Allen, M. (2004). Management style shows weaknesses. *The Washington Post*, 2 June. Online: http://www. washingtonpost.com/wp-dyn/articles/A7869-2004Jun1.html

Atwood, N. (2015). *Date like a CEO: Leadership in life and love for men*. Dallas, TX: Nina Atwood Enterprises.

Bloom, P. (2014). Back to the capitalist future: Fantasy and the paradox of crisis. *Culture and Organization*, 22 (2), 158–177.

Blyth, M. (2013a). *Austerity: The history of a dangerous idea*. Oxford: Oxford University Press.

Blyth, M. (2013b). Austerity delusion: Why a bad idea won over the West. *Foreign Affairs*, 92 (41).

Boyett, I. (1996). New leader, new culture, 'old' university. *Leadership & Organization Development Journal*, 17 (5), 24–30.

Brenner, N. (1997). Global, fragmented, hierarchical: Henri Lefebvre's geographies of globalization. *Public Culture*, 10 (1): 135–167.

Briggs, B. (2013). 10 business leaders with politics in their blood. *MSNBC*. Online: http://www.nbcnews. com/id/39800329/ns/business-us_business/t/business-leaders-politics-their-blood/#.VUj5n9NViko

Brown, W. (2015). *Undoing the Demos: Neoliberalism's stealth revolution*. Boston, MA: MIT Press.

Cannon, L., & Cannon, C. M. (2007). *Reagan's disciple: George W. Bush's troubled quest for a presidential legacy*. PublicAffairs.

Carroll, R., & Neate, R. (2015). Carly Fiorina will run for president as a successful tech CEO. Silicon Valley says that's a fantasy. *The Guardian*, May 3. Online: http://www.theguardian.com/us-news/2015/may/03/carly-fiorina-run-for-president-hewlett-packard

Corn, D. (2015). Can a CEO who laid off thousands, botched a merger, and left with $21 million become president? *Mother Jones*, May 4. Online: http://www.motherjones.com/politics/2015/05/carly-fiorina-hewlett-packard-2016-gop

Dahl, A., & Soss, J. (2014). Neoliberalism for the common good? Public value governance and the downsizing of democracy. *Public Administration Review*, 74 (4), 496–504.

Date, V. (2009). Is the CEO model of political leadership the answer? *Economic and Political Weekly*, 44 (8).

Dean, J. (2011). *Be the CEO of your own body*. Bayswater, Australia: Port Campbell Press.

Giddens, A. (1998). *The Third Way: The renewal of social democracy*. Cambridge: Polity.

Gilbert, J. (2013). What kind of thing is 'Neoliberalism'? *New Formations: A Journal of Culture/Theory/Politics*, 80 (80), 7–22.

Greenstein, F. I. (2000). *The presidential difference: Leadership style from FDR to Clinton*. New York: Free Press.

Haigh, G. (2003). Bad company: The cult of the CEO. *Quarterly Essay*, 10 (1–98).

Hansen, K. P. (1996) The mentality of management: Self-images of American top executives, in S. R. Clegg & G. Palmer (Eds) *The politics of management knowledge*. London: Sage.

Hayward, M. L., Rindova, V. P., & Pollock, T. G. (2004). Believing one's own press: The causes and consequences of CEO celebrity. *Strategic Management Journal*, 25 (7), 637–653.

Iversen, T. (1994). Political leadership and representation in West European democracies: A test of three models of voting. *American Journal of Political Science*, 38 (1), 45–74.

Kellerman, B. (Ed.) (1986). *Political leadership: A source book*. Pittsburgh, PA: University of Pittsburgh Press.

Kessler, R. (2004). *A matter of character: Inside the White House of George W. Bush*. New York: Sentinel.

Kettl, D. F. (2003). *Team Bush: Leadership lessons from the Bush White House*. New York: McGrawHill.

Kossek, E., & B. Lautsch (2007). *CEO of me: Creating a life that works in the flexible job age*. Upper Saddle River, NJ: Pearson Education.

Lee, M. J. (2015). Carly Fiorina announces presidential bid, *CNN*, May 5. Online: http://www.cnn.com/2015/05/04/politics/carly-fiorina-presidential-announcement

Littler, J. (2007). Celebrity CEOs and the cultural economy of tabloid intimacy, in S. Redmond & S. Homes (Eds) *Stardom and celebrity: A reader*. Los Angeles: Sage.

Ma, W. (2015). If Tony Abbott was CEO, would he be sacked for his performance? *The Daily Telegraph*. Online: http://www.news.com.au/finance/economy/if-tony-abbott-was-ceo-would-he-be-sacked-for-his-performance/story-e6frflo9-1227205790536

McCargo, D. (2005). Network monarchy and legitimacy crises in Thailand. *The Pacific Review*, 18 (4), 499–519.

Melville, H. (1850). *White jacket: The world in a man-of-war*. Bentley: London.

Peterman, A. E. (1891) *Elements of civil government*. New York: American Book Co.

Pfiffner, J. (2007). The first MBA president: George W. Bush as public administrator. *Public Administration Review*, January/February.

Phillips, L., & Ilcan, S. (2004). Capacity-building: The neoliberal governance of development. *Canadian Journal of Development Studies/Revue canadienne d'études du développement*, 25 (3), 393–409.

Phongpaichit, P., & Laker, C. J. (2004) *Thaksin: The business of politics in Thailand*. Copenhagen: Nordic Institute of Asian Studies.

Posner, P., & Blöndal, J. (2012). Democracies and deficits: Prospects for fiscal responsibility in democratic nations. *Governance*, 25 (1), 11–34.

Richardson, J. D. (ed.) (1911). *A compilation of the messages and papers of the presidents, 1789–1897, Vol. 7*. New York: Bureau of National Literature and Art.

Roberts, A. (2010). *The logic of discipline: Global capitalism and the architecture of government*. Oxford: Oxford University Press.

Rowley, A. (2014). Bill Clinton: Leader on the couch. *Anna Rowley.com*. Online: http://annarowley.com/leader-on-the-couch/bill-clinton

Scherer, A. G., & Palazzo, G. (2011). The new political role of business in a globalized world: A review of a new perspective on CSR and its implications for the firm, governance, and democracy. *Journal of Management Studies*, 48 (4), 899–931.

Schiller, B. (2011). The rise of the MBA politician. *Financial Times*, January 16. Online: http://www.ft.com/cms/s/2/96d634f0-1ffd-11e0-a6fb-00144feab49a.html#axzz3ZA9np4K0

Sinha, P. N., Inkson, K., & Barker, J. R. (2012) Committed to a failing strategy: Celebrity CEO, intermediaries, media and stakeholders in a co-created drama. *Organization Studies*, 33 (2), 223–245.

Strauss, S. (2013). Ask an expert: A look at leadership traits. *USA Today*, February 18. Online: http://www.usatoday.com/story/money/columnist/2013/02/18/steve-strauss-leader-entrepreneur/1927581

Thorndike, J. J. (2013). A lost age of fiscal heroes? Not so much. *Huffington Post*.

Toffel, M., & Schendler, A. (2014). The climate needs aggressive CEO leadership. *Harvard Business School*, September 24. Online: http://hbswk.hbs.edu/item/7632.html

Tucker, A. (2012). The citizen shareholder: Modernizing the agency paradigm to reflect how and why a majority of Americans invest in the market. *Seattle UL Review, 35*, 1299.

Weber, M. (1947). *Theory of social and economic organization*. Trans. A. R. Anderson & T. Parsons. New York: The Free Press.

White, L. (1926). *The city manager*. Chicago: University of Chicago Press.

Willner, A. R. (1985). *The spellbinders: Charismatic political leadership*. New Haven, CT: Yale University Press.

Wilson, S. (1955). *The man in the grey flannel suit*. New York: Cardinal.

Part V
Evaluating Leadership

Introduction

If leadership is 'everything' – widely problematized and craved for in the public sphere, feverishly theorized and investigated by academics, and offered up as both a cause of and a solution for the challenges of our turbulent times by consultants – then maybe it is 'nothing' – not as powerful a cause or not as shiny and unproblematic a solution as different species of leadership enthusiasts like to think. Perhaps the 'leadership industry' – of which this compendium inevitably is a part, too – will be seen by future historians as an emperor that had no clothes. Its ascent in the 1990s, and its growing hold on academia, business, government, consulting, and even the arts in the last 25 years may well be looked upon by future historians as a modern equivalent of the tulip craze: an intellectual dead-end sparking a bubble egged on by an odd mixture of romantic appeal and unhinged self-interest. Of course, future historians may also conclude that the early-twenty-first-century preoccupation with leadership was 'something' – that there were pockets of demonstrable human progress due to prudent, catalytic, inspiring leadership emanating from the myriad of research, training, consulting, and institutionalization efforts that we see today.

In any case, the leadership industry owes it to itself to constantly ask evaluative questions, about leadership in concrete cases and settings, about the leadership models it espouses and the evidence-based leadership practices it aims to elicit. But where to begin? There are so many different routes to arriving at criteria for evaluating public leaders and leadership. Why not keep it simple and focus the effort on what happens to the office-holders themselves as a result of the way they do their jobs? We could look at the extent to which leaders are able to consolidate their positions through (re)election and (re)appointment, based on the idea that good leaders thrive and bad leaders fail. Length of tenure, and formal judgements passed by elective, promotion, and professional bodies then become pivotal to assessing leaders, as does the reputation for influence that they develop. We could take a utilitarian perspective and ask whether leaders demonstrably help groups and organizations achieve their stated objectives, their 'bottom lines', their 'targets'. We could even ask if they manage to lift their constituencies to a higher moral plain – or at least assess whether they deal with moral dilemmas and ethical trade-offs in a responsible way. We could also adopt a follower-centric perspective and focus on the extent to which followers perceive their leaders as satisfying their needs and wants. Or we could adopt an institutional perspective, where good leadership is indicated by the legitimacy, performance, and continuity of organizations.

The list of possibilities is long, and it is probably impossible to articulate a common denominator that can be applied meaningfully to all the forms of leadership covered in this Companion. Leadership will always be hard to assess in a way that meets with universal recognition and stands the test of time. It is too complex for that; it is no doubt one of the 'essentially contested concepts' that social scientists like to go on about. But in each corner of the Byzantine maze that is leadership, it is incumbent upon its community of practice (scholars and practitioners alike) to do its bit, to take stock, ask the 'how good', 'good for who/what' questions that need to be asked, and critically and systematically assess how that particular corner of the field measures up. In this part of the Companion we present three efforts to do just that.

In Chapter 25, Burke goes right to the darkest corners of the leadership maze, providing a comprehensive literature review of the state of our knowledge about bad, destructive leadership. His conclusion is twofold. First, we should not allow our thinking about the potential negative impacts of certain types and styles of leadership to be distracted by the relatively rare but attention-grabbing examples of epically destructive leadership (the Hitlers, Stalins, Maos, Idi Amins, and in the corporate world the relatively short list of notoriously narcissistic, hubristic, incompetent, soul- and stock-destroying CEOs), because it obscures the reality that less extreme forms of destructive leadership are commonplace and can be found across all countires, cultures, and sectors. Second, popular media are way ahead of the field of leadership studies in paying sustained attention to the forms, antecedents, and impacts of destructive leadership. In other words, the leadership industry has work to do in owning up to the damage its main product can do.

In Chapter 26 on the evaluation of 'ethical leadership', Lawton first demonstrates the sheer complexity we get ourselves into when we begin to ask evaluative questions about leadership. 'Leadership', what leadership? Conceptualized how? Which aspects, skills, or relationships involved in leadership are we going to focus on? And if we are going to evaluate leadership in terms of its impact on the entity in which it is being exercised, how are we going to conceptualize that impact? What, for example, counts as 'performance'? He then focuses on the distinctive nature, challenges, and possible criteria for ethical leadership, which he argues is:

> both simple and complex. We all agree that it is a good thing and we all have our own examples of ethical and unethical leadership. We want to believe that our leaders are acting in our interests, that they will treat us fairly, enhance our well-being.

But, after surveying what research has taught us about assessing the ethical dimensions of leadership, he concludes that there is no magic bullet, nor will there ever be. What we need to do is 'recognise the complexity of balancing organizational and wider interests in ways that do no harm to us, our organizations or our societies'.

In Chapter 27, Knies *et al.* drill down further into the leadership–performance nexus introduced by Lawton. Systematically reviewing the empirical evidence on the (mostly organizational) performance impacts of, for example, transactional and transformational leadership styles as reported by five meta-analyses published between 1996 and 2011, they conclude that leadership does indeed matter for organizational performance, but that the kind and strength of impact that is being found is mediated by type of performance measure (objective versus subjective), type of research design (multi-rater or not), context (public versus private sector), and level of analysis at which the relationship is being assessed. True to their positivistic methodological colours, they conclude that:

Both in generic management studies and in public management studies, cross-sectional designs with subjective performance measures tend to find strong effects, and this reflects a need for stronger methods. The generic management literature often relies on lab experiments with low external validity, only two public management studies apply before-and-after designs, and only two studies use experimental methods, so there is a great need for contributions in this area.

Finally, in Chapter 28, Tourish critically assesses one of the more ambitious yet elusive sub-species of the leadership industry, the field of 'spirituality at work', whose proponents assert that organizations and their leaders should facilitate more holistic personal expressions by employees. Since employees increasingly expect their leaders to offer meaning in both their work and wider lives, the management of meaning-making processes is therefore held to be a crucial activity for leaders. The field is boundless in its ambitions, in that its proponents believe that, if spirituality at work gains a sufficiently strong purchase on organizational practices, personal, social, and global transformation will surely follow. Tourish does not share this enthusiasm. On the contrary, after evaluating the literature, he concludes that spiritual leadership can be:

> employed as yet another means of establishing monocultural workplace environments, in which employee dissent is demonised as the sinful antithesis of pure spiritual values, to which only morally deficient individuals could object, and which organisational leaders are uniquely qualified to articulate.

Taken together, the four chapters in this part of the Companion are a sobering reminder that dodging normative questions and fudging causal claims are not the way to make progress in leadership theory and practice, tempting though they may at times seem given the sheer complexity of the challenges of creating a field that is self-conscious and reflective about what it seeks to contribute to and down to earth about the extent to which 'leadership' can actually be part of the problem as well as part of the solution.

25

Destructive Leadership
Antecedents, Consequences and Remedies

Ronald Burke

Leadership research and writing has previously emphasized qualities and characteristics of what were presumed to be effective leaders. Organizations worldwide spend an estimated $50 billion a year on the development of leaders based on these assumptions (Fulmer & Conger, 2004). Yet many leaders fall short. It has been estimated that over half of the people holding managerial or supervisory positions fail to achieve their organization's objectives (Hogan, 1994; Hogan & Hogan, 2001). Every reader of this chapter will probably have experienced or observed a bad leader. Although thousands of research articles have discussed traits, styles and behaviors that make leaders effective, many leaders still fail. These failures are attributed to destructive, toxic and dysfunctional behaviors. The fact that so many leaders fail suggests that paying attention to ineffective and failed leaders will offer a more complete understanding of leadership and improve the practice of leading (Charan & Colvin, 1999; Clements & Washbush, 1999). This has led to increasing attention being paid to understanding why leaders fail, the dark side of leadership (Hornstein, 1996; Kaiser & Bartholomew, 2014; Kellerman, 2004), including destructive and toxic leadership. Leaders fail because of who they are and how they act, that is, there are normally a number of behavioral issues (Dotlich & Cairo, 2003). It should be noted though that not all failed or flawed leaders are necessarily destructive (Finkelstein, 2003). Based on the wide variety of terms used to describe destructive leaders, there are likely to be different forms of destructive leadership, conclude Aasland, Skogstad, Notelairs, Nielsen and Einarsen (2010).

The last decade has shown increasing interest in destructive leadership in both the academic and the popular press (Schyns & Hansborough, 2010; Namie & Namie, 2000; Einarsen, Aasland, & Skogstad, 2010; Lipman-Blumen, 2005; Naider & Schreisheim, 2010). Destructive leadership has negative effects on employees (e.g., the experience of abuse, intimidation, hostility, belittlement, humiliation) as well as on their organizations (e.g., organizational leaders being flawed, derailed, dysfunctional and impaired). In this chapter the term 'destructive leadership' serves as an umbrella term encompassing several types of dysfunctional and toxic leadership.

Let us begin with some examples of destructive leadership. Jackson (2004) describes leaders of two firms that had destructive leaders. First, Al Dunlap, CEO of Sunbeam Corporation, was dubbed "Chainsaw Al," "Rambo in pinstripes" and "The shredder" in the popular press. Byrne (2003) wrote a book on Dunlap titled *Chainsaw*. Dunlap took over failing companies, downsizing and restructuring them in a bid to make them profitable. In these efforts he terminated thousands of employees. Dunlap wrote his own book, *Mean Business*, reflecting his approach to workplaces. At Sunbeam he planned to terminate half its workforce. The Sunbeam Company was found guilty of misusing information to inflate its value. Dunlap was fired, with Sunbeam eventually filing for bankruptcy. Second, Jackson uses the case of Enron. Kenneth Lay and Andrew Fastow of Enron, besides engaging in unethical practices, created a culture of fear and "yes-men" and "yes-women," of cutting corners, of punishing employees who expressed disagreement with them with negative performance appraisals. Enron filed for bankruptcy, taking down Arthur Andersen, their accounting firm, with them in the process. Both Lay and Fastow were sentenced to prison terms, though Lay died before he started to serve his sentence.

The Nature of Destructive Leadership

Einarsen, Aasland and Skogstad (2007) first proposed a model having two dimensions (pro-subordinate and pro-organization behaviors, anti-subordinate and anti-organization behaviors) that had destructive and constructive leadership behaviors in the resulting four quadrants: pro-subordinate and pro-organization representing constructive leadership (e.g., constructive, supportive–disloyal), and anti-subordinate and anti-organization representing destructive leadership (e.g., tyrannical). Einarsen et al. define destructive leadership as "the systematic and repeated behavior by a leader, supervisor or manager that violates the legitimate interest of the organization by undermining and/or sabotaging the organization's goals, tasks, resources, and effectiveness and/or job satisfaction of subordinates" (2007, p. 208). This definition emerges as a more inclusive definition of destructive leadership than other terms that have been used.

Aasland, Skogstad, Notelaers, Nielsen and Einarsen (2010), building on the earlier Einarsen et al. (2007) model, suggest that leadership behavior is best seen on a continuum from "highly anti" to "highly pro" with five types of leadership behaviors emerging, one being constructive and three (or perhaps four) being destructive. They examined the prevalence of four types of destructive leadership behaviors in a large sample of Norwegian workers (n = 2539). The four types of destructive leadership were tyrannical, derailed, supportive–disloyal and laissez-faire. In addition, constructive leadership was also investigated. Constructive leadership was significantly and negatively correlated with the presence of tyrannical, derailed and laissez-faire leadership assessments of leadership behaviors that respondents had experienced over the past six months. The total prevalence of destructive leadership behaviors ranged from 34 to 61 percent, based on two different estimation methods. The most common destructive leadership behaviors were laissez-faire, followed by supportive–disloyal, derailed, with tyrannical being the least prevalent. Interestingly, some leaders exhibited both constructive as well as destructive behaviors; leadership can consist of both.

Destructive leadership is a term that subsumes various types of leadership having negative outcomes. Other terms that have been offered include: "petty tyranny" (Ashforth, 1994, 1997), "intolerable bosses" (Lombardo & McCall, 1984), "psychopaths" (Furnham & Taylor, 2004), "toxic leaders" (Goldman, 2009; Lipman-Blumen, 2005), "Machiavellian leaders" (Christie & Gies, 1970), "narcissistic leaders" (Rosenthal & Pittinsky, 2006) and the "dark side of leadership" (Hogan & Hogan, 2001). Destructive leadership occurs in the private sector, the public sector, in the military and among world leaders; it can also be seen in all organizational functional areas. Finally, destructive leadership can be observed at all levels of the organizational hierarchy from CEOs and country presidents to first line supervisors.

Krasikova, Green and LeBreton (2013) review the destructive leadership literature, recognizing various forms of destructive leadership, and distinguish destructive leadership from other types of leadership. Krasikova et al. (2013, p. 1310) define destructive leadership as "harmful behavior imbedded in the process of leading" (p. 1310). Destructive leadership then refers to harmful behaviors of a leader that are part of the process of leading. They propose two ways in which destructive leadership is observed: encouraging employees to pursue destructive goals, and using destructive verbal and non-verbal behaviors to influence subordinates to reach organizational goals. They distinguish destructive leadership from ineffective leadership in that destructive leadership is intentional.

Padilla, Hogan and Kaiser (2007) define destructive leadership in terms of five elements: destructive leadership is rarely entirely destructive, and typically carries both good and bad outcomes; destructive leadership involves dominance, coercion and manipulation instead of influence, persuasion and commitment; destructive leadership is selfishly oriented and focused on the leader's needs more than the organization's needs; destructive leadership reduces individual satisfaction and organizational performance; and both susceptible followers and organizational culture contribute to the presence of destructive leadership.

Lipman-Blumen (2005, p. 18) defines toxic leaders as "leaders who act without integrity by dissembling and engaging in various other dishonorable behaviors," including "corruption, hypocrisy, sabotage and manipulation, as well as other assorted unethical, illegal, and criminal acts." And she writes (p. 18):

> to count as toxic, these behaviors and qualities of character must inflict some reasonably serious harm on their followers and organizations. The intent to harm others or to enhance the self at the expense of others distinguishes seriously toxic leaders from the careless or unintentional toxic leaders, who also cause negative effects.

Walton (2007, p. 20) defines toxic leadership as "behavior which is exploitative, abusive, destructive and psychologically – and perhaps legalistically – corrupt and poisonous." Some common themes are present in these various definitions. The term "toxic leadership" encompasses various harmful consequences and is widely used in both the academic and practitioner literatures.

One dominant theme is petty tyranny. Ashforth (1994, p. 126) defines a petty tyrant as "someone who uses their power and authority oppressively, capriciously, and perhaps vindictively." Ashforth (1994) developed a model of proposed antecedents and effects of petty tyranny. Two categories of antecedents – individual predispositions and situational facilitators – were considered. Individual predispositions included: beliefs about organizations (e.g., holding a bureaucratic orientation involving being domineering, impersonal, inflexible and deserving of the rights and benefits of status and authority), beliefs about subordinates (e.g., holding Theory X views that people dislike work, are lazy, need direction and resist change); beliefs about the self (e.g., low self-esteem and self-confidence) and a preference for action (e.g., being direct, low tolerance for ambiguity). Situational facilitators included: macro-level factors (e.g., organizational norms and values, mechanistic organizational features, entrepreneurial organization features); micro-level factors (e.g., feeling powerless leading to controlling others, having power) and workplace stressors (e.g., becoming more directive under duress or in a crisis). As consequences of petty tyranny, Ashforth (1994) lists high levels of dissatisfaction with one's manager, high levels of subordinate stress and frustration, high levels of helplessness and disengagement from work, low self-esteem, low job performance and low levels of work unit cohesiveness.

Ashforth (1997), in a study of 63 sets of respondents (a set consisting of a manager and two subordinates) and 25 partial sets, examined the effects of petty tyranny on subordinate work experiences. The following results were obtained. Managers scoring higher on Theory X beliefs and intolerance of ambiguity were seen by subordinates as engaging in more petty tyranny;

managers' bureaucratic orientation was also associated with subordinate assessments of petty tyranny; petty tyranny was associated with lower satisfaction with one's manager, higher levels of subordinate stress and frustration, higher levels of subordinate helplessness and work alienation, and lower levels of work unit cohesiveness.

Another type is abusive supervision. Tepper (2000, p. 178) defines abusive supervision as "subordinates' perceptions of the extent to which supervisors engage in the sustained display of hostile verbal and nonverbal behaviors excluding physical contact." Tepper writes that the relationships that people at work have with their immediate supervisors are of vital importance, more important than any other relationship they have at work. The quality of this relationship influences employee job satisfaction and health, their job performance, pay and career progress. Managers engaging in abusive supervision create dissatisfaction, low commitment, intention to quit and psychological distress. Employees respond to abusive supervision by engaging in deviant behaviors that may hurt their organizations (poor performance, insubordination, sabotage, revenge).

Why do supervisors abuse particular subordinates? Tepper, Moss and Duffy (2011), in a study of 183 supervisor–subordinate dyads, found that supervisor perceptions of relationship conflict and subordinate job performance mediated the relationship between deep-level dissimilarity (having different values, attitudes and personality) and abusive supervision. Thus dissimilarity, relationship conflict and level of subordinate job performance influenced abuse of particular subordinates.

Two extensive reviews (Tepper, 2007; Martinko, Harvey, Brees, & Mackey, 2013) have examined antecedents and consequences of abusive supervision. Both reviews document the negative consequences of abusive supervision. Martinko, Harvey, Bees and Mackey (2013) reviewed additional studies on abusive supervision published after Tepper's review (about 60) noting again the association of abusive supervision and important organizational outcomes (e.g, more aggression, fewer organizational citizenship behaviors, poorer subordinate job performance, more counter-productive workplace behaviors) and the fact that the abuse of employees creates value and ethical concerns for employing organizations.

Narcissism is a third type. It has been associated with destructive leadership by several writers. DuBrin (2012) notes seven traits of narcissists: higher felt authority, greater self-sufficiency, feeling superior, being the center of attention, exploiting others, vanity and entitlement. Among the symptoms of narcissism, he identifies self-admiration, statements of superiority, talking a lot, interrupting others, expecting extra attention, a dependence on others to reinforce their self-image, perfection and compulsivity, and low levels of empathy. Narcissists use emotional detachment and rationalizations to justify their actions. Narcissism then results in particular behaviors and demands in the workplace such as uncivil treatment of others, arrogance, a sense of entitlement, exploiting others and a heightened sense of self-importance. Extreme levels of narcissism have been termed a psychiatric condition, narcissistic personality disorder.

DuBrin (2012), as well as others (e.g., Maccoby, 2003, 2007; Higgs, 2009), describe healthy and productive narcissists (e.g., Richard Branson of the Virgin organization) as well as dysfunctional narcissists (Angelo Mozilo, Countrywide Financial).

Narcissistic leaders are described as dominant, self-confident, having a sense of entitlement, grandiose and low on empathy. On the positive side, they are viewed by others as inspirational and leading by charisma. On the negative side they can engage in unethical behaviors, create dissatisfied subordinates, more toxic workplaces, the bullying of staff and the making of more risky decisions. Narcissists are more likely to emerge as leaders (Brunell et al., 2008). Narcissists look and act like leaders and also emerge as leaders (Judge, LePine, & Rich, 2006). People are attracted to narcissists, and narcissists make a favorable first impression (Bach, Schmulke, & Egloff, 2010).

Narcissists have an unhealthy level of self-worth as opposed to healthy levels of self-confidence and self-esteem. Campbell, Reeder, Sedikides and Elliot (2000), in two studies, reported that narcissists more than non-narcissists engaged in self-enhancement strategies.

Machiavellianism is another form. Individuals high on Machiavellianism tend to manipulate and exploit others to achieve their own goals, to control their social interactions, to resist the influence of others and are persuasive (Christie & Gies, 1970). Klazad, Restobog, Zagenczyk, Klewitz and Tang (2010), in two studies carried out in Australia and the Philippines, using supervisor–subordinate dyads, found that supervisor Machiavellianism was positively associated with subordinate ratings of abusive supervision, with subordinate assessments of authoritarian leadership behaviors fully mediating this relationship. Miska, Stahl and Fuchs (2014) examined 52 actual cases of unethical managerial behavior (Enron, WorldCom, Salomon Brothers) and found that companies involved in major scandals had leaders scoring high on Machiavellian characteristics. In a study of 122 hospital employees in Greece, Gkorezis, Petridou and Krouklidou found that employee perceptions of their mangers' level of Machiavellianism had both direct and indirect effects (through cynicism) on their levels of emotional exhaustion (2015).

Toxic leadership can also take the form of workplace bullying. Samnani and Singh (2012) reviewed 20 years of workplace bullying research. Bullying has been defined as follows:

> Bullying at work means harassing, offending, socially excluding someone or negatively affecting someone's work tasks. In order for the label bullying (or mobbing) to be applied to a particular activity, interaction, or process it has to occur repeatedly and regularly (e.g., weekly) and over a period of time (e.g., about six months). Bullying is an escalated process in the course of which the person confronted ends up in an inferior position and becomes the target of systematic negative acts.
>
> *(Einarsen, Hoel, Zapf, & Cooper, 2003, p. 15)*

Estimates of bullying suggest that about 10 percent of the workforce have experienced being bullied; other estimates suggest that 95 percent of employees have experienced bullying over a five-year period. Workplace bullying can be overt or subtle. Antecedents of workplace bullying include individual characteristics of the target (e.g., gender, ethnicity, personality traits) and of the perpetrator (e.g., gender, holding a stressful job), group-level characteristics (e.g., witnessing bullying, status inconsistency within workgroups), as well as organizational-level antecedents (e.g., authoritarian leadership and management styles, power imbalance and organizational culture and climate). Individual consequences of workplace bullying include psychological outcomes (e.g., depression, suicide), physiological (e.g., sleep problems, mood swings) and work outcomes (e.g., intent to quit, lower levels of job satisfaction), less effective work teams and higher levels of bullying at the group level, and more aggressive organizational cultures and lower levels of performance at the organizational level (Glasso, Vie, & Hoel, 2010).

Measures of Destructive Leadership

Efforts have been made to develop and validate measures of destructive leadership and related concepts. Hogan and Hogan (1997) developed and validated the Hogan Development Survey as a measure of "dark side" personality characteristics associated with failed leadership. This measure taps 11 dimensions: excitable – moody, hard to please, emotionally volatile; skeptical – suspicious, sensitive to criticism and expecting betrayal; cautious – risk-averse, resistant to change and slow to make decisions; reserved – aloof, uncommunicative and different to the feelings of others; leisurely – overly cooperative but privately irritable, stubborn and uncooperative; bold – overly self-confident, arrogant and entitled; mischievous – charming, risk taking and excitement seeking; colorful – dramatic, attention seeking and interruptive; imaginative – creative but thinking and acting in unusual or eccentric ways; diligent – meticulous, precise, hard to please and micromanaging; and dutiful – eager to please and reluctant to act independently of or against popular opinion.

Schmidt (2008) developed and validated a toxic leadership scale using both qualitative and quantitative methods. Data were collected from both civilian and military respondents. In the first qualitative phase, participants developed themes and traits underlying toxic leadership. These were then used to create a quantitative measure of the six dimensions that emerged. His final measure of toxic leadership contained five dimensions (unprofessional behavior was dropped): abusive supervision, authoritarian leadership, narcissism, self-promotion and unpredictability. His measure of toxic leadership was also clearly differentiated from measures of transformational leadership and leader–member exchange concepts. Finally, dimensions of this scale were associated with higher levels of turnover intentions, and lower levels of both job and supervisor satisfaction.

Tepper (2000) created a 15-item measure of abusive supervision in which subordinates indicated the frequency that their supervisors engaged in particular behaviors; items included "ridicules me," "gives me the silent treatment," "reminds me of my past mistakes and failures" and "expresses anger at me when he/she is mad for another reason."

Ashforth (1994) developed a 45-item measure of petty tyranny containing six dimensions (e.g., arbitrariness and self-aggrandizement, belittling subordinates, lack of consideration, a forcing style of conflict resolution, discouraging initiative, and non-contingent punishment; items included: "how often were you in circumstances when a superior belittled or embarrassed subordinates" and "how often have superiors encouraged subordinates to speak up when they disagreed with a decision" (reverse coded)).

While most writers believe that destructive leaders have negative effects on employees and their organizations, few have reported the prevalence of such leadership behaviors. Research (e.g., Hogan, Rankin, & Fazzni, 1990) has shown that between 60 and 75 percent of employees indicated that the worst aspects of their jobs were their supervisors, and abusive managers were cited as the causes of compensation claims filed against organizations in 94 percent of these claims (Wilson, 1991). Tepper (2007) estimates that the costs of employee withdrawal from abusive supervision exceed $29 billion per year. Thus destructive leadership may be fairly widespread.

Psychopathology in the Workplace

Not all psychopaths are in prison. Some are in the boardroom.

(Hare, 2002)

Smith and Lilienfeld (2013) review the literature on workplace psychopathy and various outcome measures. They note that considerably more interest has been shown in workplace psychopathy in the popular media/press than by the academic research community. Psychopathic personality, or psychopathy, refers to a cluster of personality traits and behaviors that includes "superficial charm, dishonesty, ego-centrality, manipulativeness, risk taking, and a lack of empathy and guilt masked as apparent normalcy" (Smith & Lilienfeld, 2013, p. 206). Psychopathy is moderately correlated with a diagnosis of anti-social personality disorder. It has been also suggested that psychopathy can be associated with positive outcomes. Smith and Lilienfeld conclude the following, based on the unfortunately limited amount of research on this topic. First, individuals working in business organizations may have higher rates of some psychopathic traits than do individuals in other jobs. Second, psychopathy tends to be related to aggression and counter-productive workplace behaviors, to unethical decision making, to intentions to commit white-collar crime, and to both positive (e.g., better job performance) and negative (e.g., unethical behaviors, poorer management skills) leadership behaviors.

Babiak, Neumann and Hare (2010), in a study of 293 corporate professionals, found higher levels of psychopathy in this sample than in other community samples. Professionals scoring higher on psychopathy also scored higher on company assessments of charisma/presentation style (e.g., creativity, good communication skills and strategic thinking) and lower on assessments of responsibility performance (e.g., management skills, being a good team player, overall accomplishments).

Mathieu, Neumann, Hare and Babiak (2014), in a sample of 136 employees of a large Canadian financial institution and a sample of 518 employees of a public service organization, studied the relationship of the psychopathy of supervisors as perceived by subordinates with measures of psychological well-being, work–family conflict and job satisfaction. In both samples, psychopathy levels perceived by subordinates were associated with less job satisfaction and more work–family conflict; psychopathy ratings of supervisors predicted psychological distress only in the public sector sample, however. Psychopaths are similar to sociopaths. Neither is officially a clinical disorder. The latest version of the Diagnostic and Statistical Manual of Mental Disorders (American Psychiatric Association, DSM-V) uses the term Antisocial Personality Disorder to describe an individual who is ruinous, remorseless, self-interested and reckless.

Antecedents of destructive leadership have been suggested. These include psychological traits (Hogan & Hogan, 2001), personality traits including narcissism (Rosenthal & Pittinsky, 2006), anti-social personality disorder (Goldman, 2006), and character flaws such as arrogance, selfishness, abrasiveness and compulsiveness (McCall & Lombardo, 1983).

Goldman (2006) includes borderline personality disorder as an antecedent of high toxicity/destructive leadership using a case study of a male senior executive at a US fashion house, a medium-sized organization. Goldman was hired as a consultant to improve morale, which included coaching the senior executive in question. As he got to observe this person over a longer period of time, Goldman typed him as having "borderline personality disorder" which contributed to his intrapersonal and interpersonal problems. This man was erratic, unpredictable, cruel, harassing, and diminishing of staff and increasing levels of stress among staff.

As antecedents of destructive leadership, Krasikova et al. suggest two: first, the leader's and organization's goals are different, and the leader sees subordinates as impediments to achieving their own or their organizations goals; second, the leader's characteristics, such as a lack of self-control, an emphasis on personal interests as opposed to the interests of others, and the presence of justifications for engaging in destructive leadership behaviors that harm others (e.g., a favorable view of revenge, low levels of trust, high levels of anger, previous success in using destructive leadership). Context factors such as inadequate resources, unmotivated subordinates and incompetent subordinates, along with little punishment for engaging in destructive leadership, also play a role in engaging in destructive leadership.

Understanding destructive leadership is complicated by the fact that some behaviors can produce negative outcomes, while the same behaviors in a different context may produce positive outcomes, referred to as "dark side" and "bright side" characteristics respectively (Judge and LePine, 2007). Judge, Piccolo and Kosalka (2009) examine the effects, both positive and negative, of "bright side" and "dark side" personality traits and leader effectiveness. "Bright" refers to positively valued traits while "dark" refers to negatively valued traits. It is also useful to distinguish between leader emergence and leader effectiveness. Certain traits may be associated with both leader emergence and leader effectiveness, others with leader emergence only and still others with leader effectiveness only. It is also possible that the relationship between traits and emergence and/or effectiveness may not be linear (too little or too much may be limiting).

Here are some illustrations of "bright side" and "dark side" characteristics:

Bright side of bright side traits: conscientious, extraversion, agreeableness, emotional stability, open to experience – highly conscientious leader focuses on achieving personal and organizational goals successfully;

Dark side of dark side traits: narcissism, over controlling, micro managing – over controlling leader squelches initiative of subordinates;

Dark side of bright side traits: – highly confident leader makes risky decisions that fail;

Bright side of dark side traits: – controlling leader takes charge in a crisis situation.

Furnham, Trickey and Hyde (2012), in a sample of almost 5000 British respondents, examined relationships of 11 "dark side" traits assessed by the Hogan Development Survey (listed earlier) and six indicators of work success measured by the Hogan Personality Inventory. They found some "dark side" traits were consistently related to lower work outcomes (excitable, skeptical), others had no relationship with work outcomes or were positively associated with work outcomes (bold, diligent). In addition, some "dark side" traits were positively associated with some work outcomes and negatively with others (mischievous, colorful). They conclude that "dark side" traits may not always cause problems (also see Furnham, 2007).

Consequences of Destructive Leadership

There are additional consequences of destructive leadership. Schyns and Schilling (2013) undertook a meta-analysis of 57 studies examining the effects of destructive leaders. Ratings of leader destructiveness were associated with unfavorable attitudes towards the leader, poorer psychological well-being, lower job performance, greater intentions to quit, more counter-productive workplace behaviors and more resistance towards the leader.

Padilla et al. (2007) argue that the negative consequences of destructive leadership emerge when three factors come together: destructive leaders, susceptible followers and conducive workplace environments, which they term the toxic triangle. They offer the following examples within each. Destructive leader traits include charisma, personalized power, narcissism, negative life themes and an ideology of hate. Susceptible followers include both conformers and colluders: the former encompass individuals with unmet needs, low maturity individuals and individuals having low core self-evaluations; the latter encompass highly ambitious individuals, individuals sharing the same world view and individuals having bad values. Finally conducive environments are unstable, perceive internal and external threats, lack checks, balances and accountabilities, possess particular values and are basically ineffective.

There is considerable evidence that destructive leaders, by definition, have negative effects on their subordinates. It is also likely that destructive leaders create dysfunctional organizations, a position supported by Goldman (2010) and Kets de Vries and Miller (1985a, 1985b). Goldman offers clinical case studies on how destructive leaders create dysfunctional workplaces.

Goldman describes consulting and executive coaching assignments with organizations as entailing aspects of psychological and psychotherapy. Organizations are systems so it should come as no surprise that the effects of destructive leaders will be widespread. His case studies include an international fashion house whose head designer harassed staff and increased workplace incivility, a senior manager of a Fortune 500 company treating staff with verbal and physical abuse, and the bizarre and destructive behavior of the head of a major Research and Development division. Goldman stresses how critical it is to understand destructive leaders from a psychological perspective. These leaders' pathologies affected their entire operation. In some cases, these destructive leaders exhibit psychological pathologies.

Given the negative effects of destructive and toxic leaders, why do so many of them remain in their jobs? Shapiro and Von Glinow (2007) address this question. They first conclude that more bad leaders (e.g., destructive, toxic, dysfunctional) remain in their higher-level organizational jobs than is the case for destructive, toxic or dysfunctional leaders holding lower-level organizational positions. It may be more difficult to evaluate the overall contribution of more senior leaders to organizational performance. In addition, subordinates are typically reluctant to speak up for fear of their jobs and careers. Senior toxic leaders exist in a network of supporters. Forbes and Watson (2010) use a case study of Michael Eisner's CEO tenure with the Disney Corporation to show how board loyalty allowed his destructive leadership to continue despite its negative consequences for the Disney Corporation.

Management Education and Leadership Development

One can usefully make a distinction between management education (e.g., that typically offered in MBA programs), which involves knowledge, abilities and skills, and the ability to increase performance in managerial jobs and effective performance in leadership roles, which are the real objective of leadership development. There is considerable debate about the benefits of such efforts to increase leadership effectiveness. Organizations unfortunately rarely evaluate the benefits and effects of their considerable investments in leadership development efforts (Collins & Holton, 2004; Day, 2000).

There is considerable evidence that narcissism levels among US college students have risen over the past 25 years (Twenge, Konrath, Foster, Campbell, & Bushman, 2008). In addition, business students report higher levels of cheating than do students enrolled in other programs. Schools of business and their faculty members can, however, address levels of student narcissism. Possible initiatives include: sending/suggesting that clinically narcissistic students and faculty seek counseling, educating and increasing faculty and student understanding of narcissism by including materials on narcissism in course content, offering tools for self-assessment, making more use of assessment and behavior feedback, engaging students in smaller classes, including activities where student behaviors can be observed, and one-on-one interactions with faculty members where student behavior can be observed and coaching provided. In addition, faculty teaching skills workshops should include faculty narcissism as one element.

Interestingly, potential destructive leadership behaviors associated with dark side characteristics are rarely addressed in business education, particularly in MBA programs. For example, Bedwell, Fiore and Salas (2014) do an outstanding job in proposing a taxonomy of interpersonal skills deemed critical for the future workforce and indicating how these could be incorporated into MBA education and executive education more broadly. They fail to include or address destructive leadership behaviors, however. Recent extensive reviews of leadership theories and leadership development (Day, Fleenor, Atwater, Sturm, & McKee, 2014; Dinh, Lord, Gardner, Meuser, Liden, & Hu, 2014) do not even mention destructive leadership.

Given both the pervasiveness of various types of destructive leadership and their negative effects on people and organizations, a critical question becomes whether toxic leaders' dark side characteristics can be changed. Hogan, Curphy and Hogan (1994) write that dark side characteristics can be changed but this requires more intensive efforts than are typical in most leadership development offerings. Peterson (1993) and Peterson and Hicks (1993), citing data from the Coaching for Effectiveness Program of Personnel Decisions, Inc., involving 370 mangers over a five-year period, reported that most managers changed many of their targeted behaviors.

Padilla et al. (2007) propose three broad areas for interventions to reduce levels of destructive leadership. First, destructive leaders can be identified in selection, hiring and promotion processes by including assessments of narcissism, hostility, ethics and other dark side personality characteristics. Feedback from assessment instruments including 360-degree assessments can be used in development and training initiatives. Obviously these assessments should include dark side characteristics. Second, creating a culture of employee empowerment might curtail a leader's use of autocratic power. In addition, rewarding leaders for developing leadership potential of their subordinates would also serve as a countervailing force. The development of subordinates should also be an important factor in promotion decisions. Finally, organizations need to develop checks on toxic leadership by using hierarchy and accountability to control these events at lower levels. These include performance reviews, succession management processes, promotion processes as well as opportunities to "punish" leaders who exhibit toxic behaviors. Organizations need to develop policies and practices that discourage destructive leadership behaviors. It is also possible that subordinates who observe a destructive leader will be less likely to engage in these behaviors (Baden, 2014; Sutton, 2009).

Krasikova et al. (2013) offer three recommendations. First, organizations must be aware that destructive leadership is occurring and be motivated to respond to this. The best evidence is in the experiences of subordinates so organizations need to tap into the grapevine, using focus groups and employee surveys. Second, leaders' personal traits and behavioral characteristics need to inform selection, placement and promotion decisions, and leaders need to create an organizational context that rewards constructive leadership behaviors and punishes destructive leadership behaviors. Third, organizations should limit the discretion allowed to leaders by creating policies and practices that bring leadership behaviors in line with organizational expectations and goals.

Individuals being considered for a new job can do some things to determine whether their new manager is destructive. These include asking the potential new manager to describe their approach to leadership, examining other external sources of information about the company culture (e.g., online, reports of company turnover) and observing the potential new manager's behavior and attitudes in the interview. Is the manager present and engaged (taking phone calls, etc.), how does the manger talk about other employees (e.g. negatively) and what signals can one detect from other employees in the organization when you arrive for interviews (are they dissatisfied?)

Lubit (2013) offers advice on dealing with one's own narcissism, narcissistic bosses, narcissistic peers and narcissistic subordinates, as well as organizational options. On the organizational level, organizations should take pains to avoid hiring or promoting narcissists, and foster a culture that supports and rewards narcissism. Individuals should not argue with their narcissistic bosses; deal with them tactfully and move to another position when this is possible. In dealing with narcissistic colleagues, individuals should make sure their managers know of their performance, and individuals should watch their backs. In dealing with narcissistic subordinates, individuals should also watch their backs, and when providing feedback to their subordinates make sure that positive comments are offered as well as negative ones.

Organizations need to manage petty tyranny by developing policies that support the well-being of all employees. In addition, leaders must realize how their behaviors impact their employees and their work teams. Subordinates should also be empowered to stand up to angry leaders.

360-degree feedback (also known as multi-rater feedback and multi-source feedback) is a process in which an individual receives information about how their behaviors and contributions are perceived by others with whom they interact. Individuals (typically managers) are rated on various defined behaviors by one or more managers, their peers, their subordinates and sometimes clients or customers. 360-degree programs can also include self-assessments. More information on the benefits, potential disadvantages, issues to consider and key aspects of successful 360-degree feedback programs are offered in Nikolaou, Vakola and Robertson (2006).

Goldman (2010) uses case studies of his consulting experiences with organizational leaders where destructive leadership became one focus of his work to offer illustrations of his approach to reducing levels of destructive leadership behaviors.

Although writing on executive coaching first appeared as far back as the late 1930s, it became an accepted field of organizational practice in the 1960s (O'Neill, 2000; Megginson & Clutterbuck, 2009; Kets de Vries, 2004). Several writers (Bartley, 2005; Greenberg, 2006; Simon, 2009) describe their use of Gestalt theory in their coaching practices in working with narcissistic individuals inside and outside of organizations.

Conclusions

Several observations follow from the literature reviewed in this chapter. First, various types and forms of destructive leadership exist. Second, destructive leadership, particularly in its less destructive forms, is fairly widespread, knowing no national boundaries – it is a global phenomenon. Third, relatively little attention has been devoted to understanding destructive leadership, other than to advocating more "positive" theories and models of leadership, particularly in the academic community. The popular media, however, has shown considerably more attention to it. Fourth, both college and university management education and leadership development efforts by organizations have paid little attention to destructive leadership. Fifth, the roots of destructive leadership are varied and include genetics, early family experiences and environments, social learning, personality development and workplace experiences. Antecedents of destructive leadership include both individual predispositions (beliefs) and personality factors as well as organizational factors. Sixth, destructive leadership generally has negative effects on subordinates, their families and organizations. Seventh, these effects themselves are complex in that aspects of destructive leadership (e.g., narcissism) can result in leader emergence in early career stages and other aspects (e.g., dominance) can contribute to success in specific circumstances (e.g., crisis situations). Eighth, we also need more efforts to reduce destructive leadership and an evaluation of the success of these. Finally, given the importance of understanding destructive leadership, more research attention needs to be placed here; fortunately the last decade has seen increased activity in this regard.

References

Aasland, M. S., Skogstad, A., Notelaers, G., Nielsen, M. B., & Einarsen, S. (2010) The prevalence of destructive leadership behavior. *British Journal of Management, 21*, 438–452.

Ashforth, B. E. (1994) Petty tyranny in organizations. *Human Relations, 47*, 755–778.

Ashforth, B. E. (1997) Petty tyranny in organizations: A preliminary examination of antecedents and consequences. *Canadian Journal of Administrative Sciences, 14*, 126–140.

Babiak, P., Neumann, C. S., & Hare, R. D. (2010) Corporate psychopathy: Talking the walk. *Behavioral Sciences and the Law, 28*, 174–193.

Bach, M., Schmulke, S., & Egloff, B. (2010) Why are narcissists so charming at first sight: Decoding the narcissism–popularity link at zero acquaintance. *Journal of Personality and Social Psychology, 98*, 132–145.

Baden, D. (2014) Look on the right side: A comparison of positive and negative role models in business ethics education. *Academy of Management Learning and Education, 13*, 154–170.

Bartley, T. J. (2005) Working with narcissism in organizations. *Gestalt Review, 9*, 38–52.

Bedwell, W. L., Fiore, S. M., & Salas, E. (2014) Developing the future workforce: An approach for integrating interpersonal skills into the MBA classroom. *Academy of Management Learning and Education, 13*, 171–186.

Brunell, A. B., Gentry, W. S., Campbell, W., Hoffman, B. J., Kuhnert, K. W., & DeMarree, K. G. (2008) Leader emergence: The case of the narcissistic leader. *Personality and Social Psychology Bulletin, 34*, 1663–1676.

Byrne, J. (2003) *Chainsaw: The notorious career of Al Dunlap in the era of profit-at-any-price.* Toronto: HarperCollins Canada.

Campbell, W. K., Reeder, G. D., Sedikides, C., & Elliot, A. J. (2000) Narcissism and comparative self-enhancement strategies. *Journal of Research in Personality, 34*, 329–347.

Charan, R., & Colvin, G. (1999) Why CEOs fail. *Fortune, 29*, 69–78.

Christie, R., & Geis, F. L. (1970) *Studies in Machiavellianism.* New York: Academic Press.

Clements, C., & Washbush, J. B. (1999) The two faces of leadership: Considering the dark side of leader–follower dynamics. *Journal of Workplace Learning: Employee Counseling Today, 11*, 39–48.

Collins, D. B., & Holton, E. E. (2004) The effectiveness of managerial leadership development programs: A meta-analysis of studies from 1982–2001. *Human Resource Development Quarterly, 15*, 217–248.

Day, D. V. (2000) Leadership development: A review in context. *Leadership Quarterly, 11*, 581–613.

Day, D. V., Fleenor, J. W., Atwater, L. E., Sturm, R. E., & McKee, R. A. (2014) Advances in leader and leadership development: A review of 25 years of research and theory. *Leadership Quarterly, 25*, 63–82.

Dinh, J. E., Lord, R. G., Gardner, W. L., Meuser, J. D., Liden, R. C., & Hui, J. (2014) Leadership theory and research in the new millennium: Current theoretical trends and changing perspectives. *Leadership Quarterly, 25*, 36–62.

Dotlich, D. L., & Cairo, P. (2003) *Why CEOs fail: The 11 behaviors that can derail your climb to the top and how to manage them.* San Francisco: Jossey-Bass.

DuBrin, A. J. (2012) *Narcissism in the workplace: Research, opinion and practice.* Cheltenham: Edward Elgar.

Einarsen, S., Aasland, M. S., & Skogstad, A. (2007) Destructive leadership behavior: A definition and conceptual model. *Leadership Quarterly, 18*, 207–216.

Einarsen, S., Aasland, M. S., & Skogstad, A. (2010) The nature and outcomes of destructive leadership behavior in organizations. In R J. Burke & C. L. Cooper (eds.) *Risky business: Psychological, physical and financial costs of high risk behavior in organizations.* Surrey: Gower, pp. 323–350.

Einarsen, S., Hoel, H., Zapf, D., & Cooper, C. L. (2003) The concept of bullying at work. In S. Einarsen (ed.) *Bullying and emotional abuse in the workplace: International perspectives in research and practice.* London: Taylor and Francis, pp. 3–30.

Finkelstein, S. (2003) *Why smart executives fail and what we can learn from their mistakes.* New York: Portfolio.

Forbes, W., & Watson, R. (2010) Destructive corporate leadership and board loyalty: A case study of Michael Eisner's long tenure at Disney Corporation. Paper presented at Behavioral Finance Working group Conference, Cass Business School, July.

Fulmer, R. M., & Conger, J. A. (2004) *Growing your company's leaders.* New York: AMACOM.

Furnham, A. (2007) Personality disorders and derailment at work: The paradoxical positive influence of pathology in the workplace. In J. Langan-Fox, C. L. Cooper, & R. J. Klimoski (eds.) *Research companion to the dysfunctional workplace: Management challenges and symptoms.* Cheltenham: Edward Elgar, pp. 22–38.

Furnham, A., & Taylor, J. (2004) *The dark side of behavior at work: Understanding and avoiding employees leaving, thieving and deceiving.* New York: Palgrave MacMillan.

Furnham, A., Trickey, G., & Hyde, G. (2012) Bright aspects to dark side traits: Dark side traits associated with work success. *Personality and Individual Differences, 52*, 908–913.

Gkorezis, P., Petridou, E., & Krouklidou, T. (2015) The detrimental effect of Machiavellian leadership on emotional exhaustion: Organizational cynicism as a mediator. *Europe's Journal of Psychology, 11*, 619–631.

Glaso, L., Vie, T. L., & Hoel, H. (2010) Bullying in the workplace. In R. J. Burke & C. L. Cooper (eds.) *Risky business: Psychological, physical and financial costs of high risk behavior in organizations.* Surrey: Gower, pp. 351–374.

Goldman, A. (2006) High toxicity leadership: Borderline personality disorder and the dysfunctional organization. *Journal of Managerial Psychology, 21*, 733–746.

Goldman, A. (2009) *Transforming toxic leaders.* Palo Alto, CA: Stanford University Press.

Goldman, A. (2010) *Destructive leaders and dysfunctional organizations: A therapeutic approach*. Cambridge: Cambridge University Press.

Greenberg, E. (2006) The narcissistic tightrope walk: Using Gestalt therapy field theory to stabilize the narcissistic client. *Gestalt Review, 9,* 58–68.

Hare, R. D. (2002) The predators among us. Keynote address to the Canadian Police Association, St Johns, Newfoundland, August 27.

Higgs, M. (2009) The good, the bad, and the ugly: Leadership and narcissism. *Journal of Change Management, 9,* 165–178.

Hogan, R. (1994) Trouble at the top: Causes and consequences of managerial incompetence. *Consulting Psychology Journal, 46,* 1061–1087.

Hogan, R., & Hogan, J. (1997) Hogan Development Survey manual. Tulsa, OK: Hogan Assessment Systems.

Hogan, R., & Hogan, J. (2001) Assessing leadership: A view of the dark side. *International Journal of Evaluation and Assessment, 9,* 40–51.

Hogan, R., Curphy, G. J., & Hogan, J. (1994) What we know about leadership effectiveness and personality. *American Psychologist, 49,* 493–504.

Hogan, R., Raskin, R., & Fazzini, D. (1990) The dark side of charisma. In K. E. Clark & M. B. Clark (eds.) *Measures of leadership*. West Orange, NJ: Leadership Library of America, pp. 343–354.

Hornstein, H. A. (1996) *Brutal bosses and their prey*. New York: Riverhead Books.

Jackson, K. T. (2004) *Building reputational capital: Strategies for integrity and fair play that improve the bottom line*. Oxford: Oxford University Press.

Judge, T. A., & LePine, J. A. (2007) The bright and dark sides of personality: Implications for personnel selection in individual and team contexts. In J. Langan-Fox, C. L. Cooper, & R. J. Klimoski (eds.) *Research companion to the dysfunctional workplace: Management challenges and symptoms*. Cheltenham: Edward Elgar, pp. 332–354.

Judge, T. A., LePine J. A., & Rich, B. L. (2006) Loving yourself abundantly: Relationship of the narcissistic personality to self: And other perceptions of workplace deviance, leadership, and task and contextual performance. *Journal of Applied Psychology, 91,* 762–776.

Judge, T. A., Piccolo, R. F., & Kosalka, T. (2009) The bright and dark sides of leader traits: A review and theoretical extension of the leader trait paradigm. *Leadership Quarterly, 20,* 855–875.

Kaiser, R. B., & Bartholomew, C. S. (2014) Destructive leadership in and of organizations. In D. V. Day (ed.) *Oxford handbook of leadership and organizations*. Oxford: Oxford University Press.

Kellerman, B. (2004) *Bad leadership: What it is, how it happens, why it matters*. Boston: Harvard Business School Press.

Kets de Vries, M. R. F. (2004) Putting leaders on the couch. *Harvard Business Review, 80,* March, 100–106.

Kets de Vries, M. R. F., & Miller, D. (1985a) Narcissism and leadership: An object relations perspective. *Human Relations, 38,* 583–601.

Kets de Vries, M. R. F., & Miller, D. (1985b) *The neurotic organization*. London: Jossey-Bass.

Klazad, K., Restubog, S. L. B., Zagenczyk, T. J., Kiewitz, C., & Tang, R. L. (2010) In pursuit of power: The role of authoritarian leadership in the relationship between supervisors' Machiavellianism and subordinates' perceptions of abusive supervisory behavior. *Journal of Research in Personality, 44,* 512–519.

Krasikova, D. V., Green, S. G., & LeBreton, J. M. (2013) Destructive leadership: A theoretical review, integration, and future research agenda. *Journal of Management, 39,* 1308–1338.

Lipman-Blumen, J. (2005) *The allure of toxic leaders: Why we follow destructive bosses and corrupt politicians: And how we can survive them*. New York: Oxford University Press.

Lombardo, M. M., & McCaul, M. W. J. (1984) *Coping with an intolerable boss*. Greensboro, NC: Center for Creative Leadership.

Lubit, R. (2013) The emotional intelligence response to coping with narcissism in the workplace. In R. J. Burke & C. L. Cooper (eds.) *The fulfilling workplace: The organization's role in achieving individual and organizational health*. Surrey: Gower, pp. 151–162.

Maccoby, M. (2003) *The productive narcissist: The promise and peril of visionary leadership*. New York: Broadway.

Maccoby, M. (2007) *Narcissistic leaders: Who succeeds and who fails*. Boston: Harvard Business School Press.

Martinko, M. J., Harvey, P., Brees, J. R., & Mackey, J. (2013) A review of abusive supervision research. *Journal of Organizational Behavior, 34,* 120–137.

Mathieu, C., Neumann, C. S., Hare, R. D., & Babiak, P. (2014) A dark side of leadership: Corporate psychopathy and its influence on employee well-being and job satisfaction. *Personality and Individual Differences, 59,* 83–88.

McCall, M., & Lombardo, M. (1983) *Off the track: Why and how successful executives get derailed.* Greensboro, NC: Center for Creative Leadership.

Megginson, D., & Clutterbuck, D. (2009) *Further techniques for coaching and mentoring.* Oxford: Butterworth Heinemann.

Miska, C., Stahl, G. K., & Fuchs, M. (2014) Unethical managerial behavior: The moderating roles of moral intensity and situational strength. Academy of Management Meeting, August. Philadelphia.

Naider, L., & Schriesheim, C. (2010) *Research in management: The dark side of management* (vol. 8). Charlotte, NC: Information Age Publishing.

Namie, G., & Namie, R. (2000) *The bully at work: What you can do to stop the hurt and reclaim the dignity on the job.* Naperville: Sourcebooks, Inc.

Nikolaou, I., Vakola, M., & Robertson, I. T. (2006) 360-degree feedback and leadership development. In R. J. Burke & C. L. Cooper (eds.) *Inspiring leaders.* London: Routledge, pp. 305–318.

O'Neill, M. B. (2000) *Executive coaching with backbone and heart: A systems approach to engaging leaders with their challenges.* San Francisco: Jossey-Bass.

Padilla, A., Hogan, R., & Kaiser, R. (2007) The toxic triangle: Destructive leaders, susceptible followers and conducive environments. *Leadership Quarterly, 18,* 176–194.

Peterson, D. B. (1993) Measuring change: A psychometric approach to evaluating individual training outcomes. In V. Arnold (Chair) *Innovations in training evaluation: New measures, new designs.* Symposium presented at the eighth annual conference of the Society for Industrial and Organizational Psychology, San Francisco, April.

Peterson, D. B., & Hicks, M. D. (1993) How to get people to change. Workshop presented at the eighth annual conference of the Society for Industrial and Organizational Psychology, San Francisco, April.

Rosenthal, S. A., & Pittinsky, T. L. (2006) Narcissistic leadership. *Leadership Quarterly, 17,* 617–633.

Samnani, A.-K., & Singh, P. (2012) 20 years of workplace bullying research: A review of the antecedents and consequences of bullying in the workplace. *Aggression and Violent Behavior, 17,* 581–589.

Schmidt, A. A. (2008) Development and validation of the Toxic Leadership Scale. Unpublished thesis. University of Maryland.

Schyns, B., & Hansborough, T. (2010) *Why leadership goes wrong: Destructive leadership, mistakes, and ethical failures.* Charlotte, NC: Information Age Publishing.

Schyns, B., & Schilling, J. (2013) How bad are the effects of bad leaders? A meta-analysis of destructive leadership and its outcomes. *Leadership Quarterly, 24,* 138–158.

Shapiro, D. L., & Von Glinow, M. A. (2007) Why bad leaders stay in good places. In J. Langan-Fox, C. L. Cooper, & R. J. Klimoski (eds.) *Research companion to the dysfunctional workplace: Management challenges and symptoms.* Cheltenham: Edward Elgar, pp. 90–108.

Simon, S. N. (2009) Applying Gestalt theory to coaching. *Gestalt Review, 13,* 230–240.

Smith, S. F., & Lilienfeld, S. D. (2013) Psychopathy in the workplace: The knowns and unknowns. *Aggression and Violent Behavior, 18,* 204–218.

Sutton, R. I. (2009) *Good boss, bad boss: How to be the best . . . and learn from the worst.* New York: Business Plus.

Tepper, B. J. (2000) Consequences of abusive supervision. *Academy of Management Journal, 43,* 178–190.

Tepper, B. J. (2007) Abusive supervision in work organizations: Review, synthesis, and research agenda. *Journal of Management, 33,* 261–289.

Tepper, B.J., Moss, S. E., & Duffy, M. K. (2011) Predictors of abusive supervision: Supervisor perceptions of deep-level dissimilarity, relationship conflict, and subordinate performance. *Academy of Management Journal, 54,* 279–294.

Twenge, J. M., Konrath, S., Foster, J. D., Campbell, W. K., & Bushman, B. J. (2008) Egos inflating over time: A cross-temporal meta-analysis of the Narcissism Personality Inventory. *Journal of Personality, 76,* 875–901.

Walton, M. (2007) Leadership toxicity: An inevitable affliction of organizations? *Organizations and People, 14,* 19–27.

Wilson, B. (1991) U.S. businesses suffer from workplace trauma: Here's how to protect the mental health of your workforce – and the fiscal health of your company. *Personnel Journal, 70,* 47–50.

26

Evaluating the Performance of Ethical Leadership

Alan Lawton

Paradox – *a seemingly absurd or contradictory statement, even if actually well founded* (OED).

Category Mistake – *it represents the facts of mental life as if they belonged to one logical type of category when they actually belong to another* (Ryle, 1963 [1949]).

Introduction

The notion of evaluating ethical leadership is puzzling for a number of reasons. First, evaluation itself is usually evaluation of some act or performance and may be undertaken to pass judgement and to identify how such performance might be improved upon. Thus there would need to be some independent criteria upon which to form the basis of a judgement and a sense of what constitutes improvement. In a post-modern world where agreement in ethics appears to be problematic, then where would the independent criteria come from and what would they consist of? From this point of view, no set of judgements can claim an absolute privilege (Johnston, 1999). At the same time, it is not entirely clear, from an ethical point of view, what is to count as ethical improvement. How do we become 'better' persons in the same way that we might become better at our chosen profession? And, of course, how do we define 'better'?

Second, there appears to be no universally accepted definition of leadership, although most definitions say something about both the relationship with other individuals, usually followers, and the goals to be achieved by an organization, through the activities of such individuals. This presupposes that individuals are goal seeking, and yet numerous scholars, as discussed below, question this assumption. At the same time, ethics may be found in the relationships between individuals rather than in goal-oriented behaviour, notwithstanding the arguments from a consequentialist theory of ethics. Nevertheless: 'Ethical leadership is thought to be important because of the outcomes it is thought to influence' (Brown & Treviño, 2006: 606).

And yet, Ciulla (2004) makes the point that, because we cannot always know the results of our actions, moral judgements should be based on the right moral principles and not be contingent on outcomes. Ciulla (2004: 310) argues that some leaders are ethical but not very effective and vice versa, and that 'This distinction between ethics and effectiveness is not always a crisp one.'

Thus, the relationship between ethical leadership and organizational purpose and performance remains under researched (Kempster, Jackson, & Conroy, 2011).

Third, the responsibilities of leaders are varied in their nature and scope. They have responsibilities to a wide group of stakeholders and their performance is evaluated by different types of criteria. Shareholders, employees and the public in general may have different kinds of expectations, and these will vary depending upon the type of organization within which leadership is practised. For example, political leaders may be expected to further the public interest; business leaders may be expected to create wealth for shareholders.

At the same time, according to Jackall (2010 [1988]) the primary imperative of every organization is to succeed – the logic of performance – such that its 'institutional logic' means that performance is determined solely by organizational needs. If this is the case then the needs of individual members will be subservient to those of the organization. However, if the imperative is to succeed then it does beg the question of why, in the first place, should leaders be ethical? This is a normative question, but if it could be demonstrated that ethical behaviour leads to organizational goals then the normative question could be given an empirical answer.

We are left, then, with a number of puzzling questions, which may or may not lend themselves to easy answers. At the same time we do not wish to throw the ethics baby out with the performance bathwater before we have explored more fully, to borrow a phrase, the 'perimeters of the logical geography' (Carlisle & Manning, 1996: 359). This chapter explores the contours of ethical leadership before reconfiguring its boundaries. In reconfiguring, the chapter will discuss the nature of performance itself, dimensions of leadership, ethical leadership and leadership performance and the organizational context within which such activities take place.

Evaluating Performance

Evaluation is a complex activity and takes different forms (Dahler-Larsen, 2005). One form is goal-oriented evaluation, which analyses the extent to which activities have achieved their goals. This is the approach to evaluation that is taken in this chapter. Thus, evaluation involves assessing an activity according to a set of criteria or standards with a view to forming a judgement on performance in order that it can be improved. We would also expect clear guidelines on what objectives are to be achieved, what the reasons are for doing it, who is to carry out the evaluation and what the criteria are for performance improvement.

If we take the individual as our unit of analysis, then we would focus upon the extent to which performance met an agreed-upon set of objectives concerning tasks to be achieved and objectives met. The agreement, usually with line managers, would be set out in the form of a contract or other document such as a personal development/appraisal plan. We are all familiar with the questions from our appraisers concerning what we want to achieve in the next twelve months and where we want to be in five years' time. Such questions assume that individuals in the workplace are goal oriented and have clear objectives. This assumption has been challenged; for example, Johnson (1995) has argued that the bulk of our activity is in relating, not in the rational pursuit of goals. He argues that performance is based on the assumption that human beings are essentially governed, or even determined, by an urge towards goal or purpose fulfilment. And yet:

> It is the relationships that hold us together far more than the goals to be achieved, and often enough these relationships (which will themselves change over time) do in some degree at least displace the goals ostensibly set for organizations.
>
> *(Johnson, 1994: 39)*

Where such relationships are included as part of a performance review, they are considered only insofar as they add to, or detract from, team, group or organizational performance.

If our unit of analysis is the organization, then in any performance system we need to be clear whether we are measuring inputs, processes, outputs or outcomes. Inputs are concerned with the resources, financial and human, that are then utilised through processes to produce outputs and outcomes. Processes include systems, structures or programmes. It might also include the quality of the relationships between colleagues, supervisors and staff within the organization. Criteria of performance will include efficiency – can the organization achieve the same output for less resources or increased output from the same resources? This might translate as, for example, in the case of addressing unethical behaviour, improving the time it takes to respond to complaints, the length of time to conduct any investigations and so on, i.e. the easily measurable. The outputs of an organization might be the goods and services that it provides and the outcomes might be in terms of the extent to which the organization achieves its wider goals. Different types of organizations will have different understandings of outputs and outcomes. The outputs of a hospital might be the number of operations that it performs; the outcomes might be the extent to which it improves the general health of its local population.

There are different dimensions to performance. In examining ethical performance in the public services, Lawton, Rayner and Lasthuizen (2013) identify three different dimensions that focus on philosophical, technical and implementation issues. Philosophical issues address the status of individual ethics within an organizational context and the availability of agreed-upon criteria for judging ethical conduct, a key concern for this chapter. Technical issues recognize the complexity of performance measurement generally and are concerned with such issues as specifying the unit of analysis, identifying quantitative and qualitative measures and determining the extent to which the indicators are clear, unambiguous, relevant, valid, reliable, accurate, sensitive and so on. We can break down performance into its constituent elements. The basic elements of performance management are concerned with some activity that we can measure and for which we can collect data. We apply criteria to that data and this gives us information which we can use in judging both whether that activity is successful and whether we can learn from it. From this we can work out what improves performance towards some agreed-upon goal. This begs a number of questions including:

1. Which aspects of which activities are to be measured and which are not?
2. How will activities be measured?
3. Will the measures be both qualitative and quantitative?
4. Who is going to be responsible for measurement?
5. Are there clearly identifiable causal relationships so that we can see that this behaviour/activity/policy directly led to this output or outcome?
6. Will performance indicators be relevant, timely, cost-effective, etc.?
7. Which criteria will be applied?
8. How will the information be presented?
9. Who will have access to the resulting information?
10. How will it be used?

It is generally considered that performance will consist of multiple measures consisting of a mix of quantitative and qualitative and that different stakeholders will have different criteria for judging performance (Holloway, 2009). This does of course beg the question of who the stakeholders are, whether they should be prioritised and, if so, using which criteria?

There will also be challenges of implementation and the dysfunctional aspects of performance systems have been well documented. The paradox of performance is that it builds an industry of audit and regulation and then focuses on performance indicators rather than performance itself. There has been an explosion in measuring, evaluating and holding to account, not least in the public sector (Van Thiel & Leeuw, 2002). This has involved the bureaucratization of performance in the shape of inspection and audit. They point to the dangers of perverse learning through the manipulation of assessments and suppression as differences in performance are ignored.

In summary, there are different units of analysis and we need to be clear what we are analysing. Not only that, but performance takes on multiple forms and there are multiple criteria to be considered. At the same time, demonstrating cause and effect relationships is problematic (Dahler-Larsen, 2005).

Dimensions of Leadership

The practice of leadership appears to require multiple skills and has different dimensions to it. Thus Kotter (1990), for example, argued that leadership is multi-faceted and involves different activities, including setting a direction for the organization, aligning people to move in that direction and motivating people. More recently, Yukl (2008) argues that effective strategic leadership is task oriented, relations oriented and change oriented. The role of the leader consists of different elements and these are, first, influencing relations with subordinates, peers and outsiders; second, making decisions about programmes, systems and structures; third, developing the competitive strategy of the organization.

Common to both scholars is a concern with relationships with individuals and with defining and pursuing organizational objectives. Yet relations with others take on distinct characteristics. It is different from the relationships that we define as friendship – enjoyment of a mutual relationship for its own sake. And yet our expectations of our friends may also apply to our leaders. Thus we expect our friends be honest with us, listen to us, treat us with respect, not take advantage of us and so on. We might also expect them to act in our interests and, perhaps, on occasion put our interests before their own. Our expectations of our leaders in their leadership role may include that they put the general interest above their own, that they ensure that we are treated equitably, that they are transparent with their decisions, that they take into account our interests, make decisions on our behalf and trust us to get on with our jobs. At the same time, Barker (2001) argues that 'leadership theory has been based in the understandable but incorrect perception of a direct cause–effect relationship between the leader's abilities, traits, actions and leadership outcomes' (p. 478). For Barker, leadership is a social process of adaptation and of evolution that is dynamic – much like friendship.

Thus, we need to recognize the multi-faceted nature of leadership. Lawton and Páez (2014) identify three dimensions to leadership: leadership in an activity that will require excellence; leadership of others; and leadership for some organizational or societal goal. Their framework addresses the who, the how and the why of leadership and they present a framework which reconciles these different dimensions.

However, much of the discussion of leadership has focused on the relationships with others and also with the characteristics of leaders. Thus, Yukl (2008), for example, identifies the particular characteristics that distinguish effective from ineffective leaders. They possess:

- greater energy levels and tolerance of stress
- higher self-confidence
- a stronger internal locus of control

- high power needs
- moderately high achievement needs
- low affiliation needs
- greater emotional stability and maturity
- greater personal integrity.

Indeed, Gini (1997) argues that: 'The quality and worth of leadership can only be measured in terms of what a leader intends, values, believes in or stands for – in other words, character' (p. 73). So we might have some sense of who they are, and how they relate to others but we need to ask whom leaders are responsible for, and whom they are accountable to. Leaders are responsible for steering the organisation or group towards commonly agreed-upon goals. For business leaders, depending upon whether we take a stakeholder or a shareholder view of the firm then these goals will be employment, growth, profits – sectional interests. Political leaders will promote employment, growth, equality, freedom, etc. Their goals are to promote a wider set of social as well as economic values – the public interest.

According to Price (2008), a commonly accepted feature of leadership is its instrumental nature: 'Leadership aims to achieve something considered to be valuable and worth achieving, and the success of leaders depends to a large extent on the actual achievement of these ends' (2008: 5–6).

These ends will differ, depending upon the kind of organization under analysis. Its purposes will be varied, and different types of organization will have different objectives. By way of example, we can distinguish, simply, between public and private organizations (whilst recognising that the boundaries between the two have become blurred, increasingly, and that there are now 'hybrid' organizations). Public organizations may have competing, vague or abstract goals but may still be committed to the overall goal of promoting the public interest. The goals of private organizations may need to be compatible with, or recognize, the public interest, but the objectives will be company survival and flourishing through wealth creation. Whilst there will be similarities in some of the leadership skills required, there will also be key differences (see Boyne, 2002).

However, irrespective of sector, Jing and Avery (2008) suggest that leadership is viewed as one of the key driving forces for improving performance. Yet, they argue that research findings to date are inconclusive and difficult to interpret. Different concepts of leadership have been employed in different studies making comparison difficult. Their own framework includes indices for decision making, power distance between leader and staff, staff responsibility, source of staff commitment, situation of management and leadership in the organization, diversity in the organization and control in the organization.

Depending upon what leadership is for, different skills will be required. For example, Metcalf and Benn (2013) focus on leadership qualities for the demonstration of corporate social responsibility and the achievement of sustainability. Leaders need problem-solving skills for complex situations so that they can engage with individuals and groups in dynamic situations of organizational change and can also manage the emotions that accompany such change.

Leadership is clearly complex; not only that, the extent to which leadership impact is direct or indirect is a moot point. The impact on the organization may be indirect through the direct impact on individuals. But this raises the question, 'Is leadership as a social process compatible with leadership as goal seeking and outcome oriented?'

Leadership and Ethics

Generally the discussion of ethical leadership has tended to focus on only one aspect of leadership – relationships with employees – rather than a concern with vision or purpose.

Thus, much of the literature has focused on the relationship between leadership and effectiveness in bringing about, in the language of performance systems, a number of outputs rather than outcomes. The research is extensive and the main focus of such research has been on individual outputs among employees, such as follower voice behaviour (Walumbwa & Schaubroeck, 2009), follower job satisfaction, commitment and perceptions of ethical climate (Neubert, Carlson, Kacmar, Roberts, & Chonko, 2009), or subordinate's job performance (Piccolo, Greenbaum, Den Hartog, & Folger, 2010). There has also been a concern with leaders themselves in terms of, for example, promotability (Rubin, Dierdorff, & Brown, 2010). In addition, researchers have explored group-level outcomes such as unit deviance and organizational citizenship behaviours (Mayer, Kuenzi, Greenbaum, Bardes, & Salvador, 2009), and unit counter-productive work behaviours (Detert, Treviño, Burris, & Andiappan, 2007).

It is argued that leadership behaviour, in terms of fair and considerate treatment, elicits positive responses in employees' attitudes and behaviours (Brown, Treviño, & Harrison, 2005; Brown & Treviño, 2006). According to Caldwell and Dixon (2010), leaders who develop relationships with employees based on trust, and treat them with dignity and respect, enhance employees' self-efficacy, as well as their commitment and loyalty (Cameron, Dutton, & Quinn, 2003) and performance (Cameron, Bright, & Caza, 2004).

Despite the range of research, there appears to be some agreement on a definition of ethical leadership and the most oft-quoted definition is: 'the demonstration of normatively appropriate conduct through personal actions and interpersonal relationships, and the promotion of such conduct to followers through two-way communication, reinforcement and decision-making' (Brown et al., 2005: 120)

The focus is on relationships with followers. The authors use the vague phrase 'normatively appropriate conduct' deliberately, as they recognize the importance of context. So we cannot divorce relations between individuals from the organizations within which they work. This is revisited in the next section.

However, in terms of relationships with followers, Rhodes (2012) argues that leaders face multiple ethical demands and that how leaders deal with these demands in a just manner defines ethical leadership:

> Just leadership is an ongoing engagement with the irresolvable anxieties, dilemmas, contradictions and double-binds that occur in the conflict between the ethical demands of all the others. Such justice must be inspired by an ethical caring for and generosity towards every single unique other person, while at the same time requiring a compromise between them.
>
> *(2012: 1324)*

Leadership is the practice of justice, but, Rhodes argues, justice is often reduced to the application of an instrumental formula that has as its goal not justice but organisational effectiveness. This, he suggests, is a managerialist rationality. Yet it is in the professional ethos of leaders that they will have to attend to justice. Responsibilities accrue to management by virtue of their position and these will include looking after the health, safety and welfare of employees (Carlisle & Manning, 1996). These authors argue that standards of moral conduct are enshrined in the legal regulation of the management of human resources. There is no distinct jurisdiction for professional ethics here. Assuming a liberal society, certain considerations come into play and these include avoiding prejudicial decision making in hiring and firing, support and encouragement of staff, complying with standards of professional behaviour and not abusing positions of power and influence: 'In short, certain rules of civilized behaviour are particularly relevant to the profession of business management by virtue of their relevance to the objectives of that paid employment' (Carlisle & Manning, 1996: 348).

So is there something distinctive about the ethical responsibilities of business leaders that is different from both their responsibilities as individuals and their professional ethos?

At the same time, it has been argued that a concern with such relationships has ignored the antecedents of ethical leadership (Eisenbeiß & Giessner, 2012). What are the inputs, as it were, to ethical leadership? Eisenbeiß and Giessner (2012) examine how societal characteristics in the form of values, industry characteristics such as environmental complexity and the ethical interests of stakeholders and intra-organizational characteristics, such as peer groups, might impact ethical leadership. Similarly, Brown and Treviño (2006) argue that exposure to role models, including childhood role models, contributes to the development of ethical leadership.

The Organization and Ethics

In the words of the Independent Commission Against Corruption (ICAC), the New South Wales, Australia anti-corruption commission: 'The ability to behave ethically in the workplace may be related more to aspects of the organization than to the attributes of the individual' (ICAC, 1998: 7).

So what is the organizational dimension to leadership performance? Organizations are complex social practices. For Collier (1998), the ethical character of any practice is formed by the complex interweaving of goal-related activity on the one hand and the web of human interactions on the other. In MacIntyre's (1985) virtue approach to ethics, virtues require a practice, and these practices consist of internal goods such that standards of excellence are appropriate to that particular practice, whether it be administration, farming or medicine. It is contestable whether leadership or business constitutes practices (Beadle, 2008; Moore, 2005; but see Beabout, 2012). External goods exist outside, and independently, of that practice and include fame, money, power and reputation. If we assume, for a moment, that business constitutes a practice, then the excellence of that practice will depend upon the virtues of its leaders. Virtues are those qualities that enable us to achieve internal goods. Thus, the conditions for success in the practice will depend upon how business is conducted rather than the external goods that might be achieved. At a minimum we would expect business to be conducted, at least within the liberal democratic tradition, in compliance with laws, codes and government regulations, with organizational standards of ethical behaviour and with professional standards of conduct (Carlisle & Manning, 1996).

And yet, for Aristotle, doing and becoming are parts of the same process. But have we been seduced by the Greeks into believing that the good life cannot be cultivated or practised outside of the organization or polis – it is only this particular form of association that facilitates the development of the human self? Without business achieving what might be termed external goals of wealth creation, then the practice will not survive. At the same time, the future flourishing of the company will depend upon the flourishing of the individuals who work within it. The two are inextricably linked. As Ciulla (2004) argues, leaders create the conditions for employees to flourish. The question is, is this flourishing necessarily ethical in character? The answer may be in the extent to which we believe that in certain societies organizations have replaced the community group, the clan or the tribe as the place of social activity.

In all of this we might wonder what the expectations of employees are of their leaders; are they prudential or ethical or both? Are counter arguments ever presented – 'If it came to a choice between your boss acting ethically and losing a contract and you therefore losing your job, or your boss acting illegally by offering a bribe to secure a contract, which course of action would you prefer?' As Carlisle and Manning (1996) put it when commenting upon relationships within business organizations: 'Their relationship of trust is based upon a common understanding of the priority of the task of wealth creation by the most efficient, economical and useful deployment of all the human and other resources involved' (p. 348).

Evaluating Ethical Leadership

We can and do judge leaders by ethical criteria. We are quick to assert that leaders should have done this or that. But what if one prescription is different from others? What can we do if our leaders respond by not accepting our judgement or dismissing it as inappropriate? There needs to be some agreement in what is to count as criteria and what is acceptable or unacceptable behaviour. We address these issues from different perspectives.

The Individual

There have long been debates about the importance of individual traits in leadership behaviour. In exploring ethical leadership, recourse to virtue ethics has been a common approach. As already indicated, virtue does not stand alone but requires a practice. Thus, the paradigm of human excellence will depend upon the context – the warrior (Homer), the Athenian gentleman (Aristotle), the politician or the entrepreneur. MacIntyre (1985) argues that we cannot identify, for example, the Homeric virtues until we have identified the key social roles in Homeric society. Therefore our concept of leadership comes after our understanding of key roles in our society. We will have different understandings of what constitutes excellence in leadership, depending upon the context. And yet, common attributes of ethical leadership have been found globally. Thus, some studies have found that certain dimensions of ethical leadership are cross-culturally endorsed (Resick et al., 2011; Den Hartog, House, Hanges, & Ruiz-Quintanilla, 1999). Common attributes have included honesty, a concern for justice, integrity, role-modelling and authenticity (Eisenbeiß & Brodbreck, 2014). In an attempt to bring together different religious and ethical traditions Eisenbeiß (2012) identifies four ethical orientations for leadership: humane orientation, justice orientation, responsibility and sustainability orientation and moderation orientation. The attraction of this approach is that ethical leadership is broken down into components rather than treated as a composite.

And yet, having values is not sufficient to make a leader and neither is good character. Our accounts of leadership may be purely prescriptive as observer bias favours leaders who we happen to admire (Levine & Boaks, 2014).

Relations with Others

Much of the research has focused on the relationships between leaders and their followers and a number of tools have been developed to measure such relationships. The ethical leadership at work questionnaire developed by Kalshoven, Den Hartog and De Hoogh (2010) consists of 38 items across 7 factors. These factors can be critiqued as follows:

1. people orientation – yet it is not clear that this constitutes a particularly ethical dimension as distinct from the obligations of the professional ethos that we introduced earlier;
2. fairness – are all reverse-coded and there are no items that capture fair recruitment, promotion, etc;

3. power-sharing – is not necessarily anything to do with ethics and may just be an example of good business practice;
4. concern for sustainability – consists of three items, none of them directed to individuals, unlike the other items;
5. ethical guidance – four out of the seven items are ensuring clarity in understanding rules – nothing about role-modelling;
6. role clarification – this is not necessarily ethical in character;
7. integrity – four items concerned with keeping promises and commitments.

Whilst the tool may be statistically valid, are all the items relevant and do they capture all aspects of ethical leadership? A second instrument, the ethical leadership scale developed by Brown *et al.* (2005), has ten items but is, according to Yukl, Mahsud, Hassan and Prussia (2013), missing key aspects of ethical leadership, e.g. fair allocation of rewards; also, honesty is measured with two negative items. Again the tool is statistically valid but does it capture all aspects of ethical leadership? Such surveys are also based upon perceptions. They do not ask 'Did ethical leadership affect the way that you behave and can you give me examples?' The relationship between ethical leadership and effectiveness is often perceived rather than demonstrated.

Yukl *et al.* (2013) are critical of existing measures and argue for an 'improved measure' of ethical leadership. Their measure consists of 15 items, including honesty, fairness and communication of ethical values. They do argue that ethical behaviour is only one part of a leaders' role and that it should be considered in addition to task, relations and change-oriented behaviour.

Yet, despite the difficulties of measuring leader effectiveness, De Vries (2000) suggests that we are infatuated with leadership, that we attribute success to leaders and that perceptions of leadership effectiveness will be higher when we have a strong need for leadership.

For the Organization

Studies, increasingly, are looking beyond the relationship between leadership and employee behaviours. These studies include Shin, Sung, Choi and Kim (2014), who explore the relationship between ethical leadership and ethical climate. This results in a procedural justice climate, which, in turn, mediates the effects of ethical leadership on two organisational outcomes: firm-level organizational citizenship behaviour and firm financial performance. The authors suggest that the relationship between ethical leadership and organisational outcomes is likely to be realized through various intermediate processes involving the internal and external dynamics of the firm.

Their findings were that top management and ethical climate were positively related to organization size. One key finding is that the direct effects of ethical leadership on organizational outcomes are insignificant but their effect is through intermediate organizational processes. They argue that this can be explained by a delayed effect:

> One caveat of the current study is that the link between ethical leadership and organisational outcomes is indirect and likely to unfold over time. Specifically, our analysis showed that unless top management ethical leadership affects the ethical and procedural justice climates of the firm, its influence on the firm's financial performance can be limited.
>
> *(Shin, Sung, Choi, & Kim, 2015, p. 54)*

This conclusion is supported by Jing and Avery (2008). They also argue that much of the research on leaders' behaviour relies on followers' self-reports of commitment to organizational goals, satisfaction with the leader and perceived leader effectiveness. They support using multiple performance measure to include both financial indicators such as net profits and turnover and non-financial measures such as staff and customer satisfaction.

According to Yukl *et al.* (2013), no study has examined the effect to which ethical leadership can enhance work-unit-effectiveness performance independently of relevant leadership behaviours. Indeed, they suggest that ethical leadership may have negative effects on work-unit performance in terms of task-oriented behaviours, relations-oriented behaviours and change-oriented behaviours.

Discussion

We have examined ethical leadership from different perspectives and recognize that evaluating the performance of ethical leadership cannot be a simple exercise that only considers one activity, i.e. relations with followers. This can only be the case if ethics confines itself to relations between two individuals in one-to-one relationships; in organizations, however, leaders face multiple ethical demands from both inside and outside the organization. Thus, as with all performance regimes, ethical leadership will be judged from different perspectives requiring different criteria. Societies will have different expectations of organizations, business and government and will judge them differently and with different consequences. Governments will be voted out of power; business will lose customers as they buy their products and services elsewhere. The impact of ethics on the decisions of both voters and customers will vary from society to society.

Thus, McCall (2002) argues that the ethical evaluation of leadership requires standards of assessment that are independent of leadership. He argues that a stakeholder theory may be appropriate. At the same time, he recognized that what and who is to count as a stakeholder is problematic and contested. Is there a mechanism for adjudicating between the competing claims of conflicting parties, perhaps based upon some notion of obligations or rights? Clearly ethical leadership will require practical wisdom to balance all of these expectations.

A balanced approach is recommended, increasingly, by scholars in the field. Maak and Pless (2006) identify ethical leaders as those who have the capacity to assess complex situations and problems from the perspectives of different stakeholders and recognize the diverse and conflicting interests of such stakeholders. Lawton and Páez (2014) present a holistic framework that binds practices, purposes and virtues together and where ethical leadership is found in the interplay of these different dimensions. They argue that virtues cannot be separated from the context within which they are practised, and they identify different virtues appropriate to different tasks of leadership including vision building, decision making, inspiring others and acting as role models: 'Our holistic approach to ethical leadership might best be understood in terms of distinct types of activities where the interplay of virtues, practices and purposes will lead to different forms of ethical leadership' (Lawton & Páez, 2014). They also take into consideration sectoral differences, particularly in terms of organizational purpose.

We have also sought to outline the distinctiveness of ethical leadership and contrasted ethical leadership with the professional ethos of organizational leaders. In many ways they are very similar; both are concerned to avoid prejudicial decision making in hiring and firing, comply with standards of professional behaviour and care for the health, welfare and safety of employees.

Is this enough to justify the label of ethical leadership? Perhaps as a minimum: but if we are concerned with the good as well as the right then we might expect some commitment by leaders to the human flourishing of their employees, as articulated by Ciulla (2004).

Conclusion

Commenting upon the poet Robert Conquest's line that the shifting patterns of light are 'like the complex, simple movement of great verse', Australian polymath Clive James observes: 'Combined into a single oxymoronic phrase, the two words "simple" and "complex" not only collide, they explode. Once they touch and go off, each is riddled with the other's particular shrapnel. You can't have one without the other' (James, 2014: 154).

We introduced the chapter with two concepts: the paradox and the category mistake. The paradox involved measuring ethical behaviour by its impact on individual productivity, not well-being. Thus the research has looked at the impact on job satisfaction, job performance, voice, commitment and loyalty. What makes these specifically ethical? At the same time the bulk of our activity is in building, developing and sustaining relationships, rather than the pursuit of goals. If we evaluate the relationship, we can ask was trust kept, was justice done, were obligations fulfilled, were rights protected, was individual autonomy protected (see Lawton et al., 2013)? And yet we have argued that the paradox can be resolved if we take a holistic view of ethics that recognizes that, within organizations, be they business, government or social, individual goals are inextricably tied to the organization.

In terms of the category mistake the discussion is ambiguous – on the one hand we have Arjoon (2000) arguing that true leadership is ethical leadership or that leadership that is not ethical is simply not leadership. In contrast McCall (2002), for example, argues that the ethical evaluation of leadership requires standards of assessment that are independent of leadership.

In one sense, the argument mirrors the debate between those who more generally believe that the only criterion to judge a business organization on is the creation of shareholder value and those who believe that business organizations have a wider responsibility to create stakeholder value. Clearly this latter view is compatible with those who argue that the complexity of performance evaluation requires multiple measures of performance (Holloway, 2009).

Ethical leadership is both simple and complex. We all agree that it is a good thing and we all have our own examples of ethical and unethical leadership. We want to believe that our leaders are acting in our interests, that they will treat us fairly, enhance our well-being and so on, but we recognise the complexity of balancing organizational and wider interests in ways that do no harm to us, our organizations or our societies.

References

Arjoon, S. (2000) 'Virtue theory as a dynamic theory of business', *Journal of Business Ethics*, 28 (2), 159–178.

Barker, R.A. (2001) 'The nature of leadership', *Human Relations*, 54 (4), 469–493.

Beabout, G.R. (2012) 'Management as a domain-relative practice that requires and develops practical wisdom', *Business Ethics Quarterly*, 22 (2), 405–432.

Beadle, R. (2008) 'Why business cannot be a practice', *Analyse & Kritik*, 30, 229–241.

Boyne, G.A. (2002) 'Public and private management: What's the difference?' *Journal of Management Studies*, 39 (1), 97–122.

Brown, M.E., & Treviño, L.K. (2006) 'Ethical leadership: A review and future directions', *The Leadership Quarterly*, 17, 595–616.

Brown, M.E., Treviño, L.K., & Harrison, D.A. (2005) 'Ethical leadership: A social learning perspective for construct development and testing', *Organisational Behavior and Human Decision Processes*, 97 (2), 117–134.

Caldwell, C., & Dixon, R.D. (2010) 'Love, forgiveness, and trust: Critical values of the modern leader', *Journal of Business Ethics*, 93 (1), 91–101.

Cameron, K.S., Bright, D., & Caza, A. (2004) 'Exploring the relationships between organizational virtuousness and performance', *The American Behavioral Scientist*, 47 (6), 766–790.

Cameron, K.S., Dutton, J.E., & Quinn, R.E. (2003) *Positive organizational scholarship: Foundations of a new discipline*. Berrett-Koehler Publishers, San Francisco.

Carlisle, Y.M., & Manning, D.J. (1996) 'The domain of professional business ethics', *Organization*, *3* (3), 341–360.

Ciulla, J.B. (2004) 'Ethics and leadership effectiveness' in J. Antonakis, A.T. Ciancolo, & R.J. Sternberg (eds) *The nature of leadership*. Sage, New York, pp. 302–327.

Collier, J. (1998) 'Theorising the ethical organization', *Business Ethics Quarterly*, *8* (4), 621–654.

Dahler-Larsen, P. (2005) 'Evaluation and public management' in E. Ferlie, L.E. Lynn Jr, & C. Pollitt (eds) *The Oxford handbook of public management*. Oxford University Press, Oxford, pp. 615–639.

de Vries, R.E. (2000) 'When leaders have character: Need for leadership performance, and the attribution of leadership', *Journal of Social Behaviour and Personality*, *15* (43), 413–430.

Den Hartog, D.N., House, R.J., Hanges, P.J., Ruiz-Quintanilla, S.A., & Dorfman, P. W. (1999) 'Culturally specific and cross-culturally generalizable implicit leadership theories: Are attributes of charismatic/transformational leadership universally endorsed?' *The Leadership Quarterly*, *10* (2), 219–256.

Detert, J.R., Treviño, L.K., Burris, E.R., & Andiappan, M. (2007) 'Managerial modes of influence and counterproductivity in organizations: A longitudinal business-unit-level investigation', *Journal of Applied Psychology*, *92* (4), 993–1005.

Eisenbeiβ, S.A. (2012) 'Re-thinking ethical leadership: An interdisciplinary integrative approach', *The Leadership Quarterly*, *23*, 791–808.

Eisenbeiβ, S.A., & Brodbeck, F. (2014) 'Ethical and unethical leadership: A cross-cultural and cross-sectoral analysis', *Journal of Business Ethics*, *122*, 343–359.

Eisenbeiβ, S.A., & Giessner, S.R. (2012) 'The emergence and maintenance of ethical leadership in organizations: A question of embeddedness?', *Journal of Personnel Psychology*, *11* (1), 7–19.

Gini, A. (1997) 'Moral leadership and business ethics', *Journal of Leadership & Organizational Studies*, *4* (4), 64–81.

Holloway, J. (2009) 'Performance management from multiple perspectives; Taking stock', *International Journal of Productivity and Performance Management*, *58* (4), 391–399.

Jackall, R. (2010 [1988]) *Moral mazes: The world of corporate managers*. Oxford University Press, Oxford.

James, C. (2014) *Poetry notebook 2006–2014*. Picador, London.

Jing, F.F., & Avery, G.C. (2008) 'Missing links in understanding the relationship between leadership and organizational performance', *International Business and Economics Research Journal*, *7* (5), 67–78.

Johnson, N. (1994) 'Institutions and human relations: A search for stability in a changing world', *American Behavioral Scientist*, *38* (1), 26–43.

Johnson, N. (1995) 'Vickers' *The Art of Judgement*', *Political Studies*, 43, 159–171.

Johnston, P. (1999) *The contradictions of modern moral philosophy: Ethics after Wittgenstein*. Routledge, London.

Kalshoven, K., Den Hartog, D.N., & De Hoogh, A.H.B. (2011) 'Ethical leadership at work questionnaire (ELW): Development and validation of a multidimensional measure', *The Leadership Quarterly*, *22* (1): 51–69.

Kempster, S., Jackson, B., & Conroy, M. (2011) 'Leadership as purpose: Exploring the role of purpose in leadership practice', *Leadership*, *7* (3), 317–344.

Kotter, J.P. (1990) *A force for change: How leadership differs from management*. Free Press, New York.

Lawton, A., & Páez, I. (2014) 'Developing a framework for ethical leadership', *Journal of Business Ethics*, doi: 10.1007/s10551-014-2244-2.

Lawton, A., Rayner, J., & Lasthuizen, K. (2013) *Ethics and management in the public sector*. Routledge, London.

Levine, M.P., & Boaks, J. (2014) 'What does ethics have to do with leadership?', *Journal of Business Ethics*, *124*, 225–242.

Maak, T., & Pless, N.M. (2006) 'Responsible leadership in a stakeholder society: A relational perspective', *Journal of Business Ethics*, *66* (1), 99–115.

McCall, J.J. (2002) 'Leadership and ethics: Corporate account ability to whom, for what and by what means?' *Journal of Business Ethics*, *38*, 133–139.

MacIntyre, A. (1985) *After virtue: A study in moral theory* (2nd ed.). Duckworth, London.

Mayer, D.M., Kuenzi, M., Greenbaum, R., Bardes, M., & Salvador, R. (2009) 'How low does ethical leadership flow? Test of a trickle-down model', *Organizational Behavior & Human Decision Processes*, *108* (1), 1–13.

Metcalf, L., & Benn, S. (2013) 'Leadership for sustainability: An evolution of leadership ability', *Journal of Business Ethics*, *112*, 369–384.

Moore, G. (2005) 'Corporate character: Modern virtue ethics and the virtuous corporation', *Business Ethics Quarterly*, *15* (4), 657–685.

Neubert, M.J., Carlson, D.S., Kacmar, K.M., Roberts, J.A., & Chonko, L.B. (2009) 'The virtuous influence of ethical leadership behavior: Evidence from the field', *Journal of Business Ethics*, *90* (2), 157–170.

Piccolo, R.F., Greenbaum, R., Den Hartog, D.N., & Folger, R. (2010) 'The relationship between ethical leadership and core job characteristics', *Journal of Organizational Behavior*, *31* (2/3), 259–278.

Price, T.L. (2008) *Leadership ethics: An introduction*. Cambridge University Press, Cambridge.

Resick, C.J., Martin, G.S., Keating, M.A., Dickson, M.W., Kwan, H.K., & Peng, C (2011) 'What ethical leadership means to me: Asian, American, and European perspectives', *Journal of Business Ethics*, *101*, 435–457.

Rhodes, C. (2012) 'Ethics, alterity and the rationality of leadership justice', *Human Relations*, *65* (10), 1311–1331.

Rubin, R.S., Dierdorff, E.C., & Brown, M.E. (2010) 'Do ethical leaders get ahead? Exploring ethical leadership and promotability', *Business Ethics Quarterly*, *20* (2), 215–236.

Ryle, G. (1963 [1949]) *The concept of mind*. Penguin, Harmondsworth, Middlesex.

Shin, Y., Sung, S.Y., Choi, J.N., & Kim, M.S. (2015) 'Top management ethical leadership and firm performance: Mediating role of ethical and procedural justice climate', *Journal of Business Ethics*, *129*, 43–57.

van Thiel, S., & Leeuw, F.L. (2002) 'The performance paradox in the public sector', *Public Performance and Management Review*, *25* (3), 267–281.

Walumbwa, F.O., & Schaubroeck, J. (2009). 'Leader personality traits and employee voice behavior: Mediating roles of ethical leadership and work group psychological safety', *Journal of Applied Psychology*, *94* (5), 1275–1286.

Yukl, G. (2008) 'How leaders influence organizational effectiveness', *The Leadership Quarterly*, *19*, 708–722.

Yukl, G., Mahsud, R., Hassan, S., & Prussia G.E. (2013) 'An improved measure of ethical leadership', *Journal of Leadership and Organizational Studies*, *20* (1), 38–48.

27

Leadership and Organizational Performance
State of the Art and a Research Agenda

Eva Knies, Christian Jacobsen and Lars Tummers

Introduction

A large portion of the everyday discourse about leadership and leaders takes it for granted that leaders make a big difference in terms of performance. The football managers discussion is one clear example; the wider fascination with business leaders likewise marks this association – and so too the fascination with political leaders. However, the academic literature finds it hard to find reliable evidence for a clear association, because both main concepts (leadership and performance) are broad and difficult to define and because of many confounding variables that make it difficult to demonstrate clear cause and effect. But, while some academics have seemingly abandoned the attempt to tackle this difficult but central subject, there are some who seek to trace the relationship. It can be shown that a change of leader does produce some kind of performance outcome. For example, appointments of some leaders and the dismissal of others can trigger dramatic shifts in stock prices. In this chapter we will systematically examine the relationship between leadership and performance, both theoretically (in the second section) and empirically (in the third section). In the fourth section, we will use public leadership and performance as illustrative of our analysis. We will conclude with an overview of the current state of the literature and we will outline a research agenda. Overall, we show that empirical studies have mainly found positive relationships between leadership and performance, although effect sizes vary considerably. However, cross-sectional designs with subjective performance measures tend to find relatively strong effects. Therefore, we advocate a systematic approach to studying the leadership–performance relationship with attention to research designs, and we urge that more panel designs and experimental designs are applied in future studies, because these enable scholars to assess changes over time and get a much better grasp of causality.

Background on Leadership and Performance

The goal of this section is to provide an overview of the two main concepts central to this chapter – leadership and performance – and to make these more specific so that they can be studied. We will also theoretically explore the link between leadership and performance.

Introducing Leadership

Leadership is a powerful term, but it is often weakly conceptualized. In trying to define leadership, Bennis (1959: 259) noted that:

> the concept of leadership eludes us or turns up in another form to taunt us again with its slipperiness and complexity. So we have invented an endless proliferation of terms to deal with it . . . and still the concept is not sufficiently defined.

In other words, leadership is a 'magic concept'; it is inspiring for scholars and practitioners, but it also vague, meaning everything and nothing at the same time (Pollitt & Hupe, 2011).

Various authors have tried to make sense of the apparent chaos. Yukl (2013; see for a similar analysis Northouse, 2015) studied the various definitions used by scholars and noted that these have in common that leadership is about an influencing process, more specifically a process whereby intentional influence is exercised over other people to guide, structure, and facilitate activities in groups or organizations. In this chapter, we continue on this line of thought.

In line with this general definition, scholars conceptualized more specific leadership styles, such as transformational leadership, transactional leadership, leader–member exchange, empowering leadership, and network leadership. Given space constraints, we will only discuss the background of two core leadership styles that have often been linked to performance (Piccolo & Colquitt, 2006): transformational and transactional leadership.

Transformational and Transactional Leadership

Transformational and transactional leadership are broad concepts on which various authors highlight other aspects (Yukl, 2013: 312–313). In his seminal book on political leadership, Burns (1978), for example, focuses mainly on the moral dimension of transformational leadership. According to Burns, transformational leaders offer followers a 'purpose.' They aim to motivate employees by focusing on their moral values, raising their consciousness of moral issues and mobilizing their energies to change the current situation. Followers internalize the values proposed – such as eliminating apartheid, equal rights for women and men – and become intrinsically motivated to perform. In contrast, transactional leaders aim to motivate followers by offering an 'exchange' appealing to their more narrow self-interest, such as providing jobs or subsidies (Conger & Kanungo, 1998).

Building upon the work of Burns (1978) and that of Bass and colleagues (Bass, 1985; Bass & Avolio, 1990; Bass & Riggio, 2006), transformational and transactional leadership are nowadays considered as higher order constructs composed of several components. For transformational leadership, four components have been identified. First, *idealized influence* concerns the degree to which leaders behave charismatically, so that followers identify with them and consider them to be role models. Second, *inspirational motivation* is about communicating a vision that appeals to followers. These first two dimensions are often highly correlated and therefore combined into one 'charisma' factor, often called charismatic leadership (Van Knippenberg & Sitkin, 2013). Third, transformational leaders provide *intellectual stimulation* to followers. They challenge them to view problems from a new perspective and, hence, encourage them to generate creative ideas. Fourth, *individualized consideration* is about giving support to followers, coaching them, and giving them personal attention.

For transactional leadership, three components have been distinguished: *contingent reward*, *management by exception (active)*, and *management by exception (passive)*. Contingent reward refers to setting goals and rewarding employees when these goals are achieved. In general, management by exception is the degree to which the leader takes action when the behavior of followers is not in line with the expectations. In the 'active' form, leaders actively monitor followers and take corrective actions before the behavior of followers creates serious difficulties. In the 'passive' form, leaders wait until something has gone wrong and then take corrective action.

Introducing Performance

Like leadership, performance is also a broad concept. Performance can manifest itself on different levels and in different forms (Borman & Motowidlo, 1993; Yammarino et al., 2005). Performance in general can be described as how well a person, a group of persons, or an object does a piece of work or activity (Cambridge Dictionary Online, 2015). In organizational research, performance can be conceptualized on various levels of analysis. Here, we distinguish between the organizational level, team level, and individual level.

Organizations can be defined as instruments of purpose (March & Sutton, 1997). Scholars and practitioners talk about the purposes of an organization and evaluate the success of organizations in reaching these. In essence, they are then talking about the performance of these organizations. However, when discussing organizational performance, Kirby (2005: 36) succinctly stated that 'figuring out who stands tallest is far from straightforward; it depends upon which yardstick you use.' For business firms, profit, sales, and market growth can be used as performance criteria, but also employment in a region. For schools, test scores of students can be used, but also the employment rate (and salary) of former students. Richard, Devinney, Yip, and Johnson (2009) reviewed the literature on organizational performance and found that, across 213 articles published in the top management journals, 207 different measures of performance were used. To provide some clarity, Richard et al. (2009) developed a multidimensional conceptualization of organizational performance, consisting of three specific areas: financial performance (profits, return on assets), product market performance (sales, sales growth, market share) and shareholder return (total shareholder return, economic value added, dividends). This conceptualization is useful, although it is very much focused on private organizations, and less suitable for political, administrative, or civic organizations (see for instance 't Hart, 2014 and also the fourth section of this chapter).

As with organizational performance, team performance is a broad construct. A team can be defined as two or more persons who interact interdependently and adaptively toward a common goal or objective (Salas et al., 1992). In their meta-analysis on the associations between relationship conflict, task conflict, team performance, and team member satisfaction, De Dreu and Weingart (2003) note that team performance measures in the literature have included product quality, production quality, decision quality, and team effectiveness. Furthermore, some scholars use various team outcomes and team behaviors and combine them into one team performance measure. For instance, Stewart and Barrick (2000) measured team performance using the following dimensions: knowledge of tasks, quality of work, quantity of work, interpersonal skills, commitment to the team, and overall performance. These were then summed up to tap the construct of team performance. Others used a more differentiated design. For instance, Somech (2006) makes a clear distinction between in-role team performance (the extent to which a team accomplishes its goal) and team innovation (introduction or use of new and useful ideas in a team).

Regarding individual performance, it also becomes clear that various authors define this quite differently. For instance, Welbourne, Johnson, and Erez (1996) developed the 'role-based performance scale.' Based on role and identity theory, they identify five key roles when tapping individual performance: job performance (doing things according to the job description, aligned with 'in-role' performance); career performance (obtaining necessary skills to progress); innovator performance (coming up with new ideas and implementing them); team performance (working well with co-workers); and organization performance (going beyond the call of duty in your organization). In a similar vein, Wang, Oh, Courtright, and Colbert (2011) differentiate between task performance (similar to the job performance of Welbourne et al.); contextual performance (similar to organization performance); creative performance (similar to innovator performance); and general performance (an overall performance measure).

The goal of this section was to introduce the two concepts central to this chapter – leadership and performance – and to make them more specific so that they can be empirically analyzed. We made a distinction between two leadership styles (transformational and transactional) and three levels of performance (organizational, team, and individual). We fully acknowledge that this is a partial view. There are more ways to analyze the relationship between leadership and performance, using different leadership constructs (for instance Chatterjee & Hambrick, 2007), or focusing specifically on the role of contextual leadership and performance (Pfeffer & Salancik, 2003). However, our distinction is in line with the concepts used in recent meta-analyses, as this makes it possible to summarize the empirical evidence that was generated up until now.

Connecting Leadership and Performance

Before we turn to an overview of the empirical evidence for the link between leadership and performance, we first address the fundamental conceptual debate on whether or not leadership potentially can have a significant impact on performance. In the literature there are two schools of thought: the 'constraints school' and the 'leadership school' (Pettigrew, 2013; Wasserman, Nohria, & Anand, 2001). On the one hand, there are scholars who advocate that leaders can only have a very limited impact on performance as a result of contextual constraints, either internal or external to the organization. The study by Lieberson and O'Connor (1972) is a prominent example in this line of thought, which shows that industry and company variables account for more variance in performance than leadership. Related to this, based on attribution theory, some psychologists point out that the impact of leadership on performance is a social construction. According to them, the presence of leadership does not result in high or low performance (other antecedents may be at play), but people interpret it in this way (Weber, Camerer, Rottenstreich, & Knez, 2001). This is particularly the case when studying leadership using non-experimental methods, as cause and effect are then hard to separate.

On the other hand, there are others that argue that top managers have sufficient discretion to influence performance (Ireland & Hitt, 1999; Thomas, 1988). That is, they have strategic choice (Child, 1972). These scholars argue that, by shaping the organization's strategy, structure, and culture (Wasserman et al., 2001) through sharing insights, knowledge, and responsibilities (Ireland & Hitt, 1999), leaders can have a significant impact on performance. An important point that we want to highlight with regard to this discussion is the difficulty to empirically examine the impact of leadership on performance. According to Mackey (2008), as a result of methodological problems, early research has systematically underestimated the impact of leaders on performance. Relevant methodological issues in this respect are: the order in which the independent variables are included in the analyses, the distinction within and between organization variation (Thomas, 1988), the availability of relevant control variables, and the availability of time series data (Pettigrew, 2013). Recently, the balance between the 'constraints school' and the 'leadership school' seems to have shifted in favor of the latter.

In his book *Leadership and Performance Beyond Expectations*, Bass (1985) builds a theoretical argument underlying the 'leadership school.' He argues that leaders can be simultaneously transformational and transactional and that both styles of leadership can have beneficial results for performance. Bass notes that, in the case of transformational leadership, followers feel trust, admiration, and loyalty towards the leader, and therefore are motivated to do more than they are expected to do. Hence, they are performing beyond expectations. In case of transactional leadership, there is an exchange process in which leaders set goals and rewards in exchange for in-role behavior. Such leadership behavior is important too, but is likely to result in follower compliance rather than in performance 'beyond expectations.' Therefore, based on the work of Bass it may be expected that transformational leadership is more beneficial for performance than transactional leadership.

In the next section we will present an overview of the empirical evidence for the link between leadership and performance.

Empirical Evidence for the Link between Leadership and Performance

The relationship between leadership and performance has been the subject of many empirical studies. Over the past 30 years, researchers have tried to establish the link between these two concepts. Scholars have used different conceptualizations of the independent variable, such as transactional, transformational, and laissez-faire leadership, and/or have included several related concepts such as trust in leadership, leader–member exchange, and leadership structure. In terms of the dependent variable, we also find a variety of relevant outcomes that have been studied, such as organizational citizenship behavior, employee attitudes, and performance measured using different criteria on different levels of analysis. Also, the relationship between leadership and performance has been studied in different organizational, sectoral, and national contexts. The abundance and conceptual variety of empirical studies into the relationship between leadership and performance raises the question of where to start when you want to provide a comprehensive and concise overview of the state of the art. To tackle this problem, we rely on five meta-analyses that have been published on the relationship between leadership and performance: Fuller, Patterson, Hester, and Stringer (1996), DeGroot, Kiker, and Cross (2000), Dumdum, Lowe, and Avolio (2002), Judge and Piccolo (2004), and Wang et al. (2011). The criteria for selecting relevant meta-analyses were that these should include leadership and performance as well as the relationship between the two. According to Wang et al. (2011) the five meta-analyses presented here represent a complete list of relevant studies. As such, these provide an excellent overview of this field of study, not only at present, but also over the past twenty years. Meta-analyses typically provide an understanding of the generalizability of findings of individual studies. The discussion of the successive meta-analyses will show which issues were topical at a particular point in time and give an overview of the most important empirical findings. In doing so, we will highlight how the field has matured over the past decades.

The first meta-analysis dates from 1996. At that time there was a sufficient number of empirical studies to conduct a quantitative review. Fuller et al. used 32 studies with a total of 4,611 participants. Fuller et al. (1996) focused on the effects of charismatic leadership (which is one dimension of transformational leadership) on three outcome variables: satisfaction with the leader, perceived leader effectiveness, and performance. Fuller et al. also included several potential moderators: type of performance measure (objective versus subjective), type of research design (multi-source or not), level of the leader, and sample sectoral context. Fuller et al. found positive and significant relationships between charismatic leadership and all three outcome variables. The relationship with the variable 'satisfaction with the leader' was the strongest (mean correlation of .80), followed by perceived leader effectiveness (mean correlation of .79), and overall performance (mean correlation of .45). Moreover, they found significantly stronger correlations for subjective performance measures than for objective ones, indicating that these two reflect different aspects of effectiveness. Also they found that single source studies tend to inflate the relationship between leadership and performance. The level of the leader did not moderate the relationship between leadership and performance. Finally, they showed that the relationship between leadership and performance is not generalizable across contexts: for example, military samples provided higher correlations, and student samples show stronger correlations than samples from civilian contexts.

In 2000, DeGroot et al. also conducted a meta-analysis including charismatic leadership as an independent variable. Like Fuller et al. (1996), DeGroot and colleagues included a range of outcome variables: leadership effectiveness, subordinate performance, subordinate satisfaction, subordinate effort, and subordinate commitment. The former two were also included in the meta-analysis of Fuller et al. The moderators included in this study were common method variance and level of analysis. DeGroot et al. used 36 samples in their analysis. An important finding is that the relationship between charismatic leadership and subordinate performance is weaker when the latter is measured at the individual level (mean correlation of .31), compared to subordinate performance on the group level (mean correlation of .49). Furthermore, the study advises researchers to avoid common source bias and apply measures of leadership and performance from independent sources. It must be noted that a majority of the samples used in this meta-analysis are collected in a military context, which provide higher correlations (see Fuller et al., 1996).

In 2002, Dumdum and colleagues performed a meta-analysis including transformational, transactional, and laissez-faire leadership as independent variables and performance effectiveness and satisfaction as dependent variables. Organizational type (public versus private) was included as a moderator. This study is an update of a meta-analysis by Lowe, Kroeck, and Sivasubramaniam (1996), in which they extended their initial time period to 2002. Because the two studies overlap significantly, we report only the results of the later study. The results show that transformational and transactional leadership are both positively and significantly related to the effectiveness/satisfaction criteria. The corrected coefficient are .46 and .20 respectively. Laissez-faire leadership was also significantly related to the effectiveness/satisfaction criteria, but in the opposite direction. The corrected coefficient was -.38. When decomposing the effectiveness/satisfaction criteria, the authors show that satisfaction is more strongly related to transformational and laissez-faire leadership, compared to effectiveness. For transactional leadership they found the opposite: effectiveness is slightly more strongly related to this type of leadership compared to satisfaction. Regarding the difference between public and private organizations, Dumdum et al. found mixed results. The relationship between transformational leadership and the effectiveness/satisfaction criteria is stronger in the public than in the private sector. This also holds for laissez-faire leadership, but the difference between the coefficients is much smaller. No data were available for transactional leadership in the private sector.

Another 2002 study by Judge and Piccolo focused on the effects of transformational and transactional leadership on follower leader satisfaction, follower job satisfaction, follower motivation, rated leader effectiveness, leader job performance, and group or organization performance. The latter is of particular interest for this contribution. Like Dumdum et al. (2002), Judge and Piccolo hypothesize that transformational and transactional (contingent reward) leadership show a positive relationship with group or organizational performance. Moreover, they expect that transformational leadership will predict the outcome variables, controlling for transactional leadership.

As expected, both transformational (mean correlation of .26) and contingent reward leadership (mean correlation of .16) have a positive relationship with all dependent variables, including group or organizational performance. The differences between the effects of transformational and contingent reward leadership on group or organizational performance were not significant.

The most recent study by Wang et al. (2011) is based on 117 independent samples. The main independent variable in their meta-analysis is transformational leadership. The dependent variable is performance on three levels of analysis: individual, team, and organization. Wang et al. not only distinguish various levels of analysis; they also include three types of performance: task performance, contextual performance, and creative performance. Overall, they find support for their hypotheses that transformational leadership is positively and significantly related to individual, team, and organizational performance. More specifically, they found that the relationship between transformational leadership and individual performance is stronger for contextual performance compared to task performance. They showed that transformational leadership has the strongest relationship with team-level performance (mean correlation of .33) and the weakest relationship with individual-level performance (mean correlation of .25). The mean correlation of the relationship between transformational leadership and organizational-level performance is .27. Additionally, Wang et al. looked at evidence for the augmentation effect: that is, whether or not transformational leadership adds explained variance above and beyond transactional leadership. They found evidence for such an effect for individual-level and team-level performance.

Overall, the five meta-analyses presented above show very consistent results. Without any exception, the results show a positive relationship between leadership and performance. More precisely, the first two studies by Fuller et al. (1996) and DeGroot et al. (2000) focus on the effects of one dimension of transformational leadership (i.e. charismatic leadership) on performance outcomes. Both studies find a positive effect. Dumdum et al. (2002) and Judge and Piccolo (2002) analyzed the effect of transformational and transactional leadership on performance outcomes and also found a positive effect. Additionally, Dumdum et al. found a negative effect of laissez-faire leadership on performance effectiveness. Wang et al. (2011) studied the effect of transformational leadership on individual-level, team-level, and organizational-level performance. They found that transformational leadership has a significant relationship with all performance measures, and that the relationship with team-level performance is the strongest (compare DeGroot et al., 2000). Furthermore, Wang et al. found support for the augmentation effect (see also Judge and Piccolo, 2002). However, it should be noticed that the strength of the correlations varies considerably among these five studies. Drawing from the meta-analyses, we can also conclude that the following variables are important moderators in the leadership–performance relationship: type of performance measure (objective versus subjective), type of research design (multi-rater or not), context (public versus private sector), and level of analysis. Overall, the conclusion that can be drawn from these meta-analyses is that leadership matters for performance.

Leadership and Performance in the Public Sector

In this section, we will zoom in on leadership and performance in the public sector as an illustration of our analysis. A focus on the public sector is particularly interesting because it is often said that leaders in the public sector are constrained by rules and regulations (O'Toole & Meier, 2014). That is, if leaders in the public sector can make a difference for performance, this gives hope for other sectors.

Most leadership studies have focused on private organizations, whereas the role of leadership in public organizations is less investigated and more controversial. Van Wart (2013) recently identified three approaches to public leadership: a generic approach, which highlights the underlying similarities between public and private organizations; a dissimilar approach, which highlights the particular political and societal nature of public leadership; and a convergence approach, which argues that the sectors are becoming more similar over time. These underlying assumptions relate to how leadership can be exerted, the understanding of performance, and the links between leadership and performance.

A central question is what defines public leadership. The publicness tradition has shown that in fact the public–private dichotomy is too simple (Bozeman, 1987). Thus, depending on the ownership status, share of public funding, and level of political involvement, organizations are characterized by various levels of publicness (Bozeman & Bretschneider, 1994). Publicness is associated with aspects such as complexity (e.g. multiple stakeholders), permeability (high influence from external events), instability (frequent policy changes), and lack of competitive pressure, which can affect the leaders' inclinations and possibilities for exerting leadership (Boyne, 2002). For example, leaders in high publicness organizations are expected to have weaker profit motives (Alchian & Demsetz, 1972) and face efficiency constraints defined by special interests and competing public goals (Moe, 2012). However, some empirical studies suggest the opposite – that, if at all, publicness is only weakly related with performance, and that leaders may mitigate eventual negative effects (Andrews, Boyne, & Walker 2011). Most public management scholars agree that leadership in public organizations to some extent requires distinctive skills and knowledge (Rainey, 2014: 364), and some studies have shown that the impact of leadership depends on context factors (Lim & Ployhart, 2004; Wofford, Whittington, & Goodwin, 2001; Avolio et al., 2009). In terms of theory, however, there is still need for more work on what exactly constitutes public leadership (Vogel & Masal, 2014: 15).

The classical theories on public leadership view public leaders as being tied up with red tape, vague goals, and organizational constraints (Buchanan, 1976; Warvick, 1975), and expectations towards effective public leadership are diminutive. Administrative leadership is also said to run counter to democratic governance, because accountability risks being obscured, and in terms of performance the common good can become secondary to managerial interest (Terry, 1998). However, there is scant empirical evidence for these expectations. Recent contributions have instead contemplated how public leaders can become more effective, and for example Tummers and Knies (2016) suggest that public leaders can support their employees by adhering to four leadership roles: accountability, rule-following, political loyalty, and network governance. This approach deliberately focuses on tasks that successful public leaders should attend to, and at the same time acknowledges that more generic, operational, and employee-directed leadership roles are also important in public organizations.

Another important question is what defines public performance. Performance is often conceptualized in relation to production and emphasizing aspects such as economy, effectiveness, and efficiency (Walker, Boyne, & Brewer, 2010). However, such measures will often capture only part of what is considered good performance in public organizations. Thus, allocative considerations and equity concerns are typically important prerequisites for public service provision in the first place, and aspects such as citizen and user satisfaction are of interest to, for example, re-election oriented politicians. Boyne (2003) identified seven dimensions of public performance, including quantity and quality of output, efficiency, outcomes, value for money, which resemble the production view, but also equity and satisfaction. Whereas profit is a vital goal in market-based organizations, public organizations may have more difficulty with prioritization of performance dimensions, especially when powerful actors (e.g. politicians, employee organizations, service users) disagree over the prioritization of performance dimensions (Andersen, Boesen, & Pedersen, 2014). In these instances, an important aspect of public leadership is the willingness and ability to balance performance dimensions. A related challenge is that performance dimensions are not equally measurable (Langbein, 2010), and that goals in public organizations are often ambiguous in the sense that they involve some leeway for interpretation (Chun & Rainey, 2005). Leaders are therefore likely to be held more accountable for less measurable and more ambiguous goals. This also has implications for research on public leadership. Some argue that objective performance measures are more reliable than subjective ones (O'Toole & Meier, 2014), whereas others argue that this will lead to a neglect of important performance dimensions (e.g. satisfaction) or performance in certain areas (e.g. quality of administrative work) (e.g. Brewer, 2008).

A number of empirical studies have investigated the relationship between transformational and/or transactional leadership and performance in public organizations, and we will now go through some of the most important findings. Wright and Pandey (2009) found that public organizations were less bureaucratic than commonly believed, and that bureaucratic structures had little effect on the prevalence or practice of transformational leadership. This is also backed up by earlier empirical studies, which have shown that public employees regard their leaders as more transformational than their private counterparts (Dumdum et al., 2002). Recently, public management scholars sought to explain how transformational leadership can be particularly relevant in public sector organizations (Paarlberg & Lavigna, 2010), because the articulation of values, ideologies, and visions speaks to for example public service motivation (Wright, Moynihan, & Pandey, 2012).

Several empirical studies have found positive effects of transformational leadership on performance using employee survey-based measures of both leadership and performance using cross-sectional research designs. A study of 177 Australian administrators reports strong relationships between transformational leadership and performance outcomes, collective efficacy expectancies, and organizational commitment (Muchiri, Cooksey, & Walumbwa, 2012). Chen and Cheng (2012) also found positive effects of charismatic leadership on subjectively measured performance. Another study reports a mediated effect of transformational leadership on performance through employee satisfaction in a study of 117 US schools (Griffith, 2004), and an Israeli study of 201 law enforcement agents found a mediating effect of leadership through organizational politics (Vigoda-Gadot, 2007). These studies report strong correlations, but common source bias most likely explains some of this shared variation (Podsakoff & Organ, 1986; Favero & Bullock, 2014). To remedy such challenges, Wofford et al. (2001) measured leadership and performance separately and found a positive relationship between employee-rated leadership and manager-rated performance among 157 engineering employees. Another study uses a time-series design of more than one million US federal employees over seven years and reports that there are remarkably strong intra-organizational patterns in leadership and performance assessments over time, but that improvements in leadership are also associated with improved performance (Oberfield, 2012). Other studies have sought to deal with the common source problem by applying performance measures from administrative sources. A study of 79 Danish upper-secondary schools reports that leader and employee ratings of leadership are only weakly correlated (both transformational and transactional (management-by-exception)), and that only employee-rated leadership measures are significantly related with performance measured as school value added (Jacobsen & Andersen, 2015). On the opposite side, a school study from Singapore finds no effect on objectively measured performance (Koh, Steers, & Terborg, 2013). These studies do, however, suffer from difficulties with assessing the question of causality.

To address causality better, a few studies have used before-and-after designs, where performance is measured after some inducement to leadership. One study reports the results from 28 public and 22 private Israeli middle-managers that participated in a training program.

Looking at changes during the training period, they report effects on satisfaction and effort but not on perceived effectiveness (Parry & Sinha, 2005). A study of 72 army platoon leaders found that employee-rated transformational and transactional leadership (contingent reward) predicted unit performance, which was measured by external auditors in following mission exercises (Bass, Avolio, Jung, & Berson, 2003). Two studies report findings from experimental studies. An Italian study of 138 nurses reports that nurses who were randomly assigned to a transformational leadership were significantly more effective in assembling surgical kits, but that the effect was much greater when the nurses were also randomly assigned to either a self-persuasion treatment or beneficiary contact (Bellé, 2013). Furthermore, the results of the transformational leadership treatment were much stronger for nurses with high levels of public service motivation. A study from the Israeli military reports positive effects on employee performance of a training program in which training was randomly assigned among 41 military platoon leaders (Dvir, Eden, Avolio, & Shamir, 2002).

Moving to transactional leadership, this leadership strategy is typically expected to be less useful in public organizations due to constraints on harder HRM tools such as pay, promotion, and benefits. Furthermore, public employees are portrayed as less motivated by extrinsic motives than their private counterparts (Rainey, 1982). Studies have found very mixed results for transactional leadership; some find negative effects (Muchiri et al., 2012; Chen & Cheng, 2012), whereas others find positive effects (Jacobsen & Andersen, 2015; Oberfield, 2012).

Waldman, Bass, and Yammarino (1990) argue that the best leadership is both transformational and transactional, because transformational behaviors augment the positive effect of contingent reward behaviors resulting in improved subordinate effort and performance. Their study applies a hierarchical regression model based on survey data from 186 navy officers and their 793 employees, and it supports the hypothesis that charismatic and transactional leadership explain unique variance in relation to leader effectiveness and performance. A similar pattern was found in Oberfield (2012), Jacobsen and Andersen (2015), and Chen and Chang (2012), and these studies suggest that transformational and transactional leadership are complementary rather than substitutes.

Table 27.1 sums up the empirical studies reported here on subjects, research designs, leadership strategies, and performance measures in relation to subjective/objective, level, and type. Also, the main findings are reported.

Conclusion

This chapter has presented and discussed arguments and findings about the importance of leadership for performance in general and has reviewed the research findings on leadership and performance in public organizations in particular. In popular discussions and in some parts of the business management literature, leaders are often portrayed as decisive for organizational success or failure, whereas public administration scholars have traditionally been more skeptical and have underscored that leaders in public organizations face stronger constraints, vaguer goals, and more complex political environments than their private counterparts. This review can only begin to answer the question of whether leadership is effective for performance, because this is indeed a complicated matter to investigate. Not only are both the concept of leadership and performance multi-faceted, but it is also inherently difficult to investigate how leadership affects performance over time.

As shown here, empirical studies have mainly found positive relationships between leadership and performance, although effect sizes vary considerably. Both in generic management studies and in public management studies, cross-sectional designs with subjective performance

Table 27.1 Overview of Published Studies on Leadership and Performance in Public Organizations

	Study	Subjects	RD[1]	Leadership[2]	Sub/Obj[3]	Level[4]	Type[5]	Findings[6]
1	Bellé (2013)	138 nurses	LE	TFL	O	I	OR	+ (++: Mod.)
2	Parry and Sinha (2005)	28 public and 22 private middle managers	BA	TFL	S	I	SR	0 (+ for effort)
3	Vigoda-Gadot (2007)	201 law enforcement agents	CS	TFL	S	I	SR	0 (+: Med.)
4	Griffith (2004)	117 schools	CS	TFL	O	O	OR	0 (+: Med)
5	Dvir, Eden, Avolio, and Shamir (2002)	41 military platoon leaders and 814 followers	FE	TFL	O	W	OR	+/0
6	Wofford, Whittington, and Goodwin (2001)	157 engineering employees and 96 managers	HM	TFL	S	W	OR	+
7	Bass, Jung, Avolio, and Berson (2003)	72 military platoon leaders and 1,340 soldiers	BA	TFL, PaL	O	I	OR	TFL: +, PaL: -
8	Oberfield (2012)	1,104,537 federal employees (five periods)	TS	TFL, TAL	S	W	SR	TFL & TAL: +
9	Jacobsen and Andersen (2015)	79 upper secondary schools	CS	TFL, TAL	O	O	OR	TFL & TAL: +
10	Koh, Steers, and Terborg (1995)	846 school teachers	CS	TFL, TAL	O	O	OR	0
11	Muchirie, Cooksey, and Walumbwa (2012)	177 local administrators	CS	TFL, SP	S	I, O	SR	TFL +, TAL: -
12	Waldman, Bass, and Yammarino (1990)	186 US Navy officers/793 subordinates	HM	TFL, TAL	S	I, L	SR/OR	TFL: +, TAL: +
13	Chen and Cheng (2012)	1,058 kindergarten teachers	CS	CL, TAL	S	I	SR	CL: +, TAL: -

[1] RD: Research design, CS: Cross-sectional design, BA: Before and after study, HM: Hierarchical model, LE: Lab experiment, FE: Field experiment
[2] TFL: Transformational leadership, TAL: Transactional leadership, PaL: Passive leadership, CL: Charismatic leadership, SP: Social Processes leadership
[3] S: Subjective, O: Objective
[4] I: Individual, O: Organizational, W: Work group, N: Network, L: Leader, E: Employees
[5] OR: Other-rated, SR: Self-rated
[6] Med: Mediated effects of leadership, Mod: Moderated leadership effects

measures tend to find strong effects, and this reflects a need for stronger methods. The generic management literature often relies on lab experiments with low external validity, only two public management studies apply before-and-after designs, and only two studies use experimental methods, so there is a great need for contributions in this area. Thus, despite the growing number of empirical studies, we still lack broad knowledge about the causal effects of leadership. A more systematic approach with attention to research designs would be highly useful, and we urge that more panel designs and experimental designs are applied in future studies, because these enable scholars to assess changes over time and get a much better grasp of causality. Particularly in relation to socially desirable aspects of leadership, there is a risk of endogeneity in relation to performance (Meier & O'Toole, 2013: 443). We expect that such studies will show more modest effects of leadership on performance, which will also reflect the autoregressive nature of performance, which is affected by a number of internal and external stabilizing factors (O'Toole & Meier, 2011). Thus, the role of the leader is potentially important, but it should not be exaggerated.

This also leads to the question of which aspects of leadership matter for performance. The leadership literature is immense and offers a vast number of perspectives on leadership strategies and dimensions, and, in this review, we have primarily focused on transformational and transactional leadership. These are the most studied leadership concepts in the management literature (Dinh et al., 2012). Public management studies have also applied generic leadership concepts such as transformational and transactional leadership, which have also been our focus in this chapter, but we see the beginning of specific public sector leadership theorizing. Future studies could fruitfully integrate these approaches with broader leadership theories, and perhaps even test their relevance for performance. This also touches upon the public–private differences in leadership effects on performance, which we still know very little about. One aspect of this question is which aspects of sector really matter, if at all. We know from other studies that sector can be understood as consisting of, for example, ownership, funding, and regulation, and that these aspects can have very different implications (Bozeman, 1987). Furthermore, it is important to keep the task constant in sector comparisons and at least pay attention to differences relating to, for example, service delivery versus manufacturing, which could potentially provide very different possibilities for exerting leadership. The meta-studies from the generic management literature have also shown that leadership can function very differently dependent on, for example, the level of the leader, leader characteristics, and/or follower characteristics. Most existing studies have paid relatively little attention to such moderators, and perhaps this would be an avenue of research for future meta-studies of leadership and performance.

This leads to the performance concept, which still needs to be investigated more broadly in relation to leadership effects. Existing studies have mainly focused on either broad self-assessed measures of performance or on relatively specific but also narrower measures related to effectiveness or user satisfaction. However, other aspects of performance such as cost efficiency and equity are also highly relevant performance criteria for many (public) organizations, which are aimed at creating as much value as possible. A systematic approach to investigating leadership effects on different performance dimensions would bring more nuanced knowledge on the actual performance effects of leadership. Such studies could include various leadership styles (transactional, transformational, and others) as well as performance on multiple levels of analysis. Doing so we also urge scholars to consider threats from common source bias seriously and use research designs that measure leadership and performance from independent sources.

The challenge is to systematically assess when, where, and how leadership affects performance. Based on this review, we welcome well-designed studies of leadership and performance, because we see a great potential for contributions in this field.

References

Alchian, A. A., & Demsetz, H. (1972). Production, information costs, and economic organization. *The American Economic Review*, *62* (5), 777–795.

Andersen, L. B., Boesen, A., & Pedersen, L. H. (2014). *Dimensions of performance in public organizations: Clarifying the conceptual space*. Paper presented at the PAR 75 anniversary conference, November 16–18, 2014, Guangzhou, China.

Andrews, R., Boyne, G. A., & Walker, R. M. (2011). Dimensions of publicness and organizational performance: A review of the evidence. *Journal of Public Administration Research and Theory*, *21* (suppl 3), i301–i319.

Avolio, B. J., Reichard, R. J., Hannah, S. T., Walumbwa, F. O., & Chan, A. (2009). A meta-analytic review of leadership impact research: Experimental and quasi-experimental studies. *The Leadership Quarterly*, *20* (5), 764–784.

Bass, B. M. (1985). *Leadership and performance beyond expectations*. Free Press: Collier Macmillan.

Bass, B. M., & Avolio, B. J. (1990). Developing transformational leadership: 1992 and beyond. *Journal of European Industrial Training*, *14* (5), 21–27.

Bass, B. M., & Riggio, R. E. (2006). *Transformational leadership*. Psychology Press.

Bass, B. M., Avolio, B. J., Jung, D. I., & Berson, Y. (2003). Predicting unit performance by assessing transformational and transactional leadership. *Journal of Applied Psychology*, *88* (2), 207.

Bellé, N. (2013). Leading to make a difference: A field experiment on the performance effects of transformational leadership, perceived social impact, and public service motivation. *Journal of Public Administration Research and Theory*, *24* (1), 109–136.

Bennis, W. G. (1959). Leadership theory and administrative behavior: The problem of authority. *Administrative Science Quarterly*, *4*, 259–301.

Borman, W. C., & Motowidlo, S. M. (1993). Expanding the criterion domain to include elements of contextual performance. In: N. Schmitt & W. C. Bormans (eds.). *Personnel selection in organizations*. Jossey-Bass, 71–98.

Boyne, G. (2002). Public and private management: What's the difference? *Journal of Management Studies*, *39*, 97–122.

Boyne, G. A. (2003). What is public service improvement? *Public Administration*, *81* (2), 211–227.

Bozeman, B. (1987). *All organizations are public: Bridging public and private organizational theories*. Jossey-Bass.

Bozeman, B., & Bretschneider, S. (1994). The 'publicness puzzle' in organization theory: A test of alternative explanations of differences between public and private organizations. *Journal of Public Administration Research and Theory*, *4* (2), 197–224.

Brewer, G. A. (2008). Employee and organizational performance. In: J. Perry & A. Hondeghem. *Motivation in public management: The call of public service*. Oxford University Press, 136–156.

Buchanan, B. (1974). Government managers. *Public Administration Review*, *34* (4), 339–347.

Burns, J. M. (1978). *Leadership*. Harper & Row.

Chatterjee, A., & Hambrick, D. C. (2007). It's all about me: Narcissistic chief executive officers and their effects on company strategy and performance. *Administrative Science Quarterly*, *52* (3), 351–386.

Chen, Y., & Cheng, J. (2012). Leadership behavior and job performance of teachers in public and private kindergartens: The perspectives of institutionalization, reason, and feeling. *School Effectiveness and School Improvement: An International Journal of Research, Policy and Practice*, *23* (1), 1–19.

Child, J. (1972). Organizational structure, environment and performance: The role of strategic choice. *Sociology*, *6* (1), 1–22.

Chun, Y. H., & Rainey, H. G. (2005). Goal ambiguity and organizational performance in US federal agencies. *Journal of Public Administration Research and Theory*, *15* (4), 529–557.

Conger, J. A., & Kanungo, R. N. (1998). *Charismatic leadership in organizations*. Sage Publications.

De Dreu, C. K., & Weingart, L. R. (2003). Task versus relationship conflict, team performance, and team member satisfaction: A meta-analysis. *Journal of Applied Psychology*, *88* (4), 741.

DeGroot, T., Kiker, D. S., & Cross, T. C. (2000). A meta-analysis to review organizational outcomes related to charismatic leadership. *Canadian Journal of Administrative Sciences*, *17* (4), 356–372.

Dinh, J. E., Lord, R. G., Gardner, W. L., Meuser, J. D., Liden, R. C., & Hu, J. (2012). Leadership theory and research in the new millennium: Current theoretical trends and changing perspectives. *Leadership Quarterly*, *25* (1), 36–62.

Dumdum, U. R., Lowe, K. B., & Avolio, B. J. (2002). *A meta-analysis of transformational and transactional leadership correlates of effectiveness and satisfaction: An update and extension.* In: B. J. Avolio & F. J. Yammarino (eds.). *Monographs in leadership and management,* vol. 2. Emerald Group, 67–94.

Dvir, T., Eden, D., Avolio, B. J., & Shamir, B. (2002). Impact of transformational leadership on follower development and performance: A field experiment. *Academy of Management Journal, 45* (4), 735–744.

Favero, N., & Bullock, J. B. (2015). How (not) to solve the problem: An evaluation of scholarly responses to common source bias. *Journal of Public Administration Research and Theory, 25* (1), 285–308.

Fuller, J. B., Patterson, C. E., Hester, K., & Stringer, D. Y. (1996). A quantitative review of research on charismatic leadership. *Psychological Reports, 78* (1), 271–287.

Griffith, J. (2004). Relation of principal transformational leadership to school staff job satisfaction, staff turnover, and school performance. *Journal of Educational Administration, 42* (3), 333–356.

Ireland, R. D., & Hitt, M. A. (1999). Achieving and maintaining strategic competitiveness in the 21st century: The role of strategic leadership. *The Academy of Management Executive, 13* (1), 43–57.

Jacobsen, C. B., & Bøgh Andersen, L. (2015). Is leadership in the eye of the beholder? A study of intended and perceived leadership practices and organizational performance. *Public Administration Review, 75* (6), 829–841.

Judge, T. A., & Piccolo, R. F. (2004). Transformational and transactional leadership: A meta-analytic test of their relative validity. *Journal of Applied Psychology, 89* (5), 755.

Kirby, J. (2005). Toward a theory of high performance. *Harvard Business Review, 83,* 30–39.

Koh, W. L., Steers, R. M., & Terborg, J. M. (2013). The effects of transformational leadership on teacher attitudes and student performance in Singapore. *Journal of Organizational Behavior, 16,* 319–333.

Langbein, L. (2010). Economics, public service motivation, and pay for performance: Complements or substitutes? *International Public Management Journal, 13* (1), 9–23.

Lieberson, S., & O'Connor, J. F. (1972). Leadership and organizational performance: A study of large corporations. *American Sociological Review, 37* (2), 117–130.

Lim, B. C., & Ployhart, R. E. (2004). Transformational leadership: Relations to the five-factor model and team performance in typical and maximum contexts. *Journal of Applied Psychology, 89* (4), 610.

Lowe, K. B., Kroeck, K. G., & Sivasubramaniam, N. (1996). Effectiveness correlates of transformational and transactional leadership: A meta-analytic review of the MLQ literature. *The Leadership Quarterly, 7* (3), 385–425.

Mackey, A. (2008). The effect of CEOs on firm performance. *Strategic Management Journal, 29* (12), 1357–1367.

March, J. G., & Sutton, R. I. (1997). Organizational performance as a dependent variable. *Organization Science, 8* (6), 698–706.

Meier, K. J., & O'Toole, L. J. (2013). Subjective organizational performance and measurement error: Common source bias and spurious relationships. *Journal of Public Administration Research and Theory, 23* (2), 429–456.

Moe, T. M. (2012). Delegation, control, and the study of public bureaucracy. In *The Forum, 10* (2).

Muchiri, M. K., Cooksey, R. W., & Walumbwa, R. W. (2012). Transformational and social processes of leadership as predictors of organisational outcomes. *Leadership & Organization Development Journal, 33* (7), 662–683.

Northouse, P. G. (2015). *Leadership: Theory and practice.* Sage Publications.

O'Toole, L. J. Jr., & Meier, K. J. (2011). *Public management: Organizations, governance, and performance.* Cambridge University Press.

O'Toole, L. J., & Meier, K. J. (2014). Public management, context, and performance: In quest of a more general theory. *Journal of Public Administration Research and Theory, 25* (1), 237–256.

Oberfield, Z. W. (2012). Public management in time: A longitudinal examination of the full range of leadership theory. *Journal of Public Administration Research and Theory, 24* (2), 407–429.

Paarlberg, L. E., & Lavigna, B. (2010). Transformational leadership and public service motivation: Driving individual and organizational performance. *Public Administration Review, 70* (5), 710–718.

Parry, K. W., & Sinha, P. N. (2005). Researching the trainability of transformational organizational leadership. *Human Resource Development International, 8* (2), 165–183.

Pettigrew, A. (2013). *Can leaders make a difference to organisational performance?* Presentation at the British Academy, 18 April.

Pfeffer, J., & Salancik, G. R. (2003). *The external control of organizations: A resource dependence perspective.* Stanford University Press.

Piccolo, R. F., & Colquitt, J. A. (2006). Transformational leadership and job behaviors: The mediating role of core job characteristics. *Academy of Management Journal, 49* (2), 327–340.

Podsakoff, P., & Organ, D. (1986). Self-reports in organizational research: Problems and prospects. *Journal of Management, 12*, 531–544.

Pollitt, C., & Hupe, P. (2011). Talking about government: The role of magic concepts. *Public Management Review, 13* (5), 641–658.

Rainey, H. G. (1982). Reward preferences among public and private managers: In search of the service ethic. *The American Review of Public Administration, 16* (4), 288–302.

Rainey, H. G. (2014). *Understanding and managing public organizations.* John Wiley & Sons.

Richard, P. J., Devinney, T. M., Yip, G. S., & Johnson, G. (2009). Measuring organizational performance: Towards methodological best practice. *Journal of Management, 35*, 718–804.

Salas, E., Dickinson, T. L., Converse, S. A., & Tannenbaum, S. I. (1992). Toward an understanding of team performance and training. In R. W. Swezey & E. Salas (eds.). *Teams: Their training and performance.* Ablex.

Somech, A. (2006). The effects of leadership style and team process on performance and innovation in functionally heterogeneous teams. *Journal of Management, 32* (1), 132–157.

Stewart, G. L., & Barrick, M. R. (2000). Team structure and performance: Assessing the mediating role of intrateam process and the moderating role of task type. *Academy of Management Journal, 43* (2), 135–148.

't Hart, P. (2014). *Understanding public leadership.* Palgrave MacMillan.

Terry, L. D. (1998). Administrative leadership, neo-managerialism, and the public management movement. *Public Administration Review, 58* (3), 194–200.

Thomas, A. B. (1988). Does leadership make a difference to organizational performance? *Administrative Science Quarterly, 33*, 388–400.

Tummers, L., & Knies, E. (2016). Measuring public leadership: Developing scales for four key public leadership roles. *Public Administration, 94*, 433–451.

Van Knippenberg, D., & Sitkin, S. B. (2013). A critical assessment of charismatic–transformational leadership research: Back to the drawing board? *The Academy of Management Annals, 7* (1), 1–60.

Van Wart, M. (2013). Administrative leadership theory: A reassessment after 10 years. *Public Administration, 91* (3), 521–543.

Vigoda-Gadot, E. (2007). Leadership style, organizational politics, and employees' performance: An empirical examination of two competing models. *Personnel Review, 36* (5), 661–683.

Vogel, R., & Masal, D. (2014). Public leadership: A review of the literature and framework for future research. *Public Management Review*, 1–25.

Waldman, D. A., Bass, B. M., & Yammarino, F. J. (1990). Adding to contingent-reward behavior. The augmenting effect of charismatic leadership. *Group & Organization Management, 15* (4), 381–394.

Walker, R. M., Boyne, G. A., & Brewer, G. A. (eds.). (2010). *Public management and performance: Research directions.* Cambridge University Press.

Wang, G., Oh, I. S., Courtright, S. H., & Colbert, A. E. (2011). Transformational leadership and performance across criteria and levels: A meta-analytic review of 25 years of research. *Group & Organization Management, 36* (2), 223–270.

Warvick, D. P. (1975). *A theory of public administration.* Sage.

Wasserman, N., Nohria, N., & Anand, B. N. (2001). *When does leadership matter? The contingent opportunities view of CEO leadership.* Harvard Working Paper no. 02–04.

Weber, R., Camerer, C., Rottenstreich, Y., & Knez, M. (2001). The illusion of leadership: Misattribution of cause in coordination games. *Organization Science, 12* (5), 582–598.

Welbourne, T. M., Johnson, D. E., & Erez, A. (1998). The role-based performance scale: Validity analysis of a theory-based measure. *Academy of Management Journal, 41* (5), 540–555.

Wofford, J. C., Whittington, J. L., & Goodwin, V. L. (2001). Follower motive patterns as situational moderators for transformational leadership effectiveness. *Journal of Managerial Issues, 13* (2), 196–211.

Wright, B. E., & Pandey, S. K. (2009). Transformational leadership in the public sector: Does structure matter. *Journal of Public Administration Research and Theory, 20* (1), 75–89.

Wright, B. E., Moynihan, D. P., & Pandey, S. K. (2012). Pulling the levers: Transformational leadership, public service motivation, and mission valence. *Public Administration Review, 72* (2), 206–215.

Yammarino, F. J., Dionne, S. D., Chun, J. U., & Dansereau, F. (2005). Leadership and levels of analysis: A state-of-the-science review. *The Leadership Quarterly, 16* (6), 879–919.

Yukl, G. (2013). *Leading in organizations.* Pearson.

28

Leaders as Spiritual Heroes
The Paradoxes of Unlimited Leader Agency

Dennis Tourish

Introduction: Spirituality in the Workplace

Spirituality at work (henceforth, SAW), along with associated movements promoting spiritual management and leadership development, has grown in significance over the past two decades, particularly in the USA (Tourish and Tourish, 2010). Aburdene (2005) has argued that it constitutes a 'megatrend', likely to dominate much business activity in the years ahead. Indicative of this, articles have appeared in many news outlets, including *Newsweek*, *Time* and *Fortune* magazines. The Academy of Management has a special interest group devoted to the subject with (in 2015) 581 members, a development which has created 'legitimacy and support for research and teaching in this newly emerging field' (Neal and Biberman, 2003: 363). It is scarcely surprising that some advocates have been able to note with evident satisfaction that 'Spirituality at work . . . appears to be an idea whose time has come' (Singhal and Chatterjee, 2006: 162). Within this, an enthusiastic sub-stream of researchers has urged the development of 'spiritual leadership' (SL), intended to promote the common interests and values of leaders and followers in the interests of improving organisational performance (e.g. Fry and Nisiewicz-Sadler, 2012).

Advocates of SAW challenge the notion that work should be a spirit-free zone, and assert that organisations and their leaders should facilitate more holistic personal expressions by employees (Lewis and Geroy, 2000). Since people now spend most of their waking hours at work, it is claimed that they increasingly look to their organisations 'as a communal centre' (Mirvis, 1997: 702), thereby legitimating the concern of leaders with what might previously have been considered to be the private belief systems of their employees. It is argued that SAW is 'changing the fundamental nature of work' (Konz and Ryan, 1999: 200), with employees increasingly expecting their leaders to offer meaning in both their work and wider lives. The management of meaning is therefore held to be a crucial activity for leaders (Singhal and Chatterjee, 2006), which the adoption of SAW-related practices would purportedly help them to perform. Fry (2003: 702) claims that:

> Companies as diverse as Taco Bell, Pizza Hut, BioGenenex, Aetna International, Big Six accounting's Deloitte and Touche, and law firms such as New York's Kaye, Scholer,

Fierman, Hayes and Haroller are extolling lessons usually doled out in churches, temples and mosques.

Typically, these fanciful propositions rely on stories derived from founders and/or senior managers (Bell *et al.*, 2012).

There are few limits. Thus, if SAW gains a sufficiently strong purchase on organisational practices, much of the literature asserts that personal, social and global transformation will surely follow – and for the better (Driscoll and Wiebe, 2007). Business leaders, meanwhile, are presented with a vastly expanded range of concerns, despite their evident difficulties in resolving those that they already confront. In consequence, they are invited to exercise a colonising influence on the deepest recesses of their employees' hitherto private belief and value systems (Tourish and Pinnington, 2002). The assumption that such an approach can succeed is consistent with the long-standing tendency to treat followers as though they are an undifferentiated collective (Collinson, 2006), thereby capable of adhering to a relatively simple normative framework proposed by leaders on their behalf. It is an assumption that I challenge in this chapter.

I argue that SAW has been poorly defined, and has attempted to straddle both secularism and a particular stress on religion. However, both secular and explicitly religious manifestations of it seek to extend the power of leaders. Non-spiritual, utilitarian and performative notions of productivity underlie much of its advocacy, with the assumption that, because such notions are valued by leaders, they embody priorities which either are or ought to be shared by their followers. It is also presented without sufficient acknowledgement of power differentials in the workplace, and therefore ignores the additional power which its practice may cede to a managerial elite. As a result, its claimed emancipatory agenda may serve as a vehicle for the advancement of a more controlling and oppressive leadership agenda than is normally acknowledged or may be intended. In particular, SAW can be employed as yet another means of establishing monocultural workplace environments, in which employee dissent is demonised as the sinful antithesis of pure spiritual values, to which only morally deficient individuals could object, and which organisational leaders are uniquely qualified to articulate.

SAW: A Religious or Secular Paradigm?

A key problem lies with the multiple ways in which SAW has (failed) to define itself. Karakas (2010) identified at least 70 definitions now in circulation. In one sense, the absence of a clear definition insulates its proponents from critique. Since SAW is so protean in conception, it can assume whatever form is most likely to help it escape censure. But, in another sense, both the secular and religious definitions that have abounded share an underlying performative intent. They therefore privilege the values, priorities and concerns of leaders, while affirming to employees that these capture their own immediate and seemingly homogeneous interests. I argue that a common feature of the competing definitions on offer is their tendency to reify organisations and, intentionally or otherwise, promote the desirability of a monocultural environment, in which the power of leaders is intensified, that of followers is diminished and dissent is marginalised.

In general, SAW has been defined in terms that imply a deep relationship with the core of what it means to be a human being (Hudson, 2014). It has been described as something that involves ultimate and personal truths (Wong, 1998), as the promotion of a relationship with a higher power that affects how one conducts oneself in the world (Armstrong, 1995), as being intimately bound up with religion (Dent *et al.*, 2005) and as an animating force that inspires one towards purposes beyond oneself and which in turn gives life meaning and direction

(McKnight, 1984). Mason and Welsh (1994) define it as wonder, play, spontaneity, joy, imagination, celebration, discernment, insight and creativity. This may be a revelation to those who disdain the nomenclature of spirituality and who view such terms as 'joy' and 'spontaneity' from a humanist or secular perspective. In straightforward religious terms, spiritual wellbeing has also been posited as requiring an affirmation of life in a relationship with God and the celebration and nurturing of wholeness (Ellison, 1983). Reave (2005: 677) argues that

> Most spiritual teachings urge the appreciation of others as fellow creations of God worthy of respect and praise. Praise of God's creation is widely considered to be a means of prayer, so appreciating others may similarly be considered an expression of gratitude not only to individuals but also to God.

In this view, spirituality and religion are inseparable constructs. Daniels *et al.* (2000) are among those who argue for a specifically Christian approach to management and management education, including an advocacy of the need to model a sense of Christian community on university campuses. Similarly, Cavanagh (1999) argues that spirituality includes acknowledging both God and the importance of prayer.

Such religious definitions offer a narrow, normative framework, of limited appeal when significant numbers of people have abandoned formal church attendance and the rituals of religious commitment. It is nevertheless suggested that leaders can articulate this framework in such a manner that it assumes a wide appeal, and so acts as a unifying force within their organisations. These assumptions are deeply problematic. Overt religious symbols are unwelcome in many workplaces, precisely because of their divisive potential – for example, in Northern Ireland (Hargie, 2014). There are, in addition, a multitude of legal issues around the expression of spirituality in the workplace in the United States (Schley, 2008). Such perspectives also confer considerable additional power on managers and leaders, whom it is assumed can and should encourage employees to redefine their views of God and religion in terms determined by leaders. There is little evidence that such an approach would be welcomed. In addition, attempts to pursue it may be viewed as an effort to create a monocultural environment that, by privileging particular belief systems over others, reproduces a repressive managerial agenda at odds with a claimed emancipatory intent.

While this critique can be applied to the overtly religious definitions of spirituality, the more secular notions on offer suffer from similar limitations. A seemingly humanistic approach is to the fore, although the intent is still often to produce fundamental personal change and hence create 'converts' to new ways of thinking, feeling and behaving (Cullen, 2011). SAW is nevertheless depicted in emancipatory terms, simply intended to 'help' people bring more of themselves to work, without incurring sanction or ridicule. Thus, Mitroff (2003) promotes spirituality as a transcendent force connecting people to the universe and which therefore enables them to bring the deepest essence of themselves to work, while being distinct from religion, particularly of the organised variety. Leaders who champion it are cast in the role of liberators, freeing the human spirit, but also as construction workers, demolishing outmoded barriers between people's identities at work and other important areas of their lives. So framed, this might appear an entirely benign ambition. The problem lies, however, with how it is to be translated into practice, within the power-saturated and conflicted organisations where most people work. But, driven by the conviction that positive outcomes from spiritual leadership are almost inevitable, such downsides are rarely considered (Chaston and Lips-Wiersma, 2014).

Ashmos and Duchon (2000) epitomise the difficulty. They argue that SAW encompasses three major themes: the importance of a person's inner life, the need for meaning at work and the importance of a sense of connection and community within organisations. It is commonly assumed that the promotion of 'connection' and 'community' requires employees to align their values with the organisation's larger purpose, as it has been defined by its formal leaders (Milliman *et al.*, 2003; Ashforth and Pratt, 2003). SAW is therefore advocated as a means of personal rather than organisational transformation. People's attention is directed internally to whatever obstacles block their full engagement with an unproblematic organisational agenda – rather than externally, to those systemic difficulties that might prevent the emergence of more humanistic work organisations. By contrast, a post-structuralist perspective, drawing in particular on the work of Foucault (1977, 1979), would suggest the need to acknowledge that specific regimes of power and knowledge can be inscribed on people, creating individuals who essentially participate in their own subordination through absorbing the value systems of others which may, in reality, reflect interests contrary to their own. In this way, the social control of leaders over followers becomes more deeply entrenched (Collinson, 2006). This process is not necessarily mitigated by a discourse which often asserts its intention to accomplish the opposite.

The predominant presumption within the literature is also that those at the top will have ultimate say, and that how leaders view themselves is a key ingredient behind the 'successful' development of SAW. This managerialist (or 'leaderist') bias runs through the literature, with minimal awareness of its complications. For example, Mitroff and Denton's (1999) much cited book reports on the results of a 'spirituality audit' conducted by them. It is based on a survey of 1738 people. But *all* of these were managers. Moreover, they all worked in the USA. This is sufficient for Mitroff (2003: 376) to conclude that 'people want to bring their whole selves to work . . . They are extremely frustrated with and tired of having to leave significant parts of themselves at home and pretending that one can do it.' The point is not whether this conclusion is valid; it is simply that it is an unusual research practice to extrapolate from a survey of managers in one country to the workforce of the planet. It is also questionable whether, based on their responses, it is then justified to assume that business leaders should have full control over developing a spirituality agenda for their employees, thus extending their power in ever wider directions.

The paradox is clear. On the one hand, since it is asserted that employees bring spiritual values with them to work, it follows that 'the organisation is cast neutrally as the provider of opportunities for individual spiritual expression' (Bell and Taylor, 2003: 343). But, simultaneously, spiritual values are to be defined, shaped and introduced by managers. It is rarely said that such values are merely there, awaiting discovery. The spiritual leader is therefore cast in quite a different role to that of an explorer, bringing hidden treasures to the surface. Rather, he/she assumes the demeanour of a spiritual engineer, transforming the already existing values of followers. Thus, 'The creation of spiritually oriented workplaces involves identifying and then nurturing core values among leaders and followers' (Jeon *et al.*, 2013: 343). This 'nurturing' is, of course, performed by the organisation's formal leaders. Wagner-Marsh and Conley (1999: 107) argue that:

> the president or CEO is usually the key person to initiate a process defining an organization's mission and vision, and, as stated, this should be part of his or her job description, but a governing board should be deeply involved in the process, especially in the case of religious and other non-profit institutions. Granted, the process may create new expectations for them and change their role. Similarly, staff must be consulted throughout the process in meaningful ways that take seriously their input but don't place inappropriate expectations on them to ultimately control the outcome.

Ultimately, it appears that staff must be prepared to embrace powerful value systems set for them by others, albeit with the consolation of having been 'consulted' about what these should be.

In line with this, it is routinely asserted that spiritual management leadership involves 'creating a vision wherein organization members experience a sense of calling in that their life has meaning and makes a difference' (Fry, 2003: 711). Leaders must promote a common vision and achieve value congruence at all organisational levels (Maghroori and Rolland, 1997). Much that is ostensibly positive is claimed to flow from this, including improved organisational learning (Bierly et al., 2000), unified communities in the workplace (Cavanagh et al., 2001), a greater feeling of connection between employees, and between employees and their work (Khanna and Srinivas, 2000), increased compassion, wisdom and connectedness (Maxwell, 2003) and increased corporate social responsibility – at, incidentally, no cost to key indicators of financial performance (Fry and Cohen, 2008). Fry and Nisiewicz-Sadler (2012) published *Maximizing the Triple Bottom Line through Spiritual Leadership*. Issued by the prestigious Stanford University Press, the publisher's website asserts that the book

> draws on the emerging fields of workplace spirituality and spiritual leadership to teach leaders and their constituencies how to develop business models that address issues of ethical leadership, employee well-being, sustainability, and social responsibility without sacrificing profitability, growth, and other metrics of performance excellence.

The unitarist assumption is pervasive. Thus, 'spiritual leadership concerns creating or providing meaning, purpose and value for people based on a sense of shared vision, purpose, values and beliefs' (Gill, 2014: 136). To achieve this, leaders are urged to instil a sense of the spiritual realm within individuals, teams and the organisation more widely (Cacioppe, 2000). A key proposition is that workplace spirituality is related to the leader's ability to 'enable' the worker's inner life, sense of meaningful work and community (Duchon and Plowman, 2005). Accordingly, a leader who embraces SAW will have a heightened ability to create a definition of what represents a meaningful life, to predefine employees' sense of community excessively in the direction of workplace relationships and to transform their inner life so that it is more consistent with corporate purposes.

In order to prepare for such a development, it also follows that leaders require 'development' (i.e. training/indoctrination) in its precepts. Spiritual management and leadership development is therefore increasingly offered by providers, who 'claim to enable the release of managers from their socialised selves so they can be liberated from the "negative thoughts", "fears" or "barriers", which impede the development of a successful corporate culture' (Bell and Taylor, 2004: 441). It has been suggested that this can also be accomplished through 'spiritual mentoring', by which leaders can show and then encourage spiritual behaviours in others (Weinberg and Locander, 2014). This reflects a focus on managing identity (and thus ensuring compliance through the internalisation of dominant corporate values), rather than old hierarchical structures and simple mechanisms of command and control. The focus is on the need for individuals to adapt everything they possess, body and soul, to the organisational environment in which they find themselves, in pursuit of meaning and solace. It is an imperative that can be viewed as a form of 'symbolic violence', despite the liberating rhetoric that accompanies it (Kamoche and Pinnington, 2012). The possibility that such a colonisation of people's affective domain might be oppressive, invasive or unwelcome is not generally considered.

Thus, while some texts acknowledge that there is a danger of overly 'enthusiastic' CEOs attempting to impose a particular religious belief system on others (e.g. Cavanagh, 1999), such writers generally still favour a unitarist view of organisations which privileges a managerial voice above that of other organisational members. Cavanagh (1999: 192) also posits the view that 'If handled well, common religious and spiritual beliefs in an organization can be fruitful. But if not handled well, it can lead to divisiveness and even law suits.' It is simply assumed that an organisation must have a 'common' view about such inherently contentious subjects, and that, somehow, leaders can become adept at managing whatever tensions inadvertently arise.

In opposition, paradox, contradiction, ambiguity, inconsistency and creation tensions are endemic to identity construction and maintenance (Kondo, 1990; Collinson, 2008). It may be that people have many 'spiritual' essences, none of them necessarily in harmony with each other, let alone an overarching organisational purpose, vision or mission. Cavanagh (1999) nevertheless argues in favour of prayer within 'religiously oriented business schools,' in order to bring a sense of 'perspective' to the curriculum. Meanwhile:

> Spirituality enables a businessperson to gain a better perspective on their firm, family, neigh-bours, community and themselves. Furthermore, acknowledging dependence on God gives the individual manager a more stable and helpful vision. The manager then knows that his/her success also depends on someone beyond themselves, so such a view also lessens stress. Such a vision also enables the manager to integrate their life, so that it is less segmented and compartmentalized.
>
> *(Cavanagh, 1999: 198)*

Whether non-religious employees will be likely to feel the same is not considered.

Even assuming that such a discourse is greeted by a receptive audience, we encounter a further problem. Forray and Stork (2002: 507) argue compellingly that an invocation of spirituality involves a retreat from rational thinking, to such an extent that 'in any commitment to spirit, reason is silenced'. It could therefore be suggested that leaders advocating SAW diminish the rational and hence questioning roles of their followers, arousing instead an unreflexive emotional response that is more likely to promote conformity and so further entrench leadership power. Again, this would contradict the emancipatory rhetoric with which most discourse on SAW is infused.

The Illusion of Inclusivity

Many advocates of SAW, particularly those who place less emphasis on the term's religious connotations, have been keen to stress the inclusive nature of their approach, as a means of addressing these issues. If SAW is inclusive, then it theoretically follows that it cannot be a means of advancing the sectional interests of organisational leaders to the detriment of those of their followers. In line with this approach, Mitroff and Denton (1999) argue that spirituality must be broadly inclusive by definition, since it promotes values that are 'universal and time-less'. SAW is also characterised as 'the ultimate source and provider of meaning and purpose', dealing with 'the sacredness of everything' by exploring 'the deep feeling of interconnectedness of everything'.[1] Ashmos and Duchon (2000: 634) argue that:

> spirituality is neither about religion nor about getting people to accept a specific belief system. Rather, it is about employees who understand themselves as spiritual beings at work whose souls need nourishment, a sense of purpose and meaning, and a sense of connected-ness to one another and to their workplace community.

The language seeks to articulate appealing values that lie beyond the domain of one religious world view, and which can therefore elide controversy. In line with this, Reave (2005: 655) concludes that 'there is a clear consistency between spiritual values and practices and effective leadership. Values that have long been considered spiritual ideals, such as integrity, honesty, and humility, have been demonstrated to have an effect on leadership success.'

However, many of these statements are themselves deeply ambiguous and therefore contested. For example, what does it mean to say that spirituality is 'universal and timeless'? As Hicks (2003: 165) put it:

> if citizens do hold in common a few values, such as freedom, equality, and toleration, these values are not 'thick' enough to provide the resources to settle morally challenging leadership questions such as what role religion should play in the contemporary workplace. Attempts to translate religiously particular values into common spiritual or secular values are reductionist at best and inaccurate at worst.

All such definitions of SAW suffer from a twofold problem. When couched in religious terms they exclude many and are opposed by others. Such definitions are likely to have a limited and perhaps diminishing appeal. This may not prevent leaders who have bought into such a philosophy from expending enormous energy in the pursuit of a monocultural environment that, in reality, is likely to prove elusive. On the other hand, when SAW assumes an inclusive and secular form, it lacks real regulatory power, since allegedly universal values are in reality vulnerable to multiple and contested interpretations, and hence applications. Again, despite the effort invested in its advocacy, it would therefore have a limited impact on people's thoughts, emotions and behaviour – the three main areas where it aspires to have a normative effect.

The Paradoxes of Performativity and 'Spiritual Leadership'

Spiritual leadership theory (SLT) is posited, as 'a causal leadership theory for organizational transformation designed to create an intrinsically motivated, learning organization' (Fry et al., 2005: 835). Since leaders will be enabled by this approach to integrate their personal and professional lives, it is also argued that it will improve their effectiveness (Neal, 2001). But not only leaders will gain. Tischler et al. (2002) argue that, for similar reasons, individuals who embrace SAW will have greater success at work. Within this unitarist framework, it appears that no one stands to lose – all will have prizes.

Paradoxically, organisations are urged to promote increasingly religious values, and require employees to buy into them – in order to make more money. Spirituality seems to be viewed as another means of asserting that the visions developed by an organisation's leaders have been designed to genuinely reflect their followers' interests – as opposed to, say, enhancing shareholder value. Followers should therefore comply, to boost organisational performance. Since 'managers rely on intangible resources to improve employee and organizational performance', Lee et al. (2014: 45) simply urge those running businesses in the service sector to promote workplace spirituality and then reap the benefits. It is merely a coincidence, albeit a happy one, that a preoccupation with spirituality will yield a rise in profits.

This paradox is heightened by the context in which it is occurring. Kinjerski and Skrypnek (2004: 26–27), in noting that downsizing and re-engineering failed to accomplish improvements in organisational performance, characterise SAW as being among efforts to develop 'work environments that foster employees' creativity and personal growth . . . The assumption is that such environments will foster more fulfilling lives for employees and positive outcomes for organizations.' Thus, even as the traditional psychological contract is violated, SAW is deployed in an attempt to increase loyalty, precisely in a context in which the credibility of business leaders as advocates of humanistic values has been damaged by previous, divisive and discredited fads that they have endorsed. Even that paragon of managerialism, *Harvard Business Review*, has published articles acknowledging that trust in leaders is low, and that unless this changes the future of capitalism may be in doubt (e.g. Barton, 2011).

In such a context, where leaders are being scrutinised more critically, it is doubtful whether those who pursue spirituality primarily for pecuniary ends could sustain a credible impression over the long term. Rather, it may be that such an obvious intent further undercuts the possibility of the concept taking deep root in people's minds. Instead, it may generate further cynicism about management intentions in the workplace. However, as we will now argue, even if SAW is not well placed to exercise a colonising impact by leaders on the affective domain of employees, this is clearly its intent.

SAW and Corporate Culturism: The Second Coming?

Our critique is consistent with the suggestion made by Willmott (1993: 517), to the effect that the emphasis on the importance of a strong corporate culture that was prevalent in the 1980s and 1990s 'aspires to extend management control by colonising the affective domain. It does this by promoting employee commitment to a monolithic structure of feeling and thought.' Willmott's analysis, which he fruitfully revisits in Willmott (2013), focused on the notion of 'excellence', utilised to promote the notion that employees should reframe their identity in corporate terms, so that all organisational members should 'see themselves reflected in the emerging conception of the enterprising organization and thus to come increasingly to identify with it' (du Gay, 1991: 53–54). These approaches promoted monoculturism in the workplace, at least as the ideal. Within this world view, it is no longer permissible for employees merely to do a decent job while holding a privately critical attitude towards an organisation's goals, culture or its leaders. The implied goal seems to be that behaviour will be rendered complaisant with the needs of the corporation, always and everywhere. If something such as 'spirituality' can be invoked as the basis of an organisation's culture, then it may be appropriated for the same ends as were served by the 'excellence' and 'strong cultures' movements that were critiqued by Willmott (1993), and perhaps with similar doleful results. Advocates of SAW tend to present the prerogatives of leaders in an unassailable and uncontested light, and merely assume that they have a perfectly legitimate right to determine values and beliefs for employees.

An obvious problem is the potential for such leaders, assuming that they succeed in embedding SAW, to so engage their followers that they become over-committed to the group and its values. But when people become what can be defined as 'true believers', and evince overly zealous commitment, they 'can endow a prototypical leader with overwhelming power to influence' (Hogg, 2008: 273). Such influence may be benign – or it may not (Tourish, 2013). In either eventuality, an emphasis on corporate culturism combined with an emerging focus on spirituality management and leadership may unleash precisely this dynamic, and thus constitute major mechanisms for the deep structure exercise of power and constraint in organisations, albeit couched in emancipatory and humanistic rhetoric.

Thus, Korac-Kakabadse *et al.* (2002: 172) simply assert that 'Spiritual leaders are moral leaders. Moral leaders prefer not to compromise, accommodate or collaborate in areas where core values are at stake. They prefer to challenge opinions and ideas, rather than accommodate them.' An immediate riposte to this is to ask: in how many organisations do followers have an equal right, authority and power to challenge opinions that they find objectionable, particularly when those are held by leaders? How frequently do they have access to the resources necessary to accomplish this? These authors, as with many others, simply take it for granted that leaders have special powers to determine reality for their followers, in ever wider and more personal directions.

Thus, it is axiomatic in much of the literature that leaders should seek to mould the organisation's culture, and hence the personality of those who work within it. An organisation's culture is therefore viewed as merely another resource, to be defined and moulded by its managerial elite (Smircich, 1983). It is assumed that leaders can demonstrate to those lower down the organisation how they should perform, think and feel, by a judicious combination of example and exhortation. But those who hold managerial positions are, in turn, expected to take their ideological cue from the CEO at the top, and internalise his/her values accordingly. The challenge is to frame spiritual values so that they are inclusive – but yet capable of exercising a powerful enough normative appeal to constrain behaviour. Management development programmes play a critical role in this effort. The use of programmes which have appropriated much of the rhetoric and ritual of self-discovery, faith and commitment are therefore increasingly common (Ackers and Preston, 1997).

Such programmes often just assume that leaders can and indeed should embark on the personal transformation of whatever value systems are held by their employees. An environment characterised by 'bounded choice' may then emerge, in which only a limited repertoire of feelings, attitudes and behaviour is permissible (Lalich, 2004). This view is consistent with the notion of 'concertive control' (Barker, 1993). SAW has the potential to become precisely such a form of concertive control. Within this paradigm, it is not too fanciful to see business leaders as a priestly caste, endowed with greater wisdom than other lesser mortals, and empowered with the dispensation to impart it unidirectionally to all within their orbit. It is taken for granted that they can frame productivity targets and organisational goals for everyone in a manner that secures the interests of all, that the goals of the organisation's formal leaders are intrinsically uncontentious, and that these goals can/should be linked to spirituality, in the somewhat Machiavellian calculation that profit-driven goals will become more acceptable to employees. The overall implication is that whatever prevents full engagement with the management agenda is a personal weakness to be overcome, and that organisations have the right to invade people's internal cognitive space to reshape their values ('We need a new vision around here'), in the unproblematic pursuit of corporate efficiency.

Paradoxically, the movement promoting corporate cultures that burgeoned in the 1980s and 1990s fell somewhat into abeyance, since in practice it proved difficult if not impossible to create cohesive values to which employees would unquestioningly subscribe. In analysing this process, Fleming (2013, 2014) suggests that many managers have lost interest in attempting to bind employees every closer to corporate ideals, since corporations seem to care less than ever about their internal and external legitimacy. Rather, they have reverted to much older concerns about simply ensuring that people do the work they are paid for. If that involves them expressing different values in the workplace it might be a price that must be paid. Indeed, it might even be helpful, in strengthening illusions on the prevalence of individual freedom within the straightjacket of corporate life. However, the literature on SL would seem to suggest that, even if Fleming's argument is partially or completely true, not all theorists who have drunk from the well of corporate culturism and not all management practitioners have abandoned the hope of creating unifying belief systems that will constrain behaviour and improve performance. Hope springs eternal. Thus, leaders decide – everything. In the context of asymmetrical power relations in the workplace, it is difficult to see how this agenda could genuinely serve an emancipatory purpose. Whatever the intent, SAW seems well placed to become another repressive project, expressed through the coercive exercise of power.

Yet possessing power changes the behaviour of both leaders and followers, often for the worse (Sturn and Antonakis, 2015). In particular, leaders often lose touch with reality, frequently because employees fail to openly ventilate their disagreement with organisational goals (Tourish and Robson, 2006). In particular, those with a lower level of status in organisations habitually exaggerate the extent to which they agree with the opinions and actions of higher status people, as a means of acquiring influence over them (Wu *et al.*, 2013). This calls into question the ability of leaders to invariably articulate a compelling vision that is genuinely in the interests of their followers and which is capable of engaging their support. Advocates of SAW are thus likely to encounter a working environment in which leaders have an overly privileged voice in determining the spiritual values to be embraced. Employees, meanwhile, may be reluctant to articulate their true feelings, but feel compelled to conceal this reluctance behind public statements and actions that ostensibly embrace the new value system.

Despite the espousal of an emancipatory intent by leaders intent on promoting SAW, such a conflicted stance by their followers is liable to increase the gap between their public and private selves, engendering additional alienation. It may be even more difficult to secure genuine buy-in with spiritual values, when many people traditionally see such issues as beyond the domain of work and as constituting the essence of a highly personalised self. Their promotion at work may therefore exacerbate rather than resolve the tension between people's private and public identities, even as proponents of SAW stress their intent of abolishing it. In such a context, noble-sounding ideals expressed in the language of spirituality can become another form of social control, mobilised in support of interests that are different to those implied in the surface declarations of its advocates.

This is particularly the case when the underlying purpose of such spirituality is the very down-to-earth goal of enhancing profitability. In a context of growing corporate power, and the concentration of authority within corporations in the hands of powerful CEOs, it is questionable whether society should cede them the right to abolish the distinction between employees' activities at work and their private values, and hence legitimise only those aspects of spirituality that can be depicted as serving the bottom line.

Conclusion

Advocates of SAW and SLT contend that leaders should seek to fill the void in people's lives that has been created by the well-documented decay of wider social networks. Putnam's (2000) classic study *Bowling Alone* is a powerful analysis of this process. In essence, work pressures have appropriated the time that people used to spend on sports, churches or even political parties. Altruism, philanthropy and volunteering have all declined precipitously. But there is no obvious reason to assume that business leaders would be motivated in an endeavour to address these problems by anything other than the performative norms which have been instrumental in creating this void in the first place. Rather, SAW could be employed as a convenient ideological tool to limit dissent, heighten commitment and secure a redoubled focus on profit-oriented goals. This danger is particularly acute when those who advocate such approaches are insensitive to the problem of power, and its unequal distribution in most workplaces. However, as Galbraith (1977: 259) wryly noted, 'By pretending that power is not present, we greatly reduce the need to worry about its exercise.' Seemingly unaware of such complications, most advocates of SAW take power differentials for granted, and propose measures which would, perhaps ironically, have the effect of strengthening them.

A different approach is required. In particular, I suggest that the workplace is not a useful medium for people to find the deepest meaning in their lives. Leaders of business organisations are not spiritual engineers or secular priests, charged with responsibility for the human soul, and business organisations are not a suitable forum for exploring such issues. The distinction between private and public spaces is important, and worth preservation. The notion that people's private identity, or sense of separateness, can or should be overcome through forming an emotional attachment to a larger organisational identity is highly questionable, and perhaps even delusional (Driver, 2005). Work can and should be meaningful, but only in its own terms, and not as a substitute for the creation of wider social networks, interests, commitments, values and beliefs. To suggest otherwise is to extend the power of leaders in new, inappropriate and dangerous directions. In particular, it inadvertently seeks to abolish vital distinctions between leadership and followership (since it is assumed that followers must imbibe critical core values articulated by leaders, in pursuit of a unitarist organisational framework).

In reality, such distinctions as those between leadership and followership may be vital to people's sense of their authentic inner selves and what it means to be a well-rounded human being. I suggest that the power of leaders should be limited, rather than extended in a potentially infinite number of new directions. In the post-2008 world that we now inhabit, this need is more pressing than ever. We need more responsible theorising in leadership studies that acknowledges it, in the interests of more responsible leadership practice.

Note

1 All quotations from Mitroff and Denton (1999) here are from pages 23–25 of their book.

References

Aburdene, P. (2005) *Megatrends 2010*, Charlottesville, VA: Hampton Roads Publishing.

Ackers, P. and Preston, D. (1997) Born again? The ethics and efficacy of the conversion experience in contemporary management development, *Journal of Management Studies*, 34, 677–701.

Armstrong, T.D. (1995) *Exploring spirituality: The development of the Armstrong measure of spirituality*, paper presented at the annual convention of the American Psychological Association, New York.

Ashforth, B. and Pratt, M. (2003) Institutionalized spirituality: An oxymoron? In R. Giacalone and C. Jurkiewicz (Eds.) *Handbook of Workplace Spirituality and Organizational Performance*, pp. 93–107. New York: Sharpe.

Ashmos, D. and Duchon, D. (2000) Spirituality at work: A reconceptualisation and measure, *Journal of Management Inquiry*, 9, 134–145.

Barker, J. (1993) Tightening the iron cage: Concertive control in self-managing teams, *Administrative Science Quarterly*, 38, 408–437.

Barton, D. (March, 2011) Capitalism for the long term, *Harvard Business Review*, 84–91.

Bell, E. and Taylor, S. (2003) The elevation of work: Pastoral power and the new age work ethic, *Organization*, 10, 329–349.

Bell, E. and Taylor, S. (2004) 'From outward bound to inward bound': the prophetic voices and discursive practices of spiritual management development, *Human Relations*, 57, 439–466.

Bell, E., Taylor, S., and Driscoll, C. (2012) Varieties of organizational soul: The ethics of belief in organizations, *Organization*, 19, 425–439.

Bierly III, P., Kessler, E. and Christensen, E. (2000) Organizational learning, knowledge and wisdom, *Journal of Organizational Change Management*, 13, 595–618.

Cacioppe, R. (2000) Creating spirit at work: Re-visioning organization development and leadership – Part 1, *Leadership and Organization Development Journal*, 21, 48–54.

Cavanagh, G. (1999) Spirituality for managers: Context and critique, *Journal of Organizational Change Management*, 12, 186–199.

Cavenagh, G., Hanson, B., Hanson, K., and Hinojoso, J. (2001) Toward spirituality for the contemporary organization: Implications for work, family and society. Institute for Spirituality and Organizational Leadership, Proceedings from 'Bridging the Gap', http://lsb.scu.edu/ISOL/contemporary_organization.pdf.

Chaston, J. and Lips-Wiersma, M. (2014) When spirituality meets hierarchy: Leader spirituality as a double-edged sword, *Journal of Management, Spirituality & Religion*, http://dx.doi.org/10.1080/14766 086.2014.938244.

Collinson, D. (2006) Rethinking followership: A post-structuralist analysis of follower identities, *The Leadership Quarterly*, 17, 179–189.

Collinson, D. (2008) Conformist, resistant, and disguised selves: A post-structuralist approach to identity and workplace followership, In R. Riggio, I. Chaleff and J. Lipman-Blumen (Eds.) *The Art of Followership: How Great Followers Create Great Leaders and Organizations*, pp. 309–324. San Francisco, CA: Jossey-Bass.

Cullen, J. (2011) Researching workplace spiritualization through auto/ethnography, *Journal of Management, Spirituality & Religion*, 8, 143–164.

Daniels, D., Franz, R., and Wong, K. (2000) A classroom with a worldview: Making spiritual assumptions explicit in management education, *Journal of Management Education*, 24, 540–561.

Dent, E., Higgins, M., and Wharff, D. (2005) Spirituality and leadership: An empirical review of definitions, and embedded assumptions, *The Leadership Quarterly*, 16, 625–653.

Driscoll, C. and Wiebe, E. (2007) Technical spirituality at work: Jacques Ellul on workplace spirituality, *Journal of Management Inquiry*, 16, 333–348.

Driver, M. (2005) From empty speech to full speech? Reconceptualizing spirituality in organizations based on a psychoanalytically grounded understanding of the self, *Human Relations*, 58, 1091–1110.

du Gay, P. (1991) Enterprise culture and the ideology of excellence, *New Formations*, 13, 45–61.

Duchon, D. and Plowman, D. (2005) Nurturing the spirit at work: Impact on work unit performance, *The Leadership Quarterly*, 16, 807–833.

Ellison, C. (1983) Spiritual well-being: Conceptualisation and measurement, *Journal of Psychology and Theology*, 11, 330–340.

Fleming, P. (2013) 'Down with Big Brother!' The end of 'corporate culturism?' *Journal of Management Studies*, 50, 474–495.

Fleming, P., (2014) *Resisting Work: The Corporatization of Life and Its Discontents*, Philadelphia: Temple University Press.

Forray, J. and Stork, D. (2002) All for one: A parable of spirituality and organization, *Organization*, 9, 497–509.

Foucault, M. (1977) *Discipline and Punish*, London: Allen and Unwin.

Foucault, M. (1979) *The History of Sexuality*, London: Allen and Unwin.

Fry, L. (2003) Toward a theory of spiritual leadership, *The Leadership Quarterly*, 14, 693–727.

Fry, L. and Cohen, M. (2009) Spiritual leadership as a paradigm for organizational transformation and recovery from extended work hours cultures, *Journal of Business Ethics*, 84, 265–278.

Fry, L. and Nisiewicz-Sadler, M. (2012) *Maximizing the Triple Bottom Line Through Spiritual Leadership*, Palo Alto, CA: Stanford University Press.

Fry, L., Vitucci, S., and Cedillo, M. (2005) Spiritual leadership and army transformation: Theory, measurement, and establishing a baseline, *The Leadership Quarterly*, 16, 835–862.

Galbraith, J. (1977) *The Age of Uncertainty*, London: BBC/Andre Deutsch.

Giacalone, R. and Jurkiewicz, C. (2003) (Eds.) *Handbook of Workplace Spirituality and Organizational Performance*, New York: Sharpe.

Gill, R. (2014) Spirituality at work and the leadership challenge, *Journal for the Study of Spirituality*, 4, 136–148.

Hargie, O. (2014) Communication accommodation in a divided society: Interaction patterns between Protestants and Catholics in Northern Ireland, *Studies in Communication Sciences*, 14, 78–85.

Hicks, D. (2003) *Religion and the Workplace*, Cambridge: Cambridge University Press.

Hogg, M. (2008) Social identity processes and the empowerment of followers. In R. Riggio, I. Chaleff and J. Lipman-Blumen (Eds.) *The Art of Followership: How Great Followers Create Great Leaders and Organizations*, pp. 267–276. San Francisco, CA: Jossey-Bass.

Hudson, R. (2014) The question of theoretical foundations for the spirituality at work movement, *Journal of Management, Spirituality & Religion*, 11, 27–44.

Jeon, K., Passmore, D., and Hunsaker, W. (2013) Spiritual leadership: A validation study in a Korean context, *Journal of Management, Spirituality & Religion*, 10, 342–357.

Kamoche, K. and Pinnington, A. (2012) Managing people 'spiritually': A Bourdieusian critique, *Work, Employment and Society*, 26, 497–513.

Karakas, F. (2010) Spirituality and performance in organizations: A literature review, *Journal of Business Ethics*, 94, 89–106.

Khanna, H. and Srinivas, E. (2000) Spirituality and leadership development. Presented to the roundtable conference on developing leaders, teams and organizations: Meeting the challenges of global markets and technology, Management Development Institute, Guragon.

Kinjerski, V. and Skrypnek, B. (2004) Defining spirit at work: Finding common ground, *Journal of Organizational Change Management*, 17, 26–42.

Kondo, D. (1990) *Crafting Selves: Power, Gender and Discourses of Identity in a Japanese Workplace*, Chicago: University of Chicago Press.

Konz, G. and Ryan, F. (1999) Maintaining and organizational spirituality: No easy task, *Journal of Organizational Change Management*, 12, 200–210.

Korac-Kakabadse, N., Kouzmin, A., and Kakabadse, A. (2002) Spirituality and leadership practice, *Journal of Managerial Psychology*, 17, 165–182.

Lalich, J. (2004) *Bounded Choice: True Believers and Charismatic Cults*, Berkeley, CA: University of California Press.

Lee, S., Lovelace, K., and Manz, C. (2014) Serving with spirit: An integrative model of workplace spirituality within service organizations, *Journal of Management, Spirituality & Religion*, 11, 45–64.

Lewis, J. and Geroy, G. (2000) Employee spirituality in the workplace: A cross-cultural view for the management of spiritual employees, *Journal of Management Education*, 24, 682–694.

Maghroori, R. and Rolland, E. (1997) Strategic leadership: The art of balancing organizational mission with policy, procedures, and external environment, *Journal of Leadership Studies*, 2, 62–81.

Mason, E. and Welsh, A. (1994) Symbolism in managerial decision making, *Journal of Managerial Psychology*, 9, 27–35.

Maxwell, T. (2003) Integral spirituality, deep science, and ecological awareness, *Journal of Religion & Science*, 38, 257–276.

McKnight, R. (1984) Spirituality in the workplace. In J. Adams (Ed.) *Transforming Work: A Collection of Organizational Transformation Readings*, pp. 138–153. Alexandria, VA: Miles River.

Milliman, J., Czaplewski, A., and Ferguson, J. (2003) Workplace spirituality and employee work attitudes: An exploratory empirical assessment, *Journal of Organizational Change Management*, 16, 426–447.

Mirvis, P. H. (1997) 'Soul work' in organizations, *Organization Science*, 8 (2), 193–206.

Mitroff, I. (2003) Do not promote religion under the guise of spirituality, *Organization*, 10, 375–382.

Mitroff, I. and Denton, E. (1999) *A Spiritual Audit of Corporate America: A Hard Look at Spirituality, Religion, and Values in the Workplace*, San Francisco, CA: Jossey Bass.

Neal, J. (2001) Leadership and spirituality in the workplace. In R. Lussier and C. Achua (Eds.) *Leadership Theory, Application, Skill Development*, pp. 464–473. Boston: South-Western College Publishing.

Neal, J. and Biberman, J. (2003) Introduction: The leading edge in research on spirituality and organizations, *Journal of Organizational Change Management*, 16, 363–366.

Putnam, R. (2000) *Bowling Alone*, New York: Simon and Schuster.

Reave, L. (2005) Spiritual values and practices related to leadership effectiveness, *The Leadership Quarterly*, 16, 656–687.

Schley, D. (2008) Legal aspects of spirituality in the workplace, *International Journal of Public Administration*, 31, 342–358.

Singhal, M. and Chatterjee, L. (2006) A person–organization fit-based approach for spirituality at work: Development of a conceptual framework, *Journal of Human Values*, 12, 161–178.

Smircich, L. (1983) Concepts of organizational culture and organizational analysis, *Administrative Science Quarterly*, 29, 339–358.

Sturn, R. and Antonakis, J. (2015) Interpersonal power: A review, critique, and research agenda, *Journal of Management*, 41, 136–163.

Tischler, L., Biberman, J., and McKeage, R. (2002) Linking emotional intelligence, spirituality and workplace performance: Definitions, models and ideas for research, *Journal of Managerial Psychology*, 17, 203–218.

Tourish, D. (2013) *The Dark Side of Transformational Leadership: A Critical Perspective*, London: Routledge.

Tourish, D. and Pinnington, A. (2002) Transformational leadership, corporate cultism and the spirituality paradigm: An unholy trinity in the workplace? *Human Relations*, 55, 147–172.

Tourish, D. and Robson, P. (2006) Sensemaking and the distortion of critical upward communication in organizations, *Journal of Management Studies*, 43, 711–730.

Tourish, D. and Tourish, N. (2010) Spirituality at work, and its implications for leadership and followership: A post-structuralist perspective, *Leadership*, 5, 207–224.

Wagner-Marsh, F. and Conely, J. (1999) The fourth wave: The spiritually based firm, *Journal of Organizational Change Management*, 12, 292–301.

Weinberg, F. and Locander, W. (2014) Advancing workplace spiritual development: A dyadic mentoring approach, *The Leadership Quarterly*, 25, 391–408.

Willmott, H. (1993) Strength is ignorance; slavery is freedom: Managing culture in modern organizations, *Journal of Management Studies*, 30, 515–552.

Willmott, H. (2013) 'The substitution of one piece of nonsense for another': Reflections on resistance, gaming and subjugation, *Journal of Management Studies*, 50, 443–473.

Wong, P. (1998) Implicit theories of meaningful life and the development of the personal meaning profile (PMP). In P. Wong and P. Fry (Eds.) *Handbook of Personal Meaning: Theory, Research and Practice*, pp. 111–140. Mahwah, NJ: Lawrence Erlbaum.

Wu, L., Kwan, H., Wei, L., and Liu, J. (2013) Ingratiation in the workplace: The role of subordinate and supervisor political skill, *Journal of Management Studies*, 50, 991–1017.

Part VI
Imagining Leadership

Introduction

Leadership is a timeless, universal and at the same time highly contingent, varied, ambiguous feature of human life. Depending on how it is exercised, it can inspire us, empower us, teach us, frighten us, and repel us – it hardly ever leaves us indifferent. We want to follow people who tell us believable stories about who we are and who we could be, who appeal to the better angels of our nature, challenging and empowering us to lift ourselves to a higher moral, material, or spiritual plain. Wherever and whenever we look around the globe, human groups, organizations, and societies long for leadership, particularly when the times are such that 'business as usual' approaches no longer suffice to navigate the uncertainty and dilemmas they face. In times of change and threat, or when people that are 'not us' make their entry, raise their voices, or claim their share of 'our' pie, we want protection, direction, and order – and we are only too happy to accept authority figures that provide us with just that.

Ironically, precisely because of this craving and all the expectations of being protected, lifted, and transformed, that people invest in the idea of leadership, we are often disappointed, even disillusioned, with the leadership practices we are exposed to. We see the narcissism of our bosses, our politicians, even our 'community leaders'. We sense their compulsive need for adulation, power, or control. We witness their ugly power struggles. We learn that even great leaders more often than not do not know when it is their time to go. And most of all, most of us are only too aware of the awesome and potentially destructive powers of strong leaders – and so we are keen to restrain that power and reserve the right to get rid of them when they abuse that power, exercise it imprudently, or simply overstay their welcome.

In short, our relationship with leadership is deeply important and deeply ambivalent. And so it is a pervasive – if sometimes 'under the surface' – presence in most people's everyday lives. We talk about it, criticize it, applaud it, fantasize about it, laugh at it, call it into being, and repudiate it – casually, intently, incessantly, sometimes all at the same time. Moreover, we all 'do' it – sometimes as leaders, often as followers, always as spectators. Leadership is deeply ingrained in the cultures we inhabit. It is, in fact, in considerable part a product of those cultures. For it to exist and become institutionalized in different forms, it first has to be imagined. This imagining happens not just in the corridors of corporate and political power, or on the drawing boards of constitutional scholars, governance experts, and leadership consultants, but in the arts, in popular culture, even in the way we design the buildings and spaces where leadership is supposed to happen.

In Part VI of the Companion, we have commissioned three essays examining these processes of imagining leadership outside the world of 'leadership studies' and the professional domains of business, political, and civil society governance. In Chapter 29, Kim Yost takes us to that ever imaginative and for some outright addictive corner of literature, film, and television: the world of science fiction. What narratives of leadership are enacted? Science fiction is a genre that, Yost tell us, mediates the discourses of 'science' and 'magic' and is a means of projecting a future that comments upon the fears and desires of the present. It allows us to contemplate more fully our human experiences by blurring the line of what is real or can be real. For example, the subgenre of post-apocalyptic science fiction television is about crisis leadership, about how leaders cope with threat, stress, and existential dilemmas, and how emergent leaders may sometimes trump formal ones in the process. Yost presents a fascinating *tour d'horizon* of how issues such as hierarchy, race, class, ecology, free will, and technology are tackled through leadership dramas in science fiction narratives and concludes that the alternative futures embedded in these narratives have the power to change attitudes and behaviours about social justice issues within individuals, and thus to change the psychological equation leaders face when they advocate social change.

In Chapter 30, Maja Šimunjak and John Street survey how news media and popular culture portray leadership, particularly political leadership. In a world of 24/7 media coverage and running social media commentary on every move politicians make, controlling the frame of not just the issues of the day but of the way in which people see, think about, and evaluate those very politicians themselves has become an imperative for the exercise of political leadership, indeed for leadership survival – if only because people think this is so, and because a vastly expanded army of media consultants, political marketers, and 'spin doctors' have worked their way into the fabric of political life and into the advisory courts that political leaders create around themselves. The chapter discusses the extent to which politics has become more personalized – in that parties and ideologies matter less and less, public personae and the projection of personality and character matter more – and finds only modest and variable support for that proposition. Still, American journalist Walter Lippman observed many decades ago that politics is showbusiness for ugly people, and this truism has only become much more true in the early twenty-first-century environment. Research has suggested that shows that bridge politics and entertainment – like Jon Stewart's *Daily Show* – can inform citizens as (or more) effectively than straight news. Leading politicians are reported on as if they were celebrities, and celebrities from other walks of life can easily turn their fame into the political capital required to get elected or exercise leadership on political issues. Despite noting pivotal national and systemic sources of variation and cautioning us to eschew sweeping generalizations, the authors conclude that, regardless of the specific frames they espouse, media are central to the way leadership is understood and enacted, not just in representing political leaders but in shaping the public's response to them.

Finally, Michael Minkenberg in Chapter 31 takes us to the world of architecture and urban design, based on the premise that few arenas reflect the dreams, aspirations, interests, and self-images of leadership better than their built form in architecture. Meant to endure and to inspire the population and future generations alike, architecture uniquely expresses desired forms of power and authority. The chapter looks at the planned part of capital cities and explores how it connects to those who have made the plans – political leaders and those serving the interests of the powerful. Contrasting practices of capital city planning and architecture in autocratic or democratic regimes helps us see different types and meanings that leaders in those regimes want to communicate. Covering cases such as Paris, Rome, and Berlin, and contrasting them with 'New World' capitals such as Washington, Canberra, Berlin, and the post-communist yet autocratic capital of Astana, Minkenberg uncovers the fundamental dilemma of democratic leadership as reflected in political architecture. As with the tension between leadership and democracy, there is the tension between capital cities as symbols of empowerment – 'we the people', in stone and buildings, owning as it were the symbolic space of politics – and the realities of alienation – 'we the political class', safeguarded from the people, who are reduced to spectators that can choose to be awed, entertained, or miffed by a world that at best governs for them but which they cannot fully penetrate let alone control.

29

Star-Crossed

Imagining Leadership in Science Fiction Narratives

Kimberly Yost

The purpose of this chapter is to explore the ways in which leaders and social justice are imagined in science fiction (sf) narratives, particularly visual texts. The chapter is not a critical analysis of these texts, but an introduction for leadership scholars as to the ways in which representations of leaders in sf television and film can influence the way we think about leadership. (For a comprehensive overview of science fiction history and theories, see *The Routledge Companion to Science Fiction*, 2009.) Interestingly, popular culture artifacts echo the theories and desired outcomes often associated with leadership, in that they establish "norms, social boundaries, rituals, and innovations, while also paving the way for social change" (Kidd, 2007, p. 71). Films, in general, "shape and constitute our understanding of social and organizational life . . . [and are] a powerful tool for illustrating topics and concepts and for demonstrating the application of theory" (Huczynski and Buchanan, 2004, p. 708). The intention for primarily discussing visual sf narratives is they are often more readily known and accessible to those who are not science fiction fans, and can also become a collective experience from which discussions of leadership and issues of social justice can be fostered.

To appreciate the connection between sf narratives and leadership, a brief discussion of science fiction narratives is needed. Roberts (2009) offers a 'long history' of science fiction dating back to the Ancient Greeks, but skillfully argues the Copernican revolution as elemental in the shaping of sf as "science supplanted religion and myth in the imaginative economy of European thought" (p. 5). During this period of the seventeenth century, nascent scientists and theologians "were in the process of separating themselves into rationalist Protestant and ritualist–magical Catholic religious idioms" (Roberts, 2007, p. 42). These cultural aspects form the way in which we continue to view the mechanics of the universe and our individual agency. The altering of cosmological understanding within a Copernican universe meant futurist fiction was now unfettered from religious dogma and allowed for negotiating imaginative possibilities; however, "the more science itself became an empirical, experimental discourse, and therefore the less place the speculative impulse had in the practice of science, the more important science fiction became" (Roberts, 2007, p. 60). Science fiction becomes the genre that "mediates the discourses of 'science' and 'magic'" (Roberts, 2007, p. 42), and is a means of projecting a future that comments upon the fears and desires of the present. More fully, science fiction narratives mediate the tensions between our rational and spiritual natures by projecting our fears and desires upon the future.

Contemporary leadership theory and practice is imbued with similar characteristics that seek to clarify and reconcile the duality of our natures. Analogous to science fiction narratives, leadership practice can lean toward rational data-driven decisions or to the other end of the spectrum toward spiritual self-actualization. It may be too simplistic to describe the concept as task-oriented versus people-oriented, but as effective leadership requires a balance between those orientations, so do leaders need a means by which to explore the rational and the spiritual aspects of their practice. Science fiction texts allow for these thought experiments and engagement with cultural, social, and organizational issues from a safe distance, as they evoke emotional responses and the effect is greater cognitive and emotional understanding of human actions (Oatley, 1999), including leadership behaviors.

The socio-political anxieties of the seventeenth century are eerily similar to those of the twenty-first century. In our time, we are transitioning from the view of leadership as a position of authority that is self-legitimizing to models of autonomous and collective leadership. Technological advancements, corporate hegemony, economic collapse, biological disasters, and tribal sentiments are recurrent concerns echoing the anxieties present at the genre's beginnings. In essence, sf becomes the space wherein the apprehensions of our collective psyche lurk. The rational/spiritual tensions of our daily lives are an outgrowth of our mass experiences, where access to technologies and self-determined spirituality are available to ordinary people and not only the divine right of kings. With the exponential proliferation of ordinary technology and scientific innovations, techno-scientific discoveries call into question religious orthodoxy and the concept of human exceptionalism in the universe. These tensions between the rational–technoscientific and the spiritual–transcendent offer a profound opportunity to explore human experience on individual and collective levels. And yet, the fears and desires we hold for the future cause us to embark on an ancient pursuit of looking outside of ourselves for direction: for a leader. Nonetheless, we confront the concept within contemporary sf that leaders face similar troubling external and internal challenges as ourselves. The expression is a departure from the heroic model of leadership to one that is more complex, egalitarian, and, ultimately, depicts the tensions of leading within the oscillating framework of our rational/spiritual natures.

Consequently, sf narratives offer an optimal genre for exploring leadership and the human condition and allow us to contemplate more fully our human experiences by blurring the line of what is real or can be real (Roberts, 2007). These experiences are accomplished through *cognitive estrangement*, the presentation of an alternative world that is different from our own, but wholly familiar (Suvin, 1976). Cognitive estrangement is the key concept for understanding how science fiction narratives operate as a mediating force. The depiction of a society that is like our own, but different, provides the chance for contemplation on those similarities and differences. These reflections are crucial, in that they permit science fiction narratives to play a role in how we understand our current society and ourselves. Reflection also allows us to determine whether there is an opportunity to change our current situation: to embrace the other, to care for planetary natural resources, to exercise self-determination. Moreover, Suvin (1977/2010) identifies sf narratives not as allegorical works with singular comparisons to the real world, but a *feedback oscillation* moving between the narrative reality and the reader's reality to allow for a renewed perception of both narrative and actual realities. This feedback oscillation allows authors and audiences to explore issues of contemporary society through cognitive estrangement and, ideally, develop or even change their understanding of those issues. In essence, science fiction narratives have a social function to help us make sense of our world and our future through reflecting on possible alternatives.

Science fiction can also be described as a problem-solving genre (Butler, 2011). Csicsery-Ronay (2008) considers the "imaginary worlds of sf are pretended resolutions of dilemmas insoluble and often barely perceived in the present" (p. 3). The narratives can trigger understanding that a problem exists, with the potential for activating the moral imagination of the audience and lead to changed behaviors and social systems. This approach is Gadamerian in that it is an engagement both historical and relational. In essence, "meaning is not an objective, eternal idea but something that arises in relationship" (Palmer, 1969, p. 227). As Kuhn (1990) explains, "Meanings in film texts are not already there, but are produced in a relationship between text and spectator" (p. 145). Consequently, resolutions via leadership practices to real world problems can be offered and understood through this relationship.

Models of problem-solving are often apparent in the narratives because science fiction is not really about science. As Sontag (1976) notes, science fiction is more about the imaginings of disasters. Within these imaginings of disaster, restoration of order is needed and the narratives invoke leadership as the catalyst for solving problems. Sontag (1976) also suggests science fiction is an "emblem of an *inadequate response* . . . of the inadequacy of most people's response to the unassimilable terrors that infect their consciousness" (p. 130). While Sontag considers these films as an intersection of commercial art and "the most profound dilemmas of the contemporary situation" (p. 130), they may also be considered as a depiction of the intersection between existential terror and the often flawed capacity of leaders to address those terrors.

This is not to say that science fiction narratives only illustrate incompetent leaders. The complexity of the situations leaders confront in these narratives stretches the limits of their tacit knowledge and skills, as well as their morality. Csicsery-Ronay (2008) states art, such as films, are "models for moving from customary routines to new regimes of behavior" (p. 58); thus, we can begin to fashion an idea of how science fiction narratives can support leadership studies. The important point is to understand that visual sf texts, as objects of cultural production, are an integral part of the social conversation. Commencing from an understanding that science fiction narratives function within advanced capitalist societies as a mediating force between rational and spiritual desires and fears to allow us to reflect and make sense of our world and future by shaping our self-conceptualizations and social practices, we can begin to explore science fiction visual texts for themes that encourage effective leadership practices and societal change surrounding issues of social justice.

Leadership Practices in Science Fiction Television

If we start from Sontag's perspective of science fiction film being a genre that concerns responses to disasters, we can focus the exploration of how science fiction imagines leaders within post-apocalyptic narratives. Curtis (2010) suggests, echoing Roberts's (2007) views on science fiction in general, that post-apocalyptic fiction speaks to our fears and desires and functions with a "didactic purpose of warning us away from particular behaviors . . . [and] criticizes where we are now and who and what we might wish to be" (p. 5), as well as the catharsis of imagining a total destruction leading to a new, and potentially 'better,' society. In sf television, these narratives typically examine the actions of legitimate military or political leaders under extreme stress and emergent leaders who fill the power void in the absence of or demonstrated incompetence of legitimate authority. Essentially, post-apocalyptic science fiction television is about crisis leadership and suggests a theoretical framework for discussion that includes the hierarchical needs of followers and the inevitability of emergent leaders. The complexity of crisis leadership is revealed in ways that demonstrate the tension between ordered rational decision-making and the irrationality of human behaviors and feelings. This illustration is the core challenge of leadership, but within this heightened emotional and physiological context important questions on the nature of leadership emerge, particularly questions that run counter to the positivity bias so often encountered in traditional leadership discourse.

Contemporary long-form narratives of sf television series often question the heroic ideal, either from situational diminishment of the leader or a leader's inner conflict that yearns to go beyond the binary of good/evil. This is a depiction of critical importance if we consider leadership as a process of self-discovery and development. Essentially, leaders in science fiction television are caught in the drama of what Heifetz (1994) would describe as an adaptive challenge, consisting of "the learning required to address conflicts in the values people hold, or diminish the gap between the values people stand for and the reality they face" (p. 22). This requires change in values, beliefs, or behaviors to provide new methods of learning and behaving (Heifetz, 1994). As conflict is a primary consideration for adaptive work, dramatic narratives become ideal and less dangerous methods of exploring this concept, and long-form television narratives provide greater detail and evidence of the challenges faced by leaders during times of extreme crises.

Hierarchical Needs

Hierarchical needs, as expressed by Abraham Maslow, include the lower order needs of physiological requirements such as food, shelter, water, and medicine, as well as safety and security. The higher order needs include a sense of belonging and esteem and the need for self-actualization. The implication is a linear progression from lower to higher orders as needs are met, though disagreement exists as to the predictive conditions of this sequence (Nelson and Quick, 2015).

Several science fiction television series address the concept of hierarchical needs. In *Stargate: Universe* (2009–2011), Colonel Everett Young must provide for dozens of military personnel, government scientists, and civilians when they are marooned on a derelict alien ship millions of light years from Earth after an emergency evacuation through a stargate. Indeed, the series reflects follower needs through the progression of early episode titles: "Air," "Light," "Water," "Earth," "Time," "Life," and "Justice." In *Firefly* (2002–2003), Captain Malcolm Reynolds must balance the physiological needs of his crew with their physical safety from arrest by government officials or harm from other criminals, while seeking the higher order needs of meaning and purpose through political dissent and the creation of a just society.

In *Battlestar Galactica* (2003–2009), the hierarchical needs of followers and the competing values held by leaders during the onset of a crisis are given substantial consideration. The story begins with a cataclysmic attack that destroys a system of planets known as the Colonies and leaves roughly 50,000 human survivors stranded in space with nowhere to call home. The Secretary of Education Laura Roslin is the highest-ranking government official to survive and is sworn in as President of the Colonies. She begins to gather surviving ships and make arrangements for shelter, food, fuel, and medical care. The *Galactica*'s commander William Adama takes control of the Colonial fleet as all other battlestars are considered lost and determines to gather weapons and continue to fight the enemy. When the two meet, the competing values of military and political leadership practice are exposed, as well as the individual need for power. Roslin bluntly tells Adama the war is over and humanity lost, so they need to run, hide, and start having babies. She needs Adama to be a part of that plan to move toward the level of safety and security, not risking the remaining military forces against the overwhelming forces of the enemy. Adama demurs at first, but subsequently decides to run and take all the civilian ships.

Later, Adama states he knows where the mythical planet Earth is located and insists he will lead the fleet there. But this is a lie. Roslin confronts him in private, and he justifies the lie by summarizing her own view that people need something to live for, thus envisioning their leadership practice as moving toward the higher order needs. Roslin agrees to the deception in exchange for his acceptance of her legitimate political authority.

As leaders are expected to provide vision and inspiration, those behaviors can "create meaning to reinforce legitimacy . . . but may also be a device for manipulation" (Sinclair, 2007, p. 30). This sequence of events at the opening of the narrative demonstrates the ways in which leaders during a crisis can circumvent the immediate tensions of the rational and spiritual by addressing hierarchical needs and compromising ethical behaviors, such as honesty and trust, to maintain their legitimacy and manipulate followers.

Emergent Leaders

In contrast to legitimate military and political leaders, emergent leaders often provide the ethical foundation for post-apocalyptic science fiction narratives. They frequently stand in opposition to the status quo and use their influence to enact social change. These leaders emerge based on their referent or expert power, whether people positively identify with them due to their personality or other characteristics, or whether they are seen as possessing special knowledge and skills (Northouse, 2007). Any given episode can introduce an emergent leader from the supporting cast or in a guest role and then relegate them back into obscurity once the situation is resolved. But the importance of understanding emergent leadership is that it is not solely a function of one's organizational role or a single experience that is never repeated or leveraged. Emergent leaders are developed through a process of follower identification and personal growth. Science fiction television provides a valuable means by which to track the development and effectiveness of emergent leaders, and, to fully appreciate the process of emergent leadership, we must look at characters who are central to the story throughout. Three science fiction television series that depict emergent leaders, *Battlestar Galactica* (2003–2009), *Stargate Universe* (2009–2011), and *Babylon 5* (1993–1998), are most notable.

Battlestar Galactica presents Chief Galen Tyrol as an example of an emergent leader who meets the challenge of creating an equilibrium between rational and spiritual natures in response to crises. Tyrol holds a position of authority as chief engineer, the highest-ranking non-commissioned officer, but his referent and expert power is more compelling as we see his relationships with his deck hands and civilian workers within the fleet. Tyrol employs his referent power in opposition to the status quo when he disobeys orders and calls for a work stoppage on board a fuel refinery ship in protest at the deplorable working conditions. After being jailed by Adama for mutiny and forced to call off the strike, Tyrol and Roslin discuss the problematic structure of their society that relegates workers to positions often based on their parent's occupation as a means of succession planning and disregards a person's aspirations.

Within this episode we see Tyrol, Adama, and Roslin grapple with the rational need for survival and the spiritual need for recognition and self-actualization. Their attitudes and behaviors demonstrate varied leadership styles, but we can specifically view Tyrol's emergent leadership as rather pragmatic. Jackson and Parry (2008) explain, "pragmatic leaders exercise influence by identifying and communicating solutions to significant social problems, meeting the practical needs of followers, working through elites in solution generation, creating structures to support solution implementation, and demonstrating the feasibility of these solutions" (p. 103). Although Tyrol did not win the concessions he sought, he grows in his role as an emergent leader through this pragmatic approach and the ability to acknowledge the ethical failures of the society.

Maintaining one's integrity and moral values as a depiction of the process of emergent leadership is also seen in *Babylon 5* (1993–1998) through the character of Vir Cotto, an attaché to the Centauri ambassador Londo Mollari, stationed on *Babylon 5*. Vir must overcome the political and cultural obstacles of his society to claim his legitimacy as a leader. The narrative initially presents him as timid, awkward, anxious, and lacking self-esteem, but one who performs his duties as a matter of family honor, and his fundamental compassion for others places him in opposition to Mollari and his society.

Vir pleads with Mollari not to carry out a plot to overthrow their Emperor by solidifying power with the extermination of their enemy, the Narn, but Mollari refuses to listen. As Mollari's power grows, Vir's position becomes precarious. Vir is Mollari's ever-present reminder of compromised morals and acts of genocide in the pursuit of power. Mollari has him removed from *Babylon 5* and posted to the planet Minbar as the Centauri ambassador. Ostensibly this is a promotion, but within the structure of Centauri society, Vir has been separated from the center of power, which is a diminishment of his influence. However, the Minbar posting has the unanticipated benefit of allowing Vir to operate beyond the reach of the Centauri and collaborate with other societies. Vir secretly works to redeem his society from their enslavement of the Narn by forging transit papers and death certificates in order to help thousands of Narns escape Centauri control. The plot is discovered and Mollari uses this incident to blackmail Vir into setting a trap for the execution of the Narn ambassador, which is unsuccessful. Vir remains unable to uphold his principles as Mollari also recruits him in the assassination of the Centauri Emperor, where the plot goes awry and Vir causes the fatal blow, an act that haunts him for months.

The depiction of Centauri society is one of hedonism, corruption, and maliciousness in contrast to the depiction of Vir, often described as an innocent with a good heart. Vir must mediate the tensions between the rational order of his society and his desire for their spiritual transcendence by overcoming his own tendencies for self-preservation, belonging, and timidity by speaking truth to power – even when no one listens. Initially, his efforts appear fruitless, but the series concludes with Vir becoming Emperor himself and beloved by the Centauri people. What we discover in this depiction of emergent leadership is one who is continually tested and often falls short of his own expectations, but is nevertheless able to maintain an ethical center and ultimately succeed for the benefit of his society.

Similarly, Eli Wallace in *Stargate: Universe* (2009–2011) is an awkward and obnoxious character who maintains his sense of spiritual transcendence and emerges as a leader through an initial position of expertise, though not expert power. He solves a mathematical puzzle planted online by Stargate Command and is whisked away to help the agency. After the destruction of their base and stranding on a derelict ship billions of light years from home, his expert power grows as he solves myriad technological problems that serve to maintain their physiological needs. However, he is also not accepted by the other scientists who consider him immature, inexperienced, and, worst of all, lacking a college degree. Yet his curiosity and need for belonging cause him to meet the emotional needs of others by providing a technological means for recording their thoughts and feelings, which they cannot openly express. The combination of technological expertise and concern for the emotional well-being of his fellow passengers allows Eli to create and hold both expert and referent power, which propels him into a leadership role. Through tenacity, competence, curiosity, compassion, and the desire to help others, Eli emerges as a key leader within the narrative. Indeed, it is the solitary figure of Eli contemplating the vastness of space that is the final image of the series and solidifies his leadership role.

Particularly through the long-form narratives of sf television, we glimpse the ways in which leaders are imagined and negotiate the obstacles of leadership practice during times of crises.

Not only are depictions of leader–follower relationships observed, but issues of social justice also surface, chiefly through the development of an emergent leader. Theatrical science fiction films also explore these issues and can be powerful tools for beginning conversations about leadership.

Themes of Social Justice in Science Fiction Film

For the purposes of this chapter, the exploration of themes within science fiction visual narratives that champion social justice are limited to broad categories of race, class privilege, the environment, and self-empowerment/free will, and the period of the films discussed from the mid-1970s forward. The mid-1970s saw a significant, though not absolute, transformation in the production and popularity of science fiction films, and so my interest is to explore the ways in which they support or reflect social justice and change. Again, the intention is not to critically analyze the validity or inconsistencies of their efforts within the discipline of critical science fiction studies, but to provide a general consideration of their value as points of discussion for leadership studies.

Race

The subject of race in science fiction films is more prevalent if one considers non-human sentient beings in a racial construct. One film that unequivocally discusses race is John Sayle's *The Brother from Another Planet* (1984), starring Joe Morton. Morton plays a humanoid alien whose spacecraft crash lands in Upper Bay near Ellis Island. The Brother pulls himself from the wreckage and explores the abandoned Ellis Island immigration facilities. We discover he has strong empathic skills as he touches the columns and receives fragments of distressing visual and auditory memories of those who passed through Ellis Island as immigrants. As he walks down the streets of Harlem, we see he has no shoes and displays three-toed feet, the only indication that he is not a human Black man, but he soon realizes the anatomical difference and finds some shoes to wear. Much of the film concerns The Brother's experiences of living in Harlem and trying to find others through messages coded in graffiti. When The Brother goes to a museum of African American history, we discover he was a slave on his planet and escaped. We also discover there are two bounty hunters intent on capturing him for return to their planet.

The film addresses several issues within American society through the experiences of The Brother. There are scenes in the welfare office where the impersonal bureaucracy of getting assistance is overwhelming. A subplot involves drugs and the overdose of a teenager with a White man selling the drugs to keep his legitimate business afloat. There are depictions of the underground economy of prostitution and under-the-table wage labor. The Brother finds a job fixing pinball machines and his supervisor Hector keeps up a running monologue of taken-for-granted racism.

As the bounty hunters close in on capturing The Brother, he has followed the graffiti signs and seeks safety in a building with cleaning personnel who help him to flee. When the bounty hunters are about to strike, these people, and others in the neighborhood, stand as silent witnesses and protectors of The Brother. The Brother points his thumb to the sky, mutely asking if his rescuers are from outer space like him, but one man shakes his head and points his thumb down. They are Earthlings and motivated by belief in the dignity and freedom of all beings, even though their place on Earth may be marginalized.

The Brother from Another Planet functions as a social discourse on race in America precisely because of the protagonist's journey through the unfamiliar world of Harlem. As he experiences racial intolerance, an obstructive bureaucratic social system, the underground economies, and

443

drug culture, the audience has the opportunity to see these situations with new eyes, which changes their knowledge of the issues and potentially their attitudes towards race relations.

A more recent film to explore race relations and the parameters of human existence is Neil Blomkamp's *District 9* (2009). The narrative begins 28 years after the marooning of an alien space ship above the city of Johannesburg, South Africa. The inhabitants of the ship, derogatorily called 'Prawns,' have been rescued from the ship and interned in a militarized slum on the outskirts of Johannesburg known as District 9. National and international agencies worked to provide for the non-humans, but astonishment and awe over the Prawns wore off and they are treated as little more than unwelcome refugees. To this end, a military–industrial weapons conglomerate, Multi-National United (MNU), is given control over the alien population and determines to evict the Prawns from their shacks. Wikus Van De Merwe is a mid-level executive who is to supervise the quasi-military forces in gaining the consent of the Prawns for leaving. This consent involves reading and signing a form in English, which, of course, the non-humans are not capable of doing.

During the eviction notifications, Wikus accidentally poisons himself with a biochemical hidden by Christopher, one of the non-humans, and slowly begins to transform into a Prawn. Wikus now becomes an important asset for MNU since his hand is able to fire the highly valuable alien weapons that only interact with alien bodies. Scientists for MNU want to harvest his DNA for experimentation in search of a way for humans to use the alien weapons. Wikus escapes the MNU scientists and finds himself back in District 9 pleading with Christopher to help him reverse the metamorphosis. Christopher eventually agrees to get Wikus on the mothership and to Christopher's home planet for the antidote, if Wikus can retrieve the remaining portion of the biochemical fuel now held at MNU. Wikus and Christopher retrieve the fuel, but Christopher is unable to get Wikus in the command module and on the mothership. He promises to return, which is a round trip of several years. Meanwhile, the aliens are moved to District 10 and Wikus continues his transformation as he pines for his wife.

District 9 is a powerful film that tackles racism and corporate complicity in social marginalization and genocide through a frenetic documentary style that bridges the cognitive estrangement of aliens on Earth with the familiar visuals of television news reports for audiences. The most fascinating element of this film is the journey taken by Wikus from his comfortable human existence to his terrifying transformation to the Other. Wikus is a rather nerdy middle manager who is loyal to his company and country, while trying to be understanding toward the aliens. He engages in racist jokes at the expense of the non-humans, but sees this all as harmless fun. Only when the serving of an eviction notice goes terribly wrong does he witness the truly cruel persecution of the Prawns at the hands of humans. Yet, when Wikus begins to transform into an alien, he is terrified. He may think there is nothing wrong being an alien, but he would not want to be one. As Wikus eludes the police and security forces of MNU, his family and friends simultaneously shun him and beg him to give himself up. Wikus has no choice but to turn to Christopher, whom he has already disrespected. Wikus must learn to control his human hubris, but his understanding of human superiority is so ingrained he has difficulty making the conscious decisions necessary to change his behaviors and language.

Alternatively, *District 9* could be viewed as a parable of crime and punishment. Wikus's behavior, socially acceptable as it is, remains morally repugnant. Perhaps his transformation is the penalty for his insensitivity and abuse of the aliens. The problem with this line of thought is the value judgment that human form is more desirable than alien form, thus moving beyond the themes of race and engaging in reflections on being human. There is no shame in wanting to possess one's original biological form, but the question remains as to whether other forms are inferior. *District 9* works on several levels to offer viewers the opportunity to explore their own attitudes towards the Other, the unchecked power of military corporatism, and persecution of those who are different from the dominant culture, and reflect on potential changes to social system infrastructures that would discontinue practices that demean and marginalize the powerless.

Both *The Brother From Another Planet* and *District 9* clearly purpose their themes specifically toward Black/White race relations. However, both films also offer a chance to open a space for contemplation on 'being human' that is less segregated and more inclusive. Our common culture opts for human exceptionalism regardless of the technological or spiritual advantages enjoyed by our imaginative creations of desire and fear. These science fiction narratives call into question our human arrogance and challenge the ways in which we see our reality. As viewed from a different perspective, such as a non-human, our ignorance, prejudices, and false self-conceptions are brought to the forefront. Film can be a very intimate experience for the viewer, as emotions are exploited through the narrative. Consequently, film enhances the prospect of engagement that leads to reflection on changes in personal attitudes and increases the possibility of change on a wider scale.

Class Privilege

Closely related to issues of race are those of class privilege. Particularly within science fiction, the narrative frequently involves the gap between those favored by the utopian/dystopian social system and those who are not. More typically, the gap occurs between those who are employed by the system, thus holding the power to put their own welfare and interests ahead of the larger society, and those who are set apart as 'the masses.' For Americans, these themes create a dissonance above the cognitive estrangement as they counter the American mythologies of democratic pluralism and meritocracy.

Andrew Niccol's 1997 film *Gattaca* explores the issue of class privilege and meritocracy. In the world of *Gattaca*, education, occupation, and social class are determined by genetic engineering. Those children conceived biologically without the assistance of genetic engineering are considered 'in-valid,' while genetically adjusted children are 'valid.' Only the 'valids' are allowed to attend the best schools, get the best jobs of their own choosing, and enjoy other advantages of society.

The film tells the story of Vincent Freeman, an 'in-valid' expected to have significant biological problems and die at the age of 30 based on an examination of his DNA when he is born. Vincent's parents are encouraged to have another son who is genetically perfect and able to be successful. Although the parents put most of their hopes on his brother Anton, Vincent is determined to attain his dreams of being an astronaut. To this end, Vincent illegally assumes the identity of Jerome Morrow, a paraplegic who is genetically valid and, therefore, socially acceptable and able to enjoy the privileges of genetic superiority. Vincent undergoes surgery to be taller, gets fitted for permanent contact lenses, each day must remove and burn evidence of his own DNA, such as dander, learn to be right-handed, and be prepared to provide a urine sample at any moment in order to be employed at Gattaca Corporation and become an astronaut for a mission to one of Saturn's moons.

Vincent's fraud is nearly exposed when the director of the space flight is found dead. Anton, now a police detective, is shocked to discover that Vincent has somehow surpassed him in privilege and career success and tries to persuade Vincent to flee Gattaca and hide before he is found out to be illegally working in the company. Vincent challenges his brother to a swimming contest out into the ocean, as they did when they were teenagers, and Vincent, as before, wins. Vincent explains he is able to do this with his inferior genetic structure because he risks everything and does not save anything for the swim back to shore. In other words, it is Anton's fears that keep him from rising to his potential and Vincent's fearlessness and spirit that allow him to succeed. On the day of his space launch, Vincent arrives unprepared for a DNA check. The doctor in charge of testing passes him through, as it seems the doctor has always known Vincent is posing as a valid. Vincent's efforts give the doctor hope for his own son who is considered genetically unfit.

Gattaca presents a possible future, depicting the unintended consequences of techno-scientific advances enfolded into social policy. Genetically engineered humans who will not suffer from heart disease, myopia, or any number of other diseases are certainly a desire on the part of some in our society. However, the film directly addresses the tensions caused by such advances when they interfere with the transcendent spirit of human beings. In other words, the techno-scientific codified into legal regulations and social norms refutes the inexplicable nature of humans. The ability to strive, improve, and better ourselves, which is also at the heart of the American mythology of meritocracy, is shown to be superior to the 'genetic superman' admired by the society. Again, we hear the echoes of the question of what constitutes being a human. *Gattaca* answers this question by stating it is not our creativity or ability to order our environment and our bodies to our own will, but Being lies in our frailties and our indomitable spirit.

The Environment

Admittedly, providing pressure on society to consider the consequences of genetic engineering in terms of potential marginalization of those born without technologically aided enhancements is a difficult endeavor. The issue is simply not at the forefront of American zeitgeist. However, environmental issues are increasingly a part of conversations within political, scientific, and spiritual communities. Science fiction films have historically discussed the failings of humans as stewards of the Earth. In the early 1970s, several films looked at issues of overpopulation and the stresses placed on natural resources, such as *Soylent Green* (Richard Fleischer, 1973), *Silent Running* (Douglas Trumbull, 1972), and *Logan's Run* (Michael Anderson, 1976). With the rising concern of climate change, major Hollywood films have returned to themes of preserving the Earth's natural resources, such as *Avatar* (James Cameron, 2009) and *Interstellar* (Christopher Nolan, 2014).

WALL-E (Andrew Stanton, 2008) tells the story of a robot whose purpose is to gather and bale the waste that has accumulated on Earth and forced humans to retreat to luxury space ships in outer space. WALL-E, the robot, is highly anthropomorphic and enamored of collecting human debris, such as hubcaps, lighters, and other artifacts. He also loves the film *Hello Dolly!*, repeatedly watching the video, mimicking the dancing, and coming to understand the depiction of romantic love as the characters hold hands. One day on the job, WALL-E discovers a small green plant, which he brings back to his shelter. A reconnaissance robot, EVE, arrives on Earth to search for life and determine whether the Earth is able to sustain life. EVE eventually finds the plant and sends a signal for the mothership to return. When it does, WALL-E hitches a ride to be near EVE.

The robots end up on the evacuation ship, the *Axiom*, and we begin to see how humans have devolved over the centuries. Humans are fat from non-nutritious food and beverages, have lost the use of their legs and are whisked around in motorized reclining chairs, essentially considering themselves living lives of leisure and comfort. A multi-national conglomerate, Buy n Large, has profited not only from the sale of products that are now waste, but also controls the ships that evacuated humans 700 years ago. WALL-E and EVE get into a scrape and are considered renegade robots and chased throughout the ship. EVE's programming requires that she protect the plant, but the ship's 'first mate,' a computer program named AUTO, has counter-programming to destroy any evidence of life on Earth to prevent the knowledge of Buy n Large's complicity in the destruction of the environment.

Captain McCrea, the ship's captain, through a computer archive, eventually discovers the history of Earth, including how to care for plants, and realizes all the human race has lost. He battles AUTO to keep EVE, WALL-E, and the plant safe. EVE and WALL-E battle their way to a machine in the central area of the ship and when they place the plant in the machine, the ship immediately returns to Earth. The humans begin to get used to using their legs and Captain McCrea starts to teach everyone how to care for the plant. The final image shows that other plants have begun to grow across the garbage-filled landscape.

Once again, this science fiction narrative uses the trope of corporate 'evil-doing,' technology beyond human control, and humankind's neglectful indifference to explore issues of social justice including care of the environment and the human spirit. Interestingly, an anthropomorphic robot displays the spiritual transcendence of humans, making the point more powerfully. The film provides a balance between useful and malevolent technology as embodied in WALL-E and AUTO. The film is not anti-technology per se, but explores human responsibility and accountability for the technology we create. Furthermore, the issues of consumption and waste are quite explicit and, though depicted in a humorous and exaggerated manner, provide strong images for a potential future that endangers humanity's survival.

Self-Empowerment and Free Will

Many of the films discussed above explore how characters empower themselves to change their lives and meet the challenges presented by society and their own choices. Increasingly, science fiction films overtly examine the themes of self-empowerment and free will. In a global environment of progressively expanding techno-scientific developments, science fiction films are exploring the sense of powerlessness on the part of humans: the sensibility that our technology controls us, not the other way around. Within this theme lies the tension between techno-scientific rationalism and human transcendence, demonstrating that the twenty-first century is still working through the issues first expressed during the Protestant Reformation.

A few significant films in this category of examining self-empowerment and free will include Terry Gilliam's *Brazil* (1985), Ridley Scott's *Blade Runner* (1982), Stephen Spielberg's *Minority Report* (2002), Alex Proyas's *Dark City* (2001), the Wachowski Brothers' *The Matrix* trilogy (1999–2003), and George Nolfi's *The Adjustment Bureau* (2011). At the core of each of these films is *choice*. The characters in these films are caught in societal traps founded on embedded techno-science that influence the present and the trajectory of their future. They are seemingly powerless to determine their own fates; they are forced followers. Only through the realization of their own agency in opposition to social norms and legitimate authority do they exercise their right to choose, thus substantiating the prerogative of humanity's free will, as well as their leadership potential.

Importantly, the catalyst for reclaiming the power to determine one's own destiny in all of these films is love. Love is a basic human emotion that crosses cultural and class boundaries. In many ways, the ability to love is a singular quality that defines being human. Love allows for reaching beyond one's self to embrace others, including other people, robots, and the planet. The films discussed here explore the concept of love in various ways to demonstrate how human agency is empowered by this emotion. For example, in *Blade Runner*, Deckard finds himself falling in love with a replicant, which changes his attitudes toward cyborgs and their entitlement to self-determination, allowing them to leave an urban dystopia. In *Dark City*,

John Murdoch is able to stay focused on resisting the aliens because of his love for his wife. In *The Adjustment Bureau*, David Norris fights back against the angels who are trying to design his future because of his love for Elise. Neo makes the choice of saving Trinity because he loves her more than the human race, though this choice ultimately saves humanity, in *The Matrix* trilogy.

Love. Self-empowerment. Free will. Choice. Modern science fiction narratives explore these eschatological qualities, suggesting science fiction narratives are continuing to work through the tension of our place in the cosmos and our capacity for integrating the technology we create in a way that upholds the dignity of the individual and provides for the betterment of society. The function of these films is to warn against total reliance on our technology, but, as succinctly expressed in *The Matrix Reloaded*, to understand that we benefit from this technology also. As Ruppersberg (1990) noted, the viewpoint of science fiction film toward science and technology can be confusing as "it views them as redemptive forces that can lift humanity out of the muck and mire of its own biological forces. On the other hand, it sees them as potentially destructive forces, inimical to humanity" (p. 32). Desire and fear still rule. Yet, both themes can be instructive to the ways in which spectators create meaning and enact change. The key is not to lose our humanity and our ability to choose our own destiny because we have allowed technology to usurp our agency; our rational nature should not displace our spiritual nature, but find an optimum balance.

The alternative futures discussed in the films above clearly demonstrate the power of science fiction films through cognitive estrangement to change attitudes and behaviors about social justice issues within individuals, which potentially allows for broader social change. Issues of race, class privilege, stewardship of the environment, and self-empowerment are significant matters for modern societies and the people who participate in these systems. The failure of social systems to provide equitable, safe, and clean environments where individuals can maintain their hopes and pursue their dreams is not only a possibility, but also a reality for many humans on Earth.

Narratives, in general, and science fiction narratives in particular, are exceptional means for developing epistemological and ontological understandings. These narratives accomplish this by presenting alternatives and exploring 'the big stuff' in ways that engage the imaginations and the emotions of viewers. There exists a greater potential for harnessing the power of science fiction narratives and realizing the full function of these narratives within society and for the understanding of leadership. They challenge viewers to look at issues in new ways through the eyes of the characters and experience the challenges and triumphs of those characters. More importantly, the characters provide strategies for creating individual and social change. Although these tactics usually include insurrection or defying legitimate authority, the critical notion is that we each have the capacity, if not the obligation, to order our world in an ethical manner. Herein is the significance of the practicality of science fiction films. They are useful in presenting situations for discussion and reflection. By engaging the hearts and minds of viewers, they have the ability to transform attitudes and modify behaviors. They can be educational and developmental objects that help to create our values, beliefs, and norms and are deserving of greater review within leadership studies.

References

Butler, A. M. (2011). Postmodernism, Postmodernity and the Postmodern: Telling Local Stories at the End of Time. In Sawyer, A. and Wright, P. (eds.) *Teaching Science Fiction*. Hampshire, UK: Palgrave MacMillan.

Csicsery-Ronay, Jr., I. (2008). *The Seven Beauties of Science Fiction*. Middletown, CT: Wesleyan University Press.

Curtis, C. P. (2010). *Postapocalyptic Fiction and the Social Contract: We'll Not Go Home Again*. Lanham, MD: Rowman & Littlefield.

Heifetz, R. A. (1994). *Leadership Without Easy Answers*. Cambridge, MA: Belknap Press of Harvard University.

Huczynski, A., and Buchanan, D. (2004). Theory from fiction: A narrative process perspective on the pedagogical use of feature film. *Journal of Management Education,* 28 (6), 707–726.

Jackson, B., and Parry, K. (2008). *A Very Short, Fairly Interesting and Reasonably Cheap Book About Studying Leadership*. Thousand Oaks, CA: Sage.

Kidd, D. (2007). Harry Potter and the functions of popular culture. *The Journal of Popular Culture*, 40 (1), 69–89.

Kuhn, A. (1990). *Alien Zone: Cultural Theory and Contemporary Science Fiction Cinema*. New York: Verso.

Nelson, D. L., and Quick, J. C. (2015). *Organizational Behavior*. 4th Ed. Stamford, CT: Cengage.

Northouse, P. G. (2007). *Leadership Theory and Practice*. 4th Ed. Thousand Oaks, CA: Sage.

Oatley, K. (1999). Why fiction may be twice as true as fact: Fiction as cognitive and emotional stimulation. *Review of General Psychology*, 3 (2), 101–117.

Palmer, R. E. (1969). *Hermeneutics: Interpretation Theory in Schleiermacher, Dilthey, Heidegger, and Gadamer*. Evanston, IL: Northwestern University Press.

Roberts, A. (2007). *The History of Science Fiction*. New York: Palgrave Macmillan.

Roberts, A. (2009). The Copernican Revolution. In Bould, M., Butler, A. M., Roberts, A., and Vint, S. (eds.) *The Routledge Companion to Science Fiction*. London: Routledge.

Ruppersberg, H. (1990). The Alien Messiah. In Kuhn, A. (ed.) *Alien Zone: Cultural Theory and Contemporary Science Fiction Cinema*. New York: Verso.

Sinclair, A. (2007). *Leadership for the Disillusioned: Moving Beyond Myths and Heroes to Leadership that Liberates*. Crows Nest, NSW: Allen & Unwin.

Sontag, S. (1976). The Imagination of Disaster. In Rose, M. (ed.) *Science Fiction: A Collection of Critical Essays*. Englewood Hills, NJ: Prentice-Hall.

Suvin, D. (1976). On the Poetics of the Science Fiction Genre. In Rose, M. (ed.) *Science Fiction: A Collection of Critical Essays*. Englewood Hills, NJ: Prentice-Hall.

Suvin, D. (1977/2010). *Defined by a Hollow: Essays on Utopia, Science Fiction and Political Epistemology*. Bern, Switzerland: Peter Lang.

30

Media Portrayals

From Leadership Cults to Celebrity Politicians[1]

Maja Šimunjak and John Street

Introduction

This chapter is about how various media represent leadership, in particular political leadership. Why might this be important, either for the specific case of politicians or for leadership more generally? We suggest that there are three main reasons.

First, in the case of political leadership in democratic regimes, media representations are assumed to be vital to electoral success. Managing representation, and by implication reputation, is seen as key to winning office or retaining it. The army of media advisers (or 'spin doctors') that are now part of the leadership entourage is testimony to this (Franklin, 2004; Jones, 1995).

Second and more broadly, such developments are themselves symptomatic of wider trends in which the traditional sources of party loyalty (class, community, family, religion, etc.) are increasingly attenuated. Other ways have to be found to attract voters, and one of these is the 'personality' of the leader (Swanson and Mancini, 1996). He or she is required to embody and represent the party. This is a process that depends on the creation of media images that capture the leader's 'character'. Media are taken to be intrinsically linked to the constitution and communication of the persona adopted by the leader.

Third, the focus on leaders and their media presence is further sustained by governmental politics. Many democratic regimes are marked by an increasing 'presidentialization' of political leadership (Poguntke and Webb, 2005; Webb and Poguntke, 2013). This describes the concentration of political power with the leader, and the downplaying of cabinets and other decision-making bodies. As the *Financial Times*'s political commentator wrote of the UK system: 'the government of the day is a magnification of the prime minister's character' (Ganesh, 2015). Even allowing for the journalistic hyperbole, such arguments underline the importance of media. It matters for citizens to know what kind of leader they have or might have. And media are their source of knowledge.

So for these three reasons, among others, it is apparent that political leadership is intimately tied to media. It is, however, one thing to note the increasing dependence of political leadership on media. It is quite another to ask how that relationship operates: that is, how media contribute to, as well as reflect, the exercise of leadership.

One of the obvious starting points is to ask how media represent leaders. What images, narratives and frames are used in mediated discourse about leaders and leadership? How do audiences and readers get to see and imagine their leaders? Research into this has taken a variety of forms. It has led to comparisons between the media representation of male and female leaders (Norris, 1997; Van Zoonen, 2005), and between coverage that focuses on personality rather than on policy (Langer, 2011; Stanyer, 2007). It has also compared media and political systems to establish whether coverage of leaders is dependent on either system (Stanyer, 2013), or whether for example leaders are differently represented in authoritarian and democratic regimes (Šimunjak, 2014).

Representation, though, is not the only issue. There is the further question as to whether the coverage matters. A measure of this is how citizens' judgement of leaders is determined by the coverage received by those leaders. Political leaders clearly act on the assumption that how they appear matters to their electoral success, but such assumptions may be wrong. Experimental research has indicated that the framing of leaders does indeed matter to the way that they are viewed (Cappella and Jamieson, 1997).

Media scholars and others have also highlighted the different styles of leadership that have been adopted as a result of media dependence (Corner and Pels, 2003). One symptom of this has been the emergence of the 'celebrity politician'. This has taken many guises (Marsh et al., 2010; West and Orman, 2003), but two serve to illustrate the phenomenon. The first is the rise of figures from popular culture and entertainment who assume the guise of political leadership, and who trade on their fame and their fans to establish legitimacy. Figures like Bono, George Clooney and Madonna all fit this category. The other version is the traditional politician who borrows from popular culture, either in the form of endorsements or platforms (the chat show), to validate their leadership claims. Studying how such figures operate, and how the media is intrinsic to their operation, provides a further insight into the role of media in political leadership.

Among the more famous of the 'celebrity politicians' are Ronald Reagan and Arnold Schwarzenegger, people who moved from Hollywood into political office. Besides being representative of the celebrity leader, they are also symbolic of something else: how leadership is imagined and evaluated. Popular conceptions of leadership, and particularly of 'good' and 'bad' leaders, are not simple products of performance or of media reporting of that performance. Politics is an art as much as a science, and it is a performative art (Alexander, 2011; Hajer and Uttermark, 2008). What is to be performed and the manner of its performance derive in part from popular culture, from how citizens imagine and understand leadership. The kind of roles that Reagan and Schwarzenegger played in the movies – the cowboy, the Terminator – were not incidental to their leadership: they were intrinsic to them. How works of fiction construe and construct leadership matters, as do the narratives that attach to it. Both are important to what political leadership entails in the modern world.

In this chapter, we explore these themes further. We begin by looking at how political leadership has been represented in news reporting, particularly in relation to ideas of 'personality', 'persona' and 'personalization'. We then turn to the fictional representation of leadership and the phenomenon of the celebrity politician. In this combined approach, we hope to indicate how media and leadership are linked. We would further contend that, while our focus is on political leadership in democratic settings, our analysis might apply equally to leadership in authoritarian regimes and to leadership more generally.

News Media and Leaders: The Rise of Personalization?

The media have focused on political leaders in their coverage of politics since their early days. A simple explanation for this is that, from the media perspective, individuals are seen as newsworthy. In one of the first studies of news values, Johan Galtung and Mari Holmboe Ruge (1965) claimed that the media invariably focus on individuals, as opposed to structures and processes. News is what individuals do; it is not the shifts in class relations or routine institutional practices. Subsequent studies of news values have continued to conclude that the media focuses primarily on individual political actors, and sometimes their personae, at the expense of collectives and structures (Campus, 2010; Kriesi, 2011; Mazzoleni, 1987; Stromback, 2008; Takens et al., 2013).

Current concern with the 'mediatization of politics' (Hjarvard, 2013; Esser and Stromback, 2014) has led to the view that political leaders are nowadays even more media visible than they were before, while political issues and collectives have been further marginalized. The attention is not only focused on leaders' professional acts and qualities, but on their private lives as well. The increased media visibility of political leaders is usually referred to as the 'personalization of mediated political communication' (Balmas and Sheafer, 2013; Downey and Stanyer, 2010; Stanyer, 2007; Van Aelst et al., 2011), although it has also been characterized more broadly as the 'personalization of politics' (Balmas et al., 2014; Karvonen, 2010; Langer, 2011; Maier and Adam, 2010).

One of the reasons why scholars started to examine politicians' media representation is the perceived discrepancy between what *should* be the role of political leaders in politics and their *real* role and its *media representation*. Jean Blondel (2005, 2014) argues that Western European party theory has tended to ignore the role of political leaders in studying politics until the last few decades, partly as a response to the role that leaders were seen as playing in the prelude to, during and after the Second World War. He notes that:

> not only has political leadership ostensibly led to horrible developments in countries hitherto described as 'civilized', in Europe in particular, but the emergence of new countries after the Second World War has been associated with atrocities and graft on a huge scale seemingly stemming from actions of leaders.
>
> *(2014: 705)*

Consequently, according to Blondel, Western European party theory during these periods treated political leaders as 'aberrations' (2005: 4).

The centrality accorded to leaders in the authoritarian and totalitarian regimes of the twentieth century led Western political actors and scholars alike to argue that strong political leaders were incompatible (and inconsistent) with democratic systems, and that the focus should be put on political collectives, e.g. parties and cabinets/executives (Kane et al., 2009). Although, it should be noted that there are also scholars who argue that strong leaders are necessary in an unpredictable, globalized world (e.g. Bjerling, 2012; Manin, 1997). They think that leaders and their personae can help voters feel better represented, more interested and engaged in politics (e.g. Garzia, 2011; Kruikemeier et al., 2013). Against this background, scholars became increasingly aware of the rise of the new, highly mediated leaders. As they did so, their attention fell upon the need to explain this rise in media visibility, to understand its form and to analyse its effects.

Representing Leaders

Research into how political leaders are represented in the news media can be seen as focusing on three major themes. First, the extent to which news reporting can be seen as leader centred: that is, focused on political leaders at the expense of political collectives (such as the party or the cabinet) or political issues. The second major theme concerns the extent to which, and ways in which, the leaders' private personae, their personal qualities and private life, are prominent in mediated content. And finally, there is a significant body of research that looks into the role that gender plays in politicians' media representation. The main focus here is on differences and similarities between the ways in which female and male politicians are represented in news media.

In spite of this considerable scholarly interest in the role of political leaders in news reporting and the growth of empirical evidence, questions remain as to how universal is the personalization phenomenon and what factors account for it. This gap in our knowledge can be ascribed to the problems with studying the personalization of political communication. In the first instance, there is no widespread consensus on how 'personalization' should be conceptualized. There has, however, been an emerging consensus that personalization is a multifaceted phenomenon which involves at least two dimensions. One dimension is associated with the increasing emphasis on politicians as individuals at the expense of political collectives, and hence its labelling as 'personalization', 'individualization' or 'presidentialization' (Poguntke and Webb, 2005; Rahat and Sheafer, 2007; Van Aelst et al., 2011). The other dimension can be seen as concerned with communicating information associated with the political leader's private sphere, and has been called the privatization of politics, the politicization of private personae or intimization (Holtz-Bacha, 2004; Langer, 2011; Stanyer, 2013).

Conceptualizing personalization, though, is not the only challenge that scholars face. Operationalizing the term is a problem too, especially when it comes to research that focuses on how a leader's personality, and especially their private persona, is represented in the media. Some scholars concentrate only on the mediated visibility of a leader's private life; others focus on the leader's private qualities. The main problem stems from inconsistencies in how a leader's private persona is conceptualized and operationalized. Much research fails to explain what is meant by the 'private sphere', 'private life' or 'private qualities' (for notable exceptions see Langer, 2011; Stanyer, 2013). Consequently, given the lack of consensus about the key terms, comparison of national case studies provides limited evidence of the extent to which, and ways in which, the personalization phenomenon has spread across different societies.

To establish whether we are dealing with a universal phenomenon, or whether there are significant variations between countries and systems, it is, however, important to use a comparative approach. Despite the advantages of the comparative approach, such studies are very rare. Apart from problems of agreement over the key terms, difficulties also lie in acquiring access to comparable datasets, and the language barriers which make cross-national studies of media representation of political leaders challenging.

Comparative Studies of the Representation of Leaders

Nonetheless, comparative studies do provide important indications of the state of the relationship between leadership and the media. There is evidence that political leaders have become increasingly prominent in news reporting in the past few decades in established, Western democracies. Russell Dalton and Martin Wattenberg (2000) investigated whether there is an increase in focus on leaders (as opposed to parties) in the US, France, the UK, Austria and Canada. They analysed newspaper campaign coverage from the 1950s to the 1990s, comparing the ratio of candidate to party mentions cross-temporally and cross-nationally. They revealed that over time the number of occasions on which a candidate is mentioned outnumbered the mentions made of their parties in all countries, but with a significant difference emerging between presidential and parliamentary systems. In presidential systems, such as in the US and France, the ratio of candidate to party mentions was four times higher than in parliamentary systems (the UK, Austria and Canada).[2]

However, a more recent comparison of leader-centred news reporting in the UK and Germany calls for caution in drawing conclusions about the universality of this phenomenon. Christina Holtz-Bacha *et al.* (2014) studied mediated visibility of British and German political leaders and parties in the 2009 and 2010 general elections. They found that news reporting in the UK was indeed leader-centred, meaning that the media mentioned political leaders to a greater extent than their parties, while the same was not true for Germany. The German media, by contrast, reported their 2009 general elections by focusing more on political parties than leaders. Hence, it would be wrong to assume that political leaders are central figures in the communication of politics in all Western societies.

The Media and Leaders' Behaviour

Does leader-centred news reporting affect the behaviour of leaders themselves? Some scholars think so. Analysts speak of politics being 'colonized' (Meyer, 2002) or 'mediatized' (Mazzoleni and Schulz, 1999; Stromback, 2008). In both cases, the assumption is that politicians are forced to adapt their political behaviour and style of communication to conform with 'media logic'. It is only by doing this, the argument runs, that they can be accommodated by the media and reach voters/audiences, who have become accustomed to media forms of communication. It is claimed that politicians have internalized media conventions and aesthetics in adopting media logic (Corner and Pels, 2003; Stromback, 2008).

Key to this process of adaptation has been 'personalization' (Kriesi, 2011; Mazzoleni, 1987; Stromback, 2008; Takens *et al.*, 2013). Politicians have pursued a personalized form of communication because this is what the media expect or require. The politicians put the focus on themselves, rather than on their parties, because the media put the spotlight on them as individuals (Stromback, 2008).

Despite the plausibility of such arguments, there is, in fact, little empirical evidence for the suggestion that politicians' communication has become more personalized over time, or that personalized media reporting is what has caused the change. In reviewing research into personalization, Michaela Maier and Silke Adam (2010) found very few studies that examined changes in the extent to which political actors have focused upon their individual personae in their communication. Indeed, it may be that leader-centred political communication was initiated by the politicians, rather than the media. In Germany, for example, research has revealed that, while there had been a rise in leader-centred media reporting from 1990 to 2002, this represented the *reaction* of media to the party leaders' campaigns (Schulz and Zeh, 2005). Similarly, findings from an analysis of the UK's 1992 general election campaign coverage suggest that British media responded to the political parties' communication strategies. Holli Semetko *et al.* (1994) found that party leaders were the most prominent political actors in both press and television election coverage, largely due to the parties' leader-oriented campaign communication strategies. Nonetheless, it is, again, impossible to make any generalizations from this scarce and context-specific data.

Leaders and Their Personal Lives: Who Are Our Leaders Sleeping With?

Whoever is responsible for the focus on leaders, the question remains as to whether the focus is more and more on the private lives of politicians. As we have already mentioned, it is often suggested that the media increasingly focus on matters that were typically thought to be 'private', and in doing so politics is thereby 'trivialized' or 'dumbed down' (Franklin, 2004). Others, who also see the rise of personalized communication, argue that it actually serves to enhance democracy by engaging viewers and readers (Garzia, 2011; Langer, 2011). Recent studies seem to support both points of view. In the Netherlands, Sanne Kruikemeier *et al.* (2013) conducted experiments which revealed that personalized communication increased citizens' political involvement. Meanwhile Nael Jebril *et al.*'s (2013) study, which relied on data gathered from a panel survey of respondents from the UK, Spain and Denmark, came to the conclusion that exposure to information about politicians' private lives increased cynicism among citizens in these three countries.

Comparative research into political leaders' private personae in news media has also revealed that there are significant variations in the media attention given to private lives and personal qualities. James Stanyer (2013) conducted one of the first, and most comprehensive, comparative studies of the visibility of political leaders' private lives. He did this by concentrating on the number of press references to the leader's birthday, to their spouses and to their holidays. He also tracked the number of books published about the leaders' private lives in the 1990s and 2000s. He concluded that there was an increase in the media visibility of leaders' private lives in the US, the UK and France, and to some extent in Australia. On the other hand, in Italy and Spain, similar trends were visible but very weak, while in Germany there was a decline in such coverage. Holtz-Bacha *et al.*'s (2014) study confirms these differences between the mediated visibility of British and German politicians' private lives. They showed that British media put more emphasis on their leaders' private lives and qualities in the 2010 general election than did the German media in their 2009 elections.

Interestingly, another comparative study of how/whether leaders' private lives appear in news media did not find that French politicians' private lives have become significantly more visible in the last few decades. Bas den Herder (2013) found that British and Dutch newspapers mentioned their leaders' private lives in around 24 per cent more interviews in 2010 than in 1990, while the equivalent increase in the French press was only 3 per cent. Specifically, in the UK the proportion of interviews which referred to politicians' private lives rose from 16 to 39.4 per cent, and in the Netherlands from 9.4 to 33.3 per cent. France had the lowest figures: 8.6 per cent in 1990; 11.4 per cent in 2010.

Den Herder also claims that one of the reasons why politicians' private lives feature in news media across Western democracies is because political leaders use them strategically to humanize and normalize their public image. His analysis revealed that 'politicians willingly disclose details about their family life to portray themselves as authentic people who spend time with their loved ones' (den Herder, 2013: 476). However, other research suggests that the willingness of political leaders to reveal details of their private lives differs between countries. Liesbeth Hermans and Maurice Vergeer (2013) examined the type of information that politicians from 17 European Union countries shared on their websites in the 2009 elections for the European Parliament, and came to the conclusion that there are significant differences between countries in the extent and type of personal information that political leaders communicated. According to this study, British politicians were more willing to disclose information about their home and family life and personal preferences than were Dutch and French politicians. However, what was most striking about this research is that politicians from the new democracies – the post-communist countries – shared the most personal information. Two possible explanations have been offered for this finding. On the one hand, it was suggested that such politicians needed to communicate personal information to bond with voters, in circumstances where they lacked the professional experiences of European politics. Another explanation focused on the historical political communication practices of these countries, where there was a tradition of glorifying political leaders. It was possible that 'practices of presenting professional feats are still engrained in post-communist cultures' (Hermans and Vergeer, 2013: 83).

The explanation for personalization in established Western democracies is different. It has been argued that politicians started to disclose more information about themselves because the media required it of them (Jamieson, 1988; Meyrowitz, 1985). Kathleen Jamieson (1988) noted that in the pre-television era US presidents did not mention their families, their pets or their childhood, and she claims this changed only with the introduction of television. Joshua Meyrowitz (1985) also sees television as the factor driving the rise in personalized political communication. He claims that, due to the television effect, disclosing private information has become routine because '*without* such intimate revelations [the politicians] seem stuffy and unrealistic' (1985: 179; italics in original).

However, while this might be true for the US, evidence from some Western European countries suggests otherwise. There it was the political leaders, not the media, that put the emphasis on the private realm. Traditionally, the French media were reluctant to reveal details of a politician's private life (Kuhn, 2004). It was Nicolas Sarkozy who changed this in 2007, when he revealed to the media his love life, hobbies, vacations, family and insecurities (Campus, 2010). Something similar might be observed in the United Kingdom. Despite the UK's vibrant tabloid sector and the absence of protection for privacy in common law (Deacon, 2004), it has been argued that the attention paid to politicians' private lives has been derived largely from changes in the leaders' political strategies. Based on a longitudinal content analysis of British daily newspapers and a historical qualitative analysis of politicians' communication strategies, Ana Inés Langer (2011) suggested that it was the political actors who initiated the focus on these private issues. However, she remained tentative in her conclusions, aware that no causality had been established.

What these comparative studies reveal is that there are important differences in the extent to which political leaders' private personae feature in news media, and that this has to do with the willingness of politicians from different countries to use their private lives for political purposes. Despite the temptation to attribute the changes to 'mediatization' and other such processes, we should be wary about doing so. Rather, it seems that leaders are more inclined to use the media to secure their leadership claims, as opposed to having the media dictate their behaviour.

It should, however, be noted that the reason why politicians' private personae are in the media spotlight might be much more complex. Specifically, recent research showed that this phenomenon is connected with a range of both political- and media-related factors. Several studies that have employed fuzzy-set, qualitative, comparative analysis have revealed that the focus on politicians and their personae is connected with factors such as the type of political system, size of tabloid sector, politician's age and ideological position (Downey and Stanyer, 2010, 2013; Stanyer, 2013).

Gender and the Representation of Leaders

Our argument is not that the media have no independent effect upon the conduct of contemporary political leadership. Studies examining the ways in which politicians are represented in news media frequently reveal how gender differences affect (and are affected by) reporting. Differences in the representation of female and male politicians establish 'important things about the relations between gender, power and politics' (Garcia-Blanco and Wahl-Jorgensen, 2012: 422). Female politicians are, for example, sometimes represented as less capable of performing, and less suitable to perform, leadership roles than their male colleagues.

The research on media representation of women leaders has revealed comparable findings across Western democracies, showing that the coverage of female politicians is typically centred on their private personae, especially their appearance, lifestyle, fashion sense, family life, and maternal and marital status (Everitt, 2003; Mavin *et al.*, 2010; Wasburn and Wasburn, 2011; Van Zoonen, 2006). In addition, the female politicians' private sphere is frequently politicized in such a way as to connect their appearance and marital status to their competence to perform public duties (Heflick and Goldenberg, 2009; Mavin *et al.*, 2010; Muir, 2005; Wasburn and Wasburn, 2011).

That said, comparative studies again reveal more differences than similarities, and paint a more nuanced picture of the representation of female politicians. For example, Inaki Garcia-Blanco and Karin Wahl-Jorgensen (2012) have examined how media in France, Italy, Spain and the UK reported the first majority female government in Spain. They found considerable diversity in how these women were represented. The appointment of female ministers was reported as a 'sign of normality' in French newspapers (2012: 428), while Italian newspapers offered a more conservative view. The French press focused on Carme Chacon, who was pregnant when appointed minister, and were critical of the fact that she was travelling to Afghanistan. The Italian press portrayed her as an 'uncaring mother' (2012: 434) and even questioned her 'suitability to be a mother' (2012: 437). Part of the Spanish media displayed similar prejudices. In the UK and Spain, there were papers that focused on topics such as gender equality, quota systems and the role of women in politics, and there were others that reported on the women's physical appearance and dress sense.

Another aspect of the reporting of female leaders is the discussion of their emotions. Ingrid Bachmann (2009) reports that there are differences in how news media report women politicians' displays of emotion. Her textual analysis of election coverage in Germany, Chile and the US revealed that Angela Merkel's emotions were often, but briefly, reported in German newspapers, while the emotions of Chile's Michelle Bachelot were a frequent topic of her news coverage, and were used to portray her as different from her male colleagues (as both emotional and charming). In the US, Hillary Clinton's emotional management was also frequently mentioned, but almost always in a negative way. She was portrayed as aggressive and lacking empathy. In this case, Clinton was seen as being *too like* her male colleagues.

Bachmann (2009: 23) ascribes the diversity of media representations to 'culturally bound differences', and does not acknowledge that the differences might also be attributed to differences in the personalities of the political leaders and their communication strategies. By contrast, Van Zoonen (2006: 295) argues, based on her analysis of European female leaders, that Angela Merkel and Tarja Harlonen 'both present a thoroughly political and professional persona to the public and rigidly conceal their private lives' because they do not want to give media reasons to focus on their private personae. The conclusion that Van Zoonen (2006: 299) draws is that 'women – willingly or not – may end as the last keepers of traditional modernist ideas of politics as a separate sphere in which rational actors and representatives publicly deliberate and decide on the course of society'.

This short overview of personalization research not only points to the fact that there are as many differences as similarities between Western countries in the ways in which political leaders are portrayed in news media, but also to the fact that most of this scholarship is Western-centric. We know little about how, if at all, personalized reporting in non-Western systems affected the ways in which politicians were represented in their media. There is also a gap in our knowledge about how citizens are affected by news media coverage of leaders in these countries, and about how the development of personalized media reporting might best be explained. Hence, while there is limited, and often contradictory, evidence available for established, Western democracies, there is a lack of evidence about how political leaders are represented in non-Western countries.

From News to Entertainment

In reporting on the relationship of media and leadership, we have, until now, concentrated on the 'real world' of political leadership and news reporting. But as we argued at the beginning, this is to consider only one, albeit very important, dimension of the relationship. The worlds of politics and entertainment, of political reporting and showbiz gossip, are not always discrete. Indeed, they are increasingly entwined (Corner and Pels, 2003; Jones, 2005; Richardson *et al.*, 2013; Street *et al.*, 2013; Van Zoonen, 2005). One of the more obvious examples of their entanglement emerges in the phenomenon of the celebrity politician.

The Celebrity Political Leader

The phenomenon of the 'celebrity politician' has attracted considerable attention in recent years. Typically, it has been associated with the political role assumed by stars of the entertainment industry. Towards the end of the last century, it was hard to avoid images of Bono, the lead singer of the band U2, in the company of world leaders. He was pictured with presidents, prime ministers and even popes. Following events such as Live Aid in 1985, Bono had come to be seen as the representative of global compassion, able to speak on behalf of the poor and the destitute (Browne, 2013). *Time* (2 March 2002) magazine put him on its cover with the headline 'Can Bono Save The World?' In 2005, at Live Aid's successor event Live 8, Bono and his co-activist Bob Geldof claimed that they had persuaded the G8 leaders to revise their policy on developing country debt (see: http://www.live8live.com).

Whether these rock stars actually persuaded the G8 to change tack remains a contentious issue. Many factors were in play, and it is difficult to disentangle them, and to identify the specific contribution made by the musicians (Street, 2012). What cannot be disputed is that the stars of popular culture have *appeared* to act as political representatives, and to lead their fans and a wider public to adopt causes and concerns that might have otherwise been neglected. Bono and Geldof are but two examples. Others include George Clooney, Angelina Jolie, Russell Brand and Sean Penn. Indeed, the 'celebrity politician', as we have defined it so far, is not a recent phenomenon. It has been with us for many years. During the 1960s, actors such as Jane Fonda, Donald Sutherland, Robert Redford and Warren Beatty spoke against the war in Vietnam. And before them, Charlie Chaplin and Paul Robeson spoke out against government (Chambers, 2006). Nor is it a phenomenon confined to the Anglo-American world. In Latin America and Africa, musicians and others have come to assume the guise of political leader (Peddie, 2011; Wheeler, 2013)

Accompanying the rise of celebrities as politicians has been a change in the way in which traditional political leaders present themselves. The trend towards the personalization of leadership, which we described earlier, can be seen as another form of celebrity politics. In order to reach an increasingly disengaged or disillusioned electorate, politicians have not just sought to expose and highlight their personality and their personal life. They have also adopted platforms and modes of communication that derive directly from popular culture and popular entertainment (Crouch, 2004; Meyrowitz, 1985).

This has typically meant appearing on television shows that allow, indeed require, revelations of the personal. In the UK, David Cameron, just after he had secured the leadership of the Conservative Party in 2005, appeared on the *Jonathan Ross Show* on BBC TV. He was the first politician to be a guest. His predecessors had been the usual chat show mix of film and television stars, musicians and comedians. The relatively unknown Cameron saw Ross's programme as an opportunity to present himself to a wider (and younger) audience than would have watched a standard political interview. In exchange, he had to answer questions, not about policy and party ideology, but about his personal life. At one point, it emerged that as a teenager he had had a poster of Margaret Thatcher on his wall. Ross asked whether she was, therefore, the object of Cameron's sexual fantasies. The question was rather awkwardly laughed off by the discomfited prospective prime minister.

Mrs Thatcher had herself appeared on the talk show *Aspel & Company*, a much cosier precursor of Ross's. For her, this was an opportunity to present her 'softer' side: to indicate that there was more to her than the 'Iron Lady' (Cockerell, 1988). In the same vein, George W. Bush appeared with Oprah Winfrey, and Barack Obama with Ellen DeGeneres (he danced with the host before subjecting himself to her questions).

Behind these communication strategies, and their implications for how 'leadership' is represented and conveyed, is another process. This is the increasing reliance of leaders on those with expertise in the marketing of politics (Scammell, 2014). The underlying logic is that leaders and their parties need a 'brand' in order to convey what they represent quickly and accessibly. As Anthony Downs (1957) pointed out many years ago, acquiring detailed information about a leader's or party's policies is not rational for a voter who knows that their vote will count for little. A brand reduces the voter's information costs. If branding is key to political communication, then it follows that to do this successfully requires the advice and guidance of those with the relevant knowledge and skills. These people include advertising executives and marketing professionals, but also film and video directors. They help to blur the line between politics and popular entertainment, and to turn political leaders into performers and icons of the brand.

Key to such developments is the notion that media are central to the conduct of political leadership. And this in turn prompts the argument that political leaders have to follow the dictates of 'media logic', as opposed to 'political logic'; or that the former 'colonizes' the latter (Meyer, 2002). The modes of communication adopted or required by media are those that conform to the conventions of a medium consumed in a domestic setting, rather than in a debating chamber or public meeting (Silverstone, 1994). It requires a confessional mode of address rather than a declaratory one. Leadership, and the virtues associated with it, are filtered through the expectations and demands of the medium of its communication. This, in turn, affects how leadership is received and judged by citizen audiences (Richardson *et al.*, 2013).

'Role Models' and Narratives: Imagining Leadership

While the impact of media on the thoughts and actions of their readers and audiences remains a matter of much debate, it is increasingly apparent that it cannot be discounted as it once was. Citizens' understanding of the world and their responses to it are shaped, to a significant extent, by media representations (Newton and Brynin, 2001; Ladd and Lenz, 2009; Whiteley, 2011). Media's role in the representation and communication of political leadership is not simply that of providing a platform or space in which the politician operates. It provides ways of understanding what 'leadership' is supposed to be, and how we are to understand and evaluate 'leaders'.

The framing of political leaders in news reports as either principled or strategic actors can influence our response to them. Presenting them as strategic, as acting to maximize votes only, leads to cynicism among the electorate (Cappella and Jamieson, 1997). Something similar occurs (as we have noted) in the case of the representation of women political leaders, who, insofar as they are represented as breaking with tradition, are simultaneously burdened with expectations that are not felt by their male counterparts (Norris, 1997).

It is not just news representation that matters, however. Research has suggested that shows that bridge politics and entertainment – such as Jon Stewart's *Daily Show* – can inform citizens as (or more) effectively than straight news. Those who watch 'infotainment' programmes of this kind are shown to be more knowledgeable about, and more engaged in, politics than those who do not (Baym, 2005). And even works of pure fiction, such as *The West Wing*, can provide voters with the resources to think about real world politics (Van Zoonen, 2005; Richardson *et al.*, 2013; Street *et al.*, 2013).

One of the implications of this evidence is that we need to take seriously the representation of political leadership in popular culture as much as in news and current affairs coverage. This might mean, on the one hand, being sensitive to how entertainment portrays leaders, and how the attributes of leadership are presented. In his mapping of the representation of politicians in British cinema 1944–1964, Steven Fielding (2008: 121) says that films tended to depict politicians 'as a group apart, preoccupied with advancing their own interests'. In research conducted in the UK, it was revealing to see how, when asked who, in the world of entertainment, would make a good prime minister, young people identified Jeremy Clarkson (*Top Gear*), Simon Cowell (*X Factor*) and Alan Sugar (*The Apprentice*) (Street *et al.*, 2013). (It might be rewarding to explore further how fictional leaders are portrayed and understood in these terms – from Dumbledore to the leaders of the warring factions in *Game of Thrones* or Frank Underwood in *House of Cards*.)

Key to appreciating how leadership is imagined in fiction is only partly about the character; it is also about the narrative in which they are located. In her surveys of popular cultural representations of politics, Liesbet Van Zoonen (2005; and Van Zoonen and Wring, 2012) has suggested that politics is typically portrayed – in fiction and fact – within a limited number of storylines. These include the quest, in which our hero strives for election, overcoming obstacles of various kinds en route; the conspiracy, where dark and malign forces design to thwart the ideals and ambitions of elected representatives; the bureaucracy, where the dead weight of administration thwarts the democratic will; and, finally, soap opera, where flawed but well-intentioned individuals strive to serve the people. In each of these narratives, leaders assume a different guise – from honourable success to innocent failure. And in these guises, they posit different attitudes or dispositions to leadership. Leaders might appear as warrior heroes or innocent dupes, as malign or benign. Van Zoonen's analysis chimes with that of Cappella and Jamieson's (1997) experiments with the framing (cynical vs principled) of politics and political leaders, to which we referred earlier.

The interplay between the fictional world and the 'real' world of political leadership is nicely illustrated by the leadership debates that accompanied the UK's 2010 general election campaign. Kay Richardson and her colleagues (2013: 138) write of these debates:

> by having the three major TV events at which three party leaders made their pitch alongside each other . . . the issue of leadership was projected with a new directness of comparative performance. The widely used analogy of the 'talent show' (*X Factor*) model, often employed disparagingly, but not always . . . made great imaginative play with the nature of the events.

This is suggestive of the way in which popular culture is used to understand and evaluate political leadership. One aspect of this is the recognition that political leadership has to be performed; it is art, and has to be evaluated as such.

The Art of Political Leadership

The 'art' of political leadership is not simply that of skilfully managing friends and foes, of winning elections or policy debates. It is about making and justifying claims to represent a people or a constituency. Such claims are not made on the basis of statistical data, but rather by the application of the imagination. The historian Frank Ankersmit (2002) has described political representation, and the role of leadership in it, as requiring an ability of 're-presenting' to voters a sense of themselves as 'the people'. Just as Benedict Anderson (2006) talked of nationalism as a form of 'imagined community', so representation is understood as involving an imagined people on whose behalf the politician acts. This requires the politician to be able to conjure up or evoke a sense of community to which voters are willing to subscribe. This is a cultural process as much as a political one.

The bond between leaders and those who follow them assumes a different guise by this analysis. 'Style', rather than statistics, becomes key. This is especially true of populist movements. Benjamin Moffitt and Simon Tormey (2014) argue that populism is to be understood in stylistic terms, rather than ideological ones. Populist leaders have to evoke their 'people' and the future that they can enjoy through rhetoric and gesture. The form of this rhetoric, and of the accompanying gestures, are shaped by the culture of communication in which they are expressed. Indeed, key to these views of political leadership is the suggestion that it involves cultural practice, and that these practices do not simply require the platforms offered by the media, but draw on the tropes, images and roles that media itself constructs and circulates. It is not obvious that this argument applies only to populism. Style, and hence media representation, may be key to all forms of leadership that seek the support of those to be led.

Conclusion

What we have argued in this chapter is that media are central to the way leadership is understood and enacted. We have suggested that it operates not just in representing the political leader, but in shaping the response to them. Moreover, we have argued that this process operates in both factual news and current affairs reporting, and in popular entertainment.

We have raised questions about the direction of the relationship, suggesting that it may owe as much to the strategies and tactics of leaders as it does to the demands and conventions of media. We have also pointed to how the differences in media and political systems point to the contingent factors at play. We should be wary of sweeping generalizations. At the same time, we would also emphasize the importance of studying political leaders in conjunction with the study of media representation and media processes.

What we have said has applied primarily to democratic political leadership, but we would contend that it applies also to leadership within authoritarian regimes. It applies too to leadership of social movements or unconventional political parties. We need to think only of the media reports devoted to the dress style of the Syriza leaders in the immediate aftermath of their electoral victory in early 2015. How they looked – the leather jackets and open-necked shirts – almost seemed as important as what they said.

It might be argued too that the account we offer here has application to other forms of leadership. All leaders are in the communication business. And as such, they are required to draw upon the conventions established by their mode of communication.

Notes

1 Acknowledgements: we are very grateful for the comments on an earlier version of this chapter that we received from Paul 't Hart and Toby James.
2 In the mid-1990s the ratio for the US and France was 5:6, while for the UK and Austria it was 1:3 and for Canada 1:6 (Dalton and Wattenberg, 2000: 52).

References

Alexander, J. (2011). *Performance and Power*. Cambridge: Polity.

Anderson, B. (2006). *Imagined Communities*. London: Verso.

Ankersmit, F. (2002). *Political Representation*. Stanford, CA: Stanford University Press.

Bachmann, I. (2009). Gender, Emotion, and Politics: A Comparison of National Press Coverage of Female Political Leaders' Emotional Management. Paper presented at the annual meeting of the International Communication Association. Chicago.

Balmas, M. and Sheafer, T. (2013). Leaders First, Countries After: Mediated Political Personalization in the International Arena. *Journal of Communication*, 63 (3), 454–475.

Balmas, M., Rahat, G., Sheafer, T. and Shenhav, S. R. (2014). Two Routes to Personalized Politics: Centralized and Decentralized Personalisation. *Party Politics*, 20 (2), 37–51.

Baym, G. (2005). The Daily Show: Discursive Integration and the Reinvention of Political Journalism. *Political Communication*, 22, 259–276.

Bjerling, J. (2012). *The Personalisation of Swedish Politics*. University of Gothenburg. Doctoral dissertation.

Blondel, J. (2005). The Links between Western European Parties and Their Supporters: The Role of Personalisation. *Occasional Papers*. Centre for the Study of Political Change. Available at: http://www.circap.org/uploads/1/8/1/6/18163511/occ_16.pdf.

Blondel, J. (2014). What Have We Learned? In R. A. W. Rhodes and P. 't Hart (eds.) *The Handbook of Political Leadership*. Oxford: Oxford University Press.

Browne, H. (2013). *The Frontman: Bono (In the Name of Power)*. London: Verso.

Campus, D. (2010). Mediatization and Personalization of Politics in Italy and France: The Cases of Berlusconi and Sarkozy. *The International Journal of Press/Politics*, 15 (2), 219–235.

Cappella, J. and Jamieson, K. (1997). *Spiral of Cynicism*. New York: Oxford University Press.

Chambers, C. (2006). *Here We Stand: Politics, Performers and Performance*. London: Nick Hern Books.

Cockerell, M. (1988). *Live from Number 10*. London: Faber & Faber.

Corner, J. and Pels, D. (eds.) (2003). *Media and the Restyling of Politics*. London: Sage.

Crouch, C. (2004). *Post-democracy*. Cambridge: Polity.

Dalton, R. J. and Wattenberg, M. P. (eds.) (2000). *Parties without Partisans: Political Change in Advanced Industrial Democracies*. Oxford: Oxford University Press.

Deacon, D. (2004). Politicians, Privacy and Media Intrusion in Britain. *Parliamentary Affairs*, 57 (1), 9–23.

Den Herder, B. (2013). Personal Questions, Political Answers. *Journalism Practice*, 7 (4), 465–480.

Downey, J. and Stanyer, J. (2010). Comparative Media Analysis: Why Some Fuzzy Thinking Might Help: Applying Fuzzy Set Qualitative Comparative Analysis to the Personalization of Mediated Political Communication. *European Journal of Communication*, 25 (4), 331–347.

Downey, J. and Stanyer, J. (2013). Exposing Politicians' Peccadilloes in Comparative Context: Explaining the Frequency of Political Sex Scandals in Eight Democracies Using Fuzzy Set Qualitative Comparative Analysis. *Political Communication*, 30 (3), 495–509.

Downs, A. (1957). *An Economic Theory of Democracy*. New York: Harper & Row.

Esser, F. and Stromback, J. (eds.) (2014). *Mediatization of Politics: Understanding the Transformation of Western Democracies*. Houndmills: Palgrave Macmillan.

Everitt, J. (2003). Media in the Maritimes: Do Female Candidates Face a Bias? *Atlantis*, 27 (2), 90–98.

Fielding, S. (2008). A Mirror for England? Cinematic Representations and Party Politics, circa 1944–1964. *Journal of British Studies*, 47 (1), 107–128.

Franklin, B. (2004). *Packaging Politics: Political Communications in Britain's Media Democracy* (Second edn.). London: Edward Arnold.

Galtung, J. and Ruge, M. H. (1965). The Structure of Foreign News. *Journal of Peace Research*, 2 (1), 64–91.

Ganesh, J. (2015). Policy Is Trivial – Personality Is Destiny. *Financial Times*, 30 March. Available at: http://www.ft.com/cms/s/0/93924b4c-d6c1-11e4-97c3-00144feab7de.html#axzz3XU3np6P0.

Garcia-Blanco, I. and Wahl-Jorgensen, K. (2012). The Discursive Construction of Women Politicians in the European Press. *Feminist Media Studies*, 12 (3), 422–441.

Garzia, D. (2011). The Personalization of Politics in Western Democracies: Causes and Consequences on Leader–Follower Relationships. *The Leadership Quarterly*, 22 (4), 697–709.

Hajer, M. and Uttermark, J. (2008). Performing Authority: Discursive Politics after the Assassination of Theo Van Gogh. *Public Administration*, 86 (1), 5–19

Hjarvard, S. (2013). *The Mediatization of Culture and Society*. London: Routledge.

Heflick, N. A. and Goldenberg, J. L. (2009). Objectifying Sarah Palin: Evidence that Objectification Causes Women to Be Perceived as Less Competent and Less Fully Human. *Journal of Experimental Social Psychology*, 45 (3), 598–601.

Hermans, L. and Vergeer, M. (2013). Personalisation in e-Campaigning: A Cross-National Comparison of Personalisation Strategies Used on Candidate Websites of 17 Countries in EP Elections 2009. *New Media & Society*, 15 (1), 72–92.

Holtz-Bacha, C. (2004). Germany: How the Private Life of Politicians Got into the Media. *Parliamentary Affairs*, 57 (1), 41–52.

Holtz-Bacha, C., Langer, A. I. and Merkle, S. (2014). The Personalization of Politics in Comparative Perspective: Campaign Coverage in Germany and the United Kingdom. *European Journal of Communication*, 29 (2), 153–170.

Jamieson, K. H. (1988). *Eloquence in an Electronic Age*. Oxford: Oxford University Press.

Jebril, N., Albaek, E. and de Vreese, C. H. (2013) Infotainment, Cynicism and Democracy: The Effects of Privatization vs Personalization in the News. *European Journal of Communication*, 28 (2), 105–121.

Jones, J. (2005). *Entertaining Politics: New Political Television and Civic Culture*. New York: Rowman & Littlefield.

Jones, N. (1995). *Soundbites and Spin Doctors*. London: Cassell.

Kane, J., Patapan, H. and 't Hart, P. (eds.) (2009). *Dispersed Democratic Leadership: Origins, Dynamics, and Implications*. Oxford: Oxford University Press.

Karvonen, L. (2010). Introduction. In L. Karvonen (ed.) *The Personalisation of Politics: A Study of Parliamentary Democracies*. Colchester: ECPR Press.

Kriesi, H. (2011). Personalization of National Election Campaigns. *Party Politics*, 18 (6), 825–844.

Kruikemeier, S., van Noort, G., Vliegenthart, R. and de Vreese, C. H. (2013). Getting Closer: The Effects of Personalized and Interactive Online Political Communication. *European Journal of Communication*, 28 (1), 53–66.

Kuhn, R. (2004). *Vive la difference?* The Mediation of Politicians' Public Images and Private Lives in France. *Parliamentary Affairs*, 57 (1), 24–40.

Ladd, J. and Lenz, G. (2009). Exploiting a Rare Communication Shift to Document the Persuasive Power of News. *American Journal of Political Science*, 53 (2), 394–410.

Langer, A. I. (2011). *The Personalisation of Politics in the UK: Mediated Leadership from Attlee to Cameron*. Manchester: Manchester University Press.

Maier, M. and Adam, S. (2010). Personalisation of Politics: A Critical Review and Agenda for Future Research. In C. T. Salmon (ed.) *Communication Yearbook 34*, pp. 212–257. Oxford: Routledge.

Manin, B. (1997). *The Principles of Representative Government*. Cambridge: Cambridge University Press.

Marsh, D., 't Hart, P. and Tindall, K. (2010). Celebrity Politics: The Politics of the Late Modernity. *Political Studies Review*, 8 (3), 322–340.

Mavin, S., Bryans, P. and Cunningham, R. (2010). Fed-Up with Blair's Babes, Gordon's Gals, Cameron's Cuties, Nick's Nymphets: Challenging Gendered Media Representations of Women Political Leaders. *Gender in Management: An International Journal*, 25 (7), 550–569.

Mazzoleni, G. (1987). Media Logic and Party Logic in Campaign Coverage: The Italian General Election of 1983. *European Journal of Communication*, 2 (1), 81–103.

Mazzoleni, G. and Schulz, W. (1999). 'Mediatization' of Politics: A Challenge for Democracy? *Political Communication*, 16 (3), 247–261.

Meyer, T. (2002). *Media Democracy: How the Media Colonize Politics*. Cambridge: Polity.

Meyrowitz, J. (1985). *No Sense Of Place*. Oxford: Oxford University Press.

Moffitt, B. and Tormey, S. (2014). Rethinking Populism: Politics, Mediatisation and Political Style. *Political Studies*, 62 (2), 381–397.

Muir, K. (2005). Media Darlings and Falling Stars: Celebrity and the Reporting of Political Leaders. *Westminster Papers in Communication and Culture*, 2 (2), 54–71.

Newton, K. and Brynin, K. (2001). The National Press and Party Voting in the UK. *Political Studies*, 49 (2), 265–285.

Norris, P. (ed.) (1997). *Women, Media, and Politics*. New York: Oxford University Press.

Peddie, I. (ed.) (2011). *Popular Music and Human Rights. Volume II: World Music*. Aldershot: Ashgate.

Poguntke, T. and Webb, P. (eds.) (2005). *The Presidentialization of Politics: A Comparative Study of Modern Democracies*. Oxford: Oxford University Press.

Rahat, G. and Sheafer, T. (2007). The Personalization(s) of Politics: Israel, 1949–2003. *Political Communication*, 24 (1), 65–80.

Richardson, K., Parry, K. and Corner, J. (2013). *Political Culture and Media Genre*. Houndmills: Palgrave Macmillan.

Scammell, M. (2014). *Consumer Democracy: The Marketing of Politics*. Cambridge: Cambridge University Press.

Schulz, W. and Zeh, R. (2005). The Changing Election Coverage of German Television. A Content Analysis: 1990–2002. *Communications*, 30 (4), 385–407.

Semetko, H., Scammell, M. and Nossiter, T. (1994). The Media's Coverage of the Campaign. In A. Heath, R. Jowell and J. Curtice (eds.) *Labour's Last Chance? The 1992 Election and Beyond*. Aldershot: Dartmouth.

Silverstone, R. (1994). *Television and Everyday Life*. London: Routledge.

Šimunjak, M. (2014). *The (de)personalisation of mediated political communication in communist and post-communist societies: The case of Croatia*. Doctoral thesis, University of East Anglia.

Stanyer, J. (2007). *Modern Political Communication: Mediated Politics in Uncertain Times*. Cambridge: Polity.

Stanyer, J. (2013). *Intimate Politics*. Cambridge: Polity.

Street, J. (2012). Do Celebrity Politics and Celebrity Politics Matter? *Political Studies Review*, 14 (3), 346–356.

Street, J., Inthorn, S. and Scott, M. (2013). *From Entertainment to Citizenship: The Politics of Popular Culture*. Manchester: Manchester University Press.

Stromback, J. (2008). Four Phases of Mediatization: An Analysis of the Mediatization of Politics. *The International Journal of Press/Politics*, 13 (3), 228–246.

Swanson, D. and Mancini, P. (1996). *Politics, Media, and Modern Democracy*. New York: Praeger.

Takens, J., van Atteveldt, W., van Hoof, A. and Kleinnijenhuis, J. (2013). Media Logic in Election Campaign Coverage. *European Journal of Communication*, 28 (3), 277–293.

Van Aelst, P., Sheafer, T. and Stanyer, J. (2011). The Personalization of Mediated Political Communication: A Review of Concepts, Operationalizations and Key Findings. *Journalism*, 13 (2), 203–220.

Van Zoonen, L. (2005). *Entertaining the Citizen*. New York: Rowman & Littlefield.

Van Zoonen, L. (2006). The Personal, the Political and the Popular: A Woman's Guide to Celebrity Politics. *European Journal of Cultural Studies*, 9 (3), 287–301.

Van Zoonen, L. and Wring, D. (2012). Trends in Political Television Fiction in the UK: Themes, Characters and Narratives, 1965–2009. *Media, Culture and Society*, 34 (3), 263–279.

Wasburn, P. C. and Wasburn, M. H. (2011). Media Coverage of Women in Politics: The Curious Case of Sarah Palin. *Media, Culture & Society*, 33 (7), 1027–1041.

Webb, P. and Poguntke, T. (2013). The Presidentialisation of Politics Thesis Defended. *Parliamentary Affairs*, 66 (3), 646–654.

West, D. and Orman, J. (2003). *Celebrity Politics*. Upper Saddle River, NJ: Prentice-Hall.

Wheeler, M. (2013). *Celebrity Politics*. Cambridge: Polity.

Whiteley, P. (2011). *Political Participation in Britain*. Houndmills: Palgrave Macmillan.

31

Leadership and Architecture

Michael Minkenberg

Introduction

Very few arenas reflect the dreams, aspirations, interests and self-images of leadership better than their built form in architecture. Meant to endure and to inspire the population and future generations alike, architecture uniquely expresses aspects of power and authority (see Kane and Patapan 2012: 151). In the world of politics, these aspirations are highly concentrated – and consequential – in capital cities:

> Capitals became the symbols of human greatness and political behavior. Paris, London, Vienna, and Prague all have an attitude toward life that is admired and, in a remarkable manner, beloved. Their appearance is not merely an outward one. It reflects an essence that cannot be denominated because relationships and intellectual currents have entered into it on a number of different levels. Only a part of it could be planned; a somewhat larger part may be inferred from the appearance of the city.
>
> *(Braunfels 1988: 277–278)*

This chapter looks at the planned part of capital cities and explores how it connects to those who have made the plans, i.e. political leaders and those serving the interests of the powerful.[1] That is, it inquires into the specific input of political leadership – individual as well as collective – through the appearance of the capital city. This process can be seen as "capital building" in a dual sense: (a) building a capital city to project leaders' authority by providing a particular vision and by accommodating the public's (perceived) need to identify with the larger whole of the body politic; and (b) accumulating what has been termed "political capital" or "leadership capital" that will most likely survive specific leaders' tenure in office, if not entire regimes (see Bourdieu 2005; Vale 2008; Bennister et al. 2015). In other words: if "political leaders . . . have the opportunity to shape the environment in which they operate" (Helms 2005: 20), this environment includes more than rules, institutions and political structures; it includes also the built environment in terms of public architecture in capital cities. Through reflections upon the nature of a range of capital city architectures, the chapter seeks to reveal aspects of leadership with a particular focus on the types of leadership and its regime context (democratic or autocratic) across time (mostly but not exclusively in the modern age) and space (from Europe to non-European regions). On the most general level, the argument is that capital city planning and architecture reflects the autocratic or democratic type of leadership and the different meanings leaders want to communicate (see Rapoport 1993: 35–43; Schatz 2004a: 117f.). But due to particular historical contexts and legacies, it does so in a less than straightforward way.

From ancient times into the modern age, individual autocratic rulers such as the Babylonian kings and the emperors of Rome and Constantinople or modern day autocrats such as Mussolini in Italy and Nazarbaev in Kazakhstan have shaped their capital cities by inserting their personal visions if not tastes with only minimal constraints. That is, non-democratic or autocratic regimes allow a high degree of realization of the respective leaders' imaginations, due to the absence of democratic checks and balances and the concomitant opportunity to widely use resources, patronage and coercion to overcome opposition, i.e. the highest level of political leadership in the executive encounters low barriers to realize its plans.

In contrast, the role of leadership in a democratic context is less clear. Since modern democracy can be conceived as a regime with a historically unprecedented level of complexity and differentiation in the social and political orders and relationships, the building and design of capital cities and public architecture can be expected to mirror this complexity. Many factors and deciders compete with or challenge the incumbent political leaders in the shaping of capital cities and their efforts to project authority by giving them a particular appearance, not least the municipalities themselves (see Hall 1997: 274). On a more general level, a fundamental tension exists between leadership which is indispensable in any political regime and the principle of popular sovereignty which severely limits the authority of leaders, not least because in contrast to authoritarian leaders who rule *by* or *through* law, democratic leaders must rule *under* law with multiple centers of influence (see Kane and Patapan 2012: 1f., 109; also Elgie 1995). In modern democratic regimes, leadership encounters many constraints on the process and its outcomes, the executive is confronted with opposition by parliamentary leaders (plus the relative autonomy of ministries and bureaucracies and their committees) and multiple centers of influence (see Kane and Patapan 2012: 2). Moreover, regional leaders may pose a bigger obstacle to the realization of the national leaders' ideas in a democratic polity than in autocratic circumstances, in particular if it is federally organized, but in both types of regimes local leadership in capital cities will be of more symbolic than substantial importance (see Borraz and John 2004).

Since the role of leadership is particularly consequential in times of political change such as the change of regimes and the building of states and nations, this chapter pays particular attention to such circumstances. More than older or "evolved" capitals, newly built capital cities in new or post-colonial regimes are a cornerstone in the political business of "inventing traditions," in the threefold sense as identified by Hobsbawm: the new capital as a symbol of social cohesion and national identity; the new capital's contribution to establishing or legitimizing the political institutions and hierarchies of the regime; and the function of the new capital in socializing the people into both the nation state and political system (Hobsbawm 1983: 9). Against this backdrop, the central argument can be restated in a different manner: the purity of the leadership's vision fails to materialize in the built space of new capital cities to the degree that the decision-making process is truly democratic. In other words, democracy matters but it matters more in the process than in the outcome. The less democracy there is in the building of democratic capitals, the more the purity of vision or the "dream of the rational city" (Boyer 1983) can be maintained.

To illustrate these points, the chapter focuses on a number of cases that fall into the categories of historical and new capital cities in autocratic and democratic contexts. Against the backdrop of the "model city" Paris (Braunfels 1988: 307), "old capitals" such as Rome and Berlin are discussed, with a focus on the changing regime context and the nexus between leadership and architecture. Next, new capitals in "new nations" are considered as illustrations for the architectural projection of political power in newly established nation states and democracies, covering the "post-colonial" capital cities of Washington, Canberra and Brasília. To this is added the contrasting case of Astana, also a post-colonial capital city but in an autocratic regime.

The cases are selected on the grounds that a change of regime, and with it a change of leadership in a more fundamental way, reveals most clearly the effects of leadership on public architecture, the attempts to project power and legitimacy by the building of new forms or the re-cycling and re-interpreting of old ones. In this light, Berlin is an unusually complex case in that it combines, within the time span of only two-and-a-half centuries, the widest variety of regimes and types of leadership, from monarchical to republican, from fascist to communist, including the division of the city and its reunification under democratic auspices. It thus embodies an extraordinary and constantly changing expanse of leadership and architectural aspirations (see Figure 31.1).

Across all cases, the "regime quality" of the capital city projects will be assessed, by focusing on the aspects of site selection and urban design and architecture, as well as the decision process

Figure 31.1   Berlin: A Capital City in Constant Transition – and a container of multiple regime icons: the Television Tower (1969), the "Red Townhall" (1869), the last ruins of the Palace of the Republic (1976) on the site of the old and future Royal Palace (1706/2019), and the dual spires of the Nicolai church (ca. 1250) (from left to right, as of 2008)

© Michael Minkenberg

which led to the outcomes and by addressing the relationship between the need for vision and leadership on the one hand, and the need to adapt to the new rules of the political game and expectations, on the other (see Kane and Patapan 2012, 2014).

The "Model Case" of a Capital City: Paris

Paris has variously been called the "model city," the national capital par excellence, or a multi-functional or super-capital (Braunfels 1988: 307; Sonne 2003: 141; White 2006: 38). Here, the architectural expression of political power and its spatial arrangement most clearly result from the royal past and the rulers' aspiration of monumentality. With Wolfgang Braunfels (1988: 309), we can identify four pre-modern political forces which have shaped Paris as a capital city with ongoing significance in the democratic age: the mass of the population and its growth, which resulted not only in constant revisions of the city's delimitations but also in overcrowding along with a strict class-based segregation of the residential quarters (see also Hall 1997: 55f. and White 2006: 43); the royal axis, which has existed for eight centuries but undergone significant alteration of its political meanings, currently connecting "high culture" at one end with "high capitalism" at the other (see Vale 2008: 21f.); the Seine River and the development of its banks in a classicist interpretation of symmetry and axiality (see Braunfels 1988: 323); and finally the constant efforts at embellishment of Paris since the *ancien régime* and Enlightenment across different regime types and historical eras (see also Hall 1997: 59–63; White 2006: 51–54).

It is in the fourth factor that the political ideas of the respective leaders – in the age of modernity, particularly Napoleon I and III, de Gaulle and Mitterrand – most clearly appear. And among these, the third Napoleon can claim credit for the most profound phase of (re)building – and thereby, redefining – Paris:

> This idea of Paris as a town in a class by itself is not in fact very old; it goes back to the second Empire . . . in the first half of the nineteenth century, Paris had been regarded as one of the dirtiest places in Europe. The explanation of this astonishing change lay in the radical transformation effected under Georges-Eugène Haussmann.
>
> *(Hall 1997: 55)*

But it should not be ignored that, in this project, Baron Haussmann, as *Préfet de la Seine* since 1853 directly accountable to the Emperor Napoleon III, was also motivated by a strategic motive rooted in his and his superior's repulsion of riots and revolutionary upheaval, in particular the memory of 1848 (see Hazan 2002: 137–140; see also Epstein 2013, who deemphasizes this strategic motivation). Here, the aesthetic desire to embellish the city merged with the political and military desire to control the crowds by ridding the city's center of narrow streets and the social desire to clear the slums and improve the living conditions of the urban masses. It was not only in the transformation of Paris that Napoleon III embodied a particular type of leader: "When it came to action he was a romantic: energy and drive were crucial components in the image he wanted to project. In this respect he anticipated such later rulers as Mussolini" (Hall 1997: 78).

Embodying a centuries-long process of adding ever new layers of *grandeur* and monumentality to the French capital, the royal axis connects the historical city center and current cultural center not just of Paris but of France, the Louvre, with today's center of French capitalism, La Défense (see Figure 31.2). While the palace of the French kings and emperors, the Tuileries, was demolished in the Third Republic, the grand design of the ceremonial axis

Figure 31.2   Royal Axis in Paris: View from the Place de la Concorde (bottom) to the Arc de Triomphe and La Défense (2014)

© Yann Arthus-Bertrand/Altitude

survived all revolutions and regime changes well into the Fifth Republic. From its beginning in the twelfth century until the culmination in the nineteenth with Napoleon I and Haussmann's Place de l'Étoile, the axis symbolizes a highly political meaning of the state's and the nation's greatness, rooted in pre-democratic ideas: "Every stage in this development was conditioned by the attitude of the king and, later, the emperor toward Paris and their conception of the monarchy itself" (Braunfels 1988: 318; see also Manow 2008: 55). At the intersection of the Place de la Concorde which was the biggest construction project in the mid-eighteenth century (Hall 1997: 61), a cross-cutting axis connects a church in classicist style in the north, the Madeleine, and the Assemblée Nationale, the lower house of the parliament, with an equally classicist façade in the south (left and right end on Figure 31.2). In the center of the monumental square, the largest in Paris, an ancient monument rises above the traffic: a 3,300-year-old Egyptian obelisk, a gift from the Egyptian king to France in 1833, then a constitutional–liberal monarchy as a result of the July Revolution, connecting earth with heaven in what can be considered the spatial center of today's secularist Republic and at the same time connecting Paris with Imperial Rome which also boasted a number of obelisks from Egypt in its city-scape as an ancient expression of ordering public space in a vertical fashion (see Meckseper 1996; Knell 2004; also Asendorf 2004 and Curran et al. 2009).

The monumentalism and centrality of the royal and imperial legacies in the French capital's public architecture and political space, to a large extent framed if not shaped by Haussmann's activities during the Second Empire (see Hall 1997: 55–83), stands in contrast to the inconspicu-ousness of the governmental sites and architecture of the Fifth Republic. In the current political system, the center of gravity lies with the president who is both the head of state and, together with the prime minister, head of government, fusing extensive substantial with symbolic pow-ers in his office. De Gaulle's constitution thus revived an important French tradition of leader-ship, that of Bonapartism, with the president's role bordering on being a "republican monarch" which can be seen as an effort to ease the tension between leadership and popular sovereignty (see above and Ehrman and Schain 1992: 292; also Lacroix and Lagroye 1992; Schain and Keeler 1995). But in striking contrast to the White House in Washington DC, or even the new Chancellery in Berlin (see below), the Palais de l'Elysée, the president's official residence, does not occupy a central place, nor does it sit on any of the axes that run across the inner city. With the president of the Republic also being directly elected by the people, thus embodying the nation and claiming supreme authority, his physical distance from the parliament and the cabinet members as well as his location in the vicinity of the old royal seats of power contribute to his particular legitimacy – a legacy of Bonapartism fueled by de Gaulle's dislike of party and parliamentary politics (see Ehrman and Schain 1992: 11–15; Gaïti 1998).

In several respects, the Fifth Republic breaks with the past: it does not only differ from its republican predecessor regimes with regard to the strong role of the president and the new power arrangements; it also heralded a new era of capital city planning. While the Third Republic in its rejection of the Second Empire and its excesses refrained from further plans to build up Paris and instead invested more in the provinces, a course of action that contin-ued in the Fourth Republic, it was de Gaulle and his Fifth Republic which returned to the Napoleonic approach. Paris was to become a "world city" and modern metropolis, reflecting the new ambitions of the president as a world leader and his idea of France. De Gaulle and his chief planner Delouvrier's vision of Paris was that of a new prestigious role for the city and for France, coupled with a program of modernization and integration of Paris and its region, including the creation of La Défense and new towns, new traffic systems and the manage-ment of the inner city (see White 2006: 40–47). The emphasis was increasingly on culture, and de Gaulle's successors continued the projects, especially his erstwhile opponent François Mitterrand. With several *grand projets*, including the Grand Louvre, the National Library, the Opéra at Bastille and the development of La Défense with its Great Arc, Mitterrand even more than de Gaulle continued the Bonapartist tradition in adding new and monumental landmarks to the appearance of the city (see Seidl 1996; White 2006: 51–54; Vale 2008: 22). Yet, the controversy surrounding Mitterrand's projects and the shift to more cultural than political pro-jects as well as the reluctance of Mitterrand's successors to engage in similarly grand designs (see Cohen 2010) point at the changing, that is declining, stature of the French presidency in the recent past (Cole et al. 2013).

Nation Building and Regime Change: Rome

Rome and Berlin share the fate of having become modern capital cities in processes of "late nation building" in the second half of the nineteenth century and hence having been recon-figured in their earlier roles as capital cities of different states (the Papal States, Prussia). Here national leadership, i.e. a particular alliance of nation builders consisting of the leaders of the national–liberal movements in Italy and Germany along with the military and monarchical leaders of the dominant states of Piedmont and Prussia, played a prominent role in shaping the capital cities. Also, both cities stand for the megalomaniac aspiration of fascist leaders who sought to turn a modern national capital into the center of an empire: in Rome, this led to the recovery of the Imperial Rome of ancient times by Mussolini, whereas in Berlin a whole new and gigantic city, "Germania," was dreamed up by Hitler and his chief architect, Albert Speer, to replace a large part of the nineteenth-century urban mass in central Berlin. Moreover, in both cases, Haussmann's Paris served as the (modest) model for the monumentalism to come. Hence, it is no accident that accounts of capital city building in Rome and Berlin focus largely on the fascist period (e.g. Vale 2008: 24–36).

Curiously, in several pertinent comparative studies of capital cities in Europe, Rome appears as the last or a late case rather than in the beginning (Braunfels 1988; Hall 1997; Gordon 2006). The reasoning is that:

> as an urban personality, Rome surpasses all other capitals. There is nothing to compare with the first, imperial Rome as the capital of that most perfect empire which ruled all the coasts surrounding the Mediterranean. Nor is there anything to compare with the papal city of the Renaissance and the baroque period, *Roma secunda*.
>
> *(Braunfels 1988: 340; see also Hall 1997: 255 and Vale 2008: 31)*

The legacies of the first two Romes created a particular challenge for the "Third Rome," the modern capital of unified Italy, and the national leaders' architectural aspirations.

To begin with, more than its successors, ancient Rome bore the imprint of individual rulers, i.e. its emperors, with Augustus at the beginning of imperial city planning on the grandest scale. Their leadership was the epitome of autocratic leadership in line with the above formula: the emperors' words and acts *were* the law (Ewald and Noreña 2010: 4; and see above). But their rule was nonetheless constrained because they had to balance the relationship between mass and elite, or the people and the leaders, which the republican Rome had bestowed on the empire. This was accomplished by their building programs, along with the games, food and water supply and other activities which constituted acts of public benefaction in the relationship between the emperors and the people, in particular the urban plebs of Rome (see Zanker 1997, 2010; Ewald and Noreña 2010).

While Augustus's predecessors, most notably Caesar and Pompey, had already begun to monumentalize the Forum Romanum (see Connolly and Dodge 2001: 110), Augustus set out to massively refurbish the center of the city with a number of projects such as the completion of the rearrangement of the forum begun under Caesar, the construction of his own Forum Augustum, the altar of peace (Ara Pacis) and a house on the Palatine in which the emperor himself lived. When he died, Augustus left a fully reconfigured forum as a public space (see Figure 31.3; also Figure 31.4) representing the new political regime and his family, although the end result was more the product of an incremental rearrangement than the execution of a comprehensive plan from the outset (see Muth 2014).

Augustus's successors Tiberius, Caligula and Claudius added their own palaces and more temples until Nero rebuilt the city after the fire of AD 64 which severely damaged ten of the fourteen areas of the city. More monumental structures were erected by Vespasian and Titus (such as the Colosseum and new triumphal arches), Domitian (a new imperial palace on the Palatine) and finally Trajan and Hadrian, with the latter's mausoleum (today's Castel Sant'Angelo) along with the older Pantheon being the most lasting complete edifice (see Stambaugh 1988: 67–88). In sum, the emperors, by having turned the building trade in the city of Rome into their own private monopoly (including the property of the quarries, mines and forests in the empire) and unhindered by institutional constraints were able to build on a grand scale, thus adding a thick layer of "public architecture" to the mass of private buildings. But with very few exceptions (such as Nero's Golden House) the buildings for the citizens of Rome surpassed in scale and

Figure 31.3 Imperial Rome: The Forum Romanum at the time of Augustus's death (AD14), seen from the southeast

© digitales-forum-romanum, Projekt am Winckelmann-Institut der Humboldt-Universität zu Berlin, Leitung Susanne Muth, 3D-Modell Armin Müller; www.digitales-forum-romanum.de/epochen/augusteisch-ii/

magnificence the buildings the emperors built for themselves – an aspect of patronage that survived from the republican tradition (see Zanker 2010). However, as a whole, the city of Rome was an unplanned metropolis, in contrast to many cities built in the empire. As with the royal axis in Paris 1,000 years later, the Forum remained the public center despite frequent reconstruction of the city:

> As succeeding emperors added directly to the Forum, or, like Julius Caesar, founded a new one in the vicinity, ever larger crowds would be drawn to the center for shopping, for worship, for gossip, for taking part, as spectators or actors, in public affairs or private lawsuits . . . Here in the Forum Romanum was the center of public life not merely for Rome itself, but for the Empire.
>
> *(Mumford 1961: 222)*

The monumental scale of imperial public architecture was passed on from the first Rome to the second, the papal Rome, most visibly embodied by the stadium-turned-Piazza Navona a thousand years later, to which even a Roman obelisk returned in 1651, now with new significance as a baroque symbol (see von Matt and Barelli 1980: 265; Braunfels 1988: 359; Roth and Clark 2014: 433). Prior to St. Peter's Basilica, the papal leaders engaged in the building of four monumental churches and many other places of worship but, at the same time, Rome underwent decay due to the capital's move to Constantinople. Imperial monumentality such as the Castel Sant'Angelo, the Lateran and others was either destroyed or sacralized and "inhabited" by the new leaders. Overall, "the efforts of individual popes to create zones of new architectural order were successful only to the extent that every religious endowment in the sacral area received indissoluble rights" because the city of Rome lacked economic sustenance (Braunfels 1988: 344f.).

Only after the return of the pope from Avignon in the early fifteenth century did papal Rome develop a political and architectural structure. Michelangelo's rebuilding of the Capitol Hill, with its turning away from the ancient Forum and providing a counterweight to St. Peter's Basilica, marked this new beginning as "a symbol of the imperial idea" (see Saxl 1957). The new monumental program was underlined by the re-building of St. Peter, the redevelopment of the area across the river from the Castel Sant'Angelo and the amplification of the papal residence in the early sixteenth century (see von Moos 1980: 47). These and many other projects could proceed smoothly because the popes' power was unlimited, they had extraordinary resources and they benefited from the city's self-image as eternal, unique and savior of the world. Almost all of the 45 popes from Martin V (1417–31) to Pius VI (1775–99) were engaged in the extension of the papal residence (the Vatican, the Lateran and later the summer residence on the Quirinal) and building a family residence: "As a result, Rome became the only city with numerous and very large family residences that exceed in monumentality and luxury the aristocratic palaces of all other cities" (Braunfels 1988: 345f.). In short, what the first and second Rome demonstrate is that the leadership's absolute power and limitless resources turned the city into the physical materialization of the leaders' visions, often coupled with public services for the poor masses as well.

In the age of nation building, Rome had to be converted into the Italian capital city by force. As early as 1861, when Italy minus the Papal States and Venice was unified under the leadership of Cavour and Garibaldi, Rome, then still the capital of the Vatican regime, was declared the permanent capital of Italy by a parliamentary vote in Turin. Only nine years later, with the conquest of Rome by King Victor Emmanuel's troops, did Rome become the effective capital. Under the auspices of the king of Italy, it was parliamentary governments that pursued the project of turning Rome into the new capital of the Italian nation. A plan for a new layout of the city with long boulevards engraved into the papal outline of the city was drafted by the municipality but never approved by the Italian government; due to the involvement of many persons and agencies and the lack of strong executive power, this happened only ten years later on a smaller scale (see Hall 1997: 257–259; Kirk 2005a: 222–230).

The need to build and develop a national image in a language of "the iconography of unity" (Kostof 1973) led to a number of new streets and plazas cutting across the existing road scheme and the project of a new city quarter with government buildings to the east of the old city center. With the emerging "building fever," tensions arose between the national and local leadership, in particular between the conservative national government under PM Giolitti and left-wing mayor Ernesto Nathan. Nathan left some marks (education, hygiene, transportation, etc.) but in the overall city planning, the nationalist forces prevailed and the government and its most important institutions and representatives, such as the king, the prime minister, the parliament and several ministries, moved into prestigious locations and buildings formerly inhabited by its clerical residents. Among these are the Palazzo Montecitorio, which became the seat of the lower house of parliament, and the Palazzo del Quirinale, the pope's summer palace, which turned into the permanent residence of the Italian head of state, first of the king and, after 1946, of the president (see Kirk 2005a: 226f. and Piccinato 2006: 223). To these existing edifices was added the largest institutional building constructed by the national government, the Palazzo di Guistizia, in neo-Cinquecento style, which is situated on the Vatican side of the Tiber River and houses the Italian Supreme Court (Kirk 2005a: 246).

The once all-powerful church leaders in the Vatican state exerted little influence – a powerful sign that the occupation of Rome as the new capital city was at the same time a move to secularize the city under the national leadership. Yet, while the Paris of Napoleon III served as the inspiration for the rebuilding of Rome, there was no Haussmann. Many new buildings did not acquire the monumental character they were supposed to have while, on the other hand:

the most striking addition to the urban scene, the national monument for Victor Emmanuel II . . . was not among the proposals . . . [Moreover] the ruthless exploitation of the parks and gardens round the old villas is perhaps the worst result of what Reed justifiably called "the third sack of Rome."

> *(Hall 1997: 261; the preceding two sacks having been the one by the Normans under Robert Guisdard in 1084 and that by the mutinous troops of Holy Roman Emperor Charles V in 1527)*

The massive structure in honor of the first king in the center of the old Rome, reminiscent of the ancient imperial glory, dwarfed not only Michelangelo's Capitol next to it (see Figure 31.4), but also other monuments glorifying the political and military leaders of the Risorgimento, and thereby served as "the keystone of national symbolism . . . that communicated the moral and political messages of the regime . . . while counterbalancing ecclesiastical tradition" (Kirk 2005a: 236; see also Kirk 2014: 154–157).

What the "third Rome" of the new Italian nation state was missing, Mussolini tried to make good in a "full range of Fascist symbol-mongering" (Vale 2008: 33). The plan of finishing the (re)construction of Rome led to a massive return to the imperial capital of ancient times. Here, more than in the kingdom that preceded Mussolini's regime, the executive and Mussolini himself provided the parameters. In a directive to the newly appointed mayor ("Governatore") of

Figure 31.4 Rome: Victor Emmanuel Monument, with Forum Romanum in the foreground and Michelangelo's Capitol on the left, seen from the southeast

© Dieter Minkenberg

Rome in 1925, he announced: "In five years Rome must appear to all peoples of the world vast, ordered, and powerful, as it was in the times of Augustus's first empire" (in Kirk 2014: 159). Local leadership proved no obstacle; the new office of "Governatore" was directly responsible to the dictator and more monumentality and grand design was added to the city, at the expense of the existing urban fabric:

> In a succession of Haussmannesque interventions, Mussolini's planners and designers cut through a series of straight-line avenues linking favored monuments. Perhaps the most invasive of these was the Via dell'Impero which destroyed 5,500 units of housing to expose the ruins of the imperial fora.
>
> *(Vale 2008: 35; see also Kirk 2005b: 120–127)*

Other grand projects included the new headquarters of the Fascist party, a whole city to be built for the Esposizione Univesale di Roma in the context of Mussolini's bid to host the world fair in 1942, and the Foro Mussolini as a "significantly politicized Fascist space in which architecture was enlisted to reach sophisticated governing goals, and functioned as such for at least a decade" (Kirk 2014: 169; see also Piccinato 2006: 218; Vale 2008: 35f.) In an attempt to link the past with the future, these projects combined elements of classicist style with those of modernism; yet overall, the plan to rebuild Rome as a new version of the Augustan city remained patchwork. Moreover, despite the differences of the political ideologies of the liberal and Fascist governments, both turned to monumentalism (Kirk 2014: 159) – a line which was abandoned in the new Italian Republic which emerged after the Second World War on the ruins of the Fascist state.

When comparing the three Romes, it becomes evident that leadership had the most direct effect in implementing its vision of Rome when autocratic regimes posed few obstacles: emperors, popes and, to a lesser extent, Mussolini forced their structures onto the city with little opposition – yet they could not prevent the possibility that later rulers would do away with, or significantly alter, their architecture. The post-war republican regime, on the other hand, lacked both vision and ambition to leave a mark; here leadership retreated and "changes and new developments were introduced by 'great events' [the Olympic Games in 1962, the 1990 World Cup, the Holy Year and others] rather than through regular planning" (Piccinato 2006: 223; also Kirk 2005b: 248–257). Moreover, since contemporary Rome possesses an extraordinary amount of historical heritage and archeological sites stemming from the first two, any urban planning by local or national leaders runs the risk of strong public resistance when threatening to change the fabric of the city. The last time this happened without much resistance occurred under the dictatorial circumstances of the 1930s – and even then it remained fragmentary (Kirk 2014).

Nation Building and Regime Change: Berlin

On the surface, Rome and Berlin underwent parallel developments until the collapse of fascism. With German unification in 1871, Berlin had to fulfill a promise similar to that of Rome. But from the onset, a crucial difference rested in the role of Berlin as the capital of Prussia, with a mixture of baroque and classical features promoted by the Prussian kings, most notably Frederick the Great (r. 1740–86) and Frederick William III (r. 1797–1840). In the eighteenth century, the kings encouraged house construction and a "sober, Calvinistic classicism" (Braunfels 1988: 217) was preferred. In the early nineteenth century, the king commissioned the architect Karl Frederick Schinkel to turn Berlin into an "Athens on the Spree," by widely using the architectural language of classical Athens, and borrowing inspiration, as did Frederick the Great before, from imperial architecture in Rome, in particular the Pantheon (see Asendorf 2014: 132–141).

While the reform-minded aspirations of the bourgeois elite clashed with the backward-oriented political philosophy of the rulers before and especially after the 1848 revolution, the embellishment of Berlin with a classical impulse continued. At the same time, the transformation of Prussia from a military and agrarian state into an industrial and modern one meant that Berlin had to cope with massive population growth, to which the master plan by James Hobrecht, who was appointed by the king in 1858, responded. Although the timing corresponded with Haussmann's redoing of Paris, this plan and its subsequent execution proved a different enterprise:

> In Paris it was primarily the case of redeveloping and clearing existing buildings by constructing new streets; in Berlin, on the other hand, it was entirely a question of making plans for new building. In Paris one of the fundamental goals was to create an efficient street system through the centre; in Berlin the centre was not directly involved.
>
> *(Hall 1997: 194)*

In sum, when Berlin became the capital of the unified Germany in 1871, it was already a fully functioning and planned out capital city for the largest and most powerful of the German states, and Bismarck, the first German chancellor, extended the existing city as needed. In the Wilhelmine era, the most important architectural addition was the erection and opening of the new national parliament building, the Reichstag (built from 1884 to 1894). It was the result of several parliamentary votes (and the work of a parliamentary committee) and was finally placed outside the innermost section of the city and next to the Brandenburg Gate (see Hoffmann 2000: 94–130). In all respects, this highly significant building was subordinate to the non-democratic authorities in Prussia and Germany. Officially, the building was given "to the German people" by the emperor (this inscription was only added above the entrance in 1916); architecturally, it had to subordinate itself to the Royal Palace by not exceeding the latter's size (see Asendorf 2014: 143); politically it served to add a parliamentary touch to the semi-authoritarian regime established by Bismarck, an institution with limited powers, which only grew more significant towards the end of the Wilhelmine empire. In the process of building the Imperial Diet, Bismarck and even more so the emperor William I (r. 1861–88) took interest in the project, the selection of the site and the architectural details such as the dome, the design of which was altered significantly as a result of the emperor's interventions, in line with the many conflicts between architect and parliament on the one side, and the Prussian authorities on the other (see Cullen 1999: esp. 41–62, 99–130; Hoffmann 2000: 60–68, 156–160). Attempts to add a new monumental expression to reflect the aspired greatness of the German nation resulted in a competition for a Greater Berlin prior to the First World War, but, since Berlin was not administratively unified, the plans had no consequences (see Sonne 2003: 101–140).

This situation of Berlin as an enlarged Prussian capital was to change under fascist leadership in the 1930s. Hitler's dreams of a German world empire had to be matched by a capital corresponding to them (see Schirmer 2005). His architect Albert Speer, who incorporated some of Hitler's ideas such as façades of buildings into his Berlin plan, designed the city as rearranged according to a newly built massive axis running from north to south, "a Berlin Champs-Élysées two-and-a-half times the length of the original" (Speer in Vale 2008: 25; for earlier plans of a monumental north–south axis, see Sonne 2003: 110–123; see Figure 31.5). On the northern end of this axis, the "Great Hall of the German People" was to be erected, meant to accommodate up to 180,000 people, and, as "the headquarters of the Reich," it had to surpass in size all similarly monumental buildings such as St. Peter's in Rome, the Capitol building in Washington and others (see Asendorf 2014: 144–145). The southern end of the axis was to be a new central train station, and, between these two, a monstrous triumphant arc more than twice

Figure 31.5   Model of Proposed North–South Axis for Hitler's Berlin

© Bundesarchiv

the size of the Arc de Triomphe in Paris was to be erected, an idea which Hitler had formulated as early as the 1920s (see Sonne 2006: 201). These plans were not executed, but other buildings such as Hitler's Imperial Chancellery, the Tempelhof airport and the Olympic Stadium, all bearing the signs of a monumentalized classicism (with massive rectangular columns instead of round ones) went up and even survived the devastation of the war. In sum:

> during the Third Reich, urban planning for Berlin was basically a matter of capital city planning: the new government buildings were to foster identity on the domestic front and create an impressive image to the world of the nation's foreign policy. All that remained of this new representation in urban design, however, was a massive pile of rubble.
>
> *(Sonne 2006: 203)*

Or, as playwright Bertolt Brecht described the city after the war: "Berlin, an etching by Churchill after an idea by Hitler" (quoted in Asendorf 2014: 129).

A survivor of the war, however, was the monumentalist language inscribed into the eastern half of Berlin which, after the separation of the city and country and the establishment of two German states, became the capital of the socialist German Democratic Republic. The regime under the leadership of Walther Ulbricht relentlessly remodeled the inner city according to its political program, substituting icons of the feudal and militaristic, capitalist and imperial past with new ones (see Ladd 2005). Along with all the Nazi structures such as the Reich Chancellery, the Hohenzollern city palace was demolished in 1950 to give way to a huge rallying ground which was to be crowned by a sky scraper, first in a bombastic neo-gothic and neo-classicist "Stalinist" style, later in the guise of modernism: the Central Building housing party headquarters and government functions (see Sonne 2006: 205). A new central axis was planned and meant to connect the Brandenburg Gate in the west with the Central Building and a new broad avenue, the Stalinallee, in the east. While the latter was finished, the Central Building never saw the light of day and instead, with a delay of 20 years and signaling a new era under Erich Honecker, the new General Secretary of the Party, the much more modest and politically impotent East German parliament building, the Palace of the Republic, was built on the palace's site in the mid-1970s. Although the regime did not change its political closeness, the more realistic aspirations of the new generation of leaders in the 1970s translated directly into a more utilitarian architecture (see Ladd 2005: 224–227; Sonne 2006: 206; Schirmer 2005: 153). The endpoint of the adjustments of the East German regime was the return of history into the planning of East Berlin: the rehabilitation of the Prussian past, as embodied by the re-erection of the monument of Frederick the Great in Unter den Linden, the renovation of the monumental German Cathedral built under Emperor William II and the restoration of the Forum Fridericianum, the central square in absolutist Prussia's capital (see Ladd 2005: 228f. and also Asendorf 2014: 128–132). These efforts did not prevent the growing alienation of the people from the regime and the protests that led to its downfall in the fall of 1989.

In the post-1989 period, Berlin underwent yet another phase of city planning and public architecture project. For the first time since the Wilhelmine era and the Hobrecht plan preceding it, the city experienced the implementation of a comprehensive urban plan, and, for the first time ever, it occurred under democratic conditions with many checks and balances, not least stemming from the federal nature of the German political system. The task had to be carried out by both national and local leadership, accompanied by broad public debates and always under suspicion that the leadership might give way to new imperialist temptations (see von Beyme 2014: 113–124; Sonne 2006: 206f.; Asendorf 2014). To counter such suspicions, a new federal government quarter was developed, which ran across the north–south axis fashioned by the Wilhelmine and Nazi planners; instead the idea of a new "Band des Bundes" (the Federal Row) connecting east and west along the Reichstag building and cutting across the former wall won the day (see Sonne 2006: 209, and Figure 31.6). Also, the Reichstag itself underwent a substantial overhaul by British architect Norman Forster, and the new Chancellery, the only hint at monumentality, was built in a palazzo style by Berlin architect Axel Schultes, who combined abstract elements of modernity, inspired by Le Corbusier and Louis Kahn, with traditional references such as the placement of the central building behind a forecourt (see Asendorf 2014: 146f.). These three major projects were the result of open competitions under the auspices of the two governments and ministerial committees, but the addition of the glass dome on the parliament building and the choice of Schultes's Chancellery involved the intervention of the then chancellor, Helmut Kohl (see Sonne 2006: 209).

Two more controversial large-scale projects concerned the master plan of the Berlin government's city planning administration and the reappearance of the Berlin Royal Palace right in the city center. The first suggested a critical reconstruction of the city according to the historical street plan, along with new high-rise projects at Alexanderplatz, Potsdamer Platz and City West (see Bodenschatz 2013: 111f.). While the reconstruction of Pariser Platz at the Brandenburg Gate was realized largely unhampered, projects around Alexanderplatz were put

Figure 31.6 Berlin: The Federal Row ("Band des Bundes") with Federal Chancellory (center), rebuilt Reichstag building (upper right) and the new Federal Ministry of Interior (bottom) (2013)

© euroluftbild.de/Robert Grahn

to rest due to changes in the government. The idea of the return of the Royal Palace (the Hohenzollern Stadtschloss) on the location of the Palace of the Republic was highly political and controversial from the outset. The outside appearance of this new building, officially named Humboldt Forum and the host-to-be of extra-European art collections, a library and a science museum, had been fixed prior to an international competition, not by a group of architects, urban designers or other experts, but, in 2002, by the Bundestag, the national parliament (see Asendorf 2014: 149; Minkenberg 2014b: 1–4). This project is interpreted by critics as a nostalgic return to the past and even an imperial message which does not match the current challenges of finding the right mix of capital building and other considerations such as commercial, ecological or lifestyle-related ones. Overall, the city center of Berlin is marked by the imprint of almost all the political regimes of Germany's modern era in an altogether eclectic way, bordering on a postmodern patchwork, with architectural icons of medieval times, the nation building and the communist eras as well as the current age of German reunification (see Figure 31.1). Moreover, the case of post-1989 Berlin shows that democracy matters but it matters more in the process than in the outcome. This becomes even clearer when moving to new capitals in new nations in a post-colonial and democratic context.

New Capitals in New Nations in a Democratic Context: Washington DC

The siting of the federal capital of the newly formed United States can be regarded as a model case of a democratic process – with less-than-democratic outcomes. The following political players shaped the process: Congress as the national parliament, the United States' first president, already a living legend and as such endowed with powers beyond the text of the Constitution, and some of the states, most importantly Virginia in the south and Pennsylvania in the north. The idea of creating a new capital city *and* turning it into a powerful symbol of the nation's self-image as well as a representative seat of its political institutions was initially considered utopian, or doomed or just foolish; yet it proved successful as the first case of a democratically legitimized enterprise of creating a capital – albeit at the expense of the political rights of that locality's citizens (see Wolman *et al.*, 2006).

The search process started with Congress leaving Philadelphia in a crisis situation in the spring of 1783 (see Bowling 1991: 30–64). In this search, President Washington pursued his own agenda and lobbied for a place in Virginia, on the Potomac River (see Abbott 1999: 26). This was done with great or even "feverish" expectations for regional development: "Potomac Fever, a delusion-inducing obsession with the grandeur and commercial future of the Potomac River, infected these men and the corporation they founded" (Bowling 1988: 39). While the almost ten-year-long struggle to identify the site of the future capital was a largely Congressional affair with little public involvement by the chief executive, the implementation of the Act turned into an almost exclusively presidential enterprise (see Cummings and Price 1993: 219). The Act entrusted the president with complete authority over its execution and he alone could choose the members of the planning committee as well as the precise site on the river.

The extraordinary role of the first president in the creation of the new capital affected not only site selection but also the early urban design and planning. Washington's hiring of Pierre L'Enfant brought to the United States' capital planning a dimension that, on the one hand, set in stone the political self-understanding of the new republic, while at the same time introducing a measure of grandeur oriented more at baroque European capitals than a strictly democratic vision. Lewis Mumford observes that:

> despite L'Enfant's firm republican conviction, the design he brought forth for the new capital was in every respect what the architects and servants of despotism had originally conceived . . . The sole feature that was lacking was the original sixteenth-century fortifications . . . Apart from that, the plan was an exemplary adaptation of the standard baroque principles of a new situation.
>
> *(Mumford 1961: 403f. See also Field and Gournay 2007)*

Yet, the selection of the site, the role of public space and the nature and arrangement of monuments and public buildings suggest an intended disassociation from autocratic control, as the design included an openness to the general public (see Vale 2008: 65).

In the desire to free capital planning and design from an autocratic spirit, royal or aristocratic palaces, parks and places were substituted with the buildings and places which marked the key institutions of the young republic (see also Manow 2015: 46). The principle of the separation of powers was duly applied by a physical distance between the seats of the legislature and executive, clearly a long stretch, and not only in the pre-automobile era of the nineteenth century: visitors in Washington do not walk from one of these buildings to the others; they "hike" (see Abbott 1999: 118; also Bowling 1991: 239). The street system underscores that Congress, the seat of the parliament where "the people" meet and decide through their directly elected representatives, and not the White House and its resident, signifies the center of the political universe of the United States (see Abbott 1999: 99). The centrality of the institution was underscored by the mid-nineteenth century enlargement of the Capitol and in particular by the addition of a gigantic dome which was modeled after the Renaissance dome of St. Peter's Basilica in Rome and the post-Renaissance dome on St. Isaac's Cathedral in St. Petersburg and which dwarfed any other profane building at the time (see Scott 1995: 99f.). This arrangement was intended by the founding fathers, as various plans such as the early sketch by Thomas Jefferson, the plans by L'Enfant and Ellicot, and finally the realization of these plans document.

While the city functioned as a political stage, it did not acquire a representational role until 100 years later. Again, parliamentary leadership proved central in this development. Frequent criticism of the state of the governmental center and the retreat from L'Enfant's ideas led to the forming of the Senate Park Commission in 1901. Under the chairmanship of Sen. McMillan, its task was to find ways to upgrade the city and give it a statelier outlook, and in doing so it went back to L'Enfant's original plan and its republican promises. The result was monumentalism on a grand scale (see Figure 31.7). As such, Washington was more inspired by European capitals of imperial powers such as London, Paris, Vienna, Berlin and Rome than democratic reasoning (see Abbott 1999: 117). In fact, the McMillan Commission, backed by Presidents McKinley and Roosevelt, received its inspiration on a major tour to European capital cities in 1901 before drafting its plan for the US capital (see Reps 1967: 94–138). The new arrangement of a "capital center" in the heart of DC, with the reinforcement of central axes such as the Mall, the erection of monuments such as the Washington and Lincoln Memorials, and the building of the Federal Triangle, National Archives etc., added a new layer of grandeur and monumentality as well as unresolved conflicts in city planning, such as the disparity between the economic and cultural significance of Washington, its political stature and the ill-defined responsibilities of the agencies involved (see Gournay 2006: 115f.).

Many prominent buildings, places and monuments in Washington's center are or include in a major way architectural citations of structures and styles employed by non-democratic regimes and leaders. This is above all true of the obelisk of the Washington Monument, which, like the one in Paris, is placed at the intersection of the two politically most significant axes of the capital city and, with a height of 169m, is the world's tallest obelisk-shaped building (it compares to the 23m of the obelisk in Paris and 25.5m of the one on St. Peter's Square in Rome). Other examples of such historical inspirations include the Pantheon of Imperial Rome (Jefferson Memorial), Italian Renaissance (the Library of Congress), St. Peter's Basilica in Rome (the U.S. Capitol), Roman temples in the Corinthian order (the Supreme Court), French and English *ancien régime* palaces and gardens (the White House, the Mall) and Second Empire Paris (the Old Executive Building) (see Sonne 2003: 61, and respective sections in Reps 1967; Craig et al. 1978; Scott 1995). A good portion of these aesthetic choices can be explained by the classical tastes of key political figures such as Sen. McMillan and the influential journalist Charles Moore, who were skeptical of modern architecture and for whom classical ideas of beauty and monumental public buildings represented both the values of patriotism and democracy,

Figure 31.7 Washington DC and Its Monumental Axis: The Mall with the Washington Monument and the Capitol, seen from the Lincoln Memorial (2010)

© Michael Minkenberg

even though these architectural notions were opposed and criticized as aristocratic, elitist, superficial and financially irresponsible (see Reps 1967: 192–198; Sonne 2003: 70–81). In the course of the city's and the country's history, Washington DC's monumentalism, then, transcended the early republican vision of the founding fathers and increasingly reflected ambitions of imperial dimensions, in accordance with the world power status of the United States by the beginning of the Cold War.

New Capitals in New Nations in a Democratic Context: Canberra

The case of Canberra followed its own post-colonial logic (for details, see Minkenberg 2014c: 68–72). Granted self-government by London in 1850 and after, the Australian colonies New South Wales, Victoria, Tasmania and South Australia successively drafted their own constitutions and set up bi-cameral parliaments. Moving towards independence of the entire colony, two constituent assemblies in 1891 and 1897–98 produced a constitutional draft that was approved in a referendum by the population in all colonies in 1898. In the resulting

Commonwealth of Australia Constitution Bill of 1900, section 125 stipulated that the new capital city should be "in the State of New South Wales, and be distant not less than one hundred miles from Sydney" (in Lovell et al. 1998: 887).

To a large extent, the capital issue was determined by distrust between Sydney, the oldest and largest city, and Melbourne, the second largest one, and the solution eventually emerged in the federal parliament. In the debate, a number of parliamentarians used climate as an argument for the location (see Wigmore 1963: 36; Pegrum 1988: 330–333). For example, King O'Malley, the strongman of Australian politics in those years and future Minister of Home Affairs, proclaimed:

> Cold climates have produced the greatest geniuses . . . This is the first opportunity we have had of establishing a great city of our own. I hope that the site selected will be Bombala and that the children of our children will see an Australian federal city that will rival London in population, Paris in beauty, Athens in culture and Chicago in enterprise.
>
> *(quoted in Pegrum 2003: 8; see also Wigmore 1963: 34)*

Apparently, the Potomac fever of George Washington and his supporters found more than a match in King O'Malley's vision of grandeur.

The Australian lawmakers engaged heavily in the decision about the new capital city and, after an extended tour of a bi-cameral committee into the designated region in 1902, decided on the Canberra area along the Molongo River. The legislature determined that the decisive criterion for an appropriate location was not its climate, nor water supply or scenic beauty but its geographic location, which had to be acceptable to both Sydney and Melbourne (see Pegrum 1988: 325; Fischer 1984: 13). The name was yet to be found, and many suggestions were debated but in the end, for once, the executive intervened. At the christening ceremony in 1913, the Governor General's wife, without parliamentary consultation, simply declared: "I name the capital of Australia, Canberra" (see Pegrum 1988: 333; see also Wigmore 1963: 59–63). The name Canberra is of Aboriginal origin and has been translated as "meeting place" in one of the Aboriginal languages; yet the last Aboriginal in the area had already died 16 years earlier (see Vale 2008: 84).

Concerning its public architecture and urban design, Canberra contrasts with its American predecessor in that it embodies a much more contemporary, less dramatic and less European vision. In the "bush capital," it is landscape, rather than urban design, that is pre-eminent (Vernon 2006). The international design competition of 1912 was overshadowed by political struggles and controversy, especially over the fact that a government minister, the aforementioned King O'Malley, would have the final say over the outcome (see Reid 2002: 26–45; Freestone 2007: 94–98). The winner of the competition, the American architect Walter Burley Griffin, applied the concept of the "Organic City," thus harmoniously reconciling the plan for a city with the topography of the Australian capital site. But the execution of the plan proved less harmonious. Once Griffin was selected and entrusted with the planning of Canberra, opposition arose. Not unlike the estrangement that divided L'Enfant in Washington and his presidential mentor and other political leaders, Griffin encountered political opposition from upper-level bureaucrats who preferred "a more compact" and less expensive city (Freestone 2007: 106; see also Reid 2002: chapter 6). The quarrels resulted in adjusting Griffin's ideas to those of some of his major rivals in the competition, such as Eliel Saarinen, who proposed a more monumental and axial design (see Figure 31.8). In both L'Enfant's and Griffin's cases, political scheming and lobbies for alternative visions, financial constraints and also the chief architect's lack of comprehension of the political process, in sum the complexities of democratic politics, resulted in

Figure 31.8　Capital City Axiality, Australian-Style: The "Land Axis" in Canberra from the top of the Parliament Building with the Old Parliament Building (Center), the High Court (Right) and the War Memorial in the Distance (2006)

© Michael Minkenberg

alterations and deceleration of the plan, the blurring of its underlying vision and an early retirement of its author (see Freestone 2007: 115; also Minkenberg 2014c: 86–92).

For the most important institution, the Australian parliament, Griffin chose a location below the top of Capital Hill with the top itself being designated as the true "Capitol" where the people should meet. However, from 1927 on, when parliament moved from Melbourne to Canberra, it occupied a provisional building at the foot of the hill where it remained for a good sixty years, until the new building was opened. This new building (see Figure 31.9) was literally built into Capital Hill and met massive criticism, especially with regard to the alleged betrayal of the democratic principles of transparency and openness, by lifting public circulation to a floor level separate from that of the law makers, thereby abandoning the practice of public access in the provisional building and creating an empty center in the new building (see Vale 2008: 95). But, like the glass dome of the Berlin parliament, which allows the general public to walk literally on top of the representatives, the Canberra building provides a similar connection between citizens on the roof of the building and the politicians below them in the plenary halls and lobbies.

From an international perspective, which looks at old capital cities in modern democracies as well (see above), the Australian version of a democratic capital appears in a favorable light:

Figure 31.9 Canberra's Parliament Building (2006)

© Michael Minkenberg

"Modern parliament buildings from Den Haag to Canberra have shown that a lavish architecture in parliaments is possible" (von Beyme 1998: 365; my translation). The building's modest "democratic monumentality" (Sonne 2003: 185) stands in stark contrast to the not so modest one of the high court building at the lakeshore and foot of Capital Hill (see Figure 31.8), a concrete and glass block towering above the surrounding buildings, including the nearby and equally immodest national gallery. Built in modernist style in the early 1970s and reflecting the ambitions of the Chief Justice (see Metcalf 2003: 34), its "inflated look" (Metcalf) makes it a visual and unsettling counterpoint to the new parliament. Next to the high court building, newly built plazas such as Reconciliation Place, meant to include Australia's indigenous people in the capital architecture (completed 2002), fill the area between the major governmental buildings with empty space, contrary to Griffin's vision of a parliament zone populated by numerous buildings and plazas (see Vernon 2006: 145; Vale 2008: 97–103). The project of creating the Australian capital appears unfinished, with the mighty high court and national gallery as two solitary buildings "isolated in time and space from everything around them" (Reid 2002: 299). Overall and in contrast to many other modern cases such as Washington DC or Ankara, urban and building forms correlate with the democratic principles they are meant to embody (see Taylor 1989); moreover, from beginning until the end, the planning and creation of Canberra was an entirely parliamentary process with little involvement of executive leadership.

New Capitals in New Nations in a Democratic Context: Brasília

The case of Brasília shows the polar opposite of the Australian experience, with a dominant executive setting both the agenda and pushing through the process. In the transition from the empire to the republic in 1899, Rio de Janeiro remained the national capital and survived a fundamental regime change, as it did when democracy and federalism gave way to military dictatorship in 1930 and a centralist, para-fascist state under Vargas. When democracy returned in 1946 with a nominal federalism, it did not bring back the decentralized system that had existed prior to 1930 (see Skidmore 1967: 62–64; Thibaut 1996: 113). The establishment of Brasília occurred, then, in the context of a presidential democracy with a strong executive, two legislative chambers and a weakened federal system.

While the building of Brasília took only four years after the government decided and the parliament voted in 1956 to move the capital from Rio to the hinterland, site selection preceded the actual move by about 150 years. Since independence in 1822, proposals to establish a new capital named Brasília in the center of the country appeared, and a passage entered the constitution of 1891 that reserved a territory in the Central Plateau for a future federal capital (see Holston 1989: 16–17; Avila 2000: 44–50; Vale 2008: 133). The process demonstrates that, in contrast to the United States and Australia, site selection in Brazil did not follow the logic of political haggling, regional rivalries and interstate politics. Instead of a territorial compromise solution, it reflected more utopian desires and abstract considerations (see Vale 2008: 133).

The constitutional mandate of 1891 led to several commissions to chart the site for the future capital (1892, 1946, 1953), two presidential decrees (1920, 1955), and reiterations in the constitutions of 1934 and 1937 and in the Constituent Assembly of 1946 (see Holston 1989: 17). However, it was a presidential election that finally brought the dream to fruition. In his presidential bid in 1955, Juscelino Kubitschek campaigned on a populist platform that promised "fifty years progress in five" (in Skidmore 1967: 164), five years being the term for presidential tenure. Part of his "National Plan for Development" was the pledge to make good the constitutional mandate and build a new inland capital city (see Evenson 1973: 113; Holston 1989: 18). With only the slightest margin of victory (35.7 percent of the popular vote), Kubitschek set about pushing through an impressive economic program to build a lasting legacy, part of which would be the new Brazilian capital (see Holston 1989: 18).

The case of Brasília turned out to be a model case of executive leadership in a weak democratic setting. The bill put before parliament hardly met any resistance and was readily approved, "almost to the disbelief of the Congress itself" (Skidmore 1967: 167). However, the outcome of this parliamentary vote was not a given; eye-witnesses recount that Kubitschek almost blackmailed Congress into a yes vote. Facilitated by the structures of the Brazilian presidential regime and aided by a significant economic upswing, which enabled him to massively spend public money, Kubitschek was able to "buy" parliamentary support for his capital city project by "selling" public contracts to the electorates of crucial parliamentarians (see Thibaut 1996: 129; also Fils 1996: 194). Critical voices in the national press, parliamentarian leaders and local elites concerning the costs, location and other obstacles for such a plan were countered by the government's campaign to successfully link the project to Brazilian mythology and the promise of progress (see Holston 1989: 19–20). In both its urban form and public architecture, Brasília embodies the complete implementation of its designers' plan. The purity of the vision is preserved in the built environment, although the functioning of the city itself undermines the modernist vision of a class-less urban society: it celebrates the "romantic image of the automobile in motion" but fails to implement sufficient parking lots (Evenson 1973: 173; see also Holston 1989: 160; Vale 2008: 138; Minkenberg 2014c: 92f.).

In the Brazilian case, leadership also mattered on a more personal level. In contrast to the emerging tensions between and eventual break-up of Washington and L'Enfant, or King O'Malley and Griffin, the relationship between Kubitschek and chief architect Oscar Niemeyer remained durable and intimate from the 1940s until the completion of Brasília (see Evenson 1973: 117). With the authorization of Congress for all necessary measures to build the new capital in September 1956, Kubitschek practically eliminated parliamentary control by creating a special commission, the Company for the Urbanization of the New Capital (NOVACAP) which reported directly to the president, owned almost all the land in the new Federal District and had wide-ranging powers and financial resources (see Fils 1988: 99). As its technical director in charge of all architectural designs, Kubitschek selected Niemeyer who, after a competition for Brasília's pilot plan was held, was joined by Lúcio Costa (see Batista et al. 2006: 166f.; see also Evenson 1973; Fils 1988: 41–72). It was due to the concentration of power and resources in a small group of leading architects along with NOVACAP that the city was inaugurated nine months before Kubitschek's term in office ended (April 1960).

The centerpiece of this political segment of the Brazilian capital is the Plaza of the Three Powers at the end of the monumental axis that is framed on both sides by identical ministerial buildings (see Figure 31.10). The plaza is arranged in an equilateral triangle: the Congress building with two legislative wings and the slender twin towers of the secretariat; the Planalto Palace of the President; and the building of the Supreme Federal Court, the "cockpit" of the capital city plane (see Minkenberg 2014c: 93–97). With its central location, its large structures and high towers, the parliament building strives to echo the American example by emphasizing the dominance of the legislative powers over the executive, but diverges from the realities of the Brazilian political system. Instead, with the towers hosting the offices of the legislators and the administration, it came to symbolize "the dominance of the bureaucracy over the legislature" (Vale 2008: 139). However, the visual dominance of the bureaucracy in the Brazilian Congress could also be read as a more modest symbolization of the nation's supreme lawmaking body, compared to the monumental dome in Washington (see Figure 31.7). Moreover, Brasília's legislative chambers are clearly distinguishable from the outside (unlike the American or Australian case), with the Assembly meeting under a large and elegant bowl and the Senate situated under a smaller, flat but equally elegant dome.

Despite the clarity of design and architectural order, there are several symbolic confusions in this political plaza, e.g. that of the symbolic meaning of the secretariat's monumentality, and that of the parliament overshadowing the Presidential Palace which hosts the most powerful political office in the country: "There is surely some irony in this, given the all-powerful executive needed to make Brasília a reality during one man's five year term" (Vale 2008: 142). It is equally ironic that at the intersection of the monumental axis and the cross-axis are situated the entertainment and cultural quarter and a colossal bus-terminal (see Fils 1988: 14–17). Compared with all the previous cases, Brasília is, lastly, the capital of the long distances, both within the city and to other metropolises in the country, thus keeping the contentious use of public space at a scale that can easily be managed by the authorities. Presidents and parliamentarians, military dictators and rational bureaucrats alike have benefited from the remoteness and relative quiet of the Brazilian capital: "Whatever the egalitarian tenets of its architects and planners, the economic and political realities of this iconically modern capital serve only to recapitulate an ancient theme: distancing the masses from the seat of courtly power" (Vale 2008: 145). In this regard, the vision of the founders, if it ever had been democratic, was seriously compromised by the outcome.

Figure 31.10 Brasília: Monumental Axis with Central Bus Station (Foreground), Ministry Buildings (Right and Left Margin), Parliament Building (Center) and Plaza of the Three Powers (behind Parliament Building) (2005)

© Michael Minkenberg

Nation-Building and Regime Change: Astana

If the case of Brasília demonstrates the realization of a utopian vision in a classic modernist design, helped by strong executive leadership in a democratic setting, Astana can be regarded as the post-modern incarnation of such a vision, but in an autocratic context. In contrast to the previous cases discussed, Astana is the new capital of a very new nation with no history of statehood until the breakup of the Soviet Union in 1991. Kazakhstan's president Nursultan Nazarbaev had already been the leader of the Kazakh republic in Soviet times and has held the office since independence (see Aitken 2009: 187–191). The country's abundance of natural resources (in particular oil and gas), and the absence of a strong political opposition and free media, contribute to a very personalized leadership of a president who skillfully uses patronage as a political resource in a "patrimonial–clientelist system . . . allowing virtually no place for non-insiders to enter into formal political and electoral processes" (Dave 2007: 4; see also Junisbai 2010). With the constitutional term limit (two terms of five years each) being suspended for the incumbent by parliament, Nazarbaev keeps being reelected with more than 90 percent of the vote (except for 1999 when he received 81 percent); his party Nur Otan ("Light of the Fatherland") has been the only party in parliament for a number of terms and currently holds 83 of the 107 seats in the Assembly (Mazhilis). In this system, politics is clearly carried out in a top-down fashion with the president centrally involved in all decisions and parliament without any independent power (see Schatz 2004b: 86f.).

Against this backdrop, the president announced in 1994 that the capital city would be relocated from Almaty, the capital of the Kazakh province and republic since Tsarist times, which is located in the south, to Akmola, to be named Astana (which translates into "capital" in English), in the steppe of the center north with a large ethnic Russian community (see Aitken 2009: 229). From afar, the decision was considered a matter of the leader's personal taste: "The more that Westerners observed Nazarbaev's authoritarian tendencies and personalistic style of rule, the more the decision seemed rooted in nothing more than a leader's whim" (Schatz 2004a: 111). But this view was also shared by some domestic media at the time, for example the Almaty newspaper *Karavan* which commented: "Only in conditions where there is no democracy can epoch-making projects emerge that nobody understands" (quoted in Aitken 2009: 231) and it is still criticized by oppositional leaders such as Serikbolsyn Abdildin, the first chairman of the post-Soviet Communist Party of Kazakhstan, Nazarbaev's challenger in the presidential elections of 1999 and speaker of the parliament in 1997 when the vote on the capital relocation was taken (interview with the author on September 9, 2010 in Almaty).

However, as Edward Schatz and others argue, the relocation of the capital should be seen as a highly strategic move and a substantial step in the process of state- and nation-building (Schatz 2004a: 112; Dave 2007: 122f.; see also Vale 2008: 153f.), mixed with personal motives by the country's undisputed leader. Unlike in the United States, where Congress debated and decided the issue of capital location, or in Brazil where parliament still needed to be wooed by the president, the case of Astana demonstrates the preponderance of presidential leadership in Kazakhstan: Nazarbaev put the motion before parliament in 1994 but ignored the opposition which was substantial[2] and made it an entirely executive issue to his political benefit: "The Astana move was intended to marginalize the rivals to Nursultan Nazarbaev, bolster his supporters, and simultaneously to gain access to important sources of international capital" (Schatz 2004a: 124).

Officially, the reasons given for this expensive project concerned the old capital's proximity to the Chinese border, its location in a region with seismic activity and limited potential for further urban development due to its already high population density and its being built on the slopes of the 4000 m high Zailiiski Alatau mountain range (see Aitken 2009: 228f.; also Schatz 2004a: 122f.). The move can also be interpreted as a reflection of the new country's relationship to its two big neighbors, China and Russia. Moving the central apparatus of the state away from China and closer to the 7000 km long border with Russia corresponds with Nazarbaev's official program of "Eurasianism," which promotes the country as the geographic bridge between Europe and Asia and the celebration of the country's multicultural legacy and its multi-ethnic community (see Schatz 2004b: 76; Dave 2007: 122f.). But the capital relocation may have more to do with the country's relations with Russia (and the relationship between the two countries' respective leaders) than with a balanced position between Russia and China: as of 2014, there were a dozen flights from Almaty to other parts of the former Soviet Union, none to China, and one each to Delhi, Istanbul and Dubai (Bloomfield 2015: 80).

Most importantly, however, it appears that the capital relocation is an expression of domestic power politics: with it Nazarbaev quelled secessionist tendencies in the Russian-populated areas of the northern steppe by building the governmental center in the middle of it and bringing in a large urban population of Kazakh background, thus diminishing the proportion and finally the size of the ethnic Russian community in the region, a move which has been dubbed "ethno-territorial gerrymandering" (Dave 2007: 122). Likewise, the relocation of the capital shifted the balance between the three large sub-ethnic units, or "hordes," which constitute the Kazakh population. Moving the political center from the south, which is populated by Nazarbaev's own "greater horde," to the north, where the "middle horde" resides, created a tacit alliance between the two and helped keep a check on the "lesser horde" which dominates the east with its vast oil and gas resources (Schatz 2004a: 129f).

Finally, the new capital can be seen as an instrument of integration in the project of state and nation building (see earlier in this chapter; Hobsbawm 1983: 9; Rapoport 1993: 35–43): it was to foster a stronger sense of belonging of all citizens of Kazakhstan (which the old capital failed to accomplish) and to project the plan of an ideal city with modern, representative official and residential buildings to the citizens as well as to the international community. For this, the city planners turned more to a functional design in line with Eurasian symbols than to an outright show of monumentalism (Schatz 2004a: 127) although in a number of cases, grandiose and megalomaniac designs overshadowed pragmatic considerations (see Meuser 2010: 232). With Nazarbaev centrally involved in the planning of the city and of individual landmarks, the city's development formula can be summarized as "diversity of design but under one decision maker" (see Aitken 2009: 222).

In April 1998, an international competition for the planning of Astana was initiated and the final jury, to which belonged the president and the prime minister as well as a number of experts, chose the Japanese architect Kisho Kurokawa (Kurokawa 2006). In conscious contrast to Brasília, which Kurokawa knew from visits and considered too formal and fixed in form, his plan for Astana promoted an open and growing city, following his idea of the "metabolic and symbiotic city" which leaves room for development and changes (Kurokawa 2014: 81, 1991: 189–191). The aim was that by 2030 Astana would be one of the most modern cities in the world and have a population of 1 million inhabitants (as of 2015, there are already 800,000).

Because of the envisaged openness of the city's development, the outcome in the physical cityscape does not communicate an overarching idea or design but presents a collection of solitary buildings, plazas and structures which do not correspond to each other and thus fail to form an interrelated urban ensemble (such as the geometric layout and dominant style forms in "classicist" Washington D.C. or "modernist" Brasília). Instead, the city can boast of a number of good examples of international contemporary architecture, but more often than not, important official buildings reflect particular preferences of and even direct intervention by the president who "took responsibility for the new capital by acting as if he were its proprietor as well as its President" (Aitken 2009: 232; see also Vale 2008: 154; Meuser 2010: 231f.). Hence, Astana looks like someone's vision of the future, "a city where architects have been given plots of land, no planning rules, no price limit and no need to consider the city's soul" (Bloomfield 2015: 69). This is particularly true for the new governmental, administrative and business city center (about 6 km from the old center of Akmola), which is organized around a large monumental axis from east to west, the Nurzhol Boulevard, and a high monument at the crossing point of a smaller north–south axis, thus echoing the basic idea of other planned capital cities but, unlike them, failing to provide a minimum of coherence in appearance.

In the east, the axis ends at the Presidential Palace Ak Orda which combines symmetrical classical forms, reminiscent of the White House in Washington DC but much larger, with the local language of the dome and spire in blue and gold, the colors of the national flag (see Figure 31.11) – though this edifice looks more constrained than the grandiose palaces of modern-day dictators such as Saddam Hussein, Colonel Gaddafi or Bashar al-Assad (see Wainwright 2013). Behind the palace and not visible from the central axis, Norman Foster's pyramid shaped Palace of Peace and Reconciliation emerges, in which Nazarbaev hosts the tri-annual meeting of world religious leaders and other international events. The lower chamber of the parliament (Mazhilis) and the senate building (the latter one a gift from Saudi Arabia in oriental style) are tucked away behind other government buildings such as the

Figure 31.11　Astana: The eastern end of the central axis, as seen from Baiterek Tower, with the Presidential Palace (Center) and Government Towers (the Parliament on the far left, the Government Tower with Prime Ministerial Office on the right, plus the golden cones of the House of Ministries) (2010)

© Michael Minkenberg

two golden towers where the gigantic half-circle of the house of ministries is interrupted by the central axis; appropriate to their political status, the houses of parliament are hardly visible from the axis. The same goes for the flat but monumental neo-classicist high court building, which is situated at a right angle to the Presidential Palace in due distance and in "under-complex postmodern arbitrariness" (Meuser 2014: 165), vis-à-vis a giant desert rose-shaped concert hall in blue and green and designed by renowned Italian architect Manfredo Nicoletti.

At the center of the axis rises the 97 m high Baiterek Tower (the height pointing to the year when the move to Astana was decided), which is said to have been sketched by Nazarbaev himself (see Aitken 2009: 222; Meuser 2014: 151) and which symbolizes the golden egg which the mythical bird Samruk had placed in a poplar tree (see Figure 31.12). The tower is open to the public, contains the gold-plated handprint of the president and marks the crossing of the east–west axis with the shorter north–south axis, the end-points of which are the ministries of foreign affairs and defense, respectively, both in a pseudo-classical style mix with colossal columns typical of Kazakh state architecture in the new capital (see Meuser 2014: 154). The opposite end of the east–west axis is occupied by the headquarters building of the state-owned energy corporation KazMunaiGas in the casino or holiday resort style of the Bahamas and Canary Islands (see www.atlantisbahamas.com/). The central axis continues beyond the KazMunaiGas building and ends at the monumental (and sparsely frequented) shopping center

Figure 31.12   Astana: Baiterek Tower and view of the western end of the central axis with the
headquarters of the state-owned energy corporation KazMunaiGas at the end
and Norman Foster's Khan Shatyr shopping complex beyond (2010)

© Michael Minkenberg

Khan Shatyr by Norman Foster (see Bloomfield 2015: 69) which in gigantic dimensions takes
on the form of a yurt, a nomadic living space typical of the Kazakhs' historical culture (see
Bloomfield 2015: 69; Meuser 2014: 141).

With the president's palace at one end of the axis, and the KazMunaiGas building at the
other, the axis with the country's real centers of political and economic power opposite each
other reflects, more than those in many democratic capitals, the power structure in Kazakhstan.
In this way, Astana can be considered a particularly "honest" city. All in all, the design of the
city center carries out the master planner's idea of an "open city" to the degree that architectural
eclecticism dominates with very little coherence – the only recurring theme being the generous use of domes and the national colors blue and gold (for details see Aitken 2009: 222f. and
Meuser 2014: 118–211). At the same time, the city reflects more than other newly built capitals
the nature of Kazakhstan's leadership and regime structures. While, with few exceptions such
as the presidential palace and the Baiterek Tower, issues of style were left to the architects or
originators of the buildings (as in the case of the senate building), the planning of the city as a
whole and the decision to move the capital from Almaty to Astana was entirely in the hands of
the autocratic executive, i.e. the president, his family and his advisors. In the appearance of the
city, however, a future visitor to Astana will have little information about the personal tastes
and style preferences of the founding father beyond his occasional megalomaniacal inclinations,
quite in contrast to the position in Washington DC or Brasília.

Conclusions

This chapter has taken a comparative look at the planned part of modern capital cities and explored how it reflects the ideas and interests of those who have made or implemented the plans, i.e. political leaders. By contrasting "old" and "new" as well as democratic and non-democratic capitals, the chapter tried to shed light on the relationship between leadership in various types of regimes and architecture, especially the issue of a particular tension between leadership and democratic principles (see Kane and Patapan 2012).

As a starting point, it is the institutional make-up of regimes, and in particular the difference between autocratic and democratic regimes, which is relevant for how they are translated into built space and what role leadership plays in them:

> Government buildings are . . . an attempt to build government and to support specific regimes. More than mere homes for government leaders, they serve as symbols of the state. We can, therefore, learn much about a political regime by observing closely what it builds.
>
> *(Vale 2008: 3)*

By implication, we can also learn much about leadership by observing what and how they build.

One lesson to be learned is that autocratic leadership does not necessarily translate into a coherent urban design and public architecture in capital cities but can be detected more visibly in single projects showing a particular taste. Individual autocratic leaders, from the Roman emperors and the popes to modern autocrats and dictators such as Napoleon, Mussolini and Hitler in Western Europe, Stalin and the post-communist leaders in the new states of the former Soviet Union, often had grand visions and great plans for the entire city. But in reality, they only added single pieces of their leadership's evidence in stone. For that matter, the two Napoleons left more lasting and coherent traces in Paris than either Mussolini or Hitler in their respective capital cities.

A second lesson lies in the discovery that the study of leadership and architecture suggests a typology of autocratic leadership that does not simply echo the conventional distinctions of left and right, or totalitarianism and authoritarianism. Accordingly, one type of leader follows through – or attempts to follow through – a coherent project of (re)building the capital city, occasionally embedded in a cultural–political program, with little regard to the interests or livelihood of the city's residents or historical legacies as they ruthlessly replace existing quarters by their own projects (e.g. Nero, Mussolini, Hitler; one may add Stalin and Mao, see Vale 2008: 36–41). Others build their capital cities with more consideration for the local population, usually adding new buildings or quarters without tearing down existing neighborhoods (except for those in desolate condition) (e.g. Augustus, East German leaders since the early 1970s, Nazarbaev). Napoleon III falls somewhat in between: he tore down large segments of the inner city of Paris but built new and improved neighborhoods. Only the absolutist age granted leaders nearly absolute freedom to build as they pleased following the motto "*car tel est mon plaisir*" (von Beyme 1996: 231).

A third lesson is that, ironically, it was democratic regimes with strong executive leadership that produced the most complete execution of the leaders' vision. As has been shown, there are democratic cases of strong leadership with few constraints, as in the United States with George Washington in the 1790s and Congress in the early 1900s when the democratic process produced imperial outcomes and monumental visions on a scale comparable to the monumentalism of past empires (Rome) (see Scott 2002). A similar trajectory can be observed in France with Napoleon III and, to a lesser degree, presidents in the Fifth Republic. Here the tension between leadership and popular sovereignty has been eased at the expense of democracy. But, as in Washington DC and in many other cases, even monumental architecture which seemingly betrays the democratic credo allows the return of "popular sovereignty" through the back door via the popular use of public space and buildings, provided the system grants such use (see Vale 2008: 73–75).

Lesson number four concerns the democratic exception to the rule: Brasília was built in a presidential regime with less constraints on executive leadership than in de Gaulle's France and more comparable to the Second Empire under Napoleon III. The "purity of vision" was preserved but it remains contested to what extent the vision was democratic in the first place when considering the actual personnel involved: a president intent on pushing through a forceful modernization of the country with little esteem for the parliament and a communist chief architect, the main representative of modernism in Brazil.

A final lesson is that collective leadership as in the Westminster model or in consociational democracies such as Germany encounters institutional constraints from the beginning of their planning with the effect that the outcomes can only be fragmentary expressions of the respective leadership, and reflect more the tastes of the experts and interested public than that of the leaders themselves. The rebuilding of Berlin after German reunification is a case in point: while the general mood was against overt signs of monumentalism, the particular style of any new or major renovation of an old building was left to the architects if they respected this mood. Here a legacy of post-war West Germany constrained aspirations to think bigger, a lesson to be learned by the architectural team that won the second of the two first prizes in the competition for the new chancellor's office but, due to their more classical and monumental style, were rejected in favor of Axel Schultes's postmodern entry. East Berlin before 1989 deviates from the model of collective leadership in that, in the early postwar years, monumentalism was not a problem; yet even here, the 1970s witnessed a more utilitarian approach to public buildings (such as the "people's chamber") and the effort to provide modern housing for the urban masses.

The debate on whether democracies, or democratic leaders, build or should build differently is an ancient as well as a very modern debate. For example, Frank Lloyd Wright's belief that architecture should serve the individual and not rule over him led him to distinguish between "organic architecture of and for the individual" and "the pseudo-classic order of the schools, which was mainly derived from survival of the military and monarchic order" (Wright 1945: 53). In Germany, the debate about a democratic architecture unfolded in the post-war era when both Germanys were rebuilt with old and new capitals and it centered much more narrowly on the architecture of public buildings. In conscious contrast to the closed public spaces of Wilhelmine and the manipulated spaces of Nazi architecture, some leaders in the Bonn Republic were asking for a new level of transparency (see Minkenberg 2014b; von Beyme 1996, 2014; Wise 1998). The connection between democratic leadership and architecture was most pronounced in the case of Canberra, where early on political, that is parliamentary, leaders sought to express their style of Westminster policy making in the modest monumentality of the new capital city which grew out of the garden city model and with few exceptions shied away from grandiose gestures (see Sonne 2003). In these cases, the demand for more transparency, as the hallmark of democratic regimes, has been translated into the demand for more glass and light in governmental architecture and more accessible public spaces.[3]

However, as this chapter has shown, even when conscious efforts were made to express capital-city building and public architecture in a democratic language, the syntax often stems from pre-democratic times. This is what connects "old" and "new" capital cities under democratic and autocratic leadership alike: the emphasis on axiality and geometry, on large empty spaces and vista points, from L'Enfant's Washington to Griffin's Canberra, from Niemeyer's Brasília to Le Corbusier's Chandigarh and Kurokawa's Astana; the monumentality of key public buildings such as parliaments, even the seating order in those institutions, carry on symbolic messages from a non-democratic past, most notably the monarchical approach to political space and the built environment of the baroque era (see Mumford 1961: 406; Sutcliffe 1993: 198; Manow 2008: 18f., 2015; Vale 2008: 121–156).

The democratic dilemma regarding the necessity of leadership and the promise of democratic principles such as popular sovereignty (Kane and Patapan 2012, 2014) is reflected in the democratic dilemma of building a capital city: unlike in classical Athens, modern democracies are characterized by a division of labor between the people and those institutionally entrusted with doing the work for the people and in the name of the people. They are elitist and representative, and hence capital cities in modern democracies can be configured as representative in multiple ways (see Nerdinger 1996: 17–24; Sonne 2003: 35–44, 294–315; Vale 2008: chapter 2). First, they represent the nation as a whole, i.e. the image that nation builders have provided, including the ideal site for such a city as a national, not a regional or sectional, symbol. Second, they represent the promise of democracy by communicating the values of inclusiveness and contestation in public places and buildings and a location that is not compromised by pre- or non-democratic traditions and interests. Third, they embody the practice of representation by providing the physical space for the exercise of democratic politics, for politicians, bureaucrats and the judiciary, while occupying a geographic place which facilitates these practices. And fourth, they represent the tastes, interests and visions of those who actually planned and built the cities (Jefferson in Washington, Niemeyer in Brasília, Schultes in Berlin).

For these representations to function, the promise of democracy – inclusiveness, participation, transparency, accountability – must retreat to some degree. The functional requirements of government result in a hierarchical relationship, in a vertical order of status and power, between those who govern and those who are governed – and when visiting the capital city citizens perform the role of spectator much more than that of participant. Hence, as with the tension between leadership and democracy, there is the tension between capital cities as symbols of empowerment ("we the people," in stone and buildings) and the realities of alienation ("we the political class," safeguarded from the people, removed from other power centers such as an older metropolis) (see Taylor 1989: 80).

This tension affects in a particular way the issues of size and monumentality in new democratic capitals. On the one hand, big cities typically lack a ceremonial focus, so smaller and newly created capitals can better provide for this communication for a specific political (democratic) meaning in their design and architecture (see Rapoport 1993: 40). As a result, the capital city is able to project a sense of urban unity where, as was L'Enfant's idea for Washington (and, one might add, Griffin's as well as Saarinen's for Canberra), "the axial government complex could be harmoniously embodied within, and relate to, a comprehensively ordered street fabric" (Evenson 2002: 21; see also Sonne 2003: 155–165). On the other hand, their monumentalism in public architecture, although in some cases inspired by ideas of modernity and democracy (Canberra and Brasília), risks segregating the political function of the city from other functions (residence, recreation, transport, etc.) and thereby accentuate the separation between the rulers and the ruled, even in a democratic setting and as a democratic conception. In this sense "form followed culture, and both followed structure" (Taylor 1989: 80; see also Sutcliffe 1993; Vale 2008: 8f. and Manow 2008). Hence, new capitals in democracies are not immune to pre-democratic legacies and non-democratic meanings. While specific designs may emphasize democratic values and contribute to the implementation of ideas that they represent (see Sonne 2003: 39f.), they are unsuited to communicate specific messages and thereby are open to multiple interpretations.

More specifically, in the cities under consideration in this chapter, the democratic quality of the process did not produce, by itself, democratic outcomes, an instance which becomes even clearer when including the obvious non-democratic cases of Imperial and Papal Rome as well as autocratic Paris, Fascist Rome, Nazi and Communist (East) Berlin, and autocratic Astana into our examination. Clearly, the less democracy in terms of popular control or checks and balances, the greater the chance to preserve the purity of vision in the outcome. In other words: regime type matters, as the cases of the Roman emperors or Napoleon III or today's Kazakhstan demonstrate. Against this backdrop, Wilhelmine Berlin provides an interesting case of ambivalence: the semi-democratic leadership was constrained by both a lack of vision and a fixation on the authoritarian past and left only a few (monumental) traces, most importantly the Reichstag, the Berlin Cathedral, and a number of monuments such as the victory column (see Cullen 1999; Hoffmann 2000).

It appears that in only a few cases is the tension between leadership and democracy in building capital cities resolved in favor of democracy. These include the parliamentary democracies of Australia and the Germany of the 1990s. Both Canberra and Berlin after reunification display a reluctance of leadership to use "grand design" involving (pre-democratic) monumentalism and axiality, yet both cases show some signs of a (democratic) vision (see von Beyme 1996). In Canberra, site search and layout strictly followed the logic of the parliamentary democratic process, and the new parliament in its "democratic monumentality" can be seen as an approximation to squaring the circle. In Berlin, the new planning involved an explicit attempt to counter old planning traditions of undemocratic leaders, for example the "Federal Row" instead of the traditional north–south axis, modest monumentality in the Chancellery mixed with historical reconstruction of the city center (Pariser Platz, the Hohenzollern Palace) (see Sonne 2006; Asendorf 2014).

Overall, in architecture any type of leadership and vision is constrained by two impersonal and non-systemic factors: the prevalent "zeitgeist" which rules out certain styles or fosters others (witness the prevalence of classicism in all kinds of eras and regime types; or the wave of neo-Gothic and neo-Renaissance at the end of the nineteenth century in many parts of Europe), and path-dependency which can only be broken in the rare occasion of building a new capital city, itself the beginning of a new path and new dependencies. In addition, the tension between leadership and democracy is deeply affected by the 9/11 legacies and the subsequent surge of securitization in the Western world, with democracy and the promise of transparency in architecture at the losing end (see Vale 2008: 75).

Notes

1 This contribution builds on a larger project on political power and capital city building (see Minkenberg 2014a, c). The author thanks the editors of this volume for their helpful comments.
2 Aitken (2009: 230) quotes Nazarbaev who claims that the parliamentary vote for Astana was very narrow while the then speaker of parliament Abdildin claims that the majority voted against the measure (interview with the author on September 9, 2010, in Almaty).
3 The European Parliament building in Brussels, with its large glass front, built as a conference center before the European Parliament rented and modified it, can be seen as an effort to speak the "democratic language" of transparency, in a similar way to the Berlaymont building of the Commission and the glass-fronted parliament building in Strasbourg, which is even surrounded by a large open space. Yet the abundance of glass conceals the nature of the EU's regime, which only a few would consider a truly democratic polity. Moreover, the Brussels parliament building has been interpreted as a failure rather than a success in integration and identity creation (see Hein 2014: 273f.).

References

Abbott, Carl. 1999. *Political Terrain: Washington, D.C., from Tidewater Town to Global Metropolis*. Chapel Hill, NC: University of North Carolina Press.

Aitken, Jonathan. 2009. *Nazarbayev and the Making of Kazakhstan*. London: Continuum.

Asendorf, Christoph. 2004. "In die Vertikale gestellt. Von Obelisken und Kathedralen zum Skyscraper." In: *Der Traum vom Turm. Hochhäuser: Mythos – Ingenieurkunst – Baukultur*. NRW-Forum Kultur and Wirtschaft Düsseldorf (eds.). Ostfildern-Ruit: Hatje Cantz Verlag, pp. 29–39.

Asendorf, Christoph. 2014. "Berlin: Three Centuries as Capital." In: *Power and Architecture. The Construction of Capitals and the Politics of Space*. M. Minkenberg (ed.). New York: Berghahn, pp. 128–151.

Avila, Fabio. 2000. *Guiarquitetura Brasilia*. Sao Paulo: Empresa das Artes.

Batista, Geraldo Nogueira, Sylvia Fischer, Francisco Leitão and Dionísio Alves de França. 2006. "Brasilia. A Capital in the Hinterland." In: *Planning Twentieth Century Capitals*. David Gordon (ed.). London: Routledge, pp. 164–181.

Bennister, Mark, Paul 't Hart and Ben Worthy. 2015. "Assessing the Authority of Political Office Holders: The Leadership Capital Index." *West European Politics* 38 (3): 417–440.

Bloomfield, Steve. 2015. "Reportage 1. A Tale of Two Cities: Kazakhstan." In: *The Monocle Forecast* No. 1, pp. 67–82.

Bodenschatz, Harald. 2013. *Städtebau in Berlin. Schreckbild and Vorbild für Europa*. Berlin: DOM Publishers.

Borraz, Olivier and Peter John. 2004. "The Transformation of Urban Political Leadership in Western Europe." In: *International Journal of Urban and Regional Research* 28 (1): 107–120.

Bourdieu, Pierre. 2005. "The Political Field, the Social Science Field and the Journalistic Field." In: *Bourdieu and the Journalistic Field*. Cambridge: Polity Press, pp. 29–48.

Bowling, Kenneth. 1988. *Creating the Federal City, 1774–1800: Potomac Fever*. Washington, DC: The American Institute of Architects Press.

Bowling, Kenneth. 1991. *The Creation of Washington, DC: The Idea and Location of the American Capital*. Fairfax, VA: George Mason University Press.

Boyer, Christine. 1983. *Dreaming the Rational City: The Myth of American City Planning*. Cambridge, MA: MIT Press.

Braunfels, Wolfgang. 1988. *Urban Design in Western Europe. Regime and Architecture, 900–1900*. Trans. Kenneth J. Northcott. Chicago: The University of Chicago Press.

Cohen, Jean-Louis. 2010. "Petite histoire du 'Grand Paris.'" In: *Critique: Vivement Paris!* No. 757–758: 486–492.

Cole, Alistair, Sophie Meunier and Vincent Tiberij (eds.). 2013. *Developments in French Politics 5*. Basingstoke: Palgrave Macmillan.

Connolly, Peter and Hazel Dodge. 2001. *The Ancient City: Life in Classical Athens and Rome*. Oxford: Oxford University Press.

Craig, Lois et al. 1978. *The Federal Presence: Architecture, Politics, and Symbols in United States Government Building*. Cambridge, MA: The MIT Press.

Cullen, Michael. 1999. *Der Reichstag. Parlament, Denkmal, Symbol*. Berlin: be.bra Verlag.

Cummings, Milton C. and Matthew Price. 1993. "The Creation of Washington DC: Political Symbolism and Practical Problem Solving in the Establishment of the Capital City in the United States of America." In: *Capital Cities. Les Capitales*. John Taylor, Jean G. Lengellé, and Caroline Andrew (eds.). Ottawa: Carlton University Press, pp. 213–249.

Curran, Brian A., Anthony Grafton, Pamela O. Lang and Benjamin Weiss. 2009. *Obelisk: A History*. Cambridge, MA: The MIT Press.

Dave, Bhavna. 2007. *Kazakhstan: Ethnicity, Language and Power*. London: Routledge.

Ehrman, Henry J. and Martin A. Schain. 1992. *Politics in France*. 5th edition. New York: HarperCollins.

Elgie, Robert. 1995. *Political Leadership in Liberal Democracies*. Basingstoke: Macmillan.

Epstein, Renaud. 2013. *La renovation urbaine. Démolition-reconstruction de l'Etat*. Paris: Presses de Sciences Po.

Evenson, Norma. 1973. *Two Brazilian Capitals: Architecture and Urbanism in Rio de Janeiro and Brasilia*. New Haven, CT: Yale University Press.

Evenson, Norma. 2002. "Monumental Spaces." In: *The Mall in Washington*. Richard Longstreth (ed.). New Haven, CT: Yale University Press, pp. 19–34.

Ewald, Björn and Carlos F. Noreña. 2010. "Introduction." In: *The Emperor and Rome: Space, Representation, and Ritual*. Björn Ewald and Carlos F. Noreña (eds.). Cambridge: Cambridge University Press, pp. 1–44.

Field, Cynthia R., Isabelle Gournay and Thomas P. Somma (eds.). 2007. *Paris on the Potomac: The French Influence on the Architecture and Art of Washington DC.* Athens: Ohio University Press.

Fils, Alexander. 1988. *Brasilia. Moderne Architektur in Brasilien.* Düsseldorf: Beton Verlag.

Fils, Alexander. 1996. "Politische Idealstädte. Das Beispiel Brasilia und andere Neugründungen." In: *Architektur und Demokratie.* Ingeborg Flagge and Wolfgang Jean Stock (eds.). 2nd rev. ed. Stuttgart: Hatje, pp. 186–211.

Fischer, K. G. 1984. *Canberra: Myths and Models. Forces at Work in the Formation of the Australian Capital.* Hamburg: Institute of Asian Affairs.

Freestone, Robert. 2007. *Designing Australia's Cities: Culture, Commerce, and the City Beautiful, 1900–1930.* Sydney: University of New South Wales Press.

Gaïti, Brigitte. 1998. *De Gaulle. Prophète de la Cinquième République.* Paris: Presses de la Fondation Nationale des Sciences Politiques.

Gordon, David L. A. (ed.). 2006. *Planning Twentieth Century Capitals.* London: Routledge.

Gournay, Isabelle. 2006. "Washington: The DC's History of Unresolved Planning Conflicts." In: *Planning Twentieth Century Capitals.* David Cordon (ed.). London: Routledge, pp. 115–129.

Hall, Thomas. 1997. *Planning Europe's Capital Cities: Aspects of Nineteenth Century Urban Development.* London: Taylor and Francis.

Hazan, Eric. 2002. *L'invention de Paris. Il n'y a pas de pas perdus.* Paris: Seuil.

Hein, Carola. 2014. "Building Capital Mindscapes for the European Union." In: *Power and Architecture: The Construction of Capitals and the Politics of Space.* Michael Minkenberg (ed.). New York: Berghahn, pp. 261–286.

Helms, Ludger. 2005. *Presidents, Prime Ministers, and Chancellors.* Basingstoke: Palgrave.

Hobsbawm, Eric. 1983. "Introduction: Inventing Tradition." In: *The Invention of Tradition.* Eric Hobsbawm and Terence Ranger (eds.). Cambridge: Cambridge University Press, pp. 1–14.

Hoffmann, Godehard. 2000. *Architektur für die Nation? Der Reichstag und die Staatsbauten des Deutschen Kaiserreichs.* Köln: DuMont.

Holston, James. 1989. *The Modernist City: An Anthropological Critique of Brasília.* Chicago: The University of Chicago Press.

Junisbai, Barbara. 2010. "A Tale of Two Kazakhstans: Sources of Political Cleavage and Conflict in the Post-Soviet Period." In: *Europe-Asia Studies* 62 (2): 235–269.

Kane, John and Haig Patapan. 2012. *The Democratic Leader.* Oxford: Oxford University Press.

Kane, John and Haig Patapan (eds.). 2014. *Good Democratic Leadership: On Prudence and Judgment in Modern Democracies.* Oxford: Oxford University Press.

Kirk, Terry. 2005a. *The Architecture of Modern Italy. Vol 1: The Challenge of Tradition, 1750–1900.* New York: Princeton Architectural Press.

Kirk, Terry. 2005b. *The Architecture of Modern Italy. Vol 2: Visions of Utopia, 1900–Present.* New York: Princeton Architectural Press.

Kirk, Terry. 2014. "Image, Itinerary, and Identity in the 'Third' Rome." In: *Power and Architecture: The Construction of Capitals and the Politics of Space.* Michael Minkenberg (ed.). New York: Berghahn, pp. 152–177.

Knell, Heiner. 2004. *Bauprogramme römischer Kaiser.* Darmstadt: Verlag Phillip von Zabern in Wissenschaftliche Buchgesellschaft.

Kostof, Spiro. 1973. *The Third Rome, 1870–1950: Traffic and Glory.* Berkeley, CA: University Art Museum.

Kurokawa, Kisho. 1991. *Intercultural Architecture: The Philosophy of Symbiosis.* London: Academy Editions.

Kurokawa, Kisho. 2006. "International Competition for the Master Plan and Design of Astana, Kazakhstan" (http://www.kisho.co.jp/page.php/222, last accessed July 4, 2015).

Kurokawa, Kisho. 2014. "Astana braucht eine offene Gesellschaft." Interview. In: *Architekturführer Kasachstan.* Philipp Meuser (ed.). Berlin: DOM Publishers, pp. 81–85.

Lacroix, Bernard and Jacques Lagroye (eds.). 1992. *Le Président de la République. Usages et genèse d'une institution.* Paris: Presses de la Fondation Nationale des Sciences Politiques.

Ladd, Brian. 2005. "Socialism on Display. East Berlin as Capital." In: *Berlin – Washington, 1800–2000. Capital Cities, Cultural Representations, and National Identities.* Andreas Daum and Christof Mauch (eds.). Cambridge: Cambridge University Press, pp. 216–231.

Lovell, David W., Ian McAllister, William Maley and Chandran Kukathas. 1998. *The Australian Political System.* 2nd edition. South Melbourne: Addison Wesley Longman.

Manow, Philip. 2008. *Im Schatten des Königs. Die politische Anatomie demokratischer Repräsentation.* Frankfurt/Main: Suhrkamp.

Manow, Philip. 2015. "Demokratie und Architektur." In: *Merkur* 69 (March): 45–52.

Meckseper, Cord. 1996. "Oben und unten in der Architektur. Zur Entstehung einer abendländischen Raumkategorie." In: *Architektur als politische Kultur*. Hermann Hipp and Ernst Seidl (eds.). Berlin: Dietrich Reimer Verlag, pp. 37–52.

Metcalf, Andrew. 2003. *Canberra Architecture*. Sydney: The Watermark Press.

Meuser, Philipp. 2010. "Astana, Almaty, and Aktau. Architectural Experiments in the Steppe of Kazakhstan." In: *The Post-Socialist City: Continuity and Change in Urban Space and Imagery*. Alfrun Kliems and Marina Dmitrieva (eds.). Berlin: Jovis Verlag, pp. 230–247.

Meuser, Philipp (ed.). 2014. *Architekturführer Kasachstan*. Berlin: DOM Publishers.

Minkenberg, Michael (ed.). 2014a. *Power and Architecture: The Construction of Capitals and the Politics of Space*. New York: Berghahn.

Minkenberg, Michael. 2014b. "Introduction. Power and Architecture: The Construction of Capitals, the Politics of Space and the Space of Politics." In: *Power and Architecture: The Construction of Capitals and the Politics of Space*. Michael Minkenberg (ed.). New York: Berghahn, pp. 1–30.

Minkenberg, Michael. 2014c. "A City of the People, by the People, for the People? Democracy and Capital-Building in Washington, DC, Ottawa, Canberra, and Brasília." In: *Power and Architecture: The Construction of Capitals and the Politics of Space*. Michael Minkenberg (ed.). New York: Berghahn, pp. 53–105.

Mumford, Lewis. 1961. *The City in History: Its Origins, Its Transformations, and Its Prospects*. San Diego, CA: Harcourt Inc.

Muth, Susanne. 2014. "Forum Romanum in Augusteischer Zeit II: um 14 n.Chr." http://www.digitales-forum-romanum.de/epochen/augusteisch-ii/ (September 21, 2014).

Nerdinger, Winfried. 1996. "Politische Architektur. Betrachtungen zu einem problematischen Begriff." In: *Architektur und Demokratie. Bauen für die Politik von der amerikanischen Revolution bis zur Gegenwart*. Ingeborg Flagge and Wolfgang Jean Stock (eds.). 2nd edition. Ostfildern-Ruit: Hatje, pp. 10–31.

Pegrum, Roger. 1988. "Canberra: The Bush Capital." In: *The Origins of Australia's Capital Cities*. Pamela Statham (ed.). Cambridge: Cambridge University Press, pp. 317–340.

Pegrum, Roger. 2003. "Introduction. The Dream of a Dreamer." In: *Canberra Architecture*. Andrew Metcalf (ed.). Sydney: The Watermark Press, pp. 7–15.

Piccinato, Giorgio. 2006. "Rome: Where Great Events Not Regular Planning Bring Development." In: *Planning Twentieth Century Capitals*. David Gordon (ed.). London: Routledge, pp. 213–225.

Rapoport, Amos. 1993. "On the Nature of Capitals and Their Physical Expression." In *Capital Cities. Les Capitales*. John Taylor, Jean G. Lengellé and Caroline Andrew (eds.). Ottawa: Carlton University Press, pp. 31–67.

Reid, Paul. 2002. *Canberra following Griffin: A Design History of Australia's National Capital*. Canberra: National Archives of Australia.

Reps, John W. 1967. *Monumental Washington: The Planning and Development of the Capital Center*. Princeton, NJ: Princeton University Press.

Roth, Leland and Amanda Clark. 2014. *Understanding Architecture: Its Elements, History, and Meaning*. 3rd edition. Boulder, CO: Westview Press.

Saxl, Fritz. 1957. "The Capitol during the Renaissance: A Symbol of the Imperial Idea." In: *Lectures*. Fritz Saxl (ed.). London: The Warburg Institute, Universtiy of London, pp. 200–214.

Schain, Martin A. and John S. Keeler. 1995. "Le pouvoir présidentiel aux Etats-Unis et an France: Une perspective comparative." In: *La France présidentielle*. Nicolas Wahl and Jean-Louis Quermonne (eds.). Paris: Presses de la Fondation Nationale des Sciences Politiques, pp. 237–256.

Schatz, Edward. 2004a. "What Capital Cities Say About State and Nation Building." In: *Nationalism and Ethnic Politics*, 9: 111–140.

Schatz, Edward. 2004b. *Modern Clan Politics: The Power of "Blood" in Kazakhstan and Beyond*. Seattle, WA: University of Washington Press.

Schirmer, Dietmar. 2005. "Staat, Volk, and Monumental Architecture in Nazi-Era Berlin." In *Berlin – Washington, 1800–2000. Capital Cities, Cultural Representations, and National Identities*. Andreas Daum and Christof Mauch (eds.). Cambridge: Cambridge University Press, pp. 127–153.

Scott, Pamela. 1995. *Temple of Liberty: Building the Capitol for a New Nation*. New York: Oxford University Press.

Scott, Pamela. 2002. "'This Vast Empire': The Iconography of the Mall, 1791–1848." In: *The Mall in Washington*. Richard Longstreeth (ed.). New Haven, CT: Yale University Press, pp. 37–60.

Seidl, Ernst. 1996. "Monument im Dienst der Demokratie? La Grande Arche in Paris." *Architektur als politische Kultur*. Hermann Hipp and Ernst Seidl (eds.). Berlin: Dietrich Reimer Verlag, pp. 311–326.

Skidmore, Thomas E. 1967. *Politics in Brazil 1930–1964: An Experiment in Democracy.* Oxford: Oxford University Press.

Sonne, Wolfgang. 2003. *Representing the State: Capital City Planning in the Early Twentieth Century.* Munich: Prestel.

Sonne, Wolfgang. 2006. "Berlin: Capital under Changing Political Regimes." In: *Planning Twentieth Century Capitals.* David Gordon (ed.). London: Routledge, pp. 196–212.

Stambaugh, Jonathan E. 1988. *The Ancient Roman City.* Baltimore, MD: The Johns Hopkins University Press.

Sutcliffe, Anthony. 1993. "Capital Cities: Does Form Follow Values?" In *Capital Cities. Les Capitales.* John Taylor, Jean G. Lengellé, and Caroline Andrew (eds.) Ottawa: Carleton University Press, pp. 195–212.

Taylor, John. 1989. "City Form and Capital Culture: Remaking Ottawa." In: *Planning Perspectives* 4, pp. 79–105.

Thibaut, Bernhard. 1996. *Präsidentialismus und Demokratie in Lateinamerika.* Opladen: Leske + Budrich.

Vale, Lawrence J. 2008. *Architecture, Power, and National Identity.* 2nd edition. London: Routledge.

Vernon, Christopher. 2006. "Canberra: Where Landscape is Pre-eminent." In: *Planning Twentieth Century Capitals.* David Gordon (ed.). London: Routledge, pp. 130–149.

Von Beyme, Klaus. 1996. "Parlament, Demokratie und Öffentlichkeit. Die Visualisierung demokratischer Grundprinzipien im Parlamentsbau." *Architektur und Demokratie. Bauen für die Politik von der amerikanischen Revolutin bis zur Gegenwart.* Ingeborg Flagge and Wolfgang Jean Stock (eds.). 2nd edition. Ostfildern-Ruit: Hatje, pp. 32–46.

Von Beyme, Klaus. 1998. *Die Kunst der Macht und die Gegenmacht der Kunst. Studien zum Spannungsverhältnis von Kunst und Politik.* Frankfurt (Main): Suhrkamp.

Von Beyme, Klaus. 2014. "Capital-Building in Postwar Germany." In: *Power and Architecture: The Construction of Capitals and the Politics of Space.* Michael Minkenberg (ed.). New York: Berghahn, pp. 106–127.

Von Matt, Leonard and Franco Barelli. 1980. *Rom. Kunst und Kultur der "Ewigen Stadt."* Köln: DuMont.

Von Moos, Stanislaus. 1980. "The Palace as Fortress: Rome and Bologna under Pope Julius II." In: *Art and Architecture in the Service of Politics.* Henry A. Millon and Linda Nochlin (eds.). Cambridge: The MIT Press, pp. 46–79.

Wainwright, Oliver. 2013. "Assad's Palace: An Empty, Echoing Monument to Dictator Décor." In: *The Guardian* 11 September.

White, Paul. 2006. "Paris: From the Legacy of Haussmann to the Pursuit of Cultural Supremacy." In: *Planning Twentieth Century Capitals.* David Gordon (ed.). London: Routledge, pp. 38–57.

Wigmore, Lionel. 1963. *The Long View: Australia's National Capital.* Melbourne: F.W. Cheshire.

Wise, Michael. 1998. *Capital Dilemma: Germany's Search for a New Architecture of Democracy.* New York: Princeton Architectural Press.

Wolman, Hal, Jan Chadwick and Ana Karruz. 2006. "Capital Cities and Their National Governments: Washington, DC in Comparative Perspective." Washington, DC: George Washington University Institute of Public Policy.

Wright, Frank Lloyd. 1945. *When Democracy Builds.* 2nd edition. Chicago: University of Chicago Press.

Zanker, Paul. 1997. *Der Kaiser baut fürs Volk.* Opladen: Westdeutscher Verlag.

Zanker, Paul. 2010. "By the Emperor, for the People: 'Popular' Architecture in Rome." In: *The Emperor and Rome: Space, Representation, and Ritual.* Björn Ewald and Carlos F. Noreña (eds.). Cambridge: Cambridge University Press, pp. 45–88.

Part VII
Nurturing Leadership

Introduction

Any good leader wants to be better; better leaders then make others better by investing in and upgrading the next generation of leadership. There is a seemingly endless debate about whether leaders are born or bred; nature vs nurture; placement vs development. Those on the nature/born side would invest less in developing leaders than in placing the right leader in the right position at the right time, since the individual has limited ability to develop new skills (e.g. build on your strengths). Those on the nurture/bred side of this debate would argue that, with proper development, leaders can grow new competencies to respond to the requirements of the position (be all you can be).

While advocates on both sides of this debate speak eloquently and boldly, there is actually consistent scientific evidence that leadership behavior is about 50/50. Half of what leaders know and do comes from heritable predispositions; the other half can be learned from experience and development (see some key references at end of this introduction on the subject). Nurturing leadership requires understanding how leaders are both born and bred.

So, what do the 50/50 findings mean? For an individual who wants to be a better leader, the findings put improvement within a realistic framework. Some leadership skills will come more easily and naturally to the aspiring leader, some may require extensive personal development, and some may be unlikely even with good intentions and immense personal effort. For those charged with upgrading leadership within an organization, this means that investments in leadership development programmes need to be wisely tailored to both the business requirements that the leader must face and the personal learning styles of the leader. The chapters in this part offer insights on these issues.

Cunliffe and Wilson focus on the nurture/breed end of leadership development. They do an outstanding job of describing where leadership is taught (universities, consulting firms, or leadership centres, inside organizations). They also highlight tensions in teaching leadership; for example, should one teach leaders as individuals or a collective? As behavioural or socially constructed concepts? Through rationalistic or existential assumptions? As a neutral or political activity? They propose that, rather than teach leadership, it is much better to focus on how one learns leadership. They encourage leadership learning through *phronesis*, which focuses on reflection, through relationship building, which focuses on experience, and through aesthetic embodiment, which focuses on emotional sensing. By recognizing innovative ways to learn leadership, individuals can become more effective leaders and nurture is enhanced.

Gosling and Sutherland offer a thorough overview of an array of practices in leadership development. They emphasize followership as much or more than leadership. They show that most leadership development activities are focused on individual prescriptions. They provide a wonderful history of the evolution of leadership development, starting with the Greeks through to current events. They overview the $14 billion leadership development industry. They highlight the critiques of leadership development as not attending to the context or delivering desired outcomes. They then review the standards and competencies related to building leadership and summarize approaches to learning including: experiential learning, reflection, learning spaces, and memories with momentum (application of ideas). Finally, they review pedagogical methods (case study, role plays, action learning, mindfulness, group dynamics, coaching, outdoor/adventure, roundtables, arts, and gamification). This thorough overview of approaches to leadership development demonstrates that investments in leadership will likely continue in varied ways and that individuals who want to be better leaders or companies that want to build better leadership can make informed choices to do so.

The last two chapters in this part show that leadership development is not merely mastering a new set of skills or deploying new tools, but redefining one's identity. Delaney places leadership development in a broader historical and social context (e.g. showing the National Training Laboratories T-groups and the Tavistock Institute of Human Relations as important historical precedents for leadership development). In this setting leadership development is not just about skills and tools, but helping leaders explore their unique identity (or become 'identity workspaces'). By focusing on identity more than just skills, leadership development attempts to create sustainable change in how leaders think and act. She gives an example of an 18-month leadership development experience in which participants were encouraged to work on identity not just skills. The metaphor for identity may be toolbox, book, or kaleidoscope, each of which shapes how to accomplish leadership development.

Sun makes the case that, by focusing on leadership identity more than skills, leaders exist throughout an organization, not just in formal positions of power. A focus on identity clarifies distributed leadership where each leader engages followers by socially constructing the shared role of leadership. Identity shapes and is shaped at personal, interpersonal, and organizational levels. Leaders who recognize identity as central to their leadership narrative will be more able to positively influence others. He reports on a nine-month leadership development programme in which participants focused on identity through self-reflection and were able to articulate an aspired identity. With a clearer personal identity, leaders are able to know and engage others both up and down the organization and to share information. When leadership development encourages identity, organizations are more able to secure the desired culture.

Collectively, these essays give the reader insights on how to personally become a better leader and how to build leadership development programmes within an organization.

References on Nature/Nurture Debate

Bouchard, T. J. Jr., Lykken, D. T., McGue, M., Segal, N. L. and Tellegen, A. (1990). Sources of human psychological differences: The Minnesota Study of Twins Reared Apart. *Science*, 250, 223–228.

Ceci, Stephen J. and Williams, Wendy M., eds. (1999). *The Nature–Nurture Debate: The Essential Readings*. Blackwell Publishing.

Goldhaber, Dale (2012). *The Nature-Nurture Debates: Bridging the Gap.* Cambridge University Press.

Kaiser, Robert (ed.). (2009). *The Perils of Accentuating the Positive.* Hogan Press.

Kaiser, Robert (session organizer). (2006). Symposium at Society of Industrial and Organizational Psychology in Dallas on Leadership and Evolutionary Psychology, Dallas, Texas.

Kolb, B., Gibb, R., and Robinson, T. E. (2003). Brain plasticity and behavior. *Current Directions in Psychological Science*, 12 (1), 1–5.

Van Vugt, M. (2006). Evolutionary origins of leadership and followership. *Personality and Social Psychology Review*, 10 (4), 354–371.

32
Can Leadership Be Taught?

Ann Cunliffe and Julie Wilson

While there is debate around the impact of leadership education and development on practice, the general assumption underpinning the debate is that leadership can be taught in some form. This is reflected in the number of university leadership centres across the world (e.g. Lancaster, Exeter and INSEAD in Europe; Auckland in New Zealand; and Washington, Northwestern and Pennsylvania in the US). There are also non-university organizations such as the Center for Creative Leadership (US), which has a global reach, and the Asian Leadership Institute (Thailand and Canada) that offer a variety of leadership programmes. Many business schools across the world are re-packaging MBA programmes around global, strategic or executive leadership – as opposed to management. And this is not just the purview of business schools. Kellerman (2013: 136) says that at Harvard University, where she works, 'virtually every single one of its professional schools boasts the words "leader" or "leadership" in its mission statement'. The Massachusetts Institute of Technology's Sloan Fellows programme in innovation and global leadership promises a 'deep reservoir of resources', 'expanded skills and capabilities' and a 'change-the-world toolkit',[1] which is typical of many top-ranked programmes.

In short, there is a plethora of degrees, certificates, courses, consultants and training programmes addressing various aspects of leadership. A recent 2015 survey in the *New York Times*[2] counted the number of times 'leader' and 'leadership' appeared on a *single* webpage of top US business schools: MIT Sloan and the University of Pennsylvania's Wharton School notched up 47 each. Leadership, leadership development and leadership courses appear to be 'big business' worldwide (Day & Antonakis 2012), and, because of the market saturation, business schools are searching for new ways of branding and marketing their leadership programmes. Despite this ubiquitous nature of leadership – or perhaps because of it – leadership definitions are multiple and contested, with numerous books addressing what it means to be an effective leader; proposing leadership frameworks and models; and identifying key traits, styles or behaviours. The word 'leadership' is now often preceded by an adjective – collective, transformational, relational, etc. Indeed, as Day and Antonakis state: 'leadership is often easy to identify in practice but it is difficult to define precisely. Given the complex nature of leadership, a specific and widely accepted definition of leadership does not exist and might never be found' (p. 5). We address this impact of multiple definitions later by examining the tensions around teaching leadership. Our concern is not with narrowing down leadership definitions, but with whether leadership (in its many forms) can be taught, or whether, as Antonacopoulou and Bento (2010) argue, it is more fruitful to think about leadership as learning.

In this chapter we will examine the premise that leadership can be taught by first looking at what is currently taught and where; second, exploring a number of tensions around teaching leadership; and third, reframing the 'teaching' of leadership around the notion of 'learning' leadership. We suggest that this reframing foregrounds not only the difference between learning and teaching, but also that learning to be a leader is about learning how to become a leader in situated experiential contexts, i.e. learning leadership does not necessarily mean that leadership can be taught. The latter was noted in Doh's (2003) interviews with six prominent leadership academics (all white male and mainly North American) who framed leadership as a learned capacity, as competencies, as skills/perspectives/dispositions, as a performance sport, and as incorporating both explicit and tacit knowledge. However, while the six academics all believed leadership could be learned, they argued not everyone could learn it and that only some aspects of leadership could be taught. We end by offering three alternative forms of leadership learning that seem not to be present in the leadership courses we surveyed. These forms focus on more experiential and creative ways of learning that narrow the theory–practice gap.

What Is Being Taught?

The question of whether leadership can be taught, and if so how, is of both academic and practical concern. As a 2014 Deloitte survey report, *Closing the Gap between Hype and Readiness*, noted:

> Leadership remains the No.1 talent issue facing organizations around the world, with 86 percent of respondents in our survey rating it as 'urgent' or 'important.' Only 13 percent of respondents say they do an excellent job developing leaders at all levels – the largest 'readiness gap' in [the] survey.
>
> *(Canwell, Dongrie, Neveras & Stockton, 2014: 1)*

These findings suggest an acute gap between demand and supply, one that impedes organizational growth. This shifts into focus the question of how leaders develop and whether or not leadership can be taught to meet this shortfall.

In order to understand what is currently being taught on courses that are labelled 'leadership', in December 2014 we undertook a short survey of courses across a number of worldwide geographical locations.[3] This was initially based on the *Financial Times* Top 50 MBA courses, then extended to a Google search for Master's-level courses with 'leadership' in the title and finally a general Google search for leadership courses. While MBA programmes are about management, they are often framed in terms of leadership. For example, London Business School's MBA claims 'Leave this transformational programme as a well-rounded global leader' and Spain's IESE 'Gain a new perspective on what it means to lead'.[4] In other words, leadership now appears to be a key element of many MBA and Master's in Management programmes, perhaps because being a leader is sexier, and generates higher status and reward, than being a manager.

The sample looked at predominantly UK provision, but also included centres in Europe, the US, Canada, Africa and Asia. The survey was explorative rather than representative of provision across all geographical or industrial sectors, taking data from a sample of online marketing material and downloadable course brochures. This allowed us to see whether the advertised courses gave information about what is being taught, how, and whether students are afforded opportunities to assess and apply their own skills.

The survey revealed four types of provision:

1. Universities and colleges offering academic MBA- and Master's-level courses that contain a leadership element and/or include the word 'leadership' in the title;
2. Non-degree leadership courses, accredited by a range of national and international awarding bodies, run by individual training practitioners, further education colleges and universities;
3. Non-accredited university, college or leadership centre courses for practitioners, which contain 'generic' leadership knowledge, with no specific industrial or sector focus;
4. Sector- or industry-specific leadership training: for example, local government, education and National Health Service leadership training.

Excluded from the results are the plethora of individual consultancies or consortia offering tailor-made leadership and management training that might be industry or geographical-area specific (see Mole 2010 and Antonacopoulou and Bento 2010, for discussion and critique around leadership-training provision). These are usually neither accredited by awarding bodies nor affiliated to universities or colleges. As such, no detail of their content was available, which made comparison with other providers unfeasible. An overview of the survey results is summarized in Table 32.1 (see Appendices 32.1–32.3 for details). We discuss the findings in the following section.

Leadership Content in MBA and Master's-Level Courses

Given the growing importance assigned to the need for leaders to demonstrate effective, ethical and socially responsible behaviours, especially since the 2008 global economic crisis (Stahl & De Luque 2014), we had expected to see a stronger presence of leadership topics in core (non-executive) MBA modules. In our sample of business schools in Europe, North and South America, Asia and Australasia, just 6 of 21 MBA programmes have a core module including leadership or with leadership in the module title (see Appendix 32.1). Many of the MBA programmes have a strong focus on operational and functional competencies such as finance and operations management. Leadership is often combined with other topics (e.g. organizational behaviour, teamwork, change management) and leadership theory, skills, competencies or roles are offered through additional activities such as master classes, seminars or work-based projects. Whilst the additional leadership activities might mean that students gain the opportunity to develop insights about themselves and their own leadership practices, not all universities offer leadership content as a core element of a programme. At a number of the universities in the sample (e.g. Harvard Business School) elective leadership modules compete with up to 120 other elective courses! This means that, although many MBA students will engage with leadership as an aspect of their business education, there is no guarantee that they will supplement the development of their technical capabilities (e.g. in finance or operations management) with leadership competencies or tools.

In contrast, in the Master's degrees surveyed, leadership occurred in a course title and as a core module in 15 out of 17 programmes (see Table 32.2). It is interesting to note that there is a wide variety of leadership topics – for example, leadership and society (King's College London), leadership futures (Birmingham), values-based leadership (Trinity Western, Canada), tools for leadership and personal leadership action plans (Georgetown, USA) – suggesting that more time is given to focusing on the art of leading rather than achieving functional proficiency.

Table 32.1 Leadership Modules in Sampled MBA Programmes

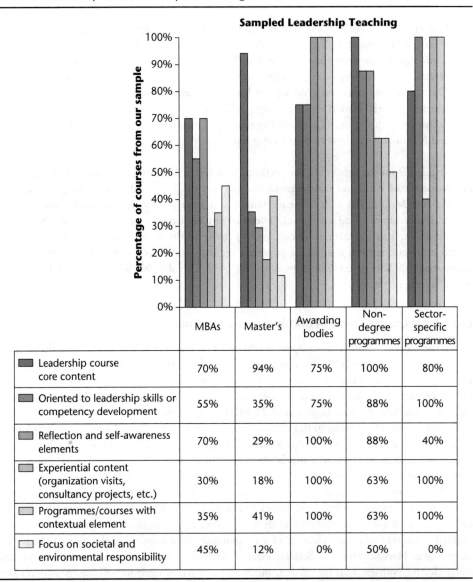

	MBAs	Master's	Awarding bodies	Non-degree programmes	Sector-specific programmes
Leadership course core content	70%	94%	75%	100%	80%
Oriented to leadership skills or competency development	55%	35%	75%	88%	100%
Reflection and self-awareness elements	70%	29%	100%	88%	40%
Experiential content (organization visits, consultancy projects, etc.)	30%	18%	100%	63%	100%
Programmes/courses with contextual element	35%	41%	100%	63%	100%
Focus on societal and environmental responsibility	45%	12%	0%	50%	0%

Non-degree Accredited Leadership Courses

Three main UK bodies accredit courses that are delivered by third parties (further education and higher education institutions and private training companies): the Chartered Management Institute (CMI), the Institute of Leadership and Management (ILM) and Skills CFA, which oversees vocational qualifications through apprenticeships and work-based learning across the UK. The sample here also includes an Australian company (Proteus) which offers a similar model to CMI and ILM and which has started to operate outside of Australia in recent years. These four organizations offer leadership and management training aimed at practitioners in all industrial sectors rather than specializing in leading in a specific environment. The courses are delivered under licence so that the content and delivery are controlled with the aim of achieving quality assurance across the large number of delivery agencies.

Three of the four organizations (see Appendix 32.1) appear to focus as much on developing and reflecting on practice as understanding theories and models of leadership. ILM, for example, has modules on developing the reflective leader and on the leadership journey. The exception is Skills CFA, which concentrates on skill development including thinking creatively and valuing others, but does not appear to include theories of leadership that might underpin its practice.

Non-degree Accredited Practitioner Programmes

Practitioner-oriented leadership programmes (see Appendix 32.2) are run by further education and higher education institutions and offer perspectives on leadership for practitioners without an accredited leadership degree at the end of the delivery. There is a diverse menu of topics and models and a focus on skills development. Course offerings cover a broader spectrum of issues, such as gender (Cranfield International Centre for Women Leaders), social and environmental sustainability (the African Leadership Centre, King's College) and young leaders (European School of Management and Technology, Berlin). Courses are also practice oriented. In particular, the Asian Leadership Institute and the US Center for Creative Leadership both focus on reflection and leadership practice to develop understanding not only of participants' own leadership behaviours but also how these influence the organizations within which they are operating.

Sector-Specific Leadership Programmes

Finally, sector-specific leadership programmes are offered by organizing bodies for industrial sectors such as the National Health Service, local government authorities and education bodies (see Appendix 32.3). These consider leadership from an industry-specific perspective and, where course content is available online, appear to offer theories and models of leadership as well as the opportunity to reflect on leadership practice. The aim of these bodies is to enhance leadership skills as they relate to a particular environment.

To summarize, our brief survey of the provision of leadership courses indicates that, in moving through the provision of leadership courses in MBA, Master's, third-party and non-accredited to specific sector courses, the focus on leadership and the content of leadership courses vary from the more functional/theoretical (MBA) to the more leadership-specific application/personal practice (non-degree, sector-specific). This is perhaps connected to the lack of definition of 'effective' leadership and to the theoretical tensions articulated in the following section. Where course content is available, it appears that, overall, knowledge-building activities are more prevalent than skill-building or practical application opportunities across all four types of provision.

Non-degree accredited practitioner courses appear to incorporate a greater diversity of leadership topics along with more opportunities to build reflective skills and for self-development than the MBA courses we sampled. Master's-level leadership programmes have more core leadership modules than the MBAs and link theoretically based content with placements or other opportunities to gain practical experience. Awarding bodies such as CMI or ILM have reflection built into the titles of their modules and attempt to link knowledge and reflective practice. Programmes with the least leadership content in our sample appear to be MBA courses. A number offer the opportunity to gain leadership experience either indirectly through functional and operational skills or through electives or additional leadership activities. However, of the four types of provision, MBAs appear the poor relation in terms of their leadership knowledge content in core modules, and Master's courses struggle to offer the same range of opportunities

Table 32.2 Survey of Master's Programmes with Leadership in the Title

Country/region	Centre	Full time programmes	Module type (core or elective)	Modules	Notes/module content	Additional leadership content	Core theoretical and/or models of leadership content	Elective theoretical and/or models of leadership content	Oriented to leadership skills or competency development	Reflection and self-awareness elements	Experiential content (organization visits, consultancy projects, etc.)	Contextual element	CSR
UK	London Business School	MBA	Core	Leadership launch	Self-awareness, careers advice, problem solving, decision making, communication skills, change management, soft-skill development	*London Talks – motivational speakers							
				Managing organizational behaviour	Skill development to predict behaviours and lead groups and individuals								
			Elective	Leading teams and organizations	Leadership theory, case studies, confidence building exercises	*Local and international visits to sucessful organizations		✓	✓	✓	✓		
				Paths to power	Negotiation, power management								
	Cambridge Judge Business School	MBA		No modules with leadership content	-	*Career accelerator programme develops self-awareness; *Leadership seminars				✓		✓	

		Type	Module	Description		✓	✓	✓	✓	✓	✓
Warwick Business School	MBA	Core	Leadership Plus	Reflective experience and self-awareness, potentially practical leadership exercises	*Leadership in action discussion groups / Business networks with seminars and workshops						
		Elective	Leading for innovation / Leadership and the art of judgement / Strategic leadership	No details of elective modules available on website		✓					
Oxford Said Business School	MBA	Core	Leadership fundamentals	Leadership theories and effective management practices	*Integrated module on responsible leadership / *Applied learning through consultancy projects / *Executive coaching						
		Elective	Leadership in the humanities / Political economy for business leaders / Reputation and leadership	Leadership as represented in literature, history and the arts / No further information available on website		✓	✓	✓	✓	✓	✓
Europe: Germany	European School of Management and Technology	MBA	Elective	Sustainable and responsible leadership / Leadership and personal development	Both elective modules part of the Management of Technology and Innovation Track / *Leadership competency development programme / *Leadership master classes		✓			✓	✓

(continued)

Table 32.2 *(continued)*

Country/region	Centre	Full time programmes	Module type (core or elective)	Modules	Notes/module content	Additional leadership content	Core theoretical and/or models of leadership content	Elective theoretical and/or models of leadership content	Oriented to leadership skills or competency development	Reflection and self-awareness elements	Experiential content (organization visits, consultancy projects, etc.)	Contextual element	CSR
France	INSEAD	MBA	Core	Organizational behaviour 1 Organizational behaviour 2	Self-awareness and team leadership Strategic design; power and politics; cultural issues	Non-credit bearing Business Ethics course runs across the first two semesters							
			Elective	Organizational behaviour	Communication and leadership element to the elective module					✓		✓	✓
	Iese Business School	MBA	Core	Leading organizations: systems, values and ethics	Leadership processes, change management, economic and social responsibilities	Responsible leadership integrated into modules	✓					✓	✓
			Elective	Managing people in organizations	Individual and group behaviours with sources of authority, management styles,	Case-based learning							

Country	School							
Switzerland	IMD	MBA	Core	Personal and leadership development	Combines classroom interactions, psychoanalytical coaching and individual reflection to develop your ability to navigate organizational contexts	leadership, hierarchical communication, inter-functional relationships, structural systems, and organizational cultures		
						Leadership challenges, contextualized assignments ✓	✓	✓	✓
USA	MIT	MBA	Core	Organizations and change	Participants choose from a range of course options to complete their courses. Leadership appears in several forms as shown here; no further detail on course content was available electronically			
				Power, influence, negotiation		*Sloan Innovation Period		
				Leadership as practice		*4 Capabilities Leadership Workshop		
				Leadership in context		*Peer-to-Peer Coaching Program		
				Leadership theories		*Leadership Development and Coaching Program ✓	✓	✓	✓
				Ethics				
				Communication				

(continued)

Table 32.2 (continued)

Country/region	Centre	Full time programmes	Module type (core or elective)	Modules	Notes/module content	Additional leadership content	Core theoretical and/or models of leadership content	Elective theoretical and/or models of leadership content	Oriented to leadership skills or competency development	Reflection and self-awareness elements	Experiential content (organization visits, consultancy projects, etc.)	Contextual element	CSR
	Harvard Business School	MBA	Core	Leadership and Organizational Behavior (LEAD)	The determinants of group culture Managing the performance of individual subordinates Establishing productive relationships with peers and seniors over whom the manager has no formal authority The intermediate modules look at successful leaders in action to see how they: *Develop a vision of the future *Align the organization behind that vision *Motivate people to achieve the vision	FIELD Foundations: Leadership workshops, reflection and small team practices	✓	✓		✓			✓

School	Program	Type	Module/Course	Description	Delivery methods
Stanford Business Schools	MBA	Elective	Leadership and Corporate Accountability (LCA)	*Design effective organizations and change them to achieve superior performance; Legal, ethical, and economic responsibilities; management and governance systems; how personal values can play a critical role in effective leadership	
		Core	Strategic Leadership	General management and leadership, culture of organizations	Leadership labs
		Elective	Becoming a leader: managing early career challenges; Compassion and leadership; Leadership and crisis management	No further details available on website	Reflective workshops and simulations
Wharton University	MBA	Core	Foundations of teamwork and leadership	No details available on website	Coaching and mentoring from leadership fellows; Learning teams

(continued)

Table 32.2 (continued)

Country/region	Centre	Full time programmes	Module type (core or elective)	Modules	Notes/module content	Additional leadership content	Core theoretical and/or models of leadership content	Elective theoretical and/or models of leadership content	Oriented to leadership skills or competency development	Reflection and self-awareness elements	Experiential content (organization visits, consultancy projects, etc.)	Contextual element	CSR
Toronto, Canada	Rotman Business School	MBA	Core	Leadership and change management	No details available on website	Self-development labs Aimed at enhancing self-awareness and communication skills, unclear leadership content							
			Elective	Organizational behaviour and human resource management	Two modules: Leading teams and Leading social innovation		✓		✓	✓			
Asia	HKUST Business School	MBA	Core	Preparing to lead	Residential programme aimed at developing practical managing skills and building team cohesiveness amongst cohort	No details available on website							
Hong Kong				Responsible leadership and ethics	Responsible leadership corporations Ethical responsibilities and decision making		✓		✓	✓			✓

Country	School	Program	Type	Module	Details						
Shanghai	Ceibs	MBA	Core	Responsible leadership and governance	Sustainable corporate social responsibility for lasting positive impacts on society						✓
					Self-awareness and governance and ethical challenges through a values-based approach	✓			✓		✓
			Elective	Proactive leadership and conflicts of interest	No details on website	✓			✓		
		Finance MBA	Core	Leadership and change	No details on website	✓					
South Korea	Sungkyunkwan University GSB	MBA	Elective	Leadership	The nature of leadership and the complexities of dealing with people who hold different values						
					Consulting projects	✓	✓				
					Careers development centre: leadership and career class					✓	
Australia	University of Melbourne	MBA	Core	Leadership orientation	No details on website	✓	✓				
					CEOs as guest speakers					✓	
					Team projects						✓
					Immersion in industry consulting assignments and internships					✓	
					Action learning						✓

(continued)

Table 32.2 (continued)

Country/region	Centre	Full time programmes	Module type (core or elective)	Modules	Notes/module content	Additional leadership content	Core theoretical and/or models of leadership content	Elective theoretical and/or models of leadership content	Oriented to leadership skills or competency development	Reflection and self-awareness elements	Experiential content (organization visits, consultancy projects, etc.)	Contextual element	CSR
South Africa, Cape Town	Graduate School of Business	MBA	Core	Leadership	Personal leadership through self-awareness and reflective development	Professional development management			✓	✓			
				Organizational behaviour and people management	No details of content available on website		✓						
			Elective	Advanced leadership	No details of content available on website			✓	✓				
Brazil	Coppead, UFRJ	MBA/MSc	Elective	Leadership and management ethics	No details of content available on website	Multi-cultural consulting projects	✓				✓		✓

Country/region	Centre	Academic programmes	Core/elective	Modules	Additional leadership content	Leadership course core content	Leadership course elective content	Oriented to leadership skills or competency development	Reflection and self-awareness elements	Experiential content (organization visits, consultancy projects, etc.)	Programmes/courses with contextual element	Focus on societal and environmental responsibility
UK	African Leadership Centre, King's College London	MSc Leadership and development; MSc Security, leadership and society	Core	Leadership and society; Emerging powers in global leadership; Natural resource governance; The State and development in Africa and Asia; Diaspora populations and developing societies	No additional information available on website	✓					✓	✓
	Birmingham University	MSc Leadership and organizational performance	Core	Service leadership and change management; Leadership and followership; Leadership futures	6-month work placement, opportunity to develop skills and identity?	✓				✓		
	Bristol Leadership Centre	MA Leadership and media production management	Elective	Leadership	No additional information available on website		✓					

(continued)

Table 32.2 (continued)

Country/region	Centre	Academic programmes	Core/elective	Modules	Additional leadership content	Leadership course core content	Leadership course elective content	Oriented to leadership skills or competency development	Reflection and self-awareness elements	Experiential content (organization visits, consultancy projects, etc.)	Programmes/courses with contextual element	Focus on societal and environmental responsibility
	Lancaster Leadership Centre	MSc Leadership practice and responsibility	Core	Responsible leadership: reflections and challenges; Responsible leadership: initiating change; Responsible leadership in action; Leadership challenge and dissertation; Global leadership	First core unit involves students' critical evaluation of their own practice. No additional information available on website	✓		✓	✓		✓	✓
	London Business School	Master's in Leadership and strategy	Core	Executive leadership; Understanding top management; Managing people and organizations	Guest speakers; Workshops; Coaching training (GROW model)	✓	✓	✓	✓			
			Electives	Choice of 70 electives								

Institution	Programme		Modules	Additional information						
Northumbria University, Newcastle	Leadership and management MSc	Core	Leader identity and leadership Creating the dynamic organization Leading for organizational performance	Guest speakers			✓			
Queen Margaret University, Edinburgh	MSc International management and leadership	Core	Leadership power and policy Contemporary issues in international management	Guest speakers International visits	✓				✓	✓
Regents University, London	MA Management and leadership	Core	Management Organizational behavior Managerial leadership Integrated studies in management	No additional information available on website	✓					
Sheffield University Management School	MSc Leadership and management	Core	Foundations of leadership and teamwork Organizational behaviour Advanced topics in leadership Leading in challenging times	Focus on skill building and action learning which may contribute towards skills facilitation and identity development?	✓	✓	✓	✓		✓
		Electives	Cultural leadership and management							

(continued)

Table 32.2 (continued)

Country/ region	Centre	Academic programmes	Core/ elective	Modules	Additional leadership content	Leadership course core content	Leadership course elective content	Oriented to leadership skills or competency development	Reflection and self-awareness elements	Experiential content (organization visits, consultancy projects, etc.)	Programmes/ courses with contextual element	Focus on societal and environmental responsibility
	York, St John's	MA Leadership and management	Core	Leadership and management coaching / Strategic leadership and management / Managing culture and leading change	No additional information available on website	✓					✓	
Europe	Redcliffe College	MA Global leadership in intercultural context	Core	Method and content in missiological study / An introduction to global leadership / Organizational development and cultural change / The mission of the church in the context of post-colonialism and globalization / Crucial issues in Asian mission and theology / Crucial issues in European mission and theology	Global leadership Initiative listed but not defined or described. Critical reflection activities are assessed	✓		✓	✓			
Czech Rep											✓	

USA	Georgetown McDonough, Washington DC	Executive Master's in Leadership	Core	Leading teams and organizations Tools for leadership Looking to the future	Capstone Project – research project Personal leadership action plan – reflective if not reflexive process runs alongside the modules There is a broad range of units within the three key themes	✓	✓	✓	✓
	Arizona State University School of Global Management and Leadership	Master's Applied leadership and management	Core	Develop organizational vision Inspire employee professional growth Foster productivity and achievement Create harmonious working environments Instil team spirit and cooperation Develop innovative and integrative solutions	No additional information available on website	✓			

(continued)

Table 32.2 (continued)

Country/ region	Centre	Academic programmes	Core/ elective	Modules	Additional leadership content	Leadership course core content	Leadership course elective content	Oriented to leadership skills or competency development	Reflection and self-awareness elements	Experiential content (organization visits, consultancy projects, etc.)	Programmes/ courses with contextual element	Focus on societal and environmental responsibility
Canada	Trinity Western University, Langley	Master of arts in leadership	Core	Transformational servant leadership Values based leadership	No additional information on website							
			Electives	Range of focus from business to Christian ministry		✓						
	Levene, University of Regina	M.Admin leadership	Core	Leadership: theory and practice Cases in leadership	'Insight' speaker series	✓					✓	
Australia	University of Notre Dame, Fremantle	Master of business leadership	Core	Leadership: theory and practice	No additional information on website	✓						
Singapore	Kaplan Higher Education Institute	MSc Management and leadership	Core	Power, authority and decision-making Leadership and organization Management and change	No additional information on website	✓						

to focus on developing reflective leadership practice. Instead, these programmes focus on a broad range of functional skills and knowledge about operational and strategic management.

The type of leadership content across all MBA, Master's and awarding body courses in the sample appears fairly homogeneous. Much of the programme focus is on quantitative, results-focused processes; leadership course content is often formulaic, and, particularly for MBA curricula, is secondary to non-leadership content. Some leadership courses include alternative approaches to mainstream theories – for example, relational leadership – but this tends to be from the instrumental perspective of 'how to get people to do what you want them to do'. Ethical leadership appears from time to time along with 'responsible' leadership, which focuses on the societal impact of business (e.g. University of Oxford, King's College London, INSEAD and Trinity Western University in Toronto).

It therefore appears that, despite the rhetoric around leadership, offerings of leadership courses are fairly limited in scope and content. Many MBA and Master's-level courses focus on learning leadership theories and models, with fewer providing opportunities to rehearse skills, learn leadership experientially or obtain feedback on practice or self-development. In our sample, the types of leadership skills, experience and wisdom noted as being essential in reports such as Camwell *et al.* (2014) are not uniformly offered at this level. Leadership content of these courses is often generic, whereas organizations are looking for leaders who are fully developed individuals who can creatively respond to a range of experiences and crises. Practitioner-oriented courses (as noted in points 2, 3 and 4 in the list above) often adopt a pedagogy that allows participants – to varying degrees – to reflect upon and evaluate their practice. Two major questions therefore arise that we will now begin to address. First, if much of what is currently being delivered does not meet organizational and societal needs, should we be re-assessing what we teach by examining tensions in the theoretical and pedagogical underpinnings of leadership course curricula? Second, what other possibilities can we explore?

From Teaching to Learning Leadership

In the remainder of the chapter we suggest there are a number of tensions underpinning the teaching of leadership that have their roots in how we research and theorize leadership. We begin by highlighting these tensions and then move on to reframe 'teaching leadership' to 'learning leadership' and offer three possibilities which emphasize learning: 'the person discovering and experiencing leadership from within' (Antonacopoulou & Bento, 2010: 82).

Tensions in Teaching Leadership

As noted previously, definitions and approaches to leadership are multiple and contested. We suggest that, although there is a body of mainstream leadership literature in which the purpose, goal and outcomes of leadership are relatively coherent, the advent of more critical and philosophically oriented perspectives over the last 20 years have revealed a number of ideological, definitional and theoretical tensions that extend into the debate about whether – and how – leadership can be taught. These tensions may be expressed in the following ways:

- Leadership as individualistic (e.g. Griffith, Connelly, Thiel, & Johnson 2015) and/or collective (e.g. Raelin 2003).
- Leadership as work, behavioural and organizational competences or skills (Battilana, Gilmartin, Sengul, Pache, & Alexander 2010); as personal qualities (Cavazotte, Moreno, & Hickmann 2012); as discursively constituted (Fairhurst 2007; Ford 2006); as a social practice

(Crevani, Lindgren, & Packendorff 2010; Raelin 2011); or as a relational way of being (Cunliffe & Eriksen 2011).

- Leadership as essentialist and rationalistic (Kaplan, Cortina, Ruark, LaPort, & Nicolaides 2014) or existential (Cunliffe 2009; Sparrowe 2005).
- Leadership as a benign/neutral or a political and moral activity.

We will begin by summarizing briefly the assumptions underpinning mainstream theories that have influenced how leadership is generally taught as theoretical and normative. After a brief critique, we will shift the focus from teaching to learning leadership in more critical, experiential and reflexive ways.

Mainstream Theories and Leadership Teaching

The mainstream leadership literature has a substantial impact on the way leadership is taught, in that its strong rationalistic assumptions, theories and findings often provide the content for leadership programmes. Mainstream approaches focus on seeking the essence of leadership (Lawler 2005), whether in terms of traits, behaviours, competencies, styles and/or situational factors. These are seen to be predictors of success, 'effective' leaders being those who possess the 'right' competences, skills and personal qualities, and are able to apply the appropriate techniques to given situations. For example, a typical study from this perspective is that of Cavazotte *et al.* (2012) who examine the effect of intelligence, personality traits and emotional intelligence on transformational leadership, using a covariance-based structural equation model to test a number of hypotheses. They conclude that intelligence and conscientiousness are the two main important factors. Similarly, Schyns, Kiefer, Kerschreiter and Tymon (2011) propose that teaching implicit leadership theories – 'images that everyone holds about the traits and behaviors of leaders in general' (p. 398) – can help individual leaders to understand how they operate in social contexts. Essentialist approaches therefore attempt to delineate the knowledge and skills that serve as antecedents to leadership and therefore organizational effectiveness.

Leadership is often perceived as individualistic, an *enduring fantasy of leadership omnipotence* in that we accord leaders heroic status in being able to realize visions and achieve miracles (Gabriel 2005: 159). This fantasy carries the assumption that, although individual leaders may differ in terms of the types of charisma or influence they display, leadership theories and competencies are generalizable across contexts and time. In doing so, they 'offer an illusory promise to rationalize and simplify the processes of selecting, measuring and developing leaders' (Bolden & Gosling 2006: 147). The individualistic heroic approach also ignores the potentially social and collective nature of leadership (Carroll, Levy, & Richmond 2008) and its contextualized nature (Mole 2010). Additionally, more critical leadership scholars critique mainstream assumptions that leadership is a benign/neutral activity, legitimated by the position itself, and that a leader's right to direct activities in the best interest of the organization is axiomatic (Collinson 2014; Ford, Harding, & Learmonth 2008).

The problem with this approach is that it assumes homogeneity both in terms of leaders themselves and their contexts; ignores differences relating to gender, race, culture and so on; and misses the mundane details and nuances of everyday experiences of being a leader (Bell, Taylor, & Thorpe 2002; Bolden & Gosling 2006; Lawler 2005; Stead & Elliot 2012; Xing & Sims 2012). It is about fitting individuals into norms, typologies and categories, rather than acknowledging the 'subtle acts of leadership' (Karp 2013).

Gabriel (2005) argues that the MBA ethos is 'antithetical to educating students in leadership' (p. 150) because it is based on a model of obedience (students as followers) that encourages hierarchical, authoritarian and narcissistic forms of leadership. Developed in a laboratory for leadership to encourage students to inquire, experiment and use their imagination, Gabriel concluded that he was not educating leaders, but educating students to be followers. This position was supported by Sinclair (2007), who, when she tried to introduce a more critical pedagogy into an EMBA leadership course by asking participants to challenge leadership orthodoxy, found that she was potentially reinforcing 'the power and legitimacy of the mainstream teaching content and process' (p. 470) because students resisted and the course in that format ceased.

More critical, philosophical and experiential approaches to leadership often focus on the relationship between identity, selfhood and leadership; issues of power and legitimacy; and differences or dialectics (Cunliffe 2009; Hawkins & Edwards 2015; Lawler 2005). For example, drawing on poststructural discursive and psychoanalytical approaches, Jackie Ford (2006) challenges the essentialist notion of the traditional unified coherent leader with core traits and competencies, arguing that leaders find themselves struggling with competing, multiple, contradictory and complex identities. We suggest that the standard taught MBA programmes we found in our survey are perhaps inadequate for 'teaching' leaders how to deal with these circumstances, which require thinking and acting in more creative, reflexive ways. We go on to explore three alternative approaches.

Learning Leadership As . . .

Given the critiques and challenges of 'teaching' leadership, what if we reframe the question to 'can we learn leadership?' What alternative issues and approaches might emerge? Cameron, one of Doh's (2003: 62) interviewees, quotes Whetten to describe a learning model for leadership: (1) skill pre-assessment, (2) skill learning (concepts and best practices), (3) skill analysis, (4) skill practice (with feedback) and (5) skill application. Although an emphasis on knowledge and skills is important, it is still an essentialist, individualist and homogeneic approach to teaching. Antonacopoulou and Bento (2010) argue that learning to become a leader means being able to learn in practice: to deal with vulnerability, be open to experience and also learn to be a good follower by learning 'with and from others' (p. 75). We argue that learning to lead is also about learning how to thoughtfully and carefully consider and address the situations one faces, which means figuring out who to be and how to negotiate the identity struggles a leader may face in their day-to-day experiences (Collinson 2003; Edwards, Elliot, Iszatt-White, & Schedlitzki 2013; Fletcher 2004; Ford 2010). This learning may take place both in the classroom and experientially if we offer students ways of learning in their lived experience.

We concur with Grint's (2007) reframing of teaching to learning leadership and that there is not a 'single form of leader-dominated rationality' (p. 232). He believes that experience alone is insufficient: drawing on Aristotle's three types of knowledge, he argues that learning leadership involves skills and principles of 'doing' (techné), rational scientific knowledge (episteme) and context-related wisdom (phronesis). So how do leaders learn these? In addition to the usual ways, Grint suggests leaders need to learn by leading in real situations because learning to lead is a social process that includes phronesis or practical wisdom (Cunliffe & Eriksen 2011). Learning leadership – in contrast to teaching leadership – is framed as a more experiential process that often involves some form of vulnerability and disruption (Mackay, Zundel, & Alkiriwi 2014; Segal 2010; Sinclair 2007). It is not about 'tightening our conceptual grasp' (Mackay et al. 2014: 433) or learning the rules of the game, but about surfacing the implicit knowing lying within action; reflecting on our place in the world; reflecting on the emergent, often opaque nature of life; and aiming for a 'good life' with others (Cunliffe 2008).

In the remainder of the chapter we will explore what forms learning leadership might take, focusing particularly on its experiential, existential and embodied nature. We organize our exploration under three headings: phronesis, a way of becoming and aesthetic embodiment, offering illustrations of each.

Phronesis (a Reflexive Experience)

Phronesis differs from rational forms of knowledge (episteme) in that it is a form of practical wisdom or practical reasoning that involves ethical and reflexive insight into both the particulars of a situation and the broader background. It recognizes our agency in an uncertain and indeterminate world and therefore can help students grapple with the issues they may face in particular circumstances. In our *Relational Leadership* study (Cunliffe & Eriksen 2011), Matthew Eriksen and Ann Cunliffe came to understand from their conversations with Federal security directors that practical wisdom is about making judgements that 'draw on a sense of who one is, one's values, and on an experiential knowing-from-within that involves acting prudently [. . .] a recognition of the need for moral community and "just institutions", a respect for others and for different world views' (p. 1442). Phronesis is therefore not about teaching abstract theoretical knowledge, which techniques to apply or how to find the right answer; it is an experiential and reflexive *knowing how to be and to act* in particular situations.

In their study of how women leaders learn to lead, Stead and Elliott (2012) found that disrupting our ways of thinking and acting plays a key role in knowing how to be. This may involve unsettling, resisting and countering traditional discourses of leadership in which lie embedded ideological, power and identity assumptions (p. 387). As educators we therefore need to consider the potential use of such discourses in helping students challenge taken-for-granted assumptions and practices and encouraging deeper learning about what it means to be a leader. In doing so, we become more reflexive about our own, others' and our organization's practices and policies and more able to learn and generate knowing in practice (Cunliffe 2009, 2014).

A number of scholars have suggested that creating disruptive reflexivity through threshold concepts can facilitate learning about self and practice (e.g. Hawkins & Edwards 2015; Hibbert & Cunliffe 2015; Yip & Raelin 2011). Articulated by Meyer and Land (2003), threshold concepts have the following characteristics. They are: *troublesome*, in the sense that they surface unfamiliar and often counter-intuitive knowledge; *integrative*, in that they help identify new connections and patterns; *irreversible*, because any retreat to previous understandings becomes impossible; and *transformative*, because they lead to changes in ways of thinking and acting. 'Such concepts lead to significant transformation, the change begins with disruption as students encounter unsettling feelings of confusion, doubt and frustration as they struggle at the edge of old and new understandings' (Hibbert & Cunliffe 2015: 181). Threshold concepts can be pivotal in helping students learn about leadership practice by exposing them to the complexity and uncertainty of situations and identities and encouraging them to question their own assumptions in relation to everyday experiences and practices of leadership (Yip & Raelin 2011). Hawkins and Edwards (2015) support this, arguing that engaging with doubt and liminal spaces of betweenness in relation to experiences can help students recognize and learn to 'try on' new ways of thinking, acting and being a leader.

These approaches also recognize the contextual and experiential nature of learning leadership . . . but not in the traditional sense of identifying contingent factors of the situation that will determine the appropriate leadership style to use. Rather, they take a more relational perspective in which meaning-making occurs within what Shotter (2008) calls an ongoing background flow of everyday activities in which relationships are fluid and shift over time. From this perspective, leaders and context are mutually constitutive in the sense that they, with others, shape their surrounding 'realities' as they continually make sense of what is going on in their conversations and actions, and in turn this becomes seemingly 'real' and shapes understanding and activities.

Leaders therefore learn practical reasoning: to be sensitive to what is going on around them and with others, and to understand that their talk is exploratory, formative and therefore crucial (Barge & Fairhurst 2008; Cunliffe & Eriksen 2011; Shotter & Cunliffe 2003).

Phronesis is about insight in particular circumstances (Dunne 1997). This means learning to act skilfully and with sensibility within unfolding moments. Statler (2014) argues that a pre-requisite to this is the need to recognize the limits of our knowledge. One way of facilitating insight and sensitivity – knowing from within – is by asking leaders to be reflexive about their ongoing experiences in reflexive journals or papers (Cunliffe 2009). This involves slowing down thinking as a means of exploring many possible interpretations within a situation. For example, in Ann's Exec MBA Leadership courses, designed around the theme of leadership as a relational, reflexive and moral activity, students wrote a final reflexive 'Self As Leader' paper, submitted six weeks after the course ended to give students time to connect ideas from the course to their experience. One student commented:

> I operated from the assumption that others view my actions as 'rational'. But I now realize that rationality is interpreted differently and embodies its opposite (Cunliffe 2009: 32). I assumed that in pushing my idea through the meeting . . . others would see it as the only possible 'rational' option – so why bother getting their input? I now feel that their unwillingness to implement my idea is perhaps associated with their perception that it was non-rational. To be dialogic is to talk *with* people not *to* them, to recognize the many voices in the conversation (polyphony).

Barge and Little (2008) take a communication perspective, proposing that phronesis can be encouraged by helping students learn to create conversational coherence in talk and action by 'holding one's tools lightly' – with 'tools' being a mix of processes, practices, policies, concepts and models of one's community of practice. This means helping students, through practice-based inquiry, to focus on how their 'conversational utterances connect with each other and unfold over time, which moves us to make judgments as to whether the placement of particular utterances within the conversational pattern are skilfully performed' (p. 526).

A Way of Being/Becoming (a Relational Experience)

In contrast to individualized and heroic models of leadership, we argue that learning leadership as a way of being/becoming means thinking and acting relationally. The relatively small amount of literature addressing this aspect draws on philosophy, particularly existential and hermeneutic philosophy. Existentialism addresses who we are and who we are becoming as embodied beings. It also questions the reasons for our existence. Lawler (2005), for example, argues that the generalizations that result from conventional forms of research into leadership fail to address the subjective, unique and contextualized experiences of leaders. He proposes the need for an existential approach which foregrounds that 'we live life as a continuous stream of events which only make sense to us in relation to each other' (p. 223). Similarly, Ashman (2007) argues that mainstream approaches to teaching leadership focus on what is present and can be seen, whereas existentialism, from a Sartrean perspective, draws attention to non-being or what is absent now that may affect our choices about the present and future. For Ashman, viewing leadership as a way of being also draws attention to a leader's moral responsibility in the world and to day-to-day experiences rather than abstract generalizations. Thus, an existential or 'philosopher leader' sees leading as a relational, reflexive and moral activity, and accepts responsibility for her/himself, for her/his actions and for others (Cunliffe 2009).

Relationality is about being able to position oneself – and different versions of self – in relation to others and to competing discourses, perhaps by disrupting gender stereotypes (Ford 2010). But how do leaders learn this way of being in the world? While this can be associated with facilitating learning through disruption, as we indicated in the previous section, it is also associated with learning within the flow of experience. Stead (2013) examines how women leaders deal with being visible and invisible (by their own and/or others' expectations), arguing that learning to do so involves becoming aware of the 'complex and relational nature of revealing and concealing (in)visibility' (p. 75) and how they relate to gender and power. She argues that, by encouraging leaders to use the lens of (in)visibility in examining their lived experiences, they can learn to read each situation and identify when to deploy advantageous forms of invisibility and visibility. She cites the example of Rebecca, who has learned to be selective about being visible by declining to be a 'token woman' on selection panels.

We suggest this not only means learning how to be reflexively aware of how we position ourselves in relation to others, but also being open and flexible. The importance of such learning was highlighted by a Federal security director in our study (Cunliffe & Eriksen 2011: 1426), who commented:

> I think that every FSD kind of became a creature of his own environment and realized right away what he had to do to survive. How he had to manage to survive – at least the successful ones. The ones who have not been successful, and there have been several of those, are the ones that came in with their own management style that they thought would work in any environment. They found that it did not.

Kempster and Stewart (2010) suggest that leaders can learn their situated practice of leading experientially through a *situated curriculum*, 'an order or pattern of activities that enable a "novice" to become a fully participating member practising a particular role' (p. 205). Stewart (a leader) kept a narrative account of his experience of becoming a leader – a chief operating officer. Kempster (an academic) examined and questioned these narratives, providing an opportunity for both to reflect and be reflexive about what was happening. This co-produced learning experience surfaced tacit knowing and exposed 'underlying issues of social, political, power and ethics embedded in contextual relationships' (p. 216).

These examples suggest that leadership can be learned in practice, in situ, as a relational experience that accounts for tensions within the workplace around gender, age, culture, etc. They also draw attention to the small, subtle acts of leadership that occur in everyday interactions and conversations – acts that are not necessarily by the formal leader but in the 'power tilts' of those assuming leadership in the interactive moment (Karp 2013). Such experiences take the learner beyond instrumental leadership education and training, which seeks to influence others to perform the leader's will, to a more constructed, contested and complex notion which requires a more integrated, aesthetic and sensual experience in which 'leaders' are reflexively aware of themselves in relation to others and their surroundings. Learning leadership is about learning how to learn in experience, as in the examples given by Stead and by Kempster and Stewart.

Aesthetic Embodiment (Sensing Leadership)

A number of scholars explore how to move away from the more instrumental, normative and dispassionate forms of learning to forms of learning leadership that emphasise the emotional, imaginative, bodily and aesthetic (Dey & Steyaert 2007; Ewenstein & White 2007; Hansen &

Bathurst 2011; Sinclair 2005; Taylor 2008). Aesthetic knowing is sensual and embodied, and such learning can be transformative in terms of helping students see, think and act differently by engaging tacit and embodied knowing, often through aesthetic disturbances (Mack 2015). Sutherland (2013: 26) argues that educators need to help leaders to 'embrace the dynamic, subjective, interactional environments of organisational life in ways that are critical, ethical, responsible and sensitive to the contemporary realities of managing and leading' and suggests that one way of doing so is through arts-based approaches to leadership learning. He held an MBA leadership masterclass where students interacted with a conductor and a choir as a means of experiencing and feeling the interactional and real time aspects of leadership. Learning was facilitated by dialogue and essays around the relationship between conducting and leadership – as participatory and involved. Sutherland develops the notion of aesthetic reflexivity, which involves recognizing their embodied selves in relation to others and, from this, challenging routine ways of thinking and acting. He notes that, in creating learning through aesthetic workspaces, 'the learning environment is purposefully framed, evocatively aestheticized and de-routinised' (p. 39).

If leadership is embodied, it is also gendered (Kelan 2013; Muhr & Sullivan 2013). The body regime in mainstream leadership is about managing impressions by dressing for success and staging theatrical performances to legitimate and convey the mission and idealized culture to which employees are expected to conform. Normative performances involve 'props designed to enlarge leadership figures to God-like proportions' (Sinclair 2005: 388). From a more critical perspective, scholars argue that the enactment of leadership is dominated by omnipotent, transcendental visions based on masculine discourses that subordinate feminine discourses of leadership (Ford 2010). To address these discourses, Sinclair (2005) argues that leadership bodies can be a means of disruption, contestation, resistance and new possibilities. She studied how two leaders – experientially – invoked their bodies as a political statement (e.g. marching in a gay and lesbian parade) to subvert and bring about change. Similarly, but in a classroom setting, Kelan uses media images of businesswomen to encourage students to question dress norms, which create a liminal space which not only makes:

> a statement about their professionalism but also how they position themselves in respect to ideal masculinity and femininity [. . .] Women will have to consider the double bind [. . .] if they are perceived as too masculine, they are seen as not enough of a woman, and if they are too feminine, they do not fulfil the role of the ideal business professional.
>
> *(2013: 46)*

She argues crucially that the issue is not about learning how to dress, but understanding how becoming a professional and a leader is a complex process. While we can 'teach' students to be alert to these issues in the classroom, they have to 'learn' how to recognize, think about and cope with the challenges of living them.

Working from a different perspective, Schedlitzki, Jarvis and MacInnes (forthcoming) encourage students to learn about leadership and themselves as leaders through the aesthetic experience of connecting stories and characters in Greek mythology to their own experience of who they are at work and how they interact with others. They argue that this approach encourages students to engage reflexively with more nuanced socially constructed views of organizations and leadership. Using characters from Greek mythology and improvised storytelling approaches, they disrupt students' thinking and provoke critical reflection on taken-for-granted assumptions as students learn from their emotional experience.

Conclusion

Our brief survey of leadership programmes indicates that 'leadership' is taught, but often in functionalist ways predicated on essentialist, rationalist and individualist assumptions. Whilst the rhetoric of leadership is ubiquitous, leadership programmes are often designed around technical and functional expertise with comparatively little 'leadership' content. This is perhaps reflective of the many attempts to define leadership and to the dominance of positivist research, which privileges rationality, quantification and techniques and aims to identify universal models (Lawler 2005). Such models ignore the complex and fluid lived experience of those learning to become leaders.

Alternative approaches focus on the need to learn – rather than teach – leadership from within: to create experiences within or outside the classroom where phronesis (or wisdom) may emerge (Cunliffe 2009; Grint 2007; Sutherland & Ladkin 2013; Yip & Raelin 2011). It is not, as Antonacopoulou and Bento (2010) note, learning about leadership; rather it is learning how to learn. We argue that it is a form of learning that aims to develop sensitivity to what is happening around us and reflexive insight into our own ways of being and acting as leaders. We are not suggesting that learning to be a leader is atheoretical, but that theories are only a part of the repertoire of leaders. Wise leaders learn to be bricoleurs (Gabriel 2002), using the resources to hand and working with others to do what must be done. We also suggest that wise leaders learn continually about themselves, others and the situations they find themselves dealing with: this involves engaging with reflexivity, situated relationality and aesthetic embodiment. A number of scholars propose that this is based on some form of disruption to current ways of thinking and acting, where taken-for-granted assumptions, conventional leadership practices and competing discourses and differences around gender, age, race and culture can be acknowledged and supported – a process that may begin in the classroom but that leaders learn to extend outside to their own lived experiences.

Notes

1 http://mitsloan.mit.edu/fellows/ (accessed 6 March 2015).
2 http:www.nytimes.com/2015/04/12/education/edlife/12edl-12leadership.html?_r=1
3 Carried out December 2014.
4 http://www.london.edu/education-and-development/masters-courses/mba?gclid=Cj0KEQjw-OCqBRDXmIWvveLE3_cBEiQAZWfImS5VsjK-ZKK2_CPybZ09txyGDK04b1Qk2h-4w X8hmfoaAszA8P8HAQ#.VVhkhkvFaII and http://formscloud.iese.edu/landings-mba-general/?utm_source=google&utm_medium=cpc&utm_term=iese%20business%20school%20MBA&utm_content=business%20School%20MBA%20IESE&utm_campaign=701b0000000A0vg&gclid=Cj0KEQ jw-OCqBRDXmIWvveLE3_cBEiQAZWfImU7xZpzeYIBbvP-OasOPEhEzy7WXuG0U7ZwRGM GVAt0aAss18P8HAQ (accessed 17 May 2015).

References

Antonacopoulou, E. P., & Bento, R. F. (2010) 'Learning leadership' in practice. In J. Storey (Ed.) *Leadership and organization: Current issues and key trends.* 2nd edition. (pp. 71–92). London: Routledge.

Ashman, I. (2007) Existentialism and leadership: A response to John Lawler with some further thoughts. *Leadership*, 3: 91–107.

Barge, J. K., & Fairhurst, G. T. (2008) Living leadership: A systemic, constructionist approach. *Leadership*, 4: 227–51.

Barge, J. K. & Little, M. (2008) A discursive approach to skillful activity. *Communication Theory*, 18: 505–34.

Battilana, J., Gilmartin, M., Sengul, M., Pache, A.-C., & Alexander, J. A. (2010) Leadership competencies for implementing planned organizational change. *Leadership Quarterly*, 21: 422–38.

Bell, E., Taylor, S., & Thorpe, R. (2002) A step in the right direction? Investors in people and the learning organization. *British Journal of Management*, 13: 161–71.

Bolden, R., & Gosling, J. (2006) Leadership competencies: Time to change the tune? *Leadership*, 2: 147–63.

Canwell, A., Dongrie, V., Neveras, N., & Stockton, H. (2014) http://dupress.com/articles/hc-trends-2014-leaders-at-all-levels/ (accessed 8 April 2015).

Carroll, B., Levy L., & Richmond, D. (2008) Leadership in practice: Challenging the competency paradigm. *Leadership*, 4: 363–79.

Cavazotte, F., Moreno, V., & Hickman, M. (2012) Effects of leader intelligence, personality and emotional intelligence on transformational leadership and managerial performance. *The Leadership Quarterly*, 23: 443–55.

Collinson, D. (2003) Identities and insecurities: Selves at work. *Organization*, 10: 527–47.

Collinson, D. (2014) Dichotomies, dialectics and dilemmas: New directions for critical leadership studies? *Leadership*, 10: 36–55.

Crevani, L., Lindgren, M., & Packendorff, J. (2010) Leadership, not leaders: On the study of leadership as practices and interactions. *Scandinavian Journal of Management*, 26: 77–86.

Cunliffe, A. L. (2008) Orientations to social constructionism: Relationally responsive social constructionism and its implications for knowledge. *Management Learning*, 39: 123–39.

Cunliffe, A. L. (2009) The philosopher leader: On relationalism, ethics and reflexivity: A critical perspective to teaching leadership. *Management Learning*, 40: 87–101.

Cunliffe, A. L. (2014) *A very short, fairly interesting and reasonably cheap book about management*. London: Sage Publications. 2nd edition.

Cunliffe, A. L., & Eriksen, M. (2011) Relational leadership. *Human Relations*, 64: 1425–49.

Day, D., & Antonakis, J. (2012) Leadership: Past, present and future. In D. Day & J. Antonakis (Eds.) *The nature of leadership*. 2nd Edition. Thousand Oaks, CA: Sage Publications.

Dey, P., & Steyaert, C. (2007) The troubadours of knowledge: Passion and invention in management education. *Organization*, 14: 437–61.

Doh, J. P. (2003) Can leadership be taught? Perspectives from management educators. *Academy of Management Learning and Education*, 2: 54–7.

Dunne, J. (1997) *Back to the rough ground: Practical judgment and the lure of technique*. Notre Dame, IN: University of Notre Dame Press.

Edwards, G., Elliott, C., Iszatt-White, M., & Schedlitzki, D. (2013) Critical and alternative approaches to leadership learning and development. *Management Learning*, 44: 3–10.

Ewenstein, B., & Whyte, J. (2007) Beyond words: Aesthetic knowledge and knowing in organizations. *Organization Studies*, 28: 689–708.

Fairhurst, G. (2007) *Discursive leadership: In conversation with leadership psychology*. Thousand Oaks, CA: Sage Publications.

Fletcher, J. K. (2004) The paradox of postheroic leadership: An essay on gender, power and transformational change. *Leadership Quarterly*, 14: 647–61.

Ford, J. (2006) Discourses of leadership: Gender, identity and contradiction in a UK public sector organization. *Leadership*, 2: 77–99.

Ford, J. (2010) Studying leadership critically: A psychosocial lens on leadership identities. *Leadership*, 6: 47–65.

Ford, J., Harding, N., & Learmonth, M, (2008) *Leadership as identity: Constructions and deconstructions*. Basingstoke: Palgrave Macmillan.

Gabriel, Y. (2002) Essai: On paragrammatic uses of organizational theory: A provocation. *Organization Studies*, 23 (1): 133–51.

Gabriel, Y. (2005) MBA and the education of leaders: The new playing fields of Eton? *Leadership*, 1 (2): 147–63.

Griffith, J., Connelly, S., Thiel, C., & Johnson, G. (2015) How outstanding leaders lead with affect: An examination of charismatic, ideological and pragmatic leaders. *Leadership Quarterly*, doi: 10.1016/j.leaqua.2015.03.004

Grint, K. (2007) Learning to lead: Can Aristotle help us find the road to wisdom? *Leadership*, 3 (2): 231–46.

Hansen, H., & Bathurst, R. (2011) Aesthetics and leadership. In A. Bryman, D. Collinson, & K. Grint (Eds.) *The Sage handbook of leadership* (pp. 255–66). London: Sage.

Hawkins, B., & Edwards, G. (2015) Managing the monsters of doubt: Liminality, threshold concepts and leadership learning. *Management Learning*, 46: 24–43.

Hibbert, P., & Cunliffe, A. L. (2015) Responsible management: Engaging moral reflexive practice through threshold concepts. *Journal of Business Ethics*, 127: 177–88.

Kaplan, S., Cortina, J., Ruark, G., LaPort, K., & Nicolaides, V. (2014) The role of organizational leaders in emotion management: A theoretical model. *Leadership Quarterly*, 25 (3): 563–80.

Karp, T. (2013) Studying subtle acts of leadership. *Leadership*, 9: 3–22.

Kelan, E. K. (2013) The becoming of business bodies: Gender, appearance, and leadership development. *Management Learning*, 44: 45–61.

Kellerman, B. (2013) Leading questions: The end of leadership – Redux. *Leadership*, 9: 135–9.

Kempster, S., & Stewart, J. (2010) Becoming a leader: A co-produced autoethnographic exploration of situated learning of leadership practice. *Management Learning*, 41: 205–19.

Lawler, J. (2005) The essence of leadership? Existentialism and leadership. *Leadership*, 1: 215–31.

Mack, K. (2015) Breaching or disturbing the peace? Organizational aesthetic encounters for informed and enlivened management learning experiences. *Management Learning*, 46: 156–74.

Mackay, D., Zundel, M., & Alkiriwi, M. (2014) Exploring the practical wisdom of metis for management learning. *Management Learning*, 45: 418–36.

Meyer, J. H. F., & Land, R. (2003). Threshold concepts and troublesome knowledge: Linkages to thinking and practising within the disciplines. In C. Rust (Ed.) *Improving student learning: Theory and practice: Ten Years On.* (pp. 412–24). Oxford: Centre for Staff and Learning Development.

Mole, G. (2010) Can leadership be taught? In J. Storey (Ed.) *Leadership and organization: Current issues and key trends.* 2nd edition. (pp. 114–26). London: Routledge.

Muhr, S. L., & Sullivan, K. R. (2013) 'None so queer as folk': Gendered expectations and transgressive bodies in leadership. *Leadership*, 9: 416–35.

Raelin, J. (2003) *Creating leaderful organizations: How to bring out leadership in everyone.* San Francisco: Berrett-Koehler.

Raelin, J. (2011) From leadership-as-practice to leaderful practice. *Leadership*, 7: 195–211.

Schedlitzki, D., Jarvis, C., & MacInnes, J. (forthcoming) Leadership development: A place for storytelling and Greek mythology? *Management Learning*, doi:10.1177/1350507614560303.

Schyns, B., Kiefer, T., Kerschreiter, R., & Tymon, A. (2011) Teaching implicit leadership theories to develop leaders and leadership: How and why it can make a difference. *Academy of Management Learning & Education*, 10: 397–408.

Segal, S. (2010) A Heideggerian approach to practice-based reflexivity. *Management Learning*, 41: 379–89.

Shotter, J. (2008) *Conversational realities revisited: Life, language, body and world.* Chagrin Falls, OH: Taos Institute Publications.

Shotter, J., & Cunliffe, A. L. (2003) Managers as practical authors: Everyday conversations for action. In D. Holman & R. Thorpe (Eds.) *Management and language* (pp. 1–37). London: Sage.

Sinclair, A. (2005) Body possibilities in leadership. *Leadership*, 1 (4): 387–406.

Sinclair, A. (2007) Teaching leadership critically to MBAs: Experiences from heaven and hell. *Management Learning*, 38: 458–71.

Sparrowe, R. (2005) Authentic leadership and the narrative self. *Leadership Quarterly*, 16: 419–39.

Stahl, G. K., & De Luque, M. S. (2014) Antecedents of responsible leader behaviour: Research synthesis, conceptual framework and agenda for future research. *The Academy of Management Perspectives*, 28: 235–54.

Statler, M. (2014) Developing wisdom in a business school? Critical reflections on pedagogical practice. *Management Learning*, 45: 397–417.

Stead, V. (2013) Learning to deploy (in)visibility: An examination of women leaders lived experiences. *Management Learning*, 44: 63–79.

Stead, V., & Elliott, C. (2012) Women's leadership learning: A reflexive review of representations and leadership teaching. *Management Learning*, 44: 373–94.

Sutherland, I. (2013) Arts-based methods in leadership development: Affording aesthetic workspaces, reflexivity and memories with momentum. *Management Learning*, 44: 25–43.

Sutherland, I., & Ladkin, D. (2013) Creating engaged executive learning spaces: The role of aesthetic agency. *Organizational Aesthetics*, 2: 105–24.

Taylor, S. S. (2008) Theatrical performance as unfreezing: Ties that bind at the Academy of Management. *Journal of Management Inquiry*, 17: 398–406.

Xing, Y., & Sims, D. (2012) Leadership, Daoist wu wei and reflexivity: Flow, self-protection and excuse in Chinese bank managers' leadership practice. *Management Learning*, 43: 97–112.

Yip, J., & Raelin, J. A. (2011). Threshold concepts and modalities for teaching leadership practice. *Management Learning*, 43: 333–54.

Appendix 32.1 Awarding Bodies Offering Leadership Course Content

Country/ region	Awarding body	Practitioner programmes	Practitioner leadership content	Notes	Core and/ or elective theoretical and/or models of leadership content	Leadership course elective content	Oriented to leadership skills or competency development	Reflection and self-awareness elements	Experiential content (organization visits, consultancy projects, etc.)	Contextual element	CSR
Various	ILM	Level 7 Strategic management and leadership core modules	Leadership in practice Developing the reflective leader The leadership journey Leading change in organizations	Aimed at practitioners from any field, executives for Level 7 Delivered through 220+ partner organizations, including universities such as Exeter	✓		✓	✓	✓	✓	
Various	CMI	Level 7 Strategic management and leadership diploma Learners choose a minimum of 8 modules from those available	Personal leadership development as a strategic manager Strategic leadership Strategic leadership practice	Aimed at practitioners from any field, executives for Level 7 Delivered through 220+ partner organizations, including universities such as Exeter	✓		✓	✓	✓	✓	

(continued)

Country/ region	Awarding body	Practitioner programmes	Practitioner leadership content	Notes	Core and/ or elective theoretical and/or models of leadership content	Leadership course elective content	Oriented to leadership skills or competency development	Reflection and self-awareness elements	Experiential content (organization visits, consultancy projects, etc.)	Contextual element	CSR
		Those related to leadership are listed here	Introduction to strategic management and leadership, developing risk management strategies								
UK	Skills CFA	National occupational management and leadership standards	Managing self Providing direction Facilitating innovation and change Working with people Using resources Achieving results	Aimed at practitioners, the management and leadership standards comprise a suite of 56 NVQ modules from level 2 (GCSE equivalent) to level 7 (equivalent to Master's level). The modules describe	?		✓	✓	✓	✓	

| Various | Proteus leadership programmess | Various levels in leadership Advanced Diploma to certificate | 'Provide leadership across the organisation' | behaviours such as persuading, managing conflict and consulting and reflective units such as thinking creatively or strategically, valuing others and involving others | Aimed at practitioners from any field – mostly based in Australia but a few delivery centres in the UK and elsewhere | ✓ | ✓ | ✓ | ✓ |

Country/ region	Centre	Practitioner programmes	Leadership content	Core theoretical and/or models of leadership content	Elective theoretical and/or models of leadership content	Oriented to leadership skills or competency development	Reflection and self-awareness elements	Experiential content (organization visits, consultancy projects, etc.)	Contextual element	CSR
UK	Lancaster Leadership Centre	International LEAD	Responsible leadership							
		Global advanced leadership programmes	Leadership and change							
		Customized programmes	Leadership in practice							
			Conscious capitalism							
			Future business models	✓		✓			✓	✓
			Responsible business development							
			Responsible business function management							
	Cranfield International Centre for Women's Leaders	Women as leaders	Doing leadership differently as a woman							
			Your aspirations and values as a leader							
			Navigating in a male dominated organization	✓		✓	✓		✓	✓
			Political skills and networking in organizations							

Organisation	Programme	Topics				
The North Leadership Centre, Newcastle University, Education Dept	Team leaders programme	Increasing personal presence				
		Creating and maintaining resilience and well-being				
		Self awareness				
		Communication				
		Self-management				
		Change management	✓	✓	✓	✓
		Developing others				
		High performance workplaces				
African Leadership Centre, King's College London	Short courses	Leadership and society				
		Emerging powers in global leadership				
		Natural resource governance	✓	✓	✓	✓
		The State and development in Africa and Asia				
		Diaspora populations and developing societies				
Centre for Leadership Performance, Cumbria University	Short courses	Strategic planning				
	Leadership at lunch	The management of change				
	Leader to leader	Problem solving				
	Learning labs	Motivating teams				

(continued)

Country/region	Centre	Practitioner programmes	Leadership content	Core theoretical and/or models of leadership content	Elective theoretical and/or models of leadership content	Oriented to leadership skills or competency development	Reflection and self-awareness elements	Experiential content (organization visits, consultancy projects, etc.)	Contextual element	CSR
		Customized courses	Going for growth / Performance management / Innovation / Collaboration / Business development	✓		✓	✓	✓		
Europe	European School of Management and Technology (ESMT), Berlin	Practitioners (executive) courses	Leading people / Psychological intelligence / Errors and crises / Change management / Leadership as practice / Young leaders	✓		✓	✓	✓	✓	
USA	Center for Creative Leadership, USA, EMEA, Asia-Pacific	Leadership at the peak / Leading for organizational impact / Leadership development programme / Maximizing your leadership potential / Leadership fundamental	Business operations / Strategy vision, direction and goals / Managing change / Boundary spanning / Talent management / Individual leadership styles / Building relationships	✓		✓	✓	✓		

Asia	Asian Leadership Institute, Hong Kong and Thailand	Individual leadership	Executive coaching and mindfulness retreats	✓	✓			
		Family-run business	Family coaching and family retreats			✓		
		Organizational development	Triad leadership programme and high performance teams				✓	
		Specialized programmes	Couples retreat, corporate health retreat and higher purpose retreat				✓	✓

Appendix 32.3 Sector-Specific Leadership Provision

Country/region	Centre	Practitioner programmes	Leadership content	Audience	Core and/or elective theoretical and/or models of leadership content	Oriented to leadership skills or competency development	Reflection and self-awareness elements	Experiential content (organization visits, consultancy projects, etc.)	Contextual element	CSR
UK	The Leadership Centre, London	Public sector, localized leadership programmes. Based in Cumbria, Norfolk and Suffolk	Improving strategic partnerships through local research	Local authority staff	✓					
	London Centre for Leadership in Learning (LCLL)	Leadership training for education: National professional qualification for headship (NPQH) National professional qualification for senior leadership (NPQSL) Subject specialist and middle-management courses	Leading in an education setting HR and appraisal Improving teaching and learning	Education sector	✓	✓		✓	✓	
						✓		✓	✓	

Provider	Courses	Content detail	Education sector	NHS – all areas
Eastern Leadership Centre	Leadership training for education: Schools, children's centres etc.	Leading an effective school		
	Courses for governors	Succeeding in headship		
	Teaching assistant courses	Leading inclusion: achievement for all	✓	
	NPQH	Leading staff and effective teams	✓	
	NPQSL	Leading change for improvement		
	Specialist and middle-management courses	Leading in diverse contexts		
		Free-school leadership	✓	
NHS Leadership Academy Regional centres offer courses	The Edward Jenner programme	No content detail available		✓
	The Mary Seacole programme	No content detail available		
	The Elizabeth Garrett Anderson programme	No content detail available		
	The Nye Bevan programme	No content detail available		✓
	The top leaders programme	No content detail available		
	ILM qualifications levels 1–5	As per ILM in Awarding Bodies Table		

NHS – all areas

(continued)

Country/region	Centre	Practitioner programmes	Leadership content	Audience	Core and/or elective theoretical and/or models of leadership content	Oriented to leadership skills or competency development	Reflection and self-awareness elements	Experiential content (organization visits, consultancy projects, etc.)	Contextual element	CSR
NZ	Leadership Development Centre	Public sector	Best practice guidance	Local authority staff					✓	
			Access to tools for talent spotting							
			Leadership development planning and implementation					✓		
			Individual assessment					✓		
			Customized programmes for identified leaders				✓			
			Information on experts in the field and accredited coaches				✓			
			Facilitators and mentors			✓				
			Information on the latest research on what works		✓					

33

Diverse Approaches to Leadership Development

Jonathan Gosling and Ian Sutherland

Introduction

Finding and developing people to lead enterprises, armies and governments has always been a challenge: this is the explicit aim of most leadership development, but sometimes it is confused with efforts to restrain and discipline current leaders who threaten to misuse power – hence contemporary emphases on 'responsible leadership', and the mechanisms of 'checks and balances' that characterize most governance arrangements.

In other words, it is as much about 'aligning' as 'inspiring' the energies of potent people. We want to encourage and enable leaders to take initiative, open new opportunities and challenge the constraints of established systems; but we also want to keep them aligned to corporate intentions and limit what we see as moral transgressions.

This dilemma exposes the extent to which we identify leadership with juxtaposed values of freedom and duty, service and glory, individualism and collectivism. It also hints at the nature of leadership development in co-creating the phenomenon of leadership.

While much leadership training is still predicated on the notion that there is a gap or lack in skills and competences to be filled, many leadership development programmes focus on enabling people, engaging them in the search for and perhaps co-creating an inner sense of authority, and encouraging in them a resolution to act on it. In sociological terms, leadership development seeks to enhance the agency of individuals. This is consonant with much current organization theory, which understands organizing to be closely allied to the 'identity work' of individuals and groups; ordinary organization members can discover 'the leader within', enhancing their contribution to the collective so long as this emerging confidence remains aligned with organizational goals and methods.

Leadership of an organization often requires one to be an employee performing functions on behalf of the principals – usually the owners or shareholders. As an employee, the leader's functions include meaning-making, direction-setting and aligning resources. While we may couch this work in diplomatic terms, at a basic level it is manipulating other people's beliefs and energies in the interests of the corporation, even calling for their sacrifice at times. So no wonder that leadership often appeals to the more power-hungry and narcissistic amongst us; or that it provokes such ambivalence amongst organizational members. In amelioration of this, some leadership development programmes are designed to encourage ambition in the modest, lessen the narcissism of the hungry and persuade the modest that they have something to offer. Such contradictory associations go some way to explaining the oft-remarked fact that a common outcome of leadership development is that participants leave their sponsoring organization in search of something more authentic, meaningful or harmonious.

The confusion implicit in the foregoing is derived from a simple but important conflation: leader vs leader*ship* development. It is possible that leadership of an organization can be improved simply by enhancing the skills and attitudes of those in authority: hence the common focus on leader development. But the willingness and ability of others to collaborate with this leadership is equally important – if career structures, incentives, corporate culture or any number of other factors are misaligned to the aspirations of leaders, it is unlikely that leader*ship* will be effective. Hence leadership development, if taken seriously, can extend to what is more usually delineated as OD (organization development). This can be further illustrated in the following formula:

$$L = I{:}F$$

where:

L   stands for 'leadership'
I   stands for the qualities of individual leaders – people in positions of authority, likely to be the subjects of 'leader development'
F   stands for 'followership' – the collective capacity to orient actions according to the guidance, inspiration or instructions of one or more leaders.

Hence this formula suggests that leadership is a product of a relationship between individual leaders and 'followership'. The qualities of individual leaders are accounted for by their traits, personalities, competencies, attitudes, mindsets and so forth – the usual foci for leadership development programmes.

Followership, in turn, is affected by many factors, principal amongst which are:

- the **Number** of people involved, which largely determines the extent to which one is dealing with the dynamics of small groups, teams, gangs, crowds, and intra-group processes of identification, splitting, competition, cooperation and so forth, and hence the modes by which leadership is communicated and fantasized about;
- the **Individual** characteristics of 'followers' – their skills, educational levels, career aspirations, extroversion, desire for order and predictability and so forth;
- **Culture**, which is an intangible but powerful influence on authority relations, and hence on how leadership and followership are enacted. Hierarchy and autonomy are obvious differentiators, and some cultures are marked by gender inequalities, distance between top management and others, fatalism, and many other features that have an obvious impact;
- **Environment** factors, which impact on the desire for leadership – most simply summarized in a distinction between stable and turbulent conditions, and more recently in the acronym 'VUCA', standing for Volatile, Uncertain, Complex and Ambiguous (Stiehm & Townsend, 2002);
- **Systems** – both hard and soft, formal and informal, institutionalized and emergent – which influence leadership and followership through the effect on, for example, the ability of front-line staff to work autonomously, transparency of information, performance management regimes and the centralization of control;

- **Technology,** which mediates all relations in the workplace. Automation can make established professions redundant almost overnight, shifting the balance of power and the prevailing leadership dynamics.

Converting these six factors into an acronym, we can present our formula as:

$$L = I:F$$

where

$$F = NICEST^1$$

Therefore developing leadership – often assumed to be solely a matter of enhancing 'I' (individuals in positions deemed to be leaderly, i.e. hierarchically superior) – may also be accomplished through changes to any of the other factors. Indeed, we often hear that improving leadership will take a change in culture; and the oft-remarked tension between leadership and management can be explained as a tussle about the dominance of 'systems'. In any case, this formula, simple as it is, explains why leader*ship* development is as much to do with shifting the ways in which people participate in collective tasks. Not all of these shifts derive from changes in beliefs, practices or behaviours: technological innovation and environmental pressures are just as powerful. Development of *leaders* is just one of many possible approaches – one that is perhaps most attractive to those who control the training budgets.

Evidently, leadership development initiatives vary in their concentration on individual or collective/organizational factors; and also on the extent to which they seek to improve leadership though prescription or emergence. If one believes that leadership arises from specified behaviours and competencies, it makes sense to prescribe training in these. But if one sees leadership emerging from improvised (sometimes inspired) responses to changing circumstances, one seeks to enhance this rather ad-hoc and complex process – usually involving reflection, coaching and so forth.

This distinction has been modelled by Rodgers, Frearson, Holden and Gold (2003) to enable a typology of leadership development (see Figure 33.1).

Reviewing a large number of leadership development programmes, Bolden, Gosling, Marturano and Dennison (2003) estimated 80 per cent lie in cell (1) and 15 per cent in cell (2). This is not surprising: it seems rational to first construct a framework of the kinds of leadership we want, then describe the leadership competencies to satisfy this framework. All that remains is to assess current leaders against these competencies and provide remedial training or recruitment to fill the gaps. Almost every major organization pursues some version of this, and 'competency-oriented leadership development' is a large part of the industry.

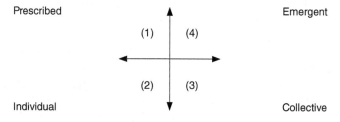

Figure 33.1 A Typology of Leadership Development
Source: Rodgers et al., 2003

However there are problems: frameworks tend to describe all the features that an organization wants, but most people have strengths in some areas; often it is the peculiar chemistry of a mix of people that makes for a successful leadership team, though none are competent in all aspects. Measuring competence is difficult, especially of values such as honesty and integrity; and the time and expense of assessing competence easily becomes excessive – and politically difficult if the CEO does not match the ideal! Nonetheless, discussion about desirable competencies is an integral part of most leadership development design processes. It becomes arguably less productive when used as a template of the 'standard leader'. (For a review and critique of leadership competencies, see Bolden *et al.*, 2003; and Bolden & Gosling, 2009.)

However if one starts out with a concept of leadership development that sees leadership as relational and open to influence by the factors of 'followership', one is likely to be alert to a much wider domain of leadership development interventions – informed by, but not reliant on, a competency framework. One might thus recognize an intervention as simple as hiring professional communications consultants might improve the perceived capability of leaders during a change process – but this would hardly count as 'leadership development' in most formal definitions.

In the sections that follow we set out a brief historical trajectory and outline of the leadership development industry; set out some of its main conceptual foundations; and provide examples of current practice. Finally we will venture some predictions about future directions.

A History of Leadership Development

Developing the next generation of leaders is a process embedded in whatever the current dominant assumptions about legitimate power and authority may be. When it is assumed that the child will inherit from the parent, caste and class norms provide experiences aimed to ensure reasonably able successors. Thus medieval Europe was characterized by assumptions about aristocratic ability and legitimacy; sons of rulers become squires to their parents' peers, and were thus tutored by example, exhortation and practice into mature leadership positions. But if inheritance gave the right to lead, it did not guarantee the ability, nor moral probity. Writing about his failure to educate the tyrant Dyonisius II, Plato writes 'Mankind . . . will find no cessation from evil until either the real philosophers gain political control or else the politicians become by some miracle real philosophers' (1973: 326d). He later set up the Academy to educate young men from patrician families, arguing that the relevant knowledge could be absorbed only by those with the right character as well as intelligence – those with 'an eye for the *eidos*'. The balance of character and competence is a theme to which we will return.

A new idea arose in the West with the French and American Revolutions, and much earlier in China: the idea of meritocracy. Meritocracy suggests that talent and achievement should take precedence over inheritance. Regardless of whether talent is inherited or tutored, meritocracy demands that it should be proven in action. Therefore measures and tests of leadership ability have become central to the leadership development process.

The need to assess and actively develop raw leadership talent came urgently to the fore during the two World Wars of the twentieth century, when the demand for officers outstripped the supply from traditional sources – in the UK and Europe, the upper-class high schools. Perhaps the most influential were the War Office selection boards developed by the British military to meet its rapid expansion in 1940. Methods included group exercises and individual psychiatric interviews (King, 2003; Murray, 1990) designed to evince a candidate's ability to command in the midst of social and operational pressures. These so-called assessment centres became the models for numerous multi-modal leadership assessments; because they were seen to be successful in selecting officers (perhaps a self-fulfilling prophecy), they had a substantial impact on the design of leadership training and development. Prominent amongst the spin-offs were the T-groups developed by Kurt Lewin and colleagues at the National Training Laboratories in the USA, and the Tavistock Institute of Human Relations 'working conferences' in the UK and later throughout Europe and beyond. Common to these approaches is a belief that the capacity to lead arises from an individual's ability to 'take up authority' derived from (a) his or her inner conviction, (b) the role or position in an organizational hierarchy or (c) the unconscious projections from a group or crowd.

This last point is important, because a group under threat – real or imagined – responds as if it will be saved by strategies of fight, flight, dependency or pairing. That is, the group seems to share such 'basic assumptions' (Bion, 1961) and seeks leadership to fulfil those assumptions. It may therefore give leadership to someone who offers to lead it in fight, someone who distracts it from the threat (flight), someone promising to take care of things (dependency) or a combination of people from whom might be expected a new and more promising future (pairing). Such group dynamics push into leadership those with a valency (available tendency) to lead in corresponding ways – with aggression, avoidance or as a kind of saviour. Leadership development in the Tavistock and NTL traditions alert participants to these group processes and to their own valencies and thus their ability to distinguish more rational and intentional purposes at personal and organizational levels.

This tradition of leadership development, derived from the War Office selection boards and evolving into multi-modal assessment centres, remains influential as a selection process in military and knowledge-intensive industries such as management consulting. They include leaderless group discussions, individual and team activities, inter-group exercises and personality tests – and are conducted over several days. As leadership development (rather than selection) for experienced and in-service employees, these traditions have had a tremendous and lasting impact in many of the experiential approaches described below.

Somewhat counter to this has been the growth of interest in leadership competencies, referring to a mixed bag of skills, behaviours and attitudes ascribed to an individual and believed to be useful in leading. The argument is simple enough: a person can be taught and incentivized to behave in required ways or to achieve required outcomes (not the same thing) – including in relation to team coordination, strategic visions, operational effectiveness and other aspects of leadership. This is a sensible approach – to be clear about what we want our leaders to be able to do. It is even possible to define collective competencies when working with a board or across an organization (for example, to critique executive recommendations, to collaborate with external stakeholders and so on). However there is a risk of reductionism – that we reduce leadership to this list, that we design and measure leadership development to do just these things – and miss the fact that leadership is always about more than can be defined in advance, that development is effective when it goes beyond its foreseeable goals. Furthermore, as we argued in the opening to this chapter, effective leadership might arise from a range of factors that influence the capacity for followership. So for example a policy of reducing team sizes to focus on projects could make good use of existing teamwork competency and thus improve the experience of an effectively led organization. Conversely, detailed performance management systems that work well in manufacturing sectors can reduce the autonomy and enthusiasm of knowledge workers, giving them a sense of impoverished leadership – however excellent the leadership development courses attended by the bosses.

So, while an eye to competencies is helpful in designing leadership development, it is perhaps more attuned to developing followers than leaders.

Does It Work?

The answer to this question rather depends on what is expected, over what time span. It is relatively easy to assess acquisition of skills, but harder to know if a person is more able to step up to leadership, to support others in leadership roles, or if a group as a whole is behaving with more purpose, efficacy and responsibility. Although there are accepted measures for these, they tend to be culture specific and it is very unusual to have a sample large enough to smooth out accidental influences such as market conditions, group-specific events and so forth. While many leadership development firms claim to be able to measure the return on investment, these invariably depend on proxies such as 'employee engagement' or project outcomes, which are not really as causally dependent on 'leadership' as their proponents might claim. People selected for leadership development are likely to be talented anyway, and would make good use of any opportunity. Furthermore, professionals in this field often comment on the large proportion of participants who opt to leave their current employment, often for a period away from corporate life. There are several possible explanations – this is a self-selecting population looking for change; once people take time to reflect on what really matters to them they no longer want to give so much of their lives to the industrial machine; leadership development is a CV-enhancing experience that improves the individual's employability beyond their current employer's expectations. Conversely, there is evidence that some people in senior leadership positions, looking back on their careers, point to insights and networks gained on leadership development programmes. It is not possible to know if these were more or less significant than other life events and relationships; it seems likely that what a person considers to be 'formative' is rather idiosyncratic. So it is probably a mistake to look for tight causal links between leadership development and leader career or impact. However, it seems highly plausible that the experiences on leadership development programmes will act as affordances of leadership outcomes, for individuals and groups. A leadership development programme cannot create leaders, but it can make leadership much more likely.

The Leadership Development Industry

As will be evident from the foregoing, leader and leadership development have been constructed in particular ways through historically specific circumstances, and this work of construction continues in the same way as any significant industry. Understood as a 'culture industry' like film, design and fashion, it has some of the same properties of creativity, elitism, branding and isomorphism. Like other services, it is not fully produced until it is consumed – when participants internalize the experience and 'learn' the lessons.

Overall it has the features of a mature and tiered industry, with players at different levels – unsurprising when $14 billion a year is spent by companies in the USA alone (Loew & Leonard, 2012). Leadership development companies vary from large global operations (e.g. the Center for Creative Leadership, headquartered on its own leafy campus in Greensborough, North Carolina with offices, staff and associates on every continent) through to one-person consultancies drawing on personal networks – often with a global reach. Companies position themselves differently: able to provide assessment and feedback on standard factors and scales; deliver a consistent product in any setting; able to customize every detail every time; deploy local experts in any language; offer personal coaching in various formats and so on. Furthermore, the industry is subject to high elasticity of demand because HR and training budgets are strongly affected by economic swings. This militates towards an organizational form featuring flexible networks of associates rather than employees – a form of organization likely to be preferable for the individualistic and 'creative' people involved in this work, many of whom are opting for post-corporate careers.

At the same time buyers vary in their sophistication, some specifying precise requirements, sometimes through professional procurement offices. This may drive improved quality along with the conformity that is common to formal tendering processes. However the demand for creativity and distinctiveness probably means there will continue to be space for the 'boutique' providers; also, while it is easy to teach leadership theories, models and tools, it is much harder to change behaviour and to solve inter-personal, inter-departmental or strategic problems – hence the blend of leadership development with OD interventions. Therefore a prior relationship and trust is a significant component of the buying decision. Even where formal tenders are managed by purchasing departments, experienced providers will often respond only when they have a prior relationship with the purchaser.

However the ability to deliver larger-scale interventions requires trust and control of quality. Some providers opt to carry larger numbers of directly employed staff for this reason; some belong to active knowledge-exchange networks and accreditation schemes, and hence drive a secondary market for 'train-the-trainers' (Guthey, Sweet & Fjalland, 2015).

General Critiques of Leadership Development

While leadership development has a history, it also has its critics. In recent years, these target its relevance to practice and its methods of delivery. Leadership thinkers, educators and practitioners have become dissatisfied with overly conceptually driven, economically derived and objectively analytical approaches to the practice of developing leaders. Within this is a critique of the contents (hyper-rationalist and conceptual), methods (top-down, sage-on-the-stage) and focus (leaders not leadership) of the traditional approaches to development (Donaldson, 2002; Ghoshal, 2005; Gioia, 2002; Khurana, 2007). To be fair, much of this critique focuses on leadership development found in business schools and executive education delivered by these lauded but conservative institutions (Bennis & O'Toole, 2005; Brocklehurst, Sturdy, & Winstanley, 2007; Buechel & Antunes, 2007a, 2007b; Garvin, 2007; Gosling & Mintzberg, 2004; Houde, 2007; Kets de Vries & Korotov, 2007; Mintzberg, 2004; Petriglieri & Petriglieri, 2010; Sinclair, 2007; Welsh & Dehler, 2007).

The myriad critics call for new and novel ways of approaching leadership development centring not so much on leaders as leadership practice, and in ways which recognize and engage the dynamic, subjective, interactional realities of organizational life. Moreover, there is a call to do so through learning methods that are more participant centred than sage-on-the-stage performances, and more impactful than entertaining team-building games. Perhaps most importantly, the calls are to re-imagine leadership development to tackle the critical, ethical, responsible, human-sensitive deficit found in contemporary environments of managing and leading (Adler, 2006; Atkinson, 2007; Clarke & Butcher, 2009; French and Grey, 1996; Gabriel, 2005; Giacalone & Thompson, 2006; Gosling & Mintzberg, 2006; Grey & Mitev, 1995; Henisz, 2011; Mintzberg, 2009; Mitroff, 2004; Reynolds, 1998; Weick, 2007).

The critiques were nicely summed up by Cunliffe in 2002 when she bemoaned the practice as failing 'to consider that practitioners deal with ill-defined, unique, emotive and complex issues' as we continue to employ normative means of teaching and learning based on applying 'objective, decontextualised theories and techniques' (p. 35). These criticisms laid at the feet of leadership development – whether new or traditional, fresh or stale – emanate from a belief in leadership's existence, importance and ability to engender positive benefits. There is a vein of critical scholarship questioning these assumptions around change, benefit and so forth (Alvesson & Sveningsson, 2003; Guthey, 2015; Kellerman, 2012). However, we leave these criticisms to elsewhere in this volume.

Response to the criticisms has come in the form of more interactive, socially co-created approaches involving experiential learning (Kolb, 1984; Kolb & Kolb, 2005), reflection and reflexivity (Cunliffe, 2002, 2004), heterotopic learning environments (Beyes & Michels, 2011; Sutherland & Ladkin, 2013; Vince, 2011), action learning (Revans, 1980; Raelin, 2007), appreciative inquiry and a focus on creating memories with momentum (Sutherland, 2013). Below we deal with these in turn.

Some Key Concepts Relevant to Leadership Development

Above we have laid out a general landscape of the purposes, directions and main contestations of leadership development.

As the field has expanded and developed, fed by the drive of corporatization, it has laboured to substantiate and further itself through theoretical, conceptual and empirical research. Here we overview key concepts focusing on those most present and active today, those that address the critiques on which we have briefly pondered above.

Standards, Frameworks and Competencies

Assuming leadership and management can be reduced to sets of behaviours and skills, a vast industry has grown around the identification, modelling, measuring and assessing of competencies. Kick-started by the work of McBer consultants for the American Management Association in the late 1970s and early 1980s, the aim was 'to explain some of the differences in general qualitative distinctions of performance (e.g. poor versus average versus superior managers) which may occur across specific jobs and organisations as a result of certain competencies which managers share' (Boyatzis, 1982: 9), with a job competency being defined as 'an underlying characteristic of a person which results in effective and/or superior performance in a job' (p. 21).

The search for a definitive list of competencies, with frameworks showing how they are related to each other and to improved performance, was often linked to national schemes for productivity improvement. For example, the UK's 2002 report by the Council for Excellence in Management and Leadership (CEML, 2002), promoted government-endorsed models, frameworks and standards that were widely adopted by public and private sector organisations.

The underlying assumption behind such frameworks is that these competencies are universally applicable. As the UK's Management Standards Centre boldly stated: 'Whatever the size of your organisation, you will find the standards have been written to meet your management needs' (MSC website, December 2003).

However their effectiveness with regards to improving actual managerial performance is unclear. Critics raise a number of objections. First, it is overly reductionist, focusing on small parts of role behaviour because these are easy to see and measure, thereby missing the holistic interplay that these frameworks often set out to describe. Leaders' experience is highly subjective and contextual, and their behaviours result from a complex interaction between internal beliefs, values, knowledge, understanding, skills, experience and many influences of which they are only partially conscious – so the whole cannot be reduced to its parts.

Second, standards are criticised for being overly universalistic. It seems obvious that competencies differ across cultures, industries and professions, and change over the length of a career, come into play in different settings, and might even be interchangeable (a chief officer might be good with people or great with details, and in either case others will adapt accordingly). So how granular and customized should we go?

Third, standard competencies focus on current 'best practice', and are in fact often based on limited research in a small group of senior personnel – as if their success is a pattern for others to follow. Where change and diversity are the norm, leadership development should hold lightly to its defined competencies.

Fourth, because they emphasize measurable behaviours and outcomes, the processes of evidence gathering and assessment may actually inhibit organizational learning and development by promoting a focus on observable behaviours and indicators to the exclusion of less overt aspects such as values, beliefs and relationships.

Fifth, they may encourage a mechanistic approach to leadership development, attending to trainable skills rather than deep-rooted wisdom.

Experiential Learning Theory

Influentially promoted by Kolb (1984) but rooted in earlier theories of Dewey (1934), experiential learning has found a strong foothold in contemporary approaches to leadership development (see Kolb & Kolb, 2005; Mainemelis, Boyatzis, & Kolb, 2002; Vince, 1996; Weick, 2007). Conceptually succinct, experiential learning theory suggests that we learn best when engaged by experiences with affective, emotional impact, and when helped to reflect on these in ways that integrate them with our current understanding. This is something we do implicitly day to day as we have experiences, think on them, and draw new understandings of ourselves, the worlds we experience, and how we are and act in those worlds (e.g. touching a hot stove, burning our finger, never touching a hot stove again; expressing an opinion, being slapped down, being more circumspect in future). As applied to leadership development, experiential learning largely falls into three categories: (1) creating opportunities for participants to study relations to authority as they happen, 'in the here and now'; and (2) activities that simulate emotional, cognitive and relational challenges of the workplace.

In all respects, learning occurs through the impact of lived experience more than rational–logical learning from texts, articles and case studies (you can read about hot stoves and human fingers, but you do not really 'know' the implications until you burn your finger). Kolb sees this process as a cycle: concrete experience, reflective observation, abstract conceptualization, active experimentation and back to concrete experience. He suggests that most of us have preferences for one or other aspect of this cycle, so good learning design will include elements of each. However Kolb's learning cycle, and many similar models along with most learning evaluations, assume that learning is a process of becoming conscious and aware of – of grasping a 'point'. But this can be only partially true: we all learn our first lesson about authority, dependency, trust and loyalty as infants, figuring out how to get along with the adults on whom we depend. We internalize personal strategies that become so integrated into our personalities that we are seldom conscious of them as optional. In adult life our encounters with authority – i.e. leadership – often excite habitual emotional responses, so leadership development is largely about developing new, less trammelled responses to authority relations. When we speak about transformative learning, we refer to changes in these deep-seated personality formations. Such changes often take a long time, evolving as one encounters new situations, experiences trust and encouragement or gains new insight into patterns in life and relationships. These evolving developments are mostly unconscious but can have profound effects in leadership (and followership) ability. So these important aspects of experiential learning actually take place without us knowing that we are experiencing them – one might say pre-experiential learning.

Through these processes we gradually develop self-awareness, rational and non-rational insights. These can be ways to surface embodied, tacit, contextual experiences arising from the sometimes sordid nexus of organizational life, sometimes described as perspectival and circumstantial incongruities in our late (post)modern age (Giddens, 1991, 2003; Lash & Urry, 1994).

Within the second category (creation of experiences for participants to have), practitioners set up scenarios, exercises, games, etc. that stimulate affective and cognitive experiences relevant to leadership – uncertainty, authority conflicts, team dynamics, competition and so forth. During and after these exercises, participants engage in reflection on the activities, form understandings of those experiences, abstract them to conceptual levels, and hopefully go out into the world to experiment and adapt their leadership practice accordingly. While hugely influential and undoubtedly impactful, such 'designed' experiences are open to a critique that they are too far removed from the day-to-day realities of organizational life, encouraging participants to learn important personal lessons, but maybe not to change their work practices.

In both cases, the learning occurs at the intersection of engaged participation within an event and making connections between that event and one's self. These connections arise through sensemaking, the activity of giving meaning to experience (Weick, 1995; Weick, Sutcliffe, & Obstfeld, 2005). It is a collaborative, socially situated practice, influenced by others and by context (Holt & Macpherson, 2010), in which, in the best cases, participants go beyond reflection (a simplifying of experience) into reflexivity (a complexifying of experience).

Reflection/Reflexivity

As the above discussion implies, reflection has become essential to contemporary leadership development, implying an ideal kind of subjectivity characterized by self-awareness (Chia, 1996; Cunliffe, 2002, 2009; Keevers & Treleaven, 2011; Reynolds, 1998; Segal, 2010). Reflection is said to constitute a transformational bridge between experience and learning (Boud, Keogh, & Walker, 1985; Gray, 2007). This, in and of itself, recognizes leadership as a practice beyond an active/passive split of downloading information from gurus, professors, books, models, YouTube videos or blogs. Reflection, it is claimed, takes the practitioner into a realm of leadership as a messy affair populated by intersecting contexts, situations, people, purposes, values and beliefs – the embodied, often messy (sometimes elegant) nature of the practice.

Reflection can be a powerful collective exercise in which leadership development focuses on the post-hoc analysis and reflection on particular challenges, usually with some attempt to articulate responses. The starting point might be as general as 'issues' such as leading in the digital age, leading innovation, economic turbulence or climate change. In this approach, the material used to discuss challenges, issues or topics comes from the participants themselves as they share with the learning community what they have observed and gone through, and what they are facing in their roles. What ultimately boils down to storytelling is a way of surfacing the rich and diverse life histories of a group of people as a multi-dimensional resource for exploring the phenomena of interest: a diversity of concrete experiences that can be brought into the learning environment, which participants can collectively reflect upon, abstractly conceptualize and then experiment with.

Reflexivity – also beginning with thinking and pondering, a kind of intensification of reflection, or a further 'fold' (flect/flex = fold in Latin) – invites questions about our own part in the events we recall, or even about current experience. What affective bias do we bring, the desires, anxieties and cognitive models that impact what we notice and what we avoid? With a reflexive mindset, the learner raises doubts, differences, discrepancies, quandaries, predicaments, paradoxes, any manner of irreconcilable, logic-defying reality. In the leadership development workspace, the participating learners are placed at the centre to question and ultimately re-orient how they have formulated problems, beliefs, values and ways of acting.

Learning Spaces

The location of learning is not the same as the quality of place. If learning is primarily subjective and emergent, it likely takes place in the ordinary course of work: maybe in quiet times between meetings, during a commute, at informal gatherings, in dreams at night. Some claim that 70 per cent of learning is from facing tough challenges, 20 per cent from other people and 10 per cent from courses and reading (Lombardo & Eichinger, 1996). Short on evidence, this claim nonetheless provokes a useful thought – different kinds of learning takes place in different ways in different places. Petrigglieri and Petrigilieri (2010), for example, argue that business schools provide 'identity workspaces' where participants can let go of habitual self-images and discover new possibilities – learning that is distinct from the formal instruction they might receive in a classroom, but made possible by the structures, dependency relations and secure authority of business school.

The concrete structures of space enable and inhibit some kinds of learning. Tiered amphitheatres focus attention on the professor, the 'sage-on-the-stage', and clearly anticipate the whole class learning the same lessons. Flat classrooms reduce apparent hierarchy and uniformity, enabling members of the development space to contribute more or less equally, and possibly to have diverse conversations and insights. Beyes and Michel's (2011) work attends to the ways in which learning environments can be constructed to encourage the diversity (heterotopic) of viewpoints present in any development group to be expressed and used as material for further learning. Others, such as Vince (2011) and Sutherland (2013), also note the importance of the way in which the physical space of the room, materials and diversity of participating agents and processes evoke responses that may be more or less conducive to different development purposes. The outdoors often features as a distinctive space in leadership development, enabling physical team activities to encourage more direct relatedness, and also eliciting holistic responses to the wildness and beauty of nature. As ecological crisis becomes a more pressing aspect of our awareness, a reawakened connection with nature may be a powerful spur to leadership activism. Similarly, many leadership development programmes feature versions of 'service learning' – engaging in work that serves the interests of less advantaged communities, eliciting an awareness of ideals and values that might have become lost or tarnished in the midst of a corporate career but are thought to be touchstones of authentic and purposeful leadership.

Whatever the place, a fruitful learning space requires development practitioners to create safe holding environments in which learners experience 'a climate or culture of support' which they 'trust to "hold" them over time' (Kolb & Kolb, 2005: 207). This is perhaps the crucial point here.

Memories with Momentum

People can have a great time on a leadership development course, but behave no differently back at work. 'Memories with momentum' is a concept that re-orients the work of leadership development to a practice of memory formation. In particular it orients leadership development towards helping participants develop learning*full* memories that impact their future leadership practice.

Sutherland (2013) suggests the aesthetics of the environment (the sights, sounds and feelings of learning environments), the quality of the interactions between all actors involved, and the processes by which the learning memories are formed and processed during *and after* the development interventions have finished. Equally important is to provide future opportunities for participants to formally re-visit and extend the leadership development done.

Leader/ship Development in Action

Case Study Method

Ubiquitous across many business school, management and leadership development programmes, the case method wraps stories and data around the challenges experienced in the past by others (the case). In a decision-forcing situation, students read, study, debate and ultimately decide courses of action to resolve the case challenges.

The case method is a bit like a mystery novel. Students are presented with the mystery, the characteristics and dynamics of the case (facts, figures, market dynamics, personality traits, etc.), up to the point where the mystery needs solving. Acting as Holmes, Poirot and Columbo, participants plumb the depths of the mystery, individually or in groups, to develop the best solution they can.

As a teaching approach, it places the teacher in a facilitation role much like that described above. As facilitation, the process is to ask probing questions, challenge student assumptions and lines of thinking, elicit argument and debate across the group, stir controversy and eventually connect theory and concepts to the practice seen in the case itself and put forward the best solutions.

The great value of case methodology is its focus on practice. While students read cases (they often also involve other materials such as videos), this is reading a story of practice, not a theoretical construct. The ensuing learning debates centre on something that *really* happened (though cases are to greater and lesser degrees fictionalizations of what really happened in the situations they depict). Lessons, concepts and theoretical explanations are derived out of the examination of the case, rather than the imposition of concepts and theories to a case. Moreover, case teaching, when done well, is a highly engaging affair. A great case study teacher has the ability to stir and develop debate and argument across a classroom, developing the complexity of real world leadership challenges from the multiple angles, perceptions, beliefs and values of the students in the class. Finally, as cases revolve around narratives, the story aspect of the material tends to stay with students. We remember stories. For example, many an MBA student will, when back at work facing a particular challenge, first remember the stories of cases related to those problems, then theories that may be applicable to solving them.

Simulation/Role Plays

A form of leadership development often used within development programmes of all types is simulations and role plays. Within these processes individuals and groups are placed within pre-defined scenarios and asked to 'act out' the scenario.

For example, a group of individuals may be asked to form a team that is tasked with completing a business plan. The goal of the exercise is not so much to complete a fantastic business plan, but to go through a group process and then critically examine that process. Another typical version, more in the line of role playing, will place an individual or group in a specific situation in which they take on the identity(ies) of a certain character or group of characters. Within the situation there will be a challenge or conflict which the participants need to navigate and negotiate their way through. A poignant example involves senior leaders role playing the positions of disadvantaged members of society – for example, a company executive role playing the part of a young, unemployed individual. The goal is to invite the role player to see and feel from a different point of view, and often in so doing people discover a degree of empathy that they had not been aware of themselves. This is personally developmental, and it also contributes to the collective effort by ensuring a wider range of concerns is expressed, albeit by proxy. Role plays can allow for cathartic moments, when participants project aspects of their own experiences – often of which they are themselves unconscious – into the roles and the role play. Thus for example someone playing the part of a subordinate might experience feelings of frustrated ambition, feelings that come from the heart but would be too unsettling to allow in daily working life. Once 'out', such experiences can be subjects for reflection, if sensitively facilitated. Equally, role-play can be an excellent means to rehearse new behaviours and techniques. It is a common way to train 'coaching styles' of leadership, for example for disciplinary and mediation processes and for performance conversations. This aspect of role rehearsal is also used in attempts to strengthen the moral fibre of organization members in programmes such as 'Giving Voice to Values' (GVV). Here people are invited to speculate about what would help them to speak up when they perceive an action to be unethical (or see an opportunity for an ethical one). By rehearsing what they would actually want to say in a role-play situation, people become clearer about their ethical positions and how to mange their emotional and physical presence in potentially difficult situations.

Action Learning

Action learning is the name given to formal procedures for reflecting on and analysing one's own managerial and leadership work, through facilitated discussions with a group of peers known as an action learning set. As such, action learning is a form of experiential learning that relies heavily on reflection, reflexivity and heterotopic learning environments. Action learning was energetically promoted by Reg Revans (1980) as an alternative to formal training and education, emphasizing the value for experienced practitioners of reflecting on their current challenges, devising strategies and sharing their progress and feedback along the way. Revans believed that an action learning group should include people from diverse sectors, suspicious of the convergent thinking that might arise if members were from the same company. He also eschewed linkages to formal education because of the privileging of conceptual and cognitive forms of knowledge, which tends to crowd out the harder-to-articulate emotional, visceral and tacit knowledge that leaders actually draw on. However, action learning has been thoroughly accommodated by management education programmes that construct an action learning set as a form of tutorial group to support members in writing class papers, project work and collaborative research that link theoretical constructs to workplace experience. This hardly qualifies as action learning, although the discursive support and critique from peers can be very productive.

This is what makes the approach pertinent to leadership development: that a commitment to listen and talk about current predicaments in a secure and confidential setting with a group of peers has the effect of constructing these predicaments as 'living experiments', objects that can be examined and analysed, and about which participants can articulate working hypotheses about the kinds of interventions they might make. In this way, members gain some relational distance from their work roles, consciously seeking to learn by observing the effects of their actions and analysing these observations with their action learning set. Simply put, this is a cycle of action and reflection (the latter incorporating analysis and interpretation too).

Mindfulness

When the 3 February 2014 issue of *Time* declared a 'Mindfulness Revolution', practices of introspection, meditation and yoga became headline discussions in managerial practice, OD and leadership development. Inspired by corporate legends of Google, Steve Jobs, Medtronic, even

Goldman Sachs (more popularly known for recklessness than mindfulness), the mindfulness path appropriates a myriad of reflective, meditative practices in the service of creating more peaceful, aware and attuned leaders.

Typically connected with notions of emotional intelligence, leadership development has sought to ameliorate the stress, turbulence, complexity and speed of contemporary professional life with age-old practices of meditation, yoga, qigong, journaling and more. Give leaders, current or future, techniques to take time, quiet the mind, develop clarity of thought and focus to deal with the challenges they face, goes the rationale. Spice that with developing more creative solutions, time to prioritize what really matters (translation: not profit, market share and growth), and to do it all with a little more compassion for others, and you have the basic belief of mindfulness as practised in leadership development.

Mindfulness practices offer illustration of the unwritten modus operandi of leadership development. First: focus on developing the individual. Meditation begins with the singular person, isolated, focused initially on centring and developing the self through reflection. Second: develop that individual's capacity to understand themselves in relation to others (followers). Many meditative practices move from a centring of self to see one's self in relation to others entering the space of reflexivity. Third: relate the individual self to the wider external world (context). Meditation moves the individual into the self, into relation with others and then outwards across externalities: time and space.

Group Dynamics

In our general introduction to leadership development, we introduced the group dynamics that have characterized the Tavistock Institute for Human Relations (TIHR) and the National Training Laboratory (NTL) approaches to leadership development – and subsequently Ron Heifetz's well-known 'case-in-point' method. This work foregrounds unconscious group and inter-group assumptions and the anxieties arising from working life and consequent strategies of fight, flight, dependency and pairing. The aim of these approaches is to help participants become aware of their own collusion in these group processes, their valencies with regards to them and consequently their abilities to form more rational and intentional purposes in leadership at personal, group and organizational levels.

While fight, flight, dependency and pairing group dynamics form the foundations of TIHR and NTL approaches, they are explored through a variety of development processes such as the T-groups and the TIHR working conferences. The former begin with self-awareness, encouraging participants to explore unconscious aspects of their experiences, including repressed feelings, which are not directly recognizable. Methodologically, the learning occurs through critical examination of personal and group experiences as they unfold in real time, 'in the here and now'. Awareness is itself a function of the psychological dynamics of the situation – not something that is gained and stored once and for all.

The TIHR working conferences have similar foundations as they explore the experiential nature of power, authority, leadership and dependency in institutional contexts. The working conferences are conceived as a temporary organization tasked with studying the unfolding dynamics and work of that organization. The organization is established by the staff who take responsibility for the direction, facilitation and the administration of the organization. Their work, along with the orientation of all participants who become part of the developing organization, becomes 'evidence' for the work of the organization, part of the here-and-now experiences of all participants. This material forms the focus of the critical examination of personal and group processes as they emerge over the course of the conference (Aram, Baxter, & Nutkevitch, 2012).

Going back to the late 1940s, these development approaches come with decades of practice, refinement and a significant amount of empirical research that underpins their methodology and outcome orientations. Their influence is significant in many aspects of group facilitation, coaching and OD.

Coaching

Coaching is a varied practice, typically happening in coach–leader dyads. As a practice it has psychological roots, but is tailored towards reflection, conversation and debate about the daily events and challenges faced in leadership roles.

Over the second half of the twentieth century, and accelerating today, coaching has grown within the upper echelons of companies and corporations. The coaching space provides a critical–conversational space in which coaches listen to, question, challenge, guide and in general facilitate learning and development of executives. One way to understand the coaching dynamic is to see it as a focused space of experiential learning. Within a coaching session, a coach creates a conversational space around which a leader (again, this is typical within business settings so the leader is most likely a senior executive) can present and discuss the challenges s/he is facing. Through questions and debate, the coach seeks to help the coachee reflect on and reflexively engage with the challenges and issues faced. As such, it is a means of surfacing experience, debating it and forming new insights on this.

Many recipients of coaching see its value as a safe, confidential space to air their concerns and frustrations and to do so through a guided process of critical examination to find new approaches to those concerns. The process often involves bringing in many experiences, recent and past. Coaches provide constructive criticism on these experiences, guiding the coachee through an interrogation of their own circumstances. It is also increasingly common, particularly with C-Suite executives, for coaches to spend increasing time with them, through which coaches may offer their own insights, gleaned through their observations of the leader at work and in interaction with their colleagues and employees.

Outdoor-Adventure

The myriad approaches to outdoor leadership development (OLD) fall within the space of experiential learning. The idea is quite simple: take groups of people out into the environment, give them team-oriented tasks, see how they do, learn by studying what they did and how they did it. As experiential learning, OLD provides the opportunity for team outdoor activities (e.g. white water rafting) and then the space to reflect through and upon those experiences to build insights into team dynamics and leadership.

The tradition developed largely through wilderness education. While sometimes the 'outdoor' component means rope games on the lawn, or treasure hunts across a park, true OLD takes participants out to forests, rivers, deserts and glaciers and places them in a variety of problem-centred team, often survival-related, activities. The premise is one of translation, that individual and team skills learned in developing outdoor skills (how to start a fire, collectively erect a tent or cross a raging river as a team) can be translated back into organizational practices.

OLD are total immersion experiences that bring participants out of their work lives into wilderness settings. In the best case scenarios, they are highly engaging, evocative and rich in interaction and learning. Participants do not soon forget the experiences. From a trainer–teacher perspective, the approach requires facilitators to have wilderness and leadership development skills. Often teams of facilitators are involved with such events, where one or more are wilderness experts and one or more are trained leadership development practitioners. Working with the experiences had, insights are drawn from how leadership gets done within the group of people present. Efforts are then made to draw this learning back into the professional environments from where the participants come. An added outcome of all of this, particularly strong if the participants are a group from a single organization, is the team bonding and spirit that gets built as individuals engage in this activity together.

Contemporary Cases

Roundtables For Practising Managers (www.embaroundtables.com)

Each year a group of Executive MBA students, the majority practising executives engaged in full-time work, come together from a variety of schools and contexts around the world. The Roundtables form a week-long journey through problem-centred learning and learning in context about how management and leadership gets done.

Participants from the programme typically come from one of a variety of partner schools spanning the globe from Europe to Asia, Africa, North, Central and South America. To the programme, each brings a key managerial challenge faced in their real professional lives. The programme begins with thinking about and problematizing those challenges. The first programme day is devoted to examining, reframing, questioning and challenging the challenge itself in the service of deepening the understanding of the challenge. Forming thematic learning groups around connections to challenges, participants then, over the course of several days, go through a variety of individual and group processes aimed at exploring and developing the challenges present and seeking new solutions to those challenges. These activities are juxtaposed with learning in context where the participants meet and enter into dialogue with managers, leaders, professionals from the context in which the programme is taking place. Each year it occurs in a different country, hosted by a partner institution. The participants also go out into the places surrounding the programme, involving company visits, cultural events, artistic performances and more. All the while, they are focused on being intrepid explorers always looking for how organizing, managing and leadership gets done.

At the end of the week, through a series of 'friendly consulting' exercises, participants find their initial challenges transformed. They may have new questions, see the challenge in a completely different way, and they may have new solutions.

Arts (Music, Visual, Role Play, Theatre)

As leadership development has sought a more reflective, creative and more human-centred approach over the last couple of decades, the arts have entered the practice. Emanating from experiential learning beliefs, the underlying assumption is that leadership development participants engage with the arts and artists, thereby having aesthetic experiences, which they then, through processes of experimenting, discussing and reflecting, transform into new forms of knowing skewed towards the aesthetics – felt, sensory emotional elements – of leadership and organizational behaviour. As this learning emerges through arts experiences, the new knowing that is formed privileges non-rational, non-logical capabilities and self-knowledge that constitute and cultivate more sophisticated approaches to complexities faced as well as the so-called softer (i.e. emotional) issues of leadership.

Often dwelling around aesthetic consciousness and embodied cognition, contextual and subjective, leadership development practitioners and researchers in the field argue they develop leadership capabilities required to navigate the perspectival and circumstantial incongruities of contemporary life. The general argument was well summarized by Ladkin and Taylor (2010):

> we live in a complex world which cannot be fully understood solely by reference to scientific forms of logic and sense-making. The arts, and art-based practices, provide different ways of both describing and relating to that complexity, thereby offering novel ways of responding.
>
> *(p. 235)*

As discussed in Sutherland and Jelinek (2015), arts-based approaches are a mixed bunch, but fall within three general categories. The first – 'mastering craft' – is largely about skills transfer. Within this vein, participants work with the arts or artists to develop skills (craft) found within the arts but also highly valuable in leadership practice. A familiar practice is learning stage presence and public speaking from theatre actors. The second category is 'metaphorical engagement'. Here metaphors are drawn between the arts and the realities of leadership practice. For example, the improvisatory and fluid structures of certain forms of jazz are used as metaphors for the ephemerality of organizational structures and organizational change. The final area revolves around the aesthetics of leadership and organizing. Here participants explore the felt, sensory and emotional nature of leading through artistic experiences and doing. Prime examples include participants conducting choirs or orchestras. When placed in these situations, what leadership feels like and is as an in-action phenomenon, fully embodied, is brought to the fore as a subject of discussion, reflection and learning.

Gamification

As an educational approach, gamification draws on our human enjoyment of and engagement with games to facilitate learning and development. The argument flows that humans enjoy games, therefore designing learning and development programmes that are carried out in a gaming environment has the potential to increase enjoyment and engagement by drawing on the interests of learners in playing games. It is a fun way to learn.

Gamification has been a growing practice over the last two decades. As an extension of simulation approaches discussed above, gamification presents participants with games, now typically video games, in which they actively play to complete a certain task or mission. Through their playing they learn new skills and knowledge and also critically examine their enacted behaviours and reactions to the events experienced in the game itself.

With regards to leadership development, gamification first came onto the scene through skills and competency development. Through the creation of games around finance, project management, marketing, accounting, etc., the subjects of leadership development learn particularly skills or knowledge relevant to the fields of activity they are responsible for. For example, a game may be designed in which an individual or team must oversee the construction of a new factory. Through the game participants learn about project management, budgeting, dealing with the challenges or crises that the game throws at them, and so on. In addition to the skills or knowledge learned, individuals would also debrief on how they played the game. There is focus on how they made decisions, what their priorities, their assumptions and so on were. In less skill or competency-based processes, and often found in military leadership training, individuals may engage in games that take them through combat missions, in which they have to make strategic decisions about allocation of resources, actions of progress or retreat and are placed in situations where life and death matters arise. In the safety of the gaming environment, participants can test their ability to lead in a variety of situations and then learn from their relative successes and failures within those environments.

Summary and Future Trends

Leadership development processes will be affected by changes in each of the factors identified in the opening section of this chapter. Individual members of organizations will (in general) become more worldly, educated, connected, less pliant to authority and more often experienced as unreliable. (Because of the higher incidences of migration, family break-up, technology changes and other disruptions, young people will learn adaptive responses and adjust their expectations accordingly.) As a consequence, some will be more inclined to what Western (2015) refers to as 'autonomist leadership', instigating and joining movements outside of traditional bureaucratic hierarchies. At the same time, many firms will reward innovation but seek to regulate risky or unethical behaviour, so this tension will become more of a feature of leadership development in large and medium-sized organizations. Programmes will therefore involve more reflection and debate on notions of 'responsible leadership' – which is as much about citizenship and general fairness.

The major changes, however, will be driven by two rather different factors. Technology will enable observations, analysis and feedback of leader and follower behaviour in real time. Already an ordinary android smartphone can collate and correlate the activity levels, wellbeing, location and mood of large numbers of people. Leadership development can move from the offsite retreat into the web. Managers wanting to improve leadership (I:F) can track the impact of changes to systems, working practices, communications and many other manipulations. There are huge opportunities for data-savvy psychologists.

On the other hand, human connectedness with nature will deepen through new sciences at quantum and systems levels and a holistic appreciation of the economy as a sub-system of ecology. This will inspire a leadership development richer in natural and humanistic engagement, with more emphasis on collective processes of decision-making and activism. These will be exciting times.

Note

1 The acronym permits other anagrams, evoking an appropriate irony when considering such a contested field.

References

Adler, N. J. (2006). The arts and leadership: Now that we can do anything, what will we do? *Management Learning, 5* (4), 486–499.

Alvesson, M., & Sveningsson, S. (2003). The great disappearing act: Difficulties in doing 'leadership'. *Leadership Quarterly,* 14, 359–381.

Aram, E., Baxter, R., & Nutkevitch, A. (Eds). (2012). *Group relations conferences: Tradition, creativity, and succession in the global group relations network.* Vol. III. London: Karnac.

Atkinson, D. (2007). *Thinking the art of management: Stepping into Heidegger's shoes.* New York: Palgrave Macmillan.

Bennis, W., & O'Toole, J. (2005). How business schools lost their way. *Harvard Business Review, 83* (5): 96–104.

Beyes, T., & Michels, C. (2011). The production of educational space: Heterotopia and the business university. *Management Learning, 42* (5), 521–536.

Bion, W. (1961). *Experiences in groups*. London: Tavistock.

Bolden, R., & Gosling, J. (2006). Leadership competencies: Time to change the tune? *Leadership, 2* (2): 147–163.

Bolden, R., Gosling, J., Marturano, A., & Dennison, P. (2003). *A review of leadership theory and competency frameworks*. Exeter, UK: Centre for Leadership Studies, University of Exeter. http://business-school.exeter.ac.uk/research/areas/centres/cls/.

Boud, D., Keogh, R., & Walker, D. (1985). What is reflection in learning? In: Boud, D., Keogh, R., Walker, D. (eds) *Reflection: Turning experience into learning*. London: Routledge, 7–17.

Boyatzis, R.E. (1982). *The competent manager: A model for effective performance*. New York: Wiley.

Brocklehurst, M., Sturdy, A., Winstanley, D., & Driver, M. (2007). Introduction: Whither the MBA? Factions, fault lines and the future. *Management Learning, 38* (4): 379–388.

Buechel, B., & Antunes, D. (2007a). From the guest co-editors: Executive education in 'TOIL'. *Academy of Management Learning & Education, 6* (3): 305–309.

Buechel, B., & Antunes, D. (2007b). Reflections on executive education: The user and provider's perspectives. *Academy of Management Learning & Education, 6* (3): 401–411.

CEML (2002). *Managers and leaders: Raising our game*. London: Council for Excellence in Management and Leadership.

Chia, R. (1996). Teaching paradigm shifting in management education: University business schools and the entrepreneurial imagination. *Journal of Management Studies, 33* (4): 409–428.

Clarke, M., & Butcher, C. (2009). Political leadership, bureaucracies and business schools: A comfortable union? *Management Learning, 40* (5): 587–607.

Cunliffe, A. (2002). Reflexive dialogical practice in management learning. *Management Learning, 1* (33), 35–61.

Cunliffe, A.L. (2004). On becoming a critically reflexive practitioner. *Journal of Management Education, 33* (1): 407–426.

Cunliffe, A.L. (2009). The philosopher leader: On relationalism, ethics and reflexivity. A critical perspective to teaching leadership. *Management Learning, 40* (1): 87–101.

Dewey, J. (1934). *Art as experience*. New York: Putnam.

Donaldson, L. (2002). Damned by our own theories: Contradictions between theories and management education. *Academy of Management Learning & Education, 1*: 96–106.

French, R., & Grey, C. (eds) (1996). *Rethinking management education*. London: SAGE.

Gabriel, Y. (2005). MBA and the education of leaders: The new playing fields of Eton? *Leadership, 1* (2): 147–163.

Garvin, D.A. (2007). Teaching executives and teaching MBAs: Reflections on the case method. *Academy of Management Learning & Education, 6* (3): 364–374.

Ghoshal, S. (2005). Destroying good management. *Management Learning, 4* (1): 75–91.

Giacalone, R.A., & Thompson, K.R. (2006). Business ethics and social responsibility education: Shifting the worldview. *Management Learning, 5* (3): 266–277.

Giddens, A. (1991). *Modernity and self-identity: Self and society in the late modern age*. Stanford, CA: Stanford University Press.

Giddens, A. (2003). *Runaway world: How globalization is reshaping our lives*. New York: Routledge.

Gioia, D.A. (2002). Business education's role in the crisis of corporate confidence. *Academy of Management Executive, 16* (3): 142–144.

Gosling, J., & Mintzberg, H. (2004). The education of practicing managers. *MIT Sloan Management Review, 45* (4): 19–22.

Gosling, J., & Mintzberg, H. (2006). Leadership education as if both matter. *Management Learning, 37* (4), 419–428.

Gray, D.E. (2007). Facilitating management learning: Developing critical reflection through reflective tools. *Management Learning, 38* (5): 495–517.

Grey, C., & Mitev, N. (1995). Management education: A polemic. *Management Learning, 26* (1): 73–90.

Guthey, E. (2016). Romanticism, antimodernism, and a pluralistic perspective on responsible leadership. In: Kempster, S., & Carroll, B. (eds) *Responsible leadership: Realism and romanticism*. London: Routledge.

Guthey, E., Sweet, P., & Fjalland, K. (2015). *The Future of the Leadership Industry Across Borders and Generations*. International Leadership Association, Barcelona.

Henisz, W.J. (2011). Leveraging the financial crisis to fulfill the promise of progressive management. *Management Learning, 10* (2): 298–321.

Holt, R., & Macpherson, A. (2010). Sensemaking, rhetoric and the socially competent entrepreneur. *International Small Business Journal, 28* (1), 20–42.

Houde, J. (2007). Analogically situated experiences: Creating insight through novel contexts. *Academy of Management Learning & Education, 6* (3): 321–331.

Keevers, L., & Treleaven, L. (2011). Organizing practices of reflection: A practice-based study. *Management Learning*. doi: 10.1177/1350507610391592.

Kellerman, B. (2012). *The end of leadership*. London: Harper.

Kets de Vries, M., & Korotov, K. (2007). Creating transformational executive education programs. *Academy of Management Learning & Education, 6* (3): 375–387.

Khurana, R. (2007). *From higher aims to hired hands: The social transformation of American business schools and the unfulfilled promise of management as a profession*. Princeton, NJ: Princeton University Press.

King, P. (ed.) (2003). *No ordinary psychoanalyst: The extraordinary contributions of John Rickman*. London: Karnac.

Kolb, A., & Kolb, D. (2005). Learning styles and learning spaces: Enhancing experiential learning in higher education. *Academy of Management Learning & Education, 4* (2), 193–212.

Kolb, D.A. (1984). *Experiential learning: Experience as the source of learning and development*. Englewood Cliffs, NJ: Prentice Hall.

Ladkin, D., & Taylor, S. S. (2010). Enacting the 'true self': Towards a theory of embodied authentic leadership. *The Leadership Quarterly, 21* (1), 64–74.

Lash, S., & Urry, J. (1994). *Economies of signs and space*. London: SAGE.

Loew, L., & O'Leonard, K. (2012). *Leadership development factbook 2012: Benchmarks and trends in U.S. leadership development*. Bersin by Deloitte, July 2012, bersin.com.

Lombardo, M.M., & Eichinger, R.W. (1996). *The career architect development planner*. Minneapolis, MN: Lominger.

Mainemelis C., Boyatzis, R.E., & Kolb, D.A. (2002). Learning styles and adaptive flexibility: Testing experiential learning theory. *Management Learning, 33* (1): 5–33.

Mintzberg, H. (2004). *Managers not MBAs*. New York: Harlow.

Mintzberg, H. (2009). Rebuilding companies as communities. *Harvard Business Review* (August), 140–144.

Mitroff, I.I. (2004). An open letter to the deans and the faculties of American business schools. *Journal of Business Ethics*, 54: 185–189.

Murray, H. (1990). The transformation of selection procedures: The war office selection boards. In: Trist, E., & Murray, H. *The social engagement of social science Vol 1: The socio-psychological perspective*. London: Free Association Books.

Petriglieri, G., & Petriglieri, J.L. (2010). Identity workspaces: The case of business schools. *Academy of Management Learning & Education, 9* (1): 44–60.

Plato (1987). *The Republic*, trans. H.D.P. Lee. London: Penguin Classics.

Raelin, J.A. (2007). Toward an epistemology of practice. *Academy of Management Learning and Education, 6* (4), 495–519.

Revans, R. (1980). *Action learning: New techniques for management*. London: Blond & Briggs, Ltd.

Reynolds, M. (1998). Reflection and critical reflection in management learning. *Management Learning, 29* (2): 183–200.

Rodgers, H., Frearson, M., Holden, R., & Gold, J. (2003). *The rush to leadership*. Presented at Management Theory at Work conference, Lancaster University, April 2003.

Segal, S. (2010). A Heideggerian approach to practice-based reflexivity. *Management Learning, 41*, 379–389.

Sinclair, A. (2007). Teaching leadership critically to MBAs: Experiences from heaven and hell. *Management Learning, 38* (4): 458–471.

Stiehm, J.H., & Townsend, N.W. (2002). *The U.S. army war college: Military education in a democracy*. Philadelphia, PN: Temple University Press.

Sutherland, I. (2013). Arts-based methods in leadership development: Affording aesthetic workspaces, reflexivity and memories with momentum. *Management Learning, 44* (1): 25–43.

Sutherland, I., & Jelinek, J. (2015). From experiential learning to aesthetic knowing: The arts in leadership development. *Advances in Developing Human Resources*, 1–18.

Sutherland, I., & Ladkin, D. (2013). Creating engaged executive learning spaces: The role of aesthetic agency. *Organizational Aesthetics, 2* (1), 105–124.

Vince, R. (1996). Experiential management education as the practice of change. In: French, R., & Grey, C. (eds) *Rethinking management education*. London: Sage.

Vince, R. (2011). The spatial psychodynamics of management learning. *Management Learning, 42*, 333–347.

Weick, K. (1995). *Sensemaking in organizations*. London: Sage.

Weick, K.E. (2007) Drop your tools: On reconfiguring management education. *Journal of Management Education*, *31* (1): 5–16.

Weick, K.E., Sutcliffe, K.M., & Obstfeld, D. (2005). Organizing and the process of sensemaking. *Organization Science*, *16* (4): 409–421.

Welsh, M.A., & Dehler, G.E. (2007). Whither the MBA? Or the withering of MBAs? *Management Learning*, *38* (4): 405–423.

Western, S. (2015). Autonomist leadership in leaderless movements: Anarchists leading the way. *Ephemera*, *14* (4), 673.

34

Identity Work in Leadership Development

Helen Delaney

Leadership development settings are framed by many scholars, practitioners, and leaders as legitimate sites for working upon one's self. This inclusion of the self in leadership development, of personal development in the name of leadership development, is perhaps no surprise given the history of leadership development, the psychologisation of contemporary life, and the 'identity turn'. What is surprising is the lack of critical studies that problematise this relationship. The majority of identity and leadership development literature tends to prescribe how self-growth or identity work should be undertaken, underlying which is a relatively unquestioned assumption that working upon the self is a necessary and positive aim for leadership development. In contrast, the purpose of this chapter is to scrutinise the targeting, framing, and treatment of the self in leadership development.

The chapter draws on contemporary scholarship, as well as empirical material from an eighteen-month leadership development programme, to consider the following questions. First, why and how has identity become a legitimate target of leadership development efforts? To answer this question I offer a brief historical analysis of institutions that preceded leadership development, and consider broader social changes to work that have shaped the rise of leadership development programmes (LDPs). Second, what assumptions underpin how identity is framed in the leadership development literature? By analysing the leadership development literature, I offer three main metaphors for how identity is conceptualised. Third, what are the variety of ways in which identity work is experienced in leadership development? I discuss how participants in LDPs can experience both identity construction and deconstruction in development and consider the consequences. The chapter ends with some concluding thoughts about what is excluded, ignored, and concealed by focusing on the self in leadership development.

Targeting the Self in Leadership Development: Historical and Social Influences

A number of leadership development scholars describe this context as a place where participants can and should work upon their identity (Carroll and Levy, 2010; Day and Harrison, 2007; Petriglieri, 2013). It seems almost common sense now to associate self-development with leadership development; however, such an assumption is deserving of more critical inquiry. Why has the self become a target of leadership development efforts? One way of answering this question is to place contemporary leadership development in a broader historical and social context – a move rarely done in the literature. Indeed, one could be forgiven for thinking that leadership development in its current form is a relatively new beast. However, leadership development did not come out of nowhere: it has been shaped by a number of institutions and social changes. Understanding these historical and social influences enables a deeper understanding of why and how leadership development has come to be seen by many as a legitimate site for self-work. It also raises questions about the interests shaping leadership development and the potential risks of doing identity work in this context.

A whole book would be needed to do justice to the historical and social context of leadership development. In this chapter, I selectively focus on the role of training groups (also called sensitivity training, encounter groups, and so on), and management education in university-based business schools. A more comprehensive history would also look at the role of civic groups, church and religious groups, the military, management gurus/self-help movements, organisational development, therapy culture, and new age spirituality, to name a few. I then turn to a discussion of how changes to the nature of work in the twentieth century have impacted upon managerial identity, and ultimately on the existence and purposes of leadership development.

One of the richest historical antecedents of contemporary leadership development is the training group (T-group) movement that originated in post World War II America. Behavioural scientist Kurt Lewin and his colleagues unintentionally created this group process during a training session for community leaders dealing with interracial problems (Gottschalk et al., 1971; Kleiner, 2008). These content-less, leader-less, and structure-less small groups focused on the 'here-and-now' interactions of the shared group experience, with particular attention paid to emotions and group dynamics (Campbell and Dunnette, 1968).

T-groups entered the realm of organisations from the 1950s onwards. Initially, the groups helped employees become more comfortable with (or, more sceptically, amenable to) organisational change. The groups were a chance for workers to listen to each other's 'fears of and feelings for each other' and to get 'a better perspective on what life in the "executive suite" at Central City was really like' (Tannenbaum et al., 1961, p. 187). National Training Laboratories (NTL), which began in the 1940s and were home to the sociopsychological theorising of Kurt Lewin, trained tens of thousands of managers during its time (Campbell and Dunnette, 1968). The groups focused on 'the worker's own private life space' in order to boost the worker's performance and productivity (Back, 1973, p. 165). Training occurred when the individual felt the uncomfortable process of examining his/her self. As a result, many participants endured high levels of anxiety in the T-group process, feeling unsettled and uncomfortable about their own opinions and comments made to them (Back, 1973). Similar to contemporary leadership development, organisational T-groups assumed a causal relationship between self-awareness, awareness of others, and improved organisational performance.

The intended outcomes of T-groups are strikingly similar to those of contemporary LDPs. Schein and Bennis (1965) list the outcomes of T-groups as: an increased awareness, sensitivity, and authenticity to oneself and others; an increased spirit of enquiry and experimentation; an advanced ability to act in collaborative and interdependent ways with peers, superiors, and subordinates; and an ability to resolve conflict through problem solving rather than coercion or manipulation. These ambitions mirror LDPs that aim to develop authentic leadership, relational leadership, collective leadership, and so on. For some behavioural scientists, the training also aspired to improve organisational life by inviting participants to learn more about their behaviour and how it impacts upon others to ultimately become more effective in interpersonal relations (Mangham and Cooper, 1969). As we will see later, this ambition mirrors more critically inclined LDPs that aim to 'emancipate' leaders and workers.

Some critics argued that the focus on the self was not necessarily leading to better organisational performance; in fact it could be detrimental. From the late 1960s onwards, T-groups fell out of favour as some critics started to question whether ripping off the 'executive mask' was actually beneficial to self-growth. Concerns were raised about the emotional damage to individuals and work relationships caused by training groups. Problems of transferability from the emotionally open group experience to the emotionally repressive organisational context were also noted (House, 1967). This history should serve as a warning to contemporary LDPs; however, surprisingly, the literature rarely considers the potentially harmful consequences of examining the self in the development setting.

Kurt Lewin had a close relationship with the Tavistock Institute for Human Relations, established in Britain in the mid-1940s. The Institute believed that industrial life could be radically transformed following World War II, primarily through social psychological interventions (Miller and Rose, 1989). Drawing on elements of the T-group method, behavioural scientists believed that, by addressing problematic group tensions, employee and organisational productivity could be improved. Hence, the 'relational life of the enterprise' was the principal focus of Tavistock's mission to transform industrial life (Miller and Rose, 1989, p. 184). The role of leadership training became increasingly important.

During the 1950s, the Tavistock Institute joined with the University of Leicester to run the first full-scale experimentation of the laboratory method of group relations training (Dicks, 1970). The primary task of these residential conferences was to provide attendees with 'opportunities to learn about leadership' (Rice, 1965, p. 5). Similar to T-groups, leaders were taught to be more aware of the feelings and attitudes of themselves and others, as well as to notice group dynamics, so they could respond in ways that improved task performance (Rice, 1965). Unlike T-groups, these conferences were highly structured and disseminated academic research through content sessions. Hence, as early as the 1950s, leadership scholarship was enlisted to help leaders not only learn about leadership, but to work upon themselves.

This brings us to a discussion about the historical influence of the university-based business school (UBBS) on contemporary leadership development. In the late 1800s and early 1900s, the rise of large corporations due to industrial capitalism gave rise to a new class of worker, the manager (Khurana, 2007). As neither labour nor capital, managers were seen as 'unfamiliar' and 'controversial' economic actors: 'it was not clear who they were, what they did, or why they should be entrusted with the task of running corporations' (Khurana, 2007, p. 3). Hence, the managerial class needed to legitimate their authority and social worth. One of the purposes of the UBBS was to legitimise management as a worthy profession (Khurana, 2007).

Aware of critics who saw managers as solely interested in making money, the earliest business schools (such as Wharton and Harvard Business School) positioned management training as involving not only the development of managerial knowledge and skills, but crucially the development of one's moral character (Khurana, 2007). The hope for some business schools was that managers would embody a social consciousness and altruism similar to the 'high' professions such as lawyers, doctors, or clergymen. Hence, the leader's character has long been targeted as a necessary element of development not only for the individual, but importantly for legitimising management as a worthy profession and ultimately for legitimising the UBBS (a failed project according to Khurana). Arguably, contemporary leadership development appears to replicate this historical ambition: it promises to train leaders in a formal (albeit contested) body of knowledge and skills, as well as develop one's morals and values via self-awareness and personal growth in order to positively impact the world (however expansively or narrowly the 'world' is defined). The focus on the leader's self in contemporary leadership development could therefore be seen as the on-going attempt to legitimise leadership/management as a 'high' profession, and in turn to legitimise those who train leaders. By failing to acknowledge this historical influence, contemporary leadership development ignores how broader political and institutional interests shape the supposed 'need' to focus on identity.

In addition to these historical influences, a series of changes to the nature of work have impacted on managerial identity and influenced the establishment and rise of leadership development. The changes brought about by new forms of capitalism (Sennett, 1998), neo-liberalism (Harvey, 2005), post-modernism (Gergen, 1991), and post-industrialism (Casey, 1995), have destabilised the worker's self. These social shifts caused significant changes to the nature of work, such as automation, job displacement and insecurity, flatter organisational structures, outsourcing and offshoring, greater surveillance of workers, a greater sense of competition in a global labour market, and the need to be a flexible and adaptable worker (Casey, 1995). Alongside heightened global competition, rising uncertainty and precarity, and the popularity of humanistic forms of management, many workers were called to bring more of their 'whole self', their mind, heart, and body, into the workplace in order to be more productive (Costea et al., 2008).

These changes to the conditions and demands of work shape the presence and purpose of leadership development in two ways. First, LDPs can be seen as organisationally sanctioned settings where managers learn how to be the 'ideal' worker who brings their 'whole self' to work. LDPs are arguably a product of what Heelas (2002) calls 'soft capitalism', which has created a new 'self-work' ethic of work that invites certain workers to see work as a setting for self-development and fulfilment. By providing a setting for identity exploration, Heelas argues that management training sessions are important arenas to train managers to adopt the belief that the workplace is a site where you can 'live a full life' (Heelas, 2002, p. 90). In doing so, the divide between public (work) and private (non-work) lives is eroded as managers are invited to give more of themselves to work. However, the work identities on offer are tied to organisational productivity and success, limiting the scope of what a good 'full' life means. LDPs can therefore be seen as settings that encourage the formation of new managerial subjectivities that 'bind the worker into the productive life of society' (Rose, 1999, p. 60).

Second, LDPs can be seen as places of 'retreat' to which workers willingly 'flee' (Scott, 2010, p. 213), in order to deal with the anxieties, insecurities, and fragmentation created by the changing conditions of work. Sennett argues that the fast, flexible, short-term nature of contemporary capitalism has set workers' 'emotional, inner life adrift' (Sennett, 1998, p. 20). Workers find it increasingly difficult to form a sustained narrative of the self in a climate characterised by increased job flexibility, insecurity, and competition. Workers are left 'longing for community' and searching out places that will meet this need where they can feel needed by others, and where they can re-form a sense of coherence and continuity (Sennett, 1998, p. 138). LDPs are one such site, what Scott (2010) calls a 'reinventive institution', which the 'worried well' can check themselves into without fear of stigmatisation. Under the watchful gaze of a new 'breed of experts', workers hope to deal with these problems of modern existence (Rose, 1999).

Indeed, some writers embrace this idea that leadership development programmes should be 'identity workspaces' (Petriglieri, 2013). An 'identity workspace' is an institution entrusted to 'hold' individual members and 'soothe their distress and facilitate sense making' (Petriglieri and Petriglieri, 2010, p. 46). It is a place where participants explore the question 'who am I as a leader' and address personal questions they have neglected due to the speed and demands of their career (Petriglieri, 2013). Echoing Sennett, the authors argue that individuals attend LDPs in order to recover or discover a 'solid narrative' of self, which they have 'lost' due to the demands of contemporary work (Petriglieri and Petriglieri, 2010, p. 57). Business schools are more likely to be entrusted with the role of an identity workspace because the commitment between corporations and individuals has become 'increasingly transient and instrumental' (Petriglieri and Petriglieri, 2010, p. 45). Business schools, and LDPs, should therefore help leaders 'stabilize a fragile identity or transition to a new one' (Petriglieri and Petriglieri, 2010, p. 54).

This argument is reflective of a general pattern in leadership development whereby identity work is seen as inherently necessary and positive. It is problematic in that it seems to repackage critiques about contemporary work in order to advocate for the necessity of leadership development. One only needs a brief knowledge of the history of T-groups to realise it is unlikely that only positive identity work (such as repair and stabilisation) will be experienced. What's more, there is very little room for LDPs to question, unsettle, or destabilise participant's knowledge, worldviews, or identities – potentially a vital capacity for developing more responsible, ethical, and critical leaders. Finally, there is no acknowledgement that viable 'public' settings already exist that workers could instead turn to for existential support and nourishment that are not as compromised by commercial imperatives, such as the church, community group, family, or even nature.

In summary, by situating leadership development within (a selected) historical and social context we can start to see how the leader's self became a target for leadership development. But how do leadership development scholars justify the 'benefit' of targeting one's identity/self?

Contemporary Rationales

Across all approaches to leadership development, positivist, interpretive, and critical, the participant's self tends to be seen as a primary avenue for provoking deep change in leadership practices and capacities. Put simply, identity is used to gain maximum effectiveness from leadership development efforts (Day and Harrison, 2007; McCollum, 1999; Pearce, 2007). It is the holy grail of leadership development: a 'frontier' in need of 'taming' (Day and Harrison, 2007, p. 370).

The belief is that in order to get people committed to leadership, change must start first with the leader's identity: 'to sustain interest for the months and years required to develop and practice complex leadership skills, it is also likely that the leadership role needs to become part of one's self-identity' (Lord and Hall, 2005, p. 592). In a leadership development programme built on the work of Warren Bennis and with links to Harvard Business School, the programme literature says that 'the intention of this course is to leave the participants actually being leaders and exercising leadership effectively as their natural self-expression' (Erhard et al., 2010, p. 2). Through identity work, leadership will become so ingrained that it permeates 'one's perceptions, emotions, creative imagination, thinking, planning, and action' (Erhard et al., 2010, p. 1).

Critical scholars also believe that by developing one's identity, leadership behaviours will come naturally. As Cunliffe (2009, p. 94) says, 'if we know who to be, then what to do falls into place'. Other critical writers argue that, by working on identity, leaders are better equipped to resist power and imagine alternative organisational realities. As Sinclair argues, if leaders can make their own identity work conscious, 'they are not only in a better position to take up or resist identities from themselves, but also to make choices about whether and how they impose identities on others' (Sinclair, 2007, p. 142).

Example from a Leadership Development Programme

I turn to empirical material from a leadership development programme to illustrate the facilitators' rationale for doing identity work. Between 2009 and 2010, I undertook an ethnography of an eighteen-month leadership development programme based in New Zealand. I have written about this programme elsewhere and refer the reader to these texts for more information about the programme's social constructionist approach to leadership and its development (see: Carroll and Nicholson, 2014; Nicholson and Carroll, 2013a, 2013b). Later in the chapter I will discuss how the programme conceptualised identity and how the participants experienced the identity work. For now, I focus on how the programme presented the purpose of doing identity work to the participants.

From the beginning of the programme, identity work was introduced as a vital leadership practice (along with others). The facilitators defined identity as 'the answer given to the question "who am I/who am I being" in any given moment'. One facilitator told the group: 'this programme gives you more selves, more to choose from. We're asking you to pay attention to who you call into existence at moments.' Developing as a leader involves 'getting new identities to add to the repertoire', in order to 'create space', 'do a different thing', and to 'change others'. As one facilitator summarises, 'if you can carry multiple identities, you have multiple options', and 'leadership work is calling in other identities for who you're with'. Corporate organisations are portrayed as 'giving rules about what identities you can bring' to work; however, leaders can resist these constraints by using identity work to open up 'infinite space'. Therefore, one of the purposes of leadership development was for the participants to experiment with their identity.

Identity work here involves increasing the number of identities in one's 'repertoire', and developing the flexibility to shift between different identities to suit the context. The role of the programme is to 'give' the leaders 'more selves'. In doing so, the leader will apparently change themselves, change others, and change the context/situation ('create space'). By working on their identities, leaders will be able to break through organisational structures, norms, and rigidities. Hence, this programme's rhetoric persuasively appeals to an individual's desire for self-fulfilment (as they get to become more than who they are currently), their desire to influence and change others (seen as an important part of leadership), and the desire to transform their work context (the ultimate peak of leadership practice for many leadership concepts) – all by developing their identity. It is not hard to see why a programme participant would not want to resist such an invitation. However, using identity in this way appears to reproduce heroic and individualised notions of leadership and change, which is problematic in the content of a 'critically oriented' programme.

In summary, working on one's self is invariably seen as a 'good thing' for many leadership development scholars and practitioners. For some, the purpose of doing identity/self-work in leadership development is purely instrumental: a leader's identity should be developed in order to improve leadership and ultimately organisational effectiveness. While there would be numerous examples of how improved self-awareness and personal growth may well improve leadership and organisations, such writing ignores the cautionary lessons of T-groups (i.e. may doing self-work in LD be harmful to both the person, their peers, and the organisation?). Few studies raise concerns about the political nature of identity work: what and whose interests are shaping this fixation upon the self? What kinds of identities are held up as ideals? Even fewer raise concerns about the power of the facilitators, the 'engineers of the human soul' and their 'expertise of subjectivity' (Rose, 1999).

Conceptualising Identity in Leadership Development: Metaphors and Assumptions

In this section, I explore three main metaphors of identity that underpin the scholarly leadership development literature: identity as a toolbox, a book, and a kaleidoscope. Each reveals a series of assumptions about the self, and therefore what methods should be used to develop it.

The Self as a Toolbox

A significant amount of leadership development research tends to see identity[1] as a toolbox: something carried internally by the leader that contains the skills, behaviours, competencies, and so on that make up one's self. Leadership development therefore involves adding more 'tools' in order to be more effective as a leader (Riggio, 2008). Hence, one of the tasks of this scholarship is to identify and prescribe the individual differences that predict effectiveness in leadership (Atwater *et al.*, 1999).

Lord and Hall's research (2005) is representative of this metaphor. Their argument assumes that leaders can be more or less 'expert' in their identity, based on how sophisticated their 'toolbox' is. They segregate identity into different levels (individual, relational, and collective) along which leaders may progress throughout their development (from novice to intermediate to expert leaders). The more 'expert' one is in their identity, the more 'inextricably integrated' leadership skills and knowledge are with 'one's self concept' (p. 592). A novice leader has an individual-level identity as they focus more on 'demonstrating uniqueness' and 'differentiating oneself' from other leaders in order to be 'recognized and accepted as leaders' (p. 596). A leader operating with an intermediate skill level has more of a relational identity as they include other individuals in their identity processing. Expert leaders apparently have collective identities that are 'sensitive to the follower context', authentic, and able to enact alternative identities (p. 597). Hence, the toolbox approach exhibits a belief in developing a 'science of the self' (Jones, 2006, p. 483), whereby leadership development participants can have their current level of 'identity' tested and measured according to a predefined category. Knowing what kind of 'toolbox' a leader has, the role of the educator/developer is to prescribe the next set of tools to advance their identity and leadership.

The Self as a Book

Primarily (although not exclusively) informed by psychological or constructivist perspectives, this research again sees identity as something contained within a person that can and should be accessed and developed. Van Velsor and Drath's (2004) lifelong developmental framework, used by the Center for Creative Leadership, is exemplary here. Based on Kegan's adult development theory, Van Velsor and Drath identify self-reading, self-authoring, and self-revising as three prime identity development stages an individual can progress along. The self is seen as a book that can be read, written, or continuously revised. Self-reading describes the 'immature' stage in which an individual's core identity is determined by the ideas and judgements of other people – they 'read the book of his identity' (p. 389). Self-authoring is the next stage in which the person writes his or her own original book of identity, independent of what others think or say – an assumption evident in authentic leadership development (Shamir and Eilam, 2005). Self-revising is the ultimate stage where the person continuously revises and rewrites their sense of self in relation to their environment.

The book metaphor is predicated on several assumptions. The first is that life is apparently far more complex and complicated than in decades gone by (when self-reading would have been sufficient). The contemporary demands and challenges of work and personal life call for a different kind of development – specifically the ability to self-author (for those in management positions), and self-revise (for those in leadership/senior management positions). Development therefore requires a life-long commitment to self-transformation, where leaders should continue to disengage from old and ingrained selves, experiment with new possible selves, and ultimately transition to new identities (Ibarra et al., 2010). Given this individualised book metaphor, leadership development methods tend to involve activities that enable participants to access and reflect upon their self, such as individual sessions with a psychotherapist (Petriglieri et al., 2011), autobiographical writing (Petriglieri, 2012), 360-degree feedback (Hall, 2004), and reflecting on one's early childhood and young adulthood (Murphy and Reichard, 2011).

The Self as a Kaleidoscope

A smaller body of leadership development research assumes that identity is fluid, fragmented, contested, and shaped by multiple forces. Usually adopting a social constructionist or critical perspective to identity, this research challenges the toolbox and individual 'authorship' journey approaches (for example, Carroll and Levy, 2010; Cunliffe, 2009; Ford et al., 2008; Ford and Lawler, 2008; Gagnon, 2008; Sinclair, 2007). This tends to view leaders as occupying a complicated discursive position with competing demands that influence their identity (Ford et al., 2008). Identity work as a leader involves building a capacity to hold multiple and contradictory selves (Parush and Koivunen, 2014). The self is not seen as existing or emanating solely from 'within' an individual; rather it is historically and socially constructed. Hence, such research may explore how identity is shaped by dominant discourses of leadership and development, as well as by power relations in the workplace and development setting (Ford and Harding, 2008; Gagnon, 2008; Nicholson and Carroll, 2013a; Sinclair, 2009).

Some of this scholarship encourages LDPs to realise the emancipatory potential of identity work. Such programmes would invite participants to 'challenge taken-for-granted organizational realities' (Cunliffe, 2009, p. 93), and release themselves from limiting, oppressive, or diminishing leadership identities (Carroll and Levy, 2010). Programmes should eliminate the unachievable 'super-hero' model of leadership and instead offer 'alternative languages that allow for different possibilities of being' (Ford et al., 2008, p. 172).

Example from a Leadership Development Programme

The LDP that I researched enacted the kaleidoscope approach to identity. Using the work of George Herbert Mead (1934), participants were invited to see themselves as a 'parliament of selves', in other words, as containing a whole host of different and potentially contradictory identities that can be 'animated' and 'foregrounded' in their leadership. Participants were encouraged to add more identities to this 'parliament' in order to bring a different energy and influence to a situation by adopting another identity. Drawing on the work of Karl Weick (1996), the programme also encouraged participants to consider what identities they hold that may need to be dropped, or held 'more lightly'.

A number of identity work techniques were used on the programme. For example, prior to an important interaction or scenario, the participants were encouraged to reflect on the question 'Who are you going to be in this interaction?' and to communicate this with their group members. Likewise, after the interaction, participants were encouraged to reflect on 'who they were' and how this impacted the interaction. Facilitators sometimes pointedly questioned participants about who they were being in certain interactions, and invited them to experiment with different identities – at times assigning them an identity to experiment with. Therefore, even critically inclined LDPs' may well contribute to the regulation and powered shaping of participants' identities in ways that feel far from 'freeing' as participants are still encouraged to enact certain emotions, behaviours, and identities. In the next section, I will go into more detail about how participants experienced this kind of identity work.

In summary, the leadership development literature views the self in a number of different ways, which is often dependent on the paradigmatic approach to personality/self/identity. Each approach is likely to have different interpretations of how the self is developed, what the role of facilitators/educators is, and what leadership theories are used, but on the whole, the majority of literature reinforces the idea that a leader's identity can and should be targeted in order to improve leadership and organisational performance. But what is it like to undergo identity work in the name of leadership development? The next section explores this question.

Experiencing Identity Work in Leadership Development

The majority of identity and leadership development research tends to offer a largely positive and unproblematised picture of doing identity work in leadership development. Perhaps this positive bias is symptomatic of a trend in leadership studies whereby many leadership scholars are also directly involved in facilitating or designing leadership development initiatives, which may make it difficult to gain critical distance (see Butler, Delaney and Spoelstra, 2015, for a more detailed discussion of this relationship between leadership scholars and practitioner engagement). Whatever the reason, leadership development literature tends to portray this setting as a place where leaders primarily repair, strengthen, and construct their identity. Only a handful of studies question this assumption (Gagnon, 2008; Ford et al., 2008; Kelly, 2013; Nicholson and Carroll, 2013a). In this section, I use the concept of 'identity undoing' to capture the multitude of ways in which identity work is experienced in both positive and debilitating ways. For a more detailed exploration of this concept, see Nicholson and Carroll (2013a).

Throughout the course of observing the eighteen-month leadership development programme previously discussed, I was struck by the different ways in which people experienced the programme's invitation to do identity work. In amongst talk about feeling more secure, validated, and confident in their leadership identity, many participants experienced significant moments of loss, doubt, destabilisation, unravelling, and even deconstruction. While there was learning and excitement in these moments, some participants also articulated feelings of fear, isolation, and severe self-doubt as a result of this identity work. We chose the word 'undoing' to capture the variety of these experiences, because the verb 'to undo' has multiple definitions: on the one hand, it refers to opening up, untying, and releasing, as in the sentence, 'to undo a knot'. It also means to reverse, annul, and do away with something, such as to undo the damage of the storm. At the more extreme end, it refers to destruction and ruination, for example, 'his lying undid him'. Finally, it means to unsettle or 'throw into confusion' (Random House Dictionary, 2010). As a concept, then, undoing contains a diversity of interpretations and movements to explore identity work which have not been strongly theorised in detail, let alone in conjunction with each other, in the identity or leadership development literature.

In our article (Nicholson and Carroll, 2013a) we propose five main manifestations of identity undoing and explore how they play out in interactions between participants and facilitators. The five forms of identity undoing are: shaking up, cutting apart, letting go, being playful, and floundering. *Shaking up* refers to the experience of having one's identity unsettled, disrupted, and agitated. Some participants desired this form of identity work, often inviting others to do it to them by posing critical questions about a person's character or offering reflective feedback. Others felt confronted or vulnerable when exposed to this type of practice. *Cutting apart* is felt in a more violent and destructive manner, whereby participants feel their sense of self is threatened or painfully attacked. The power relations are important here: cutting apart was more likely to be experienced when participants felt that the facilitators were destroying their sources of strength (i.e. foundational beliefs, world-views, valued ideas about leadership, trusted identities, etc.).

Letting go is about discarding usually familiar and entrenched whole identities, or elements of one's self. Participants often took it upon themselves to advise others about what parts of them they should 'let go of', and, at other times, participants examined their own self and identified identities they would like to 'drop'. Like the 'shaking up' form of identity work, some participants were thrilled to try to 'let go' of parts of themselves, and for peers to monitor their progress or defaulting, whereas others were more wary of dropping familiar and trusted identities. *Floundering* refers to the faltering, helpless stagnation, and frustrated thrashing about that some participants experienced in their identity work. Participants would often question whether they were 'correctly' doing identity work, and 'getting' the 'right' learning from it. They would feel frustrated with a lack of progress, and an entrenched sense of feeling stuck in a similar grind, rather than advancing to a 'new and improved' version of themselves as a leader. Finally, *being playful* refers to a form of identity work whereby an individual tries to undo a fixed identity by experimenting with a new one. While many participants were enchanted with this idea of shape-shifting, a few questioned the ethics of changing (or manipulating) who they are to suit other interests.

Remember, this programme encouraged participants to enlarge their identity 'repertoire' and to be more flexible moving between different identities in order to be more effective in their leadership. Therefore, these forms of identity undoing could be seen as techniques for creating the programme's ideal leaders/leadership. For example, the facilitators imparted the 'being playful' practice as an ideal form of identity work. Participants were required to do an 'experimentation' activity, which for some involved being allocated a different identity to experiment with. Participants had to 'reflect back' to their peers and facilitator about the results of this experiment (i.e. whether it created a different group dynamic, opened up more 'space', etc.) and receive feedback about their efforts. Hence, identity undoing operates within a disciplinary regime, where the 'observing hierarchy' (facilitators) enlist examination and confessional technologies that require the participant to visibly perform and (ideally) internalise the preferred identity work, all the while monitoring their progress (Foucault, 1977). Participants responded to these practices in a variety of unpredictable ways: some would resist, deflect, or ignore them, a few would challenge or question them, others would reshape them to suit their needs, while others would embrace and relish them. Some participants seemed to internalise the programme's approach and would encourage (and monitor) other peers to do the same.

One of the roles of the facilitators therefore was to guide participants in the ideal forms of identity work. On the surface, facilitators appeared to strongly claim the power to advance their perspective of identity and leadership/leadership development, and to challenge competing perspectives. In one-on-one interviews however, some admitted that their powerful role in shaping others' selves was a source of struggle, discomfort, and doubt suggesting that facilitators are not immune from identity undoing. However, the facilitator's identity undoing was not made visible to the participants, at least not to the extent that participants' struggles were visible, highlighting the asymmetrical power relations in leadership development.

On the one hand, identity undoing can be a positive aspect of leadership development, for example if it results in unravelling unjust, discriminatory, and harmful ideologies, identities, and behaviours – a result many critical scholars would most likely support (Alvesson, 2008). It may also validate different ways of being a leader that do not conform to narrow 'super hero' visions of leadership. Given the power relations involved in learning and identity work, as well as the feelings of vulnerability and doubt that comes with certain forms of identity undoing, participants may feel they do not have the language, voice, or power to challenge the programme's preferred identities – even on critical/social constructionist inspired programmes. If what these leaders are learning and practising is how to conform to dominant ideals, then we should be far more sceptical and critical of the 'value' of leadership development in society.

Concluding Thoughts

There is no doubt that the task of leading is difficult. In their day-to-day working life, leaders encounter a number of constraints, pressures, demands, and tensions that may disrupt and unsettle one's self. Having access to relationships and communities where leaders can go to process these struggles is important. The question this chapter raises is whether leadership development programmes (in their current form) are the most suitable settings for this self-work. Many leadership development scholars, practitioners, and even participants would argue that it is. They would agree that LDPs should embrace their role as 'identity workspaces' and provide the resources to stabilise and repair leaders' identities because the contemporary workplace no longer provides this role. Many would argue that leadership development facilitators/trainers possess an expertise about identity, leadership, business, and learning that sets them apart from counsellors, therapists, and HR practitioners. In addition, many would point to the fact that leadership development has become an accepted 'talent development' tool for improving individual and organisational performance, and is therefore mandated (and often funded) by organisations in ways that individual and group therapy may not be. Even critical leadership scholars, who one may expect to be wary of corporate sponsored development, also seem to believe in the potential of LDPs to create 'better' kinds of leaders and organisational realities. These arguments may well have merit, but they fail to acknowledge the variety of competing interests that shape leadership development.

Leadership development literature and practice tends to ignore a number of important considerations. Let us begin with what tends to be excluded and ignored in both realms (scholarship and practice). As Bell and Taylor (2004) highlight in their study of spiritual management development programmes, the workplace is quite literally excluded from development programmes. Participants are physically removed from the workplace, and transported to other locations (the seminar room, the five-star resort, the outdoor adventure setting, the orchestral pit, or as Kelly (2013) describes, the equestrian ring). While this separation from work may be beneficial as routines are disrupted and new possibilities are imagined, not only is the physical location of work excluded but more importantly the political, structural, and cultural realities and constraints of work are generally ignored. By adopting a highly individualised approach to the self, leadership development tends to ignore how identity and leadership are shaped by the realities of work. When they are alluded to, the focus tends to remain on the leader and how they will individually learn to cope with or challenge these constraints through their 'new and improved' leadership identity (Bell and Taylor, 2008). Other avenues for mobilising collective change are entirely absent (such as collective forms of representation, voice, and bargaining), and little attention is given to how difficult it is to create structural, ideological, and material change in organisations.

This points to a deeply problematic trend within leadership development literature: the encroachment of a narrow and instrumentalised form of psychology has colonised the field, crowding out perspectives from other disciplines such as political economy, sociology of work, philosophy, and industrial relations, to name a few. Leadership development seems to be suffering a similar fate to fields such as organisational behaviour and human resource management whereby working life and workplace relations are narrowly understood through the lens of psychology (Godard, 2014). No wonder it is difficult, impossible almost, to access leadership development literature that considers how leadership and organisations are shaped by the economic, political, and legal environment, or how organisational history constrains the possibilities for leadership, or how occupational identity shapes an individual leader, or how identity politics shape identity work, to name but a few. Only when leadership development seriously starts to contend with the complexity of forces shaping contemporary labour relations and workplaces will it be able to live into its ideal of creating change (regardless of whether this means improving performance or challenging power relations).

However, there are two significant barriers to doing this. First, it would require leadership development scholars and practitioners to engage with ideas from a variety of disciplines. The openness, commitment, and capacity to embark on interdisciplinary training may not be encouraged or 'incentivised' in either academia or practitioner contexts. Second, leadership development is largely funded by corporations who are guided by their own interests, and therefore may avoid or even oppose LDPs that shine too bright a light on the politics of work and organisations. Leadership development practitioners interested in more interdisciplinary approaches may well find their ethos constrained by the political economy of LDPs. If so, more scholarship that reflects upon how scholars/practitioners' values and actions are co-opted and compromised would be a welcome addition.

Finally, the identity and leadership development literature would benefit from deeper explorations of the competing interests shaping LDPs. A recent study by Tomlinson and colleagues (2013, p. 82) reminds us that some organisations use leadership development initiatives as a 'key political tool' to 'acculturate' leaders with the required 'values, beliefs and dispositions'. Far from being a benign 'identity workspace', then, leadership development is a powerful managerialist tool for creating consent and alignment amongst the elites of an organisation in order to reproduce and maintain dominant regimes of power and control (Tomlinson et al., 2013). Leaders may not be aware of this political interest, and instead (mis)recognise leadership development as a privileged chance to engage in self-work and personal growth. Hence the lure of identity work is used as a 'hook' to get leaders to consent to doing leadership development without realising how their interests are being co-opted by the organisation. This is one 'ugly truth' of leadership development, perhaps one that scholar–practitioners would rather not acknowledge, but it is precisely this kind of critical examination, of 'undoing' fundamental assumptions and biases about the purpose of leadership development, that would bring much needed scholarly depth to the field.

Helen Delaney

Note

1 Given the positivist perspective that usually characterises this research, the terms personality, individual differences, or self-concept are more common than identity.

References

Alvesson, M. (2008). The future of critical management studies. In D. Barry (Ed.), *The Sage handbook of new approaches to organization studies* (pp. 11–30). London: SAGE Publications.

Atwater, L. E., Dionne, S. D., Avolio, B. J., Camobreco, J. F., and Lau, A. W. (1999). A longitudinal study of the leadership development process: Individual differences predicting leader effectiveness. *Human Relations*, 52 (12), 1543–1562.

Back, K. (1973). *Beyond words: The story of sensitivity training and the encounter movement*. Baltimore, MD: Penguin Books.

Bell, E. and Taylor, S. (2004). From outward bound to inward bound: The prophetic voices and discursive practices of spiritual management development. *Human Relations*, 57 (4), 439–466.

Butler, N., Delaney, H. and Spoelstra, S. (2015). Problematizing 'relevance' in the business school: The case of leadership studies. *British Journal of Management*, 26 (4), 731–744.

Campbell, J. P. and Dunnette, M. D. (1968). Effectiveness of T-group experiences in managerial training and development. *Psychological Bulletin*, 70 (2), 73.

Carroll, B. and Levy, L. (2010). Leadership development as identity construction. *Management Communication Quarterly*, 24 (2), 211–231.

Carroll, B. and Nicholson, H. (2014). Resistance and struggle in leadership development. *Human Relations*, 67 (11), 1413–1436.

Casey, C. (1995). *Work, self, and society: After industrialism*. London: Routledge.

Costea, B., Crump, N. and Amiridis, K. (2008). Managerialism, the therapeutic habitus and the self in contemporary organizing. *Human Relations*, 61 (5), 661–685.

Cunliffe, A. (2009). The philosopher leader: On relationalism, ethics and reflexivity: A critical perspective to teaching leadership. *Management Learning*, 40 (1), 87–101.

Day, D. V. and Harrison, M. M. (2007). A multilevel, identity-based approach to leadership development. *Human Resource Management Review*, 17 (4), 360–373.

Dicks, H. (1970). *Fifty years of the Tavistock Clinic*. London: Routledge & K. Paul.

Erhard, W., Jensen, M. C., Zaffron, S. and Granger, K. L. (2010). Introductory reading for being a leader and the effective exercise of leadership: An ontological model. Harvard Business School Research Paper.

Ford, J. and Harding, N. (2008). Move over management: We are all leaders now. *Management Learning*, 38 (5), 475–493.

Ford, J. and Lawler, J. (2008). Blending existentialist and constructionist approaches in leadership studies: An exploratory account. *Leadership and Organization Development Journal*, 28 (5), 409–425.

Ford, J., Harding, N. and Learmonth, M. (2008). *Leadership as identity: Constructions and deconstructions*. Basingstoke: Palgrave Macmillan.

Foucault, M. (1977). *Discipline and punish*. London: Allen Lane.

Gagnon, S. (2008). Compelling identity: Selves and insecurity in global, corporate management development. *Management Learning*, 39 (4), 375–391.

Gergen, K. J. (1991). *The saturated self*. New York: BasicBooks.

Godard, J. (2014). The psychologisation of employment relations? *Human Resource Management Journal*, 24 (1), 1–18.

Gottschalk, L. A., Pattison, E. M. and Schafer, D. W. (1971). Training groups, encounter groups, sensitivity groups and group psychotherapy. *California Medicine*, 115 (2), 87.

Hall, D. T. (2004). Self-awareness, identity and leader development. In D. V. Day, S. J. Zaccaro and S. M. Halpin (Eds.), *Leader development for transforming organizations* (pp. 153–176). Mahwah, NJ: Lawrence Erlbaum Associates Inc.

Harvey, D. (2005). *A brief history of neoliberalism*. Oxford: Oxford University Press.

Heelas, P. (2002). Work ethics, soft capitalism and the 'turn to life'. In P. du Gay and M. Pryke (Eds.), *Cultural econom: Cultural analysis and commercial life* (pp. 78–96). London: SAGE Publications.

House, R. J. (1967). T-group education and leadership effectiveness: A review of the empiric literature and a critical evaluation. *Personnel Psychology*, 20 (1), 1–30.

Ibarra, H., Snook, S. and Guillen-Ramo, L. (2010). Identity-based leader development. In N. Nohria and R. Khurana (Eds.), *Handbook of leadership theory and practice* (pp. 657–678). Cambridge, MA: Harvard University Press.

Jones, A. (2006). Leading questions: Developing what? An anthropological look at the leadership development process across cultures. *Leadership*, 2 (4), 481–498.

Kelly, S. (2013). Horses for courses: Exploring the limits of leadership development through equine-assisted learning. *Journal of Management Education*, 38 (2), 216–233.

Khurana, R. (2007). *From higher aims to hired hands: The social transformation of American business schools and the unfulfilled promise of management as a profession*. Princeton, NJ: Princeton University Press.

Kleiner, A. (2008). *The age of heretics: A history of the radical thinkers who reinvented corporate management* (2nd ed.). San Francisco, CA: Jossey-Bass.

Lord, R. G. and Hall, R. J. (2005). Identity, deep structure and the development of leadership skill. *Leadership Quarterly*, 16, 591–615.

Mangham, I. and Cooper, C. L. (1969). The impact of T-Groups on managerial behaviour. *Journal of Management Studies*, 6 (1), 53–72.

McCollum, B. (1999). Leadership development and self-development: An empirical study. *Career Development International*, 4 (3), 149–154.

Mead, G. H. (1934). *Mind, self, and society*. Chicago: The University of Chicago Press.

Miller, P. and Rose, N. (1988). The Tavistock programme: The government of subjectivity and social life. *Sociology*, 22 (2), 171–192.

Murphy, S. E. and Reichard, R. (Eds.). (2011). *Early development and leadership: Building the next generation of leaders*. New York: Routledge.

Nicholson, H. and Carroll, B. (2013a). Identity undoing and power relations in leadership development. *Human Relations*, 66 (9), 1225–1248.

Nicholson, H. and Carroll, B. (2013b). So you want to be authentic in your leadership: To who and for what end? C. Spiller and D. Ladkin (Eds.), *Reflections on authentic leadership: Concepts, coalescences and clashes* (pp. 286–302). Cheltenham, UK: Edward Elgar.

Parush, T. and Koivunen, N. (2014). Paradoxes, double binds, and the construction of 'creative' managerial selves in art-based leadership development. *Scandinavian Journal of Management*, 30 (1), 104–113.

Pearce, C. L. (2007). The future of leadership development: The importance of identity, multi-level approaches, self-leadership, physical fitness, shared leadership, networking, creativity, emotions, spirituality and on-boarding processes. *Human Resource Management Review*, 17, 355–359.

Petriglieri, G. (2013). Identity workspaces for leadership development. In S. Snook, N. Nohria and R. Khurana (Eds.), *The handbook for teaching leadership*. Thousand Oaks, CA: SAGE Publications.

Petriglieri, G., Wood, J. D. and Petriglieri, J. L. (2011). Up close and personal: Building foundations for leaders' development through the personalization of management learning. *Academy of Management Learning & Education*, 10 (3), 430–450.

Petriglieri, J. L. and Petriglieri, G. (2010). Identity workspaces: The case of business schools. *Academy of Management Learning and Education*, 9 (1), 44–60.

Rice, A. (1965). *Learning for leadership: Interpersonal and intergroup relations*. London: Tavistock.

Riggio, R. E. (2008). Leadership development: The current state and future expectations. *Consulting Psychology Journal: Practice and Research*, 60 (4), 383–392.

Rose, N. (1999). *Governing the soul: The shaping of the private self*. London: Free Association Books.

Schein, E. H. and Bennis, W. G. (1965). *Personal and organizational changes through group methods: The laboratory approach*. New York: Wiley.

Scott, S. (2010). Revisiting the total institution: Performative regulation in the reinventive institution. *Sociology*, 44 (2), 213–231.

Sennett, R. (1998). *The corrosion of character: The personal consequences of work in the new capitalism*. New York: Norton.

Shamir, B. and Eilam, G. (2005). 'What's your story?' A life-stories approach to authentic leadership development. *Leadership Quarterly*, 16, 395–415.

Sinclair, A. (2007). *Leadership for the disillusioned: Moving beyond myths and heroes to leading that liberates*. Crows Nest, NSW: Allen & Unwin.

Sinclair, A. (2009). Seducing leadership: Stories of leadership development. *Gender, Work and Organization*, 16 (2), 266–284.

Tannenbaum R., Weschler, I. R. and Massarik, F. (1961). *Leadership and organization: A behavioral science approach*. New York: McGraw-Hill.

Tomlinson, M., O'Reilly, D. and Wallace, M. (2013). Developing leaders as symbolic violence: Reproducing public service leadership through the (misrecognized) development of leaders' capitals. *Management Learning*, 44 (1), 81–97.

Van Velsor, E. and Drath, W. H. (2004). A lifelong developmental perspective on leader development. In C. D. McCauley and E. Van Velsor (Eds.), *The Center for Creative Leadership handbook of leadership development* (pp. 383–414). San Francisco, CA: Jossey-Bass.

Weick, K. (1996). Drop your tools: An allegory for organizational studies. *Administrative Science Quarterly*, 41 (2), 301–313.

35

Discourse and Identity
Leader Identity at Work

Peter Sun

Leadership is seen everywhere in the organization, and is not necessarily the domain of individuals placed in formal roles or positions in an organization. This is a shift away from the traditional concept of leaders and followers as distinct individuals bound together by a chain of command (Carsten & Uhl-Bien, 2013). It is true that individuals placed in formal position of power would have greater access to resources, and could yield influence by either distributing or withdrawing resources and support to others (Oc & Bashur, 2013). Although followers may not necessarily have positional power, they can still yield considerable influence through their expertise and connections (Oc & Bashur, 2013). Their manipulation of information, their influence tactics, and their personal power can be used effectively to lead and influence change. Leadership is therefore a state of being that everyone can enter into irrespective of their position in the organization (Quinn, 1996). The emergence of such leadership is dependent on situational factors such as needs of others, threat to the group, as well as particular environmental conditions (Vught, 2006). This stream of thinking runs counter to the idea that leadership is the prerogative of a fixed few.

In this chapter, I look at how an aspiring leadership identity is created, and what narratives and discourses are involved. As stated earlier, I do not consider the leader identity to be the prerogative of those in formal positions of power. Even followers could have leader identity. Although most research on leadership and followership considers leaders and followers as static and non-transferrable, some of the recent works on followership do recognize the existence of leader identity in followers. For example, the paper by Collinson (2006) views followers as having three self-views. One self-view, the resistant self-view, portrays followers as those having leader-like qualities such as questioning the ideas of their managers. The empirical work done by Carsten, Uhl-Bien, West, Patera, and McGregor (2010) suggests three broad types of followers, with the pro-active type displaying leader-like qualities. Such followers seek out opportunities to lead, they question the underlying beliefs and assumptions of their organization, and they proactively suggest new approaches (Carsten et al., 2010). Such followers view leadership as being shared and hence mutually enacted among group members.

Research on shared leadership and self-leadership mirror the above pattern of thinking. In shared leadership, leadership is conceptualized as a shared property of the group and anyone can participate in the process (Carson, Tesluk, & Marrone, 2007; Morgeson, DeRue, & Karam, 2010; Pearce & Conger, 2003). Given the right environment (e.g., shared purpose, social support, and team member voice behavior) team members can share in the leadership, thereby reducing the need for an external leader (Carson et al., 2007). While shared leadership is often conceptualized at the team level, self-leadership is more about an individual's capacity to take initiative and to be self-directive and self-motivating (Lovelace, Manz, & Alves, 2007).

Whether it be shared leadership or self-leadership, the basic premise is that anyone can take on the role of a leader (DeRue & Ashford, 2010), requiring them to internalize their identity as a leader and externalize it through leadership actions and behaviors. DeRue and Ashford (2010) argue that the leader identity has to be "conceptualized along three levels of self-construal: individual, relational, and collective" (p. 629). At the individual level, internalization happens when the individual incorporates the identity of a leader as part of their self-concept. It means the individual places him/herself as the subject where a new aspect of self as a leader is created. However, this is not context free involving only a cognitive assessment of self. It takes place within specific contexts where social interaction plays an important role (DeRue & Ashford, 2010).

Therefore, this leader identity needs to be recognized in its interpersonal relationship with others and collectively endorsed by all. At the interpersonal level, the individual's expression of leader identity has to be reciprocally recognized by others who would take on the role of followers. This recognition can escalate to the organizational level where there is a collective endorsement by others of the individual's leader identity.

Because the identity of a leader is bound up in reciprocal relationships involving co-construction of meaning and roles (DeRue & Ashford, 2010), it is fluid. In other words, the identities of leaders and followers are not fixed states as seen in most research (DeRue & Ashford, 2010), but the role of leaders and followers can change. In this sense, I view the leader identity as a "thing in motion" (Carroll & Levy, 2011), or as Fairhurst (2007) puts it "a working subjectivity." "If identities are inherently social . . . and both leader and follower identities are available to anyone, . . . then the process by which certain people become socially constructed as leaders . . . becomes particularly important to understand" (DeRue & Ashford, 2010, p. 670).

This identity work, involving co-construction of meaning and roles, is inherently laced with discourses and narratives. How do focal individuals, through discourses and narratives in the organization, construct their leader identity?

Leader Identity Work: "A Narrative Project"

Some research posits leader identity work as "subject" orientated where the focal actor places him/herself as the subject, and then engages in reflexivity as they consciously construct a new leader identity in a context of disruption and contradictions (Carroll & Levy, 2010). This perspective is biased toward a qualitative paradigm where leader identity work happens in a context of change and subjectivity. It is intra-individual, where the narratives and discourses happen within self. However, in reality, this is not always the case. While there is the intra-individual reflexivity in creating a leader identity, in certain situations the focal individual will assume a leader identity and enact that identity by inserting themselves as "objects" within discourses or "integrated, prefabricated line(s) of language and reasoning" within the organization (Sveningsson & Alvesson, 2003, p. 1167). They position themselves as "objects" in the discourses that happen at the interpersonal and organizational levels. Therefore, the leader identity work (happening at the intrapersonal, interpersonal, and organizational levels) is an inter-play between the focal individual as subject and as object. This differs from previous works that treat identity work as grounded in an interpretive epistemology – i.e., individuals as subjects in a context of change and contradictions (e.g., Carroll & Levy, 2010; Koning & Waistell, 2012).

This leader identity construction process, where the leader is both the subject and object, where the nature of reality changes dynamically between social constructivism and positivism, is better described as a narrative identity process or an emplotment (Sparrowe, 2005; see definition below). In the hermeneutic philosophy of Ricoeur (1992), the focal individual characterizes the self as a "narrative project." The focal individual can insert themselves as objects within a series of narrative events in the organization. The narratives and discourses can be verbal (e.g., direct reference to a person as a leader or follower in situations). Verbal narratives and discourse is important for identity work, as language is an important means of confirming identities (Fiol, 2002). Language provides clarity and understanding, and individuals must dialogue and converse about themselves until they know themselves (Koning & Waistell, 2012). Narratives and discourses can also be non-verbal (e.g., playing or looking the part) (Cooper & Thatcher, 2010), where drama can become a powerful language for communication. Such discourses can either result in a grant and confirmation of the leader identity claim or result in contradictions, chaos, and discomfort when the leader identity is not granted. This claim can be influenced by:

(1) *Implicit theories of leadership and followership* (DeRue & Ashford, 2010): People have implicit cognitive assumptions as to how leaders should look and act, and this is captured in a body of literature referred to as implicit leadership theory (Lord & Maher, 1993; Schyns & Schilling, 2011). The more closely aligned the focal individual is to the implicit theories of leadership, the more likely that their claim for leadership is granted (DeRue & Ashford, 2010).

(2) *The visibility, credibility, and social power* (DeRue & Ashford, 2010; Oc & Bashur, 2013): This means that others may be more inclined to grant leader identity if the focal individual claiming such a role is visible, credible, and more powerful.

(3) *Risk and reward* (DeRue & Ashford, 2010): If the organizational culture is such that claiming leadership is seen to be negative, and any failure is met with harsh consequences, it may inhibit the motivation for individuals to claim leadership and take initiative. If the leadership culture within the organization is authoritarian and the organizational culture is bureaucratic, it might constrain the leader identity emerging (Carsten et al., 2010).

(4) *Prior history of claims and grants*: DeRue and Ashford (2010) state that a "prior history of reciprocal and reinforcing claims and grants between people will carry forward and affect those individuals' future claims and grants of leader and follower identities – especially when the situational context is relatively stable over time." Prior history of claims and grants can also mitigate the influence of implicit theories of leadership. In other words, if the focal individual has built his/her credibility through history of claims and grants, then others are less likely to use their cognitive prototypes (such as implicit theories) in recognizing the leader identity.

However, within these series of events, the focal individual can also be subject to "contradiction, disruption and confusion" (Alvesson & Willmott, 2002, p. 626), especially when a claim to leadership is not met with a grant. The focal individual then extricates him/herself from being the object and engages in intrapersonal reflexivity thus becoming the subject for change and revision. There is therefore interplay between the focal actor as the "subject" (intrapersonal construction of a leader identity) and as the "object" (inserting themselves as leaders in a series of situations/contexts). We can therefore view leader identity work as a narrative process or an emplotment.

An emplotment is constituted by a series of dynamic events (or plots) that may appear discordant when viewed independently (Sparrowe, 2005). The actor as the subject looks for ways to build a leader identity. The leader identity is regarded as the static prototype. The totality of events or plots presents a single storyline that is objectively aimed at this prototype. For example, if the aspiring self is to be a leader that empowers others, then a series of discordant events can be viewed in totality as a single storyline of a leader that empowers (or attempts to empower) others. Sparrowe says:

> We make sense of events by figuring them into brief plots – often with implied or actual actors, intentions, and outcomes. These brief plots are then retrospectively figured into larger narratives, where there is an implied or actual beginning, middle, and ending.
>
> *(2005, p. 428)*

In this sense, I view leader identity work as being related to series of events (or plots) that are sensitive to time. This same approach has been used previously to understand how individuals develop identities as ethical leaders (e.g., Koning & Waistell, 2012).

To understand more fully the narrative process, and how focal individuals are both the subjects and objects in the leader identity work, I analyze some interviews I did with participants who have gone through leadership development in a leading business school in New Zealand. Such individuals would be seeking to have their internalized leadership identity recognized and endorsed in their organization. Hence understanding how this narrative process happens will have important implications for research and practice.

Because of a lack of empirical research to draw from, and in order to understand the narrative process that occurs at the intrapersonal, interpersonal, and organizational levels, a preliminary data analysis is done and presented in this chapter. The next section briefly describes the study context.

The Study Context

Participants in the study undertook a leadership development program that spanned over a period of nine months. I focus on one organization that participated in the leadership development program. It is a large pulp and paper manufacturer in New Zealand. The organization is under constant pressure to lower its manufacturing cost, while also increasing its reliability and throughput, in order to meet world pulp and paper prices. For this reason, reliability engineers and process specialists play a vital role in the organization. Three cohorts of specialist (engineers, process people, and supply chain people) from this organization have undergone the leadership development program (from the years 2012–2014). Most of the participants have no direct reports, but yet have to influence change and decisions across several functions in the organization.

I interviewed eight participants during the month of March 2015 and analyzed the interviews to gain insight into the narrative process that happens at the intrapersonal, interpersonal, and organizational levels in the leader identity work. To maintain confidentiality, they are identified as Participant A–Participant H.

Leader Identity Work at the Intrapersonal Level

Understanding Gaps in Their Leader Identity

Leader identity work involves changes to meaning as to what leaders are, and language is an important means of effecting such transformation (Fiol, 2002). As Berger and Luckmann (1967) state "individuals must talk about themselves until they know themselves" (p. 38). The 360-degree evaluation participants underwent before the start of the workshops, and the first workshop in the program, which is designed to understand self, results in participants having an internal discourse about their life events over different time zones. They begin to understand their place in society, their place in their family, and their place in the organization as leaders, with the ability to influence decision and change. They develop a new understanding of what leadership means.

> I knew ignorantly about leadership. I thought to be a leader you got to have the right personality, to be at a particular position in the organization, and that leadership was all about managing things (Participant D).

> I thought that leaders are those with natural aptitudes only, so some are born to be leaders while others are not (Participant E).

> I know I was a leader when I was working in the Philippines. However, coming into a different culture and different country, I did not know that I could lead . . . or . . . how I could lead (Participant B).

Through internal discourses, this greater understanding of leadership has created a greater self-awareness of their leader identity gaps.

> I'm now aware that I need to display greater confidence, and at times I need to show more positive aggression in the organization as this is what people expect, and I need to be more vocal and visible. In the past I was probably timid and not vocal because I was in a different culture (Participant B).

> I used to be able to place myself in the center of people's attention. However, I have now come to realize through this program that this did not translate to good leadership because my influence was only social. . . . it did not translate to any discussion about business or organizational issues. I'm now acutely aware of this and sometimes kick myself when I engage only socially (Participant D).

> Through this program I have come to understand my strengths and weaknesses and the gaps I had to be effective in leadership (Participant G).

One may argue that this is a constructionist approach to leader identity work, in which there are sequential linear stages of identifying where the participants are at (i.e., identifying gaps) and what steps they need to take to approach the next stage of leader development (i.e., eliminating or minimizing the gaps) (Keegan & Lahey, 2001). However, while strong elements of the constructionist approach were evident from the interviews, there were also cases where individuals got to know their strengths and weaknesses and how to "order" themselves in a social situation in order to enhance their aspiring leader identity – i.e., a social construction approach to leader development (Carroll & Levy, 2010).

Aspiring Leader Identity

The internalized discourse about leader identity gaps creates what the literature refers to as a "turning" experience. Although most experiences of turning happen over a longer period (Zerubavel, 2003), in the leadership development program participants are encouraged to narrate their true self. This, through an internalized narrative process, takes them through their life journey, and thus is a temporal discontinuity talk that "discursively constructs an old/new bifurcation" (Koning & Waistell, 2012, p. 67).

This old/new bifurcation leads to participants having an aspiring leader identity, with the motivation to lead and influence in the organization. Having the proper understanding of leadership, their leader identity gaps, and a better understanding of self, enhances affective-identity factors such as ascribing to oneself certain leadership qualities. This narrative increases their motivation to lead in their organization (Chan & Drasgow, 2001; Waldman Galvin, & Walumbwa, 2012), as well as creating a desire to be a particular person and pursuing that objective (Thornborrow & Brown, 2009).

> In the past I had thought I was miles away from being a CEO, and especially when I hear senior leaders like my CEO speak. Now I realize that it is not so daunting and I now realize that I can be a senior leader. I now look at every opportunity, every dialogue with the CEO . . . as an opportunity to learn and grow (Participant D).

> When I started on the course I thought I was not a leader. I was good with machines and technical stuff but not good with people. From the course it generated an understanding that leadership can be learnt and worked on . . . I now recognize that I have the people-related skills and traits to be an effective leader, as well as traits that I need to work on. It has given me the tools I can use to be a leader (Participant E).

The understandings of gaps in the leader identity and developing an aspiring leader identity are narrative processes that take place at the intrapersonal level. In this narrative process, the participants place themselves as subjects that need revision and development. It is a process that happens within a context of contradiction and change, requiring reflexivity (Carroll & Levy, 2010). This intrapersonal narrative process, in which the participant becomes the subject, happens when they withdraw themselves from being objects in events/plots. This transition to and fro is dynamic and happens throughout the emplotment.

> I'm now more self-aware prior, during and after events. Before the meeting I think of situations and how I might and might not react. During the meeting, sometimes I mentally withdraw and quickly take stock of situations, and I do that self-evaluation after the meeting. This was not the case before but now it has almost become part of what I do (Participant G).

Leader Identity Work at the Interpersonal Level

At the interpersonal level, the narratives and discourses involve positioning themselves as objects and engaging with activities that align with their aspiring leader identity. Leader identity narratives at the interpersonal level are driven by the enhanced understanding as to what leadership means at that level.

> I now understand that success does not come only from what I do but also comes from what others do. It is about working with people, getting others involved in the "doing,"

and the quality of what you get is much higher . . . although it might be faster to do it yourself but may not be of a higher quality and effectiveness (Participant E).

> Leaders create other leaders. This is what I learnt from the program. I need to therefore relate to people and see how they can become leaders themselves (Participant B).

The participants position themselves as the leader who knows others, engages with others, engages with the upper echelon, and shares information.

Knowing Others

Getting to know others through conversations and engagement is important in trying to understand others' capabilities, strengths, and weaknesses. This knowledge helps participants to tap into their capabilities and work with others in a complementary way to achieve greater outcomes. This, to many, is a way they can influence and hence display their leader identity.

> I now make it a point to understand who people are and what they can offer and how to get the best of them. I now go with the mindset, in all of my conversations with people, how I can learn from them and how I can be of best help to that person. I now listen more and try not to have any pre-conceived ideas of who people are. For example, I had previously thought that this particular IT person was always negative. I however went to him without any preconceived ideas and surprisingly found how knowledgeable and constructive this person is (Participant D).

Knowing others is important for leadership influence, because it enables you to empower others by sharing appropriate levels of responsibilities. This enhances the leader identity in you as well as in the eyes of others.

> I now have many conversations with people, observe them at work, and take note of their strengths and weaknesses. So, when it comes to some machine problems or even during plant shut downs, I now give them the responsibility to get it done without doing everything myself. I find that people really like this and respect you for it. . . . they feel really empowered (Participant B).

Engagement with Others

Engagement with others is closely related to knowing others. This relates to the narratives and discourses involved in engaging people in their personal and social life, especially when it intersects with work life. This type of engagement builds affective trust, and displaying altruism aligns with leader identity (Vught, 2006). Vught (2006) argues, from research found in psychology literature, that leadership is linked to generosity and fairness. Past research has found that socio-emotional qualities such as empathy predicts leadership emergence (e.g., Batson, 1998).

> When talking to people and dealing with them, I try to be mindful of the pressures they face at work. People have a life outside of work. When they fall sick I try to be mindful of that in my conversations. Being mindful of their social side instead of just engaging with the issue like what engineers normally do (Participant E).

Research shows that leaders are individually considerate, showing empathy (Sun & Anderson, 2012), and often exercising ethics of care over ethics of justice (Simola, Barling, & Turner, 2010). Therefore narratives involved in such engagement are a display of the leader identity. However, in such narratives, you need to be able to have the difficult conversations when appropriate.

> Engagement with people requires you to have difficult conversations with people; especially when things are not going well, or have gone wrong, to look at things objectively and have a positive, yet difficult conversation with people. You got to talk about the bad stuff and good (Participant E).

Engagement with Upper Echelons

Engagement with upper echelons came out as a separate theme. Participants discussed the need to have conversations with senior management, so that they know who you are and would recognize the leadership potential in you.

> I now engage frequently with senior management. . . . I seek feedback, ask how things are going. . . . If there are problems they raise, I thank them for it, and I bring it to my team to see how it can be addressed (Participant E).

By engaging with the upper echelons, participants make themselves visible and hence lessen the distance from senior management. Some of the participants I interviewed state that you have to "put yourself out there," in order to ensure that your leadership potential is recognized. Frequent engagement and proximity ensures that senior leadership would not judge you based on cognitive prototyping (i.e., using implicit theories of leadership – Schyns & Schilling, 2011), or third party information, but who you are as a person and your competencies and capabilities. The narrative involved is about promoting and selling yourself to upper management.

Sharing Information

Leaders share information, and they provide the systemic and big picture thinking that enable others to better understand situations and take appropriate actions. Information is resource, and leaders are those who own and distribute such resources at their discretion (Oc & Bashur, 2013). Leaders provide big picture and systems thinking (Alexander, Comfort, Weiner, & Bogue, 2001), and have the cognitive capability to understand and differentiate various forces that impact on decisions (Sun & Anderson, 2012). Therefore, narratives involved in providing others with all the facts, relating them to the overall objectives, providing the big picture thinking, are all discourses aligned with the leader identity.

> I make sure that others know all the relevant facts and information. I provide them with this big picture by sharing with others about the impact it makes to the entire process. They therefore understand what is happening, and are able to act independently and make right decisions. It is no longer about simply repairing a fault (Participant F).

> I make sure I'm transparent with all the information necessary. By sharing information as openly as possible others are able to work on their own and make decisions. I don't have to always be there to do things . . . I tell others that they can make decisions and here are the information they need (Participant B).

Leader Identity Work at the Organizational Level

"Impression management is concerned with the behaviors people direct toward others to create and maintain desired perceptions of themselves" (Gardner & Martinko, 1988, p. 321). Leaders influence others and hence their impression management as part of their communication process is important, and this has been recognized in prior research (e.g., Gardner & Avolio, 1995; Gardner & Cleavenger, 1998).

Managing impressions is important at the collective level of the organization as people have implicit cognitive assumptions as to how leaders should look and act. This is captured in a body of literature referred to as implicit leadership theory (Lord & Maher, 1993; Schyns & Schilling, 2011). People in general tend to use a form of cognitive schemata to explain leadership behaviors (Lord & Maher, 1993), and this use is more pronounced if there is greater distance between the focal individual and the observer. Attributes that people often use, in order to implicitly attribute leadership, are: charisma, decisiveness, dedication, participation verbal skills, understanding, and intelligence (Offermann, Kennedy, & Wirtz, 1994; Schyns & Shillings, 2011). This impression management was clearly seen in the participants, at the collective level of the organization.

At this level of influence, the leader identity needs to be collectively endorsed by the wider organization. The participants do so by actively positioning themselves as leaders, taking initiatives, and building competencies. Inserting themselves into the narratives and discourses in the above areas are attempts to make their leader identity recognized at the collective level of the organization.

Actively Positioning as the Leader

Participants spoke of active insertion by deliberately walking beside their manager and not behind them, speaking louder, and showing aggression rather than timidity. One participant actively sought out graduate engineers to mentor so as to create the impression that she has direct reports in the organization.

> I make it a point to have graduates that I can mentor. While others would see it as extra work, I see it as having direct reports so that others will see me as a leader. I also make sure that I now walk beside my manager instead of being behind him. In the past, being a female, I use to walk behind my manager and I get used a lot to be their secretary to do the paper work. I have now changed my actions and I'm more louder and aggressive in my approach (Participant B).

Participants also spoke of the way they act in meetings. Participant D mentioned that he shows decisiveness by influencing the outcomes of the meeting so that there is less waffle. He deliberately ensures that minutes are taken and action points are discussed and allocated. He therefore positions himself as a leader in these situations.

Leaders are known for the size of their social networks and often occupy central positions in influence and advice networks (Bono & Anderson, 2005).

> I'm actively going around and trying to get to know more and more people (Participant B).

> I'm increasingly becoming the go-to person. If senior management wants to organize something, or get certain information, they now come to me. I see this happening more and more (Participant D).

Participants actively insert themselves as substitute for their managers.

> I now deliberately take charge when my boss is not around. When people come and ask for my boss, I say "I can sort this out for you," instead of asking them to wait for my boss to come back (Participant B).

Taking Initiative

Taking initiative is a prototypical behavior of leaders. Taking initiative can be considered as a "voice behavior," which is a form of proactive behavior that involves constructive and change-orientated narratives that intend to improve the situation (Fuller, Barnett, Hester, Relyea, & Frey, 2007). Individuals with higher voice behavior are deemed to be more attractive as leaders and therefore more promotable (Fuller et al., 2007).

> I deliberately seek opportunities to be involved in new initiatives. When I initiate something and it is successful, I make sure that I communicate this to others so that I get the required credit and recognition (Participant B).

> I offer myself to anyone who has a problem. Sometimes it may be in an area that I know nothing about. However, being available and ready to help gives the people the confidence there is someone out there willing to support them. Often when people talk about the problem, they come to the solutions themselves and all you have to do is to facilitate that process (Participant D).

Technical Competency

Because the participants involved are technical specialists, their technical identity is valuable. This technical identity (i.e., being recognized as technically competent) is closely intertwined with their leader identity, so much so that a loss (or a reduction) of this technical identity will erode their credibility as a leader.

Past research has confirmed the importance of competence for leaders. When it comes to technical abilities, past research has shown that leadership in a domain area is correlated with expertise in that area (Vught, 2006), and this is especially true for professionals such as engineers and accountants. For example, a successful head of the accounting department is often deemed to be a better accountant than his/her subordinates (Tsui, 1984). Therefore, leadership identity is enhanced if others identify that focal individual as being competent.

> You need to have technical competence so that others will trust what you say, and have confidence in your ability. Trust is important, I believe, for someone to be influential (Participant F).

> I believe you need to show confidence in your conversations. You need to ask people confidently if they have viewed the problem differently . . . rather than saying "this is the solution," to be able to facilitate the process confidently to come out with the most optimum solution . . . To be open to different ideas and different perspectives. Because of this, and a change in the approach, people are now coming to me for ideas (Participant E).

Organizational Factors

In the leader identity work, I have identified some narratives that take place at the intrapersonal level (where the participants are the subjects) and at the interpersonal and organizational levels (where the participants are the objects). Participants moved to and from being subjects to inserting themselves as objects in the narrative process, and most participants report an increased endorsement of their aspiring leader identity.

> XYZ . . . who is the senior leader for health and safety, the person in charge of the project, is increasingly turning to me and running his ideas past me before tabling it to the organization (Participant D).

> My Plant Manager, very recently, endorsed his confidence in me in a recruitment matter. This is something that rarely happened before (Participant E).

However, various organizational factors can either impede or enhance this narrative process. One organizational factor that came out clearly is the culture of leadership in the organization. In a culture of leadership, everyone would take initiatives and would have the legitimacy to lead, irrespective of their position in the hierarchy. They would be provided with a safety net for such initiative taking. DeRue and Ashford (2010) state that, if claiming leadership is seen to be risky, and any failure is met with harsh consequences, it may inhibit the motivation for individuals to claim leadership and take initiative.

However, the culture of leadership was not widespread in the organization, although there are signs that this culture is evolving. Participant E spoke of an ingrained pattern of behavior where the union is seen to be negative. The dominant narrative in the organization is that unions are anti-change and hence do not step up and take initiatives. In his personal dealings with the unions, Participant E has found that this stereotyping was not always true.

Those who have participated in the leadership development program are expected by senior management to step up and take on leadership in different situations and contexts. This legitimacy is provided through their association with the leadership program, rather than it being a culture of leadership.

> The leadership program has opened up opportunities for me to have difficult conversations with my manager with regards to his leadership and management styles. He is now more open to listen to me, to see how he can learn from what I benefited from the workshops (Participant H).

> As participants in the leadership program we are all expected to step up and display our leadership skills. We are expected to be involved in all sorts of conversations and contribute with initiatives (Participant E).

However, within the organization the culture of leadership is evolving with greater support from senior management, especially the CEO, for leadership development. There is also growing top management support for initiative taking.

> The CEO encourages people to go out and try things, to explore new ideas, and share ideas with people. This opens people's mind and they are not afraid to throw ideas in (Participant E).

Conclusion

The study argues that evolving a leader identity is a narrative process that happens at the intrapersonal, interpersonal, and organizational levels. At the intrapersonal level, the participant becomes the subject and engages in a reflexive process of identifying gaps in their leader identity. Through this intrapersonal narrative process, an aspiring leader identity is created. At the more visible interpersonal and organizational levels, the narrative process involves the participant inserting themselves as objects into various situations so that their discourse aligns with their internalized leader identity. At the interpersonal level, the narratives include getting to know others, engaging with others at a personal and social level, engaging with upper echelons, and actively sharing information. At the organizational level, the narratives include actively positioning themselves as the leader, taking initiatives, and displaying technical competencies. The individual traverses back and forth, between the intrapersonal and the more visible interpersonal and organizational levels, in their leader identity work (see Figure 35.1 for the framework of the study).

This study has important practical implications. For those who undertake leadership development and have the desire to grow in influence, it shows the dynamics at the intrapersonal, interpersonal, and organizational levels. It highlights the narrative processes that are better able to position the participants as leaders of influence in their organizations. For those in senior management, it is important that they create a culture of leadership within the organization to provide legitimacy for people to take initiatives and enable leader identity work to happen.

This study has several research implications. What would happen to the leader identity work if the focal individual emphasizes narratives only at certain levels? What perception would this create on their leader identity? Is it possible for the culture of the organization to influence the type of discourses and narratives that happens at the different levels? For example, could a more masculine culture result in more goal-orientated discourses?

Although some empirical evidence is provided, the study is not an exhaustive qualitative study of the narrative process in leader identity work. Future research work can collect data from different organizations and different contexts, and build a grounded theoretical model

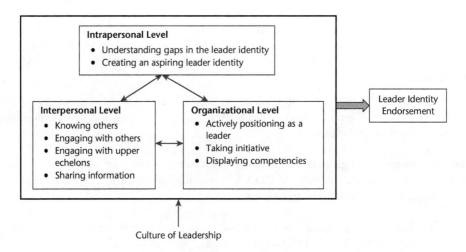

Figure 35.1 Leader Identity at Work: A Narrative Process

for the narrative process in leader-identity work. The intention of this study is to reveal some aspects of the narrative processes happening at the intrapersonal, interpersonal, and organizational levels, and to show that leader-identity work is complex, with constant interplay between participants as subjects and objects. This will, I hope, spur more studies in this area.

References

Alexander, J. A., Comfort, M. E., Weiner, B. J., & Bogue, R. (2001). Leadership in collaborative community health partnerships. *Nonprofit Management & Leadership, 12*, 159–175.

Alvesson, M., & Willmott, H. (2002). Producing the appropriate individual: Identity regulation as organizational control. *Journal of Management Studies, 39*, 619–644.

Batson, C. D. (1998). Altruism and prosocial behaviour. In D. Gilbert, S. Fiske, & G. Lindzey (Eds.), *Handbook of social psychology* (pp. 282–316). New York: McGraw-Hill.

Berger, P. L., & Luckmann, T. (1967). *The social construction of reality: A treatise in the sociology of knowledge.* Garden City, NY: Anchor Books.

Bono, J. E., & Anderson, M. H. (2005). The advice and influence network of transformational leaders. *Journal of Applied Psychology, 90*, 1306–1314.

Carroll, B., & Levy, L. (2011). Leadership development as identity construction. *Management Communication Quarterly, 24*, 211–231.

Carson, J. B., Tesluk, P. E., & Marrone, J. A. (2007). Shared leadership in teams: An investigation of antecedent conditions and performance. *Academy of Management Journal, 50*, 1217–1234.

Carsten, M. K., & Uhl-Bien, M. (2013). Ethical followership: An examination of followership beliefs and crimes of obedience. *Journal of Leadership & Organizational Studies, 20*, 49–61.

Carsten, M. K., Uhl-Bien, M., West, B. J., Patera, J. L., & McGregor, R. (2010). Exploring social construction of followership: A qualitative study. *Leadership Quarterly, 21*, 543–562.

Chan, K.Y., & Drasgow, F. (2001). Toward a theory of individual differences and leadership: Understanding the motivation to lead. *Journal of Applied Psychology, 86*, 481–498.

Collinson, D. (2006). Rethinking followership: A poststructuralist analysis of follower identities. *Leadership Quarterly, 17*, 179–189.

Cooper, D., & Thatcher, S. M. (2010). Identification in organizations: The role of self-concept orientations and identification moves. *Academy of Management Review, 35*, 516–538.

DeRue, D. S., & Ashford, S. J. (2010). Who will lead and who will follow? A social process of leadership identity construction in organizations. *Academy of Management Review, 35*, 627–647.

Fairhurst, G. T. (2007). *Discursive leadership: In conversation with leadership psychology.* Thousand Oaks, CA: Sage.

Fiol, C. M. (2002). Capitalizing on paradox: The role of language in transforming organizational identities. *Organization Science, 13*, 653–666.

Fuller, J. B., Barnett, T., Hester, K., Relyea, C., & Frey, L. (2007). An exploratory examination of voice behaviour from an impression management perspective. *Journal of Managerial Issues, 19*, 134–151.

Gardner, W. L., & Avolio, B. J. (1995). Charismatic leadership: The role of impression management. Paper presented at the Annual Meeting of the Academy of Management, Vancouver, BC.

Gardner, W. L., & Cleavenger, D. (1998). The impression management strategies associated with transformational leadership at the world-class level: A psychohistorical assessment. *Management Communication Quarterly, 12*, 3–41.

Gardner, W. L., & Martinko, M. J. (1988). Impression management in organizations. *Journal of Management, 14*, 321–338.

Keegan, R., & Lahey, L. (2001). *How the way we talk can change the way we work: Seven languages for transformation.* San Francisco: Jossey-Bass.

Koning, J., & Waistell, J. (2012). Identity talk of aspirational ethical leaders. *Journal of Business Ethics, 107*, 65–77.

Lord, R. G., & Maher, K. J. (1993). *Leadership and information processing.* London: Routledge.

Lovelace, K. J., Manz, C., & Alves, J. C. (2007). Work stress and leadership development: The role of self-leadership, shared leadership, physical fitness and flow in managing demands and increasing job control. *Human Resource Management Review, 17*, 374–387.

Morgeson, F. P., DeRue, D. S., & Karam, E. P. (2010). Leadership in teams: A functional approach to understanding leadership structures and processes. *Journal of Management, 36*, 5–39.

Oc, B., & Bashshur, M. R. (2013). Followership, leadership and social influence. *Leadership Quarterly*, *24*, 919–934.

Offermann, L. R., Kennedy, J. K., & Wirtz, P. W. (1994). Implicit leadership theories: Content, structure, and generalizability. *Leadership Quarterly*, *5*, 43–58.

Pearce, C. L., & Conger, J. A. (2003). *Shared leadership: Reframing the hows and whys of leadership*. Thousand Oaks, CA: Sage.

Quinn, R. E. (1996). *Deep change: Discovering the leader within*. San Francisco: Jossey-Bass.

Ricoeur, P. (1992). *Oneself as another*. Chicago: University of Chicago Press.

Schyns, B., & Schilling, J. (2011). Implicit leadership theories: Think leader, think effective? *Journal of Management Inquiry*, *20*, 141–150.

Simola, S. K., Barling, J., & Turner, N. (2010). Transformational leadership and leader moral orientation: Contrasting an ethic of justice and an ethic of care. *Leadership Quarterly*, *21*, 179–188.

Sparrowe, R. T. (2005). Authentic leadership and the narrative self. *Leadership Quarterly*, *16*, 419–439.

Sun, P. Y. T., & Anderson, M. H. (2012). The importance of attributional complexity for transformational leadership studies. *Journal of Management Studies*, *49*, 1001–1022.

Sveningsson, S., & Alvesson, M. (2003). Managing managerial identities: Organizational fragmentation, discourse and identity struggle. *Human Relations*, *56*, 1163–1193.

Thornborrow, T., & Brown, A. D. (2009). "Being regimented": Aspiration, discipline and identity work in the British parachute regiment. *Organization Studies*, *30*, 355–376.

Tsui, A. S. (1984). A role set analysis of managerial reputation. *Organizational Behaviour and Human Performance*, *34*, 64–96.

Vught, M. V. (2006). Evolutionary origins of leadership and followership. *Personality and Social Psychology Review*, *10*, 354–371,

Waldman, D. A., Galvin, B. M., & Walumbwa, F. O. (2012). The development of motivation to lead and leader role identity. *Journal of Leadership & Organizational Studies*, *20*, 156–168.

Zerubavel, E. (2003). *Time maps: Collective memory and the social shape of the past*. Chicago: University of Chicago Press.

36

Conclusions
Looking to the Future of Leadership

John Storey, Jean Hartley, Jean-Louis Denis,
Paul 't Hart and Dave Ulrich

The Changing Fortunes of 'Leadership': A Cautionary Tale

Most of the editors of this book grew up during an era when there was a deep suspicion of strong, heroic leadership. In post-war Europe, there was little need to be reminded of where powerful, charismatic, and inspirational but at the same time fanatical, evil, anti-moral leadership could lead, nor indeed of the complicit role that followers and other non-leaders play in paving the road to hell that it forged. The mindset was to view behaviour that in twenty-first-century settings has become associated with strong leadership as populism, zealotry, pedantry, ego-tripping – things to avoid. We collectively remember what the prior generation had perhaps forgotten, that we need a government conducted first and foremost through laws and institutions, not one dominated by the capricious dynamics of leadership and followership. In the post-war world, public trust in political institutions reached high levels.

But the move away from leaders and leadership has not lasted. Trust in political institutions has plummeted throughout the Western world as people felt that governments were unable to cope with the big challenges of the era – globalization, migration, multiculturalism, crime – or to maintain adequate levels of what people had come to regard as elementary public service delivery – education, health, and welfare. The reaction: an unprecedented call for more, better, stronger, courageous, visionary, 'leadership'. A similar dynamic occurred in the business sector, where financial collapses, ethical fiascos, globalization of trade, and relentless technological innovation have provided both a frame-breaking and a game-changing impetus to rethink traditional models of corporate governance and strategy. Moreover, not-for-profit organizations, churches, and hitherto 'untouchable' bulwarks of professional authority in sectors such as health care, higher education, and accountancy have all been confronted with the deinstitutionalization of their status quos in a world where transparency, accountability, and performativity have become the dominant makers and breakers of institutional fates.

By the last decade of the millennium, the discourse had shifted across all walks of society. Old institutional orders appeared to be caught out, tired, and simply not up to the challenges of the turbulent times the world was moving into. And yet they were persistent, recalcitrant, and resistant to change even if they were tantamount to 'permanently failing organizations' (Meyer and Zucker 1991). They strenuously tried to manage what was left of their shrinking legitimacy

(Suchman 1995). With such a diagnosis as the vantage point, the inference that it would need strong individuals to challenge, reform, and revitalize them was only just around the corner. And so, 'leadership' made a comeback – and a spectacular one it was.

In its new guise, leadership became even more firmly equated with instigating change on the back of heady statements by influential authors such as John Kotter (Kotter 1996). Moreover, to be effective agents of change, leaders needed to be outsiders rather than insiders; critics of the old system rather than exponents of it; confrontational rather than consensus seeking; decisive rather than consultative; business-like rather than collegiate; asking 'why' at least as much as wondering 'how'. There was much talk about 'empowering' leaders, releasing them from the stranglehold of institutional rules and conventions (Peters and Waterman 1982).

The new leadership talk fitted the times. It epitomizes contemporary individualism. It provides even supposedly dispassionate managers with persuasive stories about real, tangible heroes. It shows that resourceful – dynamic, wise, persistent, proactive, entrepreneurial – people can take on dark or ineffective institutions, and win. It tells people to look at themselves, improve themselves, and 'create value' as a result.

But as with any compelling story, one should ask: is it true? As often happens, the answer is: yes and no. Yes, there are kernels of truth in many of these stories. When an Iaccocca, a Gates, a Branson, a Giuliani, or a Musk talk about their own leadership experiences, they are not lying – they have tangible successes demonstrating their impact to back up their claims. When Goleman and his co-workers find that a high level of emotional intelligence correlates with certain forms of leadership success, they are on to something. When an unlikely Pope from Argentina manages to thoroughly upset the deeply entrenched conservative forces inside the Roman Catholic Church and rebuild the public credit it had lost so spectacularly through a global string of sexual abuse scandals, we cannot but note the transformative power of leaders.

But a lot of the sweeping claims found in contemporary leadership talk are quite debatable. What, then, are some of its problems? First, is the equation of leadership with instigating change. Modern leadership-speak talks down 'management' as dull, unimaginative, store-minding stuff that may have been good enough for less dynamic times – thus oddly dismissing the 1960s, 1970s, and 1980s as periods of stability, when management rather than 'leadership' was the buzzword, and 'managers' were hot property in professionalizing governance. Real leaders clean house, innovate, reform, we are told. And so they do. They come into their top positions with their MBAs and MPAs and do what they have been taught: changing things – sometimes radically. A number of scholars have used the term 're-disorganization' to refer to the wave after wave after wave of imposed change, resulting in organizational introversion, loss of institutional memory, staff demotivation, and doing precious little to improve service delivery to customers. This tale is strikingly familiar to many of us living in and observing corporations and governments in many countries. We are re-organizing ourselves to death and a large part of the reason is because people in charge of organizations are conditioned – by training, by incentive systems, by informal talk – to think that this is what they ought to do.

Second, it rests on scant evidence. There is certainly fervour in the way people advocate their preferred conception of leadership: entrepreneurial leadership, transformational leadership, coaching leadership, servant leadership, empowerment leadership, charismatic leadership. The list of slogans and catchphrases is endless. Shelves full of them stare at you in the business sections of the major bookstores. The problem is that every time you look, hordes of authors have dreamt up new adjectives and prefixes for leadership, each with its own philosophy, model, success stories, or other corroborating evidence, and the inevitable set of well-crafted maxims, lessons, or 'to-do's. Good science is cumulative: today's students possess a common language, a set of shared assumptions, and above all a widely accepted body of robust empirical knowledge produced by their predecessors. Not so in the world of leadership studies, where people cannot even agree on basic definitional issues. There are more than 10,000 notions of leadership out there. It is a field in which semantic innovation is a better road to professional advancement than patient testing and retesting of promising propositions. Such a field is essentially footloose. And when there is considerable money to be gained for whoever manages to write the next 'in-book' on the subject, such a field is hype-prone. Gurus come and gurus go in the leadership field; a great many more leadership writers see their books catch dust on warehouse shelves. What makes the difference is hard to tell, but it can hardly be the greater scientific rigour of the former.

Most of the guru books on leadership are of two kinds. One kind is written by either current or former leaders who made it big and tell their readers to act exactly as they did – a highly debatable lesson given the highly contextual nature of leadership situations and niches. The other is written by leadership scholars and observers who have deduced leadership principles from teaching courses, interviewing people, and reading other leadership books. What do they share? None of them has ever bothered seriously testing their leadership prescriptions in a variety of contexts and settings. All of them make exactly the same mistake: overgeneralization. Falling in love with one's own professional successes and one's own models is easy to do. But much of this is intellectual hubris. Peters and Waterman's *In Search of Excellence* looked very impressive when it was published (Peters and Waterman 1982); yet when most of their excellent companies came crashing down within years of the publication of their book, their recipes lost their appeal very quickly. As any serious scientist can tell you, reliable knowledge comes from testing, testing again, and testing once more. Why do we conveniently forget about this rule when it comes to knowledge claims in the area of management and leadership?

The gulf between guru-style and academically sound leadership studies could not be bigger. Studies in the latter vein – of which, fortunately there are many too, but getting much less attention than the guru books – overwhelmingly offer messages of caution rather than boldness when it comes to embracing leadership prescriptions. The simple fact is that the power of 'leadership' factors in explaining outcomes of complex organizations and policy networks is really difficult to pin down. Yet we are blinded by the aura of success that surrounds great leadership icons (as perpetuated and mimicked through mass media and in popular culture), and we are seduced by the sometime brilliant writing style of the gurus. But why is it that the true vanguard of leadership studies – people who have led the field for decades such as James MacGregor Burns (MacGregor Burns 2010), Robert House (House 2013), James Gardner (Gardner 1998), Fred Greenstein (Greenstein 2000) – have tended to shy away from holding up pet metaphors and simple sets of maxims? As we hope this volume attests, serious scholars help people gain awareness of the contingencies, predicaments, and constraints of leadership but they know better than to tell people what to do. They insist on the benefits of looking at leadership practices and leaders in context and from multiple theoretical prisms. Leadership becomes an umbrella concept to think about and to study empirically how individuals and collectives gain agency and promote some convergence in contemporary and complex organizations.

Third, the current infatuation with leadership and the industry it has called into being (Kellerman 2012) *extols people and their skills and ignores the pivotal roles of institutions and roles.* There is nothing wrong with people. We need skilful, wise, reflective, entrepreneurial, empathic, upright, humble, inspirational, decisive, and otherwise eminently 'followable' people as catalytic forces in a turbulent, uncertain era that demands permanent, perhaps even accelerating, change. And we too believe in helping people nurture their leadership skills – we would not be bothering to edit volumes like these otherwise. But we should acknowledge the risk of overdoing it: the countless courses/seminars on leadership suggest that it is all about 'you' – your drive, your skills, your attitudes, your self-confidence, your communication, your aura, your moral compass, your ego-control, your emotional intelligence.

But, as citizens, customers, and clients, we should not want to have governments, corporations, and service providers that are predominantly built upon the shaky foundations of 'a few good men or women' at the top. We want them to be embedded in adaptive yet resilient institutional fabrics, and governed by principles and rules that carve out an intelligent role play between their key office-holders, stakeholders, and accountability forums. In other words, we want them made and kept idiot-proof, dictator-proof, populist-proof, opportunist-proof. We should want them as little dependent as possible upon charismatic figures for breathing life – and change – into them. Even a cursory glance at the history of politics, for example, shows that, in the long run, open, resilient, democratic public institutions are far more important to the quality of government than any effort to groom and select an elite of wise individuals to lead the country (Kane *et al.* 2009). Paradoxically, there is a role for these agents that understand the subtleties of institutional context and the conditions for their sustainability and adaptations. This may correspond to a more realistic view of leaders while recognizing at the same time that some individuals have a unique potential to assist in transcending current institutional or organiza- tional limitations. In addition, contemporary studies of leadership suggest that it is a distributed phenomenon – in some types of organizations at least. Beyond ideologically driven discourses on leadership figures, we must recognize the importance of understanding how individuals in organizations and in politics exert leadership based on a diversity of resources such as expertise, tacit knowledge, and relational skills.

Placing so much faith in 'leadership' runs the risk of bestowing power without thinking enough about responsibility, blinded by a Platonic model of governance where all wisdom is expected to reside at the top. Yet we live in an era of *horizontalization*, citizen empowerment, networks rather than only pyramids. Shared power in partnerships, networks, and coalitions is the name of the game. The real challenge for leaders today is to remain relevant in an era in which open borders, empowered customers and citizens, complex interdependencies, and self- conscious professionals continuously serve to hollow out the power of the centre. Fortunately, the emerging work on distributed, shared, dispersed, tandem, network, and collaborative leadership – our field is as heavy as it gets on adjectives – is starting to help us to rethink what 'leadership' is really about in contexts where no one is in charge of the whole group or system but everyone has big stakes riding on joint action (Crosby and Bryson 2010).

We need a leadership studies field that is driven by careful reasoning and sound evidence rather than metaphors and slogans: one that takes on board not only the personal but also the institutional and contextual dimensions of public leadership; one that is conscious of the fact that powerful leaders may destroy as much as they create; one that avoids privileging change for change's sake, and that recognizes the need to conserve certain values and institutions may at times be stronger than the need to reform or abandon them; one that does not presume all wisdom resides at the top; one that does not tell people they should become superheroes but instead stresses the need to manage interdependence and organize complementarity in the per- formance of leadership functions; one that recognizes that exercising authority does not equate to performing leadership.

We need, in short, to come to our senses. More, stronger, even 'better' (whatever that might turn out to be) leadership by individuals is not going to be the panacea for the current crisis of confidence and spirit that many parts of the world are experiencing. To be sure, today as much as in any other era, we need prudent, creative, empowering leadership. But we also need strong institutions which control those who exercise leadership, whether rooted in formal authority roles or the sheer enthusiasm they inspire in their followers. To anyone giving it more than a passing thought, it should become clear that leadership is a deeply ambivalent phenomenon, and has always been. Scholars who study it do well to take this as their starting point.

Futures for (and beyond) Leadership

Leadership has become a big beast across a range of disciplines within and beyond the social sciences – as this Companion vividly illustrates. It has a growing number of dedicated journals of both the generic (e.g. *The Leadership Quarterly, Journal of Leadership Studies*) and niche kind (e.g. *Journal of Spirituality, Management and Leadership, International Journal of Leadership in Education, Journal of Healthcare Leadership*). But, where will this beast move in the years to come? Adjective-infested and hype-prone as the field has proven to be, can it succeed in building a body of knowledge that retains its wide reach and disciplinary diversity and yet delivers insights that are more widely shared, more robustly researched, and more enduring that much of what has been produced in its big expansion over the last twenty years? And, will it manage to address the conditions, challenges, and complexities of twenty-first-century societies, business, and governments?

To start with the latter, Table 36.1 (adapted from 't Hart, 2014, pp. 182–183) provides an overview of main trends affecting what conditions leadership will face, what challenges it will be expected to address, how it can be exercised, and how it can be legitimized. None of these is simple; all are ambiguous; few can be effectively tackled by continuing to rely on early twentieth-century presumptions underpinning the top-down, unitary leadership models in which much contemporary scholarship continues to be steeped. Hierarchy, authority, deference, persuasion,

Table 36.1 Trends and Leadership Implications

Trend	Characteristics	Leadership implications
1. The age of *networks* Key source: Castells (1996)	Rise of complex interdependencies, distributed authority, and resources, and public demand for integrated, customized services	Need to balance the reality of specialization, hierarchy and 'turf'-based 'top-down' leadership with a need for collaborative leadership in shared-power settings
2. The age of *empowerment* Key source: Ryde (2013)	Reduction of the 'power distance' between high-status and low-status people Decline of 'automatic' public deference towards authority figures and established public institutions	Need to balance a post-paternalistic, more interactive way of leaders–community/group engagement with need for authoritative leadership that remains capable of making hard calls
3. The age of *transparency* Key source: Mulgan (2014)	Increased public access to information about how institutions and organizations operate, and where they succeed and fail Rapid growth of the proportion of citizens, employees, shareholders, organization members who want to (and think they) 'know' how they are being governed	Need to balance maximum openness about conduct of public office-holders and performance of public organizations with the confidentiality and reflective space required to handle sensitive issues and craft delicate multi-actor compromises

(continued)

Table 36.1 (continued)

Trend	Characteristics	Leadership implications
4. The age of *immediacy* Key source: Gleick (2000)	Information technology and increased mobility have created time–space compression in economic, cultural and political life Rise of tightly interconnected, speeded-up, interactive forms of collective deliberation and feedback	Need to balance speed, responsiveness, and a sense of urgency with prudence, patience, and the ability to take a long-term view
5. The age of *accountability* Key source: Bovens *et al.* (2014)	Continued growth of formal and informal mechanisms of oversight, evaluation, quality control, and comparative assessment ('rankings') Legitimacy of office-holders and other authority figures is now much more contingent on (perceptions of) their 'past performance'	Need to balance production of believable, confidence-inspiring 'performances' in a high-scrutiny marketplace for public trust with the transaction costs and unintended effects of 'managing' multifaceted accountability regimes
6. The age of *fluidity* Key source: Bauman (2006)	Decline of the bonding, bridging, and socializing power of traditional identities, institutions, and social ties Growing eclecticism and ephemerality and thus declining predictability and dependability of people's values, preferences, fears, and life styles	Need to balance a form of leadership that is credible through clarity, consistency, and tenacity in values and purposes with a form of leadership that is responsive and adaptive to more changeable public moods, priorities, and loyalties
7. The age of *glocalisation* Key source: Blij (2009)	Increased salience of transnational problems and development of a deepening field of transnational forces At the same time, a growing anti-cosmopolitan cultural backlash driven by fear of losing locally based identities, values, and institutions	Need to balance institutionalizing post-national leadership capacities with keeping governance grounded in the national and local communities from which it emanates and which it affects

meaning-making, the power to decide, unilateralism, secrecy/confidentiality – all of them are becoming endangered species under the combined influence of these trends.

If, at least for the moment, we adopt an alternative set of presumptions, we arrive at a vision of leadership as a very complex balancing act (see the right-hand column of the table) that can – and will – be performed by a much greater variety of actors, who are much less concentrated at the top of pyramid-like organizations and more often can only exercise leadership when they act in concert. These actors will be embedded in much less stable, more polycentric, and much less self-evidently mandate-conferring institutions. They will come and go faster than was the case in preceding generations. The 'romance of leadership' (Meindl *et al.* 1985) cannot just be made much faster but also destroyed much faster in a 24/7 online hyper-mediatized world.

What research agendas might emerge in such a transformed world of leadership? Promising research themes can be derived from a more critical and less heroic view of leadership.

First, one may want to understand the intersection between the agentic capacity of leaders and the ability of organizations and institutions to adapt to challenging conditions. Such a research focus may help to avoid the change junkies' syndrome and the overemphasis on individual leaders that have characterized much of the writing on so-called great leaders. This alternative research approach will necessarily be contextual and processual. This will be necessary in order to gain an understanding of how the processes of change and improvement are nurtured by practices developed by numerous individuals in the day-to-day life of organizations and governments.

Second, as suggested by a more critical approach to leadership, more attention can be paid to the evolution of discourses about leadership in various sectors of the economy and public affairs. The importance of decoding the political and ideological filiation of these discourses needs to be underlined to understand the embeddedness of leadership phenomena in societies.

Third, the role of materiality in leadership should not be underestimated: how agency is gained through the use (and also mis-use) of managerial tools and policy instruments. Public reforms have often been driven by the promotion of discourses and instruments (lean and managerialism, performance management and incentives) that provide the foundations for the emergence of new leading figures. Discourses and tools appear to be a fertile ground for new sources of legitimacy and consequently a new space for the development of leadership and leaders.

Finally, alternate views of leaders and leadership should be nurtured. For example, the role of individuals and groups in resisting pressures for conformity and in generating spaces for innovations in highly institutionalized fields can provide cutting-edge insights on processes and practices involved in un-freezing detrimental and outdated organizational norms and strategies.

References

Bauman, Z. (2006). *Liquid Times: Living in an Age of Uncertainty*. Cambridge, Polity Press.

Blij, H. de (2009). *The Power of Place*. Oxford, Oxford University Press.

Bovens, M., Goodin, R. E., and Schillemans, T. (eds) (2014). *Oxford Handbook of Public Accountability*. Oxford, Oxford University Press.

Castells, M. (1996). *The Network Society*, Oxford, Basil Blackwell.

Crosby, B. C. and Bryson, J. M. (2010). Integrative leadership and the creation and maintenance of cross-sector collaborations. *Leadership Quarterly* 21 (2), 211–230.

Gardner, J. (1998). *Quality Performance in Human Services: Leadership, Values, Vision*. Baltimore, MD, Brookes.

Gleick, J. (2000). *Faster: The Acceleration of Just About Everything*. London, Vintage.

Greenstein, F. (2000). *The Presidential Difference: Leadership Style from F.D.R. to Clinton*. Cambridge, Free Press.

't Hart, P. (2014). *Understanding Public Leadership*. Basingstoke, Palgrave.

House, R. (2013). *Strategic Leadership Across Cultures: GLOBE Study of CEO Leadership Behavior and Effectiveness in 24 Countries*. New York, Sage.

Kane, J., Patapan, H., and 't Hart, P. (2009). *Dispersed Democratic Leadership*. Oxford, Oxford University Press.

Kellerman, B. (2012). *The End of Leadership*. New York, Harper Business.

Kotter, J. (1996). *Leading Change*. Cambridge, Harvard Business Press.

MacGregor Burns, J. (2010). *Leadership*. New York, Harper.

Meindl, J. R., Ehrlich, S. B., and Dukerich, J. M. (1985). The romance of leadership. *Administrative Science Quarterly*, 30 (1), 78–102.

Meyer, M. W. and Zucker, L. G. (1989). *Permanently Failing Organizations*. Newbury Park, Sage.

Mulgan, R. (2014). *Making Open Government Work*. Basingstoke, Palgrave Macmillan.

Peters, T. and Waterman, R. (1982). *In Search of Excellence*. New York, Harper & Row.

Ryde, R. (2013). *Never Mind the Bosses*. San Francisco, Jossey-Bass.

Suchman, M. C. (1995). Managing legitimacy: strategic and institutional approaches. *Academy of Management Review*, 20, 571–611.

Index